# SOCIAL PSYCHOLOGY

# SOCIAL PSYCHOLOGY
## The Heart and the Mind

**Elliot Aronson**
University of California, Santa Cruz

❖

**Timothy D. Wilson**
University of Virginia

❖

**Robin M. Akert**
Wellesley College

HarperCollins*CollegePublishers*

Acquisitions Editor: Catherine Woods
Developmental Editor: Mimi Melek
Project Coordination, Text and Cover Design:
    Thompson Steele Book Production
Cover Photo: Tim Gibson, 1987
Photo Researchers: Elsa Peterson/Rosemary Hunter
Production Manager: Willie Lane
Compositor: Thompson Steele Book Production
Prepress: Interactive Composition Corporation
Printer and Binder: R.R. Donnelley & Sons Company
Cover Printer: The Lehigh Press, Inc.

Social Psychology: The Heart and The Mind

Library of Congress Cataloging-in-Publication Data

Aronson, Elliot.
    Social Psychology : the heart and the mind / Elliot Aronson,
    Timothy D. Wilson, Robin M. Akert.
        p.  cm.
    Includes bibliographical references and indexes.
    ISBN 0-06-040294-6
    1. Social psychology.    I. Wilson, Timothy D.    II. Akert, Robin M.
    III. Title.
HM251.A794    1994
302—dc20        93-43017
                        CIP

94 95 96 9 8 7 6 5 4 3 2

*To my family, Vera, Hal, Neal, Julie,*
*and Joshua Aronson*

—E.A.


*To my family, Deirdre Smith, Christopher*
*and Leigh Wilson*

—T.D.W.


*To my mentor, colleague, and friend,*
*Dane Archer*

—R.M.A.

# BRIEF CONTENTS

# PART FOUR
## Social Interaction

# PART FIVE
## Applying Social Psychology

# DETAILED CONTENTS

PART ONE

## Chapter 1
## Introduction to Social Psychology                          2

INTRODUCTION

## PART TWO

## UNDERSTANDING OURSELVES AND THE SOCIAL WORLD

# Chapter 4
# Social Cognition: How We Think About the Social World          114

# Chapter 6
# Self-Understanding: How Do We Know Ourselves?    198

# Chapter 7
# Conformity: Influencing Behavior    242

Chapter 8
Attitudes and Attitude Change: Influencing Thoughts
and Feelings                                                              284

P A R T   F O U R

# SOCIAL INTERACTION

## Chapter 10
## Interpersonal Attraction: From First Impressions to Close Relationships    370

# Chapter 13
# Prejudice: Causes and Cures

# Chapter 15
# Law and Business                                                    578

# PREFACE

Welcome to *Social Psychology: The Heart and the Mind*. Thank you for inviting us into your classroom. As teachers, we feel honored knowing that more students than we could ever reach individually will now be studying with us. We've devoted our adult lives to the field, and while we don't expect everybody else to do so, we do strongly believe that everyone can benefit from learning about social psychology. This is the academic field that is real life. Why does prejudice exist around the world? How can people be so helpful and kind in one situation and so aggressive and violent in another? What causes people to fall in love, not to mention out of love? In short, why do people do what they do?

Whether you are alone or with other people, you are always a social being. Knowing, consciously or unconsciously, that you are part of a larger, interactive network of human beings shapes your thoughts, feelings, and behavior. What others think and say affects you—while you may agree or disagree with them, we humans are always reacting to each other. Human social behavior is an intricate blend of emotions and cognitions. Our subtitle, *The Heart and the Mind*, reflects our analysis of what social psychology is all about. As Charles Dickens put it, "There is a wisdom of the head, and . . . a wisdom of the heart." We can be logical and analytical; we can be tempestuous and moody. We can follow our heads; we can follow our hearts. Sometimes, we can please both masters at the same time. Social psychology is the study of these processes.

Working on this book was certainly a labor of both the heart and the mind. The three of us combined have taught social psychology for 65 years— and that's at least 65 times we've flipped through different textbooks, trying to decide what to order for our students, and almost without exception, feeling that our choices didn't quite hit the mark. So, we decided to write a book of our own.

*Social Psychology: The Heart and the Mind* reflects the way we teach our courses. It offers a combination of scientific rigor (for this is a wonderful empirical science) and intellectual excitement (how can real life be anything but the most exciting game in town?). Specifically, here's what we wanted in our "dream" social psychology textbook, and how we've translated those desires to real pages and print.

## A Humanistic Approach to Science

We take the aim of a liberal arts education very seriously; we want to educate people to be both artists and scientists, to be conversant with both the humanistic world view and the scientific one. Social psychology is, in our minds, the perfect meeting place for the two traditions. First, social psychology is a rich empirical science. By studying social psychology, students will learn much about the scientific method, a "blueprint" for answering cause-and-effect questions, pertinent to any field.

We believe that everyone who graduates from college should have a firm grasp of scientific methodology; in short, he or she should be scientifically literate. Because social psychology focuses on everyday life—the situations, thoughts, and actions that we all encounter daily—it constitutes an engaging way to learn how science works. Thus, in our methodology chapter (Chapter 2), we have presented a comprehensive discussion of how social psychologists conduct empirical science. Reading this chapter will give students the groundwork to understand how science "works." The discussions of social psychological research throughout the book will expand on this knowledge, leading to scientific literacy.

But what about art? Humans can not live by science alone. We believe that the methodological techniques and the real-life basis of our field help us interweave science and art. Creating a well-crafted experiment is an artistic process, requiring a great deal of creativity. When designing a study, the researcher tries out many possibilities, keeping the best ideas, while discarding others, and trying new combinations, just as an artist draws many pencil sketches before beginning an oil painting. Conducting the actual experiment is very much like directing a movie or a Broadway play: "Lights, camera, action!" Your study begins as the first research participant walks through the door. Have you, the director (writer and producer too), constructed an experimental situation that is enough like real life to evoke meaningful behavior in your participants? If not, you have not been successful as an artist or a scientist.

We have sprinkled quotations from writers, artists, and statespeople, as well as the common man or woman, throughout the text. The points made in these quotations parallel what social psychologists have pondered and discovered through experimentation. The quotations remind us that social life is not just the province of scientists but of artists as well—social psychological phenomena relate to everyone's experience.

While quotations remind us of the literary world's contribution to understanding social psychology, the book's illustrations remind us of how much the visual arts inform our social life. A picture is indeed worth a thousand words. We have carefully chosen the photographs in this book. In many cases, they come from our personal files of teaching materials. Our aim was to create visual excitement through the use of thought-provoking as well as beautiful images. In addition, we have created original cartoon art for this book that clarifies difficult or complex social psychological concepts in an eye-catching (and amusing) visual manner. We have found cartoons to be a wonderful teaching tool in our courses; they bring difficult concepts to life and help the student experience them first hand. We're particularly pleased to have had a professional artist turn our amateur renderings into the delightful art you will see.

## The Research Process as Rigorous and Exciting

When the three of us sat down to plan this book, our first and foremost aim was to present social psychological research to the reader in all its complexity and grandeur; however, we wanted the student to learn more than just the findings of studies. We hoped to communicate that doing research is an exciting and stimulating intellectual endeavor, one that is actually fun. At the same time, it is a highly rigorous process, requiring much detailed planning, painstaking decision-making, and careful execution. A major component of our identities as social psychologists is that of experimental researchers. We wanted our textbook to reflect our enthusiasm and love for the research process. It has never ceased to intrigue, amaze, and even amuse us. We wanted these sentiments to come through in our discussion of social psychology's theories and findings.

We don't believe that you have to dilute information in order to make it palatable or easy to understand. People are capable of learning very complex material, if it is presented effectively. We try not to "talk down" to our students when we teach; we have tried to avoid doing so in our prose in this book as well. We take our reader through many of the most complex (and wonderful) studies in social psychology. In most cases, we take the trouble to clearly describe how the study was set up; what the research participants perceived and did; how the research design derives from and reflects pertinent theoretical issues; and how the findings offer support for the initial hypotheses. If that communicates the rigor, how did we communicate the fun?

One way is to make clear to readers that real people, usually people we know (including ourselves), did these studies. We've used our colleagues' first names throughout the book. Real people, deeply committed to doing their work, come through more clearly when you read their full name instead of just a list of last names. The use of first names also reminds the reader of the large number of women researchers in our field, a fact that is implicitly hidden when we only use last names. Whenever pertinent, we've included anecdotal information about how a study was done or came to be; these brief stories allow the reader to see "backstage," the hitherto hidden world of creating research.

## The Application of Social Psychology to Everyday Life

We believe that social psychology is an intrinsically interesting field, one that should appeal to every student regardless of his or her interests, background, or proclivities. All people are social "actors" in their everyday lives, navigating their way through their social world, often feeling they don't have a map! The topics we study in social psychology can provide students with such a map, that is, a body of knowledge, including theories and empirical findings that explain why people do what they do.

Bringing everyday life into the social psychology classroom has several benefits. When we present students with inherently interesting information, they are more highly motivated to work with it, study it, and master it. When we tie real-life events to psychological processes, students will understand the academic material on a more sophisticated and complex level. Finally, and most importantly, linking book learning to experiential learning gives students something to take with them when the course is over—the ability to apply social psychological theories to their future experiences and to their observation of world events. In our view, a course in social psychology never really ends—you just become your own professor (and you don't have to give yourself exams!).

The challenge for the social psychology professor (and the textbook writer) is to make a clear, pertinent, and exciting connection between academic information and real-life experience. We've taken that challenge very seriously. Each chapter opens with a story that is drawn from a real-life situation, such as a recent news event, historical incident, current political debate, or popular culture phenomenon. These opening vignettes encourage students, right from the beginning of the chapter, to think about and examine their daily experiences using a social psychological perspective. Most importantly, throughout each chapter, we refer back to the opening vignette, enriching the student's understanding of it in light of the theories and research findings that we have just presented. We anticipate that this pedagogical technique will encourage students to apply the material to their own lives and to what is happening in the world around them as they read through it.

## The Promotion of Critical Thinking

There's been a great hullabaloo about "critical thinking" in higher education over the past few years. What does critical thinking mean to us? We want our students to be active consumers of information, not passive ones; we want our students to go beyond the role of consumer to that of producer. We want our students to question, challenge, and engage in the material. In short, we want students to think and not memorize mindlessly. Isn't that every professor's dream? (And shouldn't it be every student's classroom fantasy as well?) What can we do, as textbook writers, to promote this kind of thinking?

We believe the answer centers on how we present theoretical and empirical information in a social psychology textbook. Both theory and research results must be equally stressed. It is the interplay, or even the tension, between these two that creates intellectual excitement. Has the researcher translated the theory into an appropriate research design? Is the stated hypothesis testing the theory? Are the results valid and meaningful? Do the results support the theory or do they challenge some aspect of it?

To promote critical thinking, we've described a great many complex experiments in detail, so that students will understand how and why researchers do their work. How does a researcher construct a study so as to arrive at his or her hypothesized conclusion? Why are the findings pertinent, interesting, or useful? We've tried to make the link between theory and research very clear, discussing the theoretical bases of a phenomenon, illuminating the questions that arise from the theory, and then showing the empirical evidence. Such a style often includes a frank discussion of those areas where the evidence is equivocal, where the data from several studies do not yet provide a coherent or adequate answer to the initial question. We need to remind our students that science is alive—it is constantly evolving, even as they read about it.

This style of presentation encourages students to critique research and to decide for themselves whether the study's findings are relevant, valid, and reliable. Critical thinking involves questioning; it involves thinking for yourself. Students get "the big picture," the feedback loop that exists between reasoning and action—the testing of hypotheses—when they read how and why a researcher conducted a study.

We should remember that critical thinking doesn't just mean critiquing what one reads. It also refers to a style of thinking that is systematic and analytical. Presenting information in this style should promote thinking in such a style. In short, we think you can lead a student to a textbook and make him or her think! We've promoted critical thinking by planning the organization of our chapters carefully. The placement and flow of material as well as the judicious use of headings helps the reader get the "big picture."

Finally, an important aspect of critical thinking is the ability to see beyond the familiar and "known." We want students to realize that how North Americans think and act in their social world is far from the whole story of human existence. To this end, we have included cross-cultural information wherever appropriate, with the intent of encouraging students to consider the diversity both within and outside of their own cultures.

## Textbook and Lectures: Twin Children of Different Parents

A really good textbook should become part of the classroom experience, supporting and augmenting the professor's vision for his or her class. *Social Psychology: The Heart and the Mind* offers a number of supplements that will enrich both the professor's presentation of social psychology and the student's understanding of it.

First, an instructor's manual, written by Fred W. Whitford of Montana State University, accompanies our textbook. The manual includes a chapter outline, a "teacher to teacher" section, lecture lead-ins, classroom activities, teaching strategies, questions for thought and discussion, and a list of selected readings for each text chapter. Additionally, it contains some of our own classroom exercises and more listings of videotapes and films for classroom viewing.

Second, a comprehensive test bank by Kurt Holzhausen and Richard P. McGlynn, both of Texas Tech University, also accompanies our text. The test bank contains over 1,000 multiple-choice and essay questions, which have been extensively reviewed by social psychologists. Each question is cross-referenced to the corresponding text topic and page number. Approximately 15 percent of the multiple-choice questions in the test bank also appear in the student study guide, to promote greater testing flexibility.

The test bank is also available on TestMaster software for IBM or Macintosh, a computerized form that enables the professor to edit existing questions and add new questions.

For the student, Kurt Holzhausen and Richard P. McGlynn have written a study guide that contains chapter overviews and study tips, chapter outlines, learning objectives, key terms, and two practice tests that use both multiple-choice and critical thinking essay questions for each chapter. Additionally, the guide includes our comprehensive self-test on the entire book.

Thank you for selecting our book. We welcome your comments and suggestions. Please write to us in care of HarperCollins Publishers, 10 East 53rd Street, New York, NY 10022.

## Acknowledgments

Elliot Aronson would like to thank Carrie Fried, who was very helpful in researching some of the material for this book, and Vera Aronson, who, as usual, provided the inspiration and acted as the sounding board for many of his ideas.

Timothy Wilson would like to thank his graduate mentor, Richard E. Nisbett, who nurtured his interest in the field and showed him the continuity between social psychology as an academic discipline and everyday life. He thanks his graduate students, Eric Anderson, Kate Etling, Sara Hodges, Chris Houston, Kristen Klaaren, Suzanne LaFleur, and Samuel Lindsey who helped keep him a well-balanced professor: a researcher as well as a teacher and author. He thanks his parents, Elizabeth and Geoffrey Wilson, for their comments on drafts of chapters and overall support. Most of all, he thanks his wife, Deirdre, and his children, Christopher and Leigh, for their love, patience, and understanding, even when the hour was late and the computer was still on.

Robin Akert would like to thank her students and colleagues at Wellesley College for their support and encouragement. In particular, she is beholden to Professors Julie Drucker, Patricia Berman, Nancy Genero, Abigail Panter, and Jonathan Cheek. Their advice, feedback, and senses of humor were invaluable. She is deeply grateful to her family, Michaela and Wayne Akert, and Linda and Jerry Wuichet; their inexhaustible enthusiasm and boundless support have sustained her on this project as on all the ones before it. She also thanks C. Issak and G. Livet for authorial inspiration. Finally, no words can express her gratitude and indebtedness to Dane Archer, mentor, colleague, and friend, who opened the world of social psychology to her and has been her guide ever since.

No book can be written and published without the help of a great many people working with the authors behind the scenes, and our book is no exception. First, we would like to thank the many colleagues who read drafts of chapters and provided extremely valuable feedback: Jeffrey B. Adams, Saint Michael's College; John R. Aiello, Rutgers University; Charles A. Alexander, Rock Valley College; Joan W. Baily, Jersey City State College; Norma Baker, Belmont University; William A. Barnard, University of Northern Colorado; Susan E. Beers, Sweet Briar College; Thomas Blass, University of Maryland, Baltimore County; C. George Boeree, Shippensburg University; Lisa M. Bohon, California State University, Sacramento; Peter J. Brady, Clark State Community College; Kelly A. Brennan, University of Texas at Austin; Susan D. Clayton, Allegheny College; Brian M. Cohen, University of Texas at San Antonio; Steven G. Cole, Texas Christian University; Eric J. Cooley, Western Oregon State College; Keith E. Davis, University of South Carolina–Columbia; Karen G. Duffy, State University of New York at Geneseo; Steve L. Ellyson, Youngstown State University; Susan Fiske, University of Massachusetts, Amherst; Robin Franck, Southwestern College; William Rick Fry, Youngstown State University; Frederick X.

Gibbons, Iowa State University; Judith Harackiewicz, University of Wisconsin—Madison; Tracy B. Henley, Mississippi State University; David E. Hyatt, University of Wisconsin—Oshkosh; James D. Johnson, University of North Carolina—Wilmington; Lee Jussim, Rutgers University; G. Daniel Lassiter, Ohio University; Joann M. Montepare, Tufts University; W. Gerrod Parrott, Georgetown University; M. Susan Rowley, Champlain College; Connie Schick, Bloomsburg University; Richard C. Sherman, Miami University of Ohio; Randolph A. Smith, Ouachita Baptist University; T. Gale Thompson, Bethany College; Gary L. Wells, Iowa State University; Paul L. Wienir, Western Michigan University; William H. Zachry, University of Tennessee—Martin.

We also thank the expert editorial staff of HarperCollins, especially our Acquisitions Editor, Catherine Woods, and our Developmental Editor, Mimi Melek. We'd also like to thank Susan Driscoll, Editorial Director; Marcus Boggs, Editor-in-Chief; Art Pomponio, Director of Development; Paula Soloway, Project Editorial Manager; Evelyn Owens, Supplements Editor; Mark Paluch, Marketing Manager; Tony Griego, Cartoonist; Sally Steele and Thompson Steele Book Production, Design and Production Group; and Laura Pearson and Chris Olson. Finally, we thank Mary Falcon, but for whom we never would have begun this project.

Elliot Aronson<br>Timothy D. Wilson<br>Robin M.Akert

# SPECIAL TIPS FOR STUDENTS

There is then creative reading as well as creative writing."
—Ralph Waldo Emerson, 1837

"I am a kind of burr; I shall stick."
—William Shakespeare, 1604

These two quotes, taken together, sum up everything you need to know to be a proficient student: be an active, creative consumer of information and make sure it sticks! How do you accomplish these two feats? It's actually not difficult at all. Like everything else in life, it just takes some work—some clever, well-planned, purposeful work. Here's how to do it.

## Get To Know the Textbook

Believe it or not, we thought very carefully about the organization and structure of each chapter. Things are the way they appear for a reason, and that reason is to help you learn the material in the best way. Here are some tips on what to look for in each chapter:

- Important definitions or key terms are in boldface type in the text so you'll notice them. We define the terms in the text, and that definition appears again in the margin. These marginal definitions are there to help you out if you forget what something means later in the chapter. The marginal definitions are quick and easy to find. You can also look up key terms in the alphabetical glossary at the end of the textbook.
- Make sure you notice the headings (in color) and subheadings (in boldface). When reading, people have the tendency to skim past headings and not really notice them. That's why you may sometimes have the disconcerting feeling after reading several pages that you don't really know what's going on. The headings are the skeleton that holds the chapter together. They link together like vertebrae. If you ever feel lost, look back to the last heading and the headings before that one—this will give you the "big picture" of where the chapter is going. It should also help you see the connections between the material.

• The summary at the end of each chapter is a succinct, shorthand presentation of the chapter information with the key terms set in boldface. You should read it and make sure there are no "surprises" when you do so. If there is anything in the summary that doesn't ring a bell, go back to the chapter and read that section again. Most importantly, remember that the summary is purposefully brief. Your understanding of the material should be full and complete. Use the summary as a study aid before your exams. When you read it over, everything should be familiar, and you should have that wonderful feeling of knowing more than is in the summary (in which case, you are ready to take the exam).

• At the end of each chapter, we list some books or articles on the subject that we think are particularly good. These recommended readings are excellent resources for any papers you may be writing in your course. They are the first place to start in a bibliographic search for further information on your paper topic. As is always the case with literature searches, they will lead you to still other references. Good hunting!

## Just Say No to the Couch Potato Within

Because social psychology is about everyday life, you might lull yourself into believing that the material is all common sense, and easy. Don't be fooled. The material is more complicated than it might seem. Therefore, we want to emphasize that the best way to learn it is to work with it in an active, not passive, fashion. You can't just read a chapter once and expect it to stick with you. You have to go over the material, wrestle with it, make your own connections to it, question it, and think about it. Actively working with material makes it memorable; it makes it your own. Since it's a safe bet that someone is going to ask you about this material later, and you're going to have to pull it out of memory, do what you can to get it into memory now. Here are some techniques to use:

• Go ahead and be bold! Use a yellow highlighter! Go crazy, write in the margins! Draw a moustache on the photograph of William James (actually, he already has one). In other words, make this your book. If you underline, highlight, circle, or draw little hieroglyphics next to important points, you will remember them better. We remember taking exams in college where we not only remembered the material, we could actually see in our minds the textbook page it was written on and the little squiggles and stars we'd drawn in the margin. We found it very helpful.

• Read the textbook chapter before the applicable class lecture, not afterwards. This way, you'll get more out of the lecture, which will introduce new material. The chapter will give you that "big picture" as well as a lot of detail. The lecture will enhance that information and help you put it all together. If you don't read the chapter first, you may not understand some of the points made in the lecture or realize that they are important.

• Similarly, go over your class lecture notes on a regular basis, not just the day before the exam. Only by reading through them regularly will you be able to tell if you really are keeping up with the material and understanding it on the level that your professor expects. As soon as you come across something you don't understand in your notes, ask for clarification. Little misunderstandings become big ones as the term progresses. If you didn't really get an earlier point, you're going to have trouble with the more complex information that comes later. Solve problems when they're little.

• Here's a good way to study material: write out a difficult concept or a study (or say it out loud to yourself) in your own words, without looking at the book or your notes. Can you do it? How good was your version? Did you leave out anything important? Did you get stuck at some point, unable to remember what comes next? If so, you now know that you need to go over that information in more detail. You can also study with someone else, describing theories and studies to each other and seeing if you're making sense.

• If you have trouble remembering the results of an important study, try drawing your own version of a graph of the findings (you can use our data graphs for an idea of how to proceed). If all the various points in a theory are confusing you, try drawing your own flowchart of how it works. You will probably find that you remember the research results much better in pictorial form than in words, and that the theory isn't so confusing (or missing a critical part) if you've outlined it. Draw information a few times and it will stay with you.

• Remember: the more you work with the material, that is, write it in your own words, talk about it, explain it to others, or draw visual representations of it, the better you will learn and remember it.

Last, but not least, remember that this material is a lot of fun. You haven't even started reading the book yet, but we think you're going to like it. In particular, you'll see how much social psychology has to tell you about your real, everyday life. As this course progresses, you might want to remind yourself to observe the events of your daily life with new eyes, the eyes of a social psychologist, and try to apply what you are learning to the behavior of your friends, acquaintances, strangers and, yes, even yourself. When you read newspapers or magazines, or watch the nightly news, think about what social psychology has to say about such events and behaviors; we believe that you will find that your understanding of daily life is richer. If you notice a newspaper or magazine article that you think is an especially good example of social psychology "in action," please send it to us, with a full reference to where you found it and on what page. If we decide to use it in the next edition of the textbook, we'll list your name in the acknowledgments.

We suspect that ten years from now, you may not remember all the facts, theories, and names that you learn now. We hope that you will remember some of them, but our major goal is for you to take away a great many of the broad social psychological concepts with you into your future. If you open yourself to social psychology's magic, we feel it will enrich the way you look at the world and the way you live in it.

# ABOUT THE AUTHORS

## Elliot Aronson

When I was a kid, we were the only Jewish family in a virulently anti-Semitic neighborhood. I had to go to Hebrew school every day, late in the afternoon. Because I was the only youngster in my neighborhood going to Hebrew school, this made me an easy target for some of the older neighborhood toughs. On my way home from Hebrew school, after dark, I was frequently waylaid and roughed up by roving gangs shouting anti-Semitic epithets.

I have a vivid memory of sitting on a curb, after one of these beatings, nursing a bloody nose or a split lip, feeling very sorry for myself and wondering how it was that these kids could hate me so much when they didn't even know me. I thought about whether those kids were taught to hate Jews or whether, somehow, they were born that way. I wondered if their hatred could be changed; if they got to know me better, would they hate me less? I speculated about my own character. What would I have done if the shoe were on the other foot; that is, if I were bigger and stronger than they, would I be capable of beating them up for no good reason?

I didn't realize it at the time, of course, but eventually I discovered that these were profound questions. And, some thirty years later, as an experimental social psychologist, it was my great good fortune to be in a position to answer some of those questions and to invent techniques to reduce the kind of prejudice that had claimed me as a victim.

*Elliot Aronson graduated from Brandeis University and received his Ph.D. from Stanford University, working with Leon Festinger. He has done pioneering research in areas of social influence, persuasion, and prejudice reduction. Aronson has written several books, including* The Social Animal, The Jigsaw Classroom, *and* Methods of Research in Social Psychology. *He has won the American Psychological Association's Distinguished Teaching Award and the Distinguished Research Award from the American Association for the Advancement of Science. He teaches psychology at the University of California, Santa Cruz.*

## Tim Wilson

When I was eight, a couple of neighborhood friends told me, with great excitement, that they had found an abandoned house down a country road. "It's really neat," one of them said. "I broke a window, and nobody cared!" My best friend and I went to investigate and soon found the house. My friend promptly heaved a rock through a first-floor window. There was something terribly exciting about the smash-and-tingle of shattering glass, especially when we knew there was nothing wrong with what we were doing; after all, the house was abandoned. We proceeded to break nearly every window in the house, after which we climbed through one of the first-floor windows to look around. It was then that we realized something was terribly wrong. The house certainly did not look abandoned. There were pictures on the wall, nice furniture, books in bookshelves. We went home feeling very confused and more than a little afraid. We soon learned that the house was not abandoned, but that it was the residence of an elderly couple who had been on vacation. Eventually my parents found out, and paid a substantial sum to cover the damage.

For years, I pondered this incident: why did I do such a terrible thing? Was I a bad kid? I didn't think so, and neither did my parents. But then how could a good kid do such a bad thing? Even though the neighborhood kids said it was an abandoned house, why couldn't my friend and I see the clear signs that someone lived there? How crucial was it that my friend was there and threw the first rock? Though I didn't know it at the time, these reflections touched on several classic social psychological issues, such as whether it is only bad people who do bad things, whether the social situation can be so powerful as to make good people do bad things, and the way in which our expectations about an event can make it difficult to see it the way it really is. Fortunately, my career as a vandal ended with the window-breaking. This incident did, though, mark the beginning of my fascination with basic questions about how people understand themselves and the social world, questions that I continue to investigate to this day.

*Timothy D. Wilson did his undergraduate work at Williams and Hampshire Colleges. He received his Ph.D. from the University of Michigan under the guidance of Richard E. Nisbett. He is currently Professor of Psychology at the University of Virginia and has published numerous articles in the areas of introspection, judgment, and attitude change. His research has received the support of the National Science Foundation and the National Institute for Mental Health. He has been a member of the Executive Board of the Society for Experimental Social Psychology, a member of the Social and Groups Processes Review Committee at the National Institute of Mental Health, and a member of the editorial boards of several professional journals.*

## Robin Akert

One fall day, when I was about 16, I was walking with a friend along the shore of the San Francisco Bay. Deep in conversation, I glanced over my shoulder and saw a sailboat capsize. I pointed it out to my friend, who took only a perfunctory interest and went on talking. However, I kept watching as we walked, and I realized that the two sailors were in the water, clinging to the capsized boat. Again, I said something to my friend, who replied, "Oh, they'll get it upright, don't worry."

But I was worried. Was this an emergency? My friend didn't think so. And I was no sailor; I knew nothing about boats. But I kept thinking, "That water is really cold. They can't stay in that water too long." I remember feeling very confused and unsure. What should I do? Should I do anything? Did they really need help?

We were near a restaurant with a big window overlooking the Bay, and I decided to go in and see if anyone had done anything about the boat. Lots of people were watching but not doing anything. This confused me too. Very meekly, I asked the bartender to call for some kind of help. He just shrugged. I went back to the window and watched the two small figures in the water. Why was everyone so unconcerned? Was I crazy?

Years later, I reflected on how hard it was for me to do what I did next. I demanded that the bartender let me use his phone. In those days before "911," it was lucky that I knew there was a Coast Guard station on the Bay, and I asked the operator for their number. I was relieved to hear the Guardsman take my message very seriously.

It had been an emergency. I watched as the Coast Guard cutter sped across the Bay and pulled the two sailors out of the water. Maybe I saved their lives that day. What really stuck with me over the years was how other people behaved and how it made me feel. The other bystanders seemed unconcerned and had done nothing to help. Their reactions made me doubt myself and made it harder for me to decide to take action. When I later studied social psychology in college, I realized that on the shore of the San Francisco Bay that day, I had experienced the "bystander effect" fully: the presence of other, apparently unconcerned bystanders had made it difficult for me to decide if the situation was an emergency and whether it was my responsibility to help.

*Robin M. Akert graduated summa cum laude from the University of California, Santa Cruz, where she majored in psychology and sociology. She received her Ph.D. degree in experimental social psychology from Princeton University. She is currently an Associate Professor at Wellesley College, where she was awarded the Pinanski Prize for Excellence in Teaching. She publishes primarily in the area of nonverbal communication and is the co-author of the forthcoming book,* Interpretation and Awareness: Verbal and Nonverbal Factors in Person Perception.

# SOCIAL PSYCHOLOGY
## THE HEART AND THE MIND

**Elliot Aronson,** *University of California, Santa Cruz*
**Timothy D. Wilson,** *University of Virginia*
**Robin M. Akert,** *Wellesley College*

0-06-040294-6

This is a social psychology text by an author team whose versatile leader, Elliot Aronson, is one of the most creative contributors to and researchers in the field (Aronson has done pioneering research, both basic and applied, in social influence, persuasion, and prejudice reduction, and has won major awards in research, teaching, race relations, writing, and community service).

In *Social Psychology*, Aronson and co-authors Tim Wilson (a nationally-known researcher in social cognition, introspection, and attitudes) and Robin Akert (an award-winning teacher whose research focuses on nonverbal communication and sexual stereotyping), tell the story of social psychology, drawing on their great scholarship and deep understanding of the process of research. All three currently teach social psychology and have for many years. In fact, the authors' combined experience teaching this course is 65 years. Active researchers as well, they have created a comprehensive, up-to-date, and user-friendly narrative that conveys the excitement and enthusiasm they feel about social psychology.

### Clever, Original "Stick" Figure Art

Conceived by the authors, these "cartoon" drawings bring difficult social psychological concepts to life.

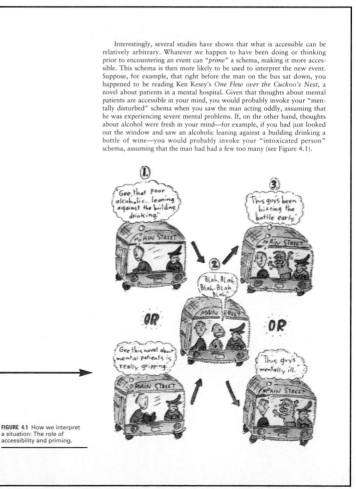

Interestingly, several studies have shown that what is accessible can be relatively arbitrary. Whatever we happen to have been doing or thinking prior to encountering an event can "*prime*" a schema, making it more accessible. This schema is then more likely to be used to interpret the new event. Suppose, for example, that right before the man on the bus sat down, you happened to be reading Ken Kesey's *One Flew over the Cuckoo's Nest*, a novel about patients in a mental hospital. Given that thoughts about mental patients are accessible in your mind, you would probably invoke your "mentally disturbed" schema when you saw the man acting oddly, assuming that he was experiencing severe mental problems. If, on the other hand, thoughts about alcohol were fresh in your mind—for example, if you had just looked out the window and saw an alcoholic leaning against a building drinking a bottle of wine—you would probably invoke your "intoxicated person" schema, assuming that the man had had a few too many (see Figure 4.1).

FIGURE 4.1 How we interpret a situation: The role of accessibility and priming.

# CHAPTER 3

## Cognitive Dissonance and the Need to Maintain Self-Esteem

**Real-Life Chapter Opening Vignettes/Situations**

Chapter-opening vignettes, drawn from such real-life situations as news events, current political debates, popular culture, and literature, introduce chapter topics and encourage students to take another look at their daily experiences from a social psychological perspective. These opening vignettes are often referred to later in the chapter as illustrative examples of social psychological concepts.

### Chapter Outline

Not long ago, Dr. Bob Arnot, medical editor of "CBS Morning News," appeared on the show to report some startling news. A group of distinguished medical researchers had just published the results of an apparently definitive study demonstrating that stretching before engaging in physical activity does not do athletes any good—and might even cause them harm. The data, based on thousands of cases, showed that people who always stretch a moderate amount suffer no fewer injuries than those who never stretch—while those who stretch deeply actually suffer more injuries than those who never stretch ("CBS Morning News," March 9, 1990).

While Dr. Arnot was reporting these data, the camera panned to New York's Central Park, where the roving reporter was interviewing several joggers. "How interesting!" exclaimed one jogger. "That's important information. Who, me? No, I almost never stretch—too much trouble." The reporter then went over to a chain-link fence, where several joggers were dutifully stretching prior to their morning run, and reported the latest finding. "I don't believe it," said one; "it can't be true." "That has to be wrong," said another; "after all, I've been stretching for over fifteen years and I have had very few muscle injuries." "That's nothing but a pack of lies!" exclaimed a third stretcher. "Why would the scientists lie?" asked the roving reporter. "To keep their jobs," answered the stretcher.

Chapter Outline

**The Nature of the Self**
  Cross-Cultural Definitions of Self
**Knowing Ourselves Through Introspection**
  Self-Awareness Theory
  Judging Why We Feel the Way We Do: Telling More
    Than We Can Know
  The Consequences of Introspecting About Reasons
**Knowing Ourselves Through Observations of Our
  Own Behavior**
  Self-Perception Theory
  The Overjustification Effect
  The Two-Factor Theory of Emotion
  Misattribution of Arousal
**Knowing Ourselves Through Self-Schemas**
  Autobiographical Memory
**Knowing Ourselves Through Social Interaction**
  The "Looking-Glass Self"
  Social Comparison Theory
**Impression Management**
  All the World's a Stage
**Summary**
**Suggested Readings**

There is one thing, and only one in the whole universe which we know more
about than we could learn from external observation. That one thing is [our-
selves]. We have, so to speak, inside information; we are in the know.

—C. S. Lewis, 1960

We are unknown, we knowers, ourselves to ourselves; this has its own good
reason. We have never searched for ourselves—how should it then come to pass,
that we should ever find ourselves?

—Friedrich Nietzche, 1918

top for a moment and think about how you feel right now. Are you happy or sad?
Tired or energetic? Calm or irritated? Questions like these are usually pretty easy
to answer; as C. S. Lewis says, we are "in the know" about ourselves. Few of us,
however, would claim to know ourselves perfectly. Sometimes our thoughts and
are a confused jumble of contradictory reactions. And even if we know how we
not always clear why we feel that way. There is a lot about ourselves that is

# CHAPTER 6

## Self-Understanding:
## How Do We Know Ourselves?

## Vivid Descriptions of Experiments

The authors offer detailed and vivid descriptions of social psychology experiments, and encourage students to place themselves in the shoes of the experiment subjects. These descriptions not only teach students about the phenomenon being studied, they also convey how and why research in social psychology is done the way it is.

more interesting question is, What happens to the students' attitudes about cheating *after* their decision? Suppose that after a difficult struggle, you decide to cheat. How do you reduce the dissonance? You can't very easily pretend you didn't cheat. That would constitute a complete denial of reality. What you could do is try to justify the action by finding a way to minimize the negative aspects of the action you chose. In this instance, an efficacious path of dissonance reduction would entail a change in your attitude about cheating. In short, you will adopt a more lenient attitude toward cheating, convincing yourself that it is a "victimless" crime that doesn't hurt anybody, that "everybody does it" so it's not really that bad, and so on.

Suppose, on the other hand, that after a difficult struggle you decide *not* to cheat. How would you reduce your dissonance? Once again, you could change your attitude about the morality of the act—but this time in the *opposite* direction. That is, in order to justify giving up a good grade, you must convince yourself that cheating is a heinous sin, that it's one of the lowest things a person can do, and that cheaters should be rooted out and severely punished.

What has come about is not merely a rationalization of your own behavior, but an actual change in your system of values; individuals faced with this kind of choice will undergo either a softening or a hardening of their attitudes toward cheating on exams, depending on whether or not they decided to cheat. The interesting and important thing to remember is that two people acting in the two different ways described above could have started out with almost identical attitudes toward cheating. Their decisions might have been a hair's breadth apart—one came within an inch of cheating but decided to resist, while the other came within an inch of resisting but decided to cheat. Once they made their decisions, however, their attitudes toward cheating will diverge sharply as a consequence of their actions.

These speculations were put to the test by Judson Mills (1958) in an experiment he performed in an elementary school. Mills first measured the attitudes of sixth-graders toward cheating. He then had them participate in a competitive exam, with prizes being offered to the winners. The situation was arranged so it was almost impossible to win without cheating. Mills made it easy for the children to cheat and created the illusion that they could not be detected. Under these conditions, as one might expect, some of the students cheated and others did not. The next day, the sixth-graders were again asked to indicate how they felt about cheating. Those children who had cheated became more lenient toward cheating, and those who had resisted the temptation to cheat adopted a harsher attitude toward cheating.

### The Justification of Effort

Most people are willing to put out a lot of effort in order to get something they really want. That's axiomatic. For example, if there's a particular job you want, you are likely to go the extra mile in order to get it. This might involve shopping for appropriate clothing, studying extra hard to meet entrance requirements, passing a battery of difficult exams, or putting up with a series of unpleasant interviews.

Let's turn that proposition inside out. Suppose you put out a great deal of effort in order to get into a particular club and it turns out to be a totally worthless organization, consisting of boring, pompous people in pursuit of

In sum, people go through two steps when making attributions (Gilbert, 1989, 1991, 1993). They begin by making an internal attribution, assuming that a person's behavior was due to something about him or her. They then attempt to adjust this attribution by taking into account the situation the person was in. As we have seen, people often do not make *enough* of an adjustment in this second step. An interesting implication of this fact is that if people are distracted or preoccupied when explaining someone's behavior, they might not get to the second step, thereby making an even *more* extreme internal attribution. Why? Because the initial step (making the internal attribution) occurs quickly and spontaneously, whereas the second step (adjusting for the situation) requires more effort and conscious attention. Daniel Gilbert has performed several experiments that support this view. Subjects in his studies are asked to explain why someone did what they did, but are distracted by having to do something else at the same time, such as remembering an eight-digit number. These subjects make even more extreme internal attributions than subjects who are not distracted, because they are unable to mentally adjust their initial impression that the person's behavior emanated solely from within him or her, uninfluenced by the situation (Gilbert & Osborne, 1989; Gilbert, Pelham, & Krull, 1988).

**The Role of Culture.** A second reason that the fundamental attribution error exists is that Western culture teaches us to *prefer* dispositional explanations. Such a preference is not found in cultures that place less emphasis on individual freedom and autonomy (Zebrowitz-McArthur, 1988). For example, Joan Miller (1984) asked people of two cultures—Hindus living in India and Americans living in the United States—to think of various examples of behaviors performed by their friends, and to explain why these behaviors occurred. Consistent with what we've said so far, the American participants preferred *dispositional* explanations for the behaviors. They were more likely to say that the causes of their friends' behaviors were the kind of people they were, rather than the situation or context in which the behaviors occurred. In contrast, Hindu participants preferred *situational* explanations for their friends' behaviors (Miller, 1984).

But, you might be thinking, perhaps the Americans and Hindus generated different kinds of examples. Perhaps the Hindus thought of behaviors that really were more situationally caused, whereas the Americans thought of behaviors that really were more dispositionally caused. To test this alternative hypothesis, Miller (1984) took some of the behaviors generated by the Hindu participants and gave them to Americans to explain. The difference in internal and external attributions was again observed: Americans preferred dispositional causes for the behaviors that the Hindus had thought were situationally caused.

For example, one of the behaviors concerned a lawyer riding to work on his motorcycle with his friend as a passenger. They got into an accident, and the friend was seriously injured. After taking his friend to the hospital, the lawyer continued on to work, rather than staying to talk with the doctors about his friend's condition. Why did he do this? Most Americans made a dispositional attribution, assuming that it was something about the lawyer (e.g., "The lawyer is obviously irresponsible"). Hindus, however, were more likely to make a situational attribution, assuming it was something about the context in which the behavior occurred (e.g., "It was the lawyer's responsi-

## Interim Summaries

In each chapter, Interim Summaries recap more difficult topics, and remind students of the social psychological theories discussed earlier in the chapter.

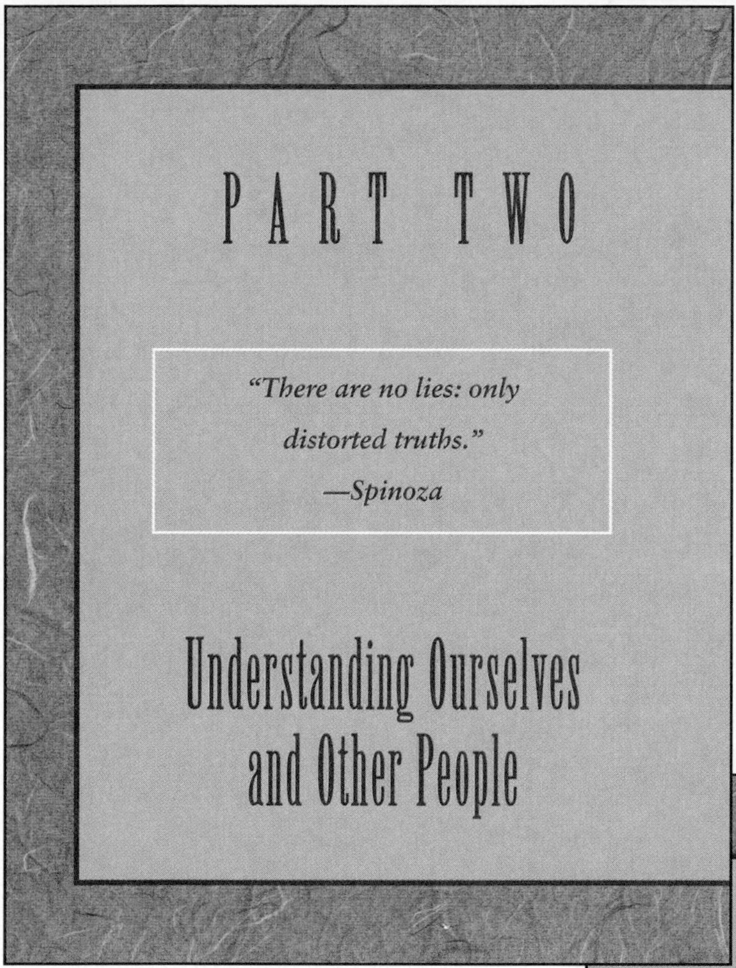

# PART TWO

"There are no lies: only
distorted truths."
—Spinoza

## Understanding Ourselves and Other People

← **Part-Opening Spreads**

Literary Part-Opening Quotes and thought provoking photos help bridge the gap between arts and sciences, and reinforce the authors' "humanistic" approach to social psychology.

## Marginal Glossary

A running Marginal Glossary defines key terms that are highlighted in the corresponding text passages.

Such an approach is only interesting, of course, to the extent that social influences actually do affect people's behavior in significant ways. If everyone went on his or her merry way, uninfluenced by what other people were doing or thinking, then we would not need a science called social psychology to understand human behavior. It is clear, however, that people *are* influenced by each other. Nonetheless, the power and extent of this influence are not always obvious to the naked eye—as we shall see.

### The Power of Social Influence

When trying to convince people that their behavior is greatly influenced by the social environment, the social psychologist is up against a formidable barrier: the inclination we all have for explaining people's behavior in terms of their personalities (as in the case of the waitress discussed above). This barrier has been discussed by several social psychologists, most notably Fritz Heider (1958), E. E. Jones (1979), and Lee Ross (1977). Ross refers to it as the **fundamental attribution error**, or the tendency to explain our own and other people's behavior entirely in terms of personality traits, thereby underestimating the power of social influence.

Because of this tendency to overlook the power of social influence, as authors of this book, we are fully aware that we face an uphill battle. If you are like most people, when you first encounter the examples of social behavior we will discuss, your initial tendency will be to explain that behavior in terms of the personalities of the people involved. All we ask is that, while reading this book, you try to suspend judgment for a short time, and consider the possibility that to understand why people do what they do, it is always important to look closely at the nature of the social situation. (See the photo on this page.)

**fundamental attribution error:** the tendency to overestimate the extent to which people's behavior is due to their personalities, and to underestimate the role of situational factors

We often assume that people behave in unusual, bizarre, or peculiar ways because of the nature of their personalities. Often, however, unusual, bizarre, or peculiar behavior is caused by powerful social influences. In the movie "Trading Places," a character played by Dan Ackroyd was extremely wealthy, comfortable, and "normal" — until he became caught in a web of social influences that changed his life dramatically.

## Marginal Quotes

Marginal Quotes from literature, philosophy, popular culture, and psychology draw parallels between the key concepts and ideas discussed in the text and real life.

We do not love people so much for the good they have done us, as for the good we have done them.

—Leo Tolstoy

### The Aftermath of Good and Bad Deeds

**How We Come to Like Our Beneficiaries: The Ben Franklin Manipulation.** It is obvious that when we like people, we tend to treat them well, speak kindly to them, do them favors, and smile at them benevolently. If we don't like them, we treat them less kindly, avoid them, say bad things about them, and perhaps even go out of our way to snub them. But what happens when we do a person a favor? Do we like them more, or less? In particular, what happens when we are subtly induced to do a favor for a person we do not like? Dissonance theory predicts that we will like that person more after doing him or her the favor.

This phenomenon was hardly discovered by dissonance theorists; in fact, it is a part of folk wisdom. Indeed, in 1736 Benjamin Franklin confessed to having utilized this bit of folk wisdom as a political strategy. While serving as a member of the Pennsylvania state legislature, Franklin was disturbed by the political opposition and apparent animosity of a fellow legislator. So he set out to win him over:

> I did not . . . aim at gaining his favour by paying any servile respect to him but, after some time, took this other method. Having heard that he had in his library a certain very scarce and curious book I wrote a note to him expressing my desire or perusing that book and requesting he would do me the favour of lending it to me for a few days. He sent it immediately and I returned it in about a week with another note expressing strongly my sense of the favour. When we next met in the House he spoke to me (which he had never done before), and with great civility; and he ever after manifested a readiness to serve me on all occasions, so that we became great friends and our friendship continued to his death. This is another instance of the truth of an old maxim I had learned, which says, "He that has once done you a kindness will be more ready to do you another than he whom you yourself have obliged." (Bigelow, J. (1916) *The Autobiography of Benjamin Franklin* (pp. 216-217. New York: Putnam)

Although he wasn't aware of it, Ben Franklin may have successfully used dissonance theory as a political strategy.

## Chapter Summaries with Key Terms Emphasized

Every chapter concludes with a summary that highlights its major points and re-emphasizes its key terms. They have been designed to serve as both a study aid and a self-quiz for students.

### SUMMARY

In this chapter, we focused on **conformity**, or how people change their behavior due to the real (or imagined) influence of others. We found that there are two main reasons people conform: because of informational and normative social influences. **Informational social influence** occurs when people do not know what is the correct (or best) thing to do or say. This reaction typically occurs in new, confusing, or crisis situations, where the definition of the situation is unclear. People look to the behavior of others as an important source of "information" and use it to choose appropriate courses of action for themselves. Informational influence usually results in **private acceptance**, wherein people genuinely believe in what other people are doing or saying.

People are most likely to use others as a source of information when the situation (and thus what they should do) is ambiguous; here a person is most open to the influence of others. Experts are powerful sources of influence, since they typically have the most information about appropriate responses. A special type of ambiguous situation is a crisis; fear, confusion, and panic increase our reliance on others to help us decide what to do.

Using others as a source of information can backfire, however, as when people panic because others are doing so. **Contagion** occurs when emotions and behaviors spread rapidly throughout a large group; one example is research on **mass psychogenic illnesses**. You can best resist the inappropriate use of others as a source of information by checking the "information" you are getting against your common sense and internal moral compass.

**Normative social influence** occurs for a different reason—we change our behavior to match that of others not because they seem to know better what is going on, but because we want to remain a member of the group, continue to gain the advantages of group membership, and avoid the pain of ridicule and rejection. Normative social influence can occur even in unambiguous situations; people will conform to others for normative reasons even if they know that what they are doing is wrong. Normative social influence usually results in **public compliance** but not **private acceptance** of other people's ideas and behaviors.

Failure to respond to normative influences can be painful. Normative pressures operate on many levels in social life: They influence our eating habits, body image, hobbies, fashion, and so on; they promote "correct" (polite) behavior in society; and they can be an agent for social change. A special type of **mindless conformity**, whereby we operate as if on automatic pilot, never questioning or thinking about the *social norms* we are following.

**Social impact theory** specifies when normative social influence is most likely to occur, by referring to the strength, immediacy, and number of group members. We are more likely to conform when the group is one we care about, when the group members are unanimous in their thoughts or behaviors, and when the group size is three or more. We can resist inappropriate conformity for normative reasons by being more mindful of normative pressures and by gathering **idiosyncrasy credits**, over time, from a group whose membership we value. Finally, **minority influence**, whereby a minority of group members influences the beliefs and behavior of the majority, can occur under certain conditions.

In the most famous series of studies in social psychology, Stanley Milgram examined the limits of obedience to authority figures. Informational and normative pressures combined to cause chilling levels of obedience, to the point where a majority of the participants administered what they thought were near-lethal shocks to a fellow human being. In addition, the participants were caught in a web of conflicting social norms, so that is was difficult to recognize that the one they started following ("Obey authority figures") was no longer appropriate. Contributing to this difficulty was the fact that people were asked to increase the level of shocks in small increments. After justifying to themselves that they had delivered one level of shock, it was very difficult for people to decide that a slightly higher level of shock was wrong. Unfortunately the conditions that produced such extreme antisocial behavior in Milgram's laboratory have been present in real-life tragedies, such as the Holocaust and the mass murders at My Lai in Vietnam.

### SUGGESTED READINGS

Cialdini, R. B. (1993). *Influence: Science and Practice* (3rd ed.). New York: HarperCollins.
An extremely readable and entertaining account of research on conformity and applications to everyday life.

Milgram, D. (1974). *Obedience to Authority: An Experimental View*. New York: Harper & Row.
A detailed description of the most famous studies in social psychology: those in which people were induced to deliver what they believed were lethal shocks to a fellow human being. Nearly twenty years after it was published, Milgram's book remains a poignant and insightful account of obedience to authority.

Sherif, M. (1936). *The Psychology of Social Norms*. New York: Harper.
An entertaining account of Sherif's study of informational social influence, wherein people judged how much a light was moving. It is still worth reading today.

Turner, J. C. (1991). *Social Influence*. Pacific Grove, CA: Brooks/Cole.
An up-to-date, in-depth account of social psychological research on social influence and conformity.

## Annotated List of Suggested Readings

The authors have carefully selected additional readings on topics related to the chapter for students to pursue on their own. Each reading is accompanied by the authors' personal descriptions and assessments of the books and journal articles recommended.

# PART

*Social psychology deals with
human interaction–the way
people relate to one another and
the way people influence one another.
How can we understand
human relations and social influence?
By studying the way people feel
and the way people think–in short,
by studying
the heart and the mind.*

—The Authors

# ONE

# Chapter 1
## Introduction to Social Psychology

he task of the psychologist is to try to understand and predict human behavior. Different kinds of psychologists go about this in different ways, and in this book we will attempt to show you how social psychologists do it. Let's begin with a few examples of human behavior. Some of these might seem important; others might seem trivial; one or two might seem frightening. To a social psychologist, all of them are interesting. As you read these examples, try to think about how you would explain why what happened, happened.

1. In the predawn hours of June, 1981, the residents of a trendy neighborhood in Los Angeles heard desperate cries for help coming from a yellow house. "Please don't kill me!" screamed one woman. Other neighbors reported hearing tortured screams and cries for mercy. And yet, not one neighbor bothered to investigate or help in any way. No one even called the police. One woman, who lived two houses away, went out onto her balcony when she heard the screams, but went back into her house without doing anything. Twelve hours later, an acquaintance arrived at the yellow house, and discovered that four people had been brutally murdered. A fifth person was critically wounded, and spent those 12 hours lying in a bedroom, bleeding from her wounds, waiting in vain for just one neighbor to lift their finger and dial the police (*New York Times*, July 3, 1981).

Why are neighbors reluctant to help?

Why do you think the neighbors failed to do anything after hearing the cries for help? Stop and think for a moment: What kind of people are these neighbors? Would you like to have them as friends? If you had a small child, would you hire one of these neighbors as a baby-sitter?

2. Recently, one of our students, Sally, told us about the following incident. Sally was watching TV with several of her acquaintances. On the tube, President Clinton was making an important policy speech. It was the first time Sally had seen President Clinton in action since the election campaign, and she was favorably impressed. There was a homey quality about the President; Sally felt he was honest, sincere, and straightforward. As soon as the speech was over, her friend Melinda said, "Boy, what a phony—I wouldn't trust that guy with my dirty laundry, let alone the nation. No wonder they call him Slick Willie!" The others quickly chimed in, voicing their agreement. Sally felt uncomfortable, and was frankly puzzled. Finally, she mumbled, "Yeah, I guess he did come off as a bit insincere."

What do you suppose was going on in Sally's mind?

3. We have a friend whom we will call Charlie. Charlie is a middle-aged executive in a computer software company. Many years ago, Charlie attended a large state university in the Midwest, where he was a member of a fraternity we will call Delta Nu. He remembers going through quite a severe and dangerous hazing ritual in order to become a member, but believes it was well worth it. Although he was terribly frightened by the hazing, he loved his fraternity brothers and was proud to be a member of Delta Nu—easily the best of all fraternities. A few years ago, his son, Sam, was about to enroll in the same university; naturally, Charlie urged Sam to pledge Delta Nu: "It's a great fraternity—always attracts a wonderful bunch of fellows. You'll really love it." Sam did in fact pledge Delta Nu and was accepted. Charlie was relieved to learn that Sam was not required to undergo a severe initiation in order to become a member; times had changed, and hazing was now forbidden. When Sam came home for Christmas break, Charlie asked him how he liked the fraternity. "It's all right, I guess," he said, "but most of my friends are outside the fraternity." Charlie was astonished.

How is it that Charlie had been so enamored of his fraternity brothers and Sam wasn't? Had the standards of old Delta Nu slipped? Was the fraternity now admitting a less desirable group of young men than in Charlie's day? Or was it just one of those inexplicable things? What do you think?

4. In the mid-1970s, several hundred members of the Peoples Temple, a California-based religious cult, emigrated to Guyana under the guidance of their leader, the Reverend Jim Jones. Their aim was to form a model interracial community, called Jonestown, based on "love, hard work, and spiritual enlightenment." In November 1978, Congressman Leo Ryan of California flew to Jonestown to investigate reports that some of the members were being held against their will. He visited the commune and found that several residents wanted to return with him to the United States. Rev. Jones agreed they could leave, but as Ryan was boarding a plane, he and several other members of his party were shot and killed by a member of the Peoples Temple, apparently on Jones's orders. On hearing that several members of Ryan's party had escaped, Jones grew despondent and began to speak over the public address system about the beauty of dying and the certainty that everyone would meet again in another place. The residents lined up at a pavilion in front of a vat

containing a mixture of Kool-Aid and cyanide. According to a survivor, almost all of the residents drank willingly of the deadly solution. At least 80 babies and infants were given the poison by their parents, who then drank it themselves. More than 800 people died, including Rev. Jones.

How is it that people can agree to kill themselves and their own children? Were they crazy? Were they under some kind of hypnotic spell? How would you explain it?

Why did the Los Angeles residents ignore the screams coming from the yellow house, when they might have averted a tragedy? Why did Sally change her opinion about the sincerity of the new president and bring it into line with her acquaintances' opinion? Why did Charlie like his frat brothers so much more than Sam did? And how could large numbers of people be induced to kill their own children and themselves in Jonestown? In this chapter, we will consider what these examples have in common and why they are of interest to social psychologists.

## What Is Social Psychology?

Social psychology is about what goes on in the hearts and minds of human beings. Although our examples differ widely, they have one thing in common: the phenomenon called social influence. In one way or another, people's thoughts, feelings, or behaviors were influenced by other people. This is the central topic of **social psychology**, which we can define as the scientific study of the way in which people's thoughts, feelings, and behaviors are influenced by the real or imagined presence of other people (Allport, 1985). But exactly what do we mean by influenced? The kinds of examples that probably first come to mind are direct attempts at persuasion, whereby one person deliberately tries to change someone else's behavior. This is what happens in an advertising campaign, when sophisticated techniques are employed to get us to buy a particular brand of toothpaste or laundry detergent, or just prior to an election, when similar techniques are used to get us to vote for a particular political candidate. Direct attempts at persuasion also occur when our friends try to get us to do something we don't really want to do ("Come on, have another shot of bourbon—everyone is doing it!"), or when the school yard bully uses force or threats to get smaller, less aggressive kids to part with their lunch money or homework.

These direct social influence attempts form a major part of social psychology and will be discussed in our later chapters on conformity, attitudes, and group processes. To the social psychologist, however, social influence is broader than attempts by one person to change another person's behavior. First, not only our behavior but also our thoughts and feelings are influenced by others. Second, social influence takes on many forms other than deliberate attempts by others to modify our behavior. As noted earlier, people are often influenced by the imagined or implied presence of others.

Even when we are not in the physical presence of other people, we are still influenced by them; thus, in a sense we carry our mothers, fathers, friends, and teachers around with us, as we attempt to make decisions that would make them proud of us. On a still subtler level, each of us is immersed in a social and cultural context. Social psychologists are interested in studying how and why our thoughts, feelings, and behaviors are shaped by the entire social environment—broadly defined—and what happens when

**social psychology:** the scientific study of the way in which people's thoughts, feelings, and behaviors are influenced by the real or imagined presence of other people

We are by all odds the most persistently and obsessively social of all species, more dependent on each other than the famous social insects, and really, when you look at us, infinitely more imaginative and deft at social living.
—Lewis Thomas,
*The Medusa and the Snail*

one of these influences comes into conflict with another. For example, when young people go to college, most of them occasionally find themselves in conflict between the beliefs and values they learned at home and the beliefs and values being expressed by their professors or peers. When this occurs, how do you handle it?

As we will see in a moment, other disciplines, like anthropology and sociology, are also interested in how people are influenced by their social environment. Social psychology is distinct, however, in several respects. First, it is concerned not with social situations in any objective sense, but with how people are influenced by their interpretation, or **construal,** of the social environment. This means that to understand how a person is influenced by the social environment, social psychologists insist that it is more important to understand how that person perceives, comprehends, or interprets the environment than it is to understand the objective environment (Lewin, 1943).

**construal:** the way in which people perceive, comprehend, and interpret the social world

Suppose, for example, that Jason is a shy high school student who admires Debbie from afar. As a budding social psychologist, it is your job to predict whether or not Jason will ask Debbie to the senior prom. One way you might do this is to observe Debbie's objective behavior toward Jason. Does she pay attention to him and smile a lot? If so, the casual observer might decide that Jason will ask her out. As a social psychologist, however, you are more interested in viewing Debbie's behavior through Jason's eyes— that is, in seeing how Jason interprets Debbie's behavior. If she smiles at him, does he construe this as mere politeness, the kind of politeness she would extend to any nerd? Or does he view her smile as an encouraging sign, one that inspires him to gather the courage to ask her out? If she ignores him, does Jason figure that she's playing "hard to get"? Or does he take it as a sign that she's not interested in dating him? To predict Jason's behavior, it is not enough to know the details of Debbie's behavior; it is imperative to know how Jason interprets Debbie's behavior.

Given the importance placed on the way people interpret the social world, social psychologists pay special attention to the origins of these interpretations. For example, when construing their environment, are most people concerned with making an interpretation that places them in the most positive light (e.g., Jason believing "Debbie is going to the prom with Eric because she is trying to make me jealous"), or with making the most accurate interpretation, even if it is unflattering (e.g., "Painful as it may be, I must admit that Debbie would rather go to the prom with a sea slug than with me")? A great deal of research in social psychology has addressed these and other determinants of people's thoughts and behaviors. We will expand on these determinants later in this chapter.

Another distinctive feature of social psychology is that it is a science that tests its assumptions, guesses, and ideas about human social behavior empirically, rather than by relying on folk wisdom, common sense, or an appeal to the opinions and insights of philosophers, novelists, political pundits, grandmothers, and others wise in the ways of human beings. Most students, when they think of an experimental science, think of the natural sciences, such as biology and chemistry—of men and women in white lab coats dissecting frogs or mixing chemicals in a beaker. The idea of social psychologists conducting carefully designed and well-controlled experiments on the behavior of human beings does not immediately conjure up available images. Yet in a very real sense, social psychology is no less an

Drawing by Handelsman; ©1991 The New Yorker Magazine, Inc.

To social psychologists, objective reality is less important than understanding how people *construe* (i.e., perceive or interpret) reality.

*"The problem is to get rid of the perception that we receive perks but not get rid of the perks."*

experimental science than biology or chemistry. But because, as experimenters, we social psychologists are trying to predict the behavior of highly complex, sophisticated organisms, we are faced with a special array of challenges as we attempt to find answers to important questions—such as what causes aggression, prejudice, and attraction, or why certain kinds of political ads work better than others. How experimental social psychologists respond to these challenges will be illustrated throughout this book, and discussed in detail in Chapter 2.

We will spend most of this introductory chapter expanding on the issues raised in the above paragraphs—of what social psychology is and how it is distinct from other, related disciplines. A good place to begin is with what social psychology is not.

## Social Psychology Compared to Folk Wisdom and Philosophy

Let's take another look at the examples at the beginning of this chapter. Why did people behave the way they did? One way to answer this question might be simply to ask them. We could question the residents in Los Angeles about why they didn't call the police, and ask Sally why she changed her opinion of Bill Clinton. The problem with this approach is that people are not always aware of the origins of their own responses (Nisbett & Wilson, 1977). For example, it is very unlikely that the neighbors know exactly why they went back to sleep without calling the police.

**Folk Wisdom.**   Alternatively, we might rely on the wisdom of the ages and sages. Philosophers, social critics, and novelists might have a great many interesting things to say about these situations, and if they do not, our grandmothers probably do. Such wisdom is generally referred to as common sense. For example, when people fail to intervene in an emergency to help their fellow humans, as in the case of the Los Angeles residents who ignored the cries for help from the yellow house, common sense tells us that these people must have some flaw in their personalities—surely a normal, caring human being would take the small step of calling the police. Similarly, the mass suicide at Jonestown received considerable media attention, and explanations of it ranged from an analysis of the so-called diabolic, messianic personal power of Jim Jones to speculation that the people who were attracted to his cult must have been disturbed, self-destructive individuals. History has a tendency to repeat itself. As we write these words, a similar array of theories is emerging from the conflagration in Waco, Texas, where some eighty-six members of an apocalyptic cult known as the Branch Davidians apparently took their own lives and the lives of their children. Then as now, these speculations are almost certainly incorrect—or, at the very least, oversimplified.

Don't get us wrong. We are convinced that a great deal can be learned about social behavior from philosophers, social critics, novelists, and grandmothers—and in this book, we will quote liberally from all these sources (except our grandmothers). There is, however, at least one problem with relying on such sources: More often than not, they disagree with one another, and there is no easy way of determining which of them is correct. Consider what folk wisdom has to say about the factors that influence how much we like other people: On the one hand, we know that "birds of a feather flock together," and we can probably all think of cases where, indeed, we liked and hung around with people who shared our backgrounds and interests. But then again, sometimes opposites attract. Which is it?

Similarly, are we to believe that "out of sight is out of mind," or that "absence makes the heart grow fonder," that "haste makes waste," or that "he who hesitates is lost"? And who is to say whether the Jonestown massacre occurred because (a) Rev. Jones succeeded in attracting the kinds of people who were psychologically depressed to begin with; (b) only people with self-destructive tendencies join cults; (c) Jones was such a powerful, messianic, charismatic figure that virtually anyone—even strong, nondepressed individuals like you or us—would have succumbed to his influence; (d) people cut off from society are particularly vulnerable to social influence; (e) all of the above; or (f) none of the above?

**Philosophy.**   Instead of relying on folk wisdom and adages, perhaps we should turn to philosophers and other great thinkers to answer questions about human nature and the effects of social influence. Throughout the history of psychology, philosophy has been a source of vast insight about human nature. Today there are many exciting examples of philosophers joining with psychologists to tackle such important psychological questions as what the nature of consciousness is (e.g., Dennett, 1991) and how people form beliefs about the social world (e.g., Gilbert, 1991). Sometimes, however, even great thinkers disagree, and it can be difficult to know who is right.

To find out, social psychologists address many of the same questions as philosophers and purveyors of folk wisdom do, but we attempt to do so scientifically. Just as a physicist performs experiments to test hypotheses about the nature of the physical world, the social psychologist performs experiments to test hypotheses about the nature of the social world. The major reason we have conflicting folk aphorisms about the kinds of people we like and the relationship between absence and liking is almost certainly that there are some conditions under which birds of a feather do flock together and others under which opposites do attract; similarly, there are some conditions under which absence does make the heart grow fonder and others under which out of sight does mean out of mind. So both can be true. Good enough? Not really, for if you really want to understand human behavior, knowing that both can be true is not sufficient. One of the tasks of the social psychologist is to design experiments sophisticated enough to demonstrate the specific situations under which one or the other applies. This enriches our understanding of human nature and allows us to make accurate predictions once we know the key aspects of the prevailing situation. In Chapter 2, we will discuss in more detail the scientific methods social psychologists use.

## Social Psychology Compared to Other Social Sciences

Social psychology's interest in social behavior is shared by several other disciplines in the social sciences, including sociology, economics, and political science. Each of these disciplines is concerned with the influence of social and societal factors on human behavior. There are important differences, however, between social psychology and the other social sciences, most notably in their level of analysis. Social psychology is a branch of psychology, and as such is rooted in an interest in individual human beings, with an emphasis on the psychological processes going on in their hearts and minds. For example, to understand why people intentionally hurt one another, the social psychologist focuses on the psychological processes that trigger aggression. To what extent is aggression preceded by a state of frustration? Is frustration necessary? If people are feeling frustrated, under what conditions will they vent their frustration with an overt, aggressive act? What factors might preclude an aggressive response by a frustrated individual? Besides frustration, what other factors might cause aggression? (We will address these questions in Chapter 12.)

Other social sciences are more concerned with broad societal, economic, political, and historical factors that influence human behavior. Sociology, for example, is concerned with such topics as social class, social structure, and social institutions. It goes without saying that, because society is made up of collections of people, some overlap is bound to exist between the domains of sociology and those of social psychology. The major difference is this: Sociology, rather than focusing on the psychology of the individual, tends toward a more macro focus—that of society at large. Although sociologists, like social psychologists, are interested in aggressive behavior, sociologists are more likely to be concerned with why a particular society produces different levels and types of aggression in its members. Why, for example, is the murder rate in America so much higher than in Canada? Within America, why is the murder rate higher in some social classes than in others? How do changes in society relate to changes in aggressive behavior?

The difference between social psychology and other social sciences in level of analysis reflects another difference between the disciplines—namely, in what they are trying to explain. The goal of social psychology is to identify universal properties of human nature that make everyone—regardless of social class or culture—susceptible to social influence. The laws governing the relationship between frustration and aggression, for example, are hypothesized to be true of most people in most places, not just members of one social class, age-group, or race. Social psychology is a young science that, until recently, has developed mostly in the United States; thus, many of its findings have not yet been tested in other cultures to see if they are indeed universal. Nonetheless, the goal of most social psychologists is to come up with such laws. And increasingly, as methods and theories developed by American social psychologists are adopted by European, Asian, African, Middle Eastern, and South American social psychologists, we are learning more about the extent to which these laws are universal. We will encounter several examples of such cross-cultural research in subsequent chapters.

## Social Psychology Compared to Personality Psychology

Within the field of psychology are other disciplines that, like social psychology, are interested in studying individuals and why they do what they do; paramount among these is personality psychology. Because personality psychology and social psychology have so much in common, it might be helpful if we try to specify how social psychology and personality psychology differ in their approach and concerns.

If you are like most people, when you read the examples presented at the beginning of this chapter and began to think about how those events might have come about, your first thoughts were about the strengths, weaknesses, flaws, and quirks of the personalities of the individuals involved. When people behave in interesting or unusual ways, it is natural to try to pinpoint what aspects of their personalities led them to respond as they did. Why did the Los Angeles residents fail to call the police when they heard the cries for help? Most of us tend to assume that they possessed some personality flaw or quirk that made them reluctant to respond. What might these be? Some people are leaders and others are followers; some people are bold and others are timid; some people are public-spirited and others are selfish. That's the way it goes. Think back: How did you answer the question about whether you would want any of these people as a friend or a babysitter?

**individual differences:** the aspects of people's personalities that make them different from other people

Personality psychologists generally focus their attention on **individual differences** as explanations of social behavior. For example, to explain why the people at Jonestown ended their own lives and those of their children by drinking poison, it seems natural to point to their personalities. Perhaps they were all "conformist types" or weak-willed; maybe they were even psychotic. Social psychologists believe that, whereas this approach adds something to our understanding of human behavior, to attempt to explain behavior primarily in terms of personality factors leads to a serious underestimation of the role played by a principal source of human behavior—social influence. In this context, it is important to bear in mind that it was not just a handful of people who committed suicide at Jonestown, but almost 100 percent of the people in the village. It is conceivable that they were all psychotic, but this is highly improbable. More likely, we need to understand the power and influence of a charismatic figure like Jim Jones, and what it is about people in general that makes them susceptible to such influence (see Figure 1.1).

| Sociology | Social Psychology | Personality Psychology |
|---|---|---|
| Provides general laws and theories about societies, not individuals. | Studies the psychological processes people have in common with one another that make them susceptible to social influence. | Studies the characteristics that make individuals unique and different from one another. |

**FIGURE 1.1 Social psychology compared to related disciplines.**

These two different approaches can perhaps be best illustrated by focusing on a more mundane example. Suppose you stop at a roadside restaurant for a cup of coffee and a piece of pie. The waitress comes over to take your order, but you are having a hard time deciding which kind of pie to order. While you are hesitating, the waitress impatiently taps her pen against her order book, rolls her eyes toward the ceiling, scowls at you, and finally snaps, "Hey, I haven't got all day, you know!"

What do you conclude about this event? When faced with such a situation, most people would conclude that the waitress is a nasty or unpleasant person. But suppose we were to tell you that she is a single parent and was kept awake all night by the moaning of her youngest child, who has a painful terminal illness; that her car broke down on her way to work and she has no idea where she will find the money to have it repaired; that when she finally arrived at the restaurant, she learned that her co-worker was too drunk to work, requiring her to cover twice the usual number of tables; and that the short order cook keeps screaming at her because she is not picking up the orders fast enough to please him. Given all of that information, you might want to revise your judgment and conclude that she is not necessarily a nasty person—just an ordinary person under enormous stress. But the fact remains that, when trying to account for a person's behavior in a complex situation, the overwhelming majority of people will jump to the conclusion that it had a lot to do with the personality of the individual involved. And this fact— that we often fail to take the situation into account—is important to a social psychologist, for it has a profound impact on how human beings relate to one another. Specifically, the way you relate to the waitress is bound to be affected by how you interpret her behavior toward you.

In sum, to explain social behavior, social psychology is located between its closest cousins, sociology and personality psychology. It shares with sociology an interest in situational and societal influences on behavior, but focuses more on the psychological makeup of individuals that renders people susceptible to social influence. It shares with personality psychology an emphasis on the psychology of the individual, but rather than focusing on what makes people different from one another, it emphasizes the psychological processes shared by most people that make them susceptible to social influence.

Such an approach is only interesting, of course, to the extent that social influences actually do affect people's behavior in significant ways. If everyone went on his or her merry way, uninfluenced by what other people were doing or thinking, then we would not need a science called social psychology to understand human behavior. It is clear, however, that people are influenced by each other. Nonetheless, the power and extent of this influence are not always obvious to the naked eye—as we shall see.

## The Power of Social Influence

When trying to convince people that their behavior is greatly influenced by the social environment, the social psychologist is up against a formidable barrier: the inclination we all have for explaining people's behavior in terms of their personalities (as in the case of the waitress discussed above). This barrier has been discussed by several social psychologists, most notably Fritz Heider (1958), E. E. Jones (1979), and Lee Ross (1977). Ross refers to it as the **fundamental attribution error,** or the tendency to explain our own and other people's behavior entirely in terms of personality traits, thereby underestimating the power of social influence.

Because of this tendency to overlook the power of social influence, as authors of this book, we are fully aware that we face an uphill battle. If you are like most people, when you first encounter the examples of social behavior your initial tendency will be to explain that behavior in terms of the personalities of the people involved. All we ask is that, while reading this book, you try to suspend judgment for a short time, and consider the possibility that to understand why people do what they do, it is important to look closely at the nature of the social situation.

Why do people tend to underestimate the power of social influence? There are a great many reasons; we will consider them in detail in Chapter 5. For now, it is important to point out that this tendency constitutes a bias that could lead to dysfunctional attitudes and behaviors; accordingly, it is a bias we should try to overcome. One of the major problems with this bias is that it produces a sense of false security. In a very real sense, by systematically underestimating the power of social influence we increase the risk of succumbing to it. For example, when trying to explain why people do repugnant or bizarre things, such as the people at Jonestown and Waco taking their own lives and those of their children, it is both tempting and comforting to write off the victims as flawed human beings. This gives the rest of us the feeling that it could never happen to us—thus increasing our personal vulnerability to social influence. Moreover, by failing to fully appreciate the power of the situation, we tend to oversimplify complex situations; oversimplification decreases our understanding of the causes of a great deal of human behavior. Among other things, this oversimplification can lead us to blame the victim, as in the Jonestown tragedy, in situations where the individual was overpowered by social forces that were difficult to resist.

Here is an example of the kind of oversimplification we are talking about. Suppose we described to you a situation in which people are playing a two-person game called the Prisoner's Dilemma. In this game, people can choose one of two strategies: They can play *competitively*, where they try to win as much money as possible and make sure their partner loses as much as possible, or they can play *cooperatively*, where they try to make sure that

**fundamental attribution error:** the tendency to overestimate the extent to which people's behavior is due to internal, dispositional factors, and to underestimate the role of situational factors

The head monkey at Paris puts on a traveller's cap, and all the monkeys in America do the same.
    –Henry David Thoreau,
    *Walden,* 1854

We often assume that people behave in unusual ways because of the nature of their personalities. Often, however, such behaviors are caused by powerful social influences. In the movie *Trading Places*, a character played by Dan Aykroyd was extremely wealthy, comfortable, and normal—until he became caught in a web of social influences that changed his life dramatically.

both they and their partner win some money. We will discuss the details of this game in Chapter 9. For now, it is important to note only that there are these two basic strategies people can use when playing the game: competition or cooperation. Now think about some of your friends. How do you think they would play this game?

Few people find this question hard to answer; we all have a feeling for the relative competitiveness of our friends. "Well," you might say, "I am certain that my friend Bob, who is a cutthroat business major, would play this game more competitively than my friend Karen, who is a really caring, loving person." That is, we think of our friends' personalities, and answer accordingly. We usually do not think much about the nature of the social situation when making our predictions. But how accurate are such predictions? Should we think about the social situation?

To find out, Steven Samuels and Lee Ross (1993) conducted the following experiment. First, they chose a group of students at Stanford University who were considered, by the resident assistants in their dorm, to be either especially cooperative or especially competitive. They did this by describing the Prisoner's Dilemma game to the resident assistants and asking them to think of students in their dormitories who would be most likely to adopt the competitive or cooperative strategy. As expected, the resident assistants had no trouble thinking of students who fit each category.

Next, Samuels and Ross invited these students to play the Prisoner's Dilemma game in a psychology experiment. There was one added twist: The researchers varied a seemingly minor aspect of the social situation—namely,

Why would any reasonable person blindly follow someone claiming to be Jesus Christ, give up personal freedoms, allow the leader to take liberties with his spouse, and dictate which personal relationships will continue? While it may be easy to dismiss the followers of a cult leader like David Koresh as foolish, such oversimplification and denial of the power of social influence can lead us to blame the victims.

what the game was called. They told half the participants that the name of the game was the "Wall Street Game," and half that it was the "Community Game." Everything else about the game was identical. Thus, people who were judged as either competitive or cooperative played a game that was called either the Wall Street or the Community game, resulting in four conditions. What do you think happened? How would your friends play this game?

Again, most of us go through life assuming that what really counts is an individual's personality—not something so trivial as what a game is called. Some people seem competitive by nature, and would thus relish the opportunity to go head to head with a fellow student. Others seem much more cooperative, and would thus achieve the most satisfaction by making sure that no one lost too much money and that no one's feelings were hurt. Right? Not so fast! As seen in Figure 1.2, even so trivial an aspect of the situation as the name of the game made a tremendous difference in how people behaved. When it was called the Wall Street Game, approximately two-thirds of the people responded competitively, whereas when it was called the Community

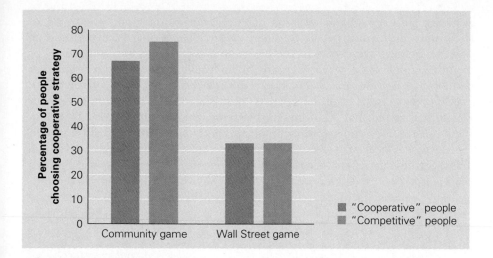

**FIGURE 1.2 What influences how cooperative people will be—their personalities or the nature of the social situation?** Samuels and Ross (1993) found that college students' personalities, as rated by the resident assistants in their dormitories, did not determine how cooperative or competitive they were in a laboratory game. The label of the game—whether it was called the Community Game or the Wall Street Game—did, however, make a tremendous difference. Such seemingly minor aspects of the social situation can have powerful effects on people's behavior, overwhelming the differences in their personalities. (Adapted from Samuels & Ross, 1993)

Game, only a third of the people responded competitively. The name of the game conveyed strong social norms about what kind of behavior was appropriate in this situation, and as we will see in Chapter 7, social norms can shape people's behaviors in powerful ways.

In this situation, a student's personality made no measurable difference in how he or she behaved. The students labeled "competitive" were no more likely to adopt the competitive strategy than the so-called "cooperative" students. This pattern of results is one we will encounter frequently in this book: Seemingly minor aspects of the social situation can have powerful effects, overwhelming the differences in people's personalities. This is not to say that personality differences do not exist or are unimportant; they do exist and frequently are of great importance. But we have learned that certain social and environmental situations are so powerful that they have dramatic effects on almost everyone. And this is the domain of the social psychologist.

## The Power of Subjective Situations: A Brief History of an Idea

To summarize, social situations often have surprising and profound effects on human behavior. But what exactly do we mean by social situations? One strategy would be to try to specify the objective properties of the situation, such as how rewarding it is to people, and then document the behaviors that follow from these objective properties.

**Behaviorism.** This was the approach taken by **behaviorism,** a school of thought that dominated American psychology in the first half of this century.

**behaviorism:** a school of psychology maintaining that to understand human behavior, one need only consider the reinforcing properties of the environment—that is, how positive and negative events in the environment are associated with specific behaviors

Behaviorism grew out of research on the lower animals and attempted to show that all learning occurs through *reinforcement*—that is, by associating positive or negative events in the environment with specific behaviors. For example, dogs come when they are called because they have learned that compliance is followed by positive reinforcement (e.g., food or fondling). Psychologists in this tradition, such as John Watson (1924) and B. F. Skinner (1938), suggested that all of human behavior could be understood by examining the rewards and punishments in the organism's environment and that there was no need to study such subjective states as thinking and feeling. Thus, to understand the behavior of the Los Angeles residents who ignored their neighbors' predawn cries for help, a behaviorist would analyze the situation to see what factors were inhibiting any attempts to help. Concepts and terms like *cognition*, *thinking*, and *feeling* were not used by behaviorists, because these were considered too vague and mentalistic and were not directly anchored to observable behavior.

Most contemporary social psychologists (like the authors of this book) have come to believe that, while the behaviorist approach has some merit, it is far too simplistic to provide a complete, accurate understanding of social behavior. Moreover, we have learned that, with a certain degree of ingenuity and attention to detail, it is possible for a scientist to be objective and precise even while working with so-called mentalistic concepts like cognition, thinking, and feeling.

In addition, we have learned that social behavior cannot be fully understood by confining our observations to the physical properties of a situation. Instead, we must look at the situation from the viewpoint of the people in it, to see how they construe the world around them (Griffin & Ross, 1991; Ross & Nisbett, 1991). As you know, by construe we mean not what is objectively out there, but what human beings make of what's out there. For example, if a person approaches us, slaps us on the back, and asks us how we are feeling, we might construe the meaning differently, depending on whether the question is asked by a close friend of ours who is deeply concerned that we might be working too hard, a casual acquaintance simply passing the time of day, or an automobile salesperson intending to sell us a used car—even if the question is worded the same and asked in the same tone of voice. It is unlikely that, responding to the salesperson's question, we will begin a detailed description of the pains we've been having in our kidney.

**Gestalt Psychology.**  This emphasis we place on construal has its roots in an approach called **Gestalt psychology.** Initially proposed as a theory of how people perceive the physical word, Gestalt psychology holds that we should study the subjective way in which an object appears in people's minds (the gestalt, or whole), rather than how the objective, physical attributes of the object combine. For example, one way to try to understand how people perceive a painting would be to break it down into its individual elements, such as the exact amounts of primary colors applied to the different parts of the canvas, the types of brush strokes used to apply the colors, and the different geometric shapes they formed, and to attempt to determine how these elements are combined by the perceiver to form an overall image of the painting. According to Gestalt psychologists, however, it is impossible to understand the way in which an object is perceived simply by studying these building blocks of perception. The whole is different from the sum of its

**Gestalt psychology:** a school of psychology stressing the importance of studying the subjective way in which an object appears in people's minds, rather than the objective, physical attributes of the object parts. One must focus on the phenomenology of the perceiver—that is, on how an object appears to people—instead of on the individual elements of the objective stimulus.

The Gestalt approach was formulated in Germany in the first part of this century by Kurt Koffka, Wolfgang Kohler, Max Wertheimer, and their students and colleagues. In the late 1930s, several of these psychologists immigrated to the United States to escape the Nazi regime, and had a major impact on American psychology. Their influence was so large that it prompted at least one astute observer to remark, "If I were required to name the one person who has had the greatest impact on the field, it would have to be Adolf Hitler" (Cartwright, 1979, p. 84).

Among these émigrés was Kurt Lewin, who took the bold step of applying Gestalt principles beyond the perception of objects to social perception—how people perceive other people and their motives, intentions, and behaviors. Lewin was the first scientist to fully realize the importance of taking the perspective of the people in any social situation to see how they construe (e.g., perceive, interpret, distort) this social environment. Social psychologists soon began to focus on the importance of considering subjective situations (how they are construed by people). These early social psychologists and their key statements are presented on the following pages.

Such construals can be rather simple, as in the example of the question "How are you feeling?" discussed earlier. They can also be remarkably complex. For example, suppose that Mary gives John a kiss on the cheek at the end of their first date. How will John respond to the kiss? We would say that it depends on how he construes the situation: Does he interpret it as a first step—a sign of awakening romantic interest on Mary's part? Or does he see it as an aloof, sisterly expression—a signal that Mary wants to be friends but nothing more? Or does he see it as a sign that Mary is interested in him, but wants things to go slowly in their developing relationship? Were John to misconstrue the situation, he might commit a serious blunder; he might turn his back on what could have been the love of his life—or he might express passion inappropriately. In either case, we believe that the best strategy for understanding John's reaction would be to find a way to determine John's construal of Mary's behavior, rather than to dissect the objective nature of the kiss itself (its length, degree of pressure, etc.). But how are these construals formed? Stay tuned!

## Where Construals Come From: Basic Human Motives

How will John determine why Mary kissed him? If it is true that subjective and not objective situations influence people, then we need to understand how people arrive at their subjective impressions of the world. What are people trying to accomplish when they interpret the social world? Again, we could address this question from the perspective of people's personalities. What is it about John, including his upbringing, family background, and unique experiences, that makes him view the world the way he does? As we have seen, such a focus on individual differences in people's personalities, while valuable, misses what is usually of far greater importance: the effects of

**Early social psychologists emphasized that to predict social behavior, you have to consider how people construe (interpret, perceive) the social world.**

*Theodore Newcomb:* "It seems to me to be a truism that no interpersonal behavior can be understood without a knowledge of how the relationship is perceived by the persons involved." (1947)

*Kurt Lewin:* "If an individual sits in a room trusting that the ceiling will not come down, should only his 'subjective probability' be taken into account for predicting behavior or should we also consider the 'objective probability' of the ceiling's coming down as determined by engineers? To my mind, only the first has to be taken into account." (1943)

*Solomon Asch:* "It is not possible, as a rule, to conduct investigations in social psychology without including a reference to the experience of persons." (1959)

*Muzafer Sherif* and *Carolyn Sherif:* "What an individual does . . . is not independent of the way in which he perceives the situation, appraises it, what he remembers at the time." (1969)

*Fritz Heider:* "Generally, a person reacts to what he thinks the other person is perceiving, feeling, and thinking, in addition to what the other person may be doing." (1958)

*Leon Festinger:* "The way I have always thought about it is that if the empirical world looks complicated, if people seem to react in bewilderingly different ways to similar forces, and if I cannot see the operation of universal underlying dynamics—then that is my fault. I have asked the wrong questions; I have, at the theoretical level, sliced up the world incorrectly. The underlying dynamics are there, and I have to find the theoretical apparatus that will enable me to reveal these uniformities." A highly influential social psychologist, Leon Festinger was part of a seminal group of people who founded modern social psychology in the 1950s. In reminiscing about this period, he discussed why social psychology has placed less emphasis on individual differences in people's personalities than on what people have in common—the "universal underlying dynamics" to which he refers—that explains how they construe the social world.

the social situation on people. And to understand these effects, we need to understand the fundamental laws of human nature, common to all, that explain why we construe the social world the way we do.

We humans are complex organisms; at a given moment, myriad intersecting motives underlie our thoughts and behaviors. Over the years, social psychologists have found that two of these motives are of primary importance: the need to be as accurate as possible and the need to justify our thoughts and actions in order to feel good about ourselves.

As we go through life, much of the time each of these motives pulls us in the same direction. For example, suppose our parent's anniversary is coming up and we want to get them the perfect gift. If they are very different kinds of people with different interests and hobbies, getting the perfect gift—one that will delight both of them—requires a great deal of thought and sensitivity to a variety of subtle social cues. If we can achieve this, we not only will have seen the social world accurately, but also will feel competent and good about ourselves. Often, however, we find ourselves in situations where these two motives tug us in opposite directions—where to see reality closely is to come to terms with the fact that we have behaved foolishly or immorally.

Leon Festinger, one of our most innovative researchers, was quick to realize that it is precisely when these two motives tug an individual in opposite directions that we social psychologists can gain our most valuable insights into the workings of the human mind. For example, imagine that you are the president of the United States and your country is engaged in a difficult and costly war in Southeast Asia. You have poured hundreds of billions of dollars into that war, and it has consumed tens of thousands of American lives as well as a great many more lives of innocent Vietnamese civilians. The war seems to be at a stalemate; there is no end in sight. You frequently wake up in the middle of the night bathed in the cold sweat of conflict: On the one hand, you deplore all the carnage that is going on; at the same time, you don't want to go down in history as the first American president to lose a war.

Social psychology focuses on how even intelligent and powerful individuals can make a grievous error when faced with conflicting advice on a monumental decision.

**self-esteem:** people's evaluations of their own self-worth—that is, the extent to which they view themselves as good, competent, and decent

Some of your advisers tell you that they can see the light at the end of the tunnel—that if you intensify the bombing, the enemy will soon capitulate and the war will be over. This would be a great outcome for you; not only will you have succeeded in achieving your military and political aims, but history will consider you to have been a hero. Other advisers, however, believe that intensifying the bombing will result only in strengthening the enemy's resolve; they advise you to sue for peace.

Which advisers are you likely to believe? As we shall see in Chapter 3, President Lyndon Johnson was faced with exactly this dilemma. Not surprisingly, he chose to believe those advisers who suggested that he escalate the war, for if he could succeed in winning the war, it would justify his prior behavior as commander in chief, whereas if he withdrew from Vietnam, he would not only go down in history as the first president to lose a war, but would also have to justify the fact that all those lives and all that money had been spent in vain. This advice, however, proved to be erroneous. Increasing the bombing served only to strengthen the enemy's resolve, thereby needlessly prolonging the war. As this example illustrates, the need for self-justification can fly in the face of the need to be accurate—and can have catastrophic consequences.

Most social psychologists agree that both of these motives are important, and that, in many situations, they can apply with varying degrees of strength. But each has a unique and interesting set of ramifications that is worth considering separately. Let's examine each of these two motives in more detail.

### The Self-Esteem Approach: The Desire to Feel Good About Ourselves

Most people have a strong need to view themselves as decent, competent, likable, honorable human beings. The reason people view the world the way they do can often be traced to this underlying need to maintain a favorable image of themselves, or, in other words, to maintain high **self-esteem** (Aronson, 1992; Baumeister, 1993; Kunda, 1990; Pyszczynski & Greenberg, 1987; Thibodeau & Aronson, 1992). Given the choice between distorting the world in order to feel good about themselves and representing the world accurately, people often take the first option.

**Justifying Past Behavior.** For example, a recently divorced man might blame the breakup of his marriage on the fact that his ex-wife was not sufficiently responsive or attentive to his needs, rather than admitting the truth: that his jealousy and overpossessiveness drove her away. His interpretation makes him feel better about himself—it is very difficult to own up to major deficiencies in ourselves, even when the cost is seeing the world inaccurately. The consequence of this distortion, of course, is that it decreases the probability of his learning from his experience; that is, in his next marriage he is apt to run into the same problems.

We do not mean to imply that people totally distort reality, denying the existence of all information that reflects badly on them; such extreme behavior is rare outside of mental institutions. Yet it is often possible for normal people like you and us to put a slightly different spin on the existing facts, one that puts us in the best possible light. Consider Roger—the guy whose shoes are almost always untied and who frequently has coffee stains on the front of his shirt or mustard stains around his lips. Most observers might consider Roger to be a slob, but Roger might see himself as casual and noncompulsive. Or, if Heather is playing basketball and has missed six or seven easy lay-ups in succession, her teammates might consider her to be untalented and might begin to think twice about passing the ball to her; on the other hand, Heather might simply feel that she hasn't yet gotten into her rhythm.

The fact that people distort things to make themselves feel better is pretty obvious, known to any casual observer of human behavior. The ways in which this motive operates, however, are often startling—and shed a great deal of light on behavior that would otherwise be mystifying.

**Suffering and Self-Justification.**   Let's go back to one of our early scenarios—the case of Charlie and his son Sam. Why was Sam less enamored of his fraternity brothers than Charlie had been when he was in college? You will recall that Charlie was quick to form the hypothesis that perhaps his fraternity was not attracting the kinds of wonderful people who were there when he was in college. This might be true. But we would assert that one powerful reason might have something to do with the hazing. Specifically, we would contend that a major factor that increased Charlie's liking for his fraternity brothers was due in part to the unpleasant hazing ritual he underwent, a ritual Sam was able to avoid. That sounds a little strange. Why would something so unpleasant cause Charlie to like his fraternity? Didn't behavioristic psychology teach us that rewards, not punishments, make us like things associated with them? Quite so. But as we indicated earlier, in recent years social psychologists have discovered that this formulation is far too simplistic to account for human thinking and motivation. Unlike rats and pigeons, human beings have a need to justify their past behavior, and this need leads them to thoughts, feelings, and behaviors that don't always fit into the neat categories of the behaviorist.

Here's how it works. If Charlie goes through a severe hazing in order to become a member of the fraternity but later discovers things about his fraternity brothers that are unpleasant, he will feel like a fool: "Why did I go through all that pain and embarrassment in order to live in a house with a bunch of jerks? Only a moron would do a thing like that." In order to avoid feeling like a fool, he will try to justify his decision to undergo the hazing by distorting his interpretation of his fraternity experience. That is, he will try to put a positive spin on his experiences.

Suppose that, having gone through all that hazing, Charlie moves into the fraternity house and begins to experience things that, to an outside observer, are not very positive: The fraternity dues make a significant dent in Charlie's budget; the frequent parties take a toll on the amount of studying he can do, and consequently his grades begin to suffer; most of the meals served in the house are only a small step up from dog chow. While an unmotivated observer (someone who didn't go through the hazing) might consider these experiences to be extremely negative, Charlie is motivated to see them differently; indeed, he considers them to be a small price to pay for the sense of brotherhood he feels toward his fraternity brothers. He focuses on the good parts of living in the fraternity, and distorts or dismisses the bad parts. The result of all this self-justification is bound to make Charlie more kindly disposed toward the fraternity than Sam was, because Sam, not having gone

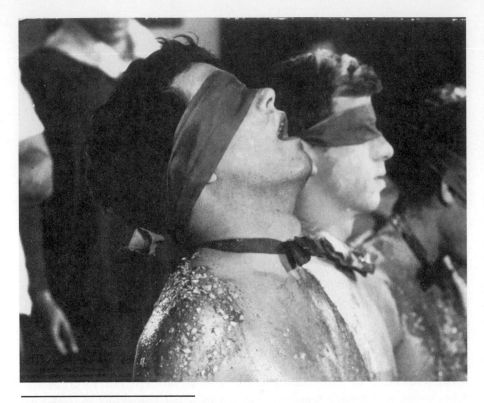

Our desire to maintain self-esteem can have surprising consequences.
Does undergoing a dangerous or embarrassing fraternity hazing increase
or decrease people's liking for the fraternity? Social psychological research
demonstrates that when people volunteer to undergo a painful or embarrassing initiation to join a group, they need to justify the experience in order
to avoid feeling foolish. One way they do this is to decide that the initiation
was worth it, because the group is so wonderful.

through the hazing, had no need to justify his behavior and thus no need to
see his fraternity experiences in a positive light. The end result? Charlie loved
his fraternity; Sam did not.

Does this sound farfetched? How do we know that the people in the fraternity were not objectively nicer when Charlie was a member than when
Sam was a member? In a series of well-controlled laboratory experiments,
social psychologists have investigated the phenomenon of hazing, holding
everything in the situation constant—including the precise behavior of the
fraternity members—except for the severity of the hazing students underwent
in order to become members. These experiments demonstrated conclusively
that the more unpleasant the procedure the participants underwent to get
into a group, the better they liked the group—even though, objectively, the
group members were the same people, behaving in the same manner
(Aronson & Mills, 1959; Gerard & Mathewson, 1966). This phenomenon
will be discussed more thoroughly in Chapter 3. The important things to
remember here are that (a) human beings are motivated to maintain a positive picture of themselves, in part by justifying their past behavior, and (b)
under certain specifiable conditions, this leads them to do things that, at first
glance, might seem surprising or paradoxical—for example, to like the things

and people for whom they have suffered better than the things and people not associated with pain or suffering.

Again, we want to make it crystal clear that the results of this research tradition should not be taken to mean that behaviorist theories are dead wrong; they explain some behavior very well (e.g., see our discussion in Chapter 10 of the research on social exchange theory). In our view, however, behavioristic approaches are inadequate to account for a huge subset of important attitudes and behaviors. This will become much clearer as you read on; in future chapters, we will try to specify the precise conditions under which one or the other set of principles is more likely to apply.

## The Social Cognition Approach: The Need to Be Accurate

As mentioned earlier, even when people are bending the facts to cast themselves in as favorable a light as they can, they do not completely distort reality. It would not be very adaptive to live in a fantasy world, believing that the car speeding toward us as we step off the curb is really a mirage, or that our future spouse will be Mel Gibson or Kim Basinger, as soon as they get done making movies and arrive at our doorstep. In fact, humans are quite skilled at thinking, contemplating, and deducing. One of the major hallmarks of being human is the ability to reason, and as a species, we have highly developed logical and computational abilities that are little short of amazing. We don't have to tell you about the extraordinary achievements humans have made in such fields as theoretical physics, philosophy, and mathematics. Pinnacles of the sophisticated reasoning of humans are occurring in our lifetimes—the invention of computers, the exploration of outer space, the conquering of many human diseases.

Moreover, on a more common (but perhaps more important) level, it is impossible to observe the cognitive development of a child without being awestruck; just think of the vast gains in knowledge and reasoning that occur in the first few years of life, as we watch our child develop from a squirming, helpless newborn who can do little but eat, cry, and sleep to a sophisticated, garrulous four-year-old who can utter complex sentences and hatch diabolic plots to frustrate a younger sibling and evoke consternation (and pride) in parents.

**Social Cognition.**  Given our species' incredible cognitive abilities, it makes sense that social psychologists, when formulating theories of social behavior, would take into consideration the way in which human beings think about the world. We call this the cognitive approach to social psychology, or **social cognition** (Fiske & Taylor, 1991; Markus & Zajonc, 1985; Nisbett & Ross, 1980). Those researchers who attempt to understand social behavior from the perspective of social cognition begin with the assumption that people try to view the world as accurately as possible. People are portrayed as amateur sleuths who are doing their best to understand and predict their social world. But this is by no means easy; we humans frequently run into problems because we almost never know all the facts we need in order to make the most accurate judgment of a given situation. Whether it is a relatively simple decision, like which breakfast cereal is

**social cognition:** how people think about themselves and the social world; more specifically, how people select, interpret, remember, and use social information

the best combination of healthfulness and tastiness; or a slightly more complex decision, like our desire to buy the best car we can for under $15,000; or a much more complex decision, like choosing a marriage partner who will make us deliriously happy for the rest of our lives, it is almost never easy to gather all the relevant facts in advance. Moreover, we are making countless decisions every day; even if there was a way to gather all the facts for each decision, we simply lack the time or the stamina to do so.

Does this sound a bit overblown? Aren't most decisions fairly easy? Let's take a closer look. We will begin by asking you a simple question: Which breakfast cereal is better for you, Lucky Charms or 100% Natural from Quaker? If you are like most of our students, you would answer 100% Natural from Quaker. After all, everybody knows that Lucky Charms is a kid's cereal, full of sugar. Besides, it has a picture of a leprechaun on the box, for goodness sakes. And 100% Natural has a picture of raw wheat on the box, the colors are light tan, and doesn't *natural* mean "good for you"? If that is the way you reasoned, you have, understandably, fallen into a common cognitive trap—you have generalized from the cover to the product. A careful reading of the ingredients (printed in small print on the package) will inform you that, although Lucky Charms has a bit more sugar in it than 100% Natural, the latter contains far more fat—so much so that the respected journal *Consumer Reports* has judged it to be less healthful than Lucky Charms. Things are not always what they appear to be; thus, coming up with an accurate picture of the social world is not always easy.

**Expectations About the Social World.**  To add to the difficulty, sometimes our expectations about the social world get in the way of perceiving it accurately, and even change the nature of the social world. Imagine, for example that you are an elementary school teacher dedicated to improving the lives of your students as best you can. You are aware at the beginning of the academic year how each student performed on standardized intelligence tests. Early in your career you were not entirely sure that these tests could gauge each child's true potential. After several years of teaching you are certain that these tests are accurate: Almost without fail, the kids who got high scores are the ones who did the best in your classroom, and the kids who got low scores simply couldn't "cut the mustard."

This scenario doesn't sound all that novel or surprising, except for one key fact: You might be very wrong about the validity of the intelligence tests. It might be that the tests weren't very accurate, but that you unintentionally treated the kids with high scores and the kids with low scores differently, making it look like the tests were accurate. This is exactly what Robert Rosenthal and Lenore Jacobson (1968) found in their investigation of a phenomenon called the *self-fulfilling prophecy*. They first entered elementary school classrooms and administered a test. They then informed each teacher that, according to the test, a few specific students were bloomers—that is, they were about to take off and perform extremely well. In actuality, the test showed no such thing; the children labeled as bloomers were chosen by drawing names out of a hat, and thus were no different, on the average, from any of the other kids. Lo and behold, on returning to the classroom at the end of the school year, Rosenthal and Jacobson found that the bloomers were performing extremely well. The mere fact that the teachers

Which of these cereals is better for you? The answer may surprise you (see the discussion in the text). Even when we are trying to make accurate judgments about the world, we often make mistakes.

were led to expect these students to do well caused a reliable improvement in their performance.

How did this happen? Though this outcome seems almost magical, it is imbedded in an important aspect of human nature. If you were one of those teachers and were led to expect two or three specific students to perform well, you would be more likely to treat those students in special ways—such as paying more attention to them, listening to them with more respect, calling on them more frequently, encouraging them, and trying to teach them more difficult material. This, in turn, would almost certainly make these students feel happier, more respected, more motivated, and smarter—and voilà—a self-fulfilling prophecy. Thus, even when we are trying to perceive the social world as accurately as we can, there are many ways in which we can go wrong, ending up with the wrong impressions. We will see why—and the conditions under which social perception is accurate—in Chapters 4 and 5.

We want to reiterate what we stated earlier: The two major sources of construals we have emphasized here—the need to maintain a positive view of ourselves (the self-esteem approach) and the need to view the world accurately (the social cognition approach)—are the most important of our social motives, but they are certainly not the only motives influencing people's thoughts and behaviors. As noted earlier, we humans are complex organisms, and there are a variety of motives that, under various conditions, influence what we think, feel, and do. Biological drives such as hunger and thirst, of course, can be powerful motivators, especially when we are under extreme

To the social psychologist, theories and speculations are not enough. It is necessary to conduct scientific experiments to test social psychological theories.

deprivation. At a more psychological level, we can be motivated by fear or by the promise of love, favors, and other rewards involving social exchange. These motives will be discussed at length in Chapters 10 and 11. Still another significant motive is the need for control (Langer, 1975; Seligman, 1975; Taylor, 1989; Thompson, 1981); research has shown that people need to feel that they exert some control over their environment. When people experience a loss of control, such that they believe they have little or no influence over whether good or bad things happen to them, there are a number of important consequences, which we will discuss primarily in Chapter 14.

## Social Psychology and Social Problems

To recapitulate, social psychology can be defined as the scientific study of social influence. Social influence can best be understood by examining the basic human motives that produce the subjective views people form about their environment.

It might have occurred to you to ask why we want to understand social influence in the first place. Who cares? And what difference does it make whether a behavior has its roots in the desire to be accurate or in the desire to bolster our self-esteem? There are several answers to these questions. The most basic answer is simple: because we are curious. Social psychologists are

> Understanding does not cure evil, but it is a definite help, inasmuch as one can cope with a comprehensible darkness.
> —Carl Jung

How effective is this message? Finding out is part of the task of the social psychologist.

fascinated by human social behavior and want to understand it on the deepest possible level. And in a sense, all of us are social psychologists. We all live in a social environment, and we all are more than mildly curious about such issues as how we become influenced, how we influence others, and why we fall in love with some people, dislike others, and are indifferent to still others.

Many social psychologists have another reason for studying the causes of social behavior—namely, to contribute to the solution of social problems. From the very beginnings of our young science, social psychologists have been keenly interested in such social problems as the reduction of hostility and prejudice and the increase of altruism and generosity. Contemporary social psychologists have continued this tradition, and have broadened the issues of concern to include such endeavors as inducing people to conserve natural resources like water and energy, educating people to practice safer sex in order to reduce the spread of AIDS, understanding the relationship between violence on television and the violent behavior of television-watchers, developing effective negotiation strategies for the reduction of international conflict, and helping people adjust to life changes like the entry to college or the death of a loved one (Harris, 1986).

The ability to understand and explain complex and dysfunctional social behavior brings with it the challenge to change it. For example, when our government began to take the AIDS epidemic seriously, it mounted an advertising campaign that seemed intent on frightening people into practicing safer sex. This seems consistent with common sense: If you want people to do something they wouldn't ordinarily do, why not scare the daylights out of them?

This is certainly not a stupid idea. As we shall see in subsequent chapters, there are many dysfunctional acts (e.g., cigarette smoking, drunk driving) for which the induction of fear can and does motivate people to take rational, appropriate action to preserve their health (Levy-Leboyer, 1988; Wilson, Purdon, and Wallston, 1988). But based on years of systematic research on persuasion, social psychologists were quick to realize that, in the specific situation of AIDS, arousing fear would almost certainly not produce the desired effect for most people. The weight of the research evidence suggests that, where sexual behavior is involved, the situation becomes infinitely more murky. Specifically, most people do not want to be thinking about dying or contracting a painful illness while they are getting ready to have sex. Such thoughts can, to say the least, interfere with the romantic aspect of the situation. Moreover, most people do not enjoy using condoms, because they feel that interrupting the sexual act to put on a condom tends to destroy the mood. Given these considerations, when people have been exposed to frightening messages, instead of engaging in rational problem-solving behavior, most tend to reduce that fear by engaging in denial ("It can't happen to me. Surely none of my friends have AIDS," etc.).

The astute reader will see that the process of denial stems not from the desire to be accurate, but from the desire to maintain one's self esteem. That is, if people can succeed in convincing themselves that their sexual partners do not have AIDS, then they can continue to enjoy unprotected sex while maintaining a reasonably good picture of themselves as a rational person. By understanding the conditions under which self-esteem maintenance prevails, social psychologists have been able to contribute important insights to AIDS education and prevention (Aronson, Fried, and Stone, 1991), as we will see in Chapters 3 and 14.

We will examine many similar examples of the applications of social psychology throughout this book. In Chapters 3 through 13, we will discuss the underlying human motives and the characteristics of the social situation that produce significant social behaviors, with the assumption that, if we are interested in changing our own or other people's behavior, we must first know something about these fundamental causes. Although most of the studies discussed in these chapters are concerned with such fundamental causes, in the process they also address critical social problems, including the effects of the mass media on attitudes and behavior (Chapter 8), violence and aggression (Chapter 12), and prejudice (Chapter 13). We devote our final two chapters (Chapters 14 and 15) to a detailed look at how social psychological principles address four important applied areas: health, the environment, law, and business. Throughout the book, our emphasis is on understanding the aspects of the human heart and mind that make people susceptible to social influence, with the assumption that by understanding these dynamics, we will make social problems more amenable to solution.

# SUMMARY

People are constantly being influenced by other people. **Social psychology** is defined as the scientific study of the way in which people's thoughts, feelings, and behaviors are influenced by the real or imagined presence of other people. Social influence is often very powerful, usually outweighing and frequently overwhelming **individual differences** in people's personalities as determinants of human behavior. To appreciate this fact, we must try to avoid making the **fundamental attribution error**—the tendency to explain our own and others' behavior entirely in terms of personality traits, thus underestimating the power of social influence.

To appreciate the power of social influence, we must understand how people form **construals** of their social environment. We are not computerlike organisms who respond directly and mechanically to environmental stimuli; rather, we are complex human beings who perceive, think about, and sometimes distort information from our environment. By emphasizing the way in which people construe the social world, social psychology has its roots more in the tradition of **Gestalt psychology** than that of **behaviorism.**

Although human behavior is complex and nonmechanical, it is not unfathomable. A person's construals of the world are rooted primarily in two fundamental motives: the desire to maintain **self-esteem** and the desire to form an accurate picture of oneself and the social world (the **social cognition** approach). Accordingly, to understand how we are influenced by our social environments, we must understand how our hearts and minds do the perceiving, thinking, and distorting. Two major concepts in social psychology can thus be stated succinctly: (a) Social influence has a powerful impact on people, and (b) To understand the power of social influence, we must examine the motives that determine how people construe the social environment.

We also discussed another important point about social psychology: It is an empirical science. Social psychologists attempt to find answers to key questions about social influence by designing and conducting research, rather than by relying on common sense or the wisdom of the ages. In Chapter 2, we will discuss the scientific methods social psychologists use when conducting such research.

# SUGGESTED READINGS

Festinger, L. (Ed.). (1980). *Retrospections on social psychology.* New York: Oxford University Press. A collection of articles by many of the most eminent scientists in the field of social psychology. Even though this book is more than a decade old, it remains an excellent source of articles about the origins of the field and its current research trends.

Jones, E. E. (1985). Major developments in social psychology during the past five decades. In G. Lindzey & E. Aronson (Eds.), *Handbook of social psychology* (3rd. ed., Vol. 1, pp. 47–107). New York: Random House. A thorough treatment of the history of social psychology from a leading researcher in the field. This chapter discusses the roots of the field, plots the changes in its emphases and trends, and details its intellectual history.

Ross, L., & Nisbett, R. E. (1991). *The person and the situation: Perspectives of social psychology.* New York: McGraw-Hill. An entertaining, insightful look at many of the ideas presented in this chapter, including the importance of considering people's construals of social situations, and how those construals are often more powerful determinants of people's behavior than their personalities.

# Chapter 2
## Methodology: The Process of Doing Research

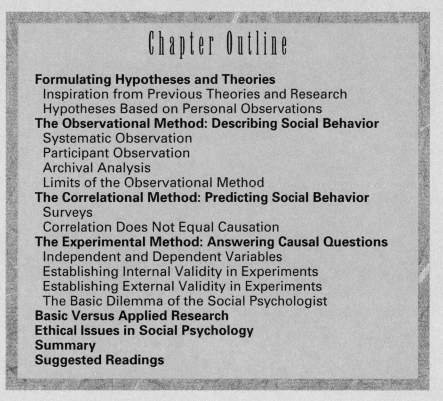

# Chapter Outline

Science is the refusal to believe on the basis of hope.

—C. P. Snow

I love games. I think I could be very happy being a chess player or dealing
with some other kinds of games. But I grew up in the Depression. It didn't seem
one could survive on chess, and science is also a game. You have very
strict ground rules in science and your ideas have to check out
with the empirical world. That's very tough and also very fascinating.

—Leon Festinger, 1977

ne of the most troubling and pressing social problems in our society is violence. Newspaper headlines report murders, assaults, and rapes virtually every day, and local news broadcasts sometimes seem like little more than a recitation of the day's body count. It is obviously of great importance to understand why violent behavior occurs and to find ways of reducing it. Social psychologists have conducted research on aggression and violence from a number of angles, and we will discuss the findings of these studies at several points (see especially Chapter 12). In this chapter, we will address how social psychologists do research, using studies on violence as an example. Once social psychologists decide on a topic of inquiry, such as violence, what tools do they have to unravel its causes?

Consider the relationship between pornography and sexual violence against women. Does reading pornography increase the likelihood that men will assault women? Is this true only of certain types of pornography, such as material that openly portrays and condones violent acts? In 1985, the attorney general of the United States, Edwin Meese III, convened a commission to answer these questions. This group, which became known as the Meese Commission, reported that pornography is a cause of rape and other violent crimes. Critics immediately disagreed, claiming that this conclusion was based more on political and moral concerns than on solid scientific evidence (Vance, 1986). In fact, the commission's conclusions were the opposite of those of the 1970 Presidential Commission on Obscenity and Pornography, which reported that pornography did not contribute significantly to sexual violence (*Time*, July 21, 1986). Who was right? How can we get beyond the rhetoric to find out if exposure to pornography does or does not have negative effects? What sort of research methodologies might we use?

This is the area where Kitty Genovese was attacked, in full view of her neighbors. Why didn't anyone call the police?

Put this question on hold for a moment, while we consider a related question about violence. In addition to examining the causes of human aggression, it is important to consider how witnesses and bystanders react to it, and the conditions under which they will come to the aid of their fellow humans. Though people might not intervene directly, out of fear for their own safety, we assume that most people will seek help in some fashion, such as by calling the police. It is because of this very assumption that people were so shocked by an incident that occurred in the early 1960s, in the Queens section of New

York City. A woman named Kitty Genovese was attacked while walking to her car and brutally murdered in the alley of an apartment complex. The attack lasted forty-five minutes. No fewer than thirty-eight of the apartment residents admitted later that they had rushed to their windows after hearing Genovese's screams for help. However, not one of the bystanders attempted in any way to help her—none of them even bothered to telephone the police. Not surprisingly, the Kitty Genovese murder received a great deal of publicity. Reporters, commentators, and pundits of all kinds came forward with their personal theories about why the bystanders had done nothing. The most popular explanation was that there is something dehumanizing about living in a metropolis that inevitably leads to apathy, indifference to human suffering, and lack of caring. The blame was laid on New York and New Yorkers; the general belief was that this kind of thing would not have happened in a small town, where people care more about each other (Rosenthal, 1964). Was big-city life the cause of the bystanders' behavior? Or was there some other explanation? Again, how can we find out?

In Chapter 1, we mentioned that it is insufficient to rely on personal beliefs, folk wisdom, or hope when answering such questions. Although novelists and social critics often provide valuable observations about why people behave as they do, ultimately such observations must be translated into hypotheses that can be tested scientifically.

This is necessary for two reasons. First, each of us is a prisoner of his or her own experience. Whereas we may have many explanations for the social behavior we observe, our implicit theories reflect our own life events, personalities, and goals, and often do not translate to another person's experience. For example, an individual who has constructed an elaborate social theory proving that pornography is harmless might have done so for highly personal reasons and goals. Second, our personal theories about why people do what they do are based on informal observations—not carefully controlled, scientific observation. For example, research has indicated that we are more likely to notice and remember the behavior of others that supports our beliefs about them, and that we tend to reinterpret the facts we once learned to make them fit our current impressions (Darley & Akert, 1991; Snyder & Uranowitz, 1978).

You might think that folk wisdom is a more trustworthy source of social theory and explanation than personal experience. Based on the accumulated observations of many people in a culture over time, these beliefs are not as susceptible to the problems cited above. However, folk wisdom is quite amusingly contradictory. Which best describes a long-distance romantic relationship—"absence makes the heart grow fonder" or "out of sight, out of mind"? Is it true that people are basically selfish and will ultimately put their own self-interest first, or are people basically altruistic, capable of self-sacrifice, and motivated to do well by others? You are probably thinking, "Well, it's both; both are true. It depends." And that is the point: Only by carefully identifying and studying the exact conditions that cause one of these contradictory sayings to be true can we tell that folk wisdom is useful or predictive.

Sometimes when people hear about the results of an experiment in social psychology, they think the findings are obvious and known by anyone who has made an effort to reflect even casually about social behavior. In a sense, many social psychology findings are obvious, and some have been anticipated by folk wisdom or the writings of novelists and philosophers. On the other hand, such findings can appear obvious because only in retrospect do most examples of human behavior seem to make sense and to have been easily predictable (Fischhoff, 1975). For example, given that much of folk wisdom is mutually contradictory, the opposite finding of an experiment could have seemed just as obvious as well.

If you want to experience what we mean when we say that not all obvious findings are easy to predict, take the quiz displayed in Figure 2.1. Each answer is based on social psychological research that we will discuss later in this book. In our experience as teachers, we have found that few of our students get all the answers correct.

Social psychology is an empirical science, with a well-developed set of methods to answer questions about social behavior, such as the ones about violence with which we began this chapter. These methods are of three types: the *observational method*, the *correlational method*, and the *experimental method*. Any of these methods could be used to explore a specific research

## Social Psychology Quiz

1. Suppose an authority figure asks college students to administer near-lethal electric shocks to another student who has not harmed them in any way. What percentage of these students will agree to do it?

2. If you give children a reward for doing something they already enjoy doing, they will subsequently like that activity (a) more, (b) the same, or (c) less.

3. Seeing someone you admire do something rather clumsy or stupid, such as spilling a cup of coffee, will make you like him or her (a) more, (b) the same, or (c) less.

4. Repeated exposure to a stimulus, such as a person, a song, or a painting, will make you like it (a) more, (b) the same, or (c) less

5. You ask an acquaintance to do you a favor—for example, to lend you $10—and he or she agrees. As a result of doing you this favor, the person will probably like you (a) more, (b) the same, or (c) less.

6. True or false: It is most adaptive and beneficial to people's mental health to have a realistic view of the future, an accurate appraisal of their own abilities and traits, and an accurate view of how much control they have over their lives.

7. Suppose that a representative of a community organization knocks on people's doors and asks them to put a small sign in their window promoting auto safety, and that most people agree to this request. A couple of weeks later, a different person from a different organization knocks on their doors and asks a much larger favor: To erect an unsightly billboard in their front yard promoting a clean environment. Do you think that agreeing to the first, smaller request will (a) make people more likely to agree to the second request, (b) make people less likely to agree to the second request, or (c) have no effect on people's agreeing to the second request?

8. Suppose that two elementary school children, Mary and Bob, take an IQ test, and Mary gets a higher score than Bob. Which of the following might have contributed to Mary's higher score? (a) On average, girls are smarter than boys; (b) IQ tests are biased so that girls do better than boys; (c) the children's teacher thought Mary was smarter than Bob, even though this is not true; or (d) the children's teacher thought Bob was smarter than Mary, so Mary tried hard to prove her wrong.

9. In public settings, (a) women touch men more, (b) men touch women more, or (c) there is no difference—men and women touch each other equally.

10. True or false: The more you pay people to make a speech against their own beliefs, the more they will change their minds and agree with the speech they made.

**Answers**

1. In studies conducted by Stanley Milgram (1974), up to 65 percent of participants in a study purportedly on learning and memory administered what they thought were near-lethal shocks to another subject. (In fact, no real shocks were administered.)

2. (c) Rewarding people for doing something they enjoy will typically make them like that activity less in the future (e.g., Lepper, Greene, & Nisbett, 1973).

3. (a) More (Aronson, Willerman, & Floyd, 1966).

4. (a) Under most circumstances, repeated exposure increases liking for a stimulus (Zajonc, 1968).

5. (a) More (Jecker & Landy, 1969).

6. False (Taylor & Brown, 1988).

7. (a) People will be more likely to agree to the second request. (Freedman & Fraser, 1966).

8. (c) If teachers have a strong expectation about how well a student can do, they can unintentionally treat the child in such a way that makes their expectation come true (Rosenthal & Jacobson, 1968).

9. (b) Men touch women more than vice versa (Henley, 1977).

10. False (Festinger & Carlsmith, 1959).

FIGURE 2.1 **Social psychology quiz.** Take a moment to answer the questions above, each of which is based on social psychological research. Though the correct answers may seem obvious in retrospect, many are hard to guess in advance.

question; each is a powerful tool in some ways and a weaker tool in others. The creativity in conducting social psychological research involves choosing the right method, maximizing its strengths, and minimizing its weaknesses.

In this chapter, we will discuss these methods in detail. We, the authors of this book, are not primarily writers of textbooks—we are social scientists who have done a great deal of experimental research in social psychology. As such, we will try to provide you with an understanding of both the joy and the difficulty of doing research. The joy comes in unraveling the clues about the causes of interesting and important social behaviors, just as a sleuth gradually unmasks the culprit in a murder mystery. Each of us finds it exhilarating that we have the tools to provide definitive answers to questions that have been debated by philosophers for centuries. At the same time, as seasoned researchers we have learned to temper this thrill of discovery with a heavy dose of humility, for creating and conducting social psychological research involves formidable practical and ethical constraints.

The starting point of research is an idea, or hypothesis, that the researcher wants to test. Thus, a good place to begin is with the question of where these hypotheses come from.

> The most incomprehensible thing about the world is that it is comprehensible.
> —Albert Einstein

## Formulating Hypotheses and Theories

### Inspiration from Previous Theories and Research

Hypotheses come from a variety of sources. Many are inspired by previous theories and research in psychology. For example, Leon Festinger was dissatisfied with the ability of behaviorist theories to explain attitude change. He formulated a new approach—dissonance theory—that made specific predictions about when and how people would change their attitudes. As we will see in an upcoming chapter, other researchers were dissatisfied with Festinger's explanation of the results he obtained, and so they conducted further research to test other possible explanations. Social psychologists, like scientists in other disciplines, engage in a continual process of theory refinement: A theory is developed; specific hypotheses derived from that theory are tested; and based on the results obtained, the theory is revised and new hypotheses are formulated.

"I THINK YOU SHOULD BE MORE EXPLICIT HERE IN STEP TWO."

### Hypotheses Based on Personal Observations

Theory is not the only way to derive a new hypothesis in social psychology. Researchers often observe a phenomenon in everyday life that they find curious and interesting. These observations can stem from their own personal experience, from literature, or from current events. Being social psychologists, these researchers then construct a theory about why this phenomenon occurred, and design a study to see if they are right.

For example, one of us was struck by a curious political phenomenon, leading him to formulate a hypothesis about some of the antecedents of interpersonal attraction. In the early 1960s, Elliot Aronson happened to be glancing through *Time* magazine and was amazed to find that a Gallup poll showed that President John F. Kennedy's personal popularity had undergone a huge increase during the week. What made this startling was that this was the week following the disastrous attempt by U.S.-sponsored forces to invade Cuba at the Bay of Pigs—known then and forever after as "the Bay of Pigs fiasco." Here was a president who admitted to being responsible for what at the time was considered to be one of our nation's most embarrassing blunders—and his popularity rating had soared. How could this be?

Some research hypotheses come from observations of everyday events. When Elliot Aronson observed that John F. Kennedy's popularity went up after admitting responsibility for the Bay of Pigs fiasco, he conceived of the hypothesis that very attractive people will be liked more after committing a blunder. This hypothesis was confirmed in a social psychological experiment (Aronson, Willerman, and Floyd, 1966).

In 1961, John F. Kennedy's personal characteristics and accomplishments made him extraordinarily attractive. Aronson reasoned that Kennedy might have seemed too wonderful, too talented, and too perfect for people to be able to identify with him; he might have seemed unapproachable. If this were the case, then perhaps some indication of fallibility—like the blunder of the Bay of Pigs invasion—served to make him more human, more real, more approachable, and hence more likable. To find out, Aronson conducted an experiment showing that indeed, an attractive person is liked more if he or she commits a blunder (Aronson, Willerman, & Floyd, 1966). We describe this study in Chapter 10 on interpersonal attraction.

As another example, consider the murder of Kitty Genovese, discussed earlier. As we saw, most people blamed her neighbors' failure to intervene on the apathy, indifference, and callousness that big-city life breeds. Two social psychologists who taught at universities in New York, however, had a different idea. Bibb Latané and John Darley got to talking one day about the general assumptions about the witnesses to the Genovese murder. Here is how Latané describes it:

> One evening after [a] downtown cocktail party, John Darley . . . came back with me to my 12th Street apartment for a drink. Our common complaint was the distressing tendency of acquaintances, on finding that we called ourselves social psychologists, to ask why New Yorkers were so apathetic. (Latané, 1987, p. 78)

Instead of trying to find out "what was wrong with New Yorkers," Latané and Darley thought it would be more interesting and more important to examine the social situation in which Genovese's neighbors found themselves:

> We came up with the insight that perhaps what made the Genovese case so fascinating was itself what made it happen—namely, that not just one or two, but thirty-eight people had watched and done nothing. (Latané, 1987, p. 78)

The researchers had the hunch that, paradoxically, the more people who witness an emergency, the less likely it is that any given individual will intervene. Genovese's neighbors might have assumed that someone else had called the police, a phenomenon Latané and Darley (1968) referred to as the *diffusion of responsibility*. Perhaps the bystanders would have been more likely to help had each thought he or she alone was witnessing the murder.

Once a researcher has a hypothesis, whether it comes from a theory, previous research, or an observation of everyday life, how can he or she tell if it is true? How could Latané and Darley tell whether the number of eyewitnesses in fact affects people's likelihood of helping a victim? In science, idle speculation will not do; the researcher must collect data to test his or her hypothesis. Let's look at how the observational method, the correlational method, and the experimental method are used to explore research hypotheses such as Latané and Darley's. These methods are summarized in Table 2.1.

**Methods of Research**

| Method | Questions Answered |
|---|---|
| 1. Observational | Description: What is the nature of the phenomenon? |
| 2. Correlational | Prediction: From knowing X, can we predict Y? |
| 3. Experimental | Causality: Is variable X a cause of variableY? |

**TABLE 2.1  A summary of research methods.**

## The Observational Method: Describing Social Behavior

As its name implies, the **observational method** involves watching people and seeing what they do. It goes without saying that observation is not the exclusive province of social scientists; it is practiced with great success by writers, filmmakers, and journalists interested in a particular social problem or the manner in which an institution works. For example, both Frederick Wiseman and Susan Sheehan spent a considerable amount of time in mental hospitals—not as patients, but as observers—Wiseman recording his obser-

**observational method:** the technique whereby a researcher observes people and systematically records measurements of their behavior

> You see, but you do not observe.
>
> —Sir Arthur Conan Doyle,
> *The Adventures of Sherlock Holmes*, 1892

vations in a documentary film (1967) and Sheehan in writing (1982). These works had a powerful effect on their audience and have been responsible for changing many people's views about the role of mental hospitals in our society.

Sometimes the observation can be in the form of a television camera, placed in a strategic location and used to record what people do in specific situations. For example, in the early days of television Allen Funt produced a show called "Candid Camera" in which people were confronted with strange situations—like a voice coming from inside a mailbox—while a hidden camera simply observed their reactions to the event. As interesting as these observations were, they are of limited value in helping us understand human behavior, because they were not done in a controlled, scientific manner. For example, for every interesting response to the talking mailbox that Funt recorded, there were almost certainly dozens of people who, suspecting it was a joke of some kind, simply shrugged and moved on. Since these behaviors do not make for interesting television viewing, Funt discarded them. There's nothing wrong with that—unless you want to draw conclusions about what people in general tend to do in such a situation. As interesting as excerpts from "Candid Camera" might be, they do not provide us with definitive answers about the intricacies of human behavior.

**systematic observation:** a form of the observational method whereby the observer is a trained social scientist who sets out to answer questions about a particular social phenomenon by observing and coding it according to a prearranged set of criteria

## Systematic Observation

With **systematic observation,** the observers are trained social scientists who set out to answer questions about a particular social phenomenon by observing and coding it according to a prearranged set of criteria. This method varies according to the degree to which the observer actively participates in the scene. At one extreme, the observer neither participates nor intervenes in any way; instead, the observer is unobtrusive and tries to blend in with the scenery as

Psychologists sometimes systematically observe their subjects through a one-way mirror. This enables the psychologist to observe telling behaviors without intervening and possibly affecting the behavior.

**THE FAR SIDE** By GARY LARSON

PRIMATE STUDIES

"For crying out loud, gentlemen! That's us! Someone's installed the one-way mirror in backward!"

The hazards of the observational method.

much as possible. For example, a researcher interested in children's social behavior might stand outside a playground fence to observe children at play. In this case, the observer would be systematically looking for particular behaviors, such as aggression, cooperation, leadership, or assertiveness. These social behaviors are concretely defined before the observation begins. For example, cooperation might be defined as a child sharing a toy with another, and as a child interacting with others to achieve a goal. The observer then notes when these behaviors occur and makes the appropriate check marks under the type of cooperation observed. If the researcher were interested in exploring possible sex and age differences in social behavior, he or she would also note the child's gender and age.

## Participant Observation

Some situations, by their very nature, require **participant observation.** In these situations, the observer interacts with the people being observed; however, the observer is careful not to alter the situation in any way because of his or her presence. For example, several years ago a group of people in the Midwest predicted that the world would come to an end in a violent cataclysm on a specific date. They also announced that they would be rescued in time by a spaceship that would land in their leader's backyard. Assuming that the end of the world was not imminent, Leon Festinger and his colleagues thought it would be interesting to observe this group closely and chronicle how they reacted when their beliefs and prophecy were disconfirmed (Festinger, Riecken, and Schachter, 1956). However, unlike the case when simply observing children at play, the researchers couldn't stand outside the fence and unobtrusively observe the subtleties of the group members' behavior. In order to monitor the hour-to-hour conversations of

**participant observation:** a form of systematic observation whereby the observer interacts with the people being observed, but tries not to alter the situation in any way

this group, the social psychologists found it necessary to join the group and pretend that they too believed the world was about to end.

## Archival Analysis

A third form of the observational method is **archival analysis.** Much can be learned about social behavior by examining the accumulated documents, or archives, of a culture. For example, diaries, novels, suicide notes, popular music lyrics, television shows, movies, magazine and newspaper articles, and advertising all tell us a great deal about how a society views itself. As long as these written and pictorial traces of the culture have been saved and are available to the researcher, they can be coded on specific variables of interest. Much like in our earlier example, specific, well-defined categories are created and then applied to the archival source. **Interjudge reliability**—the level of agreement between two or more people who independently rate the material—is measured. For example, the content analysis of magazine advertisements should not reflect the subjective opinion of one individual, but should be an objective, scientific rating of what is actually in the source document, agreed on by anyone who analyzes the advertisements.

Archival analysis is a powerful form of observational research because it allows us to examine changes in social behavior over time and across different cultures. For example, Archer, Iritani, Kimes, and Barrios (1983) and Akert, Chen, and Panter (1991) have coded portrait art and news and advertising photographs in print and television media for how they portray men and women—specifically, for how much of the pictorial image is devoted to the person's face. Their results indicate that across five centuries, across cultures, and across different forms of media, men are visually presented in a more close-up style (focusing on the head and face), whereas women are visually presented in a more long-shot style (focusing on the body). These researchers interpret their findings as indicating a subtle form of sex-role stereotyping: Men are being portrayed in a stronger style that emphasizes their intellectual achievements, whereas women are being portrayed in a weaker style that emphasizes their total physical appearance.

As another example, think back to the question of the relationship between pornography and violence. One problem with addressing this question is in defining what pornography is. Most of us have come across sexually explicit material at one time or another—for example, the centerfold photographs in magazines like *Playboy*. Does this constitute pornography? What about nudity in the movies, or newspaper ads for lingerie that show scantily clad models? For decades, the nation as a whole has been struggling to define pornography; as Supreme Court Justice Potter Stewart put it, "I know it when I see it," but describing its exact content is not easy. What is being portrayed in American "adults-only" literature and photographs?

Archival analysis is the perfect tool for answering this question, for it enables researchers to describe the content of documents present in the culture—in this case, the photographs and fictional stories that represent currently available pornography in the marketplace. Don Smith (1976) was one of the first researchers to examine the content of pornography, specifically in adults-only fiction paperback books. He purposefully chose for his study locations that were far from the pornography centers of the country (e.g.,

Archival studies have shown that news and advertising photographs typically give prominence to men's faces and women's bodies.

Many people believe that there is a causal relationship between the number of publications depicting violent pornography and the rise in sexual violence against women. They believe such publications should be illegal. Do you think reading and looking at pornography can cause people to commit violent sexual crimes against women? How can this question be answered scientifically?

cities in Nebraska and Tennessee), because he wanted to study the type of pornography that is typically and widely available. For the same reason, he studied books sold at newsstands and regular bookstores, and not those sold at special adults-only bookstores. His method involved choosing every fifth paperback on the shelves at one store in each of eight cities across five states. His content analysis covered many variables, such as how much sex was in the book, what kinds of sex occurred, and what the plots or themes were.

Smith (1976) found that the typical character in these books was young, single, white, physically attractive, and heterosexual. His data strikingly indicated that "the world of pornography is a male's world" (p. 21). Compared to the depictions of women, males' physical characteristics were given little attention; women's bodies were described in minute detail. The most disturbing finding of his study was that almost one-third of all the sex episodes coded in the books involved the use of force (physical, mental, or blackmail) by a male to make a female engage in unwanted sex. Thus, aggression against women was a major theme in these pornographic stories.

A second archival analysis, this time focusing on photographs, also found evidence of sexual violence against women. Park Dietz and Barbara Evans (1982) classified the cover photographs of magazines in adults-only bookstores in the pornography district of Forty-second Street in New York City. They randomly selected four stores in this area and coded all the magazines that had one or more women on the cover. Their categories reflected the specific sexual acts depicted, the clothes and physical appearance of the women, and so forth. Whereas two people engaged in sexual activity was the most common type of cover photograph (37.3 percent of all covers), the second most common type portrayed bondage and domination (17.2 percent of covers), wherein a woman was shown bound with ropes, handcuffs, chains, shackles, constrictive garments or other material. As Dietz and Evans (1982) describe this category:

> Gags, taped mouths, blindfolds, and hoods were also common. Torture is depicted through clothespins, clamps, and vises attached to the breasts or genitals, burning or dripping hot wax onto the skin, and extreme postures such as hanging by the wrists or ankles. Less frequently, a man is depicted threatening a woman with a gun or knife, raping her, cutting her skin with apparent bleeding, or strangling her. The degree of violence depicted ranges from a stern glance to apparent murder. Some photographs are such that it would take little suspension of belief to imagine that the woman was dead. (p. 1494)

Observational research, in the form of archival analysis, can tell us a great deal about society's values and beliefs. The prevalence in pornography of sexual violence against women suggests that these images and stories appeal to many readers (Dietz & Evans, 1982; Lowry, Love, & Kirby, 1981). These disturbing results lead us inexorably to frightening questions: Is pornography associated with sexually violent crimes against women that occur in our society? Do reading and looking at pornography cause some men to commit violent sexual acts? To answer these questions, research methods other than archival analysis must be used. Later in this chapter, we will see how the correlational method and the experimental method have been used to investigate these important questions about sexual violence against women.

## Limits of the Observational Method

The observational method is a good one if the researcher's goal is to provide a description of social behavior. This method has some significant drawbacks, however. First, certain kinds of behavior are difficult to observe because they occur only rarely or only in private. For example, had Latané and Darley chosen the observational method to study the effects of the number of bystanders on people's willingness to help a victim, we might still be waiting for an answer. In order to determine how witnesses react to a violent crime, the researchers would have had to linger on street corners throughout the city, wait patiently for assaults to occur, and then keep careful track of the responses of any and all bystanders. Obviously, they would have had to wait a very long time before an assault happened to occur in their presence, and they would have found it difficult to gather data while a real-life emergency occurred at their feet.

Instead, Latané and Darley might have used the archival analysis version of the observational method—for example, by examining newspaper accounts of violent crimes and noting the number of bystanders and how many offered assistance to the victim. However, the researchers would have quickly run into problems: Did each journalist mention how many bystanders were present? Was the number accurate? Were all forms of assistance noted in the newspaper article? Clearly, these are messy data. As is always the case with archival analysis, the researcher is at the mercy of the original compiler of the material; the journalists had different aims when they wrote their articles, and they may not have included all the information that researchers would later need.

Another limitation of the observational method is that it is confined to one particular group of people in one particular situation—one doomsaying group in the Midwest, or one group of children on a playground. This can be a problem if the goal is to generalize from the people observed in one setting to different populations and settings. Finally, social scientists usually want to do more than describe social behavior. A goal of social science is to understand relationships between variables and to be able to predict when different kinds of social behavior will occur. For example, what is the relationship between the amount of violence people see on television and how aggressive they are? How do children react when their parents get divorced? Who is most at risk for using drugs? To answer such questions, researchers frequently use a different approach—the correlational method.

## The Correlational Method: Predicting Social Behavior

The **correlational method** involves systematically measuring two or more variables and seeing if they are related. That is, if you know a person's standing on one variable, how well can you predict his or her standing on the other? This is called assessing the degree of correlation between the two variables. Whereas the goal of the observational method is to describe behavior, the goal of the correlational method is to assess relationships between variables, usually in order to test hypotheses about when and why social behavior occurs.

In correlational research, people's behavior and attitudes can be measured in a variety of ways. Just as with the observational method, researchers sometimes make direct observations of people's behavior. For example, using the correlational method, researchers might be interested in testing the relationship between children's aggressive behavior and how much violent television they watch. They too might observe children on the playground, but here the goal is to assess the relationship, or correlation, between the children's aggressiveness and other factors, like TV viewing habits, which the researchers also measure.

### Surveys

Besides observational data, the correlational method makes heavy use of surveys. Many of the social behaviors of interest to researchers are difficult if not impossible to observe, such as how much pornography people read, how knowledgeable they are about the transmission of AIDS, or how many friends they have. When the variables of interest cannot be easily observed, researchers rely on surveys, wherein people are questioned about their

**correlational method:** the method whereby two or more variables are systematically measured, and the relationship between them (i.e., how much one can be predicted from the other) is assessed

beliefs, attitudes, and behaviors. The researcher looks at the relationship between the questions he or she asked, such as whether people who know a lot about how AIDS is transmitted are most likely to engage in safer sex.

The way researchers look at such relationships is by calculating the correlation between different variables. A **positive correlation** means that increases in the value of one variable are associated with increases in the value of the other variable. Height and weight are positively correlated; the taller people are, the more they tend to weigh. A **negative correlation** means that increases in the value of one variable are associated with decreases in the value of the other. If height and weight were negatively correlated in humans, we would look very peculiar—short people, such as children, would look like penguins, whereas tall people, like NBA basketball players, would be all skin and bones! It is also possible, of course, for two variables to be completely uncorrelated, so that a researcher cannot predict one variable from the other.

**positive correlation:** a relationship between two variables wherein increases in the value of one variable are associated with increases in the value of the other variable

**negative correlation:** a relationship between two variables wherein increases in the value of one variable are associated with decreases in the value of the other variable

Correlations are expressed as numbers that can range from -1 to +1. A correlation of 1 means that two variables are perfectly correlated in a positive direction; thus, by knowing people's standing on one variable, the researcher can predict exactly where they stand on the other variable. In everyday life, of course, perfect correlations are rare. For example, one study found, in a sample of men aged eighteen to twenty-four, that the correlation between height and weight was .47 (Freedman, Pisani, Purves, & Adhikari, 1991). This means that, on average, the taller people were heavier than the shorter people, but there were exceptions. A correlation of -1 means that two variables are perfectly correlated in a negative direction, whereas a correlation of 0 means that two variables are not correlated.

Surveys have many advantages, not the least of which is the ability to sample representative segments of the population. Answers to a survey are useful only if they reflect the responses of people in general—not just the sample of people actually tested. Survey researchers go to great lengths to ensure that the people they sample are representative. They select samples that are representative of the population on a number of characteristics important to a given research question (e.g., age, educational background, religion, gender, income level). They also make sure to use a **random selection** of people from the population at large; this means that everyone in the population had an equal chance of being selected for the survey. As long as the sample is selected randomly, we can assume that the responses are a reasonable match to those of the population as a whole.

**random selection:** a way of ensuring that a sample of people is representative of a population, by making sure that everyone in the population has an equal chance of being selected for the sample

Sampling has not always been done successfully. In the fall of 1936, a weekly magazine called the *Literary Digest* conducted a large survey, asking people who they planned to vote for in the upcoming presidential election. The magazine obtained the names and addresses of its sample from telephone directories and automobile registration lists. The results of its survey of 2 million people indicated that the Republican candidate, Alf Landon, would win by a landslide. Of course, you know that there never was a President Landon; instead, Franklin Delano Roosevelt won every state in the Union but two. What went wrong with the *Literary Digest's* poll? In the depths of the Great Depression, many people could not afford telephones or cars. Those who could afford these items were, by definition, doing well financially, were frequently Republican, and overwhelmingly favored Alf Landon. However, the majority of the voters were poor—and overwhelmingly supported the

Democratic candidate, Roosevelt. By using a list of names that excluded the less affluent members of the population, the *Literary Digest* created a nonrepresentative sample. (The Literary Digest never recovered from this methodological disaster and went out of business shortly after publishing its poll.)

Modern surveys and political polls are not immune from such sampling problems. During the 1984 presidential race, polls conducted by Ronald Reagan's campaign staff found that Reagan had a comfortable lead over Walter Mondale, except when the polls were conducted on Friday nights. After an initial panic, they figured out that because Democrats tend to be poorer than Republicans, they were more likely to be home when the pollsters called on Friday nights (*Newsweek*, September 28, 1992). Despite notable glitches, or perhaps because of them, surveys have improved enormously over the years and can now accurately detect correlations between many interesting social variables.

Another potential problem with survey data is the accuracy of the responses. Straightforward questions—about what people think about an issue or what they typically do—are relatively easy to answer. However,

The importance of random selection in surveys. In 1936, the *Literary Digest* obtained a sample of names from telephone directories and automobile registration lists, and asked these people who they planned to vote for in the upcoming presidential election. Based on the results of this survey, the *Literary Digest* predicted that Alf Landon would win by a landslide. In fact, Franklin Roosevelt carried virtually every state in the union. Why was the *Literary Digest* poll so inaccurate?

*"Next question: I believe that life is a constant striving for balance, requiring frequent tradeoffs between morality and necessity, within a cyclic pattern of joy and sadness, forging a trail of bittersweet memories until one slips, inevitably, into the jaws of death. Agree or disagree?"*

asking survey participants to predict how they might behave in some hypothetical situation, or to explain why they behaved as they did in the past, is an invitation to inaccuracy (Schuman & Kalton, 1985). Often people simply don't know the answer—but they think they do. Richard Nisbett and Timothy Wilson (1977) demonstrated this saying more than you know phenomenon in a number of studies in which people often made inaccurate reports about why they responded the way they did. Their reports about the causes of their responses pertained more to their theories and beliefs about what should have influenced them than to what actually influenced them. (We discuss these studies at greater length in Chapter 6.) Finally, survey researchers have to be careful that they do not influence people's responses by the way they phrase the question (Hippler, Schwarz, and Sudman, 1987).

## Correlation Does Not Equal Causation

The major shortcoming of the correlational method is that it tells us only that two variables are related, whereas the goal of the social psychologist is to identify the psychological processes that explain why people are susceptible to social influence. To obtain this information, we must be able to infer causality. We want to be able to say that A causes B, not just that A is related, or correlated, to B.

If a researcher finds that there is a correlation between two variables, it means that there are three possible causal relationships between these vari-

There tends to be a correlation between watching violence on television and aggressive behavior in children. What are the different causal relationships that could explain this correlation?

ables. For example, researchers have found a correlation between the amount of violent television children watch and how aggressive they are (Eron, 1982). One explanation of this correlation is that watching the violent TV causes kids to become more violent themselves. It is equally probable, however, that the reverse is true: that kids who are violent to begin with are more likely to watch violent TV. Or there might be no causal relationship between these two variables; instead, both TV watching and violent behavior could be caused by a third variable, such as having neglectful parents who do not pay much attention to their kids. (In Chapter 12, we will present experimental evidence that supports one of these causal relationships.) When we use the correlational method, it is wrong to jump to the conclusion that one variable is causing the other to occur. Correlation does not imply causation.

Unfortunately, one of the most common methodological errors in the social sciences is to forget this adage. Consider, for example, the report of a resident of Los Angeles, following a severe earthquake that rocked Southern California:

> A lot of people probably think that in one way or another they caused the earthquake, but I'm here to tell you that I'm the one who really did it. At seven-forty-two this morning, I pressed the button that raises the door of my garage, and all hell broke loose. The first thing I said to myself was "I've got to get this thing fixed." (*New Yorker*, October 19, 1987)

While this account is clearly tongue-in-cheek, it underscores a trap that is very easy to fall into: jumping to the conclusion that if two variables are correlated, one must have caused the other. Other examples of this error are not nearly so comical or inconsequential, such as the conclusions drawn from a recent study of birth control methods and sexually transmitted diseases (STDs) in women (Rosenberg, Davidson, Chen, Judson, and Douglas, 1992). The researchers examined the records of women who had visited a clinic for STDs, noting which method of birth control they used and whether they had STDs. Surprisingly, the researchers found that women who used condoms had significantly more STDs than women who used diaphragms or contraceptive sponges. This result was widely reported in the popular press, with the conclusion that the use of diaphragms and sponges caused a lower incidence of disease. Some reporters urged women whose partners used condoms to switch to other methods.

Can you see the problem with this conclusion? The fact that the incidence of disease was correlated with the type of contraception women used is open to a number of causal interpretations. Perhaps the women who used sponges and diaphragms had sex with fewer partners. (In fact, condom users were more likely to have had sex with multiple partners in the previous month.) Perhaps the partners of condom users were more likely to have STDs than the partners of sponge and diaphragm users. There is simply no way of knowing. Thus, the conclusion that any of the three types of birth control was the cause of protection against STDs cannot be drawn from this correlational study.

As another example of the difficulty of inferring causality from correlational designs, let's return to the question of whether pornography causes aggressive sexual acts against women, such as rape. To address this question, Larry Baron and Murray Straus (1984) examined whether a relationship exists between the amount of pornography sold in different states and the number of rapes reported in those states. To measure the amount of pornography, they chose eight sexually explicit magazines (e.g., *Playboy*, *Hustler*, *Chic*) and gathered data on how many issues were sold in 1979 in each state. They compared this information to the incidence of rape in each state, using the FBI *Uniform Crime Reports* publication. (Since rape is an underreported crime, these data are undoubtedly conservative estimates of the actual number of rapes committed.)

The researchers' data revealed a strong, positive correlation of .63 between pornography readership and rape. (Probability theory indicates that there is only one chance in a thousand that a correlation of this size would occur by chance.) In addition, the researchers found that the amount of pornography sold was not as highly correlated with nonsexual violent crimes. Thus, they ruled out the possible explanation that pornography leads to more violent crimes in general, and not just to sexually violent crimes.

As suggestive as these findings are, they do not establish that pornography was a cause of rape. Can you think of alternative explanations for this correlation? Baron and Straus (1984) took pains to acknowledge that causality was not proved in their study. As they noted, the findings could reflect differences between states in a hypermasculine culture pattern (p. 207) that led men both to purchase more pornographic magazines and to commit rape.

Latané and Darley might also have turned to the correlational method to determine if the number of bystanders affects helping behavior. They might have surveyed victims and bystanders of crimes, and then correlated the total number of bystanders at each crime scene with the number of bystanders who helped or tried to help the victims. Let's say that a negative correlation was found in these data: The greater the number of bystanders, the less likely it was that any one of them intervened. Would this be evidence that the number of bystanders caused helping behavior to occur or not? Unfortunately, no. Any number of unknown third variables could be causing both the number of bystanders and the rate of helping to occur. For example, the seriousness of the emergency could be such a third variable, in that serious, frightening emergencies, as compared to minor mishaps, tend to draw large numbers of bystanders and make people less likely to intervene. Other examples of the difficulty of inferring causality from correlational studies are shown in Figure 2.2.

The only way to determine causal relationships is with the **experimental method,** whereby the researcher systematically controls and orchestrates the event so that some people experience it in one way (e.g., they witness an emergency along with other bystanders), while others experience it in a different way (e.g., they witness the same emergency, but they are the only bystander). As we will see, the experimental method is the method of choice in most social psychological research, because it allows the experimenter to make causal statements. The observational method is extremely useful in helping us describe social behavior; the correlational method is extremely useful in helping us understand what aspects of social behavior are related, or co-occur. However, only the experimental method allows us to make cause-and-effect statements. For this reason, the experimental method is the crown jewel of social psychological research design.

**experimental method:** the method of choice to study cause-and-effect relationships; the researcher randomly assigns participants to different conditions and ensures that these conditions are identical except for the independent variable (the one thought to have a causal effect on people's responses)

## The Experimental Method: Answering Causal Questions

The experimental method always involves a direct intervention on the part of the researcher. The variable (e.g., number of bystanders) thought to be a cause of the behavior of interest (e.g., helping behavior) is controlled by the researcher, so that some participants in the study are exposed to it in one form (e.g., they witness an emergency alone), whereas others are exposed to it in other forms (e.g., they witness the same emergency in a small group, or they witness it in a large group). By carefully changing only one aspect of the situation (e.g., group size), the researcher can see whether this aspect is the cause of the behavior in question.

Sound simple? Actually, it isn't. Stop and think for a moment how you might stage such an experiment to test Latané and Darley's hypothesis about the effects of group size. A moment's reflection will reveal that some rather severe practical and ethical difficulties are involved. What kind of emergency should be used? Ideally (from a scientific perspective), it should be as true to the Genovese case as possible. Accordingly, you would want to stage a murder that passersby could witness. In one condition, you could stage the murder so that only a few onlookers were present; in another condition, you could stage it so that a great many onlookers were present.

> Theory is a good thing but a good experiment lasts forever.
> —Peter Leonidovich Kapitsa

## Correlation Does Not Equal Causation Quiz

1. Recently, a politician extolled the virtues of the Boy and Girl Scouts organizations. In his salute to the Scouts, the politician mentioned that few teenagers convicted of street crimes had been members of the Scouts. In other words, he was positing a negative correlation between activity in Scouting and frequency of criminal behavior. Why might this be?

2. A research study found that having a pet in childhood is correlated with a reduced likelihood of becoming a juvenile delinquent in adolescence. Why is this?

3. A recent study of soldiers stationed on army bases found that the number of tatoos a soldier had is correlated positively with becoming involved in a motorcycle accident. Why?

4. Officials in the Reagan administration took credit for a reduction in the crime rate, because the crime rate went down after Reagan took office. That is, there was a negative correlation between the onset of the Reagan administration and the crime rate. What are some alternative explanations for this correlation?

5. Recently, it was reported that a correlation exists between people's tendency to eat breakfast in the morning and how long they live, such that people who skip breakfast die younger. Does eating Wheaties lead to a long life?

6. A few years ago, newspaper headlines announced, "Coffee suspected as a cause of heart attacks." Medical studies had found a correlation between the amount of coffee people drank and their likelihood of having a heart attack. Are there any alternative explanations?

7. A positive correlation exists between the viscosity of asphalt in city playgrounds and the crime rate. How can this be? When asphalt becomes viscous (softer), is some chemical released that drives potential criminals wild? When the crime rate goes up, do people flock to the playgrounds, such that the pounding of feet increases the viscosity of the asphalt? What explains this correlation?

**Answers**

1. The politician ignored third possible variables that could cause both Scout membership and crime, such as socio-economic class. Traditionally, Scouting has been most popular in small towns and suburbs among middle-class youngsters; it has never been very attractive or even available to youths growing up in densely populated, urban, high-crime areas.

2. Families who can afford or are willing to have a pet might differ in any number of ways from families who can neither afford nor are willing to have one.

3. Did tatoos cause motorcycle accidents? Or, for that matter, did motorcycle accidents cause tatoos? The researchers suggested that a third (unmeasured) variable was in fact the cause of both: A tendency to take risks and to be involved in flamboyant personal displays led to tatooing one's body and to driving a motorcycle recklessly.

4. By chance, the size of the cohort in the population that is most likely to commit crimes—teenagers—went down when Reagan took office.

5. Not necessarily. People who do not eat breakfast might differ from people who do in any number of ways that influence longevity—for example, in how obese they are, in how hard-driving and high-strung they are, or even in how late they sleep in the morning.

6. Coffee drinkers may be more likely to engage in other behaviors that put them at risk, such as smoking cigarettes or not exercising regularly.

7. Both the viscosity of asphalt and the crime rate go up when the temperature is high—for example, on a hot summer day or night.

**FIGURE 2.2 Correlation does not equal causation.** It can be rather difficult to remember that correlation does not allow us to make causal inferences, especially when a correlation suggests a particularly compelling cause. It is easy to forget that there are alternative explanations for the obtained correlation; for example, other variables could be causing both of the observed variables to occur. For each of the following examples, think about why the correlation was found. Even if it seems obvious which variable was causing the other, are there alternative explanations?

Clearly, there are some glaring ethical problems with this scenario. What is ideal from a scientific perspective can be less than ideal from an ethical perspective. It goes without saying that no scientist in his or her right mind would actually commit a murder. Perhaps, instead, we could hire some actors to fake a murder on a city street. This is somewhat better from an

NEVER THE EXPERIMENT

ALWAYS THE CONTROL

ethical perspective, but it is still problematic; it is wrong to subject unsuspecting people to such a disturbing event. A solution might be to compromise further and stage an emergency that is less upsetting and frightening to people. But how can we arrange a realistic situation that is upsetting enough to be similar to the Genovese case without it being too upsetting? In addition, how can we ensure that each bystander experiences the same emergency except for the variable whose effect we want to test—in this case, the number of bystanders?

Let's see how Latané and Darley (1968) dealt with these problems. Imagine you were a participant in their experiment. You arrive at the scheduled time and find yourself in a long corridor with doors to several small cubicles. An experimenter greets you and takes you into one of the cubicles, mentioning that five other students, seated in the other cubicles, will be participating with you. The experimenter leaves after instructing you to put on a pair of headphones with an attached microphone. You listen through the headphones as the experimenter explains that he is interested in learning about the kinds of personal problems college students currently experience. To ensure that people will discuss their problems openly, he explains, each participant will remain anonymous; each will stay in his or her separate room and communicate with the others only via the intercom system. Further, the experimenter says, he will not be listening to the discussion, so that people will feel freer to be open and honest. Finally, in order to impose some structure on the discussion, the experimenter asks that participants take turns presenting their problems, each speaking for two minutes, after which each person will comment on what the others said. To make sure this procedure is followed, he says, only one person's microphone will be turned on at a time.

The group discussion then begins. You listen as the first participant admits he has found it difficult to adjust to college. With some embarrassment, he mentions that he sometimes has seizures, especially when under stress. When his two minutes are up, you hear the other four participants discuss their problems, after which it is your turn. When you have finished, it is the first person's turn to speak again. To your astonishment, after he makes a few further comments, he begins to experience one of the seizures he mentioned earlier:

> I-er-um-I think I-I need-er-if-if could-er-er-somebody er-er-er-er-er-er-er-give me a little-er-give me a little help here because-er-I-er-I'm-er-er-h-h-having a-a-a real problem-er-right now and I-er-if somebody could help me out it would-it would-er-er s-s-sure be-sure be good . . . because-er-there-er-er-a cause I-er-I-uh-I've got a-a one of the-er-sei-------er-er-things coming on and-and-and I could really-er-use some help so if somebody would-er-give me a little h-help-uh-er-er-er-er c-could somebody-er-er-help-er-uh-uh-uh (choking sounds) . . . I'm gonna die-er-er-I'm . . . gonna die-er-help-er-er-seizure-er (chokes, then quiet). (Darley & Latané, 1968, p. 379)

Stop and think for a moment: What would you have done in this situation?

If you were like most of the participants in the actual study, you would have remained in your cubicle, listening to your fellow student having a seizure, and done nothing about it. Does this surprise you? Latané and Darley kept track of the number of people who left their cubicle to find the victim or the experimenter before the end of the victim's seizure. Only 31 percent of the participants sought help in this way. Fully 69 percent of the students remained in their cubicles and did nothing—just as Kitty Genovese's neighbors had failed to offer assistance in any way.

Does this finding prove that the failure to help was due to the number of people who witnessed the seizure? How do we know that it wasn't due to some other factor? Here is the major advantage of the experimental method: We know because Latané and Darley included two other conditions in their experiment. In these conditions, the procedure was identical to that described above, with one crucial difference: The size of the discussion group was smaller, meaning that fewer people were witnesses to the seizure. In one condition, the participants were told that there were three other people in the discussion group besides themselves (the victim plus two others). In another condition, participants were told that there was only one other person in their discussion group (namely, the victim). In this latter condition, each participant believed he or she was the only one who could hear the seizure.

## Independent and Dependent Variables

independent variable: the variable a researcher changes or varies to see if it has an effect on some other variable; this is the variable the researcher thinks will cause a change in some other variable

The number of people witnessing the emergency was the **independent variable** in the Latané and Darley study. The independent variable is under the direct control of the experimenter; it is the variable that is manipulated (presented in different ways). The independent variable is the one hypothesized to exert a causal effect on the **dependent variable,** which is what the experimenter measures to see if any such effect was present (in this case, whether or not people helped). That is, the dependent variable is hypothesized to depend on the independent variable (see Figure 2.3). Latané and Darley found that their independent variable—the number of bystanders—did have an effect on the dependent variable. When the partici-

dependent variable: the variable a researcher measures to see if it is influenced by the independent variable; the researcher hypothesizes that the dependent variable will depend on the level of the independent variable

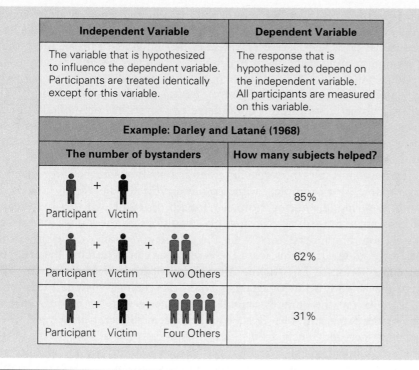

| Independent Variable | Dependent Variable |
| --- | --- |
| The variable that is hypothesized to influence the dependent variable. Participants are treated identically except for this variable. | The response that is hypothesized to depend on the independent variable. All participants are measured on this variable. |

| Example: Darley and Latané (1968) | |
| --- | --- |
| **The number of bystanders** | **How many subjects helped?** |
| Participant  Victim | 85% |
| Participant  Victim  Two Others | 62% |
| Participant  Victim  Four Others | 31% |

**FIGURE 2.3 Independent and dependent variables in experimental research.**

pants believed that four other people were witnesses to the seizure, only 31 percent offered assistance. When the participants believed that only two other people were aware of the seizure, the amount of helping behavior increased to 62 percent of the participants. When the participants believed that they were the only person listening to the seizure, nearly everyone helped (85 percent of the participants).

Whereas these results indicate that the number of bystanders strongly affects the rate of helping, it does not mean that the size of the group is the only cause of people's decision to help. After all, when there were four bystanders, a third of them still helped; conversely, when participants thought they were the only witness, some of them still failed to help. Obviously, other factors also influence helping behavior—the bystanders' personalities, their prior experience with emergencies, and so on.

Because social behavior is complex, we realize that many variables are typically the cause of any given behavior. Thus, experiments often include more than one independent variable at a time. In addition, because we know that some combinations of independent variables have particularly powerful effects on behavior, we can make sure that all the different versions of the independent variables co-occur with each other. This is called a **factorial design**—an experimental design in which (a) there is more than one independent variable; (b) each independent variable has more than one version, or level; and (c) all possible combinations of these levels occur in one study.

For example, a researcher might choose to study bystander intervention by including the following three independent variables in one study: the

**factorial design:** an experimental design in which there is more than one independent variable; each independent variable has more than one version, or level; and all possible combinations of these levels occur in one study

severity of the emergency, the number of bystanders present, and the gender of the victim, or person in need of help. The severity variable could have three levels: (a) a very severe emergency (the individual falls to the ground with blood pouring from his or her mouth); (b) a less severe emergency (the individual falls to the ground, clutching his or her sides and moaning); and (c) a minor emergency (the individual trips and falls to the ground). The number of bystanders variable could have two levels: (a) only one bystander present and (b) three bystanders present. The final independent variable, the gender of the "victim," would obviously have two levels: (a) a male victim and (b) a female victim.

This design results in twelve different combinations of the three independent variables; for example, in one condition, the female victim falls to the ground with blood pouring from her mouth, in front of three bystanders. The researcher runs all twelve possible conditions in the study and gathers data on how bystanders react when the different versions of the three variables are combined. In this way, the researcher can determine the independent contribution of each of the three independent variables (e.g., to what extent the helping behavior changes when the victim is female rather than male), as well as the unique combination or interaction of the different versions of the three variables (e.g., whether a female victim in a very severe emergency gets more help from three bystanders than a male victim in the same predicament does). The factorial design is a very powerful one, and does the best job of tearing apart the complex interplay of social variables and of allowing social psychologists to determine how these variables combine in important ways.

## Establishing Internal Validity in Experiments

How can we be sure that the differences in help across conditions in the Latané and Darley (1968) seizure study were due to the different numbers of bystanders who witnessed the emergency? Could this effect have been caused by some other aspect of the situation? Again, this is the beauty of the experimental method: We can be sure of the causal connection between the number of bystanders and helping because Latané and Darley made sure that everything about the situation was the same in the different conditions except the independent variable, the number of bystanders.

**internal validity:** making sure that nothing else besides the independent variable can affect the dependent variable; this is accomplished by controlling all extraneous variables and by randomly assigning people to different experimental conditions

Such a study is described as having high **internal validity** (Campbell & Stanley, 1967), meaning that everything was the same in the different conditions of the study except for the independent variable. Latané and Darley were careful to maintain high internal validity in their seizure study in the following ways: All of the participants received the same instructions and description of the study; all participated in the same set of cubicles; only one person participated in the experiment at a time, so that all other aspects of the situation could be carefully controlled and thus kept the same across participants; and all the comments of the supposed other participants and the victim were prerecorded and played over the intercom system, ensuring that all actual participants heard the same group discussion and witnessed the same emergency.

The astute reader will have noticed, however, that there was a key difference between the conditions of the Latané and Darley experiment other than the number of bystanders: different people participated in the different conditions. Maybe the observed differences in helping were due to characteristics of the participants instead of the independent variable. For example, maybe the participants in the sole witness condition happened to be very helpful individuals, more helpful by nature than participants in the other two conditions. They might have differed in any number of ways from their counterparts in the other conditions, making them more likely to help. Maybe they were more likely to have had loving parents, to know something about epilepsy, or to have experience helping in emergencies. Were any of these possibilities true, the study's internal validity would be seriously threatened.

Fortunately, there is a technique that allows experimenters to rule out differences among participants as the cause of the results: **random assignment to condition.** This powerful technique is a major component of the experimental method. It means that each participant in the Latané and Darley study had an equal chance of being assigned to any one of the three conditions. In practice, this is done by flipping coins, drawing names out of a hat, or consulting a random numbers table (lists of numbers that have been randomly generated by a computer). Through random assignment, researchers can be relatively certain that differences in the personalities or backgrounds of their participants are distributed evenly across conditions. For example, since the participants were assigned randomly, probability theory tells us that it is very unlikely that most of the helpful personalities ended up in one condition. Helpful personality types should be randomly (i.e., roughly evenly) dispersed across the three experimental conditions.

However, even with random assignment there is always the (very small) possibility that different characteristics of people did not distribute themselves evenly across conditions. For example, if we randomly divide a group of forty people into two groups, it is possible that the twenty who know the most about epilepsy will all end up in one group. This is a possibility we take seriously in experimental science. Thus, the statistical analyses of our data come with a **probability level (*p*-value)** that the observed findings occurred by chance (due to the failure of random assignment) and not because of our independent variable(s). The convention in science, including social psychology, is to consider results significant if the probability level is less than five in one hundred that the results might be due to chance factors and not the independent variables studied. If the results are significant, we accept the hypothesis that the independent variable, rather than differences in participants' backgrounds or personalities, caused differences in the dependent variable.

The ability to control extraneous variables that might influence the results and the ability to randomly assign people to conditions are the hallmarks of the experimental method and set it apart from the observational and correlational methods. Even if a strong correlation exists between two variables, we cannot be certain which one is causing the other, or whether some other variable is influencing both. For example, as we saw earlier, had Latané and Darley used the correlational method and found a strong correlation between the number of bystanders and helping behavior, they would not have been able to rule out the possibility that some other variable—such as the seriousness of the emergency—was influencing both the number of bystanders present and the likelihood of people intervening. However, by orchestrating the number of bystanders as an independent variable and

**random assignment to condition:** making sure that all participants have an equal chance of taking part in any condition of an experiment; through random assignment, researchers can be relatively certain that differences in their participants' personalities or backgrounds are distributed evenly across conditions

**probability level (*p*-value):** a number, calculated with statistical techniques, that tells researchers how likely it is that the results of their experiment occurred by chance (due to the failure of random assignment) and not because of the independent variable(s); the convention in science, including social psychology, is to consider results significant if the probability level is less than five in one hundred that the results might be due to chance factors and not the independent variables studied

keeping everything else (e.g., the seriousness of the emergency) constant, Latané and Darley were able to rule out such alternative explanations.

Similarly, we saw that the correlational study of pornography and sexual violence was impossible to interpret in causal terms. Larry Baron and Murray Straus (1984) found a significant correlation between the number of pornographic magazines sold and the number of rapes committed in each state, but could not rule out the possibility that some third variable was causing both of these variables. Rather than pornography causing rapes, for example, it is possible that some states have more men with disturbed, hyper-masculine personalities, and that these men are more likely both to read pornography and to commit rape.

Only the experimental method can answer the question of whether exposure to pornography causes men to commit sexually violent acts. Obviously, for ethical reasons we cannot conduct experiments in which the dependent variable is the incidence of violent sexual acts. The effects of pornography on aggression have been examined, however, in a number of clever experiments by Edward Donnerstein, Neil Malamuth, and their colleagues (Donnerstein, Linz, & Penrod, 1987; Malamuth, 1986; Malamuth & Donnerstein, 1983).

Let's take a look at one of these experiments, conducted by Edward Donnerstein (1980). All the participants were male undergraduates. In an experiment purportedly studying the effects of stress on learning, the participant and a confederate (who posed as a real participant) were partners in a learning task that involved one of them administering electric shocks to the other for every wrong answer given. The confederate was always the one who, in another room, received the shocks (no actual electric shocks were given). The gender of the confederate was the first independent variable in the study—the confederate was either a male or a female undergraduate.

Another independent variable was the type of short film the participant saw before delivering the shocks. While the participant was waiting for the confederate to finish studying for his or her upcoming test, the experimenter asked the participant if he would view a film the experimenter was thinking of using in future research and rate it on a number of dimensions. All the participants agreed. They each viewed one of three short films: (a) a film of a man who breaks into a house and rapes a woman at gunpoint (i.e., violent pornography); (b) a film of a male and female in various stages of sexual intercourse, but with no aggressive or violent content; or (c) a neutral film, with no sexual or aggressive content.

After viewing the film, the participants took part in the learning task. If the confederate gave an incorrect answer, the participant was instructed to deliver an electric shock of an intensity of his choosing—ranging from a shock level of 1 to a shock level of 8. The participants then heard the confederate make several mistakes (actually, this was a tape recording of a male or female accomplice). The dependent measure was the intensity of the shocks the participant chose to deliver. Did those who had just viewed pornography behave more aggressively (give stronger shocks) than those who had not? Did it make a difference whether the pornography was violent or nonviolent? Did the female confederate, or "victim," receive more intense shocks than the male?

The results are shown in Figure 2.4. The most striking finding was that when the male participants saw violent pornography and then had the

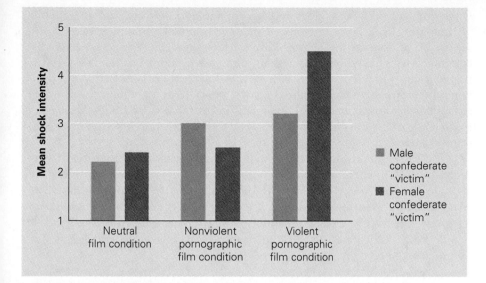

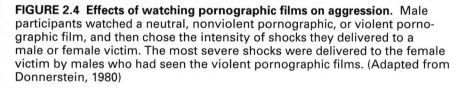

**FIGURE 2.4 Effects of watching pornographic films on aggression.** Male participants watched a neutral, nonviolent pornographic, or violent pornographic film, and then chose the intensity of shocks they delivered to a male or female victim. The most severe shocks were delivered to the female victim by males who had seen the violent pornographic films. (Adapted from Donnerstein, 1980)

opportunity to aggress against a female victim, they delivered the most severe electric shocks of all. When the victim was male, seeing either the nonviolent or the violent pornographic film led to a slight increase in aggression, possibly because these films aroused or upset people, which caused them to take it out on the victim. This increase, however, was nowhere near the intensity of the shocks delivered to the female victim by men who saw the violent pornography. This study and others like it (e.g., Linz, Donnerstein, and Penrod, 1984) suggest that when men watch pornography in which women are degraded and treated violently, they become more desensitized to violence toward women, view it as less abhorrent, and become more violent themselves.

We will discuss this issue at greater length in Chapter 12, on aggression. For now, we point out that only studies like Donnerstein's (1980), which are experiments on the effects of pornography, can definitely answer the question of whether pornography causes violence and aggression.

## Establishing External Validity in Experiments

As is always the case in life, the advantages of the experimental method are accompanied by potential costs. By virtue of gaining enough control over the situation so as to randomly assign people to conditions and rule out the effects of extraneous variables, the situation can become somewhat artificial and unlike real life. For example, one could argue that Latané and Darley went far astray from the original inspiration for their study, the Kitty

Genovese murder. What does witnessing someone having a seizure, while participating in a laboratory experiment in a college building, have to do with a brutal murder in Queens? How often in everyday life do we have discussions with other people through an intercom system? Did the fact that the participants knew they were in a psychology experiment influence their behavior? Similarly, we might question the extent to which the kind of aggression Donnerstein (1980) examined in his laboratory study—delivering electric shocks to another student—can be generalized to violent sexual crimes, such as rape.

These are interesting questions that concern the **external validity,** or generalizability, of experiments in psychology. Two kinds of generalizability are at issue: (a) the extent to which we can generalize from the situation constructed by an experimenter to real-life situations (generalizability across *situations*) and (b) the extent to which we can generalize from the kind of people who participated in the experiment to people in general (generalizability across *people*).

**Generalizability Across Situations.** A possible criticism of research in social psychology is that it is often conducted in artificial situations that cannot be generalized to real life. To address this problem, social psychologists attempt to increase the generalizability of their results by making their studies as realistic as possible. But it is important to note that there are different ways in which an experiment can be realistic. By one definition—the similarity of an experimental situation to events that occur frequently in everyday life—it is clear that many experiments are decidedly unreal. In many of the experiments we will discuss, people are placed in situations that they would rarely if ever encounter in everyday life, such as occurred in Latané and Darley's group discussion of personal problems over an intercom system. We can refer to the extent to which the experiment reflects real-life situations as the **mundane realism** (Aronson & Carlsmith, 1968) of the experiment, which is often low.

A more important kind of realism, however, is how well an experiment captures psychological processes like those occurring in everyday life. We will refer to this as the **psychological realism** of experiments. Even though Latané and Darley staged an emergency that was, in significant ways, unlike ones encountered in everyday life, was it *psychologically similar* to real-life emergencies? Were the same psychological processes triggered? Did the participants have the same types of perceptions and thoughts, make the same types of decisions, and choose the same types of behaviors as they would in a real-life situation? If so, then the results of this study are generalizable to everyday life.

Making an experiment realistic, both mundanely and psychologically, is no easy task. It is, perhaps, where the creative talents of researchers come most into play. For example, the simplest way to study bystander intervention would be to say to people, "Look, we are interested in how people react to emergencies, so at some point during this study we are going to stage an accident, and then we'll see how you respond." We think you will agree, however, that such a procedure would be very low in psychological realism and mundane realism. In everyday life, we do not know when emergencies are going to occur; we do not have time to plan our responses to them; we

**external validity:** the extent to which the results of a study can be generalized to other situations and to other people

**mundane realism:** the extent to which an experiment is similar to situations encountered in everyday life

**psychological realism:** the extent to which the psychological processes triggered in an experiment are similar to psychological processes occurring in everyday life; psychological realism can be high in an experiment, even if mundane realism is low

do not think they are staged for our benefit; and we do not think a researcher is observing our reactions to them. Thus, the situation itself and the kinds of psychological processes triggered would differ widely from those of a real emergency.

Further, as discussed earlier, people don't always know why they do what they do, or even what they will do until it happens. Thus, describing an experimental situation to participants and then asking them to respond normally will produce responses that are at best suspect. For example, after describing the Latané and Darley seizure experiment to our students, we often ask them to predict how they would respond, just as we asked you earlier. Invariably, almost all of our students think they would have helped the victim, even when they know that in the condition where the group size was six, most people did not help. Unfortunately, we cannot depend on people's descriptions of what they would do in a hypothetical situation; we can only find out what people will really do when we construct a situation that triggers the same psychological processes as occur in the real world.

To make a study psychologically real, it is often necessary to tell the participants a **cover story**—a description of the purpose of the study that is different from its true purpose. You might have wondered why Latané and Darley told people that the purpose of the experiment was to study the personal problems of college students. It certainly would have been simpler to tell them that the point of the study was to see how they would react to emergencies. However, this revealing comment would have considerably reduced the study's psychological realism, making it difficult to generalize the results to people's reactions to emergencies in everyday life. Psychological realism is heightened if people find themselves imbedded in a real event. To the extent that they are forewarned, people will plan their response, and this is not how it happens in the real world.

**cover story:** a description of the purpose of a study, given to participants, that is different from its true purpose; cover stories are used to maintain psychological realism

**Generalizability Across People.**  Recall that social psychologists study the way in which people in general are susceptible to social influence. Latané and Darley's experiment documented an interesting, unexpected example of social influence, whereby the mere knowledge that others were present inhibited helping behavior. But what have we learned about people in general? The participants in their study were fifty-two male and female students at New York University, who received course credit for participating in the experiment. It is reasonable to ask whether the same results would have been found had a different population been used. Would the number of bystanders have influenced helping behavior had the participants been middle-aged blue-collar workers instead of college students? Midwesterners instead of New Yorkers? Japanese instead of American?

The only way to be certain that the results of an experiment represent the behavior of a particular population is to ensure that the participants are randomly selected from that population. Ideally, samples in experiments should be randomly selected, just as they are in surveys. However, it is rare in social psychological experiments for participants to be selected in this way. Latané and Darley, for example, did not attempt to choose a random sample of American citizens, or even New Yorkers, or even students at New York University. As is the case in many of the experiments we will describe in this book, the participants were students who volunteered for the study.

Social psychology attempts to study psychological processes that affect all people and make them susceptible to social influence. To see if the results of an experiment are generalizable across people, the study must be replicated with diverse populations.

Unfortunately, it is impractical and expensive to select random samples for social psychology experiments. It is difficult enough to convince a random sample of Americans to agree to answer a few questions over the telephone as part of a political poll, and such polls can cost thousands of dollars to conduct. Imagine the difficulty Latané and Darley would have had convincing a random sample of Americans to board a plane to New York to take part in their study, not to mention the cost of such an endeavor. Even trying to gather a random sample of students at New York University would not have been easy, given that each person contacted would have had to agree to take time out of his or her busy schedule to spend an hour in Latané and Darley's laboratory.

Of course, concerns about practicality and expense are not good excuses for doing poor science. More importantly, given the goal of social psychology it is unnecessary to select random samples for every experiment performed. As noted in Chapter 1, social psychologists attempt to identify the basic psychological processes common to all people that make them susceptible to social influence. If we accept the premise that there are fundamental psychological processes shared by all people in all places, and that it is these processes that are being studied in social psychology experiments, then it becomes relatively unimportant to select participants from every corner of the earth. Most social psychologists assume that the processes they study—such as the diffusion of responsibility caused by the presence of others in an emergency—are basic components of human nature, common to New Yorkers, Midwesterners, and Japanese alike.

This is not to say that we should take social psychologists' word for it. How can we be certain that the diffusion of responsibility effect is universal? Ultimately, the extent to which the results of a particular study can be generalized is an empirical question, tested by replicating the study with different populations.

**Replications.** Suppose a researcher claims that his or her study is high in psychological realism, that it has thus captured psychological functioning as it occurs in everyday life, and that it doesn't matter that only college sophomores participated, because these psychological processes are universal. Should we believe the researcher?

The ultimate test of an experiment's external validity is **replication**—conducting the study over again, often with different subject populations or in different settings. Do we think that Latané and Darley found the results they did only because their participants knew they were in a psychology experiment? Then we should try to replicate their study in an experiment conducted outside of the laboratory. Do we think their results are limited to only certain kinds of emergencies? Then we should try to replicate it with an emergency different from an epileptic seizure. Do we think that only New Yorkers would be so unhelpful? Then we should try to replicate it with southerners, Californians, or Germans. Only with such replications can we be certain about how generalizable their results are.

Virtually all of the findings we will discuss in this book have been replicated in a number of different settings, with different populations, thus proving that they are not phenomena limited to the laboratory or to college sophomores. For example, Latané and Darley's original hypothesis has been supported in numerous studies. Increasing the number of bystanders has been found to inhibit helping behavior with many kinds of people, including children, college students, and future ministers (Darley & Batson, 1973; Latané & Nida, 1981); in both small towns and large cities (Latané and Dabbs, 1975); in a variety of settings, such as psychology laboratories, city streets, and subway trains (Latané & Darley, 1970; Piliavin, Dovidio, Gaertner, and Clark, 1981; Piliavin & Piliavin, 1972); and with a variety of types of emergencies, such as seizures, potential fires, fights, and accidents (Latané & Darley, 1968; Shotland & Straw, 1976; Staub, 1974), as well as with less serious events, such as having a flat tire (Hurley & Allen, 1974). Many of these replications have been conducted in real-life settings (e.g., on a subway train) where people could not possibly have known that an experiment was being conducted. We will frequently point out similar replications of the major findings we discuss in this book.

As noted in Chapter 1, experimental social psychology began primarily as an American discipline; thus, one limit on the generalizability of the results is that most research in the field has been conducted by Americans

**replication:** repeating a study, often with different subject populations or in different settings

with American participants. More and more social psychological experiments are being performed in other cultures, however, and this activity will enrich our understanding of the external validity of many findings. For example, the inhibiting effects of bystanders on helping behavior has been replicated in at least one other country (Israel; see Schwartz & Gottlieb, 1976). As more cross-cultural research is conducted, we will be able to determine which processes are universal and which are culture-bound.

## The Basic Dilemma of the Social Psychologist

**field experiments:** experiments conducted in real-life settings, rather than in the laboratory

One of the best ways to increase external validity is by conducting **field experiments.** In a field experiment, people's behavior is studied outside of the laboratory, in its natural setting. Unlike systematic observation or the correlational method, however, the researcher controls the occurrence of an independent variable (e.g., group size) to see what effect it has on a dependent variable (e.g., helping behavior), and randomly assigns people to the different conditions. Thus, a field experiment is identical in design to a laboratory experiment except that it is conducted in a real-life setting, rather than in the relatively artificial laboratory setting. The participants in a field experiment are unaware that the events they experience are in fact an experiment. The external validity of such an experiment is high, since, after all, it is taking place in the real world, with real people who are more diverse than a typical college student sample.

Many such field studies have been conducted in social psychology. For example, Latané and Darley (1970) tested their hypothesis about group size and bystander intervention in a convenience store outside of New York City. Two "robbers" (with full knowledge and permission of the cashier and manager of the store) waited until there were either one or two other customers at the checkout counter. Then they approached the cashier and asked what was the most expensive beer the store carried. The cashier named a brand and said he would check in the back to see how much was in stock. While the cashier was gone, the robbers picked up a case of beer in the front of the store; declared, "They'll never miss this"; put the beer in their car; and drove off.

Given that the robbers were rather burly fellows, no one attempted to intervene directly to stop their theft. The question was: When the cashier returned, how many people would help by telling him that a theft had just occurred? The number of bystanders had the same inhibiting effect on helping behavior as in the laboratory seizure study: Significantly fewer people reported the theft when there was another witness/customer in the store than when they were alone.

It might have occurred to you to ask why laboratory studies are conducted at all, since field experiments are obviously so much better in terms of external validity. Why not dispense with laboratory studies and do all research in the field? Indeed, it seems to us that the perfect experiment in social psychology would be one that was conducted in a field setting, with a sample randomly selected from a population of interest, and with extremely high internal validity (all extraneous variables controlled, people randomly assigned to the conditions). Sounds good, doesn't it? The only problem is that it is very difficult to satisfy all these conditions in one study—making such studies virtually impossible to conduct.

There is almost always a trade-off between internal and external validity—that is, between (a) having enough control over the situation to ensure that no extraneous variables are influencing the results and (b) making sure that the results can be generalized to everyday life. Control is best exerted in a laboratory setting, but the laboratory may be unlike real life. Real life can be best captured by doing a field experiment, but it is very difficult to control all extraneous variables in such studies. For example, the astute reader will have noticed that Latané and Darley's (1970) beer theft study was unlike laboratory experiments in an important respect: People could not be randomly assigned to the alone or in pairs conditions. Were this the only study Latané and Darley had performed, we could not be certain whether the kinds of people who prefer to shop alone, as compared to the kinds of people who prefer to shop with a friend, differ in ways that might influence helping behavior. By randomly assigning people to conditions in their laboratory studies, Latané and Darley were able to rule out such alternative explanations.

The trade-off between internal and external validity has been referred to as the basic dilemma of the social psychologist (Aronson & Carlsmith, 1968; Aronson, Ellsworth, Carlsmith & Gonzales, 1989). The way to resolve this dilemma is to not try to do it all in a single experiment. Most social psychologists opt first for internal validity, conducting laboratory experiments in which people are randomly assigned to different conditions and all extraneous variables are controlled; here there is little ambiguity about what is causing what. Other social psychologists prefer external validity to control, conducting most of their research in field experiments. And many social psychologists do both. Taken together, both types of studies meet the requirements of our perfect experiment. Through replication, a given research question can thus be studied with maximal internal and external validity.

## Basic Versus Applied Research

Now that we have discussed the three major research methodologies in social psychology, there are two remaining issues about research we need to address. First, you might have wondered how people decide which specific topic to study. Why would a social psychologist decide to study helping behavior, cognitive dissonance theory, or the effects of pornography on aggression? Is he or she simply curious? Or does the social psychologist have a specific purpose in mind, such as trying to reduce sexual violence?

In general, we can distinguish between two types of research, each having a different purpose. The goal in **basic research** is to find the best answer to the question of why people behave the way they do, purely for reasons of intellectual curiosity. No direct attempt is made to solve a specific social or psychological problem. In contrast, the goal in **applied research** is to solve a specific problem. Rather than investigating questions for their own sake, constructing theories about why people do what they do, the aim is to find ways of alleviating such problems as racism, sexual violence, and the spread of AIDS.

**basic research:** studies that are designed to find the best answer to the question of why people behave the way they do and that are conducted purely for reasons of intellectual curiosity

**applied research:** studies designed specifically to solve a particular social problem; building a theory of behavior is usually secondary to solving a specific problem

The difference between basic and applied research is easily illustrated by examples from other sciences. Some biology researchers, for example, are concerned primarily with fundamental theoretical issues, such as the role DNA plays in the transmission of genetic information, without an immediate concern with how these issues can be applied to everyday problems. Other biology researchers are concerned primarily with applied issues, such as how to develop a strain of rice that has more protein and is more resistant to disease, in order to help solve problems of world hunger.

In most sciences, however, the distinction between basic and applied research is a fuzzy one. Even though many researchers label themselves either basic or applied scientists, it is clear that the endeavors of one group are not independent of those of the other group. There are countless examples of advances in basic science that at the time had no known applied value, but later proved to be the key to solving a significant applied problem. Basic research on DNA and genetics has led to a technology that enables researchers to create new strains of bacteria, with several important real-world applications in medicine and environmental control. For example, genetically engineered bacteria are now used in oil spills to help break up and disperse the oil. The same is true in social psychology. As we will see in Chapter 14, for example, basic research done on dogs, rats, and fish to examine the importance of feeling in control of one's environment led to techniques that improved feelings of control in elderly nursing home residents, with dramatic benefits to their health (Langer & Rodin, 1976; Richter, 1957; Schulz, 1976; Seligman, 1975).

Similarly, advances in applied research often have theoretical implications, leading to the revision of basic theories about the physical world. For example, in the mid-1700s James Watt decided to conduct experiments with an applied purpose in mind: to improve the performance of steam engines. Not only did his experiments lead to more efficient engines, but they also provided the foundation for modern theories of thermodynamics.

> There is nothing so practical as a good theory.
> —Kurt Lewin, 1951

Most social psychologists would agree that in order to solve a specific social problem, it is vital to have a good understanding of the psychological processes responsible for it. Kurt Lewin (1951), one of the founders of social psychology, coined a phrase that has become a motto for the field: "There is nothing so practical as a good theory." He meant that to solve such difficult social problems as urban violence or racial prejudice, one must first understand the underlying psychological dynamics of human nature and social interaction. In the beginning of social psychology as a discipline, differences emerged in the extent to which researchers focused directly on solving a social problem versus studying basic aspects of human nature. Lewin's own research group fell into these two camps. This dichotomy is present in the field today, with some social psychologists doing basic research primarily in laboratory settings, and others doing applied research primarily in field settings.

This book reflects the first school of social psychologists, those concerned mainly with basic theoretical issues. The subject matter of social psychology, however, is such that even when the goal is to discover the psychological processes underlying social behavior, the findings often have clear applied implications. Thus, we will see many examples of research with direct, applied implications throughout the book. In our final two chapters, we will discuss how social psychology has been applied to important social problems.

## Ethical Issues in Social Psychology

Last but not least, it is important to discuss ethical issues that are endemic to research in social psychology. In their quest to create realistic, engaging situations that capture the essence of the process under study, social psychologists frequently face an ethical dilemma. On the one hand, for obvious scientific reasons we want our experiments to resemble the real world as much as possible and to be as sound and well controlled as we can make them. On the other hand, we want to avoid causing our participants undue and unnecessary stress, discomfort, or unpleasantness. These two goals are in a constant state of tension as the researcher goes about his or her business of creating and conducting experiments.

Researchers are concerned about the health and welfare of the individuals participating in the experiment. Researchers are also in the process of discovering important information about human social behavior—such as bystander intervention, prejudice, conformity, aggression, and obedience to authority. Many of these discoveries are bound to be of benefit to society. Indeed, given the fact that social psychologists have developed powerful tools to investigate such issues scientifically, many scholars feel it would be immoral not to conduct these experiments. However, in order to gain insight into such critical issues, researchers must create vivid events that are involving for the participants. Some of these events, by their very nature, are likely to produce a degree of discomfort in the participants. Thus, what is required for good science and what is required for ethical science can be contradictory. The dilemma cannot be resolved by making pious claims that no participant ever experiences any kind of discomfort in an experiment, or by insisting that all is fair in science and forging blindly ahead. Clearly, some middle ground is called for.

The dilemma would be less problematic if researchers could obtain **informed consent** from their participants prior to their participation. If the experimenter fully describes to participants the kinds of experiences they are about to undergo and asks them if they are willing to participate, then the ethical dilemma is resolved. In many social psychology experiments, this sort of description is feasible—and where it is feasible, it is done. However, in other kinds of experiments, it is impossible. Suppose Latané and Darley had told their participants that a seizure was about to be staged, that it wouldn't be a real emergency, and that the hypothesis stated they should offer help. As we saw earlier, such a procedure would be bad science. In this kind of experiment, it's essential that the participant experience contrived events as if they were real; this is called a **deception** experiment because the events that transpire differ from what the participants were led to believe would happen. (It is important to note that not all research in social psychology involves deception.)

Some degree of compromise is called for. The dignity and safety of the participants must be protected, and the research must be conducted in a scientifically rigorous manner. It is not an easy compromise to forge. However, over the years a number of guidelines have been developed to ensure the ethical treatment of participants. For example, the American Psychological Association has published a list of ethical principles that govern all research in psychology; these ethical guidelines are summarized in Figure 2.5.

**informed consent:** explaining to participants the nature of the experiment before it begins, and obtaining their consent to participate in the experiment

**deception:** misleading or concealing from participants the true purpose of a study, or the events that will actually transpire

**Ethical Principles of Psychologists in the Conduct of Research**

1. Psychologists must take steps to avoid harming their research participants.

2. When planning research, psychologists must evaluate its ethical acceptability. Because individual researchers might not be objective judges of the ethical acceptability of their studies, they should seek ethical advice from others, including Institutional Review Boards. Institutional Review Boards are a group of scientists and nonscientists who judge whether the risks to participants outweigh the potential gains of the research.

3. As much as possible, the researcher should describe the procedures to participants before they take part in a study, and obtain informed consent from participants that documents their agreement to take part in the study as it was described to them.

4. Deception may be used only if there are no other viable means of testing a hypothesis, and only if an Institutional Review Board rules that it does not put participants at undue risk. After the study, participants must be provided with a full description and explanation of all procedures, in a post-experimental interview called the debriefing.

5. All participants must be informed that they are free to withdraw from a study at any point.

6. All information obtained from individual participants must be held in strict confidence, unless the consent of the participant is obtained to make it public.

**FIGURE 2.5 Procedures for the protection of participants in psychological research.** (Adapted from *Ethical principles of psychologists in the conduct of research,* American Psychological Association, 1992)

**debriefing:** explaining to participants, at the end of an experiment, the purpose of the study and exactly what transpired

In addition, all research conducted by psychologists must be reviewed by an Institutional Review Board, or ethics committee. Any aspect of the experimental procedure that this committee judges to be stressful or upsetting must be changed or deleted before the study can be conducted. When deception is used, the postexperimental interview, called the **debriefing** session, is crucial and must occur. During the debriefing, the participants are told about the deception and why it was necessary. If they experienced any discomfort, the researchers attempt to undo and alleviate it. Finally, the debriefing session provides an opportunity to inform the participants about the goals and purpose of the research, thereby serving an important educational function. The best researchers question their participants carefully and listen to what they say, regardless of whether or not deception was used in the experiment. (For a detailed description of how debriefing interviews should be conducted, see Aronson, Ellsworth, Carlsmith, & Gonzales, 1989.)

In our experience, virtually all participants understand and appreciate the need for deception, as long as the time is taken in the postexperimental debriefing session to go over the purpose of the research and to explain why alternative procedures could not be used. Several investigators have gone a

**THE FAR SIDE**     By GARY LARSON

It is unlikely that an Institutional Review Board would have approved this study!

step further and assessed the impact on people of participating in deception studies (e.g., Christensen, 1988; Gerdes, 1979). These studies have consistently found that people do not object to the kinds of mild discomfort and deceptions typically used in social psychological research. In fact, some studies have found that the vast majority of people who participated in deception experiments said they had learned more and enjoyed the experiments more than those who participated in *non*deception experiments did (Smith & Richardson, 1983). For example, Latané and Darley had this to say about their participants' reactions to their seizure study:

> Although the subjects experienced stress and conflict during the experiment, their general reactions to it were highly positive. On a questionnaire administered after the experimenter had discussed the nature and purpose of the experiment, every single subject found the experiment either "interesting" or "very interesting" and was willing to participate in similar experiments in the future. All subjects felt they understood what the experiment was about and indicated that they thought the deceptions were necessary and justified. (Latané & Darley, 1970, p. 101)

We do not mean to imply that all deception is beneficial. Nonetheless, if mild deception is used, and time is spent after the study discussing the deception with participants and explaining why it was necessary, the evidence is that people will not be adversely affected.

## SUMMARY

The goal of social psychology is to answer questions about social behavior scientifically. The principal research designs used are the observational, correlational, and experimental methods. Each has its strengths and weaknesses and is most appropriate for certain research questions. Each method causes the researcher to make a different type of statement about his or her findings.

The **observational method,** whether it be **systematic, participant-observational,** or **archival,** primarily fulfills a descriptive function; it allows a researcher to observe and describe a social phenomenon, with the objectivitiy of the researcher's observations tested through **interjudge reliability.** The **correlational method** allows the researcher to determine if two or more variables are related—that is, whether one can be predicted from the other. If a **positive correlation** exists, increased levels of variable A are related to increased levels of variable B. If a **negative correlation** exists, increased levels of A are related to decreased levels of B. Correlations are often calculated from survey data, in which there is **random selection** of a sample from a larger population. This ensures that the responses of the sample are representative of those of the population. The major drawback of the correlational method is that it cannot determine causality. It is not possible to determine from a correlation whether A causes B, B causes A, or some other variable causes both A and B.

For this reason, the **experimental method** is the preferred design in social psychology; it alone allows the researcher to infer the presence of causality. Experiments can occur in a laboratory setting or in a **field** setting. The **independent variables** are the ones the researcher systematically manipulates; they are the ones hypothesized to have a causal effect on behavior. The **dependent variables** are the measured variables that are hypothesized to be caused or influenced by the independent variables. The researcher makes sure that participants are treated identically except for the independent variable, and randomly assigns people to the experimental conditions. **Random assignment,** the hallmark of true experimental design, ensures that different types of people are evenly distributed across conditions. A **probability level** ($p$-**value**) is calculated, telling the researcher how likely it is that the results are due to chance versus the independent variable.

Social psychologists often use **factorial designs** for their experiments. These designs involve more than one independent variable and more than one level of each; all the various combinations of levels of independent variables are present in the experiment. In this way, the researcher can determine the independent effects of each independent variable and the unique interaction, or combination, of the levels of the independent variables with each other.

Experiments are designed to be as high as possible in **internal validity** (making sure that nothing else besides the independent variables is influencing the results) and in **external validity** (making sure that the results can be generalized across people and situations). **Mundane realism** reflects the extent to which the experimental setting is similar to real-life settings. **Psychological realism** reflects the extent to which the experiment involves psychological responses like those occurring in real life. The best test of external validity is **replication**—repeating the experiment in different settings with different people, to see if the results are the same.

Researchers engage in both **basic** and **applied research.** While the line between these is often blurred, basic research aims to gain understanding of human social behavior, without trying specifically to solve a particular problem, whereas applied research aims to solve a specific problem, often one with social policy implications. Finally, a major concern in social psychological research is the ethical treatment of participants. The American Psychological Association's guidelines are followed carefully, and include such points as **informed consent,** the ability to leave the experiment at any time, ensured anonymity and confidentiality, and **debriefing** following an experiment, particularly if **deception** (involving a **cover story** about the supposed purpose of the study or the independent or dependent variables) has been used.

## SUGGESTED READINGS

Aron, A., & Aron, E. N. (1990). *The heart of social psychology* (2nd. ed.). Lexington, MA: Heath. A behind-the-scenes look at how social psychologists conduct research, based on interviews with leading researchers.

Aronson, E., Ellsworth, P., Carlsmith, J. M., & Gonzales, M. (1989). *Methods of research in social psychology* (2nd. ed.). New York: Random House. An entertaining, thorough treatment of how to conduct social psychological research.

Rosenthal, R., & Rosnow, R. L. (1991). *Essentials of behavioral research: Methods and data analysis* (2nd. ed.). New York: McGraw-Hill. A detailed guide to methodology and statistical analyses, for the advanced student and professionals.

# PART TWO

> There are no
> lies; only
> distorted truths
> —Spinoza

# Understanding Ourselves
# and the Social World

# Chapter 3
## Cognitive Dissonance and the Need to Maintain Self-Esteem

ot long ago, Dr. Bob Arnot, medical editor of "CBS Morning News," appeared on the show to report some startling news. A group of distinguished medical researchers had just published the results of an apparently definitive study demonstrating that stretching before engaging in physical activity does not do athletes any good—and might even cause them harm. The data, based on thousands of cases, showed that people who always stretch a moderate amount suffer no fewer injuries than those who never stretch—while those who stretch deeply actually suffer more injuries than those who never stretch ("CBS Morning News," March 9, 1990).

While Dr. Arnot was reporting these data, the camera panned to New York's Central Park, where the roving reporter was interviewing several joggers. "How interesting!" exclaimed one jogger. "That's important information. Who, me? No, I almost never stretch—too much trouble." The reporter then went over to a chain-link fence, where several joggers were dutifully stretching prior to their morning run, and reported the latest finding. "I don't believe it," said one; "it can't be true." "That has to be wrong," said another; "after all, I've been stretching for over fifteen years and I have had very few muscle injuries." "That's nothing but a pack of lies!" exclaimed a third stretcher. "Why would the scientists lie?" asked the roving reporter. "To keep their jobs," answered the stretcher. "They have to come up with new 'findings' every once in a while or else they'll get fired!"

Even to the casual viewer, the contrast was striking; those people who almost never stretched didn't seem at all disturbed by the findings, while those people who had spent a lot of time stretching over the years seemed to have a difficult time believing the scientific findings—even to the point of concluding that distinguished scientists would intentionally falsify

their data. How can we account for this phenomenon?

During the past half-century, social psychologists have discovered that one of the most powerful determinants of human behavior stems from the desire of most people to think highly of themselves—that is, to maintain a relatively high level of self-esteem (Aronson, 1969; Baumeister, 1993; Greenberg, Pyszczynski, and Solomon, 1986). Most of us try to believe that we are reasonable, decent folks who make wise decisions, do not behave immorally, and have integrity. In short, we try to believe that we do not do stupid, cruel, or absurd things. But as we go through life, we encounter a great many challenges to this belief. The topic of this chapter is how human beings deal with those challenges.

## The Theory of Cognitive Dissonance

> When the heart speaks, the mind finds it indecent to object.
>
> —Milan Kundera, 1989

Let's take another look at the joggers in our opening example. Suppose you are a jogger, and out of sheer laziness, you've never stretched before jogging. You then learn that stretching does no good and might even do harm. For you, that is good news. You will feel exonerated. Indeed, even if your reason for not stretching in the past was laziness, somehow, in retrospect, you feel that you have behaved reasonably. The information provided by Dr. Arnot is not a challenge to your past behavior.

Now suppose you had spent a good deal of time, over the past few years, stretching prior to every run. In this case, the news conveyed by Dr. Arnot is not very welcome. It makes you feel uncomfortable. If you believe the data, then your past behavior is not sensible—indeed, in retrospect, it is even absurd. Therefore, you will be motivated to try to find a way to dismiss these new findings—even to the point of questioning the honesty of the scientists who conducted the research, as some of the interviewees did. The feeling of discomfort caused by information that is discrepant from your conception of yourself as a reasonable and sensible person is called **cognitive dissonance** (Aronson, 1992; Brehm & Cohen, 1962; Festinger, 1957; Festinger & Aronson, 1960).

As originally conceived by Leon Festinger (1957), dissonance was defined as an inconsistency between any two **cognitions,** or thoughts. We have many thoughts about ourselves and the world, and sometimes these thoughts clash with one another. Consider people who smoke cigarettes. They are likely to have very inconsistent cognitions—the knowledge that they smoke, on the one hand, and the knowledge that smoking can cause terrible health problems, on the other. Festinger's statement holds that whenever two cognitions are inconsistent, people will experience a type of psychological tension called dissonance.

But is it really the case that any inconsistent thoughts cause dissonance? If you could open up someone's head and examine all of his or her thoughts and beliefs, you would undoubtedly find some that contradicted each other, but did not seem to arouse much dissonance or discomfort. For example, we might believe that it is desirable to be tidy and neat, but discover one day that we left the cap off the toothpaste tube. For most of us, this inconsistency would not be particularly upsetting. Other kinds of inconsistencies, such as the clash between the thoughts "I smoke" and "Smoking can kill me," are likely to cause much greater dissonance.

As this example indicates, not all cognitive inconsistencies are equally upsetting. As the theory evolved, it became increasingly clear that dissonance is most likely to occur when we do or learn something that threatens our image of ourselves, by creating an inconsistency between who we think we are and how we behave—that is, by acts or thoughts that threaten our self-esteem (Aronson, 1969; Greenwald & Ronis, 1978; Thibodeau & Aronson, 1992). In short, cognitive dissonance occurs whenever we feel absurd, stupid, or immoral.

Cognitive dissonance always produces discomfort and therefore motivates a person to try to reduce the discomfort, in much the same way as hunger and thirst produce discomfort that motivates a person to eat or drink. But unlike the case with hunger or thirst, the ways of reducing dissonance produce very interesting behaviors. How can an individual reduce dissonance? There are three basic ways we do this:

- By changing our behavior to bring it in line with the dissonant cognition
- By justifying our behavior through changing one of the cognitions to make it less dissonant (and therefore more consonant) with the behavior
- By justifying our behavior by adding new cognitions that are consonant with the behavior and thus support it. The basic ways of reducing dissonance are displayed in Figure 3.1.

To illustrate, let's return to the example of smoking. Suppose you smoke cigarettes. You are likely to experience dissonance, because it is stupid to

**cognitive dissonance:** a drive or feeling of discomfort originally defined as being caused by holding two or more inconsistent cognitions, and subsequently defined as being caused by performing an action that is discrepant from one's conception of oneself as a decent and sensible person

**cognitions:** thoughts, feelings, beliefs, or pieces of knowledge

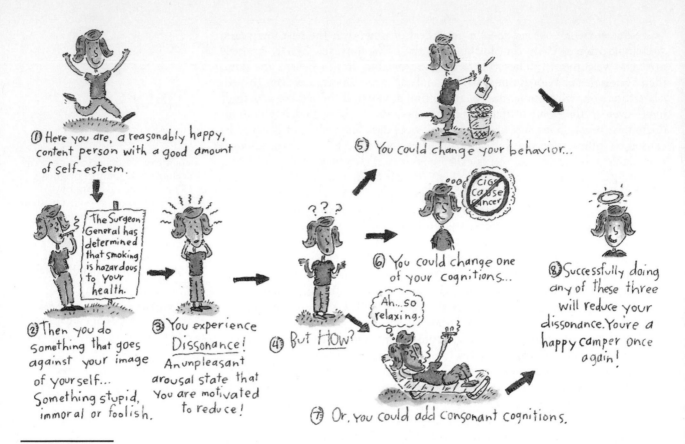

① Here you are, a reasonably happy, content person with a good amount of self-esteem.

The Surgeon General has determined that smoking is hazardous to your health.

② Then you do something that goes against your image of yourself... Something stupid, immoral or foolish.

③ You experience Dissonance! An unpleasant arousal state that you are motivated to reduce!

④ But HOW?

⑤ You could change your behavior...

⑥ You could change one of your cognitions...

Cigs Cause Cancer

Ah...so relaxing.

⑦ Or, you could add consonant cognitions.

⑧ Successfully doing any of these three will reduce your dissonance. You're a happy camper once again!

**FIGURE 3.1  How we reduce cognitive dissonance.**

engage in behavior that might lead to a painful, early death. How can you reduce this dissonance? The most direct way is to change your behavior: to give up smoking. Your behavior would then be consistent with your knowledge of the link between smoking and cancer. While many people have succeeded in doing just that, it's not easy—many have tried to quit and failed. What do these people do? It would be erroneous to assume that they simply swallow hard and prepare to die. Instead, they try to reduce their dissonance by finding some justification for their behavior.

Some smokers will try to change one of the cognitions; for example, they might try to convince themselves that the data linking cigarette smoking to cancer are inconclusive. (This is similar to what some of the stretching joggers did in our opening example.) Others will try to add new cognitions—for example, the belief that filters trap most of the harmful chemicals and thus reduce the threat of cancer. Some will add a cognition that allows them to focus on the vivid exception: "Look at old Sam Carouthers—he's ninety-seven years old and he's been smoking a pack a day since he was twelve. That proves it's not always bad for you." Still others will add the cognition that smoking is an extremely enjoyable activity—one for which it is worth risking cancer. Others may even succeed in convincing themselves that, all things considered, smoking is worthwhile because it relaxes them, reduces nervous tension, and so on.

These justifications may sound silly to the nonsmoker, and that is precisely our point. People experiencing dissonance will often go to extreme lengths to reduce it. We did not make up the examples of denial, distortion, and justification listed above; they are based on actual examples generated by people who have tried and failed to quit smoking. Similar justifications have been generated by people who have tried and failed to lose weight or who refuse to practice safer sex or who receive unwelcome information about their health (see Croyle & Jemmott, 1990; Goleman, 1982; Kassarjian & Cohen, 1965; Leishman, 1988). To escape from dissonance, people will engage in quite extraordinary rationalizing.

## Rational Behavior Versus Rationalizing Behavior

Most people proudly believe that humans are rational animals—and indeed, human beings are capable of rational behavior. But as the above examples illustrate, the need to maintain our self-esteem produces thinking that is not always rational; rather, it is rationalizing. The joggers who spent years stretching and refused to believe the antistretching research were not behaving rationally. Totally rational people would have read the report carefully, would have checked out the methodology to make sure it was sound, and, if there were no flaws, would have then ceased stretching. But people who are in the midst of reducing dissonance are so involved with convincing themselves that they are and always have been right that they frequently end up behaving irrationally and maladaptively. In this case, by continuing to justify their past behavior they would ultimately be persuading themselves to continue stretching. If the scientific methodology is sound, this would be a waste of time, at best. In the case of cigarette smoking, the end result could be tragic.

To demonstrate the irrationality of dissonance-reducing behavior, Edward E. Jones and Rika Kohler (1959) performed a simple experiment in a southern town in the late 1950s, before desegregation was widely accepted. First, they selected individuals who were deeply committed to a position on the issue of racial segregation—some of the participants were in favor of segregation, and others were opposed to it. Next, the researchers presented these individuals with a series of arguments on both sides of the issue. Some of the arguments, on each side, were plausible, and others, on each side, were rather silly. The question was, Which of the arguments would people remember best?

If Jones and Kohler's participants were behaving in a purely rational manner, we would expect them to remember the plausible arguments best and the implausible arguments the least—regardless of which side they were on. After all, why would anyone want to remember implausible arguments? What does dissonance theory predict? A silly argument in favor of one's own position arouses some dissonance, because it raises doubts about the wisdom of that position or the intelligence of the people who agree with it. Likewise, a sensible argument on the other side of the issue also arouses some dissonance, because it raises the possibility that the other side might be closer to the truth than the person had thought. Because these arguments arouse dissonance, one tries not to think about them; that is, one might not learn them very well, or one might simply forget about them. This is exactly what Jones and Kohler (1959) found. The participants in their experiment did not remember in a rational or functional manner. They tended to remember the

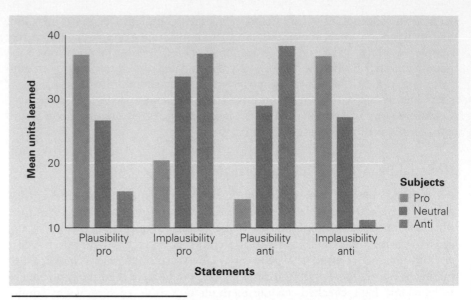

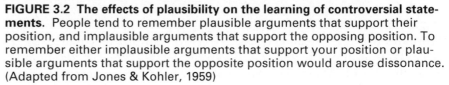

**FIGURE 3.2 The effects of plausibility on the learning of controversial statements**. People tend to remember plausible arguments that support their position, and implausible arguments that support the opposing position. To remember either implausible arguments that support your position or plausible arguments that support the opposite position would arouse dissonance. (Adapted from Jones & Kohler, 1959)

*plausible* arguments agreeing with their own position and the *implausible* arguments agreeing with the *opposing* position. Other researchers have found similar results (e.g., Lord, Ross, and Lepper, 1979; Vallone, Ross, and Lepper, 1985), all of which indicate that we humans do not process information in an unbiased manner. Rather, we distort it in a way that fits our preconceived notions. The major results of the Jones and Kohler experiment are presented in Figure 3.2.

This process probably accounts for the fact that, on issues like politics and religion, people who are deeply committed will almost never come to see things our way (the proper way!), no matter how powerful and balanced our arguments might be. The next time you watch a presidential debate, check out each viewer's opinion of who won, depending on which candidate he or she favored before the debate began. If the outcome is at all close, chances are you will find little agreement across opposing camps about which candidate was the winner.

## Decisions, Decisions, Decisions

**What Happens After a Decision.** Based on our discussion thus far, you might guess that whenever we make an important decision, we will experience dissonance. This is called **postdecision dissonance.** An important decision can be defined as a decision that is costly, is difficult to change, is effortful, or causes harm to another person. Let us illustrate what we mean with a cogent example.

A few months ago, our friend Roger traded in his eight-year-old Honda Civic and bought a brand-new Mercedes. Soon after making the purchase, Roger, who tends to be shy and unassuming, began to engage in

**postdecision dissonance:** dissonance is inevitably aroused after a person makes a decision. In this situation, dissonance is typically reduced by enhancing the attractiveness of the chosen alternative and devaluing the rejected alternatives

some uncharacteristic behaviors. He began to criticize his friends' cars, making statements like "Isn't it about time you traded in that wreck? Don't you think you deserve the pleasure of driving a well-engineered machine?" and "You know, it's really unsafe to drive little cars—if you got in an accident, it could kill you. Certainly, your life and the lives of your family members are worth an extra few thousand dollars. You have no idea how much peace of mind it brings me to know that my family is safe because I'm driving a solid, substantial automobile."

What's going on here? Why did our shy, unobtrusive friend suddenly begin imposing his views on anyone and everyone within earshot? Why did the cars we drive suddenly become so important to him? It could be that he simply got bitten by the safety or engineering bug and decided, coolly and rationally, that it would be wonderful if everyone drove a great car like the Mercedes. But there may be something else going on here. The Mercedes costs a great deal of money. It is possible that after investing all that money in a new car, Roger might have felt foolish. His thinking might have gone like this: "Gee, was it really worth it? I'll be making payments on that car for the next five years. This will really strap me. If I had settled for a new Honda Civic, I would have had a lot of money left over for other things we need. What did I do? What kind of idiot am I?"

But then, in response to his self-doubt, Roger would have begun to marshal arguments in support of his action: "The Mercedes is a wonderful car; I've worked hard all my life; I deserve it. Besides, look at the safety factor. My family's well-being is worth the extra payments." Still feeling a bit uneasy, he would then have begun to tout the Mercedes to his friends. "After all," he might have reasoned, "if sensible folks like Elliot, Tim, and Robin can be convinced to go out and buy a Mercedes, how could I ever feel that I might have done a foolish thing?" In short, if Roger could persuade others, he would feel exonerated, his dissonance would be reduced, and his self-esteem would be intact.

**When Prophecy Fails.** While our interpretation of what motivated Roger's behavior is purely speculative, a similar process of dissonance reduction through proselytizing, or trying to convince others to agree with your beliefs, has been studied closely (Festinger, Riecken, and Schachter, 1956). It all began with a newspaper article about an unusual woman and her small band of followers. Marian Keech was a charismatic, middle-aged woman living in a large midwestern city who, in the early 1950s, claimed to be receiving messages from outer space. One evening in September, she received a message from the planet Clarion informing her that on December 21 the world would be destroyed by a great flood. The message went on to say that a fleet of flying saucers would come from Clarion to rescue her and those close to her.

Keech attracted a small but loyal group of followers who fervently believed in her prophecy and who made a great many sacrifices consistent with this belief: They quit their jobs; gave away their money, houses, and possessions (who needs money and belongings on the planet Clarion?); and withdrew from their friends. A few even left their spouses.

Keech also attracted a small group of social psychologists: Leon Festinger, Henry Riecken, and Stanley Schachter. Using a participant-observation methodology, they infiltrated the movement, pretending to be believers. Their purpose was to get a precise, close-up view of what these people would do

> Fanatics have their dreams, wherewith they weave a paradise for a sect.
>
> —John Keats,
> *The Fall of Hyperion*

after December 21 when they discovered that their prophecy had (hopefully!) failed to come true. Festinger and his colleagues first noted that Keech and her followers constituted a gentle, benign, and reclusive group. One of the most interesting things about them was that they shunned publicity and discouraged converts; they were content to stick to themselves. They treated the newcomers politely, but they made it clear that it was of no consequence to them whether or not the newcomers chose to remain a part of the group. While the newspapers had picked up the story, Keech and her followers refused to grant interviews to reporters and declined to publicize their beliefs in any way.

On the morning of December 20, Marian Keech received a message from the planet Clarion instructing her group to be prepared to be picked up precisely at midnight. They were also told to remove all metal from their clothing. The group complied; zippers and clasps were dutifully removed from trousers, skirts, and blouses. When midnight passed, the members nervously checked the clock, thinking it must be running slow. As the minutes and hours dragged by, the group became increasingly engulfed by feelings of anxiety and despair. By 4:00, the group was sitting in stunned silence. Keech began to cry.

But then at 4:45, her face suddenly took on a radiant glow. She had just received a message from Clarion to the effect that there was no longer any need for the flying saucers to descend—the world had been spared a cataclysm because of the unflagging faith of this small group of believers. As you might imagine, the group was relieved and elated to hear this news. Keech's message added a new cognition that was consonant with the group members' beliefs and thus helped explain away the dissonance they were experiencing.

However, this rationalization was not enough to reduce their unease totally. Within twenty-four hours, they initiated a new rationalizing ploy. The true believers—a group of quiet, reclusive people—began calling newspapers and TV stations to talk about their prophecy. They made speeches at the drop of a hat and stood on street corners handing out leaflets, trying hard to attract new converts. The group suddenly found it of urgent importance to spread its message to as broad an audience as possible. Why? According to Festinger and his colleagues, the group, after its initial elation, experienced some doubts. Group members had given up a great deal because of their belief in the imminent end of the world. The world had not ended, and they were now devoid of their spouses, homes, jobs, and possessions. How could they be certain they had done the right thing? By convincing others, of course! In short, after their original prophecy failed to occur, the group felt motivated to attract followers as a way of convincing themselves that the sacrifices they had made were not in vain. If they could somehow persuade others that their belief had saved the world, then they could allay their misgivings that perhaps they had behaved foolishly.

**Distorting Our Likes and Dislikes.**  In the two examples, both Roger and the followers of Mrs. Keech made an important decision and were in danger of feeling foolish. In short, they were experiencing the dissonance that comes from a threat to one's self-esteem. In these situations, the easiest way to reduce dissonance was to proselytize. But there are other ways to reduce dissonance following a decision. In most situations, we can do it all by ourselves, inside our own heads, by simply distorting our perceptions of how likable something is.

Once we have committed a lot of time or energy to a cause, it is nearly impossible to convince us that the cause is unworthy.

For example, in an early experiment Jack Brehm (1956) posed as a representative of a consumer testing service and asked women to rate the attractiveness and desirability of several kinds of appliances, such as a toaster and an electric coffee maker. Each woman was told that, as a reward for having participated in the survey, she could have one of the appliances as a gift. She was given a choice between two of the products she had rated as being equally attractive. After she made her decision, her appliance was wrapped up and given to her. Twenty minutes later, each woman was asked to rerate all the products. Brehm (1956) found that after receiving the appliance of their choice, the women rated its attractiveness somewhat higher than they had done the first time. Not only that, but they drastically lowered their rating of the appliance they might have chosen, but decided to reject.

Making a decision produces dissonance. Cognitions about any negative aspects of the preferred object are dissonant with having chosen it, and cognitions about the positive aspects of the unchosen object are dissonant with not having chosen it. To reduce dissonance, people change the way they feel about both objects—cognitively spreading them apart in their own minds in order to make themselves feel better about the choice they made.

**The Permanence of the Decision.**  As we have seen, the more important the decision, the greater the dissonance. Deciding which person to marry is clearly a more important decision than deciding which car to own. Decisions also vary in terms of how permanent they are—that is, how difficult they are to revoke. It is usually a lot easier to go back to the car dealership and trade in your car for another one than it is to extricate yourself from an unhappy

Once an individual makes a final and irrevocable decision, he or she has a greater need to reduce dissonance. For example, at the racetrack, once we've placed our bet, our certainty is greater than it is immediately before we've placed our bet.

marriage. The more permanent and less revocable the decision, the greater the need to reduce dissonance.

An excellent place to investigate the significance of irrevocability is at the racetrack. Experienced bettors typically spend a great deal of time pouring over the "dope sheets" trying to decide which horse to put their money on. When they make a decision, they head for the betting windows. While they are standing in line they have already made their decision, but because it is still revocable, we would hypothesize that they have no urge to reduce dissonance. But once they get to the window and place their bet—even if it's for only $2—it is absolutely irrevocable. Thirty seconds later, one cannot go back and tell the nice person behind the window that one has changed one's mind. Therefore, if irrevocability is an important factor, one would expect greater dissonance reduction among bettors a few minutes after placing the bet than a few minutes before placing the bet.

In a simple but clever experiment, Knox and Inkster (1968) intercepted people who were on their way to place $2 bets and asked them how certain they were their horses would win. The investigators also intercepted other bettors just as they were leaving the $2 window, after having placed their bets, and asked them the same question. Almost invariably, people who had already placed their bets gave their horses a much better chance of winning than those who had yet to place their bets did. Since only a few minutes separated one group from another, nothing real had occurred to increase the probability of winning; the only thing that had changed was the finality of the decision—and thus the dissonance it produced.

The irrevocability of a decision always increases dissonance and the motivation to reduce it. Because of this, unscrupulous salespeople have devel-

Car salespeople frequently use a high-pressure technique whereby they make the customer feel like he or she has entered into an irrevocable agreement.

oped techniques for creating the illusion that irrevocability exists. One such technique, called **lowballing,** is a successful ploy used by some car sales-people. The social psychologist Robert Cialdini temporarily joined the sales force of an automobile dealership to observe this technique closely. Here's how it works: You enter an automobile showroom intent on buying a partic-ular car. Having already priced it at several dealerships, you know you can purchase it for about $13,000. You are approached by a personable, middle-aged man who tells you he can sell you one for $12,679. Excited by the bargain, you agree to the deal, and at the salesperson's request, you write out a check for the down payment, so that he can take it to the sales manager as proof that you are a serious customer.

Meanwhile, you rub your hands in glee as you imagine yourself driving home in your shiny new bargain. But alas, ten minutes later the salesperson returns, looking forlorn. He tells you that, in his zeal to give you a good deal, he made an error in calculation and the sales manager caught it. The price of the car actually comes to $13,178. You are disappointed. Moreover, you are pretty sure that you can get it a bit cheaper elsewhere. The decision to buy is not irrevocable. And yet in this situation, research by Cialdini and his col-leagues (1978) suggests that far more people will go ahead with the deal than if the original asking price had been $13,178, even though the reason for purchasing the car from this particular dealer—the bargain price—no longer exists. How come?

There are at least three reasons that lowballing works. First, while the customer's decision to buy is certainly reversible, a commitment of sorts does exist, due to the act of signing a check for a down payment. This creates the illusion of irrevocability, even though, if the car buyer really thought about it, he or she would quickly realize that it is a nonbinding contract. However,

**lowballing:** an unscrupulous strategy whereby a salesperson induces a customer to agree to purchase a product at a very low cost, subsequently claims it was an error, and then raises the price; frequently the customer will agree to make the purchase at the inflated price

in the razzle-dazzle world of high-pressure sales, even temporary illusion can have powerful consequences. Second, this commitment triggered the anticipation of an exciting event: driving out with a new car. To have had the anticipated event thwarted (by not going ahead with the deal) would have produced dissonance and disappointment. Third, although the final price is substantially higher than the customer thought it would be, it is probably only slightly higher than the price at another dealership. Under these circumstances, the customer in effect says, "Oh, what the heck. I'm already here, I've already filled out the forms, I've already written out the check—why wait?" Thus, by using dissonance reduction and the illusion of irrevocability, high-pressure salespeople increase the probability that you will decide to buy their product at their price.

**The Decision to Behave Immorally.**  Life is made up of more than just decisions about cars, appliances, and racehorses. Often our decisions involve moral and ethical issues. When is it permissible to lie to a friend, and when is it not? When is an act stealing, and when is it borrowing? Resolving moral dilemmas is a particularly interesting area in which to study dissonance because of the implications for one's self-esteem. Even more interesting is the fact that dissonance reduction following a difficult moral decision can cause people to behave either more or less ethically in the future (Mills, 1958).

Take the issue of cheating on an exam. Suppose you are a college sophomore taking the final exam in a physics course. Ever since you can remember, you have wanted to be a surgeon, and you know that your admission to medical school will depend heavily on how well you do in this physics course. The key question on the exam involves some material you know fairly well, but because so much is riding on this exam, you experience acute anxiety and draw a blank. The minutes tick away. You become increasingly anxious. You simply cannot think. You glance up and, lo and behold, you notice that you happen to be sitting behind the smartest person in the class.

You glance at her paper and notice she is just completing her answer to the crucial question. You know you could easily read her answer if you chose to. Time is running out. What do you do? Your conscience tells you it's wrong to cheat—and yet if you don't cheat, you are certain to get a poor grade. And if you get a poor grade, there goes medical school. You wrestle with your conscience.

Regardless of whether or not you decide to cheat, you are doomed to experience the kind of threat to your self-esteem that arouses dissonance. If you cheat, your cognition "I am a decent, moral person" is dissonant with your cognition "I have just committed an immoral act." If you decide to resist temptation, your cognition "I want to become a surgeon" is dissonant with your cognition "I could have acted in such a way that would have ensured a good grade and admission to medical school, but I chose not to. Wow, was that stupid!"

In this situation, some students—perhaps most—will decide to cheat; others will decide not to cheat. While that is interesting, we think an even more interesting question is, What happens to the students' attitudes about cheating after their decision? Suppose that after a difficult struggle, you decide to cheat. How do you reduce the dissonance? You can't very easily pretend you didn't cheat. That would constitute a complete denial of reality. What you could do is try to justify the action by finding a way to minimize the negative aspects of the action you chose. In this instance, an efficacious path of dissonance reduction would entail a change in your attitude about cheating. In short, you will adopt a more lenient attitude toward cheating, convincing yourself that it is a victimless crime that doesn't hurt anybody, that everybody does it so it's not really that bad, and so on.

Suppose, on the other hand, that after a difficult struggle you decide not to cheat. How would you reduce your dissonance? Once again, you could change your attitude about the morality of the act—but this time in the opposite direction. That is, in order to justify giving up a good grade, you must convince yourself that cheating is a heinous sin, that it's one of the lowest things a person can do, and that cheaters should be rooted out and severely punished.

What has come about is not merely a rationalization of your own behavior, but an actual change in your system of values; individuals faced with this kind of choice will undergo either a softening or a hardening of their attitudes toward cheating on exams, depending on whether or not they decided to cheat. The interesting and important thing to remember is that two people acting in the two different ways described above could have started out with almost identical attitudes toward cheating. Their decisions might have been a hair's breadth apart—one came within an inch of cheating but decided to resist, while the other came within an inch of resisting but decided to cheat. Once they made their decisions, however, their attitudes toward cheating will diverge sharply as a consequence of their actions.

These speculations were put to the test by Judson Mills (1958) in an experiment he performed in an elementary school. Mills first measured the attitudes of sixth-graders toward cheating. He then had them participate in a competitive exam, with prizes being offered to the winners. The situation was arranged so it was almost impossible to win without cheating. Mills made it easy for the children to cheat and created the illusion that they could not be detected. Under these conditions, as one might expect, some of the students cheated and others did not. The next day, the sixth-graders were again asked to indicate how they felt about cheating. Those children who had cheated became more lenient toward cheating, and those who had resisted the temptation to cheat adopted a harsher attitude toward cheating.

## The Justification of Effort

Most people are willing to put out a lot of effort in order to get something they really want. That's axiomatic. For example, if there's a particular job you want, you are likely to go the extra mile in order to get it. This might involve shopping for appropriate clothing, studying extra hard to meet entrance requirements, passing a battery of difficult exams, or putting up with a series of unpleasant interviews.

Let's turn that proposition inside out. Suppose you put out a great deal of effort in order to get into a particular club and it turns out to be a totally worthless organization, consisting of boring, pompous people engaged in trivial activities. You would feel pretty foolish, wouldn't you? A sensible person doesn't work hard in order to gain something trivial. Such a circumstance would produce a fair amount of dissonance; your cognition that you

What experiences might bring these recruits closer together and make them into a more cohesive unit?

**self-concept:** the sum total of one's knowledge about oneself, including one's identity, abilities and roles

are a sensible, adept human being is dissonant with your cognition that you worked hard to get into a worthless club. How would you reduce this dissonance? How would you, after the fact, justify your behavior? You could conceivably change your **self-concept** ("Perhaps I'm not a sensible, adept person, after all"), but as we shall see, the self-concept is a rather stable entity; it's the last thing a person will consider changing. A less drastic but equally effective way to reduce dissonance would be to convince yourself that the club and the people in it are nicer, more interesting, and more worthwhile than they at first glance appeared to be.

But, you're probably thinking, that would be crazy! How can you turn boring people into interesting people and a trivial club into a worthwhile one? In actuality, it's not as crazy as it might appear. Even the most boring people and trivial clubs have some redeeming qualities. Activities and behaviors are also open to a variety of interpretations; if we are motivated to see the best in people and things, we will tend to interpret these ambiguities in a positive manner. In this type of situation, dissonance aroused by the need for **justification of effort** provides the necessary motivation for this kind of distortion.

**justification of effort:** the tendency for individuals to increase their liking for something they have worked hard to attain

The classic experiment that tested the effort-dissonance link was conducted by Elliot Aronson and Judson Mills (1959). In this experiment, college women volunteered to join a group that would be meeting regularly to discuss various aspects of the psychology of sex. The women were told that if they wanted to join, they would first have to go through a screening test designed to ensure that all people admitted to the group could discuss sex freely and openly. This instruction served to set the stage for the initiation procedure. One-third of the women were assigned to a severe initiation that required them to recite aloud, in the presence of the male experimenter,

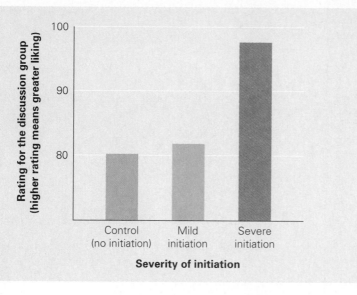

**FIGURE 3.3** The tougher the initiation the more we like the group. The more effort we put into gaining group membership, the more we like the group we have just joined. (Adapted from Aronson & Mills, 1959)

a list of obscene words and a few rather lurid sexual passages from contemporary novels. (It should be noted that this experiment was performed in the late 1950s, when this kind of procedure was far more embarrassing for most women than it would be today.) One-third of the students underwent a mild procedure, in which they recited a list of words that were sexual but not obscene. The final one-third of the participants were admitted to the group without undergoing any initiation.

Each participant was then allowed to listen in on a discussion being conducted by the members of the group she would be joining. Although the women were led to believe that the discussion was a live, ongoing one, what they actually heard was a prerecorded tape. The taped discussion was arranged so that it was as dull and bombastic as possible. After the discussion was over, each participant was asked to rate it in terms of how much she liked it, how interesting it was, how intelligent the participants were, and so forth. The major findings are shown in Figure 3.3.

The results supported the predictions: Those participants who underwent little or no effort to get into the group did not enjoy the discussion very much. They were able to see it for what it was—a dull and boring waste of time. They regretted that they had agreed to participate. Those participants who went through a severe initiation, however, succeeded in convincing themselves that the same discussion, while not as scintillating as they had hoped, was dotted with interesting and provocative tidbits and therefore, in the main, was a worthwhile experience. In short, they justified their effortful initiation process by interpreting all the ambiguous aspects of the group discussion in the most positive manner possible (see also Gerard & Mathewson, 1966).

It should be clear that we are not suggesting that most people enjoy painful experiences—they do not. Nor are we suggesting that people enjoy things because they are associated with painful experiences. What we are asserting is that, if a person agrees to go through a difficult or a painful experience in order to attain some goal or object, that goal or object becomes more attractive. Thus, if you were walking to the discussion group and a

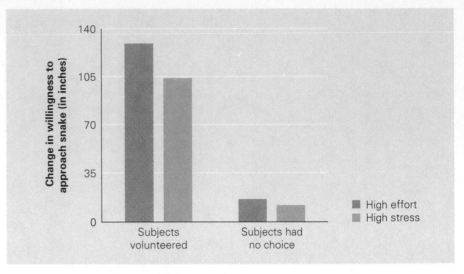

**FIGURE 3.4** The act of volunteering to be subjected to a painful or traumatic experience in order to obtain a goal (in this case, to reduce one's fear of snakes) makes it more likely that we will carry through and obtain the goal. (Adapted from Cooper, 1980)

passing car splashed mud all over you, you would not like that group any better. However, if you volunteered to jump into a mud puddle in order to be admitted to a group that turned out to be trivial and boring, you would like the group better.

The importance of volunteering to go through an unpleasant experience was demonstrated in an experiment by Joel Cooper (1980). The participants in this experiment were people who were suffering from serious snake phobias. The extent of their fear of snakes was first measured by observing how closely they dared to approach a six-foot boa constrictor that was housed in a glass tank. Participants were then put through an unpleasant set of experiences—for some, stressful, for others, effortful—which, they were informed, might have some therapeutic value in helping reduce their fear of snakes. But—and this is the crucial part—half of the participants were simply told about the procedure and then put through it. The other half were reminded of what they had all been told earlier: that they could leave the experiment at any time, that it was their choice to continue, and so on. In this manner, the sense of having volunteered for the next phase of the experiment was heightened and made salient for half of the participants. After going through the therapeutic procedure, each participant was then brought back into the presence of the boa constrictor and asked to approach it as closely as possible. Only those who had been induced to volunteer for the unpleasant therapeutic procedure showed improvement—they were able to come much closer to the boa constrictor than they had before. Those who were simply put through the unpleasant therapeutic procedure, without being strongly reminded that it was their choice and that they had volunteered, showed very little improvement (see also Axsom, 1989). The results of Joel Cooper's experiment are shown in Figure 3.4.

## The Psychology of Insufficient Justification

**Saying Is Believing.** When we were little, we were taught never to tell a lie. Indeed, our elementary school history courses were full of mythical stories (disguised as truths) like that of George Washington and the cherry tree, apparently aimed at convincing us that we had better be truthful if we aspired to the presidency. Alas, the world is a complicated place. There may be some people in the world who have never told a lie, but we have yet to meet one. At times, most of us feel that, for good reason, we need to be less than perfectly truthful. One such reason involves something else that we were taught—namely, to be kind to one another. Occasionally, in order to be kind to someone, we find it necessary to tell a lie.

For example, suppose you walk into your friend Sam's house and notice an atrocious painting on the wall. You look at it, and it's so bad you think it's a joke. You are about to burst into raucous laughter when Sam says, with considerable pleasure and excitement, "Do you like it? It cost a great deal. It's by a relatively unknown local artist named Carol Smear; I think she's very talented, so I went into hock to buy it from her. Don't you think it's beautiful?"

How do you respond? You hesitate. Chances are you go through something like the following thought process: "Sam seems so happy and excited. Why should I rain on his parade? If I were to tell him my true feelings, I would almost certainly cause him some distress. He obviously likes the painting and paid a great deal for it. Telling him my honest opinion might make him annoyed at me or might make him feel that he made a terrible mistake. Either way, it will be unpleasant. Even if I end up convincing Sam that it's a piece of garbage, he can't take it back. What's the sense in telling him the truth?"

So you tell Sam that you like the painting very much. Do you experience much dissonance? We doubt it. There are a great many thoughts that are consonant with having told this lie, as outlined in your reasoning in the above paragraph. In effect, your cognition that it is important not to cause pain to people you like provides ample **external justification** for having told a harmless lie.

But what happens if you say something you don't really believe and there is no ample external justification for doing so? What if your friend Sam was fabulously wealthy and bought paintings constantly? What if he sincerely needed to know your opinion of this purchase? What if in the past you'd told him he's bought a veritable eyesore and your friendship survived? Now the external justifications for lying to Sam about the painting are minimal. If you still refrain from giving your true opinion (saying instead, "Gee, Sam, uh, it's . . . interesting"), you will experience dissonance. When you can't find external justification for your behavior, you will attempt to find **internal justification,** by bringing the two cognitions (your attitude and your behavior) closer together. How can you do this? You begin looking for positive aspects of the painting—some evidence of creativity or sophistication that might have escaped you previously. Chances are that if you look hard enough, you will find something. Within a short time, your attitude toward the painting will have moved in the direction of the statement you made— and that is how "saying is believing." This phenomenon is generally referred to as **counterattitudinal advocacy,** a process by which individuals are induced to state publicly an opinion or attitude that runs counter to their own private attitudes. When this is accomplished with a minimum of external justification, it results in a change in the individual's private attitude in the direction of the public statement.

**external justification:** a person's reason or explanation for his or her dissonant behavior that resides outside the individual (e.g., if a person does something in order to receive a large reward or avoid a severe punishment)

**internal justification:** reducing dissonance by changing something about oneself (e.g., one's attitude or behavior)

**counterattitudinal advocacy:** the process that occurs when a person states an opinion or attitude that runs counter to his or her private belief or attitude

This proposition was first tested in a classic experiment by Leon Festinger and J. Merrill Carlsmith (1959). In this experiment, male college students were induced to spend an hour performing a series of excruciatingly boring and repetitive tasks. The experimenter then told each student that the purpose of the study was to determine whether or not people would perform better if they were told in advance that the tasks were interesting. He went on to tell the subject that he had been randomly assigned to the control condition—that is, he had not been told anything in advance. However, he explained, the next participant, who was just arriving in the anteroom, was going to be in the experimental condition. The researcher said that he needed to convince her that the task was going to be interesting and enjoyable. Since it was much more convincing if a fellow student rather than the experimenter delivered this message, would the participant do so? Thus, with his request the experimenter induced the participants to lie about the task to another student (actually a confederate).

Half of the students were offered $20 for telling the lie (a large external justification), while the others were offered only $1 for telling the lie (a very small external justification). After the experiment was over, an interviewer asked the lie-tellers how much they had enjoyed the tasks they had performed earlier in the experiment. The results validated the hypothesis: Those students who had been paid $20 for lying—that is, for saying that the tasks had been enjoyable—rated the activities as the dull and boring experiences they were. But those who were paid only $1 for saying the task was enjoyable rated the task as significantly more enjoyable. In other words, people who had received an abundance of external justification for lying told the lie but didn't believe it, whereas those who told the lie without a great deal of external justification succeeded in convincing themselves that what they said was true.

One might ask whether this phenomenon works when important attitudes are involved. Can you induce a person to change an attitude about things that matter? Subsequent research has shown that the Festinger-Carlsmith paradigm has wide ramifications in areas of great significance. Consider the experiment by A. R. Cohen (1962), for example. Cohen was a social psychologist at Yale University during a turbulent period, when the city police were often descending on the campus to control the overly exuberant behavior of the Yale students. Occasionally the police reacted with gleeful and excessive force. After one such altercation, Cohen visited a Yale dormitory, indicating he worked for a well-known research institute. He told the students there were two sides to every issue, and the institute was interested in looking at both sides of the police-student issue. He then asked the students to write forceful essays supporting the behavior of the police. Moreover, he told them that he was able to offer them an incentive for writing the essay. Depending on the condition to which the students were assigned, he offered them 50¢, $1, $5, or $10. (None of the students was aware of what the others were being offered.) After the students wrote their essays, Cohen assessed their real attitude toward the actions of the city police.

The results were clear. The smaller the incentive, the more favorable people became toward the city police. In other words, when the students were given a great deal of external justification for writing the essay, they did not need to convince themselves that they really believed what they had written. However, when they were faced with the fact that they had written positive things about the police for 50¢ or $1, they needed to convince themselves that there may have been some truth in what they had written.

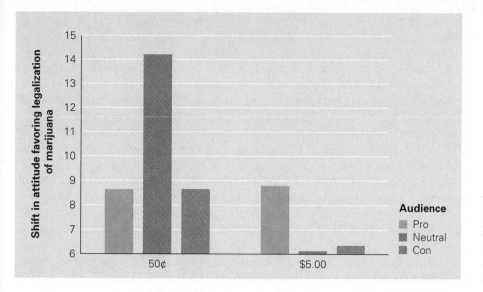

**FIGURE 3.5** Students came to believe their own speech only if their audience was persuasable and the incentive was small. (Adapted from Nel, Helmreich, and Aronson, 1969)

In a similar experiment, Elizabeth Nel, Robert Helmreich and Elliot Aronson (1969) induced college students who were opposed to the use of marijuana to compose and recite a videotaped speech favoring its use and legalization. Some were offered large incentives; others were offered small incentives. Again the findings were clear: the smaller the incentive, the greater the softening of the attitude toward the use and legalization of marijuana.

As an additional wrinkle on this paradigm, these researchers also varied the audience to whom the videotape would supposedly be played. Nel and her colleagues hypothesized that if the audience consisted of high school students who had not yet made up their minds about the desirability of smoking marijuana, the college students making the tape would experience a great deal of dissonance. They would be in grave danger of convincing naive young people to engage in behavior they personally thought was bad. In order to reduce their dissonance, and in the absence of a large external justification for their act, they would have to persuade themselves that marijuana was not so bad after all.

On the other hand, Nel and her colleagues hypothesized, if the tape was going to be played to an audience that had already made up their minds about the use of marijuana, then it would have little or no effect on the audience's behavior and, consequently, much less dissonance would be aroused. If little dissonance was present, there would be little need to change one's attitude in the direction of the speech. The results of the experiment supported the predictions. The greatest shift in attitude toward the use and legalization of marijuana was in the condition where, for a very small incentive, people recorded a promarijuana message that they believed would be shown to impressionable, persuadable young people. When the audience was believed to be strongly for or strongly against the use of marijuana, dissonance was minimal regardless of the size of the incentive. The results are illustrated in Figure 3.5.

**Hypocrisy and AIDS Prevention.** In recent years, AIDS has become an epidemic of epic proportions. Hundreds of millions of dollars have been spent on AIDS information and prevention campaigns in the mass media. While these campaigns have been effective in conveying information, they have not been nearly so successful in preventing people from engaging in risky sexual behavior. For example, although college students are aware of AIDS as a serious problem, a surprisingly small percentage use condoms every time they have sex. The reason seems to be that condoms are inconvenient and unromantic and remind people of disease—the last thing they want to be reminded of when getting ready to make love. Rather, as researchers have consistently discovered, people have a strong tendency to experience denial where sexual behavior is involved—in this case, to believe that while AIDS is a problem for most people, they, themselves, are not at risk. If the mass media have been ineffective, is there anything else that can be done?

Recently Elliot Aronson, Carrie Fried, and Jeff Stone (1991) have had some success at convincing people to use condoms, by employing a variation of the saying is believing paradigm. They asked college students to compose a speech describing the dangers of AIDS and advocating the use of condoms every single time you have sex. In one condition, the students merely composed the arguments. In another condition, the students composed the arguments and then recited them in front of a video camera, after being informed that the resulting videotape would be played to an audience of high school students. In addition, half the students in each condition were made mindful of their own failure to use condoms by making a list of the circumstances in which they had found it particularly difficult, awkward, or impossible to use them.

Essentially, then, the participants in one condition—those who made a video for high school students after having been made mindful of their own failure to use condoms—were in a state of high dissonance. This was caused by their being made aware of their own hypocrisy; they were fully aware of the fact that they were preaching behavior to high school students that they themselves were not practicing. In order to remove the hypocrisy and maintain their self-esteem, they would need to start practicing what they were preaching. And that is exactly what Aronson and his colleagues found: Students in the hypocrisy condition showed a greater willingness to increase their use of condoms, as compared to students in the control conditions. Moreover, in a follow-up experiment (Stone, Aronson, Crain, Winslow, and Fried, 1993) each student was given the opportunity to purchase condoms very cheaply. The results demonstrated that the students in the hypocrisy condition were far more likely to buy condoms than students in any of the other conditions were. Figure 3.6 illustrates the results of this experiment.

**Insufficient Punishment.**  Complex societies run, in part, on punishment or the threat of punishment. As members of society, we constantly find ourselves in situations where those who are charged with the duty of maintaining law and order are threatening to punish us if we do not comply with their rules and regulations. For example, while cruising down the highway at seventy miles an hour, we know that if we get caught, we will end up paying a substantial fine. If it happens often, we will lose our license. So we learn to obey the speed limit when there are patrol cars in the vicinity. By the same token, youngsters in school know that if they cheat on an exam and get caught, they could be humiliated by the teacher and severely punished. So they learn not to cheat while the teacher is in the room watching them. But does harsh punishment teach adults to want to obey the speed limit? Does it

**insufficient punishment:** the dissonance aroused when individuals lack sufficient external justification for having resisted a desired activity or object, usually resulting in individuals devaluing the forbidden activity or object

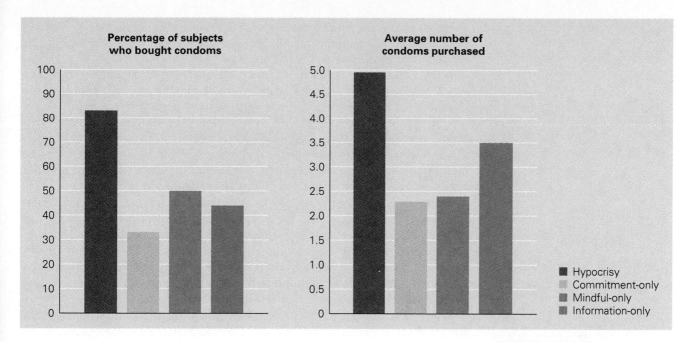

**FIGURE 3.6** People who are made mindful of their hypocrisy begin to practice what they preach. (Adapted from Stone, Aronson, Crain, Winslow, and Fried, 1993)

teach youngsters to value honest behavior? We don't think so. Rather, we believe that all it teaches us is to try to avoid getting caught. In short, the use of threats of harsh punishment as a means of getting someone to refrain from doing something he or she enjoys doing requires constant vigilance and harassment.

Let's look at bullying behavior. It is extremely difficult to persuade children that it's not right or enjoyable to beat up smaller children. But theoretically, it is conceivable that under certain conditions they will persuade themselves that such behavior is unenjoyable. Imagine that you are the parent of a six-year-old boy who often beats up his four-year-old brother. You've tried to reason with him, but to no avail. So in order to make him a nicer person (and in order to preserve the health and welfare of his little brother), you begin to punish him for his aggressiveness. As a parent, you have at your disposal a number of possible punishments, ranging from the extremely mild (a stern look) to the extremely severe (a hard spanking, forcing the child to stand in the corner for two hours, and depriving him of TV privileges for a month). The more severe the threat, the greater the likelihood the youngster will cease and desist—while you are watching him. But he may very well hit his brother again as soon as you are well out of sight. In short, just as most drivers learn to be vigilant of the Highway Patrol while speeding, your six-year-old has not lost his enjoyment of bullying his little brother; he has merely learned not to do it while you are around to punish him.

Suppose that you threaten him with a very mild punishment. In either case—under threat of severe punishment or of mild punishment—the child experiences dissonance. He is aware that he is not beating up his little brother, and he is also aware that he would very much like to beat him up. When he has the urge to hit his brother and doesn't, he implicitly asks himself, "How come I'm not beating up my little brother?" Under severe threat, he has a convincing answer in the form of a sufficient external justification: "I'm not beating him up because if I do, my parents are going to really punish me." This serves to reduce the dissonance.

The child in the mild threat situation experiences dissonance too. But when he asks himself, "How come I'm not beating up my little brother?" he doesn't have a very convincing answer, because the threat is so mild it does not provide a superabundance of justification. The child is refraining from doing something he wants to do, and while he does have a modicum of justification for not doing it, he lacks complete justification. In this situation, he continues to experience dissonance. Therefore, the child must find another way to justify the fact that he is not aggressing against his kid brother.

The less severe the threat, the less external justification; the less external justification, the greater the need for internal justification. The child can reduce his dissonance by convincing himself that he doesn't really want to beat up his brother. In time, he can go further in his quest for internal justification and decide that beating up little kids is not fun. Allowing children the leeway to construct their own internal justification is tantamount to enabling them to develop a permanent set of values.

Thus far, this has all been speculative. Will threats of mild punishment for performing any behavior diminish the attractiveness of that behavior to a greater extent than severe threats? This proposition was first investigated in an experiment with preschoolers (Aronson & Carlsmith, 1963).

In this experiment, because the researchers were dealing with very young children, ethical concerns precluded their trying to affect important values, like those concerning aggressive behavior. Instead, they attempted to change something that was of no great importance to society but was of great importance to the children: their preference for different kinds of toys. The experimenter first asked each child to rate the attractiveness of several toys. He then pointed to a toy that the child considered very attractive and told the child that he or she was not allowed to play with it. Half the children were threatened with mild punishment if they disobeyed; the other half were threatened with severe punishment. The experimenter then left the room and gave the children the opportunity to play with the other toys and to resist the temptation of playing with the forbidden toy. None of the children played with the forbidden toy.

After several minutes, the experimenter returned to the room and asked the child to rate how much he or she liked each of the toys. Initially, all of the children had wanted to play with the forbidden toy. During the temptation period, all of them had refrained from playing with it. Clearly, this disparity means that dissonance was aroused in the children. How did they respond? The children who had received a severe threat had ample justification for their restraint. They knew why they hadn't played with the attractive toy, and they thus had no reason to change their attitude about the toy. These children continued to rate the forbidden toy as highly desirable; indeed, some even found it more desirable than they had before the threat.

But what about the others? Lacking an abundance of external justification for refraining from playing with the toy, the children in the mild threat condition needed an internal justification to reduce their dissonance. They succeeded in convincing themselves that the reason they hadn't played with the toy was that they didn't really like it. They rated the forbidden toy as less attractive than they had at the beginning of the experiment. What we have here is a clear example of self-justification leading to self-persuasion in the behavior of very young children. The implications for child rearing are fascinating.

**The Permanence of Self-Persuasion.**  Let's say you've attended a lecture on the evils of cheating. It might have a temporary effect on your attitudes toward cheating. But if a week or two later you found yourself in a highly tempting situation, your recent change in attitude would probably lack the staying power to act as a deterrent. Social psychologists know that mere lectures do not usually result in permanent or long-lasting attitude change. In contrast, suppose you went through the kind of situation experienced by the children in Judson Mill's (1958) experiment on cheating, discussed earlier in this chapter. Here we would expect the attitude change to be far more deep-seated and permanent. Those children who were tempted to cheat but resisted the temptation came to believe that cheating is a dastardly thing to do, not because someone told them so, but because they persuaded themselves of this belief as a means of justifying the fact that, by not cheating, they had given up an attractive prize.

The long-lasting effects of attitudes generated by **self-persuasion** and self-justification have been clearly demonstrated in a number of contexts. To take one dramatic example, Jonathan Freedman (1965) performed a replication of Aronson and Carlsmith's (1963) forbidden toy experiment. In Freedman's version of the experiment, the forbidden toy was an attractive battery-powered robot; all the children in the experiment were eager to play with it. But Freedman forbade them from doing so, indicating that they could play with the other toys—which were pallid by comparison—if they wanted to. Just as in the original experiment, he issued either a mild threat or a severe threat for breaking the rule. And just as in the original experiment, all of the children obeyed the rule. Freedman then left the school and never returned.

Now here is the interesting part. Several weeks later, a young woman came to the school, ostensibly to administer some paper-and-pencil tests to the children. In actuality, she was working for Freedman; however, the children were totally unaware that her presence was in any way related to Freedman, the toys, or the threats that had occurred several weeks earlier. Coincidentally, she was administering her tests in the same room Freedman had used for his experiment—the room where the same toys were casually scattered about. After administering the test, she asked the children to wait for her while she went to the next room to score the test. She then casually suggested that the scoring might take a while, and that—how lucky!—someone had left some toys around, and the children could play with any of them they wanted to.

The results were striking: The overwhelming majority of the children whom Freedman had mildly threatened several weeks earlier decided, on their own, not to play with the robot; they played with the pallid toys instead. On the other hand, the great majority of the children who had been severely threatened did in fact play with the robot now that they had the opportunity to do so. Specifically, 78 percent of the children in the severe threat condition played with the toy, while only 33 percent of the children in the mild threat condition did so. Thus, a single mild threat was still very effective several weeks later, while a severe threat was not. Again, the power of this phenomenon rests on the fact that the reason the children didn't play with

**self-persuasion:** a long-lasting form of attitude change that results from attempts at self-justification

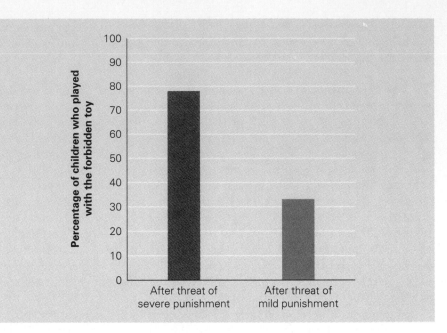

**FIGURE 3.7** Several weeks afterwards, children who received a threat of mild punishment were far less likely to play with the forbidden toy than children who received a threat of *severe* punishment. Those given a mild threat had to provide their own justification by devaluing the attractiveness of the toy. (Adapted from Freedman, 1963, 1965)

the toy was not that some adult told them the toy was undesirable; such admonitions would not have persisted for very long after the admonishing adult had left the premises. The reason the mild threat persisted for at least several weeks was that the children were motivated to convince themselves the toy was undesirable. The results of Freedman's experiment are presented in Figure 3.7.

### What Do We Mean by "Insufficient Justification"?

Throughout this chapter, we have talked about self-justification occurring in situations where there is insufficient external justification. For example, we showed how saying something you don't believe will produce a shift in belief in the direction of what you said only if there is no adequate tangible reward for having said it. Similarly, we have shown that refraining from performing a particular activity will result in a derogation of that activity only if there is not fully adequate punishment to justify continued compliance.

The term insufficient external justification needs clarification. In one sense, it is sufficient—sufficient to produce the behavior. For example, the students in Festinger and Carlsmith's (1959) experiment did agree to lie about how interesting it was to perform the boring job. The experimenter's request was just sufficient to get them to do the behavior, but it wasn't sufficient, later, for them to explain to themselves how they could have done such a mean thing to another student. After all, nobody had held a gun to their heads; they agreed, of their own free will, to lie—at least, that's how these participants saw it.

In fact, this situation, like many others in life, is characterized by the "illusion of freedom." We think we're free to choose our response, but powerful social norms and rules often dictate what we will actually do. How could these participants say no to a politely worded, fairly innocuous request from an authority figure? The cards were stacked—indeed, close to 100 percent of participants in these types of studies agree to the experimenter's request; basically, no one says no. So how much real choice could there be?

And yet the participants don't perceive the inherent restraints on their ability to truly choose between saying yes or no to the request. Later, when thinking about why they lied to an innocent person, they don't blame it on the experimenter and his or her request; they see it as their personal choice. And the best way to maintain their self-esteem is to decide that the task was sort of fun and interesting, after all; hence, it wasn't such a lie.

Thus, while we like to think of ourselves as fully rational creatures, we frequently find ourselves doing things without entirely thinking them through—saying yes when we wanted to say no, and so on. Indeed, the irony is that precisely because we like to believe that we are rational, sensible, and moral creatures, we are vulnerable to dissonance-induced self-persuasion.

**And It Isn't Just Rewards or Punishments.**  As we have seen, a sizable reward or a severe punishment is an effective way of providing external justification for an action. Accordingly, if you want a person to do something or refrain from doing something only once, the best strategy would be to promise a large reward or threaten a severe punishment. But if you want a person to develop a deep-seated attitude, the smaller the reward or punishment that will induce momentary compliance, the greater will be the eventual attitude change and therefore the more permanent the effect. Large rewards and severe punishments, because they are strong external justifications, militate against dissonance and thus prevent attitude change.

We should note that this phenomenon is not limited to tangible rewards and punishments; justifications can come in more subtle packages as well. Take friendship, for example. We like our friends; we trust our friends; we do favors for our friends. Suppose you are at a formal dinner party at the home of a close friend. Your friend is passing around a rather strange-looking appetizer. It's not quite a potato chip, but it looks like it's been fried. "What is it?" you ask warily. "Oh, it's a fried grasshopper; I'd really like you to try it," answers your friend. Because she's a good friend and you don't want to cause her any discomfort or embarrassment in front of the other guests, you gingerly pick one out of the bowl, place it in your mouth, chew it up, and swallow it. How much do you think you will like this new snack food?

Keep that in mind for a moment as we expand the example. Suppose you are a dinner guest at the home of a person you don't like very much, and he hands you, as an appetizer, a fried grasshopper and tells you that he'd really like you to try it. In much the same way, you put it in your mouth, chew it up, and swallow it. Now the crucial question: In which of these two situations will you like the taste of the grasshopper better? Common sense might suggest that the grasshopper would taste better when recommended by a friend. But think about it for a moment; which condition involves less external justification? Common sense notwithstanding, dissonance theory makes the opposite prediction. In the first case, when you ask yourself, "How come I ate that disgusting insect?" you have ample justification: You ate it because your good friend asked you to. In the second case, you lack this kind of justification for having eaten the grasshopper. Therefore, you must add some justification of your own; namely, you must convince yourself that it was tastier than you would have imagined, that as a matter of fact, it was quite good—"I'm thinking of laying in a supply myself."

While this may seem a rather bizarre example of dissonance-reducing behavior, it's not as farfetched as you might think. Indeed, Phillip Zimbardo and his colleagues (1965) conducted an experiment directly analogous to our

> We do not love people so much for the good they have done us, as for the good we have done them.
>
> —Leo Tolstoy, 1869

example. In this experiment, army reservists were asked to eat fried grasshoppers as part of a research project on survival foods. Reservists who ate grasshoppers at the request of a stern, unpleasant officer increased their liking for grasshoppers far more than those who ate grasshoppers at the request of a well-liked, pleasant officer. Those who complied with the unfriendly officer's request had little external justification for their actions. As a result, they adopted more positive attitudes toward eating grasshoppers in order to justify their otherwise strange and dissonance-arousing behavior.

## The Aftermath of Good and Bad Deeds

**How We Come to Like Our Beneficiaries: The Ben Franklin Manipulation.** It is obvious that when we like people, we tend to treat them well, speak kindly to them, do them favors, and smile at them benevolently. If we don't like them, we treat them less kindly, avoid them, say bad things about them, and perhaps even go out of our way to snub them. But what happens when we do a person a favor? In particular, what happens when we are subtly induced to do a favor for a person we do not like? Will we like them more or less? Dissonance theory predicts that we will like that person more after doing him or her the favor.

This phenomenon was hardly discovered by dissonance theorists; in fact, it is a part of folk wisdom. Indeed, in 1736 Benjamin Franklin confessed to having utilized this bit of folk wisdom as a political strategy. While serving as a member of the Pennsylvania state legislature, Franklin was disturbed by the political opposition and apparent animosity of a fellow legislator. So he set out to win him over:

> I did not . . . aim at gaining his favour by paying any servile respect to him but, after some time, took this other method. Having heard that he had in his library a certain very scarce and curious book I wrote a note to him expressing my desire of perusing that book and requesting he would do me the favour of lending it to me for a few days. He sent it immediately and I returned it in about a week with another note expressing strongly my sense of the favour. When we next met in the House he spoke to me (which he had never done before), and with great civility; and he ever after manifested a readiness to serve me on all occasions, so that we became great friends and our friendship continued to his death. This is another instance of the truth of an old maxim I had learned, which says, "He that has once done you a kindness will be more ready to do you another than he whom you yourself have obliged." (Bigelow, pp. 216–217)

Benjamin Franklin was clearly pleased with the success of his blatantly manipulative strategy. As skeptical scientists, we should not be fully convinced by this anecdote. It is not entirely clear whether Franklin's success was due to this particular gambit or simply to his charm. In order to be certain, it is important to design and conduct an experiment that controls for such things as charm. Such a study was conducted by Jon Jecker and David Landy (1969), more than 230 years after Franklin's more casual experiment.

In the Jecker and Landy (1969) experiment, students participated in a concept-formation task that enabled them to win a substantial sum of money.

After the experiment was over, one-third of the participants were approached by the experimenter, who explained that he was using his own funds for the experiment and was running short, which meant he might be forced to close down the experiment prematurely. He asked, "As a special favor to me, would you mind returning the money you won?" The same request was made to a different group of subjects—except this time, not by the experimenter but by the departmental secretary, who asked them if they would return the money as a special favor to the psychology department's research fund, which was running low. The remaining participants were not asked to return their winnings. Finally, all of the participants were asked to fill out a questionnaire, which included an opportunity to rate the experimenter. Those participants who had been cajoled into doing a special favor for the experimenter found him the most attractive—they had convinced themselves he was a wonderful, deserving fellow. The others thought he was a pretty nice guy, but not anywhere near as wonderful as the people who had been asked to do him a favor. Figure 3.8 shows the results of this experiment.

**How We Come to Hate Our Victims.**   Several years ago, during the height of the war in Vietnam, one of us hired a young man to help paint his house. Here are Elliot's reminiscences:

> The painter was a gentle and sweet-natured person who had graduated from high school, joined the army, and fought in Vietnam. After leaving the army, he took up housepainting and was a good and reliable craftsman and an honest businessman. I enjoyed working with him. One day while we were taking a coffee break, we began to discuss the war and the intense opposition to it, especially at the local university. It soon became apparent that he

Without realizing it, Ben Franklin may have been the first dissonance theorist.

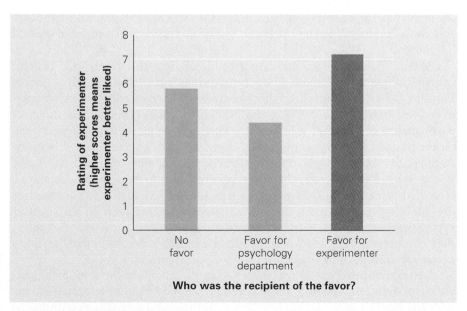

**FIGURE 3.8**  If we have done someone a favor, we are more likely to feel more positively toward that person. (Adapted from Jecker & Landy, 1969)

and I were in sharp disagreement on this issue. He felt that the American intervention was reasonable and just and would "make the world safe for democracy." I argued that it was a terribly dirty war, that we were killing, maiming, and napalming thousands of innocent people: old people, women, children—people who had no interest in war or politics. He looked at me for a long time; then he smiled sweetly and said, "Hell, Doc, those aren't people; those are Vietnamese! They're gooks." He said it matter-of-factly, without obvious rancor or vehemence. I was astonished and chilled by his response. I wondered how it could be that this apparently good-natured, sane, and gentle young man could develop that kind of attitude. How could he dismiss an entire national group from the human race?

Over the next several days, as we continued our dialogue, I got to know more about him. It turned out that during the war he had participated in actions in which Vietnamese civilians had been killed. What gradually emerged was that initially he had been wracked by guilt—and it dawned on me that he might have developed this attitude toward the Vietnamese people as a way of assuaging his guilt. That is, if he could convince himself that the Vietnamese were not fully human, it would make him feel less awful about having hurt them, and it would reduce the dissonance between his actions and his self-concept as a decent person.

It goes without saying that these speculations about the causes of the housepainter's attitude are far from conclusive. While it is conceivable that he derogated the Vietnamese people as a way of reducing dissonance, the situation is complex; for example, he might have always had a negative and prejudiced attitude toward the Vietnamese, and this might have made it easier for him to behave brutally toward them. To be certain that the justification of cruelty can occur in such situations, it is essential for the social psychologist to temporarily step back from the helter-skelter of the real world and test the proposition in the more controlled setting of the experimental laboratory.

Ideally, if we want to measure attitude change as a result of dissonant cognitions, we should know what the attitudes were before the dissonance-arousing behavior occurred. Such a situation was produced in an early experiment performed by Keith Davis and Edward E. Jones (1960). Each student's participation consisted of watching a young man being interviewed and then, on the basis of this observation, providing him with an analysis of his shortcomings as a human being. Specifically, the participants were told to tell the young man (a confederate) that they believed him to be a shallow, untrustworthy, boring person. The participants succeeded in convincing themselves they didn't like the victim of their cruelty—after the fact. In short, after saying things they knew were certain to hurt him, they convinced themselves that he deserved it. They found him less attractive than they had prior to saying the hurtful things to him.

Let us return to our housepainter example. Suppose for a moment that all the people he killed and injured in Vietnam had been fully armed enemy soldiers, instead of a sizable number of noncombatants. Do you think he would have experienced as much dissonance? We think it is unlikely. When engaged in combat with an enemy soldier, it is a "you or me" situation; if the

During wartime, especially when defenseless civilians such as old people, women, and children are targets of military violence, the soldiers committing such acts of violence will become inclined to derogate or dehumanize their victims—after the fact—to reduce their dissonance.

housepainter had not killed the enemy soldier, the enemy soldier might have killed him. Thus, while hurting or killing another person is probably never taken lightly, it is not nearly so heavy a burden as it would be if the victim was an unarmed civilian—a child, a woman, an old person.

These speculations are supported by the results of an experiment by Ellen Berscheid and her colleagues (Berscheid, Boye, and Walster, 1968). In this study, college students volunteered for an experiment in which each of them administered a (supposedly) painful electric shock to a fellow student. As one might expect, these students derogated their victim as a result of having administered the shock to him or her. However, half of the students were told there would be a turnabout—the other student would be given the opportunity to retaliate against them at a later time. Those who were led to believe that their victim would be able to retaliate later did not derogate the victim. In short, because the victim was going to be able to even the score, there was very little dissonance, and therefore the harm-doers had no need to belittle their victim in order to convince themselves that he or she deserved it.

The results of these laboratory experiments lend credence to our speculations about the behavior of the housepainter; the results suggest that during a war, military personnel have a greater need to derogate civilian victims (because these individuals can't retaliate) than military victims. Moreover, several years after Elliot's encounter with the housepainter, a similar set of

Dehumanizing their victims provides the aggressor with justification for brutal acts that feeds into a horrifying, endless chain of escalating violence against their victims.

events emerged during the court-martial of Lieutenant William Calley for his role in the slaughter of innocent civilians at My Lai in Vietnam. In a long and detailed testimony, Lieutenant Calley's psychiatrist made it clear that the lieutenant had come to regard the Vietnamese people as less than human.

As we have seen, systematic research in this area demonstrates that people do not perform acts of cruelty and come out unscathed. We can never be completely certain of how the housepainter, Lieutenant Calley, and thousands of other American military personnel came to regard the Vietnamese as subhuman, but it seems reasonable to assume that when people are engaged in a war where a great number of innocent people are being killed, they might try to derogate the victims in order to justify their complicity. They might poke fun at them, refer to them as "gooks," and dehumanize them. Ironically, success at dehumanizing the victim virtually guarantees a continuation or even an escalation of the cruelty. It becomes easier to hurt and kill subhumans than to hurt and kill fellow human beings. Thus, reducing dissonance in this way has sobering future consequences: It increases the likelihood that the atrocities people are willing to commit will become greater and greater through an endless chain of violence followed by self-justification (in the form of dehumanizing the victim), followed by greater violence and still more intense dehumanization. In this manner, unbelievable acts of human cruelty—such as the Nazi "Final Solution" that led to the murder of 6 million European Jews—can occur. Needless to say, atrocities are not a thing of the past but are as recent as today's newspaper.

> There's nothing people can't contrive to praise or condemn and find justification for doing so.
> –Molière, *The Misanthrope*

## The Evidence for Motivational Arousal

The phenomenon of discomfort or arousal is crucial to the formulation of the theory of cognitive dissonance. Arousal is what drives the engine, what motivates the individual to change his or her attitude or behavior. Is there any independent evidence indicating that people who experience dissonance are in a state of discomfort or arousal? A fascinating experiment by Mark Zanna and Joel Cooper (1974) provides just such evidence. Participants in their study were given a placebo—a milk-powder pill having no physiological effect whatever. Some were told that the pill would arouse them and make them feel tense. Others were told that the pill would make them feel calm and relaxed. Participants in the control condition were told that the pill would not affect them in any way. After ingesting the pill, each person voluntarily wrote a counterattitudinal essay, thus creating dissonance.

Dissonance theory predicts that such participants will change their attitudes, bringing them in line with their essays in order to reduce their uncomfortable arousal state, only if they actually feel aroused. However, if some of the participants think the arousal they are experiencing is due to the pill, they won't need to alter their attitudes to feel better about themselves. At the opposite end of the spectrum, if some of the participants think they should be feeling relaxed due to the pill, any arousal they experience should be very salient to them and they should change their attitudes a great deal. Thus, the theory predicts that attitude change will come or go across conditions, depending on whether the arousal due to dissonance is masked by an alternative explanation ("Oh, right—I took a pill that's supposed to make me feel tense; that's why I'm feeling this way") or magnified by an alternative explanation ("Oh no—I took a pill that's supposed to make me feel relaxed and I feel tense").

Zanna and Cooper's (1974) results supported these predictions. Participants in the control condition underwent considerable attitude change, as would be expected in a typical dissonance experiment. Participants in the aroused condition, however, did not change their attitudes—they attributed their discomfort to the pill, not their counterattitudinal essay. Finally, participants in the relaxed condition changed their attitudes even more than the control participants did. They inferred that writing the counterattitudinal

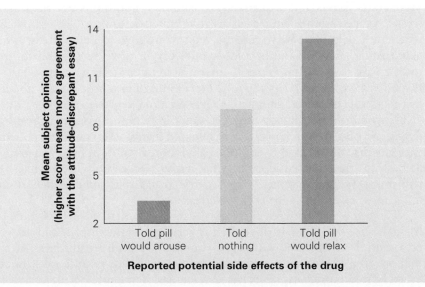

**FIGURE 3.9** If subjects can misattribute the arousal associated with the dissonance, they do not show the typical attitude change following a counterattitudinal essay. This is strong support for the notion that dissonance causes physiological arousal. (Adapted from Zanna & Cooper, 1974)

essay had made them very tense, since they were feeling aroused despite a relaxing drug. Thus, they inferred that their behavior was very inconsistent with their perception of themselves as decent and reasonable people, and they changed their attitude to bring it into line with their essay contents. These data are illustrated in Figure 3.9.

## New Directions in Research on Self-Esteem Maintenance

Throughout this chapter, we've indicated that humans have a need to see themselves as generally intelligent, sensible, and decent folks who behave with integrity. Indeed, what triggers the attitude change and distortion that can take place in the process of dissonance reduction is precisely the need people have to maintain this picture of themselves. At first glance, much of the behavior described in this chapter seems startling: people coming to dislike others more after doing them harm, people liking others more after doing them a favor, people believing a lie they've told only if there is little or no reward for telling it, and so on. These behaviors would be difficult for us to understand if it weren't for the insights provided by the theory of cognitive dissonance.

In recent years, social psychologists have taken this basic premise—that people have a fundamental need to maintain their self-esteem—in fascinating new directions. For example, most dissonance research has been concerned with how our self-image is threatened by our own behavior, such as lying to someone or acting contrary to our attitudes. Abraham Tesser (1988) has explored how other people's behavior can threaten our self-image in ways that have important implications for our interpersonal relationships.

### Self-Evaluation Maintenance Theory

Suppose you consider yourself to be a very good cook—in fact, the best cook of all your friends and acquaintances. You love nothing better than playing with a recipe, adding your own creative touches, until voilà!—you have a wonderful, delectable new creation. Then you move to another town, make new friends, and—lo and behold!—your very favorite new friend turns out to be a superb cook, far better than you. How does that make you feel? We suspect you will agree that you might feel more than a little uneasy about the fact that your friend outdoes you in your area of expertise.

Now consider a slightly different scenario. Suppose your new best friend is, instead of a superb cook, a very talented artist. Are you likely to experience any discomfort in this situation? Undoubtedly not; in fact, you are likely to bask in the reflected glory of your friend's success. "Guess what?" you will probably tell everyone. "My new friend has sold some of her paintings in the most exclusive New York galleries."

The difference between these two scenarios is that in the first one, your friend is superior at an attribute that is very important to you, and may even be a central part of how you define yourself. We all have abilities and traits that we treasure—we are especially proud of being good cooks, talented artists, gifted musicians, or inventive scientists. Whatever our most treasured

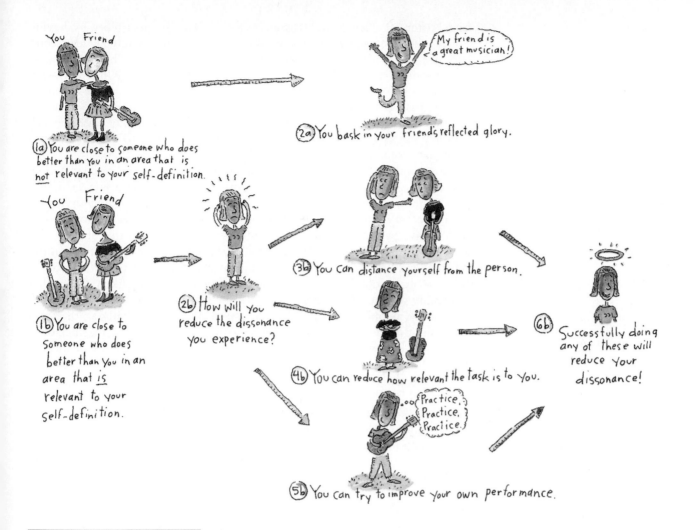

**FIGURE 3.10 Self-evaluation maintenance theory.**

ability, if we encounter someone who is better at it than we are, there is likely to be trouble—trouble of the dissonance variety. It is difficult to be proud of our ability to cook if our closest friend is a far better chef than we are.

This is the basic premise of Tesser's (1988) **self-evaluation maintenance theory,** which says that there are three important predictors of dissonance in interpersonal relationships: how we perform on a task relative to another person, how close we are to this person, and how relevant the task is to our self-definition. As seen in Figure 3.10, there is no problem if a close friend outperforms us on a task that is not that relevant to us. In fact, we bask in the person's reflected glory, and feel even better about ourselves. Dissonance occurs when a close friend outperforms us on a task that is relevant to our self-definition.

**How Do We Reduce This Dissonance?** We can try to change any one of the three components that produced it. First, we can distance ourselves from the person who outperforms us, deciding that he or she is not such a close

**self-evaluation maintenance theory:** the theory that one's self-concept can be threatened by another individual's behavior, and that the level of threat is determined by both the closeness of the other individual and the personal relevance of the behavior

friend after all. Pleban and Tesser (1981) tested this possibility by having college students compete against another student, who was actually an accomplice of the experimenter, on general knowledge questions. They rigged it so that in some conditions, the questions were on topics that were highly relevant to people's self-definitions, and the accomplice got many more of the questions correct. Just as predicted, this was the condition in which people distanced themselves the most from the accomplice, saying they would not want to work with him again. It is too dissonance producing to be close to someone who is better than we in our treasured areas of expertise (Wegner, 1986).

A second way to reduce such threats to our self-esteem is to change how relevant the task is to our self-definition. If our new friend is a far better cook than we are, we might lose interest in cooking, deciding that auto mechanics is really our thing. To test this prediction, Tesser and Paulus (1983) gave people feedback about how well they and another student had done on a test of a newly discovered ability, *cognitive-perceptual integration*. When people learned that the other student was similar to them (high closeness) and had done better on the test, they were especially likely to say that this ability was not very important to them—just as the theory predicts.

Finally, people can deal with self-esteem threats by changing the third component in the equation, their performance relative to the other person's. If our new best friend is a superb cook, we could reduce the dissonance by trying to make ourselves an even better cook. This won't work, however, if we are already performing to the best of our abilities. If so, we can take a more diabolic route, wherein we try to undermine our friend's performance so that it is not as good as ours. If our friend asks for a recipe, we might leave out a critical ingredient, so that his or her *salmon en brioche* is not nearly as good as ours.

**Why Might We Help a Stranger more than a Friend?**   Are people really so mean-spirited that they try to sabotage their friends' performance? Surely not always; there are many examples of times when we are extremely generous and helpful toward our friends. If our self-esteem is on the line, however, there is evidence that we are not as helpful as we would like to think. Tesser and Smith (1980) asked students to play a game of Password wherein one person gave clues to another to guess a word and to do so with both a friend and a stranger. The students could choose to give clues that were very helpful, making it easy for the other player to guess the word, or very obscure, making it hard for the other player to guess the word. The researchers set it up so that people first performed rather poorly themselves and then had the opportunity to help the other players by giving them easy or difficult clues. The question was, who would they help more—the strangers or their friends?

By now, you can probably see what self-evaluation maintenance theory predicts. If the task is not very self-relevant to people, they should want their friends to do especially well, so they can bask in the reflected glory. If the task is self-relevant, however, it would be threatening to people's self-esteem to have their friends outperform them. So they might make it difficult for their friends, by giving them especially hard clues. This is exactly what Tesser and Smith found. They made the task very self-relevant for some participants, by telling them that performance on the game was highly correlated with their intelligence and leadership skills. Under these conditions, people gave more difficult clues to their friends than to the strangers, because they

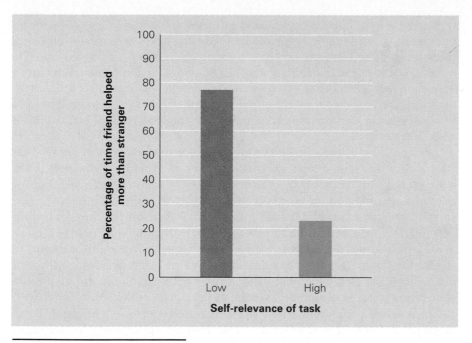

**FIGURE 3.11 Self-relevance of task**. People are more inclined to be helpful to a friend if the friend's success does not pose a threat to their own self-esteem. (Adapted from Tesser & Smith, 1980)

did not want their friends to shine on a task that was highly important to them. When the task was not self-relevant, people gave more difficult clues to the strangers than to their friends (see Figure 3.11).

In sum, research on self-evaluation maintenance theory has shown that threats to our self-esteem have fascinating implications for our interpersonal relationships. Though much of the research has been with college students in laboratory settings, the theory has been confirmed in field and archival studies as well. Tesser (1980), for example, examined biographies of male scientists, noting how close these scientists were to their fathers. As the theory predicts, when the scientists' field of expertise was the same as their fathers', they had a more distant and strained relationship with their fathers. Similarly, the greatest amount of friction between siblings was found to occur when the siblings were close in age and one sibling was significantly better on key dimensions, such as popularity or intelligence. When performance and relevance are high, it can be difficult to avoid conflicts with family members. Consider how the novelist Norman Maclean (1983) describes his relationship with his brother in the story "A River Runs Through It": "One of the earliest things brothers try to find out is how they differ from each other. . . . Undoubtedly, our differences would not have seemed so great if we had not been such a close family."

## Self-Affirmation Theory

As we have seen, people will go to great lengths to maintain a good image of themselves, by changing their attitudes, their behavior, or their relationships with other people. In each case, people try to restore a sense of integrity by warding off a specific threat to their self-esteem. If we smoke cigarettes, we

self-affirmation theory: a theory suggesting that people will reduce the impact of a dissonance arousing threat to their self-concept by focusing on and affirming their competence on some dimension unrelated to the threat

try to deal with the specific threat to our health by quitting, or by convincing ourselves that smoking is not really bad for our health. Sometimes, however, threats to our self-esteem can be so strong and difficult to avoid that the normal means of reducing dissonance do not work. It can be very difficult to stop smoking, as millions of people have discovered. It is also difficult to ignore all the evidence indicating that smoking is bad for us and might even kill us. So what can we do? Are smokers doomed to wallow in a constant state of dissonance?

Research by Claude Steele (1988) on **self-affirmation theory** shows that people are creative and flexible when it comes to avoiding dissonance. Even if we cannot rationalize away a threat to our self-esteem, we can avoid dissonance by affirming our competence and integrity in some other area. "Yes, I smoke," you might say. "But I am a great cook" (or a terrific poet, or a wonderful friend, or a promising scientist). Self-affirmation is defined as the following: When our self-esteem is threatened, we will, if possible, attempt to reduce the dissonance by reminding ourselves of some irrelevant aspect of our self-concept that we cherish, as a way of feeling good about ourselves in spite of some stupid or immoral action we have just committed.

In a series of fascinating experiments, Steele and his colleagues have demonstrated that if you provide people with an opportunity for self-affirmation, they will grab it and avoid reducing dissonance in more direct ways, such as by changing their attitudes (Steele, 1988; Steele, Hoppe, & Gonzales, 1986; Steele & Liu, 1981). For example, Steele, Hoppe, and Gonzales (1986) performed a replication of Jack Brehm's (1956) classic experiment on postdecision dissonance reduction. They asked students to rank-order ten record albums, ostensibly as part of a marketing survey. As a reward, the students were then told that they could keep either their fifth- or sixth-ranked album. Ten minutes after making their choice, they were asked to rate the albums again. You will recall that in Brehm's (1956) experiment, after selecting one of the kitchen appliances, the participants spread apart their ratings of the appliances, rating the one they had chosen much higher than the one they had rejected. In this manner, they "convinced" themselves that they had made a smart decision. And that is exactly what most of the students did in Steele and his colleagues' (1986) record album experiment.

But Steele and his colleagues built an additional set of conditions into their experiment. Half of the students were science majors, and half were business majors. Half of the science majors and half of the business majors were asked to put on a white lab coat while participating in the experiment. Why the lab coat? As you know, a lab coat is associated with the idea of science. Steele and his colleagues suspected that the lab coat would serve a "self-affirmation function" for the science majors but not for the business majors. The results supported their predictions. Whether or not they were wearing a lab coat, business majors reduced dissonance just as the people in Brehm's (1956) experiment did: After their choice, they increased their evaluation of the chosen album and decreased their evaluation of the one they had rejected. Similarly, in the absence of a lab coat, science majors reduced their dissonance in the same way. However, science majors who were wearing the lab coat resisted the temptation to distort their perceptions; the lab coat reminded these students that they were promising scientists, and thereby short-circuited the need to reduce dissonance by changing their attitudes toward the albums. In effect, they said, "I might have made a dumb choice in record albums, but I can live with that because I have other things going for

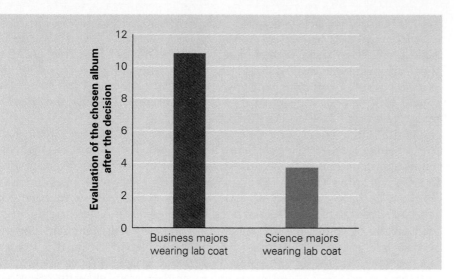

**FIGURE 3.12 Graph of dissonance and self-affirmation.** People who were allowed the opportunity to affirm their values (science majors wearing lab coats) were able to avoid the pressures to reduce dissonance by increasing the attractiveness of the chosen album. (Adapted from Steele, Hoppe, and Gonzales, 1986)

me; at least I'm a promising scientist!" A simplified version of these findings is presented in Figure 3.12.

Abraham Tesser and David Cornell (1991) showed that self-affirmation can also short-circuit the need to reduce the kind of dissonance described by self-evaluation maintenance theory—that is, wherein people feel threatened by another person's outstanding performance in their own area of expertise. Tesser and Cornell replicated the Tesser and Smith (1980) study we reviewed earlier, wherein people played Password with friends and strangers. As you recall, when people felt that Password was highly self-relevant, they tried to undermine their friends' performance by giving them difficult clues. Tesser and Cornell added a condition: People were first given the opportunity to affirm themselves in an area unrelated to the Password game. In this condition, people first completed a questionnaire that enabled them to express their most treasured values, such as how honest or religious they were. Once again, this opportunity to self-affirm short-circuited the need to deal with the self-esteem threats more directly: These participants did not try to undermine their friends' performance by giving them hard clues, even when the task was self-relevant. They seemed to have said to themselves, "It's OK if my friend does better than me on this test of intelligence, because I have a lot of other things in my favor, such as my overall honesty and integrity." In short, people are very flexible at maintaining their self-esteem. If we cannot ward off a threat directly, we can affirm ourselves in some unrelated domain if provided with the opportunity and the cues to do so.

## Self-Enhancement or Self-Verification?

We have said repeatedly that people will experience dissonance whenever they feel a threat to their self-esteem—namely, whenever they do something that makes them feel absurd, stupid, or immoral. The astute reader may have

**self-verification theory:** a theory suggesting that people have a need to seek confirmation of their self-concept, whether the self-concept is positive or negative. In some circumstances, this tendency can conflict with self-enhancement and self-justification

> The mind is a strange machine which can combine the materials offered to it in the most astonishing ways.
> —Bertrand Russell, *The Conquest of Happiness*, 1930

noticed that this prediction becomes tricky when applied to people who have a poor opinion of themselves. Consider Jason, who has always thought of himself as a lousy writer with poor verbal skills. One day he is working on a term paper with a friend, who remarks that she thinks his paper is skillfully crafted, beautifully written, and superbly articulate. How will Jason feel? He should feel pleased and gratified, we might predict, because the friend's praise gives Jason's self-esteem a boost.

On the other hand, Jason's friend has given him feedback that challenges a long-standing view of himself as a poor writer, and he might be motivated to maintain this negative view. Why? For two reasons, according to **self-verification theory** (Swann, 1984, 1990). First, it is unsettling and confusing to have our views of ourselves disconfirmed; if we changed our self-concept every time we encountered someone with a different opinion of us, it would be impossible to maintain a coherent, consistent self-concept. Second, interacting with people who view us differently from the way we view ourselves can be embarrassing. People who don't know us might have unrealistic expectations, and we might be embarrassed when they find out that we are not as smart or as artistic or as creative as they think we are. Better to let them know our faults at the outset.

In short, when people with negative self-views receive positive feedback, opposing needs go head to head: the desire to feel good about themselves by believing the positive feedback (*self-enhancement needs*) versus the desire to maintain a consistent, coherent picture of themselves and avoid the embarrassment of being found out (*self-verification needs*). Which needs win out?

Throughout this chapter, we have been telling you that humans have a powerful need to feel good about themselves—in short, that the need for self-enhancement is a powerful determinant of our attitudes and behaviors. We now have to qualify this statement. Several studies suggest that under certain conditions, self-verification needs overpower self-enhancement needs (Aronson & Carlsmith, 1962; Brock et al., 1965; Marecek & Mettee, 1972; Swann, 1990). For example, William Swann and his colleagues have found that people prefer to remain in close relationships with those friends, roommates, and romantic partners whose evaluations of their abilities are consistent with their own (sometimes negative) self-evaluations (Swann, Hixon, & De La Ronde, 1992; Swann & Pelham, 1988). In other words, people prefer to be close to someone whose evaluations of them are not more positive than their self-concept. In a close relationship, most people find it better to be known than to be overrated.

The need to self-verify, however, appears to dominate our behavior only under a limited set of circumstances. First, if the consequences of being improperly evaluated are not too great—for example, if our contact with these individuals is rare so that it is unlikely that they will discover we are not who we appear to be—then even people with negative views prefer positive feedback (Aronson, 1992). Second, if people feel there is nothing they can do to improve their abilities, then they prefer positive feedback to accurate feedback. Why remind ourselves that we are terrible if there is nothing we can do about it? If, however, people feel that a negative self-attribute can be changed with a little work, they prefer accurate feedback, because this information can help them figure out what they need to do to get better (Steele, Spencer, and Josephs, 1992).

## Avoiding the Rationalization Trap

Dissonance-reducing behavior is ego-defensive behavior. It can be useful because it keeps our egos from being continually battered; it provides us with a feeling of stability and high self-esteem. But as we have seen, dissonance-reducing behavior can be dangerous as well. The tendency to justify our past behavior can lead us into an escalation of rationalizations that can be disastrous. The irony, of course, is that in order to avoid thinking of ourselves as stupid or immoral, we set the stage for increasing our acts of stupidity or immorality. We call this phenomenon the **rationalization trap**: Through the reduction of dissonance, there is a tendency to trap ourselves in a web of distortion that prevents us from seeing things as they really are.

**rationalization trap:** the potential for dissonance reduction to produce a succession of self-justifications which ultimately result in a chain of stupid or immoral actions

**Humans Cannot Live by Consonance Alone.** If we human beings did not learn from our mistakes, we would get stuck within the confines of our narrow minds and never grow or change. If we were to spend all of our time and energy defending our egos, we would never learn from our mistakes. Instead, we would sweep our mistakes under the rug, or, worse still, we would try to turn them into virtues. As we have seen throughout this chapter, this process frequently serves to perpetuate error and can lead to tragedy. For example, people who hurt others can derogate their victims to the point where not only do their actions seem just, but they might even become heroic in their own eyes (we will elaborate on this phenomenon in our chapters on aggression and prejudice). Similarly, we have seen how people who say something they don't really believe will come to believe the statement—and some of those beliefs might be tragically erroneous. The memoirs of some of our most beleaguered former presidents are full of the kind of self-serving, self-justifying statements that can best be summarized as "If I had it all to do over again, I would not change anything important" (Johnson, 1971; Nixon, 1990; Reagan, 1990).

Following the debacle in Waco, Attorney General Janet Reno did not expend much energy on self justification; instead, she expressed genuine remorse, and took full responsibility for the problem. Our guess is that this stance significantly increased the possibility of her learning from the event thereby reducing the possibility of similar tragedies in the future.

Occasionally human beings do learn and change. How does this come about? In order to learn from our mistakes, we must be able to tolerate dissonance long enough to examine the situation critically and dispassionately. We then stand a chance of breaking out of the cycle of action, followed by **self-justification,** followed by more intense action. For example, suppose Mary has acted unkindly toward a fellow student. In order to learn from that experience, she must be able to resist the need to derogate her victim. Ideally, it would be effective if she were able to stay with the dissonance long enough to say, "OK, I blew it; I did a cruel thing. But that doesn't necessarily make me a cruel person. Let me think about why I did it." We are well aware that this is easier said than done. But a clue as to how such behavior might come about is contained in some of the research on self-affirmation that we discussed previously (Steele, 1988). Suppose that, immediately after Mary acted cruelly and before she had an opportunity to derogate her victim, she was reminded of the fact that she had recently donated several pints of blood to the Red Cross to be used by earthquake victims, or that she had recently gotten a high score on her physics exam. This self-affirmation would be likely to provide her with the ability to resist engaging in typical dissonance-reducing behavior. In effect, Mary might be able to say, "It's true—I just did a cruel thing. But I am also capable of some really fine, intelligent, and generous behavior."

**self-justification:** the tendency to justify one's actions in order to maintain one's self-esteem

*The self is one's chief interest.*

Indeed, self affirmation can serve as a cognitive buffer, protecting a person from caving into temptation and committing a cruel or immoral act. This was demonstrated in an early experiment on cheating (Aronson & Mettee, 1968). In this experiment, college students were first given a personality test and then given false feedback that was either positive (aimed at temporarily raising self-esteem) or negative (aimed at temporarily lowering self-esteem), or they received no information at all. Immediately afterward, they played a game of cards in which, to win a large pot, they could easily cheat without getting caught. The results were striking. Students in the high self-esteem condition were able to resist the temptation to cheat to a far greater extent than the students in the other conditions. In short, a temporary boost in self-esteem served to inoculate these students against cheating, because the anticipation of doing something immoral was more dissonant than it would have been otherwise. Thus, when they were put in a tempting situation, they were able to say to themselves, "Terrific people like me don't cheat." And they didn't (see also Spencer, Josephs, & Steele, 1993; Steele, Spencer, & Lynch, in press). We find these results encouraging, inasmuch as they suggest a viable way of reversing the rationalization trap.

# SUMMARY

One of the most powerful determinants of human behavior is the need to maintain a high level of *self-esteem*. In this chapter, we have seen that this need has intriguing consequences for people's attitudes and behaviors. According to **cognitive dissonance theory,** people experience discomfort (dissonance) whenever they are confronted with **cognitions** about some aspect of their behavior that is inconsistent with their **self-concept**. People are motivated to reduce this dissonance by either changing their behavior or justifying their past behavior, bringing it into line with a positive view of themselves. The resulting change in attitude stems from a process of **self-persuasion.**

Dissonance inevitably occurs after important decisions (**post–decision dissonance**), because the thought that "I chose alternative X" is inconsistent with the thought that "I might have been a lot better off with alternative Y." People reduce this dissonance by increasing their liking for the chosen alternative and decreasing their liking for the negative alternative. Unscrupulous salespeople have been known to take advantage of this human tendency through the utilization of a strategy called **lowballing** which creates the illusion in the customer's mind that a commitment has been made to purchase the product, when, in fact, no such commitment exists.

Dissonance also occurs after people choose to exert a lot of effort to attain something boring or onerous. A **justification of effort** occurs, whereby people increase their liking for what they attained.

A third source of dissonance occurs when people commit foolish, immoral, or absurd acts for insufficient justification. For example, when people say something against their attitudes (**counterattitudinal advocacy**) for low **external justification,** they find an **internal justification** for their behavior, coming to believe what they said. Similarly, if people avoid doing something desirable for **insufficient punishment,** they will come to believe that the activity wasn't really all that desirable. And if people find themselves doing someone a favor for insufficient justification, they assume that they did so because the person is likable. The flip side of this kind of dissonance reduction has sinister effects: If people find themselves acting cruelly toward someone for insufficient justification, they will derogate the victim, assuming he or she must have deserved it. Finally, consistent with the idea that dissonance is an uncomfortable state people are motivated to reduce, there is evidence that dissonance is accompanied by physiological arousal.

In recent years, social psychologists have taken the idea that people are motivated to maintain their self-esteem in fascinating new directions. **Self-evaluation maintenance theory** argues that dissonance is produced in interpersonal relationships, whenever someone close to us outperforms us on a task that is highly relevant to our self-definition. People can reduce this dissonance by distancing themselves from the person, improving their performance, lowering the other person's performance, or reducing the relevance of the task. **Self-affirmation theory** argues that people are very flexible at dealing with threats to their self-esteem. When dissonance cannot be reduced by dealing with a specific threat, people can feel better about themselves by affirming themselves in some other area. Research on **self-verification theory** suggests that the need to bolster our self-esteem sometimes conflicts with the need to verify our self-views. When people with nega-tive self-views are concerned that other people will discover that they are not who they appear to be, and when they think that it's possible to change and improve the less desirable side of themselves, they will prefer feedback that confirms their low opinion of themselves to feedback that is self-enhancing.

The problem with reducing dissonance in ways that make us feel better about ourselves is that it can result in a **rationalization trap,** whereby we set the stage for acts of increasing stupidity or immorality. As suggested by self-affirmation theory, we can avoid this trap by reminding ourselves that we are good and decent people, so that we do not have to justify and rationalize every stupid or immoral act we perform.

## SUGGESTED READINGS

Aronson, E. (1969). The theory of cognitive dissonance: A current perspective. In L. Berkowitz (Ed.), *Advances in experimental social psychology* (Vol. 4, pp 1–34). New York: Academic Press, 1969. A revision of the original theory in terms of self-esteem and the self-concept.

Aronson, E. (1992). The return of the repressed: Dissonance theory makes a comeback. *Psychological Inquiry*, 3, 303–311. A brief attempt to bring dissonance theory up to date by discussing the linkage between the theory of cognitive dissonance and recent developments in cognitive psychology.

Festinger, L. (1957). *A theory of cognitive dissonance.* Evanston, IL: Row, Peterson. The original presentation of dissonance theory. A classic in social psychology—clear, concise and engagingly written.

Wicklund, R., & Brehm, J. (1976). *Perspectives on cognitive dissonance.* Hillsdale, NJ: Earlbaum. A scholarly, readable presentation of dissonance theory some two decades after its inception. Contains a description of much of the early research as well as some of the more important conceptual modifications of the theory.

# Chapter 4
## Social Cognition: How We Think
## About the Social World

uly 3, 1988. A hot, humid day in the Persian Gulf. Crew members of the USS *Vincennes* are defending their ship from the persistent fire of several Iranian gunboats. For months, Iranian ships and planes have attacked international oil tankers in the gulf, prompting President Reagan to send an American fleet to keep the vital shipping lanes open. Already, there have been serious skirmishes between Iranian and U.S. forces. An Iranian plane recently fired a missile on the USS *Stark*, killing thirty-seven soldiers and nearly sinking the ship. The captain of the *Stark* was accused of not defending his ship adequately and was forced to resign from the navy.

Acrid smoke fills the air as the Iranian gunboats fire machine guns and rocket launchers at the *Vincennes*. Suddenly the *Vincennes*'s advanced radar system shows that a plane has taken off from an Iranian airfield and is heading toward the ship. The radar technicians hurry to identify the plane. With the attack of the *Stark* on their minds, they scan the incoming data and conclude that it is an Iranian F-14 fighter, following a descending flight pattern toward the *Vincennes*. Ominously, this is the flight pattern followed by planes about to launch an air-to-ship missile. The *Vincennes* immediately sends radio messages to the plane, warning it to change its path, but receives no reply. To add to the confusion, the *Vincennes*'s rear gun jams and the ship has to make a sudden turn at full rudder going thirty knots, causing the ship to list at a thirty-two-degree angle. Lights flicker and everything that is not lashed down flies through the air.

Captain Rogers has only a moment to decide what to do about the approaching plane. He considers the information his technicians have given him: The plane is an Iranian F-14 flying in an attack pattern directly toward the ship, and has not responded to radio warnings. Deciding he can wait no longer, he turns the firing key that launches two surface-to-air missiles. Seconds later, the plane is destroyed in midair.

To the horror of Rogers and the rest of the world, Iran soon announces that the plane was not an F-14 fighter, but a civilian airliner, Iran Air Flight 655, with 290 innocent passengers aboard. There are no survivors. How could such a tragic error have occurred? Navy investigators considered the possibility that the new, state-of-the art radar equipment on the *Vincennes* had failed, falsely identifying the plane as an F-14. The investigators discovered, however, that the radar equipment had operated flawlessly. Tapes of the radar signals showed clearly that the plane was ascending, not descending toward the *Vincennes*, that it was not an F-14, and that it was within the commercial air corridor. Somehow, the radar technicians had misidentified the plane, even with clear evidence to the contrary. How could this tragic mistake have been made by highly trained radar technicians drilled in performing under combat conditions?

That is the subject of this chapter.

**social cognition:** how people think about themselves and the social world; more specifically, how people select, interpret, remember, and use social information to make judgments and decisions

**W**e all make decisions every day of our lives. Sometimes these decisions are of little consequence, such as deciding whether we should eat lunch at the local greasy spoon or at the fast-food joint on the corner. Sometimes they are very important, such as deciding where to go to college, whether we should become a psychologist or a lawyer, or whether we should marry Billy or Jim. The subject of this chapter is how people make decisions such as these. More formally, the topic is **social cognition:** the study of how people select, interpret, and use information to make judgments and decisions about the social world. We will see that human beings are often excellent decision makers, more sophisticated than the most powerful computer. We will also see that, under some conditions, people are prone to make consequential mistakes in reasoning, such as the radar technicians' judgment that the blip on their radar screen was an F-14 fighter.

The radar technicians were faced with a great deal of information, and had very little time to make a quick, crucial decision. Fortunately, when we make decisions in our everyday lives, we are usually not under such tremendous pressure. There are, however, some parallels between how radar technicians interpret the signals on their screens and everyday decision making. In both cases, people have to sift through a lot of information, deciding what is relevant and what can be ignored. Think about how much information you process every time you talk to another person or walk into any social setting, whether it's a party or a train station. There are literally thousands of bits of information present in the scene—can you notice, think about, and respond to all of them? If every time you talked to other people you had to notice in minute detail every word they said (and consider every word they didn't choose to say), every nuance in their voice, facial expression, and gestures, every aspect of their physical appearance, every characteristic of the social setting in which you are conversing, and everything you have ever known about these people and this social setting . . . well, you'd be paralyzed. You would be so busy noticing and thinking that you wouldn't have any time or energy left to respond.

Clearly, we humans have figured out a way to solve this dilemma: by relying on mental shortcuts. By doing so, we have to attend to only some of that dizzying amount of information in order to answer our fundamental questions: What's going on here, and how should I behave? We deal with the vast amount of information that constantly surrounds us by being **cognitive misers** (Fiske & Taylor, 1991). We typically follow the route of least resistance and the law of least effort, taking in only as much information as we need in order to get something done—make decisions, choose how to respond, and so on.

> It is the mind which creates the world about us, and even though we stand side by side in the same meadow, my eyes will never see what is beheld by yours.
> —George Gissing, *The private papers of Henry Ryecroft*, 1903

**cognitive misers:** the idea that people have developed efficient mental shortcuts and rules of thumb to help them understand the social world, because they have a limited capacity to process all of the social information impinging on them

*Drawing by Weber; © 1987 The New Yorker Magazine, Inc*

*"Our real first line of defense, wouldn't you agree, is our capacity to reason."*

As we shall see in this chapter, these mental shortcuts are useful. But we rely on them at some peril, for sometimes they are just plain wrong. Whenever we rely on only some information and disregard the rest, we run the risk of disregarding what is really important. Our "cognitive miser" techniques can make us inaccurate, and even bias how we view and make sense of the social world. To compound the problem, we often don't realize that we are wrong. Thus, while the cognitive theories and shortcuts we will discuss help us move through the social world with the fluidity and grace of ballet dancers, it is also true that because of them, we sometimes step on other people's toes and stub our own as well.

## People as Everyday Theorists: Schemas and Their Influence

In formal science, scientists formulate many theories and hypotheses about their topic of interest, be it the behavior of subatomic particles or of witnesses to an emergency. We each, in our everyday lives, also have theories about ourselves and the surrounding social world. Social psychologists are interested in these theories because they play a significant role in how people understand and interpret themselves, other people, and all the interactions and social settings in which they find themselves.

Our theories about the social world, called **schemas** (Bartlett, 1932; Markus, 1977; Taylor & Crocker, 1981), have a profound effect on what information we notice, think about, and later remember. As noted by Norman Maclean in his story "A River Runs Through It," "I know that often I would not see a thing unless I thought of it first." Schemas are the cognitive structures in our heads that organize information around themes or topics. We have schemas about many things—other people, ourselves, social roles (e.g., what a librarian or an engineer is like), and specific events (e.g., what kinds of things usually happen when people eat a meal in a restaurant). In each case, our schemas contain our basic knowledge and impressions. For example, our schema about the members of the Animal House fraternity might be that they're loud, obnoxious partiers with a propensity for projectile vomiting.

Once people have developed a schema, it has interesting effects on how they process and remember new information. If you see a member of the Animal House acting in a calm, polite, and studious manner, this information will be inconsistent with your schema and you are likely to not notice it, to ignore it, or to not remember it later. Thus, schemas act as filters, straining out information that is contradictory to or inconsistent with the prevailing theme (Higgins & Bargh, 1987; Stangor & Ruble, 1989).

Sometimes, of course, a fact can be so inconsistent with a schema that it sticks out like a sore thumb, and we are likely to remember it. If we encounter a member of the Animal House who is actively campaigning to raise the drinking age to twenty-five, and prefers poetry readings to raucous parties, he is such a glaring exception to our schema that he will stick in our minds—particularly if we spend time pondering how he could ever have ended up in the same house as his party-loving brothers (Hastie, 1980; Srull, 1981). In most

**schemas:** cognitive structures people have to organize their knowledge about the social world by themes or subjects; schemas powerfully affect what information we notice, think about, and remember

Theory helps us to bear our ignorance of facts.
—George Santayana,
*The Sense of Beauty,* 1896

cases, however, we are likely to notice and think about the behavior of the Animal House frat members that fits our preconceptions about them. In this way, our schemas become stronger and more impervious to change over time. For example, Claudia Cohen (1981) showed people a videotape of a woman engaged in various activities and identified her as a librarian or a waitress. When later asked to recall scenes from the video, the participants more accurately recalled information that was consistent with the occupational label, for example, that the librarian had been listening to classical music.

In addition, human memory is *reconstructive*. We don't remember exactly what occurred in a given setting, as if our minds were a film camera recording the precise images and sounds. Instead, we remember some information (particularly that which our schema leads us to notice and pay attention to) and we remember other information that was never there but that we have unknowingly added later (Loftus & Palmer, 1974; Markus & Zajonc, 1985). For example, if you ask people what is the most famous line of dialogue in the classic Humphrey Bogart and Ingrid Bergman movie *Casablanca*, they will probably say, "Play it again, Sam." Similarly, if you ask them what is one of the most famous lines from the original (1966–69) "Star Trek" television series, they will probably say, "Beam me up, Scotty."

Here is a piece of trivia that might surprise you: Both of these lines of dialogue are reconstructions—the characters in the movie and the television series never said those lines. Not surprisingly, memory reconstructions tend to

"Beam me up, Scotty." Did the characters in the original Star Trek television series ever speak this line?

be consistent with our schema. For example, in Cohen's (1981) librarian/waitress study, participants misremembered what beverage the librarian had been drinking in the videotape. They reconstructed the scene in memory so that she was drinking wine, not beer, because that fit their schema of what a librarian would drink. As we will discuss in Chapter 13, the very way in which our schemas operate makes prejudiced attitudes highly resistant to change.

In the rest of this chapter, we will discuss in detail how mental shortcuts affect how we make sense out of the social world. As we shall see, in a very real sense, beliefs can create reality.

### The Function of Schemas: Why Do We Have Them?

What would it be like to have no schemas about your social world? What if everything you encountered was inexplicable, confusing, and unlike anything else you'd ever known? It would be like visiting another planet, where you didn't have a clue about what anything meant. As an example, read the following paragraph and try to figure out what it means:

> The procedure is quite simple. First you arrange things into different groups. Of course, one pile may be sufficient, depending on how much there is to do. If you have to go somewhere else due to lack of facilities, that is the next step; otherwise you are pretty well set. (Bransford & Johnson, 1973, p.400)

Sounds pretty strange, doesn't it? What on earth does it mean to say that "one pile may be sufficient"? But suppose we told you that the paragraph is about how to do your laundry. Once you have this schema with which to interpret the paragraph, it makes perfect sense. Schemas help us categorize stimuli by providing answers to the question, "What is it"? when we encounter something new. Relating new experiences to what we already know is an efficient way of trying to understand the social world, particularly if those new experiences are ambiguous or difficult to decipher.

Consider, for example, how people interpreted ambiguous information in a classic study by Harold Kelley (1950). Students in different sections of a college economics class were told that their instructor was out of town and that a guest lecturer would fill in that day. In order to create a schema about what the guest lecturer would be like, Kelley told the students that the economics department was interested in how different classes reacted to different instructors, and the students would thus receive a brief biographical note about the instructor before he arrived. The note contained information about the instructor's age, background, and teaching experience. It also gave one of two descriptions of his personality. One version said that "people who know him consider him to be a rather cold person, industrious, critical, practical, and determined." The other version was identical, except that the phrase "a rather cold person" was replaced with "a very warm person." The students were randomly given one of these personality descriptions.

The guest lecturer then conducted a class discussion for twenty minutes, after which the students rated their impressions of him. How humorous was he? How sociable? How considerate? Given that there was some ambiguity in this situation—after all, the students had seen him for only a brief amount of time—Kelley hypothesized that they would use their schema about the

People who know him consider him to be a rather cold person, industrious, critical, practical, and determined.

People who know him consider him to be a very warm person, industrious, critical, practical, and determined.

instructor, provided by the biographical note, to fill in the blanks. This hypothesis was confirmed: The students who expected the instructor to be warm gave him significantly higher ratings than the students who expected him to be cold, even though all the students had observed the same teacher behaving in the same way. Students who expected the instructor to be warm were also more likely to ask him questions and participate in the class discussion. Think for a minute if this has ever happened to you. Has what you've known about a professor prior to the first day of class affected your impressions of him or her? Did you find, oddly enough, that the professor acted just as you'd expected? Next time, ask a classmate who had a different expectation about the professor what he or she thought. See if the two of you have different perceptions of the instructor based on the different schemas you were using.

Of course, people are not totally blind to what is actually out there in the world. Sometimes what we see is relatively unambiguous, and we do not need to use our schemas to help us interpret it. For example, in one of the classes in which Kelley conducted his study, the guest instructor happened to be unambiguously self-confident, even cocky. Given that cockiness is a relatively unambiguous trait, the students did not need to rely on their expectations to fill in the blanks. They rated him as being immodest in both the warm and cold conditions. However, when they rated this instructor's sense of humor, which was less clear-cut, the students fell back on their expectations. The students in the warm condition thought he was more humorous than the students in the cold condition did. Thus, people are more likely to use schemas to fill in the blanks when they are not completely sure about what it is they are observing.

It is important to note that there is nothing wrong with what Kelley's students did. As long as people have reason to believe that their schemas are accurate, it is perfectly reasonable to use them to resolve ambiguity. If a sus-picious-looking character comes up to you in a dark alley and says, "Take out your wallet," your schema about such encounters tells you that the person wants to steal your money, not admire pictures of your family. This schema helps you avert a serious and perhaps deadly misunderstanding. Schemas also provide useful guidelines for our behavior so that we do not have to stop and think about every action we perform. For example, when we go out to eat, we invoke a "restaurant" script—a schema that describes what sort of events are likely to occur and in what order. We do not have to spend time wondering if we should tip the waitress before or after the meal, or whether we should order dessert or a main course first. Both our own behavior and the waitress's behavior are heavily "scripted" in this situation, and a common understanding of this script facilitates effortless and smooth social interaction (Abelson, 1976).

### Which Schema Do We Use? The Role of Accessibility and Priming

Sometimes only one schema fits a situation, so we have no problem knowing which one to use. When we enter a restaurant, we know we should invoke the "restaurant script," because no other script is appropriate. (Next time you're in a restaurant, try invoking the "dinner party" script instead. After you've finished your meal, thank your host [waiter], and then get up and head for the door—and see what happens!) Other times it is not nearly so clear which schema we should use to understand a situation or another person. Suppose that you are sitting next to a fellow on a bus who is acting a little strangely. He mutters incoherently to himself, covers his face with his hands, and then suddenly turns to you and asks, "Is there really a point to any of this?" What kind of schema will you call up to try to understand what this man is all about? Recent research shows that it depends on the **accessibility** of schemas, which we can define as the ease with which people can bring to mind thoughts and ideas (i.e., those which happen to be at the forefront of our minds; Higgins, 1989; Wyer & Srull, 1989).

Interestingly, several studies have shown that what is accessible can be relatively arbitrary. Whatever we happen to have been doing or thinking prior to encountering an event can prime a schema, making it more acces-sible. This schema is then more likely to be used to interpret the new event. Suppose, for example, that right before the man on the bus sat down, you happened to be reading Ken Kesey's *One Flew over the Cuckoo's Nest*, a novel about patients in a mental hospital. Given that thoughts about mental patients are accessible in your mind, you would probably invoke your "men-tally disturbed" schema when you saw the man acting oddly, assuming that he was experiencing severe mental problems. If, on the other hand, thoughts about alcohol were fresh in your mind—for example, if you had just looked out the window and seen an alcoholic leaning against a building drinking a bottle of wine—you would probably invoke your "intoxicated person" schema, assuming that the man had had a few too many (see Figure 4.1).

Thus, recent experiences can prime the schemas people use to interpret ambiguous situations. Tory Higgins, Stephen Rholes, and Carl Jones (1977) illustrated this priming effect in the following experiment. Imagine that you are a participant. When you arrive, you are told that you will be partici-

**accessibility:** the ease with which different thoughts and ideas can be brought to mind; an idea that is accessible is already on our minds, or can easily be brought to mind

**FIGURE 4.1 How we interpret an ambiguous situation: The role of accessibility and priming.**

pating in two unrelated studies. The first is a perception study, in which you will identify different colors, while at the same time memorizing a list of words. The second is a reading comprehension study, in which you will read a paragraph about someone named Donald and then give your impressions of him. This paragraph is shown in Figure 4.2. Take a moment to read it. What do you think of Donald?

You might have noticed that many of Donald's actions are ambiguous, interpretable in either a positive or a negative manner. Take the fact that he piloted a boat without knowing much about it, and wants to cross the Atlantic in a sailboat. It is possible to put a positive spin on these acts, deciding that Donald has an admirable sense of adventure. It's just as easy, however, to put a negative spin on these acts, assuming that Donald is a rather reckless and dangerous fellow. The researchers deliberately made this paragraph ambiguous, interpretable in either a positive or a negative manner.

How did the participants interpret it? Higgins and his colleagues (1977) found, as expected, that it depended on whether a positive or a negative

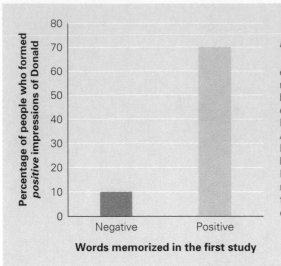

**Description of Donald**

Donald spent a great deal of time in his search of what he liked to call excitement. He had already climbed Mt. McKinley, shot the Colorado rapids in a kayak, driven in a demolition derby, and piloted a jet-powered boat—without knowing very much about boats. He had risked injury, and even death, a number of times. Now he was in search of new excitement. He was thinking, perhaps, he would do some skydiving or maybe cross the Atlantic in a sailboat. By the way he acted one could readily guess that Donald was well aware of his ability to do many things well. Other than business engagements, Donald's contacts with people were rather limited. He felt he didn't really need to rely on anyone. Once Donald made up his mind to do something it was as good as done no matter how long it might take or how difficult the going might be. Only rarely did he change his mind even when it might well have been better if he had.

**FIGURE 4.2 Priming and accessibility**. People read the above paragraph about Donald, and formed an impression of him. In a prior study, some people had memorized words that could be used to interpret Donald in a negative way (e.g., *reckless, conceited*). Others memorized words that could be used to interpret Donald in a positive way (e.g., *adventurous, self-confident*). As seen in the graph, those who had memorized the negative words formed a much more negative impression of Donald than those who had memorized the positive words. (Adapted from Higgins, Rholes, and Jones, 1977)

**priming:** the process by which recent experiences increase a schema's accessibility

All thought is a feat of association: having what's in front of you bring up something in your mind that you almost didn't know you knew.
—Robert Frost, interview, *Writers at Work: Second Series*, 1963

schema was accessible. In the first study, the researchers divided people into two groups and gave them different words to memorize. People who had memorized the words *adventurous, self-confident, independent,* and *persistent* formed positive impressions of Donald, viewing him as a likable fellow who enjoyed new challenges. People who had memorized the words *reckless, conceited, aloof,* and *stubborn* formed negative impressions of Donald, viewing him as a stuck-up person who took needlessly dangerous chances. This is an example of **priming,** whereby the words learned in the first study made different schemas more accessible, thereby influencing what people thought of Donald.

We should note that it was not memorizing just any old positive or negative words that influenced people's impressions of Donald. In other conditions, people memorized words that were equally positive or negative, such as *neat* (in one condition) or *disrespectful* (in another). These words did not influence people's impressions of Donald, because they had little to do with Donald's actions. For example, when trying to decide whether to put a positive or negative spin on the fact that Donald wants to sail across the Atlantic, having the thoughts "neat" or "disrespectful" on one's mind are of little help, because piloting a boat has little to do with how neat or respectful someone is. Having the thoughts "adventurous" or "reckless" are germane, however, and thus influenced people's impressions. A schema has to be both relevant and accessible in order to be used when forming impressions of the social world.

Let's return for a moment to our opening example, the tragic mistake on the part of the crew of the USS *Vincennes*. Accessibility and priming can help us understand how this error in reasoning and decision making occurred. What thoughts would have been most accessible to the crew members right before the Iranian plane was sighted? Given that they were currently under attack by Iranian gunboats, their most accessible schema would have been that this plane was also an enemy, about to attack them. The fact that the plane failed to answer their radio messages would fit well into this schema—attacking F-14s don't make radio contact with their prey. Primed to see an enemy plane, the radar technicians misperceived the pattern of data as a descending plane and not an ascending one—again, the prevailing, accessible schema led them to interpret the ambiguous data in a way that was consistent with that schema. The captain, when faced with a decision, no doubt remembered the USS *Stark*, which had failed to take action and was hit by the enemy. With that memory primed (as well as, perhaps, the memory of what happened to the *Stark* captain), the *Vincennes* captain acted on the information he was given by his subordinates and ordered the missiles to be fired. It all would have seemed so logical at the time, to all the participants. The schema—being attacked by an enemy plane—was so readily accessible and well primed that it is almost impossible, in retrospect, to imagine they could have made any other decision.

We should emphasize that there are myriad advantages to viewing the world through schema-tinted glasses. Eating at a restaurant involves little cognitive effort on our part, because our schema enables us to sail right through the experience with little thought. Compare your behavior to that of a very young child. Restaurants are often difficult for toddlers, because they do not have the correct schema to help them interpret the situation. Young children have only the "eating at home" script to understand dinnertime, and thus do not understand why the food doesn't come immediately, why they can't have seconds, and why they can't leave the table as soon as they're finished. Eating at a restaurant violates every aspect of the one script they do know, and until they develop a new, special schema for this setting, eating out will be an unpleasant experience for them (as well as for everybody else!).

At the same time, viewing the world through schema-tinted glasses can cause problems. If a schema is incorrect, it will obviously lead to some faulty judgments, as it did among the crew of the *Vincennes*. We are often overzealous theorists, clinging too long to schemas that have not proved to be accurate representations of the world. We turn now to the problems an overreliance on schemas can cause.

## Revising Schemas: How Easily Do People Change Their Minds?

Most of us know an old curmudgeon or two who has firm, unyielding views on virtually all topics. What is wrong with the country today? Our Old Curmudgeon (O.C.) knows the answer. Why are our schools in bad shape? What does the local baseball team need to do to win the pennant? What is the best car on the road today? Just ask O.C. If we dared to present such a person with evidence that contradicted his or her beliefs, we would no doubt be greeted by a lecture on the fallibility of statistics, on the attempt by soft-headed liberals (or harebrained conservatives) to obscure the issue, or maybe a homily like "It's the exception that proves the rule."

It is easy to smile at such know-it-alls, secure in the knowledge that we are not nearly so rigid and unyielding in our views of the world. There is considerable evidence, however, that most people do not easily change their schemas or beliefs, even in the face of contradictory information. Perhaps we are not as rigid as our Old Curmudgeon, but neither are we very likely to revise our schemas, even when the evidence suggests we should. For example, after Mikhail Gorbachev became general secretary of the Soviet Union, it became increasingly clear that he was no ordinary Soviet leader. He presided over the end to the cold war and the breakup of the Soviet Union. Unlike his predecessors, he did not resist—and he even encouraged—the end of Communist rule in Eastern Europe. Under Gorbachev's leadership, the West and the Soviet Union had never been on better terms. Conservative politicians and commentators, however, found it difficult to abandon the view that the Soviet Union was, in President Reagan's words, an "evil empire." One said that "the real question is not whether [Gorbachev] will pursue a course different from that taken by his predecessors, but whether he will pursue it more effectively." Another suggested that "it is very dangerous to think that Gorbachev will be any more 'liberal' or 'flexible' on foreign relations." As late as 1989, Vice-President Quayle said, "I don't think they've changed much in foreign policy. . . . You're still dealing with a totalitarian government."

Why do people cling to their preconceptions, even when faced with clear-cut contradictory information? We saw one reason in Chapter 3: It is dissonance-arousing to admit we are wrong, and pleasing to our egos to see the world as consistent with our needs, wishes, and cherished beliefs. Another reason is that our minds work in such a way that evidence confirming our beliefs is more likely to be noticed, recalled, and given greater weight, whereas contradictory information is more likely to be overlooked, forgotten, or discounted, even when the evidence has relatively few implications for our self-esteem. In the next sections, we will see several examples of people's tendency to cling to their schemas, some of which can be traced back to motivational forces such as dissonance, and others that can be traced back to the way our minds notice and remember information.

> It is a capital mistake to theorize before you have all the evidence. It biases the judgement.
> —Sherlock Holmes (Sir Arthur Conan Doyle), 1988

**People View New Evidence Through Schema-Tinted Glasses.**  It is one thing to use a schema to interpret the meaning of an ambiguous behavior, as did the students who evaluated the instructor in Harold Kelley's (1950) experiment. It is quite another when our schemas dictate what we see. If we distort the evidence to make it consistent with our schemas, there is little chance that any truly inconsistent information will register.

A classic demonstration of such distortion was performed by Al Hastorf and Hadley Cantril (1954). They showed a film of a football contest between Dartmouth and Princeton to students from both schools, and asked them to record the number of infractions committed by each team. The game had been a particularly rough one, generating heated protests on both campuses; each school blamed the other for the injuries that had occurred. Hastorf and Cantril conjectured that one reason for this difference of opinion was that the students from the two universities actually saw a different game, due to their partisanship. This hypothesis was confirmed in their study: The Princeton students who watched the film saw more infractions committed by the Dartmouth team than the Princeton one, whereas the Dartmouth students saw just the reverse. It is important to note that the students were perfectly sincere about their perceptions—they really saw two different realities in the same film.

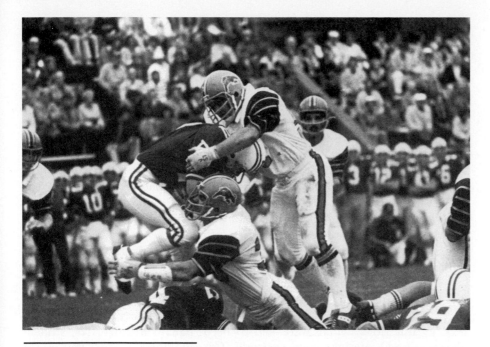

People view reality through schema-tinted glasses. Students from Princeton and Dartmouth watched the same film of a rough football game between the two schools. The Princeton students saw more penalties committed by the Dartmouth team, whereas the Dartmouth students saw more penalties committed by the Princeton team.

Because of the way in which our schemas bias what we see, there is a tendency for us to view the world in black-and-white terms, wherein our own side is the hero and the other side is the villain. Interestingly, this biased view can make partisans think that most other people are interpreting reality incorrectly. For example, what would have happened had the Princeton and Dartmouth students seen a balanced, neutral newscast that reported that both football teams had exhibited rough, unsportsmanlike behavior? Each side would think the newscast was biased against their school, because it did not present the extreme view that they knew to be the truth. Vallone, Ross, and Lepper (1985) demonstrated this **hostile media phenomenon** by showing news broadcasts about conflicts in the Middle East (reporting the massacre of civilians in refugee camps in Lebanon in 1982) to students who were either very pro-Arab or very pro-Israel. As expected, each group believed that the newscasts were biased in favor of the other side, because the newscasts did not present the one-sided viewpoint that they believed to be the truth.

The participants in the Hastorf and Cantril (1954) and Vallone and colleagues (1985) studies were highly involved in the issues, and had a big investment in viewing their side as the good guys. It is likely that motivational forces such as dissonance came into play in these studies. For example, when the Princeton students saw one of their own players commit a questionable act, they were likely to interpret it as a rough but sportsmanlike play that was well within the rules, due to their investment in the belief that their school was blameless. The students from Dartmouth were likely to interpret

**hostile media phenomenon:** the finding that opposing partisan groups both perceive neutral, balanced media presentations as hostile to their side, because the media have not presented the facts in the one-sided fashion the partisans "know" to be true

the same act as a ruthless, unsportsmanlike attempt to injure one of their players, so that they could maintain the view that their side was blameless. One need only attend a few sessions of divorce court to witness this kind of distortion of the facts in the service of people's egos.

There are, however, conditions under which people will interpret the facts as consistent with their schemas and expectations even when they have relatively little investment in the issues. Consider research on what has been called the **primacy effect**. Several experiments have demonstrated that first impressions are often very important, because these impressions influence the way in which later information is interpreted. (While there are circumstances under which *recency effects* occur—whereby information received last has the greatest impact—such effects appear to be the exception.) The primacy effect occurs because people form schemas on the basis of the first information they receive, and these schemas then influence the interpretation of later information. That is, people often cling to their first impression, and later information that contradicts it is ignored, discounted, or reinterpreted.

This dominance of first impressions was demonstrated in a simple, elegant experiment by Jones, Rock, Shaver, Goethals, and Ward (1968). Participants watched a male student trying to solve thirty multiple-choice analogy questions, which were said to be of equal difficulty. The student always solved half of the items correctly. The only difference was that in one condition, he started off very well, getting most of the first items right, and then he began to do poorly, getting most of the last items wrong. In the other condition, this sequence was reversed: He got most of the first items wrong, and then he got most of the last ones right. After observing the student, the participants were asked to judge his intelligence and to recall how many items he had solved correctly.

As predicted, the participants were strong theorists who distorted the data to fit their first impressions. Those who observed the student solve most of the initial items correctly thought he was more intelligent, and recalled that he had solved a higher number of items on the test, than those who saw him get most of the first items wrong did. Remember, in both cases the student solved fifteen of the thirty items, all of which were of equal difficulty. Even so, the participants exhibited a strong primacy effect: What they saw first dominated their impressions, leading them to discount (and indeed to misrepresent) what came later (see Figure 4.3).

Why? It seems unlikely that participants distorted reality in order to feel better about themselves, as self-esteem approaches (e.g., dissonance theory) would suggest. The participants were judging another student, who was a stranger to them, and whom they would probably never encounter again. Given that these people had little investment in the situation, it is unlikely that self-esteem needs were responsible for their distortion of what they observed. Instead, it appears that once formed, people's schemas take on a life of their own, influencing how new information is viewed, regardless of whether their self-esteem has been threatened.

**People Maintain Schemas Even After the Original Evidence for Them Is Discredited.** Sometimes we hear something about an issue or another person that later turns out not to be true. We might hear that Bob is guilty of insider trading, that Susan is an alcoholic, or that Philip and Jane are breaking up, only to find out later that these rumors are false. Similarly, a jury might hear

**primacy effect:** the process whereby our first impression of another person causes us to interpret his or her subsequent behavior in a manner consistent with the first impression

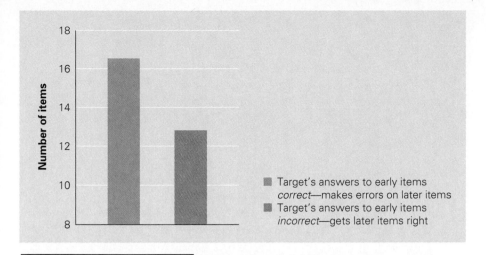

**FIGURE 4.3 The primacy of first impressions.** People observed a student's work on thirty test questions and then recalled how many he answered correctly. Those who saw him get most of the first ones right overestimated the total number, whereas those who saw him get most of the first ones wrong underestimated the total number (in both cases, he got fifteen out of thirty correct). (Adapted from Jones et al., 1968)

something in the courtroom about a defendant that is untrue or labeled "inadmissible evidence," and be told by the judge to disregard that information. How easy is it to abandon our beliefs or schemas after the evidence proves them to be false?

Not so easy, according to research by Lee Ross, Mark Lepper, and Michael Hubbard (1975). Imagine you were a subject in their study. You are given a stack of cards containing both real and fictitious suicide notes. Your job is to guess which ones are real, supposedly to study the effects of physiological processes during decision making. After each guess, the experimenter tells you whether you are right or wrong. As you do the task, you find out that you are rather good at it. In fact, you guess right on twenty-four of the twenty-five cards, which is much better than the average performance of sixteen correct.

At this point, the experimenter tells you the study is over, and explains that it was actually concerned with the effects of success and failure on physiological responses. You learn that the feedback you received was bogus; that is, you had been randomly assigned to a condition where the experimenter said you were correct on twenty-four of the cards, regardless of how well you actually did. The experimenter then gives you a final questionnaire, which asks you how many answers you think you really got correct, and how many times you think you would guess correctly on a second, equally difficult test with new cards. What would you say? Now pretend you were in the other condition of the study. Here everything would be identical, except that as you did the task, you would learn that you were not good at it. You would be told that you got only ten of the twenty-five answers correct, which is much worse than the average performance of sixteen correct, only to discover later that this feedback was bogus. How would you respond to the questionnaire, once you found out that the feedback was bogus?

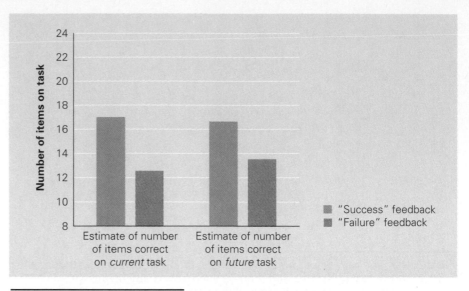

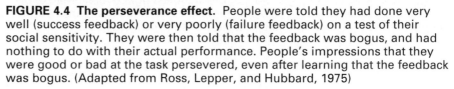

**FIGURE 4.4  The perseverance effect**. People were told they had done very well (success feedback) or very poorly (failure feedback) on a test of their social sensitivity. They were then told that the feedback was bogus, and had nothing to do with their actual performance. People's impressions that they were good or bad at the task persevered, even after learning that the feedback was bogus. (Adapted from Ross, Lepper, and Hubbard, 1975)

**perseverance effect:** the finding that people's beliefs about themselves and the social world persist even after the evidence supporting these beliefs is discredited

Depending on which condition you were in, you would have formed a schema that you were either very good or very poor at the task. What happens when the evidence for this schema is discredited? Ross and colleagues (1975) went to some pains to make sure that the participants believed the feedback had been randomly determined and had nothing to do with their actual performance. Even though the participants believed this, those who had received the "success" feedback still thought they had gotten more of the items correct, and would do better on a second test, than subjects who had received the "failure" feedback. In addition, when asked how they would do on a new test, success participants said they would do better than failure participants did (see Figure 4.4).

This result is called the **perseverance effect,** because people's beliefs persevered even after the original evidence for them was discredited. Why do people do this? Again, one possibility is our old friend self-esteem maintenance: People may persist in their beliefs in order to feel good about themselves. This interpretation cannot, however, explain the fact that people in the failure condition persisted in believing they were not very good at the task, for this belief was not very flattering to their self-esteem. That is, if people's overriding goal was to maintain the belief that was most flattering, then those who learned that they had done poorly should have been more than willing to accept the fact that the feedback was false. Why didn't they? Because the schema they invoked shaped their perceptions of reality. When people received the feedback, they explained to themselves why they were doing so well or so poorly, bringing to mind evidence from their past that was consistent with their performance (e.g., "I really am very perceptive.

After all, I was the only one who realized last week that Jennifer was depressed," or "Well, I'm not so good at this stuff; my friends always say I'm the 'last to know'"). Even after learning that the feedback was false, these thoughts were still fresh in people's minds, making them think they were particularly good or bad at the task.

The perseverance effect is not limited to beliefs about ourselves—our schemas about other people persevere as well. Suppose you were told that research has shown that people who are rather conservative by nature make the best firefighters. Stop for a moment and think about why this is true. If you are like the participants in a study by Craig Anderson, Mark Lepper, and Lee Ross (1980), you probably did not have much trouble thinking of reasons. A burning building is a dangerous, unpredictable place, one where it is important to proceed with caution. Indeed, if you were a firefighter, who would you rather have by your side—a reckless, foolhardy person who was swinging an ax in a wild, devil-may-care fashion, or someone who was by nature cautious and mindful of potential dangers?

Suppose, however, that we had asked you to explain the opposite fact—namely, that people who are rather risky by nature make the best firefighters. Again, if you were like Anderson and colleagues' (1980) participants, you would have no trouble explaining this fact either. Firefighters sometimes have to take risks to save lives and prevent property loss. If you were trapped in a fire, would you prefer that a fearless, risk-loving firefighter was dashing through the flames to save you, or that a timorous, fainthearted person was outside deliberating whether it was worth the risk?

The point is that people are adept at explaining all sorts of facts about themselves and the social world. Even if the basis of these facts happens to be discredited, the explanations people generated to explain them remain in force, causing people's beliefs to persevere. This is precisely what Anderson and his colleagues found. After giving people evidence that the best firefighters are conservative (or risky), they told people that this evidence was actually bogus. Even so, people persisted in believing the relationship between personality and firefighting ability that they had originally been given, due to the plausibility of the schemas they had generated to explain it.

## Making Our Schemas Come True: The Self-Fulfilling Prophecy

The preceding studies have shown that when people encounter new evidence or have old evidence discredited, they tend not to revise their schemas as much as we might expect. People are not always passive recipients of information, however. People often act on their schemas, and in doing so can change the extent to which their schemas are supported or contradicted. Research on this process—called **the self-fulfilling prophecy**—has found that people sometimes inadvertently behave in a way that creates evidence in support of their schema. This research is perhaps the most pessimistic in its portrayal of people's ability to change their schemas and beliefs.

A classic demonstration of this effect was performed by Robert Rosenthal and Lenore Jacobson (1968) in an elementary school in the mid-1960s. They administered an IQ test to all of the students in the school, and told the teachers that some of the students had scored so well that they were sure to "bloom" academically in the upcoming year. In fact, however, this

**self-fulfilling prophecy:** the case whereby people (a) have an expectation about what another person is like, which (b) influences how they act toward that person, which (c) causes that person to behave in a way consistent with people's original expectations

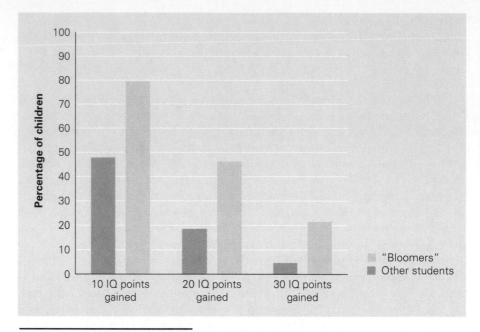

**FIGURE 4.5  The self-fulfilling prophecy: Percentage of first- and second-graders who improved on an IQ test over the course of the school year.** Those who the teachers expected to do well actually improved more than the other students. (Adapted from Rosenthal & Jacobson, 1968)

Prophecy is the most gratuitous form of error.
—George Eliot,
(Mary Ann Evans Cross), 1871

was not necessarily true. The students identified as "bloomers" were chosen randomly by the researchers. As we discussed in Chapter 2, the use of random assignment means that, on the average, the students designated as bloomers were no smarter or more likely to bloom than any of the other kids. The only way in which these students differed from their peers in the classroom was in the minds of the teachers (neither the students nor their parents were told anything about the results of the test).

After creating the expectations in the teachers that some of the kids would do especially well, Rosenthal and Jacobson waited to see what would happen. They observed the classroom dynamics periodically over the school year, and at the end of the year they tested all of the children again with an actual IQ test. Did the prophecy come true? Indeed it did—the few students in each class who had been labeled as bloomers showed significantly higher gains in their IQ scores than the other students did (see Figure 4.5). How could this have happened? How did the teachers' expectations become reality?

It is important to note that the teachers did not callously decide to direct their limited time and resources to the bloomers, writing off the rest of the class as not worth the trouble. Actually, the teachers reported that they had spent slightly more time with the students who were not labeled as bloomers. Instead, the teachers challenged the bloomers more, assuming that they were more capable of learning. They gave the bloomers more material to learn, gave them material that was more difficult, gave them more feedback on their work, and gave them more opportunities to respond in class. In addition, the teachers created a warmer emotional climate for those they expected to do well, giving them more personal attention, encouragement, and support (Rosenthal, 1974). These behaviors on the part of the teachers caused the bloomers to try harder and to learn more, and also raised their confidence and self-esteem. Thus, the bloomers responded to the special attention and instructions they received and, in fact, bloomed (Brophy, 1983; Jussim, 1986; Snyder, 1984).

Subsequent research has reinforced the idea that self-fulfilling prophecies are not the result of a deliberate attempt by people to confirm their schemas; rather, they occur inadvertently and unconsciously. Even when people try to treat others in an evenhanded, unbiased manner, their expectations can creep in and change their behavior, which in turn changes the behavior of the person with whom they are interacting (Darley & Gross, 1983; Word, Zanna, and Cooper, 1974). For example, Myra and David Sadker (1985) observed a classic self-fulfilling prophecy toward boys and girls in several middle schools. The teachers behaved in a way that encouraged boys to be more assertive and contribute more in class than girls. Most of the teachers denied, however, that they were behaving this way. In fact, they did not even realize that the boys were talking more. At one point, the teachers were shown a film of an actual classroom discussion, and asked who had talked more. They said the girls had. In fact, the boys in the film had talked three times as much as the girls. Sadker and Sadker (1985) suggest that sex-role stereotypes can be insidious, influencing teachers' perceptions and behaviors without their awareness.

Nor are self-fulfilling prophecies limited to the way teachers treat students. Each of us has all sorts of schemas about what other people are like, and anytime we act on these schemas in a way that makes the schema come true, a self-fulfilling prophecy results (Darley & Fazio, 1980). Self-fulfilling prophecies have been found with such diverse populations and expectations as college students' schemas about what a potential dating partner is like, mothers' schemas about what premature babies are like, and supervisors' expectations about the performance of assembly-line workers (King, 1971; Snyder & Swann, 1978; Stern & Hildebrandt, 1986).

A distressing implication of research on the self-fulfilling prophecy is that our schemas may be resistant to change because we see a good deal of false evidence that confirms them. Suppose a teacher has the schema that boys possess some innate ability that makes them superior in math to girls. "But Ms. Jones," we might say, "how can you hold such a belief? There are plenty of girls who do very well in math." Ms. Jones would probably be unconvinced, because she would have data to support her schema. "In my classes over the years," she might note, "nearly three times as many boys as girls have excelled at math." Her error lies not with her characterization of the evidence, but in failing to realize her role in producing it. Robert Merton referred to this process as a "reign of error," whereby people can "cite the actual course of events as proof that [they were] right from the very beginning" (1948, p. 195).

Stop for a moment and examine some of your own schemas and expectations about other social groups, especially ones you don't particularly like. These might be members of a particular race or ethnic group, of a rival fraternity, of a political party, or people with a particular sexual orientation. Why don't you like members of this group? "Well," you might think, "one reason is that whenever I interact with blacks [substitute whites, Jews, gentiles, gays, straights, Sigma Chis, Democrats, Republicans, or any other

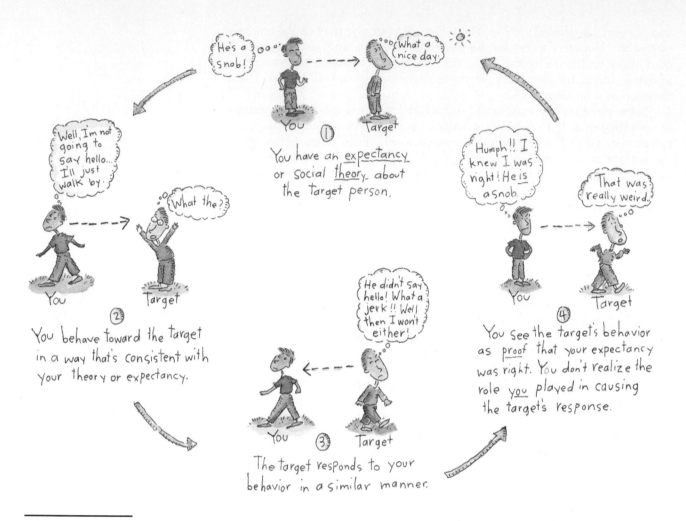

**FIGURE 4.6 The self-fulfilling prophecy: A sad cycle in four acts.**

social group], they seem cold and unfriendly." And you might be right. They do respond to you in a cold and unfriendly fashion. Not, however, because they are this way by nature, but because they are responding to the way you have treated them. Figure 4.6 demonstrates this sad, self-perpetuating cycle of a self-fulfilling prophecy.

We often ask our students to try an experiment to counteract this process. The next time you interact with a member of a group you dislike, try to imagine that this individual is the friendliest, kindest, sweetest person you ever met. Be as charming and outgoing as you can be. You might be surprised by the results. People you thought were cold and unfriendly by nature might suddenly behave in a warm and friendly manner themselves, in response to the way you have treated them. Give it a try!

## Do We Ever Disconfirm Our Schemas or Change Our Views?

We do not mean to exaggerate the extent to which people are stubborn, unyielding theorists. First, under certain conditions, people will focus on or even seek out information that is inconsistent with their schemas. For example, as we mentioned earlier, if a new piece of information is so inconsistent with a schema that people spend time trying to explain it or reconcile it with their prior beliefs, they have quite accurate recall of this information (Hastie, 1980; Srull, 1981). Second, if people are in a situation where it is important to them to hold accurate and defensible beliefs (e.g., if they have to justify publicly why they think the way they do), they will be more likely to notice and take into account inconsistent information, instead of ignoring or discounting it (Kruglanski & Freund, 1983; Tetlock, 1983). Third, several conditions have been identified in which people will seek out information that has an equal chance of confirming or disconfirming their hypotheses, thereby avoiding a self-fulfilling prophecy. People have been found to treat people in an unbiased way if they are uncertain about whether their schema is true, if there is a clear alternative to their schema, or if they are specifically asked to disconfirm the schema (Higgins & Bargh, 1987; Swann & Ely, 1984; Trope & Bassok, 1983).

Our point is simply that people are usually reluctant to change their views, and under most conditions take considerably longer to do so than logic would demand. For example, Carreta and Moreland (1982) found that in the summer of 1972, when congressional hearings on the Watergate scandal were revealing more and more negative information about President Richard Nixon, people who had voted for Nixon persevered in their positive opinions of him. There comes a point, however, when contradictory evidence is of such quantity and strength that it cannot be ignored, and people adopt new beliefs. This is especially likely to be the case if there are strong pressures from others to adopt new views. For example, Theodore Newcomb (1963) studied the attitudes of women entering Bennington College in the mid-1930s. When these women began college, most of them held the conservative political views of their parents. By the time they graduated, however, a remarkable shift had occurred—most of them now held extremely liberal views. This shift was due in part to the fact that Bennington was a close-knit community where liberal views were the norm; the women undergraduates were subjected to a considerable amount of peer pressure to be liberal. Thus, whereas people seem to treasure their schemas and beliefs, and often cling to them even in the face of contradictory evidence, there are circumstances under which change will occur.

To summarize, we have seen that the amount of information with which we are faced every day is so vast that we have to reduce it to a manageable size. In addition, much of this information is ambiguous or difficult to decipher. One way we deal with these problems is by relying on schemas, which help us reduce the amount of information we need to take in, and help us interpret ambiguous information. We turn now to other, more specific mental shortcuts that people use.

## Judgmental Heuristics

Think about how chess players decide which chess moves to make. Good players ponder several possible moves, taking into account how their opponent is likely to respond, how they would respond to this response, and so on. However, it is impossible for even the best chess players to consider all the possible patterns of future moves. For example, to begin a game, you can move one of ten pieces. For each of these ten moves, your partner could respond by moving ten of his or her pieces. You then need to consider how you would respond to each of these one hundred possible combination of moves. The permutations quickly become extremely large, so large that not even the most powerful computers in the world can process them all.

What, then, do master-level chess players do? They select only the possible moves that are the most promising, and then play out in their minds the moves and countermoves of these few possibilities. That is, they use strategies or well-honed rules of thumb to reduce to a manageable size the amount of information with which they are faced. This is exactly what people do in their everyday lives as well. Think about how you made your decision about which college to attend. You could have thoroughly investigated everything there was to learn about the more than 2,000 colleges and universities in the United States, reading their catalogs from cover to cover, visiting each one, interviewing students, and so on. To do so, however, would have been time-consuming and costly. Instead, you probably narrowed down your choice to a small number of colleges, following a set of rules of your own devising, and found out what you could about those schools. In other words, you relied on mental shortcuts. These shortcuts do not always lead to as good a decision as you would have made had you considered every piece of information. For example, if you had exhaustively studied all 2,000 colleges in the United States, maybe you would have found one that you liked better than the one where you are now. Mental shortcuts are efficient, however, and usually lead to good decisions in a reasonable amount of time.

What are these shortcuts? We have already seen that using schemas is one. Another shortcut was discussed in Chapter 3: Choose the alternative that makes you feel the best about yourself. The basic assumption of self-esteem approaches, such as dissonance theory, is that our judgments and decisions are driven by a need to maintain our self-esteem. When trying to decide to which college to apply, we might consider only those which make us feel the best about ourselves, such as Harvard or Stanford. Clearly, however, this strategy will get us only so far. It can be highly maladaptive to see only what we want to see, and to think only pleasant, esteem-building thoughts. Imagine that all high school seniors applied only to Harvard or Stanford, overlooking the fact that most of them would not be admitted. It is often necessary to form as accurate a picture of the world as we can, even if it does not stroke our egos to do so.

**judgmental heuristics:** mental shortcuts people use to make judgments quickly and efficiently

We will examine three shortcuts people use to help them form an accurate picture of the world. These shortcuts are called **judgmental heuristics.** The word *heuristic* comes from the Greek word meaning "to discover"; in the field of social cognition, heuristics refer to the rules people follow to make judgments quickly and efficiently. Before discussing these heuristics, we should note that they do not guarantee that people will make accurate inferences about the world. Sometimes heuristics are inadequate for the job at hand or are misapplied, leading to faulty judgments. In fact, a good deal of research in social cognition has focused on just such mistakes in reasoning; we will document many such mental errors in this chapter, such as the *Vincennes* radar technicians' misidentification of the Iranian airliner. As we discuss the mental strategies that sometimes lead to errors, however, it is important to keep in mind that people use heuristics for a reason: Most of the time, they are highly functional and serve us well.

## The Availability Heuristic: What Comes to Mind?

Suppose a friend is giving you a lift to a party. You climb into the car and pause for a moment, deliberating whether or not to put on your seatbelt. Your decision will probably be influenced by how likely you think it is that you will get into an accident that night. This judgment, in turn, will be influenced by how easily you can bring to mind examples of car accidents. For example, suppose that a friend of yours has just been seriously injured in an automobile accident, or that you have just read about a particularly grisly accident in the paper. Automobile accidents will easily come to mind, making you more likely to wear your seatbelt. This mental rule of thumb is called the **availability heuristic,** which refers to judgments based on the ease with which we can bring something to mind (Schwarz et al., 1991; Tversky & Kahneman, 1973).

**availability heuristic:** a mental rule of thumb whereby people base a judgment on the ease with which they can bring something to mind

There are many situations in which the availability heuristic is a good strategy to use. Suppose we asked you to estimate the percentage of doctors in the United States who are women. You could obtain a list of all M.D.s from the American Medical Association, or you could make a wild guess. Alternatively, you could use the availability heuristic: You could think of examples of doctors you have met, see how many of them are women, and make an educated guess from this sample of MDs. Such a strategy would probably lead to a reasonably close answer.

The trouble with the availability heuristic is that sometimes what is available in our memories is atypical, leading to faulty judgments. If four of the last five doctors you saw happened to be women, you might well overestimate the percentage of doctors in the United States who are women, because so many instances of female doctors are available in your memory. Or consider this question: Which kind of word is more common—words that begin with the letter *R*, or words that have the letter *R* as the third letter? Most people estimate that there are more words with *R* as the first letter, when in fact there are far more words with *R* as the third letter. This error occurs because of the way we store words in our memories: Words that start with *R* are more available in memory and thus easier to recall than words with *R* in the third position.

Tversky and Kahneman (1973) and others have performed several interesting demonstrations of when the availability heuristic can lead to incorrect inferences. Many of these studies have involved judgments and behaviors that are much more important to people than how many words start with *R*. For example, many people believe that deaths resulting from fire are more common than deaths due to drowning. This belief stems from the fact that the former type of fatality is more likely to be covered by the news media, and is thus more available in people's memory (Slovic, Fischhoff, and Lichtenstein, 1976). In fact, people are much more likely to drown than they are to perish in a fire. Similarly, if you ask people to estimate the number of violent crimes committed each year in the United States, you will get very different answers, depending on how much prime-time television they watch. Those who watch a great deal of television—and hence see a great deal of fictionalized violence—vastly overestimate the amount of real crime that occurs in the country (Gerbner, Gross, Morgan and Signorielli, 1980). Here's an example of the availability heuristic that you can try yourself: What's the

People overestimate the percentage of people who die in fires and under- estimate the percentage of people who perish by drowning. Examples of deaths in fires are more likely to be reported by the media, and are thus more available in people's memories.

ratio of homicides to suicides in the United States? Our students invariably believe that homicides outnumber suicides, as would anyone who reads the newspaper or watches TV news. In fact, suicides consistently outnumber homicides by nearly 40 percent year after year.

Availability effects are not just idle inferences of little consequence; rather, they can influence people's behavior in significant ways. Though the importance of regular health checkups is well known, many people do not see doctors as often as they should. For example, fatalities from breast cancer would be reduced if more women had regular mammograms. One way to increase the frequency of mammograms would be to disseminate more widely the statistics about the likelihood of getting breast cancer. Another way, however, is to present people with vivid cases of one individual who had breast cancer. If one vivid case is highly available in people's memories, they are more likely to think about the possibility that they are at risk. This is what happened when the wives of two U.S. presidents—Betty Ford and Nancy Reagan—were discovered to have breast cancer. When these cases were publicized, there was a marked increase in the number of women around the country who had mammograms.

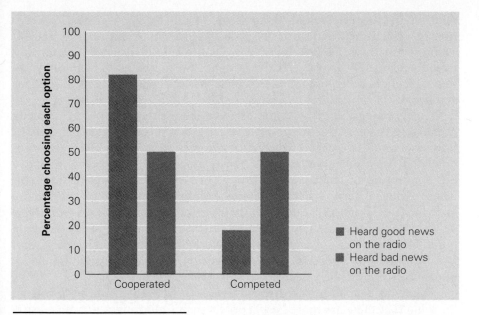

**FIGURE 4.7  Availability and how we treat others.** People heard either a good or a bad news story on the radio while waiting to participate in an experiment. Those who heard the good news were more likely to act cooperatively toward another participant in the experiment than those who heard the bad news. Those who heard the bad news were more likely to act competitively toward the other participant than those who heard the good news. (Adapted from Hornstein et al., 1975)

The effects of a highly available case on people's behavior was demonstrated experimentally by Harvey Hornstein and his colleagues (1975). Imagine you arrive for this experiment, and are asked to have a seat in a waiting room for a few minutes. A radio happens to be on, playing popular music. After a few moments, a newscaster describes either a brutal murder or an extremely generous act—wherein a complete stranger donated a kidney to a man with kidney disease. The experimenter then arrives and explains that you will be playing a game for money with another participant. In this game, you can choose to be cooperative—trying to maximize the amount of money that both you and your partner win—or competitive—trying to win most of the money for yourself. What will you do? In the actual study, people's behavior in the game was influenced by which news broadcast they had overheard (see Figure 4.7). Those who heard about the kidney donation behaved more cooperatively toward their partner than those who heard about the murder did, because these broadcasts increased the availability, respectively, of prosocial or antisocial events in people's minds. (The researchers ruled out other interpretations of this finding—e.g., the possibility that the newscasts influenced people's moods, which then influenced their behavior in the game.)

## The Representativeness Heuristic: How Similar Is A to B?

Suppose you attend a state university in New York. At the student union one day, you meet a student named Brian. Brian has blond hair, seems to be very mellow and laid-back, and likes to go to the beach. What state do you

representativeness heuristic: a mental shortcut whereby people classify something according to how similar it is to a typical case

base rate information: information about the frequency of members of different categories in the population

think Brian is from? Because Brian seems similar to many people's conception of what Californians are like, you might guess California, or at least seriously entertain this possibility. If so, you would be using the **representativeness heuristic**—that is, classifying things on the basis of their similarity to a typical case (e.g., how similar Brian is to your idea of what Californians are like).

Categorizing things by virtue of their representativeness is a perfectly reasonable thing to do. If we did not use the representativeness heuristic, how else would we decide where Brian comes from? Should we just randomly choose a state, without making any attempt to judge his similarity to our conception of students from New York State versus out-of-state students? Actually, there is another source of information we might use. If we knew nothing about Brian, it would be wise to guess that he was from New York State, because at state universities there are many more in-state than out-of-state students. If we guessed New York State, we would be using what is called **base rate information**, or information about the relative frequency of members of different categories.

What do people do when they have both base rate information (e.g., knowing that there are more New Yorkers than Californians at a university) and contradictory information about the person in question (e.g., knowing that Brian is blond and mellow and likes to hang out at the beach)? Kahneman and Tversky (1973) have found that people ignore the base rate, judging only how representative the information about the specific person is of the general category (e.g., Californians). While this is not a bad strategy if the information about the person is very reliable, it can get us into trouble when the information is rather flimsy. Given that the base rate of Californians attending state universities in New York is so low, you would need to have good evidence that this person was a Californian before ignoring the base rate and guessing that he is one of the few exceptions. Given that it is not that unusual to find people from eastern states who have blond hair, are laid-back, and like to go to the beach, you would be wise not to ignore the base rate in this instance.

Let's look at another example of how our reliance on the representativeness heuristic can cause us to make a mistaken judgment. Consider the following description of a woman named Linda:

> Linda is 31 years old, single, outspoken and very bright. She majored in philosophy. As a student, she was deeply concerned with issues of discrimination and social justice, and also participated in anti-nuclear demonstrations. (Tversky and Kahneman, 1983, p. 297)

Now guess which of the following descriptions of Linda is more probable: "Linda is a bank teller" or "Linda is a bank teller and is active in the feminist movement." If you are like Tversky and Kahneman's (1983) research participants, you rated the second description as much more probable than the first. After all, a bank teller who is active in the feminist movement is more representative of (similar to) someone who was concerned with discrimination in college than someone described simply as a bank teller is. The careful reader, however, will note that this judgment violates a basic law of probability: Logically, two independent events cannot be more probable than one of them alone. Because the category of "bank tellers" includes those who are active in the feminist movement as well as those who are not, it cannot be less likely than the category of "bank tellers who are active feminists."

Thus, people's use of the representativeness heuristic can lead to problematic inferences. Throughout history, for example, people have assumed that the cure for a disease must resemble the symptoms of the disease:

> The lungs of a fox must be a specific remedy for asthma, because that animal is remarkable for its strong powers of respiration. Turmeric has a brilliant yellow color, which indicates that it has the power of curing the jaundice. (Mill, 1974, p. 767)

This reliance on representativeness has sometimes impeded the discovery of the actual cause of a disease. Around the turn of the century, an editorial in a Washington newspaper denounced the foolhardy use of federal funds on ridiculous, farfetched ideas about the causes of yellow fever, such as the absurd idea of one Walter Reed that yellow fever was caused by, of all things, a mosquito.

## Anchoring and Adjustment: Taking Things at Face Value

Suppose that one day your economics professor asks the class to estimate the percentage of families in the United States who have an income of $40,000 or more. Someone in the front row suggests the answer is 25 percent; the professor says that figure is incorrect and asks you to make a guess. In this situation, most people will use the other student's guess of 25 percent as an anchor, or starting point. People often make judgments by considering an initial value, and then determining how much they need to adjust their answer from this value. Several studies have found that people make estimates that are fairly close to an anchor (DePaulo, Stone, and Lassiter, 1985; Edwards, 1968; Jones, 1990; Ross, 1977; Slovic & Lichtenstein, 1971). That is, your estimate would probably be fairly close to 25 percent, at least closer than if you began by considering some other number, such as 50 percent. This mental shortcut has been called the **anchoring/adjustment heuristic** by Tversky and Kahneman (1974).

**anchoring/adjustment heuristic:** a mental shortcut that involves using a number or value as a starting point, and then adjusting one's answer away from this anchor; people often do not adjust their answer sufficiently

It is often a good strategy to stick close to an initial anchor when making judgments, particularly if you have reason to believe that the value of the anchor is close to the truth. If you knew, for instance, that the student who guessed 25 percent was a bright economics major whose favorite pastime was perusing government statistics, you might assume that his or her guess was close to being right, and therefore stick pretty close to it. Yet as with the other heuristics we have considered, people sometimes rely too heavily on the anchoring heuristic, leading to faulty judgments. People have been found to adjust their judgments from an anchor insufficiently, even when they know that the anchor is incorrect.

Many demonstrations of the anchoring heuristic involve giving people numerical judgments. For example, Tversky and Kahneman (1974) asked people to estimate what percentage of countries in the United Nations are in Africa. They asked people first to estimate whether this percentage was higher or lower than an arbitrary starting point, determined by spinning a roulette wheel. For some subjects, the wheel stopped on the number 10; thus, they first estimated whether the correct answer was higher or lower than 10 percent. In this condition, the subjects estimated, on average, that the correct answer was 25 percent. For the other subjects, the wheel stopped on the number 65, and they estimated, on average, that the correct answer was 45 percent. Thus, people's estimates were anchored by the initial value they considered, even though they knew this number was chosen arbitrarily.

The tendency to stick close to an initial value or belief, and sometimes to insufficiently adjust one's judgments, is a deep-seated and fundamental characteristic of human thought. The philosopher Benedict Spinoza made an important observation about human cognitive processing three centuries ago: When people initially see, hear, or learn something, they take it at face value and assume it is true. Only after accepting the veracity of a fact do people go back and decide whether it might be false (Gilbert, 1991, 1993).

Although other philosophers (e.g., René Descartes) disagreed, research on the anchoring heuristic shows that Spinoza knew exactly what he was talking about. If people assume initially that everything they see or hear is true, this would explain why they often insufficiently adjust their beliefs from an initial anchor. For example, the crew members operating the advanced radar warning system on the *Vincennes* might have allowed what happened to the USS *Stark* to anchor their judgments too much. The fact that an Iranian fighter plane had launched a missile at a U.S. ship earlier may have made it more difficult for them to consider alternative scenarios—such as that this blip on the radar screen might be a civilian aircraft.

This example illustrates that it is not just numerical judgments that are influenced by the anchoring heuristic. When we form judgments about the world, we often allow our personal experiences and observations to anchor our impressions, even when we know our experiences are unusual. Suppose, for example, that you go to a popular restaurant that all your friends rave about. As luck would have it, your entree is burned and the waiter is rude. At one level, you know your experience is atypical—all your friends have had great meals at this restaurant. Nonetheless, your experiences are likely to anchor your impression of the restaurant, making you reluctant to return. We will see more examples of how the anchoring heuristic influences social judgments shortly.

To summarize, we have discussed two kinds of mental shortcuts people use: schemas and judgmental heuristics. There is a close relationship between these two types of cognitive processing. Schemas are organized bits of knowledge about people and situations, like books in a library. Which schema is called up (which book is retrieved from the stacks) depends on judgmental heuristics. The more available a particular schema is in memory—the easier a book is to find in the stacks—the more likely we are to use that book. The more a person or situation is representative of a particular schema (the more similar the contents of the book are to the situation we are in), the more likely we are to use it. And once we call up a particular schema and use it as a starting point to interpret a situation, the more it will anchor our impressions, making it difficult to call up alternative schemas (once a book has been retrieved and read, it is hard to completely forget it and send it back to the stacks, replacing it with another book). Now that we have reviewed the basic workings of social cognition—the role of schemas and judgmental heuristics—we turn to how people use these mental shortcuts when making specific kinds of judgments about the social world.

## Using Mental Shortcuts When Forming Social Judgments

We consider here two kinds of judgments: (a) making generalizations from samples of information and (b) judging the relationship between two variables, that is, how well one variable can be predicted from the other. Both kinds of judgments reflect a bias in human cognitive processing; we don't always weigh information in a totally logical and rational fashion.

### Biased Sampling: Generalizing from Samples to Populations

After visiting New Jersey for a few days, most people feel they have learned something about what the state is like. We form opinions about homeless people after seeing a few interviewed on television or encountering a few on the street. We feel that we have a pretty good idea about our acquaintances' personalities based on a few observations of their behavior. In each of these examples, we are not familiar with everything about the city or person: We have not visited every part of New Jersey, met every homeless person, or observed all of our acquaintances' behaviors. Just as scientists make inferences about populations from samples of data, however, we often fill in the blanks by assuming that what we have not observed is similar to what we already have observed.

As we discussed in Chapter 2, when scientists select samples they try to ensure that the sample is representative of the population at large. A political

Biased sampling: How would you feel about the entire state of New Jersey if you visited only one of these locations? People have been found to generalize from small samples of information, even when they know these are not typical or representative.

pollster would be unwise to try to predict the outcome of an election from a small sample of extremely wealthy people; instead, pollsters try to select samples that are representative of the entire electorate. In everyday life, however, people usually do not try to select representative samples. In fact, we often want our samples to be biased in various ways. When inviting people to a party, we do not want a random sample of all our acquaintances; we want people who are particularly fun and interesting, and who will get along well with each other. When sightseeing in Chicago, we do not take out a street map, close our eyes, and visit those locations on which our finger happens to fall; we try to select a biased sample of sites that are particularly noteworthy.

Given that people often deliberately select biased samples, we might expect that they would be reluctant to generalize from these samples. If we know that we have visited only the noteworthy parts of Chicago, presumably we will be careful about assuming that all of Chicago is like what we have seen. Interestingly, however, people are often remarkably insensitive to sample bias, and are quite willing to generalize from their limited experiences—a process called **biased sampling.**

For example, one day a social psychologist was eating lunch with several colleagues, one of whom remarked, "Say, did you see the story in the current *New Yorker* about the typical welfare mother? Boy, what a picture of social pathology. Makes you wonder about the welfare system, doesn't it?" It just so happened that another person at the lunch table was a prominent economist who was an expert on the welfare system. "What makes you think she is typical?" he asked. "In fact, she is anything but typical. For one thing, the average amount of time on welfare in her state is two years, whereas she has been on welfare for more than a decade."

The fact that the social psychologist had assumed that the welfare mother was typical was the inspiration for a study one of us performed with two colleagues (Hamill, Wilson, and Nisbett, 1980). We gave subjects a condensed version of the *New Yorker* article. The article was a vivid portrayal of Carmen Santana, a welfare mother living in New York City. Though Santana was friendly and warm, she lived a life that was, by most people's standards, irresponsible and bleak. She often squandered her welfare check on state lotteries and the numbers racket; what was left she spent on rent, food from an overpriced corner market, and monthly payments on over-priced, cheap, plastic-covered furniture. She lived in a rat-infested building with broken doors and mailboxes, cracked walls and ceilings, and broken appliances. The youngest of her eight children (who were the result of relationships with three different men) wore old tattered clothing, and their attendance at school was irregular at best. One had not yet started school, because Ms. Santana did not have a copy of the child's birth certificate. The older children were involved in numbers running, heroin, and prostitution. All in all, it was a bleak, depressing picture.

We were curious whether people would become more negative toward people on welfare as a result of reading the article about Ms. Santana—that is, whether they would draw an inference about the population of welfare recipients based on the sample of one person they had read about. Logically, this should depend on how typical or representative of all welfare recipients people thought Ms. Santana was. To see if people would follow this logic, we explicitly told some of them that Ms. Santana was highly atypical, in that

**biased sampling:** making generalizations from samples of information that are known to be biased or atypical

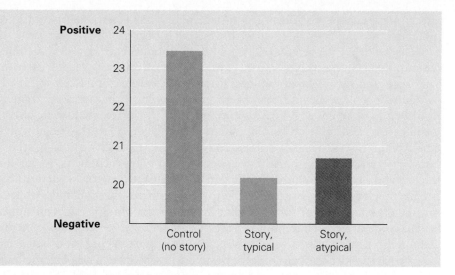

**FIGURE 4.8  Attitudes toward welfare recipients.**  People who read a story about one unlikable welfare recipient had more negative attitudes toward welfare recipients in general, regardless of whether they believed she was typical or atypical. (Adapted from Hamill, Wilson, & Nisbett, 1980)

she had been on welfare much longer than the average welfare recipient. We told others that she was typical, in that she had been on welfare for about the same length of time as the average recipient. We then observed whether these two groups changed their attitudes toward welfare, by comparing their views with those of a control group who did not read the story.

When people were told that Ms. Santana was typical, they became more negative toward welfare recipients (see Figure 4.8). This is not, perhaps, very surprising; people knew that Ms. Santana was similar in at least one respect to the average welfare recipient, and thus generalized from her to the group as a whole. Surprisingly, however, people were equally willing to generalize when they knew she was atypical. Even though people in this condition were able to recall the fact that she was atypical, this information had little impact on their willingness to generalize from what they had read: They became as negative toward welfare recipients as did the people who believed she was typical.

Even when we know that a piece of information is biased or atypical, it can be hard to ignore it completely. At some level, we all know that reporters, television producers, and authors seldom present information that is typical, for their job is to present what is unusual, interesting, and attention-grabbing, not what is average. (How often do we hear a TV anchorperson say something like, "Leading the news tonight: Barbara Kowalski did not have a car accident on her way to the office, and Stan Smith had an average day driving his city bus up and down Main Street"?) Nonetheless, we seem to find it hard not to make generalizations from what we see. Sound familiar? This is another example of the anchoring/adjustment heuristic. People have a starting point, or an anchor ("Ms. Santana was really a mess"), from which they should adjust their judgment ("She is not representative of the population at large; therefore, I should not draw inferences about welfare recipients in general"). As with many other kinds of anchoring effects, however, people do not adjust their judgments sufficiently, and are influenced too much by the case with which they began.

This tendency is not limited to judgments about other people. Sometimes we may even make unwarranted generalizations about ourselves from samples of our own behavior. Jones, Rhodewalt, Berglas, and Skelton (1981) instructed people to behave toward an interviewer in either (a) an extremely positive, competent, and sensitive manner or (b) an extremely negative, incompetent, and insensitive manner. After complying with this request, the participants rated their self-esteem, supposedly as part of another study. Now, you might think that these people would view their behavior in the interview as a biased sample that had no implications for what kind of person they really were; after all, they were simply doing what the experimenter instructed them to do. However, as in the Hamill and colleagues (1980) study of the welfare mother, the participants seemed to make generalizations from what they knew to be a biased sample. Those who had been asked to respond positively reported that their self-esteem was significantly higher than those who had been asked to respond negatively did.

People also overgeneralize from biased samples of observations of cities. For example, John Steinbeck vividly illustrated this problem in the following passage:

> In this report I do not fool myself into thinking I am dealing with constants. A long time ago I was in the ancient city of Prague and at the same time Joseph Alsop, the justly famous critic of places and events, was there. He talked to

In his book *Travels with Charley*, John Steinbeck reports his impressions of America, after traveling several thousand miles in a camper with his dog, Charley. One purpose of this journey, Steinbeck said, was to answer the question, "What are Americans like today?" However, he was well aware of the problems of biased sampling.

informed people, officials, ambassadors; he read reports, even the fine print and figures, while I in my slipshod manner roved about with actors, gypsies, vagabonds. Joe and I flew home to America on the same plane, and on the way he told me about Prague, and his Prague had no relation to the city I had seen and heard. It just wasn't the same place, and yet each of us was honest, neither one a liar, both pretty good observers by any standard, and we brought home two cities, two truths. (p. 77)

## Covariation Assessment: Predicting One Variable from Another

Jim is a nice guy when you see him in class. Would he make a good roommate? Does the fact that you enjoy your social psychology class mean that you will enjoy a class in developmental psychology? Is it true that blonds have more fun, or that redheads have hot tempers? Each of these questions concerns the extent to which you can predict one variable (Jim's behavior in class) to another (Jim's behavior as a roommate). This is called **covariation assessment,** which involves judging the correlation between two variables. Without an understanding of covariation—knowing how well we can predict one variable from another—we would live in a confusing, unpredictable world where all future events would be unexpected and surprising. For example, imagine that we did not understand the relationship between turning a key in the ignition and a car starting, and had to rediscover this relationship every time we wanted to go somewhere. Not a very pleasant world to live in!

People's ability to detect covariations has been found to be quite good, at least when they do not have a prior schema or expectation about the nature of the covariation. For example, Jennings, Amabile, and Ross (1982) gave people several pictures of men with walking sticks, and asked them to judge whether there was a relationship between the height of the men and the length of their walking sticks. People did a creditable job of estimating the covariation. When there was a strong relationship between height and length of the sticks, people were likely to notice this relationship. When there was no relationship between these two variables, people reported that there was no correlation. This is not to say that people are perfect covariation detectors. However, under most circumstances people do a fairly good job. This is not terribly surprising, given the adaptive value of making such judgments correctly. After all, even animals are adept at learning many correlations, such as the relationship between coming when they are called and the receipt of a doggy treat.

Nonetheless, it would be difficult for each of us to have to learn every covariation from scratch. Imagine that we had no idea which plants are edible and which are poisonous, or whether smoking cigarettes is correlated with cancer and heart disease. Eventually we might figure out such relationships on our own, but only after a lot of trial and error and (possibly fatal) mistaken assumptions. Fortunately, we do not have to learn every covariation for ourselves, because our culture furnishes us with schemas and expectations about many covariations. We have the benefit of centuries of accumulated knowledge to teach us such relationships.

Occasionally, however, the covariations our culture teaches us are themselves in error. Consider the following theories about covariation: People are in better moods on weekends than on Mondays; eating chocolate increases

**covariation assessment:** judgment as to the extent to which two variables are correlated; that is, predicting one variable (e.g., a person's friendliness) from another variable (e.g., his or her gender)

people's chance of getting pimples; going out in damp, chilly weather increases the likelihood that people will catch a cold. Sound reasonable? Actually, there is research indicating that all these assumptions are wrong (e.g., Williams, 1983; Wilson, Laser, and Stone, 1982). Given that some of the covariations we learn are wrong, the best approach might be to learn what the culture has to say about the association between such things as eating chocolate and getting acne, and then seeing for ourselves whether these covariations are true or not. We could test for ourselves whether the chocolate-acne covariation is true for us, by eating large amounts of chocolate (being good scientists, we want a big sample size) and then making note of how much our complexion suffers.

You might hear bells going off at this point. "Wait a minute," you say. "Didn't you just get done telling us that once people have a schema, they are not so hot at disconfirming it?" Indeed we did, and indeed this is another situation where people tend to be stubborn, unyielding theorists. Several studies have found that when people judge the covariation between two variables, if they expect there to be a relationship, they will see one there. For example, one of us conducted a study in which college students kept track of their moods every day for five weeks (Wilson, Laser, and Stone, 1982). The students also kept track of several factors that might have been correlated with their moods, such as how much sleep they had gotten the night before and what the weather was like. From these data, we could see which variables (e.g., the weather) actually correlated with people's moods. We then compared these actual correlations to people's estimates of what they thought the correlations were, to see how accurate people were at knowing what variables their mood covaried with.

It is important to note that in this study, people had prior theories about the variables they were judging—unlike the participants who judged the relationship between the heights of men and the length of their walking sticks. There are many common ideas about what influences moods, such as the idea that our moods are worse at the beginning of the week, and that a lack of sleep puts us in a bad mood. In the Wilson and colleagues (1982) study, people's theories seemed to determine, to a large extent, their judgments about what had covaried with their mood, even when their theories were wrong. For example, most subjects said that a lack of sleep was followed by a bad mood the next day, when in fact this was not true for most of them.

Other studies have also found that people's schemas can overwhelm their judgments of covariations, leading them to see **illusory correlations** (Alloy & Tabachnik, 1984; Berman & Kenny, 1976; Crocker, 1981; Kunda & Nisbett, 1986; Nisbett & Ross, 1980; Trolier & Hamilton, 1986; Wright & Murphy, 1984). Loren Chapman and Jean Chapman (1967) found that many clinical psychologists continue to believe in the validity of certain diagnostic tests that have repeatedly been shown to be invalid indicators of mental illness. One such test is the "Draw-a-Person Test," wherein the psychologist makes inferences about a client's personality from the way in which he or she draws a picture of a human being. Several studies have shown that this test has no validity: The kinds of pictures people draw have no bearing on the kind of people they are. Why, then, do many clinical psychologists continue to use this test? According to Chapman and Chapman (1967), many clinical psychologists have the schema that certain kinds of responses

**illusory correlations:** the belief that two variables are correlated when they actually are not, because of a schema that says the variables are related

The "Draw-a-Person Test," which asks a client to draw a picture of a person, has not been shown to have any validity. In study after study, researchers have found that the kind of picture people draw is not related to their personalities. Many psychotherapists, however, persist in believing that the test is valid, because of their schema that certain kinds of drawings (e.g., those with big eyes) are a sign of certain kinds of problems (e.g., paranoia).

on these tests—say, drawing someone with big eyes—are a sign of certain kinds of pathology—say, paranoia—and this schema dictates what covariations they observe in their clients. Thus, they are probably much more likely to remember a time when someone drew big eyes and was paranoid than the times when people drew big eyes and were not paranoid.

## Are People Really Such Bad Thinkers?

So far, we have discussed quite a few foibles in human reasoning. We have shown that people rely too heavily on mental rules of thumb, let their schemas do the talking even in the face of contradictory information, and make rash generalizations from atypical experiences. Sometimes these shortcomings in human inference have tragic consequences, as when the radar technicians on the *Vincennes* mistakenly believed they were under attack by an Iranian fighter plane even when their radar equipment indicated otherwise.

But can it really be the case that our thought processes are so flawed? After all, most of us make it through the day quite well, without stumbling too badly. Some people argue that social psychologists exaggerate the extent to which human reasoning is flawed. According to this view, social psychologists have cleverly devised tasks that trip people up and cause them to make errors, when in fact people's performance on these tasks is unrepresentative of how they make inferences in everyday life. Those holding this view maintain that the experimental tasks are similar to parlor tricks: Just because a magician can trick us into believing that he or she has disappeared in a puff of smoke does not mean that our perceptions of everyday events are fundamentally flawed. Others argue just the opposite: Even though people are capable of making sophisticated inferences, they are also capable of making errors that have important real-life consequences.

> The greatest of all faults, I should say, is to become conscious of none.
>
> —Thomas Carlyle

## A Portrayal of Human Inference

A major difficulty in this debate is defining what a "correct" inference is. Are people at fault for not making inferences in the same way as trained logicians? Should we aspire to be like computers, processing information rationally at all times, devoid of any feeling or emotion? Who is the final arbiter of human thought? These are thorny philosophical issues that cannot be done justice here. (See Cohen, 1981; Kahneman & Tversky, 1983; Nisbett & Ross, 1980; Stich, 1990; Stich & Nisbett, 1980, for an in-depth discussion of these issues.) We offer what in our view is the best resolution of the debate about how good people are as inference makers.

**People Do What They Do for Good Reasons.**   The rules of inference (e.g., judgmental heuristics) that have evolved over the millennia are functional and for the most part serve us well. Though these rules sometimes lead us astray, more often they are helpful. For example, one lesson of this chapter is that people are unyielding theorists, clinging to their schemas even when contradictory data are staring them in the face. This sounds pretty bad. But do we want people to abandon all their prior expectations and schemas when entering a new situation? Surely not, because it is highly adaptive to approach new situations armed with expectations that will help us interpret what we'll see. Several philosophers have argued that it is better to assign less weight to data that conflict with a prior schema than to totally alter our world view each time we encounter a contradictory piece of evidence (e.g. Kuhn, 1962; Polanyi, 1958).

As another example, consider the anchoring/adjustment heuristic. We have seen several cases where people do not sufficiently adjust their judgments from a starting point, as when assuming that biased samples are representative of a general population. Like many other mistakes people make, this may be a byproduct of a useful inferential strategy: the tendency to take what we see at face value. It is adaptive to assume that the world is as it appears to be, rather than doubting every new piece of information we receive ("Is that a car swerving into my path? Perhaps I should wait for further information before I decide what it is . . . CRASH!"). After all, most of what we see and hear probably is as it appears to be (Gilbert, 1991).

**The Evidence for Inferential Errors May Be Exaggerated.**   Experiments on inferential errors may have exaggerated, at least slightly, the extent to which these errors occur in everyday life. In many experiments, people have been asked to make judgments that are of little importance to them. When faced with such a task, people might not bother to make the more effortful, accurate inferences of which they are capable. This is illustrated by several studies showing that when more consequential tasks are used, people do make more complex and accurate inferences (Borgida & Howard-Pitney, 1983; Chaiken, Liberman, and Eagly, 1989; Darley, Fleming, Hilton, and Swann, 1988). For example, Allan Harkness, Kenneth DeBono, and Eugene Borgida (1985) gave female participants information about a person named Tom Ferguson, whom they had never met. The participants learned how interested Tom was in dating each of several women, and learned several things about these women, such as how good a sense of humor they had.

They were asked to judge the covariation between the qualities of the women (e.g., their sense of humor) and Tom's willingness to date them. As with many other studies that have examined people's ability to judge covariations, Harkness and colleagues (1985) found that the women used simple strategies to figure out the covariations, and made estimates that, while not totally wrong, were not particularly accurate.

Unless, that is, they were highly motivated to make careful judgments. Some of the participants thought they were taking part in a dating study, and that they themselves would be dating Tom for several weeks. Under these conditions, when the women were more motivated to figure out what Tom liked and disliked in a dating partner, they used more complex strategies to assess the covariations, and made judgments that were more accurate. (See also Dunn & Wilson, 1990; Flink & Park, 1991; Kruglanski, 1989; Petty & Cacioppo, 1986; Tetlock, 1985).

**There Is Plenty of Room for Improvement in Human Inference.**  Even though some laboratory demonstrations of errors in human inference might have overestimated the extent to which these errors occur in everyday life, we and numerous others believe that many of these errors can have consequential effects (e.g., Gilovich, 1991; Nisbett & Ross, 1980; Quattrone, 1982; Slusher & Anderson, 1989). For example, in Chapter 13 we will see that racial prejudice can be traced back, in part, to faulty reasoning processes. Another example is the tragic case of the *Vincennes*, where the decision to shoot down the Iranian airplane can be traced back to several inferential errors.

> Modest doubt is called the beacon of the wise.
> —William Shakespeare

## Correcting Human Inference

Given that the shortcomings of human cognition can have unpleasant and even tragic consequences, it is important to consider how these mistakes can be corrected. Is it possible to teach people to make better inferences, thereby avoiding some of the mistakes we have discussed in this chapter? If so, what is the best way to do it? Educators, philosophers, and psychologists have debated this question for decades, and recently some fascinating experiments have provided encouraging answers.

One approach is to make people a little more humble about their reasoning abilities. Often we have greater confidence in our judgments than we should. The crew members operating the radar system on the *Vincennes* placed too much faith in their interpretations of the blips on the screen, and failed to check computer printouts showing that the Iranian plane was ascending, not descending. To illustrate people's overconfidence, several studies have asked participants how certain they are that they know the answer to a question, and have then compared their certainty to their actual performance. For example, Vallone, Griffin, Lin, and Ross (1990) asked students questions about how they would behave in the future and how confident they were that their answers were correct. In this and many similar studies, participants were overconfident, in that their answers were not as correct as they thought they would be. When people are 100 percent certain that they know the answer, typically they are correct only 85 percent of the time. When people think there is a 75 percent chance that they know the

overconfidence barrier: the
finding that people usually have
too much confidence in the accuracy of their judgments; people's
judgments are usually not as
correct as they think they are

answer, typically they are correct only 60 percent of the time (Lichtenstein, Fischhoff, and Phillips, 1982).

Anyone trying to improve human inference is thus up against an **over-confidence barrier.** Many people seem to think that their reasoning processes are just fine the way they are, and hence there is no need for any remedial action. One approach, then, might be to address this overconfidence directly, getting people to consider the possibility that they might be wrong. This tack was taken by Lord, Lepper, and Preston (1984). They found that when they asked people to consider the opposite point of view to their own, people realized that there were other ways to construe the world than their own way, and were less likely to make errors in their judgments (see also Anderson, Lepper, and Ross, 1980; Anderson & Sechler, 1986; Koriat, Lichtenstein, and Fischhoff, 1980).

Another approach is to teach people directly some basic principles about how to reason correctly, with the hope they will apply these principles in their everyday lives. Many of these principles are already taught in courses in statistics and research design, such as the idea that if you want to generalize

## Questions Testing Statistical Reasoning

1. The city of Middleopolis has had an unpopular police chief for a year and a half. He is a political appointee who is a crony of the mayor and he had little previous experience in police administration when he was appointed. The mayor has recently defended the chief in public, announcing that in the time since he took office, crime rates decreased by 12 percent. Which of the following pieces of evidence would most deflate the mayor's claim that his chief is competent?

a. The crime rates of the two cities closest to Middleopolis in location and size have decreased by 18 percent in the same period.

b. An independent survey of the citizens of Middleopolis shows that 40 percent more crime is reported by respondents in the survey than is reported in police records.

c. Common sense indicates that there is little a police chief can do to lower crime rates. These are for the most part due to social and economic conditions beyond the control of officials.

d. The police chief has been discovered to have business contacts with people who are known to be involved in organized crime.

2. In general, the major league baseball player who wins Rookie of the Year does not perform as well in his second year. This is clear in major league baseball in the past 10 years. In the American League, eight Rookies of the Year have done worse their second year; only two have done better. In the National League, the Rookie of the Year has done worse the second year 9 times out of 10. Why do you suppose the Rookie of the Year tends not to do as well in his second year?

**Answers**

1. (a)

2. A typical nonstatistical answer for this question would be, "The Rookie of the Year doesn't do as well because he's resting on his laurels; he's not trying as hard in his second year." A good statistical answer would be, "A player's performance varies from year to year. Sometimes you have good years and sometimes you have bad years. The player who won the Rookie of the Year award had an exceptional year. He'll probably do better than average in his second year, but not as well as he did when he was a rookie."

**FIGURE 4.9** Sample questions from the test of people's reasoning abilities. (Adapted from Lehman, Lempert, & Nisbett, 1988)

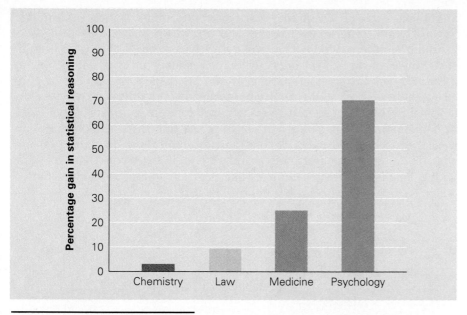

**FIGURE 4.10 Performance on a test of statistical reasoning abilities by graduate students in different disciplines.** After two years of graduate study, students in psychology and medicine showed more improvement on statistical reasoning problems than students in law and chemistry. (Adapted from Nisbett et al., 1987)

from a sample of information (e.g., one welfare mother) to a population (e.g., all welfare mothers), you must have a large, unbiased sample. Do people who take these courses apply these principles in their everyday lives? Are they less likely to make the kinds of mistakes we have discussed in this chapter? Do people have to take a semester-long course to learn these principles, or can they be taught in a single lesson? A recent series of studies by Richard Nisbett and his colleagues have provided encouraging answers to these questions. Nisbett has shown that people's reasoning processes can be improved by college statistics courses, graduate training in research design, and even brief, one-time lessons (Cheng, Holyoak, Nisbett, and Oliver, 1986; Fong, Krantz, and Nisbett, 1986; Nisbett, Fong, Lehman, and Cheng, 1987; Nisbett, Krantz, Jepson, and Kunda, 1983).

One set of studies, for example, examined how different kinds of graduate training influenced people's reasoning on everyday problems involving statistical reasoning—that is, problems testing mistakes similar to the ones we have considered in this chapter, such as their understanding of covariation (see Figure 4.9 for sample questions). The researchers predicted that students in psychology and medicine would do better on the statistical reasoning problems than students in law and chemistry would, because graduate programs in psychology and medicine include more training in statistics than programs in the other two disciplines do. These predictions were confirmed, as seen in Figure 4.10.

After two years of graduate work, students in psychology and medicine improved on the statistical reasoning problems more than students in law and chemistry did. The improvement among the psychology graduate students was particularly impressive. Interestingly, the students in the different

> The sign of a first-rate intelligence is the ability to hold two opposed ideas at the same time.
>
> —F. Scott Fitzgerald

disciplines performed equally well on sample items from the Graduate Record Exam, suggesting that they did not differ in overall intelligence. Instead, the different kinds of training they had received appeared to influence how accurately and logically they reasoned on everyday problems (Nisbett, Fong, Lehman, and Cheng, 1987). Thus, there is reason to be optimistic about people's ability to overcome the kinds of mistakes we have documented in this chapter. And you don't have to go to graduate school to do it. Sometimes it helps simply to consider the opposite, as Lord and colleagues' (1984) subjects did. Beyond this, formal training in statistics helps, at both the graduate and undergraduate levels. So if you were dreading taking a college statistics course, take heart: It might not only satisfy a requirement for your major, but improve your reasoning as well!

## SUMMARY

Social cognition is the study of how people select, interpret, and use information to make judgments and decisions about the social world. The social world is composed of far too much information for us to perceive, interpret, and react to all of it. We respond to this informational overload by being cognitive misers: we use schemas and judgmental heuristics to help us interpret and respond to people and situations. Schemas are cognitive structures in our heads that organize information around themes or subjects. Schemas have a powerful effect on what information we notice, think about, and later remember. When we encounter an ambiguous situation, we interpret it according to our schema. Under most conditions, we are more likely to notice and remember information that is consistent with our schemas, ignoring or forgetting inconsistent information. Because human memory is a reconstructive process, we remember information that is consistent with our schemas even when we never saw this information. Because schemas bias what we see, a hostile media phenomenon can result, whereby opposing partisan groups both perceive a neutral, balanced media presentation as hostile to their side. Because the media have not presented the facts in the one-sided fashion that partisans perceive to be true, each group believes the media is biased against them.

Sometimes many schemas apply to a given situation; the one we actually use can be affected by accessibility and priming. Recent thoughts or experiences can make one schema more available or accessible in our memory. These recent events can thus prime a specific schema and cause us to think along those lines. Relying on schemas is adaptive and functional up to a point, but people can be overzealous theorists. For example, sometimes we persevere in our beliefs even when they're disproved, as shown in research on the perseverance effect. At times, we distort information so that it fits our schemas; for example, the primacy effect shows how our first impression of a person causes us to interpret his or her subsequent behavior in a schema-consistent manner. Finally, schemas also affect our behavior— we act on the basis of our schemas. The most fascinating example of this is the self-fulfilling prophecy, wherein we make our schemas come true by unconsciously treating others in such a way that their response proves to us that our schema about them was right.

In addition to schemas, we use judgmental heuristics to help us deal with the large amount of social information with which we are faced. Heuristics are rules of thumb people follow in order to make judgments quickly and efficiently. The availability heuristic refers to the ease with which we can think of something, which has a strong effect on how we view the world. The representative heuristic helps us decide how similar one thing is to another; we use it to classify people or situations on the basis of their similarity to a typical case. When using this heuristic, we have a tendency to ignore base rate information—that is, the prior probability that something or someone belongs in that classification. People also rely on the anchoring/adjustment heuristic, wherein an initial piece of information acts as an anchor, or starting point, for subsequent thoughts on the topic. Whereas all three heuristics are useful, they can also lead to incorrect conclusions.

We also discussed how people use mental shortcuts when making two specific kinds of judgments. First, people often commit the fallacy of **biased sampling,** wherein they make generalizations from samples of information they know are biased or atypical. Second, judgments that require us to predict one variable from another, or **covariation assessment,** are often inaccurate as well. If we expect a correlation to exist between two variables in the social world, we will tend to see proof that it does, resulting in an **illusory correlation.**

Schemas and judgmental heuristics exist because, most of the time, they are adaptive and functional. However, they are used at some peril—sometimes, they lead us to highly inaccurate conclusions. Further, people are up against an **overconfidence barrier,** whereby they are too confident in the accuracy of their judgments. Fortunately, recent research has indicated that some of the shortcomings of human reasoning can be improved, particularly by training in statistics.

## SUGGESTED READINGS

Fiske, S. T., & Taylor, S. E. (1991). *Social cognition* (2nd ed.). New York: McGraw-Hill. A recent, encyclopedic review of the literature on social cognition by two experts in the field.

Gilovich, T. (1991). *How we know what isn't so: The fallibility of human reason in everyday life.* New York: Free Press. An entertaining overview of the many ways in which mental shortcuts can get us into trouble.

Kahneman, D., Slovic, P., & Tversky, A. (1982). *Judgment under uncertainty: Heuristics and biases.* New York: Cambridge University Press. A classic collection of chapters by researchers in the area of human inference.

Nisbett, R. E., & Ross, L. (1980). *Human inference: Strategies and shortcomings of human judgment.* Englewood Cliffs, NI: Prentice Hall. A lively, poignant review of mental shortcuts and biases in human reasoning by the people who discovered many of them.

# Chapter 5
## Social Perception: How We Come to Understand Other People

## Chapter Outline

**Nonverbal Behavior**
Facial Expressions of Emotion
Other Channels of Nonverbal Communication
Multichannel Nonverbal Communication
Gender Differences in Nonverbal Communication
**Implicit Personality Theories: Filling in the Blanks**
**Causal Attribution: Answering the "Why" Question**
The Nature of the Attributional Process
Correspondent Inference Theory: From Acts to
  Dispositions
The Covariation Model: Internal Versus External
  Attributions
**Using Mental Shortcuts When Making Attributions**
Using Schemas and Theories
The Fundamental Attribution Error: People as Personality
  Psychologists
The Actor/Observer Difference
Self-Serving Attributions
**How Accurate Are Our Attributions and Impressions?**
Why Are Our Impressions of Others Sometimes Wrong?
Why Does It Seem Like Our Impressions Are Accurate?
**Summary**
**Suggested Readings**

In a recent television ad, a woman discovers, as she finishes serving dinner to her guests, that she is out of coffee. She quickly runs next door and borrows some from her new neighbor. She lingers a bit, and he smiles flirtatiously. We start to wonder—is something developing here? Will he ask her out? To find out, we need only tune in to the next installments of these ads for Taster's Choice coffee. In the next episode, the woman returns the coffee and the man still seems interested, but—uh oh—someone is in his apartment, probably another woman. A little while later, the neighbors run into each other at a dinner party, and he asks her out. Then we see their first date, after which the man asks if he can come in for (what else?) a cup of coffee. What will happen? Will they kiss? Despite the fact that this is an advertisement trying to sell us something, we find ourselves "hooked" by the story it tells.

157

Consider as well a newspaper ad for Benson & Hedges cigarettes—one that came to be known as "the Jammy man" in the trade. In this ad, a man is standing in a doorway clad only in pajama bottoms, facing a table full of smiling men and women who are smoking (of course) and drinking wine. The ad is attention-getting because it needs explaining—why is the man in his pajamas during what appears to be a fancy dinner party? Is he sick? (He sure looks robust and healthy!) Is this his house, or is he a dinner guest? Why is a fellow at the table toasting "the Jammy man" with his wine glass? And why are the women laughing?

A scene from a Taster's Choice television commercial.

Readers' interest in "the Jammy man" grew to such proportions that the company actually ran a national contest for the best explanation of his behavior ("Jammy Man," 1988).

These ad campaigns succeeded because of a basic fact about human nature: People are endlessly curious about other people. Each of us expends a great deal of time and energy trying to explain the behavior of others. Why? Because doing so helps us understand and predict our social worlds (Heider, 1958; Kelley, 1967). In this chapter, we will discuss social perception—the study of how we form impressions of other people and how we reach judgments about them.

**social perception:** the study of how we form impressions of and make inferences about other people

**O**ne interesting thing about **social perception** is that we form impressions quickly and effortlessly. To be sure, other people can be a mystery, their feelings obscure and their motives hard to decipher. Still, it's nearly impossible to meet someone without forming some kind of impression of him or her. Look at the advertisement for Taster's Choice on this page. What do you think about the man and woman? Do you like them? How much do you think they like each other? Chances are that you formed impressions of these people even after looking at the picture for only a few seconds.

How? In this chapter, we will consider how people decide what other people are like, such as what kind of personality they have and what they are feeling. One important source of information people use is nonverbal behavior, such as other people's facial expressions and body movements. Sometimes people wear their hearts on their sleeves (or on their faces), making it relatively easy to tell how they are feeling. There is a considerable amount of research on how people read each other's nonverbal behaviors, to which we now turn.

## Nonverbal Behavior

What do we know about people when we first meet them? We know what we can see and hear, and even though we know we should not judge a book by its cover, this kind of easily observable information is critical to our first impressions. Physical characteristics such as people's attractiveness and facial configuration (e.g., how much of a baby face they have) influence others' judgments of them (Berry & McArthur, 1986; Hatfield & Sprecher, 1986; McArthur, 1990). We also pay a great deal of attention to what people say. After all, our most noteworthy accomplishment as a species is the development of language; the verbal channel of communication contains an extraordinary amount of information.

But people's words are not the full story. Pretend you are an actor in an improvisational class, and say the following sentence out loud in as many different ways as you can: "I don't know her." Try it with an angry tone of voice, a loving one, a sarcastic voice, a fearful tone, and a surprised one. Try emphasizing different words in the sentence, first stressing the word *I*, then the word *her*. The words stay the same—but the message changes dramatically.

This example illustrates that there is a rich source of information about people other than their words: the ways they communicate nonverbally. **Nonverbal communication** refers to a large body of research on different aspects of communication without words. Facial expressions, tone of voice, gestures, body positions and movement, the use of touch, and eye gaze are the most frequently used and diagnostic channels of nonverbal communication (Henley, 1977; Knapp, 1980). How does nonverbal communication work?

Nonverbal cues serve many functions in communication. Michael Argyle (1975) describes the primary uses of nonverbal behavior as: (a) *expressing emotion* (your eyes narrow, your eyebrows lower, you stare intensely, your mouth is set in a thin, straight line—you're angry), (b) *conveying attitudes* (e.g., "I like you"—smiles, extended eye contact—or "I don't like you"—eyes averted, flat tone of voice, body turned away), (c) *communicating one's personality traits* ("I'm outgoing"—broad gestures, a change in inflection when speaking, an energetic tone of voice), and (d) *facilitating verbal communication* (you lower your voice and look away as you finish your sentence so that your conversational partner knows that you are done and that it is his or her turn to speak).

In addition, Paul Ekman (1965) notes that some nonverbal cues repeat or complement the spoken message, as when you smile while saying, "I'm so happy for you!" Others actually contradict the spoken words. Com-

**nonverbal communication:** the way in which people communicate, intentionally or unintentionally, without words; nonverbal cues include facial expressions, tone of voice, gestures, body position and movement, the use of touch, and eye gaze

> An eye can threaten like a loaded and leveled gun, or can insult like hissing or kicking; or, in its altered mood, by beams of kindness, it can make the heart dance with joy.
>
> —Ralph Waldo Emerson, *The Conduct of Life*, 1860

ESOTERIC BODY LANGUAGE

Meaning: Please, can I have an English muffin?

Meaning: My childhood was as dull as a doornail.

Meaning: Do you still have any servants?

R. Chast

© Roz Chast. Used with permission.

municating sarcasm is the classic example of verbal/nonverbal contradiction. Think about how you'd say, "I'm so happy for you," sarcastically. (You could use your tone of voice, stressing the word *so* with an ironic twist, or you could roll your eyes as you speak, a sign of sarcasm in this culture.) Nonverbal cues can also substitute for the verbal message. You can have a miniconversation with another person without using words at all: Imagine you are on the telephone and a friend sticks her head into your room. Now imagine how, without speaking to her, you'd communicate the following: "Hi! I'm on the phone. I'll be on the phone for another ten minutes or so. I'll call you, OK?" (Here's how we'd do it: "Hi"—smile, wave hand. "I'm on the phone"—point to phone, roll eyes for dramatic emphasis. "I'll be on the phone for another ten minutes"—point to wrist [where a watch would be] and then flash your ten fingers—". . . or so"—hold one hand out, palm down, and "waggle" it right, left, right. "I'll call you"—point to yourself, the phone, and then the other person, and look at her with your eyebrows raised, as if asking a question. "OK"—nod head and smile, and make emphatic hand gesture in which your index finger and thumb form a circle.)

Nonverbal forms of communication have typically been studied individually, in their separate "channels" (e.g., eye gaze or gestures), even though in everyday life nonverbal cues of many kinds occur all at the same time in a quite dazzling orchestration of information (Archer & Akert, 1980, 1984). Let's focus on a few of these channels and then turn to how we interpret the full symphony of nonverbal information as it naturally occurs.

## Facial Expressions of Emotion

Without doubt, the crown jewel of nonverbal communication is the facial expressions channel. This aspect of communication has the longest history of research, beginning with Charles Darwin's (1872) book, *The Expression of the Emotions in Man and Animals*; its primacy is due to the exquisite communicativeness of the human face. Look at the photographs on the next page; we bet you can decode (read or interpret) the meaning of these expressions with very little effort.

Darwin's research on facial expressions has had a major impact on the field in many areas; we will focus on his belief that the primary emotions conveyed by the face are universal—all humans everywhere express (or "encode") these emotions in the same way, and all humans can interpret (or "decode") them with equal accuracy. Given Darwin's (1872) interest in evolution, it is not surprising that he believed nonverbal forms of communication to be "species-specific" and not "culture-specific." He stated that facial expressions were vestiges of once-useful physiological reactions—for example, if early hominids ate something that tasted terrible, they would have wrinkled their noses in displeasure (from the bad smell) and expelled the food from their mouths. Note that the photograph showing the disgusted expression demonstrates this sort of reaction. Darwin (1872) states that such facial expressions then acquired evolutionary significance; being able to communicate such emotional states (e.g., the feeling of disgust, not for food, but for another person or a situation) had survival value for the developing species (Hansen & Hansen, 1988; McArthur & Baron, 1983). Was Darwin right? Are facial expressions of emotion universal?

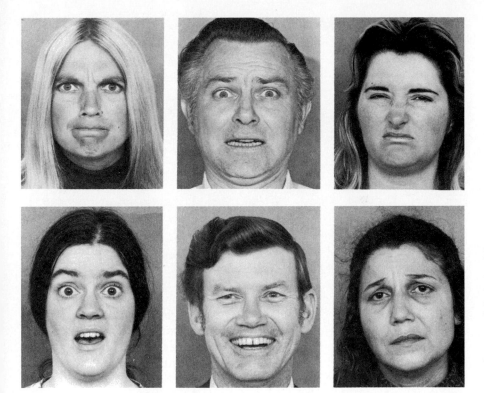

The photographs depict facial expressions of the six major emotions. Can you guess the emotion expressed on each face? The answers are printed below. (Adapted from Ekman & Friesen, 1975)
*Answers (clockwise, beginning with upper left photo):* Anger, fear, disgust, sadness, happiness, and surprise.

The answer is yes, for the six major emotional expressions: anger, happiness, surprise, fear, disgust, and sadness (Buck, 1984; Ekman, Friesen, and Ellsworth, 1982a, 1982b; Izard, 1977). For example, in a particularly well-designed study, Paul Ekman and Walter Friesen (1971) traveled to New Guinea, where they studied the decoding ability of the Fore, a preliterate tribe that had had no contact with Western civilization. They told the Fore people brief stories with emotional content and then showed them photographs of American men and women expressing the six emotions; the Fore's job was to match the facial expressions of emotion to the stories. They were as accurate as Western subjects had been. The researchers then asked the Fore people to demonstrate, while being photographed, facial expressions that would match the stories they were told. These photographs, when later shown to American research participants, were also decoded accurately. Thus, there is considerable evidence that the ability to interpret at least the six major emotions is cross-cultural—part of being human and not a product of people's cultural experience (Ekman et al., 1987; Izard, 1969).

However, we should note that culture does play a role as to when and how you display emotions on your face. Ekman and Friesen (1969) note that **display rules** are particular to each culture and dictate what kind of emotional expression people are supposed to show. For example, American cultural norms discourage emotional displays in men, such as grief or crying, whereas women are allowed to display such facial emotions. In Japan, traditional cultural rules dictate that women should not exhibit a wide, uninhibited smile (Ramsey, 1981); Japanese women will often hide their wide smiles behind their hands, whereas in Western cultures women are allowed—indeed

**display rules:** culturally determined rules about the nonverbal behaviors that are appropriate to display

Often, people express more than one emotion at the same time. Can you tell which emotions these people are expressing? The answers are printed below. (Adapted from Ekman & Friesen, 1975)

*Answers*: The man is expressing a blend of anger and disgust. The woman is expressing a blend of surprise and happiness.

> When the eyes say one thing, and the tongue another, a practiced man relies on the language of the first.
> —Ralph Waldo Emerson, *The Conduct of Life*, 1860

encouraged—to smile broadly and often (Henley, 1977). In fact, the cultural display rules that govern Japanese nonverbal expression are surprisingly different from Western ones. Japanese norms lead people to cover up negative facial expressions with smiles and laughter, and to display fewer facial expressions in general than is true in the West (Friesen, 1972; Morsbach, 1973). This is undoubtedly what lies behind the Western stereotype that Asians are "inscrutable" and "hard to read."

A final note about decoding facial expressions accurately: This situation is more complicated than it appears, because people frequently display affect blends (Ekman & Friesen, 1975), wherein one part of their face is registering one emotion and another part is registering a different emotion. Take a look at the photographs on this page and see if you can tell which two emotions are being expressed in each face. In the photograph on the left, we see a blend of anger (the eye and eyebrow region) and disgust (the nose and mouth region). (It may help to cover half of the photograph with your hand to see each emotional expression clearly.) This is the sort of expression you might display if a person told you something that was both horrible and inappropriate—you'd be disgusted with the content and angry that the person told you.

Clearly, affect blends are more difficult to decode than straight facial expressions. In addition, research has indicated that people express "micromomentary" facial expressions (Haggard & Issacs, 1966), extremely quick flashes of facial expression that cross their faces in fractions of a second. For example, a person might very briefly flash anger across his or her face while talking to you; if that expression lasts longer than two-fifths of a second, you have a chance of noticing and interpreting it (Haggard & Issacs, 1966).

## Other Channels of Nonverbal Communication

There are, of course, other channels of nonverbal communication. Eye contact and gaze are particularly powerful nonverbal cues; we become suspicious when a person doesn't "look us in the eye" while speaking, and people wearing dark sunglasses can be quite disconcerting to talk to. Gestures of the hands and arms are also a fascinating means of communication. We are very adept at understanding certain gestures, like those we used in our telephone example above. Gestures like these, for which there are clear, well-understood definitions, are called **emblems** (Ekman & Friesen, 1975). For example, emblems include the OK sign, in which one forms a circle with the thumb and forefinger and the rest of the fingers curve above the circle, and "flipping the bird," in which one bends all the fingers down at the first knuckle except the longest, middle finger. The important point about emblems is that they are not universal; each culture has devised its own emblems, and these need not be understandable to people from other cultures. Thus, "flipping the bird" will be a clear communicative sign in American society, whereas in some parts of Europe you'd need to make a quick gesture with a cupped hand under your chin to convey the same message. The photos on this page illustrate some French emblems, ones that are different from our American emblems.

**emblems:** nonverbal gestures that have well-understood definitions within a given culture; they usually have direct verbal translations, such as the OK sign

## Multichannel Nonverbal Communication

Except for certain specific situations (e.g., talking on the telephone), everyday life is made up of social interaction in a multichannel nonverbal sense.

*La barbe! Rasoir!:* How dull. "Beard! Razor!" acquired the meaning "boring" in the nineteenth century.

*Mon oeil*—My eye: You can't fool me!

These photographs depict French nonverbal emblems. These gestures are clearly understood in France, but might be difficult for an American to interpret. (Adapted from Wylie, 1977)

*Il est bourrè!*—He's stuffed; he's potted; he's drunk.

Typically, there are many nonverbal cues available to us when we talk to or observe other people. How do we use this information? And how accurately do we use it?

Robert Rosenthal and his colleagues began research in this area with the development of their Profile of Nonverbal Sensitivity (PONS), a videotape instrument that asks viewers to answer questions about a woman after watching two-second clips of her nonverbal behaviors (e.g., only her facial expressions; Rosenthal, Hall, DiMatteo, Rogers, and Archer, 1979). For each scene, the viewer chooses between two possible descriptions of what the woman is feeling or doing—for example, "criticizing someone for being late" or "talking to someone about the death of a friend." The correct answer is the type of scene in which the actress was acting while being filmed (e.g., the death of a friend). Rosenthal and colleagues (1979) have shown this video-tape to thousands of people all over the world and have found that people are quite impressively accurate.

In a more recent approach to multichannel nonverbal decoding, one of us and Dane Archer (Archer & Akert, 1991) have constructed a nonverbal com-munication decoding task that more closely mirrors real-life interpretative situ-ations. The Social Interpretations Task (SIT) videotape is composed of twenty scenes of naturally occurring nonverbal behavior (Archer & Akert, 1977a, 1977b, 1980, 1984). Real people, not actors, are seen and heard having real conversations, not scripted ones. The scenes last a minute or so, giving the viewer a slice of a real interaction. Following each scene, the viewer is asked a question about the people in the scene or their relationship to each other. For example, in one scene two women are seen playing with a baby. The viewer is asked, "Which woman is the mother of the baby?" A clear criterion for accu-racy exists for each of the scenes; one of the women really is the mother of the baby. However, neither of the women states this fact out loud; nor did they realize this would be the interpretative question paired with their scene. In order to get this and the other scenes right, the viewer must pay attention to and interpret the nonverbal behavior of the people in the scenes. We have found that people are able to decode these scenes accurately, at a level signifi-cantly above chance (which would mean they were only guessing). For example, the scene "Who is the mother?" has been decoded accurately by 64 percent of the more than 1,400 people tested (because there were three possible answers—see the photo on the facing page—the chance level of accuracy is only 33 percent for this scene).

In further research with the SIT videotape, we have found that the important, or diagnostic, nonverbal information is actually diffused throughout each scene (Archer & Akert, 1980). In other words, it is not typi-cally the case that there is only one significant clue that signals the right answer. Instead, useful nonverbal information is present across many chan-nels in each scene. This makes the decoder's job easier: If you fail to notice the eye gaze behavior, you may notice the tone of voice, or unusual gesture, and still arrive at an accurate judgment. We have also found that some people are particularly talented at decoding nonverbal cues accurately, while others are dismally poor at this task. One of us, with Abigail Panter, has explored various personality traits to see if they predict who the good decoders are; for example, we have found some evidence that extraverts are more accu-rate decoders of nonverbal cues on a SIT-like task than introverts are (Akert & Panter, 1986).

1. Which one of these two women is the mother of the baby?  a. The woman on the left.  b. The woman on the right.  c. Neither woman.

2. Are these two people:  a. Friends who have known each other for at least six months?  b. Acquaintances who have had several conversations?  c. Strangers who have never talked before?

3. All three of these men claim to have won the poker game. Who really won the game?  a. Person 1    b. Person 2    c. Person 3

The above photographs provide examples of the Social Interpretations Task. The answers are printed below. (Adapted from Archer & Akert, 1977)
*Answers*: 1—b; 2—c; 3—c.

A final multichannel area of research focuses on a specific type of judgment—can we tell when people are lying to us? Detecting deception is tricky; after all, someone is actively trying to mislead us. In a typical study, research participants are shown videotapes of people describing how much they like several acquaintances. The participants are told that some of these people are lying and some are telling the truth. Their job is to tell which is which (e.g., DePaulo & Rosenthal, 1979). How well do people detect deception? They are better than chance; that is, they are right more often than if they just flipped a coin to decide who was lying. Overall, however, people's ability to detect deception is not very good. People tend to give others the benefit of the doubt, assuming they are telling the truth (DePaulo, 1992).

Further, even when the research participants know someone is lying, they are usually unable to tell how the person really feels—in other words, what is the truth under the lie (DePaulo, Stone, and Lassiter, 1985; Ekman, 1985; Knapp & Comadena, 1979; Zuckerman, DePaulo, and Rosenthal, 1981). The problem with detecting lies is not just that it is so difficult; we also tend to look for clues in the wrong place, particularly the face. The face is not a good channel on which to focus; liars know how to control their eye gaze and facial expressions in order to look honest. Instead, research has indicated that deception is most accurately detected from a combination of body and voice cues, completely ignoring cues in the facial channel (DePaulo, 1992; DePaulo, Stone, and Lassiter, 1985).

## Gender Differences in Nonverbal Communication

It may have occurred to you to wonder whether some people are better than others at understanding nonverbal cues. As we mentioned earlier, there is some evidence that extraverts are better at this than introverts. By far the most heavily researched difference, however, is between women and men. Who is better at understanding nonverbal cues—males or females? Who is better at expressing their feelings nonverbally?

If you answered "women" to both questions, you are right. A large number of studies show that when it comes to nonverbal behavior, women are better at both reading (deciphering other people's nonverbal cues) and sending (behaving nonverbally in ways that are easy for other people to understand; Hall, 1984). Differences in reading other people's nonverbal cues are especially well researched. In eleven different countries, including the United States, women have been found to be better at understanding nonverbal behavior (Hall, 1979; Rosenthal & DePaulo, 1979).

As with most rules, however, there is an exception. Though women are superior to men at deciphering someone's nonverbal cues when that person is telling the truth, they lose their superiority when the person is lying. Rosenthal and DePaulo (1979) found that women were more likely to take deceptive communications at face value, assuming that if Sam says he likes Jill, then surely he must. Men were more likely to pick up on the nonverbal cues that indicated people were not telling the truth—seeing that Sam doesn't really like Jill as much as he says he does. What's curious about this finding is that women are far superior at reading nonverbal cues in general. Why, then, do they seem to lose this ability when deciphering deceptive communications? Rosenthal and DePaulo (1979) suggest that the answer is that women are more polite than men. They have the ability to read someone's nonverbal cues, including the ones indicating the person is lying. Out of politeness, though, they turn off this skill when listening to a deceptive statement, taking the statement at face value.

This interpretation fits nicely with a theory of sex differences offered by Alice Eagly (1987). According to Eagly's **social-role theory,** in most societies there is a division of labor on the basis of gender. Typically, women are more likely than men to occupy certain familial and occupational roles, such as being the primary caregiver to children. There are two important consequences of this division of labor, according to Eagly: First, gender-role expectations arise, wherein members of the society expect men and women to have attributes consistent with their role. Because of the social roles they occupy, women are expected to be more nurturing, friendly, expressive, and sensitive—and so they are. Second, men and women develop different sets of skills and attitudes, based on their gender roles. Because of their position in many societies, it is more important for women to learn skills such as sensitivity and communication—and, it might be argued, to learn how to be more polite. That is, because women are less powerful in many societies and are less likely to occupy roles of higher status, it is more important for women to learn to be accommodating and polite (Deaux & Major, 1987; Henley, 1977). According to Eagly (1987), gender-role expectations and sex-typed skills combine to produce sex differences in social behavior, such as the differences in nonverbal behavior we have just discussed.

**social-role theory:** the theory that sex differences in social behavior are due to society's division of labor between the sexes; this division leads to differences in gender-role expectations and sex-typed skills, which are responsible for differences in men's and women's social behavior

One way to test this theory would be to examine sex differences in cultures that have different gender-role expectations and sex-typed skills. If women are more polite in reading nonverbal cues because of the social roles they occupy in society, then this tendency to be polite should be especially strong in those cultures where women are most oppressed. This is exactly what Judith Hall (1979) found in her cross-cultural study of nonverbal behavior. First, she classified each of eleven countries as to the level of oppression of women, based on such statistics as the number of women who go to college and the prevalence of women's groups in each country. She then examined how likely women in each country were to show the "politeness pattern" when reading other people's nonverbal behaviors—focusing on nonverbal cues that convey what people want others to see and ignoring nonverbal cues that "leak" people's true feelings. Sure enough, women's tendency to be polite in this manner was especially strong in those cultures where women are most oppressed. This finding is consistent with a social-role interpretation, which argues that the more oppressed women are, the greater the likelihood that they will learn to be accommodating and polite toward others.

To summarize, we can learn plenty about people from their nonverbal behavior, including their attitudes, emotions, and personality traits. There are several channels of nonverbal communication, and people are reasonably accurate at reading these channels, especially when they see several channels at once, and when others are not deliberately trying to deceive them. Still, there is a lot we do not know about a person when we first meet him or her. It may be clear, from the person's nonverbal behavior, that he or she is warm and friendly. But what about the many other facets of the individual's personality? Is he or she intelligent? honest? trustworthy? Without spending a great deal of time with the person over the course of weeks or even months, it can be difficult to fill in all the blanks. We turn now to shortcuts people take to accomplish this.

> Others are to us like the "characters" in fiction, external and incorrigible; the surprises they give us turn out in the end to have been predictable—unexpected variations on the theme of being themselves.
>
> —Mary McCarthy,
> *On the Contrary*, 1961

## Implicit Personality Theories: Filling in the Blanks

As we saw in Chapter 4, when people are unsure about the nature of the social world, they use their schemas to fill in the gaps. An excellent example of this use of schemas is when we form impressions of other people. If we know someone is kind, we use an important type of schema called an **implicit personality theory** to determine what else the person is like. These theories consist of our ideas about what kinds of personality traits go together (Anderson & Sedikides, 1990; Schneider, 1973). If a person is kind, our implicit personality theory tells us he or she is probably generous as well; if a person is stingy, we believe he or she is probably irritable as well.

These implicit theories about personality serve the same function as any schema: As "cognitive misers," we can extrapolate from a small to a much larger amount of information (Markus & Zajonc, 1985; Fiske & Taylor, 1991). In this case, we can use just a few observations of a person as a starting point, and then, using our schema, create a much fuller under-

**implicit personality theory:** schemas that people use to group various kinds of personality traits together; for example, many people believe that if someone is kind, he or she is generous as well

standing of what that person is like (Kim & Rosenberg, 1980). This way, we can form impressions quickly, without having to spend weeks with people to figure out what they are like.

Implicit personality theories are interesting in that there are shared components to them—many of us have very similar theories—and there is also room for idiosyncratic variation—some of our personality theories could be very different from yours (Hamilton, 1970; Kuusinen, 1969; Pedersen, 1965). These social theories are developed over time and with experience. Not surprisingly, they often have a strong cultural component: In a given society, most people will share some implicit personality theories because these are cultural beliefs passed on in that society. For example, Rosenberg, Nelson, and Vivekananthan (1968) asked college students to think of a number of people they knew who were quite different from each other. The students were then asked to sort a stack of sixty personality traits into separate piles, each pile representing their personality description of a separate person. Though all of the participants were using the same sixty traits, they

**FIGURE 5.1 Implicit personality theories.** People have theories about which personality traits go together in a person. The traits that are close together in this figure are considered to be likely to exist in the same person. For example, if someone is known to be helpful, we assume he or she is sincere as well (see lower right-hand corner of figure). (Adapted from Rosenberg, Nelson, and Vivekananthan, 1968)

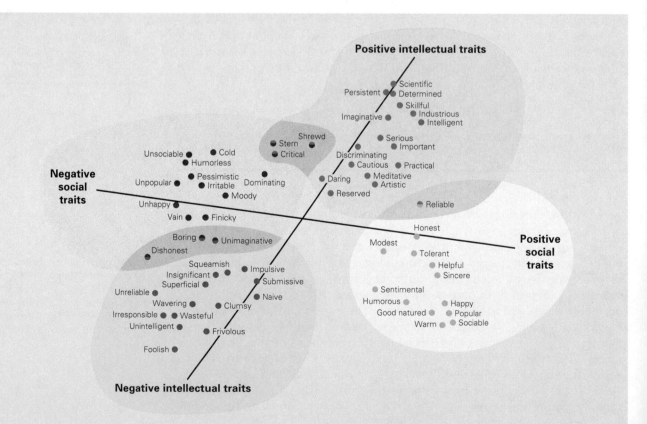

were each thinking about and describing different people. Would they group the personality traits into similar piles?

Rosenberg and colleagues (1968) found strong evidence for such similarity, or shared implicit personality theories. Figure 5.1 shows a kind of map of participants' responses. Personality traits that are close together on this map are the ones the students thought went together in the same person. For example, if someone was seen as helpful, they rated the person as sincere as well. The two axes, "Positive/Negative social traits" and "Positive/Negative intellectual traits," are a way of summarizing the implicit personality theories people used.

Cultural variation in implicit personality theories was demonstrated in an intriguing study by Curt Hoffman, Ivy Lau, and David Johnson (1986). They noted that different cultures have different ideas about personality types—that is, the kinds of people for which there are simple, agreed-on verbal labels. For example, in Western cultures we agree that there is a kind of person who has an artistic personality; this is a person who is creative, intense, and temperamental, and who has an unconventional lifestyle. The Chinese, however, do not have a schema or implicit personality theory for an artistic type. There are no labels in the Chinese language to describe someone with this collection of traits. Granted, there are words in Chinese to describe the individual characteristics of such people, such as the word for creative, but there are no labels like "an artistic type" or "a bohemian" that describe the whole constellation of traits we mean in English. Similarly, in China

Implicit personality theories differ from culture to culture. Westerners assume that there is an artistic type of person—namely, someone who is creative, intense, temperamental, and unconventional. The Chinese have no such implicit personality theory. The Chinese have a category of a *shi gú* person— someone who is worldly, devoted to his or her family, socially skillful, and somewhat reserved. Westerners do not have this implicit personality theory.

there are categories of personality that do not exist in Western cultures. For example, a *shi gú* person is someone who is worldly, devoted to his or her family, socially skillful, and somewhat reserved.

Hoffman and colleagues (1986) hypothesized that these cultural implicit personality theories influence the way people form impressions of others. To test this hypothesis, they wrote stories that described a person behaving like an artistic type of person or *shi gú* type of person, without using those labels to describe them. These stories were written in both English and Chinese. The English versions were given to a group of native English speakers who did not speak any other language, and to a group of Chinese-English bilinguals. Another group of Chinese-English bilinguals received the versions written in Chinese.

If people were using their cultural theories to understand the stories they read, what would we expect to happen? One measure of the use of theories (or schemas) is the tendency to fill in the blanks—that is, to believe that information fitting the schema was observed when in fact it was not. Hoffman and colleagues (1986) asked their participants to write down their impressions of the characters in the stories; they then looked to see whether the participants listed traits that were not used in the stories but did fit the artistic or *shi gú* personality type. For example, "unreliable" was not mentioned in the "artistic personality type" story, but it is consistent with that implicit personality theory.

As seen in Figure 5.2, when the native English speakers read about the characters in English, they were much more likely to form an impression that was consistent with the artistic type than with the *shi gú* type. Similarly, when the Chinese-English bilinguals read the descriptions of the characters in English, they too formed an impression that was consistent with the artistic type but not with the *shi gú* type, because English provides a convenient label for the artistic type. In comparison, Chinese-English bilinguals who read the descriptions in Chinese showed the opposite pattern of results. Their impression of the *shi gú* character was more consistent with the schema than their impressions of the artist, because the Chinese language provides a convenient label or implicit personality theory for this kind of person. These results are consistent with a well-known argument by Whorf (1956) that the language people speak influences the way they think about the world. Characters described identically were perceived differently by the bilingual research participants, depending on the language (and therefore the implicit personality theory) that was used. Thus, one's culture and one's language produce widely shared implicit personality theories, which can influence the kinds of impressions people form of each other.

Implicit personality theories can also be quite idiosyncratic (Hamilton, 1970). Given your personal experience and life events, you may believe that one set of traits is associated with a beautiful woman or handsome man, while a friend of yours might have a totally different theory. For example, you may be following the "what is beautiful is good" social theory (Dion, Berscheid, and Walster, 1972), whereby physically attractive people are assumed to have many other highly positive traits—warmth, charm, generosity, industriousness, and so on. Your friend, on the other hand, may have a more pessimistic view, believing that highly attractive people are likely to be self-centered, cold, manipulative, and lazy. Such differences, of course, point out the potential problem with implicit personality theories: They can

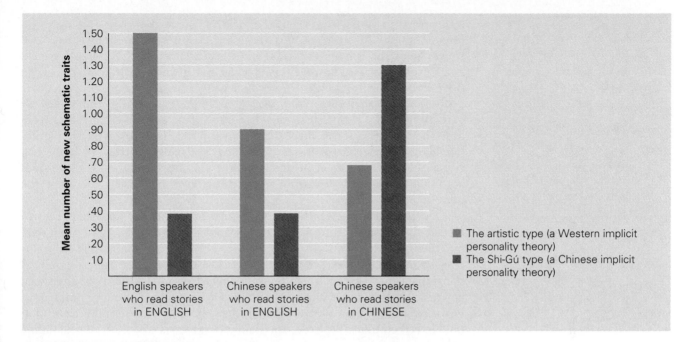

**FIGURE 5.2  Implicit personality theories: How our culture and language shape our impressions of other people.** People formed an impression of other people that was consistent with the implicit personality theory contained in their language. For example, when Chinese-English bilinguals read stories about people in English, they were likely to form impressions consistent with a Western implicit theory, the artistic personality. When Chinese-English bilinguals read the same stories in Chinese, they were likely to form impressions consistent with a Chinese implicit theory, the *shi gú* personality. (Adapted from Hoffman, 1986)

be wrong. As with any schema, information we encounter that is consistent with our personality theory is more memorable than inconsistent information, making it more difficult for us to realize our theory needs to be changed (Cohen, 1981, 1983; Park & Rothbart, 1982).

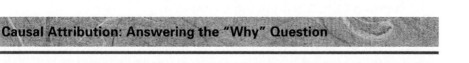

## Causal Attribution: Answering the "Why" Question

We have seen that when we observe other people, we have a rich source of information—their nonverbal behavior—on which to base our impressions. Often simply by observing people's facial expressions or their behaviors, we can tell how they feel (Newtson, 1990). From their nonverbal behavior, we can also make guesses about people's personalities, such as how friendly or outgoing they are. And once we get this far, we use our implicit personality theories to fill in the blanks: If a person is friendly, he or she must be sincere as well.

One reason their nonverbal behaviors often tell us how people feel is that these behaviors cannot be completely controlled, and thus sometimes

In the beginning was not the word, not the deed, not the silly serpent. In the beginning was *why*? Why did she pluck the apple? Was she bored? Was she inquisitive? Was she paid? Did Adam put her up to it? If not, who did?

—John le Carrè,
*The Russia House*, 1989

leak people's true feelings (DePaulo, 1992). Think about the last time you attended a surprise party. Was the guest of honor genuinely surprised? Unless he or she is a very talented actor, it was probably pretty easy to tell. For better or worse, however, people do not always wear their hearts on their sleeves. As we saw earlier, when people are trying to deceive other people about their feelings, they can often do so successfully. Sometimes it's hard to tell how people feel, or what kind of person they truly are, from how they behave. If we meet a woman for the first time and she smiles warmly and says, "Great to see you!" does she really mean it, or is she just being polite? If we meet a man who scowls and barely says hello, does he dislike us, or is he a sourpuss who treats even his closest friends in the same manner?

The point is that even though nonverbal behaviors are sometimes easy to read, giving us direct information about how someone feels, more often than not there is a fair amount of ambiguity about what someone's behavior means (Schneider, Hastorf, and Ellsworth, 1979). This is true not only of nonverbal behaviors, such as a person's smile, but more broadly of any social behavior. In fact, overt, deliberate actions are usually even more ambiguous in their meaning than nonverbal behaviors, because they usually have multiple interpretations. Suppose, for example, that you saw Bob reprimanding and yelling at his five-year-old son. What does this tell you about Bob? Does it mean he is an irresponsible person with poor parenting skills? A responsible parent reprimanding his child for a dangerous transgression? Or is he simply at the end of his rope after a long, frustrating day?

To answer these questions, we need to go "beyond the information given," inferring, from what we observe, what people are like and what they are feeling. To do so, we ask ourselves, either implicitly or explicitly, a critical question: Why are people doing what they are doing? We ask ourselves this question because people's motives are the key that unlocks the door to their personalities. If we decide that Bob exploded at his son for no particular reason, our impression of him will be different from the one we'd form if we learned that his son had just stepped into the street without looking, right after Bob told him not to. The way in which people answer "why" questions is the focus of **attribution theory**, which is concerned with how we infer the causes of other people's behavior.

## The Nature of the Attributional Process

Fritz Heider (1958) is frequently referred to as "the father of attribution theory." His influential book defined the field of social perception, and his legacy is still very much evident in current research. Heider (1958) discussed what he called "naive" or "commonsense" psychology. In his view, people were like amateur scientists, trying to understand other people's behavior by piecing together information until they arrived at a reasonable explanation or cause. Heider (1958) was intrigued by what seemed reasonable to people and by how they arrived at their conclusions.

One of Heider's (1958) most valuable contributions is a simple dichotomy: When trying to decide why people behave as they do—for example, why Bob yelled at his son—we can make either an **internal** (dispositional) **attribution** or an **external** (situational) **attribution**. We can decide that the cause of Bob's observed behavior was something about him—his personality, attitudes, or character—an explanation that assigns the causality of his

**attribution theory:** a description of the way in which people explain the causes of their own and other people's behavior

**internal attribution:** the inference that a person is behaving a certain way because of something about him or her, such as the person's attitudes, character, or personality

**external attribution:** the inference that a person is behaving a certain way because of something about the situation he or she is in; the assumption is that most people would respond the same way in that situation

In order to form impressions of other people, we often need to know why they are doing what they are doing. The impression we form of this parent will depend on how we explain why he is reprimanding his child.

behavior *internally*. For example, we might decide that Bob has poor parenting skills, and disciplines his child in inappropriate ways. Conversely, we can decide that the cause of his behavior was something about the situation—such as the fact that his son just stepped into the street without looking—an explanation that assigns the causality of his behavior *externally* (i.e., it was the child's actions that triggered Bob's behavior, not something distinctive about Bob's personality or character).

Notice that our impression of Bob will be very different depending on the type of attribution we make. If we make an internal attribution, we'll have a negative impression of him. If we make an external attribution, we won't learn much about him—after all, most parents would have done the same thing if they were in that situation and their child had just disobeyed them by stepping into the street. Quite a difference!

Another of Heider's (1958) important contributions was his discussion of our preference for internal attributions over external ones. While either type of attribution is always possible, Heider (1958) noted that we tend to see the causes of a person's behavior as residing in that person. We are perceptually focused on people—they are who we notice—and the situation, which is often hard to see and hard to describe, can be overlooked. This observation of Heider's, that internal attributions are particularly attractive to perceivers, is the starting point for one of the basic theories of how people make attributions: correspondent inference theory (Jones & Davis, 1965).

## Correspondent Inference Theory: From Acts to Dispositions

Edward Jones and Keith Davis developed **correspondent inference theory** to describe the process by which we arrive at an internal attribution: how we *infer dispositions*, or internal personality characteristics, from *corresponding behaviors* or actions (Jones, 1990; Jones & Davis, 1965; Jones & McGillis, 1976). Suppose, for example, we learn that Karen has accepted a job in an advertising agency in New York City. Why? Did Karen accept the job because

**correspondent inference theory:** the theory that we make internal attributions about a person when there are (a) few noncommon effects of his or her behavior and (b) the behavior is unexpected

she is interested in advertising? Because she wants to live in New York? Because the job pays well? Correspondent inference theory is concerned with how we narrow down these possibilities to a specific conclusion about why Karen did what she did.

**The Role of Noncommon Effects.** The main way we do this, according to the theory, is by comparing what people could accomplish by the behavior they chose to perform with what they could have accomplished with alternative actions (comparing the effects of the different choices, in the words of the theory). For example, to determine why Karen accepted the advertising job, we would consider what Karen accomplished by accepting this job, compared to what she could have accomplished by making a different choice. An internal attribution is easier to the extent that there are few **noncommon effects** of these different choices—that is, if by accepting the job in New York Karen could accomplish only one or two things that she could not accomplish by accepting other jobs.

For instance, suppose we knew that when Karen accepted the advertising job, she turned down an offer to teach history in a rural high school in Wyoming. Here it would be hard to know why she chose the advertising job, because by taking this job she could accomplish so many things that she could not accomplish by accepting the teaching job—starting a career in advertising, living in a large city, earning more money (see Figure 5.3). In this situation, there would be many noncommon effects of the two options. Suppose, however, we knew that Karen had narrowed down her choices to two options: (a) a job with the Hook 'Em Advertising Agency, which specializes in cigarette ads, and (b) a job with the Help 'Em Agency, which specializes in public service ads designed to get people to engage in healthier behaviors. Suppose, further, that we knew the two jobs paid the same and had the same opportunities for advancement. If we learn that Karen accepted

**noncommon effects:** effects produced by a particular course of action that could not be produced by alternative courses of action

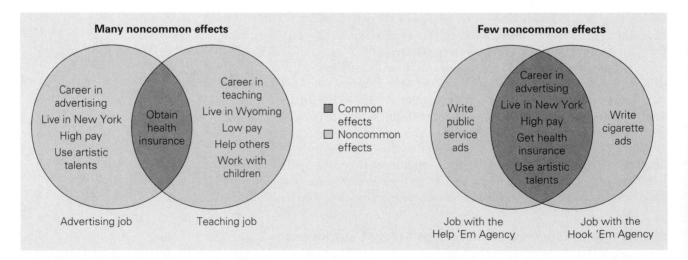

**FIGURE 5.3  The role of noncommon effects.** When people can accomplish many things by one action that they cannot accomplish by an alternative action, it can be difficult to tell why they did what they did (see left side of figure). When there are few noncommon effects—when people can accomplish very few things by one action that they cannot accomplish by the other action—it is easier to make an internal attribution for why they did what they did (see right side of figure).

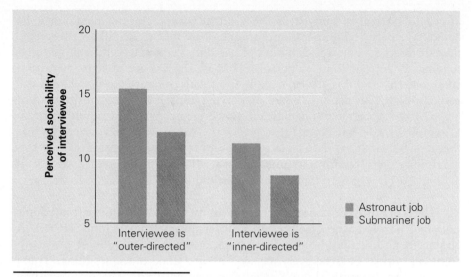

**FIGURE 5.4 People's ratings of the sociability of an applicant for a job as an astronaut or a submariner.** People made the most extreme ratings when the applicant behaved in a way that was not what the job demanded—that is, when he behaved in an "outer-directed" manner during his interview for the astronaut job (see far left-hand side of the figure), and when he behaved in an "inner-directed" manner during his interview for the submariner job (see far right-hand side of the figure). When the applicant behaved in a way consistent with what the job demanded, it was more difficult for people to tell what kind of person he really was. (Adapted from Jones, Davis, and Gergen, 1961)

the job at the Help 'Em Agency, we can be more confident about why Karen made the choice she did, because there is only one noncommon effect between the two options: their areas of specialization. Clearly, Karen must have wanted to work on public service ads more than cigarette ads.

To demonstrate how people make attributions based on noncommon effects, Edward Jones, Keith Davis, and Kenneth Gergen (1961) made tape recordings of two job interviews. In one, the interviewee was pretending to apply for a job as an astronaut; in the other, he was pretending to apply for a job as a submarine crew member. In the two taped versions, the interviewee responded with answers that either fit the job prerequisites well or did not. For example, in one interview he stressed his ability to work well with others and his social and easygoing manner. These "outer-directed" traits fit the submariner job (where one works closely with others in a confined space). In the other interview, he stressed his preference for working alone, his self-reliance, and so on. These "inner-directed" traits fit the astronaut job. (During this early phase of the space program, astronauts were sent into space alone.) The research participants were told that the interviewee had been instructed to say whatever he needed to in order to impress the interviewer and get the job—even if that meant lying about his personality and habits.

As can be seen in Figure 5.4, the research participants made more correspondent inferences when the interviewee's responses did not match the type of job for which he was being interviewed. The interviewee was seen as the most sociable when he was an outgoing astronaut candidate, and the least sociable when he was a reserved submariner candidate. Why? When the applicant portrayed himself as the kind of person the job demanded, he could have been trying to accomplish one of two different things: expressing the fact that he really was that kind of person, or trying to get the job by pretending to be that kind of person. That is, there were at least two noncommon effects of this action, making it difficult to figure out which one was responsible for his actions. When portraying himself as the opposite kind of person from what the job demanded, however, he could have been trying to accomplish only one thing: to express the kind of person he really was (because he surely wouldn't get the job under these circumstances). In this condition, there is only one noncommon effect to the person's choice of action; thus, it is easy to figure out why he did it.

**The Role of Expectations.**  There is another kind of information people take into account when making attributions, according to Jones (1990). A course of action may be uninformative even when it involves few noncommon effects, because everyone would have done the same thing. Think back to our example about Karen. Suppose we know she was deciding between two jobs that were nearly identical, except that one paid $50,000 a year and the other paid $10,000 a year. Since the only noncommon effect is the amount of pay, we should be able to make a confident, internal attribution about Karen when we learn that she chose the one that pays more. Or can we? Actually, we learn almost nothing about Karen, because anyone would have done the same thing. We learn more about people when the noncommon effects are something that not everyone would have chosen to accomplish. If Karen chose the $10,000 job, for example, this action would be so unexpected—and so unlike what most people would do—that we would learn a lot about her.

We learn more about people when they behave in unexpected ways than when they behave in expected ways.

There are two different types of expectations that come into play here: category-based expectancies and target-based expectancies (Jones & McGillis, 1976). **Category-based expectancies** refer to expectations about people based on groups to which they belong. If you were told that Mick Jagger graduated from the London School of Economics, a very prestigious institution, you would be surprised, for this is not the typical background or behavior of a rock-and-roll star. **Target-based expectancies** refer to how you expect a particular person to behave, based on his or her past actions. If Madonna called a news conference to state that she now believes sex, nudity, and rock and roll are evil, you would be surprised, because this has certainly not been her attitude in the past. In both examples, you would make a correspondent inference—the assumption that Mick Jagger's and Madonna's behaviors match their dispositions.

In sum, making attributions, according to correspondent inference theory, is kind of like being a detective. When we try to deduce why someone behaves the way they do, the culprits are the various things the person might have been trying to accomplish (the effects of his or her actions). We reduce the number of possibilities by examining what the person could have accomplished by behaving in some alternative manner (Jones, 1990; Newtson, 1974). We also take into account how much we expected people to do what they did: Unexpected actions are much more diagnostic of what someone is really like.

**category-based expectancies:** expectations about people based on the groups to which they belong, such as expecting someone to love going to parties because he or she belongs to a party-loving fraternity or sorority

**target-based expectancies:** expectations about a person based on his or her past actions, such as expecting someone to go to the beach on vacation because he or she has always gone to the beach in the past

## The Covariation Model: Internal Versus External Attributions

Harold Kelley (1967) took a somewhat different approach when he developed his theory of attribution. Whereas Jones and Davis (1965) focused on the information people use to make a dispositional (internal) attribution, Kelley (1967) focused on the first step in the process of social perception—how people decide whether to make an internal or an external attribution. Another difference between the two theories is that correspondent inference theory applies to a single observation of a behavior (e.g., your friend refuses to lend you his car), whereas Kelley's (1967) **covariation model** applies to multiple instances of behavior, occurring across time and across different situations (e.g., Did your friend refuse to lend you his car in the past? Does he lend it to other people? Does he dislike lending you other possessions of his?).

Kelley assumes (like Heider before him) that when we are in the process of forming an attribution, we gather information, or data, that will help us reach a judgment. The data we use, according to Kelley, are how a person's behavior *covaries* across time, place, different actors, and different targets of the behavior. By discovering covariation in people's behavior (e.g., your friend's refusal to lend his car "co-occurs" with you, in that he is happy to lend it to others), you are able to reach a judgment about what caused their behavior.

What kinds of information do we examine for covariation when forming an attribution? Kelley (1967) states there are three important types of information: *consensus*, *distinctiveness*, and *consistency*. Let's describe these three through an example: You are at a party, and you see John stumble and trip while dancing with Mary. He looks pretty ridiculous; in fact—oops, there he goes again—he just stomped on her foot. Without any conscious effort on your part, you pose that attributional question: "Why is John stumbling and

**covariation model:** the idea that we make causal attributions about a person's behavior by observing the things that covary with his or her behavior—for example, the extent to which the person's clumsy dancing occurs only with certain partners

**Why Did John Step on Mary's Feet?**

People are likely to make an *internal attribution*—it was something about John—if they see this behavior as
   *low* in consensus: John is the only one who steps on Mary's feet
   *low* in distinctiveness: John steps on all women's feet when he dances with them
   *high* in consistency: John steps on Mary's feet whenever he dances with her

People are likely to think it was something about Mary (to make an external attribution) if they see this behavior as
   *high* in consensus: Everyone who dances with Mary steps on her feet
   *high* in distinctiveness: John does not step on anyone else's feet when he dances with other people
   *high* in consistency: John steps on Mary's feet whenever he dances with her

People are likely to think it was something peculiar about the particular circumstances in which John stepped on Mary's feet if they see this behavior as
   *low or high* in consensus
   *low or high* in distinctiveness
   *low* in consistency: This is the only time John has ever stepped on Mary's feet

The covariation model. Why did John step on Mary's feet? To decide whether a behavior was caused by internal, dispositional factors or external, situational factors, people use consensus, distinctiveness, and consistency information.

**consensus information:** information about the extent to which other people behave the same way toward the same stimulus as the actor does

**distinctiveness information:** information about the extent to which one particular actor behaves in the same way to different stimuli

tripping and stepping on Mary's toes?" Is it something about John, or is it something about the situation that surrounds and affects him?

Now let's look at how Kelley's (1967) model of covariation assessment answers this question. **Consensus information** refers to how other people behave toward the same stimulus—in this case, Mary. When other people dance with Mary, do they also trip and stumble? **Distinctiveness information** refers to how the actor (the person whose behavior we are trying to explain) responds to other stimuli. Does John trip and stumble when he dances with other people? **Consistency information** refers to the frequency with which the observed behavior between the same actor and the same stimulus occurs across time and circumstances. Does John trip every time he dances with Mary? Does he trip when he dances with her at different types of parties and to different kinds of music?

According to Kelley's theory, when these three sources of information combine into one of two distinct patterns, a clear attribution can be made. People are most likely to make an *internal attribution* (deciding the behavior was due to something about John) when the consensus and distinctiveness of the act are low but its consistency is high (see the example on page 178). We would be pretty confident that John stumbled because he is a clumsy dancer if we knew that no one else stumbles when dancing with Mary, that John stumbles when dancing with other women, and that John stumbles every time he dances with Mary. People are likely to make an *external attribution* (in this case, about Mary) if consensus, distinctiveness, and consistency are all high. Finally, when consistency is low, we cannot make a clear internal or external attribution, and we resort to a special kind of external or *situational attribution*, inferring that John stumbled because of something peculiar about the particular circumstances, such as a wet spot on the dance floor.

Both correspondent inference theory and the covariation model assume that people make causal attributions in a rational, logical fashion. People observe the clues, such as the distinctiveness of the act, and then draw a logical inference about why the person did what he or she did. Several studies have confirmed that people often do make attributions the way that Jones and Davis's (1965) and Kelley's (1967) models say they should (Fosterling, 1989; Hazelwood & Olson, 1986; Hewstone & Jaspars, 1987; Major, 1980; Ruble & Feldman, 1976; Zuckerman, 1978).

For example, Leslie McArthur (1972) presented people with descriptions of behavior like our example (e.g., "John stepped on Mary's feet while dancing"), along with information about the distinctiveness, consistency, and consensus of this behavior, which she varied as in our example on page 178. She then asked the participants to make an attribution about the cause of the behavior. McArthur (1972) found that, in general, the participants did make an internal, external, or situational attribution when the three types of information were in the pattern predicted by Kelley's theory. McArthur, however, discovered one wrinkle: Participants didn't use consensus information as much as Kelley's theory predicted; they relied more on consistency and distinctiveness information when forming attributions.

To summarize, both correspondent inference theory and the covariation model portray people as master detectives, deducing the causes of behavior as systematically and logically as would Sherlock Holmes. And research has found that, at least under some conditions, people do just that. As we saw in Chapters 3 and 4, however, people do not always come up with the most accurate or rational answer when forming judgments about other people. Sometimes they distort information to satisfy their need for high self-esteem (see Chapter 3). Other times they use mental shortcuts that, while helpful, can lead to inaccurate judgments (see Chapter 4). Is the same true when people make inferences about why other people do what they do? We turn now to evidence that, under some conditions, people use mental shortcuts when making attributions.

**consistency information:** information about the extent to which the behavior between one actor and one stimulus is the same across time and circumstances

## Using Schemas and Theories

You may have noticed that the McArthur study testing the covariation model was rather unlike everyday life in one respect: People were given detailed descriptions of the circumstances under which the behaviors occurred, without having to determine this information for themselves. For example, people were told how often John stepped on other people's feet, rather than having to figure out this covariation for themselves. This raises the question of how accurately people perceive covariations between variables, such as how often John stumbles when dancing with different partners.

As you may recall, we addressed this question in Chapter 4. People are not bad at perceiving covariations between variables, we saw, except when they have a strong schema or theory suggesting what the covariation should be. When people have a theory that two variables are related, they tend to see them as related even if they are not (Chapman & Chapman, 1967). For example, if we strongly suspected that John was an extremely clumsy person, we would be likely to remember those times he stepped on people's feet and stumbled while dancing, even if he were no worse a dancer than anyone else. Thus, in everyday life we let our schemas do the talking when we make causal attributions, so that we end up with the attribution we expected (e.g., "See, just as I thought—John is a clumsy dancer"; Nisbett & Wilson, 1977). This is true both of our theories about specific people—such as about John—and of our theories about why people in general do what they do. In fact, one kind of general theory is very pervasive, at least in Western cultures: the idea that people do what they do because of the kind of people they are, not because of the situation they are in. This has been termed the fundamental attribution error.

## The Fundamental Attribution Error: People as Personality Psychologists

It has always struck us as remarkable how easily people can suspend disbelief when watching films and plays. At one level, we know these are actors and actresses reciting lines they have memorized. And yet when we hear King Lear give an anguished cry at the end of the final act as he clutches Cordelia's body, we do not think, "Oh, the actor is doing this because he is being paid to play a part written by Shakespeare, and that is what the script says he should do." We see a sorrowful king gone mad over the loss of his daughters and his kingdom, and maybe even shed a tear with him.

Sometimes the tendency to see actors as the people they are portraying has amusing consequences. When the actor Robert Young played a kindly, caring doctor in the old television series "Marcus Welby," he was said to receive daily mail from his fans detailing their physical ailments and asking for medical advice. We may snicker at such absurdity, but think about your reactions to movies and plays. After seeing the movie *Taxi Driver*, would you leave the actor Robert De Niro alone with your teenage daughter? How many of us were dry-eyed when Debra Winger said goodbye to her children as she lay dying of cancer in *Terms of Endearment*, even though we knew this was an actress being paid a lot of money to pretend she was dying?

Well, you might say, we choose to suspend disbelief when watching a film or a play because doing so adds to our enjoyment. But it is clear that this is not something most of us can control very easily. When we see a particularly sappy television ad, like one where a father watches his daughter grow from an infant to a schoolgirl to an adult, finally sending her off on her wedding day, we know the ad is trying to manipulate our emotions to sell us insurance or long-distance service. Nonetheless, it can still be difficult not to see the actors as real people who really believe what they are saying, and not to be affected emotionally by the story. This is one reason that the ads for Taster's Choice coffee and Benson & Hedges cigarettes, discussed at the beginning of the chapter, are so effective.

These are examples of a pervasive, fundamental theory most of us have about the causes of human behavior: We assume that people do what they do because of the kind of people they are, not because of the situation they are in or the role (husband, mother, professor, student) they are playing. We are strongly predisposed to see a correspondence between what people do and what they really think or feel, even when it is clear that their behavior was constrained by the situation (e.g., they were reciting the lines of a play). In this way, we are more like personality psychologists, who see behavior as stemming from internal dispositions and traits, than social psychologists, who focus on the impact of social situations on behavior. This bias toward being personality psychologists is so pervasive that social psychologist Lee Ross (1977) termed it the **fundamental attribution error** (Heider, 1958; Jones, 1990).

There have been many empirical demonstrations of the tendency to see people's behavior as a reflection of their dispositions and beliefs, rather than as influenced by the situation. Jones and Harris (1967), for example, asked college students to read an essay written by a fellow student that either supported or opposed Fidel Castro's rule in Cuba, and then to guess how the author of the essay really felt about Castro (see Figure 5.5). In one condition, the researchers told the students that the author freely chose which position to take in the essay, thereby making it easy to guess how he really felt. If he

**fundamental attribution error:** the tendency to overestimate the extent to which people's behavior is due to internal, dispositional factors, and to underestimate the role of situational factors

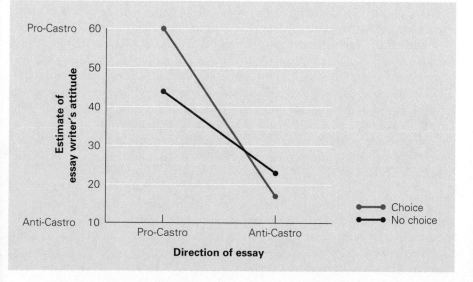

**FIGURE 5.5  The fundamental attribution error.** Even when people knew that the author's choice of an essay topic was externally caused (i.e., in the no-choice condition), they assumed that what he wrote reflected how he really felt about Castro. That is, they made an internal attribution for his behavior. (Adapted from Jones & Harris, 1967)

*Drawing by M. Stevens; © April 22, 1991 The New Yorker Magazine, Inc.*

The attributions people make, and the impressions they form of others, depend on their visual perspective (i.e., what is perceptually salient).

*Fascinating, aren't they?*

chose to write in favor of Castro, then clearly he must indeed be sympathetic to Castro. In another condition, however, the students learned that the author did not have any choice about which position to take—he had been assigned the position as a participant in a debate. Logically, if we know someone could not choose the topic, we should not assume the writer believes what he or she wrote. Yet the participants in this study, and in the dozens of others like it, assumed that the author really believed what he wrote, even when they knew he could not choose which position to take. As seen in Figure 5.5, people moderated their guesses a little bit—there was not as much difference in people's estimates of the author's attitude in the pro-Castro and anti-Castro conditions—but they still assumed that the content of the essay reflected the author's true feelings.

We should address the question of why the tendency to explain behavior in terms of people's dispositions is called the fundamental attribution error. This does not mean that it is always wrong to make an internal attribution; clearly, people often do what they do because of the kind of people they are. There is ample evidence, however, that social situations can have a large impact on behavior—indeed, the major lesson of social psychology is that these influences can be extremely powerful. The point of the fundamental attribution error is that people tend to underestimate these influences when explaining other people's behavior. Even when a situational constraint on behavior is obvious, as in the Jones and Harris (1967) experiment, people persist in making internal attributions (Ross, Amabile, and Steinmetz, 1977). Thus, whereas it can be difficult to tell whether an internal attribution is appropriate for a given instance of behavior, it is clear that, in general, people underestimate the power of social (external) influences (Ross, 1977; Ross & Nisbett, 1991).

**The Role of Perceptual Salience.** Why do people commit the fundamental attribution error? One reason is that when we try to explain someone's behavior, our focus of attention is usually on the person, not on the surrounding situation, and our attributions tend to follow our focus of attention (Heider, 1958; Jones & Nisbett, 1971). Human beings are perceptually salient—they are what our eyes and ears notice. And as Heider (1958) pointed out, what we notice seems to be the reasonable and logical cause of the observed behavior.

Several studies have confirmed the importance of perceptual salience—in particular, an elegant one by Shelley Taylor and Susan Fiske (1975). In this study, two male students engaged in a get acquainted conversation. (They were actually both accomplices of the experimenters and were following a specific script during their conversation.) At each session, six actual research participants also took part. They sat in assigned seats, surrounding the two conversationalists (see Figure 5.6). Two of them sat on each side of the actors; they had a clear, profile view of both individuals. Two observers sat behind each actor; they could see the back of one actor's head but the face of the other. Thus, who was visually salient—that is, who the participants could see the best—was cleverly manipulated in this study.

After the conversation, the research participants were asked questions about the two men—for example, who had taken the lead in the conversation, and who had chosen the topics to be discussed? As you can see in Figure 5.7, the person whom they could see the best was the person who they thought had the most impact on the conversation. Even though all the observers heard the same conversation, those who were facing student A thought he had taken the lead and chosen the topics, whereas those who were facing student B thought he had taken the lead and chosen the topics. In comparison, those who could see both students equally well thought both were equally influential.

**Perceptual salience,** or our visual point of view, helps explain why the fundamental attribution error is so prevalent. We focus our attention more on people than on the surrounding situation, and thus underestimate the influence of the situation when explaining human behavior. But this is only part of the story. In a way, it begs the question: Why are our attributions influenced by perceptual salience? Why should the simple fact that we are

> Be not swept off your feet by the vividness of the impression, but say "Impression, wait for me a little. Let me see what you are and what you represent."
> —Epictetus, *Discourses*

**perceptual salience:** information that is the focus of people's attention; people tend to overestimate the causal role of perceptually salient information

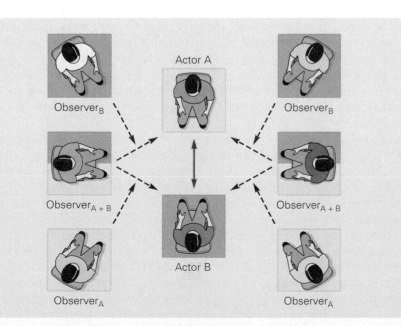

**FIGURE 5.6 Manipulating perceptual salience.** This is the seating arrangement for two actors and the six research participants in the Taylor and Fiske study. Participants rated each actors' impact on the conversation. Researchers found that people rated the actor they could see most clearly as having the largest role in the conversation. (Adapted from Taylor & Fiske, 1975)

Actor A

Observer_B

Observer_B

Observer_{A + B}

Observer_{A + B}

Observer_A

Actor B

Observer_A

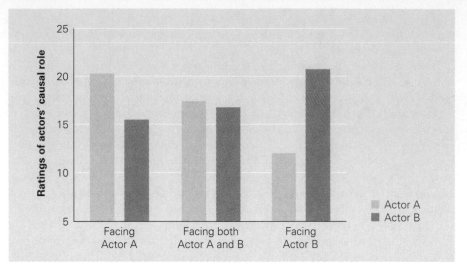

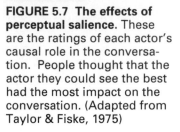

**FIGURE 5.7 The effects of perceptual salience**. These are the ratings of each actor's causal role in the conversation. People thought that the actor they could see the best had the most impact on the conversation. (Adapted from Taylor & Fiske, 1975)

focused on a person make us exaggerate the extent to which that person is the cause of his or her actions?

The culprit is one of the mental shortcuts we discussed in Chapter 4, the *anchoring/adjustment heuristic*. We saw several examples in which people began with a reference point when making a judgment, and then did not adjust sufficiently away from this point. The fundamental attribution error is another byproduct of this shortcut. When making attributions, people use the focus of their attention as a starting point. For example, when we hear someone argue strongly in favor of Castro's regime in Cuba, our first inclination is to explain this in dispositional terms: "This person must hold radical political views." We realize this explanation might not be the whole story, however. We might think, "On the other hand, I know he was assigned this position as part of a debate," and adjust our attributions more toward the situation. For example, in the Jones and Harris (1967) experiment cited earlier, people did adjust their attributions to some extent when they knew that the author could not choose his topic; they were somewhat less likely to assume that the essay reflected his beliefs than when they were told he could choose his topic. The problem is that they did not adjust their judgments enough. Even when they knew the author did not have a choice, the observers still thought he believed what he had written, at least to some extent. They adjusted insufficiently from their anchor, the position advocated in the essay.

In sum, people go through two steps when making attributions (Gilbert, 1989, 1991, 1993). They begin by making an internal attribution, assuming that a person's behavior was due to something about him or her. They then attempt to adjust this attribution by taking into account the situation the person was in. As we have seen, people often do not make enough of an adjustment in this second step. An interesting implication of this fact is that if people are distracted or preoccupied when explaining someone's behavior, they might not get to the second step, thereby making an even more extreme internal attribution. Why? Because the initial step (making the internal attribution) occurs quickly and spontaneously, whereas the second step (adjusting for the situation) requires more effort and conscious attention. Daniel Gilbert has performed several experiments that support this view.

Subjects in his studies are asked to explain why someone did what they did, but are distracted by having to do something else at the same time, such as remembering an eight-digit number. These subjects make even more extreme internal attributions than subjects who are not distracted, because they are unable to mentally adjust their initial impression that the person's behavior emanated solely from within him or her, uninfluenced by the situation (Gilbert & Osborne, 1989; Gilbert, Pelham and Krull, 1988).

**The Role of Culture.**  A second reason that the fundamental attribution error exists is that Western culture teaches us to prefer dispositional explanations. Such a preference is not found in cultures that place less emphasis on individual freedom and autonomy (Zebrowitz-McArthur, 1988). For example, Joan Miller (1984) asked people of two cultures—Hindus living in India and Americans living in the United States—to think of various examples of behaviors performed by their friends, and to explain why these behaviors occurred. Consistent with what we've said so far, the American participants preferred dispositional explanations for the behaviors. They were more likely to say that the causes of their friends' behaviors were the kind of people they were, rather than the situation or context in which the behaviors occurred. In contrast, Hindu participants preferred situational explanations for their friends' behaviors (Miller, 1984).

But, you might be thinking, perhaps the Americans and Hindus generated different kinds of examples. Perhaps the Hindus thought of behaviors that really were more situationally caused, whereas the Americans thought of behaviors that really were more dispositionally caused. To test this alternative hypothesis, Miller (1984) took some of the behaviors generated by the Hindu participants and gave them to Americans to explain. The difference in internal and external attributions was again observed: Americans preferred dispositional causes for the behaviors that the Hindus had thought were situationally caused.

For example, one of the behaviors concerned a lawyer riding to work on his motorcycle with his friend as a passenger. They got into an accident, and the friend was seriously injured. After taking his friend to the hospital, the lawyer continued on to work, rather than staying to talk with the doctors about his friend's condition. Why did he do this? Most Americans made a dispositional attribution, assuming that it was something about the lawyer (e.g., "The lawyer is obviously irresponsible"). Hindus, however, were more likely to make a situational attribution, assuming it was something about the context in which the behavior occurred (e.g., "It was the lawyer's responsibility to be in court to represent his client. . . . [H]is friend's condition might not have looked as serious as it was"; Miller, 1984). Thus, people in Western cultures appear to be more like personality psychologists, viewing behavior in dispositional terms, whereas people in Eastern cultures seem to be more like social psychologists, viewing behavior in situational terms.

## The Actor/Observer Difference

An interesting twist on the fundamental attribution error is that it does not apply to our attributions about ourselves to the same extent that it applies to our attributions about other people. Whereas we tend to see others' behavior as dispositionally caused (the fundamental attribution error), we are less likely

The letter depicts actor/observer differences in attribution. Schoeneman and Rubanowitz (1985) examined letters to the "Dear Ann Landers" and "Dear Abby" advice columns and found strong evidence for actor/observer differences. Letter writers tended to attribute their problems to external factors (e.g., the letter writer above says her biggest problem is her mother), whereas the advice columnists tended to make dispositional attributions to the letter writers (e.g., "Get into counseling at once"). (From the *Boston Globe*, Sept. 10, 1991, p. 52)

**Dear Ann Landers:**

I'm writing you in desperation, hoping you can help me with a problem I'm having with my mother.

A little over a year ago, I moved in with my boyfriend despite my mother's protests. She has never liked "Kevin." I'll admit he's far from perfect and we've had our problems. He's an alcoholic, has a bad temper, is mentally abusive, is a compulsive liar and cannot hold a job. I am in debt over my head because of him but my biggest problem is that my mother is obsessed with my situation. I understand her concern, but I can take only so much. . . .

*OVER-MOTHERED IN MICHIGAN*

*Dear Over-Mothered:*
*Your mother didn't write to me. You did. So you're the one who is going to get the advice. Get into counseling at once and find out why you insist on hanging on to an alcoholic, abusive, unemployed liar. . . .*

**actor/observer difference:** the tendency to see other people's behavior as dispositionally caused, while focusing more on the role of situational factors when explaining one's own behavior

to do so when explaining our own behavior. This is called the **actor/observer difference.** For example, Nisbett, Caputo, Legant, and Maracek (1973) asked college students to explain why they chose their major and why their best friend had chosen his or her major. In both cases, people listed more reasons that concerned things internal to the person (e.g., "I am interested in psychology," "She is the kind of person who is good at math") than they did reasons that had to do with things external to the person (e.g., "It is a field with good career opportunities"). This preference for internal reasons, however, was less pronounced when people explained their own choice.

Observers (people explaining someone else's behavior) have been found in many studies to be strong personality theorists, seeing other people's behavior as emanating from their internal traits and attitudes. Actors (people explaining their own behavior), while still preferring internal explanations, are more likely to see that there are external influences on their behavior as well. Hence, the actor/observer difference (Jones & Nisbett, 1972; Schoeneman & Rubanowitz, 1985; Watson, 1982; West, Gunn, and Chernicky, 1975; see the letter to Ann Landers on this page for an interesting demonstration of the actor/observer difference). Why are people more likely to see their own behavior as caused by the situation?

**Perceptual Salience Revisited.** One reason is our old friend perceptual salience (Jones & Nisbett, 1972). Just as we said earlier—that we notice the behavior of other people more than their situation—so do we notice our own situation more than our own behavior. None of us is so egotistic or self-centered that we walk through life holding up a full-length mirror so we can observe ourselves constantly. We are looking outward; what is perceptually salient to us is other people, objects, the events that unfold, and so on. We don't (and can't) pay as much attention to ourselves. Thus, when the actor and the observer think about what caused a given behavior, they are swayed

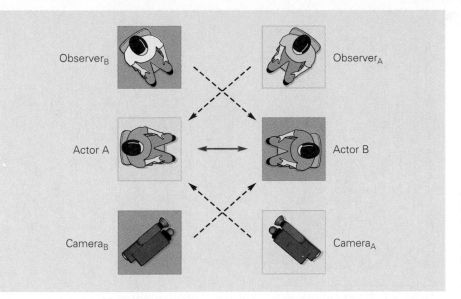

**FIGURE 5.8 Seating arrangements in the Storms study.** People's behavior was videotaped, so that some of them could view it later from a different perspective. (Adapted from Storms, 1973)

by the information that is most salient and noticeable to them: the actor for the observer, and the situation for the actor.

Michael Storms (1973) conducted a fascinating experiment that demonstrates the role of perceptual salience in both the fundamental attribution error and the actor/observer difference. In a design reminiscent of the Taylor and Fiske (1975) study presented earlier, Storms (1973) seated groups of four research participants in a special way (see Figure 5.8). Two of them were going to chat with each other (Actor A and Actor B), and two of them would observe this conversation, focusing on one of the conversationalists (Observer of A and Observer of B). In addition, two video cameras were present; one filmed Actor A's face, and the other filmed Actor B's face.

Following the conversation, the four participants were asked to make attributions about themselves (for actors) or about the actor they were watching (for observers). For example, they were asked to what extent the actor's behavior was due to personal characteristics or to characteristics of the situation (the topic of conversation, the behavior of the conversational partner, etc.). Storms (1973) found that the observers attributed more *dispositional* characteristics to the actor they were watching (demonstrating the fundamental attribution error as in the Taylor & Fiske, 1975, study), whereas the actors made more *situational* attributions about the same behavior—their own (see the left-hand side of Figure 5.9).

In a particularly elegant addition to the study's design, Storms (1973) showed the videotapes to some of the participants before they made their ratings. Some of them saw on tape what they had experienced live—Actor A saw a tape of Actor B's face, and Actor B saw the videotape of Actor A's face; Observer A saw a tape of Actor A, and Observer B saw a tape of Actor B. When asked to make causal attributions, these participants showed the same actor/observer difference as before, although the actors made even stronger situational attributions about themselves when they had the chance to sit back and observe their situation again (see middle of Figure 5.9).

Another group of participants were placed in the most interesting position of all. After the conversation, they saw a videotape that had the opposite visual orientation to the one they had experienced in real life. Actor A and

Resemblances are the shadows of differences. Different people see different similarities and similar differences.
—Vladimir Nabokov, *Pale Fire*, 1962

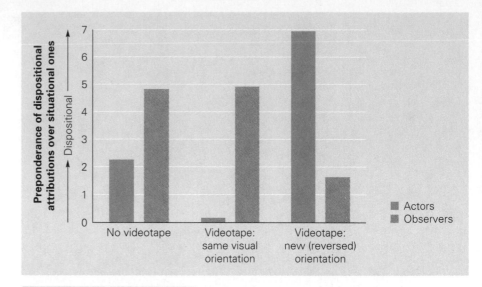

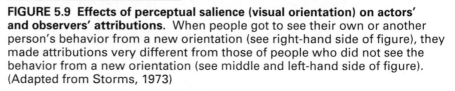

**FIGURE 5.9 Effects of perceptual salience (visual orientation) on actors' and observers' attributions**. When people got to see their own or another person's behavior from a new orientation (see right-hand side of figure), they made attributions very different from those of people who did not see the behavior from a new orientation (see middle and left-hand side of figure). (Adapted from Storms, 1973)

actor B each saw his or her own face; observer A saw the videotape of actor B; and observer B saw the tape of actor A. Now the object of perceptual salience was completely reversed. How did these participants assign causality? As can be seen on the far right of Figure 5.9, this change in perceptual salience erased the typical actor/observer difference. After looking at themselves, actors made more dispositional attributions. After looking at their actor's (the conversational partner's) situation, observers made more situational attributions about their actor.

**The Role of Information Availability.** The actor/observer difference occurs for another reason as well. Actors have more information about themselves than observers do (Jones & Nisbett, 1972). Actors know how they've behaved over the years; they know what happened to them that morning. They are far more aware than observers of both the similarities and the differences in their behavior across time and across situations. In Kelley's (1967) terms, actors have far more consistency and distinctiveness information about themselves than observers do. For example, if you are behaving in a quiet, shy fashion at a party, an observer is likely to make a dispositional attribution about you—"Gee, that person is quite an introvert." In fact, you may know that this is not your typical way of responding to a party setting. Perhaps you are particularly tired that evening and simply don't have the energy to party. Perhaps an hour before the party, your lover broke up with you. Perhaps you are shy only at parties where you don't know anyone, and that's true of this party. Thus, it is not surprising that actors' self-attributions often reflect situational factors, because they know more about how their behavior varies from one situation to the next than most observers, who see them in limited contexts, do.

So far, our discussion of the mental shortcuts people use when making attributions has covered the role of schemas, perceptual salience, and information availability. But what about a person's needs, desires, hopes, and fears? Do these more emotional factors also create biases in our attributions? Are you motivated to see the world in certain ways because these views make you feel better, about both yourself and life in general? The answer is yes. The shortcuts we will discuss below have a *motivational basis*; they are attributions that protect our self-esteem and our belief that the world is a safe and just place (see Chapter 3).

## Self-Serving Attributions

Imagine that Bill goes to his chemistry class one day with some apprehension, because this is the day he will find out how he did on the midterm. As the professor goes from person to person handing back the exam, Bill feels a knot in his stomach slowly begin to tighten. The professor gives him his exam. Bill turns it over. With disbelief, he sees that he has received a D. How is Bill likely to explain why he got such a poor grade? It probably will come as no surprise that people tend to take credit for their successes and to explain away their failures as due to external events that were outside their control. Thus, Bill is likely to think that it wasn't his fault—the test was unfair. The professor, however, is likely to believe that the test was perfectly fair, but that Bill did not study hard enough or is a poor student.

How can we explain this departure from the typical actor/observer pattern of attributions? The answer is that when people's self-esteem is threatened, they often make **self-serving attributions.** Simply put, these attributions refer to our tendency to take credit for our successes but to blame others (or the situation) for our failures (Miller & Ross, 1975). Many studies have shown that people make internal attributions when they do well on a task, but make external attributions when they do poorly (Arkin & Maruyama, 1979; Carver, DeGregorio and Gillis, 1980; Davis & Stephan, 1980; Elig & Frieze, 1979; Whitley & Frieze, 1985).

Perhaps you have experienced this bias yourself. Have you ever worked on a group project with a few other classmates whereby all of you shared the same project grade? If the project received an A, you probably made many positive dispositional attributions about your contribution (perhaps even thinking you worked harder and did more than your classmates). If instead the project received a C–, we bet you had some choice comments about the lackluster energy and intelligence of your classmates.

Self-serving attributions don't just involve academic grades. For example, Lau and Russell (1980) examined the explanations made by professional athletes and coaches for why their team won or lost a game. When explaining their victories, the athletes and coaches overwhelmingly pointed to aspects of their own teams or players; in fact, 80 percent of the attributions for wins were to such internal factors. When explaining why the New York Yankees defeated the Los Angeles Dodgers in game 4 of the 1977 World Series, the Yankees' manager, Billy Martin, attributed it to a player on his team: "Piniella has done it all" (Lau & Russell, 1980). Losses were more likely to be attributed to things external to one's own team. For example, members of the Dodgers attributed their loss not to their inferior ability or poor play, but instead to such things as luck or the superior play of the

**self-serving attributions:** explanations for one's successes that credit internal, dispositional factors, and explanations for one's failures that blame external, situational factors

Self-serving attributions. People tend to take credit for their successes but to blame others for their failures. Baseball managers are not immune from this tendency, such as Billy Martin (on the left) and Tommy Lasorda (on the right).

Yankees. In the words of Tommy Lasorda, the Dodgers' manager, "It took a great team to beat us, and the Yankees definitely are a great team" (Lau & Russell, 1980).

Why do people make self-serving attributions? As pointed out in our discussion of cognitive dissonance theory in Chapter 3, people try to maintain their self-esteem whenever possible, even if that means distorting reality by changing a cognition. Here we see a specific attributional strategy that can be used to maintain or raise self-esteem—just locate "causality" where it does you the most good (Greenberg, Pyszczynski, and Solomon, 1982; Ickes & Layden, 1978; Snyder & Higgins, 1988).

A second reason is a little more subtle, and has to do with our earlier discussion about the kinds of information that are available to people. Suppose that Bill was trying to come up, not with the most flattering explanation of why he did poorly on the chemistry test, but with the most accurate explanation. Suppose also that Bill is a good student, and has gotten A's and B's on all other chemistry tests he has taken. Plus, he knows that he studied hard for the midterm. What is the most logical conclusion he should reach about why he got a D on it? Given the information he has about his past performances, it is perfectly logical for him to conclude that it was something peculiar about this particular test—not his ability or effort. The professor, on the other hand, knows that some people did very well on the test; thus, given the information that is available to the professor, it is logical for him or her to conclude that Bill, and not the fact that it was a difficult test, was responsible for the poor grade (Miller & Ross, 1975; Nisbett & Ross, 1980). In short, people often make different attributions because they have different information available to them, and thus reach different conclusions about why the behavior occurred. Self-serving attributions, then, can result from either of two processes: (a) the differences in availability of information or (b) the need to bolster our self-esteem.

People also alter their attributions to deal with other kinds of threats to their self-esteem. One of the hardest things to understand in life is the occurrence of tragic events, such as rapes, terminal diseases, and fatal accidents. Even when they happen to strangers we have never met, they can be upsetting. They remind us of our own mortality: If they can happen to someone else, they can happen to us. Of all the kinds of self-knowledge we have, the knowledge that we are mortal and that bad things can happen to us is perhaps the hardest to accept (Greenberg, Pyszczynski, and Solomon, 1986). We thus take steps to deny this fact. One way is by making **defensive attributions,** which are explanations that defend us from feelings of vulnerability and mortality.

One form of defensive attribution is **unrealistic optimism** about the future. Suppose we asked you to estimate how likely each of the following things is to happen to you, compared to how likely each is to happen to other students at your college or university: owning your own home, liking your postgraduate job, living past age eighty, having a drinking problem, getting divorced, and being unable to have children. When Weinstein (1980) asked college students these and similar questions, he found that people were too optimistic: Virtually everyone thought that the good things were more likely to happen to them than to their peers, and that the bad things were less likely to happen to them than to their peers. Surely we will own a home and live to a ripe old age! Being overly optimistic is one way people try to protect themselves from unpleasant feelings of mortality.

Sometimes, of course, it's hard to deny that bad things happen in life. We have only to pick up a newspaper to see that people suffer terrible misfortunes every day. How do we deal with these unsettling reminders that bad things happen? One way is by explaining them in such a way as to make it seem like they could never happen to us. We do so by believing that bad things happen only to bad people. Melvin Lerner (1980) has called this a **belief in a just world**—the assumption that people get what they deserve. Because most of us view ourselves as decent, good human beings, then surely bad things couldn't happen to us. It is very threatening to believe President John Kennedy's famous statement that "Life's not fair." If life's not fair, then, hey, bad things don't just happen to bad people, they happen to . . . oh no . . . good people like me!

The "just world belief" has some sad and even tragic consequences. Think about this situation: An article in your campus newspaper reports that a female student was the victim of a date rape by a fellow male student. How do you think you and your friends would react? Would you wonder if she'd done something to trigger the rape? Would you make the attribution that she was responsible, at least in part? For example, would you wonder if she was acting suggestively earlier in the evening? Would you note that she had invited the man into her room?

Research by Elaine Walster (1966) and others has focused on such attributions, which these investigators call "blaming the victim" (e.g., Burger, 1981; Lerner & Simmons, 1966; Shaver, 1970). In several experiments, they have found that the victims of crimes or accidents are often seen as causing their fate. For example, not only do people tend to believe that rape victims are to blame for the rape (Burt, 1980), but battered wives are often seen as responsible for their abusive husbands' behavior (Summers & Feldman, 1984). By using this attributional bias, the perceiver does not have to acknowledge that there is a certain randomness in life, that an accident or criminal may be waiting just around the corner for an innocent person—like oneself. The belief in a just world keeps anxious thoughts about one's own safety at bay.

**defensive attributions:** explanations for behavior that avoid feelings of vulnernability and mortality

**unrealistic optimism:** a form of defensive attribution wherein people think that good things are more likely to happen to them than to their peers, and that bad things are less likely to happen to them than to their peers

**belief in a just world:** a form of defensive attribution wherein people assume that bad things happen to bad people and that good things happen to good people

The strategy of blaming the victim does not work, however, if misfortune befalls someone who is very similar to us. If something terrible happens to Sue, and we are similar to Sue, then blaming her for her misfortune is even more threatening: If it can happen to her, it can happen to us. Under these circumstances, people are likely to believe that the victim was not responsible, and to attribute the cause of the event to chance factors. For example, in a study by Thornton (1984), female college students read about a sexual assault that had supposedly happened to another student on their campus. Half the participants believed the victim was similar to them in terms of her attitudes and beliefs, whereas the others believed she was dissimilar. When the victim was viewed as dissimilar, people blamed her for the assault, saying she was relatively unintelligent, irresponsible, and poorly adjusted; that is, they blamed the victim. When the victim was viewed as similar, people were more likely to blame the assault on chance factors, rather than on the character of the victim.

## How Accurate Are Our Attributions and Impressions?

When we make attributions, our goal is to be able to understand other people and predict what they will do. If we successfully sift through the complex layers of social behavior, accurately concluding that the reason Jake was mean to us is that he is insecure and aggressive at the office (but quite relaxed and kind at home), we are in a good position to know what to expect from Jake in the future—regardless of where we see him. To be able to predict how people will act toward us, it is obviously to our advantage to make attributions that are as accurate as possible. On balance, how accurate are our attributions and impressions? When we decide why people do what they do, and make conclusions about the kind of people they are, are we right?

We have already touched on this question when discussing the kinds of mental shortcuts people use. People's theories can lead them astray (e.g., the fundamental attribution error), as can people's needs to bolster their self-esteem and avoid feelings of mortality. Our main concern, however, has been with how people make causal attributions and form impressions of other people. We turn now to a more detailed look at the next logical question: Once we have made an attribution and formed an impression of another person, how accurate are we?

To find out, Bella DePaulo, David Kenny, and their colleagues asked groups of college students, who were strangers to each other, to meet and work on various laboratory games and tasks (DePaulo et al., 1987). Each person got to spend some time alone with three other members of the group. All the participants rated how much they liked each of their partners, and guessed how much their partners liked them. Surprisingly, these impressions were not very accurate. Participants' impressions about who liked them the best and who liked them the least were no more accurate than if they had guessed by flipping a coin or rolling a die. Nor are our first impressions about another person's personality traits very accurate. Funder and Colvin (1988) found that when people watched a videotape of a student talking about him- or herself for five minutes, their impressions of the student's personality were surprisingly inaccurate.

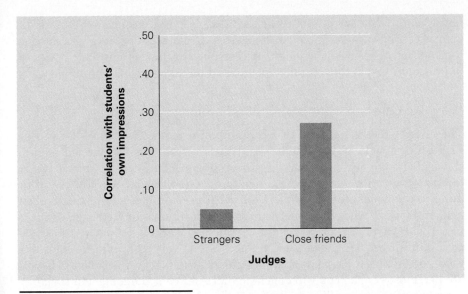

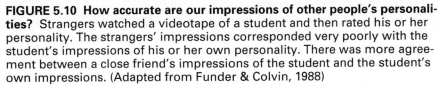

**FIGURE 5.10 How accurate are our impressions of other people's personalities?** Strangers watched a videotape of a student and then rated his or her personality. The strangers' impressions corresponded very poorly with the student's impressions of his or her own personality. There was more agreement between a close friend's impressions of the student and the student's own impressions. (Adapted from Funder & Colvin, 1988)

Both of these studies concerned people's first impressions of others based on very little information. In the DePaulo and colleagues (1987) study, people spent a total of only twenty minutes with their partners, and in the Funder and Colvin (1988) study, people saw the student on videotape for only five minutes. Not surprisingly, our impressions of others become more accurate the more we get to know them. Funder and Colvin demonstrated this by also asking close friends of the students to rate the students' personalities. As seen in Figure 5.10, the friends, who had known the students for an average of a year and a half, made more accurate assessments of the kind of people the students were.

It is not particularly earthshaking to conclude that the longer we know someone, the more accurate we are at judging his or her personality. There are, however, some surprising twists to these results. First, even though friends are more accurate than strangers at knowing what someone is like, their overall level of accuracy is still not very impressive. Look again at Figure 5.10 to see how accurate the close friends were in the Funder and Colvin study. The measure of accuracy was the correlation between the friends' impressions and the students' own impressions of their personalities. Recall from Chapter 2 that correlations can range from –1 to +1. A correlation of +1 would mean that there was perfect agreement between the students and their friends. The fact that the average agreement was only .27 suggests that there is considerable room for improvement in the accuracy of the friends' ratings.

Second, people are not as accurate as they think they are. Dunning, Griffin, Milojkovik, and Ross (1990) found that whereas college roommates were fairly accurate at predicting each other's behavior, they were overconfident, believing their predictions to be more correct than they were. Thus, even people who know each other quite well form impressions that are less than perfect, and they have too much confidence in the accuracy of their

Things are seldom as they seem, skim milk masquerades as cream.

—W. S. Gilbert,
*H.M.S. Pinafore*, 1878

impressions. These are important findings, because wrong impressions of people can have undesirable consequences. If we are interviewing someone for a job or choosing a roommate, it is to our advantage to have an accurate impression of what these people are like and how they feel about us.

## Why Are Our Impressions of Others Sometimes Wrong?

The answer to the question of why our impressions are wrong lies in our earlier discussion, in this chapter and the previous one, about the mental shortcuts people use when forming social judgments. The first culprit is our familiar friend the fundamental attribution error. People are too ready to jump to the conclusion that others did what they did because of the kind of person they are, when in fact it may have been the situation that caused them to act that way. For example, suppose you meet Andrea at a party, and she is acting in an outgoing, sociable manner. She is very animated as she talks with you, smiles a lot, and makes emphatic gestures with her hands. If you are like most people, you will conclude that Andrea is outgoing and sociable. How accurate are you likely to be?

Not too accurate, if it is the social situation that is causing her to act this way. Maybe Andrea really isn't, as a rule, very outgoing or sociable. In fact, she may be rather shy and reserved, but happens to be in a situation where most people would act sociably. Maybe she just found out she was accepted to a top graduate school, or maybe she has had a little too much to drink. If so, our conclusion that she is outgoing and sociable will be wrong, due to the fundamental attribution error: overestimating the extent to which Andrea's behavior reflects the way she always acts, rather than something about the situation.

Another reason our impressions can be wrong concerns our use of schemas. As we have seen, people use implicit personality theories to fill in the gaps in their knowledge about other people, and use theories to decide why other people do what they do. Thus our impressions are only as accurate as our theories. Whereas many of our theories are likely to be correct, there are some dramatic illustrations of how they can lead us astray.

Consider what happened to David Rosenhan (1973). He and several volunteers, who were, as far as anyone could determine, perfectly sane, went to the admissions departments of local mental hospitals. They pretended that they had been hearing voices, and all were admitted to the hospitals, most with a diagnosis of schizophrenia. From that point on, all behaved in a perfectly normal way. They chatted amiably with the staff and other patients, read, and watched television. Once they had been labeled as a schizophrenic and admitted to the hospitals, though, it was very difficult for the staff—including psychiatrists, psychologists, nurses, and aides—to tell that they were normal individuals. Once the staff had the schema that these people had severe mental problems, they seemed unable to tell that this theory was wrong. Not one of the volunteers was identified as a fake, and all were kept in the hospitals for several days. (One person had to spend more than seven weeks in the hospital before being released.) Interestingly, the staff often interpreted behaviors that were perfectly normal as confirmations of their schemas about the hapless volunteers. For example, all the volunteers kept diaries during their stay, and this writing behavior was sometimes viewed as an indication that they were psychologically disturbed.

## Why Does It Seem like Our Impressions Are Accurate?

We have seen that our impressions of other people become more accurate the more we get to know them, but there is still considerable room for improvement. Even experienced psychiatrists sometimes think that perfectly normal individuals have severe mental problems. As we have stressed again and again, people appear to underestimate the extent to which actors' behavior is due to situational factors, and often rely too much on schemas and theories that are inaccurate.

You may be treating this conclusion, however, with a healthy dose of skepticism. It sure doesn't seem like all our impressions are so off-base. If they were, wouldn't the social world be confusing and unpredictable, a place where people were constantly behaving in ways that surprised us? To the contrary, it seems like most of us can predict our friends' behavior pretty well. We know who is most likely to be the life of the party, who would rather go to a professional wrestling match than the ballet, and who will be there for us when we need a friend to lean on.

Why is it that it seems like our impressions of other people are pretty accurate if, as we have just reviewed, there is evidence that we often form incorrect impressions? One reason has to do with the number of different situations in which we see someone. If we underestimate the extent to which it is the situation that is causing someone's behavior, this will not matter much so long as we always see that person in the same situation. For example, stop and think for a moment about what your social psychology professor is like. How frivolous and fun-loving a person do you think he or she is? More likely than not, you have a sense that your professor is a serious scholar devoted to the field, and not someone who does frivolous things like eat ice cream cones, play pinball, or dance to rock music.

But—is it possible you have committed the fundamental attribution error? The fact that you never see your professor eat an ice cream cone, play pinball, or dance to rock music in the classroom probably says more about the nature of the classroom situation than it does about your professor. And yet people often assume that the behavior they observe is a good indication of the kind of person the actor is. (At least our students do, as evidenced by the look of surprise on their faces when they run into us outside the classroom eating an ice cream cone.)

Suppose students do commit the fundamental attribution error about their professors. Does this mean their predictions about how their professors will behave are inaccurate? Suppose we asked you, "How likely is it that your social psychology professor will eat an ice cream cone during your next class?" You probably would say, "Not very likely," and would undoubtedly be correct. But why? You might be right for the wrong reasons, if you assume that the reason your professor will not eat an ice cream cone is that he or she is a serious intellectual who never bothers with the small pleasures of life. The real reason may be that the situation in which you observe your professor—the classroom—is not conducive to the experience of such pleasures.

Thus, making the fundamental attribution error does not affect the accuracy of our predictions about people so long as we see them in a limited number of situations. Where we get into trouble is when we try to generalize someone's behavior from one situation to a very different one. This can be demonstrated by seeing how well you can predict the behavior of your professor in situations in which you do not normally see him or her. How likely is it that your social psychology professor dances to rock music at parties with his or her peers? You might be surprised at the answer. Because we see many people in limited situations (e.g., only in the classroom, only at work, or only with their families), however, it often doesn't matter that we have overestimated the extent to which their behavior is due to their personalities (Ross & Nisbett, 1991).

There is a second reason we might be able to predict somebody's behavior well, even if our impressions of his or her personality are wrong. This reason concerns the nature of self-fulfilling prophecies, discussed in Chapter 4. Even if an initial impression is incorrect, we often make it come true by the way we treat the person. Thus, if we think that Jane is conceited and aloof, we are unlikely to make much of an effort to be nice to her, and as a result, guess what? She is aloof in our presence. If we think Maria is warm and friendly, we are likely to be all smiles when we are around her, and guess what? She is warm and friendly to us. The mistake we make is assuming that Jane and Maria are always this way, because we do not realize how much our own reactions are influencing their behavior. You may have discovered this if you ever compared notes with a friend about a mutual acquaintance and discovered that you and your friend had very different impressions. You may have found it hard to believe you were talking about the same person. In fact, you were not: The mutual acquaintance may have been warm and friendly around you, but withdrawn and competitive in the presence of your friend, due to the operation of self-fulfilling prophecies.

In order to improve the accuracy of your attributions and impressions, remember that the fundamental attribution error and self-fulfilling prophecies exist, and try to counteract these biases. For example, the next time you hear about the victim of a crime or accident, stop yourself from immediately attributing responsibility to him or her. The world is not always a just place; bad things do happen to good people. Watch out for the other kinds of biases we have discussed as well, such as relying too much on implicit personality theories.

Now that we've delivered the sermon, let's cut to the chase. Yes, we are quite accurate perceivers of other people. We do very well indeed most of the time. We are adept at reading and interpreting nonverbal forms of communication; in fact, most of us are actually better at this than we realize. We become more accurate at perceiving others as we get to know them better, and since most of our truly important social interactions involve people we know well, this is good news. In short, we are capable of making both blindingly accurate assessments of people and horrific attributional mistakes—it's up to you to determine the difference in your life.

## SUMMARY

**Social perception** is the study of how people form impressions and make inferences about other people. People constantly form such impressions, because doing so helps them understand and predict their social worlds. One source of information people use is the nonverbal behavior of others. **Nonverbal communication** is used to express emotion, convey attitudes, communicate personality traits, and facilitate and regulate verbal speech. Many studies show that people are accurate decoders of subtle nonverbal cues. For example, the six major facial expressions of emotion are perceived accurately around the world. Other expressions vary according to culturally determined **display rules.** These rules dictate which expressions are appropriate to display. **Emblems,** nonverbal gestures that have specific meanings, are also culturally determined. In general, women are better at understanding and conveying emotion nonverbally. One exception, though, is that women are less accurate at detecting deception when observing nonverbal behavior. According to the **social-role theory** of sex differences, this may be because in many societies women have learned different skills, one of which is to be polite in social interactions, overlooking the fact that someone is lying.

Often it is difficult to tell how someone feels, or what kind of person he or she is, solely from the person's nonverbal behavior. As a result, we go beyond the information given in people's behavior, making inferences about their feelings, traits, and motives. One way we do this is with **implicit personality theories** to fill in the blanks. These are the general notions we have about which personality traits go together in one person. Second, according to **attribution theory,** we try to determine why people do what they do, in order to uncover the feelings and traits that are behind their actions. **Correspondent inference theory** focuses on how we make **internal attributions,** or how we infer dispositions from corresponding behavior. We do so by observing the number of **noncommon effects** produced by a person's behavior, and observing how much the behavior is inconsistent with our **category-based expectancies** and **target-based expectancies.** The **covariation model,** another theory of attribution, focuses on observations of behavior across time, place, different actors, and different targets of the behavior, and examines how the perceiver chooses either an internal or an **external attribution.** We

do so by using **consensus, distinctiveness,** and **consistency information.**

People also use various mental shortcuts when making attributions, including the use of schemas and theories. One common shortcut is the **fundamental attribution error,** which is the tendency to overestimate the extent to which people do what they do because of internal, dispositional factors. A reason for this error is that a person's behavior often has greater **perceptual salience** than the surrounding situation does. The **actor/observer difference** is a qualification of the fundamental attribution error: We are more likely to commit this error when explaining other people's behavior than when explaining our own behavior. People's attributions are also influenced by their need to protect their self-esteem (**self-serving attributions**) and their need to avoid feelings of mortality (**defensive attributions**). One form of defensive attribution is **unrealistic optimism** about the future, whereby we think that good things are more likely to happen to us than to other people. Another is the **belief in a just world,** whereby we believe that bad things happen to bad people and good things happen to good people.

How accurate are people's attributions and impressions of others? Not surprisingly, the more we get to know someone, the more accurate we are. Even when judging people we know well, however, the shortcuts we use sometimes lead to mistaken impressions. For example, we tend to make more dispositional attributions about other people than is warranted. Often, however, we do not realize that our impressions are wrong, because we see people in limited situations, and because the way we treat people causes them to behave the way we expect them to (the self-fulfilling prophecy).

## SUGGESTED READINGS

Fiske, S. T., & Taylor, S. E. (1991). *Social cognition* (2nd ed.). New York: McGraw-Hill. A recent, encyclopedic review of the literature on social perception by two experts in the field.

Jones, E. E. (1990). *Interpersonal perception.* New York: Freeman. An up-to-date review of social perception (with an emphasis on attribution theory) by one of the pioneers in the field.

McArthur, L. Z. (1990). *Social perception.* Pacific Grove, CA: Brooks/Cole. A general review of social perception and impression formation.

Ross, L., & Nisbett, R. E. (1991). *The person and the situation: Perspectives of social psychology.* New York: McGraw-Hill. A lively, in-depth discussion of many of the aspects of social perception we have discussed, such as the fundamental attribution error.

# Chapter 6
## Self-Understanding: How Do We Know Ourselves?

## Chapter Outline

**The Nature of the Self**
Cross-Cultural Definitions of Self
**Knowing Ourselves Through Introspection**
Self-Awareness Theory
Judging Why We Feel the Way We Do: Telling More
 Than We Can Know
The Consequences of Introspecting About Reasons
**Knowing Ourselves Through Observations of Our
Own Behavior**
Self-Perception Theory
The Overjustification Effect
The Two-Factor Theory of Emotion
Misattribution of Arousal
**Knowing Ourselves Through Self-Schemas**
Autobiographical Memory
**Knowing Ourselves Through Social Interaction**
The "Looking-Glass Self"
Social Comparison Theory
**Impression Management**
All the World's a Stage
**Summary**
**Suggested Readings**

There is one thing, and only one in the whole universe which we know more about than we could learn from external observation. That one thing is [ourselves]. We have, so to speak, inside information; we are in the know.

—C. S. Lewis, 1960

We are unknown, we knowers, ourselves to ourselves; this has its own good reason. We have never searched for ourselves—how should it then come to pass, that we should ever find ourselves?

—Friedrich Nietzche, 1918

top for a moment and think about how you feel right now. Are you happy or sad? Tired or energetic? Calm or irritated? Questions like these are usually pretty easy to answer; as C. S. Lewis says, we are "in the know" about ourselves. Few of us, however, would claim to know ourselves perfectly. Sometimes our thoughts and feelings are a confused jumble of contradictory reactions. And even if we know how we feel, it is not always clear why we feel that way. There is a lot about ourselves that is inscrutable and difficult to determine, as Nietzsche implies.

For example, have you ever been sure you knew exactly how you were going to feel about something, but then when it actually happened, found yourself feeling very differently indeed? The novelist Marcel Proust described just such a situation in his semiautobiographical novel *Remembrance of Things Past*. The narrator, Marcel, is convinced that he has no feelings left for his lover, Albertine. For months, he broods and plots about ways of leaving her. Then one day, his housekeeper brings him the news: Albertine has left him. At this instant, Marcel realizes how poorly he understood himself:

> A moment ago, as I lay analyzing my feelings, I had supposed that this separation without a final meeting was precisely what I wished, and, as I compared the mediocrity of the pleasures that Albertine afforded me with the richness of the desires which she prevented me from realizing, . . . [I] concluded that I did not wish to see her again, that I no

longer loved her. But now these words: "Mademoiselle Albertine has gone!" had expressed themselves in my heart in the form of an anguish so keen that I would not be able to endure it for any length of time. And so what I had supposed to mean nothing to me was the only thing in my whole life. How ignorant we are of ourselves. . . . Yes, a moment ago . . . I had supposed that I was no longer in love with Albertine, I had supposed I was leaving nothing out of account; a careful analyst, I had supposed that I knew the state of my own heart. But . . . I had been mistaken in thinking that I could see clearly into my own heart. (Proust, 1934, pp. 675–676)

The fact that Marcel had such little insight into his own feelings raises many interesting questions about self-knowledge. How do we understand our own thoughts and feelings? Are we more like the person with self-insight

*Self-Discovery*

Drawing by W. Steig; © April 1, 1991 The New Yorker Magazine, Inc.

described by C. S. Lewis, or more like the strangers to ourselves described by Nietzsche? And how do we obtain whatever self-knowledge we do possess? In this chapter, we will see how social psychologists answer these age-old questions.

## The Nature of the Self

Who are you? How did you come to be this person you call "myself"? The founder of American psychology, William James (1842–1910), described the basic duality that is the heart of our perception of self. First, the self is composed of our thoughts and beliefs about ourselves, or what James (1890 called the "known", or, more simply, the "me". Second, the self is also the active processor of information, the "knower," or "I". In modern terms, we refer to the known aspect of the self as the **self-concept** or the definition of self and to the knower aspect of the self as awareness or consciousness. Together, these two psychological processes combine to create a coherent sense of identity; your self is both a book (full of fascinating contents collected over time) and

**self-concept:** the contents of the self; that is, our perception of our own thoughts, beliefs, and personality traits

William James (1842–1910) wrote extensively about the nature of the self.

the reader of the book (who at any moment can access a specific chapter or add a new one).

Besides the knower and the known, James (1890) stressed the importance of social relationships in our definition of self. As he put it, "a man has as many social selves as there are individuals who recognize him and carry an image of him in their minds" (1910, vol. 1, p. 294). Thus, some aspects of your self are prominent when you are with one group of people and other aspects are prominent when you are with another group (Cantor & Kihlstrom, 1987; Gergen, 1971; Markus & Nurius, 1986). For example, when one of us is at the stable, training her horse and chatting with other riders and stablehands, she presents a different aspect of self than when she is at a national psychology conference with her colleagues. Her "barn self" is more colloquial, less intellectual. She alters her vocabulary, her topics of conversation, and even her manner of walking and standing when in this setting. These multiple selves are all known, but it is up to the knower to recognize when it is appropriate to exhibit one self and not another.

The development of a sense of self requires the realization that one is a knower and that there is, in fact, something to be known. This feat is not so simple, as shown by research on different species of mammals (Povinelli, 1993). Do animals have a sense of self? One way to find out is to place an animal in front of a mirror—does it realize that the reflection is itself, or does it think another animal is present? In a fascinating series of studies, Gordon Gallup (1977; Gallup & Suarez, 1986) placed an animal—a great ape (chimpanzees, gorillas, orangutans), a primate (rhesus monkeys, macaques), and lower mammals (dogs, rats)—in a room with a large mirror. The animals initially reacted to their reflected image with some curiosity and with "social displays"—the vocalizations, facial expressions, and postures that each uses to communicate with another member of its species. However, the animals quickly tired of the mirror image and ignored it—except for the great apes. Gallup (1977) found that over the course of several days, the great apes

Research by Gordon Gallup (1977) has found that the great apes (chimpanzees, gorillas, orangutans) have a sense of self, where as other mammals do not.

began to use the mirror to assist them in grooming themselves (e.g., picking food out of their teeth) or for entertainment (e.g., making faces, blowing bubbles with their saliva).

While this behavior suggested that the great apes, unlike other, lesser mammals, had a sense of self and could recognize their mirror image as themselves, Gallup (1977) tested the proposition carefully. He anesthetized chimpanzees briefly and painted an odorless red dye on one brow and one ear. When the chimps looked into the mirror, they immediately reached for their red brow and ear—proof that they realized the image in the mirror was themselves and not another ape, and also proof that they knew they looked differently from how they looked before.

Research with human infants indicates that self-recognition, and thus the beginnings of a self-concept, develops gradually. It is believed that the concept of the self emerges in a child at about two years of age (Bertenthal & Fischer, 1978; Lewis, 1986). A variation on the red-dye test has been used with infants; for example, a dot of red rouge is placed on a baby's nose and then his or her response to a mirror is noted. Lewis and Brooks (1978) found that 75 percent of twenty-one- to twenty-five-month-old infants touched their rouged noses, while only 25 percent of the nine- to twelve-month-old infants did so.

It is a big step, however, from recognizing yourself in a mirror to having the type of multifaceted, complex definition of self that characterizes adult humans. Psychologists have studied how people's self-concept changes from childhood to adulthood, by asking people of different ages to answer the simple question, "Who am I?" Typically, our self-concepts start out being concrete, with references to clear-cut, easily observable characteristics like age, sex, neighborhood, and hobbies. In a study by Montemayor and Eisen

(1977), for example, a nine-year-old answered the "Who am I?" question this way: "I have brown eyes. I have brown hair. I have brown eyebrows. . . . I'm a boy. I have an uncle that is almost 7 feet tall" (Montemayor & Eisen, 1977, p. 317). As we mature, we place less emphasis on physical characteristics and more emphasis on psychological states (e.g., our thoughts and feelings) and on considerations of how other people judge us (Hart & Damon, 1986; Livesley & Bromley, 1973; Montemayor & Eisen, 1977). Consider this twelfth-grade high school student's answer to the "Who am I" question:

> I am a human being. . . . I am a moody person. I am an indecisive person. I am an ambitious person. I am a very curious person. I am not an individual. I am a loner. I am an American (God help me). I am a Democrat. I am a liberal person. I am a radical. I am a conservative. I am a pseudoliberal. I am an atheist. I am not a classifiable person (i.e., I don't want to be). (Montemayor & Eisen, 1977, p. 318)

## Cross-Cultural Definitions of Self

Before we leave our discussion of the nature of the self, we should note that we have been describing a particular kind of self: one anchored in Western culture at the end of the twentieth century. Do people everywhere conceptualize the self as we do? Is it possible for something seemingly so basic to differ across peoples? The answer is yes: Recent psychohistorical and cross-cultural research demonstrates clearly that the self-concept is shaped by both culture and historical epoch.

For example, Roy Baumeister (1987) traced the history of the self-concept through ten centuries of Western civilization, relying on historical and literary sources. The self-concept of an inhabitant of the late medieval period (eleventh through fifteenth centuries) would hardly be recognizable to us. The evidence suggests that these people rarely, if ever, engaged in introspection (thinking about one's self, what one wants, etc.), and rarely, if ever, were torn by inner doubts or struggles. As Baumeister (1987) put it, "self-knowledge was not regarded as an important problem" (p. 165), because medieval identity was fixed at birth. One's social rank, kinship network, and especially gender mandated who and what one could be. The emergence of a definition of self similar to our modern one did not occur until the seventeenth century, when Puritans became self-conscious and self-aware. Because their religious belief of predestination decreed that one was a member of the saved or the damned at birth, Puritans were highly motivated to scrutinize themselves for clues (hidden in their deep, inner nature) as to their future fate (Baumeister, 1987). Thus, for the first time the concept that one has a hidden, deep inner self came into being.

Just as the self-concept has evolved and changed in Western culture over time, non-Western definitions differ from our own (Markus & Kitayama, 1991). The anthropologist Dorothy Lee (1959), for example, mapped the nature of the self among the Wintu Native American culture of Northern California. Using linguistic analysis, biography, and recollections of descendants, Lee (1959) found striking evidence for the absence of a sense of the self as a separate entity among the Wintu. She says, "When speaking about Wintu culture, we cannot speak of the self and society, but rather the self in society" (p. 132). The Wintu did not have a word for self. Wintu words were based on observations of things outside the self, rather than on introspection

The self-concept is dependent, in part, on the culture in which we grow up. Historically, for example, some Native American cultures view the self as deeply embedded within the larger social group.

or one's own thoughts. There was no separation between a person and, for example, what he or she was wearing. "You are wearing a pretty striped dress" would translate in Wintu into "You are pretty dress striped." For the Wintu, the self had no clear boundaries or demarcations; it merged and faded in and out of all other things. To paraphrase William Shakespeare, in our society "the self is the measure of all things." However natural we consider this conception of the self to be, it is important to remember that it is only a construction and not an inherent reality.

Regardless of the exact nature of the self, where does information about ourselves come from? How do we learn about ourselves? What are the sources of data that we depend on to build this sense of self? In the following sections, we will discuss four ways we come to know ourselves: through introspection, or thinking about ourselves; through observation of our own behavior; through self-schemas; and through social interaction.

## Knowing Ourselves Through Introspection

When we told you we were going to describe the sources of information you use to construct a self-concept, you probably thought, "Good grief! I don't need a social psychology textbook to tell me that! It's not exactly a surprise; I just think about myself. No big deal." In other words, you rely on **introspection,** where you look inward and examine the "inside information" that you, and you alone, have about your thoughts, feelings, and motives. And indeed, you do find some answers when you introspect. But there are two interesting things about introspection: (a) People do not rely on this source of information as often as you might think—surprisingly, people spend very little time thinking about themselves—and (b) even when

**introspection:** the process whereby people look inward and examine their own thoughts, feelings, and motives

people do introspect, the reasons they feel or behave the way they do can be hidden from conscious awareness. In short, self-scrutiny isn't all it's cracked up to be, and if this was our only source of knowledge about ourselves, we would be in big trouble.

How often do people think about themselves? To find out, Mihaly Csikszenmihalyi, and Thomas Figurski (1982) asked 107 employees, who ranged in age from nineteen to sixty-three and worked at five different companies, to wear beepers for one week. The beepers went off at random intervals between 7:30 A.M. and 10:30 P.M., for a total of seven to nine times a day. At the sound of the beeper, the participants each answered a series of questions about their activity, thoughts, and mood at that time. The responses were content-analyzed into categories, including thoughts about oneself (e.g., "How lazy I've been all day," "It hurts," or "Why did I get this fat?"). As you can see in Figure 6.1, people thought about themselves surprisingly infrequently. Only 8 percent of the total thoughts recorded (4,721) were about the self; more often, the participants thought about work, chores, and time. In fact, the response of "no thoughts" was more frequent than that of thoughts about the self. Thus, while we certainly engage in introspection at times, it is not a frequent cognitive activity. Mundane thoughts about everyday life, and indeed thoughts about other people and our conversations with them, account for the vast majority of our daily thoughts (see Figure 6.1).

> I have often wished I had time to cultivate modesty. . . . But I am too busy thinking about myself.
>
> —Dame Edith Sitwell

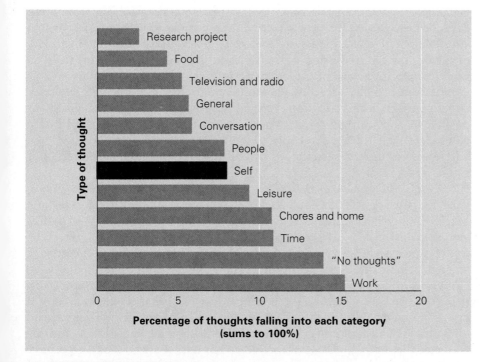

**FIGURE 6.1 "What are you thinking about?"** For a week, people wore beepers that went off at random intervals several times a day. Each time the beepers went off, people described what they had just been thinking about. Thoughts about the self were surprisingly infrequent. (Adapted from Csikszenmihalyi & Figurski, 1982)

## Self-Awareness Theory

When we are thinking about ourselves, what happens? What are the consequences of turning the spotlight of consciousness on ourselves, instead of focusing our attention on the world around us? As we just saw from the Csikszenmihalyi and Figurski (1982) study, we do not focus on ourselves very often. Sometimes, however, we encounter something in the environment that triggers self-awareness, such as knowing that people are watching us, hearing our tape-recorded voice, seeing ourselves on videotape, or staring at ourselves in a mirror. For example, if you are watching a home video taken by a friend with her new camcorder and you are the featured attraction, you will be in a state of self-awareness, where you become the focus of your attention.

**self-awareness theory:** the idea that when people focus their attention on themselves, they evaluate and compare their behavior to their internal standards and values

According to **self-awareness theory,** when we focus on ourselves we evaluate and compare our current behavior against our internal standards and values (Carver & Scheier, 1981; Duval & Wicklund, 1972; Wicklund, 1975; Wicklund & Frey, 1980). In short, we literally become self-conscious, in the sense that we become objective, judgmental observers of ourselves. Are we behaving as we think we should? Let's say that you believe it is important for you to be honest with your friends. One day, while conversing with a friend, you lie to him. In the midst of this conversation, you catch sight of yourself in a large mirror. There you are, staring back at yourself, you worthless worm who just lied to your good friend!

According to Shelley Duval and Robert Wicklund (1972), you will suddenly become aware of this disparity between your behavior and your standard, or expectation, for yourself. If you can change your behavior to match your internal guidelines (e.g., say something particularly nice to your friend, or admit you lied and ask for forgiveness), you will do so. If you feel you can't change your behavior, then being in a state of self-awareness will be very uncomfortable, for you'll be confronted with disagreeable feedback about yourself. In this situation, you will stop being self-aware as quickly as possible (e.g., by turning so your back is to the mirror, or saying good-bye to your friend and leaving the room). Figure 6.2 illustrates this process: how self-awareness makes us conscious of our internal standards and directs our subsequent behavior.

Several studies have examined the link between self-awareness and moral behavior (Carver, 1975; Gibbons, 1978). For example, Edward Diener and Mark Wallbom (1976) gave research participants an anagrams test, which was described as a good predictor of intelligence and academic ability. The test was purposefully very difficult, designed so that no one could complete more than half the items in the time allotted. Thus, the participants were motivated to do well (and look smart) but had been given a fiendishly difficult test, one on which they could not do well. What would they do? If given the opportunity to cheat, would they do so? Since prior research had found that the vast majority of college students sampled agreed that cheating was morally wrong, these research participants were presumed to have an internal standard that told them not to cheat. But would they refrain from cheating only if this standard was salient—that is, only if they were self-aware?

Diener and Wallbom (1976) presented an opportunity to cheat by telling all the participants they had five minutes to complete the test—at which point, a timer would go off—but that the experimenter wouldn't be back for

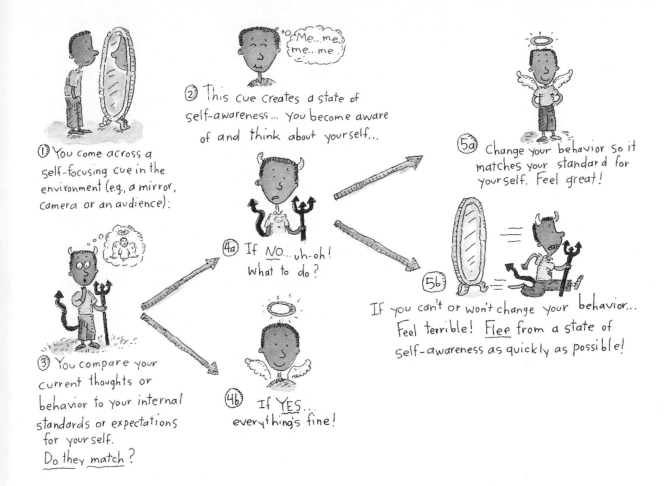

① You come across a self-focusing cue in the environment (e.g. a mirror, camera or an audience):

② This cue creates a state of self-awareness... You become aware of and think about yourself...

③ You compare your current thoughts or behavior to your internal standards or expectations for yourself. Do they <u>match</u>?

④a If <u>NO</u>...uh-oh! What to do?

④b If YES... everything's fine!

⑤a Change your behavior so it matches your standard for yourself. Feel great!

⑤b If you can't or won't change your behavior... Feel terrible! <u>Flee</u> from a state of self-awareness as quickly as possible!

**FIGURE 6.2** Self-awareness theory: The consequences of self-focused attention. (Adapted from Carver & Scheier, 1981)

about ten minutes, as he was starting another participant on the test in another room. Half of the participants were placed in a state of self-awareness during the test in the following way: A large mirror covered most of the wall directly in front of them, and they listened to an audiotape of their own voice, ostensibly to see how distraction affected performance. For the other half of the participants, the mirror was behind them—they could not see themselves—and they heard another person's voice on the audiotape. Would the participants stop when the timer bell rang, or would they keep on working? Would self-awareness affect the likelihood of cheating? As predicted, self-aware people resisted temptation; only 7 percent of them cheated. On the other hand, non-self-aware people did not resist temptation; 71 percent of them cheated. Similarly, in a study of children "trick-or-treating," researchers found that children were less likely to break the rules and take more than one piece of candy from an unattended bowl when a large mirror was behind the bowl (Beaman, Klentz, Diener, and Svanum, 1979).

Self-awareness is not always an enjoyable state, because it can remind us of how we have not lived up to our expectations. This dissatisfaction with ourselves can be painful (witness cognitive dissonance), and we will often escape from such self-scrutiny by getting involved in other activities, surrounding ourselves with distracting stimuli like television or music, or even blunting our internal voice with drugs or alcohol (Hull, 1981; Hull & Young, 1983). In studies where people have failed at a task, they will purposefully avoid situations that induce self-awareness; for example, they do not want to sit in a room with a mirror and a TV camera (Archer, Hormuth, and Berg, 1979; Duval & Wicklund, 1972).

There is, however, one side benefit of being self-aware. The quotation from Nietzsche at the beginning of the chapter suggests that we often do not search for ourselves in any great depth, and that if we did, we would uncover hidden thoughts and feelings. Consistent with this view, there is evidence that when people are self-aware, they make more accurate assessments of their feelings and personalities (Carver & Scheier, 1981). John Pryor and his associates (1977), for example, found that people made more accurate judgments about their own personalities when they were seated in front of a mirror (see also Millar & Tesser, 1986; Snyder, 1982; Wicklund, 1982).

## Judging Why We Feel the Way We Do: Telling More Than We Can Know

When people are in a state of self-awareness, then, they make relatively accurate judgments about how they feel or what their personality is. Another kind of self-knowledge, however, is much more difficult to obtain, even when we are self-aware and introspect to our heart's content: knowing why we feel the way we do. Imagine trying to decide why you love someone. Being in love typically makes you feel giddy, euphoric, and preoccupied; in fact, the ancient Greeks thought love was a sickness. But why do you feel this way? Exactly what is it about your sweetheart that made you fall in love? Most of us would be tongue-tied when trying to answer this question. We know that it is something about our loved one's looks, personality, values, and background. But precisely what? How can we possibly verbalize the special chemistry that exists between two people? A friend of ours once claimed that he was in love with a woman because she played the saxophone. Was this really the only reason? or even an important one? The heart works in such mysterious ways that it is difficult to tell.

Unfortunately, it's not just love that is difficult to explain. A major tenet of cognitive psychology holds that many of our basic mental processes occur outside of awareness (Kihlstrom, 1987; Mandler, 1975; Neisser, 1976). This is not to say that we are thinkers without a clue—we are aware of the final result of our thought processes (e.g., that we are in love), but typically unaware of the cognitive processing that led to the result. It's as if the magician pulled a rabbit out of a hat: You see the rabbit, but you don't know how it got there.

How do we deal with this rabbit problem? While we often don't know why we feel a certain way, it seems we are always able to come up with an explanation. Why? We're the proud owners of the most powerful cortex to evolve on this planet, and we certainly put it to use. (Unfortunately, it didn't come with an owner's manual.) Thus, introspection may not lead us to the true causes of our feelings and behavior, but we'll manage to convince ourselves that it did.

Richard Nisbett and Timothy Wilson explored this phenomenon, or how we tell more than we know (Nisbett & Ross, 1980; Nisbett & Wilson, 1977; Wilson, 1985; Wilson & Stone, 1985). For example, recall the study by Wilson, Laser, and Stone (1982), mentioned in Chapter 4. College students kept journals of their moods every day for five weeks; they also kept track of other variables, such as what the weather was like and how much sleep they had gotten the night before. When asked, the participants reported that several things correlated with their moods. However, an analysis of the data indicated that in many cases people were wrong. For example, most people believed that their moods were related to how much sleep they had gotten the night before, when in fact there were no such correlations in the data. The participants had introspected and found or generated some logical-sounding theories that in fact weren't right. (See also Bargh & Pietromonaco, 1982; Kihlstrom, 1987; Lewicki, 1986; Weiss & Brown, 1977)

What these participants had relied on, at least in part, was a kind of schema called a **causal theory**. People have many theories about what influences their feelings and behavior (e.g., "My mood should be affected by how much sleep I got last night") and often use these theories to help them explain why they feel the way they do (e.g., "I am in a bad mood; I bet the fact that I only got six hours of sleep last night has a lot to do with it"). We learn many of these theories from the culture in which we grow up, such as the idea that absence makes the heart grow fonder, that people are in bad moods on Monday, or that people who have been divorced are a poor choice for a successful second marriage. The only problem is that, as discussed in Chapter 4, our schemas and theories are not always correct, and can thus lead to incorrect judgments about the causes of our actions.

**causal theory:** a theory about the causes of one's own feelings and behaviors, many of which we learn from our culture (e.g., "absence makes the heart grow fonder")

Consider this example of causal theories in action from the researchers who have studied them: One night, Nisbett and Wilson were meeting in an office at the University of Michigan. They were trying to think of ways to test the hypothesis that introspection often can't tell us why we feel the way we do, and that we rely on causal theories when trying to uncover the reasons for our feelings, judgments, and actions. Brilliant insights were not forthcoming, and the researchers were becoming frustrated by their lack of progress. Then they realized that a source of their frustration (or so they thought) was the annoying whine of a vacuum cleaner that a custodial worker was operating right outside their office. Because it took them a while to realize that the background noise of the vacuum was disrupting their meeting, they experienced what seemed like an inspiration—maybe distracting background noises are more bothersome than people think. Maybe this was an example of the very kind of stimulus they were looking for—one that would influence people's judgments but, because their causal theories did not adequately cover this possibility, would be overlooked when people explained their behavior.

Nisbett and Wilson (1977) designed a study to test this possibility (after shutting the door). They showed people a documentary film and asked them to rate how interesting they thought it was. In one condition, a construction worker (actually, Richard Nisbett) ran a power saw right outside the door to the room. The irritating burst of noise began about a minute into the film. It continued intermittently until Tim Wilson, the experimenter, went to the door and shouted to the worker to please stop sawing until the film was over. The participants rated how much they enjoyed the film, and then the experimenter asked them to indicate whether the noise had influenced their evaluations. To see if the noise really did have an effect, Nisbett and Wilson included a control condition where participants viewed the film without any distracting noise. The researchers' hypothesis was that the noise would lower people's evaluation of the film, but that people would not realize that the noise was responsible for the negative evaluation.

As it happened, this hypothesis was completely wrong. The participants who watched the film with the annoying background noise did not rate it any lower than participants who saw the film without the distracting noise (in fact, they liked the film slightly more). When the participants were asked how much the noise had influenced their ratings, however, their theories agreed with Nisbett and Wilson's. Even though the noise had no detectable effect on people's ratings, most people reported that it had lowered their ratings of the film. In this case, both the participants and the researchers had the same causal theory, but the theory wasn't true—at least, not when it came to watching a documentary while hearing construction noise.

In further studies, other factors that seem like they should not influence people's judgments—that is, factors that are not part of people's causal theories—actually did have an effect. For example, in one study people evaluated the quality of items of clothing, such as pantyhose, in a shopping mall (Nisbett & Wilson, 1977). Much to the surprise of the researchers, the position of the items on the display table had a large effect on people's preferences. The more to the right an item was, the more people liked it. The researchers knew that it was the position and not something distinctive about the different pairs of pantyhose that influenced people's judgments, because in fact all four pairs were identical. However, the participants were completely in the dark about this effect of position on their judgments. Such an odd reason for their choice of pantyhose was not evident when they introspected about the reasons for their choice.

We do not mean to imply that people rely solely on their causal theories when introspecting about the reasons for their feelings and behaviors. In addition to culturally learned causal theories, we have a great deal of information about ourselves, such as how we have responded in the past and what we happen to have been thinking about before making a choice (Gavanski & Hoffman, 1987; Wilson & Stone, 1985). The fact remains, however, that introspecting about our past actions and current thoughts does not always yield the right answer about why we feel the way we do.

## The Consequences of Introspecting About Reasons

Not only is it difficult to uncover all of our reasons by introspecting; it may not be a good idea to even try to do so. Have you ever, when faced with a difficult decision, spent time reflecting about why you felt the way you did about each alternative? Perhaps when you decided where to go to college, you were faced with two or more attractive alternatives and had trouble making up your mind. Maybe you couldn't decide which courses to take this year. In situations like these, people sometimes analyze the alternatives very carefully, maybe even making a list of the pluses and minuses of each choice. Benjamin Franklin argued that this is the best way to make a decision:

> My way is to divide half a sheet of paper by a line into two columns, writing over the one Pro, and over the other Con. Then, during three or four days

> We can never, even by the strictest examination, get completely behind the secret springs of action.
> —Immanuel Kant

consideration, I put down under the different heads short hints of the different motives, that at different times occur to me, for or against each measure. . . . I find at length where the balance lies; and if, after a day or two of further consideration, nothing new that is of importance occurs on either side, I come to a determination accordingly. . . When each [reason] is thus considered, separately and comparatively, and the whole lies before me, I think I can judge better, and am less likely to make a rash step. (Quoted in Goodman, 1945, p. 746)

Timothy Wilson has recently found, however, that analyzing the reasons for our feelings is not always the best strategy, and in fact can make matters worse (Wilson, 1990; Wilson, Dunn, Kraft, and Lisle, 1989; Wilson & Hodges, 1992). The problem is that because it is difficult to know exactly why we feel the way we do about something, we bring to mind reasons that sound plausible and come to mind easily (i.e., reasons that are available in our memories; see Chapter 4). The reasons that sound plausible and are available, however, may not be the correct reasons. Even worse, we might convince ourselves that these reasons are correct, thereby changing our minds about how we feel to match our reasons.

Suppose, for example, we asked you to take out a piece of paper and write down exactly why you feel the way you do about a romantic partner. When we ask people to do this, we find **reasons-generated attitude change**, whereby people change their attitudes toward their partners (Wilson, Dunn, Bybee, Hyman, and Rotondo, 1984; Wilson & Kraft, 1993). Why? It is difficult to know exactly why we love someone; thus, we latch onto reasons that sound good and that happen to be on our minds. In our studies, the reasons people report are such things as how well they communicate with their dating partner and how similar they are to him or her in their interests and backgrounds. Whereas these reasons may often be correct, people probably overlook other reasons that are not as easy to verbalize, such as that "special chemistry" that can exist between two people.

The trouble comes when the reasons that are available in people's memories and are easy to verbalize imply a different attitude than people had before. Suppose, for instance, that things are going well between you and your dating partner, but you have trouble verbalizing exactly why this is so. What comes to mind is the fact that you have rather different backgounds and interests. Consequently, you are likely to change your mind about how you feel, assuming that your feelings must match your reasons. "We really don't have much in common," you might say. "I guess this relationship doesn't have much of a future." We have found just this sequence of events in a number of studies (e.g., Wilson & Kraft, 1993).

It's difficult to know, of course, which attitude is the right one—the positive feelings you had before analyzing reasons or the more negative ones you have afterward. We have found, however, that the attitudes people express immediately after analyzing reasons should not be trusted too much. When people make decisions based on these attitudes, they come to regret what they have chosen (Wilson, Lisle, Schooler, Hodges, Klaaren, and LaFleur, 1993). Why? The determinants of your feelings that are hard to verbalize (e.g., that "something special" your sweetheart has) do not go away, and are likely to shape your feelings in the future. Thus, if you focus only on the reasons that are easy to verbalize (e.g., the fact that you and your sweetheart have different backgrounds), you might behave in ways—such as breaking

**reasons-generated attitude change:** attitude change resulting from thinking about the reasons for one's attitudes; people assume that their attitudes match the reasons that are plausible and easy-to-verbalize

up with your sweetheart—that you later regret. Consistent with this view, several studies have found that the attitudes people express after analyzing their reasons do not predict their future attitudes and behavior very well (Millar & Tesser, 1986; Wilson et al., 1984; Wilson & LaFleur, 1993).

We have seen that introspection can be problematic in a couple of ways: It is difficult to discover why we feel the way we do through introspection, and in trying to do so, we might talk ourselves into feelings that are based only on what comes to mind and is easy to verbalize. "Well, fine," you might think, "I guess the solution is simply to try not to introspect too much." However, we need to raise an additional note of caution about attempts to avoid introspection. If by doing so you try hard not to think about certain things, these efforts might backfire, causing you to think even more about the things you were trying to suppress.

To illustrate this point, try the following exercise. When we give you the signal, we want you to try your best not to think about something—say, a dating partner or a close friend—for the next minute. Ready? Begin. How did you do? If you are like the participants in studies by Daniel Wegner (1989, 1992, in press), during the last minute thoughts about your friend popped into your mind at least once or twice. Even more interesting is that people in Wegner's studies continue to think about the forbidden topic at a high rate after the restriction is lifted—more so than people who initially were not asked to avoid thoughts about it. That is, **thought suppression**—trying hard not to think about something—can lead to an obsession with the very thought people are trying to suppress. When there is something you would really rather not think about—the D you got on your calculus test, the chocolate ice cream beckoning you from the freezer, or why you love your boyfriend or girlfriend—the best strategy is, oddly, not to try too hard to avoid these thoughts.

To summarize, thinking about how we feel and what kind of person we are can lift the veil from hidden feelings, making them easier to detect, especially when we are in a state of self-awareness. It is quite another thing to reflect about why we feel that way. Many studies show that people's judgments about the reasons for their feelings and actions are often incorrect. Further, the act of thinking about reasons can cause us to change our attitudes, convincing us that our feelings match the reasons that happen to come to mind.

If introspection has its limits, how else might we find out what sort of person we are and what our attitudes are? We turn now to another source of self-knowledge—observations of our own behavior.

**thought suppression:** an effort not to think about something; research shows that the more people try not to think about something, the more that very thought pops into their minds

## Knowing Ourselves Through Observations of Our Own Behavior

### Self-Perception Theory

How do we figure out other people—what they are like, what they want, and what they'll do next? By observing them, of course. Because we can't look inside other people's heads, we figure out what kind of people they are by seeing how they behave. Suppose you saw a woman walk into a cafeteria, carefully scrutinize all the vegetables on display, select a large bowl of

How can I tell what I think
'till I see what I say?
—E. M. Forster

*Drawing by Frascino; © September 2, 1991 The New Yorker Magazine, Inc.*

"I don't sing because I am happy. I am happy because I sing."

According to self-perception theory, people often infer their attitudes and emotions from their behavior.

brussels sprouts, and begin to eat them ravenously. What would you conclude? Simple: "She must love brussels sprouts." Given that she has freedom of choice and numerous options, why else would she have chosen that strange vegetable?

According to Daryl Bem's (1972) **self-perception theory,** we often discover what kind of people we are and what our own attitudes are in the same way we discover things about other people: by observing our own behavior, just as another person would. Suppose that you walked into a cafeteria, selected a large bowl of brussels sprouts, and began to eat them ravenously. What would you conclude from your own actions? Simple: "I must love brussels sprouts; why else would I be eating them?"

That self-observation is an important source of knowledge about the self was introduced by the British philosopher Gilbert Ryle (1949). Realizing that introspection was a rather paltry source of knowledge, Ryle argued that people come to view themselves in certain ways based on their memories of how they typically behave. If you recall that you often eat brussels sprouts, you will perceive yourself as a brussels sprouts lover.

Daryl Bem (1972) developed this idea into self-perception theory. First, Bem stated that "individuals come to 'know' their own attitudes, emotions, and other internal states partially by inferring them from observations of their own overt behavior and/or the circumstances in which this behavior occurs" (p. 5). Why does Bem say "partially"? Because sometimes we do know exactly how we feel or exactly what our attitude is. For example, as authors of this book, we know that we really like social psychology and that we're really enjoying writing this book. We don't have to wait until midnight to see how much we wrote that day—we know now. This brings us to Daryl Bem's (1972) second postulate: "To the extent that internal cues are weak,

**self-perception theory:** the theory that when our attitudes and feelings are uncertain or ambiguous, we infer these states by observing our behavior and the situation in which it occurs

ambiguous, or uninterpretable, the individual is functionally in the same position as an outside observer, an observer who must necessarily rely upon those same external cues [behavior and circumstances] to infer the individual's internal states" (p. 5; emphasis added).

For any given person, some traits or characteristics will be weak or ambiguous and others will not. You may know you are very extraverted, and thus do not need to observe your behavior to figure this out. For many of us, however, it is not always clear how extraverted or introverted we are—sometimes we are very outgoing, and sometimes we feel kind of shy. If asked how extraverted we are, we will rely on self-perception processes (How outgoing have we been recently? How many people did we talk to at the party last week?) and draw a conclusion from our behavior just as an outside observer would (Akert, 1991).

If we do rely on such self-observation, the answer we come up with will depend on whether more examples of extraversion or introversion come to mind. This notion was illustrated in a study by Russell Fazio, Edwin Effrein, and Victoria Falender (1981). They asked research participants a series of questions about their personalities. Unbeknownst to the participants, these were trick questions designed to get people in one condition to give all extraverted answers, and people in the other condition to give all introverted answers—regardless of the kind of people they really were. For example, in the extravert condition, the experimenter asked questions like "What would you do if you wanted to liven things up at a party?" Virtually everyone answers this leading question in a way that makes him or her look extraverted. In the introvert condition, the experimenter asked questions like "What things do you dislike about loud parties?" Virtually everyone answers this question in a way that makes him or her look introverted.

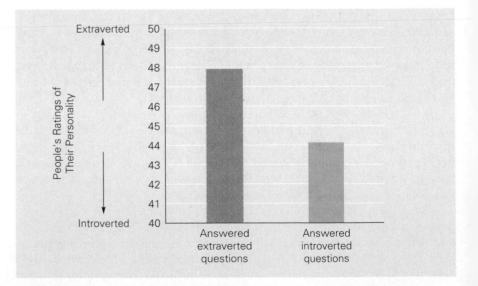

FIGURE 6.3 Self-perceptions of extraversion and introversion. People were induced by an experimenter to give examples of times they acted in either an extraverted or an introverted fashion. Those who gave extraverted answers inferred that they were more extraverted people than those who gave introverted answers. (Adapted from Fazio, Effrein, and Falender, 1981)

But did these research participants come to view themselves as extraverted or introverted people? Self-perception theory says they should have done so, to the extent that their self-perceptions in this area were not already crystal-clear and unambiguous. As can be seen in Figure 6.3, the participants did rely on self-perception processes to decide how extraverted or introverted they were: The type of questions they were asked produced a significant difference in how they perceived themselves. The people who had answered extraverted questions viewed themselves afterward as somewhat more extraverted; the people who had answered introverted questions, as somewhat more introverted.

A subtler example of self-perception theory in action is a study conducted by Fritz Strack and his colleagues (Strack, Martin, and Stepper, 1988). They asked research participants to hold a pen in their mouths—using either their teeth or their lips. The photos on this page demonstrate these two techniques. Try it yourself; notice how the muscles in your face, particularly those around your mouth, feel differently depending on how you hold the pen. Next, Strack and colleagues (1988) showed the participants (with their pens in their mouths) a series of amusing cartoons and asked them to rate how funny they were. Participants who held the pen with their teeth found the cartoons significantly more amusing than those who held the pen with their lips! Why? According to self-perception theory, to infer how we feel we observe not only our overt actions (e.g., whether we are eating brussels sprouts) but also our facial expressions. The pen-in-teeth maneuver involves some of the same muscles that we use when smiling; the pen-in-lips maneuver uses nonsmiling muscles. Thus, we have a very subtle—in fact, unconscious—example of self-perception in action: Muscle movements affected people's reactions to the cartoons without their realizing it. This finding, part of the **facial feedback hypothesis** (Laird, 1974; Laird & Bressler, 1992), indicates that facial expressions can trigger corresponding emotions. In other words, "putting on a happy face" can actually make you perceive yourself as happy.

**Self-Perception Versus Dissonance Theory.** As we mentioned in Chapter 1, two fundamental human motives influence how people perceive the social world. First is the need to be correct—that is, to form an accurate picture of the world. Bem's self-perception theory argues that this need for accuracy is what drives people's inferences about themselves. Our attitudes and emotions are said to be the result of an honest attempt to infer how we feel from how we behave. In this sense, self-perception theory is part of the same tradition as attribution theory (see Chapter 5), which portrays people as rational perceivers trying to make sense, as logically as they can, of themselves and the social world.

Second—as we saw in Chapters 1 and 3—is the desire to maintain our self-esteem. In Chapter 3, we discussed dissonance theory, which argues that people's goal is to avoid threats to their self-esteem, even if this means making some rather surprising, illogical inferences about themselves. Our need to view ourselves as decent, moral human beings causes us to hate others more after doing them harm, to like others more after doing them a favor, and to believe lies we have told, because by doing so, we avoid feeling silly, stupid, or immoral.

Several years ago, there was a lively controversy among social psychologists about which view was the correct one: Bem's theory, which argues that

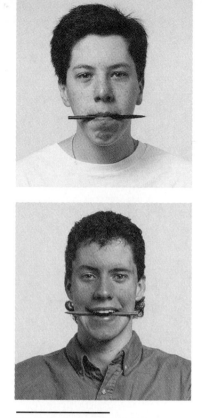

The facial feedback hypothesis: People found cartoons to be funnier when they held a pen with their teeth, because this forced them to smile while watching the cartoons. (Adapted from Strack et al., 1988)

**facial feedback hypothesis:** the hypothesis that people's facial expressions can determine the emotions they experience

we are rational perceivers trying to form accurate pictures of the world, or dissonance theory, which argues that we are primarily concerned with protecting our self-esteem. One reason for this controversy was that Bem claimed self-perception theory could explain the results of most dissonance experiments. Consider the studies we discussed in Chapter 3 on insufficient justification, where people are given small incentives to do something (e.g., write an essay) against their beliefs. Dissonance theory holds that this situation makes people feel silly and uncomfortable, and that in order to reduce these dissonant feelings, people come to believe what they are saying.

Bem (1967, 1972) argued that his self-perception theory could explain these same findings in a much simpler way—without needing to deal with such concepts as emotion, pain, discomfort, or the self-concept, which are at the root of dissonance theory. Bem believed that people simply try to make accurate inferences about their behavior in a cool and logical manner, rather than assuming that people change their attitudes to reduce the pain of dissonance or to justify their past behavior. There is a world of difference between the two theories.

For example, here is how Bem would approach Cohen's experiment that we discussed in Chapter 3. Suppose you observed Sara, a student at Yale, writing an essay favoring the hostile actions of the New Haven police during a student demonstration, and you knew she was being paid only 50 cents to write it. Wouldn't you conclude that Sara must really believe that the actions of the New Haven police were right and reasonable? Why else would she say so? Surely not for the measly little 50 cents.

Now suppose you found yourself writing an essay favoring the fierce actions of the New Haven police after being paid only 50 cents. What would you do? According to Bem, you would make the same, logical conclusion: "I can't be doing it for the money; it's only a measly 50 cents. I must believe what I am saying." The key part of Bem's explanation is that there is no need to assume people are driven by a desire to maintain their self-esteem or reduce dissonance when making such inferences. People are simply trying to come up with the most logical, reasonable explanation for their behavior.

Who was right—Bem or the dissonance theorists? After years of controversy, the answer is clear: Bem lost the battle about who could best explain dissonance findings, but won the war about whether self-perception processes occur in other areas. Bem's attempt to show that this kind of attitude change typically occurs in the absence of pain, discomfort, or other strong feelings proved to be erroneous. As we saw in Chapter 3, when people behave in ways contrary to their attitudes, they do become upset and aroused (i.e., they experience dissonance), and change their attitudes in order to relieve these unpleasant feelings (Croyle & Cooper, 1983; Fazio, Zanna, and Cooper, 1977; Pallak & Pittman, 1972; Zanna & Cooper, 1976). On the other hand, clearly Bem's theory does provide a good explanation of other findings that dissonance theory does not cover—namely, how people change their attitudes when they behave in ways that are inconsistent with their initial attitudes, but not so much so that people find their behavior objectionable or a threat to their self-esteem. Under these circumstances, no dissonance is aroused, and yet people still draw inferences about themselves from their behavior, as self-perception theory suggests.

For example, consider Fazio and colleagues' (1981) study where the experimenter asked people questions that elicited either extraverted or introverted answers. People did not give answers that were terribly discrepant or dissonant with their self-conceptions; in fact, they were drawing on their own past experiences to answer the questions. Because they were coming up with selective examples, however—say, ones that were all extraverted—they inferred that they were more extraverted than they had thought they were—just as Bem's theory predicts. In sum, Bem's self-perception theory explains a wide range of cases whereby people do not act in an objectionable or dissonance-arousing way, but still infer that their internal states match their behavior. We turn now to some fascinating examples of such self-perception processes.

## The Overjustification Effect

According to self-perception theory, when people realize their behavior is caused by an external factor, they do not assume it reflects their internal feelings. This is pretty logical; if you know that the only reason you are waiting on tables over the summer is that the pay is good, you will not assume you are doing it because it is your favorite pastime. In other words, after looking at your behavior and the situation, you will make an external attribution ("I'm doing it for the money") and not an internal attribution ("I love doing this so much I would do it for free"). The problem is that, when external causes for our behavior are conspicuous, we go overboard, **discounting** the extent to which internal factors played a role (Kelley, 1972; Nisbett & Valins, 1972). This process of discounting has important implications for a major area of life: our motivation to engage in activities and our subsequent interest in and enjoyment of those activities.

**discounting:** underestimating the effects of one cause of our behavior when another cause is conspicuous and salient

Let's say you love to play the guitar. You spend many hours happily practicing, simply enjoying the act of making music and the feeling that you are getting better. We would say that your interest in playing the guitar stems from **intrinsic motivation.** Your reasons for engaging in the activity have to do with you—the enjoyment and pleasure you feel when playing the guitar. In other words, playing the guitar is play, not work. According to Mihaly Csikszentmihalyi (1975, 1979), intrinsically motivated behavior creates an optimal experience called flow. When in a state of flow, the individual centers his or her attention on the task, blocks out other stimuli, and concentrates intently. The individual feels competent and is unconcerned about how well he or she is doing; feedback about performance is clear and unambiguous. Finally, the individual experiences a lack of self-awareness. Think about some recent activity of yours that you really enjoyed; you were probably experiencing this state of flow, as with our example of the guitar player.

**intrinsic motivation:** engaging in an activity because we enjoy it or find it interesting, not because of external rewards or pressures

Now let's say your guitar teacher gets the brilliant idea of rewarding you for learning new material and techniques. She figures that this will make you practice even harder. After all, rewards work, don't they? However, your teacher has now added a second reason for you to play the guitar: getting a reward. Your playing, hitherto stemming from intrinsic motivation, now stems from **extrinsic motivation** as well: If you do well, you'll receive a prize. Unfortunately, extrinsic rewards can undermine intrinsic motivation. Whereas before you played the guitar because you loved it, now you're playing it so you'll get the reward. What was once play is now work. The sad outcome is that replacing intrinsic motivation with extrinsic motivation (through the use of rewards) makes people lose interest in the activity they

**extrinsic motivation:** engaging in an activity because of external rewards or pressures, not because we enjoy the task or find it interesting

**the overjustification effect:** the case whereby people view their behavior as caused by compelling extrinsic reasons, making them underestimate the extent to which their behavior was caused by intrinsic reasons

initially enjoyed. This result is called **the overjustification effect,** where people overjustify their behavior by focusing on its external causes (e.g., getting a reward) and underestimate their intrinsic interest in the behavior (Boggiano, Barret, Weiher, McClelland, and Lusk, 1987; Deci & Ryan, 1985; Harackiewicz, 1979, 1989; Lepper & Greene, 1978; Pittman & Heller, 1987; Ross, 1976).

The overjustification effect applies not just to our hobbies and recreational interests, but to our work as well. Consider basketball great Bill Russell's description of how becoming a professional affected his love for the game:

> I remember that the game lost some of its magical qualities for me once I thought seriously about playing for a living. This first happened in 1955, in my junior year, after USF [the University of San Francisco] won the NCAA national championship. As a result, all through my senior year at USF I played with the idea of turning professional, and things began to change. Whenever I walked on the court I began to calculate how this particular game might affect my future. Thoughts of money and prestige crept into my head. Over the years the professional game would turn more and more into a business. (Russell & Branch, 1979, p. 98)

The overjustification effect has been found in dozens of laboratory and field experiments, with several kinds of rewards, activities, and age-groups. For example, in a study by David Greene, Betty Sternberg, and Mark Lepper (1976), fourth- and fifth-grade teachers at an elementary school introduced four new math games to their students. During a thirteen-day baseline period, the researchers simply noted how long each child played with each math game. For the next several days, a reward program was introduced, whereby the children could earn credits toward certificates and trophies, to be given out at an "Awards Assembly," by playing with the math games. The more time they spent playing with the games, the more credits they would earn. Figure 6.4 shows the data thus far. The children had some intrinsic interest in the math games initially, playing with them for several minutes during the baseline period. During the reward program, the amount of time spent on the games increased, showing that the rewards were an effective motivator.

However, the most interesting question concerns the effects of these rewards on the children's *intrinsic interest* in the games. What did the children learn about themselves by virtue of participating in the awards program? According to the overjustification hypothesis, the children should have concluded that they were playing with the math games only to earn prizes, thereby undermining any intrinsic interest they had at the outset; as a result, when the rewards were taken away, the children should have spent significantly less time with the games than they had during the baseline period (e.g., "I can't earn prizes playing with these games anymore—why play with them at all?"). This is exactly what happened, as you can see on the right-hand side of Figure 6.4. After the reward program ended, the children spent significantly less time with the math games than they had initially, before the rewards were introduced. (Greene et al. determined, by comparing these results to those of a control condition, that it was the reward that made people like the games less, and not the fact that everyone became bored with the games as time went by.)

"I remember that the game lost some of its magical qualities for me once I thought seriously about playing for a living."—Basketball great Bill Russell (Russell & Branch, 1979, p. 98)

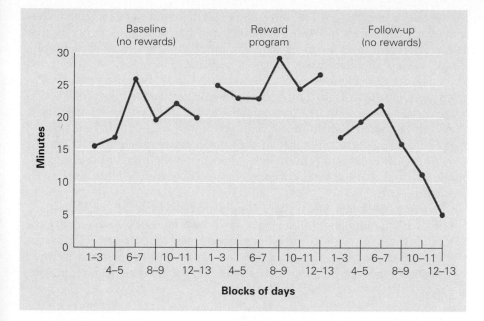

**FIGURE 6.4  The overjustification effect.** DURING the initial baseline phase, the researchers measured how much time elementary school children played with math games. During the reward program, they rewarded the children with prizes for playing the games. When the rewards were taken away (during the follow-up), the children played with the games even less than they had during the baseline phase, indicating that the rewards had lowered their intrinsic interest in the games. (Adapted from Greene, Sternberg, and Lepper, 1976)

The results of overjustification studies are distressing, given the wide use of rewards and incentives by parents and educators. As we write this, one of us has a son in the second grade. His school, in conjunction with a restaurant chain, rewards kids for reading. For every twenty-two books they read, they get a certificate for a free pizza—a great motivator for most kids. The danger of such a program is that the kids will begin to think that they are reading to earn pizzas, not because reading is an enjoyable thing to do in its own right. Rewards are a powerful motivator, and our society dispenses them freely. But we tend not to realize that our well-intentioned efforts to reward children might actually reduce their enjoyment of these activities, by encouraging them to think they are doing it for the money (or the pizzas).

What can we do to protect intrinsic motivation from the slings and arrows of our society's reward system? Fortunately, there is room for some optimism, as recent research has identified some conditions under which overjustification effects can be avoided. First, rewards will undermine interest only if interest was high initially (Calder & Staw, 1975). If you think a task is excruciatingly boring, rewards obviously can't reduce your interest any further. Similarly, if a child has no interest whatsoever in reading, then getting him or her to read by offering free pizzas is not a bad idea, because there is no initial interest to undermine. The danger arises when a child already likes to read, because then offering free pizzas is likely to convince the child that he or she is reading to earn pizzas, not because reading is interesting in its own right.

Second, it may be possible to teach people to avoid the damaging effects of rewards. Research by Beth Hennessey and her colleagues suggests that direct intervention or training can immunize children (and presumably, adults) against the deleterious effects of rewards (Hennessey, Amabile, and Martinage, 1989; Hennessey & Zbikowski, 1993). Because rewards can never be eliminated from our society, Hennessey and Zbikowski (1993) focused on how to help children operate within the system—that is, how to maintain their intrinsic motivation while rewards dangled all around them. The researchers hypothesized that direct training might work, in the form of explicitly teaching children to (a) focus on their intrinsic reasons for doing tasks and (b) distance themselves in their minds from externally imposed rewards.

Fourth-graders in a Massachusetts public school were randomly assigned to one of two conditions. In one, they saw videotapes of an eleven-year-old boy and girl talking with an interviewer about their schoolwork. This immunization video presented the fourth-graders with ways to maintain intrinsic motivation in the face of rewards. For example, the child-actor gave answers like this:

> Well, I like social studies the best. I like learning about how other people live in different parts of the world. . . . I like doing projects because you can learn a lot about something on your own. I work hard on my projects, and when I come up with good ideas, I feel good. . . . I like to get good grades, and when I bring home a good report card, my parents always give me money. But that's not what's really important. I like to learn a lot. . . .[So] I work hard because I enjoy it. (Hennessey et al., 1989, pp. 216-217)

The other group of children also watched a videotape, but it had nothing to do with intrinsic motivation, rewards, or immunization.

The day after watching the videotapes, the children met with another experimenter, ostensibly as part of a different study. They were asked to make up a story to accompany a series of pictures. Half of the children were offered a reward: They could paint a T-shirt and take it home (a fun task if you're eleven years old) only if they told the story to the experimenter first. The other half were simply told that T-shirt painting was the second in a series of things to do. In other words, the T-shirt had no bearing on the storytelling task; it was simply what would come next.

Hennessey and Zbikowski (1991) hypothesized that the use of the reward would undermine children's creativity on the storytelling task. The reward, looming before them, would lessen their intrinsic motivation for what is typically an enjoyable task, and they would produce stories that were less creative than those produced by nonrewarded children (Amabile, Hennessey, and Grossman, 1986). But Hennessey & Zbikowski (1991) also hypothesized that the intrinsic motivation training videotape would immunize children against the deleterious effects of reward. Even though they knew they'd get a reward for telling the story, the information they'd learned from the immunization video should keep them focused on their intrinsic interest in the task (and not on the reward), and they should produce creative stories. The children's stories were judged on creativity by three grade-school teachers who did not know them or what videos they had seen.

As you can see in Figure 6.5, children who had received intrinsic motivation training did produce more creative stories, both when they received a

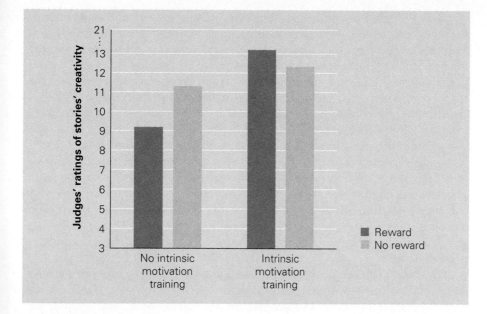

**FIGURE 6.5 Avoiding the overjustification effect**. As seen on the left-hand side of the graph, children who were rewarded told stories that were less creative, demonstrating the standard overjustification effect. As seen on the right-hand side of the graph, children who were immunized—by watching a videotape that stressed the importance of intrinsic motivation—did not demonstrate the overjustification effect. That is, when they received a reward, they still wrote creative stories. (Adapted from Hennessy & Zbikowski, 1991)

reward and when they did not, than the children who were not immunized did. In fact, the combination of a reward and intrinsic motivation training produced the most creative stories. This research suggests an encouraging solution to the dilemma posed by our society's use of rewards: Your intrinsic interest in an activity, as well as your creativity when engaged in that activity, can be maintained, and may even be increased, by the knowledge that you will receive a reward for your performance—if you focus on your intrinsic interest in the task and block out the existence of the reward. So the next time you feel that you are losing interest in a task you once enjoyed, or are performing less well than you used to, try to ignore the reward you are supposed to be working toward and instead remind yourself of how much you enjoy doing the task for its own sake.

## The Two-Factor Theory of Emotion

We have just seen that people often use observations of their behavior to determine what they think and what kind of person they are. You may have wondered whether the same is true of other kinds of views of yourself. For example, what about your emotions, such as how happy, angry, or afraid you feel at any given time—how do you know which emotion you are experiencing? Think about a time you felt angry—how did you know you felt that way? This question probably sounds pretty silly; it seems like we just know how we feel, without having to think about it or, as self-perception theory suggests, observing our behavior to see how we feel.

"[When experiencing symptoms of arousal] . . . you keep trying to find an explanation for them, an emotion to account for them, a feeling of joy or pain. . . ." "Yes, yes," Joachim said, sighing. "It is the same thing, I suppose, as when you have a fever—there are pretty lively goings-on in the system then too; . . . it may easily be that one involuntarily tries to find an emotion which would explain, or even half-way explain the goings-on."

—Thomas Mann,
*The Magic Mountain*

**two-factor theory of emotion:** the idea that emotional experience is the result of a two-step self-perception process in which people first experience physiological arousal and then seek an appropriate explanation for it; if they attribute the arousal to an emotional source, they experience that emotion (e.g., if people attribute their arousal to someone pointing a gun at them, they experience fear)

Though it may seem like we simply know how we feel, the experience of emotion is not as uncomplicated as it appears. Stanley Schachter (1964) proposed a theory of emotion that says we infer what our emotions are in the same way that we infer what kind of person we are or how interested we are in math games: by observing our behavior and then explaining why we are behaving that way. The only difference is in the kind of behavior we observe. Just like the characters in Thomas Mann's novel (quoted in the margin), Schachter says we observe our internal behaviors—namely, how physiologically aroused we feel. If we feel aroused, we then try to figure out what is causing this arousal. For example, let's say your heart is pounding, and your body feels tense. Is it because you just saw your professor—the one from whom you got a paper extension because supposedly you had to go to your grandmother's funeral that day—or is it because you just saw the person standing next to the professor—the one on whom you have the most amazing crush in the universe? Are you feeling unholy fear or stomach-churning love?

Schachter's theory is called the **two-factor theory of emotion,** because understanding our emotional states requires two factors, or steps: First, we must experience physiological arousal and be aware of it, and second, we must seek an appropriate explanation or label for it. Because our physical states are difficult to label on their own, we use information in the situation to help us make an attribution about why we feel aroused. Figure 6.6 illustrates the two-factor theory of emotion.

Stanley Schachter and Jerome Singer (1962) conducted an experiment to test this provocative theory. Imagine you were a participant; here's how the study was set up: When you arrive, the experimenter tells you he is studying the effects of a vitamin compound called Suproxin on people's vision. After a physician injects you with a small amount of Suproxin, the experimenter asks you to wait while the drug takes effect. He introduces you to another participant, who, he says, has also been given some Suproxin. The experimenter gives each of you a questionnaire to fill out, saying he will return in a little while to give you the vision tests. You look at the questionnaire, and notice that it contains some highly personal and insulting questions. For example, one question asks, "With how many men (other than your father) has your mother had extramarital relationships?" (Schachter & Singer, 1962, p. 385). The other participant comments on how offensive the questions are. He becomes angrier and angrier, finally tearing up his questionnaire in a rage, throwing it on the floor, and stomping out of the room. How do you think you would feel? Would you feel angry as well?

As you have no doubt gathered, the real purpose of this experiment was not to test people's vision. The researchers set up a situation where the two crucial variables—arousal and an emotional explanation for that arousal—would be present or absent, and then observed which, if any, emotions people experienced. The participants did not really receive an injection of a vitamin compound. Instead, the arousal variable was manipulated in the following way: Some participants received epinephrine, a drug that causes arousal (body temperature and heart and breathing rates increase), and the other half received a placebo that had no physiological effects at all.

Imagine how you would have felt had you received the epinephrine: As you read the invasive, insulting questionnaire, you begin to feel aroused. (Remember, the experimenter didn't tell you the drug was epinephrine, so

**FIGURE 6.6** The two-factor theory of emotion: How physiological arousal and observations of environmental cues result in emotional states.

you don't realize that it's the drug that's making you aroused.) The other participant (who was actually an accomplice of the experimenter) reacts with rage. You are likely to infer that you are feeling flushed and aroused because you too are angry. You have met the conditions that Schachter (1964) argues are necessary to experience an emotion—you are aroused, and you have sought out and found a reasonable explanation for your arousal in the situation that surrounds you. Ergo, you become furious. This is indeed what happened—participants who had been given epinephrine reacted much more angrily than participants who had been given the placebo did.

A fascinating implication of Schachter's theory is that people's emotions are somewhat arbitrary, depending on what the most plausible explanation for their arousal happens to be. Schachter and Singer (1962) demonstrated this idea in two ways. First, they showed that they could prevent people from becoming angry by providing a nonemotional explanation for why they felt aroused. The researchers did this by informing some of the people who received epinephrine that the drug would increase their heart rate, make their face feel warm and flushed, and cause their hands to shake slightly. When people actually began to feel this way, they inferred that it was not because they were angry, but because the drug was taking effect. As a result, these participants did not react angrily to the questionnaire.

Even more impressively, Schachter and Singer showed that they could make subjects experience a very different emotion by changing the most plausible explanation for their arousal. In other conditions, participants did not receive the insulting questionnaire, and the other subject did not respond angrily. Instead, the other subject acted in a joyful, devil-may-care fashion, playing basketball with rolled-up pieces of paper, making paper airplanes, and playing with a Hula-Hoop he found in the corner. How did the real participants respond? If they had received epinephrine but had not been told of its effects, they inferred that they must be feeling happy and euphoric as well, and often joined the accomplice's impromptu games.

The Schachter and Singer (1962) experiment has become one of the most famous studies in social psychology, because it shows that emotions can be the result of a self-perception process whereby people look about them for the most plausible explanation for their arousal. Sometimes the most plausible explanation is not the right explanation, so people end up experiencing a mistaken emotion. The people who became angry or euphoric in the Schachter and Singer (1962) study did so because they felt aroused, and thought that this arousal was due to the obnoxious questionnaire or to the infectious, happy-go-lucky behavior of the accomplice. The real cause of their arousal, the epinephrine, was hidden from them; all they had to go on were situational cues to explain their behavior.

Subsequent research has expanded and refined the two-factor theory of emotion. For example, if people experience strong levels of arousal, they tend to react negatively, because such levels represent an unpleasant bodily state. Thus, situational cues for happiness may not influence them, for they simply feel too negative to accept the happy label as appropriate (Marshall & Zimbardo, 1979; Maslach, 1979). In addition, the situational cue or label must be encountered before the person experiences arousal (Schachter & Singer, 1979). Feeling your stomach go all aflutter will lead you to think it's because you're attracted to the handsome stranger standing next to you only if the sequence is "first see stranger, then feel stomach fluttering."

## Misattribution of Arousal

To what extent do the results found by Schachter and Singer (1962) generalize to everyday life? Do people form mistaken emotions in the same way as participants in that study? Maybe not, because people are not often misinformed about the effects of a drug that arouses them. In everyday life, one might argue, people usually know why they are aroused. If a mugger points a gun at us and says, "Stick 'em up!" we feel aroused, and correctly label this arousal as fear. If our heart is thumping while we walk on a deserted moonlit beach with the man or woman of our dreams, we correctly label this arousal as love or sexual attraction.

Many everyday situations, however, present more than one plausible cause for our arousal, and it is difficult to identify how much of the arousal is due to one source versus another. Imagine that you go to see a scary movie with an extremely attractive date. As you are sitting there, you notice that your heart is thumping and you are a little short of breath. Is this because

> I could feel all the excitement of losing the big fish going through the transformer and coming out as anger at my brother-in-law.
>
> —Norman Maclean,
> *A River Runs Through It*

you are wildly attracted to your date, or because the movie is terrifying you? It is unlikely that you could say, "Fifty-seven percent of my arousal is due to attraction to my date, 32 percent is due to the scary movie, and 11 percent is due to indigestion from all the popcorn I ate." Because of this difficulty in pinpointing the precise causes of our arousal, we sometimes form mistaken emotions. You might think that most of your arousal is a sign of attraction for your date, when in fact a lot of it is due to the movie (or maybe even due to indigestion from the popcorn).

For example, consider this anecdote that Robin Akert relates from graduate school:

> A fellow graduate student and good friend, Ann, comes into the office one afternoon and relates her experiences of the day to the rest of us. That morning, in rush-hour traffic, she'd driven off to an important professional appointment. The traffic was horrible, and because of it, she was running late. Then, to her dismay, she got a flat tire. There she was, all dressed up, silk blouse, suit, high heels—the whole nine yards—with a disabled car on the New Jersey Turnpike. Life looked pretty grim. Then, amazingly, a truck pulled over and an incredibly nice man got out and changed her tire for her. After profuse thanks, she sped off to her appointment and was only a little late.

> The fascinating part of Ann's story was her description of her helper and her perception of him. Obviously, he was extraordinarily kind in helping her—a true masked stranger like the Lone Ranger—but she also found him very attractive and interesting. In fact, as she related the story, she laughed at herself in the sense of letting us know that she sort of, you know, felt that little spark of attraction for him. Well, you can't relate a story like this to a group of friends-cum-social-psychology-graduate-students without having us interpret your behavior! Which, of course, we did. Amid much whooping and hollering, we told our friend that she was a victim of misattribution of arousal. Granted, the man had been very nice and might very well have been attractive, but if she had just been driving to the office on a normal day, would she have had the same reaction to him? We suggested that the important appointment that morning had made her feel tense and aroused, the rush-hour traffic only exacerbated these emotions, and the flat tire probably put her over the top. Enter an attractive male—and gee, she's got an awful lot of unspecified arousal floating around, and gee, here's an aspect of the situation that could explain it. Our friend agreed with our interpretation, and we all had a good laugh over how the social psychology we were studying explained our lives.

In recent years, many studies have demonstrated the occurrence of such **misattribution of arousal,** whereby people make mistaken inferences about what is causing them to feel the way they do (Ross & Olson, 1981; Storms & McCaul, 1976; Schachter, 1977; Storms & Nisbett, 1970; Valins, 1966; Zillmann, 1978). Consider, for example, an intriguing field experiment by Donald Dutton and Arthur Aron (1974). Imagine you were one of the participants, who were all men. You are visiting a park in British Columbia. An attractive young woman approaches you and asks if you could fill out a questionnaire for her, as part of a psychology project on the effects of scenic attractions on people's creativity. You decide to help her out. After you complete the

**misattribution of arousal:** attributing one's arousal to the wrong source, resulting in a mistaken or exaggerated emotion

Misattribution. When people are aroused for one reason, such as occurs when they cross a scary bridge, they often attribute this arousal to the wrong source—such as attraction to the person they are with.

questionnaire, the woman thanks you, and says that she would be happy to explain her study in more detail when she has more time. She tears off a corner of the questionnaire, writes down her name and phone number, and tells you to give her a call if you want to talk with her some more. How attracted do you think you would be to this woman? Would you telephone her and ask for a date?

This is a hard question to answer. Undoubtedly, it depends on whether you are dating someone else, how busy you are, and so on. It might also depend, however, on how you interpret any bodily symptoms you are experiencing. If you are aroused for some extraneous reason, you might mistakenly think that some of the arousal was the result of attraction to the young woman. To test this idea, Dutton and Aron (1974) had the woman (a confederate) approach males in the park under two very different circumstances. Again, imagine you were a participant. As you are walking in the park, you come to the edge of a deep canyon. Spanning the canyon is a narrow, 450-foot-long suspension bridge, made of wooden planks attached to wire cables. You decide to walk across it. As you do, you have to stoop to hold onto the handrails, which are very low. When you get a little way across, the wind picks up and causes the bridge to wobble and sway from side to side. You feel like you are about to tumble over the edge, and hold on for dear life. Then you make the mistake of looking down. You see nothing but a sheer 200-foot drop to a rocky raging river. You become more than a little aroused—your heart is thumping, you breathe rapidly, and you begin to perspire. At this point, the attractive woman asks you to fill out her questionnaire. How attracted do you feel toward her?

Think about this for a moment, and now imagine that the woman approaches you under different circumstances. You make it across the bridge, and have been resting awhile on a bench in the park. You have had a chance to calm down—your heart is no longer pounding against your chest, and your breathing rate has returned to normal. You are peaceably admiring the scenery when the woman asks you to fill out her questionnaire. How attracted do you feel toward her now? The prediction from Schachter's two-factor theory is clear: If you were on the bridge, you would be considerably aroused, and should mistakenly think that some of this arousal is the result of attraction to the beautiful woman. This is exactly what happened in the actual experiment. A large proportion of the men approached on the bridge telephoned the woman later to ask her for a date, whereas relatively few of the men approached on the bench telephoned the woman (see Figure 6.7). The moral is this: If you encounter an attractive man or woman and your heart is going thump-thump, think carefully about why you are aroused—you might fall in love for the wrong reasons.

To summarize, in this section we have seen that one way people learn about themselves is by observing their own behavior and trying to explain it. Often our behavior is a reliable guide to our inner feelings. If we aren't sure how much we like coffee ice cream, the fact that we are always eating it is a pretty good indication that we do. Sometimes, however, we make mistakes about the reasons for our behavior, leading to mistaken inferences about ourselves. This is likely to occur under three conditions: (a) when external influences on our behavior are subtle, so that we mistakenly think our behavior reflects our attitudes or personality (as in the study where people assumed they were extraverted after answering the experimenter's questions in an extraverted fashion); (b) when external influences on our behavior are so conspicuous that we overestimate how much they are influencing our behavior (as in the overjustification effect, wherein people assume they are performing a task only to obtain a reward); and (c) when the causes of our

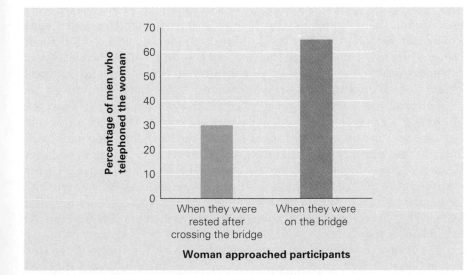

**FIGURE 6.7 Misattribution of arousal.** When a woman approached men on a scary bridge and asked them to fill out a questionnaire, a high percentage of them were attracted to her, and called her for a date. When the same woman approached men after they had crossed the bridge and were rested, relatively few called her for a date. (Adapted from Dutton & Aron, 1974)

arousal are unclear, so that we form mistaken emotions (as in the study examining attraction on the bridge). Research on these phenomena falls under the general heading of attributional biases, or errors in reasoning. In other words, we're doing the best we can as attributional animals, but as we saw in Chapter 5, we're often a bit off the mark in figuring out the exact causes of our feelings and actions.

We should not exaggerate, however, the extent to which observations of our behavior provide us with misleading or incomplete information about ourselves. Our own behavior is frequently a useful guide to our thoughts and feelings. If we are constantly eating brussels sprouts, we probably do like them! The same goes for introspection, as reviewed earlier: It is imperfect, and can mislead us, but it is not an ability we would want to get rid of. Using both introspection and observations of our own behavior, we can acquire a great deal of information about ourselves.

What do we do with all of this information once we have it? Are our minds a mumbo-jumbo collection of thoughts and feelings about ourselves? Not surprisingly, we organize our self-knowledge in much the same way that we organize our knowledge about the external world: into schemas.

## Knowing Ourselves Through Self-Schemas

In Chapter 4, we noted that people organize information about the social world into *schemas*—that is, knowledge structures about a person, topic, or object. We do not have a random, helter-skelter collection of thoughts about the world; we organize our knowledge into schemas, which help us understand and interpret new experiences. It should come as no surprise that we form **self-schemas** as well: organized knowledge structures about ourselves, based on our past experiences, that help us understand, explain, and predict our own behavior (Markus, 1977; Markus & Sentis, 1982; Markus & Zajonc, 1985). Thus, we do not have a random, helter-skelter collection of thoughts about ourselves either: we organize our self-views into coherent schemas, which influence how we interpret new things that happen to us.

To see how self-schemas operate, consider this example. Let's say you are playing a game of Trivial Pursuit with your friends. You get a question that asks who the first American was to orbit the earth, and you say, "Jack Glenn." Your opponent says that the correct answer is John Glenn, and thus you are wrong. "Come on," you say, "don't be so technical. Jack Glenn, John Glenn—it's all the same." The argument becomes heated and unpleasant, until finally you both agree that you will take your turn over again. What have you learned about yourself from this incident? How do you feel about it?

The answer depends on the nature of your self-schemas. Suppose you are the kind of person who views yourself as an independent soul who sticks up for your rights. If so, we would say that independence is an important part of your self-schema, and would predict that the importance of the Trivial Pursuit argument to you is not whether you won or lost the point, but whether you succeeded in asserting yourself when your friend challenged your answer. Other people may not view independence as a significant part

**self-schemas:** organized knowledge structures about ourselves, based on our past experiences, that help us understand, explain, and predict our own behavior

The sense of our own personal identity . . . is exactly like any of our other perceptions of sameness among phenomena.

—William James, 1910

of their personalities, but instead view themselves as competitive. To such people, the importance of the incident would be not whether they really were right or wrong, but whether they won the point. Still others may not have self-schemas related to independence or competitiveness, and thus would attach no importance to the incident: They simply got an answer wrong—that's all. Hence, the same event can mean different things to different people, depending on the nature of their self-schemas.

As children develop, their shallow, concrete self-concept progresses to a unique, complex one, based on the formation of increasingly sophisticated self-schemas. At this time, it is not entirely clear how this evolution occurs, or why certain traits and characteristics become central aspects in some people's self-schemas but not in others' (Markus, 1980). One line of research, conducted by William McGuire and his colleagues, suggests that people develop self-schemas for those aspects of self which make them distinct from other people (McGuire & McGuire, 1981; McGuire, McGuire, Child, and Fujioka, 1978; McGuire & Padawer-Singer, 1976). Thus, red-haired children are more likely to mention their hair color when asked to describe themselves, since this physical trait sets them apart from most other people. Similarly, an African American child in a predominantly white school is more likely to mention his or her ethnicity than the white children are, because this aspect of the individual is distinct in this setting.

## Autobiographical Memory

A great deal of our self-knowledge consists of our memories of our past attitudes, feelings, and behaviors. Psychologists use the term **autobiographical memory** to refer to our memories about ourselves. Whereas these memories define us, it is also the case that we define our memories. It is certainly not possible to remember everything that has happened in our lives, or to remember it perfectly. Distortions, fabrications, and outright forgetting occur over time; as Anthony Greenwald (1980) says, if historians revised and distorted history to the same extent that we do with our own lives, they'd lose their jobs! Such distortion and revision of autobiographical memory are often not accidental—we rewrite our history. How? Just as self-schemas help us organize new information about ourselves, they also help us organize memories about our past actions. If being independent is part of your self-schema but being competitive is not, you will probably remember more times when you acted independently than competitively (Akert, 1993; Markus, 1977).

A key part of our schemas about ourselves is our theory about the stability of our thoughts and feelings. Michael Ross and his colleagues (Conway & Ross, 1984; Ross, 1989; Ross & McFarland, 1988) have shown that people have implicit theories about how their thoughts and feelings change, and that these theories can influence our autobiographical memories in intriguing ways. First, when trying to remember something we once thought or did, we access from memory our current attitude or behavior. For example, if we are trying to remember how we felt about the death penalty a year ago, we first consider how we feel today. Second, we consider whether our present state is similar to or different from our past one, using our theories about whether this attitude is the type that is usually stable over time or is the type that frequently changes.

**autobiographical memory:** memories about one's own past thoughts, feelings, and behaviors

Herein lies a difficulty in any autobiographical sketch.... It is a story of oneself in the past, read in light of one's present self. There is much supplementary inference—often erroneous inference—wherein "must have been" masquerades as "was so."
—Lloyd Morgan

According to Ross (1989), people have many such theories about how stable attitudes and behaviors are over time. Some feelings, like our moods or how happy we are in a new romantic relationship, are expected to fluctuate over time. Other responses, like our attitudes about social issues (e.g., the death penalty), are expected to be relatively stable; consequently, people will assume that the way they feel now is how they felt in the past. An important implication of this view is that the accuracy of our memories depends on the accuracy of our theories about how we change. Interestingly, these theories are not always correct, leading to distortions in memory. For example, Ross has found that people's attitudes toward social issues sometimes do change, but because people's theories are that these attitudes remain stable, people underestimate the amount of change that occurs. "I've always been against the death penalty," we might think, underestimating the extent to which our attitude has evolved over the years.

People do not, of course, believe that all of their attitudes and behaviors are carved in granite. In fact, we have faith that some of our habits change over time, such as how much we study for tests, or how healthy our diets are. Ross (1989) has also shown, however, that some of these theories about changes in our behaviors are wrong as well, causing us to exaggerate the amount of change that has occurred. Consider this question: Why do many people swear by such self-improvement programs as weight-loss clinics and gimmicky programs to stop smoking, when the objective evidence suggests that most of these programs are ineffective? Conway and Ross (1984) demonstrated that one explanation is the way in which people's memories work. After participating in such programs, people observe their current standing on the relevant variable (e.g., how much they are smoking). Given their theory that the program was effective, they overestimate the extent to which they were engaging in the undesired behavior before the program (e.g., how much they were smoking before participating), thereby exaggerating how much they were helped by participating.

In sum, we learn about ourselves through introspection and observations of our behavior, and then organize this information into self-schemas. We also interpret our past using schemas and theories about how our attitudes and behaviors are likely to change. As important as these sources of self-knowledge are, though, there is still something missing. These views portray people as solitary seekers of self-knowledge, with no consultation with or comparison to other people. We turn now to two other ways in which we gain self-knowledge; both are distinctly and emphatically social, in the sense that we rely on other people to learn about who we are.

## Knowing Ourselves Through Social Interaction

We learn a great deal about ourselves from other people. This can certainly occur on a subtle level ("Everybody seems to like me; I must be a likable person"), but it occurs on an explicit level too. People tell you what they think you're like. These messages occur in our earliest childhood and continue through our lifespan; family, friends, and sometimes even strangers give you an appraisal of yourself. It's as if they've held up a mirror and reflected their image of you back at you to see. Sometimes this image is reassuring, reinforcing your own beliefs about yourself. Sometimes this image is a surprise, maybe even a jarring or unpleasant one. Have you ever had a friend make a comment about you that came as a surprise ("I'm like that?") and was all the more puzzling because your friend acted like it was obvious? Perhaps your friend said, "You get really angry at someone and talk like you're going to do something about it, but you never confront the person," whereupon you thought, "I do? Am I like that? Do I do that, really?" Maybe you said meekly, "What do you mean?" And after your friend explained at length, you perhaps admitted to yourself that there was truth in what she said—that here you'd always thought you had a big bark and a big bite, whereas your friends viewed you as a real softie at heart.

## The "Looking-Glass Self"

Charles Horton Cooley (1902) and George Herbert Mead (1934), two early and influential theorists in social psychology, discussed at length the crucial role other people play in our construction of a self-concept. Cooley (1902) used the term **the looking-glass self** to stress the extent to which our definition of self depends on the feedback and evaluations we receive from others. Mead (1934) elaborated on this idea, stating that the ability to take the perspective of other people is crucial to developing a sense of self. Taking the perspective of others means you understand that they may see the world differently from how you do and that they have a perspective on you that may be different from your own. The looking-glass self is constructed as we adopt, over time, other people's views of us (Mead, 1934).

**the looking-glass self:** seeing ourselves through the eyes of other people, and incorporating their views into our self-concept

What would it be like to have no access to others' perspectives? Oddly, if we cannot see ourselves through the eyes of other people, our own image will be a blur, because we have no social looking glass in which to view ourselves. Remember the mirror and red-dye test we discussed earlier, used to determine if animals and young children have a self-concept? You'll recall that children nine to twelve months of age do not react to their red nose when they see it in a mirror, whereas two-year-olds do. The younger children do not understand that this image is themselves. Why? One reason is that children at one year of age have far less experience with social interaction than two-year-olds do.

Experiments conducted with great apes have indicated that social contact is indeed crucial to the development of a self-concept. For example, Gordon Gallup (1977) compared the behavior of chimpanzees raised in normal, family groupings with that of chimps who were raised alone, in complete social isolation. Both types of chimps were painted with the red dye, as described earlier, and placed alone in a room without a mirror. The frequency with which they touched their marked but unseen browridge and ear was noted; these are the pretest data shown in Figure 6.8. Then a mirror was brought into the room. Now the chimps could see themselves and their new "cosmetics." The socially experienced chimps showed the typical response of great apes (and humans)—they immediately used their mirrored image to explore the red areas of their heads. However, the socially isolated chimps did not react to their reflections at all—they did not act as if the chimp in the mirror was themselves (see Figure 6.8). In primates as well as humans, social interaction is crucial for developing a sense of self.

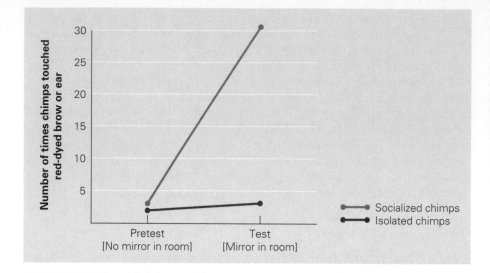

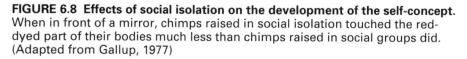

---

**FIGURE 6.8 Effects of social isolation on the development of the self-concept.** When in front of a mirror, chimps raised in social isolation touched the red-dyed part of their bodies much less than chimps raised in social groups did. (Adapted from Gallup, 1977)

## Social Comparison Theory

We also come to know ourselves by comparison to other people (Brown, 1990; Kruglanski & Mayseless, 1990; Pyszczynski, Greenberg, & LaPrelle, 1985; Wood, 1989). If you are trying to determine your feelings, traits, and abilities, other people and their feelings, traits, and abilities are a valuable source of information. Suppose, for example, we gave you a test that measured your social sensitivity, or how aware you are of other people's problems. The test involves reading excerpts from autobiographies and guessing the nature of the authors' personal problems, if any. After you've taken the test, we tell you that you achieved a score of 35. What have you learned about yourself? Not much, because you don't know what a score of 35 means. Is it a good score or a bad score? Suppose we told you that the test is scored on a scale from 0 to 50. Now what have you learned? A little more than you knew before, perhaps, because you know that although you did not achieve a perfect score, you did score above the middle of the scale. This is still pretty uninformative, however, without knowing how other people did on the test. If we told you that everyone else in your class scored between 0 and 20, you would deduce that you are a very sensitive person, at least as measured by this test. And you would feel pretty good about it—certainly more so than if we told you that everyone else scored between 45 and 50.

This example illustrates Leon Festinger's (1954) **social comparison theory.** The theory begins with the supposition that people have a need to evaluate their opinions and abilities, to figure out their strengths and weaknesses, so as to have an accurate view of themselves. Festinger (1954) stated that, when possible, people will rely on objective criteria, such as the reading on their stopwatch after they've run a mile. However, this kind of objective feedback is rather hard to come by in life. There are all sorts of interesting aspects of yourself that you would probably like to know more about, ones

**social comparison theory:** the idea that we learn about our own abilities and attitudes by comparing ourselves to other people for which objective measurements do not exist. Are you physically attractive? How good a cello player are you? Are you a particularly empathic person? Are you calm and steady in the face of a crisis? Are you conservative in matters of private or political life? How much do you lie? Just how good at math are you? To answer such questions, you need to compare yourself to other people on the relevant dimension—how do you stack up?

Social comparison theory revolves around two important questions (Goethals, 1986; Latané, 1966): (a) *When* do you engage in social comparison, and (b) *with whom* do you choose to compare yourself? As Festinger (1954) indicated, you socially compare when there is no objective standard for you to measure yourself against, and when you experience some uncertainty about yourself in a particular area (Suls & Fletcher, 1983; Suls & Miller, 1977).

Thus, when you're not sure how well you're doing or what exactly you're feeling, you'll observe other people and compare yourself to them. For example, Jerry Suls and Barbara Fletcher (1983) examined the social comparison process in scientists, using the archival method of research. It is customary when preparing to publish a research article to ask esteemed colleagues for comments and feedback on the manuscript. When it is published, these readers are thanked in an acknowledgments section. Suls and Fletcher (1983) hypothesized that in sciences with more objective standards, scientists do not have as great a need to engage in social comparison as those fields with less objective standards. The natural sciences were defined as having more objective standards—in the sense of the research designs used and the highly defined areas of study—than the social sciences. Accordingly, the researchers predicted that natural scientists would thank fewer people in their paper, indicating that they had asked fewer people for feedback about their work prior to submitting it for publication. Content-analyzing several hundred articles, Suls and Fletcher (1983) found that physicists and chemists thanked, on average, 0.5 people per article, psychologists thanked 1.2 people, and sociologists thanked 2.0 people.

> Envy, like fire, soars upward.
> —Livy (59 B.C.–A.D.17)

The second question is, With whom should you compare yourself? You have quite a choice here: If you're wondering about your artistic ability, should you compare yourself to Picasso, your little sister, or your fellow students in your drawing class? Not surprisingly, the answer is that people most frequently choose to compare themselves to others who are similar to them on the important attribute, or dimension (Goethals & Darley, 1977; Miller, 1982; Wheeler, Koestner, and Driver, 1982). Observing the ability of your classmates in drawing class will tell you what kind of artistic talent you might have. Comparing yourself to Picasso is aiming too high; you'll only become discouraged if, as a beginner, you compare yourself to one of the great artists of the twentieth century. While research has shown that people sometimes make **upward social comparisons** (i.e., to people more accomplished than they), they do this only to determine what excellence or the best really is. It is more important to them, in terms of self-knowledge, to compare themselves to someone who is similar (Thornton & Arrowood, 1966; Wheeler et al., 1982; Zanna, Goethals, & Hill, 1975). Likewise, comparing your artistic talent to that of your little sister is aiming too low; her fingerpainting and scribbles tell you little about your abilities.

**upward social comparisons:** comparing ourselves to people who are better than we are on a particular trait or ability, in order to determine the standard of excellence

However, Festinger (1954) noted that constructing an accurate image of ourselves is only one reason, albeit the principal one, that we engage in social comparison. When we are trying to assess our standing on a trait that is very

*"Of course you're going to be depressed if you keep comparing yourself with successful people."*

**downward social comparison:** comparing ourselves to people who are worse than we on a particular trait or ability, in order to feel better about ourselves

important to us, we also use social comparison in order to boost our egos. Is it very important to you to believe that you are a fabulous artist-in-the-making? Then compare yourself to your little sister—you have her beat! This use of **downward social comparison** is a self-protective, self-enhancing strategy (Pyszczynski et al., 1985; Taylor & Lobel, 1989; Willis, 1981). If you compare yourself to people who are less smart, talented, or kind than you are, you'll feel very good about yourself. Similarly, you can compare your health to that of people who are worse off than you, thereby bolstering your self-esteem. For example, Joanne Wood, Shelley Taylor, and Rosemary Lichtman (1985) found evidence of downward comparison in their interviews with cancer patients. The vast majority of patients spontaneously compared themselves to other cancer patients who were in worse shape than they were, presumably as a way of making them feel more optimistic about the course of their own disease. In sum, to whom we compare ourselves depends on the nature of our goals. When we want an accurate assessment of our abilities and opinions, we compare ourselves to people who are similar to us. When we want information about what we can strive toward, we make upward social comparisons. Finally, when our goal is self-enhancement, we compare ourselves to those who are less fortunate; such downward comparisons make us look better by comparison.

## Impression Management

Now that you've come to know yourself, what do you do with all that knowledge? Being a member of a highly social species, you present yourself to others. You have many aspects to your self-concept; you can be many selves. Thus, a basic aspect of your social existence is **self-presentation,** whereby you present who you are (or who you want people to believe you are) through your words, nonverbal behavior, and actions (DePaulo, 1992; Goffman, 1959; Schlenker, 1980; Tedeschi, 1981). However, self-presentation is not always a simple, straightforward process; there are times when you want people to form a particular impression of you. At these times, you engage in **impression management,** consciously or unconsciously orchestrating a carefully designed presentation of self that will create a certain impression, one that fits your goals or needs in a social interaction (Goffman, 1959; Schlenker, 1980).

## All the World's a Stage

The concepts of self-presentation and impression management were eloquently discussed by Erving Goffman (1955, 1959, 1967, 1971). His theory of social interaction was based on a dramaturgical model: the theater as a metaphor for social life. On the stage, the actors present certain aspects of self (or their roles) to each other; Goffman says that in everyday life, we do the same thing in our social interactions. Similarly, just as in the theater, real life is made up of backstage and frontstage areas. Frontstage is when you're on, when you are actively presenting a particular self to others so as to create or maintain a certain impression in their eyes. Thoroughly cleaning your room, apartment, or house before company arrives (and saying, "Oh, it's nothing," when they compliment you on how lovely it looks) is preparing for and being on frontstage. In contrast, backstage is when you are not actively managing or creating a particular impression. We become uncomfortable when people invade our backstage areas, for we are, by definition, unprepared. Witness how annoying it is when people you'd like to impress drop by to visit you unannounced and your place is a slovenly pigsty and you are looking your grungiest!

An amusing example of impression management is Stephen Potter's (1971) notion of one-upmanship, or the art of appearing to be much more than you are. For example, Potter (1971) described two self-presentational tactics for college students: One must give the impression of doing nothing but one's work, or one must give the impression of never doing any work at all. The first impression, which he calls "to Edinburgh" (after the University of Edinburgh, in Scotland), is created like this:

> J. Reid . . . specializes in striding into the reading-room . . . going straight to the shelves of a subject he is not necessarily studying (Wider Interests Ploy), taking a book out as if he knew where to look for it, running down a reference, and walking out again *quietly but plonkingly.*

> Over the faces of student watchers nervousness runs like a whisper; though in fact Reid has just picked up a book of quotations to verify a clue in a crossword puzzle. By an accumulation of such featherweight ploys as these . . . Reid was able to oppress his fellow students with a sense of hopelessness of any effort of theirs in the face of such competition. (p. 12)

The second strategy, which Potter (1971) calls "to Harvard," is meant to strike fear in the hearts of peers by never appearing to study and still receiving As.

**self-presentation:** the attempt to present who we are, or who we want people to believe we are, through our words, nonverbal behaviors, and actions

**impression management:** consciously or unconsciously orchestrating a carefully designed presentation of self that will create a certain impression, that fits our goals or needs in a social interaction

> Keep up appearances whatever you do.
> —Charles Dickens, 1843

> To succeed in the world, we do everything we can to appear successful.
> —La Rochefoucauld, 1678

Impression management in action: In the 1970s, David Duke was a leader in the Ku Klux Klan; in 1991, he ran for governor of Louisiana as a mainstream conservative Republican. A remarkable change occurred in Duke's presentation of self during this time. Besides undergoing facial cosmetic surgery to improve his appearance, he claimed during his campaign that he no longer supported Nazi ideology or the Ku Klux Klan.

J. FitzJames disappeared suddenly from college midway through January Reading Period, just about the time his friends began studying in earnest. Then, on the day of his first exam, he would return, strolling into the examination room five minutes late, dressed in a light Palm Beach suit and heavily tanned. Sitting down next to a friend, he would inspect his papers casually, and begin to write slowly.

Later it becomes known that FitzJames has received an A in the course. What is the explanation? FitzJames has been holing himself up in a miserable rented room in Boston surrounded by the total reading assignment including the optional books, and has been working like a dog for three weeks, stripped to the waist between two sun lamps. (p. 13)

Another, far more disturbing example of impression management is David Duke's manipulation of his image during his 1991 campaign for governor of Louisiana (see the photos on this page). Duke, an open white supremacist and anti-Semite for most of his adult life, who sold Nazi literature from his legislative office in 1989, was, in November 1991, running for governor as a mainstream conservative Republican (*"Duke"*, 1991, p. 1). A remarkable change had occurred in Duke's presentation of self. Besides having undergone facial cosmetic surgery to improve his appearance, he claimed during the campaign that he no longer supported Nazi ideology or the Ku Klux Klan, of which he was the leader (or Grand Wizard) in the 1970s. However, his campaign rhetoric was correctly perceived by the majority of Louisiana voters as the same racist message disguised in new clothes, and he was defeated by the Democratic candidate, Edwin Edwards.

Most of us, of course, do not go to quite these lengths to manage the impressions we convey. All of us, however, attempt to manage our impressions to some extent. Edward Jones and Thane Pittman (1982) have described several strategic self-presentational techniques that people use in everyday life. As we describe them, think about your own behavior and that of the people you know; see if you can recognize these strategies in action. First is **ingratiation,** where you flatter, praise, and generally make yourself likable to another, often higher-status person (Jones & Wortman, 1973). One can ingratiate through compliments, by agreeing with another's ideas, by commiserating and offering sympathy, and so on. If your professor's three-year-old spits on you and kicks you in the shin, and you say, "Oh, what an adorable child!" you are probably ingratiating. Ingratiation is a powerful technique, since we all enjoy having someone be nice to us—which is what the ingratiator is good at. However, such a ploy can backfire if the recipient of your ingratiation figures out what you're doing (Jones, 1964; Kauffman & Steiner, 1968).

A second strategy is **self-promotion**—actively "blowing your own horn" by describing your talents, exhibiting your knowledge, and generally setting out to impress people (Arkin, 1981; Godfrey, Jones, and Lord, 1986). Self-promoters must be careful, however; if the audience knows they are less than perfect in some areas, they should mention their weaknesses honestly and then move on to their strengths (Baumeister & Jones, 1978; Jones, Gergen, and Jones, 1963). Of course, self-promotion can go too far; no one likes a pompous, arrogant braggart (Godfrey et al., 1986).

The flip side of self-promotion is **basking in reflected glory.** You can't be good at everything, and so you can't self-promote successfully in all areas—but you can become close to talented or successful people and bask in their glory and fame. In other words, you can appear impressive to others because you know or associate with impressive people. For example, Robert Cialdini and his colleagues (1976) found that people referred to the outcome of the local football games as "we won" as compared to "they lost."

A final self-presentational strategy, and the one that has attracted the most research attention, is **self-handicapping.** This strategy is a blend of self-serving attributions (which we discussed in Chapter 5) and impression management. Doing poorly or failing at a task is damaging to your self-esteem. In fact, just doing less well than you expected or than you have in the past can be upsetting, even if it is a good performance. How can you deal with this disappointment attributionally? Self-handicapping is the rather surprising solution: You can set up reasons, before the fact, for your failure. That is, before you even engage in the task, you can make sure that you have a ready-made excuse to explain your (potentially) poor performance (Arkin & Baumgardner, 1985; Jones & Berglas, 1978).

Let's say it's the night before the final exam in one of your courses. It's a difficult course, required for your major, and one in which you'd like to do well. A sensible strategy would be to eat a good dinner, study for a while, and then go to bed early and get a good night's sleep. The self-handicapping strategy would be to pull an all-nighter, studying (or partying), then wandering into the exam the next morning bleary-eyed and muddle-headed. If you don't do well on the exam, you have an excuse. In other words, you

**ingratiation:** the process whereby people flatter, praise, and generally try to make themselves likable to another, often higher status person

**self-promotion:** the process whereby people try to impress other people by describing their talents and exhibiting their knowledge

**basking in reflected glory:** trying to enhance our image by associating ourselves with successful or famous people

**self-handicapping:** creating obstacles and excuses for ourselves, so that if we do poorly on a task, we have ready-made excuses

*Drawing by W. Steig: © December 9, 1991 The New Yorker Magazine, Inc.*

*Know Thyself*

have an external attribution to offer to others to explain your performance, one that deflects the potential negative, internal attribution they might otherwise make (you're not smart). And if you do ace the exam, well, all the better—you did it under adverse conditions (no sleep), which suggests that you really are smart and talented.

There are two major ways in which people self-handicap. In its most extreme form, people create obstacles that reduce the likelihood they will succeed on a task, so that if they do fail, they can blame it on these obstacles rather than on their lack of ability. The obstacles people have been found to use include drugs, alcohol, reduced effort on the task, and failure to practice for an important sporting event (Berglas & Jones, 1978; Greenberg, 1983; Higgins & Harris, 1988; Koditz & Arkin, 1982; Rhodewalt & Davison, 1984; Tucker, Vuchinich, and Sobell, 1981).

The second kind of self-handicapping is less extreme. People do not create obstacles to success, but do devise ready-made excuses in case they fail (Baumgardner, Lake, & Arkin, 1985; Greenberg, Pyszczynski, and Paisley, 1984; Smith, Snyder, and Perkins, 1983; Snyder, Smith, Augelli, and Ingram, 1985). Thus, we might not go so far as to pull an all-nighter the night before an important exam, but we might complain that we are sick. People have been found to arm themselves with all kinds of excuses, such as blaming their shyness, test anxiety, bad moods, physical symptoms, and adverse events from their pasts. One problem with preparing ourselves with excuses in advance, however, is that doing so may make us exert less effort on the task. Whereas self-handicapping may prevent unflattering attributions for our failures, it often has the adverse effect of causing the poor performance that is so feared.

## SUMMARY

In this chapter, we have explored how people come to know themselves. The "self" we come to know is made up of both awareness and consciousness (the "knower") and the **self-concept** (the "known"). We share this awareness of self with the great apes; human children acquire a sense of self at about two years of age, and as they mature, their self-perceptions become more complex, abstract, and psychological. The definition of self that we have discussed is primarily a Western cultural phenomenon. At different times and in different cultures, the self has been defined very differently.

There are four basic ways in which we come to know ourselves: through **introspection,** observations of our own behavior, self-schemas, and social interaction. Introspecting about how we feel and what kind of person we are can improve our access to our own feelings and traits, especially when we focus attention on ourselves, as found by research on **self-awareness theory.** It is quite another thing to reflect about why we feel that way. Many studies show

that people's judgments about the reasons for their feelings and actions are often incorrect, in part because people rely on **causal theories** when explaining their behavior. Further, the act of thinking about reasons can cause **reasons-generated attitude change,** convincing us that our feelings match the reasons that happen to come to mind. Trying not to introspect about something—engaging in **thought suppression**—is also problematic, in that it can cause people to focus on the very thought they are trying to suppress.

**Self-perception theory** discusses how we come to know ourselves through observation of our own behavior, just as an outsider would. This occurs in particular when we lack clear evidence for how we think or feel. According to the **facial feedback hypothesis,** for example, people infer from their facial expressions what emotion they are feeling. Another interesting application of self-perception theory is **the overjustification effect,** which is the **discounting** of our **intrinsic motivation** in a task, as a result of inferring that we are engaging in the task because of **extrinsic motivation.**

That is, rewards and other kinds of external influences can undermine our intrinsic interest; an activity we once liked will seem like work instead of play. The **two-factor theory of emotion** is an elaboration of self-perception theory; we come to know our emotions by inferring what they should be, given the situation we are in. Because physiological arousal is difficult to label, **misattribution of arousal** can occur, whereby people attribute their arousal to the wrong source (to the wrong aspect of the situation).

People organize information about themselves into **self-schemas**, which are knowledge structures about ourselves, based on our past experiences, that help us understand, explain, and predict our own behavior. People also use implicit theories about the stability of their thoughts and behaviors to organize their **autobiographical memories,** which are memories about one's own past thoughts, feelings, and behaviors. The fourth way we come to know ourselves is through social interaction. By interacting with other people, we develop a **looking-glass self,** whereby we determine who we are based on others' perceptions of us. We also know ourselves through comparison with others.

**Social comparison theory** states that we will compare ourselves to others when we are unsure of our standing on some attribute and there is no objective criterion we can use. Typically, we choose to compare ourselves to similar others, for this is most diagnostic. When we want to find out what the best is, we engage in **upward social comparisons,** comparing ourselves to those who are superior on the relevant attribute. When we want to feel better about ourselves, we engage in **downward social comparisons,** comparing ourselves to those who are inferior on the relevant attribute.

Once we know ourselves, we often attempt to manage the self we present to others through the processes of **self-presentation** and **impression management**. Social life is much like the theater, where we present selves (or roles) to others. There are four essential self-presentational strategies: **ingratiation, self-promotion, basking in reflected glory,** and **self-handicapping.** Self-handicapping involves lining up a behavior, trait, or situational event before a performance so that we can later use it as an excuse if we don't do well.

## SUGGESTED READINGS

Deci, E. L., & Ryan, R. M. (1985). *Intrinsic motivation and self-determination.* New York: Plenum. A review of research on intrinsic motivation and overjustification that presents an alternative to the attributional perspective we discussed in this chapter.

Fiske, S. T., & Taylor, S. E. (1991). *Social cognition* (2nd ed.). New York: McGraw-Hill. A recent, encyclopedic review of the literature on social cognition by two experts in the field. Includes a chapter on social cognition and the self, which covers in greater detail much of the same material we discussed in this chapter.

Olson, J., & Zanna, M. P. (Eds.). (1990). *Self-inference: The Ontario Symposium* (Vol. 6). Hillsdale, NJ: Erlbaum. A collection of chapters on self-perception theory and related formulations, by top researchers in the field.

Schlenker, B. R. (1980). *Impression management: The self-concept, social identity, and interpersonal relations.* Monterey, CA: Brooks/Cole. A classic look at research on impression management and self-presentation.

# PART THREE

> *To swallow and follow,*
> *whether old doctrine*
> *or new propaganda, is a*
> *weakness still dominating*
> *the human mind.*
> —*Charlotte Perkins Gilman,*
> *Human Work, 1904*

# Social Influence

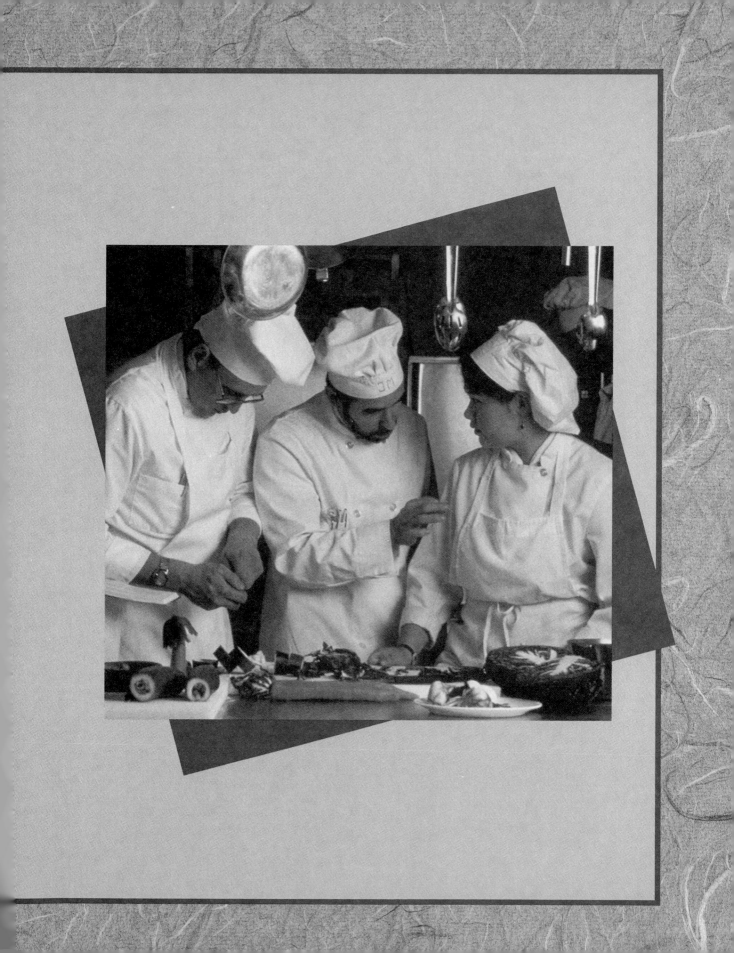

# Chapter 7
## Conformity:
## Influencing Behavior

## Chapter Outline

 n the late 1960s, Jim Jones founded a church, the Peoples Temple, preaching racial tolerance and acceptance. In 1977, following the publication of an unfavorable magazine article about the church, Jones and his congregation immigrated to an isolated jungle in Guyana. There they constructed "Jonestown." Over the years, Jones had become a messiahlike figure to his followers. He demanded and received total loyalty, devotion, and obedience. Interviews with defectors from the church indicated that Jones had also implemented strong punishments, from public humiliation to severe beatings, for any adult or child who disagreed with him.

In November 1978, California congressman Leo Ryan flew to Jonestown and investigated charges that church members were being held there against their will. As Ryan and his entourage boarded their plane to leave, Temple gunmen ambushed them and killed five, including Congressman Ryan. While these murders were occurring, Jones gathered the community together and told them that their enemies were everywhere and that the time had come to commit "revolutionary suicide." While his most trusted followers armed themselves and stood guard, others passed out cyanide-laced Kool-Aid. Jones instructed parents to first give the poison to their children and then drink it themselves. A few people tried to argue with Jones against the mass suicide, but they were shouted down by the rest of the congregation. When authorities reached the scene, they found the members of the congregation dead, lying in each other's arms. More than 800 people died that day by their own hand (Osherow, 1988).

The world was shocked and horrified by the events at Jonestown. How could people mindlessly follow a leader, conforming to his wishes and obeying his orders to such an extent that they killed their children and committed suicide? We know that such destructive conformity and

The mass suicide at Jonestown.

obedience are not unheard of. Sadly, we saw history repeat itself in 1993, when David Koresh, the spiritual leader of the Branch Davidians, prompted an armed standoff for fifty-one days with

government law enforcement officers at his compound in Waco, Texas. On April 20, a cataclysmic fire swept through the buildings, and nearly all inside died. At the time of this writing, not all the facts are known about what happened at Waco that day. Government officials state that the Branch Davidians set fire to the compound themselves; it is clear that several individuals, including Koresh, died from gunshot wounds to the head and not from fire or smoke inhalation. While we do not yet know about those final hours, it is clear that David Koresh had created such strong bonds of conformity and obedience among his followers that over eighty adults and children remained inside the buildings and burned to death. How could such conformity occur? Under what conditions and for what reasons do people fall under the influence of others?

## Conformity: When and Why

Think about the word *conformity* for a moment. Now, which one of the two quotations below do you find more appealing? Which one best describes your immediate reaction to the word?

Do as most do, and [people] will speak well of thee.—Thomas Fuller

It were not best that we should all think alike; it is difference of opinion that makes horse races.—Mark Twain

We wouldn't be surprised if you chose the second quotation. American culture stresses the importance of not conforming. We think of ourselves as a nation of rugged individualists, people who think for themselves, who stand up for the underdog, who go against the tide for what they think is right. This cultural self-image has been shaped by the manner in which our nation was founded, by our very system of government, and by our society's historical experience with Western expansion—the "taming" of the Wild West (Turner, 1932). The men and women who shaped this country had the self-reliance and tenacity to turn dreams into reality.

American mythology has celebrated the rugged individualist in many ways. For example, one of the longest-running and most successful advertising campaigns in American history is the "Marlboro Man." Since 1955, the photograph of a cowboy alone on the range has been an archetypal image. It has also sold a lot of cigarettes. People who have never seen a horse, let alone the American West, have responded for more than thirty-five years to this simple, evocative image. Clearly, it tells us something about ourselves that we want and like to hear: We make up our own minds; we're not spineless, weak conformists; we're not puppets, but players.

But are we, in fact, nonconforming creatures? Is every decision we make always based on what we think, or do we sometimes use other people's behavior to help us decide what to do? Do we sometimes go along with the crowd so that we won't stand out, cause trouble, or be the target of criticism or rejection? Of course we do! All of us, at times, exhibit signs of **conformity,** which we can define as a change in behavior due to the real or imagined influence of others (Kiesler & Kiesler, 1969). Nor, despite the American emphasis on rugged individualism, is it always best to be a nonconformer. Would you rather be thought of as a team player, or as someone who never cooperates? Conformity is not simply "good" or "bad" in and of itself.

Rather than labeling conformity as good or bad, the social psychologist is interested in why people conform. Knowing why people are influenced by others, and when, will help us understand if a given act of conformity in our own lives is wise . . . or foolish. To begin our discussion of why people conform, let's look at some very different examples of conformity. As you read each of these examples, think about the social forces that were pressuring these people to conform, and why they succumbed to those pressures.

> **conformity:** a change in behavior due to the real or imagined influence of other people

In 1930, Mohandas Gandhi organized a massive protest against British colonial rule in India. Gandhi's principles of nonviolent protest required his followers to submit passively to whatever violence the British authorities meted out. Despite their own personal reactions to being arrested, beaten, or shot at, hundreds of thousands of Gandhi's followers answered his call for a nonviolent response. This new form of protest was a success. In 1947, the British formally ended their colonial rule of India, and a new, autonomous nation, governed by Indians, was born (Kytle, 1969).

In 1961, the American civil rights movement incorporated Gandhi's principles of nonviolent protest and trained its "Freedom Riders" in the passive acceptance of violent treatment. Thousands of southern African Americans, joined by a smaller number of northern whites, many from college campuses, demonstrated against the segregationist laws of the South. In one confrontation after another, the civil rights activists reacted nonviolently as they were beaten, clubbed, hosed, whipped, raped, and even killed by southern sheriffs and police (Powledge, 1991). Their powerful show of conformity to

Sometimes different groups have very different ideas about what behavior is proper and appropriate. In the early 1960s, the Freedom Riders in the South deliberately violated segregation laws, incurring the wrath of many white southerners.

the ideal of nonviolent protest helped usher in a new era in America's fight for equality—the Civil Rights Act of 1964.

In late March of 1954, Seattle newspapers began to carry intermittent reports of damage to automobile windshields, involving pitted marks and small bubbles. In the next three weeks, reports of suspected vandalism to windshields spread across the county, as thousands of citizens called the police to report damage to their cars. On April 15, the mayor of Seattle declared that the damage was no longer a police matter, and asked the governor and President Eisenhower for assistance. As evidence of pitted windshields mounted, people took to covering their windshields with newspapers and floor mats, or kept their cars in the garage. Rumors spread that the pitting was caused by meteoric dust or by radioactive fallout from recent H-bomb tests. A few weeks later, newspaper articles suggested that what was occurring was mass hysteria—for the first time, people were looking closely at their (always pitted) windshields, instead of through them. The "Seattle windshield–pitting epidemic" ended just as suddenly as it had begun (Medalia & Larsen, 1969).

In the 1970s, a strange and risky game developed at an eastern state university. Undergraduate students would dare each other to scramble under tractor-trailers that were stopped at traffic lights. To raise the stakes, the runner started across the road just as the light was changing to green. The point was to reach the other side without being run over by the truck. One night, a female student, egged on by her friends, decided to accept the dare. As she ran, stooped, beneath the truck, she tripped and fell. Completely unaware of her presence, the truck driver put his foot on the gas and accelerated. The young woman was killed instantly.

Victims of the My Lai massacre.

In 1968, in the midst of the Vietnam War, a company of American soldiers prepared to enter the village of My Lai. The soldiers had been in Vietnam for only three months, and this was to be their first combat experience. They were particularly apprehensive because the village was rumored to be occupied by the Forty-eighth Vietcong Battalion, one of the most feared units of the enemy. On the morning of March 16, the first army assault helicopters sped toward the village. One pilot radioed that he saw Vietcong soldiers below, so the American soldiers jumped off the helicopters with rifles firing. They soon realized the pilot was wrong—there was no return fire. The first platoon to enter the village, led by Lieutenant William Calley, also encountered no resistance. Several villagers, all women, children, and elderly men, were cooking their breakfast over small fires. Suddenly, the quiet morning was shattered by the sound of gunshots. Calley had ordered one soldier to kill the civilians he was guarding; other soldiers began firing as well, and the carnage spread. The members of C Company rounded up and systematically murdered all the villagers of My Lai. They shoved women and children into a ravine and shot them; they threw hand grenades into huts filled with cowering villagers. Though no one knows the exact number of deaths, the estimates range from 450 to 500 Vietnamese civilians (Hersch, 1970; *Time*, 1969).

In all of these examples, individuals found themselves caught in a web of social influence. In response to explicit or implicit demands, they changed their behavior and conformed to the expectations of others. Certainly, the end result of their conforming behavior differs across our examples—from usefulness, to nobility, to hysteria, to tragedy. But much more is happening here than just the positive or negative outcome of the conforming act. The most important question is: Why did people conform? What is it that a group of people offers us that is so compelling and even seductive that we change our behavior to match theirs?

Some of these people conformed because they did not know what to do in a confusing or unusual situation. The behavior of the people around them served as useful information, and they decided to respond in a similar manner. Other people in these examples conformed because they did not wish to be ridiculed or punished for being different from everybody else. They chose to act the way in which the group expected them to so that they wouldn't be rejected or thought less of by group members. Let's see how each of these reasons for conforming operates.

## Informational Social Influence: The Need to Know What's "Right"

One of the important things we get from interacting with other people is information. You won't be surprised to hear that sometimes people don't know what to do in a situation, or even what is happening. Unfortunately, life, unlike your clothing, does not come with little labels attached, telling us what is going on and how we should respond. Instead, the social world is frequently ambiguous and ill-defined.

For example, how should you address your psychology professor—as Dr. Berman, Professor Berman, Ms. Berman, or Patricia? Which of three forks, two knives, and four spoons do you use when the first course arrives at a fancy French restaurant? How should you vote in the upcoming college referendum that would raise your tuition in order to increase student services? What combination of physical features best describes a beautiful woman or a handsome man? Is that scream you heard outside coming from a person joking with friends, or from the victim of a mugging?

In these and many other everyday situations, we feel uncertain about what to think or how to act. We simply don't know enough to make a good or accurate choice. Luckily, we have a powerful and useful source of knowledge available to us—the behavior of other people. Asking others what they think or watching what they do helps us reach a definition of the situation (Deutsch & Gerard, 1955; Kelly, 1955; Thomas, 1928). When we subsequently act like everyone else, we are conforming, but not because we are weak, spineless individuals with no self-reliance. Instead, we act like others because their behavior is informative; it defines an ambiguous situation for us and helps us choose appropriate courses of action. This is called **informational social influence.**

As an illustration of how other people can be a source of information, imagine you are a participant in the following experiment by Muzafer Sherif (1936). In the first phase of the study, you are seated alone in a dark room and asked to focus your attention on a dot of light fifteen feet away. The experimenter asks you to estimate in inches how far the light moves. You stare earnestly at the light, and yes, it moves a little. You say, "About two inches," though it is not easy to tell exactly. The light disappears and then comes back; you are asked to judge again. The light seems to move a little more, and you say, "Four inches." After several of these trials, the light seems to move about the same amount each time—about two to four inches.

Now, the interesting thing about this task is that the light was not actually moving at all. It looked like it was moving, because of a visual illusion

---

"It's always best on these occasions to do what the mob do."

"But suppose there are two mobs?" suggested Mr. Snodgrass.

"Shout with the largest," replied Mr. Pickwick.
—Charles Dickens,
*Pickwick Papers*

---

**informational social influence:** the influence of other people that leads us to conform because we see them as a source of information to guide our behavior; we conform because we believe that others' interpretation of an ambiguous situation is more correct than ours

called the *autokinetic effect*. If you stare at a bright light in a uniformly dark environment (e.g., a star on a dark night), the light will appear to waver back and forth. This occurs because you have no stable reference point to anchor the position of the light. The distance that the light appears to move varies from person to person but becomes consistent for each person over time. In Sherif's (1936) experiment, the subjects all arrived at their own, stable estimate during the first phase of the study, but these estimates differed from person to person. Some people thought the light was moving only an inch or so, whereas others thought that it was moving as much as ten inches.

Sherif chose to use the autokinetic effect because he wanted a situation that would be ambiguous—where the correct definition of the situation would be unclear to his participants. In the second phase of the experiment, a few days later, the participants were paired with two other people, each of whom had had the same prior experience alone with the light. Now the situation became a truly social one, as all three made their judgments out loud. Remember, the autokinetic effect is experienced differently by different people; some see a lot of movement, some not much at all. After hearing their partners give judgments that were different from their own, what did people do?

Over the course of several trials, people reached a common estimate, and each member of the group conformed to that estimate. These results indicate that people were using each other as a source of information, coming to believe that the group estimate was the correct one (see Figure 7.1). An important feature of informational social influence is that it can lead to **private acceptance**, where people come to believe the definition of the situation they have learned from others.

**private acceptance:** conforming to other people's behavior out of a genuine belief that what they are doing or saying is right

It might seem equally plausible that people publicly conformed to the group but privately maintained the belief that the light was moving only a small amount. For example, maybe someone privately believed that the light was moving ten inches but announced that it had moved three inches, the group estimate, to avoid looking silly or foolish. (This would be a case of **public compliance** without *private acceptance*.) Sherif casted doubt on this interpretation, however, by asking people to judge the lights once more by themselves, after participating in groups. Even though they no longer had to worry about looking silly in front of other participants, they continued to give the answer the group had given earlier. One study even found that people still conformed to the group estimate when they participated by themselves a year later (Rohrer, Baron, Hoffman, and Swander, 1954). These results suggest that people were relying on each other to define reality, and came to privately accept the group estimate.

**public compliance:** conforming to other people's behavior publicly, without necessarily believing in what we are doing or saying

In everyday life, of course, we are rarely asked to judge how much a stationary light is moving. It is thus important to note that there are many everyday situations in which we rely on other people to help us define what is going on. Think about the first time you were at the symphony or ballet. You knew that applause was going to figure in sometime, but exactly when? For how long? What about standing ovations, or shouting "Encore!" or "Bravo!"? No doubt, you looked to others in the audience to help you interpret the appropriate way of showing approval in this quite formal setting. That the audience's behavior can be affected through conformity is not unknown in the performing arts. Davies (1988) describes the use of the claque (hired applause) in early nineteenth-century opera:

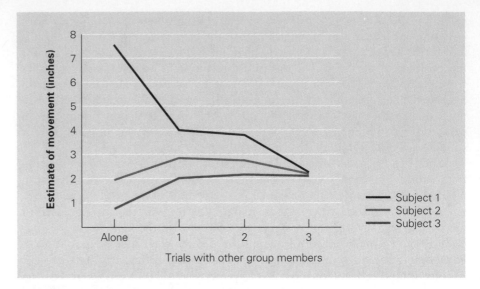

FIGURE 7.1 **One group's judgments in Sherif's (1936) autokinetic studies.** People estimated how far a point of light appeared to move in a dark room. When they saw the light by themselves, their estimates varied widely. When brought together in groups and hearing other people announce their estimates, people conformed to the group's estimate of how much the light moved. (Adapted from Sherif, 1936)

An opera audience must contain people who know the work intimately. Nobody will dare to applaud if they don't know where, and when, and why. They might make an embarrassing mistake [and] look foolish. . . . [A] claque is a small body of experts; applause, certainly, but not an unorganized row; you must have your *bisseurs* who call out loud for encores; your *rieurs* who laugh at the right places—but just appreciative chuckles to encourage the others, not from the belly; your *pleureurs* who sob when sobs are needed. . . . And all of this must be carefully organized—yes, orchestrated—by the *capo di claque.* . . . [W]e give [the composer] a success! (Davies, 1988, pp. 390-391)

Using other people to define social reality can also have a large impact on our emotions. Consider what happened to a friend of ours when he was flying from New York to Texas. He was idly reading a newspaper when he happened to glance out the window. He saw a ribbon of what looked like steam or smoke trailing from the engine. "That's odd," he thought. "Maybe it's just some sort of routine exhaust or condensation." Because he had never seen anything like it, though, our friend was a little nervous. Was something wrong? Should he alert the pilot? Like Sherif's participants, he relied on other people to help him define what was going on. "Maybe I'll just glance at the flight attendants," he decided, "to see if they look at all concerned."

At first, our friend didn't see any of the flight attendants. Craning his neck, he checked the back of the plane. There he saw one flight attendant staring out of the window, with fear frozen on her face. Two others were hugging each other and crying. How would this make you feel, were you in our friend's shoes? Not surprisingly, he was immediately gripped by terror. It turned out that the engine was on fire, and the plane was in grave danger. Fortunately, the pilot was able to make an emergency landing, and no one was injured.

This example illustrates that not just our judgments of such things as the movement of light or the way to behave at an opera are influenced by other people. As we saw in Chapter 6, other people can be a principal source of information about our emotions as well (Schachter, 1959; Schachter & Singer, 1962). Our friend was not sure whether or not to be afraid when he first saw the smoke; a glance at the flight attendants immediately told him how to feel. This reliance on others to define our emotions begins early in life. When toddlers fall down and scrape their knees, the first thing they do is look at their parents. If the parent looks alarmed and says, "Oh, honey, did you get hurt?" the child will burst into tears. If the parent smiles and acts unconcerned, the child will usually get up and continue playing (Campos & Sternberg, 1981). In either scenario, the child's response is based on the parent's definition of the situation. Other people are a tremendous source of potential information; we never outgrow our need to check reality by watching what other people are doing.

## Conversions and Crises

Informational social influence is certainly a part of everyday life. But this form of social influence also impinges on us in far more dramatic ways. For example, it comes into play when people experience a *conversion*—a sudden shift in the meaning of their lives based on new knowledge they have received from a group (Berger, 1963; Berger & Luckmann, 1967). People may experience conversion to a religion, to a political ideology, or to any one of the many cults that have arisen over recent decades. Often before the conversion experience, the individual feels indecisive and confused, dissatisfied with his or her life, and even despairing. On meeting members of the new group, the individual is exposed to a whole new definition of the situation, radically different from the one he or she knew before. These new beliefs are perceived by the individual to be more powerful and useful than his or her former convictions; conversion involves the individual conforming to the belief system of the new reference group. For example, Arthur Koestler (1959), a former Communist, describes his conversion to communism in the 1930s:

> To say that one had "seen the light" is a poor description of the mental rapture which only the convert knows (regardless of what faith he has been converted to). . . . [T]he whole universe falls into a pattern like the stray pieces of a jigsaw puzzle assembled by magic at one stroke. There is now an answer to every question; doubts and conflicts are a matter of the tortured past. (p. 19)

Another dramatic form of informational social influence occurs during crises. Here an individual is confronted with a frightening, potentially dangerous situation to which he or she is ill-equipped to respond (Killian, 1964). Literally, the person may have no idea of what is really happening or what he or she should do. When one's personal safety is involved, the need for information is acute—and the behavior of others is very informative.

The *New York Times* headlined the *War of the Worlds* incident. Many listeners believed that a fictional radio broadcast about an invasion by Martians was true, in part because of informational social influences.

Consider what happened on Halloween Night in 1938. Orson Welles, the gifted actor and film director, and the Mercury Theater broadcast a radio play based loosely on H. G. Wells's science fiction fantasy *The War of the Worlds*. (Remember, this was the era before television; radio was a source of entertainment, with music, comedy, and drama programs, and the only source for fast-breaking news.) That night, Welles and his fellow actors put on a radio drama of cataclysm—the invasion of Earth by hostile Martians—that was so realistic and effective that at least a million American listeners became frightened and several thousand were panic-stricken (Cantril, 1940).

Why were so many Americans convinced that what they heard was a real news report of an actual invasion by aliens? One reason was that the play parodied existing radio news shows very well, and many listeners missed the beginning of the broadcast (when it was clearly labeled as a play) because they had been listening to the nation's number-one-rated show, "Charlie McCarthy." Another culprit, however, was informational social influence. Many people were listening with friends and family, and naturally turned to each other, out of uncertainty, to see whether they should believe what they heard. Seeing looks of concern and worry on their loved ones' faces added to the panic people were beginning to feel. "We all kissed one another and felt we would all die," reported one listener (Cantril, 1940, p. 95).

In addition, many frightened listeners misinterpreted actual events so that they fit the news on the radio program: "We looked out the window and Wyoming Avenue was black with cars. People were rushing away, I figured," or "No cars came down my street. Traffic is jammed on account of the roads being destroyed, I thought" (Cantril, 1940, p. 93). When a situation is highly ambiguous and people begin to believe they know what is happening, they will even reinterpret potentially disconfirming evidence so that it fits their definition of the situation.

> Ninety-nine percent of the people in the world are fools and the rest of us are in great danger of contagion.
> —Thornton Wilder

Gustav LeBon (1895) was the first researcher to document how emotions and behavior can spread, seemingly out of control, through a crowd—an effect he called **contagion**. As we have learned, anytime an individual is faced with a truly ambiguous situation, he or she will most likely rely on the interpretation of others. Unfortunately, in a truly ambiguous and confusing situation, other people may be no more knowledgeable or accurate than we are.

**contagion:** the rapid transmission of emotions or behaviors through a crowd

## When Informational Conformity Backfires

The *War of the Worlds* incident reminds us that using other people as a source of information can be dangerous. If other people are misinformed, we will adopt their mistakes and misinterpretations. Depending on others to help you reach a definition of the situation can sometimes lead to an inaccurate definition indeed. Recall the Seattle windshield-pitting epidemic (Medalia & Larsen, 1969) presented earlier. On day 1, the inhabitants of western Washington state are going about their business (including driving their cars), with no worry that anything "funny" is happening to their car windshields. By day 2, these same residents are reacting to new information that something ominous and strange is going on. An ambiguous situation presents itself: Is some peculiar force at work that is pitting windshields? People check their cars . . . and see tiny blemishes they had never noticed before. They discuss the matter with friends. More people report windshield damage. Needing to find an explanation for the event, people circulate various theories; a particularly popular one is radioactive fallout from recent H-bomb tests. By now, informational social influence is riding high—people begin taking precautionary measures to protect their cars, and these actions serve as a new source of information to which others conform. Mass silliness results, until a convincing explanation is offered and widely disseminated. With a new definition of the situation, the panic or hysteria dies down just as quickly as it had begun (Medalia & Larsen, 1969).

Another example of extreme and misdirected informational social influence is **mass psychogenic illness** (Colligan, Pennebaker, and Murphy, 1982), the occurrence of similar physical symptoms, with no known physical cause, in a group of people. This form of contagion usually begins with just one or a few people reporting physical symptoms; typically, these people are experiencing some kind of stress in their lives. Other people around them construct what seems to be a reasonable explanation for their illness. This explanation, a new definition of the situation, spreads, and more people begin to think that they have symptoms too. As the number of afflicted people grows, both the physical symptoms and their supposed explanation become more credible and thus more widespread (Kerckhoff & Back, 1968).

**mass psychogenic illness:** the occurrence, in a group of people, of similar physical symptoms with no known physical cause

Several social psychologists have studied naturally occurring cases of mass psychogenic illness (e.g., Colligan & Murphy, 1979; Kerckhoff & Back, 1968; Schuler & Parenton, 1943; Singer, Baum, Baum, and Thew, 1982; Stahl & Lebedun, 1974). Donald Johnson (1945) examined a particularly fascinating case, that of the "phantom anesthetist" of Mattoon, Illinois. Here is Johnson's (1945) description of the panic:

The story of the "phantom anesthetist" begins in Mattoon, Illinois, on the first night of September, 1944, when a woman reported to the police that someone had opened her bedroom window and sprayed her with a sickish

An example of mass psychogenic illness.

sweet-smelling gas which partially paralyzed her legs and made her feel ill. Soon other cases with similar symptoms were reported, and the police organized a full-scale effort to catch the elusive "gasser." Some of the Mattoon citizens armed themselves with shotguns and sat on their doorsteps to wait for him; some even claimed that they caught a glimpse of him and heard him pumping his spray gun. As the number of cases increased—as many as seven in one night—and the facilities of the local police seemed inadequate to the size of the task, the state police . . . were called in, and scientific crime detection experts went to work, analyzing stray rags for gaseous chemicals and checking the records of patients recently released from state institutions. Before long the "phantom anesthetist" of Mattoon had appeared in newspapers all over the United States. . . . After ten days of such excitement, when all the victims had recovered and no substantial clues had been found, the police began to talk of "imagination" and some of the newspapers ran columns on "mass hysteria"; the episode of the "phantom anesthetist" was over. (p. 175)

How did the contagion spread? How did some people come to believe that their physical ailments were symptoms of a bizarre attack? Johnson (1945) determined that informational social influence had occurred primarily via newspaper articles. Few of the victims knew each other, so they had not spread the information interpersonally. Instead, blaring headlines and sensationalist articles in the town newspapers were the means by which a new definition of the situation was communicated.

What is particularly interesting about modern cases of mass psychogenic illness (as well as other bizarre forms of conformity) is the powerful role that the mass media play in their dissemination. Through television, radio, newspapers, and magazines, information is spread quickly and efficiently to all segments of the population. While in the Middle Ages it took 200 years for the "dancing manias" (a kind of psychogenic illness) to crisscross Europe (Sirois, 1982), today it takes only minutes for most of the inhabitants of the planet to learn about a strange or even bizarre event. Luckily, the mass media also have the power to quickly squelch these uprisings of contagion by introducing more logical explanations for ambiguous events.

## When Will People Conform to Informational Social Influence?

Let's review the situations that are the most likely to produce conformity because of informational social influence.

**When the Situation Is Ambiguous.** This is the most crucial variable for determining if people use each other as a source of information. When you are unsure of the correct response, the appropriate behavior, or the right idea, you will be most open to influence from others. The more uncertain you are, the more you will rely on others (Allen, 1965). Some of the situations we discussed at the beginning of the chapter were ambiguous ones for the people involved. If you wanted to completely change the existing political and social order of your society, what would be the best way to do it? How should you and your colleagues react to the confrontations with government authorities that would no doubt occur? Whether in India or in the southern United States, the principles of nonviolent action represented a new definition of the situation, actively taught to the followers. In both historical examples, it was the mass conformity to this new information that made the demonstrations so powerful and ultimately so effective.

In comparison, the conformity that occurred at Jonestown and My Lai was horrible and tragic in its consequences. However, informational social influence was at work here as well, because the situation was ambiguous for the participants. At Jonestown, for example, Rev. Jones had achieved such power that people allowed him to define reality for them. Over time, the residents of Jonestown came to entirely believe whatever Jones told them; they had no independent definition of the situation in any area of their lives. They believed him when he said their situation was hopeless and that their enemies were closing in on them. They believed him when he said that suicide was the correct course of action. Instances of mind control or "brainwashing" can actually be extreme cases of informational social influence—so extreme that, in this case, Jones was able to convince nearly an entire village to commit suicide.

**When the Situation Is a Crisis.** Two other variables—which often co-occur with ambiguous situations—also promote the use of others as a source of information. First, when the situation is a crisis, we usually do not have time to stop and think about exactly which course of action we should take. We need to act, and act now. If we feel scared and panicky and are uncertain what to do, it is only natural for us to look and see how other people are responding—and to do likewise. Unfortunately, the people we imitate may also feel scared and panicky, and not be behaving rationally.

The soldiers at My Lai, for example, expected to experience combat for the first time, and were undoubtedly scared and on edge. Further, it was not easy to tell who the enemy was. In the Vietnam War, Vietnamese civilians who were sympathizers of the Vietcong were known to have laid mines in the path of U.S. soldiers, fired guns from hidden locations, and thrown or planted grenades. In a guerrilla war like Vietnam, it was often difficult to tell if civilians were in fact civilians or combatants, allies or enemies. Thus, when one or two soldiers began firing on the villagers in My Lai, it is perhaps not surprising that others followed suit, believing this to be the proper course of action. Had the soldiers not been in a crisis situation, and had more time to think about their actions, perhaps the tragedy would have been avoided.

**When Other People Are Experts.** Typically, the more expertise or knowledge a person has, the more valuable he or she will be as a guide in an ambiguous situation (Bickman, 1974). For example, a passenger who sees smoke coming out of an airplane engine will probably look around for the flight attendants to check their reaction; they have more expertise than the vacationer in the next seat. However, the experts are not always reliable sources of information. Imagine the fear felt by the young man listening to the "War of the Worlds," who called his local police department for an explanation—and discovered that the police too thought the events described on the radio were actually happening.

### Resisting Informational Social Influence

As we have seen, relying on others to help us define what is happening can be an excellent idea, or it can be a tragedy in the making. How can we tell when other people are a good source of information, and when we should resist other people's definition of a situation?

First, it is important to remember that it *is* possible to resist illegitimate or inaccurate informational social influence. In all of our examples, some people resisted conforming to what they perceived to be incorrect information. At My Lai, not all the soldiers took part in the atrocity. One sergeant said he'd been ordered to "destroy the village," but he simply refused to follow the orders. Another soldier, watching as the others fired on civilians, purposefully shot himself in the foot so that he would have an excuse to be evacuated from the killing scene. One helicopter pilot, looking down on the grisly sight, landed and scooped up fifteen Vietnamese children and ferried them off to safety deep in the forest. Thus, some soldiers rejected the behavior of others as a correct definition of what they should do. Instead, they relied on what they knew was right and moral; they refused to take part in the massacre of innocent people.

Similarly, during the "War of the Worlds" broadcast, not all of the listeners panicked (Cantril, 1940). Some engaged in rational problem solving; they checked other stations on the radio dial and discovered that no other station was broadcasting the same news. Instead of relying on others and being caught up in the contagion and mass panic, they searched for and found information on their own.

The next time you are in an ambiguous situation and find yourself watching and listening to other people, ask yourself these key questions: Do these people know any more about what is going on than I do? Is there an expert handy, someone who should know more? Do the actions of these people or experts seem sensible? If I behave this way too, will it go against my

Yes, we must, indeed, all hang together or, most assuredly, we shall all hang separately.
—Benjamin Franklin to John Hancock, at the signing of the Declaration of Independence

common sense, or against my internal moral compass that tells me what is right and wrong? By knowing how informational social influence works in daily life, you are in a better position to know when it is useful and when it is not.

## Normative Social Influence: The Need to Be Accepted

There is another side to conformity, another reason, besides the need for information, that we change our behavior to be like that of others. We also conform so that we will be liked and accepted by other people. We conform to the group's **social norms,** which are implicit (and sometimes explicit) rules for acceptable behaviors, values, and beliefs (Deutsch & Gerard, 1955; Kelley, 1955). Groups have certain expectations about how the group members should behave, and "members in good standing" conform to these rules. Members who do not are perceived as different, difficult, and eventually deviant. Deviant members can be ridiculed, punished, or even rejected by other group members (Miller & Anderson, 1979; Schachter, 1951).

**social norms:** the implicit or explicit rules a group has for the acceptable behaviors, values, and beliefs of its members

Humans are by nature a social species. Few of us could live happily as hermits, never seeing or talking to another person. Through interactions with others, we receive emotional support, affection, and love, and we partake of enjoyable experiences. Other people are extraordinarily important to our sense of well-being. Research on individuals who have been isolated for long amounts of time indicates that being deprived of human contact is stressful and traumatic (Curtiss, 1977; Schachter, 1959; Zubek, 1969).

Given this fundamental human need for social companionship, it is not surprising that we often conform in order to be accepted by others. Conformity for normative reasons occurs in those situations where we do what other people are doing not because we are using them as a source of information, but because we won't attract attention, be made fun of, get into trouble, or be rejected. We conform so that we can continue to belong and reap the benefits of group membership. This is called **normative social influence.**

**normative social influence:** the influence of other people that leads us to conform in order to be liked and accepted by them; this type of conformity results in public compliance with, but not necessarily private acceptance of, the group's beliefs and behaviors

You probably don't find it too surprising that people sometimes conform in order to be liked and accepted by others. After all, if the group is important to us, and it is a matter of wearing the right kind of clothing or using the "hip" slang words, why not go along? But when it comes to more important kinds of behaviors, such as hurting another person, surely we will resist such conformity pressures. And surely we won't conform when we are certain of what the correct way of behaving is, and the pressures are coming from a group that we don't care all that much about. Or will we? Remember that image of Americans as rugged individualists? Are we really like the Marlboro Man, setting trends instead of following them? How much will we conform to normative pressures?

To find out, Solomon Asch conducted a series of classic studies exploring the parameters of normative social influence (Asch, 1951, 1956). Asch initiated this program of research because he believed that there are limits to how much people will conform. Naturally, people conformed in the Sherif studies, he reasoned, given that the situation was highly ambiguous—trying to guess how much a light was moving. Asch believed, however, that

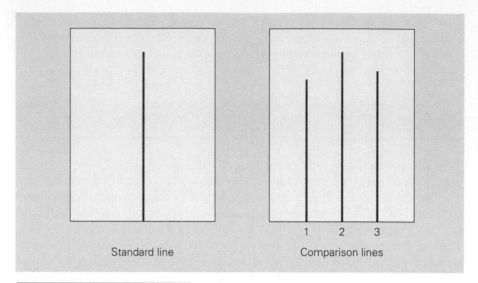

**FIGURE 7.2  The judgment task in Asch's line studies**. Participants judged which of the three comparison lines on the right was closest in length to the standard line on the left. (Adapted from Asch, 1956)

when a situation was completely unambiguous, people would act like rational, objective problem-solvers. When the group said or did something that contradicted an obvious truth, surely people would reject social pressures and decide for themselves what was going on.

To find out, Asch conducted the following study. Had you been a participant, you would have been told that this was an experiment on perceptual judgment, and that you would be taking part with seven other students. Here's the scenario: The experimenter shows everyone two cards, one with a single line on it, the other with three lines labeled 1, 2, and 3. He asks each of you to judge, and then announce aloud, which of the three lines on the second card is closest in length to the line on the first card (see Figure 7.2).

It is crystal-clear that the correct answer is the second line. Not surprisingly, each participant says, "Line 2." Your turn comes next to last, and, of course, you say, "Line 2" as well. The last participant concurs. The experimenter then presents a new set of cards and asks the group to again make their judgments and announce them out loud. Again, the answer is obvious, and everyone gives the correct answer. At this point, you are probably thinking to yourself, "What a boring experiment. How many times will we have to judge these silly lines? I wonder what they're serving for dinner in the dining hall tonight."

As your mind starts to wander, something surprising happens. The experimenter presents the third set of lines, and again the answer is obvious—line 3 is clearly the closest in length to the target line. But the first participant announces that the correct answer is line 1! "Geez, this guy must be so bored that he fell asleep," you think. Then the second person announces that he also believes that line 1 is the correct answer. The third, fourth, fifth, and sixth participants concur; then it is your turn to judge. By now, startled, you are probably looking at the lines very closely to see if you missed something. But no, line 3 is clearly the correct answer. What will

Participants in an Asch line study. The real participant is seated in the middle. He is surrounded by accomplices of the experimenter, who have just given the wrong answer on the line task.

you do? Will you bravely blurt out, "Line 3," or will you go along with the group and give the obviously incorrect answer, "Line 1"?

As you can see, Asch set up a situation to see if people would conform even when the right answer was cut-and-dried. The other participants were actually accomplices of the experimenter, instructed to give the wrong answer on twelve of the eighteen trials. Contrary to what Asch thought would happen, a surprising amount of conformity occurred: Seventy-six percent of the participants conformed on at least one trial. On average, people conformed on about a third of the twelve trials on which the accomplices gave the incorrect answer (see Figure 7.3).

Why did people conform so much of the time? One possibility is that people genuinely had a hard time with the task, and thus assumed that other people were better judges of the length of lines than they were. If so, this would be another case of informational social influence, as we saw in the Sherif study. This interpretation doesn't make much sense, however, because the correct answers were obvious—so much so that when people in a control group made the judgments by themselves, they almost never made a mistake. Instead, normative pressures came into play. Even though the other participants were strangers, the fear of being the lone dissenter was very strong, causing people to conform, at least occasionally. One participant, for example, had this to say about why he conformed: "Here was a group; they had a definite idea; my idea disagreed; this might arouse anger. . . . I was standing out as a sore thumb. . . . I didn't want particularly to make a fool of myself. . . . I felt I was definitely right . . . [but] they might think I was peculiar" (Asch, 1955, p. 46).

These are classic normative reasons for conforming: People know that what they are doing is wrong, but go along anyway so as not to feel peculiar or look like a fool. These reasons illustrate an important fact about normative pressures: In contrast to informational social influence, normative pressures usually result in public compliance without private acceptance—that is, people go along with the group, even if they do not believe in what they are doing or they think it is wrong.

What is especially surprising about Asch's results is that people were concerned about looking foolish in front of complete strangers. It is not as if the participants were in danger of being ostracized by a group that was important to them. Nor was there any risk of open punishment or

It isn't difficult to keep alive, friends—just don't make trouble—or if you must make trouble, make the sort of trouble that's expected.
—Robert Bolt, *A Man for All Seasons*, 1962

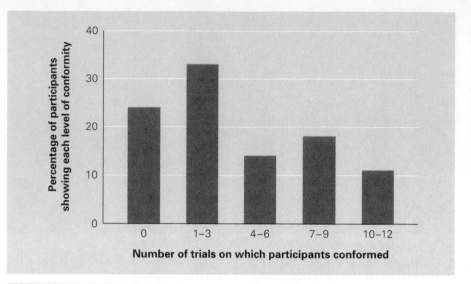

**FIGURE 7.3  Results of the Asch line study**. Seventy-six percent of the participants conformed on at least one trial. (Adapted from Asch, 1957)

disapproval for failing to conform, or of losing the esteem of people they really cared about, such as friends and family members. And yet decades of research indicate that conformity for normative reasons can occur simply because we do not want to risk social disapproval, even from complete strangers we will never see again (Crutchfield, 1955; Tanford & Penrod, 1984). As Moscovici (1985) comments, the Asch studies are "one of the most dramatic illustrations of conformity, of blindly going along with the group, even when the individual realizes that by doing so he turns his back on reality and truth" (p. 349).

Asch (1957) did a variation of his study that demonstrates the power of social disapproval in shaping a person's behavior. The confederates gave the wrong answer twelve out of eighteen times, as before, but this time the participants wrote their answers on a piece of paper, instead of saying them out loud. Now people did not have to worry about what the group thought of them, because the group would never find out what their answers were. Conformity dropped dramatically, occurring on an average of only 1.5 of the 12 trials.

Normative social influence most closely reflects the pejorative stereotype of conformity we referred to earlier. At times, conforming for normative reasons can be spineless and weak; it can have negative consequences. For example, the college students who played the truck/traffic-light game did not conform to their peers' definition of the situation for informational reasons. If you were egged on by your friends to run under a large Mack truck just as the light turned green, you would not say, "Gee, what an ambiguous situation. I don't know what to do. I guess I'll do what they're doing—it seems like a good idea." Instead, like the people in Asch's study, you would know it was a very dangerous thing to do, but might go ahead anyway—because normative social pressures can be difficult to resist. The desire to be accepted is part of human nature, but it can have tragic consequences.

## The Consequences of Resisting Normative Social Influence

One way to observe the power of normative social pressures is to see what happens when people manage to resist them (Milgram & Sabini, 1978). If a person refuses to do as the group asks and thereby violates its norms, what happens? Think for a moment about the norms that operate in your group of friends. Some friends have an egalitarian norm for making group decisions. For example, when choosing a movie such groups will make sure that everyone gets to state a preference; the choice is then discussed until agreement is reached on one movie. Think about what would happen if, in a group with this kind of norm, you stated at the outset that you only wanted to see *Rebel Without a Cause* and weren't going with them otherwise. Your friends would be surprised by your behavior; they would also be annoyed with you or even angry. If you continued to flout the friendship norms of the group by failing to conform to them, two things would most likely occur. First, the group members would attempt to "bring you back into the fold," chiefly through increased communication with you. Teasing comments and long discussions would ensue, as your friends tried to figure out why you were acting so strangely and also tried to get you to conform to their expectations (Garfinkle, 1967). If these discussions didn't work, your friends would most likely curtail communication with you (Festinger & Thibaut, 1951; Gerard, 1953). At this point, you have effectively been rejected.

This process of monitoring, convincing, and eventually rejecting the deviant was demonstrated in a study by Stanley Schachter (1951). He asked groups of college students to read and discuss a case history of "Johnny Rocco," a juvenile delinquent. Most of the students took a middle-of-the-road position about the case, believing that Rocco should receive a judicious mixture of love and discipline. Unbeknownst to the participants, however, Schachter had planted an accomplice in the group, who was instructed to disagree with the group's recommendations. He consistently argued that Rocco should receive the harshest amount of punishment, regardless of what the other group members argued.

How was the deviant treated? He received the most comments and questions from the real participants throughout the discussion, until near the end, when communication with him dropped sharply. The group had tried to convince the deviant to agree with them; when it appeared that wouldn't work, they ignored him. In addition, they punished the deviant. After the discussion, they were asked to fill out questionnaires that supposedly pertained to future discussion meetings of their group. The participants were asked to nominate one group member who should be eliminated from further discussions if the size had to be reduced. They nominated the deviant. They were also asked to assign group members to various tasks in future discussions. They assigned the unimportant or boring jobs, such as taking notes, to the deviant. Social groups are very well versed in how to bring a nonconformist into line. No wonder we respond as often as we do to normative pressures!

## Normative Social Influence in Everyday Life

Normative social influence operates on many levels in our daily lives. The clothes we wear are but one example. While few of us are slaves of fashion, we nonetheless tend to wear what is considered appropriate and stylish at a

> Customs do not concern themselves with right or wrong or reason. But they have to be obeyed; one reasons all around them until [one] is tired, but [one] must not transgress them, it is sternly forbidden.
> —Mark Twain

> Success or failure lies in conformity to the times.
> —Machiavelli

given time. Men wore ties that were wide in the 1970s; then they wore ties that were narrow in the 1980s; and undoubtedly they'll be wearing wide ties again within a decade. Similarly, women's hemlines have gone up and down with alacrity over the past century. Normative social influence is at work whenever you notice a "look" shared by people in a certain group. The "bobby-soxer" teenage girls of the 1940s and 1950s had such a look; so did the "zoot-suiter" young men of the 1940s. No doubt, twenty years from now, the current, early 1990s women's look of leggings and baggy tops will seem dated and silly, and none of us will conform to it.

Another fairly frivolous example of normative social influence is fads. Certain activities or objects can suddenly become popular and sweep the country. College students in the 1930s ate goldfish; in the 1950s, crammed as many people as possible into telephone booths; and in the 1970s, "streaked" at (ran naked through) official gatherings.

Hula-Hoops were the toy you had to have in the 1950s or risk social ostracism. One of us, Robin Akert, remembers a Saturday afternoon with the family in 1958.

> We drove from store to store, trying to find Hula-Hoops. Everywhere we went, they were all sold out. My sister and I sat in the backseat, sobbing with disappointment. Much to our parents' chagrin, we were praying in little, high-pitched voices for help in finding Hula-Hoops before nightfall!

A more sinister form of normative social influence involves women's attempts to conform to cultural definitions of an attractive body. While many, if not most, world societies consider plumpness in females attractive

Below: The "zoot suiter" look in 1942. The jacket had six inches of shoulder pads, and the balloon trousers were hitched chest-high.

Above: The "bobby-soxer" look: Teenage fashion from 1944.

Below: Female fashion today.

Fads from the 1970s: "Streaking."

The Hula-Hoop craze, Union, New Jersey, 1958.

(Ford & Beach, 1952; Rudofsky, 1972), Western culture and particularly American culture currently value thinness in the female form (Garner, Garfinkel, Schwartz, and Thompson, 1980).

For example, Silverstein, Perdue, Peterson, and Kelley (1986) analyzed photographs of women appearing in *Ladies' Home Journal* and *Vogue* magazines from 1901 to 1981, by measuring their busts and waists in centimeters and forming a bust-to-waist ratio. A high score indicates a heavier, more voluptuous body, while a lower score indicates a thin, lean body type. Their results show a startling series of changes in the cultural definition of female bodily attractiveness during the twentieth century (see Figure 7.4).

At the turn of the century, an attractive woman was voluptuous and heavy; by the "flapper" period of the 1920s, the correct look for women was rail-thin and flat-chested. The normative body changed again in the 1940s, when World War II "pinup girls" like Betty Grable exemplified a heavier standard. The curvaceous, heavier female body remained popular during the 1950s; witness, for example, Marilyn Monroe. However, the "swinging 1960s" fashion look, exemplified by the reed-thin British model Twiggy, introduced a very thin silhouette again. As Brett Silverstein and his colleagues (1986) point out, the average bust-to-waist ratio has been very low since 1963. This is the longest period of time in this century that women have been exposed to an extremely thin standard of feminine physical attractiveness.

Whereas informational social influence may be the mechanism by which women learn what kind of body is considered attractive at a given time in their culture, normative social influence helps to explain their attempts to create that body through dieting and, more disturbingly, through eating

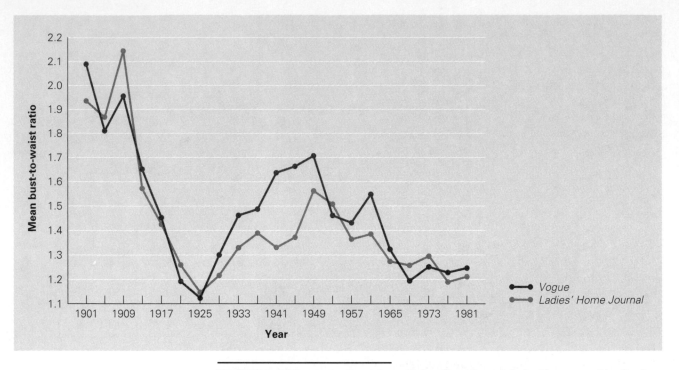

**FIGURE 7.4** **The mean bust-to-waist ratios of models in *Vogue and Ladies' Home Journal* advertisements during this century**. What has been considered an attractive female body has changed dramatically over the past one hundred years: from heavy women at the beginning of the century, to rail-thin women during the 1920s, to somewhat heavier, curvaceous women during the 1940s and 1950s, to a return to overly thin women in the 1960s and continuing. (Adapted from Silverstein, Perdue, Peterson, and Kelley, 1986)

disorders like anorexia nervosa and bulimia (Bruch, 1973, 1978; Palazzoli, 1974). As early as 1966, researchers found that 70 percent of the high school girls surveyed were unhappy with their bodies and wanted to lose weight (Heunemann, Shapiro, Hampton, and Mitchell, 1966). In 1991, Elissa Koff and Jill Rierdan found that, when asked if they'd "ever felt overweight in their lives," 72 percent of the eleven- and twelve-year-old girls surveyed answered yes (*Boston Globe*, 1992). The sociocultural pressure for thinness that is currently operating on women (and not to the same extent on men; see Silverstein et al., 1986) is a potentially fatal form of normative social influence. The last time that a very thin standard of bodily attractiveness for women existed—the mid-1920s—an epidemic of eating disorders appeared (Silverstein, Peterson, and Perdue, 1986).

Another type of normative social influence is apparent at the societal level when social change produces new rules for acceptable social behavior. For nearly one hundred years, from the Reconstruction period following the Civil War through the 1950s, African Americans in the southern states lived under an American version of apartheid—the "Jim Crow" laws. For example, blacks could not eat at most restaurants or stay in most hotels; they could not attend white schools or universities; they could not ride on public transportation unless they sat in the back of the bus; and they could not use public water fountains or restrooms except those labeled "Negro." While some southern whites found these social norms to be detestable, the vast majority lived out their lives in this milieu, rarely saying or doing anything that would challenge conformity to these social norms.

In 1955, Rosa Parks boarded a nearly full bus in Montgomery, Alabama, and sat in the "Negroes" section in the back. When the bus driver told her to give up her seat to a white man, she refused. Parks was led off the bus by police and arrested. In response, the white passengers simply murmured quietly or giggled (Toch, 1965). Parks's heroic act was a clear violation of the then operating norm; by refusing to conform, she gave impetus to the growing civil rights movement and the repeal of Jim Crow laws in the South.

> You cannot make a man by standing a sheep on its hind-legs. But by standing a flock of sheep in that position you can make a crowd of men.
> —Sir Max Beerbohm

## Mindless Normative Conformity: Operating on Automatic Pilot

As we have seen, normative pressures to conform can be very strong, and violating these norms can have severe consequences. By refusing to follow the segregation norms in the South, the Freedom Riders subjected themselves to vicious verbal and physical abuse. It is not surprising that many people conform in the face of such persecution. Many people in the South did not approve of segregation, and yet they went along with it to be liked and accepted. Similarly, Solomon Asch's participants knew that the majority was giving the wrong answer when judging the lengths of the lines, but conformed to avoid looking foolish and "standing out like a sore thumb."

There is another important reason that people obey social norms. Sometimes norms become so ingrained that people have internalized them, privately believing they are the correct way to behave. Consequently, people obey these norms even if no one is pressuring them to do so. We have learned that the "proper" thing to do is to wear socks of the same color and to greet people by shaking their hands, not patting their heads; we have learned that grasshoppers are a pesky insect, not a food delicacy. People growing up in other societies, however, have internalized different norms; in Japan, for example, toasted grasshoppers are quite a delicacy!

Many norms become so internalized that we **conform mindlessly** to them, without thinking about what we are doing or why—as if we were operating on automatic pilot. There is a great advantage to being able to respond automatically, knowing exactly what the right thing to do is, without having to waste our time deliberating about every little act we perform. When we dress in the morning, we do not have to spend time debating what color of each sock we should wear; we wear two of the same color because that is the norm.

**mindless conformity:** obeying internalized social norms without deliberating about one's actions

However, there are some definite disadvantages to following norms too mindlessly. Some norms are restrictive and unfair. In many subcultures in this country, it is the norm to hold prejudiced attitudes toward minority groups—such as African Americans, Hispanics, Asian Americans, and Jews—and unfortunately, many members of these subcultures internalize these views. It can be difficult to overcome such ingrained norms, even if we realize they are unjust (Devine, 1989).

There is another disadvantage to following norms too mindlessly: By putting ourselves on automatic pilot without carefully monitoring what we are doing, we sometimes end up following the wrong social norm (Cialdini, 1988; Langer, 1989). As a result, we get ourselves into trouble by behaving inappropriately. For example, the atomic scientist Robert Oppenheimer is said to have been so engrossed in his newspaper at breakfast one morning that he put a tip down on the table when he got up, forgetting that he was eating at home and not at a restaurant (needless to say, his wife was not amused). The consequences of this kind of mindless conformity are sometimes humorous, and sometimes very frightening.

For example, consider a study conducted by Ellen Langer and her colleagues (1978). These researchers sent a memo to forty secretaries at a New York university asking them to return the memo immediately to room 238. This was a pretty silly thing to ask: If whoever sent the memo wanted it, why did he or she send it in the first place? The researchers wondered if the secretaries would go ahead and return the memo by mindlessly following the norm that says, "Do what memos tell you to do." The researchers hypothesized that the secretaries would comply only if the memo looked like the ones they were used to receiving. If a quick glance at the memo indicated that it was like the hundreds of other memos they had seen, people were expected to do what it said rather mindlessly. If the memo looked different, however, people might stop and think more carefully about what they were doing.

To test this hypothesis, one group of secretaries received a memo that looked like the dozens of memos they received every week. It was worded impersonally—"This paper is to be returned immediately to Room 238 through interoffice mail"—and was not signed. (The researchers knew, from rummaging through old memos in trash cans, that unsigned, impersonal memos were the norm at this university.) Another memo deviated from this norm by being worded personally—"I would appreciate it if you would return this paper immediately to Room 238 through interoffice mail"—and was signed, "Sincerely, John Lewis." When the form of the memo was like the ones the secretaries normally received, it triggered the "follow instructions" norm: Ninety percent of the secretaries dutifully returned it to room 238. When the memo was different from the ones the secretaries typically received, they were more likely to turn off their automatic pilot and think about what they were doing, thereby realizing that it was a silly request: Only 60 percent of the secretaries returned the memo in this condition.

One norm that we often follow too mindlessly is the **reciprocity norm,** which says that if people do something nice for us, we should reciprocate by doing something nice for them. If someone invites us to his or her house, we feel we should reciprocate by inviting the person to ours. If someone gives us a gift, we feel obligated to get him or her a gift as well. To illustrate how strong this norm is—and how mindlessly people follow it—one researcher chose some names at random out of the telephone book and sent each person a Christmas card, signed with his name (Kunz & Woolcott, 1976). Most people sent a card back to him, even though he was a complete stranger!

Salespeople and charities often capitalize on this tendency for people to follow the reciprocity norm mindlessly. They give us a small gift, such as greeting cards or personalized address labels, making us feel obligated to reciprocate by buying their product or giving money to their cause. Retailers also capitalize on the reciprocity norm by giving free samples of their products as a gift. Suppose, for example, that you are at the grocery store one day and notice that the store is offering free samples of a new brand of cheese. A woman behind an attractive display table asks if you would like to try a piece. You agree, and she gives you a thin sliver on a toothpick. It is a sharp,

**reciprocity norm:** a social norm, which states that receiving anything positive from another person requires you to reciprocate (or behave similarly) in response

strong-tasting cheese, of a kind you do not particularly like. The woman asks expectantly, "How do you like it?" "It's OK," you say politely. You hesitate, then pick up a package of the cheese and put it in your cart, even though you know it will probably remain in your refrigerator for months, growing all sorts of strange molds before you finally throw it out.

People feel obligated to return the favor by purchasing some of the cheese, forgetting that the reciprocity norm does not apply here. You are not in a friend's living room eating an hors d'oeuvre made from a treasured family recipe; you are the target of a sales promotion in a grocery store. Nonetheless, people follow the reciprocity norm. One supermarket owner reported that he sold more than 1,000 pounds of cheese in a few hours after offering people free samples (Packard, 1957).

Shortly we will see how mindless conformity to another norm—the rule that we should obey authority figures—can have tragic consequences. First, though, let's consider when people are most likely to conform to normative social influences.

## When Will People Conform to Normative Social Influence?

People don't always cave in to peer pressure, or mindlessly follow inappropriate norms. Although conformity is commonplace, we are not lemmings who always do what everyone else is doing. And we certainly do not agree on all issues, as evidenced by the spirited public debates on such topics as abortion, family values, and affirmative action. (One need only tune in to a television or radio talk show to appreciate how much people disagree on topics such as these.) Exactly when are people most likely to conform to normative pressures?

The answer to this question is provided by Bibb Latané's (1981) **social impact theory.** According to this theory, the likelihood that you will respond to social influence from other people depends on three things: strength, referring to how important the group of people is to you; immediacy, referring to how close the group is to you in space and time during the influence attempt; and number, referring to how many people are in the group.

**social impact theory:** the theory that conforming to social influence depends on the strength, immediacy, and number of other people in a group

Social impact theory predicts that conformity will increase as strength and immediacy increase. Clearly, the more important a group is to us and the more we are in its presence, the more likely we will be to conform to its normative pressures. For example, the college students' dangerous game with trucks at stoplights involved very high degrees of strength and immediacy, with tragic consequences.

Number, however, operates in a different manner. As the size of the group increases, each additional person has less of an influencing effect—going from three people to four people makes more of a difference than going from fifty-three to fifty-four people. It is like the law of diminishing returns in economics, where increasing one's total wealth by $1 seems much greater if we have only $1 to start with than if we already have $1,000. Similarly, if we feel pressure from a group to conform, adding another person to the majority makes much more of a difference if the group consists of three people rather than fifteen people. Latané (1981) constructed a mathematical model that captures these hypothesized effects of strength, immediacy, and number, and has applied this formula to the results of many conformity studies. It has done a good job of predicting the actual amount of

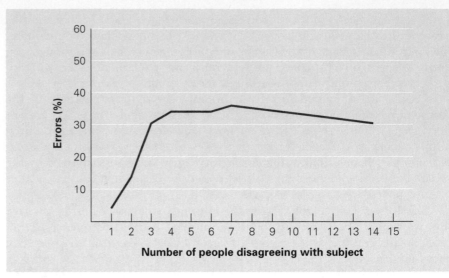

**FIGURE 7.5  Effects of group size on conformity.** Asch varied the size of the unanimous majority, and found that after the majority consisted of four people, adding more people had little influence on conformity. (Adapted from Asch, 1955)

conformity that occurred (Latané, 1981; Latané & Wolf, 1981; Tanford & Penrod, 1984).

Social impact theory covers conformity to all kinds of social influence. For present purposes, let's see in more detail what it says about the conditions under which people will conform to normative social pressures.

**When the Group Size Is Three or More.**  As we just saw, conformity increases as the number of people in the group increases—up to a point. Imagine you are a participant in Solomon Asch's study where you judged the length of lines. If there are only you and one other participant, and the latter gives a blatantly wrong answer about the length of the lines, will you be less likely to cave in and conform to the other participant's response than if there were five other participants all giving the wrong answer? What if there were fifteen people in the majority? Asch (1955) studied this question, and as we can see in Figure 7.5, conformity increased as the number of people in the group increased, but only up to a point.

Asch's (1955) initial research and that of later researchers has established that in this kind of group situation, conformity does not increase much after the group size reaches four or five other people (Gerard, Wilhelmy, and Conolley, 1968; McGuire, 1968; Rosenberg, 1961)—just as social impact theory suggests. In short, it does not take an extremely large group to create normative social influence. As Mark Twain wrote in *The Adventures of Huckleberry Finn*, "Hain't we got all the fools in town on our side? And ain't that a big enough majority in any town?"

**When the Group Is One We Care About.**  Another tenet of social impact theory is that the strength of the group makes a difference, defined as how important the group is to you. Normative pressures are much stronger when they come from people whose friendship, love, and respect we cherish, because there is a large cost to losing this love and respect. Thus, groups to which we are highly attracted and with which we strongly identify will exert more normative influence on us than groups for which we have little or no attachment (Clark & Maass, 1988; Lott & Lott, 1961; Nowak, Szamrej, and Latané, 1990; Sakurai, 1975; Wolf, 1985). One consequence of this fact is that it can be dangerous to have policy decisions made by highly cohesive groups, because they care more about pleasing each other and avoiding conflict than arriving at the most logical, sound decision. We will see several examples of this phenomenon in Chapter 9 (on group processes).

**When the Group Is Unanimous.**   Normative social influence is most powerfully felt when everyone in the group says or believes the same thing— for example, when your group of friends all believe that *101 Dalmations* was the greatest movie ever made. Resisting such unanimous social influence is difficult or even impossible—unless you have an ally. If another person disagrees with the group—say, by nominating *Citizen Kane* as the best movie ever—this behavior will help you to buck the tide as well.

To illustrate the importance of having an ally, Asch (1955) conducted another version of his conformity experiment. In this variation, he had six of the seven confederates give the wrong answer, whereas one confederate gave the right answer on every trial. Now the subject was not alone. While he or she still disagreed with the majority of the group, having one ally helped him or her to resist normative pressures. People conformed on an average of only 6 percent of the trials in this study, compared to 32 percent in the version where all of the confederates gave the wrong answer. Several other studies have found that observing another person resist normative social influence emboldens the individual to do the same (Allen & Levine, 1969; Morris & Miller, 1975; Nemeth & Chiles, 1988).

This effect of allies produces some interesting anomalies in everyday life—people who hold unpopular beliefs are able to maintain them in the face of group pressure if they can convince at least a few others to agree with them. In Chapter 3, we saw the members of a small cult persevere in their belief that the world was going to end (even when it didn't). Clearly, the fact that the other cult members continued to believe helped every individual in the group to ignore the ridicule with which outsiders viewed them. Similarly, a man in Lancaster, California, believes that the earth is flat— despite proof from scientific experiments over a few centuries that it is not (see the newspaper article reprinted on p. 270). It is difficult to hold such an unpopular (and wrongheaded!) view; not surprisingly, this man has actively recruited followers and attempts to convince others of his views through his *Flat Earth Newsletter*.

**When You Grow up in Certain Cultures.**   Does the society in which one is raised affect the frequency of normative social influence? Perhaps not surprisingly, the answer is yes. Stanley Milgram (1961, 1977) replicated the Asch studies in Norway and France. He found that the Norwegian participants conformed to a greater degree than the French participants did; he describes Norwegian society as "highly cohesive . . . [with] a deep feeling of

## Still a Hoax to Flat-Earth Group

Most people have come to accept the idea that the sun, the earth and the moon are all spheres, and that eclipses occur because of the rotation of the earth around the sun and of the moon around the earth. But one group of people, the International Flat Earth Research Society, contends that such an explanation is merely part of a gigantic hoax.

The president of the Flat Earth Society, Charles K. Johnson of Lancaster, Calif., believes that photographs taken from space, accounts of space travel and virtually everything else connected with modern science are all part of the hoax.

"Ever since Copernicus, the new religion — science, they call it — has been trying to fool the people with this notion that the earth is a ball," Mr. Johnson said in an interview.

"Starting around 1600, the facts were cast away by the priests of the new religion," he said, "and the vast, global con game began. They got most people to accept their hoax, but not us."

Nicolaus Copernicus was a Polish astronomer whose 1543 publication describing the motion of planets around the sun revolutionized astronomy. Formerly, the views of Ptolemy had prevailed, that the earth was the center of the universe around which everything else circled.

Mr. Johnson said that the society he heads, which was founded in 1888, now has about 1,600 formal members in the United States, in addition to some 2,000 believing outsiders. Members pay a $10 annual fee, for which they receive copies of the society's quarterly magazine, Flat Earth News.

The society president said he planned to "call President Carter's attention to the fact" that in 1959 a movie was made by the Three Stooges about a comic rocket trip to the planet Venus. "Purported photographs taken since then about space travel should be considered in the same category, as entertainment, rather than fact," he said.

"Only 10 or 20 percent of the people in the United States believe the hoax that men have traveled to the moon," Mr. Johnson said.

Asked how he would explain the eclipse of the sun, Mr. Johnson said, "We don't really go into all that. The Bible tells us that the heavens are a mystery."

If you can get a few allies to agree with you, it's easier to buck the majority and believe some rather strange things. (New York Times, February 26, 1979)

group identification," while French society, in comparison, "show[s] far less consensus in both social and political life" (1961, p. 51). While we might think of Japanese culture as more highly conforming than our own, an Asch-type study found that when the group unanimously gave the correct answer, some Japanese students purposefully chose the wrong one. In Japan, independence is highly prized in students; it appears that these participants went against the tide just to prove that they weren't conforming (Frager, 1970).

In another cross-cultural study of normative social influence, James Whittaker and Robert Meade (1967) found that people in Lebanon, Hong Kong, and Brazil conformed to a similar extent (both to each other and to the American sample), while participants from the Bantu tribe of Zimbabwe conformed to a much greater degree. As the researchers point out, conformity has a very high social value in Bantu culture. Finally, there is some intriguing evidence that conformity is actually decreasing. For example, replications of the Asch study conducted twenty-five to thirty years after the original, in Great Britain and the United States, have found lower percentages of conformity (Nicholson, Cole, and Rocklin, 1985; Perrin & Spencer, 1981).

**When You Are a Certain Type of Person.** While the prior conditions under which normative conformity occurs involve the group, this last condition involves aspects of the individual. Is a certain sort of person more likely to conform to normative pressures than another? Research in this area has focused on two aspects of the individual: personality and gender.

It seems reasonable to propose that some people are just conforming types, while others' personalities make them highly resistant to normative pressures. Solomon Asch (1956) suggested that people who have low self-esteem may be particularly conforming, because they fear rejection or punishment by the group. In the first study examining personality traits and conformity, Richard Crutchfield (1955) found evidence for this relationship between self-esteem and normative conformity; similarly, Mark Snyder and William Ickes (1985) found that people who perceived themselves as having a strong need for approval from others were more likely to demonstrate normative conformity.

Unfortunately, the relationship between personality traits and conforming behavior is not always so clear-cut. Some studies have found the relationship to be weak or nonexistent (Marlowe & Gergen, 1970). The reason is that, quite often, people are not very consistent in how they respond in different social situations (McGuire, 1968; Mischel, 1968). In other words, they don't always conform, across time and in different situations, the way they should if their personalities alone were affecting their behavior. Instead, the situation affects their behavior as well, so that in some situations they conform, and in other situations they don't, regardless of what type of person they are. You may recall from Chapter 1 that this is a fundamental principle of social psychology: Often the social situation is more important in understanding how someone behaves than is his or her personality.

The second person variable that has been studied is gender. Is it the case that women and men differ in how readily they conform to social pressures? For many years, the prevailing wisdom has been to answer this question in the affirmative: Women are more conforming than men (Crutchfield, 1955). When all three of your authors studied social psychology in college, this finding was presented as a fact. Recent reviews of the literature, however, have shown that matters are not so simple.

In the past few years, researchers have taken an objective look at this question by conducting *meta-analyses*. A meta-analysis is a statistical technique that allows you to combine results across a large number of studies and come up with a meaningful statistical summary. Alice Eagly and Linda Carli (1981), for example, performed a meta-analysis of 145 studies of influenceability that included more than 21,000 participants. Consistent with previous reviews of this literature, they found that, on average, men are less influenceable than women. But they found the size of the difference to be very small. A difference in influenceability shows up when you average across thousands of participants, but that does not mean that every man you encounter will be less influenceable than every woman. In fact, Eagly and Carli (1981) found that only 56 percent of men are less influenceable than the average woman, which means, of course, that a sizable proportion of men are more influenceable than the average woman.

Not only are sex differences in influenceability small, they depend on the type of conformity pressures impinging on people. Eagly (1987) and Becker (1986) report that gender differences are especially likely to be found in group-pressure situations, where an audience can directly observe how much you conform (e.g., the Asch study, where everyone can tell whether you give the same answer as the other participants). When faced with this kind of social pressure, women are especially more likely to conform than men are. In other situations, we are the only ones who know whether we conform, such as when we listen to someone give a speech against our views and then decide, privately, how much we agree with the speech. In this kind of situation, sex differences in influenceability virtually disappear. Eagly (1987) suggests that this pattern of results stems from the social roles men and women are taught in our society. Women are taught to be more agreeable and supportive, whereas men are taught to be more independent in the face of direct social pressures. And, Eagly suggests, both women and men are more likely to exhibit such gender-consistent behaviors in public situations, where everyone can see how they respond (e.g., the Asch-type conformity study). But remember, the size of these differences is relatively small.

One other finding in this area is surprising and controversial. Eagly and Carli (1981) took note of the gender of the researchers who conducted conformity studies, and found that male authors were more likely than female authors to find that males were less influenceable. Though the reason for this finding is not yet clear, Eagly and Carli (1981) suggest one possibility: Researchers may be more likely to use experimental materials and situations that are familiar to their gender. Male authors, for example, may be more likely to see how people conform to persuasive messages about sports, whereas female authors may be more likely to see how people conform to persuasive messages about topics of greater familiarity to women. As we saw earlier, people are more likely to conform when confronted with an unfamiliar, ambiguous situation; thus, women may be more likely to conform in the unfamiliar situations designed by male experimenters.

To summarize, there appears to be a small tendency for women to be more influenceable, especially in group-pressure situations. Further, the already small magnitude of this difference may be exaggerated in studies conducted by male researchers, who are more likely than female researchers to find that women are more influenceable than men.

### Resisting Normative Social Influence

Whereas normative social influence is often useful and appropriate, there are times when it is not. What can we do to resist inappropriate normative social influence? The best way to prevent ourselves from mindlessly following the wrong social norm is to become more mindful of what we are doing. If we stopped and thought carefully about whether the norm that seems to be operating is really the right one to follow, we would be more likely to recognize those times when it is not.

If becoming aware of normative influence is the first step to resistance, taking action is the second. Why do we fail to take action? Because of the possible ridicule, embarrassment, or rejection we may experience. However, we know that having an ally helps us resist normative pressures. Thus, if you are in a situation where you don't want to go along with the crowd, but you fear the repercussions if you don't, try to find another person (or better yet, a group) who thinks like you do.

In addition, the very act of conforming to normative influence most of the time earns you the right to deviate occasionally without serious consequences. This interesting observation was made by Edwin Hollander (1958, 1960), who stated that conforming to a group over time earns you **idiosyncrasy credits,** much like putting money in the bank. Thus, your past conformity allows you to deviate from the group (or act idiosyncratically) at some point in the future without getting into too much trouble. If you refuse

**idiosyncrasy credits:** the credits a person earns, over time, by conforming to group norms; if enough idiosyncrasy credits are earned, the person can, on occasion, behave deviantly without retribution from the group

to lend your car, for example, your friends may not become upset with you if you have followed their friendship norms in other areas in the past, for you've earned the right to be different, to deviate from their normative rules in this area. Thus, resisting normative influence may not be as difficult (or scary) as you might think, if you have earned idiosyncracy credits with the group.

## Minority Influence: When the Few Influence the Many

We shouldn't leave our discussion of normative social influence with the impression that the individual never has an effect on the group. As Serge Moscovici (1985) says, if groups really did succeed in silencing nonconformists, rejecting deviants, and persuading everyone to go along with the majority point of view, then how could change ever be introduced into the system? We would all be like little robots, marching along with everyone else in monotonous synchrony, never able to adapt to changing reality. Instead, Moscovici (1985) argues that the individual, or the minority, can affect change in the majority; Rosa Parks and her courageous behavior on a segregated bus in Alabama are one such example. This is called **minority influence**. The key is consistency: People with minority views must express the same view over time, and different members of the minority must agree with each other. If a person in the minority wavers between two different viewpoints or if two individuals express different minority views, then the majority will dismiss them as people who have peculiar and groundless opinions. If, however, the minority expresses a consistent, unwavering view, the majority is likely to take notice, and maybe even adopt the minority view (Moscovici & Nemeth, 1974).

**minority influence:** the case where a minority of group members influence the behavior or beliefs of the majority

Though there is some difference of opinion about why consistent minorities influence majorities, recent research suggests a possible answer. As we saw earlier in the Asch experiments, people in the majority cause public compliance in minority group members but not private acceptance. The minority members still believe they are right; they're simply unwilling to express their opinion publicly. When minorities do air their views publicly, however, they have little power to force the majority to conform to these views. Nonetheless, the majority might conform due to the informational consequences of hearing these views. Majority members might come to realize that there are different perspectives from their own, and thus examine the issues more carefully. As a result, they are likely to develop a much more thoughtful, in-depth position on the issue, often coming to believe that the minority view has merit (Latané & Wolf, 1981; Levine & Russo, 1987; Maass & Clark, 1984; Moscovici, 1980; Nemeth, 1986; Nemeth, Mayseless, Sherman, and Brown, 1990). In short, majorities often cause public compliance because of normative social influence, whereas minorities often cause private acceptance because of informational social influence.

To summarize, we have seen three reasons that people conform: because other people serve as a useful source of information (informational social influence), because of pressures to follow social norms (normative social influence), and because we have internalized social norms and follow them mindlessly. To what extent have we satisfactorily explained the different examples of social behavior with which we began the chapter?

Victims of the Holocaust, Nordhausen, April 1945.
According to social psychologists, most of the German
guards and citizens who participated in the Holocaust
were not madmen, but ordinary people exposed to extraordinary social influences.

Let's take another look at the My Lai massacre. We suspect that all three
of the reasons that people conform combined to produce this atrocity. The
behavior of the other soldiers made the killing seem like the right thing to do
(informational influence); the soldiers wanted to avoid rejection and ridicule
from their peers (normative influence); and the soldiers followed the obedience to authority social norm too readily, without questioning or taking personal responsibility for what they were doing. It was the power of these
conformity pressures that lead to the tragedy, not personality defects in the
American soldiers. This makes the incident all the more frightening, because
it implies that similar incidents can occur with any group of soldiers if
similar conformity pressures are present.

Nor are the tragic consequences of conformity limited to soldiers. The
philosopher Hannah Arendt (1965) argues that most participants in the
Holocaust were not sadists or psychopaths who enjoyed the mass murder of
innocent people, but ordinary citizens subjected to complex and powerful
social pressures. She covered the trial of Adolf Eichmann, the Nazi official
responsible for the transportation of Jews to the death camps, and concluded
that he was not the monster that many people made him out to be, but a
commonplace bureaucrat like any other bureaucrat, who did what he was
told without questioning his orders.

Our point is not that Eichmann or the soldiers at My Lai should be
excused for the crimes they committed. The point is that it is too easy to

explain their behavior as the acts of madmen. It is more fruitful—and indeed more frightening—to view their behavior as the acts of ordinary people exposed to extraordinary social influence. But how do we know whether this interpretation of the Holocaust and My Lai is correct? How can we be sure that it was social influence that produced these atrocities, and not the work of evil people? The way to find out is to study social pressure in the laboratory under controlled conditions. We could take a sample of ordinary citizens, subject them to various kinds of social influence, and see to what extent they will conform and obey. Can an experimenter influence ordinary people to commit immoral acts, such as inflicting severe pain on an innocent bystander? Stanley Milgram (1963, 1974, 1976) decided to find out, in what has become the most famous series of studies in social psychology.

## Obedience to Authority

Imagine that you were a participant in one of Milgram's studies, and think about how you would have responded: You answer an ad in the paper asking for participants in a study on memory and learning. (The other participants ranged from twenty to fifty years of age and were blue-collar, white-collar, and professional workers.) When you arrive at the laboratory, you meet another participant, a forty-seven-year-old, somewhat overweight, pleasant-looking fellow. The experimenter explains that one of you will play the role of a teacher and the other a learner. You draw a slip of paper out of a hat and discover that you will be the teacher. It turns out that your job is to teach the other participant a list of word pairs (e.g., blue-box, nice-day) and then test him on the list. The experimenter instructs you to deliver an electric shock to the learner whenever he makes a mistake, as the purpose of the study is to examine the effects of punishment on learning.

You watch as the other participant—the learner—is strapped into a chair in an adjacent room and electrodes are attached to his arm. You are seated in

Left: The shock generator used in the Milgram experiments. Right: The learner (an accomplice of the experimenter) is strapped into the chair, and electrodes are attached to his arm. (Adapted from Milgram, 1974)

**Transcript of Learner's Protests in Milgram's Obedience Experiment**

75 volts Ugh!
90 volts Ugh!
105 volts Ugh! (louder)
120 volts Ugh! Hey this really hurts.
135 volts Ugh!!
150 volts Ugh!!! Experimenter! That's all. Get me out of here. I told you I had heart trouble. My heart's starting to bother me now. Get me out of here, please. My heart's starting to bother me. I refuse to go on. Let me out.
165 volts Ugh! Let me out! (shouting)
180 volts Ugh! I can't stand the pain. Let me out of here! (shouting)
195 volts Ugh! Let me out of here. Let me out of here. My heart's bothering me. Let me out of here! You have no right to keep me here! Let me out! Let me out of here! Let me out! Let me out of here! My heart's bothering me. Let me out! Let me out!
210 volts Ugh!! Experimenter! Get me out of here. I've had enough. I won't be in the experiment any more.
225 volts Ugh!
240 volts Ugh!
255 volts Ugh! Get me out of here.
270 volts (Agonized scream) Let me out of here. Let me out of here. Let me out of here. Let me out. Do you hear? Let me out of here.
285 volts (Agonized scream)
300 volts (Agonized scream) I absolutely refuse to answer any more. Get me out of here. You can't hold me here. Get me out. Get me out of here.
315 volts (Intensely agonized scream) I told you I refuse to answer. I'm no longer part of this experiment.
330 volts (Intense and prolonged agonized scream) Let me out of here. Let me out of here. My heart's bothering me. Let me out, I tell you. (Hysterically) Let me out of here. Let me out of here. You have no right to hold me here. Let me out! Let me out! Let me out of here! Let me out!

**Instructions used by Experimenter to Achieve Obedience**

Prod 1: Please continue. *or* Please go on.
Prod 2: The experiment requires that you continue.
Prod 3: It is absolutely essential that you continue.
Prod 4: You have no other choice, you *must* go on.
The prods were always made in sequence: Only if Prod 1 had been unsuccessful, could Prod 2 be used. If the subject refused to obey the experimenter after Prod 4, the experiment was terminated. The experimenter's tone of voice was at all times firm, but not impolite. The sequence was begun anew on each occasion that the subject balked or showed reluctance to follow orders.
Special prods. If the subject asked if the learner was liable to suffer permanent physical injury, the experimenter said:
Although the shocks may be painful, there is no permanent tissue damage, so please go on. [Followed by Prods 2, 3, and 4 if necessary.]
If the subject said that the learner did not want to go on, the experimenter replied: Whether the learner likes it or not, you must go on until he has learned all the word pairs correctly. So please go on. [Followed by Prods 2, 3, and 4 if necessary.

**FIGURE 7.6** Transcript of the learner's protests in Milgram's obedience study (left). Transcript of the prods used by the experimenter to get people to continue giving shocks (right). (Adapted from Milgram, 1963, 1974)

front of a shock generator whose thirty switches deliver varying levels of shock in 15-volt increments, from 15 to 450 volts. There are labels accompanying these switches, from "Slight Shock," to "Danger: Severe Shock," to an ominous "XXX" next to the highest levels (see the photos on the previous page). The experimenter tells you that the first time the learner makes a mistake, you should give him a shock of 15 volts—the smallest amount—and then increase the amount by 15 volts for each subsequent mistake he makes. So that you will know what the shocks are like, the experimenter gives you a sample shock of 45 volts, which is rather painful.

You read the list of word pairs to the learner, and then you begin the testing phase. After announcing the first word of a pair, you give four possible answers; the learner responds by pressing one of four switches, which illuminates a light on the answer box in front of you. Everything begins smoothly, as the learner gets the first few right. Then he gets some wrong, and as instructed, you deliver the shocks. You are probably getting concerned about the number and severity of the shocks you will have to give. When you get to the 75-volt level, the learner, whom you can hear over an intercom, emits a painful "Ugh!" At this point, perhaps, you pause and ask the experimenter what you should do. "Please continue," he responds. As the learner continues to make mistakes, you deliver a few more shocks. The learner protests, shouting, "Ugh! Experimenter! That's all! Get me out of here!" You look at the experimenter with grave concern. He tells you, "It is absolutely essential that you continue." (See Figure 7.6.)

What would you do? How many people do you think would continue to obey the experimenter and increase the levels of shock until they had delivered the maximum amount—450 volts?

When this question was posed to psychology majors at Yale University, they estimated that only about 1 percent of the population would go to this extreme. A sample of middle-class adults and a panel of psychiatrists made similar predictions. However, from our discussion of conformity thus far, you are probably not so optimistic. Whereas no one would have believed that such travesties as the Holocaust or My Lai could have occurred, they did. Like the soldiers at My Lai, most of Milgram's participants succumbed to the pressure of an authority figure. The average maximum amount of shock delivered was 360 volts, and 62.5 percent of the participants delivered the 450-volt shock—the maximum amount. A full 80 percent of the participants continued giving the shocks even after the learner, who earlier had mentioned that he had a heart condition, screamed, "Let me out of here! Let me out of here! My heart's bothering me. Let me out of here! . . . Get me out of here! I've had enough. I won't be in the experiment any more" (Milgram, 1974, p. 56).

It is important to note that the learner was actually an accomplice of the experimenter and playacted his role; he did not receive any actual shocks. It is equally important to note that the study was very convincingly done, so that people believed they really were shocking the learner. Here is Milgram's description of one participant's response to the teacher role:

> I observed a mature and initially poised businessman enter the laboratory smiling and confident. Within 20 minutes he was reduced to a twitching, stuttering wreck, who was rapidly approaching a point of nervous collapse. He constantly pulled on his earlobe, and twisted his hands. At one point he pushed his fist into his forehead and muttered, "Oh God, let's stop it." And yet he continued to respond to every word of the experimenter, and obeyed to the end. (Milgram, 1963, p. 377)

Why did so many research participants (ranging in age from the twenties to fifties) conform to the wishes of the experimenter, to the point where they (at least in their own minds) were inflicting great pain on another human being? And why were the college students, middle-class adults, and psychiatrists so wrong in their predictions about what people would do? Each of the three reasons that people conform combined in an insidious way, causing Milgram's participants to obey—just as the soldiers did at My Lai. Let's take a close look at how this worked in the Milgram experiments.

First, it is clear that *normative pressures* made it difficult for people to refuse to continue. As we have seen, if someone really wants us to do something, it can be difficult to say no. This is particularly true when the person is in a position of authority over us. Milgram's participants probably believed that if they refused to continue, the experimenter would be dis-

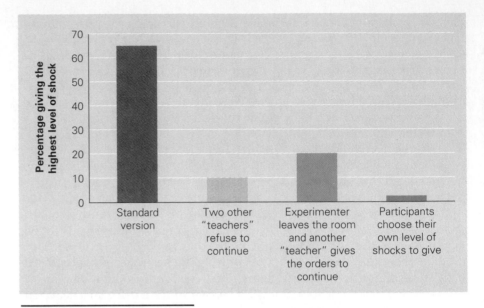

**FIGURE 7.7  The results of different versions of the Milgram experiment.**
Obedience is highest in the standard version, where the participant is ordered
to deliver increasing levels of shock to another person (left panel). Obedience
drops when other participants model disobedience or when the authority
figure is not present (two middle panels). Finally, when no orders are given to
increase the shocks, almost no participants do so (right panel). The contrast in
behavior between the far left and right panels indicates just how powerful the
social norm of obedience is. (Adapted  from Milgram, 1974)

appointed, hurt, or maybe even angry—all of which put pressure on them
to continue. It is important to note that this study, unlike the Asch study,
was set up so that the experimenter actively attempted to get people to
conform, giving such stern commands as "It is absolutely essential that you
continue." When an authority figure is so insistent that we obey, it is difficult
to say no.

The fact that normative pressures were present in the Milgram experiments is clear from a variation of the study that he conducted. This time,
there were three teachers, two of whom were confederates of the experimenter. One confederate was instructed to read the list of word pairs; the
other, to tell the learner whether his response was correct. The (real) participant's job was to deliver the shocks, increasing their severity with each error,
as in the original experiment. At 150 volts, when the learner gave his first
vehement protest, the first confederate refused to continue, despite the experimenter's command that he do so. At 210 volts, the second confederate
refused to continue. The result? Seeing their peers disobey freed participants
from their conformity, making it much easier for them to disobey too. Only
10 percent of the participants gave the maximum level of shock in this experiment (see Figure 7.7). Thus, people felt a great deal of pressure to conform
when they were all alone with the authority figure, but found it easier to
rebel when someone else did so. This result is the same as Asch's finding that
people did not conform nearly so much when one accomplice bucked the
majority and consistently gave the correct answer.

Despite the power of the normative pressures in Milgram's original study, they are not the sole reason people complied. The experimenter was authoritative and insistent, but he was not pointing a gun at anyone and telling them to "conform or else." The participants were free to get up and leave anytime they wanted to. Why didn't they, especially when the experimenter was a stranger they had never met before and probably would never see again?

As we saw earlier, when people are in a confusing situation and unsure of what they should do, they use other people to reach a definition of the situation. *Informational social influence* is especially powerful when the situation is ambiguous, when it is a crisis, and when the other people in the situation have some expertise. The situation faced by Milgram's participants was clearly confusing and unfamiliar, as well as upsetting. It all seemed straightforward enough when the experimenter explained it to them, but then it turned into something else altogether. The learner cried out in pain, but the experimenter told the participant that, while the shocks were painful, they did not cause any permanent tissue damage. The participant didn't want to hurt anyone, but he or she had agreed to be in the study and to follow the directions. When in such a state of conflict, it was only natural for the participants to use an expert—the experimenter—to help them decide what was the right thing to do.

Another version of the experiment that Milgram performed supports the idea that informational influence was present. This version was identical to the original one except for three critical changes: First, the experimenter never said which shock levels were to be given, leaving this decision up to the teacher (the real participant). Second, before the study began the experimenter received a telephone call and had to leave the room. He told the participant to continue without him. Third, there was a confederate playing the role of an additional teacher, whose job was to record how long it took the learner to respond. When the experimenter left, this other teacher said that he had just thought of a good system: How about if they increased the level of shock each time the learner made a mistake? He insisted that the real participant follow this procedure.

Note that in this situation, the expertise of the person giving the commands has been removed: He was just a regular person, no more knowledgeable than the participants themselves. Because he lacked expertise, people were much less likely to use him as a source of information about how they should respond. As seen in Figure 7.7, in this version compliance dropped from 65 percent giving the maximum amount of shock to only 20 percent. (The fact that 20 percent still complied suggests that some people were so uncertain about what to do that they used even a nonexpert as a guide.)

An additional variation conducted by Stanley Milgram underscores the importance of authority-figures-as-experts in eliciting such conformity and obedience. In this experiment, two experimenters gave the real participant his orders. At 150 volts, when the learner first cries out that he wants to stop, the two experimenters began to disagree about whether they should continue the study. At this point, 100 percent of the participant-teachers stopped responding. Note that nothing the victim ever did caused all the participants to stop obeying; however, when the authorities' definition of the situation became unclear, the participants broke out of their conforming role.

Thus, both normative and informational social influences were very strong in Milgram's experiments. However, these reasons for complying still fall short of fully explaining why people acted so inhumanely. They seem to account for why people initially complied, but after it became increasingly obvious to people what they were doing to the learner, why didn't they realize that what they were doing was terribly wrong and stop? Just as the soldiers at My Lai persisted in killing the villagers long after it was obvious that they were unarmed and defenseless civilians, many of Milgram's participants pulled the shock levers time after time after time, despite the cries of anguish from a fellow human being.

To understand this continued compliance, we need to consider additional aspects of the situation. First, as we saw earlier, people sometimes follow the wrong social norm, such as the secretaries in Ellen Langer's study who followed the "do what memos tell you to do" norm, even when it was pretty pointless. Sometimes we are on automatic pilot, and don't realize that the social norm we are following is inappropriate or nonapplicable to the situation we are in.

We don't mean to imply that Milgram's participants were completely mindless, or unaware of what they were doing. All were terribly concerned about the plight of the victim. The problem was that they were caught in a web of conflicting norms, and it was difficult to determine which one to follow. At the beginning of the experiment, it was perfectly reasonable to obey the norm that says, "Obey expert, legitimate authority figures." The experimenter was confident and knowledgeable, and the study seemed like it was a reasonable test of an interesting hypothesis. So why not cooperate and do as you are told?

But gradually the rules of the game changed, and this "obey authority" norm was no longer appropriate. The experimenter, who seemed so reasonable before, was now asking people to inflict great pain on their fellow participant. But once people are following one norm, it can be difficult to switch midstream, realizing that this norm is no longer appropriate and that another norm, "Do not inflict needless harm on a fellow human being," should be followed. For example, suppose the experimenter had explained, at the outset, that he would like people to deliver possibly fatal shocks to the other participant. How many people would have agreed? Very few, we suspect, because it would have been clear that this violated an important social and personal norm about inflicting harm on others. Instead, the experimenter pulled a kind of "bait-and-switch" routine, whereby he first made it look like an "obey authority" norm was appropriate and then gradually violated this norm.

It was particularly difficult for people to abandon the obey authority norm because of two key aspects of the situation. First, the experiment was fast-paced, preventing the participants from reflecting about what they were doing. They were busy recording the learner's responses, keeping track of which word pairs to test him on next, and determining whether his responses were right or wrong. Given that they had to attend carefully to these details, and move along at a fast pace, it was difficult for them to realize that the norm that was guiding their behavior—cooperating with the authority figure—was, after a while, no longer appropriate. We suspect that if halfway through the experiment, Milgram's participants had been told to take a fifteen-minute break and go sit in a room by themselves, many more would have successfully redefined the situation and refused to continue.

Second, it is important to remember that the experimenter asked people to increase the shocks in very small increments. The participants did not go from giving a small shock to giving a potentially lethal one. Instead, at any given point they were faced with the decision about whether to increase the amount of shock they had just given by 15 volts. As we saw in Chapter 3, every time a person makes an important or difficult decision, dissonance is produced, with resultant pressures to reduce it. An effective way of reducing dissonance produced by a difficult decision is to decide that the decision was fully justified. But because reducing dissonance provides a justification for the preceding action, in some situations it makes a person vulnerable to pressures leading to an escalation of the chosen activity.

Thus, in the Milgram study, once the participants agreed to administer the first shock, it created pressure on them to continue to obey. As the participants administered each successive level of shock, they had to justify it in their own minds. Once a particular shock level was justified, it became very difficult for them to find a place where they could draw the line and stop. How could they say, in effect, "OK, I gave him 200 volts, but not 215—never 215!"? Each succeeding justification laid the groundwork for the next shock and would have been dissonant with quitting; 215 volts is not that different from 200, and 230 is not that different from 215. Those who did break off the series did so against enormous internal pressure to continue.

In sum, Milgram's participants were in a complex social situation, and several factors contributed to their decision to flick the shock switches. Normative and informational social influences were very strong; people were reluctant to pay the social cost of disobeying an authority figure, and looked to the experimenter as an expert source of information. Further, they were caught in a web of conflicting social norms, and found it difficult to recognize that the one they started following—the obey authority norm—was no longer appropriate. Contributing to this difficulty was the fact that they were asked to increase the level of shocks in small increments. After justifying to themselves that they had delivered one level of shock, it was very difficult for participants to decide that a slightly higher level of shock was wrong.

Before leaving our discussion of the Milgram studies, we should mention one other possible interpretation of his results: Did the participants act so inhumanely because there is an evil side to human nature, lurking just below the surface, ready to be expressed with the flimsiest excuse? After all, it was socially acceptable to inflict harm on another person in the Milgram experiment; in fact, subjects were ordered to do so. Perhaps this allowed the expression of a universal aggressive urge. To test this hypothesis, Milgram conducted another version of his study. Everything was the same except that the experimenter told the participants that they could choose any level of shock they wished to give the learner when he made a mistake. Milgram gave people permission to use the highest levels, telling them that there was a lot to be learned from all levels of shock. This instruction should have allowed any aggressive urges to be expressed unchecked. Instead, the participants chose to give very mild shocks (see Figure 7.7). Only 2.5 percent of the participants gave the maximum amount of shock. Thus, the Milgram studies do not show that people have an evil streak that shines through when the surface is scratched. Instead, these studies demonstrate that social pressures can combine in insidious ways to make humane people act in an inhumane manner. Let us conclude this chapter with the words of Stanley Milgram:

> Even Eichmann was sickened when he toured the concentration camps, but, in order to participate in mass murder he had only to sit at a desk and shuffle papers. At the same time the man in the camp who actually dropped Cyclon-B into the gas chambers is able to justify his behavior on the grounds that he is only following orders from above. Thus there is fragmentation of the total human act; no one man decides to carry out the evil act and is confronted with its consequences. The person who assumes full responsibility for the act has evaporated. Perhaps this is the most common characteristic of socially organized evil in modern society. (1976, pp. 183-184)

## SUMMARY

In this chapter, we focused on **conformity,** or how people change their behavior due to the real (or imagined) influence of others. We found that there are two main reasons people conform: because of informational and normative social influences. **Informational social influence** occurs when people do not know what is the correct (or best) thing to do or say. This reaction typically occurs in new, confusing, or crisis situations, where the definition of the situation is unclear. People look to the behavior of others as an important source of information and use it to choose appropriate courses of action for themselves. Informational influence usually results in **private acceptance,** wherein people genuinely believe in what other people are doing or saying.

People are most likely to use others as a source of information when the situation (and thus what they should do) is ambiguous; here a person is most open to the influence of others. Experts are powerful sources of influence, since they typically have the most information about appropriate responses. A special type of ambiguous situation is a crisis; fear, confusion, and panic increase our reliance on others to help us decide what to do.

Using others as a source of information can backfire, however, as when people panic because others are doing so. **Contagion** occurs when emotions and behaviors spread rapidly throughout a large group; one example is research on **mass psychogenic illnesses.** You can best resist the inappropriate use of others as a source of information by checking the information you are getting against your common sense and internal moral compass.

**Normative social influence** occurs for a different reason—we change our behavior to match that of others not because they seem to know better what is going on, but because we want to remain a member of the group, continue to gain the advantages of group membership, and avoid the pain of ridicule and rejection. Normative social influence can occur even in unambiguous situations; people will conform to others for normative reasons even if they know that what they are doing is wrong. Normative social influence usually results in **public compliance** but not private acceptance of other people's ideas and behaviors.

Failure to respond to normative influences can be painful. Normative pressures operate on many levels in social life: They influence our eating habits, body image, hobbies, fashion, and so on; they promote correct (polite) behavior in society; and they can be an agent for social change. A special type is **mindless conformity,** whereby we operate as if on automatic pilot, never questioning or thinking about the **social norms** we are following, such as the **reciprocity norm.**

**Social impact theory** specifies when normative social influence is most likely to occur, by referring to the strength, immediacy, and number of group members. We are more likely to conform when the group is one we care about, when the group members are unanimous in their thoughts or behaviors, and when the group size is three or more. We can resist inappropriate conformity for normative reasons by being more mindful of normative pressures and by gathering **idiosyncrasy credits,** over time, from a group whose membership we value. Finally, **minority influence,** whereby a minority of group members influence the beliefs and behavior of the majority, can occur under certain conditions.

In the most famous series of studies in social psychology, Stanley Milgram examined the limits of obedience to authority figures. Informational and normative pressures combined to cause chilling levels of obedience, to the point where a majority of the participants administered what they thought were near-lethal shocks to a fellow human being. In addition, the participants were caught in a web of conflicting social norms, so that it was difficult to recognize that the one they started following ("obey authority figures") was no longer appropriate. Contributing to this difficulty was the fact that people were asked to increase the level of shocks in small increments. After justifying to themselves that they had delivered one level of shock, it was very difficult for people to decide that a slightly higher level of shock was wrong. Unfortunately, the conditions that produced such extreme antisocial behavior in Milgram's laboratory have been present in real-life tragedies, such as the Holocaust and the mass murders at My Lai in Vietnam.

## SUGGESTED READINGS

Cialdini, R. B. (1993). *Influence: Science and practice* (3rd ed.). New York: HarperCollins. An extremely readable and entertaining account of research on conformity with applications to everyday life.

Milgram, S. (1974). *Obedience to authority: An experimental view*. New York: Harper & Row. A detailed description of the most famous studies in social psychology: those in which people were induced to deliver what they believed were lethal shocks to a fellow human being. Nearly twenty years after it was published, Milgram's book remains a poignant and insightful account of obedience to authority.

Sherif, M. (1936). *The psychology of social norms*. New York: Harper. An entertaining account of Sherif's study of informational social influence, wherein people judged how much a light was moving. It is still worth reading today.

Turner, J. C. (1991). *Social influence*. Pacific Grove, CA: Brooks/Cole. An up-to-date, in-depth account of social psychological research on social influence and conformity.

# Chapter 8

## Attitudes and Attitude Change:
## Influencing Thoughts and Feelings

n the summer of 1988, Vice-President George Bush was far behind Governor Michael Dukakis in the race for the presidency. Some observers were convinced that Dukakis's lead was insurmountable. But surprisingly, within a few short months the lead had all but evaporated, and on Election Day, Bush won handily. A great many political analysts credit Willie Horton with playing a major role in this turnaround. Indeed, *Time* magazine referred to Willie Horton as "George Bush's most valuable player."

Who was Willie Horton? He was not one of Bush's campaign advisers; nor was he a major financial contributor. In fact, the two men had never met. As some of you may remember, Willie Horton was a convict who had been released from a Massachusetts prison before the end of his sentence, as part of a furlough program. While on furlough, Willie Horton escaped to Maryland, where he raped a woman after wounding her male companion. Michael Dukakis was governor of Massachusetts at the time of Horton's furlough.

Accusing Dukakis of being soft on crime, Bush ran a series of television and print ads showing mug shots of a scowling Willie Horton and depicting criminals going in and out of prison through a revolving door. These ads struck a responsive chord in many Americans, who feared street crime and harbored deep-seated suspicions that the criminal justice system favors criminals at the expense of victims. That the ads also indicated that Willie Horton was black may have led to stereotyped thinking and prejudiced attitudes on the part of white viewers.

Michael Dukakis fought back—with facts and figures. He pointed out that Massachusetts was only one of many states with a furlough program and that even the federal government (of which George Bush was then vice-president) furloughed inmates from its prisons. He stated that

The Willie Horton ad used in George Bush's 1988 presidential campaign.

furlough programs were generally very effective and that in 1987, of the 53,000 inmates receiving furloughs, only a small percentage got into trouble. On other issues, he also had an arsenal of facts: "Balanced ten budgets in a row," read one of his ads. "Cut taxes five times. Created 400,000 jobs, put 20 percent more cops on the street."

Are you getting bored yet? So was the American public. If Michael Dukakis had had a social psychologist on his staff, this researcher would have advised him that people who are deeply frightened and angry at the

thought of themselves or their loved ones being beaten or raped do not want to hear facts and figures. They want to be reassured—for example, by George Bush's "get tough on crime" approach, as well as his appeal for "a kinder and gentler nation." This lesson seems to have been learned by Bill Clinton, who did not use the same "facts and figures" approach as did Dukakis. In 1992, the country was in the midst of a recession, and many families were suffering severe economic hardships. Bill Clinton presented ads that emphasized the need for "change"—a word he used repeatedly—and portrayed him as a caring, compassionate man who could better solve the nation's problems. In short, his ads attempted to convey reassurance and compassion, rather than reciting facts and figures.

**S**ometimes facts and figures *are* persuasive. Consider antismoking campaigns. In the past twenty years, there has been a concerted effort to educate Americans about the dangers of smoking cigarettes, by making people more aware of the facts—that smoking is linked to a host of serious, life-threatening diseases. This campaign has been very successful: The percentage of adult Americans who smoke has dropped to the lowest level ever since the government began keeping count in 1955—24 percent in 1993, down from 43 percent in 1973 (*USA Today*, March 12, 1993). Note that this drop has occurred despite cigarette advertisements that try to make us ignore the facts, by associating smoking with sex, fun, and eternal youthfulness.

Neither Bush's Willie Horton ads nor antismoking messages were controlled experiments. Thus, we cannot be sure exactly what was responsible for causing people to vote for George Bush or to stop smoking. These examples

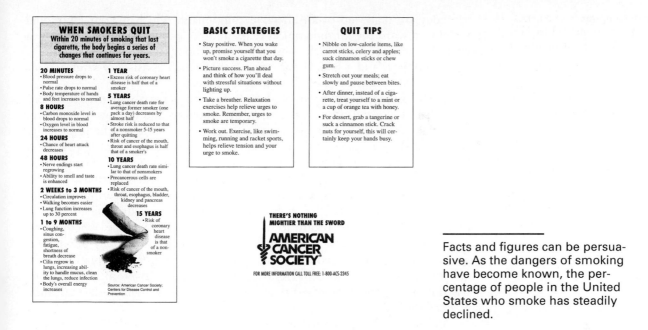

Facts and figures can be persuasive. As the dangers of smoking have become known, the percentage of people in the United States who smoke has steadily declined.

suggest, however, that people's attitudes can be influenced in quite different ways. Under some conditions, people are swayed by a logical consideration of the facts; under other conditions, people are swayed by appeals to their fears, hopes, and desires. But what are these conditions? What exactly is an attitude, and how is it changed? These questions, which are some of the oldest in social psychology, are the subject of this chapter.

## The Definition of Attitudes

Though there is not complete agreement among social psychologists over the precise definition of an **attitude**, most agree that it consists of an enduring evaluation—positive or negative—of people, objects, and ideas (Eagly & Chaiken, 1993; Olson & Zanna, 1993). Attitudes are enduring in the sense that they often persist over time. A momentary annoyance at something somebody says is not an attitude, but a lasting, negative impression of the person is. Attitudes are evaluative in the sense that they consist of a positive or negative reaction to something. People are not neutral observers of the world, but constant evaluators of what they see. For example, it would be very unusual to hear someone say, "My feelings toward anchovies, snakes, chocolate cake, and my roommate are completely neutral."

**attitude:** an enduring evaluation—positive or negative—of people, objects, and ideas

### Affective, Cognitive, and Behavioral Components

We can elaborate further on our definition of an attitude by stating more precisely what we mean by an "evaluation." Attitudes are made up of different components, or parts (Breckler, 1984; McGuire, 1985). Specifically,

**affective component of an attitude:** the emotions and feelings people associate with an attitude object

**cognitive component of an attitude:** people's beliefs about the properties of an attitude object

**behavioral component of an attitude:** people's actions toward an attitude object

attitudes are made up of an **affective component,** which is your emotional reaction toward the attitude object (e.g., another person or a social issue); a **cognitive component,** which consists of your thoughts and beliefs about the attitude object; and a **behavioral component,** which consists of your actions or observable behavior toward the attitude object.

For example, consider your attitude toward a particular model of car. First, there is your affective reaction, or the emotions and feelings the car triggers. These feelings might be a sense of excitement and aesthetic pleasure when you see the car, or feelings of anger and resentment (e.g., if you are a U.S. autoworker examining a new foreign-made model). Second, there is your cognitive reaction, or the beliefs you hold about the car's attributes. These might involve your thoughts about the car's gas mileage, steering and handling, appearance, roominess, and so on. Third, there is your behavioral reaction, or how you act in regard to this type of car. For example, whether you go to the dealership to test-drive the car and whether you actually purchase it are behaviors related to your attitude. Whereas attitudes are evaluations with affective, cognitive, and behavioral components, any given attitude can be based more on one component than on another—as we will see later (Zanna & Rempel, 1988).

Even though attitudes are more enduring than momentary whims or fancies, they do sometimes change. The American electorate, for example, seems to have undergone a dramatic change of attitude toward George Bush between 1988 and 1992. Attitudes are of great interest to social psychologists because when they do change, they often do so in response to social influence—that is, in response to the "imagined or implied presence of others" (Allport, 1985, p. 3), as we discussed in Chapter 1. Thus, something as personal and internal as an attitude is, in fact, a highly social phenomenon.

Think for a moment how often, in a given day, someone attempts to change your attitudes. American businesses spend billions of dollars a year on advertising, in an attempt to sell us everything from laundry detergent to

Car advertisements attempt to persuade you to like (and then buy) a given car by aiming their message at each of the three components that make up your attitude. In these two advertisements, which of the components—affective, cognitive, and behavioral—do you think the advertisers have targeted in their persuasion attempt?

condoms. There are entire cable television channels that do nothing but advertise and sell commercial products. Governmental officials attempt to persuade us that the economic outlook is rosy and that the bleak conditions of our inner cities are improving. Hardly a moment goes by without someone trying to change our attitude about something. Under what conditions are attitudes most likely to change?

## Changing Attitudes by Changing Behavior: Cognitive Dissonance Theory Revisited

The astute reader will remember that we have already discussed one condition under which attitudes change: when people behave inconsistently with their attitudes, and cannot find external justification for their behavior. We refer, of course, to *cognitive dissonance theory*. Because we discussed this theory at length in Chapter 3, we will give only a brief summary here.

*Cognitive dissonance* was originally defined as an inconsistency between two thoughts, or cognitions, such as "I am an honest person" and "I just lied to my best friend." As the theory evolved, it became clear that not just any inconsistency causes dissonance—the discomfort is caused by an inconsistency between an action or thought and one's self-concept (Aronson, 1969; Thibodeau & Aronson, 1992). People experience dissonance when they do something that threatens their image of themselves as decent, kind, and honest, particularly if there is no way they can explain away this behavior as due to external circumstances.

Consider an example we gave in Chapter 3. You walk into your friend Sam's house and notice an atrocious painting on the wall. You are about to burst into raucous laughter when Sam says, with a great deal of pleasure and excitement, "Do you like it? It's by a relatively unknown artist named Carol Smear; I think she is very talented, so I went into hock to buy it. Don't you think it's beautiful?"

How do you respond? You hesitate, your mind racing. "Sam seems so happy with his painting. Why should I rain on his parade? If I tell him my honest opinion, I'll hurt his feelings; he might get mad. I might make him feel that he made a terrible mistake. Anyway, he can't take it back. What's the sense in telling him the truth?" So you tell Sam that you like the painting very much. Do you experience much dissonance? We doubt it. A great many thoughts are consonant with having told this lie, as outlined in your reasoning in the above sentences. For example, your cognition that it is important not to cause pain to people you like provides ample *external justification* for having told a harmless lie.

But what happens if you say something you don't really believe and there is no ample external justification for doing so? What if your friend Sam was fabulously wealthy and bought paintings constantly? In addition, what if you were a noted art historian whose opinion Sam valued? What if, in the past, you'd told him he'd bought a veritable eyesore and your friendship had survived? Now the external justifications for lying to Sam about the painting are minimal or close to nonexistent. If you still refrain from giving your true opinion (saying instead, "Gee, Sam, it's, uh . . . interesting"), you will experience dissonance.

When you can't find external justification for your behavior, you will attempt to find *internal justification*—by bringing the two cognitions (your attitude and your behavior) closer together. How do you do this? You begin looking for positive aspects of the painting—some evidence of creativity or sophistication that might have escaped you previously. Chances are that if you look hard enough, you will find something. Within a short time, your attitude toward the painting will have moved in the direction of the positive statement you have made, and that is how "saying is believing." This phenomenon is generally referred to as *counterattitudinal advocacy:* a process by which individuals are induced to state publicly an opinion or attitude that runs counter to their own private attitudes. When this is accomplished with a minimum of external justification, it results in a change in the individual's private attitude in the direction of the public statement.

As we saw in Chapter 3, there is substantial evidence that counterattitudinal advocacy is a powerful way to change someone's attitudes. If you wanted to change a friend's attitude toward smoking, you might succeed by getting him or her to give an antismoking speech, under conditions of low external justification. But what if your goal was to change attitudes on a mass scale? Suppose you were hired by the American Cancer Society to come up with an antismoking campaign that could be used nationwide. Though dissonance techniques are powerful, they are very difficult to carry out on a mass scale (e.g., it would be impossible to have all Americans who smoke make antismoking speeches under just the right conditions of low external justification). In order to change as many people's attitudes as possible, you would have to resort to other techniques of attitude change. You probably would construct some sort of **persuasive communication** that could be broadcast or published in the mass media. How should you construct your message so that it would really change people's attitudes?

> By persuading others, we convince ourselves.
>
> —Junius, 1769

**persuasive communication:** communication (e.g., a speech or television ad) advocating a particular side of an issue

> The ability to kill or capture a man is a relatively simple task compared with changing his mind.
>
> —Richard Cohen, *Washington Post*, Feb. 28, 1991

**Yale Attitude Change Approach:** the study of the conditions under which people are most likely to change their attitudes in response to persuasive messages; researchers in this tradition focus on "who said what to whom"—that is, on the source of the communication, the nature of the communication, and the nature of the audience

## Persuasive Communications and Attitude Change

Let's say the American Cancer Society has given you a five-figure budget to develop your advertising campaign. You have a lot of decisions ahead of you. Should you pack your public service announcement with information—facts and figures? Should you grab people's attention with frightening visual images of diseased lungs? Should you hire a famous movie star to deliver your message, or a Nobel Prize–winning medical researcher? Should you take a friendly tone and acknowledge that it is hard to quit smoking, or should you take a hard line and tell smokers to (as the Nike ads put it) "Just do it?" You can see the point—it's not easy to figure out how to construct a truly persuasive communication.

Luckily, social psychologists have conducted many studies over the past fifty years on what makes a persuasive communication effective, beginning with Carl Hovland and his colleagues (Hovland, Janis, and Kelley, 1953). Because these researchers were at Yale University, this approach to the study of persuasive communications is known as the **Yale Attitude Change Approach.** Drawing on their experiences during World War II, when they worked for the U.S. armed forces to increase the morale of U.S. soldiers

(Stouffer et al., 1949), Hovland and his colleagues conducted many experiments on the conditions under which people are most likely to be influenced by persuasive communications. They studied three main factors: the *source of the communication* (e.g., how expert or attractive the speaker is), *the communication itself* (e.g., the quality of the arguments; whether the speaker presents both sides of the issue), and *the nature of the audience* (e.g., which kinds of appeals work with hostile versus friendly audiences).

## Who Says What to Whom

The research of the Yale Attitude Change Group as well as many subsequent studies succeeded in showing that all three factors—*who* says *what* to *whom*—influence when and to what degree people will change their attitudes (McGuire, 1985; Petty & Cacioppo, 1981). For example, several studies have shown that the more expert and credible a communicator is, the more people will be swayed by his or her speech. In an early demonstration of the importance of expertise, Carl Hovland and Walter Weiss (1951) presented people with persuasive arguments on several topics, while varying the supposed author of the arguments. One speech argued that it was currently feasible to build nuclear-powered submarines (a position that was implausible at the time the researchers conducted this study). Half the participants believed that the author of the persuasive communication was someone with great credibility—namely, J. Robert Oppenheimer, a well-known and highly respected nuclear physicist. The others believed that the source of the communication was decidedly lacking in credibility—namely *Pravda*, the official newspaper of the Communist party in the former Soviet Union. People were much more likely to be swayed by the speech—believing that

> Of the modes of persuasion furnished by the spoken word there are three kinds. The first kind depends on the personal character of the speaker; the second on putting the audience into a certain frame of mind; the third on the proof, or apparent proof, provided by the words of the speech itself.
>
> —Aristotle, *Rhetoric*

If you were buying a guitar, you would probably be more persuaded by Flea, a member of the Red Hot Chili Peppers, than by a less credible source.

atomic submarines were just around the corner—when the author was J. Robert Oppenheimer.

Similarly, numerous studies have been conducted on the content of the communication itself. If you want to convince an audience on a particular issue, should you present only arguments supporting your position (a one-sided communication), or should you present your side and the other side's arguments (a two-sided communication), and then knock holes in the other side's arguments? There's a risk here—mentioning the opposing viewpoint is, after all, giving them airtime; maybe you should just present your own side. On the other hand, presenting both sides makes you look fair and evenhanded, and if you close with compelling arguments about why they're wrong and you're right, it could be a powerful combination. Carl Hovland and his colleagues (Hovland, Lumsdaine, and Sheffield, 1949) found that when the audience was generally supportive of the speaker's position, one-sided arguments worked best. However, when the audience disagreed with the speaker's position, they were more persuaded by the two-sided approach. A two-sided message is more convincing to people initially opposed to your ideas because it acknowledges their position (but offers good arguments for your side). A one-sided message is best for people who already support your position—don't confuse them by bringing up the other side's points.

The Yale Attitude Change approach yielded a great deal of useful information on how people change their attitudes in response to persuasive com-

**TABLE 8.1 The Yale Attitude Change approach.** The effectiveness of persuasive communications depends on *who* says *what* to *whom*.

## The Yale Attitude Change Approach

### Who: The Source of the Communication

■ Credible speakers (e.g., those with obvious expertise) persuade people more than speakers lacking in credibility (Hovland & Weiss, 1951).

■ Attractive speakers (whether due to physical or personality attributes) persuade people more than unattractive speakers (Eagly & Chaiken, 1975).

### What: The Nature of the Communication

■ People are more persuaded by messages that do not seem to be designed to influence them (Walster & Festinger, 1962).

■ When the audience generally supports your position, it is best to present a one-sided communication (one that presents only arguments favoring your position). When the audience disagrees with your position, it is best to present a two-sided communication and then refute the arguments that are opposed to your position (Hovland, Lumsdaine, & Sheffield, 1949).

■ Is it best to give your speech before or after someone arguing for the other side? If the speeches are to be given back to back and there will be a delay before people have to make up their minds, it is best to go first. Under these conditions, there is likely to be a *primacy effect*, wherein people are more influenced by what they hear first. If there is a delay between the speeches and people will make up their minds right after hearing the second one, it is best to go last. Under these conditions, there is likely to be a *recency effect*, wherein people remember the second speech better than the first one (Miller & Campbell, 1959).

### To Whom: The Nature of the Audience

■ An audience that is distracted during the persuasive communication will often be persuaded more than one that is not (Festinger & Maccoby, 1964).

■ People are particularly susceptible to attitude change during the impressionable ages of eighteen to twenty-five. Beyond those ages, people's attitudes are more stable and resistant to change (Krosnick & Alwin, 1989; Sears, 1981).

munications, some of which is summarized in Table 8.1. As the research mounted, however, a problem became apparent. Many aspects of persuasive communications turned out to be important, but it was not clear which were more important than others, or when one factor should be emphasized over another.

For example, let's return to that job you have with the American Cancer Society—they want to see their ad next month! If you were to read the many Yale Attitude Change studies, you would find lots of useful information about who should say what to whom in order to construct a persuasive communication. However, you would also find yourself saying, "Gee, there's an awful lot of information here, and I'm not sure where I should place the most emphasis: Should I worry most about who delivers the ads? Or should I worry more about the content of the message itself?"

## The Central and Peripheral Routes to Persuasion

If you asked these questions, you would be in very good company. Some well-known attitude researchers have wondered the same thing: When is it best to stress factors central to the communication—such as the strength of the arguments—and when is it best to stress factors peripheral to the logic of the arguments—such as the credibility or attractiveness of the person delivering the speech? This question has been answered by two influential theories of persuasive communication: Richard Petty and John Cacioppo's (1986) **elaboration likelihood model,** and Shelly Chaiken's (1987) systematic-heuristic persuasion model. These theories specify when people will be influenced by what the speech says (i.e., the logic of the arguments) and when they will be influenced by more superficial characteristics (e.g., who gives the speech or how long it is). The theories are very similar; to avoid confusion, we will use the language of the elaboration likelihood model.

Both theories state that, under certain conditions, people are motivated to pay attention to the facts in a communication, so that they will be most persuaded when these facts are logically compelling. That is, sometimes people elaborate on what they hear, carefully thinking about and processing the content of the communication. Petty and Cacioppo (1986) call this the **central route to persuasion.** Under other conditions, however, people are not motivated to pay attention to the facts; instead, they notice only the surface characteristics of the message, such as how long it is and who is delivering it. Here people will not be swayed by the logic of the arguments, because they are not paying close attention to what the communicator says. Instead, they are persuaded if the surface characteristics of the message make it seem like a reasonable one, such as the fact that it is long or is delivered by an expert or attractive communicator. Petty and Cacioppo (1986) call this the **peripheral route to persuasion,** because people are swayed by things that are peripheral to the message itself.

What are the conditions under which people take the central versus the peripheral route to persuasion? In other words, when will people be swayed by the logic of the arguments, and when will they be swayed more by the peripheral cues? The key, according to Richard Petty, John Cacioppo, and Shelly Chaiken, is whether people have the motivation and ability to pay attention to the facts. To the extent that people are truly interested in the topic, and thus

> Now, what I want is, facts. . . .
> Facts alone are wanted in life.
> —Charles Dickens, *Hard Times*

**elaboration likelihood model:** the theory that there are two ways in which persuasive communications can cause attitude change; the central route occurs when people are motivated and have the ability to pay attention to the arguments in the communication; the peripheral route occurs when people do not pay attention to the arguments but are instead swayed by surface characteristics (e.g., who gave the speech)

**central route to persuasion:** the case whereby people elaborate on a persuasive communication, listening carefully to and thinking about the arguments; this occurs when people have both the ability and the motivation to listen carefully to a communication

**peripheral route to persuasion:** the case whereby people do not elaborate on the arguments in a persuasive communication but are instead swayed by peripheral cues

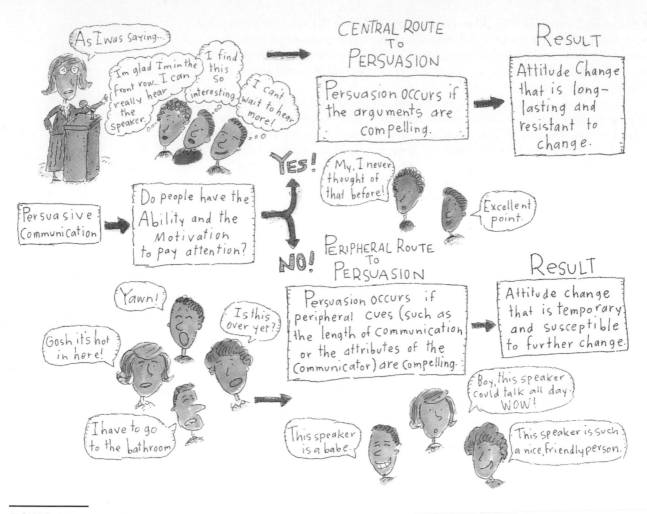

**FIGURE 8.1** The elaboration likelihood model describes how people change their attitudes when they hear persuasive communications.

personal relevance: the extent to which a topic has important consequences for people's well-being

He that goeth about to persuade a multitude, that they are not so well governed as they ought to be, shall never want attentive and favourable hearers.

—Richard Hooker, *Ecclesiastical Polity*

motivated to pay close attention to the arguments, they are more likely to take the central route. Similarly, if people have the ability to pay attention—for example, if there is nothing distracting them or keeping them from paying attention—they are more likely to take the central route (see Figure 8.1).

**Personal Relevance: The Motivation to Pay Attention to the Arguments.** An important determinant of whether people are motivated to pay attention to a communication is the **personal relevance** of the topic, which we can define as the extent to which a topic has important consequences for a person's well-being. For example, consider the issue of whether Social Security benefits should be reduced. How personally relevant is this to you? If you are a seventy-two-year-old woman whose sole income is from Social Security, this issue is obviously extremely relevant; if you are a twenty-year-old from a well-to-do family, the issue has little personal relevance.

The more personally relevant an issue is, the more willing people are to pay attention to the arguments in a speech, and thus the more likely people are to take the central route to persuasion. Richard Petty, John Cacioppo, and Rachel Goldman (1981) demonstrated this point by asking college students to listen to a speech arguing that all college seniors should be required to pass a comprehensive exam in their major before they graduate. Half of the participants were told that their university was currently giving serious thought to requiring comprehensive exams—thus for these participants, the issue was personally relevant. For the other half, the issue was of the "ho-hum" variety—the students were told that their university was considering requiring the exams, but not for ten years.

The researchers then introduced two variables that might influence whether people would agree with the speech. The first was the strength of the arguments presented. Half the participants heard arguments that were strong and persuasive (e.g., "The quality of undergraduate teaching has improved at schools with the exams"), whereas the others heard arguments that were weak and unpersuasive (e.g., "The risk of failing the exam is a challenge most students would welcome"). The second variable concerned the prestige of the source of the speech: Half the participants were told that the author was an eminent professor at Princeton University, whereas the others were told that the author was a high school student.

Thus, when deciding how much to agree with the position advocated by the speaker, the participants could use one or both of these different kinds of information. They could listen carefully to the arguments and scrutinize how persuasive they were, or they could simply go by who said them (i.e., how prestigious the source was). As predicted by the elaboration likelihood model, the way in which people were persuaded depended on the personal relevance of the issue. The left-hand panel of Figure 8.2 shows what happened when the issue was highly relevant to the listeners. These students

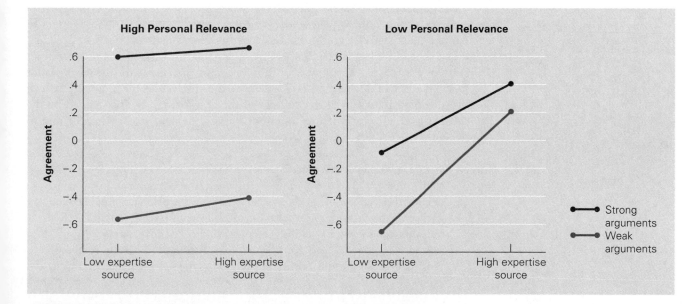

FIGURE 8.2 **Effects of personal relevance on type of attitude change.** The higher the number, the more people agreed with the persuasive communication—namely, that their university should adopt comprehensive exams. *Left panel*: When the issue was highly relevant, people were swayed by the quality of the arguments more than the expertise of the speaker. This is the central route to persuasion. *Right panel*: When the issue was low in relevance, people were swayed by the expertise of the speaker more than the quality of the arguments. This is the peripheral route to persuasion. (Adapted from Petty & Cacioppo, 1986, based on a study by Petty, Cacioppo, and Goldman, 1981)

> I'm not convinced by proofs but signs.
>
> —Coventry Patmore

were very much influenced by the quality of the arguments (i.e., persuasion occurred via the central route). Those who heard strong arguments agreed much more with the speech than those who heard weak arguments did. They were decidedly unimpressed by who presented the arguments (the Princeton professor or the high school student). A good argument was a good argument, even if it was written by someone who lacked prestige.

What happens when a topic is of low relevance to people? As seen in the right-hand panel of Figure 8.2, what mattered was not the strength of the arguments, but who the speaker was. Those who heard the strong arguments agreed with the speech only slightly more than those who heard the weak arguments, whereas those who heard the Princeton professor were much more swayed than those who heard the high school student.

This finding reflects a general rule: When an issue is personally relevant, people will pay attention to the arguments in a speech, and will be persuaded to the extent that the arguments are sound—the "proof" of the speech, in Aristotle's words. When an issue is of low relevance, people will not pay as close attention to the arguments. Instead they will take a mental shortcut, following such peripheral rules as "Prestigious speakers can be trusted" or "Length implies strong arguments" (Chaiken, 1987; Chaiken, Liberman, and Eagly, 1989; Petty & Cacioppo, 1986).

**The Ability to Pay Attention to the Arguments.** Even when an issue is personally relevant, people will take the peripheral route if it is difficult to pay attention to the speech (Festinger & Maccoby, 1964; Petty & Brock, 1981; Petty, Wells, and Brock, 1976). Sometimes it's difficult to figure out if the arguments have merit, particularly when the issue is complex and hard to evaluate. For example, a few years ago there was an exchange of letters in Ann Landers's advice column about whether drugs such as cocaine and marijuana should be legalized. Readers from across the country wrote in with all sorts of compelling arguments on both sides of the issue, and it was difficult to evaluate which arguments were most meritorious. One reader resolved this dilemma by ignoring the content of the arguments, relying instead on the prestige and expertise of the source of the arguments—a peripheral route to persuasion:

> When I can't make up my mind about an issue, I try to read everything I can on the subject and see who is in favor of it and who is against it. I decided to support the legalization of drugs after reading an article in the publication *Science* by . . . Princeton professor Ethan Nadelmann. More recently, I have read that economist and Nobel Laureate Milton Friedman favors decriminalization, as does Mayor Kurt Schmoke of Baltimore, brilliant columnist William F. Buckley and former secretary of state George Schultz. ("Ann Landers", 1990)

At other times it's difficult to pay close attention because there are competing demands on your attention—annoying noises, other people's comments and behaviors, your own feelings of tiredness or hunger, and so on. Several studies have found that distractions such as these make it more difficult to pay attention to the merit of the arguments in a persuasive communication. As a result, communications that have strong arguments will have less of an effect when people are distracted, whereas communications that have weak arguments will have more of an effect under such circumstances

(Lammers & Becker, 1980; Petty, Wells, and Brock, 1976). In short, it's hard for people to take the central route to persuasion—where they are convinced by the merit of the arguments—when they are so distracted that they cannot easily evaluate those arguments. Thus, if you are worried that your message is rather weak, you might consider distracting your audience—maybe by arranging for some construction noise just outside the room in which you are speaking. If your arguments are strong and convincing, however, make sure you have your audience's full attention.

**How to Achieve Long-Lasting Attitude Change.** Now we know that a persuasive communication can change people's attitudes in two ways—via the central or the peripheral route. You may wonder what difference it makes. Does it really matter whether it was the logic of the arguments or the expertise of the source that changed students' minds about comprehensive exams in the Petty and colleagues (1981) study? Given the bottom line—they changed their attitudes—why should we care how they got to that point?

If we are interested in creating long-lasting attitude change, then we should care a lot. People who base their attitudes on a careful analysis of the arguments will be more likely to maintain this attitude over time, more likely to behave consistently with this attitude, and more resistant to counterpersuasion than people who base their attitudes on peripheral cues. For example, Shelly Chaiken (1980) conducted an experiment in which people changed their attitudes either by analyzing the logic of the arguments or by using peripheral cues. She accomplished this in the same way Petty, Cacioppo, and Goldman (1981) did—namely, by making the issue relevant to the former group but not to the latter. Chaiken telephoned the research participants ten days later to see if their attitude change had persisted. As predicted, people were more likely to have maintained their new attitude if they had formed it by analyzing the strength of the arguments in the communication—that is, if their attitude change had occurred via the central route.

Thus, if you are trying to create long-lasting attitude change, construct strong arguments and then choose a method that causes people to scrutinize and think about these arguments so that change occurs via the central route.

*Drawing by Ed Fisher; © 1976 The New Yorker Magazine, Inc.*

*"It is a superb vision of America, all right, but I can't remember which candidate projected it."*

When attitudes change via the peripheral route—such as basing an attitude on the attractiveness of a speaker or the vision he or she evokes—the change is less likely to last.

As reasonable as this sounds, it is not always easy to accomplish in everyday life. Before people will consider your arguments, you first have to get their attention. If you are going to show your antismoking ad on television, for example, you have to somehow make sure that people pay attention, rather than changing the channel or heading for the refrigerator. How can you do this? One commonly used technique is to grab people's attention by arousing their fears and anxieties.

## Fear-Arousing Communications

OK, the American Cancer Society is happy with the ad you have devised (based on what you've read so far), but has raised the concern we have just voiced: How can you make sure that your audience will pay attention to the arguments against smoking? Say you are going to target adolescents: The problem is that they do not want to think about death and dying, or hear yet another adult lecture about how they should lead their lives. Because they might just tune out your snappy presentation of graphs and statistics, maybe you should first grab their attention by showing a gory, vivid film depicting the horrors of lung cancer. If you can arouse their fears and anxieties about what might happen to them, surely they will pay attention to your message and take it to heart—deciding to never start smoking or to kick the habit. Note that this was the approach George Bush took with his Willie Horton ads in the 1988 presidential campaign. He aroused people's fears about crime and personal safety, and then attempted to reassure voters by implying that they would be safer if he were president.

The assumption that fear appeals are a good way to cause attitude change is a common one. You have probably seen many ads that use such appeals, such as the one on TV that shows a fried egg with the message "This is your brain on drugs," or scary films designed to get you to stop smoking, use condoms, and wear your seatbelt.

This public service advertisement uses fear as a persuasion technique. By arousing anxiety and worry, it hopes to get and keep people's attention and cause them to think about the issues.

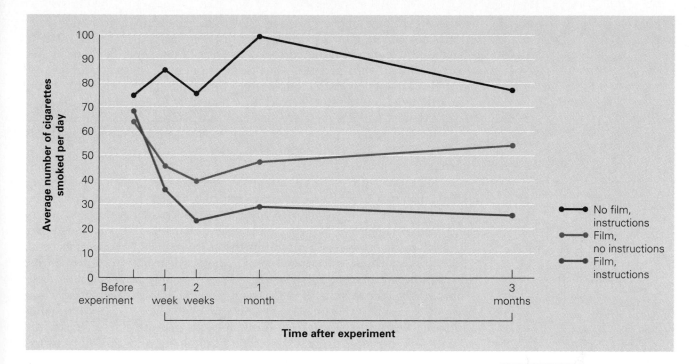

**FIGURE 8.3 Effects of fear appeals on attitude change.** People were shown a scary film about the effects of smoking, instructions about how to stop smoking, or both. Those who were shown both reduced the number of cigarettes they smoked the most. (Adapted from Leventhal, Watts, and Pagano, 1967)

**fear-arousing communications:** persuasive messages that attempt to change people's attitudes by arousing their fears

Do **fear-arousing communications** work? Several experiments suggest that they do (e.g., Janis, 1967; Leventhal, 1970; Rogers, 1983). There has been some disagreement, however, over exactly when and why fear succeeds in changing people's attitudes. Virtually all researchers agree that arousing fear can be threatening, and that people will be motivated to reduce this threat. But when will people do so by changing their attitudes and behaviors?

One way of addressing this question is in terms of the elaboration likelihood model of attitude change. As we have seen, long-lasting change is most likely to occur when people change via the central route, which occurs when people carefully analyze a set of compelling arguments. Short-term change will occur if people simply go by peripheral cues, such as what a headline says, without thinking much about the content of the message. Therefore, a key question is, do fear appeals foster or inhibit change via the central route?

A clue can be found in one of the first experiments conducted on this question, by Howard Leventhal and his colleagues (Leventhal, Watts, and Pagano, 1967). The participants received one of three combinations of anti-smoking information, all from the Public Health Service. One group saw a scary film about the dangers of smoking that included, along with graphs and figures about the relationship between smoking and cancer, a very graphic lung cancer operation. A second group saw the same film, and also received a pamphlet that gave specific instructions about how to stop smoking. Finally, a third group did not see the scary film, but did receive the pamphlet. To gauge the effects of these interventions, the researchers called people at several points after the experiment and asked them how many cigarettes a day they were smoking.

As seen in Figure 8.3, people who saw the scary film reduced their cigarette consumption more than people who did not see the scary film. This was especially the case among those who saw the scary film *and* received instruction about how to quit. After three months, these participants were smoking significantly less than those who saw the scary film alone. Why might this be? Recall that when people change their attitudes via the central route, the attitude change is especially long-lasting. Given that the people who saw the scary film and received the instructions about how to quit showed the most lasting change, perhaps these are the ones who changed via the central route.

This interpretation is consistent with recent theorizing about the effects of fear appeals. According to this view, fear can cause change via either the central or the peripheral route, depending on what people believe is the best way to reassure themselves (Gleicher & Petty, 1992; Jepson & Chaiken, 1990). The idea here is that, first, people who are fearful want to be reassured—they want something or someone to reduce their feelings of worry and arousal (Rogers, 1983). If people believe that the best way to reassure themselves is to pay close attention to the content of the message (e.g., because the message will contain specific hints about how to deal with the threat), then people will analyze the message carefully, changing their attitudes via the central route. If the message is not in any way reassuring about how to solve the problem—for example, if it presents a scary film about smoking with no suggestions about how to protect oneself from the disease—then people are likely to tune out, paying attention only to the peripheral cues.

To cause lasting change via the central route, then, the key is to scare people and to convince them that paying attention to your message will help them reduce this fear. This is exactly what Howard Leventhal and his colleagues (1967) did in the condition of their study where people saw the scary film and received the pamphlet with instructions about how to quit smoking. As we saw in Figure 8.3, this is the group that reduced their smoking the

Here are two fear-arousing communications that differ in the extent to which they offer recommendations about how to change your behavior. Which one is most likely to cause lasting changes in behavior?

most. If a message raises fears but does not give information to allay that fear—as in the other condition, where people saw the scary film but did not receive the pamphlet—the message is less likely to cause lasting change, as seen in Figure 8.3. This may explain why some attempts to frighten people into changing their attitudes and behaviors have not been very successful: They succeed in scaring people but do not provide specific recommendations for people to follow so that they can reduce their fear (Becker & Josephs, 1988; DeJong & Winsten, 1989; Job, 1988; Soames, 1988).

## Changing Attitudes of Different Strengths and Different Origins

A question we have not considered so far is whether persuasive communications are equally effective with different kinds of attitudes. For example, imagine that you are about to listen to a speech, filled with facts and figures, that is opposed to one of your attitudes. Suppose that you are at a college that does not require seniors to take comprehensive exams, and the speech is going to try to convince you that it should—in time for you to take the exams before you graduate. Because this is an issue of considerable personal relevance, you are likely to listen to the speech carefully. According to what we have seen so far, if the arguments are logically sound you are likely to change your attitude, becoming more favorable toward the idea of comprehensive exams. Indeed, this is what Petty, Cacioppo, and Goldman (1981) found (see Figure 8.2).

Now imagine the same scenario, except that the speech is concerned with a different topic: your choice of religion. The speech will challenge your religious orientation, and again, is filled with facts and figures. How likely do you think you are to change your religion after listening to the speech? Probably not very likely. But why? After all, this topic is certainly personally relevant. What exactly is it about your attitude toward religion that makes it more resistant to change than your attitude toward comprehensive exams?

### The Different Origins of Attitudes

This example illustrates that to understand how attitudes change, we need to consider the fact that attitudes differ from each other in a number of ways, such as how they were formed initially and how strong they are. We have already seen that people who change their attitudes via the central route end up with stronger attitudes—in the sense that their attitudes are more resistant to change, and more stable over time—than people who change via the peripheral route. Thus, one consequence of the different kinds of attitude change we have discussed is that people end up with relatively strong or weak attitudes.

But what about when people first hear a persuasive communication? Surely the strength and basis of the attitude at the outset makes a difference, as in the example of attitudes toward comprehensive exams versus your religion. Attitudes come in different stripes and colors. Some are stronger than others, and some, like people's attitudes about crime (as aroused by George Bush's Willie Horton ad), are based more on fear and emotion than a logical examination of the facts. How do the effects of persuasive communications differ according to the type of attitude people have?

**Cognitively Based Attitudes.**  Sometimes we base our attitudes on a perusal of the relevant facts, such as the objective merits of a car. How many miles to the gallon does it get? Does it have an air bag? To the extent that people's evaluation is based on beliefs such as these, we can say that it is a **cognitively based attitude.** The function of such an attitude is "object appraisal," which means we classify objects according to the rewards and punishments they can provide (Katz, 1960; Smith, Bruner, and White, 1956). In other words, the function of this kind of attitude is to classify the pluses and minuses of an object so we can quickly tell whether it is worth our while to have anything to do with it. Consider your attitude toward a utilitarian object like a vacuum cleaner. Your attitude is likely to be based on your beliefs about the objective merits of particular brands, such as how well they vacuum up dirt and how much they cost. If the objective merits of brand X are superior to those of brand Y, you will have a more positive attitude toward brand X.

How do cognitively based attitudes change? Because people are most concerned with the objective merits of the attitude object, then clearly a communication that stresses these merits will be most persuasive—as long as people have the motivation and ability to pay attention to the communication (Petty & Cacioppo, 1986; Shavitt, 1989). In short, if an attitude is based on beliefs about the pluses and minuses of an attitude object, then a good way to change it is to attack those beliefs with compelling arguments.

**Affectively Based Attitudes.**  Other attitudes are based more on emotions and values than on an objective appraisal of pluses and minuses. Let's return to the 1988 presidential campaign. If people had cognitively based attitudes toward the candidates, why were President Bush's Willie Horton ads so effective, and why did Dukakis's use of facts and figures seem to fall so flat? There is a good deal of evidence that people vote more with their hearts than their minds—that is, that they have an **affectively based attitude** toward political candidates (Abelson, Kinder, Peters, and Fiske, 1982; Granberg & Brown, 1989). In fact, Wattenberg (1987) estimates that one-third of the electorate knows virtually nothing about specific politicians, but nonetheless has strong feelings about them!

Affectively based attitudes stem more from people's feelings and values than from their rational thoughts about the merits of the attitude object (Breckler & Wiggins, 1989; Zanna & Rempel, 1988). Sometimes we simply like a certain brand of car, regardless of how many miles to the gallon it gets or whether it has an air bag. Occasionally we even feel very positively about something—such as another person—in spite of having negative beliefs. You have probably heard many songs about such feelings, such as Smokey Robinson's *You've Really Got A Hold On Me*:

> I don't like you, but I love you.
> Seems that I'm always, thinking of you.
> You treat me badly, I love you madly.
> You've really got a hold on me.

**cognitively based attitude:** an attitude based primarily on people's beliefs about the properties of the attitude object

I only ask for information.
—Charles Dickens

**affectively based attitude:** an attitude based more on people's feelings and values than on beliefs about the nature of the attitude object

We never desire passionately what we desire through reason alone.
—La Rochefoucauld, *Maxims*, 1678

Prolife and prochoice activists argue in front of the U.S. Supreme Court. Some attitudes are based more on emotions and values than on facts and figures.

If affectively based attitudes do not come from an examination of the facts, where do they come from? They have a variety of sources. First, they can stem from people's values, such as their basic religious and moral beliefs. People's feelings about such issues as abortion, the death penalty, and premarital sex are often based more on their values than on a logical examination of the facts. The function of such attitudes is not so much to paint an accurate picture of the world as to express and validate one's basic value system (Katz, 1960; Shavitt, 1989; Smith, Bruner, and White, 1956).

Other affectively based attitudes can be the result of a sensory reaction, such as liking the taste of chocolate (despite how many calories it has!), or an aesthetic reaction, such as the appeal of a painting or the lines and color of a car. Still others can be the result of conditioning. **Classical conditioning** is the case where a stimulus that elicits an emotional response is repeatedly experienced along with a neutral stimulus that does not, until the neutral stimulus takes on the emotional properties of the first stimulus. For example, suppose that when you were a child, you experienced feelings of warmth and love when you visited your grandmother. Suppose also that there was always a faint smell of mothballs in the air at your grandmother's house. Eventually, the smell of mothballs themselves will trigger the emotions you experienced during your visits, through the process of classical conditioning.

In **instrumental conditioning,** behaviors that we freely choose to perform increase or decrease in frequency, depending on whether they are followed by positive reinforcement or punishment. How does this apply to attitudes? Imagine that a four-year-old white girl goes to the playground with her father and chooses to play with an African American girl. Her father expresses strong disapproval, telling her, "We don't play with that kind of child." It won't take long before the child associates interacting with minorities with punishment, thereby adopting her father's racist attitudes. Attitudes can take on positive or negative affect through either classical or instrumental conditioning, as shown in Figure 8.4 (Cacioppo et al., 1992; Kuykendall & Keating, 1990).

> That is the way we are made; we don't reason; where we feel, we just feel.
> —Mark Twain, *A Connecticut Yankee in King Arthur's Court*

**classical conditioning:** the case whereby a stimulus that elicits an emotional response is repeatedly experienced along with a neutral stimulus that does not, until the neutral stimulus takes on the emotional properties of the first stimulus

**instrumental conditioning:** the case whereby behaviors that people freely choose to perform increase or decrease in frequency depending on whether they are followed by positive reinforcement or punishment

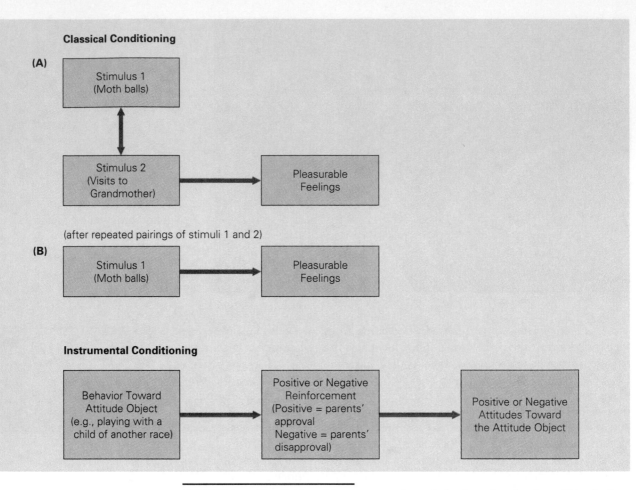

**Classical Conditioning**

(A)

Stimulus 1
(Moth balls)

Stimulus 2
(Visits to
Grandmother)

Pleasurable
Feelings

(after repeated pairings of stimuli 1 and 2)

(B)

Stimulus 1
(Moth balls)

Pleasurable
Feelings

**Instrumental Conditioning**

Behavior Toward
Attitude Object
(e.g., playing with a
child of another race)

Positive or Negative
Reinforcement
(Positive = parents'
approval
Negative = parents'
disapproval)

Positive or Negative
Attitudes Toward
the Attitude Object

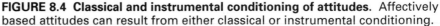

**FIGURE 8.4 Classical and instrumental conditioning of attitudes.** Affectively based attitudes can result from either classical or instrumental conditioning.

Thus, affectively based attitudes can have a variety of sources. We can group them into one family, however, because they have certain key features in common: (a) They do not result from a rational examination of the issues; (b) they are not governed by logic (e.g., persuasive arguments about the issues seldom change an affectively based attitude); and (c) they are often linked to people's values, so that trying to change them challenges these values (Katz, 1960; Smith, et al., 1956).

Our discussion of the 1988 presidential campaign ads indicates that facts and figures are unlikely to be persuasive when the attitudes in question are based on values and emotions more than on cognitions (Johnson & Eagly, 1989, 1990). How can we change affectively based attitudes? This is an important question, because many consequential attitudes are affectively based. Prejudiced feelings toward minority groups are often based on values and emotions, as are people's views on such controversial issues as abortion, premarital sex, and politics. As a guide to which attitudes are likely to be affectively based, consider the topics that etiquette manuals suggest should not be discussed at a dinner party: politics, sex, and religion. If presenting people with logical arguments won't work, what will?

One technique is to stress values and emotions instead of facts and figures, as in George Bush's Willie Horton ads (Edwards, 1990; Shavitt, 1990). Sharon Shavitt (1990) demonstrated this in a study of the effectiveness of different kinds of advertisements. Some ads, she notes, stress the objective merits of a product, such as an ad for an air conditioner that discusses its price, energy efficiency, and reliability. Other ads stress emotions and values, such as ones for perfume, beer, or designer jeans that try to associate their brands with sex, beauty, and youthfulness, rather than saying anything about the objective qualities of the product. Which kind of ad is most effective?

To find out, Shavitt gave people different kinds of advertisements for different consumer products. Some of the items were ones Shavitt called utilitarian products, such as air conditioners and coffee. People's attitudes toward such products tend to be based on an appraisal of the utilitarian aspects of the products (e.g., how energy-efficient an air conditioner is), and thus are cognitively based. The other items were ones Shavitt called social identity products, such as perfume and greeting cards. People's attitudes toward these types of products are based more on their values and concerns about their social identity, and thus are more affectively based. Thus, people received advertisements that were either cognitively based (stressing the utilitarian functions of the product) or affectively based (stressing values and social identity concerns), for products about which people had either cognitively or affectively based attitudes.

As seen in Figure 8.5, people reacted most favorably to the ads that matched the type of attitude they had. If people's attitudes were cognitively based (e.g., toward air conditioners or coffee), then the ads that focused on

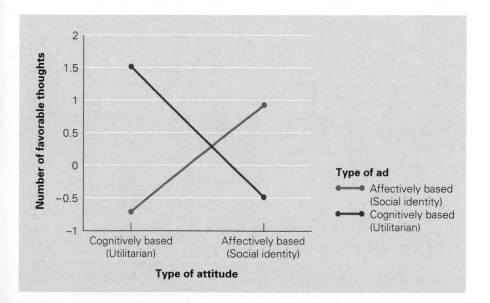

FIGURE 8.5 **Effects of affective and cognitive information on affectively and cognitively based attitudes.** When people had cognitively based attitudes (e.g., toward air conditioners and coffee), then cognitively based advertisements that stressed the utilitarian aspects of the products worked best. When people had more affectively based attitudes (e.g., toward perfume and greeting cards), then affectively based advertisements that stressed values and social identity worked best. (The higher the number, the more favorable thoughts people listed about the products after reading the advertisements). (Adapted from Shavitt, 1990)

If people's attitudes are cognitively based (as they probably are for the printer), then persuasive communications should focus on cognitions. If the attitudes are affectively based (as they probably are for perfume), then the persuasive communications should play on the viewer's emotions.

> It is useless to attempt to reason a man out of a thing he was never reasoned into.
> —Jonathan Swift

the utilitarian aspects of these products, such as the features of the air conditioner, were most successful. If people's attitudes were more affectively based (e.g., toward perfume or greeting cards), then the ads that focused on values and social identity concerns were most successful. The graph displayed in Figure 8.6 shows the number of favorable thoughts people had in response to the different kinds of ads. Similar results were found on a measure of how much people intended to buy the products. Thus, if you ever get a job on Madison Avenue, the moral is to know what type of attitude most people have toward your product and then tailor your advertising accordingly.

**Behaviorally Based Attitudes.** Earlier we noted that attitudes have three components—cognitions, affect, and behavior. Just as attitudes can be based primarily on cognitions or affect, they also can be based primarily on behavior. This may seem a little odd—how do we know how to behave if we don't already know how we feel? According to Daryl Bem's (1972) *self-perception theory*, however, there are circumstances under which people don't know how they feel until they see how they behave (see Chapter 6). For example, suppose you asked a friend how much she enjoys exercising. If she says, "Well, I guess I like it, because I always seem to be going for a run or heading over to the gym to work out," we would say she has a **behaviorally based attitude.** Her attitude is based more on an observation of her behavior than on her cognitions or affect.

**behaviorally based attitude:** an attitude based on observations of how one behaves toward the attitude object

## IN A QUANDARY

The Voice of Reason: It's not such a big thing; just put the galoshes on.

The Voice of Conscience: Mom will be mad if you don't put them on.

The Voice of Practicality: It's raining. Why don't you just wear 'em?

The Voice of Binky: Toss them out of the window.

R. Chast

Some persuasive communications will try to change your attitudes by appealing to logic; others will go straight for your emotions.

As noted in Chapter 6, people infer their attitudes from their behavior only under certain conditions. First, their initial attitude has to be weak or ambiguous. If your friend already has a strong attitude toward exercising, she would not have to observe her behavior to infer how she feels about it. Second, people infer their attitudes from their behavior only when there are no other plausible explanations for their behavior. If your friend believes that she exercises in order to lose weight, or because her doctor has ordered her to, she is unlikely to assume that she runs and works out because she enjoys it. We discussed the research evidence for self-perception theory in detail in Chapter 6. Of current interest is evidence—which we will discuss shortly—that behaviorally based attitudes are stronger and more resistant to change than those based on less hands-on experience with the attitude object.

> How can I know what I think till I see what I say?
> —Graham Wallas, *The Art of Thought*

### Attitude Strength and Accessibility

Not only do attitudes differ in their affective, cognitive, or behavioral origins, but they also differ in how strong they are. This probably does not come as a surprise; for most of us, our attitude toward the current price of rutabagas is of much less importance, and held with much less conviction, than our religious views or our feelings toward our loved ones. What might come as a surprise is that there is considerable disagreement among social psychologists about how best to define attitude strength. Some believe that the key is how easily the attitude comes to mind (how accessible it is), whereas others believe that the key is how important people think their attitude is or how knowledgeable they are about the attitude object (Krosnick & Abelson, 1991; Petty & Krosnick, 1993; Wood, 1982). Regardless of how attitude strength is measured, however, strong attitudes are more resistant to change than weak attitudes are. Let's see how this applies to attitude accessibility.

Consider this example: In a moment, we are going to give you the name of an object. When we do, simply think about that object for a few seconds. Ready? Here is the object: a StairMaster exercise machine. What did you think about? Did your attitude toward a StairMaster come to mind (i.e., thoughts about how much you like or dislike it)? Or did you think about the machine without bringing to mind how much you like it? These questions concern **attitude accessibility,** which Russell Fazio (1989, 1990, in press) defines as the strength of the association between an object and your evaluation of that object. If an attitude is highly accessible, then whenever you

**attitude accessibility:** the strength of the association between an object and a person's evaluation of that object; accessibility is measured by the speed with which people can report how they feel about an issue or object

encounter the object your attitude comes to mind. For example, if your attitude toward StairMasters is highly accessible, then as soon as you read the words on the previous page, thoughts about how much you like or dislike these machines came to mind. If an attitude is relatively inaccessible, then it is much less likely to come to mind when you encounter the object—in which case, all you may have thought of was a visual image of the machine.

Why is the accessibility of an attitude important? For one thing, as we will see toward the end of this chapter, it determines how likely people are to behave consistently with their attitude. Relevant to our current concern with attitude change, accessibility also influences people's resistance to persuasive communications. Suppose we told you about a new study showing that exercise on StairMaster machines is superior to all other forms of exercise—better for the heart, better for weight control, less stressful on the knees, and so on (actually, we know of no such study). Suppose further that your attitude toward StairMasters is relatively inaccessible. "That sounds pretty good," you are likely to think. "Maybe I'll go to the gym tomorrow and give it a try." Now suppose that you have a highly accessible and negative attitude toward StairMaster. As soon as you hear about the study, thoughts of how awkward and uncomfortable you were when you tried one come to mind. These negative feelings are likely to influence how you interpret the results of the study. "There has to be something wrong with that study," you might think. "It was probably conducted by the company that makes those machines, and thus was biased."

This is precisely what David Houston and Russ Fazio (1989) found in a recent study. First, they measured the accessibility of people's attitudes toward the death penalty (by seeing how quickly they responded to questions about their attitudes on this topic, which is a good measure of accessibility). Next, they presented people with two research studies—one that supported the death penalty as a deterrent to murder and one that did not—and asked people to judge the validity of each study. People whose attitudes were accessible tended to be the most biased in how they evaluated the studies. That is, their highly accessible attitudes colored their interpretation of the validity of the research studies, making them the most critical of the one that was inconsistent with their views (see Figure 8.6). People with inaccessible attitudes took a more open-minded approach, evaluating the merit of the studies without being biased by their own views on the subject. An important implication of this research is that people with accessible attitudes are more resistant to persuasion attempts, because they are more likely to discount or ignore evidence that contradicts their own views.

How does an attitude become accessible? One way is through direct, repeated experience with the attitude object (Fazio & Zanna, 1981). The more times you have tried a StairMaster, the more likely you are to associate positive or negative experiences with it, forming a strong association in your mind between "StairMaster" and these positive or negative feelings. Note that accessible attitudes can be positive or negative. After using a StairMaster you might feel that it is only slightly preferable to a medieval torture machine, or, you might become a StairMaster junkie, preferring it to all other forms of exercise—or somewhere in between. The point is that when your attitude is behaviorally based, then whatever your feelings are, they will be accessible. In comparison, if you have only read about StairMasters or watched other people use them, you might have positive or negative reactions ("Gee, that looks like something I would enjoy"), but these feelings will

When an attitude is behaviorally based—such as these people's attitudes toward exercise machines—it is highly accessible and thus resistant to change.

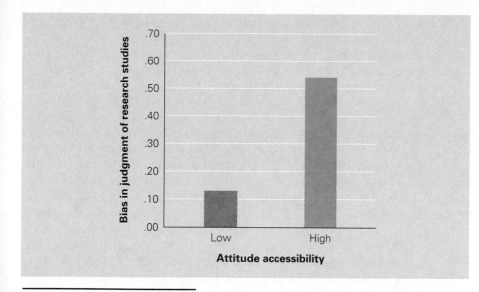

**FIGURE 8.6 Effects of attitude accessibility on the interpretation of new evidence.** Participants evaluated two research studies—one finding that the death penalty acts as a deterrent and one finding that it does not. The numbers in this figure are the correlations between people's attitude and their evaluation of how valid the studies were. The lower the number, the more open-minded people were—that is, the more their judgments of the validity of the studies were independent of their attitude. Compared to people with accessible attitudes, those with inaccessible attitudes evaluated the studies without being biased by how they felt about the issue. (Adapted from Houston & Fazio, 1989)

be much less accessible than those resulting from direct experience. In general, the more an attitude is behaviorally based, the more accessible and resistant to change it will be.

## How to Make People Resistant to Attitude Change

By now, you are no doubt getting nervous (and not just because the chapter hasn't ended yet): With all these clever methods available to change your attitudes, are you ever safe from persuasive communications? Yes indeed you are, or at least you can be, if you initiate some clever strategies of your own. Here's how to make sure all of those persuasive messages that bombard you don't turn you into a quivering mass of constantly changing opinion.

### Reinforcing Values

Let's start with the case where someone challenges an attitude with a speech that uses well-reasoned, logical arguments. For example, suppose you have a friend who believes that abortion is wrong and should be illegal. You know your friend is about to listen to a speech arguing for the opposite, prochoice position, and you want to reduce the likelihood that he or she will be persuaded by the speech. Suppose further that you know the speaker is going to present a series of thoughtful, logical arguments. What might you do?

We have seen that one type of attitude that is resistant to logical, fact-based appeals is an affectively based attitude, particularly one based on deep-seated values and moral views. Thus, one thing you might do is to try to ensure that your friend's initial attitude is affectively based, by reminding him or her of basic prolife values that underlie this position. Both sides in the abortion debate often take this approach; the very terms *prolife* and *pro-choice* are designed to call up values that are dear to everyone. Who is against life or freedom of choice? In fact, a major reason the abortion debate is so difficult to resolve is that both sides can call on fundamental human values to support their position. If you want to convince someone of your views on this issue, and make them resistant to logical arguments for the opposite view, try to convince them that the value on your side of the debate—be it freedom of choice or the right to life—is the one that is most applicable.

This approach is likely to be powerful—if it is successful. Religious leaders and parents try their best to instill a set of values in us, and they often succeed, making us relatively immune to persuasive messages that attack attitudes related to these values. The problem is that it is not so easy to instill core values in someone who does not already have them. Simply telling someone, "Believe this because it is important to my value system, and my value system is best" is unlikely to be very effective.

## Attitude Inoculation

If you do not succeed in instilling the "right" set of values in a person, there is another approach that might work: Get people to consider the arguments for and against their attitude before someone attacks it. The more people have thought about pro and con arguments beforehand, the better they will be able to ward off attempts to change their minds using logical arguments. If people have not thought much about the issue—that is, if they formed their attitude via the peripheral route—they are particularly susceptible to an attack on that attitude using logical appeals.

For example, consider cultural truisms—beliefs that most members of a society accept uncritically, without much thought about why. Examples include "Democracy is the best form of government" and "You should brush your teeth after every meal." What would happen if you presented people with a set of logical, persuasive arguments contrary to one of these truisms—for example, that it is actually a bad idea to brush your teeth too much, because doing so can damage the gums? Because most people have not thought much about the logic behind cultural truisms, attitudes based on truisms are particularly susceptible to change by presenting people with opposing arguments. Such change can be prevented, however, by giving people arguments underlying these attitudes—and possible counterarguments—before their attitudes are attacked.

**Inoculating People Against Persuasive Messages.** William McGuire (1964) demonstrated this fact by using what he called **attitude inoculation.** His idea was that to prevent people from being influenced by a persuasive speech, they should be "inoculated" against the arguments they were likely to hear by receiving a small dose of these arguments in advance. Having considered the arguments beforehand, people should be relatively immune to the

**attitude inoculation:** making people immune to attempts to change their attitudes by initially exposing them to small doses of the arguments against their position

effects of the communication, just as exposing people to a small amount of a virus can inoculate them against exposure to the full-blown viral disease.

In one study, for example, McGuire presented people with a brief argument against a cultural truism—namely, the one about brushing your teeth after every meal—and gave participants some arguments refuting this argument. Two days later, people came back and read a much stronger attack on the truism, one that contained a series of logical arguments about why brushing your teeth too frequently is a bad idea. These people were much less likely to change their attitudes than a control group that had not been inoculated by receiving the initial attack. The control group, never having considered why people should brush their teeth frequently, was particularly susceptible to the strong communication arguing that they should not.

Thus, there are two ways of immunizing people against messages that rely on logical arguments: Either make sure that the initial attitude is affectively based (e.g., by trying to instill important values), or make people think about the pros and cons beforehand, so that they can more easily refute the arguments in the communication (as William McGuire did in his studies). Often, however, attacks on our attitudes consist not of logical arguments but of appeals to our emotions. Is there some way of warding off this kind of opinion change, just as we can ward off the effects of logical appeals?

**Inoculating People Against Peer Pressure.** This is an important question, because many critical changes in attitudes and behaviors occur not in response to logic but via more emotional appeals. Consider the way in which many adolescents begin to smoke, drink, or take drugs. Often they do so in response to pressure from their peers, at an age when they are particularly susceptible to such pressure. For example, one study found that the best predictor of whether an adolescent smokes marijuana is whether he or she has a friend who does so (Yamaguchi & Kandel, 1984).

Think about how this occurs. It is not as if peers present a set of logical arguments ("Hey, Jake—did you know that recent studies show that moderate drinking may have health benefits?"). Instead, peer pressure is linked more to people's values and emotions, playing on their fear of rejection and desire for freedom and autonomy. In adolescence, peers become an important source of social approval—perhaps the most important—and can dispense powerful rewards for holding certain attitudes or behaving in certain ways, such as using drugs or engaging in unprotected sex. What is needed is a technique that will make young people more resistant to attitude-change attempts via peer pressure, so that they will be less likely to engage in dangerous behaviors.

One possibility is to extend the logic of McGuire's (1964) inoculation approach to more affectively based persuasion techniques, such as peer pressure. That is, besides inoculating people with doses of logical arguments that they might hear, we could also inoculate them with samples of the kinds of appeals to their emotions that they might encounter. Consider Jake, a thirteen-year-old who is hanging out with some classmates, many of whom are smoking cigarettes. The classmates begin to make fun of Jake for not smoking, calling him a wimp and a mama's boy. One of them even lights a cigarette and holds it in front of Jake, daring him to take a puff. Many thirteen-year-olds, faced with such pressure, would go ahead and comply. But suppose we had immunized Jake to such social pressures by exposing him to mild versions of

> The chief effect of talk on any subject is to strengthen one's own opinions and, in fact, one never knows exactly what he does believe until he is warmed into conviction by the heat of the attack and defense.
>
> —Charles Dudley Warner, *Backlog Studies*, 1873

> A companion's words of persuasion are effective.
>
> —Homer

Attitudes spread by peer pressure can be very persuasive because they appeal to people's emotions—to their desire to be liked and accepted. By being inoculated against such appeals, young people may learn to resist persuasion via peer pressure.

them, and showing him ways to combat these pressures. We might have him role-play a situation where a friend calls him a chicken for not smoking a cigarette, and teach him to respond by saying, "I'd be more of a chicken if I smoked it just to impress you." Would this help him to resist the more powerful pressures exerted by his classmates?

Several programs designed to prevent smoking in adolescents suggest that it would. For example, McAlister and his associates (1980) used a role-playing technique with seventh-graders, very much like the one described above. He found that these students were significantly less likely to smoke three years after the study, compared to a control group that had not participated in the program. This result is encouraging, and has been replicated in similar programs designed to reduce smoking (Chassin, Presson, and Sherman, 1990; Falck & Craig, 1988; Killen, 1985).

We should point out, however, that it is sometimes difficult to determine precisely why programs such as these are effective. They usually involve several interventions, making it difficult to tell which of the interventions was most responsible for the program's success. For example, McAlister's prevention program was multifaceted. In addition to the role-playing procedure to inoculate people against peer pressure, the participants made public commitments not to use tobacco, and created antismoking skits and slogans (for which they received prizes). Thus, though promising, it will take further research to illuminate which of these activities was most responsible for the success of the program.

### When Persuasion Attempts Boomerang: Reactance Theory

We have just seen that it is possible to immunize people against attempts to change their attitudes and behaviors. It is important to note, however, that these and other techniques to manage people's attitudes should not be used with too heavy a hand. For example, suppose you want to make sure that your child never smokes. "Might as well err on the side of giving too strong a message," you might think, absolutely forbidding him or her to even look at a pack of cigarettes. "What's the harm?" you might think. "At least this way, my child will get the point about how serious a matter this is."

Actually, there is harm to administering strong prohibitions—the stronger they are, the more likely they will boomerang, causing an increase in interest in the prohibited activity. According to **reactance theory** (Brehm, 1966), people do not like to feel that their freedom to do or think whatever they want is being threatened. They will feel this way if an action is strongly prohibited, and they will respond by rebelling against the threat. This often involves an increased interest in performing the forbidden behavior, as well as anger and aggression toward the person who forbade it.

**reactance theory:** the idea that when people feel their freedom to perform a certain behavior is threatened, an unpleasant state of reactance is aroused; people can reduce this reactance by performing the threatened behavior

For example, James Pennebaker and Deborah Sanders (1976) tried a couple of ways of getting people to stop writing graffiti on the walls of restrooms, one using a strong prohibition and the other a mild prohibition. They placed one of two signs in the bathrooms on a college campus. One sign read, "Do not write on these walls under any circumstances." The other gave a milder prohibition: "Please don't write on these walls." The researchers returned two weeks later, and observed how much graffiti had been written since they posted the signs. What do you think they observed? If you read these signs, which one would create more reactance, threatening your freedom to do whatever you want—including writing a message on the bathroom wall? The one with the severe prohibition, of course. And as night follows day, significantly more people wrote graffiti in the bathrooms with the "Do not write . . . ." sign than the "Please don't write . . . ." sign, just as the researchers predicted. Similarly, people who receive strong admonitions against smoking, taking drugs, or dating the seventeen-year-old runaway from across the tracks become more likely to perform these behaviors, in order to restore their sense of personal freedom and choice.

## Intrinsic Versus Extrinsic Reasons: The Overjustification Effect

There is another, more subtle reason why strong admonitions can backfire. Consider people who have no initial desire to take drugs. When they receive strong admonitions, they can explain their behavior in two ways: "I do not take drugs because I have no desire to do so" or "I do not take drugs because my parents and teachers would kill me." The first reason is an intrinsic one—namely, the lack of an interest in drugs. The second reason is an extrinsic one—a concern with how other people would react. A curious thing can happen when people have both an intrinsic and an extrinsic reason for doing something. When the external reason is strong and vivid, people begin to think that this is the only reason they are doing what they are doing, and the internal reason gets lost in the process. This is called the *overjustification effect*, which we discussed in Chapter 6. In this example, people might end up thinking that they are not taking drugs only because of how other people would react, not because they dislike drugs. As a result, their interest in drugs may actually increase.

For example, Finckenauer (1979) evaluated the effectiveness of a "scared straight" program, wherein kids who are at risk for becoming juvenile offenders visit state prisons and have harrowing confrontations with inmates who do their best to convince the kids that there are terrible consequences to leading a life of crime. He found that the juveniles who took part in this program were significantly more likely to commit crimes in the six months after its completion than a group of juveniles who did not take part but were comparable in terms of age, sex, and race. Similarly, Duryea and Okwumabua (1988) found that ninth-graders who took part in an alcohol prevention program were significantly more likely to report drinking to excess, three years later, than a similar group of students who did not take part in the program.

Neither of these studies was an experiment in which people were randomly assigned to condition, making them difficult to evaluate. There is, however, some experimental evidence that when people have little interest in a forbidden activity to begin with, giving them strong prohibitions can backfire, causing an increase in the forbidden behavior (Wilson & Lassiter, 1982). The moral is that programs designed to prevent people from doing undesirable things, such as smoking, drinking, or practicing unsafe sex, should be designed with extreme care. Ideally, they should inoculate people against social influence attempts, but they should not present strong admonitions and threats that might cause the programs to backfire by arousing reactance or an overjustification effect, whereby people's interest in the forbidden activity increases.

## When Will Attitudes Predict Behavior?

Now that we have seen how attitudes change, it is important to discuss the consequences of this change. Attitude change is a significant topic in part because of the relationship between attitudes and people's actual behavior. Many people bank on the fact that people act consistently with their attitudes. Advertisers assume that changing people's attitudes toward their products will result in increased sales. Politicians assume that positive feelings toward a candidate will result in a vote for that candidate on Election Day. And we all assume that people who like brussels sprouts will be more likely to eat them than people who do not, and that people who enjoy ballet will be more likely to go see the local company perform *Swan Lake* than people who do not. Sounds pretty straightforward, right?

Actually, the relationship between attitudes and behavior is not so straightforward, as indicated by a classic study by Richard LaPiere (1934). In the early 1930s, LaPiere embarked on a cross-country sightseeing trip with a young Chinese couple. Because prejudice against Asians was commonplace in the United States at this time, he was apprehensive about how his Chinese friends would be treated. At each hotel, campground, and restaurant they entered, LaPiere worried that anti-Asian prejudice would rear its ugly head and his friends would be refused service. Much to his surprise, this almost never happened. Of the 251 establishments he and his friends visited, only one refused to serve them.

Struck by this apparent lack of prejudice, LaPiere decided to explore people's attitudes toward Asians in a different way. After his trip, he wrote a letter to each establishment he and his friends had visited, asking if it would serve a Chinese visitor. Of the many establishments who replied, only one said it would. More than 90 percent said they definitely would not; the rest said they were undecided. People's attitudes—as expressed in their response to LaPiere's written inquiry—stood in stark contrast to their actual behavior toward LaPiere's Chinese friends.

LaPiere's study was not, of course, a controlled experiment. As LaPiere acknowledged, there are several reasons why his results may not show an inconsistency between people's attitudes and behavior. For example, he had no way of knowing whether the proprietors who answered his letter were the same people who had served him and his friends. Further, people's attitudes may have changed in the months that passed between the time they served the Chinese couple and the time they received the letter.

Nonetheless, the lack of correspondence between people's attitudes and what they actually did was so striking—with almost every proprietor acting against his or her attitudes—that we might question our earlier assumption that behavior routinely follows from attitudes. This is especially the case in light of research that followed LaPiere's study. Allan Wicker (1969) reviewed the dozens of more methodologically sound studies that followed LaPiere's, and reached the same conclusion: People's attitudes are poor predictors of their behavior.

But how can this be? Does a person's attitude toward Asians or political candidates or the ballet really tell us nothing about how he or she will behave? How can we reconcile the LaPiere findings—and other studies like it—with the obvious notion that many times people do act in accord with their attitudes? Fortunately, in recent years social psychologists have learned a great deal about when and how attitudes will predict behavior. It is now clear that Wicker's conclusions about attitude-behavior consistency were too pessimistic. Attitudes do predict behavior, but only under certain specifiable conditions. Most importantly, we need to know whether the behavior we are trying to predict is spontaneous, or deliberative and planned (Fazio, 1990).

> We give advice but we do not influence people's conduct.
> —La Rochefoucauld, *Maxims*, 1678

## Predicting Spontaneous Behaviors

Sometimes we act spontaneously, giving little forethought to what we are going to do. When LaPiere and his Chinese friends entered a restaurant, the manager did not have a lot of time to reflect on whether to serve them; he or she had to make a snap decision. Similarly, when someone approaches us at a shopping mall and asks us to sign a petition in favor of a change in the local zoning laws, we usually make a split-second decision. Typically, we do not stop and deliberate for several minutes about what to do.

The extent to which attitudes predict spontaneous behaviors depends on a quality of the attitude we discussed earlier: its accessibility (Fazio, 1990, in press). As you recall, accessibility refers to the strength of the association between an object and your attitude toward that object. When accessibility is high, your attitude comes to mind whenever you see the object. When accessibility is low, your attitude is much less likely to come to mind. It follows that highly accessible attitudes will be more likely to predict spontaneous behaviors, because people are more likely to be thinking about their attitude when called on to act.

Russell Fazio, Martha Powell, and Carol Williams (1989) demonstrated the role of accessibility in a study of people's attitudes and behaviors toward consumer items. People first rated their attitudes toward several products, such as different brands of gum and candy bars. The accessibility of these attitudes was assessed by measuring how long it took people to respond to the attitude questions. People's actual behavior was measured by placing ten of the products on a table (in two rows of five), and telling people they could choose five of them to take home as a reward for being in the study. To what extent did people's attitude toward the products determine which ones they chose?

As predicted, it depended on the accessibility of their attitudes. Attitude-behavior consistency was high among people with accessible attitudes, and relatively low among people with inaccessible attitudes. That is, people acted in accord with their attitudes only if their attitude came quickly to mind when making their choice. What about people with inaccessible attitudes—what determined which products they chose? Interestingly, they were more influenced by an arbitrary aspect of the situation—which products happened to be in the first row on the table in front of them. This is consistent with the idea that when attitudes are inaccessible, people are more influenced by situational variables—in this case, how noticeable and within reach the products were.

## Predicting Deliberative Behaviors

Sometimes behavior is not spontaneous, but deliberative and planned. Most of us give a good deal of thought about where to go to college, whether to accept a new job, or where to spend our vacation. Under these conditions, the immediate accessibility of our attitude is not as important. Given enough time to think about an issue, even people with inaccessible attitudes can bring to mind how they feel. It is only when we have to decide how to act on the spot—without time to think it over—that accessibility matters (Eagly & Chaiken, 1993; Fazio, 1990).

**The Importance of Specific Attitudes.**  The best-known theory of how attitudes predict deliberative behaviors is Martin Fishbein and Icek Ajzen's **theory of reasoned action** (Ajzen & Fishbein, 1980; Fishbein & Ajzen, 1975). According to this theory, when people have time to contemplate how they are going to behave, the best predictor of their behavior is their intention: Does Sam intend to go to the concert? Does Sue intend to get a dog? Note that these are planned, deliberate actions, not the spontaneous kind covered by Fazio's notion of accessibility.

As seen in Figure 8.7, to know what a person's intentions are we need to know two things: (a) his or her attitude and (b) his or her beliefs about the subjective norms that operate in the situation. As you can see in the figure, however, what is important here is not people's general attitude about something but their specific attitude toward the behavior in question. According to the theory of reasoned action, only specific attitudes toward the behavior in question can be expected to predict that behavior.

For example, suppose you are organizing a blood drive at your college and want to predict how many people will agree to donate blood. You decide to do a survey in which you ask people their attitudes, and from that, predict their behavior. But what question should you ask? You might ask a very general question, such as how much people are willing to help others. Because giving blood is one way of helping others, this might enable you to predict who will give blood. The problem is that even if people are willing to help others, they might fail to give blood because of a host of other factors—

**theory of reasoned action:** a theory holding that the best predictors of people's planned, deliberate behaviors are people's attitudes toward the specific behavior and their subjective norms

If actions are to yield all the results they are capable of, there must be a certain consistency between them and one's intentions.

—La Rochefoucauld, *Maxims*, 1678

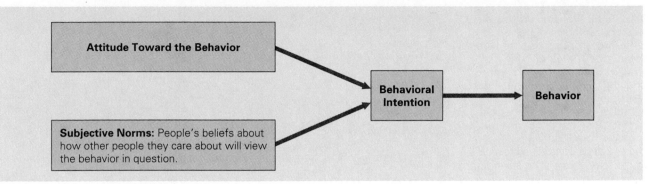

FIGURE 8.7  **The theory of reasoned action.** According to this theory, the best predictor of people's planned, deliberative behaviors are their behavioral intentions. The best predictors of their intentions are their attitudes toward the specific behavior and their subjective norms. (Adapted from Ajzen & Fishbein, 1980)

they are busy at the time of the blood drive, they are worried they will faint in front of their friends, they mistakenly believe they can catch AIDS from giving blood. To increase predictability, it is better to measure people's attitude toward the specific act in question—namely, how they feel about donating blood at the student union next Wednesday at 2:00 P.M.

This may be one reason LaPiere (1934) found such inconsistency between people's attitudes and behaviors in his study. His question to the proprietors—whether they would serve "members of the Chinese race"—was stated very generally. Had he asked a much more specific question—such as whether they would serve an educated, well-dressed, well-to-do Chinese couple accompanied by a white American college professor—they might have given a different answer.

In a study of married women's use of birth control pills, Andrew Davidson and James Jaccard (1979) demonstrated that attitudes toward specific behaviors are better predictors of people's actions than more general attitudes are. A sample of women were asked a series of attitude questions, ranging from the general (their attitude toward birth control) to the specific (their attitude toward using birth control pills during the next two years; see Table 8.2). Two years later, they were asked whether they had used birth control pills at any time since the last interview. As seen in Table 8.2, the women's general attitude toward birth control did not predict their use of birth control at all. This general attitude did not take into account other factors that could have influenced their decision, such as the women's concern about the long-term effects of the pill and their attitude toward other forms of birth control. The more specific the question was about the act of using birth control pills, the better this attitude predicted their actual behavior.

**The Importance of Subjective Norms.**  In addition to measuring attitudes toward the behavior, however, we also need to measure people's **subjective norms.** Subjective norms are defined as people's beliefs about the kinds of social pressures they might succumb to, causing them to perform or not perform the behavior. More specifically, they are people's beliefs about how

**subjective norms:** people's beliefs about how people they care about will view the behavior in question

**TABLE 8.2 Specific attitudes are better predictors of behavior.** Different groups of women were asked about their attitudes toward birth control. The more specific the question, the better it predicted their actual use of birth control. *Note*: If a correlation is close to 0, it means that there is no relationship between the two variables. The closer the correlation is to 1, the stronger the relationship between attitudes and behavior. (Adapted from Davidson and Jaccard, 1979)

| Specific attitudes are better predictors of behavior | |
| --- | --- |
| **Attitude Measure** | **Attitude-Behavior Correlation** |
| Attitude toward birth control | .08 |
| Attitude toward birth control pills | .32 |
| Attitude toward using birth control pills | .53 |
| Attitude toward using birth control pills during the next two years | .57 |

people they care about will view the behavior in question. To predict someone's intentions, knowing these beliefs can be as important as knowing their attitudes.

For example, suppose we want to predict whether Malcolm intends to go to a heavy-metal concert, and we know that he has a negative attitude toward this behavior—he can't stand heavy-metal music. We would probably say he won't go. Suppose we also know, though, that Malcolm's best friend, Kristen, really wants him to go and that Malcolm wants very much to please her. Knowing this subjective norm—his belief about how a close friend views his behavior and his motivation to go along with this person's wishes—we might make a different prediction. A considerable amount of research supports the idea that asking people about their subjective norms increases the ability to predict their planned, deliberative behaviors, such as the decision of what job to accept, whether to wear a seatbelt, and whether to check oneself for disease (Sheppard, Hartwick, and Warshaw, 1988; Stasson & Fishbein, 1990; Steffen, 1990).

> You can tell the ideals of a nation by its advertisements.
> —George Norman Douglas, *South Wind*

## Advertising: Why Does It Work?

Up to this point, we have discussed several principles of attitude and behavior change. As you have seen in many of our examples, we all encounter these principles practically every day of our lives, in the form of advertisements that attempt to change our attitudes and behavior. American businesses spend billions of dollars a year trying to sell us their products. Advertising has invaded our homes via TV, radio, magazines, and newspapers, as well as in the form of mail ads and telemarketing calls. The average American receives more than 200 pieces of direct-mail advertisements each year, and 50 telephone calls from telemarketers (Pratkanis & Aronson, 1991). As you can imagine, based on the principles we have examined, advertising can be very successful in shaping and changing our attitudes. In Chapter 15, in the section on social psychology and business, we will discuss studies showing that advertising can be powerful indeed. For now, we will look at why advertising works.

The average American watches over 37,000 television commercials a year.

We have talked about various kinds of advertisements in this chapter. Which types work the best? The answer to this question follows from our earlier discussion of attitude change. By way of review, advertisers should consider the kind of attitude they are trying to change. If they are trying to change an affectively based attitude, then as we have seen, it is best to fight emotions with emotions. Many commercial advertisements take the emotional approach—for example, ads for different brands of soft drinks. Given that different brands of colas are not all that different, many people do not base their purchasing decisions on the objective qualities of the different brands. Consequently, soda advertisements do not stress facts and figures. As noted by one advertising executive, "The thing about soda commercials is that they actually have nothing to say" ("The battle for your brain," *Consumer Reports*, August 1991, p. 521). Instead of presenting facts, soda ads play to people's emotions, trying to associate feelings of excitement, youth, energy, and sexual attractiveness with their brand.

If people's attitudes are more cognitively based, then we need to ask an additional question: How personally relevant is the issue? Does it have important consequences for people's everyday lives, or is it a remote issue that does not directly affect them? Consider, for example, the problem of heartburn. This is not a topic that evokes strong emotions and values in most people. Thus, it is more cognitively based. To people who suffer from frequent heartburn, however, it clearly is of direct personal relevance. In this case, the best way to change people's attitudes is to use logical, fact-based arguments (Chaiken, 1987; Petty & Cacioppo, 1986).

What if you are dealing with a cognitively based attitude that is not of direct personal relevance to people? Here you have a problem, because people are unlikely to pay close attention to your advertisement. You might succeed in changing their attitudes via the peripheral route, such as having attractive movie stars endorse your product. The problem here, as we saw, is that attitude change triggered by simple peripheral cues is not very long-lasting (Chaiken, 1987; Petty & Cacioppo, 1986). Thus, if you have a product that does not engage people's emotions and is not of direct relevance to people's everyday lives, you are in trouble.

But don't despair. The trick is to *make* your product personally relevant. Let's take a look at some actual ad campaigns to see how this is done. Consider the case of Gerald Lambert, who, in the early part of this century,

Many ads try to associate positive emotions with the product.

She bags the *bouquets* but never a *Beau*

You never have it? – *what colossal conceit!*

End halitosis with LISTERINE  THE SAFE ANTISEPTIC

This ad is one of the most famous in the history of advertising. Today, it is easy to see how sexist and offensive it is. When it appeared in 1936, however, it succeeded in making a problem (bad breath) personally relevant, by playing to people's fears and insecurities about personal relationships. Can you think of any contemporary ads that try to raise similar fears?

inherited a company that made a surgical antiseptic that was used to treat throat infections—Listerine. Seeking a wider marker for his product, Lambert decided to promote it as a mouthwash. The only problem was that no one at the time used a mouthwash or even knew what one was. So, having invented the cure, Lambert invented the disease. Look at the ad on this page, which appeared in countless magazines over the years.

Even though today we would find this ad incredibly sexist, at the time most Americans did not find it offensive. Instead, the ad very successfully played on people's fears about social rejection and failure. The phrase, "She was often a bridesmaid but never a bride" became one of the most famous in the history of advertising. In a few cleverly-chosen, manipulative words, it succeeded in making a problem—halitosis—personally relevant to millions of people. Listerine became a best-selling product that has since earned a fortune. Incidentally, you might think that halitosis is the official term of the American Medical Association for bad breath. In fact, it is nothing more than a fancy, medical-sounding term, invented by Gerald Lambert and his advertising team, to sound like a dreadful disease that we must avoid at all costs—by going to the nearest drugstore and stocking up on mouthwash.

Gerald Lambert's success with playing to people's fears and sense of shame was not lost on other advertisers. Similar ads have been designed to create new markets for many new products, most having to do with personal hygiene or health: under-arm deodorants, deodorant soaps, vitamin supplements, oat bran, fish oil, and more. These campaigns work by convincing people they have problems of great personal relevance, and that the advertised product can solve these problems.

*Drawing by Hamilton; © 1984 The New Yorker Magazine, Inc.*

Advertising agencies are masters at linking emotional images and words to products.

*"How about one of those sunny old grandpas who make things look honest?"*

Many advertisements also try to make people's attitudes more affectively based, by associating the product with important emotions and values (see our earlier discussion of classical conditioning). Consider, for example, advertisements for long-distance telephone service. This is not a topic that, for most of us, evokes deep-rooted emotional feelings—until, that is, we see an ad where a man calls his long-lost brother to tell him he loves and misses him, or an ad where a man calls his mother to tell her he has just bought her a plane ticket so she can come visit him. There is nothing logically compelling about these ads. Logically, there is no reason to believe using AT&T service will magically make you closer to your family than using MCI or Sprint. However, by associating positive emotions with a product, an advertiser can turn a bland product into one that evokes feelings of nostalgia, love, warmth, and general goodwill.

Interestingly, some advertisers have taken this approach to absurd lengths. They create ads that evoke positive feelings, but forget to associate

Some ads succeed in associating positive feelings with a product, through the process of classical conditioning. To do so, however, you have to present an ad that evokes positive feelings along with your product—a lesson that was forgotten by the creators of ads for Infiniti cars, who used pictures similar to this one, but did not show the car.

these feelings with the product they are trying to sell. If you flipped through a magazine in the summer of 1989, you may have come across a rather strange advertisement that looked like the photograph on the previous page. The ad showed an attractive enough picture, but oddly, it is not clear what the ad was selling. No product was displayed, nor did the ad say anything, other than one lone word in the corner: *Infiniti.* Around the same time, similar ads appeared on television. The viewer saw scenes of natural beauty, such as a single tree standing in the mist. In the background, a hushed, tranquil voice talked about the definition of luxury: "In Japan, . . . where true luxury is a spare, natural idea and beauty a close personal experience, there is a new concept of luxury—Infiniti." As the ad campaign progressed, it gradually became clear what an Infiniti was—a new luxury car manufactured by Nissan. The goal of the campaign was to get people to associate the name of the car with natural beauty, tranquillity, and a sense of Asian aesthetics. Unfortunately, the ad violated a basic principle of classical conditioning: You have to present the stimulus that evokes emotions (e.g., the attractive pictures and soothing words) with the stimulus you want to take on those emotions (e.g., a photograph of the car). By failing to show a picture of the car, or even tell the viewer what an Infiniti was, the ad gave the viewer nothing to associate the positive feelings with. It appears that the makers of the Infiniti eventually learned this lesson; in later ads, they pictured the car prominently.

# SUMMARY

**Attitudes** are people's enduring evaluations of people, objects, and ideas. All attitudes have **affective, cognitive,** and **behavioral** components, though they can be based more on one of these components than on the others.

Attitudes can be changed in a number of ways. As shown by research on *cognitive dissonance theory*, attitudes change when people engage in *counterattitudinal advocacy* for low *external justification.* When this occurs, people find *internal justification* for their behavior, bringing their attitudes in line with their behavior.

Another way attitudes change is when people receive **persuasive communications.** According to the **Yale Attitude Change approach,** the persuasiveness of a communication depends on aspects of the communicator, or source of the message; aspects of the message itself (e.g., its content); and aspects of the audience. The **elaboration likelihood model** specifies when people are persuaded by the strength of the arguments in the communication, and when they are persuaded by more surface characteristics, such as the attractiveness of the speaker. People will take the **central route to persuasion** when they have both the motivation and the ability to pay close attention to the arguments. This is

likely to occur when the topic of the communication is high in **personal relevance.** People will take the **peripheral route to persuasion** when they either do not want to or cannot pay close attention to the arguments. Under these conditions, they are persuaded by such peripheral cues as the attractiveness of the speaker or the length of the speech. Attitude change is longer-lasting and more resistant to attack when it occurs via the central route.

**Fear-arousing communications** can cause attitude change via either the central or the peripheral route. They will cause change via the central route when the communication arouses people's fears and people believe that they will be reassured by the content of the message.

The effectiveness of persuasive communications also depends on the origins and strength of people's attitudes. **Cognitively based attitudes** are based mostly on people's beliefs about the properties of the attitude object. **Affectively based attitudes** are based more on people's emotions and values; they can be created through **classical** or **instrumental conditioning. Behaviorally based attitudes** are based on people's actions toward the attitude object. For example, research on *self-perception theory* shows that when people's attitudes are weak or ambiguous, they infer how they feel by observing how they behave. Behaviorally based attitudes are likely to be high in **accessibility,** which is the strength of the association between an object and the person's attitude toward that object.

It is possible to make people resistant to attacks on their attitudes in two ways. First, you can try to make an attitude affectively based by reinforcing people's values, which should make them relatively immune to persuasive communications that use logical arguments. The second approach involves **attitude inoculation,** whereby you expose people to small doses of arguments against their position, making it easier for them to refute these arguments when they hear them later. This approach may also inoculate people against attacks that play on their emotions and values, if people are first given small doses of these kind of attacks.

Attempts to manage people's attitudes, however, should not be used with too heavy a hand. Strongly prohibiting people from engaging in certain behaviors can actually cause an increase in liking for that activity, for two reasons. First, **reactance** can be aroused, which is an unpleasant state people experience when their freedom of choice is threatened. One way people can reduce reactance is to perform the behavior that was threatened. Second, when people have an extrinsic and intrinsic reason for avoiding an activity, an overjustification effect can occur. This is the process whereby people focus on the extrinsic reason for their behavior and overlook the intrinsic one. Consequently, an interest in the forbidden activity can increase.

One reason it is important to understand when attitudes change has to do with their relationship to behavior. The relationship between attitudes and behavior, however, is not as straightforward as once thought. We need to distinguish between behaviors that are spontaneous versus those that are more planned and deliberative. Attitudes predict spontaneous behaviors only when they are relatively accessible. When attitudes are inaccessible, they are more likely to be influenced by situational and social factors. The **theory of reasoned action** specifies how we can predict people's planned and deliberative behaviors. Here it is necessary to know people's attitude toward the specific act in question, as well as their **subjective norms**—people's beliefs about how others view the behavior in question. Knowing these two things allows us to predict well people's behavioral intentions, which are highly correlated with their planned behaviors.

We concluded with a discussion of advertising and why it works. When an attitude is affectively based, as are many political attitudes, it is best to fight emotions with emotions, rather than using fact-based ad campaigns. When an attitude is more cognitively based and the issue is personally relevant, fact-based ad campaigns work well. What if people's attitudes toward your product are not affectively based and your product is not personally relevant to many people? In this case, ad campaigns succeed if they create a need for the product, convincing people that it is of substantial personal relevance.

## SUGGESTED READINGS

Ajzen, I. (1988). *Attitudes, personality, and behavior.* Chicago, IL: Dorsey Press. An in-depth discussion of the relationship between attitudes and behaviors, with an emphasis on the theory of reasoned action.

Eagly, A., & Chaiken, S. (1993). *The psychology of attitudes.* Fort Worth, TX: Harcourt Brace Jovanovich. An extremely thorough, up-to-date, and insightful look at current social psychological research on attitudes.

Petty, R. E., & Cacioppo, J. T. (1986). *Communication and persuasion: Central and peripheral routes to attitude change.* New York: Springer-Verlag. An in-depth discussion of the elaboration likelihood model of attitude change.

Pratkanis, A. R., & Aronson, E. (1991). *Age of propaganda: The everyday use and abuse of persuasion.* New York: Freeman. An engaging account of how our attitudes are shaped by the mass media.

# Chapter 9
## Group Processes

n a cold January day in 1961, John F. Kennedy was inaugurated as the thirty-fifth president of the United States. The author of a romance novel could not have written a better script: Kennedy was young, bright, and handsome; he came from a wealthy, well-connected family; he was a war hero. He had an intelligent, beautiful wife and two adorable children. In his election victory over Richard Nixon, Kennedy proved to be a master political strategist whose dashing good looks, wit, and charm were perfect for the new medium of television. He surrounded himself with advisers and cabinet members who were so talented that one writer dubbed them "the best and the brightest" (Halberstam, 1972).

As Kennedy took the helm in these heady times, he was immediately faced with a major foreign policy decision. Should he go ahead with a plan, initiated by the Eisenhower administration, to invade Cuba? Fidel Castro had led a revolution in Cuba a few years before, and his Communist government was considered a threat to U.S. security. The idea was to land a small force of CIA-trained Cuban exiles on the Cuban coast, who would then instigate and lead a mass uprising against Castro.

Kennedy assembled his advisers to examine the pros and cons of such a decision. The group became a tightly knit, cohesive unit that could not have brought more expertise to the topic. After a lengthy deliberation, they decided to go ahead, and on April 17, 1961, a force of 1,400 exiles invaded an area of Cuba known as the Bay of Pigs. The result was a complete disaster. Castro's forces captured or killed nearly all the invaders. Friendly Latin American countries were outraged that the United States had invaded one of their neighbors. Ironically, Cuba became even more closely allied with the Soviet Union as a result of the botched invasion. President Kennedy was later to ask, "How could we have been so stupid?" (Sorenson, 1966).

J.F.K. and his advisors in 1961.

What went wrong? How could such a remarkably talented group of people, who met at great length to analyze the options, come up with such a disastrous plan? Most of us assume that groups make better decisions than individuals. However, in this case a committee of experts made an astonishing number of errors. Would President Kennedy have been better off making the decision by himself, without consulting his advisers?

Though you might think so, consider Kennedy's next foreign policy crisis, which also involved Cuba. The following October, the CIA discovered that the Soviet Union had placed nuclear missiles in Cuba, a scant ninety miles from the coast of Florida. The missiles were aimed toward U.S. cities. Kennedy and his advisers plotted a brilliant strategy of threats, naval blockades, and conciliatory gestures that succeeded in getting Khrushchev, the leader of the Soviet Union, to back down and remove the missiles. What did Kennedy and his advisers do differently this time? Did they simply stumble onto a good strategy, or had they learned from their earlier mistakes at the Bay of Pigs? In this chapter we will focus on how people interact in groups, specifically, how being in a group alters their decision-making processes and their productivity. Let's begin by defining what a group is.

## Definitions: What Is a Group?

In its most basic form, a group is two or more people who are in the same place at the same time. According to this broad definition, people do not have to be interacting with each other to be considered a group; they simply need to be in each other's presence. Examples include students taking a test together, passengers on an airplane, and fans at a baseball game. In the first section of this chapter, we will consider how being in such a **nonsocial group**—where other people are around but we are not interacting with them—influences an individual's behavior. This is the most fundamental question concerning groups: What are the effects of the mere presence of other people?

Though the effects of nonsocial groups are interesting, most of us, when thinking about groups, mean something more than a bunch of people who

**nonsocial group:** a group in which two or more people are in the same place at the same time but are not interacting with each other (e.g., fans at a baseball game)

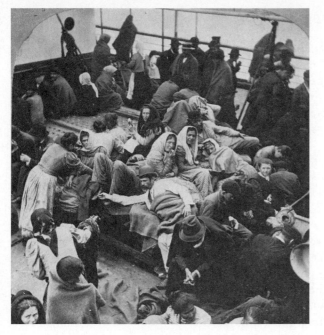

In this photograph, taken in 1902, immigrants wait to disembark at Ellis Island, New York. The entire group of people represent a *nonsocial group*; within the group, you can see *social groups* operating as well (e.g., the group of women in the center).

happen to be occupying the same space. We think of people who have assembled for some common purpose, such as Kennedy's advisers working together to reach a foreign policy decision, citizens meeting to solve a community problem, or people who have gathered to blow off steam at a party. Two variables distinguish such gatherings from nonsocial groups: (a) People interact with each other, and (b) they are interdependent, in the sense that their needs and goals lead them to rely on each other and to influence each other's behavior (Lewin, 1948). When two or more people meet these conditions, we refer to them as **social groups.** A common function of social groups is to work toward a mutual goal—for example, by making decisions. In the second part of this chapter, we will examine how groups make decisions. Do they always make better decisions than individuals acting alone? Why did President Kennedy's advisers make so many errors when deciding to invade Cuba, but plot a brilliant response to the Cuban missile crisis? These questions concern how people in a group interact when they have a common purpose; however, there are also times when members of a group have different goals, placing them in conflict with each other. In the final section of the chapter, we will examine how conflict between individuals and groups develops and how it can be reduced.

**social groups:** groups in which two or more people are interacting with each other and are interdependent, in the sense that to fulfill their needs and goals they must rely on each other

## Nonsocial Groups: The Effects of the Mere Presence of Others

Do you behave differently when other people are around? Simply being in the presence of other people can have a variety of interesting effects on our behavior. Let's begin by looking at how a group affects your performance on something with which you are very familiar: taking a test in a class.

## Social Facilitation: When the Presence of Others Energizes Us

It is time for the final exam in your psychology class. You have spent count-less hours studying the material, and you feel ready. When you arrive, you see that the exam is scheduled in a tiny, packed room. You squeeze into an empty desk, elbow to elbow with your classmates. The professor arrives and says that if any students are bothered by the close quarters, they can take the test by themselves in one of several smaller rooms down the hall. What should you do?

The answer concerns **social facilitation,** or how the mere presence of others affects individuals' performance (Geen, 1989; Harkins & Szymanski, 1987; Zajonc, 1965). The mere presence of other people can mean one of two things: performing a task with co-workers who are doing the same thing you are, or performing a task in front of an audience who is not doing any-thing except observing you. The point is that in either case, you are not inter-acting with these other people—they're just present in the same room, constituting a nonsocial group. Does their presence make a difference? If you take your exam in the crowded room, will you feel nervous and have trouble recalling the material? Or will the presence of classmates motivate you to do even better than if you took the test alone?

To answer this question, we need to talk about insects . . . cockroaches, in fact. Believe it or not, a classic study using cockroaches as research partici-pants suggests an answer to the question of how you should take your psy-chology test. Robert Zajonc and his colleagues (1969) built a contraption to see how cockroaches' behavior was influenced by the presence of their peers. The researchers placed a bright light, which is a noxious stimulus for cock-roaches, at the end of a runway, and timed how long it took a roach to escape the light by running to the other end, where it could scurry into a darkened box (see the left-hand side of Figure 9.1). The question was, did roaches perform this simple feat faster when they were by themselves or when they were in the presence of other cockroaches?

You might be wondering how the researchers managed to persuade other cockroaches to be spectators. They did so by placing extra roaches in clear plastic boxes next to the runway. These roaches were in the bleachers, so to speak, observing the solitary cockroach do his or her thing (see Figure 9.1). As it happened, the individual cockroaches performed the task faster when they were in the presence of other roaches than when they were by themselves; their behavior was facilitated (or improved) by the mere presence of their peers.

Now, we would not give advice on how you should take your psy-chology test based on one study that used cockroaches. But the story does not end here. There have been dozens of studies on the topic of social facili-tation, involving humans as well as other species, such as ants and birds (Bond & Titus, 1983; Guerin, 1986; Rajecki, Kidd, & Ivins, 1976; Zajonc & Sales, 1966). There is a remarkable consistency to the findings of these studies. As long as the task is a relatively simple, well-learned one—as escaping a light is for cockroaches—the mere presence of others improves performance. For example, in one of the first social psychology experiments ever done, Norman Triplett (1898) asked children to wind up fishing line on a reel, either by themselves or in the presence of other children. They did so faster when in the presence of other children than when by themselves.

**social facilitation:** the arousal that results when other people are present and our performance can be evaluated; this arousal enhances our performance on simple tasks but impairs our performance on complex tasks

Mere social contact begets . . . a stimulation of the animal spirits that heightens the effi-ciency of each individual workman.
—Karl Marx (1818–1883)

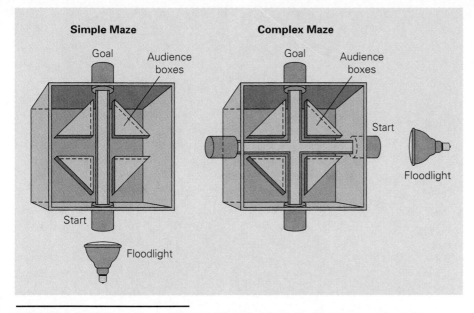

**FIGURE 9.1  Cockroaches and social facilitation.** In the maze on the left, cockroaches had a simple task: to go from the starting point down the runway to the darkened box. They performed this feat faster when other roaches were watching than when they were alone. In the maze on the right, the cockroaches had a more difficult task. It took them longer to solve this maze when other roaches were watching than when they were alone. (Adapted from Zajonc, Heingartner, and Herman, 1969)

**Simple Versus Difficult Tasks.**  Before concluding that you should stay in the crowded classroom to take your exam, we need to consider a different set of findings. Remember that we said the presence of others enhances performance on simple, well-learned tasks. Escaping a light is old hat for a cockroach, and winding fishing line on a reel is not difficult, even for a child. What happens when we give people a more difficult task to do, and place them in the presence of others? To find out, Zajonc and his colleagues (1969) included another condition in the cockroach experiment. This time, the cockroaches had to solve a maze that had several runways, only one of which led to the darkened box (see the right-hand side of Figure 9.1). When working on this more difficult task, the opposite pattern of results occurred: the roaches took longer to solve it when other roaches were present than when they were alone. Many other studies have also found that people and animals do worse in the presence of others when the task is difficult (Bond & Titus, 1983; Geen, 1989).

**Arousal and the Dominant Response.**  In an influential article published in 1965, Robert Zajonc offered an elegant theoretical explanation for why the presence of others facilitates a well-learned or dominant response, but inhibits a less practiced or new response. His argument has two steps: First, the presence of others increases physiological arousal (i.e., our bodies become more energized), and second, when such arousal exists, it is easier to do things that are simple but harder to do something complex or learn something new. Consider, for example, something that is so easy that it is second

In this photograph from the 1890s, sightseers visit the herring storage pens at Mattapoisett, Massachusetts. Social facilitation theory would predict that the man in the stream would work harder at sorting fish (a well-learned task) while being watched by an audience than when he was alone.

nature to you, such as riding a bicycle or writing your name. Arousal, caused by the presence of other people watching you, should make it even easier to perform these well-learned behaviors. On the other hand, let's say you have to do something more complex, such as learning a new sport or working on a difficult math problem. Now arousal will lead you to feel flustered, make mistakes, and do less well than if you were alone (Schmitt, Gilovich, Goore, and Joseph, 1986).

James Michaels and his colleagues (1982) demonstrated this phenomenon in the pool hall of a college student union. A team of four college students observed several different players from a distance, until they found ones who were experienced players (defined as those who made at least two-thirds of their shots) or novices (defined as those who made no more than one-third of their shots). The researchers then casually walked up to the table and observed them play. Imagine that you were one of the players. There you are, shooting a little pool, when suddenly you notice four strangers standing around watching you. What will happen to your performance? The prediction made by social facilitation theory is clear: If you have played so much pool that you would feel comfortable challenging Minnesota Fats, then the arousal caused by the presence of others should improve your game. If you are a novice and feel as if you have four thumbs, then the arousal caused by the presence of others should make your game go to pieces. This is exactly what Michaels and his colleagues (1982) found, as you can see in Figure 9.2. The experts made significantly more of their shots when they were observed, whereas the novices made significantly fewer shots.

**Why the Presence of Others Causes Arousal.**   We have seen that the mere presence of others leads to arousal, and that our performance is facilitated by such arousal if it is simple or well learned. But why should the presence of others lead to arousal? Researchers have developed three theories to explain the role of arousal in social facilitation: Arousal can cause us to

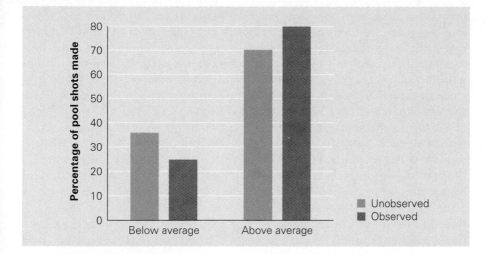

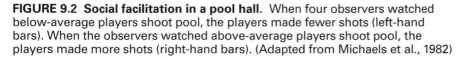

**FIGURE 9.2  Social facilitation in a pool hall**. When four observers watched below-average players shoot pool, the players made fewer shots (left-hand bars). When the observers watched above-average players shoot pool, the players made more shots (right-hand bars). (Adapted from Michaels et al., 1982)

become particularly alert and vigilant; it can make us apprehensive about how we're being evaluated; and it can distract us from the task at hand.

The first explanation suggests that the presence of other people makes us more alert. When we are by ourselves reading a book, we don't have to pay attention to anything but the book; we don't have to worry that the rug will start talking to us or that the sofa will offer us some tea. When someone else is in the room, however, we have to be alert to the possibility that he or she will do something that requires us to respond. Because other people are less predictable than rugs and sofas, we are in a state of greater alertness in their presence. This alertness, or vigilance, causes mild arousal. The beauty of this explanation (which is the one preferred by Robert Zajonc, 1980) is that it explains both the animal and the human studies. A solitary cockroach need not worry about what the cockroach in the next room is doing. However, it needs to be alert when in the presence of another cockroach—and the same goes for humans.

The second explanation focuses on the fact that people are not cock-roaches, and often have other concerns about the presence of others. One concern involves what other people think of us. "Evaluation apprehension" refers to feeling worried and nervous (i.e., aroused) because you know that someone is making a judgment about how well you are doing. According to this explanation, what causes arousal is not the mere presence of others but the presence of others who are evaluating us.

Social psychologists have done some rather creative experiments to test this idea. In a typical study, people perform a task by themselves, in the presence of others who are watching them, or in the presence of others who are blindfolded and thus cannot evaluate them (Cottrell et al., 1968). If it is the mere presence of others that arouses people, social facilitation effects should be found whether the audience is blindfolded or not; if it is evaluation apprehension that arouses people, social facilitation effects should be found only when the audience is not blindfolded. The research results in this area are mixed, favoring both the mere presence explanation (Schmitt et al., 1986) and the evaluation apprehension explanation (Cottrell et al., 1968). However, given that the evaluation apprehension interpretation has a hard time explaining the results of the animal studies (presumably, cockroaches do not have the same concerns about being evaluated as humans do), we can conclude that evaluation apprehension is one source of arousal, but that it is not the sole explanation of social facilitation effects.

A third explanation for why the presence of others arouses us has to do with how distracting other people can be (Baron, 1986; Sanders, 1983). It is similar to Robert Zajonc's (1980) notion that we need to be alert when in the presence of others, except that it focuses on the idea that any source of distraction—be it the presence of other people or noise from the party going on in the apartment upstairs—will put us in a state of conflict, because it is difficult to concentrate on what we are doing. Trying to pay attention to two things at once produces arousal, as anyone knows who has ever tried to read the newspaper with a two-year-old clamoring for attention. Consistent with this interpretation, Robert Baron (1986) found that nonsocial sources of distraction, such as a flashing light, cause the same kinds of social facilitation effects as the presence of other people.

We have summarized the research on social facilitation in the top half of Figure 9.3 (we will discuss the bottom half in a moment). This figure illustrates that there is more than one reason that the presence of other people is arousing. The consequences of this arousal, however, are the same: When

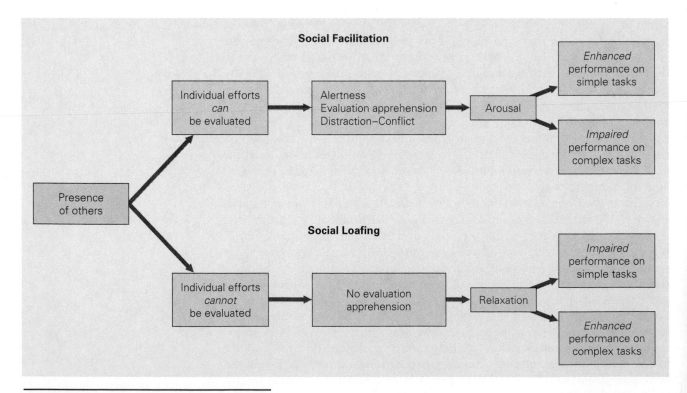

**FIGURE 9.3 Social facilitation and social loafing.** The presence of others can lead to social facilitation or social loafing. The important variables that distinguish the two are evaluation, arousal, and the complexity of the tasks. (Adapted from Cottrell, Wack, et al., 1968)

people are around other people, they do better on tasks that are simple and well learned, but worse on tasks that are complex and require them to learn something new.

We can now conclude that you should take your psychology exam in the presence of your classmates, assuming you know the material well, so that it is relatively simple for you to recall it. The arousal produced by being elbow to elbow with your classmates should improve your performance. We also can conclude, however, that when you study for an exam—that is, when you learn new material—you should do so by yourself, and not in the presence of others. In this situation, the arousal caused by others will make it more difficult to concentrate on the new material.

## Social Loafing: When the Presence of Others Relaxes Us

When you take your psychology exam, your individual efforts will be evaluated. This is typical of the research on social facilitation we have reviewed: People are doing their own thing (either alone or in the presence of others), and these individual efforts are easily observed and evaluated. Often when we are in the presence of others, however, we are working cooperatively on a joint project, and our efforts cannot be distinguished from those of the other people in our group. Such is the case when we cook dinner with a group of friends, work as a team on a class project, or help a group of neighbors push a car out of a ditch.

These situations are just the opposite of the kinds of social facilitation settings we have just considered. In social facilitation, the presence of others puts the spotlight on you, making you aroused. But if being with other people means we can merge into a group, becoming less noticeable than when we are alone, then we should become relaxed. Because no one can tell how well we are doing, we should feel less evaluation apprehension. What happens then? Will this relaxation produced by becoming lost in the crowd lead to better or worse performance? Once again, the answer depends on whether we are working on a simple or a complex task.

Let's first consider simple tasks, such as trying to pull as hard as we can on a rope. The question of how working with others would influence performance on such a task was first studied in the 1880s by a French agricultural engineer, Max Ringelmann. He found that when a group of men pulled on a rope, each individual exerted less effort than when he did it alone. A hundred years later, social psychologists Bibb Latané, Kipling Williams, and Stephen Harkins (1979) called this reduction of individual effort in a group **social loafing.** "Many hands make light work," as the proverb says, and social loafing in groups has since been found for a variety of simple tasks, such as clapping your hands, cheering loudly, and thinking of as many uses for an object as you can (Ingham, Levinger, Graves, and Peckham, 1974; Latané, 1981; Latané, Williams, and Harkins, 1979).

To what extent is social loafing due to the relaxation that results from feeling that our performance cannot be evaluated? One way of finding out is to put people in a group but then arrange things so that each individual's performance can be evaluated. Evaluation apprehension should return under these conditions, eliminating social loafing. This is just what Kipling Williams, Stephen Harkins, and Bibb Latané (1981) found. They asked college students to shout as loudly as they could, supposedly to study the

**social loafing:** the relaxation that results when people are in a group and their individual performance cannot be evaluated; this relaxation impairs performance on simple tasks but enhances performance on complex tasks

effects of sensory feedback on the noise production in groups. In some conditions, the participants thought they were shouting alone; in others, they thought they were shouting along with five other people. (Because the participants were blindfolded and wore earphones, they could not tell whether other people were really shouting along with them or not.) Social loafing occurred when people thought they were one voice in a crowd; that is, their shouts weren't as loud as when they thought they were shouting by themselves. The researchers then told people that they would be shouting in groups again, but that this time there would be a microphone in front of each person that measured the loudness of each person's shout. Under these conditions, no social loafing occurred. Because people believed the researchers were evaluating their individual performance, they shouted as loudly in the group as they did by themselves.

Pulling on a rope or shouting as loudly as we can is a pretty simple task. What happens to our performance on complex tasks when our performance is lost in the crowd? Recall that when our performance in a group cannot be identified, we become more relaxed. Recall also this chapter's earlier discussion of the effects of arousal on performance: Arousal enhances performance on simple tasks, but impairs performance on complex tasks. By the same reasoning, becoming relaxed should impair performance on simple tasks—as we have just seen—but improve performance on complex tasks. The idea is that when people are not worried about being evaluated, they are more relaxed, and should thus be less likely to "clam up" on a difficult task and do it better as a result.

To test this idea, Jeffrey Jackson and Kipling Williams (1985) asked participants to work on mazes that appeared on a computer screen. The mazes were either simple or complex. Another participant worked on identical mazes on another computer in the same room. The researchers either said that they would evaluate each person's individual performance (causing evaluation apprehension) or stated that a computer would average the two participants' scores and no one would ever know how well any one person performed (reducing evaluation apprehension). What should we expect to happen? When people think their score is being averaged with another person's, they should be more relaxed. This should lead to social loafing on the easy mazes, when the task is simple. When the task is difficult, however, being relaxed should be an advantage, leading to better performance. As seen in Figure 9.4, this is exactly the pattern of results the researchers found.

### Social Facilitation or Social Loafing: Which One When?

We now know that many variables affect your behavior when working with or in a group. But you are no doubt wondering, "How can I know ahead of time whether the presence of others will improve a group member's performance or hinder it?" To summarize, you need to know how two important variables are operating in the situation: the possibility of individual evaluation and the simplicity or complexity of the task. If your efforts can be evaluated, the presence of others will make you alert and aroused. This will lead to social facilitation effects, where people do better on simple tasks but worse on complex tasks (see Figure 9.3). If other people are present but your individual efforts cannot be evaluated (i.e., you are one cog in a machine), you are likely to become more relaxed. This leads to social loafing effects, where people do worse on simple tasks but better on complex tasks (see Figure 9.3).

Which of us . . . is to do the hard and dirty work for the rest—and for what pay?
—John Ruskin

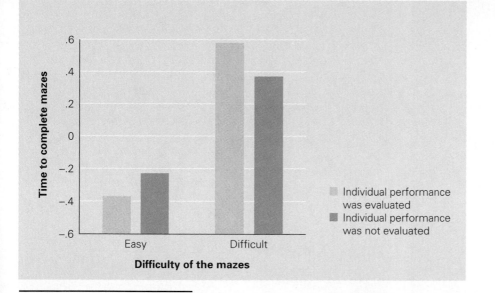

**FIGURE 9.4  Social loafing.** When students worked on easy mazes, those who thought their individual performance would not be evaluated did worse (they took more time to complete them, as seen on the left of the graph). When students worked on difficult mazes, those who thought their individual performance would not be evaluated did better (they took less time to complete them, as seen on the right of the graph). (Adapted from Jackson & Williams, 1985)

These findings have numerous implications for the way in which groups should be organized. If you are a manager who wants your employees to work on a relatively simple problem, a little evaluation apprehension is not such a bad thing—it should improve performance. You shouldn't place your employees in groups where their individual performance cannot be observed, because social loafing (lowered performance on simple tasks) is likely to result. On the other hand, if you want your employees to work on a difficult, complex task, then lowering their evaluation apprehension—by placing them in groups in which their individual performance cannot be observed—is likely to result in better performance.

## Deindividuation: Getting Lost in the Crowd

If you are going to make people more anonymous, you should be aware of other consequences of being a nameless face in the crowd. So far, we have discussed the ways in which a group affects how hard we work and how successfully we learn new things. Being in the presence of others can also cause **deindividuation,** which is defined as a feeling of anonymity and a reduced sense of ourselves as individuals. These feelings lead to the loosening of normal constraints on behavior, resulting in an increase in impulsive, atypical, and deviant acts. In other words, getting lost in a crowd can lead to an unleashing of behaviors that we would never dream of doing by ourselves.

Throughout history, there have been many examples of groups of people committing horrendous acts that no individual would do on his or her own. In Chapter 7, we discussed the My Lai incident in the Vietnam War, where a group of soldiers systematically murdered hundreds of defenseless women,

**deindividuation:** the loosening of normal constraints on behavior, leading to an increase in impulsive and deviant acts

Exactly when, where, and by whom this photograph was taken is not known. It is a moving testament to the extraordinary evil of the deindividuated lynch mob.

The robes and hoods of the Ku Klux Klan cloak them in anonymity; their violent and murderous behavior supports the predictions of deindividuation theory.

There is an accumulative cruelty in a number of men, though none in particular are ill-natured.
—George Savile, Lord Halifax

children, and elderly men. In Europe, mobs of soccer fans regularly attack and bludgeon each other, both before and after the game. In the United States, hysterical fans at rock concerts have trampled each other to death. And the United States has a shameful history of whites lynching African Americans, often cloaked in the anonymity of white robes.

Brian Mullen (1986) content-analyzed newspaper accounts of sixty lynchings committed in the United States between 1899 and 1946, and discovered an interesting fact: The more people there were in the mob, the greater the savagery and viciousness with which they killed their victims. Why do you think this was so? Here is a clue: Robert Watson (1973) content-analyzed ethnographic files on twenty-four cultures and found that warriors who changed their appearance before going into battle—for example, through face and body paint or the wearing of face masks—were significantly more likely to kill, torture, or mutilate captive prisoners than were warriors in cultures that did not mask their identity in battle.

As you might guess, when a mob consists of a large number of people or when warriors disguise their identities, people feel more anonymous and feelings of deindividuation are likely to result. But exactly what is it about deindividuation that leads to impulsive (and often violent) acts? Research by Prentice-Dunn and Rogers (1989) and Diener (1980) points to two factors: First, the presence of others (or the wearing of disguises) makes people feel less accountable for their actions, because it reduces the likelihood that any individual will be singled out and blamed. Second, the presence of others lowers self-awareness, thereby shifting people's attention away from their moral standards. Let's take a look at how these two factors lead to impulsive acts.

**The Role of Reduced Accountability.** It is perhaps obvious that the more likely we are to be caught, the less likely we are to do something that is frowned on or illegal. One researcher illustrated this point by asking people to describe what they would do if they were totally invisible for twenty-four hours, with no chance of being detected. More than half said they would commit a deviant or illegal act, such as robbing a bank or slipping into a locker room to check out the nude bodies (Dodd, 1985). (Interestingly, college students were as likely to say they would commit an illegal act as criminals incarcerated in a maximum security prison.) Being anonymous, either because you are part of a huge crowd or because your identity is somehow concealed, means that you can divorce yourself from the consequences of your actions. The larger a lynch mob, for example, the less personally accountable any one member feels for his or her actions.

Lynch mobs, of course, are hardly controlled experiments. It is possible that people who are naturally more cruel or aggressive are attracted to large mobs, rather than that being in a large crowd makes all of us feel less accountable and freer to act impulsively. Laboratory experiments, however, have confirmed the role of reduced accountability in deindividuation. In an experiment by Philip Zimbardo (1970), for example, female undergraduates participated in one of two conditions. In the deindividuated condition, the participants were asked to put on lab coats and hoods as soon as they arrived. No names were used, and the room was darkened to prevent identification of who was who. In the comparison condition, the participants wore their normal clothes, put on large name tags, were in a brightly lit room, and thus were easily identifiable. All the participants were then asked to deliver (supposed) electric shocks to another woman. Those in the anonymous, deindividuated condition were considerably more aggressive toward the experiment's confederate, delivering more and longer shocks, than were those who could be easily identified.

**accountability:** the likelihood that you will be held responsible for your actions

> If you can keep your head when all about you are losing theirs . . .
> —Rudyard Kipling

The women research participants in Zimbardo's (1970) experiment who wore concealing costumes delivered more electric shock to a victim than did women who did not wear such costumes and were clearly identifiable.

In everyday life, of course, it is rare for us to be asked to put hoods over our heads and deliver shocks to another person. It is not so uncommon, however, to be asked to wear uniforms that make us look like everyone else in the vicinity, an arrangement that might also make us feel less accountable for our actions and hence more aggressive. Does wearing a uniform, such as on a sports team, increase aggressiveness? A study by Jurgen Rehm, Michael Steinleitner, and Waldemar Lilli (1987) indicates that it does. They randomly assigned fifth-graders in German schools to various five-person teams and then watched the teams play handball against each other. In every game, all the members of one team wore orange shirts, and all the members of the other team wore their normal street clothes. Those who wore the orange shirts (and were thus harder to tell apart) played the game significantly more aggressively than the children who wore their everyday clothing did (and were thus easier to identify).

There are many other real-life examples of times when we feel anonymous and lost in the crowd, situations that may make us more aggressive. It is no accident that members of the military wear uniforms and are often required to get haircuts that make them look like everyone else. And as you no doubt noticed, the costumes worn by Zimbardo's research participants resembled Ku Klux Klan hoods and robes—another example of deindividuation leading to violence. Anytime people become more anonymous—and thus less accountable for their actions—they are more likely to commit impulsive, antisocial acts.

**The Role of Reduced Self-Awareness.** In addition to reducing accountability, the presence of others can cause a shift in attention that can also lead to impulsive acts. It is difficult to pay attention both to ourselves and to the world around us simultaneously. To illustrate this point, try thinking about something that is on your mind, such as your relationship with a close friend, while you are reading this book—it's hard to do both simultaneously. Consequently, at any given point we vary in how self-aware we are (Carver & Scheier, 1981; Duval & Wicklund, 1975), as discussed in Chapter 6. When we are tempted to behave in some deviant or antisocial manner, the more self-aware we are, the more our moral principles and values will keep our actions in check. That is, when we are self-aware we are more likely to be reminded of our personal values, such as "Cheating is wrong." When we are in a reduced state of **self-awareness,** we do not think about our values as much, and thus are more likely to act inconsistently with those values.

When are we likely to be in a state of reduced self-awareness? First, the less we feel that other people are focusing their attention on us, the less self-aware we will be. For example, you will be much more self-aware when giving a report in front of a large class than when you are a member of the class listening to someone else give a report. Second, the more stimulation there is in the environment to capture our attention, the less self-aware we will be. Our attention is focused outward; we are not paying attention to ourselves or feeling self-conscious. For example, in the study on lynch mobs (Mullen, 1986), the behavior of the large, violent crowd would be the focus of everyone's attention—people would not be focusing their thoughts on themselves in the midst of a wild mob. Finally, there is evidence that getting high on alcohol or other drugs reduces our self-awareness as well (Hull, 1981).

**self-awareness:** focusing our attention on our feelings, attitudes, and values

Deindividuation, then, is most likely to occur when people feel they are not accountable for their actions (i.e., when there is little chance they will be caught) and when they are in a state of reduced self-awareness (Harkins & Szymanski, 1987; Mullen & Baumeister, 1987; Prentice-Dunn & Rogers, 1989). The conditions that lower accountability and self-awareness are precisely those in which mob violence and other deviant acts tend to occur.

Before leaving this topic, we need to mention one important qualification. We said that deindividuation leads to impulsive, atypical, and deviant acts, and have given several examples of deindividuation that result in violence and aggression. Not all impulsive acts, however, are negative or violent. Other examples include eating too much and dancing wildly at a party. Deindividuation increases these sorts of impulsive acts as well.

But what determines whether deindividuation will lead to positive or negative behaviors? Being good social psychologists, you can probably guess the answer: It depends on whether the context or situation encourages negative or positive behavior (Gergen, Gergen, and Barton, 1973). If we feel angry toward someone, then being deindividuated will lower our inhibitions, making us more likely to act aggressively. If we are hungry and are at a party where there is lots of good food, then being deindividuated will increase the likelihood that we will scarf down large portions of it. In other words, if our inhibitions are preventing us from doing something nonaggressive (e.g., eating) or something pleasant (e.g., hugging someone), the more we are deindividuated, the more we will overcome these inhibitions.

Consider Figure 9.5, for example, depicting a study by Robert Johnson and Leslie Downing (1979), who used the original costume manipulation of Zimbardo's study (1970) but turned it on its ear. In their experiment, participants wore a costume that resembled that of the Ku Klux Klan or a nurse's uniform. The researchers told the participants that the purpose of the costumes was to obscure individual differences; the actual look of the costumes

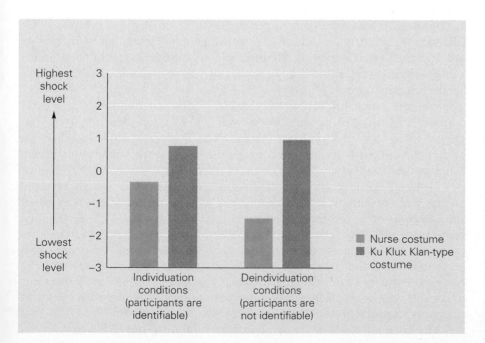

**FIGURE 9.5  Average shock level as a function of deindividuation and costume cue.** Deindividuation can result in prosocial or antisocial behavior—it depends on the context or situational cues present. In this study, once deindividuated, participants became more aggressive if they were wearing Ku Klux Klan-type uniforms, and much less aggressive if they were wearing nurses' uniforms. (Adapted from Johnson & Downing, 1979)

was presented as a kind of convenient accident—the researchers weren't too good at sewing, so the robes came out looking sort of Ku Klux Klannish, or the local hospital was really nice and loaned them nurses' gowns. After putting on their costume, the participants were then individuated (by having a Polaroid taken of them with their name attached) or deindividuated (no name tag attached). The rest of the procedure was like Zimbardo's, wherein the participants had to administer (supposed) electric shocks to a confederate. Did the costumes provide a situational cue, producing more aggressive behavior in one case and more kindly behavior in the other? As you can see in Figure 9.5, the answer is yes. When participants were individuated, the clothes they wore had little effect on the amount of shock they delivered, whereas when participants were deindividuated, the situational cue provided by the clothes made a difference: Those wearing the Ku Klux Klan costume, with its negative connotations, administered higher shocks than those wearing the nursing uniform, with its prosocial connotations of caregiving and nurturance.

The moral? If you're going to deindividuate a person (by placing her in a large crowd, or clothing him in a concealing outfit, or making mood-altering substances available), be sure that the context or situational cues present are positive and peaceful ones—otherwise, you might have trouble on your hands.

## Social Groups: How Decisions Get Made

Multitudes in the valley of decisions.
—Old Testament

So far, we have considered how the mere presence of others can influence an individual's behavior. When we are in a group, however, we are usually more than passive observers of each other's behavior—we socialize, mingle, hobnob, deliberate, and argue. In short, we interact with each other. We have already discussed many of the consequences of social interaction, such as conformity (e.g., other people pressuring us to change our behavior—see Chapter 7) and attitude change (e.g., other people persuading us to change our attitudes—see Chapter 8). We turn now to another aspect of social interaction: group decision making, in which two or more individuals put their heads together to reach a decision.

When it comes to decision making, is it true that two heads are better than one? Most of us assume the answer is yes. A lone individual may be subject to all sorts of whims and biases, whereas several people together can exchange ideas and reach better decisions. This is the assumption of the American judicial system, in which many verdicts are determined by groups of individuals (juries), not single individuals. And juries do not simply vote on the guilt or innocence of a defendant, with no deliberation; they meet, sometimes at great length, to exchange ideas until they reach a unanimous verdict (we will discuss jury decision making in Chapter 15). Similarly, governmental and corporate decisions are often made by groups of people who meet to discuss the issues, and all U.S. presidents have a cabinet and the National Security Council to advise them. It would be foolish for leaders not to consult with others before making important decisions, and to act without examining a problem from many angles.

Many common assumptions about the value of group decision making, however, turn out not to be true. For example, who is it that makes more

*"I'm a sucker for group dynamics."*

moderate, coolheaded decisions: individuals acting alone, or groups of people who discuss the issues? At the beginning of this chapter, we saw that President Kennedy and his advisers, after lengthy deliberations, made a risky and foolhardy decision to invade Cuba. We will see shortly that, contrary to what you might think, groups often make more extreme judgments than individuals. And who makes better, more creative decisions: individuals or groups? As we will see, contrary to common sense, groups are often less creative and clever than individuals working alone.

## Group Versus Individual Decision Making

Suppose you are president of Daisy Dairy, a small company that makes ice cream distributed to local grocery stores. By sticking to this one product line, your company has managed to earn a modest but reliable profit for the past several years. One day, your chief food engineer comes to you with an inspiration: She has been tinkering with the recipes and has invented a new health food ice cream that contains seaweed. All her friends love the taste, she says, and it is much better for people than regular ice cream. You take a taste, and to your surprise it's pretty good. You've been thinking about expanding, and, given how health-conscious people are becoming, the time seems right for such an innovative product.

The problem is that it would require a large investment of capital to perfect the recipe, get approval from the Food and Drug Administration, and mount an advertising campaign. Because there is no guarantee that people would buy it, substantial losses could result. Given the importance of the decision, you decide to appoint a committee of your top executives to examine the options and make a recommendation. Seems like a wise move, doesn't it? Not necessarily. Under many conditions, groups do not make superior decisions (Hackman & Morris, 1978; McGrath, 1984). Let's see what these conditions are.

**The Type of Task.** Whether or not a group will achieve its goal successfully depends on the type of task with which it is faced. Ivan Steiner (1972) divides tasks into three types. An **additive task** is one in which all group members perform basically the same job and the final product (or group performance) is a sum of all their contributions, such as the total amount of noise made by a group of cheerleaders. Such groups should perform better

> Nor is the people's judgement always true: The most may err as grossly as the few.
> —John Dryden

**additive task:** a group task in which performance depends on the sum of each individual's effort (e.g., the total noise made by a group of cheerleaders)

than a lone individual, and will do so—as long as all members do their share. However, as we have seen, social loafing is likely to occur in this type of situation. Thus, a group of four people performing an additive task can be less successful than four individuals working alone, if some members of the group engage in loafing (see Figure 9.6 on page 344).

The second type of task is a **conjunctive task,** in which group performance is defined by the skills of the least capable member of the group, or "the weak link in the chain." In this kind of task, everyone's performance depends on everyone else's. A mountain-climbing team can climb only as fast as its slowest member, the chamber-music group can produce a sound only as good as the least gifted player, and a doubles tennis team can play only as well as the least proficient member of the pair. Groups typically do worse on conjunctive tasks than lone individuals do, since the weakest member brings the performance of the group down to his or her level (Steiner & Rajaratnam, 1961, see Figure 9.6 on page 344).

The most common type of group task is a **disjunctive task,** in which group performance is defined by how well the best member of the group does. Consider a group trying to solve a difficult math problem. If there is one mathematician in the group who knows how to solve the problem, he or she can provide the others with the answer; thus, one gifted individual can dominate the group, raising the performance of average and below-average individuals to his or her level. For example, Larry Michaelson, Warren Watson, and Robert Black (1989) asked students to take a multiple-choice test individually. After they handed in their own answer sheets, the students met with a group of other students and went over the exam again, handing in one answer sheet for the entire group. First, as one would expect on a disjunctive task, the group's performance was better than that of the average member. People who did not know the answers to difficult questions deferred to those who did, allowing experts to answer them. Second, virtually every one of the groups did better than the best individual in the group.

**conjunctive task:** a group task in which performance depends on how well the least talented member does (e.g., how fast a team of roped-together mountain climbers can climb a mountain)

**disjunctive task:** a group task in which performance depends on how well the most talented member does (e.g., a group of people trying to solve a difficult math problem)

Additive tasks are those in which group members' contributions are each added together to create the group product. The Harvard 1888 tug-of-war team (for some unknown reason, pictured here lying down!) and the Wellesley 1882 crew team represent groups engaged in additive tasks.

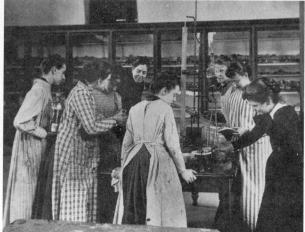

(Below) In disjunctive tasks, group performance is defined by the skills of the most talented member of the group. When working on a difficult chemistry problem, for example, the group will do as well as the person who knows the most about chemistry—assuming that this person convinces the others that he or she knows the right answer.

(Above) In conjunctive tasks, group performance is defined by the skills of the least talented member of the group. A team of mountain climbers, for example, can go only as fast as its least proficient member.

Even the most talented member didn't always know all the answers; working with others on the problems produced the best possible performance.

In general, then, groups are more likely to outperform individuals on disjunctive tasks than on additive or conjunctive ones. However, we must remember that people are not computers, putting together information in a logical, unemotional fashion. Groups are social phenomena. Group members bring their attitudes, feelings, needs, and so on, to the group setting. In Chapter 8, we discussed how people attempt to pressure or persuade others to change their attitudes, and in Chapter 7, we discussed how people conform for both informational and normative reasons. Thus, the group working on a disjunctive task will perform well only if the most talented member can convince the others that he or she is right—which is not always easy, given that many of us bear a strong resemblance to mules when it comes to admitting we are wrong (Laughlin, 1980; Maier & Solem, 1952). Several factors, as we will see, can make groups do worse on disjunctive tasks.

**Process Loss.** You undoubtedly know what it's like to try to convince a group to follow your idea, be faced with opposition and disbelief, and then have to sit there and watch the group make the wrong decision. Ivan Steiner (1972) has called this phenomenon **process loss,** defined as any aspect of group interaction that inhibits good problem solving. Process loss can occur because the most competent member has low status in the group; nobody really takes this person's ideas seriously, and his or her important contribution is thus lost. Or the most competent member might have concerns about being evaluated by others and therefore keeps silent, or he or she might find it difficult to break free from normative conformity pressures that discourage

**process loss:** any aspect of group interaction that inhibits good problem solving

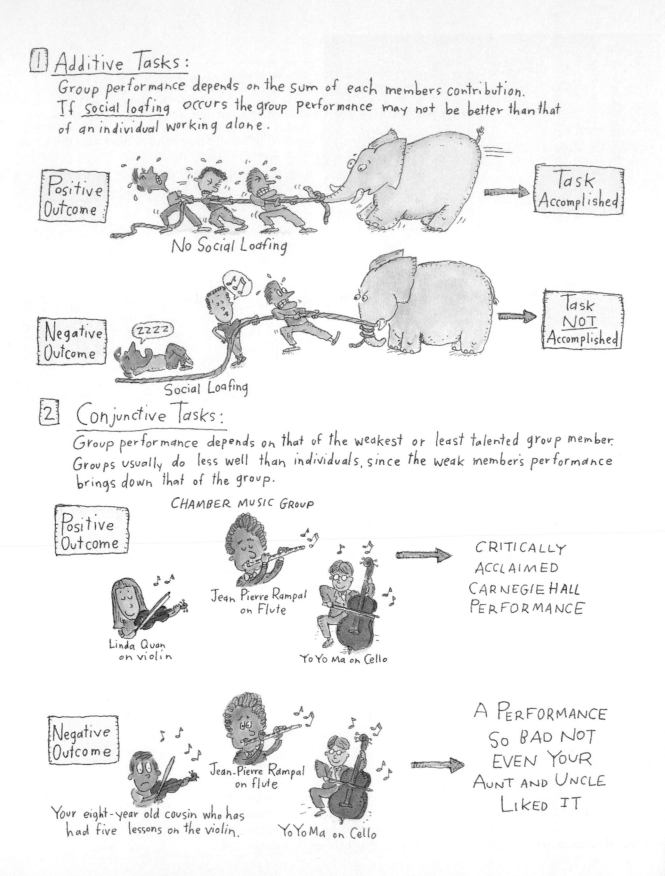

1 Additive Tasks:
Group performance depends on the sum of each members contribution.
If social loafing occurs the group performance may not be better than that
of an individual working alone.

Positive Outcome — No Social Loafing → Task Accomplished

Negative Outcome — ZZZZ — Social Loafing → Task NOT Accomplished

2 Conjunctive Tasks:
Group performance depends on that of the weakest or least talented group member.
Groups usually do less well than individuals, since the weak member's performance
brings down that of the group.

CHAMBER MUSIC GROUP

Positive Outcome — Linda Quan on violin, Jean-Pierre Rampal on Flute, Yo Yo Ma on Cello → CRITICALLY ACCLAIMED CARNEGIE HALL PERFORMANCE

Negative Outcome — Your eight-year old cousin who has had five lessons on the violin, Jean-Pierre Rampal on flute, Yo Yo Ma on Cello → A PERFORMANCE SO BAD NOT EVEN YOUR AUNT AND UNCLE LIKED IT

3. Disjunctive Tasks:

Group performance depends on how well the best or most talented member does. Group's can outperform individuals if the group has a highly talented member, if that member can convince the others that he or she is right, and if that member (and others) presents to the group unique information only he or she knows.

**Positive Outcome** — Group Solving a Physics Problem: Bob, Suzy, Albert Einstein. "WOW! Awesome AL!" "So you see it has to come out to $E=mc^2$" "Cool! Way to go AL!" → Group Solution: $E=mc^2$

**Negative Outcome** — "Albert, I really don't think you know what you're talking about here..." Suzy, Bob. "I agree with Suzy." Albert: "They won't listen to me! I can't convince them!" → Process Loss → Group Solution: $E=ABC^2$

**Negative Outcome** — Bob: "I don't think this squiggle on the handout is a typo! I think it means something!" Suzy: "Yes! It clearly means we should take the square root of the denominator." Albert: "So if the clock is in the spaceship moving at the speed of light, then—" → Failure To Share Unique Information → Group Solution: $E=mc^3 \sqrt{1/ABC}$

**FIGURE 9.6** (Opposite and above) Will groups perform better than lone individuals? It depends on the type of task.

disagreement with the whole group. Other causes of process loss involve communication problems within the group—in some groups, people don't listen to each other (see Figure 9.6); in others, one person is allowed to dominate the discussion while the others tune out. Finally, process loss is most likely to occur with tasks for which the correct answer is not clear-cut or obvious. If a group is arguing about the answer to a math problem, for instance, it is relatively easy for an expert to convince the others that his or her answer really is correct. When arguing about how to lower the national deficit, however, or what might be the consequences of invading Cuba, it is more difficult for an expert to make his or her case. On these kinds of problems, for which the answers are not obvious, groups typically do not perform as well as the best individual would have by him- or herself (Hill, 1982).

**Failure to Share Unique Information.** Another reason groups often don't do as well as individuals is that group members fail to share unique information (that only they know) with each other. Frequently, no one member of a group is an expert on all aspects of the problem. One executive of Daisy Dairy might be an expert in market analysis, whereas another might be an expert on getting approval from the Food and Drug Administration. To reach the best decision, the group must pool their resources, so that each member shares his or her particular expertise with the rest of the group.

As straightforward as it sounds, groups often fail to accomplish this rudimentary condition of good decision making. Garold Stasser and his col-

**FIGURE 9.7 When people are in groups, do they share information that only they know?** Participants in a study met to discuss candidates for an election. In the shared-information condition (top half of figure), each person was given the same positive and negative facts about the candidates. Candidate A was clearly the superior candidate, and most groups preferred him. In the unshared-information condition (bottom half of figure), each person was given the same four negative facts about candidate A, and two unique positive facts. In discussion, these people focused on the information they all shared and failed to mention their unique information; these groups no longer saw candidate A as superior. (Adapted from Stasser & Titus, 1985)

leagues have found that groups have a distressing tendency to spend their time discussing information that is shared by all the group members, instead of focusing on unique or unshared information (Stasser, Taylor, and Hanna, 1989, see Figure 9.6). In one study, for example, participants met in groups of four to discuss which candidate for political office would be most effective (Stasser & Titus, 1985). In the shared-information condition, each participant had been given the same packet of information to read; it indicated that candidate A was the best choice for office. As seen at the top of Figure 9.7, each participant knew that candidate A had eight positive qualities and four negative qualities, making him superior to the other candidates. Not surprisingly, when this group met to discuss the candidates, almost all of the members chose candidate A.

In the unshared-information condition, each participant received a different packet of information. As seen as the bottom of Figure 9.7, each person knew that candidate A had two positive qualities and four negative qualities. However, the two positive qualities cited in each person's packet were unique—different from those listed in other participants' packets. Everyone learned that candidate A had the same four negative qualities;

thus, if the participants shared with each other the information that was in their packets, they would learn that candidate A had a total of eight positive qualities and four negative qualities—just as people knew in the shared-information condition.

Interestingly, however, in the group discussions people tended to focus on the information they shared, rather than on the information each person had that the others did not. As a result, most of the groups in the unshared-information condition never realized that candidate A had more good than bad qualities, and few picked him as their candidate. This focus on shared information occurs even when group members are told that each person has knowledge the others do not possess (Stasser, Taylor, and Hanna, 1989; Stasser & Titus, 1987). In conclusion, even on disjunctive tasks groups often do not outperform the most expert individual, because of process loss and the tendency to focus on information that everyone has in common.

**Brainstorming.**  As you have seen, groups do not always make decisions as well as they should. The studies that have reached this conclusion, however, have mostly used participants having little or no knowledge of group problem-solving skills. Perhaps if we gave groups specific instructions about how to reach good, creative decisions, they would do better than individuals. For example, what would happen if we explicitly instructed a group to be open to all possible ideas, to share whatever crossed group members' minds, to be accepting and noncritical of others' suggestions—in short, to be creative? Would group productivity exceed that of an individual?

An advertising man, A. F. Osborn (1957), thought so, and he dubbed this technique **brainstorming.** The goal of brainstorming is to increase the quality and quantity of solutions by encouraging the free exchange of ideas and by removing criticism from self and others. People are given six rules to follow during the group discussion: The more ideas generated the better; the wilder and more creative the ideas the better; express ideas without concern for their quality or fear of others' reactions; don't evaluate people's ideas

**brainstorming:** a technique designed to improve group decisions by encouraging the free exchange of ideas and the elimination of criticism

The goal of brainstorming is to increase the quality and quantity of solutions by encouraging the free exchange of ideas and by removing criticism from self and others. Research suggests, however, that it is not a very successful technique.

until all possible solutions have been advanced; elaborate and improve on ideas already suggested; and don't be critical (Shaw, 1971). Osborn claimed that when people followed these rules, they generated twice as many ideas as they could by themselves. Brainstorming has become a popular technique in business and industry, where there is widespread belief that it is an effective means of finding creative solutions to problems (Paulus, Dzindolet, Poletes, and Camacho, 1993).

Unfortunately, controlled studies testing this technique suggest otherwise. There is substantial evidence that individuals receiving similar instructions but working by themselves outperform brainstorming groups, due largely to process loss (Bouchard, Barsalous, and Drauden, 1974; Cohen, Whitmyre, and Funk, 1960; Mullen, Johnson, and Salas, 1991). For example, Donald Taylor, Paul Berry, and Clifford Block (1958) gave brainstorming instructions to people in four-person groups and compared their output to that of four persons working alone. People in the brainstorming groups produced only half as many ideas as people working independently, and these ideas were of inferior quality. Why? Michael Diehl and Wolfgang Stroebe (1987) discuss the following reasons. First, only one person can talk at a time in a group, while others sit and listen; people forget important contributions while listening to others, or are led off track by points other people make, lowering productivity. Second, knowing that they are not in the spotlight, group members tune out, spending time thinking about unrelated matters while others are speaking (similar to social loafing); an individual working alone is less likely to be distracted in these ways. Brainstorming can work, if the following procedures are implemented: Give people practice at brainstorming in a group; allow them to generate ideas on their own before the group meeting; and allow them to take notes on their and others' ideas during the meeting (Bouchard, 1972; Street, 1974; Philipsen, Mulac, and Dietrich, 1979).

## Groupthink: Many Heads, One Mind

A possible limitation of research on group problem solving is that most studies use people who have never met before, and give people tasks that are unfamiliar and sometimes trivial. Would groups do better if their members were used to working with each other, and if they were dealing with important, real-world problems? Our opening example of President Kennedy and his advisers deciding to invade Cuba at the Bay of Pigs suggests not. Let's see why.

Using real-world events, Irving Janis (1972, 1982) developed an influential theory of group decision making that he called **groupthink**, defined as a kind of thinking in which maintaining group cohesiveness and solidarity is more important than considering the facts in a realistic manner. According to Janis's theory, groupthink is most likely to occur when certain preconditions are met, such as when the group is highly cohesive, isolated from contrary opinions, and ruled by a directive leader who makes his or her wishes known. Kennedy and his advisers were riding high on their close victory in the 1960 election, and were a very tight-knit, homogenous group. Since they had not yet made any major policy decisions, they lacked well-developed methods for discussing the issues. Moreover, Kennedy made it clear that he favored the invasion, and asked the group to consider only details of how it should be executed, instead of questioning whether it should proceed at all.

> We think so because other people all think so, or because—or—because—after all we do think so, or because we were told so, and think we must think so.
>
> —Henry Sidgwick

**groupthink:** a kind of thinking in which maintaining group cohesiveness and solidarity is more important than considering the facts in a realistic manner

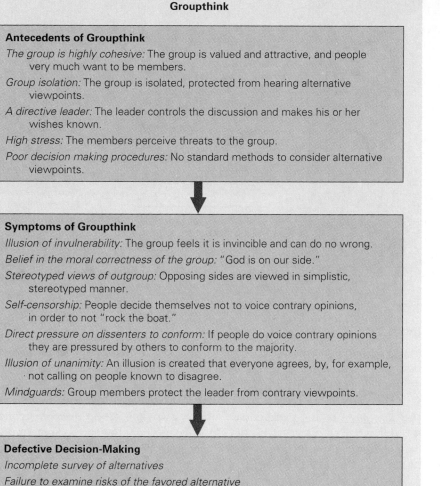

**Groupthink**

**Antecedents of Groupthink**

*The group is highly cohesive:* The group is valued and attractive, and people very much want to be members.

*Group isolation:* The group is isolated, protected from hearing alternative viewpoints.

*A directive leader:* The leader controls the discussion and makes his or her wishes known.

*High stress:* The members perceive threats to the group.

*Poor decision making procedures:* No standard methods to consider alternative viewpoints.

**Symptoms of Groupthink**

*Illusion of invulnerability:* The group feels it is invincible and can do no wrong.

*Belief in the moral correctness of the group:* "God is on our side."

*Stereotyped views of outgroup:* Opposing sides are viewed in simplistic, stereotyped manner.

*Self-censorship:* People decide themselves not to voice contrary opinions, in order to not "rock the boat."

*Direct pressure on dissenters to conform:* If people do voice contrary opinions they are pressured by others to conform to the majority.

*Illusion of unanimity:* An illusion is created that everyone agrees, by, for example, not calling on people known to disagree.

*Mindguards:* Group members protect the leader from contrary viewpoints.

**Defective Decision-Making**

*Incomplete survey of alternatives*

*Failure to examine risks of the favored alternative*

*Poor information search*

*Failure to develop contingency plans*

**FIGURE 9.8 Groupthink: Antecedents, symptoms, and consequences.** Under some conditions, maintaining group cohesiveness and solidarity is more important to a group than considering the facts in a realistic manner (see antecedents). When this happens, certain symptoms of groupthink occur, such as the illusion of invulnerability (see symptoms). These symptoms lead to defective decision making. (Adapted from Janis, 1982)

When these preconditions of groupthink are met, several symptoms appear; these are outlined in Figure 9.8. The group begins to feel that it is invulnerable and can do no wrong. People do not voice contrary views (self-censorship), because they are afraid of ruining the high morale or esprit de corps of the group, or because they are afraid of being criticized by the others. For example, Arthur Schlesinger, one of Kennedy's advisers, reported that he had severe doubts about the Bay of Pigs invasion, but did not bring up any of these concerns during the discussions, out of a fear that "others would regard it as presumptuous of him, a college professor, to take issue with august heads of major government institutions" (Janis, 1982, p. 32). If anyone does voice a contrary viewpoint, the rest of the group is quick to criticize that person, pressuring him or her to conform to the majority view. Schlesinger did voice some of his doubts to Dean Rusk, the secretary of state. When Robert Kennedy (the attorney general and the president's brother) got wind of this, he took Schlesinger aside at a party and told him that the presi-

The decision to launch the space shuttle *Challenger*, which tragically exploded due to defective O-ring seals, appears to have been a result of groupthink on the part of NASA officials, who disregarded engineers' concerns about the quality of the seals.

dent had made up his mind to go ahead with the invasion, and that his friends should support him. This kind of behavior creates an illusion of unanimity, where it looks as if everyone agrees. On the day the group voted on whether to invade, President Kennedy asked all those present for their opinion except one: Arthur Schlesinger.

The pernicious state of groupthink causes people to implement an inferior decision-making process (see Figure 9.8). The group does not consider the full range of alternatives, does not develop contingency plans, and does not adequately consider the risks of its preferred choice. Can you think of other governmental decisions that were plagued by groupthink? Janis (1972, 1982) discusses several, such as the failure of the U.S. military commanders in Pearl Harbor to anticipate the Japanese attack in 1941; President Truman's decision to invade North Korea in 1950, despite explicit warnings from the Chinese that they would attack with massive force; President Johnson's decision to escalate the Vietnam War in the mid-1960s; and the Watergate cover-up by President Nixon and his advisers. Another, more recent example was the fateful decision by NASA to go ahead with the launching of the space shuttle *Challenger*, despite the objections of engineers who said that the freezing temperatures presented a severe danger to the rubber O-ring seals (the ones that eventually failed during the launch, causing the rocket to explode and killing all aboard). All these decisions were plagued by many of the symptoms and consequences of groupthink outlined in Figure 9.8.

We should note that groupthink is not limited to decisions made by U.S. presidents or governmental agencies. Anytime a cohesive group meets to make a decision, there is the danger that groupthink will occur, be it a family deciding where to go on vacation, a social club selecting new members, or a school board working on next year's budget. Groupthink processes like those described by Janis have been found in laboratory studies (Callaway & Esser, 1984; Courtright, 1978; McCauley, 1989), as well as in laboratory simulations of international crisis situations (Druckerman, 1968; Guetzkow, 1968).

Nevertheless, we should not conclude that groupthink is inevitable whenever cohesive groups meet to make a decision. A wise leader can take several steps to ensure that his or her group is immune to this style of decision making. The leader should not take a directive role, but should remain impartial. He or she should invite outside opinions from people who are not members of the group and who are thus less concerned with maintaining group cohesiveness. He or she should divide the group into subgroups that meet separately, then meet together to discuss their different recommendations. The leader also might take a secret ballot, or ask group members to write down their opinions anonymously; doing so would ensure that people give their true opinions, uncensored by a fear of recrimination from the group (Flowers, 1977; McCauley, 1989).

Fortunately, President Kennedy learned from his mistakes with the Bay of Pigs decision, and took many of these steps to avoid groupthink when faced with his next major foreign policy decision, the Cuban missile crisis. When his advisers met to decide what to do about the discovery of Soviet missiles in Cuba, Kennedy often absented himself from the group, so as not to inhibit their discussion. He also brought in outside experts (e.g., Adlai Stevenson) who were not members of the in-group. That Kennedy successfully negotiated the removal of the Soviet missiles was almost certainly due to the improved methods of group decision making he adopted.

## Group Polarization: Going to Extremes

Before leaving the topic of decision making, we need to discuss one other possible advantage of groups: Surely they will make more moderate, less extreme decisions than a lone individual—or will they? Consider our example of the Daisy Dairy and the idea of marketing seaweed-based ice cream. A single executive might be willing to bet the ranch (or the dairy, as it were) on this risky venture, but we would expect a committee to take a more moderate position, proceeding only if there was a good chance of success (especially if precautions against groupthink were implemented). Would we be right?

Nathan Kogan and Michael Wallach (1964) compared how groups and individuals make decisions when an element of risk is involved. Such studies typically give participants the Choice Dilemmas Questionnaire (CDQ), a series of stories that present a dilemma for the main character and ask the reader to choose how much probability of success there would have to be before the reader would recommend the risky alternative (Kogan & Wallach, 1964). An example of a CDQ item about a chess player appears in Figure 9.9. People choose their answers alone, and then meet in a group to discuss them, arriving at a unanimous group decision for each dilemma. How do these two sets of answers compare? Who makes the riskier decisions—groups or individuals?

In what is called the risky shift, Wallach and his colleagues found that groups make riskier decisions than individuals do. For example, individuals said, on average, that the chess player should make the risky gambit if there was at least a 30 percent chance of success; groups, after discussing the dilemma, said, on average, that he should go for it when there was only a 10 percent chance of success (Wallach, Kogan, and Bem, 1962). Many studies have replicated this risky shift in decision making on the part of groups of Americans, and a great deal of evidence supports its occurrence in other

> The bitter change of fierce extremes, extremes by change more fierce.
> —John Milton

---

**An Example of an Item from the Choice Dilemmas Questionnaire**

A low-ranked participant in a national chess tournament, playing an early match against a highly favored opponent, has the choice of attempting or not trying a deceptive but risky maneuver that might lead to quick victory if it is successful or almost certain defeat if it fails.

Please indicate the lowest probability of success that you would accept before recommending that the chess player play the risky move:

___ 1 chance of success in 10

___ 3 chances of success in 10

___ 5 chances of success in 10

___ 7 chances of success in 10

___ 9 chances of success in 10

___ I would not recommend this alternative, no matter how high its likelihood of success

**FIGURE 9.9 The Choice Dilemmas Questionnaire.** (Adapted from Wallach, Kogan, and Bem, 1962)

Western countries as well (Bateson, 1966; Bell & Jamieson, 1970; Kogan & Doise, 1969; Lamm & Kogan, 1970; Pruitt, 1971; Rim, 1963).

Yet with increased research, it became clear that the risky shift was not the full story. Several researchers noted that the dilemmas used in earlier research were ones in which people were leaning in the direction of being risky, even when by themselves (Brown, 1965; Myers & Arenson, 1972; Teger & Pruitt, 1967). The group discussions caused them to make more extreme recommendations in the same direction as their initial inclination—namely, to be risky. What would happen if people were initially inclined to be conservative? Consider this problem: Roger, a young married man with two children, has a secure but low-paying job and no savings. Someone gives him a tip about a company stock that will triple in value if the firm's new product is successful, but will plummet if the new product fails. Should Roger sell his life insurance policy and invest in the company? Most people recommend a safe course of action here: Roger should buy the stock only if the new product is very certain to succeed. What happens when they talk it over in a group? They become even more conservative, deciding that the new product would have to have a nearly 100 percent chance of success before recommending that Roger buy stock in the company.

Thus, it is not that people in groups will always make riskier decisions. They tend to make decisions that are more extreme in the same direction as the individual's initial predispositions, whether those predispositions be risky or conservative. This pattern of results has become known as **group polarization,** a phrase capturing the idea that a group strengthens the initial inclinations of its members, pushing their decisions to the extreme—toward greater risk if people's initial tendency is to be risky, and toward greater caution if people's initial tendency is to be cautious.

**group polarization:** the tendency for groups to make decisions that are more extreme than the initial inclinations of its members

**Cognitive and Motivational Factors.** Why does group polarization occur? Groups strengthen the resolve of the members' initial inclinations for two reasons: one involving cognitive processes; the other, motivational factors. First, all individuals bring to the group a set of arguments supporting their initial recommendation, some of which other individuals have not considered. For example, one person might stress that cashing in the life insurance policy is an unfair risk to Roger's children, should he die prematurely. Another person might not have considered this possibility; thus, he or she becomes more conservative as well. A series of studies by Eugene Burnstein and Amiram Vinokur (1977) supports this persuasive argument interpretation of group polarization, whereby each member presents arguments that other members had not considered. Thus, gaining new information is an important factor in group polarization effects (Ebbesen & Bowers, 1974).

The persuasive arguments interpretation suggests that people care only about coming up with the most logical recommendation that is best supported by the facts. Though people do care about the facts, they have social concerns as well, such as wanting to be liked by the other group members. When people discuss an issue in a group, they first check out how everyone else feels. What does this group value—being risky or being cautious? In order to be liked, many people then take a position that is similar to everyone else's but a little more extreme. In this way, the individual supports the group's values and also presents him- or herself in a positive light—a person in the vanguard, an impressive thinker. Thus, both cognitive factors (hearing new persuasive arguments) and motivational factors (wanting to be liked by the group) prod group members toward a more extreme version of their initial opinion (Blaskovich, Ginsburg, and Veach, 1975; Brown, 1986; Isenberg, 1986; Myers, 1982).

**The Culture-Value Theory.** While group polarization can go either way, Roger Brown (1965) has proposed that, relatively speaking, Americans value risk more than caution. In his culture-value theory, Brown discusses how American culture, based on the economic system of capitalism, requires a willingness to take risks and try new approaches. In comparison, other cultures operate under a dominant cultural value of caution—a relatively high level of wariness and conservatism. Hence, the hypothesis derived from culture-value theory is that some cultures should be more likely to evince risky shifts, while others should evince cautious shifts.

In support of Brown's theory, research has indicated that Americans perceive people who take risks more positively than those who make cautious decisions (Madaras & Bem, 1968); find the riskier alternatives more admirable than the cautious ones (Lamm, Schaude, and Trommsdorff, 1971); and believe high-risk takers are more competent than those who choose cautious alternatives (Jellison & Riskind, 1970). Thus, it appears that risk does have value in the United States. In comparison, two cross-cultural studies have found evidence for a general cultural value of caution in African countries. In both Uganda and Liberia, groups made choices on the CDQ that were typically more cautious than those made by the individual members alone, and were more cautious than those made by Western research participants (Carlson & Davis, 1971; Gologor, 1977). Thus, when group discussion occurs, it reinforces whichever cultural value predominates in that society—for example, group polarization toward caution occurs when individuals learn they are not as cautious as others in the group and caution is valued in their culture.

STRANGE MATTER
*Roz Chast*

OLYMPICS for the CAUTIOUS

© Roz Chast. Used with permission.

This cartoon strikes us as humorous in part because we belong to a culture that values risk. (Note that the cartoon would not be so funny if it depicted people doing very risky/silly things.)

In conclusion, groups often make decisions that are no better (and even worse) than individuals alone. This is especially true if the group is working on (a) an additive task and social loafing occurs; (b) a conjunctive task and the performance of the least skilled individual drags the group down; or (c) a disjunctive task and process loss occurs, so that people do not heed the advice of the most expert member (Littlepage, 1991). It is also true if the group is highly cohesive and groupthink occurs. Groups will make better decisions if they avoid process loss, avoid groupthink, and seek out from individuals information that the rest of the group does not have. Finally, groups also tend to make more extreme decisions than individuals acting alone do, in the direction that each group member was initially leaning.

## Group Interaction: Conflict and Cooperation

We have just examined how group members work together to solve problems; in these situations, group members have a common goal. Often, however, people have incompatible goals, placing them in conflict with each other. This can be true of two individuals, such as romantic partners who disagree about who should clean the kitchen, or two groups, such as a labor union and company management who disagree over wages and working conditions. It also can be true of two nations, such as the long-standing conflict between Israel and its Arab neighbors. The opportunity for interpersonal conflict exists whenever two or more people interact. Freud (1930) went so

My own belief is that Russian and Chinese behavior is as much influenced by suspicion of our intentions as ours is by suspicion of theirs. This would mean that we have great influence over their behavior—that, by treating them as hostile, we assure their hostility.

—J. William Fulbright

far as to argue that conflict is an inevitable byproduct of civilization. The goals and needs of individuals often clash with the goals and needs of their fellow humans.

Many conflicts are resolved peacefully, with little rancor. Couples can find a way to resolve their differences in a mutually acceptable manner, and labor disputes are sometimes settled with a friendly handshake. All too often, however, conflict erupts into open hostilities. The divorce rate in the United States is distressingly high. People are increasingly resorting to violence to resolve their differences, as shown by the skyrocketing murder rate in the United States, "the murder capital of the civilized world" (*Newsweek*, July 16, 1990). On a grander scale, warfare between nations remains an all-too-common solution to international disputes. In fact, when wars over the past five centuries are examined, the twentieth century ranks first in the severity of wars (defined as the number of deaths per war) and second in their frequency (Levy & Morgan, 1984). It is therefore of great importance to find ways of resolving conflicts peacefully. Given our capability to destroy ourselves many times over with nuclear weapons, humanity's need to study the causes and cures of interpersonal conflict is more pressing than ever.

Let's begin by defining our terms. Our concern is with interpersonal, not intrapersonal conflict. **Intrapersonal conflict** is tension created by incompatible goals within one individual, such as a parent's desire to pursue a career but also to be the primary caregiver for his or her children. (We discussed intrapersonal conflict in Chapter 3). **Interpersonal conflict** is tension between two or more individuals or groups who have incompatible goals; this kind of conflict can be divided into two types. In **zero-sum conflict,** one party's gain is always the other person's loss. The two sides cannot both win or both lose in this kind of dispute. Examples include athletic contests in which there is always a clear winner and loser, and games such as chess and poker. The reason for the term *zero-sum* is that if we think of people's rewards in numerical terms (e.g., the amount of money they win or lose in a poker game), then the sum of what one side wins and the other side loses always equals zero. If Janice is playing poker with Bob and she wins $5, then Bob has lost $5.

**intrapersonal conflict:** tension within one individual due to two or more incompatible goals (e.g., a parent's desires to stay home with his or her children and to pursue a career)

**interpersonal conflict:** tension between two or more individuals or groups who have incompatible goals

**zero-sum conflict:** conflict in which one side's gain is always the other side's loss, as in athletic contests

Intergroup conflict is clearly one of the most pressing problems confronting us today. For example, as we write this chapter, Bosnia is being torn apart by ethnic conflict. In this photograph, refugees at a Bosnian checkpoint are seen hiding in a ditch during the shelling.

In everyday life, zero-sum conflicts are relatively rare. When people have conflicting goals, there are often solutions that are satisfactory to both parties, so that both come out ahead. Unfortunately, there are also solutions that are unattractive to both parties, so that nobody wins. Consider the arms race between the United States and the former Soviet Union. Both countries could win if they agreed to disarm, each reducing the number of costly, destructive missiles in their arsenal. Both could lose by continuing to spend a large proportion of their budgets on expensive weapons systems, neither achieving superiority over the other. Or one side could win by gaining so much military superiority that the other side was forced to capitulate to its demands.

Social psychologists refer to this latter kind of dispute as a **mixed-motive conflict,** defined as any conflict in which both parties can gain by cooperating, but in which an individual can gain even more by competing against his or her partner. The term *mixed-motive* comes from the fact that people have two choices: They can compete (resulting in the most positive personal gain), or they can cooperate (maximizing the joint gain of both parties). Most social psychological research has examined mixed-motive conflicts (rather than zero-sum conflicts) for two reasons. First, mixed-motive conflicts are more common in everyday life than zero-sum conflicts. Second, mixed-motive conflicts are more interesting, because it is not as obvious how each side should respond. Whereas in a zero-sum conflict people should compete with their adversary as hard as they can, because there is no way both sides can win, in a mixed-motive conflict it is not always clear whether one should adopt a cooperative or a competitive strategy.

There are many perspectives on how people respond to mixed-motive conflicts, including sociological studies of social movements and historical, economic, and political analyses of international relations. The social psychological approach is unique in its attempt to study conflict experimentally, testing both its causes and its resolutions in the laboratory. Researchers bring two or more people together and ask them to compete in some manner, studying how conflict develops. There are, of course, ethical and practical limitations to the kinds of conflict that can be studied experimentally. For example, if we are interested in how the use of threats influences the way in which nations resolve international conflicts, we cannot randomly assign world leaders to different conditions, giving some of them sophisticated weapons systems and others none at all.

Because of such ethical and practical difficulties, social psychologists rely on laboratory games to study conflict. For instance, researchers have developed some interesting mixed-motive games that pit the desire to cooperate against the desire to compete. A possible limitation of this approach, of course, is the difficulty of generalizing from people's behavior in a laboratory game to conflict in everyday life. Most social psychologists feel, however, that the conflict played out in these games is very similar to everyday conflict, so that a great deal can be learned. The most commonly used game is one called the Prisoner's Dilemma.

## The Prisoner's Dilemma

Suppose that two men, Billy and Jesse, have been arrested for armed robbery, but the police have only enough evidence to convict them of the lesser crime

**mixed-motive conflict:** conflict in which both sides can gain by cooperating, but in which an individual can gain even more by competing against his or her partner

I wonder men dare trust themselves with men.
—William Shakespeare

**Consequences of Decisions in Mixed-Motive Conflicts**

**The Prisoner's Dilemma Game**

| Billy: | Jesse Doesn't Confess | | Jesse Confesses | |
|---|---|---|---|---|
| | Billy's Sentence | Jesse's Sentence | Billy's Sentence | Jesse's Sentence |
| Doesn't Confess | 3 years | 3 years | 30 years | released |
| Confesses | released | 30 years | 10 years | 10 years |

**A Mixed-Motive Game**

| Student A Chooses: | Student B Chooses Option X | | Student B Chooses Option Y | |
|---|---|---|---|---|
| | Student A's Points | Student B's Points | Student A's Points | Student B's Points |
| Option X | +3 | +3 | –6 | +6 |
| Option Y | +6 | –6 | –1 | –1 |

**FIGURE 9.10 Laboratory games used to study interpersonal conflict.** The top panel shows the Prisoner's Dilemma. The sentence each defendant receives depends both on whether he confesses and on whether the other person confesses. Billy's sentences are listed first in each cell of the table, followed by Jesse's sentences. For example, if Billy confesses but Jesse does not, Billy is released and Jesse receives a thirty-year sentence. The bottom panel shows a similar mixed-motive game that is used in laboratory studies. The numbers represent the points that will be added or subtracted to a student's score on the final exam. Student A's points are listed first in each cell of the table, followed by student B's points. For example, if student A chooses option Y and student B chooses option X, student A receives 6 extra points and student B loses 6 points. (Adapted from Rapoport & Chammah, 1965)

of breaking and entering. The police take the defendants to separate interrogation rooms and offer each of them a deal: If they agree to testify against their partner, they will be released with no jail time. What should they do? Should they confess or remain silent? The top of Figure 9.10 illustrates the consequences of each course of action. If both defendants remain silent, they will be convicted of breaking and entering and will receive sentences of three years. (The sentence Billy gets is listed first in each cell of the table, whereas the sentence Jesse gets is listed second.) Here both defendants are relatively well-off. If Billy confesses but Jesse remains silent, then Billy is released and Jesse gets a thirty-year sentence. If both defendants confess, however, then there is no reason for the police to use one as a witness against the other, and both will receive sentences of ten years.

This is a classic mixed-motive conflict, because it pits people's desire to look out for their own interests against their desire to look out for their partner as well. To find out how people resolve this conflict, social psychologists have asked participants to play this and similar games in hundreds of studies(Kelley & Thibaut, 1978; Pruitt & Kimmel, 1977; Rapoport & Chammah, 1965). Instead of using prison sentences, researchers typically use money or points on an exam as payoffs, and ask participants to play the game for several trials. Consider, for example, the payoff matrix shown at the bottom of Figure 9.10. Imagine that the numbers in this matrix represent points that will be added to or subtracted from your score on a final exam. You are playing against another student in the class, and you have to decide whether to choose option X or option Y, without knowing which option the other student will choose. Just as in the Prisoner's Dilemma, your payoff—the number of points you earn or lose—depends on the choices both you and your partner make. What would you do if you were playing?

If you are like most people, you will start out by choosing option Y. At worst you would lose only one point, and at best you would win the highest possible number. Choosing option X raises the possibility that both sides will win some points, but this is also a very risky choice. If your partner chooses Y while you choose X, you stand to lose a great deal. Because people often do not know how much they can trust their partners, option Y frequently seems like the safest choice (Rapoport & Chammah, 1965). The rub is that both players will probably think this way, ensuring that both sides lose (see the lower right-hand corner of Figure 9.10).

People's actions in these games seem to mirror many conflicts in everyday life. To find a solution desirable to both parties, people must trust each other. Often they do not, which leads to an escalating series of competitive moves, so that in the end, no one wins. Two countries locked in an arms race may feel they cannot afford to disarm, out of fear that the other side will take advantage of their weakened position. The result is that both sides add furiously to their stockpile of weapons, neither gaining superiority over the other, and both spending money they could use to solve domestic problems (Deustch, 1973). Such an escalation of conflict is also seen all too often among couples who are divorcing. Sometimes the goal seems more to hurt the other person than to further one's own needs (or the children's). In the movie *The War of the Roses*, for example, a husband and wife begin having disagreements that soon escalate

Conflict often escalates so that neither side wins.

into a major battle. The spouses find increasingly creative ways of hurting the other, even though they often hurt themselves in the process. In the end, both suffer, because metaphorically, they spend too much time in option Y at the bottom of Figure 9.10. Such conflicts can even span generations, as with the famous feud between the Hatfields and the McCoys in West Virginia and Kentucky.

Such escalating conflict, though common, is not inevitable. Many studies have found that when people play a Prisoner's Dilemma game they will, under certain conditions, adopt the more cooperative response (option X), ensuring that both sides end up with a positive outcome.

**The Nature of You and Your Opponent.**  For example, people are more inclined to be cooperative under some conditions than under others. Not surprisingly, if people are playing the game with a friend, or if they expect to interact with their partner in the future, they are more likely to adopt a cooperative strategy that maximizes both their and their partner's profits (Pruitt & Kimmel, 1977). In addition, growing up in some societies, such as Asian cultures, seems to foster a more cooperative orientation than growing up in the West does (Leung, 1987; Markus & Kitayama, 1991). Finally, even within the same culture some people have more of a cooperative orientation than others, and this influences their behavior in the Prisoner's Dilemma game.

Even if one person is very cooperative, however, it is the competitive person who dominates conflict, often forcing his or her opponent to act competitively as well (Kelley & Stahelski, 1970; McClintock & Liebrand, 1988). The reason is that if your partner continues to act competitively—choosing option Y in Figure 9.10—you have little choice but to defend yourself, choosing option Y as well. Otherwise, you will loose the maximum amount. An interesting byproduct of this fact is that a competitive person tends to overestimate the percentage of people in the world who are also competitive. This individual observes that most people match his or her own competitive actions with a competitive response, and assumes that the world is full of competitive people ("It's a dog-eat-dog world out there—you have to look out for yourself, because if you don't, people will jump all over you"). The person doesn't realize that often it was his or her own behavior that forced other people to respond competitively, and not the fact that everyone is competitive by nature (Kelley & Stahelski, 1970).

**The Tit-for-Tat Strategy.**  If you want your partner to cooperate, you could begin with option X and stick with it as the game goes on, thereby showing your partner that you are not trying to exploit him or her. The problem is that you become an easy mark, and your partner knows he or she can nail you at any time by choosing option Y. A better strategy is known as the **tit-for-tat strategy:** Start out making the cooperative response (option X), then choose whichever option your partner chose on the last trial. If your partner chooses the competitive response (option Y), you respond in kind on the next trial. If your partner chooses the cooperative response (option X), then you respond cooperatively on the next trial. This strategy communicates a willingness to cooperate and an unwillingness to sit back and be exploited if the partner does not cooperate. The tit-for-tat strategy is usually successful in getting the other person to respond with the cooperative, trusting response

**tit-for-tat strategy:** a means of encouraging cooperation by acting cooperatively at first, but then always responding the way your opponent did (cooperatively or competitively) on the previous trial

(Axelrod, 1984; McClintock & Liebrand, 1988). The analogy to the arms race would be to match any military buildup made by an unfriendly nation, but also to match any conciliatory gesture, such as a ban on nuclear testing.

**Individuals Versus Groups Competing.** People are more likely to act cooperatively when playing against another individual than when playing against a group of people (Insko, Schopler, Hoyle, Dardis, and Graetz, 1990; McCallum, Harring, Gilmore, Drenan, Chase, Insko, and Thibaut, 1985). Interestingly, we are more likely to assume that a given individual is cooperative at heart and can be trusted, but that most groups of individuals will, given the opportunity, stab us in the back. As we saw in our earlier discussion of deindividuation, this assumption is often on the mark—people feel less accountable for their actions when in groups, and are more likely to behave in an antisocial (e.g., competitive) manner. The implication is that world leaders might be more cooperative when negotiating one on one than when groups of advisers from the two nations meet.

## The Use of Threats

You may have noticed that there is an important way in which the Prisoner's Dilemma game does not approximate conflict in everyday life: the inability to communicate with your adversary. In most versions of this game, no communication is allowed, and the only thing you know about your partner is whether he or she chose option X or option Y on each trial. What would happen if you could speak with your adversary? What would you say? When caught in a conflict, many of us are tempted to use threats to get the other party to give in to our wishes. Many people seem to endorse the strategy that we should "walk quietly and carry a big stick." Parents commonly use threats to get their children to behave, and teachers often threaten their students with demerits or a visit to the principal. More alarming is the increasing number of youths in the United States who carry guns and use them to resolve conflicts that used to be settled with a playground scuffle. Threats are commonly used on an international scale as well, to further the interests of one nation over another.

A series of classic studies by Morton Deutsch and Robert M. Krauss (1960, 1962) indicates that threats are not an effective means of reducing conflict. These researchers developed a game in which two participants imagined they were in charge of trucking companies named Acme and Bolt. The goal of each company was to transport merchandise as quickly as possible to a destination. The participants were paid 60¢ for each "trip," but had 1¢ subtracted for every second it took them to make the trip. The most direct route for each company was over a one-lane road on which only one truck could travel at a time. This placed the two companies in direct conflict, as seen in Figure 9.11. If Acme and Bolt both tried to take the one-lane road, then neither truck could pass and both would lose money. Each company could take an alternate route, but this was much longer, guaranteeing that they would lose at least 10¢ on each trial. The game lasted until each side had made twenty trips.

How did the participants respond to this dilemma? After a while, most of them worked out a solution that allowed both trucks to make a modest

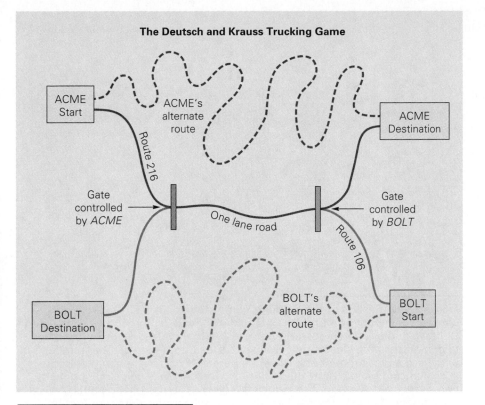

### The Deutsch and Krauss Trucking Game

ACME Start

ACME's alternate route

ACME Destination

Route 216

Gate controlled by ACME

One lane road

Gate controlled by BOLT

Route 106

BOLT Destination

BOLT's alternate route

BOLT Start

**FIGURE 9.11 The trucking game.** Participants play the role of the head of either Acme or Bolt Trucking Company. In order to earn money, they have to drive their truck from the starting point to their destination as quickly as possible. The quickest route is the one-lane road, but both trucks cannot travel on this road at the same time. In some versions of the studies, participants were given gates they could use to block the other's progress on the one-lane road. (Adapted from Deutsch & Krauss, 1960)

amount of money. They took turns waiting until the other person crossed the one-lane road; then they would take that route as well. They did so, that is, when neither had any weapons with which to threaten the other. In another version of the study, the researchers gave Acme a gate that could be lowered over the one-lane road, thereby blocking Bolt from using that route. You might think that using force—the gate—would increase Acme's profits, because all Acme had to do was to threaten Bolt, telling him or her to stay off the one-lane road or else. In fact, quite the opposite happened. When one side had the gate, both participants lost more than when neither side had the gate—as seen in the left-hand panel of Figure 9.12, on the next page. This figure shows the total amount earned or lost by both sides. (Acme won slightly more than Bolt when it had the gate, but won substantially more when neither side had a gate.) Bolt did not like to be threatened and often retaliated by parking its truck on the one-lane road, blocking the other truck's progress. Meanwhile, the seconds ticked away and both sides lost money.

   What would happen if the situation were more equitable, with both sides having gates? Surely they would learn to cooperate very quickly, recognizing

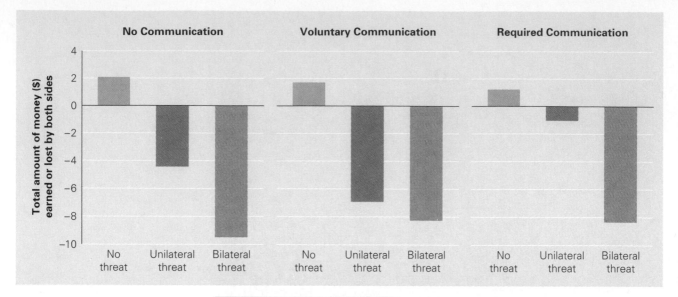

**FIGURE 9.12  Results of the trucking game studies.** The left-hand panel shows the amount of money the participants made (summed over Acme and Bolt) when they could not communicate. When threats were introduced by giving one or both sides a gate, both sides lost more money. The middle panel shows the amount of money the participants made when they could communicate as little or as much as they wanted. Once again, giving them gates reduced the amount of money they won. The right-hand panel shows the amount of money the participants made when they were required to communicate on every trial. Once again, giving them gates reduced their winnings. (Adapted from Deutsch & Krauss, 1962)

the stalemate that would ensue if both of them used their gates. To the contrary (as you can see in the left-hand panel of Figure 9.12), both sides lost more money in the bilateral threat condition than in any of the others. The owners of the trucking companies both threatened to use their gates and did so with great frequency. Once Acme used the gate to block Bolt, Bolt retaliated and blocked Acme the next time its truck came down the road—producing a stalemate that was in neither of their interests. Sound familiar? For the past few decades, the United States and the former Soviet Union were locked in an escalating nuclear arms race, each threatening the other with destruction.

## Effects of Communication

There is a way in which the Deutsch and Krauss (1960, 1962) trucking game does not approximate real life: The two sides could use behavioral threats (closing their gates), but were not allowed to communicate with each other. Would the two adversaries work out their differences if they could talk them over? To find out, Deutsch and Krauss allowed the participants to communicate over an intercom. In one condition, the participants were allowed to speak as often or as little as they liked. As seen in the middle of Figure 9.12, this communication had very little effect (compare the middle panel with the left-hand panel in the figure). Interestingly, people chose not to say much to each other in this condition, communicating on only about five of the twenty trials.

In another condition, the researchers decided to require the participants to communicate on every trial. Surely if people were forced to talk to each other they would cooperate more. As seen in the right-hand panel of Figure 9.12, however, no dramatic increase in profits occurred in the "required communication" condition. Requiring people to communicate reduced losses somewhat when Acme alone had the gate (the unilateral threat condition), but the required communication did not increase cooperation in either of the other two conditions (no threat, or bilateral threat). Overall, requiring people to communicate did not raise profits dramatically. Why not?

The problem with the communication in the trucking studies is that it did not foster trust. To the contrary, people used the intercom to convey threats and their feelings of mistrust, as illustrated in the following exchange:

> Bolt: Your gate is locked.
> Acme: I know it's locked.
> Bolt: That wasn't very fair.
> Acme: Anything's fair. . . .
> Bolt: Look's like we don't trust each other . . . Are you going to open your gate?
> Acme: Why should I?
> Bolt: I'll do the same next time.
> Acme: Is that a threat?
> Bolt: You playing tricks? (Deutsch, 1973, pp. 241–242)

It's not surprising that verbal threats fail to enhance cooperation! Why should you respond nicely and generously to someone who is so clearly untrustworthy? Cooperation will occur only if mutual trust is present. If communication succeeds in establishing trust, then communication will increase cooperation (e.g., Deutsch, 1973; Voissem & Sistrunk, 1971). Robert Krauss and Morton Deutsch demonstrated this fact in a later version of their trucking study, in which they specifically instructed people in how to communicate, telling them to work out a solution that was fair to both parties and that they would be willing to accept if they were in the other person's shoes. Under these conditions, verbal communication increased the amount of money both sides won, because it fostered trust, instead of adding fuel to the competitive fires (Krauss & Deutsch, 1966).

## Negotiation and Bargaining

In the laboratory games we have discussed so far, people's options are limited. They have to choose option X or Y in Prisoner's Dilemma, and they have only a couple of ways of getting their truck to its destination in the trucking game. In contrast, people often have a wide array of options in everyday conflicts. Consider two people haggling over the price of a car. Both the buyer and the seller can acquiesce to all of the other's demands, to some of them, or to none of them. Either party can walk away from the deal at any time. Given that there is considerable latitude in how people can resolve the conflict, communication between the parties is all the more important. By talking, bargaining, and negotiating, people can arrive at a satisfactory settlement. **Negotiation** is defined as a form of communication between opposing sides in a conflict, wherein the parties make offers and counteroffers and a solution occurs only when both parties agree (Rubin &

**negotiation:** a form of communication between opposing sides in a conflict, in which offers and counteroffers are made and a solution occurs only when it is agreed on by both parties

If the right strategies are used, negotiation can lead to successful resolutions of conflicts.

Brown, 1975; Thompson, 1990). What strategies do people use when they negotiate? Which strategies are most successful?

**Look for Integrative Solutions.** Too often, people assume that they are locked in a zero-sum conflict, where only one party can come out ahead. They don't realize that, as in the mixed-motive conflicts we have reviewed, solutions favorable to both parties are available to them. Such outcomes are known as **integrative solutions.** Consider the two people who are negotiating the purchase of a new car. Leigh Thompson (1991) asked pairs of students to play the roles of buyer and seller of a new car, negotiating over the financing, tax, warranty, and delivery date, each of which could take on several alternatives (e.g., the warranty on the car could range from six to thirty months). Many participants simply compromised on all four issues, splitting them down the middle (e.g., agreeing on an eighteen-month warranty). Doing so, however, was not the optimal solution, because the buyer and seller had different views on which issues were the most important: It was most important to the buyer to get a long-term warranty, whereas this was relatively unimportant to the seller; it was most important to the seller to get a high interest rate on the financing, whereas this was less important to the buyer. Thus, the best solution was for the buyer to agree to the highest interest rate and for the seller to agree to the longest warranty. Few of Thompson's (1991) participants reached this optimal solution, however, unless they were explicitly told to find out what the other person's priorities were. The moral is to ascertain which issues are most important to each party, so that a mutually beneficial solution can be reached.

**integrative solutions:** solutions to conflicts that find outcomes favorable to both parties

**Make Concessions.** As we saw earlier, one of the best ways to get an opponent to respond cooperatively in a Prisoner's Dilemma game is to adopt a tit-for-tat strategy, matching his or her competitive responses with competitive responses of your own, and matching his or her cooperative responses with cooperative responses of your own. A related strategy is to invoke the reciprocity norm we discussed in Chapter 7, whereby you concede on an issue, placing pressure on the other side to concede as well. In formal negotiation, it is often best to do this in a careful, structured way, using a procedure called **GRIT, or graduated and reciprocated initiatives in tension-reduction** (Lindskold, 1978; Osgood, 1962). This strategy involves four steps: (a) Communicate your willingness to cooperate; (b) act in a cooperative way to show that you mean what you say; (c) wait until the other side acts cooperatively as well, and then quickly reciprocate with a further cooperative act; and (d) should the other side try to exploit you by acting competitively, respond with the same level of competitiveness, as the tit-for-tat strategy suggests. Note that GRIT is similar to the tit-for-tat strategy, except that it involves explicitly communicating your intentions to your adversary. The GRIT strategy is useful when opponents are communicating directly, as when two nations are negotiating an arms settlement, or the police are negotiating with terrorists who have taken hostages. GRIT has proved to be an effective technique for eliciting cooperation, even when one is dealing with a hostile opponent (Linskold & Han, 1988).

**Consider Mediation or Arbitration.** Sometimes communication breaks down, deteriorating into threats and name-calling. When this occurs, it can be useful to bring in a third party to facilitate communication. Robert M. Krauss and Morton Deutsch (1966) found that communication increased cooperation when a third party (the experimenter) intervened and instructed people to use the opportunity to communicate to seek out a cooperative solution. More formally, people sometimes use mediators to help resolve a conflict. Professional mediators are often used in labor disputes, legal battles, and divorce proceedings. Although they are unable to impose a settlement on the parties, they can facilitate a solution by searching for mutually agreeable solutions, persuading one or both parties to lower their demands, and determining when it is best to let the parties talk through their disagreements by themselves (Carnevale, 1986; Emery & Wyer, 1987; Kressel & Pruitt, 1989). If **mediation** breaks down, the two parties can agree to binding **arbitration,** wherein both parties present their cases to a neutral third party and agree to accept whatever solution he or she imposes; an example is the arbitration sometimes used by major league baseball owners and players to resolve disputes about player salaries. Finally, all parties in a dispute have resorted to the legal system, telling it to the judge. Interestingly, in individualistic cultures like the United States, people prefer conflict resolution methods in which a third party imposes binding decisions, such as arbitration and legal proceedings, whereas in collectivist cultures like China and Japan, people prefer methods in which the parties themselves make the final decisions, such as bargaining and mediation (Leung, 1987).

We should note that some researchers have questioned how much we can generalize from the conflicts studied in experimental games to the conflicts occurring in everyday life (Gallo, 1966; Nemeth, 1972). Can we apply

**GRIT,** or graduated and reciprocated initiatives in tension-reduction: a strategy for reducing conflict in real-life situations, in which you (a) communicate your willingness to cooperate, (b) act cooperatively, (c) reciprocate any cooperative acts your opponent makes, but (d) if your opponent acts aggressively, retaliate with the same level of aggression

**mediation:** allowing a neutral third party to help the disputing parties resolve a conflict

**arbitration:** a system of conflict resolution in which a neutral third party imposes a decision on the disputing parties, after hearing both of their arguments

the lessons learned from two people playing an imaginary trucking game to a dispute between a landlord and a tenant, between a couple arguing over child custody, or between two nations on the brink of war? As we discussed in Chapter 2 (on methods), this is largely an empirical question. The laboratory offers the great advantages of experimental control and the ability to randomly assign people to different conditions. The lessons learned, however, should be carefully tested in real-world settings to ensure that they apply more generally. Numerous recent studies on conflict are moving in this direction, by using laboratory games that are more similar to real-world disputes and by examining conflict resolutions in real-life settings, such as the effects of mediation on actual child custody disputes (Emery, Matthews, and Wyer, 1991).

# SUMMARY

We began this chapter by examining the effects of being in a **nonsocial group,** where there is no interaction between you and the people around you. We saw that when your individual efforts can be evaluated, the mere presence of others leads to **social facilitation:** Your performance is enhanced on simple tasks but impaired on complex tasks. When your individual efforts cannot be evaluated, the mere presence of others leads to **social loafing:** Your performance is impaired on simple tasks but enhanced on complex tasks. Finally, the mere presence of others can lead to **deindividuation,** or a sense of anonymity, which involves the loosening of normal constraints on people's behavior. Prosocial and certainly antisocial group behavior occurs when people are deindividuated. This change in behavior is caused by reduced **accountability** and reduced **self-awareness.**

When other people are around, we often interact with them in **social groups.** We examined whether such groups are better or worse than individuals at making decisions. Surprisingly, groups often do worse, especially if they are working on **additive tasks** or **conjunctive tasks.** Groups also will do worse on **disjunctive tasks** if **process loss** occurs—whereby the most expert individual is unable to sway the rest of the group—and if groups fail to share unique information. Unfortunately, even techniques such as **brainstorming,** which are designed to help groups improve decision making, have not been shown to be very effective. Tightly knit, cohesive groups are also prone to **groupthink,** in which maintaining group cohesiveness and solidarity is more important than considering the facts in a realistic manner. Finally, **group polarization** indicates that groups are prone to make more extreme decisions in the direction toward which its members were initially leaning; these group decisions can be more risky or more cautious, depending on which attitude is valued in the group.

When people interact, often the result is **interpersonal conflict**—tension between two or more individuals—as opposed to **intrapersonal conflict**—tension within one individual due to incompatible goals. There are two types of interpersonal conflict: **zero-sum conflict** and **mixed-motive conflict.** The most commonly studied form of mixed-motive conflict is the Prisoner's Dilemma, a game in which two people must decide whether to look out only for their own interests or for their partner's interests as well. The **tit-for-tat strategy** is a useful way of dealing with mixed-motive conflict, allowing one to respond cooperatively or competitively, given the other person's response. Creating trust is crucial in solving this kind of conflict. We examined the conditions under which hostilities are likely to increase or decrease, including how the use of threats and the inability to communicate can exacerbate a conflict. In **negotiation,** it is important to look for **integrative solutions** and to make concessions. The **GRIT** procedure is particularly useful in resolving conflict; **mediation** and **arbitration** can be relied on when the two parties are deadlocked.

Much of the research discussed in this chapter points to ways to avoid the unpleasant consequences of group processes, making our associations with others more pleasant and fulfilling than they might otherwise be. Given the widespread incidence of conflict between individuals, groups, and nations, there is much to be learned from social psychological research on how to reduce hostilities.

## SUGGESTED READINGS

Hendrick, C. (Ed.). (1987). *Group processes and inter-group relations*. Newbury Park, CA: Sage. Chapters by researchers in social psychology reviewing the current state of the field, including such topics as social loafing, groups in organizations, and the social psychology of terrorist groups.

Janis, I. (1982). *Groupthink: Psychological studies of policy decisions and fiascoes* (2nd ed.). Boston: Houghton Mifflin. Janis argues persuasively that many important policy decisions, from the Bay of Pigs fiasco to the escalation of the Vietnam War, were flawed by groupthink, wherein maintaining group cohesiveness and solidarity was more important than considering the facts in a realistic manner.

Paulus, P. B. (Ed.). (1989). *Psychology of group influence* (2nd ed.). Hillsdale, NJ: Erlbaum. Researchers in the area of group processes discuss the current theories and findings of their field; chapter topics include social facilitation, social loafing, and deindividuation..

Pruitt, D. G., & Rubin, J. Z. (1986). *Conflict*. New York: Random House. A review of research on conflict, including such topics as the sources of conflict, conflict resolution, bargaining, and mediation.

# PART

> I mean, think if there were
> no Jews or Catholics,
> or everyone else were white
> or German or American,
> if the earth was one country , one
> color; then endless new, creative
> rationalizations would emerge
> to kill other people—the left-
> handed, those who prefer vanilla
> to strawberry, all baritones,
> any person who wears
> saddle shoes.
>
> —Woody Allen

# FOUR

# Chapter 10

## Interpersonal Attraction:
## From First Impressions to Close Relationships

# Chapter Outline

**Major Antecedents of Attraction**
  The Person Next Door: The Propinquity Effect
  The Effects of Physical Attractiveness on Liking
  Similarity: Birds of a Feather Flock Together
  Complementary: Don't Opposites Attract?
  Doling out Praise Lavishly
  Liking and Being Liked
  Theories of Interpersonal Attraction: Social Exchange and
    Equity
**Close Relationships**
**The Causes of Love**
  Social Exchange in Long-Term Relationships
  Equity: Is It Always Tit-for-Tat?
  Physical Attractiveness and Long-Term Relationships
  Attachment Styles and Intimate Relationships
  Trouble in Paradise
**Summary**
**Suggested Readings**

ometimes love blossoms at the most unexpected times. Consider Hilda Vogel and Nathan Serlin, who met on January 21, 1940—right after Hilda had fallen down an elevator shaft. Here is how columnist Andrew Malcolm describes it:

The whole thing started because Hilda Vogel got hungry. A 23-year-old medical secretary and recent German refugee, Miss Vogel was visiting her brother's sixth-floor photo studio on East 48th Street. He took forever to close. To save time en route to dinner, Miss Vogel summoned the elevator.

The elevator door opened. She stepped in to pull the string on the light bulb. Oops! There was no elevator. Just a black void. She began plummeting to her death.

Over at City Hospital, the duty intern was hungry too. The call came in: Woman falls down elevator shaft. The intern begged a colleague, Nathan Serlin, to take that ambulance run. "It's probably a D.O.A.," he said. "You'll be done in no time." . . .

[Because it was] 9 degrees that day, . . . Miss Vogel was wearing her thickest gloves. She grabbed the elevator cable. She slid down. She landed hard. But not as hard as a free fall.

It was the arriving Dr. Serlin who really fell. "She was sitting on those stairs," he recalls. "People hovered around. She was mortified. Her hands were greasy and burned. But all I could see were those blue eyes, the brightest blue I'd ever seen. They shined so in that dark hallway." (*New York Times*, September 29, 1992, p. B5)

After treating her hands, Dr. Serlin made careful note of Miss Vogel's address and phone number. Two days later, he called and asked her for a date. To his amazement, she said yes. Long walks and chats over coffee led to spaghetti dinners for 65¢, and soon, to marriage. Now, more than fifty years later, they are still happily married, with two daughters and several grandchildren. "I still love that lady I met

Hilda and Nathan Serlin in a 1941 snapshot.

on those stairs," says Dr. Serlin.

Why were Nathan Serlin and Hilda Vogel initially attracted to each other? Why did they fall in love? And why has their marriage lasted so long, when so many other marriages fail? These questions are of great interest to the social psychologist, because of all the different twists and turns of social interaction, liking and loving are perhaps the most important. When Ellen Berscheid asked people of various ages what made them happy, at or near the top of their lists were making and maintaining friendships and having positive, warm relationships (Berscheid, 1985; Berscheid & Peplau, 1983). The feelings of loneliness that come from the absence of meaningful relationships with other people make people feel worthless, hopeless, helpless, powerless, and alienated (Gerstein & Tesser, 1987; Peplau & Perlman, 1982; Weiss, 1973).

**W**e would all agree on the importance of finding close friends and companions. But what about our more casual acquaintances? Is it important to be well regarded by people we meet for the first time? It would seem so. In 1937, a successful businessman named Dale Carnegie wrote a simple little book called *How to Win Friends and Influence People*. This recipe book for quick and effective interpersonal relations was an instant success; indeed, it made publishing history by dominating the best-seller list, week in and week out, for a stupefying ten years. In addition, it was translated into thirty-five languages and read avidly by people in almost every corner of the globe.

The desire to be liked by others goes deeper, however, than simple recipes to help us succeed in the business world. As Ellen Berscheid (1985) has noted, we humans, being the most social of social animals, have survived as a species largely because of our ability to know whether another creature or human was good or bad for us. "Matters of interpersonal attraction," she argues, "are, quite literally, of life and death importance, not just to the individual but to all of humankind" (Berscheid, 1985, p. 414). In this chapter, we will discuss the antecedents of attraction, from the initial liking of two people meeting for the first time, to the attraction between two close friends, to the love that develops in close relationships.

## Major Antecedents of Attraction

Stop for a moment and think about why you like some acquaintances more than others. When we ask our students this question, the most typical responses are that they like the most (a) those whose beliefs and interests are similar to their own; (b) those who have some skills, abilities, or competencies; (c) those with some pleasant or admirable qualities, such as loyalty, reasonableness, honesty, and kindness; and, perhaps most important, (d) those who like them in return.

Research from well-controlled laboratory and field experiments suggests that these informal statements are in the ballpark. As we will see, such things as people's similarity to us, their admirable qualities, and their liking for us can influence our liking for them. As in previous chapters, however, we will see that people's intuitions about the causes of their behavior are not always accurate. We begin with one cause that is so obvious that people rarely mention it, but that, despite its obviousness, does not always work in obvious ways.

### The Person Next Door: The Propinquity Effect

There are approximately 5 billion people in the world. As hard as Dale Carnegie might try to win the friendship of all of them, he would be doomed to fail. In your lifetime, you have the opportunity to meet and interact with only a minuscule percentage of the people on this planet. Thus, it will not surprise you to learn that one of the simplest determinants of interpersonal attraction is proximity—sometimes called "propinquity." The people who, by chance, are the ones you see and interact with the most often are the most likely to become your friends and lovers (Newcomb, 1961; Priest & Sawyer, 1967; Segal, 1974). Now, this might seem obvious; you are no doubt thinking, "Of course—how can I become best friends with someone I've never met who is currently residing 3,000 miles away?" But the striking

> Contrary to popular belief, I do not believe that friends are necessarily the people you like best, they are merely the people who got there first.
> —Sir Peter Ustinov, 1977

Close friendships often are made in college, in part, because of prolonged propinquity.

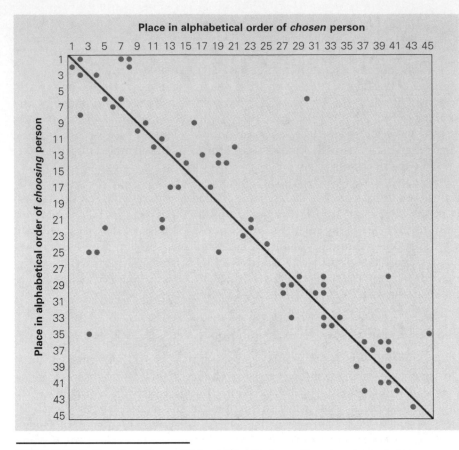

**Place in alphabetical order of *chosen* person**

*Place in alphabetical order of choosing person*

**FIGURE 10.1 Propinquity and friendship choices**. People whose last names were very close in the alphabet were best friends (as indicated by the number of data points that are close to the diagonal line), reflecting the fact that classroom seating and dormitory rooms were assigned according to alphabetical order. (Adapted from Segal, 1974)

**propinquity effect:** the finding that the more we see and interact with people, the more likely they are to become our friends

thing about proximity and attraction, or the **propinquity effect,** as social psychologists call it, is that it works on a very micro level. For example, Mady Segal (1974) demonstrated the propinquity effect among the entering class of the Maryland State Police Training Academy. The trainees were assigned to their classroom seats and to their dormitory rooms by the alphabetical order of their last names. Segal (1974) asked the trainees to name their three best friends in the group; as you can see in Figure 10.1, their choices followed the rules of alphabetization almost exactly. Larsons were friends with Lees, not with Abromowitzes or Ziernickes, even though they were separated from the Abromowitzes and Ziernickes by only a few yards (Byrne, 1961; Kipnis, 1957).

Similar research has shown that the power of propinquity affects people of all ages, from toddlers in nursery schools, to adults in housing developments, to the elderly in nursing homes (Nahemow & Lawton, 1975). Consider a classic study conducted in a married-student housing complex at MIT. Leon Festinger, Stanley Schachter, and Kurt Back (1950) tracked friendship formation among the couples in the various apartment buildings. For example, one section of the complex, Westgate West, was composed of

This is a photograph of the Westgate West apartment complex, where Leon Festinger and his colleagues conducted their now-classic study on how propinquity (or proximity) affects liking.

seventeen two-story buildings, each having ten apartments (see the photo on this page). The residents had been assigned to their apartments at random, as a vacancy opened up, and nearly all of them were strangers when they moved in. The researchers asked the residents to name their three closest friends in the entire housing project. Just as the propinquity effect would predict, 65 percent of the friends mentioned lived in the same building, even though the other buildings were not far away. Even more striking was the pattern of friendships within a building. Each Westgate West building was designed like the drawing in Figure 10.2; nineteen feet separated the majority of the front doors, while the greatest distance between apartment doors was only eighty-nine feet. The researchers found that 41 percent of the next-door neighbors indicated they were close friends, 22 percent of those who lived two doors apart did so, and only 10 percent of those who lived on opposite ends of the hall indicated they were close friends.

Festinger and his colleagues (1950) demonstrated that attraction and propinquity rely not only on actual physical distance, but on the more psychological, functional distance as well; this is defined as certain aspects of architectural design that make it more likely that some people will come into contact with each other more often than with others. For example, more friendships were made with people on the same floor than on the other floor, presumably because having to navigate the stairs to go visiting required more effort than just walking down the hall. A fascinating example of the power of functional distance is the friendship choices of the residents of apartments 1 and 5 (see Figure 10.2). Living at the foot of the stairs and in one case near the mailboxes meant that these couples saw a great deal of upstairs residents. Sure enough, apartment dwellers in apartments 1 and 5 throughout the complex had more friends upstairs than dwellers in the other first-floor apartments did, and they in turn were designated as friends more often by upstairs residents than by those on the first floors.

Even in a choice as important as a marriage partner, propinquity plays a major role. Researchers have found that most people marry someone who sits nearby in the same classroom, lives in the same neighborhood, or works

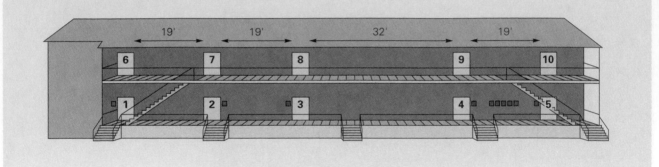

FIGURE 10.2 **The floor plan of a Westgate West building**. All the buildings in the housing complex had the same floor plan. (Adapted from Festinger, Schachter, and Back, 1950)

**mere exposure:** the finding that the more exposure we have to a stimulus, the more apt we are to like it

in the same office or factory (Bossard, 1932; Burr, 1973; Clarke, 1952; Katz & Hill, 1958). You see the point: Had you just sat in the first row instead of the last, lived a few blocks over, or taken that other job at IBM, your whole life might have been different. Of course, if you are not happy with the relationships you have, the propinquity effect suggests a useful solution: Place yourself in a new locale, even if it's just down the hall in your dormitory or apartment building.

The propinquity effect works because of familiarity, or the **mere exposure** we have to individuals who are close by. We see them a lot, and the more familiar people become, the more friendship blooms. But doesn't this fly in the face of common sense and folk wisdom? After all, we all know the saying "Familiarity breeds contempt." Is the folk wisdom wrong in this case? The answer is almost a total and unqualified yes. We say "almost" because if the person in question is a complete jerk who behaves in an obnoxious or unpleasant manner, the more exposure you have to him or her, not surprisingly, the greater your dislike (Swap, 1977). But in the absence of such negative qualities, familiarity breeds not contempt but attraction and liking.

In a classic series of experiments, Robert Zajonc and his colleagues showed that whether the stimulus was a drawing, an unfamiliar word, or an unfamiliar person, the more frequent contact people had with the stimulus, the more they grew fond of it (Moreland & Zajonc, 1982; Zajonc, 1968). For example, in one experiment, students were exposed to a photograph of either person A or person B. The photograph was flashed on a screen at such a rapid speed that the students were not even aware of having seen it. The students then entered into a brief discussion with the real persons A and B, and were subsequently asked to evaluate each of these people. Those who were previously exposed to the photo of person A tended to like person A better than person B; those who were exposed to the photo of person B tended to like person B better than person A (Bornstein, Leone, and Galley, 1987). Familiarity is indeed powerful stuff—and it almost always increases attractiveness.

As a final note on the effects of familiarity on attraction, we should point out that we even like those images of ourselves with which we are most familiar. In a clever experiment, researchers took photographs of several

By flipping a negative, photographers can print an image and its mirror image, as demonstrated above. As the *mere exposure effect* predicts, people prefer the image of themselves to which they are most frequently exposed—the mirror image, as one's face appears in a mirror—while their close friends prefer the other photo—the view of the person to which they are most frequently exposed.

students and then showed them that photo, along with a reversed, or mirror, image of the same photograph (see the photo on this page). Asked which picture they liked better, the overwhelming majority preferred the mirror image (Mita, Dermer, and Knight, 1977). Why? A moment's reflection and you will see that it's the mirror image of ourselves that we are most familiar with—that's what we look at whenever we comb our hair, brush our teeth, or sneak a peek at ourselves as we pass a shop window. To further test their interpretation of these results, the researchers showed the two types of photographs to close friends of the subjects. Guess what? The friends liked the original photograph better than the mirror image—after all, that's the view of their friend they were most familiar with.

## The Effects of Physical Attractiveness on Liking

Of course, propinquity is not the only determinant of how much we like someone. Sometimes when we meet a person for the first time, we take an instant liking or disliking to the person, even when we know little about him or her. Why? Well, one thing we do know when we first meet someone is how the person looks. Nathan Serlin says that the moment he saw Hilda Vogel's blue eyes, he fell in love. Exactly how important is physical appearance to our first impressions of people?

When asked what they looked for in a potential date, most college students in one study put "physical attractiveness" at the very bottom of the list (Tesser & Brodie, 1971). But alas, this is almost certainly a reflection of what students think they ought to believe—not the way they actually behave. How come? Most of us would be appalled by the suggestion that physical beauty plays a major role in how much we like another person. We don't want to think that we're so superficial as to like a person who is pretty or handsome better than we would were he or she not so attractive. What

> It is only the shallow people who do not judge by appearances.
>
> —Oscar Wilde, 1891

should be important about another person is his or her character and personality. We like to think that looks don't matter . . . but do they?

In field experiments investigating people's actual behavior (rather than what they say they will do), college students overwhelmingly go for physical attractiveness. For example, in one study Elaine Hatfield (Walster) and her colleagues (1966) randomly matched 752 incoming students at the University of Minnesota for a blind date at a computer dance during freshman orientation week. While the students had previously taken a battery of personality and aptitude tests, the researchers paired them up totally at random. On the night of the dance, the couples spent a few hours together dancing and chatting. They then evaluated their date and indicated the strength of their desire to date that person again. Of the many possible characteristics that could have determined whether people liked each other—such as their partner's intelligence, masculinity, femininity, dominance, submission, dependence, independence, sensitivity, or sincerity—the overriding determinant was physical attractiveness. What's more, there was no great difference between men and women on this score; these data explode the popular myth that it is only men who are interested in physical attractiveness. The general similarity of men and women in this domain has been demonstrated in numerous experiments (Andersen & Bem, 1981; Crouse & Mehrabian, 1977; Hatfield & Sprecher, 1986; Stretch & Figley, 1980). This is also the predominant finding in research involving commercial dating services (Lynn & Shurgot, 1984; Woll, 1986).

Nor is this general phenomenon limited to blind dates. Gregory White (1980) studied courting among young couples at UCLA. Like Elaine Hatfield (Walster) and her colleagues, White found that physical attractiveness was a key factor, but in this situation it was the *similarity* of the attractiveness of the members of the couple that was crucial in determining whether or not a relationship had staying power. Specifically, some nine months after the couples started dating, those pairs who were well matched in terms of physical attractiveness (as rated by the experimenter) were more deeply involved with each other than the members whose degree of physical attractiveness didn't match. Matching physical attractiveness may play a role in friendships as well. Thomas Cash and Valerian Derlaga (1978) found that same-sex friends (both male and female) were more similar to each other in physical attractiveness than to other research participants to whom they were compared randomly.

**Assumptions We Make About Attractive People.**  One of the striking things about the physical attraction phenomenon is that most people assume physical attraction is highly correlated with other desirable traits. For example, in one study Karen Dion and her colleagues (1972) showed college students photographs of three college-age people. The photos were especially selected for differing degrees of attractiveness: One was attractive, one average, and one unattractive. The research participants were asked to rate each of the people depicted in these photographs on twenty-seven different personality traits, and were asked to predict the person's future happiness. By far, the participants assigned to the physically attractive people the most desirable traits and the greatest prognosis for happiness. This was true whether it was men rating men, men rating women, women rating men, or

> Beauty is a greater recommendation than any letter of introduction.
> —Aristotle, fourth century B.C.

## The "what is beautiful is good" stereotype

Male and female subjects judged that physically attractive people (males and females) were more likely than physically unattractive people to have the following characteristics:

| | |
|---|---|
| Sexually warm and responsive | Sensitive |
| Kind | Interesting |
| Strong | Poised |
| Modest | Sociable |
| Outgoing | Exciting dates |
| Nurturant | Better character |

These same subjects also believed that the future for physically attractive people would differ in the following ways from the future of physically unattractive individuals:

| | |
|---|---|
| More prestige | Be more competent in marriage |
| Have a happier marriage | Have more fulfilling lives |
| Have more social and professional success | |

FIGURE 10.3 The "what is beautiful is good" stereotype. People believe that a host of positive attributes are associated with physical attractiveness. (Adapted from Dion, Berscheid, and Walster, 1972)

women rating women. From this and a host of subsequent studies, it is abundantly clear that men and women believe that attractive people are more successful, more intelligent, better adjusted, more socially skilled, more interesting, more poised, more exciting, more independent, and more sexual than their less attractive counterparts (Brigham, 1980; Calvert, 1988; Eagly, Ashmore, Makhijani, and Longo, 1991; Hassebrauck, 1988; Moore, Graziano, and Millar, 1987). The results of this research indicate that beauty constitutes a powerful *stereotype*—that is, we assume that an array of desirable traits go along with being beautiful. Karen Dion, Ellen Berscheid, and Elaine Walster (1972) have called this the "what is beautiful is good" stereotype (see Figure 10.3).

However, while most of the stereotypical traits and abilities we assign to beautiful people are positive and desirable, we should mention that the picture is not completely rosy for beautiful people. For example, people are more likely to think beautiful women are more vain and egotistic than less attractive women; handsome men are thought to be less intelligent than less attractive men (Bar-Tal & Saxe, 1976; Dermer & Thiel, 1975). In addition, most of us are wary of being manipulated by people who seem too friendly, too eager to please us, too full of compliments—and a similar concern applies to attractive people. In a sense, we see beautiful people as having a certain power, and we are a little worried that they might use that power to manipulate us. In one experiment, for example, Harold Sigall and Nancy Ostrove (1975) showed male and female college students an account of a criminal case in which the defendant, an attractive woman, was clearly guilty

> Oh, what a vileness human beauty is, corroding, corrupting everything it touches.
> —Orestes, 408 B.C.

of a crime, and asked them to recommend a prison term they considered appropriate. When the crime was unrelated to the defendant's attractiveness (burglary), participants recommended much more lenient sentences than when the crime was related to her attractiveness (a swindle in which the defendant induced a middle-aged bachelor to invest in a nonexistent corporation)—and in the latter instance, both male and female participants recommended harsher penalties. People tend to give a beautiful person the benefit of the doubt, but they will come down harder on a beautiful person if they believe he or she has used that beauty to gain an advantage.

**What Is Beautiful, Anyway?** These studies demonstrate that, in one way or another, physical attractiveness plays an important role in determining who likes whom in both the short and the long run. Moreover, these studies

There are clear cultural standards of beauty in the U.S. for any given era. But the standards of beauty shift more rapidly for women than for men. The top photos are cultural icons for the 1940s and 1950s; the bottom photos are current cultural icons.

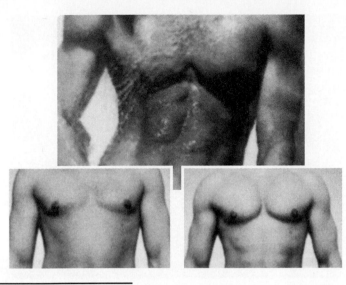

The desire to have a body that meets the current cultural standards of beauty has kept American plastic surgeons busy. Although most plastic surgery is performed on women, men often resort to it as well. The top photo (taken from a Calvin Klein ad) suggests what an ideal man's chest should look like. Below are photos taken before and after a silicon implant. The "after" photo now looks more like the ad.

indicate the existence of rather clear cultural standards for physical attractiveness in the United States and in other countries as well. Judges in all parts of this country had no difficulty rating people on physical attractiveness, and their ratings showed a high level of agreement. Moreover, the results of the experiments using photographs of "beautiful" people indicate that individuals are influenced differently, in predictable ways, by people whom the experimenter regards as beautiful versus those whom the experimenter regards as not so beautiful.

Does it surprise you to learn that most people seem to agree on both the physical characteristics and the concomitant personality traits of so-called beautiful people? Perhaps it shouldn't. From early childhood on, the media tell us what is beautiful and they tell us that this specific definition of beauty is associated with goodness. For example, illustrators of most traditional children's books, as well as the people who draw the characters in Disney movies, have taught us that gentle and charming heroines like Snow White, Cinderella, Beauty (in *Beauty and the Beast*), and Sleeping Beauty—as well as the princes who woo and win them (and in the case of *Beauty and the Beast*, the prince the beast eventually turns into)—all look alike. They all have regular features; small, pert noses; big eyes; shapely lips; blemish-free complexions; and slim, athletic bodies—pretty much like Barbie and Ken dolls.

Is it any wonder, then, that cosmetic surgery aimed at shortening or straightening noses, correcting thin lips, adding to or subtracting from the size of breasts, or straightening teeth is flourishing in this country? And such surgery is apparently effective. Michael Kalick (1977) asked students to rate photographs of several women either before or after cosmetic surgery, and the after photos not only were rated as more beautiful but also were rated as warmer, more sensitive, and more sexually responsive.

Children learn what is beautiful from TV, movies, and the dolls they play with.

**The Cultural Standards for Beauty Are Learned Early.**  One of the implications of all this is that cultural standards of beauty are learned by everyone, and especially young children, who, after all, are the major consumers of Barbie dolls and Disney cartoons. In a fascinating study, Karen Dion and Ellen Berscheid (1974) found that, even as early as nursery school, children are responsive to the physical attractiveness of their peers. In their study, Dion and Berscheid first had several independent judges (graduate students) rate the physical attractiveness of the nursery school children. They then determined who liked whom among the children themselves. They found that physical attractiveness was an important determinant of popularity.

If children favor attractive children, part of the reason might be that they are merely aping adult models—who also display such favoritism (Berkowitz & Frodi, 1979; Dion, 1972). For example, Karen Dion (1972) asked adult women to read teachers' reports of classroom disturbances; attached to each report was a photo of the child who was said to have initiated the disturbance. The reports were rigged so that in some instances, the photo was that of a physically attractive boy or girl, and in other instances, the photo was that of a less attractive boy or girl. The results? The women tended to place more blame on the less attractive children and to infer that this was typical of their everyday behavior. When a child was pictured as physically attractive, however, the women tended to excuse the disruptive behavior. As one woman put it, "She plays well with everyone, but like anyone else, a bad day can occur. Her cruelty . . . need not be taken seriously." When a physically unattractive girl was pictured as the culprit in the same situation, described in the same way, a typical respondent said, "I think the child would be quite bratty and would probably be a problem to teachers. She would probably try to pick a fight with other children her own age. . . . All in all, she would be a real problem." (p. 211)

**The Self-Fulfilling Prophecy.**  One of the most disconcerting aspects of the physical attractiveness stereotype is the strong possibility that it might produce a *self-fulfilling prophecy* (which we discussed in Chapter 4). Specifically, the way we treat people affects the way they behave and come to think of themselves. Strong evidence for this phenomenon comes from an experiment conducted by Mark Snyder, Elizabeth Decker Tanke, and Ellen Berscheid (1977). These researchers gave college men a packet of information about another research participant, including her photograph. The photograph was rigged; it was either of a very attractive woman or of an unattractive woman. The men were told that they would have a telephone conversation with this woman, since they were in the experimental condition where only verbal communication (no gestures or facial expressions) would be used. The purpose of the photograph was to invoke the men's stereotype that "what is beautiful is good"—that the woman would be more warm, likable, poised, and fun to talk to if she were physically attractive than if she were unattractive. In fact, the photograph the men were given was not a photo of the woman with whom they spoke. Did the men's beliefs create reality?

Yes: The men who thought they were talking to an attractive woman responded to her in a warmer, more sociable manner than the men who thought they were talking to an unattractive woman did. Not only that, but the men's behavior influenced how the women themselves responded. When independent observers listened to a tape recording of only the woman's half of the conversation (without looking at the photograph), they rated the women whose male partners thought they were physically attractive as more attractive, confident, animated, and warmer than the women whose male partners thought they were unattractive. In short, because the male partner thought he was talking to an attractive woman, he spoke to her in a way that brought out her best and most sparkling qualities.

This study was later replicated with the roles switched: Susan Andersen and Sandra Bem (1981) showed women participants a photograph of an attractive or an unattractive man; the women then had a phone conversation with him. The men on the other end of the line were unaware of the women's belief about them. Just as in the Snyder, Tanke and Berscheid (1977) study, the women acted on their "prophecy" and the unknowing men responded accordingly.

These studies suggest that physically attractive people may come to think of themselves as good or lovable because they are continually treated that way. Conversely, less attractive people may begin to think of themselves as bad or unlovable because they are continually treated that way, even in childhood. Ultimately, people may begin to behave in a way consistent with this self-concept—a way that is consistent with how they were treated to begin with.

If you were not born looking like Barbie or Ken, take heart. A study by Richard Nisbett and Timothy Wilson (1977) showed that it works both ways: Yes, it is true that we like people more if they are physically attractive, but it is also true that how much we like people can influence how physically attractive we think they are. In this study, students watched a videotaped interview of a college instructor who was discussing his teaching philosophy. In the "cold" condition, the instructor was aloof and autocratic, criticizing students for their lack of insights and preparation. As expected, students who watched this tape did not like the instructor much at all. In the "warm" condition, the same instructor was friendly and approachable, saying how much he cared about his students and valued their input. Students who watched this tape liked the instructor a lot.

"When I fell in love with you, suddenly your eyes didn't seem close together. Now they seem close together again."

Research shows that our liking for a person can influence how physically attractive we think he or she is.

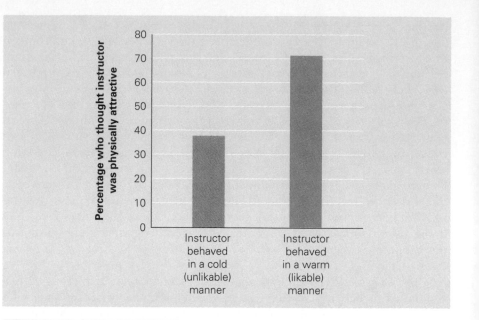

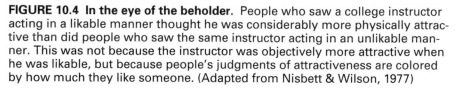

**FIGURE 10.4  In the eye of the beholder.** People who saw a college instructor acting in a likable manner thought he was considerably more physically attractive than did people who saw the same instructor acting in an unlikable manner. This was not because the instructor was objectively more attractive when he was likable, but because people's judgments of attractiveness are colored by how much they like someone. (Adapted from Nisbett & Wilson, 1977)

The question was, Would the two groups of students differ in how physically attractive they thought the instructor was, or is physical attractiveness an objective quality that does not depend on how much we like someone? As seen in Figure 10.4, those who saw the instructor being "cold" thought he was considerably less physically attractive than those who saw him being "warm." Now, the astute reader will recognize the possibility that in the cold version, the instructor may have frowned and grimaced more, making him objectively less attractive. Nisbett and Wilson ruled out this possibility by showing a separate group of participants the tapes with the sound turned off, so they could not hear the instructor express his views on teaching. These participants did not like him any less in the cold version than in the warm version, and most importantly, they did not find him any less physically attractive in the cold version. It was only when people formed different opinions of the instructor based on what he said that they differed in how attractive they thought he was. Thus, though no doubt there are objective qualities of a person that make him or her physically attractive to others, it is also true that beauty is in the eye of the beholder. The more we like someone, the more pleasing we will find his or her appearance.

## Similarity: Birds of a Feather Flock Together

So far, we have seen that the more contact we have with people, the more apt we are to like them (propinquity and familiarity), and that physical attractiveness is a significant determinant of liking. The more we get to know someone, however, the more other factors come into play. True, physical appearance is often the first thing we notice about people, but eventually we learn much more about them, such as how kind, honest, extraverted, and creative they are, their political preferences, and their favorite TV shows. To what extent do these qualities of a person influence how much we like him or her? One key is not what these exact qualities of the person are, but how similar they are to our own qualities.

Consider Chia-Ann, an attorney who attends the office holiday party and finds herself chatting with Rebecca, a fellow attorney whom she barely knows. While the two are conversing, it turns out that they are in close agreement on several important issues, including the merits of the various presidential candidates, whether or not the death penalty should be revoked, and the inequity of the income tax structure. On returning home, Chia-Ann tells her husband that while she talked with Rebecca for only fifteen minutes, she feels she has made a new friend. What Chia-Ann has experienced is the strong pull of *similarity*—the sense that aspects of oneself are similar to aspects of the other person.

One way we perceive similarity is through shared attitudes or values, as Chia-Ann did with Rebecca. Literally dozens of tightly controlled experiments have shown that if all you know about a person are his or her opinions on several issues, the more similar those opinions are to yours, the more you will like the person. For example, in an experiment by Donn Byrne and Don Nelson (1965), research participants learned that another student agreed with their attitudes to varying degrees. When asked how much they liked this person (whom they had never met), participants indicated that the degree of liking was closely related to the perceived similarity between their attitudes and those of the other student. As you can see in Figure 10.5, liking increased linearly with the percentage of attitudes shared.

Theodore Newcomb (1961) conducted a classic long-term study that examined the correlation between similarity and attraction. He randomly assigned male college students at the University of Michigan to be roommates

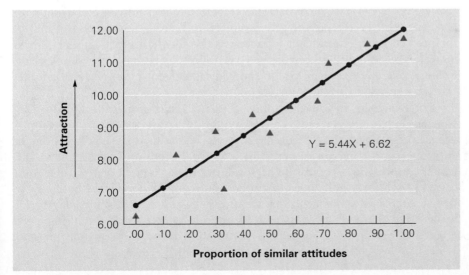

**FIGURE 10.5 Similarity and attraction.** The data in this figure summarize the results of eight studies conducted by Donn Byrne and his colleagues, who found that a strong, linear relationship exists between attraction and similarity in attitudes. The more the proportion of similar attitudes increased between research participants, the more they liked each other. (Adapted from Byrne & Nelson, 1965)

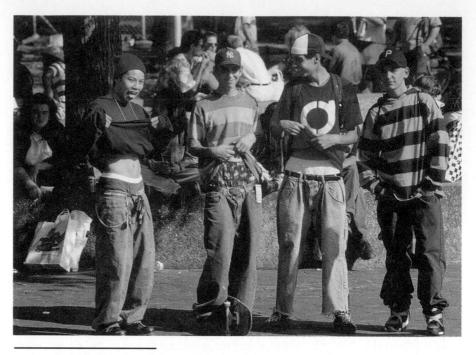

Similarity is one of the major determinants of attraction.

in a particular dormitory at the start of the school year. Would similarity predict friendship formation? The answer was yes: Men became friends with those who were demographically similar (e.g., shared a rural background) as well as with those who were similar in attitudes and values (e.g., were also engineering majors or also held liberal political views).

Why is similarity so important in attraction? There are at least two possibilities. First, people who are similar provide us with important social validation for our characteristics and beliefs—that is, they provide us with the feeling we are right (Byrne & Clore, 1970). It simply feels good and reassuring to be validated; thus, we like those who agree with us. Second, it is likely that we make certain negative inferences about the character of someone who disagrees with us on important issues—not necessarily out of the need to be validated, but because we suspect the individual's opinion is indicative of the kind of person we have found in the past to be unpleasant, immoral, weak, or thoughtless. In short, disagreement on important attitudes leads to repulsion (Rosenbaum, 1986).

For example, if you are opposed to the death penalty and you meet someone who is in favor of it, you might conclude that such a person is vengeful and aggressive. If you are in favor of the death penalty, you might conclude that a person opposed to it is weak and soft on crime. In this instance, you would regard the person's attitude as merely one possible indication of what an unlikable person he or she might be. Thus, the desire to be validated and the conclusions we draw about character both play a role in boosting the attractiveness of a like-minded person and diminishing the attractiveness of someone who is dissimilar (Byrne, Clore, and Smeaton, 1986; Condon & Crano, 1988; Griffitt & Veitch, 1974).

## Complementary: Don't Opposites Attract?

As we have seen, the venerable adage seems to be true: Birds of a feather do flock together. But where does this leave the equally venerable adage "Opposites attract"? There has been considerable speculation about the kinds of situations and characteristics where this potential rule of attraction might apply. For example, Winch (1958) suggests that a dependent person might be attracted to someone who loves to nurture others, a shy person might be attracted to someone who is outgoing and social, and a nonstop talker might be attracted to someone who is relatively quiet and loves to listen. The idea that opposites attract is the complementarity hypothesis, which states that we are attracted to people whose characteristics are not similar to ours but opposite to our characteristics. Research in this area has focused primarily on complementarity in personality characteristics, as when a shy person is paired with an extravert.

The research evidence for complementarity is mixed at best, and based on only a few studies. Whereas one researcher found that opposites in personality do indeed attract (Wagner, 1975), other researchers have found that similarity, not complementarity, describes the basis for relationship development (Levinger, 1964; Meyer & Pepper, 1977). Some researchers have argued that similarity is important early in a relationship, while complementarity becomes important later on, as the relationship lengthens (Campbell, 1980; Kerckhoff & Davis, 1962); however, other researchers have not found support for this role of complementarity over time (Levinger, Senn, and Jorgensen, 1970). In short, it's a muddle. While the idea of personality and need complementarity is appealing, the vast amount of research evidence strongly supports similarity over complementarity as the more significant predictor of attraction. Tom Boyden and his colleagues (1984), for example, found strong support for similarity in personality in gay men's relationships. Gay men who scored high on a test of stereotypical male traits desired a partner who was most of all logical—a stereotypical masculine trait. Gay men who scored high on a test of stereotypical female traits desired a partner who was most of all expressive—a stereotypical feminine trait. Further research is needed in this area—for example, studies that focus on a more varied list of personality traits and interpersonal needs.

*Drawing by Koren; © March 23, 1992 The New Yorker Magazine, Inc.*

Despite folklore about how "opposites attract," people are almost always more attracted to people who are similar to them.

## Doling out Praise Lavishly

We have now seen that several attributes of people influence how much we like them, primarily their physical appearance and how similar their attitudes are to ours. This is only a small part of the story, however. How people act toward us is crucial as well. For example, do we like others who give us praise and compliment us? Dale Carnegie thought so, giving this simple advice to win friends: "Dole out praise lavishly." Social psychological research indicates that, in general, this *is* a good strategy. Several experiments have shown that in most situations, we tend to like people better if they evaluate us positively than if they evaluate us negatively (Aronson & Worchel, 1966; Jones, 1964; Jones, Gergen, and Davis, 1961; Sigall & Aronson, 1969).

Does this mean that we always like those people who are forever running around offering praise? No. We human beings are far more complicated than that. We also tend to assume that people who are discerning and can see flaws in things are sharper and more interesting than people who see only the positive side. For example, research by Theresa Amabile (1983) shows that, all other things being equal, when we encounter a negative, critical evaluation, it generally increases the admiration we feel for the evaluator. In her experiment, Amabile asked college students to read excerpts from two reviews of novels, which, they were told, had appeared in the *New York Times* book review section. Both reviews were similar in style and quality of writing—but one was extremely favorable, and the other, extremely unfavorable. Students rated the negative reviewer as considerably more intelligent, competent, and expert than the positive reviewer.

Of course, in Amabile's experiment the critical person was being critical of someone else's work; will we react so positively to someone who is critical of our own work? This is a complicated issue. On the one hand, most people would rather be praised than criticized. On the other hand, we want to be sure that the praise is both sincere and intelligent. For example, suppose Sally is an engineer and she produces an excellent set of blueprints. Her boss says, "Good work, Sally." Generally speaking, that is nice to hear—and according to Dale Carnegie, this should increase Sally's liking for her boss. But suppose Sally is having an off-day and produces a less than stellar set of blueprints—and knows it. Will the boss's praise function as a reward in this situation?

Perhaps. Sally may interpret the statement as her boss's attempt to be encouraging and nice, even in the face of a poor performance; because of the boss's display of thoughtfulness, Sally may come to like him even more than she would have had she in fact done a good job. But this is a complex situation, and more may be going on than meets the eye. For example, Sally may attribute all kinds of characteristics or ulterior motives to her boss. She may conclude that her boss is being sarcastic, manipulative, dishonest, undiscriminating, patronizing, seductive, or stupid—any one of which could reduce Sally's liking for him.

Research in this area has found that although people like to be praised and tend to like the praiser, they also dislike feeling that they are being manipulated. If the praise is too lavish, if it seems unwarranted, or (most importantly) if the praiser is in a position to benefit from the act of giving praise, then he or she is not liked very much by the recipient. Edward E. Jones (1964, 1990) has carried out a great deal of research on the phenomenon of **ingratiation**—the

> Mountains of gold would not seduce some men, yet flattery would break them down.
> —Henry Ward Beecher, 1877

**ingratiation:** the use of strategies (e.g., offering praise, flattery and positive feedback) to manipulate people or gain their favor

deliberate attempt to manipulate people by offering them praise and positive feedback. In a typical experiment, a confederate watched a student being interviewed, and then proceeded to evaluate her. The evaluations were prearranged so that some students were given a positive evaluation, some were given a negative evaluation, and some were given a neutral evaluation. In one experimental condition, the evaluator (the confederate) was ascribed an ulterior motive—specifically, the students were told that the evaluator was a researcher who needed volunteers to participate in her own experiment and would be asking the student to volunteer later. The results showed that the students liked the evaluators who praised them better than those who provided them with a negative evaluation—but there was a sharp drop in how much they liked the praiser with the ulterior motive. In this condition, they believed the evaluator was giving them praise—or "buttering them up"—just so they'd be more likely to do her a favor later; her praise seemed not a genuine response, but an attempt to manipulate them through ingratiation. Thus, the old adage "Flattery will get you nowhere" is clearly wrong. Flattery works—but it has limitations; as Edward Jones put it, "Flattery will get you somewhere"—but not everywhere.

## Liking and Being Liked

The extent to which people flatter us is not the only behavior that is important to our liking of them. The extent to which they act friendly and warm to us—in short, how much they like us—is of obvious importance as well. We all like to be liked. It simply feels good to walk up to a person and see his or her eyes light up with pleasure, excitement, anticipation, or warmth. This is a powerful feeling and one of the prime determinants of interpersonal attraction; indeed, it is so powerful that it can even make up for the absence of similarity. For example, in one experiment, when a young woman expressed interest in male subjects simply by maintaining eye contact, leaning toward them, and listening attentively, the men expressed great liking for her despite the fact that they knew she disagreed with them on important issues (Gold, Ryckman, and Mosley, 1984). Whether the clues are nonverbal or verbal, perhaps the most crucial determinant of whether we will like person A is the extent to which we believe person A likes us (Berscheid & Walster, 1978; Condon & Crano, 1988; Hays, 1984; Kenny & La Voie, 1982; Kenny & Nasby, 1980; Secord & Backman, 1964).

Of course, what we think influences what we do. Believing that a new person likes us encourages us to act in a friendlier, more outgoing manner than we might otherwise do. And what effect do you think our actions will have? The other person will undoubtedly respond warmly to our friendly behavior, and this response in turn will reinforce and encourage our friendly behavior back. This is yet another example of the self-fulfilling prophecy, wherein the initial belief that one will be liked creates friendly behavior in oneself, prompting friendly behavior in return, encouraging more friendly behavior on one's part, and so on.

To illustrate this process, Rebecca Curtis and Kim Miller (1986) performed a clever experiment. College students took part in the study in pairs; they had not known each other prior to meeting at the study. One member of each pair was randomly chosen to receive special information. Curtis and

> Life is to be fortified by many friendships. To love, and to be loved, is the greatest happiness of existence.
> —Sydney Smith, 1855

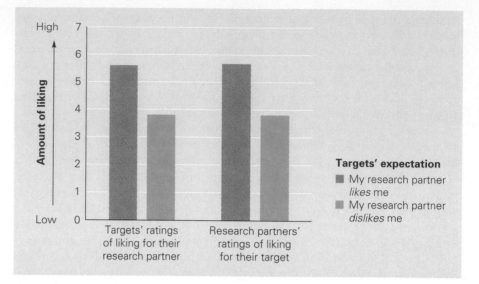

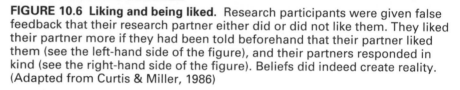

**FIGURE 10.6 Liking and being liked.** Research participants were given false feedback that their research partner either did or did not like them. They liked their partner more if they had been told beforehand that their partner liked them (see the left-hand side of the figure), and their partners responded in kind (see the right-hand side of the figure). Beliefs did indeed create reality. (Adapted from Curtis & Miller, 1986)

Miller led some college students to believe that the other student liked them, and others to believe that the other student disliked them. The pairs of students were then allowed to meet and talk to each other again. Just as predicted, those individuals who thought they were liked behaved in more likable ways with their partner; they disclosed more about themselves, disagreed less about the topic under discussion, and generally behaved in a warmer, more pleasant manner toward the other student than those individuals who thought they were disliked. Moreover, those who believed they were liked came to be liked by the other student to a far greater extent than those who believed they were disliked. In short, the partner tended to mirror the behaviors of the person with whom he or she was paired (see Figure 10.6). These results suggest that if you behave as if you believe you are lovable and everyone around will like you, you will increase the probability that the people around you will like you. "Smile, and the world smiles with you" has some truth to it.

**The Effects of Changes in a Person's Liking for Us: The Gain-Loss Effect.** As we have seen, being liked by a person is a powerful determinant of our liking for that person. One obvious question is, Does this mean that the more intense the liking or the more frequently the other person expresses liking for us, the more we will like that person? The answer is not as straightforward as you might think.

Let's say you meet Alberto at a party and talk with him for a few minutes, and subsequently run into him on campus several times over the next weeks, producing seven conversations with him in all. Four possible

Hatred which is completely vanquished by love passes into love, and love is thereupon greater than if hatred had not preceded it. For he who begins to love a thing which he was wont to hate or regard with pain, from the very fact of loving, feels pleasure.

—Spinoza, 1663

outcomes of these conversations are particularly interesting to a social psychologist: (a) Alberto's behavior toward you is exclusively positive on all seven occasions; (b) Alberto's behavior toward you is exclusively negative on all seven occasions; (c) his behavior during the first couple of conversations is negative, but gradually becomes more positive; and (d) his behavior during the first couple of conversations is positive, but gradually become more negative. In which of these situations will you like Alberto the most?

To answer this question, Elliot Aronson and Darwyn Linder (1965) set up exactly the kind of situation described above. College women met with a fellow student on a number of occasions and spoke about a variety of topics. After each encounter, the participants were allowed to eavesdrop on a conversation between the experimenter and the other student, in which the student evaluated the participant on a number of dimensions. In actuality, however, the student/evaluator was a confederate of the experimenters, instructed to evaluate the participant in one of the four sequences outlined above: (a) entirely positive, (b) entirely negative, (c) gain (beginning negative but gradually becoming more positive), and (d) loss (beginning positive but gradually becoming more negative). The research participant was then asked how much she liked the student/evaluator.

You might think that the more positive feedback people got from the confederate, the more they would like her. In fact, however, participants in the gain condition liked the confederate significantly better than participants in the positive condition. By the same token, participants in the loss condition disliked the confederate more than those in the negative condition. These results are referred to as the **gain-loss effect**. But why is a gain construed as more appealing than constant praise? And why is a loss more devastating than constant negative evaluation?

There are several possible reasons for this phenomenon. One was suggested more than 300 years ago by the philosopher Benedict de Spinoza, whom we quoted earlier. Indeed, it was Spinoza's insight that first inspired Aronson and Linder (1965) to devise the experiment described above. Aronson and Linder reasoned that two conditions are necessary for the gain-loss effect to operate. First, it is not just any sequence of positive or negative statements that constitutes a gain or loss; there must be an integrated sequence implying a change of heart. In other words, if you initially indicate that you think we are stupid and insincere and later indicate that you think we are generous and athletic, this does not constitute a gain, because different attributes are being discussed. But if you first indicate that we are stupid and insincere and subsequently indicate that you've changed your mind—you now believe we are smart and sincere—this is a true gain, because it indicates a reversal, a replacement of a negative attitude with its opposite. David Mettee and his colleagues (1973) performed an experiment that demonstrated this distinction. A gain effect occurred only when a change of heart occurred.

Second, in order for the gain-loss effect to occur, the change in attitude must be gradual. As David Mettee and Elliot Aronson (1974) showed in their research, an abrupt about-face, or reversal, is viewed by the target person with confusion and suspicion, especially if it occurs on the basis of little evidence. For example, if someone thinks you're stupid after one encounter, but brilliant after the second encounter, such a dramatic shift is bound to arouse

**gain-loss effect:** the finding that we like people the most if we feel we have gained in their estimation of us (i.e., if they initially disliked us but now like us), and that we dislike people the most if we feel we have lost their favor (i.e., if they initially liked us but now dislike us)

suspicion on your part. Is this person after something? Is this an attempt at ingratiation (Jones, 1964)? On the other hand, a gradual change in the other person's evaluation of you (the gain condition) makes sense; your suspicion is not aroused, and you like the person even more because you've won him or her over.

Moreover, as we saw earlier in this chapter, people who are capable of being critical seem more intelligent, more competent, and more discerning than people who always see the positive side (Amabile, 1983). To be liked by someone who likes everybody is certainly better than not being liked at all, but it doesn't make us feel special. To be liked by someone who is discriminating, who has high standards, who is not deeply committed to saying nice things about everybody—that makes us feel special. For example, Elaine Walster and her colleagues (1973) examined the "playing hard to get" ploy in dating relationships. They found that a person using this ploy was not attractive to others—too much fear of rejection was involved. However, the preferred date was the "selectively hard to get" individual—one who expresses interest in you but is not impressed by other potential dating partners. In terms of the gain-loss effect, one way a person can show us that he or she is capable of discernment is by expressing negative things about us early in the relationship, making the subsequent positive evaluation all the more valuable.

Finally, let's examine the other side of the coin: the loss condition. A series of unabated negative evaluations of us, while painful, can be explained away by calling the person a misanthrope—a sour, angry person who doesn't like anyone or anything. However, if a person begins by expressing positive feelings about you, and then, after a while, gradually sours on you (the loss condition), it is more difficult to dismiss that person as a complete idiot. After all, he or she was nice to you at first. Thus, the loss condition is more upsetting and produces more dislike than the totally negative condition.

## Theories of Interpersonal Attraction: Social Exchange and Equity

The determinants of attraction we have discussed so far concern aspects of the situation (propinquity, repeated exposure), the individual's attributes (physical attractiveness, similarity, complementarity), and the individual's behavior (giving praise, conveying liking). We turn now to theories of interpersonal attraction that link these different phenomena together.

**Social Exchange Theory.** Many of the variables we have discussed can be thought of as examples of social rewards. It is pleasing to have our attitudes validated; thus, the more similar a person's attitudes are to ours, the more rewarded we feel. Likewise, it is rewarding to be around someone who is physically attractive, who praises us, and who likes us. Hence, one way of summarizing much of our discussion so far is to say that the more social rewards a person provides us with (and the fewer costs), the more we will like him or her.

This point of view was expressed more than 300 years ago by the French essayist and social gadfly François La Rochefoucauld, who wryly defined friendship as "a scheme for the mutual exchange of personal advantages and favors." While La Rochefoucauld was perhaps overly cynical in this definition, there is certainly an element of truth in it. If a relationship costs (e.g., in terms

Love is often nothing but a favorable exchange between two people who get the most of what they can expect, considering their value on the personality market.
—Erich Fromm, 1955

*Drawing by Zeigler; © September 23, 1991 The New Yorker Magazine, Inc.*

"O.K., who *can* put a price on love? Jim?"

of emotional turmoil) far more than it gives (e.g., in terms of validation or praise), chances are that it will not last very long.

This simple notion that relationships operate on an economic model of costs and benefits, much like the marketplace, has been expanded by psychologists and sociologists into complex theories of social exchange (Blau, 1964; Homans, 1961; Kelly & Thibaut, 1978; Thibaut & Kelley, 1959). **Social exchange theory** states that how people feel (positively or negatively) about their relationships will depend on their perception of the rewards they receive from the relationship and their perception of the costs they incur, as well as their perception of what kind of relationship they deserve and the probability that they could have a better relationship with someone else. In other words, we buy the best relationship we can get, one that gives us the most value for our emotional dollar. The basic concepts of social exchange theory are reward, cost, outcome, and comparison level (Secord & Backman, 1964).

Rewards are the positive, gratifying aspects of the relationship that make it worthwhile and reinforcing. They include the kinds of personal characteristics and behaviors of our relationship partner that we have already discussed, and our ability to acquire external resources by virtue of knowing this person (e.g., gaining access to money, status, activities, or other interesting people; Lott and Lott, 1974). Costs are, obviously, the other side of the coin, and all friendships and romantic relationships have some costs attached to them (e.g., putting up with those annoying habits and characteristics of the other person). The outcome of the relationship is a direct comparison of its rewards and costs; you can think of it as a mathematical formula where outcome equals rewards minus costs. (If you come up with a negative number, your relationship is not in good shape.)

However, as Harold Kelley and John Thibaut (1978; Thibaut & Kelley, 1959) state, how satisfied you are with your relationship depends on another variable: your **comparison level,** or what you expect the outcome of your relationship to be in terms of costs and rewards. Over time, you have amassed a long history of relationships with other people, and this history has led you to have certain expectations as to what your current and future relationships should be like. Some people have a high comparison level, expecting to receive lots of rewards and few costs in their relationships. If a given relationship doesn't match this expected comparison level, they will be

**social exchange theory:** the theory holding that how people feel about a relationship depends on their perceptions of the rewards and costs of the relationship, the kind of relationship they deserve, and their chances for having a better relationship with someone else

**comparison level:** people's expectations about the level of rewards and punishments they are likely to receive in a particular relationship

**comparison level for alternatives:**
people's expectations about the level of rewards and punishments they would receive in an alternative relationship

unhappy and unsatisfied. In contrast, people who have a low comparison level would be happy in the same relationship, because they expect relationships to be difficult and costly.

Finally, your satisfaction with a relationship also depends on your perception of the likelihood that you could replace it with a better one—or your **comparison level for alternatives.** There are a lot of people out there—could a relationship with a different person give you a better outcome, or greater rewards for fewer costs, than your current one? People who have a high comparison level for alternatives, either because they believe the world is full of fabulous people dying to meet them or because they know of a fabulous person dying to meet them, are more likely to get into circulation and make a new friend or find a new lover. People with a low comparison level for alternatives will be more likely to stay in a costly relationship, because to them, what they have is not great, but better than their expectation of what they could find elsewhere (Simpson, 1987).

Social exchange theory has received a great deal of empirical support; friends (and, as we shall see later, romantic couples) do pay attention to the costs and rewards in their relationships, and these affect how positively people feel about the status of the relationship (Jacobson, Waldron, and Moore, 1980; Rusbult, 1983; Wills, Weiss, and Patterson, 1974). Like all generalizations, however, there are some interesting exceptions. We have already seen one: In the Aronson and Linder (1965) gain-loss study, people liked the person whose liking for them increased over the course of the study more than the person who praised them consistently. This finding is difficult to explain with social exchange theory, because the person who gave the most rewards (praise) was liked less than one who gave fewer rewards.

We saw another exception in Chapter 3, in the study that found we like others for whom we have suffered. Specifically, recall the experiment by Elliot Aronson and Judson Mills (1959). In this experiment, it was found that college students who underwent an unpleasant initiation in order to become members of a group were more enamored of that group than those who became members without undergoing all that unpleasantness were. Where is the reward? Why would somebody associated with pain or unpleasantness be viewed as more attractive than someone who isn't? As we saw in Chapter 3, dissonance can be produced when we perform unpleasant behavior for low rewards, and we can reduce this dissonance by increasing our liking for a task (or person).

By the same token, although we generally like people who have a variety of skills and abilities and who are competent at what they do, one might speculate that if they are too skillful, they can make us feel uncomfortable. Such a person may seem unapproachable, distant, superhuman. In this circumstance, we might like the person more were he or she to show some evidence of fallibility (e.g., have some costs). For example, if Sam were a brilliant mathematician, a great basketball player, and a fastidious dresser, you might like him better if, every once in a while, he misadded a column of numbers, blew an easy lay-up, or appeared in public with a gravy stain on his tie.

As you may recall from Chapter 2, this speculation was confirmed in an experiment by Elliot Aronson, Ben Willerman, and Joanne Floyd (1966). In this experiment, college students listened to a tape recording featuring one of four stimulus persons: (a) a nearly perfect person, (b) a nearly perfect person

*"Dear God, give Mr. Perfect a tiny flaw."*

Research has shown that if people are virtually perfect in all respects, we like them more if they have a flaw or commit a blunder.

who committed a clumsy blunder (he spilled a cup of coffee on himself), (c) a mediocre person, and (d) a mediocre person who committed the clumsy blunder. Which of these four people was liked the most? It was not the person with the most rewards—in this case, the most positive characteristics. Instead, people liked the superior person who committed the blunder the most. Spilling a cup of coffee added an endearing dimension to the nearly perfect person, making him more attractive. Interestingly, the same action served to make the mediocre person appear even more mediocre, and hence less attractive.

To summarize, although it is generally true that we like people whose behavior is rewarding to us, such a generalization, when given close scrutiny, is far too simple, partly because it is not always easy to know in advance what will be the most rewarding. Thus, as we have seen, there are specific situations in which we like people more if they initially criticize us or if we suffer for them, and there are specific circumstances in which we like clumsy people better than graceful people.

**Equity Theory.** Some researchers have criticized social exchange theory for ignoring an essential variable in relationships: the notion of fairness, or *equity*. Equity theorists such as Elaine Walster, Ellen Berscheid, and George Homans argue that people are not just out to get the most rewards for the least cost; they are also concerned about equity in their relationships, wherein the rewards and costs they experience and the contributions they make to the relationship are roughly equal to the rewards, costs, and contributions of the other person (Homans, 1961; Walster, Walster, and Berscheid, 1978). These theorists describe equitable relationships as the most happy and stable type. In comparison, inequitable relationships result in one person feeling overbenefited (getting a lot of rewards, incurring few costs, having to devote little time or energy to the relationship) or underbenefited (getting few rewards, incurring a lot of costs, having to devote a lot of time and energy to the relationship).

According to equity theory, both underbenefited and overbenefited partners should feel uneasy about this state of affairs, and both should be motivated to restore equity to the relationship. This makes sense for the underbenefited person (who wants to continue feeling miserable?), but why should the overbenefited individual want to give up what social exchange

**equity theory:** the theory holding that people are happiest with relationships in which the rewards and costs a person experiences and the contributions he or she makes to the relationship are roughly equal to the rewards, costs, and contributions of the other person

theory indicates is a cushy deal—lots of rewards for little cost and little work? Elaine Hatfield (Walster) and her colleagues argue that equity is a powerful social norm—people will eventually feel uncomfortable or even guilty if they get more than they deserve in a relationship. However, let's face facts—being overbenefited just doesn't seem as bad as being underbenefited, and research has borne out that inequity is perceived as more of a problem by the underbenefited individual (Hatfield, Greenberger, Traupmann, and Lambert, 1982; Traupmann, Petersen, Utne, and Hatfield, 1981).

When stripped to the bare bones, the rules of social exchange and equity may seem to be sterile and even crass ways to describe friendly and intimate relationships. Nevertheless, they operate—at least at some level of consciousness—in all relationships. But because they do seem crass, most people strive to avoid the appearance of a rigid tit-for-tat social exchange in their relationships. As we will see later, this avoidance is more likely to occur in long-term relationships, where people are less concerned with a daily tally of rewards and costs.

## Close Relationships

After getting to this point in the chapter, you should be in a pretty good position to make a favorable first impression the next time you meet someone. Suppose you want Claudia to like you. You should hang around her so that you become familiar, act in ways that are rewarding to her, and emphasize your similarity to her. Flattery is likely to get you somewhere, though if you want to be especially clever, you should be a little critical to start with, and then compliment her profusely. We make no guarantee that you and Claudia will become best friends, but all else being equal, these techniques work pretty well.

The causes of initial attraction are not always the same as the causes of love and long-term intimacy.

"It's as though everything nice about you had been just some kind of introductory offer."

You may have noticed, however, that all of this advice concerns the first impressions we make on another person. A first impression can be incredibly important; if we make a bad one, we may well not get a second chance to do better. On the other hand, we are frequently interested in more than just making a good first impression. We all want to develop relationships that go beyond the superficial, initial impressions we convey. Sometimes our goal is to become close friends or even lovers with another person, achieving lasting intimacy, love, and commitment. A valid question is whether the techniques we have discussed so far are as successful at developing close relationships as they are at winning new friends. Surely, you might ask, there is more to falling in love with someone and developing a lasting, intimate relationship with him or her (as did Hilda Vogel and Nathan Serlin in our opening example) than such things as propinquity, similarity, and social rewards?

Until recently, social psychologists have had little to say in answer to this question; research on interpersonal attraction focused almost exclusively on first impressions. Why? Primarily because long-term, close relationships are much more difficult to study scientifically than first impressions. As you might imagine, several difficulties arise when putting close relationships under the microscope of the scientific social psychologist. First, it's hard to use the scientist's most valuable tool—the experimental method—when studying long-term relationships. In Chapter 2, we saw that the only way to establish whether one variable causes another is to use the experimental method, whereby the researcher randomly assigns people to conditions that receive different treatments. While this method is, as we have seen, easily adapted to the study of first impressions, imagine the plight of the researcher interested in whether similarity leads to love and a long-term commitment: Large practical and ethical problems are raised in assigning people to conditions where they meet similar or dissimilar others, and have to interact with these people for weeks until love blossoms or they can no longer stand each other!

In addition, the feelings and intimacy associated with close relationships can be difficult to measure. As put so well by Beilby Porteus,

> Love is something so divine,
> Description would but make it less;
> 'Tis what I feel, but can't define,
> 'Tis what I know, but can't express.

Psychologists face a daunting task when trying to measure such inchoate feelings as love and passion.

Though the difficulties in studying close relationships are severe, they are not insurmountable. In the past decade, social psychologists have made significant strides in studying the nature of love, how it develops, and how it flourishes. Let's begin with perhaps the most difficult of these questions: Exactly what is love?

If you have ever been in love, think back to how you felt about your sweetheart when you first got to know him or her. You probably felt a combination of giddiness, longing, joy, and despair: "He noticed me tonight—I could barely catch my breath!" "When she kissed me, you could have knocked me over with a feather!" "I think he loves someone else—I could just curl up and die!" The ancient Greeks considered this strange, bewildering set of feelings to be a form of madness, causing all sorts of irrational

> Try to reason about love and you will lose your reason.
> —French proverb

There are different forms of love, some "hotter" and more passionate than others.

and obsessional acts. Though times have changed, we are all familiar with the torment—and exhilaration—that comes with falling in love.

A number of psychologists have developed measures of love (Aron, Aron, and Smollan, 1990; Berscheid, 1988; Berscheid, Snyder, and Omoto, 1989; Henrick & Henrick, 1986; Kelley, 1983; Lee, 1977, 1988; Rubin, 1970, 1973; Shaver, Schwartz, Kirson, and O'Connor, 1987). Initial attempts tried to distinguish between liking and loving, showing that, as you might expect, love is something different from "lots of liking," and it isn't just sexual desire either (Rubin, 1970). Later attempts dove deeper into the phenomenon by addressing what we all know intuitively is true: There seem to be different kinds of love. Consider the love between Herb and Mary, two septuagenarians who are celebrating their fiftieth wedding anniversary. They have deep feelings of devotion and intimacy, but their love is cooler than Jane and Frank's, also in their seventies, who have just met and fallen in love. Herb and Mary would probably not say they are "giddy" about each other, or that their feelings for each other are "like being on a roller coaster." But surely they can be every bit as much in love as Jane and Frank; in fact, we might even think they are more so. And what about the kind of nonsexual affection and warmth that close friends feel toward each other? We might want to use the term *love* to describe these feelings as well, though surely it is of a different variety than the kind of feelings that our two couples feel for each other.

Social psychologists have recognized that a good definition of love must encompass its myriad forms, including passionate, giddy feelings as well as deep, long-term devotion. One well-known distinction is between companionate love and passionate love (Hatfield, 1988; Hatfield & Walster, 1978). **Companionate love** is defined as the feelings of intimacy and affection we

**companionate love:** the feelings of intimacy and affection we feel for another person when we care deeply for the person but do not necessarily experience passion or arousal in his or her presence

## The Passionate Love Scale

Please think of the person whom you love most passionately right now. If you are not in love right now, please think of the last person you loved passionately. If you have never been in love, think of the person whom you came closest to caring for in that way.

1. I would feel deep despair if _____ left me.

2. Sometimes I feel I can't control my thoughts; they are obsessively on _____ .

3. I feel happy when I am doing something to make _____ happy.

4. I would rather be with _____ than anyone else.

5. I'd get jealous if I thought _____ were falling in love with someone else.

6. I yearn to know all about _____ .

7. I want _____ —physically, emotionally, mentally.

8. I have an endless appetite for affection from _____ .

9. For me, _____ is the perfect romantic partner.

10. I sense my body responding when _____ touches me.

11. _____ always seems to be on my mind.

12. I want _____ to know me—my thoughts, my fears, and my hopes.

13. I eagerly look for signs indicating _____ 's desire for me.

14. I possess a powerful attraction for _____ .

15. I get extremely depressed when things don't go right in my relationship with _____ .

Responses to each item are made along the following scale:

| Not at all true | Moderately true | Definitely true |
|:---:|:---:|:---:|
| 1  2  3 | 4  5  6 | 7  8  9 |

**FIGURE 10.7 The passionate love scale.** These items are part of a questionnaire designed to measure passionate love. Note that the questions measure the extent to which people have strong, uncontrollable thoughts; intense feelings; and overt acts toward the target of their feelings. (Adapted from Hatfield & Sprecher, 1986)

feel toward someone that are not accompanied by passion or physiological arousal. People can experience companionate love in nonsexual relationships, such as close friendships, or in sexual relationships, where they experience great feelings of intimacy (companionate love) but not a great deal of the heat and passion they may once have felt.

**Passionate love** involves an intense longing for another person. When things are going well—the other person loves us too—we feel great fulfillment and ecstasy. When things are not going well—our love is unrequited—we feel great sadness and despair. This kind of love is characterized by the experience of physiological arousal, wherein we actually feel shortness of breath and a thumping heart in our sweetheart's presence. Elaine Hatfield and Susan Sprecher (1986) developed a questionnaire to measure passionate love (see Figure 10.7). Passionate love, as measured by this scale, consists of strong, uncontrollable thoughts; intense feelings; and overt acts toward the target of one's affection. Clearly, this kind of love is distinguishable from cooler, less passionate love, such as that between Herb and Mary.

**passionate love:** the feelings of intense longing, accompanied by physiological arousal, we feel for another person; when our love is reciprocated, we feel great fulfillment and ecstacy, but when it is not, we feel sadness and despair

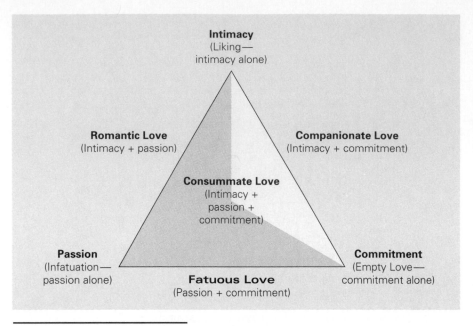

**FIGURE 10.8  The triangle of love.** According to the triangular theory of love, there are seven different forms of love, each made up of varying degrees of intimacy, passion, and commitment. (Adapted from Sternberg, 1988)

**triangular theory of love:** the idea that different kinds of love consist of varying degrees of three components: intimacy, passion, and commitment

Other researchers are not satisfied with a simple dichotomy of two kinds of love. Robert Sternberg (1986, 1988), for example, presents a **triangular theory of love,** which depicts love as consisting of three basic ingredients: intimacy, passion, and commitment. Intimacy refers to feelings of being close to and bonded with a partner. Passion refers to the "hot" parts of a relationship—namely, the arousal you experience toward your partner, including sexual attraction. Commitment consists of two decisions—the short-term one that you love your partner, and the long-term one to maintain that love and stay with your partner. Sternberg (1988) developed a scale to measure the three components of love, including such questions as "I have a relationship of mutual understanding with _____ " (intimacy), "I find myself thinking about _____ frequently during the day" (passion), and "I expect my love for _____ to last for the rest of my life" (commitment).

These three ingredients—intimacy, passion, and commitment—can be combined in varying degrees to form any of the different kinds of love (see Figure 10.8). Love can consist of one component alone, or of any combination of these three parts. For example, a person may feel a great deal of passion or physical attraction for another (infatuation love), but not know the person well enough to experience intimacy, and not be ready to make any kind of commitment. As the relationship develops, it might blossom into romantic love, characterized by passion and intimacy, and maybe even consummate love—the blending of all three components. Sternberg uses the term *companionate love* in the same way we depicted earlier, to describe love characterized by intimacy and commitment but not passion. Some of the heat may have gone out of Herb and Mary's relationship, for example, while their feelings of intimacy and commitment continued to grow.

By William Hamilton. Used with permission.

"Oh, I know you *like* me—but if you *loved* me, this would
be in slow motion with lots of backlighting."

## The Causes of Love

Now that scales have been developed to measure love, social psychologists
have begun addressing the more important question of how love develops
and how it is maintained. Are the causes of love similar to the causes of
initial attraction? As you might imagine, some of the same principles apply,
but they become more complicated and involved when it comes to developing a close relationship with someone. In our opening example, we saw
that Nathan Serlin was initially attracted to Hilda Vogel by her blue eyes. It
is doubtful, however, that beautiful eyes are enough to sustain a long-term
relationship. We will review some of the factors we discussed in the beginning of the chapter as determinants of first impressions, to see how they play
out in intimate relationships.

### Social Exchange in Long-Term Relationships

We saw earlier that, in general, everyone likes rewarding relationships. When
we meet new acquaintances, we are more attracted to those who reward us—
that is, those who are nice to us, are friendly, and so on. And if we want
other people to like us, it is important that we dole out social rewards to
them as well (Blau, 1964; Homans, 1961). This is the rule of social
exchange, which we discussed earlier in the chapter. But how does this play
out in long-term, intimate relationships? Do people pay attention to rewards
and costs in their most intimate relationships? Do they compare their current
relationships to what they think they should be getting in a close relationship, what we defined earlier as their comparison level? And finally, are they
keeping track of their options for other possible relationships, or their comparison level for alternatives?

    Research has shown ample support for social exchange theory in intimate
relationships. For example, Caryl Rusbult (1983) found that college-age
dating couples focused much more on rewards during the first three months

> What, after all, is our life but
> a great dance in which we are
> all trying to fix the best going
> rate of exchange?
> —Malcolm Bradbury, 1992

of their relationships. If the relationships were perceived as offering a lot of rewards, the people reported feeling happy and satisfied. The perception of rewards continued to be important over time; at seven months, couples who were still together, as compared to those who'd broken up, believed their rewards had increased over time. The perception and importance of costs came into play a few months into the relationships; this is when the glow created by all those rewards begins to be dimmed by the realization that costs are involved too. Not surprisingly, Rusbult found that satisfaction with the relationship decreased markedly over time for those who reported that costs were increasing in their relationships. Thus, rewards are always important to the outcome; costs become increasingly important over time.

Now, you may find this description of intimate relationships somewhat objectionable because it portrays people as coldhearted accountants who treat their relationships like they do their possessions, such as a stereo or a computer. They tally the pros and cons of their partner, and compare these to the pros and cons of alternative partners. If a relationship goes into the red—"Sorry, dear, but according to my latest tally, your negatives outweigh your positives, compared to what I can find down the street"—then that's it. The partner is gone. Not only is this portrayal distasteful, but it cannot explain the fact that many people do not leave their partners, even when they are dissatisfied and their other alternatives look bright.

Caryl Rusbult and her colleagues would agree, and go on to suggest that we need to consider at least one additional factor to understand close relationships: a person's level of investment in the relationship (Kelley, 1983; Rusbult, 1980, 1983, 1991). In her **investment model** of close relationships, Rusbult defines investments as anything people have put into a relationship that will be lost if they leave it. Examples include tangible things, such as financial resources and possessions (e.g., a house), as well as intangible things, such as the emotional welfare of one's children, the time and emotional energy spent building the relationship, and the sense of personal integrity that will be lost if one gets divorced. As seen in Figure 10.9, the greater the investment individuals have in a relationship, the less likely they are to leave, even if satisfaction is low and other alternatives look promising. In short, to predict whether people will stay in an intimate relationship, you need to know (a) how satisfied they are with the relationship, (b) what they think of the alternatives, and (c) how great their investment in the relationship is.

**investment model:** the theory holding that people's commitment to a relationship depends on their satisfaction with the relationship in terms of rewards, costs, and comparison level; their comparison level for alternatives; and how much they have invested in the relationship that would be lost by leaving it

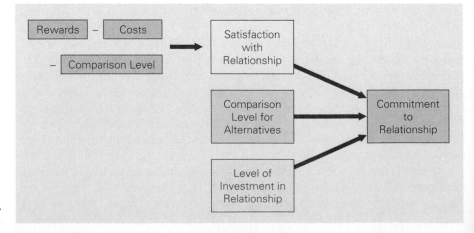

**FIGURE 10.9 The investment model of commitment.** People's commitment to a relationship depends on their satisfaction with the relationship in terms of rewards, costs, and comparison level; their comparison level for alternatives; and how much they have invested in the relationship. (Adapted from Rusbult, 1983)

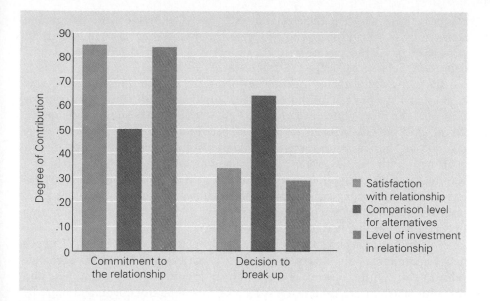

**FIGURE 10.10  A test of the investment model.** This study examined the extent to which college students' satisfaction with a relationship, their comparison level for alternatives, and their investment in the relationship predicted their commitment to the relationship and their decision about whether to break up with their partner. The higher the number, the more each variable predicted commitment and breakup, independently of the other two variables. All three variables were good predictors of how committed people were and whether they broke up or not. (Adapted from Rusbult, 1983)

To test this model, Rusbult (1983) asked college students involved in heterosexual dating relationships to fill out questionnaires for seven months. Every three weeks or so, people answered questions about each of the components of the model shown in Figure 10.9. Rusbult also kept track of whether the students stayed in the relationships or broke up with their partner. As you can see in Figure 10.10, people's satisfaction, alternatives, and investments all predicted how committed they were to the relationship and whether it lasted. (The higher the number on the scale, the more each factor predicted the commitment to and length of the relationship.) Subsequent studies have found results similar to those shown in Figure 10.10 for married couples of diverse ages, for lesbians and gays, for close (nonsexual) friendships, and for residents of both the United States and Taiwan (Rusbult, 1991). Thus, when it comes to long-term relationships, commitment is more than just the amount of rewards and punishments people dole out.

## Equity: Is It Always Tit-for-Tat?

Earlier we discussed equity theory, which argues that what matters in a relationship is not the total amount of rewards and costs but the fairness of how those rewards and costs are distributed. The argument here is that people strive for equity so that there is roughly an equal ratio of rewards to costs for each partner. Many early studies found that people use this rule, and are dissatisfied if the ratio is imbalanced, tipped in the direction of one partner. For example, in research on college-age dating couples and on older married

> The friendships which last are those wherein each friend respects the other's dignity to the point of not really wanting anything from him.
> —Cyril Connolly

couples, those who felt their relationships were equitable were happy and content; by contrast, those who felt underbenefited reported feeling angry or depressed, and those who felt overbenefited reported feeling guilty or depressed (Schafer & Keith, 1980; Walster, Walster, and Traupmann, 1978).

But does equity theory operate in long-term relationships the same way it does in new or less intimate relationships? The more we get to know someone, the more reluctant we are to believe that we are simply exchanging favors, and the less inclined we are to expect immediate compensation for a favor done. For instance, early in a relationship, when Sam drops by our apartment with his class notes, we might pour him a beer immediately as a way of showing our appreciation. Later on in the relationship, we may feel less of a need to repay such a favor immediately. In other words, long-term, intimate relationships seem to be governed by a looser, give-and-take notion of equity, rather than a rigid tit-for-tat strategy.

According to Margaret Clark and Judson Mills, interactions between new acquaintances are governed by equity concerns, and are called **exchange relationships.** Interactions between close friends, family members, and romantic partners are governed less by a tit-for-tat equity norm, and more by a desire to help each other in times of need (Clark, 1984, 1986; Clark & Mills, 1979; Mills & Clark, 1982). In exchange relationships, people keep track of who is contributing what, and feel taken advantage of when they feel they are putting more into the relationship than they are getting out of it. In **communal relationships,** people give in response to the other's needs, regardless of whether they are paid back. A good example of a communal relationship is parenting. As a friend of ours recently put it, "You spend years catering to your child's every need—changing diapers, sitting up with her in the middle of the night when she is throwing up, coaching her soccer team—knowing full well that sooner or later, she will reach an age when she will prefer to spend her time with anyone but you!"

**exchange relationships:** relationships governed by the need for equity (i.e., for an equal ratio of rewards and costs)

**communal relationships:** relationships in which people's primary concern is being responsive to the other person's needs

*"Son, you're all grown up now. You owe me two hundred and fourteen thousand dollars."*

Which of these groups of people would you say have an exchange relationship, and which a communal relationship?

In a series of clever experiments, Clark and her colleagues varied whether people desired an exchange or a communal relationship with another person, and then observed the extent to which people were concerned with equity in the relationship. The type of relationship is typically altered by having people interact with someone who is quite attractive, and telling half of the participants that this person is new to the area and interested in making new friends—thereby increasing people's interest in establishing a communal relationship. The remaining participants are told that the other person is married and visiting the area for only a brief time—thereby making people more inclined to favor an exchange relationship with this person. As predicted, people in the exchange condition operated according to the equity norm, as summarized in Figure 10.11. People in the communal condition, thinking there was a chance for a long-term relationship, were relatively unconcerned with a tit-for-tat accounting of who was contributing what (Clark, 1984; Clark & Mills, 1979; Clark & Waddell, 1985; Williamson & Clark, 1989). These results are not limited to exchange and communal relationships created in the laboratory. Other studies show that ongoing friendships are more communal than relationships between strangers are (Clark, Mills, and Corcoran, 1989).

Are people in communal relationships completely unconcerned with equity? No; as we saw earlier, people do feel distressed if they believe their intimate relationships are inequitable (Walster et al., 1978). However, equity takes on a somewhat different form in communal relationships than it does in less intimate ones. In communal relationships, the partners are more relaxed about what constitutes equity at any given time; they believe that things will eventually balance out and a rough kind of equity will be achieved. For any given day, week, or month, one partner might be feeling underbenefited, but in a good communal relationship, one can trust that this situation will change and even reverse itself. Thus, in the short run there are differences in how closely people adhere to the equity norm. In new acquaintanceships, people keep much more careful track of the debits and with-

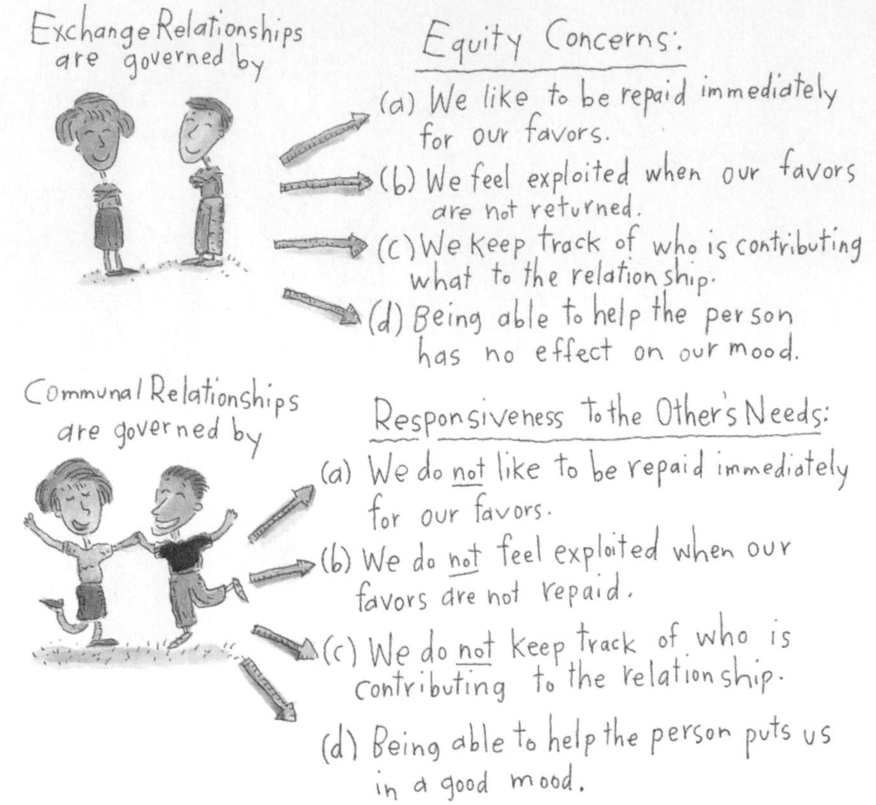

Exchange Relationships are governed by

Equity Concerns:

(a) We like to be repaid immediately for our favors.

(b) We feel exploited when our favors are not returned.

(c) We keep track of who is contributing what to the relationship.

(d) Being able to help the person has no effect on our mood.

Communal Relationships are governed by

Responsiveness to the Other's Needs:

(a) We do not like to be repaid immediately for our favors.

(b) We do not feel exploited when our favors are not repaid.

(c) We do not keep track of who is contributing to the relationship.

(d) Being able to help the person puts us in a good mood.

**FIGURE 10.11 Exchange versus communal relationships.**

> If Jack's in love, he's no judge of Jill's beauty.
>
> —Benjamin Franklin

drawals of each partner. In communal relationships, people are much more relaxed, and even resent a careful accounting of who is contributing what.

## Physical Attractiveness and Long-Term Relationships

We have already seen that physical attractiveness makes a big difference in the early stages of a relationship. People tend to assume that "what is beautiful is good," and prefer blind dates who are attractive. What about long-term relationships? Are unattractive people doomed to failure in the interpersonal domain, so that only attractive people form satisfying, long-term relationships? Earlier we saw a hint that this is not the case. In a study of dating relationships over a period of several months, White (1980) found that the couples who were most likely to be deeply involved were those who were similar in attractiveness. This suggests that physically attractive people do not have romantic relationships that are happier than other people's—what matters is dating someone who is approximately as attractive as you are.

When it comes to the everyday kinds of conversations and interactions college students have with their friends, though, attractive people may be better off. In a study by Harry Reis, Ladd Wheeler, and their colleagues (1982), college students answered questions about every interaction they had with another person (defined as a conversation that lasted for more than ten minutes) over a two-week period. The students answered questions about whom they spoke with, how they felt about this person, how long the conversation lasted, and so on. At the end of the study, the researchers photographed each student, and a separate group of students rated how physically attractive each participant was.

The main result of the study was that attractive men and women reported that they had better interactions with others (i.e., conversations that were more intimate and pleasant) than their unattractive counterparts did. We should interpret this result with caution, though, because there is no way of knowing whether attractiveness per se or some other variable associated with attractiveness caused the students to have more satisfying interactions. These results do show, however, that among college students, attractiveness is associated with interactions of higher quality.

Before you become discouraged about the advantage that attractiveness bestows on people, we should hasten to add that this advantage may be limited to the college years. Berscheid, Walster, and Campbell (cited in Brehm, 1992) examined the association between attractiveness and life satisfaction over a much longer time span. They obtained yearbook pictures of middle-aged college graduates, to see how physically attractive they had been in college. They then interviewed each person, to see if youthful attractiveness had given people a leg up in life. They found that though the attractive people were more likely to have married, they were no more satisfied with their marriages than unattractive people, and no more satisfied with their lives in general. There is no denying that attractiveness is highly valued in our society, and that beautiful people have certain advantages. It would be wrong to conclude, however, that attractiveness guarantees happy relationships or happy lives.

## Attachment Styles and Intimate Relationships

All of the determinants of love and intimacy we have discussed so far have been in the here-and-now of a relationship: the attractiveness and similarity

Attachment theory predicts that the attachment style we learn as infants and young children stays with us throughout life, and generalizes to all of our relationships with other people.

**attachment styles:** the expectations people develop about relationships with others, based on the relationship they had with their primary caregiver when they were infants

**secure attachment style:** an attachment style characterized by trust, a lack of concern with being abandoned, and the view that one is worthy and well liked

**avoidant attachment style:** an attachment style characterized by a suppression of attachment needs, because attempts to be intimate have been rebuffed; people with this style find it difficult to develop intimate relationships

**anxious/ambivalent attachment style:** an attachment style characterized by a concern that others will not reciprocate one's desire for intimacy, resulting in higher-than-average levels of anxiety

of the partners, how they treat each other, and so on. A recent theory of love emphasizes what each person brings to the relationship—namely, the **attachment styles** the person learned beginning when he or she was an infant. This research draws on the ground-breaking work of John Bowlby (1969, 1973, 1980) and Mary Ainsworth (Ainsworth, Blehar, Waters, and Wall, 1978) on how infants form bonds to their primary caregivers (e.g., their mothers or fathers), suggesting that the kinds of bonds we form early in life influence the kinds of relationships we form as adults.

Mary Ainsworth and her colleagues (1978) identified three types of relationships between infants and their mothers. Infants with a **secure attachment style** typically have caregivers who are responsive to their needs and who show positive emotions when interacting with them. These infants trust their caregivers, are not worried about being abandoned, and view themselves as worthy and well liked. Infants with an **avoidant attachment style** typically have caregivers who are aloof and distant, rebuffing the infant's attempts to establish intimacy. These infants desire to be close to their caregiver but learn to suppress this need, as if they know that attempts to be intimate will be rejected. Infants with an **anxious/ambivalent attachment style** typically have caregivers who are inconsistent and overbearing in their affections. These infants are unusually anxious, because they can never predict when and how their caregivers will respond to their needs.

The key assumption of attachment theory is that the particular attachment style we learn as infants and young children stays with us throughout life, and generalizes to all of our relationships with other people: The securely attached person is able to develop mature, lasting relationships; people who have avoidant attachment styles are less able to trust others and find it difficult to develop close, intimate relationships; and people who have anxious/ambivalent attachment styles want to become close to their partners but worry that their partners will not return their affections. In short, the kinds of expectations about other people that we literally learned at our mother or father's knee stay with us, and influence our adult relationships throughout our lives.

We do not mean to imply that if you had an unhappy relationship with your parents, you are doomed to repeat this same kind of unhappy relationship with everyone you meet. People can change, and learn to have healthier and more fulfilling relationships than they had as a child. If you had an avoidant or anxious/ambivalent relationship with your parents, however, there is a greater likelihood that you will have these same kinds of relationships with romantic partners, as well as with your own children (Feeney & Noller, 1990; Hazan & Shaver, 1987; Main, Kaplan, and Cassidy, 1985). This has been shown in several studies that measure adults' attachment styles with questionnaires or interviews, and then correlate these styles with the quality of their romantic relationships.

For example, Cindy Hazan and Philip Shaver (1987) asked adults to choose one of the three statements shown in Figure 10.12, according to how they typically felt in romantic relationships. Each of these statements was designed to capture the three kinds of attachment styles we described above. The researchers also asked people questions about their current relationships. The results of this study—and several others like it—were consistent with an attachment theory perspective. Securely attached adults report that they easily become close to other people, readily trust others, and have satisfying

**Measuring Attachment Styles**

1. I find it relatively easy to get close to others and am comfortable depending on them and having them depend on me. I don't often worry about being abandoned or about someone getting too close.

   (*secure* style; 56 percent)

2. I am somewhat uncomfortable being close; I find it difficult to trust them completely, difficult to allow myself to depend on them. I am nervous when anyone gets close, and often, love partners want me to be more intimate than I feel comfortable being.

   (*avoidant* style; 25 percent)

3. I find that others are reluctant to get as close as I would like. I often worry that my partner doesn't really love me or won't stay with me, I want to merge completely with another person, and this desire sometimes scares people away.

   (*anxious* style; 19 percent)

**FIGURE 10.12 Measuring attachment styles.** As part of a survey of attitudes toward love published in a newspaper, people were asked to choose the statement that best described their romantic relationships. The attachment style each statement was designed to measure and the percentage of people who chose each alternative are listed after each statement. (Adapted from Hazan & Shaver, 1987)

romantic relationships. People with an avoidant style report that they are uncomfortable becoming close to others, find it hard to trust others, and have less satisfying romantic relationships. And people with an anxious/ambivalent style tend to have less satisfying relationships, but of a different type: They are likely to be obsessive and preoccupied with their relationships, fearing that their partners do not want to be as intimate or close as they desire them to be (Collins & Read, 1990; Feeney & Noller, 1990; Kobak & Hazan, 1991; Shaver, Hazan, and Bradshaw, 1988; Simpson, 1990; Simpson, Rholes, and Nelligan, 1991).

Other investigators have asked research participants to describe (a) their childhood relationships with their parents, to determine their early attachment style, and (b) their current romantic relationships, to provide an even more exact test of the attachment hypothesis. For example, Judith Feeney and Patricia Noller (1990) found that securely attached individuals reported positive early family relationships, and as adults, had the most enduring, long-term romantic relationships in the sample. Anxious/ambivalently attached individuals reported that as children, they did not feel supported by their parents; their adult romantic relationships were the most short-lived of the sample. Finally, avoidant individuals stated that, when young, they were distanced from and mistrustful of their parents; as adults, these individuals were the most likely to report never having been in love or not being in love at the time of the study, and the love relationships they had experienced were the least intense in the sample.

Using a similar approach, Nancy Collins and Stephen Read (1990) found that for heterosexual, college-age dating couples, childhood attachment styles are correlated with the type of romantic partner chosen and the outcome of the relationship. In particular, the participants' descriptions of their attachment history with their opposite-sex parent was related to their current choice of romantic partner. For example, men who felt their mothers were cold or inconsistent were more likely to be dating women who were anxious. Women who felt their fathers were warm and responsive were most likely to be dating men who were able to express intimacy.

At this point, we feel the need to issue a caveat. As interesting as the results in this section might be, we must remind you that they are correlational rather than experimental. As we saw in Chapter 2, it is risky to infer causation from correlational data. Moreover, these studies rely in part on self-reports about recollections of the past—not on actual behavior observed by impartial researchers in response to carefully controlled scientific procedures. Accordingly, they are subject to several alternative causal explanations, by dint of the fact that one's recollections can be influenced by one's present situation. For example, consider the women who were currently dating men who were able to express intimacy. It may be that these women were made so happy by this situation that, when they thought about the past, it was primarily the most pleasant memories that were triggered. Accordingly, when asked to describe their fathers they might selectively have remembered more instances of warmth and responsiveness. Thus, it might not be that women with warm and responsive fathers are more likely to choose men who can express intimacy; it may be that happy women remember more happy incidents from their past.

Taken as a whole, however, these studies are highly suggestive and do lend some support to the contention that the kind of relationship we had with our parents is likely to repeat itself in adulthood. Research on attachment theory in adults is relatively new, but at this point we can summarize it as follows: If you ever place a personal ad in a newspaper seeking a romantic partner, you might want to say, "Only securely attached people need apply!"

## Trouble in Paradise

As the old saying states, "What goes up must come down," and we all know what that means in intimate relationships: Oftentimes, they end. The current American divorce rate is holding at nearly 50 percent of the current marriage rate; in addition, many romantic relationships involving heterosexuals, lesbians, and gays are terminated every day. In short, there's a whole lot of breaking up going on. After several years of studying what love is and how it blooms, social psychologists are now beginning to explore the end of the story—how it dies. We will focus on research on the jealousy in romantic relationships, and on how people experience the termination of their most intimate relationships.

**Jealousy in Close Relationships.** Just about everyone has experienced what Shakespeare called the "green-eyed monster": that anxious, gnawing feeling of jealousy when we believe a romantic partner is interested in someone else. As much as we don't want to feel jealous, sometimes we just can't help it. But where does jealousy come from? It is commonly believed

> Jealousy is . . . a tiger that tears not only its prey but also its own raging heart.
> —Michael Beer

that the people who are most likely to be jealous are those who think least highly of themselves; after all, if people are secure and feel good about themselves, there is less reason to worry that they will lose a loved one to a rival (Mead, 1977). It turns out, however, that this conclusion is only partly true. The relationship between jealousy and a person's overall self-esteem has been found to be small, at best (Buunk, 1982; Pines & Aronson, 1983; Salovey & Rodin, 1989; White, 1981b). Instead, people are most likely to feel jealous when they feel threatened in areas that are especially relevant to their feelings of self-worth (Salovey & Rodin, 1989, 1991).

You may recall our discussion in Chapter 3 of self-evaluation maintenance theory, which holds that people are most likely to feel bad about a relationship if they are (a) very close to a person who (b) outperforms them (c) in an area central to their self-definitions (Tesser, 1978). For example, if it is important to us to become a doctor and our best friend is accepted at a top medical school, whereas we are rejected, we are likely to feel more than a little pang of discomfort. On the other hand, if becoming a doctor is unimportant to us, we are likely to be pleased for our friend and even to bask in his or her reflected glory.

Peter Salovey and Judith Rodin (1989) suggest that the same reasoning applies to romantic jealousy. People are most likely to feel jealous, they argue, when they experience competition from a rival in an area that they especially value. Suppose, for example, that your lover likes to bowl. One night, he or she goes to the lanes with the local bowling champion, who has a 220-pin average. Are you likely to feel jealous? It depends on how central bowling is to your self-definition. If your life dream has been to turn professional and appear on "Bowling for Dollars," you are likely to feel pangs of jealousy. If, however, you couldn't care less about bowling, you are unlikely to feel jealous; you might even be pleased that your lover has found someone else to go bowling with, so you don't have to go yourself.

But what if your lover begins to show signs of a romantic interest in the local bowling champion? Virtually everyone will feel at least a little jealous in this situation, because for most of us, feeling desirable sexually is a central part of our self-definition. This is especially likely to be true if it is important to us to have an exclusive relationship with our lover (Bringle, 1981; Buunk, 1982; Salovey & Rodin, 1989).

It is perhaps obvious that people will feel the most threatened about things that are the most important to them. However, what people find important, and thus are most likely to get jealous about, is sometimes surprising, and differs across cultures. For example, college-age participants in the former Yugoslavia reported a strong jealousy reaction to the idea of their lover flirting with another person; in contrast, students in Hungary had a mild reaction to this jealousy scenario. And whereas students in the Netherlands said they would experience strong feelings of jealousy if they knew their partner had sexual fantasies about someone else, this scenario didn't bother the Yugoslav students at all (Buunk & Hupka, 1987). Thus, most of us are likely to feel jealous when we feel threatened in a domain that is important to us, but what that domain is differs from person to person and across cultures.

**Termination: Breaking up Is Hard to Do.**   Ending a romantic relationship is one of life's more painful experiences. How do people go about ending a relationship? During the past decade, researchers began to examine the disengagement strategies people use to exit their relationships (Baxter, 1986; Rusbult & Zembrodt, 1983). For example, Cody (1982) asked research participants to describe in detail how they had ended a romantic relationship. Their accounts revealed five basic categories: *positive tone* (e.g., telling the partner you care about him or her, but . . . ), *verbal de-escalation* (e.g., telling the partner you no longer feel in love), *behavioral de-escalation* (e.g., avoiding contact with the partner), *negative identity management* (e.g., telling the partner you should both start dating other people), and *justification* (e.g., telling the partner that the relationship isn't meeting your needs).

At the same time, Steve Duck (1982) reminds us that relationship dissolution is not a single event but a process with many steps. Duck theorizes that four stages of dissolution exist, ranging from the intrapersonal (the individual thinks a lot about how he or she is dissatisfied with the relationship), to the dyadic (the individual discusses the breakup with the partner), to the social (the breakup is announced to other people), and back to the intrapersonal (the individual recovers from the breakup and forms an account, or version, of how and why it happened). In terms of the last stage in the process, John Harvey and his colleagues (1986) have found that the version of "why the relationship ended" that we present to close friends can be very different from the official (i.e., cleaned-up) version that we present to co-workers or neighbors.

If a romantic relationship is in bad shape, can we predict who will end it? Much has been made about the tendency in heterosexual relationships for one sex to end the relationship more than the other; for example, it was commonly believed that women ended relationships more often than men (Rubin, Hill, and Peplau, 1981). Recent research has found, however, that one sex doesn't end romantic relationships any more frequently than the other (Akert, 1992; Hagestad & Smyer, 1982; Rusbult, Johnson, and Morrow, 1986).

Can we predict the different ways people will feel when their relationship ends? One key is the role people play in the decision to end the relationship (Akert, 1992; Lloyd & Cate, 1985). For example, Robin Akert asked 344 college-age men and women to focus on their most important romantic relationship that had ended, and to respond to a questionnaire focusing on their experiences during the breakup. One question asked to what extent they, as compared to their partner, had been responsible for the decision to break up. Participants who indicated a high level of responsibility for the decision were labeled *breakers*; those who reported a low level or responsibility, *breakees*; and those who shared the decision making with their partners about equally, *mutuals*.

Akert found that the role people played in the decision to end the relationship was the single most powerful predictor of their breakup experiences. Not surprisingly, Breakees were miserable—they reported high levels of loneliness, depression, unhappiness, and anger, and virtually all reported experiencing physical disorders in the weeks after the breakup as well. Breakers found the end of the relationship the least upsetting, the least painful, and the least stressful of the three; although Breakers did report feeling guilty and unhappy, they had the fewest negative physical symptoms (39 percent), such as head- and stomachaches, and eating and sleeping irregularities.

The Mutual role, which carries with it a component of shared decision making, helped individuals evade some of the more negative emotional and

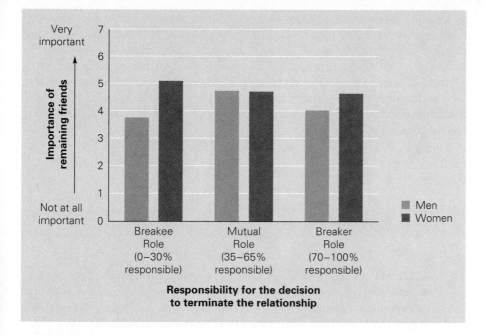

**FIGURE 10.13 Importance of remaining friends after the breakup.** After ending a romantic relationship, do people want to remain friends with their ex-partner? It depends on both the role they played in the decision to break up and on their gender. Women are more interested than men in staying friends when they are in the breakee or breaker role; men and women are equally interested in staying friends if their relationships end by mutual decision.

physical reactions to breaking up. Mutuals were not as upset or hurt as Breakees, but they were not as unaffected as Breakers. Some 60 percent of the Mutuals reported physical symptoms, indicating that a mutual conclusion to a romantic relationship is a more stressful experience than simply deciding to end it on one's own. Finally, gender played a role as well in the emotional and physical responses of the respondents, with women reporting somewhat more negative reactions to breaking up than men.

Do people want to stay friends when they break up? It depends on the role one plays in the breakup, as well as one's gender. Akert (1992) found that men are not very interested in remaining friends with their ex-girlfriends when they are in either the breaker or the breakee role, while women are more interested in remaining friends, especially when they are breakees (see Figure 10.13). Interestingly, the mutual role is the one where men's and women's interest in future friendship matches the most. These data suggest that when men experience either great control (breaker) or little control (breakee) over the ending of the relationship, they want to "cut their losses" and move on, severing ties with their ex-partner. In comparison, women wish to continue feeling connected to their ex-partner and hope to reshape the intimate relationship into a platonic friendship. The mutual breakup is the one in which each effectively plays the breaker and breakee roles simultaneously, and this equality in roles appears to be important in producing an equivalent interest in future friendship for men and women (see Figure 10.13).

The breakup moral? If you find yourself in a romantic relationship and your partner seems inclined to break it off, try to end it mutually. Your experience will be less traumatic because you will share some control over the process (even if you don't want it to happen). Unfortunately for your partner, if you are about to be in the role of breaker, you will experience less pain and suffering if you continue to play that role; however, changing your role from the breaker to the mutual would be an act of kindness toward your soon-to-be ex-loved one.

## SUMMARY

In the first part of this chapter, we discussed the variables that cause initial attraction between two people. One such variable is physical proximity, or the **propinquity effect:** People who, by chance, you come into contact with the most are the most likely to become your friends and lovers. This occurs because **mere exposure** to any stimulus, in general, produces liking for it. Though most people are reluctant to admit it, physical attractiveness also plays an important role in liking. The "what is beautiful is good" stereotype indicates that people assume physical attractiveness is associated with all kinds of other desirable traits. On a happy note, research shows that how much we like people influences how physically attractive we think they are.

Similarity between people, whether in attitudes and values, personality traits, or demographic characteristics, is also a powerful cause of attraction and liking. Similarity appears to be a far stronger predictor of attraction than complementarity—the idea that opposites attract. How people behave toward us is also of obvious importance, as when we receive praise from another person. Flattery can be overdone, however, especially if it suggests an ulterior motive. If we believe someone is flattering us because of an attempt at **ingratiation**—the deliberate attempt to manipulate us—we will like them less. In general, we like others who act in ways that indicate they like us. One exception, though, is the **gain-loss effect,** which indicates that we like people more if they initially are somewhat critical of us and then come to like us (we gain their esteem) than if they like us all along.

Many of these determinants of attractiveness can be explained by **social exchange theory,** which argues that how people feel about their relationships depends on their perception of the rewards they receive from the relationship (e.g., praise) and the costs they incur. In addition, in order to determine whether people will stay in a relationship, we

also need to know their **comparison level**—their expectations about the outcomes of their relationship—and their **comparison level for alternatives**—their expectations about how happy they would be in other relationships. There are, however, exceptions to the rule of social exchange. Under some conditions, people do not prefer the person who is most rewarding. For example, some theorists argue that the most important determinant of satisfaction is the amount of equity in a relationship. **Equity theory** states that we are happiest when the ratio of rewards and punishments we receive is roughly equal to the ratio of rewards and punishments the other person experiences.

In the second part of the chapter, we examined the causes of attraction in long-term, intimate relationships. Social psychologists have offered several definitions of intimacy and love. One important distinction is between **companionate love**—feelings of intimacy that are not accompanied by intense longing and arousal—and **passionate love**—feelings of intimacy that are accompanied by intense longing and arousal. The **triangular theory of love** distinguishes among three components of love: intimacy, passion, and commitment.

Many of the causes of love are similar to the causes of initial attraction, though there are differences in how these causes operate. Social exchange theories of close relationships, such as the **investment model,** say that to predict whether a couple will stay together, we need to know each person's level of investment in the relationship, as well as each person's comparison level and comparison level for alternatives. The notion of equity of rewards and costs is different in long-term versus short-term relationships. Short-term associations are usually **exchange relationships,** in which people are concerned about a fair distribution of rewards and costs. Long-term, intimate associations are usually **communal relationships,** in which people are less concerned with an immediate accounting of who is contributing what, and more concerned with helping their partner when he or she is in need.

The theory of **attachment styles** points to people's past relationships with their parents as a significant determinant of the quality of their close relationships as adults. Infants can be classified as having one of three types of attachment relationships with their primary caregiver: **secure, avoidant,** and **anxious/ambivalent.** There is evidence that people who as infants were securely attached have more intimate and satisfying romantic relationships than people with either of the other attachment styles.

Jealousy in intimate relationships occurs when people feel threatened that they will lose their loved one. People are most likely to be jealous when they feel threatened in areas especially relevant to their feelings of self-worth; the specific behaviors that meet these conditions differ across cultures. Unfortunately, intimate relationships end; the breaking-up process is composed of stages, not just a single event. A powerful variable that predicts how a person will weather the breakup is the role he or she plays in the decision to terminate the relationship; people differ in their behavior and reaction to breaking up, depending on whether they are in the *breaker*, *breakee*, or *mutual* role.

## SUGGESTED READINGS

Brehm, S. S. (1992). *Intimate relationships* (2nd ed.). New York: McGraw-Hill. A comprehensive overview of the entire field of interpersonal attraction, from first impressions to intimate relationships.

Duck, S. (1991). *Understanding relationships*. New York: Guilford. An overview of the field of close relationships by an eminent researcher in this area.

Hatfield, E., & Rapson, R. L. (1993). *Love, sex, and intimacy: Their psychology, biology, and history*. New York: HarperCollins. A fascinating look at love and intimacy, including both current scientific studies and historical comparisons between concepts of love in other eras and cultures.

Hendrick, C. (Ed.). (1989). *Close relationships: Review of personality and social psychology* (Vol. 10). Newbury Park, CA: Sage. Chapters on close relationships by the leading researchers in the field, including many whose work we discussed in this chapter.

Sternberg, R. J., & Barnes, M. L. (Eds.). (1988). *The psychology of love*. New Haven, CT: Yale University Press. Chapters on love by the leading researchers in the field, including many whose work we discussed in this chapter.

# Chapter 11

## Prosocial Behavior:
## Why Do People Help?

I am not interested in why man commits evil. I want to know why
he does good (here and there), or at least feels that he ought to.
— Vaclav Havel, 1982

uman beings have an amazing capacity to act in selfish, uncaring ways. All too often, people resort to confrontation, violence, and force to resolve their differences, sometimes becoming locked in spiraling conflicts that harm everyone involved, as we will see in Chapter 12, on aggression. Sometimes people simply appear not to care about their fellow human beings. In Chapter 2, on research methods, we discussed the tragic case of Kitty Genovese, who screamed in terror as she was assaulted, and eventually murdered, by an assailant outside an apartment building in the Queens section of New York City. Thirty-eight residents of the apartment building heard her cries, yet not one of them came to her aid. None of them even lifted a finger to dial the police. Unfortunately, such coldhearted acts are not uncommon. A few years ago, a nineteen-year-old woman was attacked by a rapist in the foyer of her apartment building in Greenbelt, Maryland. The woman screamed and struggled for several minutes as the assailant dragged her in front of a neighbor's apartment and raped her. Residents of the apartment building heard her screams but did nothing to help her. "It certainly sounds inhuman, doesn't it?" said Dorothy Piles, one resident. "It has made me ill. It has made all of us ill, not wanting to get involved, if that was the reason that they did not call the police" (*Washington Post*, September 19, 1986).

Fortunately, there is also a brighter side to human nature. A recent Gallup poll revealed that 80 million Americans engage in volunteer work, with many spending several hours a week helping those less fortunate. Countless citizens, including social workers, nurses, firefighters, and teachers, devote their lives to serving others.

Sometimes people help in dramatic, selfless ways that capture the attention of the entire nation. Consider what happened in January of 1982, when Air Florida Flight 90 crashed while attempting to take off in Washington, D.C. The plane lifted off the runway at National Airport during an icy, swirling snowstorm, but was unable to gain altitude. It clipped a bridge spanning the Potomac River and slammed through the ice into the dark water, making a swishing sound as it sank. Most of the passengers and crew were killed by the impact, but a few survivors clung desperately to the tail section of the plane in the frigid waters of the Potomac. A helicopter from the National Park Service flew quickly to the scene. Every second counted, because no one could survive for long in the thirty-degree water. The helicopter crew dropped a rescue line, hoping

Lenny Skutnik saves Priscilla Triado after she drops the rescue line.

to tow the survivors to waiting rescue workers on the shore. But most of the survivors were in shock and could not grab the line as it swung back and forth in the gale-force winds. One passenger, a balding man in his fifties, was more alert than the others and managed to grab the line. But instead of letting the helicopter pull him to safety, he passed the line to another passenger. Each time the helicopter returned, he grabbed the line and passed it to a fellow passenger.

One survivor, Priscilla Triado, lost her grip as the helicopter towed her to the shore. She dropped, semiconscious, into the icy water. Lenny Skutnik, a clerk at the Congressional Budget

Office, was watching from the shore. Without hesitation, he tore off his coat and boots and dove into the freezing river, dragging Triado to waiting rescue workers. Doctors later found that Triado's body temperature was 81 degrees Fahrenheit, estimating that she was moments away from death when Skutnik reached her. Meanwhile, the helicopter continued to tow the other survivors to the shore. When it returned at last for the selfless man who had been passing the line to the other passengers, he was nowhere to be found. He had succumbed to the freezing temperatures, slipping wordlessly beneath the black surface of the river.

The horror of the crash of Flight 90 was tempered by these extraordinary acts of self-sacrifice. Lenny Skutnik easily could have died in the freezing temperatures while trying to rescue Priscilla Triado. Instead, he thought, "Somebody had to go into the water," and decided without hesitation that that somebody would be him (*Time*, January 25, 1982). The entire country applauded his courageous, selfless act, as well as that of the unknown passenger who passed the rope to others, paying for his generosity with his life. The fact that he could not be identified added to his mystique. He seemed to represent the capacity in us all to act in selfless, altruistic, even heroic ways.

These strikingly different examples of human helpfulness—and the lack of it—raise some perplexing questions about human nature. Why is it that sometimes people perform acts of great self-sacrifice and heroism, whereas at other times they act in uncaring, heartless ways, ignoring the desperate pleas of those in need? In this chapter, we will consider the major determinants of **prosocial behavior,** which we define as any act performed with the goal of benefiting another person. We will begin by considering the basic origins of prosocial behavior. Why do people help others?

**prosocial behavior:** any act performed with the goal of benefiting another person

## Basic Motives Underlying Prosocial Behavior: Why Do People Help?

### Sociobiology: Instincts and Genes

According to Charles Darwin's (1859) theory of evolution, natural selection favors genes that promote the survival of the individual. Any gene that furthers our survival and increases the probability that we will produce offspring is likely to be passed on from generation to generation. Genes that lower our chances of survival, such as those producing life-threatening diseases, reduce the chances that we will produce offspring, and thus are less likely to be passed on. In recent years, evolutionary biologists like E. O. Wilson (1975) and Richard Dawkins (1976) have used these principles of evolutionary theory to explain such social behaviors as aggression and altruism, spawning the field of **sociobiology.** Sociobiologists make two fundamental assumptions: first, that many social behaviors have genetic roots, so that people who have certain genes are more likely to perform these behaviors, and second, that evolutionary pressures have favored some of these social behaviors over others, so that they are now a fixed part of our genetic heritage.

**sociobiology:** the application of evolutionary theory to social behavior

Darwin realized early on that a potential problem exists with evolutionary theory: How can it explain prosocial behavior? Why should people help others, particularly at a cost to themselves, if their overriding goal is to ensure their own survival? One way that modern sociobiologists attempt to explain prosocial behavior is with the notion of **kin selection** (Hamilton, 1964). We can increase the chances that our genes will be passed along not only by having children, but also by ensuring that our genetic relatives survive. Since all our blood relatives share some of our genes, the more we ensure their survival, the greater the chance that our genes will flourish in future generations. Thus, natural selection should favor altruistic acts directed toward genetic relatives. There is support for this notion in the animal kingdom, particularly among social insects. Greenberg (1979), for example, released bees near a nest protected by guard bees, and observed which ones the guards admitted to the nest and which ones they rebuffed. He had bred the intruders to be of varying genetic similarity to the guards. Some were siblings, some were cousins, and some were more distant relatives. Consistent with the idea of kin selection, the guard bees were much more likely to admit bees that were close relatives. They could tell how related the bees were to them by their odors, and essentially told their more distant relatives that there was no more room at the inn.

**kin selection:** the idea that behaviors that help a genetic relative are favored by natural selection

Altruism based on kin selection is the enemy of civilization. If human beings are to a large extent guided to favor their own relatives and tribe, only a limited amount of global harmony is possible.
—E. O. Wilson, 1978

Does kin selection operate in humans as well? Are we more likely to help those who share our genes? According to J. Philippe Rushton (1989), the answer is yes. It seems reasonable to suggest that you would be more likely to put your life in jeopardy by running into a burning building to save a child who was your son or daughter, as opposed to a total stranger. Rushton (1989) argues that we can recognize genetic similarity in nonrelatives as well. For example, many genes have physical markers that are easily observable (e.g., hair, eye, and skin color), allowing people who share them to recognize each other and give preferential treatment—such as by offering help. Rushton (1989) goes so far as to suggest that conflict between different ethnic groups may have a genetic basis, stemming in part from evolutionary pressures to help only those who can pass along our genes. One problem with this explanation of prosocial behavior, however, is that it has difficulty explaining why complete strangers sometimes help each other, even when there is no reason for them to assume that they share some of the same genes. For example, it seems extremely unlikely that Lenny Skutnik dove into the Potomac to save Priscilla Triado because he calculated on the spot that she shared enough of his genes to be worth saving.

To explain why people sometimes help strangers, sociobiologists point to another reason people help: the **norm of reciprocity.** This is the idea that people help others with the understanding that such behavior will be reciprocated at some point in the future. Sociobiologists suggest that as humans were evolving, a group of completely selfish individuals, each living in his or her own cave, would have found it more difficult to survive than a group who had learned to cooperate with each other. Of course, if people cooperated too readily, they might have been exploited by an adversary who never helped in return. Those who were most likely to survive, the argument goes, were people who developed an understanding with their neighbors about reciprocity: "I will help you now, with the agreement that when I need help, you will return the favor." Because of its survival value, such a norm of reciprocity may have become genetically based.

In sum, sociobiologists believe that people help others because of two factors that have become ingrained in our genes: kin selection and the norm of reciprocity. Sociobiology is a challenging and creative approach to understanding prosocial behavior, though it is important to note that not all psychologists accept its claims. Many are skeptical of the claim that all social behaviors can be traced back to our ancestral roots, becoming instilled in our genes because of their survival value, and this view is hotly debated (Economos, 1969; Gangestad, 1989). We turn now to other motives behind prosocial behavior that do not necessarily originate in our genes.

**norm of reciprocity:** the assumption that others will treat us the way we treat them (e.g., if we help someone, he or she will help us)

## Social Exchange: The Costs and Rewards of Helping

Though many social psychologists disagree with sociobiological approaches to prosocial behavior, they share the view that altruistic behavior can be based on self-interest. In fact, a principal theory in social psychology, **social exchange theory,** argues that much of what we do stems from the desire to maximize our rewards and minimize our costs (Homans, 1961; Thibaut & Kelley, 1959). The difference from sociobiological approaches is that there is neither an attempt to trace this desire back to our evolutionary roots nor an assumption that the desire is genetically based. We reviewed this theory in

**social exchange theory:** the theory that social relationships are best understood by people's desire to maximize their benefits and minimize their costs

According to social exchange theory, people help others if the rewards outweigh the costs (presumably, this is true for the helper in the left photograph). According to sociobiological theory, prosocial behavior occurs in part because of kin selection, as in the photograph on the right where a young woman helps her little brother.

some depth in Chapter 10, on interpersonal attraction, and thus will only summarize it here. Social exchange theorists assume that a basic aspect of human nature is to look out for one's own interests. Just as people in an economic marketplace try to maximize the ratio of their monetary profits to their monetary losses, so do people, in their relationships with others, try to maximize the ratio of social rewards to social costs.

This does not mean that we keep a little notebook handy, entering a plus or minus each time our friends do something good or bad. Social exchange theory does argue, however, that we keep track, at a more implicit level, of the rewards and costs in social relationships. What might these costs and rewards be in a helping situation? Irving Piliavin, Judith Rodin, and Jane Piliavin (1969) have succinctly outlined the issues at stake for a potential help-giver (Piliavin, Piliavin, and Rodin, 1975; Piliavin, Dovidio, Gaertner, and Clark, 1982). As described in Table 11.1, the rewards are both psychological and practical, and so are the costs. The rewards for helping are quite easy to think of—we feel good about ourselves, others think well of us, we've done "the right thing," and so on—but the importance of Table 11.1 is to remind us that costs are involved as well. When Lenny Skutnik dove into the freezing river to save the drowning passenger of Flight 90, he placed himself in direct physical danger. We would expect that it crossed his mind, as he tore off his coat and boots, that he was about to do something very dangerous. However, it appears that for Skutnik, the rewards of helping (e.g., feeling good about himself) as well as the costs of not helping (e.g., having to stand by and watch a person die) outweighed the potential costs to himself of helping.

Social exchange theorists describe helping behavior as rewarding in three ways. First is the concept of reciprocity, the idea that we should do unto others as they do unto us. Helping someone is an investment in the future,

## Costs and Rewards Theory

| | FOR HELPING | FOR NOT HELPING |
|---|---|---|
| **COSTS** | Short-term loss of time (e.g., late to appointment)<br><br>Long-term loss of time (e.g., court appearance)<br><br>Potential injury to self, immediate (e.g., in assault case)<br><br>Legal liability if injured person further hurt by self<br><br>Person who was aided becomes dependent on self<br><br>Potential injury to self, long-term (e.g., assailant seeks revenge) | Loss of self-esteem<br><br>Social disapproval from witnesses who helped<br><br>Legal liability (in some states, person who knows first aid must help or risk suit)<br><br>Not helping promoted, increasing the likelihood oneself will not be helped |
| **REWARDS** | Improved self-esteem<br><br>Social approval by witnesses<br><br>Avoidance of legal liability for failure to help<br><br>Helping behavior promoted<br><br>Monetary rewards available in some cities<br><br>Favorable publicity for self in some cases<br><br>Criminals brought to justice in some cases | Avoidance of short-term time loss<br><br>Avoidance of long-term time loss<br><br>Avoidance of injury to self, immediate<br><br>Avoidance of injury to self, long-term<br><br>Avoidance of dependency by victim<br><br>Avoidance of liability for further harming victim |

**TABLE 11.1  The costs and rewards of helping.** While we typically think of helping behavior in terms of its rewards, costs too are involved. Piliavin, Rodin, and Piliavin (1969) have outlined the costs and rewards of *helping* versus the costs and rewards of *not helping*. According to social exchange theory, we help only when the perceived rewards outweigh the perceived costs. (Adapted from Piliavin, Rodin, and Piliavin, 1969)

> Let him who neglects to raise the fallen, fear lest, when he falls, no one will stretch out his hand to lift him up.
> —Saadi (1184–1291)

the social exchange being that someday, someone will help you when you need it. If this sounds a bit farfetched or even naive, think about how deeply this idea permeates our society on both a secular and religious level. Being a good person and treating others with compassion (and receiving such treatment in return) are the hallmark of a civilized society, part of what early philosophers called the social contract. Few of us would want to live in a "dog-eat-dog" society; we need to believe that kindness will be reciprocated, at least some of the time.

A second reason that helping is rewarding is that it relieves the personal distress of the bystander. There is considerable evidence that people are aroused and disturbed when they see another person suffer, and that they help at least in part to relieve their distress (Dovidio, Piliavin, Gaertner, Schroeder, and Clark, 1991; Eisenberg & Fabes, 1991). Thus, helping is often rewarding because it decreases the discomfort and anguish we feel when someone in our presence is suffering.

In 1992, a white truck driver named Reginald Denny was driving through South Central Los Angeles just as the riots broke out. Two black males pulled Denny from his truck; they beat him, kicked him, and hit him in the head repeatedly with a fire extinguisher. A news crew flying overhead in a helicopter filmed the entire attack—but did nothing to stop it or to aid the victim. Left for dead in the street, Denny was saved by a black couple who drove by in the midst of the riot. They pulled Denny into their car, covering him with a blanket so no one could detect his race, and sped off to the hospital. Think about how social exchange theory would describe the costs and rewards of helping for the news crew and the couple.

Finally, helping is rewarding because it allows an individual to obtain recognition and positive feedback at low cost. As we have seen, the decision about whether to help someone can involve a calculated consideration of the costs and benefits of doing so (Dovidio et al., 1991). Helping decreases when the costs are high, as when it would result in pain or embarrassment. Helping increases if the rewards are high, as when it would result in praise from others, or if the helper can obtain the gratification of seeing how beneficial his or her help was (Smith, Keating, and Stotland, 1989).

In sum, social exchange theory challenges the idea that prosocial behavior reflects **altruism**—that is, behavior prompted by a concern for the welfare of others, with no thoughts about oneself. According to the theory, such altruism does not exist. People help when it is in their interests to do so, but not when the costs outweigh the benefits.

If you are like many of our students, you may be experiencing discomfort over this view of helping behavior, finding it to be a rather cynical portrayal of human nature. Is true altruism, motivated only by the desire to help someone else, really such a mythical act? Must we trace all prosocial behavior back to the self-interest of the helper? Such a view seems to demean prosocial behavior. When someone behaves generously, as by saving another person's life or donating a huge sum to charity, should we reduce it to a mere act of self-interest that deserves no plaudits or praise?

**altruism:** any act that benefits another person but does not benefit the helper, and often involves some personal cost to the helper

What seems to be generosity is often no more than disguised ambition.
—La Rochefoucauld, 1678

Well, a social exchange theorist might reply, there are many ways in which people can obtain gratification, and we should be thankful that one way is by helping others. After all, wealthy people could decide to get their pleasure only from lavish vacations, expensive cars, and gourmet meals at fancy restaurants. We should applaud their decision to give money to the disadvantaged, even if, ultimately, it is just another way for them to obtain gratification. Prosocial acts are doubly rewarding, in that they help both the giver and the recipient of the aid. Thus, it is to everyone's advantage to promote and praise such acts. Still, many people are dissatisfied with the argument that all helping stems from self-interest. How can it explain why people give up their lives for others, as in the passing of the rope by the unknown hero of Air Florida Flight 90? According to some social psychologists, people do have hearts of gold, helping only for the sake of helping—as we will see now.

### Empathy and Altruism: The Pure Motive for Helping

C. Daniel Batson (1991) is the strongest proponent of the idea that people often help purely out of the goodness of their hearts. Batson does not deny that sometimes we help for selfish reasons. But, he argues, as long as we feel **empathy** for the person in need of help—that is, if we experience some of the pain and suffering the person is experiencing—we will help, regardless of whether it is in our interests to do so. Suppose, for example, that you are grocery-shopping one day. As you walk down the cereal aisle, you see a man holding a baby and a bag full of diapers, toys, and rattles. As the man

**empathy:** the ability to put oneself in the shoes of another person—to experience events and emotions (e.g., joy and sadness) the way that person experiences them

This touching story of early hominid prosocial behavior is intriguing to interpret via our three theories of helping behavior. *Sociobiological theory* would argue that the caregivers helped the dwarf because he was a relative; however, since dwarfism in this early population would be genetically problematic, the theory would also suggest that the individual would not receive aid. *Social exchange theory* would maintain that the dwarf's caregivers received sufficient rewards from their actions so as to outweigh the costs of caring for him. And the *empathy-altruism hypothesis* would hold that the caregivers helped out of strong feelings of empathy and compassion for him—an interpretation supported by the article's final paragraph.

## Study: Cavemen helped disabled

United Press International
NEW YORK—The skeleton of a dwarf who died about 12,000 years ago indicates that cave people cared for physically disabled members of their communities, a researcher said yesterday.

The skeleton of the 3-foot-high youth was initially discovered in 1963 in a cave in southern Italy but was lost to anthropologists until American researcher David W. Frayer reexamined the remains and reported his findings in the British journal Nature.

Frayer, a professor of anthropology at the University of Kansas at Lawrence, said in a telephone interview that the youth "couldn't have taken part in normal hunting of food or gathering activities so

he was obviously cared for by others."

Archaeologists have found the remains of other handicapped individuals who lived during the same time period, but their disabilities occurred when they were adults, Frayer said.

"This is the first time we've found someone who was disabled since birth . . . .", Frayer said. He said there was no indication that the dwarf, who was about 17 at the time of his death, had suffered from malnutrition or neglect.

He was one of six individuals buried in the floor of a cave and was found in a dual grave in the arms of a woman, about 40 years old.

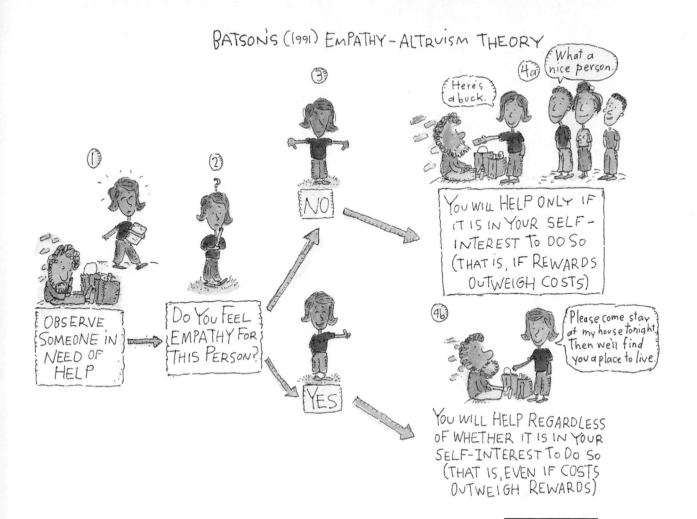

**FIGURE 11.1 Batson's (1991) empathy-altruism theory.**

reaches for a box of Wheaties, he loses his grip on the bag, and all of its contents spill on the floor. Will you stop and help him pick up his things? According to Batson's **empathy-altruism hypothesis**, it depends first on whether you feel empathy for him. If you do—if the man looks distressed or embarrassed, and watching him makes you feel the same way—you will help, regardless of what you have to gain.

What if you do not feel empathy? If, for whatever reason, you do not share the man's distress or embarrassment, then, Batson says, social exchange concerns come into play. What's in it for you? If there is something to be gained, such as obtaining approval from the man or from onlookers, then you will help the man pick up his things. If you will not profit from helping, you will go on your way without stopping. Batson's empathy-altruism hypothesis is summarized in Figure 11.1. When we feel empathy for another person, we help in order to relieve the other person's suffering, without regard to our self-interest; this is the truly altruistic response. When we do not feel empathy, we help only out of self-interest—that is, because we gain some reward that outweighs any cost involved.

One problem with this view is trying to identify exactly which motive is at work. If you saw someone else help the man pick up his possessions, how

**empathy-altruism hypothesis:** the theory holding that when we feel empathy for a person, we will attempt to help him or her, regardless of what we have to gain

> It is a feeling common to all mankind that they cannot bear to see others suffer . . . . This feeling of distress (at the suffering of others) is the first sign of humanity
> —Mencius, fourth century B.C.

could you tell whether he or she was acting out of empathic concern or to gain some sort of social reward? Consider a famous story about Abraham Lincoln. One day, while riding in a coach, Lincoln and a fellow passenger were debating the very question we are considering: Is helping ever truly altruistic? Lincoln argued that helping always stems from self-interest, whereas the other passenger took the view that true altruism exists. As the men discussed this issue, they were interrupted by the screeching of a sow, whose piglets were stuck in a creek and were in danger of drowning. Lincoln promptly called out, "Driver, can't you stop for just a moment?" He jumped out of the coach, ran down to the creek, and lifted the piglets to the safety of the bank. When he returned, his companion said, "Now, Abe, where does selfishness come in on this little episode?" "Why, bless your soul, Ed," Lincoln replied. "That was the very essence of selfishness. I should have had no peace of mind all day had I gone on and left that suffering old sow worrying over those pigs. I did it to get peace of mind, don't you see?" (Sharp, 1928)

As this example shows, an act that seems truly altruistic is sometimes motivated by self-interest. So how can we tell which is which? Daniel Batson and his colleagues have devised some clever experiments to unravel people's motives (Batson, Duncan, Ackerman, Buckley, and Birch, 1981). Imagine you were a participant in one of them. You learn that the study is about how well people perform a task under stressful conditions. There are two participants, you and a student named Elaine. One of you will be asked to memorize some numbers, for ten different trials, while receiving electric shocks. The other will play the role of an observer, watching the study over closed-circuit television. You draw lots, and find that you will be the observer.

As you watch the TV, you see the experimenter attach electrodes to Elaine's arm. As she starts to get the shocks, she grimaces and jerks her body, and it is obvious that Elaine finds the shocks to be very unpleasant. Soon the experimenter stops the procedure, and suggests to Elaine that they end the experiment. Elaine says that even though she is finding the shocks to be extremely unpleasant, she is willing to go on. Then the experimenter has an idea: Would the observer—you—be willing to help by trading places with Elaine? The experimenter enters your room, says you are under no obligation to trade places, but asks if you would be willing to do so. What would you do?

As you have probably guessed, this experiment was designed not to study memory, but to see whether people agreed to help Elaine (who was an accomplice of the experimenter). No one really received electric shocks. The question was, under what conditions would people help? Batson and his colleagues pitted two motives against each other—self-interest and empathy—in the following ways. First, they varied how costly it would be to fail to help Elaine. Half the participants were told that they would have to watch only the first two memory trials, and the experimenter interrupted the procedure during the second trial. In this condition, then, people thought they would not have to watch Elaine receive any more shocks, even if they refused to trade places with her. The other participants were told that they would have to watch all the trials. In this latter condition, it was more in people's self-interest to help, because if they refused to trade places, they would have to sit there and watch Elaine suffer through eight more trials, knowing that they could have prevented her discomfort. In other words, when there was an easy escape—the participants wouldn't have to watch Elaine receive shocks—there was less cost to their decision not to help her; they could go on their way without feeling much guilt or discomfort. However, when they had to watch all the trials, it was more in their self-interest to help, in order to avoid the unpleasantness of watching Elaine suffer.

According to the empathy-altruism hypothesis, such self-rewards should come into play only when people do not feel much empathy for Elaine (see Figure 11.1). When empathy is high, people should be motivated by genuine altruistic concerns, helping regardless of what is in it for them. To test this hypothesis, Batson varied how much empathy people felt, by altering how similar people thought Elaine was to them. Half the participants discovered, from reading a questionnaire Elaine had filled out, that her personal values and interests were similar to theirs. The others discovered that her values and interests were the opposite of theirs. Batson reasoned that those who thought Elaine was similar to them would feel more empathy for her than those who thought she was different from them.

As you can see in Table 11.2, the results were exactly as predicted by the altruism-empathy hypothesis. When people felt a lot of empathy for Elaine— that is, when they believed she was similar to them—almost everyone agreed to trade places, relieving her of the need to receive shocks by agreeing to take the shocks themselves. Most importantly, they agreed to help regardless of whether it was easy or difficult to escape the situation, suggesting that people were motivated more by a concern for Elaine than by their own self-interest. What about when empathy was low? Here, as Batson suggests, social exchange concerns came into play. Most people helped when it was in their interest to do so—namely, when they thought they could not escape having

| Altruism versus Self-Interest | | |
| --- | --- | --- |
| | **EMPATHY FOR ELAINE** | |
| | **Low** | **High** |
| Ease of escape from watching her suffer | | |
| **Easy** | 18% | 91% |
| **Difficult** | 64% | 82% |

**TABLE 11.2 Proportion of those helping.** What percentage of people agreed to trade places with Elaine, taking the shocks themselves? As predicted by the empathy-altruism hypothesis outlined in Figure 11.1, it depended on how much empathy people felt for her and on how rewarding it was to help. When empathy was high (when people viewed Elaine as similar to themselves), they helped regardless of the rewards for them (how easy it was to escape). When empathy was low, people were more concerned with the rewards and costs for them—they helped only if they could not escape having to watch her suffer through the next several trials. (Adapted from Batson et al., 1981)

*Drawing by Maslin; © 1992 The New Yorker Magazine, Inc.*

*"Just seeing you happy is my reward—I'm not
in it for the biscuits."*

to watch Elaine suffer through the next eight trials. When there were no costs for them—when they did not have to watch Elaine take the shocks—few people agreed to trade places with her.

This study by Batson and his colleagues (1981) illustrates that true altruism can exist. Indeed, the empathy-altruism approach is the only one that can explain extreme acts of self-sacrifice, such as the incredible generosity of the unknown hero of Air Florida Flight 90. Neither the sociobiological nor the social exchange approaches can explain why someone would give up his or her life for a stranger: Such heroic acts obviously lower the chances that the person will propagate his or her genes, and clearly such behavior is not motivated by self-interest.

As illustrated by our example of Abraham Lincoln and the pigs, it can be exceedingly difficult, however, to disentangle people's exact motives when they help someone. Consider those people in the Batson and colleagues (1981) experiment who thought Elaine was similar to them, and thus felt more empathy for her. Was their behavior really untainted by their own interests? Maybe not, according to social psychologist Robert Cialdini (Cialdini et al., 1987). People who thought Elaine was like them liked her more, and might thus have experienced greater sadness at the thought that she would suffer. Consequently, they might have been motivated by the egoistic desire to relieve their sadness, not by a completely altruistic concern for Elaine. Just as Abe Lincoln sought peace of mind by helping the pigs, those who felt empathy for Elaine might have been primarily concerned with relieving their own feelings of guilt and sadness, even if they knew they did not have to watch her suffering.

This possibility—along with other possible selfish motives of people who experience empathy—has led to a lively and spirited debate between social psychologists who endorse the empathy-altruism hypothesis and those who do not (Batson, 1991; Cialdini & Fultz, 1990; Schroeder, Dovidio, Sibicky, Matthews, and Allen, 1988; Shaffer, 1986). In a subsequent series of studies, Batson and his colleagues (1988, 1989) have ruled out many of the alternatives to his empathy-altruism hypothesis that apply to the Elaine study we described. However, just when the research seems to show that genuine altruism exists, other researchers report disconfirming data (e.g., Smith, Keating, and Stotland, 1989). The purity of our motives when we help others is a fascinating question about the fabric of human motivation, and one that social psychologists continue to address.

In summary, we have discussed three basic motives underlying prosocial behavior: the idea that helping is an instinctive reaction to protect and promote the welfare of those genetically similar and that we have evolved genetically to follow the norm of reciprocity (sociobiology); the notion that the rewards of helping outweigh the costs, making it in people's self-interest to help (social exchange theory); and the concept that under some conditions, powerful feelings of empathy and compassion for the victim prompt selfless giving (the empathy-altruism hypothesis). Each of these approaches has vocal proponents and vociferous critics.

It is important to note, however, that whatever the nature of people's basic motives, these motives are not the sole determinants of whether people help, for many personal and situational factors can suppress or trigger these motives. If basic human motives were all there was to it, how could we explain the fact that some people are much more helpful than others? Clearly, we need to consider the personal determinants of prosocial behavior that can override or enhance a desire to help someone. Nor should we ignore situational influences on prosocial behavior. We should not assume that the reason Kitty Genovese's neighbors did not help was that they were selfish, coldhearted people. Was there something about the social situation that night that kept them from helping, even though they were decent, caring human beings? Helping is almost always multidetermined, influenced not only by the kinds of human motives we have just discussed, but also by the personal and situational factors to which we now turn.

## Personal Determinants of Prosocial Behavior: Why Do Some People Help More than Others?

### Individual Differences: The Altruistic Personality

When you read the examples at the beginning of this chapter, did you think about the different personalities of the people involved? It is natural to assume that Kitty Genovese's neighbors happened to be particularly uncaring, heartless people. In comparison, perhaps Lenny Skutnik and the man who passed the rope to his fellow passengers were cut from a different cloth: selfless, caring people who would never dream of ignoring someone's pleas for help. Had they heard Kitty Genovese's screams, she might be alive today. Had Kitty Genovese's neighbors been standing on the shore of the Potomac watching the flight attendant lose hold of the rescue line, perhaps they would have stood there and done nothing, allowing Priscilla Triado to perish. More recently, there have been Mother Teresas who devote their lives to others, and Saddam Husseins who are bent on destruction and mayhem. And, of course, there are lots of people between these extremes of sainthood and wickedness. Social psychologists are very interested in how people develop an altruistic approach to life, as well as the extent to which individual differences in altruism determine prosocial behavior.

> On reflecting at dinner that he had done nothing to help anybody all day, he uttered these memorable and praiseworthy words: "Friends, I have lost a day."
>
> —Suetonius

Adult approval serves as a powerful reward for children when they behave prosocially.

**Instilling Helpfulness with Rewards and Models.** Developmental psychologists have discovered that prosocial behavior occurs early in life. Even children as young as eighteen months frequently help others, by assisting a parent with household tasks or trying to make a crying infant feel better (Rheingold, 1982; Zahn-Waxler, Radke-Yarrow, and King, 1979). One powerful way to encourage prosocial behavior is for parents and others to reward such acts with praise, smiles, and hugs. Several studies suggest that these kinds of rewards do increase altruistic behavior in children (Grusec, 1991). Rewards should not, however, be emphasized too much. If children decide to help others only to obtain praise from their parents, they will not come to view themselves as helpful, altruistic people; instead, they will believe it is valuable to help others only when they can get rewarded for it. The same is true for adults—believing we are helping someone in order to get a reward diminishes our view of ourselves as altruistic, selfless people (Batson, Coke, Jasnoski, and Hanson, 1979; Uranowitz, 1975).

This undermining effect of rewards is identical to the *overjustification effect* we discussed in Chapter 6: Rewarding people too strongly for performing a behavior can lower their intrinsic interest in it, because they come to believe that they are doing it only to get the reward. The trick is to encourage children to act altruistically, but not to be too heavy-handed with rewards. One way of accomplishing this is to tell children, after they have helped, that they did so because they are kind and helpful people. Such comments encourage children to perceive themselves as altruistic people, so that they will help in future situations even when no rewards are forthcoming (Grusec, Kuczynski, Rushton, and Simutis, 1979).

Another way for parents to increase altruism in their children is to behave altruistically themselves. Children often model behaviors they observe in others, including altruistic behaviors (Dodge, 1984; Mussen & Eisenberg-Berg, 1977). Children who observe their parents acting altruistically (e.g., volunteering time to help the homeless) learn that helping others is a valued act. Interviews with people who have gone to great lengths to help others—such as Christians who helped Jews escape from Nazi Germany during World War II, and civil rights activists in this country—indicate that their parents too were dedicated helpers (London, 1973; Rosenhan, 1970).

Children learn prosocial behavior by imitating others, as in this family, where the children help their parents carry in the groceries.

Children imitate other adults, besides their parents. Teachers, relatives, and even television characters can serve as models for children. J. Philippe Rushton (1975) demonstrated this fact in an interesting study of elementary school children. He asked the children to play a bowling game in which they could win tokens. The tokens could be either exchanged for prizes or donated to a needy child named Bobby as part of a "Save the Children" fund. Before playing the game, the children watched an adult—who was said to be a future teacher at the school—play the game. In one condition, the adult kept all the tokens, refusing to donate any to Bobby. In another condition, the adult took half the tokens he or she won and put them in a jar for Bobby. All the children then played the game by themselves, and the researchers kept track of how many tokens the kids donated to Bobby.

The children who watched the generous adult were much more likely to follow suit, donating some of their tokens. Does this finding surprise you? Probably not. The children who saw the generous adult may have felt some pressure to donate, even if they didn't want to. Instead of teaching the kids to be more altruistic, perhaps the generous adult simply made it more difficult for them to act selfishly in that one situation. For example, has someone ever asked you to donate money—say, to buy a collective birthday present for an acquaintance? You might not have really wanted to chip in, but if everyone else was donating, you probably felt pressured to throw in a few dollars too.

Rushton (1975) conducted a second phase of his experiment to demonstrate that the children who saw the generous adult became more genuinely altruistic themselves. Two months after the first session, a different experimenter took the children to a room and left them to play the bowling game again. This time, they could choose to keep the tokens they won or donate some to a different charity—namely, a fund for starving Asian children. The kids who had seen the adult give tokens to Bobby two months earlier gave more of their tokens to the fund for Asian children than the kids who had seen the adult keep all the tokens did. This suggests that these children came to value altruism for its own sake, causing them to act generously several weeks later in a new situation, where no models were present.

Thus, children are good imitators, and learn what is a valued and desired act from observing other people. Is this kind of modeling limited to prosocial behavior? You may be wondering if children also imitate people they see acting aggressively and violently, such as their favorite characters on television. We will see in the next chapter, on aggression, that such modeling does indeed occur.

**Is Personality the Whole Story?**    As we have just seen, parents and other adults can influence how altruistic a child becomes. We should be careful, however, about the kinds of conclusions we draw from this fact. True, some people have learned to be more altruistic than others. We can all think of people who are consistently helpful, such as our saintly Aunt Sarah, who always puts other people's needs ahead of her own, or our cousin Tom, who has just joined the Peace Corps. But this does not mean that when we want to predict how helpful someone will be, all we need to know is how much of an altruistic personality he or she has. If this were all there was to it, then we should be able to divide the world into different types of people: helpers, who regularly come to the aid of their fellow humans, regardless of the situation, and selfish people, who consistently sit on their duffs when others need help.

As we saw in Chapter 1, however, people's personalities are not the sole determinant of how they behave. According to social psychologists, to understand human behavior—such as how altruistically people will behave in a given situation—we need to consider the situational pressures impinging on them. Predicting how altruistically people will behave is no exception to the rule. Consider, for example, a classic study by Hugh Hartshorne and Mark May (1929). They observed how altruistic 10,000 elementary and high school students were in a variety of situations, including the students' willingness to find stories and pictures to give to hospitalized children, donate money to charity, and give small gifts to needy children. If personality differences are all there is to it, then we should expect to see a good deal of consistency in how each child acted in these different situations. If Nicole is one of those people with an **altruistic personality,** she should be more likely than the others to be altruistic in all the situations. If Philip tends to be self-centered, then he should be less willing than the others to do any of the altruistic acts. Makes sense, doesn't it?

Surprisingly, the extent to which the children acted altruistically in one situation (e.g., finding many stories and pictures for the hospitalized children) was not highly related to how altruistically they acted in another. The average correlation between helping in one situation and helping in another was only .23. This means that if you knew how altruistic a child was in one situation, you could not predict with much confidence how altruistic he or she would be in another. Moreover, researchers who have studied both children and adults have not found much evidence that people with high scores on personality tests of altruism are more likely to help than those with lower scores.

Does this mean that any two people we pick off the street—be they Mother Teresa or Saddam Hussein—are equally likely to help the survivors of a plane crash or a neighbor who is seriously ill? Of course not. It's just that individual differences in personality are not all we need to know when trying to predict how altruistically someone will behave. We need also to know several other critical factors, such as what mood the person is in and what kinds of situational pressures are impinging on the person. Even Mother Teresa is probably more likely to help in some situations than in others. And surely Saddam Hussein is not always evil—perhaps some situations are more likely to bring out his diabolic nature than others.

**altruistic personality:** those aspects of a person's makeup which are said to make him or her likely to help others in a wide variety of situations

In short, to predict how altruistic someone will be, it is most useful to know a lot about his or her personality and the nature of the situation he or she is in. Several studies have demonstrated that certain kinds of people are more likely to help in some situations, whereas other kinds of people are more likely to help in other situations (e.g., Batson, Bolen, Cross, and Neuringer-Benefiel, 1986; Clark, Ouellette, Powell, and Milberg, 1987; Deutsch & Lamberti, 1986). Consider, for example, how helpful you think people would be in these two situations: (a) People are standing on the shores of the Potomac, watching the rescue of Flight 90, and see Priscilla Triado lose hold of the rescue line, and (b) a retarded boy befriends a neighbor, and asks the neighbor to take him to the movies. Who is most likely to help in the first situation, and who is most likely to help in the second situation?

## Gender Differences in Prosocial Behavior

According to a recent review by Alice Eagly and Maureen Crowley (1986; Eagly, 1987), who focused on differences in helping between males and females, the answer is males in the first situation, and females in the second situation. In virtually all cultures, there are different norms for males and females, so that men and women learn to value different traits and behaviors. In Western cultures, part of the male sex role is to be chivalrous and heroic, whereas part of the female sex role is to be nurturant and caring, valuing close, long-term relationships. As a result, we might expect men to help more in situations that call for brief chivalrous and heroic acts, such as Lenny Skutnik's decision to dive into the Potomac and save Priscilla Triado, and women to help more in long-term relationships that involve less danger but more commitment, such as volunteering at a nursing home.

In a review of more than 170 studies on helping behavior, Eagly and Crowley (1986) found that men are indeed more likely to help in chivalrous, heroic ways. For example, of the 7,000 people who received medals from the Carnegie Hero Fund Commission, for risking their lives to save a stranger, 91 percent of them have been men. Social psychologists have been remiss in not studying helping in long-term, nurturant relationships as much as they have the chivalrous, heroic kind. There is evidence, however, that women are more likely to make long-term commitments to help in this way, such as volunteering to help a retarded child (Otten et al., 1988; Smith, Wheeler, and Diener, 1975).

## The Effects of Mood on Helping: Feel Good, Do Good

Another reason personality alone is an insufficient predictor of people's helping behavior is that helping depends on a person's current mood. Sometimes we're in a great mood, sometimes a lousy one, and these transitory emotional states are another key determinant of prosocial behavior. For example, imagine you are at your local shopping mall. As you walk from one store to another, a fellow in front of you suddenly drops a manila folder, and papers go fluttering in all directions. He looks around with some dismay, then bends down and starts picking up the papers. Would you stop and help him? What do you think the average shopper would do? One way to answer this question is to think about how many altruistic people there are in the world (or at least in shopping malls). But as we have just seen, it is not

> Both men and women belie their nature when they are not kind.
> —Gamaliel Bailey (1807–59)

Whereas men are more likely to perform chivalrous and heroic acts, women are more likely to be helpful in long-term relationships that involve greater commitment.

enough to consider only differences in personality. The mood people happen to be in at the time can strongly affect their behavior—in this case, whether or not they will offer help.

Alice Isen and Paul Levin (1972) explored the effect of mood on prosocial behavior in shopping malls in San Francisco and Philadelphia. They boosted the mood of shoppers in a clever way—namely, by leaving dimes in the coin-return slot of a pay telephone at the mall—and waited for someone to find them. (Remember the year this study was done—it would be like finding a quarter today.) As the lucky shoppers left the phone with their newly found dime, an assistant of Isen and Levine played the role of the man with the manila folder. He purposefully dropped the folder a few feet in front of the shopper, to see whether he or she would stop and help him pick up his papers. It turned out that finding the dime had a dramatic effect on helping. When people left a phone that had not been planted with a dime, only 4 percent of them helped the man pick up his papers. In comparison, when people found a dime in the coin-return slot, fully 84 percent of them helped.

Researchers have found this "feel good, do good" effect in diverse situations, and have shown that it is not limited to the little boost we get when we find some money. People are more likely to help others when they are in a good mood for a number of reasons, including doing well on a test, receiving a gift, thinking happy thoughts, and listening to pleasant music. And when people are in a good mood, they are more helpful in many ways, including contributing money to charity, helping someone find a lost contact lens, tutoring another student, and donating blood (Carlson, Charlin, and Miller, 1988; Salovey, Mayer, and Rosenhan, 1991).

What is it about being in a good mood that makes people more altruistic? It turns out that good moods can increase helping for three reasons. First, good moods make us look on the bright side of life. If you saw the man drop his manila folder full of papers, you could view this incident in at least two ways. "What an idiot," you might think. "This guy is really clumsy. I'll just let him clean up his own mess." Or you might have more sympathy for him, thinking, "Oh, that's too bad. I bet he was in a hurry and lost his grip. The poor guy; he probably feels terrible." When we are in a good mood, we tend to see the good side of other people, giving them the benefit of the doubt. A victim who might normally seem clumsy or annoying will, when we are feeling cheerful, seem like a decent, needy person who is worthy of our help (Forgas & Bower, 1987; Carlson, Charlin, and Miller, 1988).

Second, "feel good, do good" occurs because it is an excellent way of prolonging our good mood. If we see someone in need of help, then being a Good Samaritan will spawn even more good feelings, and we can walk away continuing to feel like a million bucks. In comparison, not helping when we know we should is a surefire "downer," deflating our good mood (Clark & Isen, 1982; Isen, 1987; Williamson & Clark, 1989).

Finally, good moods increase self-attention. As we noted in Chapters 6 and 9, at any given time people vary in how much attention they pay to their feelings and values versus the world around them. Sometimes we are particularly attuned to our internal worlds, and sometimes we are not. Good moods increase the amount of attention we pay to ourselves, which in turn makes us more likely to behave according to our values and ideals. Because most of us value altruism, and because good moods increase our attention to this value, good moods increase helping behavior (Berkowitz, 1987; Carlson, Charlin, and Miller, 1988; Salovey & Rodin, 1985).

**Negative-State Relief: Feel Bad, Do Good.** What about when we are in a bad mood? Suppose that when you saw the fellow in the mall drop his folder, you were feeling down in the dumps. Would this influence the likelihood that you would help the man pick up his papers? One kind of bad mood clearly leads to an increase in helping: feeling guilty. People often act on the idea that good deeds cancel out bad deeds. When they have done something that has made them feel guilty, helping another person balances things out, reducing their guilty feelings. For example, Mary Harris and her colleagues found that churchgoers were more likely to donate money to charities before attending confession than afterward, presumably because confessing to a priest reduced their guilt (Harris, Benson, and Hall, 1975). Thus, if you just realized you had forgotten your best friend's birthday, and felt guilty about it, you would be more likely to help the fellow in the mall to repair your guilty feelings.

But suppose you just had a fight with a friend, or just found out you did poorly on a test, and were feeling sad and blue. Given that feeling happy leads to greater helping, it might seem that feeling sad will decrease helping. Surprisingly, however, sadness can also lead to an increase in helping, at least under certain conditions (Carlson & Miller, 1987; Salovey et al., 1991). Because helping is rewarding and makes us feel good, it can lift us out of the doldrums. If people are in a bad mood—say, they just broke up with their romantic partner—they often offer help to someone to improve their mood (Cialdini & Fultz, 1990; Cialdini, Schaller, Houlihan, Arps, Fultz, and Beaman, 1987).

This view, called the **negative-state relief hypothesis** by Robert Cialdini (Cialdini et al., 1973), is an example of the social exchange theory approach to helping that we discussed earlier. People help someone else with the goal

**negative-state relief hypothesis:** the idea that people help in order to alleviate their own sadness and distress

of helping themselves—namely, to relieve their own sadness and distress. This is pretty obvious if we help in a way that deals with the cause of our sadness. If our best friend is depressed, we might feel a little depressed as well. As a result, we might bake our friend a batch of cookies. If this cheers up our friend, we have alleviated the cause of our own sadness. Cialdini argues, however, that when we feel blue we are also more likely to help in some totally unrelated way. If we are feeling down because our best friend is unhappy, we are more likely to donate money to a charity. The warm glow of helping the charity reduces our gloom, even though the charity and our friend's unhappiness are unrelated.

If the negative-state relief hypothesis is true, then it should be possible to show that people in a bad mood will not be extra helpful if they can repair their moods in some other way. Imagine, for example, that you were a participant in a study by Robert Cialdini, Betty Lee Darby, and Joyce Vincent (1973). The experimenter greets you and takes you to a graduate student's office. When she pulls out a chair for you, three boxes of computer cards come crashing down, spilling all over the floor. "Oh no!" she says. "I think it's the data from Tom's master's thesis! And I know he doesn't have time to put the cards back in order because he's studying for his qualifying exams" (Cialdini et al., 1973, p. 507).

At this point, you are probably feeling a bit distressed. Even though it wasn't your fault that the cards spilled onto the floor, you probably feel bad for this guy, Tom. You and the experimenter pick up the cards as best you can, but it is clear they are hopelessly out of order. The experimenter then goes on with the study, asking you to rate some photographs. When she leaves to get your research participation credit slip, another experimenter enters the room. "Oh," she says. "Isn't Betty here? I'm in the same class she's in and she said it would be all right if I asked her subjects to help me out with my class project." She explains that she needs people to help her do a telephone survey. "I can't give you any experimental credit for doing this," she says, "but I would appreciate your help. Would you make some interview calls for me? Any number of calls up to 15 would help" (Cialdini et al., 1973, p. 507). What would you say?

As you have probably gathered, Cialdini and his colleagues were interested in how much people would help the second experimenter after experiencing the distress of seeing Tom's computer cards spilled all over the floor. To find out, they also included a condition where the experimenter did not spill the cards. In this condition, people agreed to make an average of about three calls for the second experimenter. As predicted by the negative-state relief hypothesis, those who saw the cards spill (and were thus feeling a little bad) helped even more, agreeing to make more than twice as many calls (see Figure 11.2). But how can we be sure they did so to repair their distress at seeing Tom's cards spilled on the floor? The researchers reasoned that if people could repair their mood in some other way, they would not have to repair it by helping the second experimenter. To test this hypothesis, they included a third condition, where people saw Tom's cards spilled but then were rewarded for doing the first experiment: The first experimenter gave them $1, in appreciation for completing her study. Then the second experimenter came in and asked them to help her make the phone calls. As Cialdini and his colleagues predicted, getting $1 eliminated participants' need to feel

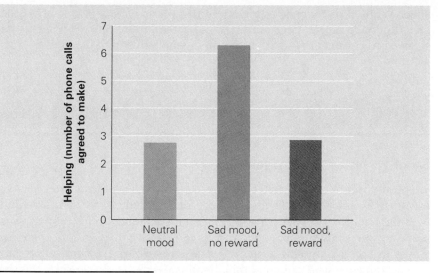

**FIGURE 11.2 The negative-state relief hypothesis.** Does sadness lead to an increase in helping? In this study, it did so only when people's moods were not already repaired by receiving a reward. When people had received no reward, those in a sad mood (middle bar) helped substantially more than those in a neutral mood (left-hand bar). When sad people had received a reward, how-ever, they did not help any more than people in a neutral mood (right-hand bar). (Adapted from Cialdini et al., 1973)

better by helping the second experimenter. Because people's moods were already repaired by getting a surprise payment of money, they didn't need the mood boost they would get from helping (see Figure 11.2).

A potential problem with the negative-relief state hypothesis is its focus on the short-term benefits of helping someone. "I will help only if there are immediate benefits for me," it seems to say—"namely, if it makes me feel good." It is important to point out, however, that sometimes people are more concerned with the long-term benefits of helping than with the imme-diate effects (Salovey et al., 1991). Consider the parent of a young child who is clamoring for attention, demanding to be helped with a difficult puzzle. The parent may be exhausted, wanting nothing more than to drink a cup of coffee and read the newspaper in peace. Stopping to help the child may have few short-term benefits—the coffee gets cold, and the newspaper goes unread. Even when help is momentarily aversive, however, it can reap large long-run rewards. Parents who sit around sipping coffee and reading the newspaper while ignoring their children are less likely to obtain the long-term satisfaction of having a good relationship with their kids. Thus, parents might get down on their knees and play with their children with this long-term goal in mind, enduring the short-term annoyance of being interrupted.

To summarize, in this section we have considered three personal deter-minants of prosocial behavior: personality differences, gender differences, and people's moods. People differ in how altruistic they are, and the way in which they are altruistic, depending on their upbringing, their gender, and their mood. This does not mean, however, that to predict how altruistically people will act, all you need to know is their standing on these three variables. While each contributes a piece to the puzzle of why people help others, they do not complete the picture. To understand more fully why people help, we need to consider the social situation in which they find themselves.

### Rural Versus Urban Environments

Suppose you are riding your bike one day, and as you turn a corner, your front wheel suddenly slams into the side of a pothole, sending you tumbling over the handlebars. You sit there stunned for a moment, then notice a sharp pain in your shin. Sure enough, you have broken your leg, and there is no way you can get up and walk to a phone by yourself. You look around, hoping someone who can give you a hand is nearby. Now consider this question: Where would you rather have this accident—on the main street of a small, rural town, or in the downtown area of a large city? In which place would passersby be more likely to offer you help?

If you said the small town, you are right. Several researchers have compared the likelihood that people will help in rural versus urban areas, and have consistently found that people in rural areas help more (Korte, 1980; Steblay, 1987). Paul Amato (1983), for example, staged an incident where a man limped down the street, suddenly falling down with a cry of pain. The man lifted the leg of his pants, revealing a heavily bandaged shin that was bleeding profusely (with theatrical blood that looked real). In small towns, about half the pedestrians who witnessed this incident stopped and offered the man help. In large cities, however, only 15 percent of such pedestrians stopped and helped. People in small towns have been found to help more in a multitude of ways, including helping a stranger who has had an accident, helping a lost child, giving directions, participating in a survey, and returning a lost letter. The same relationship between size of town and helping has been found in several countries, including the United States, Canada, Israel, Australia, and Turkey (Steblay, 1987).

Why are our chances of being helped greater in small towns? One possibility is that people who grow up in small towns learn to be more neighborly, and that this neighborliness makes them more trusting and altruistic. In comparison, people who grow up in large cities might learn that you can't trust strangers, and that it is often best to mind your own business. Alternatively, it might be something about the urban environment, and not the kinds of values people learned while they were growing up, that causes people to be less likely to help in large cities. Stanley Milgram (1970), for example, argued in his **urban-overload hypothesis** that people living in cities are constantly being bombarded with stimulation, with the result that they keep to themselves so as to avoid being overloaded by it. If you put urban dwellers in a calmer, less stimulating environment, they should be as likely as anyone else to reach out to others.

Interestingly, a review of the literature by Nancy Steblay (1987) supports the view that people's unwillingness to help stems from the urban environment, not from the upbringing people in cities receive. If such unwillingness

> Do not wait for extraordinary circumstances to do good actions; try to use ordinary situations.
> —John Paul Richter (1763–1826)

**urban-overload hypothesis:** the theory suggesting that people living in cities are likely to keep to themselves in order to avoid being overloaded by all the stimulation they receive

People are less helpful in big cities than in small towns, not because of a difference in values, but because the stress of urban life causes them to keep to themselves.

could be explained by the values people learn when growing up, then the key to whether or not people will help should be their birthplace, not the location of the incident providing an opportunity for helping. However, this explanation was found not to hold true in the dozens of studies Steblay reviewed. When an opportunity for helping arises, it matters more whether the incident occurs in a rural or urban area than which kind of person happens to be there. In short, it would be better to have a city slicker witness your bicycle accident in a small town than to have a small-town person witness it in New York City. The hustle and bustle in cities can be so overwhelming that even caring, altruistic people turn inward, responding less to the people around them.

## The Number of Bystanders: The Bystander Effect

Remember Kitty Genovese? We have just seen one reason that her neighbors turned a deaf ear to her cries for help. The murder took place in New York City, one of the most populated areas in the world. Perhaps her neighbors were so overloaded with urban stimulation that they dismissed Genovese's cries as one small addition to the surrounding din. While it is true that people help less in urban environments, this explanation is not the only reason Genovese's neighbors failed to help. Her desperate cries surely must have risen above the everyday noises of garbage trucks and car horns. And there have been cases where people ignored the pleas of their neighbors in small towns. Greenbelt, Maryland, where the woman was raped in front of her neighbor's apartment, has only 16,000 residents.

Bibb Latané and John Darley (1970) are two social psychologists who taught at universities in New York at the time of the Genovese murder. They too were unconvinced that the only reason her neighbors failed to help was the stresses and stimulation of urban life. They focused on the fact that so many people heard her cries. Paradoxically, they thought, it might be that the greater the number of bystanders who observe an emergency, the less

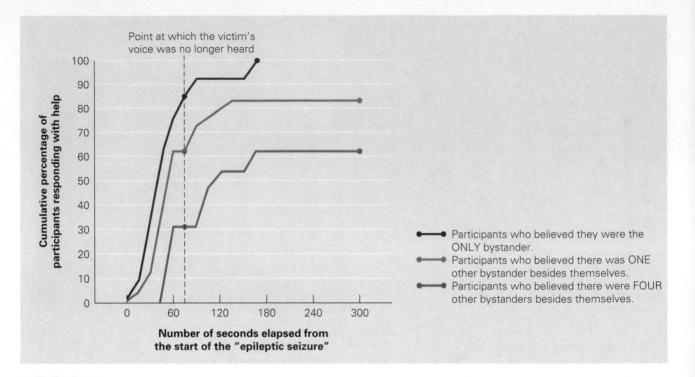

**FIGURE 11.3 Bystander Intervention: The presence of bystanders reduces helping.** When people believed they were the only one witnessing a student having a seizure—when they were the lone bystander—most of them helped him immediately, and all did within a few minutes. When they believed someone else was listening as well—that there were two bystanders—they were less likely to help and did so more slowly. And when they believed four others were listening—that there were five bystanders—they were even less likely to help. (Adapted from Darley & Latané, 1968)

likely any one of them is to help. As Bibb Latané put it, "We came up with the insight that perhaps what made the Genovese case so fascinating was itself what made it happen—namely, that not just one or two, but thirty-eight people had watched and done nothing" (1987, p. 78).

How can this be? Surely, the more people who witness an emergency—such as your hypothetical bicycle accident—the greater one's chance of receiving help. In a series of now-classic experiments, Latané and Darley (1970) found that just the opposite was true: In terms of receiving help, there is no safety in numbers. Think back to the seizure experiment we discussed in Chapter 2. In this study, people sat in individual cubicles, participating in a group discussion of college life (over an intercom system) with students in other cubicles. One of the other students suddenly had a seizure, crying out, "I could really-er-use some help so if somebody would-er-give me a little h-help-uh-er-er-er-er- c-could somebody-er-er-help-er-uh-uh-uh (choking sounds) . . . I'm gonna die-er-er-I'm . . . gonna die-er-help-er-er-seizure-er (chokes, then quiet)" (Darley & Latané, 1968, p. 379). There was actually only one real participant in the study. The other participants, including the one who had the seizure, were prerecorded voices. The point of the study was to see whether the real participant tried to help the seizure victim, by trying to find him or by summoning the experimenter, or whether, like Kitty Genovese's neighbors, he or she simply sat there and did nothing.

As Latané and Darley anticipated, the answer depended on how many people the participant thought witnessed the emergency. When people believed that they were the only ones listening to the student have the seizure, nearly all of them (85 percent) helped within sixty seconds. By two and a half minutes, 100 percent of the people who thought they were the only bystander had offered assistance (see Figure 11.3). In comparison, when

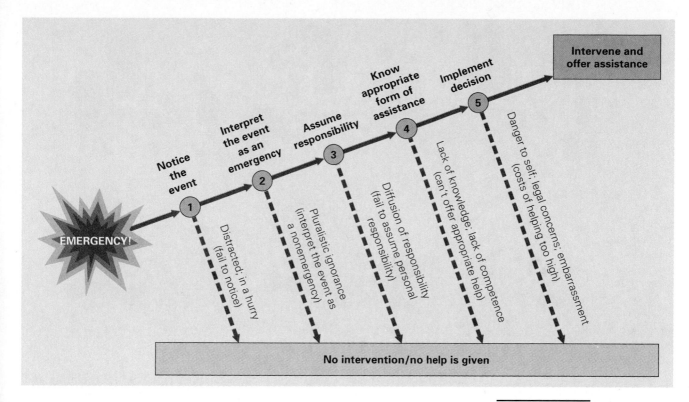

The figure shows a decision tree with the following labels:

EMERGENCY!

1. Notice the event
2. Interpret the event as an emergency
3. Assume responsibility
4. Know appropriate form of assistance
5. Implement decision

Intervene and offer assistance

Reasons for no intervention:
- Distracted; in a hurry (fail to notice)
- Pluralistic ignorance (interpret the event as a nonemergency)
- Diffusion of responsibility (fail to assume personal responsibility)
- Lack of knowledge; lack of competence (can't offer appropriate help)
- Danger to self; legal concerns; embarrassment (costs of helping too high)

No intervention/no help is given

the research participants believed that there was one other student listening, fewer people helped: only 62 percent within sixty seconds. As you can see in Figure 11.3, helping occurred more slowly when there were two bystanders, and never reached 100 percent, even after six minutes, when the experiment was terminated. Finally, when the participants believed there were four other students listening in addition to themselves, the percentage of people who helped dropped even more dramatically. Only 31 percent helped in the first sixty seconds, and after six minutes, only 62 percent had offered help. Dozens of other studies, conducted in the laboratory and in the field, have found the same thing: The greater the number of bystanders who witness an emergency, the less likely any one of them is to help the victim—a phenomenon called the **bystander effect.**

Why is it that people are less likely to help when other bystanders are present? Latané and Darley (1970) developed a step-by-step description of how people decide whether to intervene in an emergency (see Figure 11.4). Part of this description, as we will see, is an explanation of how the number of bystanders can make a difference. But let's begin with the first step—whether people notice that someone needs help.

**Noticing an Event.** Sometimes it is very clear that an emergency has occurred, as in the seizure experiment, where it was obvious that the other student was in danger. Other times, however, it is not so clear. If you are late for an appointment and are hurrying down a crowded street, you might not notice that someone has collapsed in the doorway of a nearby building. Obviously, if people don't notice that an emergency has occurred, they will not intervene and offer to help.

**FIGURE 11.4 Bystander Intervention Decision Tree: Five steps to helping in an emergency.** Latané and Darley (1970) showed that people go through five decision-making steps before they help someone in an emergency. If bystanders fail to take any one of the five steps, they will not help. Each step, as well as the possible reasons for why people decide not to intervene, is outlined above. (Adapted from Latané & Darley, 1970)

**bystander effect:** the finding that the greater the number of bystanders who witness an emergency, the less likely any one of them is to help

*Drawing by B. Tobey; © 1972 The New Yorker Magazine, Inc.*

*"Are you all right, Mister? Is there anything I can do?"*

*"Young man, you're the only one who bothered to stop! I'm a millionaire and I'm going to give you five thousand dollars!"*

What determines whether people notice an emergency? John Darley and C. Daniel Batson (1973) demonstrated that something as seemingly trivial as how much of a hurry people are in can make more of a difference than what kind of person they are. These researchers conducted a study that mirrored the parable of the Good Samaritan, wherein many passersby failed to stop to help a man lying unconscious on the side of the road. The research participants were people we might think would be extremely altruistic: seminary students preparing to devote their lives to the ministry. The students were asked to walk to another building, where the researchers would record them making a brief speech. Some were told that they were late and should hurry to keep their appointment. Others were told that there was no rush, because the assistant in the other building was a few minutes behind schedule. As they walked to the other building, each of the students passed a man who was slumped in a doorway. The man (an accomplice of the experimenters) coughed and groaned as the students each walked by. Did the seminary students stop and offer to help him? If they were not in a hurry, most of them (63 percent) did. If they were hurrying to keep their appointment, however, very few of them (10 percent) did. Many of the students who were in a hurry did not even notice the man.

It is perhaps unsurprising that when people are in a rush, they pay less attention to what's going on around them, making them less likely to help someone in need. What is surprising is that such a seemingly trivial matter as how much of a hurry we are in can overpower the kind of people we are. Darley and Batson (1973) tested the seminary students on a variety of personality measures that assessed how religious they were, and found that people who scored high on these measures were no more likely to help than those who scored low. The researchers also varied the topic of the speech they asked the students to give. Whereas some students were asked to discuss the kinds of jobs seminary students would like to have, others were asked to discuss the parable of the Good Samaritan. It might seem that seminary students who were thinking about the parable of the Good Samaritan would be likely to stop and help a man slumped in a doorway, given the similarity of this incident to the parable. However, the topic of the speech made little difference in whether they helped. If the students were in a hurry, they were unlikely to help, even if they were very religious individuals about to give a speech about the Good Samaritan.

**Interpreting the Event as an Emergency.** Just because people notice someone slumped in a doorway does not mean they will help him or her. The next determinant of helping is whether the bystander interprets the event as an emergency—in other words, as a situation where help is needed (see Figure 11.4). It is often unclear whether an event is an emergency or not. Is the person in the doorway drunk, or seriously ill? If we see white smoke coming out of a vent, is it something innocuous, such as mist from an air conditioner, or a sign that the building is on fire? Is that couple having a particularly loud argument, or is one partner about to beat up the other? If people assume nothing is wrong when an emergency is taking place, obviously they will not help.

Interestingly, people are more likely to assume that an emergency is something innocuous when other bystanders are present. To understand why, think back to our discussion of *informational social influence* in Chapter 7. This type of social influence occurs when we use other people to help us define reality. When we are uncertain about what's going on, such as whether the smoke we see is a sign of a fire, one of the first things we do is look around to see how other people are responding. If other people look up, shrug, and go about their business, we are likely to assume there is nothing to worry about. If other people look panic-stricken and yell "Fire!" we immediately assume the building is indeed on fire. As we saw in Chapter 7, it's often a good strategy to use other people as a source of information when we are uncertain about what's going on. The danger in doing so, however, is that sometimes no one is sure what is happening. Since an emergency by definition is a sudden and confusing event, bystanders tend to freeze, watching and listening with blank expressions as they try to figure out what's going on. When they glance at each other, they see an apparent lack

Emergency situations can be confusing. Does this man need help? Have the bystanders failed to notice him, or has the behavior of the others led each of them to interpret the situation as a non-emergency—an example of pluralistic ignorance?

**pluralistic ignorance:** the phenomenon whereby bystanders assume that nothing is wrong in an emergency, because no one else looks concerned

of concern on the part of everyone else. This state of **pluralistic ignorance,** where bystanders mislead each other by their blank response, leads to the assumption that there must not be any danger, since no one else looks panic-stricken.

Pluralistic ignorance was demonstrated in another classic experiment by Latané and Darley (1970). Imagine that you have agreed to take part in a study of people's attitudes toward the problems of urban life, and arrive at the appointed time. A sign instructs you to fill out a questionnaire while you are waiting for the study to begin. You take a copy of the questionnaire, sit down, and work on it for a few minutes. Then something odd happens: White smoke starts coming into the room through a small vent in the wall. Before long, the room is so filled with smoke that you can barely see the questionnaire. What will you do?

In fact, there was no real danger—the experimenters were pumping smoke into the room to see how people would respond to this potential emergency. Not surprisingly, when people were by themselves, most of them took action. Within two minutes, 55 percent of the participants left the room and found the experimenter down the hall, reporting that there was a potential fire in the building; by four minutes, 75 percent of the participants left the room to alert the experimenter. But what would happen if people were not alone? Given that 75 percent of the participants who were by themselves reported the smoke, it would seem that the larger the group, the greater the likelihood that someone would report the smoke. In fact, this can be figured mathematically: If there is always a 75 percent probability that any one person will report the smoke, then there is a 98 percent chance that at least one person in a three-person group will do so.

To find out if there really is safety in numbers in this situation, Latané and Darley (1970) included a condition in which three participants took part at the same time. Everything was identical, except that three people sat in the room as the smoke began to seep in. Surprisingly, in only 12 percent of the three-person groups did someone report the fire within the first two minutes. After the full six minutes (when the experiment was terminated), in only 38 percent of these groups did someone report the smoke to the experimenter. In the remainder of the groups, the participants sat there filling out questionnaires, even when they had to wave away the smoke with their hands to see what they were writing. What went wrong?

Because it was not clear that the smoke constituted an emergency, the participants used each other as a source of information. If the people next to you glance at the smoke and then go on filling out their questionnaires, you will feel reassured that nothing is wrong; otherwise, why would they be acting so unconcerned? The problem is that they are probably looking at you out of the corner of their eyes, and seeing that you appear to be not overly concerned, they too are reassured that everything is okay. Group members gain false reassurance from each other whenever each person assumes the others know more about what's going on than he or she does. This is particularly likely to happen when the event is ambiguous. If an event is clearly an emergency, as in the case of Kitty Genovese's cries for help, then we do not need to rely on other people to interpret it for us; however, the more ambiguous an event is, the more likely people are to look to each other to define what's going on. As a result, it is in ambiguous situations—such as seeing smoke coming from a vent—that people in groups will be in a state of

Kitty Genovese and the alley in which she was murdered. Ironically, she would probably be alive today had fewer people heard her cries for help.

pluralistic ignorance, convincing each other that nothing is wrong (Clark & Word, 1972; Solomon, Solomon, & Stone, 1978).

**Assuming Responsibility.** Let's say that as a potential help-giver, you have successfully navigated the first two steps in the decision tree (see Figure 11.4): You have noticed something odd, and you have correctly interpreted it as an emergency where help is needed. What's next? Now you must decide that you will help. Even when an emergency clearly exists, people sometimes fail to help. After hearing Kitty Genovese cry out, "Oh my God, he stabbed me! Please help me! Please help me!" (Rosenthal, 1964, p. 33), Genovese's neighbors must have believed that something terrible was happening, and that she was desperately in need of assistance. That they did nothing indicates that even if we interpret an event as an emergency, we have to decide that it is our responsibility—not someone else's—to do something about it. When dealing with issues of personal responsibility, the number of bystanders is again a crucial variable, but for different reasons. Consider the condition in the Latané and Darley (1968) seizure experiment where participants believed they were the only one listening to the student while he had a seizure. The responsibility was totally on their shoulders. If they didn't help, no one would, and the student might die. As a result, in this condition most people helped almost immediately, and all helped within a few minutes.

But what happens when there are many witnesses? Here a **diffusion of responsibility** occurs: Because other bystanders are present, no individual bystander feels a strong sense that it is his or her personal responsibility to take action. Recall from our earlier discussion that helping often entails costs—we can place ourselves in danger; we can risk looking foolish by over-reacting or doing the wrong thing; and so on. Why should we risk these costs

**diffusion of responsibility:** the phenomenon whereby each bystander's sense of responsibility to help decreases as the number of witnesses increases

when many other people who can help are present? The problem is that everyone is likely to feel this way, making all the bystanders less likely to help. This is particularly true if people cannot tell whether someone else has already intervened. When participants in the seizure experiment believed that other students were witnesses as well, they couldn't tell whether another student had already helped, because the intercom system allowed only the voice of the student having the seizure to be transmitted. Each student probably assumed that he or she did not have to help, because surely someone else had already done so. Similarly, Kitty Genovese's neighbors had no way of knowing whether someone else had called the police. Most likely, they assumed that there was no need to do so, because someone else had already made the call. Tragically, everyone assumed that it was somebody else's responsibility to take action, thereby leaving Kitty Genovese to fight her assailant alone. The sad irony of Kitty Genovese's murder is that she probably would be alive today had fewer people heard her cries for help.

**Knowing How to Help.** Even if a person has made it this far in the helping sequence—noticing that an event has occurred, interpreting it as an emergency, and taking responsibility—an additional condition must still be met. The person must decide what form of help is appropriate. Suppose, for example, that you see a woman collapse in the street, and decide she is gravely ill. No one else seems to be helping, so you decide it is up to you. But what should you do? Has the woman had a heart attack? Or did she faint for some other reason? If people don't know what form of assistance to give, obviously they will be unable to help.

**Deciding to Implement the Help.** Finally, even if you know exactly what kind of help is appropriate, there are reasons for why you might decide not to intervene. For one thing, you might not be qualified to deliver the right kind of help. It may be clear, for instance, that the woman has had a heart attack and is in desperate need of CPR, but if you don't know how to administer CPR, you'll be unable to help her. Or you might be afraid of making a fool of yourself, of doing the wrong thing and making matters worse, or even of placing yourself in danger by trying to help. Consider, for example, the fate of three CBS technicians who, in 1982, encountered a man beating a woman in a parking lot on the west side of Manhattan, tried to intervene, and were shot and killed by the assailant. Even when we know what kind of intervention is needed, we have to weigh the costs of trying to help.

In sum, five steps have to be taken before people will intervene in an emergency: They have to notice the event, interpret it as an emergency, decide that it is their responsibility to help, know how to help, and decide to act. If people fail to take any one of these steps, they will not intervene. Given how difficult it can be to take all five steps, it is not surprising that incidents like the Kitty Genovese murder are all too common.

## Characteristics of the Victim

There is one more important aspect of the situation that determines whether or not people will help: who the victim is. If you think back about the times you have been a responsive bystander, you might find that something about the victim made you decide to help. Was the person in need somehow like you?

Let's see how characteristics of the victim affect whether or not help is given.

A basic finding in research on prosocial behavior is that if the victim is similar to us, we are more likely to help. Tim Emswiller and his colleagues (1971), for example, had accomplices in the student union at Purdue University politely ask a fellow student to lend them a dime to make a phone call. At the time this study was done, students could be easily classified, by their hairstyle and dress, as "hippies" (long hair, jeans) or "straights" (short hair, conservative clothes). It turned out that people were more likely to help a student who was similar to themselves: Hippies were more willing to lend a dime to the accomplices dressed as a fellow hippie, whereas straights were more willing to lend a dime to the accomplices dressed as a fellow straight. And it is not just physical appearance that matters. On Election Day, Stuart Karabenick and his colleagues (1973) stationed campaign workers outside polling places. When a voter approached the campaign worker (who was clearly identified as working for either the Republican or the Democratic presidential candidate), the worker dropped a pile of leaflets. The result? Voters who favored the Republican candidate were most likely to stop and help the Republican campaign worker, whereas voters who favored the Democratic candidate were most likely to stop and help the Democratic campaign worker.

Why do people prefer to help those who are similar to themselves? Sociobiologists argue that this is kin selection in action. One clue to the fact that someone shares some of our genes is that the person is physically similar to us (Rushton, 1989). Thus, we prefer to help similar others because doing so promotes the propagation of our genes. Though this argument may have some merit, it seems a bit farfetched to say that hippies and Republicans helped people similar to them because they believed these persons shared many of their genes. There is another, simpler explanation. As we saw in Chapter 10, people have a strong tendency to like others who have similar attitudes. Similarity leads to liking, and people are more motivated to help

We are more likely to offer help to people who are similar to us than dissimilar.

people they like. Not surprisingly, people are not very motivated to come to the aid of people they scorn or hold in contempt.

Does this mean that people are more likely to help a friend than a stranger? After all, we like our close friends, and thus should want to help them the most. As plausible as this sounds, research by Abraham Tesser (1988) on self-esteem maintenance (see Chapter 3) shows that it is true only under certain circumstances. When the task is of little relevance to us, we do indeed help friends more than strangers. But suppose that the most important thing in the world for you is to be a doctor, that you are struggling to pass a difficult premed physics course, and that two other people in the class—your best friend and a complete stranger—ask you to lend them your notes from a class they missed. According to Tesser's research, you will be more inclined to help the stranger than your friend (Tesser & Smith, 1980). Why? Because it hurts to see a close friend do better than us in an area of keen importance to our self-esteem. Consequently, we are less likely to help a friend in these important areas than in those we don't care as much about.

In summary, given the amount of conflict and suffering in the world today, it is critical to understand the conditions under which people will help their fellow humans. We have just seen that it is necessary to consider a number of key aspects of the social situation, including where the incident occurs (in a rural or urban environment), how many bystanders are present, and the relationship between the bystanders and the victim. Taking these factors into account, along with the personal determinants of helping we discussed earlier, allows us to predict with some certainty when people are likely to help and when they are likely to turn their backs on a person in distress.

## What Are the Consequences of Helping?

> I once knew a man out of courtesy help a lame dog over a stile, and [the dog] for requital bit his fingers.
> —William Chillingworth

Is helping always a good thing, an equally positive experience for both the receiver and the giver of help? We saw earlier that there are usually several positive consequences for the helper. For example, helping makes people feel good about themselves, improves their moods, and earns them recognition and praise from others. Indeed, one of the major theories about why people help—social exchange theory—argues that people help only when it is in their best interests to do so. On the other side of the coin, there are obviously benefits to receiving help as well. In extreme cases, help can mean the difference between life and death. And in less dramatic instances, help furthers our progress toward our goals—for example, if we are doing poorly in a course, receiving extra tutoring can mean the difference between passing and failing. Ironically, however, under some conditions helping is more beneficial to the person giving the help than to the person receiving it.

One sign of this fact is that people are often reluctant to ask for help. Many students who are doing poorly in a course struggle on their own, refusing to ask their classmates or the instructor for assistance. People often do not want to be helped, because receiving aid is a two-edged sword: It can further our progress toward our goals, but it can also be damaging to our self-esteem, making us feel inadequate and dependent. Asking for help lets

Receiving help is not always a positive experience. When people very similar to you help you, it may threaten your self-esteem, for example, by making you feel incompetent.

someone know we cannot fend for ourselves. Because people do not want to appear incompetent, they often decide to suffer in silence—even if doing so lowers their chances of successfully completing a task (DePaulo, 1983; Nadler, 1991; Nadler & Fisher, 1986).

Because people are ambivalent about asking for help, they will not always react positively when someone offers them aid. Imagine, for example, that a stranger approaches as you are practicing your tennis stroke against a backboard one afternoon. "I noticed you're having a lot of trouble with your backhand," the stranger says. "I think I could help you. Would you like me to give you some pointers?" How would you feel about this offer? According to Arie Nadler and Jeffrey Fisher (1986), our response to such an offer depends on how threatened it makes us feel, which in turn depends on how similar the stranger is to us. If the stranger is a professional tennis player who just got back from Wimbledon, the fact that he or she is a better player than we are is not very threatening. After all, virtually no one is as good as the professionals, so why should we feel bad that our backhand looks pretty pathetic compared to a pro's? Under these circumstances, we will probably accept the person's offer of help gratefully, without any dent in our self-esteem.

Suppose, however, that the stranger is a member of our tennis class for beginners, and is the same age and sex as we are. An offer of help from this person is unlikely to make us feel very good, because the fact that we are not as skilled as someone similar to us highlights our incompetence—and is thus more threatening to our self-esteem. "Who do you think you are," we are likely to think, "telling me that you're a better tennis player than I am?" Consistent with this reasoning, Jeffrey Fisher and Arie Nadler (1974) found that when people received an offer of help from another person, they felt worse about it if the person was highly similar to themselves.

Receiving help can be particularly devastating if it threatens people's self-esteem and they feel unable to change their behavior in such a way as to help themselves. Under these conditions, people feel there is little they can do to improve their lot, and they are likely to give up. If they do feel they can change their behavior, they are likely to react to an offer of help quite differently—for example, by trying even harder on their own, to show the help-giver that, thank you very much, no help is needed.

Consider, for example, a study by Bella DePaulo and her colleagues (1989) of how fourth-graders responded to peer tutoring. Peer-tutoring programs, in which children are tutored by other children in their class, have become popular in many schools, because of the assumption that it is less threatening for children to be tutored by a peer than by an authority figure. Research on reactions to help, however, suggests otherwise. In the DePaulo and colleagues study, kids who were tutored by classmates similar to them in ability felt the most threatened. How did the kids react to this threat? Those who felt they had control over their performance had an "I'll show 'em" reaction, trying even harder on the task and doing very well; those who felt they had little control over their performance were the most likely to give up, doing especially poorly on the task. The moral is to offer people help in ways that do not threaten their self-esteem, particularly when people feel they don't have much control over their performance.

## How Can Helping Be Increased?

Most religions stress some version of the Golden Rule, urging us to do unto others as we would have them do unto us. There are many saintly people in the world who succeed in following this rule, devoting their lives to the welfare of others. The world would be a better place, however, if prosocial behavior was more common than it is. How can we get people, when faced with an emergency, to act more like Lenny Skutnik and less like Kitty Genovese's neighbors? How can we increase everyday acts of kindness, such as looking out for an elderly neighbor or volunteering at the local school?

The answers to these questions lie in our discussion of the causes of prosocial behavior. For example, we saw that several personal characteristics of potential helpers are important, and promoting those factors can increase the likelihood that these people will help. Personal factors, however, are not the sole cause of prosocial behavior. Even kind, altruistic people will fail to help if certain situational constraints are present, such as being in an urban environment or witnessing an emergency in the presence of numerous bystanders. Another important situational factor is the similarity of the victim to the potential helper. The role of similarity is troubling, for people have a basic tendency to draw distinctions between other people based on their gender, age, physical appearance, religion, national origin, skin color, or any other way in which they can be distinguished (see Chapter 13). Research on prosocial behavior strongly suggests that we should find ways to ignore these distinctions, because if we view someone as different from us, we are less likely to help him or her. Put another way, if others view you as different—you are the "wrong" race, believe in the "wrong" religion, or wear the

In order to increase prosocial behavior, we must remind ourselves not to fall prey to such tendencies as only helping those similar to us. Here, an Anglo-American tourist receives help from a Korean family.

"wrong" clothing—you may not receive help at a time when you need it badly. Rather than viewing each other as blacks versus whites, Christians versus Jews, or Americans versus foreigners, we should try to view each other as fellow human beings, whose similarities outweigh our differences.

As we will see in Chapter 13 (on prejudice) and as witnessed by the long-standing, seemingly irresolvable conflicts between different national and ethnic groups, perceiving similarities instead of differences is by no means an easy task. There is some evidence, however, that simply being aware of the barriers to helping can increase people's chances of overcoming them. This was demonstrated in a striking experiment by Arthur Beaman and his colleagues (1978), who randomly assigned students to listen to a lecture on Latané and Darley's (1970) bystander intervention research or a lecture on an unrelated topic. Two weeks later, all the students participated in what they thought was a completely unrelated sociology study, during which they encountered a student lying on the floor. Was he in need of help? Had he fallen and injured himself, or was he simply a student who had fallen asleep after pulling an all-nighter? As we have seen, when in an ambiguous situation such as this people look and see how other people are reacting. Because an accomplice of the experimenter (posing as another participant) purposefully acted unconcerned, the natural thing to do was to assume nothing was wrong. This is exactly what most of Beaman's participants did, if they had not heard the lecture about bystander intervention research; in this condition, only 25 percent of them stopped to help the student. However, if the participants had heard the lecture about bystander intervention, many more decided to help: 43 percent acted like the Good Samaritan, stopping to help the victim. Thus, knowing how we can be unwittingly influenced by others can by itself help us overcome this type of social influence. We can only hope that knowing about other barriers to prosocial behavior will make them easier to overcome as well.

We conclude with the reminder that we should not impose help on everyone we meet, whether the person wants it or not. Research on reactions to help indicates that under certain conditions, receiving help can have damaging effects on a person's self-esteem. The goal is to make the help supportive, highlighting your concern for the recipient, rather than threatening him or her by highlighting your superior knowledge and skill.

## SUMMARY

We began by discussing three major theories of **prosocial behavior. Sociobiology** describes helping behavior as an instinctive reaction to protect and promote the welfare of those genetically similar to us (**kin selection**); according to this theory, we have also evolved to instinctually follow the **norm of reciprocity**, whereby we help strangers in the hope that we will receive help when we need it. **Social exchange theory** views helping behavior as an analysis of rewards and costs; helping occurs due to self-interest—that is, in situations where the rewards of helping outweigh the costs. Rewards include the relief of personal distress, and recognition and praise. Neither of these theories sees helping behavior as a form of **altruism;** there is always self-gain involved. In comparison, the **empathy-altruism hypothesis** sees prosocial behavior as often purely altruistic, motivated only by **empathy** and compassion for those in need.

Prosocial behavior is multidetermined, and both personal and situational factors can override or facilitate basic motives to help. Personal determinants of helping include the **altruistic personality,** the idea being that some people are more helpful than others. Children can develop this personality by being rewarded for helping by their parents, and by modeling people that they observe help. Rewards must be used carefully, however, or they will undermine the child's intrinsic interest in helping—causing an *overjustification effect*. Gender is another personal factor that comes into play. Though one sex is not more altruistic than the other, the ways in which men and women help often differs, with men more likely to help in heroic, chivalrous ways, and women in ways that involve commitment over the long run.

Finally, mood affects helping. Interestingly, being in either a good or a bad mood—compared to being in a neutral mood—can increase helping. Good moods increase helping for several reasons, including the fact that they make us see the good side of other people, making us more willing to help them. Bad moods increase helping because of the **negative-state relief hypothesis,** which maintains that helping someone makes us feel good, lifting us out of the doldrums.

Social determinants of prosocial behavior include rural versus urban environments, with helping behavior more likely to occur in rural settings. One reason for this is the **urban-overload hypothesis,** which says that cities bombard people with so much stimulation that they keep to themselves to avoid being overloaded. The **bystander effect** points out the impact of the number of bystanders on whether help is given—the fewer the bystanders, the better. The bystander decision tree indicates that a potential helper must make five decisions before providing help: notice the event, interpret the event as an emergency (here **pluralistic ignorance** can occur, whereby everyone assumes nothing is wrong, because no one else looks concerned; pluralistic ignorance is an example of *informational social influence*); assume personal responsibility (here **diffusion of responsibility** created by several bystanders may lead us to think it's not our responsiblity to act); know how to help; and implement the help. In addition, characteristics of the victim are another social determinant of helping behavior—we are more likely to help those who are in some way similar to us.

Helping can have positive or negative consequences for the recipient; it is important that an offer of help does not threaten the recipient's self-esteem. Finally, research has indicated that teaching people about the determinants of prosocial behavior makes them more aware of why they sometimes don't help, with the happy result that they help more in the future.

## SUGGESTED READINGS

Clark, M.S. (1991). *Prosocial behavior: Review of personality and social psychology* (Vol. 12). Newbury Park, CA: Sage. A resource containing up-to-date chapters by top researchers in the field of prosocial behavior, many of whom were cited in this chapter. Topics include the development of altruism, the debate about whether people are ever truly altruistic or are always concerned with their self-interest, the effects of mood on helping, and the consequences of helping.

Latané, B., & Darley, J. M. (1970). *The unresponsive bystander: Why doesn't he help?* Englewood Cliffs, NJ: Prentice Hall. A classic look at why bystanders often fail to help victims in emergencies, including an in-depth discussion of the "seizure" and "smoke" studies described in this chapter.

Rushton, J. P., & Sorrentino, R. M. (1981). *Altruism and helping behavior: Social, personality, and developmental perspectives.* Hillsdale, NJ: Erlbaum. The chapters present many perspectives on prosocial behavior, including how prosocial behavior develops, personality differences in altruism, and social determinants of altruism.

DePaulo, B. M., Nadler, A., & Fisher, J. D.(1983). *New directions in helping: Help seeking* (Vol. 2). New York: Academic Press. Chapters address the conditions under which people are likely to seek out help from others, and the consequences of receiving help.

# Chapter 12
## Aggression: Why We Hurt Other People

It don't matter what you say about gangbangin', you know, don't matter if anybody understand it or not. We just bringin' home the hate.

—A Los Angeles gang member, 1992

 n the spring of 1992, following the acquittal of several members of the Los Angeles Police Department on charges of savagely beating a black motorist named Rodney King, angry blacks went on a rampage of rioting, arson, and looting. When the smoke cleared, forty-four people had been killed, some 2,000 were seriously injured, and entire city blocks in South Central Los Angeles were in flames, resulting in more than $1 billion in property damage.

In the aftermath of the rioting, there was no shortage of explanations. Some members of Congress attributed it to simple lawlessness. Others blamed it on grinding poverty. Former vice-president Dan Quayle blamed it on a breakdown in "family values" and pointed an accusing finger at "Murphy Brown," a TV sitcom in which the leading character decided to have a child as a single parent. Marlin Fitzwater, speaking for the Bush administration, laid the blame on frustration caused by the failure of the antipoverty programs initiated during a Democratic presidency some twenty-five years earlier. Democrats attributed it to twelve years of the neglect of inner cities and their residents by the Reagan and Bush administrations.

What is aggression? What causes it? Are humans instinctively aggressive? Can aggression be prevented or reduced? These are questions of the utmost importance.

It seems as though humans have always been aggressive. When we reach back into ancient times, to the golden age of antiquity, when ancient Greece was graced by such humane and exciting thinkers as Socrates, Plato, Aristotle, Sophocles, and Aristophanes, there were nevertheless a great many barbarous wars in which thousands were killed or maimed, cities were sacked, and noncombatant women and children were slaughtered, raped, or forced into slavery. Needless to say, humans have progressed since then—but progress isn't always for the better. Along with our astonishing creativity has come the propensity to invent ever more efficient weapons of destruction; thus, the

Angry rioters in South Central Los Angeles

bloodiest war in history was fought just five decades ago, when in the course of about seven years, an estimated 55 million humans were killed. As we write these words, current news broadcasts reverberate with stories of atrocities in Bosnia, Africa, and the Middle East. Moreover, these events are not confined to wars or riots. It is difficult to pick up a newspaper without learning of some dramatic example of aggressiveness, some gruesome event like that involving a serial killer who allegedly buried some fifty of his victims in shallow graves across the country, or that involving a mild-mannered loner in Milwaukee who habitually killed

and devoured his acquaintances.

Admittedly, those are extreme examples. Most of us would like to believe that the majority of our fellow human beings are gentle types who love their neighbors (and even their enemies) and reach out with love to people in trouble. Yet we are constantly reminded that the world isn't that benevolent, and we find it discouraging when we are bombarded by evidence of minor league aggressiveness all around us, even among the very young— for example, when we observe toddlers fighting over who owns which toys or when we notice the high degree of taunting that takes place in a typical school yard, as well as the fact that most children tend to settle their disputes by fighting rather than by reasoning. In a moment, we will examine the important questions of what causes aggression and how it might be reduced. But first, let's be sure we know what we mean by the term.

## What Is Aggression?

**aggressive action:** a behavior aimed at causing either physical or psychological pain

Defining aggression is not as simple as it might seem, because in the vernacular, most people use the term very loosely. Social psychologists define **aggressive action** as behavior aimed at causing either physical or psychological pain. It is not to be confused with assertiveness—even though people sometimes loosely refer to others as "aggressive" if they stand up for their rights, write letters to the editor complaining about real or imagined injustices, work extra hard, display a great deal of ambition, or are real "go-getters." Similarly, in a sexist society a woman who simply speaks her mind or picks up the phone and makes the first move by inviting a male acquaintance to dinner might be called aggressive by some—but not by the authors of this book. Our definition is clear—aggression is an intentional action aimed at doing harm or causing pain. The action might be physical or verbal; it might succeed in its goal or not. It is still aggression. Thus, if someone throws a beer bottle at your head and you duck, so that the bottle misses your head, it is still an aggressive act. The important thing is the intention. By the same token, if someone is a careless driver and unintentionally runs you down while you're attempting to cross the street, that is not an act of aggression, even though the damage would be far greater than that caused by the beer bottle that missed.

It is also useful to make a distinction between **hostile aggression** and **instrumental aggression.** Hostile aggression is the result of anger; the goal is to inflict pain or injury. While the result of instrumental aggression might be pain or injury, that is not the goal—here, the aggressive act is a means to some other end. For example, in a professional football game, a defensive lineman will use whatever force he deems necessary to thwart his opponent and tackle the ball carrier. This is instrumental aggression. On the other hand, if he feels that his opponent has been playing dirty, he might become angry and set out to hurt his opponent, irrespective of whether or not it increases his opportunity to tackle the ball carrier. This is hostile aggression.

## Is Aggression Inborn, or Is It Learned?

Scientists, philosophers, and other serious thinkers are not in complete agreement with one another about whether aggression is an innate, instinctive phenomenon or whether such behavior must be learned. This controversy is not new; it has been raging for centuries. For example, Thomas Hobbes, in his classic work *Leviathan* (first published in 1651), took the view that we humans, in our natural state, are brutes and that only by enforcing the law and order of society could we curb what to Hobbes was a natural instinct toward aggression. On the other hand, Jean-Jacques Rousseau's concept of the noble savage (a theory he developed in 1762) suggested that we humans, in our natural state, are benign, happy, and good creatures and that it is a restrictive society that forces aggression and depravity on us.

Hobbes's more pessimistic view was elaborated in the twentieth century by Sigmund Freud (1930), who theorized that humans are born with an instinct toward life, which he called **Eros,** and an equally powerful death instinct, **Thanatos.** According to Freud, when turned inward, the death instinct manifests itself in self-punishment, which in the extreme becomes suicide; when turned outward, this instinct manifests itself in hostility, destructiveness, and murder. "It is at work in every living being," Freud said, "and is striving to bring it to ruin and to reduce life to its original condition of inanimate matter" (p. 67). Freud believed this aggressive energy must come out somehow, lest it continue to build up and produce illness. This notion can be described as a **hydraulic theory**—that is, the analogy is one of water pressure building up in a container: Unless aggression is allowed to drain off, it will produce some sort of explosion. According to Freud, society performs an essential function in regulating this instinct and in helping people to sublimate it—that is, to turn the destructive energy into acceptable or useful behavior.

> Man's inhumanity to man
> Makes countless thousands
> mourn.
> —Robert Burns, *Man Was Made to Mourn*

**hostile aggression:** an act of aggression stemming from feelings of anger and aimed at inflicting pain

**instrumental aggression:** aggression as a means to some goal other than causing pain

**Eros:** the instinct toward life, posited by Freud

**Thanatos:** according to Freud, an instinctual drive toward death, leading to aggressive actions

**hydraulic theory:** the theory that unexpressed emotions build up pressure and must be expressed to relieve that pressure

**Breeding Organisms for Aggression.**  Much of the evidence on whether or not aggression is instinctive in humans is based on the observation of and experimentation with species other than humans. The idea behind this research is that if one can succeed in demonstrating that certain so-called instinctive aggressive behaviors in the lower animals are not rigidly preprogrammed, then surely aggression is not rigidly preprogrammed in humans. For example, consider the prevalent belief about cats and rats. Among the general public, it is considered axiomatic that cats will instinctively stalk and kill rats. After all, don't all cats go after rats? Biologist Zing Yang Kuo (1961) attempted to demonstrate that this was a myth. So he performed a simple little experiment: He raised a kitten in the same cage with a rat. What did he find? Not only did the cat refrain from attacking the rat, but the two became close companions. Moreover, when given the opportunity the cat refused either to chase or to kill other rats; thus, the benign behavior was not confined to his buddy, but generalized to rats the cat had never met before.

While this is a charming experiment, it fails to prove that aggressive behavior is not instinctive; it merely demonstrates that the aggressive instinct can be inhibited by early experience. What if an organism grows up without any experience with other organisms? Will it or won't it show normal aggressive tendencies? Irenaus Eibl-Eibesfeldt (1963) showed that rats raised in isolation (i.e., without any experience in fighting other rats) will attack a fellow rat when one is introduced into the cage; moreover, the isolated rat uses the same pattern of threat and attack that experienced rats use. Thus, although aggressive behavior can be modified by experience (as shown by Kuo's experiment), Eibl-Eibesfeldt showed that aggression apparently does not need to be learned. On the other hand, one should not conclude from this study that aggression is necessarily instinctive, for, as John Paul Scott (1958) pointed out, in order to draw this conclusion there must be physiological evidence of a spontaneous stimulation for fighting that arises from within the body alone. The stimulus in Eibl-Eibesfeldt's experiment came from the outside—that is, the sight of a new rat stimulated the isolated rat to fight. Scott concluded from his survey of the evidence that there is no inborn need for fighting: If an organism can arrange its life so there is no outside stimulation to fight, then it will experience no physiological or mental damage as a result of not expressing aggression. This view contradicts Freud's contention and in effect asserts that there is no instinct of aggression.

The argument continues to go back and forth. Scott's conclusion was called into question by the Nobel Prize–winning ethologist Konrad Lorenz (1966), who observed the behavior of cichlids—highly aggressive tropical fish. Male cichlids will attack other males of the same species to establish and defend their territory. In its natural environment, the male cichlid does not attack female cichlids; nor does it attack males of a different species—it attacks only males of its own species. What happens if all other male cichlids are removed from an aquarium, leaving only one male alone with no appropriate target? According to the hydraulic theory of instinctive aggression (mentioned above), the need to aggress will build up to the point where the cichlid will attack a fish that doesn't usually serve as an appropriate stimulus for attack. And that is exactly what happens. In the absence of other males, the cichlid will attack males of other species—males it previously ignored. Moreover, if all other males are removed, the male cichlid will eventually attack and kill females.

Aggressive behavior may make sense among animals such as these elephant seals because it has survival value. Specifically, during the mating season the biggest, strongest, and most aggressive male will achieve dominance in the rookery, and will therefore account for a high proportion of the breeding, passing along its genes to the next generation.

More recently, Richard Lore and Lori Schultz (1993) have reported that the apparent universality of aggression among vertebrates strongly suggests that aggressiveness has evolved and been maintained because it has survival value. At the same time, these researchers are quick to point out that nearly all organisms also seem to have evolved strong inhibitory mechanisms that enable them to suppress aggression when it is in their best interests to do so. Thus, even in the most violence-prone species, aggression is an optional strategy—whether or not it is expressed is determined by the animal's previous social experiences, as well as by the specific social context in which the animal finds itself.

## Of Mice and "Men"

Social psychologists are in general agreement with the interpretation of the animal research offered by Lore and Schultz. And where humans are concerned, the social situation becomes even more important (Bandura, 1973; Baron, Lysak, Rule, and Dobbs, 1989; Baron & Richardson, 1992; Berkowitz, 1968). In short, where humans are concerned, while the tendency toward aggression may be inborn, whether or not it gets expressed is a function of a complex interplay between these innate propensities, a variety of learned inhibitory responses, and the precise nature of the social situation. For example, although it is true that many animals, from insects to apes, will usually attack another animal that invades their territory, it is a gross oversimplification to imply, as some popular writers have, that humans are likewise programmed to protect their territory and behave aggressively in response to highly specific stimuli. Rather, much evidence supports the contention held by most social psychologists that, for humans, innate patterns of behavior are infinitely modifiable and flexible. This is illustrated by the fact that human cultures vary widely in their degree of aggressiveness. For example, certain primitive tribes, such as the Lepchas of Sikkim, the Pygmies

THE FAR SIDE                    By GARY LARSON

Neither rain nor snow nor sleet nor
hail, they said, could stop the mail. ...
But they didn't figure on Rexbo.

What makes this cartoon amusing underscores an important point for the scientist: Aggression in animals is very different from aggression in humans. Therefore, we need to be cautious about drawing conclusions about human aggression from studies involving animals.

of Central Africa, and the Arapesh of New Guinea, live in apparent peace and harmony, wherein acts of aggression are extremely rare (see Baron & Richardson, 1992). Meanwhile, just a short time ago in a more "civilized" society, our own government, already heavily in debt, spent billions of dollars on a brief military encounter against a relatively small and impoverished country in the Persian Gulf—killing tens of thousands in the process. In the aftermath of that brief war, the overwhelming majority of the citizens of the victorious country were pleased and proud of that accomplishment.

In addition, within a given culture, changing social conditions frequently lead to striking changes in aggressive behavior. For example, for hundreds of years the Iroquois Indians lived in benign peacefulness as a hunting nation; they simply did not engage in aggressive behavior. But in the seventeenth century, barter with the newly arrived Europeans brought the Iroquois into direct competition with the neighboring Hurons over furs, which dramatically increased in value, because they could now be traded for manufactured goods. A series of skirmishes with the Hurons ensued, and within a short time the Iroquois developed into ferocious warriors. It would be hard to argue that they were spectacular warriors because of uncontrollable aggressive instincts; rather, their aggressiveness almost certainly came about because a social change produced increases in competition (Hunt, 1940).

To sum up, after reviewing all of these findings we believe that one cannot draw a firm conclusion—aggression may or may not have an instinctual component in humans. But whether or not aggression has an instinctual component, we know that, in humans as well as in the lower animals, aggression is not caused entirely by instinct—that there are important situational and social events that frequently lead to aggressive behavior. And even more importantly, we know that, in humans, such behavior is infinitely modifiable by situational and social factors. In short, aggressive behavior can be changed. This makes the study of aggression a prime interest for social psychologists.

Although the Iroquois Indians have a reputation for being fierce warriors, they developed aggressive tendencies only after a change in their social situation was induced by increased competition with another tribe.

**Situational Causes of Aggression**

## Neural and Chemical Causes of Aggression

Some of the so-called situational causes of aggression result from situations inside the body. For example, an area in the core of the brain called the **amygdala** seems to control aggression, in humans as well as in the lower animals. When that area is stimulated, docile organisms become violent; similarly, when neural activity in that area is blocked, violent organisms become docile (Moyer, 1976). But it should be noted that there is flexibility here also: The impact of neural mechanisms can be modified by social factors, even in subhumans. For example, if a male monkey is in the presence of other, less dominant monkeys, he will indeed attack the other monkeys when the appropriate area of his brain is stimulated. But if the same area is stimulated while the monkey is in the presence of more dominant monkeys, then he will not attack but will run away instead.

**amygdala:** an area in the core of the brain that is associated with aggressive behaviors

**Testosterone.**   Certain chemicals have been shown to influence aggression. For example, the injection of **testosterone,** a male sex hormone, will increase aggression in animals (Moyer, 1983). Among humans, there is a parallel finding: Naturally occurring testosterone levels are significantly higher among prisoners convicted of violent crimes than among those convicted of nonviolent crimes. Interestingly enough, this is true for both male and female prisoners (Dabbs, Ruback, Frady, Hopper, and Sgoutas, 1988).

**testosterone:** a hormone associated with aggression

If testosterone level affects aggressiveness, does that mean men are more aggressive than women? Apparently so; in their exhaustive survey of research on children, Eleanor Maccoby and Carol Jacklin (1974) demonstrate convincingly—in dozens of laboratory experiments and field observations and in several cultures and across social classes—that boys are consistently more

*"Lizzie Borden took an ax
And gave her mother forty whacks;
When she saw what she had done
She gave her father forty-one!"*

While extreme violence is not unknown in women, it is infrequent relative to men. The trial of Lizzie Borden for the murder of her parents was one of the most famous court cases of the nineteenth century.

aggressive than girls. Similarly, among adults worldwide, the great majority of persons arrested for criminal offenses of all kinds are men. Further, when women are arrested, it is usually for property crimes (forgery, fraud, larceny), rather than for violent crimes (murder, aggravated assault). Are these differences due to biological differences or to social differences? We cannot be sure, but there is some evidence of a biological difference. Specifically, in our own country, the enormous social changes affecting women during the past thirty-five years have not produced concomitant increases in the incidence of violent crimes committed by women relative to those committed by men, yet when one looks at the comparative data between men and women involving nonviolent crimes, women have shown a far greater increase relative to men (Wilson & Herrnstein, 1985). Needless to say, this should not be construed to mean that aggressiveness among women is unknown or even that it is rare. As Eagly and Steffen (1986) have shown in their review of many of the controlled experiments on aggression, the differences between men and women are not great.

**Alcohol.**  As most socially active college students know, alcohol tends to lower our inhibitions against committing behaviors frowned on by society, including acts of aggression (see Desmond, 1987; Taylor & Leonard, 1983). The linkage between the consumption of alcoholic beverages and aggressive behavior is a common observation. For example, we are well aware of the fact that fistfights frequently break out in bars and nightclubs and that family violence is often associated with the abuse of alcohol; in addition, the "belligerent drunk" is a cliché in films and on TV. A wealth of hard data support these casual observations and cultural clichés. For example, crime statistics reveal that 75 percent of those individuals arrested for murder, assault, and other crimes of violence were legally drunk at the time of their arrest (see, e.g., Shupe, 1954). In addition, controlled laboratory experiments demonstrate that when individuals ingest enough alcohol to make them legally drunk, they tend to respond more violently to provocations than those who have ingested little or no alcohol (Taylor & Leonard, 1983).

This does not mean that alcohol automatically increases aggression; people who have ingested alcohol are not necessarily driven to go around picking fights. Rather, the results of well-controlled laboratory experiments indicate that alcohol serves as a disinhibitor—that is, our social inhibitions are reduced; thus, under the influence of alcohol, a person's primary tendencies will be evoked, so that people prone to affection will become more affectionate, and people prone to violence will become more aggressive. By the same token, after ingesting alcohol people who are subjected to social pressure to aggress or who are frustrated or provoked will experience fewer restraints or inhibitions to commit violent acts (Jeavons & Taylor, 1985; Steele & Josephs, 1990; Steele & Southwick, 1985; Taylor & Sears, 1988).

## Pain and Discomfort as a Cause of Aggression

If an animal experiences pain and cannot flee the scene, it will almost invariably attack; this is true of rats, mice, hamsters, foxes, monkeys, crayfish, snakes, raccoons, alligators, and a host of others (Azrin, 1967; Hutchinson, 1983). Such animals will attack members of their own species, members of different species, or anything else in sight, including stuffed dolls and tennis balls. Do you think this is true of humans as well? A moment's reflection

Drawing by Dana Fradon: © 1975 The New Yorker Magazine, Inc.

Alcohol, by lowering inhibitions, tends to increase the likelihood of aggression.

*"Oh, that wasn't me talking. It was the alcohol talking."*

might help you guess that it may very well be. Most of us have experienced becoming irritable when subjected to a sharp, unexpected pain (e.g., when we stub our toe) and hence being prone to lash out at the nearest available target. In a systematic experiment, Leonard Berkowitz (1983, 1988) showed that students who underwent the pain of having their hand immersed in very cold water showed a sharp increase in their likelihood to aggress against another student.

By the same token, it has long been speculated that other forms of bodily discomfort, such as heat, humidity, air pollution, and offensive odors, might act to lower the threshold for aggressive behavior. During the late 1960s and early 1970s, when a great deal of tension existed in the United States concerning issues of national policy involving the war in Vietnam, racial injustice, and the like, national leaders worried a lot about a phenomenon they referred to as "the long, hot summer"—that is, the assumed tendency for riots and other forms of civic unrest to occur with greater frequency in the heat of summer than in the fall, winter, or spring. Was this actually true, or mere speculation? It turns out to be true. In a systematic analysis of disturbances occurring in seventy-nine cities between 1967 and 1971, J. Merrill Carlsmith and Craig Anderson (1979) found that riots were far more likely to occur during hot days than during cool days. This is nicely illustrated in Figure 12.1 on the next page. Similarly, in major American cities, from Houston, Texas, to Des Moines, Iowa, the hotter it is on a given day, the greater the likelihood that violent crimes will occur (see, e.g., Anderson & Anderson, 1984; Cotton, 1981, 1986; Harries & Stadler, 1988; Rotton & Frey, 1985).

As the reader knows by this time, one has to be cautious about interpreting events that take place in natural settings. For example, the scientist in you might be tempted to ask whether increases in aggression are due to the temperature itself or merely to the fact that more people are apt to be outside (getting in one another's way!) on hot days than on cool or rainy days. So how might we determine that it's the heat itself that caused the aggression—and not merely the greater opportunity for contact? We can bring it into the laboratory. This is remarkably easy to do. For example, in one such experiment William Griffitt and Roberta Veitch (1971) simply administered a test to students, some of whom took it in a room with normal temperature, while others took it in a room where the temperature was allowed to soar to ninety

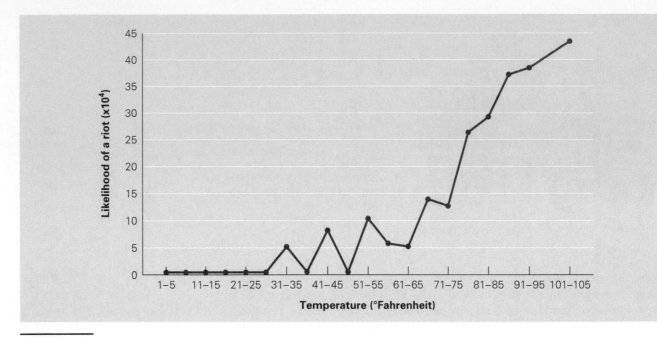

**FIGURE 12.1 The long, hot summer**. Warm temperatures increase the likelihood that violent riots and other aggressive acts will occur. (Adapted from Carlsmith & Anderson, 1979)

degrees. The students in the hot room not only reported feeling more aggressive but also expressed more hostility to a stranger whom they were asked to describe and rate. Similar results have been reported by a number of investigators (see, e.g., Bell, 1980; Rule et al., 1987). Additional evidence from the natural world helps bolster our belief in the cause of this phenomenon. For example, it has been shown that in major league baseball games, significantly more batters are hit by pitched balls when the temperature is above ninety than when it is below ninety (Reifman, Larrick, and Fein, 1988). And in the desert city of Phoenix, Arizona, drivers without air-conditioned cars are more likely to honk their horns in traffic jams than drivers with air-conditioned cars (Kenrick & MacFarlane, 1986).

## Social Situations Leading to Aggression

**Frustration as a Cause of Aggression.** Imagine that your friend Sam is driving you to the airport so you can take a plane home for the Christmas holidays. Sam is starting out a bit later than you feel comfortable with, but when you mention it, he accuses you of being overly anxious and assures you that he knows the route well and that you will arrive there with a good thirty minutes to spare. Halfway to your destination, Sam's car grinds to a halt in bumper-to-bumper traffic. You glance at your watch. Once again, Sam assures you that there is plenty of time—but this time you detect less confidence in his tone. After a few minutes, you notice that your palms are sweating and you are beginning to wring your hands. A few minutes later, you open your car door and survey the road ahead: nothing but gridlock as far as the eye can see. You get back in the car, slam the door, and glare at your friend. Sam smiles lamely, and says, "How was I supposed to know there would be so much traffic?" Should he be prepared to duck?

Feelings of frustration arise when a person is thwarted on the way to a goal. All of us have experienced some degree of frustration from time to

Feelings of frustration can occur when we are blocked or delayed as we strive to reach a goal. For example, being stuck in a sea of cars can elicit aggressive responses, ranging from honking pointlessly to fistfights, and even shootings.

time; indeed, it's unlikely we can get through a week without experiencing it. Research has shown that the experience of frustration can increase the probability of an aggressive response. This tendency is referred to as the **frustration-aggression theory.** As we shall see in a moment, this is not meant to imply that frustration always leads to aggression—but it frequently does. In a classic experiment by Roger Barker, Tamara Dembo, and Kurt Lewin (1941), young children were shown a roomful of very attractive toys, which were kept out of their reach. The children stood outside a wire screen looking at the toys—fully expecting to play with them—but were unable to reach them. After a painfully long wait, the children were finally allowed to play with the toys. In a control condition, a different group of children were allowed to play with the toys directly, without first being frustrated. This second group of children played joyfully with the toys. But the frustrated group, when finally given access to the toys, were extremely destructive: They tended to smash the toys, throw them against the wall, step on them, and so forth.

**frustration-aggression theory:** the theory that frustration—the perception that you are being prevented from obtaining a goal—will increase the probability of an aggressive response

Several factors can accentuate this frustration, and accordingly, will increase the probability that some form of aggression will occur. One such factor involves your closeness to the goal or the object of your desire. The greater the closeness, the greater the frustration; the greater the frustration, the more likely the aggression. This was demonstrated in a field experiment by Mary Harris (1974), who instructed her confederate to cut in front of people who were waiting in line in a variety of places—for movie tickets, outside crowded restaurants, or at the checkout counter of a grocery store. On some occasions, the confederates were instructed to cut in front of the second person in line; on other occasions, they cut in front of the twelfth person in line. The results were clear: The responses of the people standing behind the intruder were much more aggressive when the confederate cut into the second place in line.

Aggression also increases when the frustration is unexpected or seems illegitimate. James Kulik and Roger Brown (1979) hired students to telephone strangers and ask for donations to a charity. The students were hired on a commission basis—that is, they received a small fraction of each dollar pledged. Some of the students were led to expect a high rate of contributions; others, to expect far less success. The experiment was rigged so that none of the potential donors agreed to make a contribution. The experimenters found that the callers with high expectations directed more verbal aggression toward the nondonors, speaking more harshly and slamming down the phone with more force than the callers with low expectations.

As mentioned above, frustration does not always produce aggression. Rather, it seems to produce anger or annoyance and a readiness to aggress if other things about the situation are conducive to aggressive behavior (see Berkowitz, 1978, 1988, 1989, 1993; Gustafson, 1989). What are those other things? Well, one obvious other thing would be the size and strength of the person responsible for your frustration—as well as that person's ability to retaliate. It is undoubtedly easier to slam the phone down on a reluctant donor who is miles away and has no idea who you are than to take out your anger against your frustrator if he turned out to be the middle linebacker of the Chicago Bears and was staring you right in the face. Similarly, if the frustration is understandable, legitimate, and unintentional, it usually does not lead to aggression. For example, in an experiment by Eugene Burnstein and Philip Worchel (1962), when a confederate unwittingly sabotaged the problem solving of his groupmates because his hearing aid stopped working, the resulting frustration did not lead to aggression. In other words, most people, when frustrated, are better able to control their aggressive responses if the source of the frustration is a person trying to do his or her best.

We should also point out that frustration is not the same as deprivation. Children who simply don't have toys do not necessarily aggress. In the experiment by Barker and his colleagues, discussed above, frustration and aggression occurred because the children had every reason to expect to play with the toys, and that reasonable expectation was thwarted; this thwarting was what caused the children to behave destructively. In accord with this distinction, Rev. Jesse Jackson (1981), with great insight, pointed out that the race riots of 1967 and 1968 occurred "in the middle of rising expectations and the increased, though inadequate, social spending." In short, Jackson was suggesting thwarted expectations were largely responsible for the frustration and aggression. This is consistent with the earlier observations of psychiatrist Jerome Frank (1978), who pointed out that the most serious riots in this era occurred not in the geographic areas of greatest poverty but in Watts and Detroit, where things were not nearly so bad for blacks as they were in some other sections of the country. The point is that things were bad, relative to the blacks' perception of how white people were doing and relative to the positive changes many of the blacks had a right to expect. Thus, what causes aggression is not deprivation but **relative deprivation.**

**relative deprivation:** the perception that you (or your group) have less than you deserve, less than you have been led to expect, or less than people similar to you have

A similar phenomenon occurred in Eastern Europe in 1991, when serious rebellion against the Soviet monolith took place only after the chains had been loosened somewhat. In the same vein, Primo Levi (1985, p. 203), a survivor of Auschwitz, contends that even in concentration camps, the few instances of rebellion were performed not by the inmates at the very bottom of the camp totem pole—the suffering victims of unrelenting horror—but "by prisoners who were privileged in some way."

To sum up this section, frustration does not automatically lead to aggression. And frustration is not simply the result of deprivation; it is the result of relative deprivation—the feeling that comes from knowing that you have less than what you deserve, what you have been led to expect, or what people similar to you have. It is reasonable to speculate that, as bad as things were, the citizens of Romania, Latvia, Estonia, and what was once Yugoslavia did not fully experience frustration until after they'd found reason to begin to hope for something better.

**Direct Provocation and Reciprocation.**  So there you are, at your part-time job behind the counter, flipping hamburgers in a crowded fast-food restaurant. You are working harder than usual, because the other short-order cook went home ill, and the customers are lining up at the counter, clamoring for their burgers. In your eagerness to speed up the process, you spin around too fast and knock over a large jar of pickles, which smashes on the floor just as the boss sticks his head in. "Boy, are you clumsy!" he yells at you. "I'm gonna dock your pay $10 for that one; grab a broom and clean that up! I'll take over here!" You glare at him. If looks could kill! You feel like throwing something at him or at least telling him what he can do with this lousy job!

One obvious cause of aggression stems from the need to reciprocate after being provoked by aggressive behavior from another person. While the Christian plea to "turn the other cheek" is wonderful advice, it is not an apt description of what most humans in the world do. This has been illustrated in countless experiments in and out of the laboratory. Typical of this line of research is an experiment by Robert Baron (1988) in which subjects prepared an advertisement for a new product; their ad was then evaluated and criticized by an accomplice of the experimenter. In one condition, the criticism, while strong, was done in a gentle and considerate manner ("I think there's a lot of room for improvement"); in the other condition, the criticism was given in an insulting manner ("I don't think you could be original if you tried"). When provided with an opportunity to retaliate, subjects who were treated harshly were far more likely to do so than those in the "gentle" condition.

Just as in our responses to frustration, we do not always reciprocate when provoked. One determinant of reciprocation is the intentionality of the provocation; if we think it was unintentional, most of us will not reciprocate (Kremer & Stephens, 1983). Similarly, if there are mitigating circumstances, counteraggression will not occur. But in order to be effective at curtailing an aggressive response, these mitigating circumstances must be known at the time of the provocation. This was neatly demonstrated in an experiment by Johnson and Rule (1986). Students were insulted by the experimenters' assistant, but half of them were first told that the assistant was upset after receiving an unfairly low grade on a chemistry exam, whereas the other students were given this information only after the insult was delivered. All subjects later had an opportunity to retaliate by choosing the level of unpleasant noise to zap the assistant with. Those students who knew about the mitigating circumstances before being insulted delivered less intense bursts of noise. How can we account for this difference? Apparently, at the time of the insult the informed students simply did not take it personally, and therefore had no strong need to retaliate. This interpretation is bolstered by evidence of their physiological arousal: At the time of the insult, the heartbeat of the insulted students did not increase as rapidly if they knew about the assistant's unhappy state of mind beforehand.

> Nothing is more costly, nothing is more sterile, than revenge.
> —Winston Churchill
> (1874-1965)

*"There's a burglar prowling in the Blue Room, sir. Would you care to have a crack at him before I notify the police?"*

Does the finger pull the trigger, or does the trigger pull the finger?

**aggressive stimulus:** an object that is associated with aggressive responses (e.g., a gun) and whose mere presence can increase the probability of aggression

**Aggressive Objects as a Cause of Aggressive Behavior.** As we have seen, we humans are complex creatures. Our cognitive ability is awesome, enabling us to solve difficult problems by allowing us to make creative leaps. This same cognitive ability can, however, get us into trouble. In the realm of aggression, the mere presence of an **aggressive stimulus**—an object usually associated with aggression—can act in a way that increases the probability of an aggressive response. In a classic experiment by Berkowitz and LePage (1967), college students were made angry. Some of them were made angry in a room in which a gun was left lying around (ostensibly from a previous experiment), and others were made angry in a room in which a neutral object (a badminton racket) was substituted for the gun. Subjects were then given the opportunity to administer some electric shocks to a fellow college student. Those individuals who had been made angry in the presence of the gun administered more intense electric shocks than those made angry in the presence of the badminton racket. The results are illustrated in Figure 12.2. This experiment is indeed provocative; it points to an opposite conclusion from the slogan often seen on bumper stickers—"Guns don't kill; people do." As Leonard Berkowitz (1981) puts it, "An angry person can pull the trigger of his gun if he wants to commit violence; but the trigger can also pull the finger or otherwise elicit aggressive reactions from him, if he is ready to aggress and does not have strong inhibitions against such behavior" (p. 12).

Does the presence of guns increase the aggressive behavior of people in the real world? We think so. Consider this tale of two cities: Seattle, Washington, and Vancouver, British Columbia, are virtually twin cities in a lot of ways; they have very similar climates, populations, economies, general crime rates, and rates of physical assault. They differ in two respects: (a) Vancouver severely restricts handgun ownership, while Seattle does not, and (b) the murder rate in Seattle is more than twice as high as that in Vancouver

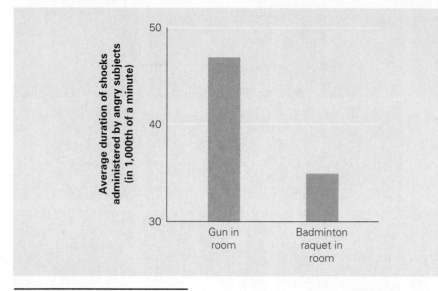

**FIGURE 12.2  The trigger can pull the finger.** Aggressive cues, such as weapons, tend to increase levels of aggression. (Adapted from Berkowitz & LePage, 1967)

(Sloan et al., 1988). Is the one the cause of the other? We cannot be sure. But laboratory experiments by Berkowitz and his colleagues strongly suggest that the ubiquitous presence of that aggressive stimulus in the United States might be a factor. This is consistent with the findings of Dane Archer and Rosemary Gartner (1984), who, in an exhaustive cross-national study of violence, found that the homicide rate in countries all over the world is highly correlated with the availability of handguns; Britain, for example, where handguns are banned, has one-fourth the number of people as the United States, and one-sixteenth as many homicides.

**Social Learning Theory: Imitation and Aggression.**  A major cause of aggression is social learning. Children frequently learn to solve conflicts aggressively by imitating adults and their peers, especially when they see that the aggression is rewarded. For example, in most high-contact sports (e.g., football and hockey) it is frequently the case that the more aggressive players achieve the greatest fame (and the highest salaries) and the more aggressive teams win more games. In these sports, it usually doesn't pay to be a gentle soul—or, as famed baseball manager Leo Durocher once said, "Nice guys finish last!" The data bear him out. For instance, in one study it was found that among hockey players, those most frequently sent to the penalty box for overly aggressive play tended to be the ones who scored the most goals (McCarthy & Kelley, 1978). To the extent that athletes serve as role models for children and adolescents, what is being modeled might be that fame and fortune go hand in hand with excessive aggressiveness.

It is also the case that a large percentage of physically abusive parents were themselves abused by their own parents when they were kids (Silver, Dublin, and Lourie, 1969; Strauss & Gelles, 1980). The speculation is that when children experience aggressive treatment at the hands of their parents, they learn that violence is the proper way to socialize their own kids. But, of

> Children have never been very good at listening to their elders, but they have never failed to imitate them.
> —James Baldwin, *Nobody Knows My Name*, 1961

It is clear from the Bandura and colleagues studies' (1961, 1963) that children learn aggressive behavior through imitation and modeling.

**social learning theory:** the theory that we learn social behavior (e.g., aggression) by observing others and imitating them

course, that is not the only conclusion one might draw from these family data. As mentioned earlier, aggressiveness may have a strong genetic component; if so, perhaps aggressive parents simply breed aggressive children. How can one determine whether or not imitation might be operating here? As you might guess, we could bring it into the laboratory. In a classic series of experiments, Albert Bandura and his associates (1961, 1963) demonstrated the power of **social learning theory:** Simply seeing another person behave aggressively serves to increase the aggressive behavior of young children. The basic procedure in these studies was to have an adult knock around a plastic, air-filled "Bobo" doll (the kind that bounces back after it's been knocked down). The adult would smack the doll around with the palm of his or her hand, strike it with a mallet, kick it, and yell aggressive things at it. The kids were then allowed to play with the doll. In these experiments, the children imitated the aggressive models and treated the doll in a very abusive manner. Children in a control condition, who did not see the aggressive adult in action, almost never unleashed any aggression against the hapless doll. Moreover, the children who watched the aggressive adult used the same actions and the same aggressive words as the adult. In addition, many went beyond mere imitation—they also engaged in novel forms of aggressive behavior.

## The Effects of Watching Violence in the Media

**Effects On Children.**    If children can be influenced to imitate adult violence against a doll, what does this say about the effects of TV and movie violence on their behavior? This is an interesting question, with important societal implications. A number of long-term studies indicate that the more violence individuals watch on TV as children, the more violence they exhibit years later as teenagers and young adults (Eron, 1982, 1987;

Television has brought back murder into the home — where it belongs.
—Alfred Hitchcock, *The Observer*, December 19, 1965

Huesmann, 1982; Turner, et al., 1986). In a typical study of this kind, teenagers are asked to recall which shows they watched on TV when they were kids and how frequently they watched them; the shows are independently rated by judges as to how violent they are; and the general aggressiveness of the teenagers is independently rated by their teachers and classmates. Not only is there a high correlation between the amount of violent TV watched and the viewer's subsequent aggressiveness, but the impact also accumulates over time—that is, the strength of the correlation increases with age. While these are fairly powerful data, they do not definitively prove that watching a lot of violence on TV causes children to become violent teenagers. After all, it is at least conceivable that the aggressive kids were born with a tendency to enjoy violence, and that this enjoyment shows itself in both their aggressive behavior and their liking for watching violence on TV. Once again, we see the value of the controlled experiment in helping us to understand what causes what. In order to demonstrate conclusively that watching violence on TV actually causes violent behavior, the relationship must be shown experimentally.

Because this is an area of great importance to society, it goes without saying that it has been well researched. While not all of the research is consistent (for a review, see Hearold, 1986), the overwhelming thrust of the experimental evidence demonstrates that watching violence does indeed cause aggressive behavior in children. For example, in an early experiment on this issue Robert Liebert and Robert Baron (1972) exposed a group of children to a television production of "The Untouchables," an extremely violent cops-and-robbers type of program that was popular in the 1960s and 1970s. In a control condition, a similar group of children were exposed to a television production of an exciting but nonviolent sporting event for the same length of time. Each child was then allowed to play in another room with a group of other children. Those who had watched the violent television program showed far more aggression against their playmates than those who had watched the sporting event. The results of this experiment are depicted in Figure 12.3. A subsequent experiment (Josephson, 1987) showed, as one

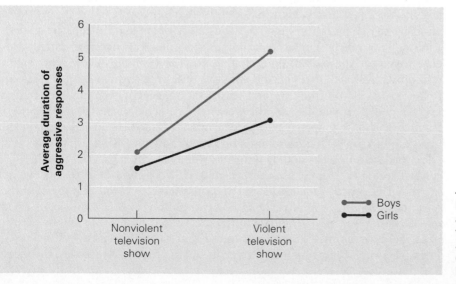

FIGURE 12.3 **TV violence and aggression.** Being exposed to violence on TV increases aggressive behavior in children. (Adapted from Liebert & Baron, 1972)

might expect, that watching TV violence has the greatest impact on youngsters who are somewhat prone to violence to begin with. In this experiment, youngsters were exposed to either a film depicting a great deal of police violence or an exciting, nonviolent film about bike racing. The youngsters then played a game of floor hockey. Watching the violent film had the effect of increasing the number of aggressive acts committed during the hockey game—primarily by those youngsters who had previously been rated as highly aggressive by their teachers. These kids hit others with their sticks, threw elbows, and yelled aggressive things at their opponents to a much greater extent than either the kids rated as nonaggressive who had also watched the violent film or the kids rated as aggressive who had watched the nonviolent film. Thus, it may be that watching media violence in effect serves to give aggressive kids permission to express their aggression. Josephson's experiment suggests that youngsters who do not have aggressive tendencies to begin with do not necessarily act aggressively—at least, not on the basis of seeing only one violent film.

And that last phrase is an important one—because it may be that even youngsters who are not prone toward aggression will become more aggressive if exposed to a steady diet of violent film fare over a long period. And that is exactly what was found in a set of field experiments (Leyens et al., 1975; Parke et al., 1977) wherein different groups of children were exposed to differing amounts of media violence over a longer period than typically happens in the "one-shot" laboratory experiments described above. In these field experiments, the great majority of the kids (even those without strong aggressive tendencies) who were exposed to a high degree of media violence over a long period were shown to have a strong tendency to be more aggressive than those who watched more benign shows. We might mention, in passing, that at a congressional hearing on TV violence conducted in the summer of 1993, it was estimated that the average twelve-year-old has witnessed over 100,000 acts of violence on television.

**What About Adults?**  Thus far, we have focused much of our attention on children in discussing the effects of media violence—and for good reason. Youngsters are by definition much more malleable than adults—that is, it is generally assumed that their attitudes and behaviors can be more deeply influenced by the things they view. But the effect of media violence on violent behavior may not be limited to children. On numerous occasions, adult violence seems to be a case of life imitating art. For example, a few years ago a man drove his truck through the window of a crowded cafeteria in Killeen, Texas; emerged from the cab; and began shooting people at random. By the time the police arrived, he had killed twenty-two people, making this the most destructive shooting spree in American history. He then turned the gun on himself. In his pocket, police found a ticket stub to *Fisher King*, a film depicting a deranged man firing a shotgun into a crowded bar, killing several people.

Did seeing the film cause the violent act? We cannot be sure. But we do know that violence in the media can and does have a profound impact on the behavior of adults. Several years ago, David Phillips (1983, 1986) performed an interesting analysis of homicides in the United States. He simply scrutinized the daily homicide rates and found that they almost always increased during the week following a heavyweight boxing match. Moreover, the more

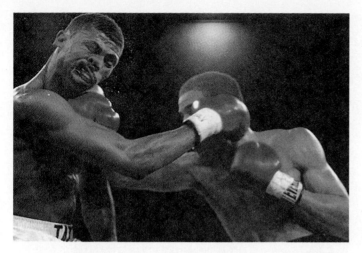

Do violent sports events increase homicide rates?

publicity surrounding the fight, the greater the subsequent increase in homicides. Still more striking is that the race of prizefight losers was related to the race of victims of murders after the fights. After white boxers lost fights, there was a corresponding increase in murders of white men, but not of black men; conversely, after black boxers lost fights, there was an increase in murders of black men, but not of white men. Phillips's results are convincing; they are far too consistent to be dismissed as merely a fluke. Again, this should not be construed as indicating that all people or even a sizable percentage of people are motivated to commit violence through watching media violence. But the fact that some people are influenced—and that the results can be tragic—cannot be denied.

**The Numbing Effect of TV Violence.** It seems to be the case that repeated exposure to horrifying events has a numbing effect on our sensitivity to those events. One of the authors of this book, Elliot Aronson, offers the following personal example:

> Several years ago, I moved to Manhattan for a few months. Soon after my arrival, I was walking down Fifth Avenue with a friend who is a native New Yorker. I was struck and touched by the great number of obviously homeless people, living in cardboard boxes, carrying their meager possessions in paper bags or wheeling them around in broken-down supermarket shopping carts. I was both deeply moved and appalled. All during our walk, I kept reaching into my pockets and dropping coins into the hands of those unfortunate souls. My friend was appalled—at my behavior. "You'll have to learn to ignore these people," my friend said. "Never," I replied, indignantly and self-righteously. Yet sure enough, within a few weeks I found myself walking down the streets of Manhattan staring straight ahead and keeping my hands out of my pockets. Amazingly, I had gotten so accustomed to the sight that, for all intents and purposes, I had become virtually indifferent to it.

Is it possible that, by a similar process, being constantly exposed to violence on TV tends to make people more tolerant of real violence? There is good evidence that this is so. In one experiment, Victor Cline and his associ-

> Death has been tidied up, cleansed of harmful ingredients, and repackaged in prime-time segments that pander to baser appetites but leave no unpleasant aftertaste. The Caesars of network television permit no mess on the living room floor.
> —Donald Goddard, *The New York Times*, February 27, 1977

Does watching violence on TV promote violence and aggression in children? What about in adults?

ates (1973) measured the physiological responses of several young men while they were watching a rather brutal and bloody boxing match. Those who watched a lot of TV in their daily lives seemed relatively indifferent to the mayhem in the ring—that is, they showed little physiological evidence of excitement, anxiety, or the like. They treated the violence in a lackadaisical manner. On the other hand, those who typically watched relatively little TV underwent major physiological arousal. The violence really got to them. In a related vein, Margaret Hanratty Thomas and her colleagues (1977) demonstrated that viewing television violence can subsequently numb people's reactions when they are faced with real-life aggression. Thomas had her subjects watch either a violent police drama or an exciting (but nonviolent) volleyball game. After a short break, they were allowed to observe a verbally and physically aggressive interaction between two preschoolers. Those who had watched the police show responded less emotionally than those who had watched the volleyball game. It seems that viewing the initial violence served to desensitize them to further acts of violence—they were not upset by an incident that by all rights should have upset them. While such a reaction may psychologically protect us from upset, it may also have the unintended effect of increasing our indifference to victims of violence and perhaps render us more accepting of violence as a necessary aspect of life in the modern era.

**Why Does Media Violence Affect Viewers' Tendencies to Aggress?**  As suggested throughout this section, there are four distinct reasons that exposure to violence via the media might increase aggression.

1. **"If they can do it, so can I."** When people watch characters on TV expressing violence, it might simply weaken their previously learned inhibitions against violent behavior.

2. **"Oh, so that's how you do it!"** When people watch characters on TV expressing violence, it might trigger imitation, providing them with ideas as to how they might go about it.

3. **"I think it must be aggressive feelings that I'm experiencing."** There is a sense in which watching violence makes feelings of anger more easily available and makes an aggressive response more likely simply through priming. Thus, an individual might erroneously construe his or her own feelings of mild irritation as anger—and might be more likely to lash out.

**4. "Ho hum, another brutal beating; what's on the other channel?"** Watching a lot of mayhem seems to reduce both our sense of horror about violence and our sympathy for the victims, thereby making it easier for us to live with violence and perhaps easier for us to act aggressively.

## Violent Pornography and Violence Against Women

A particularly troubling aspect of aggression in this country is the staggering increase in reports of violence expressed by some men against women—especially in the form of rape. In 1990, approximately 103,000 American women are known to have been raped. This is more than one rape every five minutes. According to the FBI, the number of reported rapes has increased fourfold since the mid-1960s. The actual occurrences are obviously much higher, since a great many rapes go unreported, particularly those involving "date rape," in which the victim is acquainted with the assailant.

Coincidental with the increase in rape during the past few decades has been an increase in the availability of magazines, films, and videocassettes depicting vivid, explicit sexual behavior. For better or worse, in recent years our society has become increasingly freer and more tolerant of pornography. If the viewing of violence in films and on television contributes to violence, doesn't it follow that viewing pornographic material would increase the incidence of rape? Although this possibility has been presented as an undeniable fact by some of our nation's self-appointed guardians of our morality, it turns out to be incorrect. In 1970, after carefully studying all the evidence, the Presidential Commission on Obscenity and Pornography concluded that explicit sexual material, in and of itself, does not contribute to sexual crimes, violence against women, or other antisocial acts. But as you will recall, in Chapter 2 we discussed the fact that in 1985, Edwin Meese, while serving as Ronald Reagan's attorney general, convened a commission that disagreed with the findings of the earlier report and concluded that pornography does indeed contribute to violent crimes against women. Which commission was right? Or were both right—that is, was new evidence uncovered during the intervening fifteen years that led the Meese Commission to a different conclusion?

After carefully analyzing the available evidence, we can find no foundation for the conclusions drawn by the Meese Commission. Rather, those conclusions appear to have been politically and ideologically motivated, rather than the result of dispassionate scientific inquiry. This is not to say that the issue is simple, for it is not. Indeed, the reader should note that the key phrase in our description of the findings of the 1970 report is "in and of itself." That is, now as in 1970, we would conclude that viewing explicit sexual material, in and of itself, is harmless. But we would also conclude that there are clearly undesirable effects caused by viewing materials that combine sex with violence. During the past several years, Neil Malamuth, Edward Donnerstein, and their colleagues have conducted careful studies, both in naturalistic and laboratory settings, to determine the effects of violent pornography. Taken as a whole, these studies indicate that exposure to violent pornography promotes greater acceptance of sexual violence toward women and is almost certainly a factor associated with actual aggressive behavior toward women (Donnerstein, 1980; Donnerstein & Berkowitz, 1981; Malamuth, 1981, 1986; Malamuth & Briere, 1986). In one experiment (Donnerstein & Berkowitz, 1981), male subjects were angered by a female accomplice. They were then shown one of three films—

In the United States, we try to protect children from erotic films. But research shows that violent movies are far more harmful.

**"AT LAST, A MOVIE WITHOUT ALL THOSE FILTHY SEX SCENES!"**

an aggressive-erotic one involving rape, a purely erotic one without violence, or a film depicting nonerotic violence against women. After viewing one of these films, the men took part in a supposedly unrelated experiment that involved teaching the female accomplice by means of administering electric shocks to her whenever she gave incorrect answers. They were also allowed to choose whatever level of shock they wished to use. (Needless to say, no shocks were actually received.) Those men who had earlier seen the violent pornographic film subsequently administered the most intense shocks; those who had seen the pornographic but nonviolent film administered the lowest level of shocks. There is also evidence showing that, under these conditions, subjects who view violent pornographic films will administer more intense shocks to a female confederate than to a male confederate (Donnerstein, 1980).

Similarly, Neil Malamuth (1981) conducted an experiment in which male college students viewed one of two erotic films. One version portrayed two mutually consenting adults engaged in lovemaking; the other version portrayed a rape incident. After viewing the film, the men were asked to engage in sexual fantasy. Those men who had watched the rape version of the film created more violent sexual fantasies than those who had watched the mutual-consent version.

Further, just as we saw with violence, prolonged exposure to depictions of sexual violence against women (so-called slasher films) makes viewers more accepting of this kind of violence and less sympathetic toward the victim (Linz, Donnerstein, and Penrod, 1984, 1988; Zillmann & Bryant, 1984). Interestingly, this applies to female viewers as well as male viewers. Again, it should be underscored that these experiments do not support the conclusion of the Meese Commission. That is, if anything, they demonstrate that pornographic films, by themselves, are not harmful, even in those cases where the film depicted women as sexual objects. These experiments make it clear that it is only the films depicting explicit sexual violence against women that produce measurable harmful effects.

## How to Reduce Aggression

### Does Punishing Aggression Reduce Aggressive Behavior?

Much folk wisdom is aimed at the curbing of overly aggressive behavior. It is important to scrutinize this wisdom and, where possible, to subject it to objective scientific inquiry. For example, "Spare the rod, and spoil the child," the old saying goes. Following on that advice, if your little boy tends to aggress—especially against younger, smaller children—then give him a sound spanking and he will soon learn not to aggress. By the same token, if we increase the penalties for aggression in this society—say, by adding decades to the aggressor's prison term or even by invoking the death penalty—this might be a great way to reduce aggression—or would it?

Punishment is a complex event, especially as it relates to aggression. On the one hand, one might guess that punishing any behavior, including aggression, might reduce its frequency. On the other hand, since severe punishment itself usually takes the form of an aggressive act, then the punisher is actually modeling aggressive behavior for the person whose aggressive behavior he or she is trying to stamp out, and might induce that person to imitate the action. This seems to be true—for children. As we have seen earlier in this chapter, children who grow up with punitive, aggressive parents tend to be prone toward violence when they grow up.

Moreover, as we saw in Chapter 3, several experiments with children in kindergarten have demonstrated that the threat of relatively severe punishment for committing a transgression has little impact on diminishing the attractiveness of the transgression. On the other hand, the threat of mild punishment—of a degree just powerful enough to get the child to cease the undesired activity temporarily—serves to induce the child to try to justify his or her restraint, and as a result, can produce a diminution in the attractiveness of the action (Aronson & Carlsmith, 1963; Freedman, 1965). Recently, David Olweus (1991), working in the Norwegian school system, was able to sharply

> All punishment is mischief; all punishment itself is evil.
> —Jeremy Bentham, *Principles of Morals and Legislation*

If a parent wants to curb the aggression of his or her child, threats of severe punishment will have only a temporary effect.

curtail the prevalence of bullying behavior by as much as 50 percent by training teachers and administrators to be vigilant to the problem and to make reasonable and swift interventions. This research indicates that children, who have not yet formed their values, are more apt to develop a distaste for aggression if the punishment for aggressive actions is swift and not severe.

But what about adults—especially adults who already manifest a tendency to commit aggressive acts? Here a slightly different picture emerges. On a societal level, the criminal justice system of most cultures administers harsh punishments as a means of deterring violent crimes. Does the implicit threat of harsh punishments for crimes like murder, manslaughter, and rape diminish the occurrence of such crimes? Do people who are about to commit such crimes say to themselves, "I'd better think twice about this, because if I get caught, I'll be severely punished"? Here the scientific evidence is mixed. Under ideal conditions, laboratory experiments indicate that punishment can act as a deterrent (Bower & Hilgard, 1981). By "ideal conditions," we mean that the punishment must be both very prompt and virtually certain; that is, it must come close on the heels of the commission of the violent act, and the chances of escaping punishment must be very remote. Alas, these ideal conditions are almost never met in the real world—especially in a complex society with a high crime rate like our own. In most American cities, the probability of a person committing a violent crime and being apprehended, charged, tried, and convicted is not high. Moreover, given the clogged calendars that exist in our courts, as well as the necessary care and caution with which the criminal justice system must operate, promptness is rarely possible—punishment is typically delayed by months or even years. Consequently, in the real world of the criminal justice system, severe punishment is unlikely to have the kind of deterrent effect that it does in the laboratory.

And indeed, the societal data indicate that severe punishment does not seem to deter violent crimes. For example, countries that invoke the death penalty for murder do not have fewer murders per capita than those which do not invoke the death penalty; similarly, within our own country, states that have abolished the death penalty have not experienced the increase in capital crimes that some experts predicted (Archer & Gartner, 1984; Nathanson, 1987). In a similar vein, Ruth Peterson and William Bailey (1988) examined a period in our nation just after a national hiatus on the death penalty, resulting from a Supreme Court ruling that found it to constitute cruel and unusual punishment; when the Court reversed itself in 1976, there was no indication that the return to capital punishment produced a decrease in homicides. Some representative homicide data, comparing the United States with other countries, are shown in Figure 12.4.

It should be pointed out that mild punishment, firmly and consistently meted out, can and does have a deterrent effect on some adult acts of aggression. Here we are referring to a serious and all-too-common problem in our nation—family violence, or, more specifically, wife-battering. This has been a thorny problem for the police, who traditionally have been reluctant to intervene in family disputes. In the past, when the police have intervened, they typically would almost never arrest the husband but instead would either give him on-the-spot counseling or ask him to leave the scene for a few hours until he cooled off.

How effective is this kind of intervention? Would arresting the violent husband be more effective? To find out, the Minneapolis Police Department

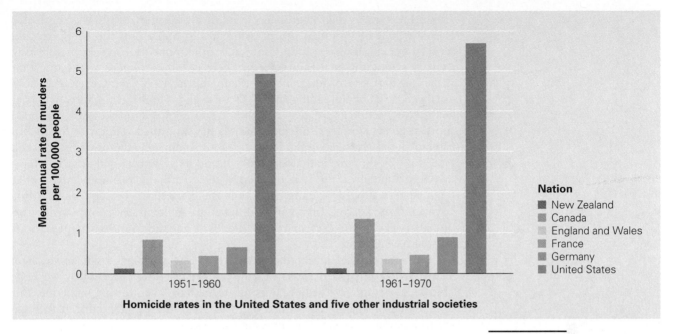

Homicide rates in the United States and five other industrial societies

conducted a simple but powerful field experiment (Sherman & Berk, 1984). In this experiment, police officers were randomly assigned to one of three conditions: In the first condition, they performed brief on-the-spot counseling; in the second condition, they asked the perpetrator to leave the scene for eight hours; and in the third condition, they placed the perpetrator under arrest. Police reports were then carefully monitored over the next six months. The results indicated that, during those months, 19 percent of the perpetrators given counseling and 24 percent of those asked to leave the premises repeated their aggressive actions, whereas only 10 percent of those placed under arrest (and made to spend a night or two in jail) repeated their actions. These data show that when law enforcement officers demonstrate they are taking the offense seriously by hauling the perpetrator off to jail, domestic violence is diminished. The findings led the Minneapolis Police Department to revamp its policies regarding the arrest of perpetrators of domestic violence and have attracted national attention. Similar results have been reported by Langer (1986) and Sherman (1992).

## Catharsis and Aggression

It is generally believed that one way for an individual to reduce his or her feelings of aggression is to do something aggressive. "Get it out of your system" has been a common piece of advice for a great many years. So if you are feeling angry (the belief goes), don't try to ignore it, but instead yell, scream, curse, throw some crockery at the wall—and then you'll be rid of it and it won't fester and grow into something truly uncontrollable. This common belief is based on an oversimplification of the psychoanalytic notion of **catharsis** (see Freud, 1933; Dollard, 1939) that has filtered down to the popular culture. As we mentioned earlier in this chapter, Freud held a "hydraulic" idea of aggressive impulses; he believed that unless people were

**FIGURE 12.4  America leads the way.** The homicide rate in the U.S. far outstrips that of other industrial countries. (Adapted from Archer & Gartner, 1984)

> Something of vengeance I had tasted for the first time; as aromantic wine it seemed, on swallowing, warm and racy; its after-flavour, metallic and corroding, gave me a sensation as if I had been poisoned.
> —Charlotte Brontë,
> *Jane Eyre*, 1847

**catharsis:** the notion that "blowing off steam"—by doing something physically exerting, watching others engage in aggressive behaviors, or actually engaging in direct aggression—relieves built-up aggressive energies and hence reduces the likelihood of further aggressive behavior

allowed to express their aggression in relatively harmless ways, the aggressive energy would be dammed up, pressure would build, and the energy would seek an outlet, either exploding into acts of extreme violence or manifesting itself as symptoms of mental illness. There is some evidence suggesting that stifled feelings can produce illness (Pennebaker, 1990). However, this does not necessarily mean that venting those feelings indiscriminately is either healthy or useful. Freud was a brilliant and complex thinker who stopped short of giving simplistic advice. Alas, as the simplified version of his theory filtered down to the popular culture, it took on the mantle of established fact; thus, by the time catharsis theory found its way to famed advice columnist Ann Landers (1969), it translated itself into the pronouncement that "Youngsters should be taught to vent their anger." The idea behind this advice is that blowing off steam will not only make angry people feel better but also serve to make them less likely to engage in subsequent acts of destructive violence.

On a superficial level, this seems to square with our own experience. Many of us, when frustrated or angry, have felt less tense when we have "blown off steam" by yelling, cursing, or perhaps even hitting someone. But does an act of aggression reduce the need for further aggression? Before we try to answer that question, let's first consider some of the ways in which aggressive energy could conceivably be discharged: (a) by expending it in the form of physical activity (e.g., playing competitive games), (b) by watching other people engage in aggressive play and thus vicariously discharging aggressive energy, and (c) by engaging in direct aggression (e.g., lashing out at someone, hurting the person, getting the person into trouble, saying nasty things about him or her).

Let's take the first one: engaging in socially acceptable aggressive behavior through physical activity. There is widespread belief—even among professional psychologists—that this procedure is effective. For example, William Menninger (1948), the distinguished therapist and cofounder of the justly famous Menninger Clinic, tells us that "competitive games provide an unusually satisfactory outlet for the instinctive aggressive drive" (p. 344). Alas, we can find no evidence to support this contention. In fact, a field study by Arthur Patterson (1974) leads to quite the opposite conclusion. He measured the hostility of high school football players, rating them both one week before and one week after the football season. If it is true that the intense physical activity and aggressive behavior that are part of playing football serve to reduce the tension caused by pent-up aggression, then the players could be expected to exhibit a decline in hostility over the course of the season. Instead, the results of the measures showed a significant increase in feelings of hostility. Similarly, in a detailed study of college athletes Warren Johnson (1970) found no evidence to support the notion of catharsis. This is not to say that people do not get pleasure out of these games; they do. But engaging in these games does not decrease the aggressive feelings of the participants—if anything, it increases them.

Even though engaging in competitive and aggressive games does not result in less aggression, perhaps watching these kinds of games does. Gordon Russell (1983), a Canadian sports psychologist, tested this proposition by measuring the hostility of spectators at an especially violent hockey game. As the game progressed, the spectators became increasingly belligerent; toward the end of the final period, their level of hostility was enor-

Fans watching aggressive sports do not become less aggressive.

mous and did not return to the pregame level until several hours after the game was over. Similar results have been found among spectators at football games and wrestling matches (Arms, Russell, and Sandilands, 1979; Goldstein & Arms, 1971). Thus, as with participating in an aggressive sport, watching one serves to increase aggressive behavior.

Now let's take a look at research on acts of direct aggression against the source of your anger. Do such actions reduce the need for further aggression? The overwhelming majority of experiments on the topic have failed to find such effects (see Geen & Quanty, 1977). In fact, by far the most common finding resembles the research on watching violence, as cited above—namely, when people commit acts of aggression, such acts increase the tendency toward future aggression. For example, in an experiment by Russell Geen and his associates (1975), each of the subjects in their experiment (male college students) was paired with another student, who was actually a confederate of the experimenters. First, the subject was angered by the confederate; during this phase, which involved the exchanging of opinions on various issues, the subject was given electric shocks when his partner disagreed with his opinion. Next, during a bogus study of "the effects of punishment on learning," the subject acted as a teacher, while the confederate served as learner. On the first learning task, some of the subjects were required to deliver electric shocks to the confederate each time he made a mistake; other subjects merely recorded his errors. On the next task, all the subjects were given the opportunity to deliver shocks. If a cathartic effect were operating, we would expect the subjects who had previously given shocks to the confederate to administer fewer and less intense shocks the second time. This didn't happen; in fact, the subjects who had previously delivered shocks to the confederate expressed even greater aggression when given the subsequent opportunity to attack him. This phenomenon is not limited to the laboratory; the same tendency has also been systematically observed in naturally occurring events in the real world, where verbal acts of aggression served to facilitate further attacks. In one such "natural experiment," several technicians who had recently been laid off were given a chance to verbalize their hostility against their ex-bosses; later, when asked to describe that person, these technicians were much more punitive in their descriptions than those technicians who had not previously voiced their feelings (Ebbesen, Duncan, and Konecni, 1975).

In summary, the weight of the evidence does not support the catharsis hypothesis. Again, on the surface, it appears to be a reasonable idea, in a limited way. That is, when somebody angers us, venting our hostility against that person does indeed seem to relieve tension and make us feel better. But "feeling better" should not be confused with a reduction in our hostility. With humans, aggression is dependent not merely on tensions—what a person feels—but also on what a person thinks. Put yourself in the place of a subject in the previous experiments: After once administering shocks to another person or expressing hostility against your old boss, it becomes easier to do so a second time. Aggressing the first time can reduce your inhibitions against committing other such actions; in a sense, the aggression is legitimized, making it easier to carry out such assaults. Further, and more importantly, the main thrust of the research on this issue indicates that committing an overt act of aggression against a person changes one's feelings about that person, increasing one's negative feelings toward the target and therefore increasing the probability of future aggression against that person.

Does this material begin to sound familiar? It should. As we have seen in Chapter 3, when one person does harm to another person, it sets in motion cognitive processes aimed at justifying the act of cruelty. Specifically, when you hurt another person, you experience cognitive dissonance. The cognition "I have hurt Charlie" is dissonant with the cognition "I am a decent, reasonable person." A good way for you to reduce dissonance is somehow to convince yourself that hurting Charlie was not an indecent, unreasonable, bad thing to do. You can accomplish this by blinding yourself to Charlie's virtues and emphasizing his faults, by convincing yourself that Charlie is a terrible human being who deserved to be hurt. This would especially hold if the target is an innocent victim of your aggression. Thus, as discussed in Chapter 3, in experiments by David Glass (1964) and by Keith Davis and Edward E. Jones (1960) the subjects inflicted either psychological or physical harm on an innocent person who had done them no prior harm. The subjects then proceeded to derogate their victims, convincing themselves they were not very nice people and therefore deserved what they got. This reduces dissonance, all right—and it also sets the stage for further aggression, for once a person has succeeded in derogating someone, it makes it easier for him or her to do further harm to the victim in the future.

What happens if the victim isn't totally innocent? That is, imagine that the victim has done something that hurts or disturbs you, and is therefore deserving of your retaliation. Here the situation becomes more complex and more interesting. One of several experiments to test this idea was performed several years ago by Michael Kahn (1966). In Kahn's experiment, a young man posing as a medical technician, taking some physiological measurements from college students, made derogatory remarks about the students. In one experimental condition, the subjects were allowed to vent their hostility by expressing their feelings about the technician to his employer—an action that looked as though it would get the technician into serious trouble, perhaps even cost him his job. In another condition, the subjects were not given the opportunity to express any aggression against the person who had aroused their anger. Those who were allowed to express their aggression subsequently

During World War II, we derogated the Japanese by depicting them as less than human. This helped to justify our own destructiveness—as in the bombing of Nagasaki.

felt greater dislike and hostility for the technician than those who were inhibited from expressing their aggression did. In other words, expressing aggression did not inhibit the tendency to aggress; rather, it tended to increase it—even when the target was not simply an innocent victim.

These results suggest that when people are made angry, they frequently engage in overkill. In this case, costing the technician his job is much more devastating than the minor insult delivered by the technician. The overkill produces dissonance in much the same way hurting an innocent person produces dissonance. That is, if there is a major discrepancy between what the person did to you and the force of your retaliation, that discrepancy must be justified by derogating the object of your wrath.

If our reasoning is correct, it might help to explain why it is that when two nations are at war, a relatively small percentage of the members of the victorious nation feel much sympathy for the innocent victims of the nation's actions. For example, near the end of World War II, American planes dropped atom bombs on Hiroshima and Nagasaki. More than 100,000 civilians—including a great many children—were killed, and countless thousands suffered severe injuries. Shortly thereafter, a poll taken of the American people indicated that less than 5 percent felt we should not have used those weapons, whereas 23 percent felt we should have used many more of them before giving Japan the opportunity to surrender. Why would so many Americans favor the wanton death and destruction of innocent victims? Our guess is that, in the course of the war, a sizable proportion of Americans gradually adopted increasingly derogatory attitudes toward the Japanese that made it increasingly easy to accept the fact that we were causing them a great deal of misery. And the more misery we inflicted on them, the more these Americans derogated them—leading to an endless spiral of aggression and the justification of aggression, even to the point of favoring a delay in the ending of the war so that still more destruction might be inflicted.

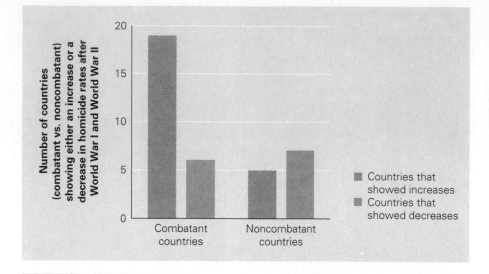

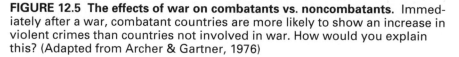

**FIGURE 12.5 The effects of war on combatants vs. noncombatants.** Immediately after a war, combatant countries are more likely to show an increase in violent crimes than countries not involved in war. How would you explain this? (Adapted from Archer & Gartner, 1976)

Does this sound like ancient history? We hasten to remind you that, in this decade, our nation won a swift and stunning victory over Iraq in a lopsided war in which American casualties were few but tens of thousands of Iraqis—including a great many civilians—lost their lives. The vast majority of U.S. citizens were elated by the outcome of the war; there were celebrations, parades, and a huge—if temporary—increase in the popularity of our former president. Please note that we are not raising the question of whether or not the war was just or necessary. The only question we are raising is, what percentage of the American population, do you suppose, paused for a few moments to feel sadness or regret about the Iraqi civilians who were killed in that war? The polls indicate very little sympathy for the innocent victims. How come? Are we a particularly callous, unsympathetic nation? We don't believe so. You now have the tools to begin to understand that phenomenon.

Interestingly, when a nation is at war the impact of that situation extends even beyond feelings of hostility toward the enemy. Specifically, being at war makes the population—even the noncombatants—more prone to commit aggressive actions against one another. Dane Archer and Rosemary Gartner (1976, 1984) compared the crime rates for 110 countries since 1900. The data can be found in Figure 12.5. They found that, compared with similar nations that remained at peace, countries that fought wars exhibited substantial postwar increases in their homicide rates. This should not be surprising; it is consistent with everything we have been saying about the social causes of aggression. In a sense, when a nation is at war it's like one big, all-pervasive, violent TV drama. Thus, just as with overexposure to TV violence, the fact that a nation is at war (a) weakens the population's inhibitions against aggression, (b) leads to imitation of aggression, (c) makes aggressive responses more available, and (d) numbs our senses to the horror of cruelty and destruction, making us less sympathetic to the victims. In addi-

In war, the state is sanctioning murder. Even when the war is over, this moral corruption is bound to linger for many years.

—Erasmus, 1514

tion, being at war serves to legitimize to the population the use of violent solutions to address difficult problems.

## What Are We Supposed to Do with Our Anger?

**Venting Versus Self-Awareness.**  If violence leads to self-justification, which in turn breeds more violence, then if we are feeling angry at someone, what are we to do with our angry feelings—stifle them? Surely, Sigmund Freud and Ann Landers were not totally wrong when they indicated that stifled anger might be harmful to the individual. Indeed, as mentioned earlier, recent research suggests that stifling powerful emotions can lead to physical illness (Pennebaker, 1990). But if it is harmful to keep our feelings bottled up and harmful to express them, what are we supposed to do with them? It isn't as difficult a dilemma as it might seem. We would suggest that there is an important difference between being angry and expressing that anger in a violent and destructive manner. To experience anger in appropriate circumstances is normal and almost invariably harmless. It is certainly possible to express that anger in a nonviolent manner—for example, by making a clear and simple statement indicating that you are feeling angry and why. Indeed, such a statement in itself is a vehicle for self-assertion and probably serves to relieve tension and to make the angered person feel better. At the same time, because no actual harm befalls the target of your anger, such a response does not set in motion those cognitive processes which would lead you to justify your behavior by ridiculing or derogating the target person. Moreover, when such feelings are expressed among friends or acquaintances in a clear, open, nonpunitive manner, greater mutual understanding and a strengthening of the friendship can result. It almost seems too simple. Yet we have found such behavior to be a reasonable option that will have more beneficial effects than shouting, name-calling, and throwing crockery, on the one hand, or suffering in silence as you grin and bear it, on the other.

While it is probably best to reveal your anger to the friend who caused it, you may also derive some benefit from sharing your anger with a third party. Although he did not work specifically with anger, James Pennebaker's (1990) research indicates that when we are experiencing emotional stress, it is helpful to reveal that emotion to anyone. In Pennebaker's experiments with people undergoing a wide range of traumatic events, those who were induced to reveal the details of the event, as well as their feelings at the time they were experiencing the event, felt healthier and suffered fewer physical illnesses six months later than either people who were allowed to suffer in silence or those who were induced to talk about the details of the events but not the underlying feelings.

Pennebaker suggests that the beneficial effects of "opening up" are due not simply to the venting of feelings but at least in part to the insights and self-awareness that usually accompany such self-disclosure. Some independent corroboration of this suggestion comes from a rather different experiment by Leonard Berkowitz and Bartholmeu Troccoli (1990). In this experiment, young women listened to another woman talk about herself as part of a job interview. Half of the listeners did so while extending their nondominant arm, unsupported (causing discomfort and mild pain), while the others listened with their arms resting comfortably on the table. In each con-

> To jaw-jaw is better than to war-war.
> —Winston Churchill, 1954

> I was angry with my friend:
> I told my wrath, my wrath did end.
> —William Blake (1757–1827)

Using our ability to communicate
can help diffuse aggression.

*"I'll make a deal with you. You don't push my buttons,
and I won't pull your strings."*

dition, half of the subjects were asked to rate their feelings while they were listening to the job interview; according to the researchers, this procedure provided those subjects with a vehicle for understanding their discomfort and a way to gain insight into it. The results were striking: Those subjects who experienced pain and discomfort during the interview but were not given the opportunity to process it experienced the most negative feelings toward the interviewee—and the more unpleasant it was for them, the more negatively they felt toward the interviewee. On the other hand, those subjects who were given the opportunity to process their pain were able to avoid being unfairly harsh to the interviewee.

**Defusing Anger Through Apology.** An effective way to reduce aggression in another person is to take some action aimed at diminishing the anger and annoyance that cause it. For example, earlier in this chapter we learned that when people had been frustrated by someone and then learned that he or she simply couldn't do any better, that frustration did not bubble over into anger or aggression. This suggests that one way to reduce aggression is for the individual who caused the frustration to take responsibility for the action, apologize for it, and indicate that it is unlikely to happen again. Suppose you are scheduled to be at your friend's house at 7:30 P.M. in order to drive her to a concert scheduled to start at 8:00. The concert is an exciting one for her—it involves one of her favorite soloists—and she has been looking forward to it for several weeks. You rush out of your house with just barely enough time to get there, but after driving for a few minutes, you discover that you have a flat tire. By the time you change the tire and get to her house, you are already twenty minutes late for the concert. Imagine her response if you (a) casually walk in, grin at her, and say, "Oh well, it probably wouldn't have been an interesting concert anyway. Don't take it so seriously; it's not such a big deal. Where's your sense of humor?" or (b) run in with a sad and anguished look on your face, show her your greasy and dirty hands, tell her you left your house in time to make it but unaccountably got this flat, apologize sincerely and profusely, and vow to find a way to make it up to her.

Our guess is that your friend would be prone toward aggression in the first instance but not in the second. This guess is supported by the results of several experiments (Baron, 1988, 1990; Weiner, Amirkhan, Folkes, and Verette, 1987). Typical of these experiments is one by Ohbuchi, Kameda, and Agarie (1989), in which college students performed poorly on a complex task because of errors made by the experimenter's assistant while presenting the materials. In three conditions, the assistant apologized publicly, apologized privately, or did not apologize at all. In a fourth condition, the senior experimenter removed the harm by indicating that he surmised there was an administrative blunder and therefore did not hold the students responsible for their poor performance. The results were clear: The students liked the assistant better and showed far less tendency to aggress against him if he apologized than if he didn't apologize, even if the harm was subsequently removed by the experimenter. Moreover, whether the apology was public or private made little difference; any apology—sincerely given, and in which the perpetrator took full responsibility—proved to be an effective way to reduce aggression.

With this in mind, one of the authors of this book (Elliot Aronson) has occasionally speculated about the great advantages that might be gained by equipping automobiles with "apology" signals. Picture the scene: You stop at a stop sign and then proceed, but too late, you realize you have taken the right of way that wasn't really yours. What happens? In most urban centers, the offended driver will honk his or her horn angrily at you, or open the window and give you that near-universal symbol of anger and contempt that consists of the middle finger pointed skyward. Because nobody likes to be the recipient of such abuse, you might be tempted to honk back—and the escalating anger and aggression could be very unpleasant. Such escalation might be avoided, though, if in addition to the horn (which throughout the world is most often used as an instrument of aggression), every car were equipped with an apology signal—perhaps at the push of a button, a little flag could pop up, saying, "Whoops! Sorry!" In the foregoing scenario, had you pushed such a button as soon as you became aware of your transgression, doing so might well have defused the cycle of anger and retaliation that is all too frequently a part of the driving experience.

**The Modeling of Nonaggressive Behavior.**  We have seen that children will be more aggressive (toward dolls as well as other children) if they witness examples of aggressive behavior in similar situations. What if we were to turn that inside out and expose children to nonaggressive models—to people who, when provoked, expressed themselves in a restrained, rational, pleasant manner? This has been tested in several experiments (Baron, 1972; Donnerstein & Donnerstein, 1976) and found to work. In those experiments, children were first allowed to witness the behavior of youngsters who behaved nonaggressively when provoked; when the children were subsequently placed in a situation in which they themselves were provoked, they showed a much lower frequency of aggressive responses than children who were not exposed to the nonaggressive models.

**Training in Communication and Problem-Solving Skills.**  It is impossible to go through life—or in some circumstances, to get through the day—without experiencing frustration, annoyance, anger, or conflict. As we have indicated earlier, there is nothing wrong with anger—it is part of being human. What causes the problem is the expression of anger in violent ways. Yet we are not born with the knowledge of how to express anger or annoy-

Martin Luther King, Jr., was effective in reducing and preventing violence by using and modeling nonviolence. Being nonviolent in the face of violence is difficult but effective.

> Man must evolve for all human conflict a method which rejects revenge, aggression and retaliation.
>
> —Martin Luther King, Jr., *Nobel Prize Acceptance Speech*, Dec. 11, 1964

ance in constructive, nonviolent, nondisruptive ways. Indeed, as we have seen, it seems almost natural to lash out when we are angry. As Hans Toch (1980) has indicated, in most societies it is precisely the people who lack proper social skills who are most prone to violent solutions to interpersonal problems. Thus, one way to reduce violence is to teach people how to communicate anger or criticism in constructive ways, how to negotiate and compromise when conflicts arise, how to be more sensitive to the needs and desires of others, and so on. There is some evidence that such formal training can be an effective means of reducing aggression (see Aronson, 1992; Davitz, 1952). In Joel Davitz's experiment, children were allowed to play in groups of four. Some of these groups were taught constructive ways to relate to one another and were rewarded for such behavior; others were not so instructed but were rewarded for aggressive or competitive behavior. Next, the youngsters were deliberately frustrated. This was accomplished by building up the expectation that they would be shown a series of entertaining movies and be allowed to have fun. The experimenter began to show a movie and to hand out candy bars, but then he abruptly terminated the movie at the point of highest interest and took the candy bars away. Now the children were allowed to play freely. As you have learned, this was a setup for the occurrence of aggressive behavior. But those children who had been trained for constructive behavior displayed far more constructive activity and far less aggressive behavior than those in the other group.

**Building Empathy.**    Let's look at horn-blowing again. Picture the following scene: A long line of cars is stopped at a traffic light at a busy intersection; the light turns green; the lead car hesitates for ten seconds. What happens? Almost inevitably, there will be an eruption of horn-honking. We're not talking about one little jab of the horn (which might be a way of informing the lead car that the light has changed), but loud and persistent honking. In a controlled experiment, Robert Baron (1976) found that when the lead car failed to move after the light turned green, almost 90 percent of

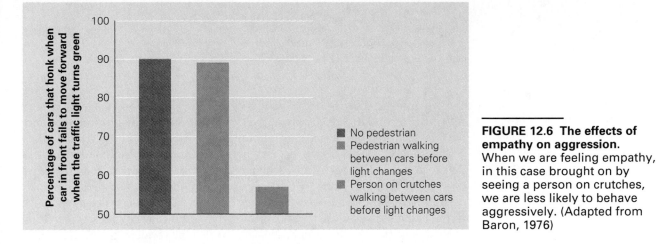

**FIGURE 12.6  The effects of empathy on aggression.** When we are feeling empathy, in this case brought on by seeing a person on crutches, we are less likely to behave aggressively. (Adapted from Baron, 1976)

the drivers of the second car honked their horn in an aggressive manner. As part of the same experiment, a pedestrian crossed the street between the first and the second car while the light was still red and was out of the intersection by the time the light turned green. As you might imagine, this did not have an effect on the behavior of the drivers of the next car in line—almost 90 percent honked their horn when the light turned green. But in another condition, the pedestrian was on crutches. Even though he was on crutches, he was able to hobble across the street before the light turned green. Interestingly, however, in this condition only 57 percent of the drivers honked their horn. How come? Apparently, seeing a person on crutches evoked an empathic response, and the feeling of empathy overwhelmed the desire to be aggressive. The results of this experiment are shown in Figure 12.6.

Empathy is an important phenomenon. As Seymour Feshbach and Norma Feshbach (1969, 1971, 1978) have observed, most people find it difficult to inflict pain purposely on another human being unless they can find some way of dehumanizing their victim. Thus, when our nation was fighting wars against Asians (Japanese in the 1940s, Koreans in the 1950s, Vietnamese in the 1960s), our military personnel frequently referred to them as "gooks." We see this as a dehumanizing rationalization for acts of cruelty; it's easier to commit violent acts against a gook than against a fellow human being. But as you know from reading this book, this kind of rationalization not only makes it possible for us to aggress against another person but also guarantees we will continue to aggress against him or her. Why? Because once we succeed in convincing ourselves that our enemy is not really a human being at all, but just a gook, it lowers our inhibitions for committing all kinds of atrocities. The photos on page 483 illustrate this point.

**Dehumanization** is not a rare phenomenon. Indeed, almost every week we read something in the newspapers or magazines illustrating dehumanization in action. For example, as we were writing an early draft of this chapter, one of us read the item on the next page in the *New Yorker* magazine.

**dehumanization:** the act of seeing victims as nonhumans (e.g., "gooks" instead of fellow human beings); dehumanization lowers inhibitions against aggressive actions and makes continued aggression easier and more likely

In a two-day period in New York City recently, a homeless man, a train maintenance worker and a dog were killed on the subway tracks. Ninety people telephoned the Transit Authority to express concern about the dog, but only three called about the worker and no one about the homeless man. (*New Yorker*, November 4, 1991, p. 106)

An understanding of the process of dehumanization is the first step toward reversing it. Specifically, if it is true that most individuals must dehumanize their victims in order to commit an extreme act of aggression, then by building empathy among people, aggressive acts will become more difficult to commit. Feshbach and Feshbach (1969) have demonstrated a negative correlation between empathy and aggression in children: The more empathy a child has, the less he or she resorts to aggressive actions. They have also developed a successful method of teaching children to take the perspective of others. Specifically, they taught children to be able to identify different emotions in people by having them act out roles in various emotionally laden situations, and these "empathy training activities" led to significant decreases in these children's aggressive behaviors. This kind of process will be discussed in greater detail in the next chapter, on prejudice.

## SUMMARY

We define **aggression** as an intentional action aimed at doing harm or causing physical or psychological pain to another person. **Hostile aggression** involves having the goal of inflicting pain; **instrumental aggression** involves inflicting pain on the way to some other goal. Aggression has become an increasingly serious concern to Americans because of the rapid increase in violent crimes, especially in major urban centers.

Over the centuries, there has been a great deal of disagreement among scholars over whether aggressiveness is primarily instinctive or learned. Sigmund Freud theorized that humans are born with an instinct toward life, called **Eros,** and a death instinct, **Thanatos.** The death instinct manifests itself as suicide when turned inward, and as hostility, destructiveness, and murder when turned outward. Freud's **hydraulic theory** states that aggressive energy must be released to avoid buildup resulting in an explosion.

Because aggressiveness has had survival value, most contemporary social psychologists accept the proposition that it is part of our evolutionary heritage. At the same time, we know that humans have developed exquisite mechanisms for controlling their aggressive impulses, and that human behavior is flexible and adaptable to changes in the environment. Thus, whether or not aggression is actually expressed depends on a complex interplay between our biological propensities, our innate and learned inhibitory responses, and the precise nature of the social situation.

There are many situational causes of aggression, ranging from the neurological and chemical to the social. The area in the core of the brain called the **amygdala** is thought to control aggression. It is reasonably clear that the hormone **testosterone** is correlated with aggressive behavior—for example, prisoners convicted of violent crimes tend to have higher levels of testosterone than those convicted of nonviolent crimes. This is consistent with the more general finding that men are more aggressive than women. At least one other chemical, alcohol, is associated with increases in aggression, due to the fact that alcohol acts as a general disinhibitor, lowering a person's inhibitions against violent behavior, as well as a variety of other behaviors frowned on by society. It has also been shown that pain and other physical discomforts (e.g., the proverbial "long, hot summer") will increase aggressive behavior.

There are also many social causes of aggression. Among these, frustration is prominent. The **frustration-aggression theory** states that the experience of frustration can increase the probability of an aggressive response. However, frustration alone does not automatically lead to aggression; it is more likely to produce aggression if one is thwarted on the way to a goal in a manner that is either illegitimate or unexpected. In addition, frustration is the result not simply of deprivation, but of **relative deprivation**—the feeling that comes from knowing that you have less than what you deserve, less than what you have been led to expect, or less than what people similar to you have.

Aggression can also be produced by social provocation or the mere presence of **aggressive stimuli** or objects associated with aggressive responses, such as guns. **Social learning theory** states that aggression can also be produced through the imitation of aggressive models—either in face-to-face situations or by viewing violence on film or TV. The possible effects of viewing violence in the media are of particular interest to social psychologists in our country because of the pervasiveness of violent programming. Violence in the media has been shown not only to lead to greater aggressiveness in the viewer but also to create a numbing effect, making us more accepting of violence in society. The viewing of pornographic material appears to be relatively harmless; however, if the pornographic material is of a violent nature, it promotes greater acceptance of sexual violence toward women and is almost certainly a factor associated with actual aggressive behavior toward women.

Aggression can be reduced in a number of ways. These include discussing the reasons for anger and hostility, the modeling of nonaggressive behavior, specific training in the use of nonviolent solutions to conflict, communication and negotiation skills, and the building of empathy toward others. Building empathy is particularly useful as a means of thwarting the human tendency to **dehumanize** one's victim.

Punishing aggressive behavior in order to reduce it is tricky; punishment can be effective if it is not too severe and if it follows closely on the heels of the aggressive act. But severe or delayed punishment is not an effective way to reduce aggression. Similarly, there is no evidence to support the notion of **catharsis**—the idea that committing an aggressive action or watching others behave aggressively is a good way to get the impulse toward aggression out of one's system. On the contrary, careful research has shown that committing an act of aggression can trigger the tendency to justify that action, which might eventually produce an increase in aggressive behavior.

## SUGGESTED READINGS

Baron, R. A. (1992). *Human Aggression*. New York: Plenum. A penetrating analysis of the social psychology of aggression.

Berkowitz, L. (1993). *Aggression: Its causes, consequences, and control*. New York: McGraw-Hill. One of the greatest living experts on aggression summarizes his thinking in this up-to-date revision of his classic work.

Tavris, C. (1989). *Anger: The misunderstood emotion*. New York: Touchstone/Simon & Schuster. An interesting and well-written analysis of anger.

# Chapter 13
## Prejudice: Causes and Cures

## Chapter Outline

**Prejudice: The Ubiquitous Social Phenomenon**
**Prejudice, Stereotyping, and Discrimination Defined**
   Prejudice: The Affective Component
   Stereotypes: The Cognitive Component
   Discrimination: The Behavioral Component
**What Causes Prejudice?**
   The Way We Think: Social Cognition
   The Way We Assign Meaning: Attributional Biases
   The Way We Allocate Resources: Realistic Conflict Theory
   The Way We Conform: Normative Rules
**How Can Prejudice Be Reduced?**
   The Contact Hypothesis
   When Contact Reduces Prejudice: Six Conditions
   Cooperation and Interdependence: The Jigsaw Classroom
**Summary**
**Suggested Readings**

f all the social behaviors we discuss in this book, prejudice is probably the most widespread and certainly the most dangerous. Prejudice touches nearly everyone's life. Many of us are victims of stereotyping and even violence, all because of a particular group to which we belong. Those who hold the prejudiced beliefs are affected negatively as well; living a life punctuated by active dislike or hatred for other groups of people is surely not a life-affirming, positive experience. Consider one of Thurgood Marshall's favorite stories:

When he was a young lawyer working for the NAACP, Mr. Marshall recalls, he journeyed to a small town in the South to defend a black man who was accused of a serious crime. When he arrived, he was shocked and dismayed to learn that the defendant was dead—lynched by an angry white mob. With a heavy heart, Mr. Marshall returned to the railroad station to wait for a train back to New York. Not having eaten for several hours, he realized that he was very hungry; luckily, there was a small food stand on the platform. As he walked toward the stand, he debated with himself whether to go right up to the front and order a sandwich (as was his legal right) or to go around to the back of the stand (as was the common practice for blacks in the South at that time). However, before he reached the stand, he was approached by a large, bulky man, who looked at him suspiciously. Mr. Marshall took him to be a lawman of some sort; while the man wore no badge or special uniform, he walked with an air of authority and Marshall noticed a telltale bulge in his pants pocket that could only have been made by a handgun.

"Hey, boy," the man shouted at Marshall, "What are you doing here?" "I'm just waiting for a train," Marshall replied.

The man scowled, took a few steps closer, glared at him menacingly, and said, "I didn't hear you. What did you say, boy?"

Marshall realized that his initial reply had not been sufficiently obsequious. "I beg your pardon, sir, but I'm waiting for a train."

There was a long silence, during which the man slowly looked Marshall up and down, and then said, "You'd better catch that train, boy—and soon, because in this town, the sun has never set on a live nigger."

As Marshall recalls, at that point his internal debate about

Thurgood Marshall, NAACP Chief Counsel, in front of the Supreme Court in 1954.

how to get the sandwich proved academic. He decided not to get a sandwich at all but to catch the very next train out—no matter where it was headed. Besides, somehow he didn't feel hungry anymore (NPR, June 28, 1991).

Thurgood Marshall went on to become chief counsel for the NAACP; in 1954, he successfully argued the Supreme Court case of *Brown v. Board of Education*, the celebrated, landmark case that overturned the doctrine of "separate but equal" and put an end to legalized racial segregation in public schools. Subsequently, Marshall was appointed to the Supreme Court, where he served with distinction until his retirement in 1991.

Many years have passed since the incident recounted by Justice Marshall. There hasn't been a lynching in the South for a long time, and the civil rights movement has made enormous progress in the second half of the twentieth century. However, while contemporary manifestations of prejudice tend to be less flagrant than they used to be, they continue to exact a heavy toll on their victims—in terms of extreme anxiety, diminished self-esteem, curtailed opportunities, and sometimes, physical violence.

## Prejudice: The Ubiquitous Social Phenomenon

Who are the targets of prejudice? Just about everyone. One of the most superordinate groups to which you belong is your nationality, and as you know, Americans have been the target of prejudice around the world. For example, in the 1960s and 1970s North Vietnamese Communists referred to Americans as the "running dogs of capitalist imperialism." In the 1980s, the Iraqi regime under the Ayatollah Khomeini depicted America as a ruthless, power-hungry, amoral nation—referring to us as "the great Satan."

On a more subtle level, even our political allies see us as stereotypically American. British research participants labeled Americans as intrusive, forward, and pushy. Conversely, American participants labeled the British as cold and unfriendly (Campbell, 1967).

Hatred and stereotypes of Americans have
become a familiar sight.

Anyone can be the target of prejudice.

Besides your nationality, many other aspects of your identity cause you
to be labeled. Racial and ethnic identity is a major focal point for prejudiced
attitudes. As you know, Americans who are African American, Asian,
Hispanic, or Native American are targets of prejudice. So are some groups of
Anglo or white Americans: Note the long-standing popularity of Polish
jokes, or the negative stereotypes used throughout this century to describe
Italian and Irish Americans. Other aspects of your identity also leave you
vulnerable to prejudice—for example, your gender, your sexual preference,
and your religion. Your appearance or physical state can arouse prejudice as
well; obesity, disabilities, and diseases like AIDS, for instance, cause people
to be treated unfairly by others. As we write this chapter, a new type of joke
is sweeping the country: "dumb blond" jokes. The old stereotype that blonds
are ditzy bimbos has been given a new life. Finally, even your profession or
hobbies can lead to your being stereotyped. We all know the "dumb jock"
and the "computer nerd" stereotypes. Some people have negative attitudes
about blue-collar workers; others, about Fortune 500 CEOs. The point is
that none of us emerges completely unscathed from the effects of prejudice; it
is a problem of and for all humankind.

Besides being widespread, prejudice is dangerous. Simple dislike of a group can lead to hatred of it, to thinking of its members as less than human, and to torture, murder and even genocide.

But even when murder or genocide is not the culmination of prejudiced beliefs, the targets of prejudice will suffer in less dramatic ways. One nearly inevitable consequence of being the target of prejudice is a diminution of one's self-esteem. As we discussed in Chapter 3, self-esteem is a vital aspect of a person's life. Who we think we are is a key determinant of how we behave and who we become. A person with low self-esteem will, by definition, conclude that he or she is unworthy of a good education, a decent job, an exciting romantic partner, and so on. Thus, a person with low self-esteem is more likely to be unhappy and unsuccessful than a person with high self-esteem. In a democracy, such a person is also less likely to take advantage of available opportunities.

For those who are the targets of prejudice, the seeds of low self-esteem are sown early in life. In a classic experiment conducted in the late 1940s, social psychologists Kenneth Clark and Mamie Clark (1947) demonstrated that black children—some of them only three years old—were already convinced that African American was not a good thing to be. In this experiment, the children were offered a choice between playing with a white or black doll. The great majority of them rejected the black doll, feeling that the white doll was prettier and generally superior.

In his argument before the Supreme Court in 1954, Thurgood Marshall cited this experiment as evidence that psychologically, segregation did irreparable harm to the self-esteem of African American children. Taking this evidence into consideration, the Court ruled that separating black children from white children on the basis of race alone "generates a feeling of inferiority as to their status in the community that may affect their hearts and minds in a way unlikely ever to be undone. . . . [S]eparate educational facilities are therefore inherently unequal" (Justice Earl Warren, speaking for the majority in the case of *Brown v. Board of Education*, 1954, quoted in Stephan, 1978).

This diminution of self-esteem affects other oppressed groups as well. For example, Philip Goldberg (1968) demonstrated that, like African Americans, women in this culture have learned to consider themselves intellectually inferior to men. In his experiment, Goldberg asked female college students to read scholarly articles and to evaluate them in terms of their competence and writing style. For some students, specific articles were signed by male authors (e.g., "John T. McKay"), while for others, the same articles were signed by female authors (e.g., "Joan T. McKay"). The female students rated the articles much higher if they were attributed to a male author than if the same articles were attributed to a female author. In other words, these women had learned their place; they regarded the output of other women as necessarily inferior to that of men, just as the African American youngsters learned to regard black dolls as inferior to white dolls. This is the legacy of a prejudiced society.

Clark and Clark's experiment was conducted some fifty years ago; Goldberg's was conducted some thirty years ago. As we have indicated, significant changes have taken place in our society since then. For example, the number of blatant acts of overt prejudice and discrimination has decreased sharply; legislation on affirmative action has opened the door to greater opportunities for women and minorities, and the media have increased our

> A little black girl yearns for the blue eyes of a little white girl, and the horror at the heart of her yearning is exceeded only by the evil of fulfillment.
>
> —Toni Morrison,
> *The Bluest Eye*, 1970

Fifty years ago African American children considered black dolls to be undesirable. This is no longer the case. Why?

exposure to women and minorities doing important work in positions of power and influence. And as one might expect, these changes are reflected in the gradual increase in self-esteem of people in these groups, an increase underscored by the fact that most recent research has failed to replicate the results of those earlier experiments. Black children are now more content with black dolls than they were in 1947 (Porter, 1971; Porter & Washington, 1979), and people no longer discriminate against a piece of writing attributed to a woman (Swim et al., 1989). Similarly, recent research suggests that there might not be any major differences in global self-esteem between blacks and whites or between men and women (Crocker & Major, 1989; Steele, 1992).

While this progress is real, it would be a mistake to conclude that prejudice has ceased to be a serious problem in our country. Prejudice exists in countless subtle and not-so-subtle ways. For the most part, here in America at the close of the twentieth century, prejudice has gone underground and become less overt (Pettigrew, 1985). But occasionally it is flagrant enough to capture national headlines—as when Yusuf Hawkins, a young African

American, was brutally beaten and murdered by a gang of youths while peacefully going about his business in Bensonhurst, a largely Italian American section of Brooklyn. The reason? He was mistakenly identified as someone who was dating a white woman.

During the past half-century, social psychologists have contributed greatly to our understanding of the psychological processes underlying prejudice, and have begun to identify and demonstrate some possible solutions. What is prejudice? How does it come about? And why is it so difficult to change?

## Prejudice, Stereotyping, and Discrimination Defined

Prejudice is an attitude. As we discussed in Chapter 8, attitudes are made up of three components: an affective or emotional component, representing both the type of emotion linked with the attitude (e.g., anger, warmth) and the extremity of the attitude (e.g., mild uneasiness, outright hostility); a cognitive component, involving the beliefs or thoughts (cognitions) that make up the attitude; and a behavioral component, relating to one's actions—people don't simply have attitudes; they also act on them.

### Prejudice: The Affective Component

> Prejudice: A vagrant opinion without visible means of support.
> —Ambrose Bierce, 1911

**prejudice:** a hostile or negative attitude toward a distinguishable group of people, based solely on their membership in that group

The term *prejudice* refers to the general attitude structure and its affective component. Technically, there are positive and negative prejudices. For example, you could be prejudiced against Texans or prejudiced in favor of Texans. In one case, your emotional reaction is negative; when a person is introduced to you as "This is Bob from Texas," you will expect him to act in particular ways that you associate with "those obnoxious Texans." Conversely, if your emotional reaction is positive, you will be delighted to meet another one of "those wonderful Texans," and you'll expect Bob to demonstrate many positive qualities, such as warmth and friendliness. While prejudice can involve either positive or negative affect, social psychologists (and people in general) reserve the word prejudice for use only when it refers to negative attitudes about others. Specifically, **prejudice** is defined as a hostile or negative attitude toward people in a distinguishable group, based solely on their membership in that group. For example, when we say an individual is prejudiced against blacks, we mean that he or she is primed to behave coolly or with hostility toward blacks and that he or she feels that all blacks are pretty much the same. Thus, the characteristics this individual assigns to blacks are negative and zealously applied to the group as a whole—the individual traits or behaviors of the target of prejudice will either go unnoticed or be dismissed.

### Stereotypes: The Cognitive Component

Close your eyes for a moment and imagine the looks and characteristics of the following people: a high school cheerleader; a New York cab driver; a Jewish doctor; a black musician. Our guess is that this task was not difficult. We all walk around with pictures in our heads. The distinguished journalist

Walter Lippman, who introduced the term *stereotype* more than seventy years ago in his book *Public Opinion* (1922), wrote about the distinction between the world out there and stereotypes—"the little pictures we carry around inside our heads." Within a given culture, these pictures tend to be remarkably similar. For example, we would be surprised if your image of the high school cheerleader was anything but bouncy, full of pep, pretty, nonintellectual, and (of course!) female. We would also be surprised if the Jewish doctor or the New York cab driver in your head was female—or if the black musician was playing classical music.

It goes without saying that there are male cheerleaders, female doctors, and black classical musicians, and it goes without saying that New York cab drivers come in every size, shape, race, and gender. But we tend to categorize according to what we regard as normative. And within a given culture, what people regard as normative is very similar, in part because these images are perpetuated and broadcast widely by the media of that culture. Stereotyping, however, goes a step beyond simple categorization. A **stereotype** is a generalization about a group of people in which identical characteristics are assigned to virtually all members of the group, regardless of actual variation among the members. Once formed, stereotypes are resistant to change on the basis of new information.

It is important to point out that stereotyping is not necessarily emotional and does not necessarily lead to intentional acts of abuse. Frequently, stereotyping is merely a way we have of simplifying how we look at the world—and we all do it to some extent. For example, Gordon Allport (1954) described stereotyping as "the law of least effort." According to Allport, the world is just too complicated for us to have a highly differentiated attitude about everything. Instead, we maximize our cognitive time and energy by developing elegant, accurate attitudes about some topics, while relying on simple, sketchy beliefs for others. (This should remind you of the many facets of social cognition that we discussed in Chapter 4.) Given our limited information-processing capacity, it is reasonable for humans to behave like "cognitive misers"—to take shortcuts and adopt certain rules of thumb in our attempt to understand other people (Fiske, 1989; Jones, 1990; Taylor, 1981). To the extent that the resulting stereotype is based on experience and is at all accurate, it can be an adaptive, shorthand way of dealing with complex events. On the other hand, if the stereotype blinds us to individual differences within a class of people, it is maladaptive, harmful, and potentially abusive.

**stereotype:** a generalization about a group of people in which identical characteristics are assigned to virtually all members of the group, regardless of actual variation among the members

**Stereotypes, Attribution, and Gender.** A particularly ubiquitous manifestation of stereotyping takes place as a function of gender roles. For example, it is almost universal for women to be seen as genetically more nurturant and less assertive than men. As Alice Eagly and Valerie Steffen (1984) suggest, this perception may be role-related—that is, traditionally women have been assigned the role of homemaker.

The phenomenon cuts deeper still. In one experiment, when confronted with a highly successful female physician, male undergraduates perceived her as being less competent and having had an easier path toward success than a successful male physician (Feldman-Summers & Kiesler, 1974). Female undergraduates saw things differently: Although they saw the male physician and the female physician as being equally competent, they saw the male as having had an easier time of it. Both males and females attributed higher

In this cartoon, while the teacher may not intend to be hurtful, his sexism is damaging, nonetheless.

motivation to the female physician. It should be noted that attributing a high degree of motivation to a woman can be one way of implying she has less skill than her male counterpart (i.e., "She's not very smart, but she tries hard"). This possibility comes into clear focus when we examine a similar study by Kay Deaux and Tim Emsweiler (1974), in which they found that if the sexual stereotype is strong enough, even members of the stereotyped group tend to buy it. Specifically, male and female students were shown a highly successful performance on a complex task by a fellow student and were asked how it came about. When it was a man who succeeded, both male and female students attributed his achievement almost entirely to his ability; when it was a woman who succeeded, students of both genders thought the achievement was largely a matter of luck.

In subsequent research, it has been shown that young girls have a tendency to downplay their own ability; specifically, while fourth-grade boys attributed their own successful outcomes on a difficult intellectual task to their ability, girls tended to derogate their own successful performance. Moreover, this experiment also showed that while boys had learned to protect their egos by attributing their own failures to bad luck, girls took more of the blame for failures on themselves (Nichols, 1975).

Gender-related attributions can cut both ways—that is, men are expected to succeed, but if they fail, they are treated more harshly than women who fail. This was demonstrated in an experiment by Kay Deaux and Janet Taynor (1973), who had participants listen to a taped interview with a college student, a candidate for a prestigious scholarship. If the candidate did well in the interview and was male, participants rated him as being more competent than a female who had done just as well. However, if the male candidate did poorly in the interview, they rated him as considerably less competent than a female candidate who had done as poorly. To summarize the research on gender-related stereotypes, we would conclude that society is particularly tough on men when they fail, and particularly ungenerous toward women when they succeed. More specifically, because men are expected to succeed in our society, they are treated harshly when they do not do so. Because women are not expected to succeed, when they do succeed, they are seen by others (and by themselves) either as the rare person with an extraordinarily high degree of motivation or as simply lucky. When women fail, they are treated more leniently; after all, if you don't expect much from a person, how can you judge the person's failure harshly?

## Discrimination: The Behavioral Component

This brings us to the final component of prejudice: when beliefs are translated into behavior. In this case, stereotyped beliefs, combined with a negative emotional reaction, translate into unfair treatment or even violence—in other words, into **discrimination,** defined as unjustified negative or harmful action toward the members of a group, simply because of their membership in it.

An excellent example of discrimination is a study conducted by Charles Bond and his colleagues (1988), who departed from the friendly confines of the college campus to compare the treatment of black versus white patients in a psychiatric hospital run by an all-white professional staff. This study is illustrated in Figure 3.1. The researchers examined the two most common methods used by staff members to handle patients' violent behavior: (a) secluding the individual in a time-out room and (b) restraining the individual in a straitjacket and administering tranquilizing drugs. An examination of hospital records over eighty-five days revealed that the harsher method— physical and chemical restraint—was used against black patients nearly four times more often than against white patients. This was the case despite the virtual lack of differences in the number of violent incidents committed by the black and the white patients. Moreover, this discriminatory treatment occurred even though the black patients, on being admitted to the hospital, had on average been diagnosed as less violent than the white patients.

**discrimination:** unjustified negative or harmful action toward a member of a group, simply because of his or her membership in that group

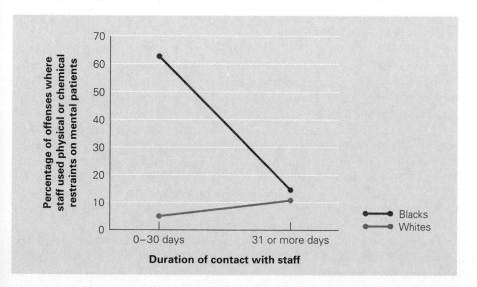

**FIGURE 13.1 Use of Extreme Measures Against Black Mental Patients.** During the first 30 days of confinement, there appeared to be an assumption that blacks would be more violent than whites. (Adapted from Bond et al., 1988)

This study did uncover an important positive finding: After several weeks, reality managed to overcome the effects of the existing stereotype. The staff eventually noticed that the black and the white patients did not differ in their degree of violent behavior, and they began to treat black and white patients equally. While this is encouraging, the overall meaning of the study is both clear and disconcerting: The existing stereotype resulted in undeserved, harsher initial treatment of black patients by trained professionals. At the same time, the fact that reality overcame the stereotype is a tribute to the professionalism of the staff, because, as we shall see, in most cases deeply rooted prejudice, stereotypes, and discrimination are not easy to change.

## What Causes Prejudice?

> Prejudices are the props of civilization.
> —André Gide, 1939

What makes people prejudiced? Is it part of our biological survival mechanism to favor our own family, tribe, and race and to express hostility to outsiders? As noted in Chapter 11, sociobiologists have suggested that all organisms have a tendency to feel more favorably toward genetically similar others and to express fear and loathing toward dissimilar organisms, even if the latter have never done them any harm (Rushton, 1989; Trivers, 1985). Conversely, are we taught by our culture (e.g., by our parents, peers, the local community, and the media) to assign negative qualities and attributes to people who are different from us? Psychologists and sociologists know that prejudice is easy to learn and that young children tend to hold the same prejudiced attitudes as their parents. While we humans might have inherited biological tendencies that predispose us toward prejudicial behavior, no one knows for sure whether or not prejudice is a part of our biological makeup. We do know that prejudice is not confined to such biologically obvious aspects of human difference as race and gender; it also exists among biologically similar people who happen to hold slightly different beliefs—for example, in religion, as with Protestant and Catholic Northern Irish. Indeed, prejudice can even be fostered in schoolchildren over such trivial differences as eye color, length of hair, and style of dress. Let's take a close look at some of the known causes of prejudice.

In the late 1960s, a third-grade teacher in Riceville, Iowa, Jane Elliot, grew concerned that her young students had no real idea of what racism or prejudice was. The children all lived in rural Iowa, they were all white, and they were all Christian. How could Elliot teach them what stereotyping and discrimination felt like?

One day, Elliot divided her class by eye color. She told her students that blue-eyed people were better than brown-eyed people—smarter, nicer, more trustworthy, and so on. The brown-eyed kids had to wear cloth collars around their necks so that they would be instantly recognizable as one of the inferior group. The blue-eyed kids got to play longer at recess, could have second helpings at the cafeteria, were praised in the classroom, and so on. How did the children respond?

In less than a half-hour, Elliot had created a microcosm of society in her classroom: a prejudiced society. While before, the children had been a cooperative, cohesive group, now they were indeed divided. The superior kids, the blue-eyed ones, made fun of the brown-eyed kids, refused to play with them, tattled on them to the teacher, thought up new restrictions and punishments for them, and even started a fistfight with them in the school yard. The inferior kids, the brown-eyed ones, were depressed and demoralized. They did significantly less well on classroom tests that day. They became shadows of their formerly happy selves.

The next day, Elliot switched the stereotypes about eye color. She said she'd made a mistake—that brown-eyed people were really the better ones. She told the brown-eyed kids to put their collars on the blue-eyed kids. They gleefully did so. The tables had turned—and the brown-eyed kids exacted their revenge.

On the morning of the third day, Elliot explained to her students that they had been learning about prejudice and discrimination and how it feels to be a person of color in this society. The children discussed the two-day experience and clearly understood its message. In a follow-up, Elliot met with these students at a class reunion, when they were in their midtwenties. Their memories of the exercise were startlingly clear—they each said it had had an amazing effect on their lives. They felt that they were less prejudiced and more aware of discrimination against others because of this childhood experience. They said they thought every child in America should experience the eye-color exercise.

> The world is full of pots jeering at kettles.
> —La Rochefoucauld, 1678

## The Way We Think: Social Cognition

Our first explanation for what causes prejudice is that it is the inevitable byproduct of the way we process and organize information—in other words, it is the dark side of human *social cognition* (as discussed in Chapter 4). Our tendency to categorize and group information together, to form schemas and to use these to interpret new or unusual information, to rely on potentially inaccurate *heuristics* (shortcuts in mental reasoning), and to depend on what are often faulty memory processes—all of these aspects of social cognition can lead us to form negative stereotypes and to apply them in a discriminatory fashion. Let's examine this dark side of social cognition more closely.

**Social Categorization: Us Versus Them.** The first step in prejudice is the creation of groups—that is, the categorization of some people into one group based on certain characteristics, and of others into another group based on their different characteristics. The underlying theme of human social cognition is such categorization—grouping stimuli according to their similarities and contrasting stimuli according to their disparities (Rosch & Lloyd, 1978; Taylor, 1981; Wilder, 1986). For example, we make sense out of the physical world by grouping animals and plants into taxonomies; we make sense out of our social world by grouping people by gender, nationality, ethnicity, and so on. We do not react to each stimulus we encounter as new and completely unknown. Instead, we rely on our perceptions of what similar stimuli have been like in the past to help us determine how to react to this particular stimulus (Andersen & Klatzky, 1987). Thus, social categorization is both useful and necessary; however, this simple cognitive process has profound implications.

For example, in Jane Elliot's third-grade classroom, children grouped according to eye color began to act differently based on that social categorization. Blue-eyed children, the superior group, stuck together and actively promoted and used their higher status and power in the classroom. They formed an **in-group,** defined as the group with which an individual identifies

**in-group:** the group with which an individual identifies and feels he or she is a member of

and of which he or she feels a member. The blue-eyed kids saw the brown-eyed ones as outsiders—different and inferior. To the blue-eyed children, the brown-eyed kids were the **out-group**, defined as the group with which the individual does not identify.

Kurt Vonnegut captures this concept beautifully in his novel *Cat's Cradle*. A woman discovers that a person she has just met, casually, on a plane, is from Indiana. Immediately, a bond is formed between them:

"My God," she said, "are you a Hoosier?"

I admitted I was.

"I'm a Hoosier too," she crowed. "Nobody has to be ashamed of being a Hoosier."

"I'm not," I said. "I never knew anybody who was."

What is the mechanism that produces this **in-group bias**—that is, positive feelings and special treatment for people we have defined as being part of our in-group, and negative feelings and unfair treatment for others simply because we have defined them as being in the out-group? The British social psychologist Henri Tajfel (1982) believed that the major underlying motive is self-esteem: Individuals seek to enhance their self-esteem by identifying with specific social groups. Yet self-esteem will be enhanced only if the individual sees these groups as superior to other groups. Thus, for members of the Ku Klux Klan, it is not enough to believe that the races should be kept separate; they must convince themselves of the supremacy of the white race in order to feel good about themselves.

To get at the pure, unvarnished mechanisms behind this phenomenon, Tajfel and his colleagues have created entities that they refer to as **minimal groups** (Tajfel, 1982; Tajfel & Billig, 1974; Tajfel & Turner, 1979). In these experiments, complete strangers are formed into groups using the most trivial criteria imaginable. For example, in one experiment participants watched a coin toss that randomly assigned them to either group X or group W. In another experiment, participants were first asked to express their opinions about artists they had never heard of and were then randomly assigned to a group that appreciated either the "Klee style" or the "Kandinsky style," ostensibly due to their picture preferences. The striking thing about the Tajfel research is despite the fact that the participants were strangers prior to the experiment and didn't interact with one another during it, they behaved as if those who shared the same meaningless label were their dear friends or close kin. They liked the members of their own group better; they rated the members of their in-group as more likely to have pleasant personalities and to have done better work than out-group members. Most striking, the participants allocated more money and other rewards to those who shared their label and did so in a rather hostile, cutthroat manner—that is, when given a clear choice, they preferred to give themselves only $2, if it meant giving the out-group person $1, over giving themselves $3 if that meant the out-group member received $4 (Abrams et al., 1990; Brewer, 1979; Oakes & Turner, 1980; Wilder, 1981).

In short, even when the reasons for differentiation are minimal, being in the in-group makes you want to win against members of the out-group and leads you to treat the latter unfairly, because such tactics serve to build your self-esteem. And when your group does win, it strengthens your feelings of pride and identification with that group. For example, our casual observa-

This whimsical poster captures the idea of out-group homogeneity. While one's own city is depicted in great detail (in-group hetero-geneity), the rest of the country is perceived as being all the same.

tion suggests that there was much more flag-waving and many more parades and patriotic speeches by politicians following the victorious Desert Storm war against Iraq than there was following the less than victorious war in Vietnam. In a more systematic observation, Robert Cialdini and his colleagues (1976) simply counted the number of college insignia T-shirts and sweatshirts worn on the Monday following a football game at seven universities that take football very seriously: Arizona State, Louisiana State, Notre Dame, Michigan, Ohio State, Pittsburgh, and the University of Southern California. The results? You guessed it: Students were more likely to wear their university's insignia after victory than after defeat.

Besides the in-group bias, there is another consequence of social categorization: the perception of **out-group homogeneity** (Linville, Fischer, and Salovey, 1989; Quattrone, 1986). This is the familiar "They're all alike" belief, which you've undoubtedly encountered before. In-group members tend to perceive those in the out-group as being more homogeneous than they really are, as well as more homogeneous than the in-group members are.

Does your college have a traditional rival, whether in athletics or academics? As an in-group member, you probably value your institution more highly than this rival (thereby raising and protecting your self-esteem), and you probably perceive students at this rival school as more similar to each other (e.g., as a given type) than you perceive students at your own institution to be. George Quattrone and Edward E. Jones (1980) studied this phenomenon using rival universities: Princeton and Rutgers. The rivalry between these colleges is based on athletics, academics, and even class-consciousness, with Princeton being private and Rutgers public. Male research participants at the two schools watched videotaped scenes in which three different young

**out-group homogeneity:** the perception that those in the out-group are more similar (homogeneous) to each other than they really are, as well as more similar than the members of the in-group

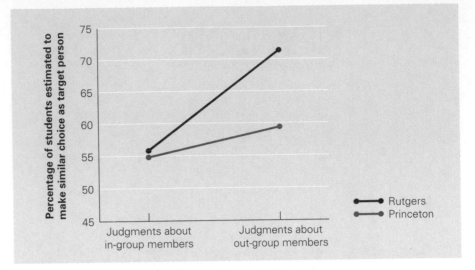

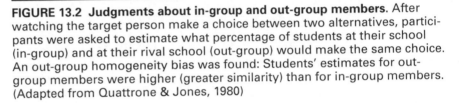

**FIGURE 13.2  Judgments about in-group and out-group members.** After watching the target person make a choice between two alternatives, participants were asked to estimate what percentage of students at their school (in-group) and at their rival school (out-group) would make the same choice. An out-group homogeneity bias was found: Students' estimates for out-group members were higher (greater similarity) than for in-group members. (Adapted from Quattrone & Jones, 1980)

> Our minds thus grow in spots; and like grease spots, the spots spread. But we let them spread as little as possible; we keep unaltered as much of our old knowledge, as many of our old prejudices and beliefs, as we can.
>
> —William James, 1907

men were asked to make a decision—for example, in one videotape an experimenter asked a man whether he wanted to listen to rock music or classical music while he participated in an experiment on auditory perception. The participants were told that the man was either a Princeton or a Rutgers student; thus, for some of them the student in the videotape was an in-group member, and for others, an out-group member. The participants' job was to predict what the man in the videotape would choose. After they saw the man make his choice (e.g., rock or classical music), they were asked to predict what percentage of male students at that institution would make the same choice. Did the predictions vary due to the in- or out-group status of the target men? As you can see in Figure 13.2, the results support the out-group homogeneity hypothesis: When the target person was an out-group member, the participants believed that his choice was more predictive of what his peers would choose than when he was an in-group member (a student at their own school). In other words, if you know something about one out-group member, you are more likely to feel you know something about all of them. Knowing something about an in-group member is not so diagnostic; after all, you know how different and unique your in-group members are (Judd & Park, 1988; Park & Rothbart, 1982).

**The Failure of Logic.**  Anyone who has ever tried to argue with people who hold a deep-seated prejudice against some group knows that it is difficult to get them to change their minds. Even people who are usually sensible and reasonable about most topics become relatively immune to rational, logical arguments when it comes to the topic of their prejudice. Why is this so? There are two reasons, involving the affective and cognitive aspects of an attitude. First, it is primarily the emotional aspect of attitudes that makes a prejudiced person so hard to argue with; as you well know, logical arguments are not effective in countering emotions. The difficulty of using reason to change prejudiced attitudes is beautifully illustrated by Gordon Allport in his landmark book *The Nature of Prejudice* (1954). Allport reports a dialogue between Mr. X and Mr. Y:

> Mr. X: The trouble with the Jews is that they only take care of their own group.
>
> Mr. Y: But the record of the Community Chest campaign shows that they gave more generously, in proportion to their numbers, to the general charities of the community than did non-Jews.
>
> Mr. X: That shows they are always trying to buy favor and intrude into Christian affairs. They think of nothing but money; that is why there are so many Jewish bankers.
>
> Mr. Y: But a recent study shows that the percentage of Jews in the banking business is negligible, far smaller than the percentage of non-Jews.
>
> Mr. X: That's just it; they don't go in for respectable business; they are only in the movie business or run night clubs. (Allport, 1954, pp. 13–14)

Because Mr. X is emotionally involved in his beliefs about Jews, he does not feel particularly bound by the usual confines of a logical discussion. In effect, the prejudiced Mr. X is saying, "Don't trouble me with facts; my mind is made up." He makes no attempt to refute the powerful data presented by Mr. Y. Either he proceeds to distort the facts in order to make them support his hatred of Jews, or he ignores them and simply initiates a new area of attack. The prejudiced attitude remains intact, despite the fact that the specific arguments Mr. X began with are now lying in tatters at his feet.

Second, the cognitive component of a prejudiced attitude in and of itself presents difficulties for the person trying to reduce a friend's prejudice, because as we discussed in earlier chapters, an attitude tends to organize the way we process relevant information about the targets of those attitudes. None of us is a 100 percent reliable accountant when it comes to processing social information we care about; the way the human mind works, we simply do not tally events objectively. Accordingly, individuals who hold specific opinions (or schemas) about certain groups will process information about those groups differently from the way they process information about other groups. Specifically, information consistent with their notions about these target groups will be given more attention, will be rehearsed (or recalled) more often, and therefore will be remembered better than information that is not consistent with these notions (Bodenhausen, 1988; Bodenhausen & Lichtenstein, 1987; Dovidio, Evans, and Tyler, 1986; O'Sullivan & Durso, 1984; Wyer, 1988). These are the familiar effects of schematic processing that we discussed in Chapter 4. Applying these effects to the topic of prejudice, we can see that whenever a member of a group behaves as we expect him or her to, the behavior confirms and even strengthens our stereotype. Thus, stereotypes become relatively impervious to change; after all, proof that they are accurate is always out there—that is, when our beliefs guide us to see it.

**The Activation of Stereotypes.** Stereotypes reflect cultural beliefs—that is, they are descriptions of people in a certain out-group that are widely known by many members of society. We all know the stereotype of the woman driver or the overemotional female, for example. Even if we don't

> The mind of a bigot is like the pupil of the eye; the more light you pour upon it the more it will contract.
> —Oliver Wendell Holmes, Jr., 1901

| Consistency and Change Among Stereotypes | | | |
|---|---|---|---|
| **GROUP** | **1933** | **1951** | **1969** |
| **Americans** | industrious | materialistic | materialistic |
| | intelligent | intelligent | ambitious |
| | materialistic | industrious | pleasure-loving |
| | ambitious | pleasure-loving | industrious |
| | progressive | individualistic | conventional |
| **Japanese** | intelligent | imitative | industrious |
| | industrious | sly | ambitious |
| | progressive | extremely | efficient |
| | shrewd | nationalistic | intelligent |
| | sly | treacherous | progressive |
| **Jews** | shrewd | shrewd | ambitious |
| | mercenary | intelligent | materialistic |
| | industrious | industrious | intelligent |
| | grasping | mercenary | industrious |
| | intelligent | ambitious | shrewd |
| **Negroes (African-Americans)** | superstitious | superstitious | musical |
| | lazy | musical | happy-go-lucky |
| | happy-go-lucky | lazy | lazy |
| | ignorant | ignorant | pleasure-loving |
| | musical | pleasure-loving | ostentatious |

**FIGURE 13.3 Some common stereotypes held by Princeton students over the years.** Note the general stability as well as the changes in these stereotypes. (Adapted from Gilbert, 1951; Karlins, Coffman, and Walters, 1969; Katz & Braly, 1933)

believe these stereotypes, we know them. For instance, in a series of studies conducted at Princeton University over a period of some thirty-six years, students were asked to assign traits to members of various ethnic and national groups (Gilbert, 1951; Karlins, Coffman, and Walters, 1969; Katz & Braly, 1933). The participants could do so easily, and to a large extent they agreed with each other. They knew the stereotypes, even for groups about whom they had little real knowledge, such as Turks. Figure 13.3 shows some of the results of these studies conducted in 1933, 1951, and 1969. Note how negative the early stereotypes were in 1933 and how they became somewhat less negative over time. What is particularly interesting about these studies is that participants in 1951 began to voice discomfort with the task (a problem, by the way, that didn't exist in 1933). By 1969, many participants did not want to label the various groups, because they did not believe the stereotypes; they performed the task only after making clear that their choice of labels reflected the stereotypes present in society (and thus were known to them) but did not reflect their own beliefs (Karlins et al., 1969).

This brings us to an interesting social cognition puzzle: If you know a stereotype, will it affect your cognitive processing about a target person, even if you neither believe the stereotype nor consider yourself prejudiced against this group? Imagine this scenario: You are a member of a group, judging another person's performance. Someone in your group makes an ugly, stereotypical comment about the individual. Will the comment affect your judgment of his or her performance? "No," you are probably thinking; "I'd disregard it completely." But would you be able to do so? Would the comment trigger in your mind all the other negative stereotypes and beliefs about people in that group, and affect your judgment about this particular individual?

Jeff Greenberg and Tom Pyszczynski (1985) decided to find out. They had two confederates, one black and one white, stage a debate about nuclear energy for groups of research participants. For half the groups, the black debater presented far better arguments and clearly won the debate; for the other half, the white debater performed far better and won the debate. The participants were asked to rate both debaters' skill. However, right beforehand the critical experimental manipulation occurred. A confederate planted in the group did one of three things: (a) He made a highly racist remark about the black debater—"There's no way that nigger won the debate"; (b) he made a nonracist remark about the black debater—"There's no way the pro [or con] debater won the debate"; or (c) he made no comment at all.

The researchers reasoned that if those participants who heard the racist comment were able to disregard it completely, they would not rate the black debater any differently from the way participants in the other conditions, who had not heard such a comment, rated him. Was that the case? The data presented in Figure 13.4 clearly show that the answer is no. The data compared the ratings of skill given to the black and white debaters when they were each in the losing role. As you can see, the participants rated the black and white debaters as being equally skillful when no comment was made; similarly, when a nonracist, nonstereotypical comment was made about the black debater, he was rated as being just as skillful as the white debater. However, after the racial stereotype was activated in participants' minds by the racist comment, they rated the black debater significantly lower than participants in the other groups did. In other words, this derogatory comment activated other negative, stereotypical beliefs about blacks, so that the participants who heard it rated the same performance by the debater as less skilled than those who had not heard the racist remark.

These results suggest that anything that activates a stereotype can have dire consequences for how a particular member of that out-group is perceived. How does this activation process work? Patricia Devine (1989) has done some fascinating work on how stereotypical and prejudiced beliefs

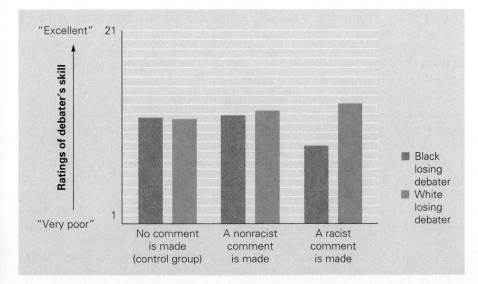

**FIGURE 13.4  The activation of a stereotypic belief.** When a derogatory comment was made about the black debater, it activated the latent stereotype held by the observers causing them to lower their rating of his performance. (Adapted from Greenberg & Pyszczynski, 1985)

affect cognitive processing. Devine differentiates between *automatic processing* of information and *controlled processing* of information. An automatic process is one over which we have no control. For example, even if you score very low on a prejudice scale, you are certainly familiar with certain stereotypes that exist in the culture, such as "Blacks are hostile," "Jews are materialistic," or "Homosexual men are effeminate." These stereotypes are automatically triggered under certain conditions—they just pop into one's mind. Since the process is automatic, you can't control it, or stop it from occurring. You know the stereotypes, and thus they come to mind—say, when you are meeting someone or rating a person's performance. However, for people who are not deeply prejudiced, their controlled processes can suppress or override these stereotypes. For example, such a person can say to him- or herself, "Hey, that stereotype isn't fair and it isn't right—blacks are no more hostile than whites. Ignore the stereotype about this person's ethnicity."

What Patricia Devine's theory suggests, therefore, is a two-step model of cognitive processing: The automatic processing brings up information—in this case, stereotypes—but the controlled (or conscious) processing can refute or ignore it. But what happens if you are busy, overwhelmed, distracted, or not paying much attention? You may not initiate that controlled level of processing, meaning that the information supplied by the automatic process—the stereotype—is still present in your mind and unrefuted. Devine (1989) set out to study exactly this process: A stereotype is automatically activated when a member of an out-group is encountered, and the stereotype can be ignored through conscious processing—for example, by people who are not prejudiced (see Figure 13.5).

First, Devine administered a test of prejudice to a large number of students and, according to their scores, divided them into high-prejudice and low-prejudice groups. Next, she demonstrated that both high- and low-prejudiced people possessed equal knowledge of racial stereotypes. Next came the test of automatic and conscious processing: She flashed stereotyped words (e.g., *black, hostile, lazy, welfare*) and neutral words (e.g., *however, what, said)* on a screen so quickly that the words were just below the participants' perceptual (conscious) awareness. They saw something, but they weren't sure what—that is, their conscious processing couldn't identify the words. However, their automatic processing could recognize the words. How could Devine be sure?

After flashing the words, she asked the participants to read a story about "Donald" (his ethnicity was not mentioned) and to rate their impressions of him. Donald was described somewhat ambiguously; he did some things in the story that could be interpreted either positively or negatively. The participants who had seen the words reflecting the stereotype of black Americans interpreted Donald significantly more negatively than those who had seen the neutral words did. Thus, for one group, the negative stereotype had been primed (activated unconsciously through automatic processing); the participants were affected by these hostile and negative words, without their awareness, as indicated in their ratings of the Donald character. Because these stereotypes were operating outside their conscious cognitive control, white students who were low in prejudice were just as influenced by the cultural stereotype (e.g., that blacks are hostile) as the prejudiced students.

In her final experiment, Devine (1989) gave the students a task that involved their conscious processing: She asked them to list all the words they

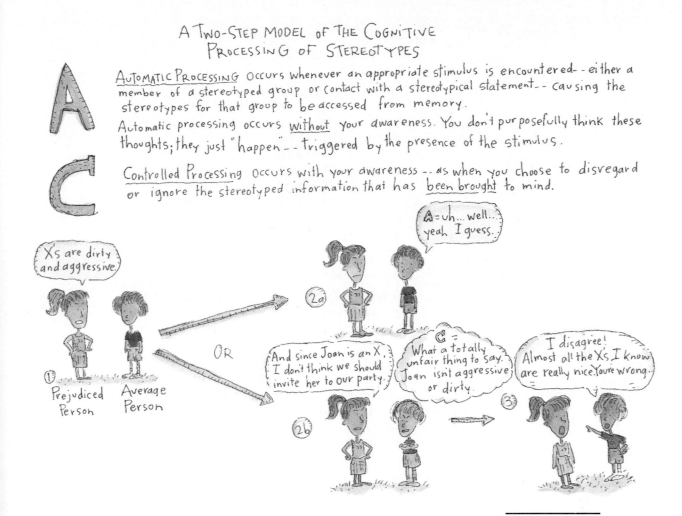

**FIGURE 13.5  A Two-Step Model of the Cognitive Processing of Stereotypes.**

could think of that are used to describe black Americans. The high-prejudiced students listed significantly more negative words than the low-prejudiced students did. In other words, the less prejudiced participants used their conscious processing to edit out the negative stereotype and therefore to respond in a manner that was free of its influence.

Remember the host of a children's TV show who used to tell us, "Put on your thinking caps"? Patricia Devine's research suggests how important it is that we wear our conscious processing thinking cap and not our automatic one. Only by doing so can we combat the stereotypes we have learned by virtue of being a member of our culture.

**The Illusory Correlation.**   Another way that our cognitive processing perpetuates stereotypical thinking is through the phenomenon of **illusory correlation** (Chapman, 1967). We have a strong tendency to see correlations where they don't exist. When we expect two things to be related, we fool ourselves into believing that they are—even when they are actually unrelated. Many illusory correlations exist in our society. For example, there is a common belief that couples who haven't been able to have children will conceive a child after they adopt a child—apparently because after the adoption, they feel less anxious and stressed. Guess what? This correlation is entirely

**illusory correlation:** the tendency to see relationships, or correlations, between events that are actually unrelated

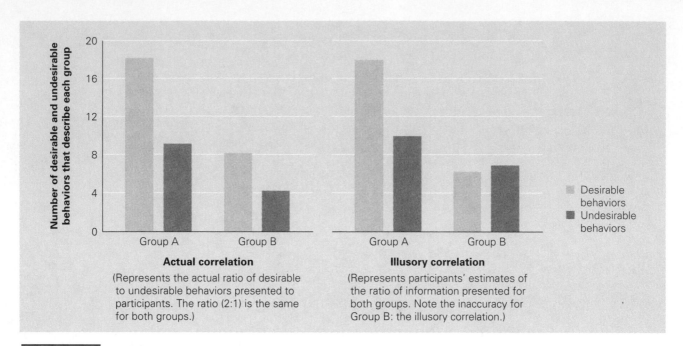

**FIGURE 13.6 The illusory correlation.** The less information you have about a group, the more likely it is that you will fall victim to the illusory correlation. (Adapted from Hamilton & Gifford, 1976)

A fanatic is one who can't change his mind and won't change the subject.
—Winston Churchill, 1944

illusory. Occasionally, an apparently infertile couple conceives after adopting a child, but this occurs with no greater frequency than for apparently infertile couples who do not adopt. The former event, because it is so charmingly vivid, simply makes more of an impression on us when it happens, creating the illusory correlation (Gilovich, 1991).

What does all this have to do with prejudice and stereotypes? Illusory correlations are most likely to occur when the events or people are distinctive or conspicuous—that is, when they are different from the run-of-the-mill, typical social scene we are accustomed to (Hamilton, 1981; Hamilton & Gifford, 1976). Minority group members—for example, as defined by race—are by definition distinctive, since fewer of them than of majority group members—in this case, whites—are present in the society. Other groups, who are not distinctive in terms of numbers—such as women, who make up 50 percent of the species—may nonetheless become distinctive or conspicuous because of a nonstereotypical profession or talent—for example, a woman member of the U.S. Senate.

David Hamilton and Robert Gifford (1976) have shown that such distinctiveness leads to the creation of and belief in an illusory correlation—that is, a relationship between the distinctive target person and the behavior he or she displays. This illusory correlation is then applied to all members of the target group. Hamilton and Gifford (1976) presented information to research participants about two hypothetical groups of people: the A's and the B's. Of the information presented, two-thirds was positive about both groups, and one-third was negative about both groups. However, more information in general was presented about group A than about group B. Thus, while the ratio of desirable to undesirable information was the same for both groups, over twice as much information of both types was given about the A's than about the B's. When asked to estimate how much information of both types was presented about each group, the participants over-estimated the number of times the two most distinctive (less frequent) variables were paired—group B and undesirable behavior. Figure 13.6 depicts this finding. B's were more distinctive because there were fewer of them; undesirable behavior was more distinctive because there was less of it; and—voilá!—an illusory correlation was perceived between the two.

How does this work in everyday life? Let's say you don't know many Jews, so for you, interacting with a Jew is a distinctive event and for you, Jews in general are distinctive people. Let's say this individual is an investment broker. Let's say a second Jew you meet is a bond trader. An illusory correlation between Jews and money is created. If you also know the stereotype that Jews are materialistic, the correlation you perceived based on your personal experiences seems all the more sound. The result is that you will be more likely to notice future situations in which Jews are behaving materialistically; you will be less likely to notice situations in which Jews are not behaving materialistically; and you will be less likely to notice situations in which non-Jews are behaving materialistically. You will have processed new information guided by your illusory correlation, seeing what you expect to see. You will also have strengthened your illusory correlation, confirming in your mind that your stereotype is right (Hamilton & Gifford, 1976; Hamilton & Sherman, 1989; Mullen & Johnson, 1988). We should note that illusory correlations are created in a far more passive fashion too. It is not necessary to have personal experience with people in a distinctive group —television, newspapers, and other forms of media create illusory correlations when they portray women, minorities, and other groups in stereotypical roles (Busby, 1975; Friedman, 1977; McArthur & Resko, 1975).

**Revising Stereotypical Beliefs.** All this discussion of the perils of information processing has probably left you quite depressed. How do you get people to change their stereotypical beliefs? Is it possible to override these social cognition processes? What sort of information would refute a stereotype? Let's say our next-door neighbor harbors two pet stereotypes that we find particularly annoying: He thinks that professors are lazy and that African Americans and Asian Americans are unpatriotic. What would happen if we provided him with evidence that his stereotypes are incorrect? For example, what if we showed him data based on the random observation of 27,000 professors across the country, demonstrating that professors work a fifty-hour week? What if we pointed out that General Colin Powell, former chairman of the Joint Chiefs of Staff and the most influential military figure in the country, happens to be African American? What if we told him that the most highly decorated combat unit in World War II was composed solely of Asian Americans? Would this information affect our neighbor's stereotypes?

According to Renee Webber and Jennifer Crocker (1983), it depends on how the disconfirming information is presented. Webber and Crocker proposed three possible theories, or models, for revising stereotypical beliefs: (a) the **bookkeeping model,** wherein each piece of disconfirming information modifies the stereotype; (b) the **conversion model,** wherein the stereotype radically changes in response to a powerful, salient piece of information; and (c) the **subtyping model,** wherein new subtype or subcategory stereotypes are created to accommodate the disconfirming information.

Webber and Crocker (1983) then conducted several experiments to see which model(s) might be right. They presented participants with information that disconfirmed their stereotypes about two occupational groups—librarians and corporate lawyers. In one condition, the participants received infor-

**bookkeeping model:** information inconsistent with a stereotype that leads to a modification of the stereotype

**conversion model:** information inconsistent with a stereotype that leads to a radical change in the stereotype

**subtyping model:** information inconsistent with a stereotype that leads to the creation of a new substereotype to accommodate the information without changing the initial stereotype

Colin Powell and the Joint Chiefs of Staff. Was Powell viewed as the exception that proves the rule?

mation in the bookkeeping style, one disconfirming fact after another. In another condition, the participants received conversion information, a fact that strongly disconfirmed their stereotype. In the final condition, the participants received information that could lead them to create a subtype of their stereotype. Did these three styles of disconfirming information change people's minds about their stereotypes?

Webber and Crocker (1983) found that the bookkeeping information and the subtyping informaton did weaken the participants' stereotypes, but that the conversion information did not. Why? Here is what occurred. When the information inconsistent with the stereotype was dispersed, with many members of the categorized group exhibiting the disconfirming traits, participants employed a bookkeeping strategy and gradually modified their beliefs. In other words, if our neighbor found out, on many occasions, that numerous professors worked a fifty-hour week, this would slowly but eventually lead him to abandon the notion that professors are lazy. In contrast, when the disconfirming traits were concentrated among only a few individuals of the group, participants used a subtyping model. In other words, if our neighbor was confronted with the undeniable patriotism of General Powell, this would lead to the persistence of the old stereotype about African Americans, plus the creation of a new substereotype to the effect that "There may be a few exceptions, like Colin Powell"; thus, General Powell becomes the well-known exception that proves the rule, leaving the original stereotype pretty much intact. Finally, the conversion approach just didn't work: One fact about an out-group that is evidence against the stereotype was just not powerful enough to change people's minds—which shouldn't surprise you, given our discussion of social cognition processes.

Two points need to be emphasized: (a) We all stereotype others to some extent—it is part of being a cognitive miser—and (b) emotional attitudes are harder to change than nonemotional ones. Thus, a strongly prejudiced person engages in stereotyping in a deeper, more thorough manner than the rest of us. Through this process, prejudiced attitudes become like a fortress— a closed circuit of cognitions, if you will—and this fortress drastically reduces the effectiveness of logical argument or disconfirming information.

## The Way We Assign Meaning: Attributional Biases

As we discussed in Chapter 5, the people and situations we encounter in our social world are not labeled with neon signs telling us everything we need to know about them. Instead, we must rely on one aspect of social cognition—*attributional processes*—to determine why people behave as they do. Just as we form attributions to make sense out of one person's behavior, so too do we make attributions about whole groups of people. As you shall see, the attributional biases we discussed in Chapter 5 come back to haunt us now in a far more damaging and dangerous form: prejudice and discrimination.

**Dispositional and Situational Explanations.**   One reason stereotypes are so insidious and persistent is the human tendency to make dispositional attributions—that is, to leap to the conclusion that a person's behavior is due to some aspect of his or her personality, rather than due to the other possibility: some aspect of the situation. This is the familiar *fundamental attribution error* we discussed in Chapter 5. Although attributing people's behavior to their dispositions is often accurate, human behavior is also shaped by situational forces. Thus, an overreliance on dispositional attributions frequently leads us to make attributional mistakes. We hear Dawn make an insulting remark to Kristen, and we form a dispositional attribution about Dawn: that she's a rude, arrogant person. In doing so, we haven't taken into account what else might have been going on in the situation to have caused Dawn's behavior. (What did Kristen say to her first? Did something terrible happen to Dawn today, so that she's in a tense, upset mood?) Making dispositional attributions when they are not warranted can get us into trouble. Your opinion of Dawn will certainly be different after making that dispositional attribution than if you had made a situational one. Seeing her behavior as dispositionally caused will lead you to expect her to be mean-spirited in the future; you may suspect you can't trust her. Given that this sort of process operates on an individual level, you can only imagine the problems and complications that arise when we overzealously act out the fundamental attribution error for a whole group of people—an out-group.

Stereotypes are dispositional attributions—negative ones. Thomas Pettigrew (1979) has called our making dispositional attributions about a whole group of people (as occurs when we stereotype them) the **ultimate attribution error.** For example, some of the stereotypes that characterize anti-Semitism are the result of Christians committing the fundamental attribution error when interpreting the behavior of Jews. These stereotypes have a long history, extending over several centuries. When the Jews were first forced to flee their homeland during the third Diaspora, some 2,500 years ago, they were not allowed to own land or become artisans in the new regions in which they settled. Needing a livelihood, some took to lending money—a profession they were allowed to have. Although this choice of occupation was an accidental byproduct of restrictive laws, it led to a dispositional attribution about Jews: that they were interested only in money and not in honest work, like farming. As this attribution became an ultimate error, Jews were labeled usurious, conniving moneylenders, vicious parasites of the kind dramatized and immortalized by Shakespeare in the character of Shylock in *The Merchant of Venice*. This dispositional stereotype contributed greatly to the barbarous consequences of anti-Semitism in Europe during the 1930s and 1940s, and has persisted even in the face of clear, disconfirming evidence—

> The cause is hidden, but the result is known.
>
> —Ovid

**ultimate attribution error:** our tendency to make dispositional attributions about an entire group of people

Unfortunately, classic works such as *The Merchant of Venice* may have helped perpetrate negative stereotypes of Jews.

such as that produced by the birth of the State of Israel, where Jews tilled the soil and made the desert bloom.

Dispositional attributions are easy to see in action. As mentioned earlier, Alice Eagley and Valerie Steffen (1984) suggest that women are thought of as genetically more nurturant and less assertive than men because women have traditionally been assigned the role of homemaker. Thus, the attributions about what women are like become dispositional (e.g., nurturant, submissive), while the situational causes for their behavior (the demands and constraints of the homemaker role) are ignored or simply not noticed.

Similarly, many Americans have a stereotype about African American and Hispanic men that involves aggression and the potential for violence—a very powerful dispositional attribution. Galen Bodenhausen (1988) found that college students, playing the role of jurors in a mock trail, were more likely to find a defendant guilty of a given crime simply if his name was Carlos Ramirez rather than Robert Johnson. Thus, any situational information or extenuating circumstances that might have explained the defendant's actions were ignored when the powerful dispositional attribution was stereotypically triggered—in this case, by the Hispanic name.

In a further study, Galen Bodenhausen and Robert Wyer (1985) set up another dispositional versus situational possibility, wherein college students read fictionalized files on prisoners who were being considered for parole, and used the information contained in the files to make a parole decision. Sometimes the crime matched the common stereotype of the offender—for example, when a Hispanic male, Carlos Ramirez, committed assault and battery, or when an upper-class Anglo-Saxon, Ashley Chamberlaine, committed embezzlement. In other instances, the crimes were inconsistent with the stereotypes. When the prisoners' crimes were consistent with participants' stereotypes, the students were harsher in their recommendations for parole. In addition, they tended to ignore other information that was relevant to a parole decision but was inconsistent with the stereotype, such as evidence of good behavior in prison. Thus, when people behave in a way that conforms to our stereotype, we tend to blind ourselves to information that would provide clues about why they might have behaved as they did. Instead, we assume that something about their character or disposition, and not their situation or life circumstances, caused their behavior. In other words, when the fundamental attribution error raises its ugly head, we make dispositional attributions (based on our stereotypical beliefs about an ethnic or racial group) and not situational ones.

**Expectations and Distortions.**  As we noted above, when a member of an out-group behaves as we expected him or her to behave, it confirms and even strengthens our stereotype. But what happens when an out-group member behaves in an unexpected, nonstereotypical fashion? Attribution theory provides the answer: We can simply engage in some attributional fancy footwork and emerge with our dispositional stereotype intact. Principally, we can make situational attributions about the exception—for example, that the person really is like that, but it just isn't apparent in this situation.

This phenomenon was beautifully captured in the laboratory by William Ickes and his colleagues (1982). College men were scheduled, in pairs, to participate in this experiment. In one condition, the experimenter casually informed one participant that his partner was extremely unfriendly; in the other condition, the experimenter told one participant that his partner was extremely friendly. In both conditions, the participants went out of their way to be nice to their partner, and their partner returned their friendliness—that is, he behaved warmly and smiled a lot, as college men tend to do when they are treated nicely. The difference was that those participants who expected their partner to be unfriendly interpreted his friendly behavior as phony—as a temporary, fake response to their own nice behavior. They were convinced that underneath it all, he really was an unfriendly person. Accordingly, when the observed behavior—friendliness—was unexpected and contrary to their dispositional attribution, participants attributed it to the situation: "He's just pretending to be friendly." The dispositional attribution emerged unscathed.

The cartoon on this page demonstrates this ability to explain away disconfirming situational evidence and maintain a dispositional stereotype. This cartoon, from 1951, is a racist depiction using the stereotype of Mexicans as lazy. While ten Mexicans are seen in the background working hard, the cartoon focuses on the stereotypical image in the foreground. The cartoon's message is that the lazy individual is the true exemplar of his ethnic group. No matter how many others refute the stereotype, the cartoon is implying that it is still true. (Note that some forty years ago, not only was this considered an acceptable message, but this cartoon was chosen as one of the best of the year.)

> I will look at any additional evidence to confirm the opinion to which I have already come.
> —Lord Molson, British politician

**Blaming the Victim.**  Try as they might, it is not always easy for people who have rarely been discriminated against to fully understand what it's like to be a target of prejudice. Well-intentioned members of the dominant majority will sympathize with the plight of African Americans, Hispanic Americans, Asian Americans, Jews, women, homosexuals, and other groups who are oppressed in our society, but true empathy does not come easily to those who are accustomed to being judged on the basis of their own merit and not their racial, ethnic, religious, or other group membership. And when empathy is absent, it is sometimes hard to avoid falling into the trap of **blaming the victim** for his or her plight. This may take the form of the "well-

**blaming the victim:** our tendency to blame individuals (make dispositional attributions) for their victimization, typically motivated by a desire to see the world as a fair place

deserved reputation." It goes something like this: "If the Jews have been victimized throughout their history, they must have been doing something to deserve it," or "That woman who got herself raped should have been more suspicious of her date." Such suggestions constitute a demand that members of the out-group conform to more stringent standards of behavior than those set for the majority.

Ironically, as we discussed in Chapter 5, this tendency to blame victims for their victimization—attributing their predicaments to deficits in their abilities and character—is typically motivated by an understandable desire to see the world as a fair and just place, one where people get what they deserve and deserve what they get. As Melvin Lerner (1980) has shown, most people, when confronted with evidence of an inequitable outcome that is otherwise difficult to explain, find a way to blame the victim. For example, in one experiment Lerner and his colleagues found that if two people worked equally hard on the same task and by the flip of a coin, one received a sizable reward and the other received nothing, observers—after the fact—tended to reconstruct what happened and convince themselves that the unlucky person must have worked less hard. Similarly, negative attitudes toward the poor and the homeless—including blaming them for their own plight—are more prevalent among individuals who display a strong belief in a just world (Furnham & Gunter, 1984).

How does the belief in a just world lead to derogation of a victim? When something bad happens to another person (e.g., the person is mugged or raped), we will undoubtedly feel sorry for him or her, but at the same time, we will also feel relieved that this horrible thing didn't happen to us. In addition, we will also feel scared that such a thing might happen to us in the future. How can we cope with these fears and worries? The best way to protect ourselves from the fear we feel when we hear about someone else's tragedy is to convince ourselves that the person must have done something to bring it on him- or herself. Therefore, in our own minds we are safe, because we would have behaved more cautiously (Jones & Aronson, 1973).

Most of us are quite adept at reconstructing situations after the fact, in order to support our belief in a just world. It just requires making a dispositional attribution—to the victim—and not to the situation—the scary, random events that can happen to anyone at any time. In a fascinating experiment by Ronnie Janoff-Bulman and her colleagues (1985), college students who were provided with a description of a young woman's friendly behavior toward a man judged that behavior as completely appropriate. Yet in another condition of the experiment, students were given the same description, plus the information that the encounter ended with the young woman being raped by the man. In this condition, the students rated her behavior as inappropriate, as her having brought the rape on herself. Such findings are not limited to American college students reading hypothetical cases. For example, in a survey conducted in England, a striking 33 percent of the population were found to believe that victims of rape are almost always to blame for it (Wagstaff, 1982). How can we account for such harsh attributions? Most of us find it frightening to think that we live in a world where people, through no fault of their own, can be raped, discriminated against, deprived of equal pay for equal work, or denied the basic necessities of life. By the same token, if 6 million Jews are exterminated for no apparent reason, it is, in some strange way, comforting to believe they must have done something to bring those events on themselves. The irony is overwhelming: Such thinking makes the world seem safer to us.

**Self-Fulfilling Prophecies Revisited.** All other things being equal, if you believe that Amy is stupid and treat her accordingly, chances are that she will not say a lot of clever things in your presence. This is the well-known *self-fulfilling prophecy*, discussed in Chapter 4. How does this come about? If you believe Amy is stupid, you probably will not ask her interesting questions and you will not listen intently while she is talking; indeed, you might even look out the window or yawn. You behave this way because of a simple expectation: Why waste energy paying attention to Amy if she is unlikely to say anything smart or interesting? This is bound to have an important impact on Amy's behavior, for if the people she is talking to aren't paying much attention, she will feel uneasy and will probably clam up and not come out with all the poetry and wisdom that is within her. This serves to confirm the belief you had about her in the first place. The circle is closed; the self-fulfilling prophecy is complete.

The relevance of this phenomenon to stereotyping and discrimination was elegantly demonstrated in an experiment by Carl Word, Mark Zanna, and Joel Cooper (1974). They asked white college undergraduates to interview several job applicants; some of the applicants were white, and others were black. Unwittingly, the college students displayed discomfort and lack of interest when interviewing black applicants. For example, they sat farther away, they tended to stammer when talking, and they terminated the inter-

**FIGURE 13.7 An experiment demonstrating self-fulfilling prophecies.**

STUDY #1:
Interviewer sits far away and has short interview.
Applicant's judged nervous, ineffective, and less competent.
Interviewer sits closer and has longer interview.
Applicant's judged poised, effective, and competent.

White interviewer treats job applicants differently during interview, based on their race. Independent judges later rate black applicants as performing more poorly than white applicants.

STUDY #2:
Sits far away and has short interview.
Applicant's judged nervous, ineffective, and less competent.
Sits closer and has longer interview.
Applicant's judged poised, effective, and competent.

When white interviewers were trained to use one of the two interviewing "styles" from study #1, white applicants were judged as performing more poorly when they received the style previously used for Blacks than when they received the style previously used for whites.

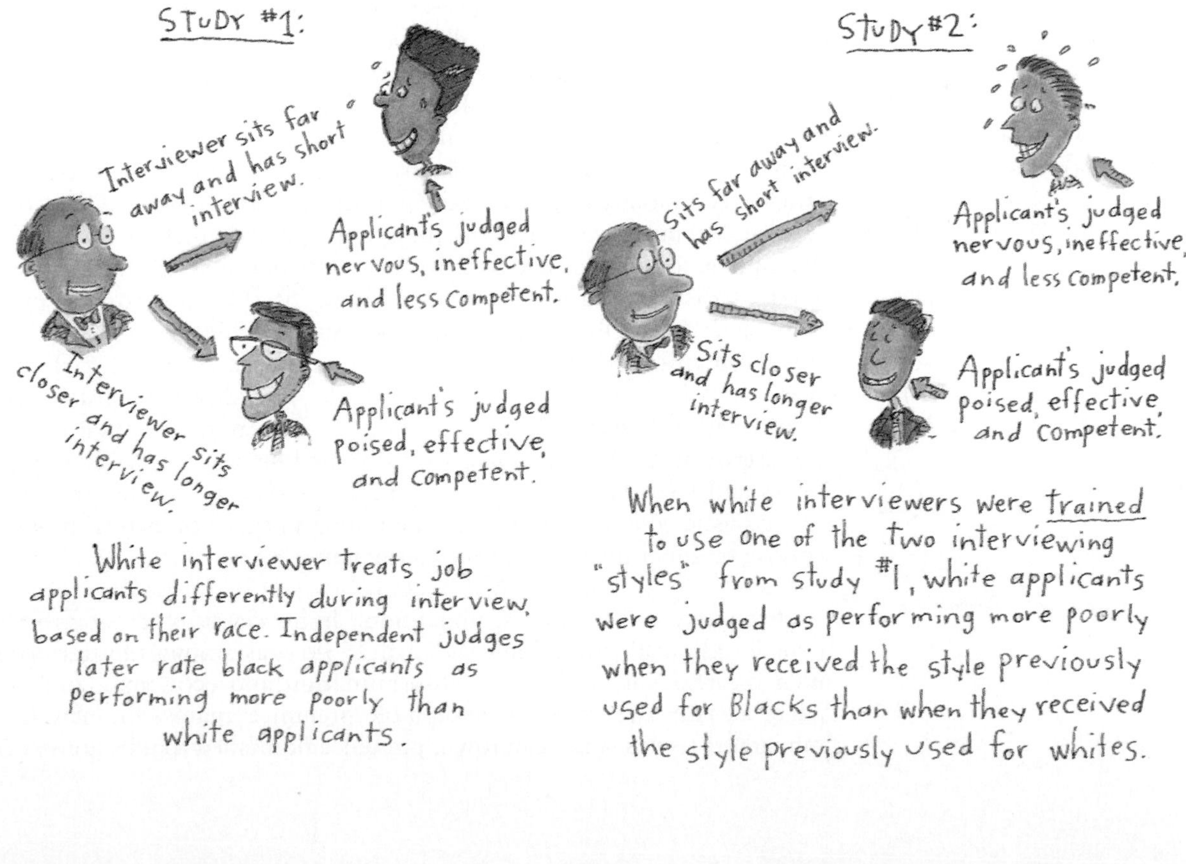

view far sooner than was the case when they were interviewing white applicants. Can you guess how this behavior might have affected the black applicants? To find out, the researchers, in a second experiment, systematically
varied the behavior of the interviewers (actually confederates) so that it coin-
cided with the way the real interviewers had treated the black or white interviewees in the first experiment. But in the second experiment, all of the
interviewees were white. The researchers videotaped the proceedings and
had the applicants rated by independent judges. They found that those applicants who were interviewed the way blacks had been interviewed in the first
experiment were judged to be far more nervous and far less effective than
those who were interviewed the way whites had been interviewed in the first
experiment. In sum, these experiments demonstrate clearly that when blacks
are interviewed by whites, they are unintentionally placed at a disadvantage
and are likely to perform more poorly than their white counterparts (see
Figure 13.7).

On a societal level, the insidiousness of the self-fulfilling prophecy goes
even further. Suppose there is a general belief that a particular group is irre-
deemably stupid, uneducable, and fit only for menial jobs. Why waste educational resources on them? Hence, they are given inadequate schooling. Thirty
years later, what do you find? An entire group that, with few exceptions, is
fit only for menial jobs. "See? I was right all the time," says the bigot. "How
fortunate that we didn't waste our precious educational resources on such
people!" The self-fulfilling prophecy strikes again.

## The Way We Allocate Resources: Realistic Conflict Theory

**realistic conflict theory:** the
theory that limited resources lead
to conflict between groups and
result in increased prejudice and
discrimination

One of the most obvious sources of conflict and prejudice is competition—
for scarce resources, for political power, and for social status. Indeed, it can
be said that whatever problems result from the simple in-group versus out-
group phenomenon, they will be magnified by real economic, political, or
status competition. **Realistic conflict theory** states that when resources are
limited, a real conflict between groups exists; there simply isn't enough of the
valuable commodity to go around. Competition results, and not surprisingly,
negative feelings develop toward the group against which one is competing.
From there, it's a short step to derogatory attributions, ugly stereotypes, and
outright discrimination against members of the out-group (Levine &
Campbell, 1972; Olzak & Nagel, 1986; Sherif, 1966; White, 1977). Thus,
prejudiced attitudes tend to increase when times are tense and conflict exists
over mutually exclusive goals. For example, prejudice has existed between
Anglos and Mexican American migrant workers over a limited number of
jobs, between Arabs and Israelis over disputed territory, and between north-
erners and southerners over the abolition of slavery. At the present time,
such realistic conflict in Germany is erupting in violence against residents of
Turkish origin at the hands of the German neo-Nazis.

**Economic and Political Competition.** In his classic study of prejudice in
a small industrial town, John Dollard (1938) was among the first to document the relationship between discrimination and economic competition.
While initially there was no discernible prejudice against the new German
immigrants to this American town, prejudice flourished as jobs grew scarce.

Local whites largely drawn from the surrounding farms manifested considerable direct aggression toward the newcomers. Scornful and derogatory opinions were expressed about these Germans, and the native whites had a satisfying sense of superiority toward them. . . . The chief element in the permission to be aggressive against the Germans was rivalry for jobs and status in the local woodenware plants. The native whites felt definitely crowded for their jobs by the entering German groups and in case of bad times had a chance to blame the Germans, who by their presence provided more competitors for the scarcer jobs. There seemed to be no traditional pattern of prejudice against Germans unless the skeletal suspicion against all outgroupers (always present) can be invoked in its place. (Dollard, 1938)

In a similar fashion, the prejudice, violence, and negative stereotyping directed against Chinese immigrants in the United States fluctuated wildly throughout the nineteenth century, as a result of changes in economic competition. For example, when the Chinese joined the gold rush in California, in direct competition with miners of Anglo-Saxon origin, they were described as "depraved and vicious . . . gross gluttons, . . . bloodthirsty and inhuman" (Jacobs & Landau, 1971, p. 71). However, only a few years later, when they were willing to accept backbreaking work as laborers on the transcontinental railroad—work few white Americans were willing to do—they were regarded as sober, industrious, and law-abiding. They were so highly regarded, in fact, that Charles Crocker, one of the great tycoons financing the railroad, wrote, "They are equal to the best white men. . . . They are very trusty, very intelligent and they live up to their contracts" (Jacobs & Landau, 1971, p. 81). With the end of the Civil War came an influx of former soldiers into an already tight job market. This was immediately followed by a dramatic increase in negative attitudes toward the Chinese: The stereotype changed to criminal, conniving, crafty, and stupid (Jacobs & Landau, 1971).

These changes suggest that when times are tough and resources are scarce, members of the in-group will feel more threatened by members of the out-group, and will therefore show more of an inclination toward prejudice, discrimination, and violence toward the latter. How might this hypothesis be tested? We might look for increases in violent acts directed at minority group members during times of economic hardship. Carl Hovland and Robert Sears (1940) did just that, by correlating two sets of very different data: (a) the price of cotton in the southern states from 1882 to 1930 and (b) the number of lynchings of southern African Americans during that same period. During this period, cotton was by far the most important crop in the South; as cotton went, so went the economy. Hovland & Sears (1940) found that a significant correlation existed between the two variables, $r = -.72$. As you'll recall from Chapter 2, this is both a large correlation, meaning that the two variables are highly related, and a negative correlation, meaning that increases in one variable are related to decreases in the other variable. In other words, as the price of cotton dropped, the number of lynchings increased (see Figure 13.8 on the next page). In short, as members of the in-group experienced the hardships of an economic depression, they became more hostile toward out-group members, whom they almost certainly perceived as a threat to their livelihood. This hostility led to an increase in the number of violent acts. (Although these data were gathered more than fifty

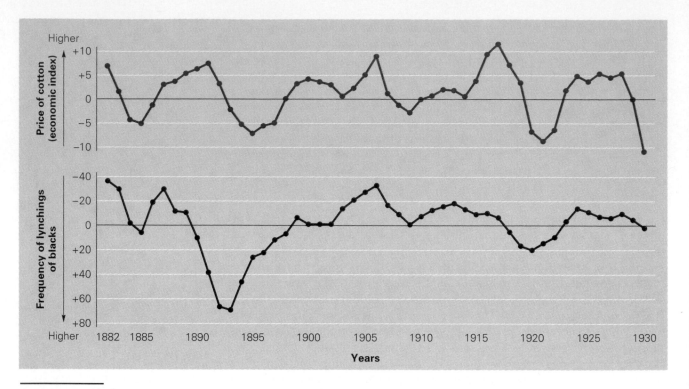

**FIGURE 13.8  Relation of total lynchings to the price of cotton.** Note that the lynching scale shows greatest frequency at the bottom of the graph. (Adapted from Hovland & Sears, 1940)

years ago, we hasten to add that they are extremely reliable; modern investigators, using more sophisticated statistical techniques, have recently confirmed the accuracy of the original research; Hepworth & West, 1988.)

Similarly, in a survey conducted in the 1970s, most antiblack prejudice was found among people who were just one rung above the blacks socioeconomically. And as we might expect, prejudice was most pronounced when whites and blacks were in close competition for jobs (Simpson & Yinger, 1985; Vannemann & Pettigrew, 1972). We should note, however, that this research is correlational; as we discussed in Chapter 2, experimental research designs allow us to make cause-and-effect statements with far more confidence than we can on the basis of correlational research. How might we study the relationship between competition and prejudice experimentally?

In a classic experiment, Muzafer Sherif and his colleagues (1961) tested group conflict theory using the natural environment of a Boy Scout camp. The participants in the camp were normal, well-adjusted twelve-year-old boys who were randomly assigned to one of two groups, the Eagles or the Rattlers. Each group stayed in its own cabin; the cabins were located quite a distance apart in order to reduce contact between the two groups. The youngsters were placed in situations designed to increase the cohesiveness of their own group. This was done by arranging enjoyable activities like hiking and swimming, and by having the campers work with their group on various building projects, preparing group meals, and so on.

After feelings of cohesiveness developed within each group, the researchers set up a series of competitive activities in which the two groups were pitted against each other—for example, in games like football, baseball, and tug-of-war, where prizes were awarded to the winning team. These competitive games aroused feelings of conflict and tension between the two groups. In addition, the investigators created other situations to further intensify the conflict. For example, a camp party was arranged, but each group was told it started at a different time, thereby ensuring that the Eagles would arrive well before the Rattlers. The refreshments at the party consisted of two different kinds of food: Half the food was fresh, appealing, and appetizing, while the other half was squashed, ugly, and unappetizing. As one might expect, the early arriving Eagles grabbed most of the appealing refreshments, leaving only the less interesting, less appetizing, squashed, and damaged food for their adversaries. When the Rattlers finally arrived and saw what had happened, they became angry—so angry, in fact, they began to call the exploitive group rather uncomplimentary names. Because the Eagles believed they deserved what they got (first come, first served), they resented the name-calling and responded in kind. Name-calling escalated into food-throwing, and within a short time, punches were thrown and a full-scale riot ensued.

Following this incident, the investigators tried to reverse the hostility they had promoted. Competitive games were eliminated, and a great deal of non-conflictual social contact was initiated. Once hostility had been aroused, however, simply eliminating the competition did not eliminate the hostility. Indeed, hostility continued to escalate, even when the two groups were engaged in such benign activities as watching movies together. Eventually, the investigators did manage to reduce the hostility between the two groups; exactly how this was accomplished will be discussed at the end of this chapter.

**The Role of the Scapegoat.**    A special case of the conflict-competition theory is the scapegoat theory (Allport, 1954; Berkowitz & Green, 1962; Miller & Bugelski, 1948). As indicated above, if times are tough and things are going poorly, individuals have a tendency to lash out at members of an out-group with whom they are in direct competition for scarce resources. But there are situations in which a logical competitor does not exist. For example, in Germany following World War I, inflation was out of control and people were extremely poor, demoralized, and frustrated. When the Nazis gained power in the 1930s, they managed to focus the frustration of the German population on the Jews, an easily identifiable, powerless out-group. The Jews were not the reason the German economy was in such bad shape, but who was? It's hard to fight back against world events, or one's government—particularly when one's government is evading responsibility by blaming someone else. Thus, the Nazis created the illusion that if the Jews could be punished, deprived of their civil rights, and ultimately eliminated, all of the problems then plaguing Germany would disappear. The Jews served as a convenient scapegoat because they were easily identifiable and were not in a position to defend themselves or strike back (Berkowitz, 1962).

It is not always easy to separate prejudice due entirely and directly to economic competition from prejudice due to general scapegoating. For example, the correlation we discussed between the price of cotton and the number of lynchings in the South probably had elements of both. Another example of the combination of these two elements is the tragic case of a young Asian American who was beaten to death by several white Americans in Detroit several years ago. The murderers were unemployed autoworkers, angry at the Japanese auto industry because they felt that competition from this industry was the main reason for their unemployment. So in their frustration, their irrational hostility toward all people of Japanese origin erupted, and they took it out on this unfortunate young man (who, ironically, was a Chinese American).

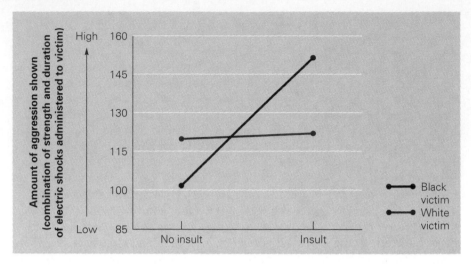

**FIGURE 13.9  Scapegoating.**
When insulted, people are more prone to aggress against minorities. (Adapted from Rogers & Prentice-Dunn, 1981)

Does scapegoating occur whenever people are feeling frustrated and angry, even in the absence of direct competition or conflict? In an experiment by Ronald Rogers and Steven Prentice-Dunn (1981), white students at the University of Alabama were instructed to administer a series of electric shocks to another student as part of a learning experiment. The students were free to adjust the level of intensity of the shocks. In actuality, the learner was a confederate who was not really connected to the shock apparatus. There was no conflict or competition involved in this study; however, for some participants, feelings of frustration and anger were aroused. The confederate was trained to be either friendly or insulting to the participant. In addition, the confederate was either black or white. Would angry white students respond more aggressively toward a black peer than a white one? The answer is yes. When the confederate insulted them, the students administered far more intense shocks to the black student than to the white student; when the confederate was friendly, the students administered slightly less intense shocks to the black student. The results of this experiment are shown in Figure 13.9.

This experiment produced findings almost identical with those of an earlier experiment performed by Donald Weatherly (1961). In Weatherly's experiment, college students were subjected to a great deal of frustration. Some of these students were highly anti-Semitic; others were not. The subjects were then asked to write stories based on pictures they were shown. For some subjects, the characters in these pictures were assigned Jewish names; for others, they were not. Two major findings emerged: (a) After being frustrated, anti-Semitic subjects wrote stories that directed more aggression toward the Jewish characters than people who were not anti-Semitic did, and (b) no difference between the anti-Semitic students and the others was found when the characters they were writing about were not identified as Jewish. In a conceptually similar experiment performed in Canada, English-speaking Canadians, after undergoing a frustrating failure experience, rated members of the out-group (French-speaking Canadians) more negatively than those who had not undergone the frustrating experience (Meindl & Lerner, 1985).

Once again, the laboratory experiments help to clarify the dynamics that underlie real-world events. What all three of the above experiments have in common is **scapegoating.** The general picture emerges that individuals, when frustrated or unhappy, tend to displace aggression onto groups that are disliked, are visible, and are relatively powerless. Moreover, the form the aggression takes depends on what is allowed or approved by the in-group in question. In the past forty years, lynchings of blacks and pogroms against Jews have diminished dramatically, because these are now deemed illegal by the dominant subculture. But not all progress is linear. In the past few years, we have seen the former Soviet Union lose its grip on several Eastern European countries, and indeed on its own Soviet republics. Although we are cheered by the new freedom that exists in this region, that freedom has been accompanied by increased feelings of nationalism ("us versus them"), which in turn have produced intensified feelings of rancor and prejudice against out-groups. Thus, in the Baltics and Balkans the rise in nationalistic feelings has been accompanied by eruptions of hostility (and war) among Serbs, Muslims, and Croats, between Azerbaijanis and Armenians, and so on. And, of course, over the past few years we have also seen increases in the inevitable hostility toward the world's favorite scapegoat, with anti-Semitism on the rise throughout Eastern Europe (Singer, 1990).

**scapegoating:** the tendency for individuals, when frustrated or unhappy, to displace aggression onto groups that are disliked, visible, and relatively powerless

## The Way We Conform: Normative Rules

As we have seen, prejudice is created and maintained by many forces in the social world. Some we can observe operating within the individual, such as the ways we process information and assign meaning to observed events. Some we can observe operating on whole groups of people, such as the effects of competition, conflict, and frustration. Our final explanation for what causes prejudice is also observed on the group level: conformity to normative standards or rules in the society. As we discussed in Chapter 7, conformity is a frequent part of social life, whether we conform to gain information (informational conformity) or to fit in and be accepted (normative conformity). Again, a relatively innocuous social behavior—in this case, conformity—becomes particularly dangerous and debilitating when we enter the realm of prejudice.

**Social Learning Theory.** Norms are beliefs held by a society as to what is correct, acceptable, and permissible. Obviously, norms vary widely across cultures; they are socially constructed standards or rules attached to certain aspects of human behavior (Berger & Luckman, 1967). For example, in the United States unwed pregnancies are frowned on and avoided when possible, whereas in Sweden about 50 percent of all births occur outside of marriage, and being an unwed parent is socially acceptable—no one even raises an eyebrow. There are also important regional differences in norms within the same country. For example, until recently, the racial segregation of hotels, eating places, motion picture theaters, drinking fountains and toilet facilities was normative in the American south but not in the north. Indeed, it can be said that, prior to 1954, segregation controlled most aspects of social life in the south.

How do we learn the norms of our culture? It's very simple, really. As social learning theory explains, everyone teaches us, beginning in our earliest childhood. For example, parents, the school system, peers, and the media both subtly and openly instruct us in how to behave and what to think (Kelly, Ferson, and Holtzman, 1958). Norms are then passed on, generation

Until the middle of the twentieth century, visible examples of prejudice and discrimination were common in the United States. Beginning in 1948, when President Truman integrated the armed forces and the Supreme Court struck down restrictions that were used to maintain residential segregation, visible symbols of segregation began to fall.

**institutionalized racism:** racist attitudes that are held by the vast majority of us because we are living in a society where stereotypes and discrimination are the norm

**institutionalized sexism:** sexist attitudes that are held by the vast majority of us because we are living in a society where stereotypes and discrimination are the norm

to generation. Clearly, stereotypes and prejudiced attitudes are part of this normative package (Ashmore & DelBoca, 1976). A newborn does not know who the out-groups are; he or she must be taught—who to distrust, who to dislike, who to hate.

Normative prejudice need not be as blatant as that depicted in the photograph of the young neo-Nazi mother, who presumably is teaching her children to hate blacks, Jews, and other groups. Simply by living in a society where stereotypical information abounds and where discriminatory behavior is the norm, the vast majority of us will develop prejudiced attitudes and discriminatory behavior to some extent. We can refer to this as institutional discrimination, or, more specifically, as **institutionalized racism** and **institutionalized sexism.** For example, if you grow up in a society where minority and female professors, business executives, or physicians are few but where most people in these groups tend to hold menial jobs, then simply living in that society will increase your likelihood for developing certain (negative) attitudes about the native abilities of minorities and women. This state of affairs can come about without anyone actively teaching you that minorities and women are inferior, and without any law or decree banning minorities and women from college faculties, boardrooms, or medical schools. Instead, societal barriers have created a lack of opportunity for these groups that makes their success extremely unlikely.

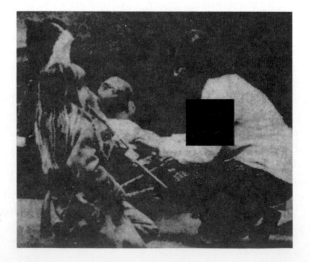

Here is a happy scene, showing an attentive young mother with her three children. But is all as it appears? See the next page for the full story.

How does normative prejudice work? As you'll recall from our discussion of **normative conformity** in Chapter 7, being accepted and feeling part of the group are important to us; in contrast, being the deviant or nonconformist can be painful. Thus, as Thomas Pettigrew (1958, 1985) has noted, many people hold prejudiced attitudes and engage in discriminatory behaviors in order to conform to, or fit in with, the prevailing majority view of their culture. It's as if people say, "Hey, everybody else thinks X's are bad; if I behave cordially toward X's, people will think I'm crazy. They won't like me. They'll say things about me. I don't need the hassle. I'll just go along with everybody else." Thus, Pettigrew (1958) argues convincingly that while economic competition, frustration, and social cognition processes do account for some prejudice, by far the greatest determinant of prejudice is slavish conformity to social norms.

For example, Ernest Campbell and Thomas Pettigrew (1959) studied the ministers of Little Rock, Arkansas, after the 1954 Supreme Court decision ushered in desegregation. As religious people, the ministers favored integration and equality for all American citizens. However, they kept these views to themselves. They were afraid to support desegregation from their pulpits, because they knew that their white congregations were violently opposed to it. Going against the prevailing norm would have meant losing church members and contributions, and under such normative pressure, even ministers found it difficult to do the right thing.

Another way to see the role of normative conformity is to track progress or change in prejudice and discrimination over time. As social norms change, so too should the strength of prejudiced attitudes and the amount of discriminatory behavior. For example, what happens when people move from one part of the country to another? If conformity is a factor in prejudice, we would expect individuals to show dramatic increases in their prejudice when they move into areas in which the norm is more prejudicial, and to show dramatic decreases when they move to an area with a less prejudicial norm. And that is just what happens. In one study, Jeanne Watson (1950) found that people who had recently moved to New York City and had come into direct contact with an anti-Semitic norm became more anti-Semitic themselves. In another study, Tom Pettigrew (1958) found that when southerners entered the army and came into contact with a less prejudiced set of social norms, their prejudice against blacks gradually decreased. A somewhat different

**normative conformity:** the tendency to go along with the group in order to fulfill their expectations and gain acceptance

> Passion and prejudice govern the world; only under the name of reason.
> —The Rev. John Wesley, 1770

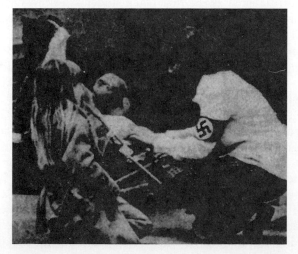

As the full photograph is revealed, what was a happy scene becomes a chilling one. This mother is a member of the American Nazi Party. As social learning theory describes, her prejudiced attitudes and hatred will almost certainly be passed on to her young children.

What a difference a decade makes. On the left, in 1963, Governor George Wallace defies a federal order by physically blocking the entrance of the first black student to the University of Alabama. On the right, 10 years later, Governor Wallace happily congratulates the University of Alabama homecoming queen.

example of shifting norms was found by researchers in a small mining town in West Virginia: Black miners and white miners developed a pattern of living that consisted of total integration while they were under the ground, and total segregation while they were above the ground (Minard, 1952; Reitzes, 1953).

Moreover, surveys conducted over the past fifty years make it clear that what is going on inside the minds of Americans has changed a great deal. For example, in 1942 the overwhelming majority of white Americans believed that it was a good idea to have separate sections for black and white people on buses. Two out of every three white Americans surveyed believed that schools should be segregated. In the South, the numbers were even more striking: In 1942, fully 98 percent of the white population was opposed to desegregating schools (Hyman & Sheatsley, 1956). In contrast, by 1988 only 3 percent of white Americans said they wouldn't want their child to attend school with black children. That is a dramatic change indeed!

Shifting cultural norms are well illustrated by the two photographs on this page, each depicting Governor George Wallace of Alabama. In one, the governor, along with his state militia, is attempting to block the doors of the University of Alabama as the first black students seek to register for college. Only the presence of federal troops and telephone intervention by President John Kennedy caused Governor Wallace to back down. And yet just a decade later, the normative climate of Alabama had changed to the extent that Governor Wallace could be seen—as in the second photograph congratulating the young woman selected by the University of Alabama student body to be homecoming queen. She happens to be black.

**Modern Racism.**  While normative changes in our own country have led to decreases in discrimination over the past fifty years, prejudice is in no way eradicated. Instead, it has become more subtle. As the norm changes to become one of tolerance for out-groups, many people simply become more careful—outwardly acting unprejudiced, yet inwardly maintaining their stereotyped views. This phenomenon is called **modern racism:** people's prejudice is typically revealed in subtle, indirect ways; they have learned to hide their prejudice in situations where it would cause them to be labeled as racists.

**modern racism:** prejudice revealed in subtle, indirect ways because people have learned to hide prejudiced attitudes in order to avoid being labeled as racist

When the situation becomes a safe one, their prejudice will be revealed (McConahay, 1986; Kinder & Sears, 1981; Gaertner & Dovidio, 1986).

For example, while it is true that few Americans say they are generally opposed to school desegregation, it is interesting that most white parents oppose busing their own children to achieve racial balance. When questioned, these parents insist that their opposition has nothing to do with prejudice; they simply don't want their kids to waste a lot of time on a bus. But as John McConahay (1982) has shown, most white parents are quite tranquil about busing when their kids simply are being bused from one white school to another—most show vigorous opposition only when the busing is interracial in nature.

Given the properties of modern prejudice, racism and sexism can best be studied with subtle or unobtrusive measures (Crosby, Bromley, and Saxe, 1980). For example, Edward E. Jones and Harold Sigall (1971) created an ingenious contraption, the bogus pipeline, to get at the real attitudes—not the socially desirable ones—of their research participants. The bogus pipeline is an impressive-looking machine that is described to research participants as a kind of lie detector. In fact, it is just a pile of electronic hardware whose dials the experimenter can secretly manipulate. Here's how researchers use the pipeline: Participants are randomly assigned to one of two conditions, in which they indicate their attitudes either on a paper-and-pencil questionnaire (where it is easy to give socially correct responses) or by using the bogus pipeline (where they believe the machine will reveal their true attitudes if they lie). Sigall and Richard Page (1971) found that more racial prejudice was present in students' responses when the bogus pipeline was used. In a similar experiment, college men and women expressed almost identical positive attitudes about women's rights and women's roles in society on a paper-and-pencil measure. However, when the bogus pipeline was used, most of the men displayed far less sympathy to women's issues than the women did.

> We all decry prejudice, yet are all prejudiced.
> —Herbert Spencer, 1873

We can also find examples of racism and sexism in overt behavior—although it is often subtle. For example, Ian Ayers and his colleagues (1991) visited ninety automobile dealerships in the Chicago area, and using a carefully rehearsed, uniform strategy to negotiate the lowest possible price on a new car (one that cost the dealer approximately $11,000), they found that white males were given a final price that averaged $11,362; white females, $11,504; black males, $11,783; and black females, $12,237. Thus, all other things being equal, when it comes to buying a new car, being black or female puts a person at a disadvantage. This also seems to be the case in a great many economic endeavors, even though such discrimination is technically illegal.

Sometimes subtle, sometimes brutally overt—prejudice is indeed ubiquitous. What can we do to eliminate, or at least reduce, this noxious aspect of human social behavior?

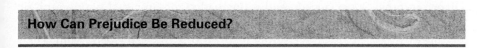

## How Can Prejudice Be Reduced?

Is it indeed too late to give up our prejudices? Never! We believe Thoreau was right. (See quote on next page.) People can change. But how?

Because stereotypes and prejudice are based on erroneous information, for many years social observers believed that all one needed to do was educate people—expose them to accurate information—and their prejudice would disappear. But this has proved to be a naive hope (Lazarsfeld, 1940). After reading this chapter thus far, you can see why this might be the case. Because of the underlying emotional aspects of prejudice, as well as some of the cognitive ruts we get into (e.g., attributional biases, biased expectations, and illusory correlations), stereotypes based on misinformation are difficult to modify simply by providing people with correct information. On the other hand, there is hope. As you have perhaps experienced in your own life, repeated contact with members of an out-group can have a positive effect on stereotypes and prejudice. But as we shall see, mere contact is not enough; it must be a special kind of contact (Pettigrew, 1958).

## The Contact Hypothesis

In 1954, when the U. S. Supreme Court ordered an end to segregated schools, there was widespread excitement among social psychologists. Because segregation lowered the self-esteem of minority children, most social psychologists believed that desegregating the schools would lead to increases in these youngster's self-esteem. In addition, social psychologists hoped that the desegregation of schools would be the beginning of the end of prejudice. The idea was that by bringing children of different races and ethnicities together, this contact would eventually erode prejudice.

There was good reason for this optimism, for not only did it make sense theoretically, but empirical evidence supported the power of contact among races. For example, as early as 1951 Morton Deutsch and Mary Ellen Collins examined the attitudes of whites toward blacks in two public housing projects that differed in their degree of racial integration. Specifically, in one housing situation, black and white families had been randomly assigned to buildings in a segregated manner—that is, they were assigned to separate buildings in the same project. In another situation, their assignment was to integrated buildings—black and white families were placed in the same building. After several months, residents in the integrated project reported a greater positive change in their attitudes toward blacks than residents of the segregated project did, even though the former had not chosen to live in an integrated building initially.

But the desegregation of schools did not work so smoothly. Far from producing the hoped-for harmony, school desegregation frequently led to tension and turmoil within the classroom. In his careful analysis of the research on desegregated schools, Walter Stephan (1978) was unable to find a single study demonstrating a significant increase in self-esteem among black children, whereas 25 percent of the studies showed a significant decrease in the self-esteem of black children following desegregation. In addition, prejudice was not reduced. Stephan (1978) found that in 53 percent of the studies, prejudice actually increased; in 34 percent of the studies, no change in prejudice occurred. And if one had taken an aerial photograph of the school yards of most desegregated schools, one would have found that there was very little true integration: White kids tended to cluster with white kids, black kids tended to cluster with black kids, Hispanic kids tended to cluster with Hispanic kids, and so on (Aronson, 1978; Aronson & Gonzalez, 1988; Schofield, 1986). Clearly, mere contact did not work.

What went wrong? Why did desegregated housing work better than desegregated schools? Let's take a closer look at the contact hypothesis. A

> It is never too late to give up our prejudices.
> —Henry David Thoreau, 1854

moment's reflection will make it obvious that not all kinds of contact will reduce prejudice and raise self-esteem. For example, in the South, blacks and whites have had a great deal of contact, dating back to the time when blacks first arrived from Africa on slave ships, but prejudice flourished nonetheless. Obviously, the kind of contact they were having was not the kind that would lead to pleasant outcomes. In his strikingly prescient masterwork *The Nature of Prejudice*, Gordon Allport (1954) stated the contact hypothesis this way:

> Prejudice may be reduced by equal status contact between majority and minority groups in the pursuit of common goals. The effect is greatly enhanced if this contact is sanctioned by institutional supports (i.e., by law, custom or local atmosphere), and provided it is of a sort that leads to the perception of common interests and common humanity between members of the two groups. (1954, p. 281)

In other words, Allport is not talking about mere contact; he is clear that contact must be between people of equal status, who are in pursuit of common goals. Note that implicit in the Deutsch & Collins (1951) housing study was the fact that the two groups were of equal status within the project, and that no obvious issues of conflict existed between them. A few decades of research have substantiated Allport's early claim that these conditions must be met before contact will lead to a decrease in prejudice between groups (Cook, 1985). Let's now turn to a discussion of these conditions.

## When Contact Reduces Prejudice: Six Conditions

Remember Muzafer Sherif's (1961) study at the boys camp—the "Eagles" and the "Rattlers"? Stereotyping and prejudice were created by instigating conflict and competition between the boys. As part of the study, Sherif and his colleagues also staged several events to reduce the prejudice they had created. Their findings at the boys camp tell us a great deal about what contact can and cannot do.

First, the researchers found that once hostility and distrust were established, harmony between the boys could not be restored simply by removing the conflict and the competition. As a matter of fact, all attempts to bring the two groups together in neutral situations served only to increase the hostility and distrust. For example, the children in these groups had trouble with each other even when they were simply watching a movie together.

How did Sherif succeed in reducing their hostility? By placing the two groups of boys in situations where they were mutually interdependent—situations in which they were forced to cooperate with each other in order to accomplish their goal. For example, the investigators set up an emergency situation by damaging the water supply system. The only way the system could be repaired was if all the Rattlers and Eagles cooperated immediately. On another occasion, the camp truck broke down while the boys were on a camping trip. In order to get the truck going again, it was necessary to pull it up a rather steep hill. This could be accomplished only if all the youngsters pulled together, regardless of whether they were Eagles or Rattlers. Eventually, these sorts of situations brought about a diminution of hostile feelings and negative stereotyping among the campers. In fact, after these cooperative situations were introduced, the number of boys who said their

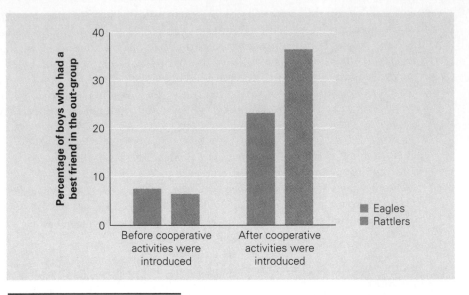

**FIGURE 13.10** Intergroup tensions were eased only after members engaged in cooperative activities. (Adapted from Sherif et al., 1961)

closest friend was in the other group increased dramatically (see Figure 13.10). Thus, two of the key factors in the success of contact are mutual interdependence and a common goal—a situation where two or more groups need each other and must depend on each other in order to accomplish a goal that is important to each of them (Amir, 1969, 1976).

The third condition is equal status. At the boys camp (Sherif et al., 1961) and in the public housing project (Duetsch & Collins, 1951), the group members were very much the same in terms of status and power. For example, no one was the boss, and no one was the less powerful employee. When status is unequal, interactions can easily follow stereotypical patterns. The whole point of contact is to allow people to learn that their stereotypes are inaccurate; contact and interaction should lead to disconfirmation of negative, stereotyped beliefs. However, if status is unequal between the groups, their interactions will be shaped by that status difference—the bosses will act like stereotypical bosses, the employees like stereotypical subordinates—and no one will learn new, disconfirming information about the other group (Pettigrew, 1969; Wilder, 1984).

Fourth, contact must occur in a friendly, informal setting, where in-group members can interact with out-group members on a one-to-one basis (Brewer & Miller, 1984; Cook, 1984; Wilder, 1986). Simply placing two groups in contact in a room where they can remain segregated will do little to promote their understanding or knowledge of each other. Fifth, through friendly, informal interactions with multiple members of the out-group, an individual will learn that his or her beliefs about the out-group are wrong. It is crucial for the individual to believe that the out-group members he or she comes to know are typical of their group; otherwise, the stereotype can be maintained by labeling one out-group member as the exception (Wilder, 1984). For example, a study of male police officers assigned female partners in Washington, D.C., found that although the men were satisfied with their female partner's performance, they still felt strongly that more women should not be hired as police officers. They perceived their partner as an

We must recognize that beneath the superficial classification of sex and race the same potentialities exist, recurring generation after generation, only to perish because society has no place for them.

—Margaret Mead, *Male and Female*, 1948

exception; their stereotypes about women's ability to do police work remained unchanged, and in fact were identical with those of male officers with male partners (Milton, 1972).

Sixth and last, contact is most likely to lead to reduced prejudice when social norms that promote and support equality among groups are operating in the situation (Amir, 1969; Wilder, 1984). We know the power of social norms; here they can be harnessed to motivate people to reach out to members of the out-group. For example, if the boss in a work setting or the professor in a classroom creates and reinforces a norm of acceptance and tolerance, group members will modify their own behavior to fit the norm.

To conclude, when these six conditions of contact—**mutual interdependence;** a common goal; equal status; informal, interpersonal contact; multiple contacts; and social norms of equality—are met, suspicious or even hostile groups will reduce their stereotyping, prejudice, and discriminatory behavior (Aronson & Bridgeman, 1979; Cook, 1984; Riordan, 1978).

**mutual interdependence:** a situation where two or more groups need each other and must depend on each other in order to accomplish a goal that is important to each of them

## Cooperation and Interdependence: The Jigsaw Classroom

Now that we know what conditions must exist for contact to work, we can better understand the problems that occurred when schools were integrated. Let's paint a typical scenario. Imagine a sixth-grader of Mexican American origin, whom we will call Carlos. Carlos has been attending schools in an underprivileged neighborhood for his entire life. Because the schools in his neighborhood were not well equipped or well staffed, his first five years of education were somewhat deficient. Suddenly, without much warning or preparation, he is bused to a school in a predominantly white middle-class neighborhood.

As you know from experience, the traditional classroom is a highly competitive environment. The typical scene involves the teacher asking a question; immediately, several hands go into the air as the children strive to show the teacher that they know the answer. When a teacher calls on one child, several others groan, because they've missed an opportunity to show the teacher how smart they are. If the child who is called on hesitates or comes up with the wrong answer, there is a renewed and intensified flurry of hands in the air, perhaps even accompanied by whispered, derisive comments directed at the student who failed. Thus, Carlos finds he must compete against white middle-class students who have had better preparation than he, and who have been reared to hold white middle-class values, which include working hard in pursuit of good grades, raising one's hand enthusiastically

> Two are better than one because they have a good reward for their toil. For if they fail, one will lift up his fellow, but woe to him who is alone when he falls and has not another to lift him up. Again, if two lie together, they are warm; but how can one be warm alone?
>
> —Ecclesiastes 4:9–12

"I WISH WE COULD HAVE MET UNDER DIFFERENT CIRCUMSTANCES . . ."

*Drawing by Oliphant, An Informal Gathering, © 1978, Simon & Shuster.*

The caption is amusing but, in actuality, a cooperative effort enhances liking.

whenever the teacher asks a question, and so on. In effect, Carlos has been thrust into a highly competitive situation for which he is unprepared, and in which payoffs are made for abilities he has not yet developed. He is virtually guaranteed to lose. After a few failures, Carlos, feeling defeated, humiliated, and dispirited, stops raising his hand and can hardly wait for the bell to ring to signal the end of the school day.

In the typical desegregated classroom, to use Allport's (1954) terms, the students were not of equal status and were not pursuing common goals. Indeed, one might say that they were in a tug-of-war on an uneven playing field. When one examines the situation closely, it is easy to see why Stephan (1978) found a general decrease in the self-esteem of minority youngsters following desegregation. Moreover, given the competitive atmosphere of the classroom, it is likely that the situation would have exacerbated whatever stereotypes were present in the youngsters' minds prior to desegregation. Specifically, given that the minority kids were ill-prepared for the competitiveness of the classroom, it is not surprising that some of the white kids quickly concluded that the minority kids were stupid, unmotivated, and sullen—just as they had suspected (Wilder & Shapiro, 1989). Moreover, it is likely that the minority kids might conclude that the white kids were arrogant show-offs. This is an example of the self-fulfilling prophecy we discussed earlier.

How could we change the atmosphere of the classroom so that it comes closer to Gordon Allport's prescription for the effectiveness of contact? Specifically, how could we get white students and minority students to be of equal status, mutually dependent, and in pursuit of common goals? One of the authors of this textbook got to find out. In 1971, the school system of Austin, Texas, was desegregated. Within a few weeks, the schools were in turmoil. Black, white, and Mexican American children were in open conflict; fistfights broke out between the various racial groups in the corridors and school yards. The school superintendent invited Elliot Aronson, who was then a professor at the University of Texas, to enter the system with the mandate to do anything within reason to create a more harmonious environment. After spending a few days observing the dynamics of several classrooms, Elliot and his graduate students were strongly reminded of the situation that existed in the Sherif (1961) camp experiment. With the findings of that study in mind, they developed a technique that created an interdependent classroom atmosphere, designed to place the students of various racial and ethnic groups in pursuit of common goals. They called it the **jigsaw classroom,** because it resembled the assembling of a jigsaw puzzle (Aronson, Stephan, Sikes, Blaney, and Snapp, 1978; Aronson & Bridgeman, 1979; Aronson & Gonzalez, 1988; Aronson & Thibodeau, 1992).

Here is how the jigsaw classroom works: Students are placed in six-person learning groups. The day's lesson is divided into six paragraphs, so that each student has one segment of the written material. For example, if the students are to learn the life of Eleanor Roosevelt, her biography is arranged in six parts. Each student has possession of a unique and vital part of the information, which, like the pieces of a jigsaw puzzle, must be put together before anyone can learn the whole picture. The individual must learn his or her own section and teach it to the other members of the group—who do not have any other access to that material. Thus, if Debbie wants to do well on the ensuing exam about the life of Eleanor Roosevelt, she must pay close attention to Carlos (who is reciting on Roosevelt's girl-

**the jigsaw classroom:** a classroom setting designed to reduce prejudice and raise the self-esteem of children by placing them in small, desegregated groups and making each child dependent on the other children in his or her group to learn the course material and do well in the class

The structure of the jigsaw technique requires students to pay attention to each other and to be supportive rather than to compete against each other.

hood years), to Natalie (who is reciting on Roosevelt's years in the White House), and so on.

Unlike the traditional classroom, where students are competing against each other, the jigsaw classroom has students depending on each other. In the traditional classroom, if Carlos, because of anxiety and discomfort, is having difficulty reciting, the other students can easily ignore him (or even put him down) in their zeal to show the teacher how smart they are. But in the jigsaw classroom, if Carlos is having difficulty reciting, it is now in the best interests of the other students to be patient, make encouraging comments, and even ask friendly, probing questions to make it easier for Carlos to bring forth the knowledge within him.

Through the jigsaw process, the children begin to pay more attention to each other and to show respect for each other. As you might expect, a child like Carlos would respond to this treatment by simultaneously becoming more relaxed and more engaged; this would inevitably produce an improvement in his ability to communicate. In fact, after a couple of weeks, the other students were struck by their realization that Carlos was a lot smarter than they had thought he was. They began to like him. Carlos began to enjoy school more and began to see the Anglo students in his group not as tormentors but as helpful and responsible teammates. Moreover, as he began to feel increasingly comfortable in class and started to gain more confidence in himself, Carlos's academic performance began to improve. As his academic performance improved, so did his self-esteem. The vicious circle had been broken; the elements that had been causing a downward spiral were changed—the spiral moved dramatically upward.

The formal data that Aronson and his colleagues gathered from the jigsaw experiments were clear and striking. Compared to students in traditional classrooms, students in jigsaw groups showed a decrease in prejudice and stereotyping, as well as an increase in their liking for their groupmates, both within and across ethnic boundaries. In addition, children in the jigsaw classrooms performed better on objective exams and showed a significantly greater increase in self-esteem than children in traditional classrooms. Children in the jigsaw classrooms also showed far greater liking for school than those in traditional classrooms. Moreover, children in schools where the jigsaw technique was practiced showed substantial evidence of true integration—that is, in the school yard there was far more intermingling among the various races and ethnic groups than in the yards of schools using more traditional classroom techniques. Finally, children in the jigsaw classrooms developed a greater ability to empathize with others and to see the world through the perspective of others than children in traditional classrooms did. Recently, Samuel Gaertner and his colleagues (1990) have demonstrated that the process of cooperation works so well in part because the mere act of participating in a cooperative group succeeds in breaking down in-group versus out-group perceptions, and allows the individual to develop the cognitive category of one group.

The jigsaw approach was first tested in 1971; in recent years, several similar cooperative techniques have been developed (see Cook, 1985; Johnson & Johnson, 1987, 1989; Sharan, 1980; Slavin, 1980). The striking results described above have been successfully replicated in thousands of classrooms in all regions of the country and abroad. The cooperative movement in education, as a way of achieving the goals of school desegregation, has grown by leaps and bounds and now constitutes something of a revolution within the field of public education. Alfie Kohn (1986) estimates that more than 25,000 teachers are now using some form of cooperative learning in the United States alone—and hundreds more are adopting it every year. John McConahay (1981), one of our nation's foremost experts on race relations, has called the cooperative learning revolution the single most effective practice for improving race relations in desegregated schools.

In sum, although the initial optimism about eliminating prejudice that occurred after the 1954 Supreme Court decision was a bit premature, we now have good evidence that we are on the right track. Research on cooperative learning groups is extremely encouraging and demonstrates beyond a doubt that, with proper care and in a sensible environment, integrated contact can produce a significant decrease in prejudice and marked improvements in students' self-esteem and classroom performance. The jigsaw experiments have taught us that under the proper conditions, contact is a viable and powerful tool in the battle against prejudice.

## SUMMARY

Prejudice is a widespread phenomenon, present in all societies of the world. Social psychologists define **prejudice** as the affective component of the attitude—specifically, a hostile or negative attitude toward a distinguishable group of people based solely on their group membership. **Stereotypes,** the cognitive component of the attitude, are defined as generalizations about a group whereby identical characteristics are assigned to virtually all members, regardless of actual variation among the members. **Discrimination,** the behavioral component, is defined as unjustified negative or harmful action toward members of a group based on their membership in that group.

As a broad-based and powerful attitude, prejudice has many causes. We discussed four aspects of social life that bring about prejudice: the way we think, the way we assign meaning or make attributions, the way we allocate resources, and the way we conform to social rules.

Social cognition processes are an important element in the creation and maintenance of stereotypes and prejudice. Categorization of people into groups leads to the formation of **in-groups** and **out-groups.** The **in-group bias** means that we will treat members of our own group more positively than members of the out-group, as demonstrated by the research on **minimal groups.** The perception of **out-group homogeneity** is another consequence of categorization: In-group members perceive out-group members as being more similar to each other than the in-group members are. Stereotypes are widely known in a culture; even if you do not believe in them, they can affect your cognitive processing of information about an out-group member. For example, recent research has shown that stereotypes are activated by automatic processing; they must be ignored or suppressed by conscious, controlled processing. The **illusory correlation** is another way that cognitive processing perpetuates stereotypical thinking; we tend to see correlations where they don't exist, particularly if the events or people are distinctive. Social cognitive research has indicated that stereotypes can be revised; the **bookkeeping model** and the **subtyping model** (but not the **conversion model**) describe such a process.

The fundamental attribution error applies to prejudice—we tend to overestimate the role of dispositional forces when making sense out of others' behavior. Stereotypes can be described as the **ultimate attribution error**—making negative dispositional attributions about an entire out-group. When out-group members act nonstereotypically, we tend to make situational attributions about them, thereby maintaining our stereotypes. In addition, our belief in a just world leads us to derogate victims as well as members of out-groups—we see them as causing their fate and circumstances. This is commonly known as **blaming the victim**. Finally, *self-fulfilling prophecies* are an attributional process by which we find confirmation and proof for our stereotypes by unknowingly creating stereotypical behavior in out-group members through our treatment of them.

The **realistic conflict theory** states that prejudice is the inevitable byproduct of real conflict between groups for limited resources—whether involving economics, power, or status. Competition for resources leads to derogation of and discrimination against the competing out-group. **Scapegoating** is a process whereby frustrated and angry people tend to displace their aggression from its real source to a convenient target—an out-group that is disliked, visible, and relatively powerless.

Social learning theory states that we learn the appropriate norms of our culture—including stereotypes and prejudiced attitudes—from adults, peers, the media, and so on.

**Institutionalized racism and sexism** are norms operating throughout the society's structure. **Normative conformity,** or the desire to be accepted and "fit in," leads us to go along with stereotyped beliefs and not challenge them. **Modern racism** is an example of a shift in normative rules about prejudice: Nowadays, many people reveal their prejudice in subtle, indirect ways; they have learned to hide their prejudice in situations where it would lead them to be labeled as racist. Given the more hidden nature of prejudice today, techniques like the bogus pipeline are used to study people's real attitudes about out-groups.

How can prejudice be reduced? The most important way to reduce prejudice is through contact—bringing in- and out-group members together. However, mere contact, as occurred when public schools were first desegregated, is not enough and can even exacerbate the existing negative attitudes. Instead, contact situations must include the following conditions: **mutual interdependence;** a common goal; equal status; informal, interpersonal contact; multiple contacts; and social norms of equality. **The jigsaw classroom,** a learning atmosphere in which children must depend on each other and work together to learn and to reach a common goal, has been found to be a powerful way to reduce stereotyping and prejudice among children of different ethnicities.

## SUGGESTED READINGS

Allport, G. (1954). *The nature of prejudice.* Reading MA: Addison-Wesley. Written the same year of the landmark Supreme Court decision on desegregation, this classic work remains an exciting and penetrating analysis of the social psychology of prejudice.

Aronson, E., Stephan, C., Sikes, J., Blaney, N., & Snapp, M. (1978). *The Jigsaw Classroom.* Beverly Hills: Sage Publications. The story of the classroom experiment that helped make school desegregation work—and that contributed to the launching of the trend toward cooperative education.

Pettigrew, T. F. (1969). Racially separate or together? *Journal of Social Issues,* 2, 43–69. A highly influential defense of desegregation, written by one of the leading experts in the field.

Stephan, W. G. (1985). Intergroup relations. In G. Lindzey & E. Aronson (Eds.), *Handbook of social psychology* (Vol. 3, pp. 599–658). Reading, MA: Addison-Wesley. Perhaps the most accessible brief introduction to the areas of prejudice and prejudice reduction; both scholarly and engagingly written.

# P A R T

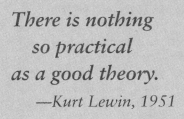

*There is nothing
so practical
as a good theory.*
—Kurt Lewin, 1951

# F I V E

# Chapter 14
## Health and the Environment

et us introduce you to a woman named Beatrice Cole. Ms. Cole has very much enjoyed the past ten years of her life—those between ages eighty and ninety, that is. Ms. Cole, now in her ninety-first year, greets each day "as a gift that I unwrap with anticipation, and live each day as if it were the last" (Cole, 1991, p. 20). She keeps a busy schedule, arising early every morning to take her dog, Pierre, for a long walk. After returning to her Manhattan apartment, she eats a large breakfast, reads the newspaper, and does some housecleaning. Then she often ties Pierre to a shopping cart and goes to the market. She spends one day a week doing volunteer work at a local synagogue, and another in the public relations department of a museum. Every night she prepares a four-course dinner, serving herself as if she were a guest. And she entertains regularly, treating her friends to a fancy dinner and a game of Scrabble.

Ms. Cole's life is not free of misfortune. Recently she found herself asking people to repeat what they had said, and realized that her hearing was failing. When she was eighty-

541

eight, she kept turning her ankle and falling, due to nerve damage in her spine. Characteristically, however, she treats these hardships as minor inconveniences. "Deafness is not a bad handicap," she says. "At night when I remove my hearing aids . . . the silence is delicious" (p. 21). She obtained a brace for her leg, and now, with the help of a cane, is as mobile as ever. She regularly takes buses around Manhattan, and frequently travels outside the city to visit friends and family. Her personal philosophy is that you should always look on the bright side, and never brood about anything for more than twenty minutes.

How does Ms. Cole feel about the fact that her life is drawing to a close? Far from feeling depressed

Ms. Cole relaxes with her dog, Pierre.

or apprehensive, she approaches her impending death with characteristic optimism:

There is still one adventure ahead of me that is the greatest experience of all—the only perfect happenstance in life, with no strings attached, no loose ends. Absolute perfection. That is death. I think of it as the perfect end to a long, happy life. (p. 21)

Beatrice Cole does not seem like the typical elderly person, does she? How has she managed to respond to the stress associated with growing old and physically ill (as well as the stress of living in a highly urban environment) with such optimism and happiness? What can we learn from social psychologists about our health and environment to increase our chances of being like Beatrice Cole when we are ninety-one?

## The Role of Applied Social Psychology

Throughout this book, we have seen how social psychological research can be applied to solve real-world problems. Examples include preventing errors in reasoning (Chapter 4), changing undesirable attitudes (Chapter 8), improving group decision making (Chapter 9), increasing prosocial behavior (Chapter 11), reducing aggression (Chapter 12), and eliminating prejudice (Chapter 13). In our final two chapters, we turn to a more specific discussion of additional applied topics that touch all our lives: health and the environment in this chapter, and law and business in the next. Each of these applied areas involves a number of interesting psychological issues. For example, few would deny that our minds and bodies are intricately linked, and that the way in which we perceive and interpret the world has important implications for our physical health.

Psychological research in the areas of health, environment, law, and business has blossomed in recent years, growing into separate subareas within psychology. These subareas are called *health psychology* (Pennebaker, 1982; Taylor, 1985), *environmental psychology* (Darley & Gilbert, 1985; Stokols & Altman, 1987), *law and psychology* (Wrightsman, 1987), and *organizational and consumer psychology* (Cafferata & Tybout, 1989; Kolb,

Rubin, and McIntyre, 1984). Each of these fields draws on many subdisciplines of psychology, including clinical, social, personality, developmental, cognitive, and physiological psychology.

What do social psychologists have to offer to such applied fields? First, as we have discussed throughout this book, social psychologists believe that, when trying to understand social behavior, it is often more important to examine the nature of the social situation than the nature of the person. Thus, social psychologists believe, in the words of Judith Rodin, that "it is not bad people but . . . bad situations that create social problems" (Rodin, 1985, p. 808). Further, as we emphasized in Chapter 1, it is not objective but subjective situations that cause behavior. That is, to understand why people behave the way they do in a particular situation, we must view that situation through their eyes, understanding how they interpret and define it. This principle will be important in understanding many of the applications of social psychology we will examine in this and the next chapter.

In this chapter, we will discuss how people interpret and understand social situations that are directly relevant to their health and to environmental threats. Consider one such social situation that might have an impact on people's health: the upheavals that occur when they get divorced. Will such a major life change increase people's susceptibility to physical illness? The answer, as we will see, is that it depends, in some interesting ways, on how people interpret and perceive this event.

It is also important, in the arenas of health and the environment, to change people's attitudes and behaviors. Getting people to behave in healthier ways, such as not smoking, is of obvious benefit. Similarly, it is imperative that we convince people to behave in ways that are less harmful to the environment. As we have seen, when it comes to influencing attitudes and behaviors, social psychologists are the ones to call (see Chapters 7–10). In this chapter, we will see how social psychologists have changed social behaviors relevant to both health and the environment.

> There is not one big cosmic meaning for all, there is only the meaning we each give to our life.
>
> —Anaïs Nin, 1967

## Social Psychology and Health

Why has Beatrice Cole lived such a long and satisfying life? Was she simply blessed with good genes and good luck? Or is the fact that she is so upbeat and optimistic due to more than just luck or coincidence? A considerable amount of research suggests that there is an important link between people's social perceptions—the way they understand themselves and the social world—and their physical health.

### Social Perception and Health: Interpreting Negative Life Events

There is a great deal of anecdotal evidence indicating that people's beliefs about the world can have dramatic effects on their physical well-being. Consider these examples, reported by the psychologist W. B. Cannon (1942): After eating some fruit, a New Zealand woman learns that it came from a forbidden supply, reserved only for the chief. Horrified, her health deteriorates, and she dies the next day. A man in Africa has breakfast with a friend, eats heartily, and goes on his way. A year later, he learns that his friend made the breakfast from a wild hen, a food strictly forbidden in his culture. The man immediately beings to tremble, and is dead within twenty-four hours. After a witch doctor in Australia casts a spell on a man, the man's health deteriorates, and he recovers only when the witch doctor removes the spell.

These examples are easy to dismiss as bizarre tales, on par with something we might read in "Ripley's Believe It or Not" column in the Sunday paper. Though they are extreme cases, they illustrate the close connection that exists between our bodies and minds, a connection that exists for all of us. Think for a moment about the plight of an older person who is institutionalized in a long-term health care facility in the United States. In many institutions, the residents have little responsibility for or control over their own lives. They cannot choose what to eat, what to wear, or even when to go to the bathroom. Residents in such institutions often become passive and withdrawn, and fade into death as if they had simply given up. Quite a contrast to the zest shown by Beatrice Cole as she begins her tenth decade of life!

These examples suggest that there is more to our physical health than germs and disease—we also need to consider people's psychological reactions to what is going on in their lives. And these psychological reactions will depend in large part on how people understand and interpret their social world. Two people might experience the same event—such as losing their hearing or getting a divorce—but experience it quite differently. This, of course is a fundamental assumption of social psychology, as discussed in Chapters 1 and 5. Below we will examine three aspects of people's understanding of the social world that are of great importance to their physical health: how people view stressful events, the amount of control people feel they have over their environment, and the way people explain the causes of negative events.

**The Connection Between Stress and Health.**  Obviously life can be difficult, and the more difficult it is, the harder it is for us to cope. People who are under a great deal of strain—a loved one has died, they have lost their job, or they are in the midst of a divorce—might be more susceptible to illness than those not under such strain. After all, not everyone who is exposed to an illness gets sick. Some people seem to catch every cold that comes along, whereas others go through the year without missing a single day of work. Does stress affect our immune system, making us more likely to become ill?

Among the first to investigate the effects of stress was Hans Selye (1956, 1976), who defined stress as the body's physiological response to threatening events. Later researchers have focused on exactly what it is about a life event that makes it threatening. Holmes and Rahe (1967), for example, suggested that stress is the degree to which people have to change and readjust their lives to an external event. The more change required, the more stress that occurs. For example, if a spouse or partner dies, just about every aspect of a person's life is disrupted, leading to a great deal of stress. This definition of stress applies to happy events in one's life as well, if the event causes a person to change his or her daily routine. Graduating from college, for example, is a happy occasion, but it can be stressful because of the major changes it creates in one's life.

It is the mind that makes the body.
—Sojourner Truth, c. 1877

Ay, there's the thing! The body pays for the mind.
—Maria Edgeworth, 1812

Some of these events are happy, yet they cause stress. Which of these situations might make you experience stress?

To assess such life changes, Holmes and Rahe (1967) developed a measure called the Social Readjustment Rating Scale (see Table 14.1). Some events, such as the death of a spouse or partner, have many "life change units," because they involve the most change in people's daily routines. Other events, such as getting a traffic ticket, have relatively few life change units. Here's how the scale works: Participants check all the events that have occurred to them in the preceding year, and then get a score for the total number of life change units caused by these events. These scores are then correlated with the frequency with which the participants become sick or have physical complaints. Several studies have found that the more life changes people report, the more likely they are to have been sick (Elliot & Eisdorfer, 1982).

There are, however, two problems with this finding. First, as you may have recognized, it is a correlational finding, not an experimental one. Just because life changes are correlated with health problems does not mean that the life changes caused the health problems (see our discussion of correlation and causality in Chapter 2). Can you think of any other interpretations of these findings? Some researchers have argued persuasively for the influence of "third variables" like neuroticism, in that people who are neurotic are

Reality is the leading cause of stress amongst those in touch with it. I can take it in small doses, but as a life-style I find it too confining.

—Jane Wagner, *The Search for Signs of Intelligent Life in the Universe*, 1986 (performed by Lily Tomlin)

## The social readjustment scale

| Rank | Life Event | Life Change Units |
|------|------------|-------------------|
| 1 | Death of spouse | 100 |
| 2 | Divorce | 73 |
| 3 | Marital separation | 65 |
| 4 | Jail term | 63 |
| 5 | Death of close family member | 63 |
| 6 | Personal injury or illness | 53 |
| 7 | Marriage | 50 |
| 8 | Fired at work | 47 |
| 9 | Marital reconciliation | 45 |
| 10 | Retirement | 45 |
| 11 | Change in health of family member | 44 |
| 12 | Pregnancy | 40 |
| 13 | Sex difficulties | 39 |
| 14 | Gain of new family member | 39 |
| 15 | Business readjustment | 39 |
| 16 | Change in financial state | 38 |
| 17 | Death of close friend | 37 |
| 18 | Change to different line of work | 36 |
| 19 | Change in number of arguments with spouse | 35 |
| 20 | Mortgage over $10,000 | 31 |
| 21 | Foreclosure of mortgage or loan | 30 |
| 22 | Change in responsibilities at work | 29 |
| 23 | Son or daughter leaving home | 29 |
| 24 | Trouble with in-laws | 29 |
| 25 | Outstanding personal achievement | 28 |
| 26 | Wife begin or stop work | 26 |
| 27 | Begin or end school | 26 |
| 28 | Change in living conditions | 25 |
| 29 | Revision of personal habits | 24 |
| 30 | Trouble with boss | 23 |
| 31 | Change in work hours or conditions | 20 |
| 32 | Change in residence | 20 |
| 33 | Change in schools | 20 |
| 34 | Change in recreation | 19 |
| 35 | Change in church activities | 19 |
| 36 | Change in social activities | 18 |
| 37 | Mortgage or loan less than $10,000 | 17 |
| 38 | Change in sleeping habits | 16 |
| 39 | Change in number of family get-togethers | 15 |
| 40 | Change in eating habits | 15 |
| 41 | Vacation | 13 |
| 42 | Christmas | 12 |
| 43 | Minor violations of the law | 11 |

**TABLE 14.1 The social readjustment rating scale.** According to Holmes and Rahe (1967), the greater the number of "life change units" you are experiencing right now, the greater the likelihood that you will become physically ill. (Adapted from Holmes & Rahe, 1967)

more likely to report that they are ill and to be experiencing difficult life changes (Schroeder & Costa, 1984; Watson & Pennebaker, 1989). According to these researchers, it is not life changes that cause health problems, but neuroticism that causes both of these variables.

The second problem is that measuring the occurrence of objective events—such as whether people have gotten married or lost their job—violates a basic principle of social psychology: Subjective situations have more of an impact on people than objective situations (Griffin & Ross, 1991). It is important to consider how people perceive and interpret an event. Some people view getting a traffic ticket as a major hassle, whereas others view it as a minor inconvenience. Some people view a major life change such as getting divorced as a liberating escape from an abusive relationship, whereas others view it as a devastating personal failure. As recognized by Richard Lazarus (1966) in his pioneering work on **stress,** it is subjective, not objective, stress that causes problems. An event is stressful for people only if they interpret it as stressful—which occurs whenever people feel that they cannot cope with demands from their environment (Lazarus & Folkman, 1984).

Consider, for instance, our opening example of ninety-year-old Beatrice Cole. If she were filling out the Social Readjustment Rating Scale, she would check item 6, "personal injury or illness," given that she was experiencing a number of health problems. She would thus receive a large number of life change units. According to the theory, she should be at high risk for further physical problems, due to the stress caused by her hearing loss and problems with her spine. There is only one catch: Ms. Cole is not particularly bothered by these problems. With her characteristic optimism, she looks on the bright side, welcoming the fact that her deafness blocks out annoying sounds at night. Because she finds these events relatively easy to cope with, they do not fit our definition of stress.

To demonstrate that the key to stress is how people interpret an event, Richard Lazarus (1966) conducted a series of classic studies. In one, he asked people to watch a safety film for woodmill workers that depicted a series of grisly accidents. One careless worker had his finger cut off by a saw; another worker was operating a circular saw the wrong way, causing a wooden plank to fly off and hit a co-worker, killing him. Would you enjoy watching this film? Here, it seems, is an objective event that everyone would find at least mildly stressful.

Lazarus (1966) demonstrated, however, that it all depends on how people interpret the experience. He instructed some participants to adopt an intellectual stance while watching the film, concentrating on the relationships between the workers, such as the way in which the foreman tried to communicate the importance of safety to the workers. Participants in a second condition watched the film with no special instructions. As expected, the participants in this second group were disturbed by the film, as evidenced by a substantial increase in their heart rate while watching it. In comparison, the participants who intellectualized the experience were relatively unaffected. Just as a physician reacts to blood and gore very differently from how most other people do, these participants adopted a more detached, clinical view of the accidents portrayed in the film, turning a stressful experience into a relatively neutral one.

Lazarus's study shows that people's interpretation of an aversive event influences how disturbing they find it. It does not show, however, that there is a link between subjectively interpreted stress and physical illness. This link has recently been demonstrated by Sheldon Cohen, David Tyrrell, and Andrew Smith (1991) in a study of who catches the common cold. When people are exposed to the cold virus, only 20 to 60 percent of them become sick. Is it possible that stress is one determinant of who this 20 to 60 percent will be? To find out, Cohen and his colleagues asked volunteers to spend a week at a research institute in southern England. They measured stress by asking the participants to make a list of recent events that had had a negative impact on their lives. That is, consistent with our definition of stress, the participants listed only those events which they felt had been difficult to cope with.

The researchers then gave participants nasal drops that contained either the virus that causes the common cold or saline (salt water). The participants

**stress:** the negative feelings and beliefs that occur whenever people feel they cannot cope with demands from their environment

> The greatest griefs are those we cause ourselves.
> —Sophocles (c. 496–406 B.C.), *Oedipus Rex*

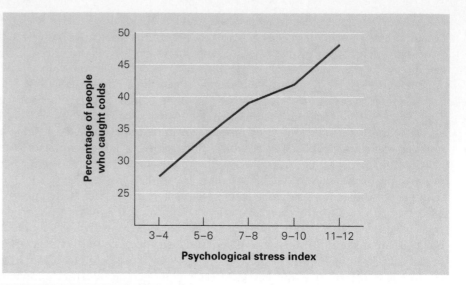

**FIGURE 14.1 Stress and the likelihood of catching a cold.** People were exposed to the virus that causes the common cold, and then isolated. The greater the amount of stress they were experiencing, the greater the likelihood that they caught a cold from this virus. (Adapted from Cohen et al., 1991)

were subsequently quarantined for several days, so that they had no contact with other people. Were the people who were experiencing a great deal of stress in their lives more likely to catch a cold from the virus than those who were experiencing less stress? As you can see in Figure 14.1, the answer was a definite yes. Among people who reported the least amount of stress, about 27 percent came down with a cold. This rate increased steadily the more stress people reported, topping out at a rate of nearly 50 percent in the group that was experiencing the most stress. (This effect for stress was found even when several other factors that influence catching a cold were taken into account, such as the time of year people participated and the participants' age, weight, and gender.) This study provides some of the best evidence yet that stress can lower people's resistance to infectious agents. In general, the more stress people experience, the lower their immunity to disease (Cohen & Williamson, 1991; Krantz, Grunberg, and Baum, 1985; O'Leary, 1990).

We have just seen that it is subjective, not objective, stress that leads to health problems. This is an important point, but it begs a significant question: What is it that makes an event easy to cope with for one person but stressful for another? We turn next to two key determinants of whether an event will be stressful: (a) how much control people believe they have over their environment and (b) how people explain the causes of the event. Let's consider **perceived control** first.

**perceived control:** the belief that we can influence our environment in ways that determine whether we experience positive or negative outcomes

**The Importance of Perceived Control.** A striking quality of Beatrice Cole's life is that she has a great deal of control over her life. She is responsible for taking care of her dog, Pierre; she decides when to entertain guests; and she determines when to take out-of-town trips to visit friends and family. Is it possible that this feeling of control over her life is partly responsible for her hardiness?

Studies with the chronically ill suggest that it is. Shelley Taylor and her colleagues (1984), for example, interviewed women with breast cancer, and found that many of them believed they could control whether their cancer returned. Here is how one man described his wife: "She got books, she got pamphlets, she studied, she talked to cancer patients. She found out everything that was happening to her and she fought it. She went to war with it. She calls it 'taking in her covered wagons and surrounding it'" (quoted in Taylor, 1989, p. 178). The researchers found that women like this, who believed their cancer was controllable, were better adjusted psychologically than women who felt their cancer was uncontrollable. And there is some evidence that people who try to control their cancer and its treatment live slightly longer than those who do not (Taylor, 1989).

It is important to note that the beliefs of at least some of the women about their control over their cancer were probably incorrect. One woman, who worked in a dress shop, said that for years she carried dresses from the racks to the fitting room over her left arm, so that the hangers banged against her left breast. When she developed a tumor in her left breast, she assumed these repeated blows had caused it. From that point on, she put the dresses on a rack and rolled them to the fitting room. According to the experts, blows to the breast are not a cause of cancer. Nonetheless, this woman gained a sense of control by believing she knew the cause of her tumor and by doing something she believed helped—which suggests that the illusion of control can be as important as real control.

> The knowledge that one has a remedy within reach is often as effectual as the remedy itself.
>
> —F. Anstey, 1900

It should be noted that studies of perceived control in the chronically ill by necessity use correlational rather than experimental designs. Researchers measure the amount of control people are experiencing, and correlate this with their psychological and physical adjustment to the disease. These studies cannot prove that feelings of control cause one's health to improve; for example, it is possible that improving health causes one to feel more in control. To address the question of whether feelings of control have beneficial and causal effects, we need to conduct experimental studies where people are randomly assigned to conditions of "high" versus "low" perceived control.

Fortunately, a number of such experimental studies have been conducted. Interestingly, this line of research began not with humans but with animals. Martin Seligman and his colleagues, for example, conducted a series of classic studies on perceived control in dogs (Overmeier & Seligman, 1967; Seligman & Maier, 1967). In one condition, the researchers placed dogs in a harness and observed how long it took them to discover that pressing a button with their noses turned off a mild electric shock. Most dogs learned this very quickly. Dogs in a second condition received the same number and duration of shocks, except that nothing happened when they pressed the button. Thus, the objective event—the number and duration of shocks—was identical in the two groups of dogs. Psychologically, however, the experience was quite different, because the first group could control the shocks (they ended when the button was pressed), whereas the second group could not (the shocks just came and went, outside of their control).

The researchers then put all of the dogs in a new situation, where they could all learn to escape the shocks. The dogs were placed in a large box with a shoulder-high wall down the middle. When a signal was given, shocks were delivered ten seconds later unless the dog jumped over the barrier to the

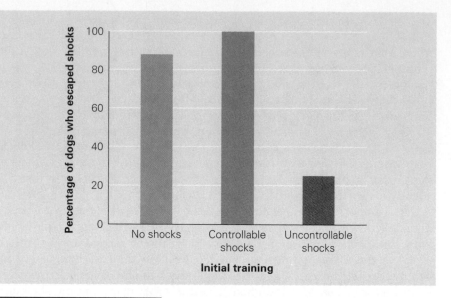

**FIGURE 14.2 Debilitating effects of the lack of control on learning.** After experiencing no shocks, controllable shocks, or uncontrollable shocks, dogs were placed in a situation where they had to learn a new way of avoiding shocks. Fewer of those who had experienced uncontrollable shocks learned how to escape the new shocks. (Adapted from Seligman & Maier, 1967)

other side of the box. How did the dogs in the high versus low perceived control conditions respond? The dogs who could control the earlier shocks learned to avoid the new ones quite well. In fact, performance in this group was slightly better than the performance of a group of dogs who had never been shocked (see Figure 14.2). However, the dogs who could not control the earlier shocks reacted quite differently: They seemed to assume they could not control the new ones either, and most of them helplessly endured the shocks without trying to find a way to escape them; they simply seemed to give up (see Figure 14.2). Similar reactions to the loss of control have been documented in other species, including rats, cats, and fish (Richter, 1957; Seligman, 1975).

Several experiments have shown that having a sense of control is beneficial for people as well. For example, Albert Bandura (1986) and his colleagues found that strengthening people's beliefs that they could control negative events had positive effects on their immune systems. In one study, people who were terrified of snakes took part in sessions where they learned to control their behavior in the presence of a live snake. They first watched another person demonstrate how to approach the snake without fear, and then, with the help of this model, gradually learned to approach the snake themselves. Through a series of such exercises, people gained a sense of mastery over their fear. Before and after the training sessions, the researchers measured the participants' immunological responses from blood samples. They found that the more the participants learned to control their fears, the better their immunological response. This study shows directly that the more control people feel over a stressful event, the better able their bodies will be to ward off disease (Wiedenfeld, O'Leary, Bandura, Brown, Levine, and Raska, 1990).

Giving senior citizens a sense of control over their lives has been found to have positive benefits, both physically and psychologically.

**Perceived Control in the Elderly.** Increasing people's feelings of control has been shown to have even more dramatic effects with older people in nursing homes. Many people who end up in nursing homes and hospitals feel they have lost control of their lives (Raps, Peterson, Jonas, and Seligman, 1982). People are often placed in long-term care facilities against their wishes, and once there, have little say in what they do, whom they see, or what they eat. Ellen Langer and Judith Rodin (1976) reasoned that it would be beneficial to such residents to boost their feelings of control. In these researchers' study, the director of a nursing home in Connecticut gathered some of the residents together and told them that, contrary to what they might think, they had a lot of responsibility for their own lives. Here is an excerpt of his speech:

> I was surprised to learn that . . . many of you don't realize the influence you
> have over your own lives here. Take a minute to think of the decisions you
> can and should be making. For example, you have the responsibility of
> caring for yourselves, of deciding whether or not you want to make this a
> home you can be proud of and happy in. You should be deciding how you
> want your rooms to be arranged—whether you want it to be as it is or
> whether you want the staff to help you rearrange the furniture. You should
> be deciding how you want to spend your time. . . . If you are unsatisfied
> with anything here, you have the influence to change it. It's your responsi-
> bility to make your complaints known, to tell us what you would like to
> change, to tell us what you would like. These are just a few of the things you
> could and should be deciding and thinking about now and from time to time
> every day. (Langer & Rodin, 1976, pp. 194–195)

The director went on to say that a movie would be shown on two nights the next week, and that the residents should decide which night they wanted to attend. Finally, he gave each resident a gift of a house plant, emphasizing that it was up to him or her to take care of it.

The director also gave a speech to residents assigned to a comparison group. This speech was different in one crucial way—all references to making decisions and being responsible for oneself were deleted. The director

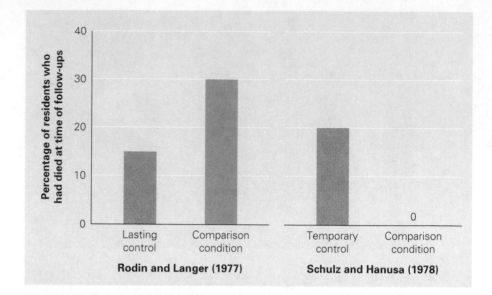

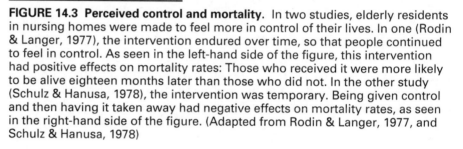

**FIGURE 14.3 Perceived control and mortality.** In two studies, elderly residents in nursing homes were made to feel more in control of their lives. In one (Rodin & Langer, 1977), the intervention endured over time, so that people continued to feel in control. As seen in the left-hand side of the figure, this intervention had positive effects on mortality rates: Those who received it were more likely to be alive eighteen months later than those who did not. In the other study (Schulz & Hanusa, 1978), the intervention was temporary. Being given control and then having it taken away had negative effects on mortality rates, as seen in the right-hand side of the figure. (Adapted from Rodin & Langer, 1977, and Schulz & Hanusa, 1978)

emphasized that he wanted the residents to be happy, but did not say anything about the control they had over their lives. He said that a movie would be shown on two nights the next week, but that they would be assigned to see it on one night or the other. He gave plants to these residents as well, but said that the nurses would take care of them.

This may not seem like a major intervention in the lives of the residents. The people in the induced control group heard one speech about the responsibility they had for their lives and were given one plant to water. That doesn't seem like very strong stuff, does it? The important point to keep in mind is that to an institutionalized person, who feels helpless and constrained, even a small boost in control can have a dramatic effect. Langer and Rodin (1976) found that the residents in the induced control group became happier and more active than residents in the comparison group. Most dramatically of all, the induced control intervention affected the residents' health and mortality (Rodin & Langer, 1977). Eighteen months after the director's speech, 15 percent of the residents in the induced control group had died, compared to 30 percent in the comparison condition (see the left-hand side of Figure 14.3).

Richard Schulz (1976) also examined the link between control and health in the elderly; he increased feelings of control in residents of nursing homes in a different way. Schulz started a program in a North Carolina nursing home wherein undergraduates visited the residents once a week for two months. In the induced control condition, the residents decided when the visits would occur and how long they would last. In a randomly assigned comparison condition, it was the students, not the residents, who decided when the visits would occur and how long they would last. Thus, the residents received visits in both conditions, but in only one could they control the visits' frequency and duration. This may seem like a minor difference, but again, giving the residents some semblance of control over their lives had dramatic effects. After two months, those in the induced control condition were happier, healthier, more active, and taking fewer medications than those in the comparison group.

Schulz returned to the nursing home several months later to assess the long-term effects of his intervention, including its effect on mortality rates. Based on the results of the Langer and Rodin (1976) study, we might expect that those residents who could control the students' visits would be healthier and more likely to still be alive than those residents who could not. But there is a crucial difference between the two studies that should affect how durable the interventions were. The residents in the Langer and Rodin study were given an enduring sense of control. They could continue to choose which days to participate in different activities, continue to take care of their plant, and continue to feel they could make a difference in what happened to them—even after the study ended. By contrast, when Schulz's study was over, the student visits ended. The residents who could control the visits suddenly had that control taken away. The question is, What happens when people are given a sense of control, only to have it eliminated? Unfortunately, Schulz's intervention had an unintended effect: Over time, the people in the induced control group did worse (Schulz & Hanusa, 1978). Compared to people in the comparison group, their health and zest for life were more likely to deteriorate, and they were more likely to have died (see the right-hand side of Figure 14.3). This study has striking implications for the many college-based volunteer programs in which students visit residents of nursing homes, prisons, and mental hospitals. These programs might be beneficial in the short run, but do more harm than good after they end.

In sum, we have seen that having a sense of control over what happens to us is beneficial, helping us cope with a world that is often uncontrollable and harsh. Perceived control is associated with better adjustment to chronic illnesses, greater immunity to disease, and, among residents of nursing homes, better health and adjustment (Rodin, 1986; Taylor & Brown, 1988). The Schulz (1976) study suggests that the effects of perceived control are so powerful that we should be very careful not to introduce it and then take it away. It is not better to have controlled and lost than never to have controlled at all.

We end this section with a word of caution. Though there is evidence for a relationship between perceived control and physical health, it can be dangerous to exaggerate that relationship. As noted by Susan Sontag (1978, 1988), when a society is plagued by a deadly but poorly understood disease, such as tuberculosis in the nineteenth century and AIDS today, the illness is often blamed on some kind of human frailty, such as a lack of faith, a moral weakness, or a broken heart. As a result, people sometimes blame themselves for their illnesses, even to the point where they do not seek out effective treatment.

The extent to which feelings of control determine physical health is therefore somewhat paradoxical. On the one hand, it is beneficial for people

> To be discouraged is to yield to misfortune.
> —Daniel DeFoe, *Moll Flanders*, 1722

to feel that they are in control of their illnesses, like the cancer patient we described earlier. But on the other hand, the risk with this strategy is that if a person does not get better, he or she may feel a sense of self-blame and failure. Tragically, diseases such as cancer can be fatal no matter how much control a person feels. It only adds to the tragedy if people with serious diseases feel a sense of moral failure, blaming themselves for a disease that was unavoidable. Thus, even if there is a psychological component to a disease, it is best to avoid self-blame and seek out the best available treatment.

**Explaining Negative Events: Learned Helplessness.** We have just seen that life events are perceived as more stressful when the individual feels he or she has little or no control over them. The second important determinant of stress is how people explain to themselves what caused the event. For example, consider two college sophomores who both got poor grades on their first calculus test. Student 1 says to herself, "I bet that the professor deliberately made the test difficult, to motivate us to do better. I'll just have to study harder. If I really buckle down for the next test, I'll do better." Student 2 says to himself, "Wow—I guess I can't really cut it here at State U! I was worried that I wasn't smart enough to make it in college, and boy, was I ever right!" Which student do you think will do better on the next test? Clearly the first one, because she has explained her poor performance in a way that is more flattering to herself and makes her feel more in control. In contrast, the second student is likely to settle into a state of **learned helplessness,** believing there is nothing he can do to improve his performance.

Learned helplessness is a pessimistic, maladaptive way of explaining negative events (Abramson, Seligman, and Teasdale, 1978). There are three ways in which an explanation can be pessimistic: viewing the cause of a bad event as stable (long-lived), as opposed to unstable (short-lived); internal (something about you), as opposed to external (something not about you); and global (something that will affect you in a wide variety of situations), as opposed to specific (something that will affect you in only one situation). According to learned helplessness theory, making **stable, internal,** and **global attributions** for negative events leads to depression, reduced effort, and difficulty in learning (see Figure 14.4).

Student 2, for example, believes that the cause of his poor grade is stable (being unintelligent will last forever), internal (something about him is to blame), and global (being unintelligent will affect him in many situations other than calculus classes). This kind of explanation will lead to learned helplessness, thereby producing depression, reduced effort, and the inability to learn new things. Student 1, on the other hand, believes that the cause of her poor grade is unstable (the professor will make the tests easier, and she can study harder next time), external (the professor purposefully made the test hard), and specific (the things that caused her poor calculus grade are unlikely to affect anything else, e.g., her grade in English). People who explain bad events in this more optimistic way are less likely to be depressed, and more likely to do better on a wide variety of tasks (Peterson & Seligman, 1984; Sweeney, Anderson, and Bailey, 1986).

You have no doubt noted that learned helplessness theory is intimately related to attribution theory, which we discussed in Chapter 5. Attribution theorists assume that your attitudes and behaviors depend on how you interpret the causes of events, an assumption that learned helplessness shares. Note that

**learned helplessness:** the state of pessimism that results from explaining a negative event as due to stable, internal, and global factors; learned helplessness causes depression, reduced effort, and difficulty in learning new material

**stable attribution:** the belief that the cause of an event is due to factors that will not change over time (e.g., your intelligence), as opposed to unstable factors that will change over time (e.g., the amount of effort you put into a task)

**internal attribution:** the belief that the cause of an event is due to things about you (e.g., your own ability or effort), as opposed to factors that are external to you (e.g., the difficulty of a test)

**global attribution:** the belief that the cause of an event is due to factors that apply in a large number of situations (e.g., your intelligence, which will influence your performance in many areas), as opposed to the belief that the cause is specific and applies in only a limited number of situations (e.g., your music ability, which will affect your performance in music courses but not in other courses)

**FIGURE 14.4  The theory of learned helplessness.**

we do not know the real reason our hypothetical students did poorly on their calculus test. Instead, learned helplessness theory states that it is more important to consider people's perceptions of these causes. The real causes, of course, are not irrelevant. If the students lack ability in calculus, they are likely to do poorly on future calculus tests. However, often in life, what actually causes our behavior is not so clear-cut or so fixed. In such situations, people's attributions about the causes of their problems can be very important.

To explore this link between learned helplessness and academic performance, Tim Wilson and Patricia Linville (1982) conducted a study with first-year college students. We assumed that many first-year students experience academic difficulties because of a damaging pattern of attributions. Due to the difficulty of adjusting to a new academic and social environment, the first year of college has its rough spots for nearly everyone. The problem is that many first-year students do not realize how common such adjustment problems are, and instead blame them on personal predicaments that are unlikely to change—just the kind of attribution that leads to learned helplessness.

We tried to combat this pessimism by presenting students with objective information about the unstable nature of initial academic problems. At Duke University, first-year students who were concerned about their academic per-

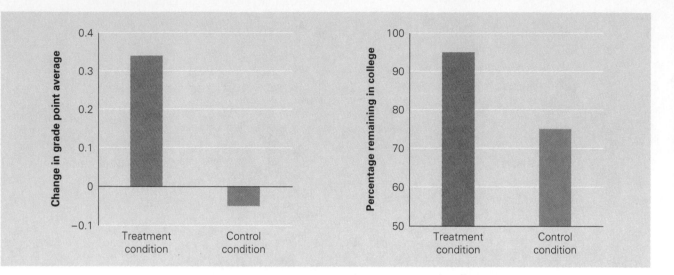

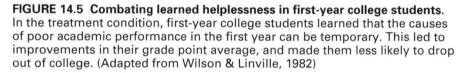

**FIGURE 14.5 Combating learned helplessness in first-year college students.** In the treatment condition, first-year college students learned that the causes of poor academic performance in the first year can be temporary. This led to improvements in their grade point average, and made them less likely to drop out of college. (Adapted from Wilson & Linville, 1982)

formance took part in what they thought was a survey of college experiences. The experimenter told the students in the treatment condition that she would show them the results of an earlier survey, to familiarize them with the kinds of questions they would be asked. The research participants looked over a page of statistics showing that academic performance is often poor in the first year of college but improves thereafter. To make these statistics more vivid, the experimenter also had participants watch videotaped interviews of four upper-class students who, during the interviews, each mentioned that their grades were poor or mediocre during the first year but had improved significantly since then.

In short, our message to the students was that the causes of poor performance are often temporary. We hypothesized that this simple message would help prevent learned helplessness, increasing the students' motivation to try harder and removing needless worries about their abilities. Judging by the students' future performance, this is just what happened. Compared to students in a control group who participated in the study but did not see the statistics or watch the videotaped interviews, students in the treatment condition improved their grades more in the following year and were less likely to drop out of college (see Figure 14.5). Similar results have been found in later studies with University of Virginia students (Wilson & Linville, 1985) and with Belgian students (Van Overwalle & De Metsenaere, 1990).

Because people's attributions were not directly measured in the Wilson and Linville (1982) study, we can only infer that the students improved their academic performance because of a beneficial change in their attributions. However, several other studies have directly measured people's attributions and found that people who explain bad events in optimistic ways are in better health and do better in school and in their careers. For example, Peterson, Seligman, and Vaillant (1988) examined the records of male

Harvard University graduates who have been studied for the past fifty years. In 1946, when the men were twenty-five years old, they filled out a questionnaire about their experiences in World War II. The researchers coded the extent to which these questionnaire responses reflected a pessimistic attributional style (i.e., attributing negative events to stable, internal, global causes), versus an optimistic attributional style (i.e., attributing negative events to unstable, external, specific causes). Interestingly, the men who exhibited the pessimistic style at age twenty-five were more likely to be in poor health in their forties, fifties, and sixties (see also Nolen-Hoeksema, Girgus, and Seligman, 1986; Scheier et al., 1990; Seligman & Schulman, 1986; Snyder, Irving, and Anderson, 1991).

In conclusion, we have seen that when people initially experience a negative event, such as failing a test, two kinds of social perceptions will determine how stressful that event will be: (a) the amount of control they feel they have over the event and (b) how they explain the causes of the event. Feelings of control and optimistic attributions are associated with better psychological and physical adjustment. People who feel a lack of control or who explain events in pessimistic terms (i.e., who experience learned helplessness) are more likely to be in poor health and experience academic and professional problems. The power of our minds over our bodies is, of course, limited. But research shows that both perceived control and the absence of learned helplessness are beneficial, making it easier for us to cope with the hardships life deals us.

## Using Social Psychology to Improve Health Habits

In addition to reducing stress, it would be beneficial to get people to change their health habits more directly—to stop smoking, lose weight, eat a healthier diet and so forth. As we mentioned earlier, this is an area in which

> Twixt the optimist and the pessimist the difference is droll:
> The optimist sees the doughnut
> But the pessimist sees the hole.
> —McLandburgh Wilson, 1915

Americans are making progress in improving some health habits, but are not doing very well in other areas. How can social psychology help people act in healthier ways?

Public smoking, like public spitting, is becoming a socially unacceptable habit.
—Ellen Goodman, 1988

social psychology can be especially helpful, given what we know about social influence and social interaction.

Americans are doing a pretty good job of improving some of their health habits. A 1993 Harris poll found that only 24 percent of adults smoked cigarettes, the lowest smoking rate ever recorded (*USA Today*, March 12, 1993). People are more likely today to avoid high-cholesterol foods than they were a few years ago, and more women are getting Pap smears to detect cancer than ever before. In many other important health areas, however, people are not doing nearly so well. The same Harris poll found that 66 percent of Americans are overweight—more than ever before. Another poll found that people drink more alcohol, exercise less, and get fewer hours of sleep than they did five years earlier (*Scientific American*, September, 1986). Finally, a recent national survey found that people who are at risk for getting AIDS are not taking as many precautions as they should. Of those who said they had more than one sex partner in the prior year, the vast majority had not used condoms at least some of the time. Only 17 percent said they had used condoms in all their sexual encounters (*Science News*, August 31, 1991).

How can we persuade people to change their health habits? Think for a moment, based on what you have already learned, how you would go about trying to do this. One approach, as we discussed in Chapter 8, on attitude change, would be to try to scare people into adopting better health habits. For example, we could show people vivid pictures of someone dying of AIDS, sending the message that if they don't practice safer sex, this could happen to them. As we saw in Chapter 8, fear appeals can work, at least to some extent, if they are accompanied by reassuring information about how best to deal with the problem.

When it comes to changing intractable, ingrained health habits, however, fear appeals may be of limited success. Many smokers have seen ads trying to scare them into throwing their cigarettes into the trash but still find it difficult to do so. The problem is that with many health problems, there are overwhelming barriers to change. Consider the use of condoms. Most people are aware that AIDS is a serious problem, and that using condoms provides some protection against AIDS. Still, a surprisingly small percentage of people use condoms. One reason is that many people find condoms to be inconvenient and unromantic, as well as a reminder of disease—something they don't want to be reminded of when they are having sex. Where sexual behavior is involved, there is a strong tendency to go into denial—in this case, to decide that whereas AIDS is a problem, we are not at risk. What can be done to change this potentially fatal attitude?

One of the most important messages of social psychology is that to change people's behavior, you need to challenge their self-esteem in such a way that it becomes to their advantage—psychologically—to change their behavior. By doing so, they feel good about themselves, maintaining their self-esteem. Sound familiar? This is a basic tenet of dissonance theory, discussed in Chapter 3. And as you may recall, one of us has recently shown that the principles of dissonance theory can be used to get people to behave in healthier ways, including using condoms more. To review briefly, Aronson, Fried, and Stone (1991; Stone, Aronson, Crain, Winslow, and Fried, in press) asked college students to compose a speech that described the dangers of AIDS and advocated the use of condoms "every single time you have sex." The students gave their speech in front of a video camera, after being informed that the resulting videotape would be played to an audience of high school students. Was giving this speech sufficient to change their own behavior, making the students more likely to use condoms themselves?

As we saw in Chapter 3, the answer is, only when the students were also made mindful of their own failures to use condoms by making a list of the circumstances in their own lives when they found it particularly difficult, awkward, or "impossible" to use condoms. These students were most aware of their own hypocrisy—namely, that they were preaching behavior to high school students that they themselves were not practicing. Because no one likes to feel like a hypocrite, these participants needed to take steps to fix their damaged self-esteem. A clear way of doing this would be to start practicing what they were preaching! This is exactly what Aronson and his colleagues found: Students in the hypocrisy condition showed the greatest willingness to use condoms in the future, and, when given the opportunity, actually purchased significantly more condoms for their own use than students in the nonhypocrisy conditions did.

The Aronson and colleagues (1991) condom study is yet another illustration of a familiar point: Sometimes the best way to change people's behavior is to change their interpretation of themselves and the social situation. No attempt was made to modify the research participants' behavior (their use of condoms) directly. They were not rewarded for using condoms; nor were they given any information about what would happen if they didn't. Instead, the researchers altered the way in which the participants interpreted their failure to use condoms. In the hypocrisy condition, the failure to use condoms took on a new meaning. Before the study, the students probably viewed failing to use a condom as no big deal; after all, surely they would never contract AIDS. After creating a speech for high school students and thinking about their own past actions, not using a condom took on a very different meaning: It became an unprincipled, hypocritical act, and—presto!—the students now wanted to use condoms more. We cannot overemphasize this important social psychological message: One of the best ways to solve applied problems is often to change people's interpretation of the situation. We turn now to how this message applies to another important influence on our health and well-being, the environment in which we live.

> Future shock . . . the shattering stress and disorientation that we induce in individuals by subjecting them to too much change in too short a time.
> —Alvin Toffler, *Future Shock*, 1970

## Social Psychology and the Environment

Earlier in this chapter, we discussed the effects of stress on people's health and examined what it is about an event that makes it stressful. It may have occurred to you, during this discussion, that a major source of stress is the environment in which we live. As we humans continue to populate the earth at an alarming rate, our physical world is becoming an increasingly difficult place in which to live.

Have you ever been stuck in rush-hour traffic, venting your anger and frustration by leaning on your car horn? Or been bothered by the noise we humans generate from cars, planes, construction, and loud parties? If so, you have found your environment to be a source of stress. But what makes our environments stressful? Why is it that the identical event—such as loud

> The earth we abuse and the living things we kill, in the end, take their revenge; for in exploiting their presences we are diminishing our future.
>
> —Marya Mannes, 1958

music—can be enjoyable on some occasions but highly stressful on others? By now, you probably know the answer to this question: It depends on how people perceive and interpret their environment—for example, how much control they feel they have over the music.

Paralleling our discussion of social psychology and health, we will first examine the role of social perceptions in determining whether the environment is a source of stress to people, such as the role of perceived control. In addition to considering the effects of the environment on people, however, it is also important to discuss the effects people are having on the environment. Few problems are as pressing as the damage we are doing to the world around us, including air and water pollution, toxic waste, overflowing landfills, global warming, and the destruction of rain forests. Just as we discussed ways in which social psychologists have attempted to change people's health habits in beneficial ways, we will discuss ways in which social influence techniques can be used to get people to behave in more environmentally sound ways.

### Social Perception and the Environment: Interpreting Environmental Stressors

In one sense, the environment has always been a source of stress to human beings. We sometimes forget, as we sit in our comfortable, well-heated homes, eating food we purchased at the grocery store, how tenuous our existence has been throughout most of our history. Starvation was no stranger to our ancestors, no further away than one bad harvest or unlucky hunting season. Severe winters claimed many victims, as did diseases that spread unchecked due to contaminated drinking water, poor sanitation, and close living quarters.

As we approach the twenty-first century, we have learned to master most of the harsh environmental hazards that plagued our ancestors (though, tragically, in many areas of the world starvation and preventable diseases are still

Whereas the environment can exert stress on us, we also exert stress on our environment.

a major cause of death). But the irony is that, as humans have learned to master the environment, they have also learned how to destroy it. As we will see later in this chapter, the human race is systematically poisoning the planet, and there is an urgent need to find ways of halting this destruction.

Further, as civilization has progressed we have created new environmental stressors that our ancestors did not have to face. Consider, for example, the lives of a group of people called the Mabaan, who live in the Republic of Sudan in Africa, near the equator. When studied by Samuel Rosen and his colleagues in 1962, this culture was relatively untouched by modern civilization. They lived in bamboo huts, wore little clothing, and thrived on a diet of grains, fish, and small game. Their environment was quiet and uncrowded, free of many of the stressors associated with modern urban life. There were no sleep-jarring noises from sirens and trucks, no traffic jams to endure at the end of the day, and little fear of crime. Rosen and his colleagues found that, compared to adults in the United States, the Mabaan had less hypertension (high blood pressure), less obesity, and superior hearing.

We cannot be sure, of course, that the absence of modern environmental stressors, such as the problems with urban life, was responsible for the excellent health of the Mabaan. Even if it was, we might not want to conclude that living in modern, urban areas is always stressful, inevitably causing health problems—just look at the way Beatrice Cole, in our opening example, thrives in New York City. As we saw earlier, the same objective event, such as doing poorly on a college test, is experienced as stressful under some conditions but not under others. When will modern environmental conditions like noise and crowding be stressful? Social psychologists have conducted numerous studies to find out.

**Noise.**  Michael and Jeanne Schatzki longed to escape the hustle and bustle of urban life. After a long search, they finally found what seemed like an idyllic spot—a house at the end of a cul-de-sac in a peaceful, secluded neighborhood in Far Hills, New Jersey. "Then spring came," says Mr. Schatzki, "and we were sitting on the porch out back. And I said to Jeannie, 'You know, there are an awful lot of airplanes overhead.' And I looked up, and it was one after another" (*New Yorker*, October 21, 1991, p. 31). It turned out that the Federal Aviation Administration (FAA) had just changed the landing patterns at Newark Airport, thirty-five miles away. Whereas the planes landing and taking off at Newark Airport used to fly some distance from Far Hills, as many as 300 jets a day now roared directly over the Schatzkis' house.

It is well known that repeated exposure to loud noises eventually causes hearing loss. Samuel Rosen and his colleagues (1962), for example, attributed the superior hearing of the Mabaan in part to the fact that the environment in which they lived was, compared to modern, urban areas, extremely quiet. Are loud noises always psychologically stressful? The answer, as you can guess from our earlier discussion of stress and health, is that it depends on how people interpret the noise and how much control they feel they have over it. Many people voluntarily go to rock concerts where the music is extremely loud, louder than the sounds of jets flying overhead. Many people thrive on the hustle, bustle, and noise of urban life, as long as they can escape to a quiet corner of their apartment when they choose to do so. In

> Noise, n. A stench in the ear . . . The chief product and authenticating sign of civilization.
> —Ambrose Bierce, *Devil's Dictionary*, 1911

contrast, Michael and Jeanne Schatzki did not choose to hear the jets screaming over their house, and could not escape this noise.

As compelling as our examples may be, we cannot be sure that perceived control eliminates the stressful effects of noise without conducting well-controlled experiments. Fortunately, David Glass and Jerome Singer (1972) have performed just such a series of studies. A typical experiment went like this: Participants were given several problems to solve, such as complex addition problems and a proofreading task. While they worked on these problems, they heard very loud bursts of noise. The noise was of such things as a mimeograph machine, a typewriter, and two people speaking in Spanish. It was played at 108 decibels, about what you would hear if you were operating a riveting machine, or if you were standing near the runway when a large commercial jet took off.

In one condition, the bursts of noise occurred at unpredictable lengths and at unpredictable intervals over the course of the twenty-five-minute session. In a second condition, people heard the same sequence of noises but were given a sense of control over them. The experimenter said they could stop the noise at any point by pressing a button. "Whether or not you press the button is up to you," explained the experimenter. "We'd prefer that you do not, but that's entirely up to you" (Glass & Singer, 1972, p. 64). A key fact to remember is that no one actually pressed the button. Thus, people in this condition heard the same amount of noise as people in the uncontrollable noise condition; the only difference was that they believed they could stop the noise whenever they wanted. Finally, a third condition was included wherein people worked on the problem in peace and quiet. After the twenty-five-minute session was over, people in all conditions worked on new problems without any noise being played.

Interestingly, the noise had little effect on people during the initial twenty-five-minute session. As long as a task was not too complex, people could bear down and ignore unpleasant noises, doing just as well on the problems as people who worked on them in quiet surroundings. A different picture emerged, however, when people worked on problems in the next session, in which everyone could work in peace and quiet. As you can see in Figure 14.6, those who had endured the uncontrollable noises made significantly more errors during this session than people who had not heard noises during the first session did. And what about the people who heard the noises but believed they could control them? As Figure 14.6 shows, these people did almost as well on the subsequent problems as the people who heard no noise at all. When people knew they could turn off the noise at any point, the noise was much easier to tolerate, and did not impair later performance—even though people never actually turned it off.

Why did noise lower performance after it ended, and why did this occur only in the condition where the noise couldn't be controlled? The answer lies in our earlier discussion of learned helplessness theory. As we saw, when people are initially exposed to uncontrollable, negative events, they often attempt to overcome them as best they can. Many of the people who lived under the new landing pattern at Newark Airport initially fought back, repeatedly contacting officials at the FAA to protest the din of the jets. As long as they felt progress was being made, the noise was probably less stressful. Similarly, in Glass and Singer's (1972) study, people initially were able to overcome the noxious effects of the noise by bearing down and concentrating as best they could.

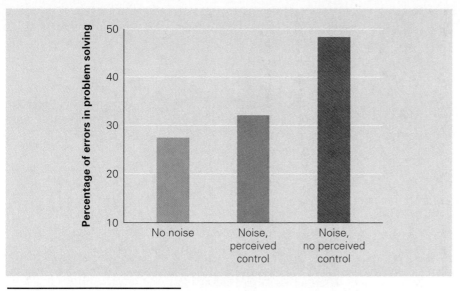

**FIGURE 14.6 Noise and perceived control**. People who believed that they could control the noxious noise did about as well on a subsequent task as people who heard no noise at all. (Adapted from Glass & Singer, 1972)

However, if negative, uncontrollable events continue despite our best efforts to overcome them, helplessness sets in (Abramson et al., 1978; Wortman & Brehm, 1975). One consequence of learned helplessness is reduced effort and difficulty in learning new material. Thus, those participants who could not control the noise in the Glass and Singer (1972) experiment were able to deal with it and do well on the problems initially, but the lack of control they experienced eventually took its toll, causing them to do poorly on the second task. In contrast, those participants who believed they could control the noise never experienced learned helplessness, and thus were able to do well on the second set of problems.

Unfortunately, in modern, urban life loud noises are often not controllable, and they last a lot longer than the twenty-five-minute initial sessions in the Glass and Singer (1972) research. Sheldon Cohen and his colleagues have shown that people who are exposed to such real-life noises respond like the participants in the uncontrollable noise condition of Glass and Singer's (1972) studies. For example, these researchers studied children living in a New York City high-rise apartment building located right next to a busy highway (Cohen, Glass, and Singer, 1973). The children who lived on the lower floors, and thus were subjected to the most traffic noise, did poorer on reading tests than children living on the upper floors did.

In a later study, Cohen and his colleagues (1980, 1981) studied children who attended schools in the air corridor of Los Angeles Airport. More than 300 jets roared over these schools every day, causing an extremely high level of noise. Compared to children who attended quiet schools (matched on the basis of their race, ethnic group, economic background, and social class), the children at the noisy schools had higher blood pressure, were more easily distracted, and were more likely to give up when working on difficult puzzles. These deficits are classic signs of learned helplessness. Many of these problems were still there when the researchers tested the kids again a year later, suggesting that long-term exposure to loud, uncontrollable noise can cause

Frequent, loud noise is an unavoidable fact of urban life. Studies have shown that children who are exposed to constant noise from airplanes have higher blood pressure, are more easily distracted, and are more likely to give up when working on difficult puzzles than other children are.

> [Describing London:] Crowds without company and dissipation without pleasure.
> —Edward Gibbon, *Memoirs*, 1796

serious problems in children. Due in part to these studies, attempts have recently been made to reduce the amount of noise to which people are subjected—for example, by adding soundproofing materials to schools and devices to jet engines to make them less noisy.

**Crowding.** As we write, 5.4 billion human beings inhabit the earth—more people than the total number of all humans who have ever lived before. The world's population is increasing at the rate of a quarter of a million people every day. At our current rate of growth, the world population will double by the year 2025, and double again at increasingly shorter intervals. Two hundred years ago, the English clergyman Thomas Malthus warned that the human population was expanding so rapidly that soon there would not be enough food to feed everyone. He was wrong about how soon such a calamity would occur, largely because of technological advances in agriculture that have vastly improved grain yields. The food supply is dwindling, however, and the number of malnourished people in the world is increasing (Sadik, 1991). Malthus's timing may have been a little off, but many scientists fear that his predictions are becoming more true every day.

Even when there is enough food to feed everyone, overcrowding can be a source of considerable stress, to both animals and humans. When animals are crowded together, in either their natural environments or the laboratory, they reproduce more slowly, take inadequate care of their young, and become more susceptible to disease (Calhoun, 1973; Christian, 1963). Studies of crowding in humans show similar negative effects. As crowding increases in prisons, for example, disciplinary problems, suicides, and overall death rates increase as well (Paulus et al., 1981). Studies of crowding in college dormitories find that students living in crowded dorms (e.g., ones that have long corridors with common bathroom and lounge facilities) are more withdrawn socially and are more likely to show signs of learned helplessness than students living in less crowded dorms (e.g., ones with smaller suites that have their own bathrooms; Baum & Valins, 1977, 1979).

As the human population explodes, our planet is becoming more and more crowded. Under what conditions will crowding be stressful?

What is it about crowding that is so aversive? To answer this question, we must first recognize that the presence of other people is not always unpleasant. Many people—such as Beatrice Cole, the woman we described at the beginning of this chapter—love living in large cities. And when Saturday night arrives, many of us are ready to join our friends for an evening of fun, feeling that the more people we round up, the merrier. This fact has led researchers to distinguish between two terms: **Density** is a neutral term that refers to the number of people in a given space. A classroom with twenty students has a lower density of people than the same classroom with fifty students. **Crowding** is defined as the subjective feeling that there are too many people in a given space; it is the stress we feel when density becomes unpleasant. Under some circumstances, the class with twenty students might be experienced as more crowded than the class with fifty students.

When will density turn into crowding? One factor, as you might expect, pertains to how people interpret the presence of others, including how much control they feel they have over the crowded conditions (Baron & Rodin, 1978; Schmidt & Keating, 1979; Sherrod & Cohen, 1979). If the presence of others lowers our feelings of control—for example, making us feel that it is harder to move around as freely as we would like, or harder to avoid running into people we would just as soon avoid—then we are likely to experience a crowd as stressful. If we feel we have control over the situation—for example, if we know that we can leave the crowd at any point and find solace in a quiet spot—then we are unlikely to experience it as stressful.

To test this hypothesis, Drury Sherrod (1974) performed a study that was very much like the one Glass and Singer (1972) conducted on the effects of noise. He asked high school students to work on some problems in a room that was jam-packed with other people. In one condition, he told the students that they were free to leave at any point. "In the past, some people who have been in the experiment have chosen to leave," he said. "Others have not. We would prefer that you do not, but that's entirely up to you" (Sherrod, 1974, p. 176). Students in a second condition worked under identical crowded conditions, but were not given the choice to leave at any point. Finally, students in a third condition worked in uncrowded conditions. After

**density:** the number of people who occupy a given space

**crowding:** the subjective feeling of unpleasantness due to the presence of other people

The thing which in the subway is called congestion is highly esteemed in the night spots as intimacy.
—Simeon Strunsky, 1954

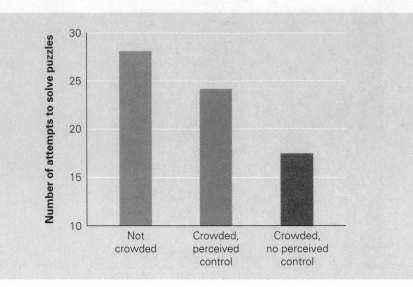

**FIGURE 14.7 Crowding and perceived control.** People who believed they had control over the crowded conditions tried almost as hard on a subsequent task as people who were not crowded at all. (Adapted from Sherrod, 1974)

working on the initial set of problems, the participants were moved to uncrowded quarters, where they worked on a series of difficult puzzles.

The results mirrored those of Glass and Singer (1972). First, students who were crowded—regardless of whether or not they had a sense of control—solved as many problems as students who were not crowded. Initially, they were able to concentrate, ignoring the fact that they were shoulder to shoulder with other people. However, in the condition where the students thought they could not escape, the lack of control eventually took its toll. As seen in Figure 14.7, those students who had no control over the crowded conditions in the first session tried to solve significantly fewer puzzles in the second session, as compared to students in the other conditions. The students who had a sense of perceived control over the crowded conditions worked on almost as many difficult puzzles as the students who had not been crowded at all.

Thus, the effects of noise and crowding appear to be similar. If we feel we have control over these environmental conditions, they do not bother us very much. If we do not have control over them, we can, in the short run, concentrate on our tasks and ignore the unpleasant effects of these stressors. Eventually, however, they take their toll, impairing our ability to cope.

In addition to perceived control, other factors determine how aversive people will find crowded conditions. It is well known, for example, that the presence of others makes people physiologically aroused (Zajonc, 1965). As we have seen elsewhere in this book, arousal can have intriguing consequences. It can lead to quite different emotions, depending on the attributions people make about its source (Schachter & Singer, 1962). Thus, as we might expect, an important determinant of how aversive crowding will be is the nature of the attributions people make for the arousal caused by crowding. If people attribute their arousal to the presence of the other people, they will interpret it as a sign that the setting is too crowded and will feel uncomfortable, cramped, and irritated. If they attribute the arousal to another source, they will not feel crowded (Aiello, Thompson, and Brodzinsky, 1983; Schmidt & Keating, 1979). For example, if a student in a class of 300 people attributes

Density or crowding? Are large groups of people always stress-provoking? Would you say the people in this photo are experiencing crowding?

the arousal she is experiencing to the stimulating and fascinating lecture she is hearing, she will feel less crowded than a bored student who attributes his arousal to the fact that he feels like a sardine in a can.

Finally, crowding will be aversive if it leads to **sensory overload** (Cohen, 1978; Milgram, 1970), a term referring to our being bombarded by more stimulation from the environment than we can reasonably pay attention to. Since other people are a key source of stimulation, one instance in which sensory overload can occur is when so many people are around that we cannot pay attention to everyone. For example, if you were being interviewed for a job by a committee of ten persons, you'd feel that you had to pay close attention to everything each interviewer said and did. The result? A severe demand placed on your attentional system—and most likely negative consequences for you.

**sensory overload:** the situation in which we receive more stimulation from the environment than we can pay attention to or process

In sum, as the human race has evolved, it has learned to master many environmental hazards but in the process has produced new ones, such as noise and crowding. We turn now to another consequence of having become a crowded and technologically advanced society: People are harming the physical environment in multiple ways. Changes in attitudes and behaviors are urgently needed in order to avert environmental catastrophe. As we mentioned earlier, social psychologists have studied a number of techniques involving social influence and social interaction that encourage people to behave in more environmentally sound ways.

## Using Social Psychology to Change Environmentally Damaging Behaviors

Humans have been treating the planet as a humongous garbage can, rapidly filling up the ground, water, and atmosphere with all sorts of pollutants. Pollution in the Los Angeles area, for example, is so bad that children who grow up there have lungs that function 10 to 15 percent less efficiently than the lungs of children who grow up in less polluted areas (Basu, 1989). When humans lived in small groups of hunters and gatherers, they could get away

In addition to polluting the physical environment, humans are crowding out (or systematically extinguishing) many other living species.

"*Help!*"

with discarding their trash wherever they pleased; now that there are more than 5 billion of us (and counting), and we have developed toxic wastes that will remain poisonous for centuries, we have to change our ways (Gilbert, 1990).

How can we get people to treat the environment better? Naturally, you will recognize this as a classic social psychological question, in that it concerns how we can change people's attitudes and behaviors. Let's see what solutions social psychologists have come up with for the planet's pressing environmental problems.

**Social Dilemmas.** The first step is to realize that we are dealing with a special kind of mixed-motive conflict (see Chapter 9) called a **social dilemma.** A social dilemma exists when it is to an individual's benefit to act in a certain way, but if most people act that way, everyone suffers. Consider the case of water conservation in states that often experience severe water shortages, such as California. Water has become so scarce in some areas that residents are urged to take very brief showers, shutting off the water while they lather their hair with shampoo. Watering the lawn is viewed as an outdated, even obscene waste of a precious resource. Many communities employ "water police," who patrol the neighborhoods, ready to pounce on residents who have dared to turn on a garden hose.

Interestingly, it is to every individual Californian's benefit to shower to his or her heart's content, to wash the car as often as he or she pleases, and to soak his or her garden regularly, with the knowledge that these actions will have a minuscule effect on the total water supply. What's a few gallons here or there? However, if everyone adopted this selfish attitude, the water supply would drop precipitously and everyone would suffer. This is a classic social dilemma, because what is good for the individual is bad for the group as a whole (Dawes, 1980; Hardin, 1968; Messick & Brewer, 1983). We are faced with increasingly important environmental social dilemmas, wherein the needs and desires of the individual conflict with the needs and desires of humans in general. How can we resolve social dilemmas? How can we convince people to abandon the selfish course of action and act for the greater good of everyone?

**social dilemma:** a situation in which the most beneficial action for an individual will, if chosen by most people, have harmful effects on everyone

To waste, to destroy, our natural resources, to skin and exhaust the land . . . will result in undermining in the days of our children the very prosperity which we ought by right to hand down to them amplified and developed.

—Theodore Roosevelt, *message to Congress,* 1907

Social psychologists have devised some fascinating laboratory games to try to answer this question. As an example, imagine you were a participant in a game developed by John Orbell, Alphons van de Kragt, and Robin Dawes (1988). You arrive for the study and discover that you will be taking part with six other participants you have never met before. The experimenter gives you and the other participants $6 and says that each of you can keep the money. There is, however, another option. Each person can donate his or her money to the rest of the group, to be divided equally among the other six members. If anyone does so, the experimenter will double its value. For example, if you donate your money, it will be doubled to $12 and divided evenly among the other six participants. If other group members donate their money to the pot, it will be doubled and you will get a share.

Think about the dilemma with which you are faced. If everyone (including you) cooperates by donating his or her money to the group, once it is doubled and divided up, your share will be $12—double what you started with. Donating your money is risky, however; if you are the only one who does so, you will end up with nothing, while having increased everyone else's winnings (see Table 14.2). Clearly, the most selfish (and safest) course of action is to keep your money, hoping that everyone else donates theirs. That way, you would make up to $18—your $6, plus your share of the money that everyone else threw into the pot. Of course, if everyone thinks this way, you'll make only $6, because no one will donate any money to the group. Note that this dilemma is similar to the one faced by Californians over water usage. Individuals gain by hoarding water for their own use, but if everyone hoards water, everyone suffers.

What would you do if you were in the Orbell and colleagues (1988) study? If you are like most of the actual participants, you would keep your six bucks. After all, as you can see in Table 14.2, you will always earn more money by keeping your $6 than by giving it away (i.e., the winnings in the top row of Table 14.2 are always higher than the winnings in the bottom row). The only problem with this strategy is that because most people

> We abuse land because we regard it as a commodity belonging to us. When we see land as a community to which we belong, we may begin to use it with love and respect.
> —Aldo Leopold, 1949

**A social dilemma in the laboratory**

| Your Decision | Other People's Decision | | | | | | |
|---|---|---|---|---|---|---|---|
| | 6 Keep<br>0 Give | 5 Keep<br>1 Give | 4 Keep<br>2 Give | 3 Keep<br>3 Give | 2 Keep<br>4 Give | 1 Keep<br>5 Give | 0 Keep<br>6 Give |
| Keep Your $6 | $6 | $8 | $10 | $12 | $14 | $16 | $18 |
| Give Your $6 | $0 | $2 | $4 | $6 | $8 | $10 | $12 |

**TABLE 14.2 Amount of money you stand to win in the Orbell, van de Kragt, and Dawes experiment.** You can either keep your $6 or donate it to the six other group members. If you donate it, the money will be doubled, so that each group member will receive $2. Most people who play this game want to keep their money, to maximize their own gains. The more people who keep their money, however, the more everyone loses. (Adapted from Orbell et al., 1988)

adopted it, everyone suffered. That is, the total pool of money to be divided remained low, because few people allowed the experimenter to double the money by donating it to the group. As with many social dilemmas, most people looked out for themselves, and as a result, everyone lost.

How can people be convinced to trust their fellow group members, cooperating in such a way that everyone benefits? It is notoriously difficult to resolve social dilemmas, as indicated by the difficulty of getting people to conserve water when there are droughts, recycle their waste goods, and clean up a common area in a dormitory or apartment. In another condition of their experiment, however, John Orbell and his colleagues (1988) found an intriguing result: Simply allowing the group to talk with each other for ten minutes dramatically increased the number of people who donated money to the group, from 38 percent to 79 percent. The increase in the number of donators led to a larger pool of money to be divided, from an average of $32 to $66. Communication works because it allows each person to find out whether the others are planning to act cooperatively or competitively, as well as to persuade others to act for the common good (e.g., "I'll donate my money if you donate yours").

This finding is encouraging, but it may be limited to small groups that are able to communicate face to face. What happens when an entire community is caught in a social dilemma? It would be impossible for all the residents of California to gather together and talk about water conservation, or even for all the residents of one city to communicate in this way. When large groups are involved, alternative approaches are needed. One approach is to make people's behavior as public as possible. If people can take the selfish route privately, undiscovered by their peers, they will often do so. But if their actions are public, then the kinds of normative pressures we discussed in Chapter 7 come into play, making people's behavior more consistent with group norms. For example, some Californians might be tempted to water their gardens on the sly, but if they believe they will become the object of derision and scorn from their neighbors, they will most likely refrain from doing so.

According to social psychological research, what is the best way to get people to change behaviors that damage the environment?

Another proven technique is to change the way in which people perceive themselves and their social behavior. Earlier in this chapter, we saw that Aronson, Fried, and Stone (1991) succeeded in getting people to behave in healthier and more socially responsible ways—purchasing (and presumably using) more condoms—by making them see their own past actions as hypocritical. Would it be possible to use similar techniques to convince people to behave in more environmentally sound ways?

**Conserving Water.** Several years ago, the administrators at one campus of the University of California realized that an enormous amount of water was being wasted by students utilizing the university athletic facilities. The administrators posted signs in the shower rooms of the gymnasiums, exhorting students to conserve water by taking briefer, more efficient showers. The signs appealed to the students' conscience by urging them to take brief showers and to turn off the water while soaping up. The administrators were confident that the signs would be effective because the vast majority of students at this campus were ecology-minded and believed in preserving natural resources. However, systematic observation revealed that less than 15 percent of the students complied with the conservation message on the posted signs.

The administrators were puzzled—perhaps the majority of the students hadn't paid attention to the sign? After all, a sign on the wall is easy to ignore. So the administrators made each sign more obtrusive, putting it on a tripod at the entrance to the showers so that the students needed to walk around the sign in order to get into the shower room. While this increased compliance slightly (19 percent turned off the shower while soaping up), it apparently made a great many students angry—the sign was continually being knocked over and kicked around, and a large percentage of students took inordinately long showers, apparently as a reaction against being told what to do. The sign was doing more harm than good—time to call in the social psychologists.

Elliot Aronson and his students (Dickerson, Thibodeau, Aronson, and Miller, 1992) decided to apply the hypocrisy technique they had used in the condom study to this new situation. The procedure involved intercepting female students who were on their way from the swimming pool to the women's shower room, introducing the experimental manipulations, then having a research assistant casually follow them into the shower room, where she unobtrusively timed their showers. Research participants in one condition were asked to respond to a brief questionnaire about their water use, a task designed to make them mindful of how they sometimes wasted water while showering. In another condition, research participants made a public commitment, exhorting others to take steps to conserve water. Specifically, these participants were asked to sign their names to a public poster that read, "Take Shorter Showers. Turn Shower Off While Soaping Up. If I Can Do It, So Can YOU!" In the crucial condition—the "hypocrisy" condition—the participants did both; that is, they were made mindful of their own wasteful behavior and they indicated publicly (on the poster) that they were practicing water conservation. In short, they were made aware that they were preaching behavior they themselves were not practicing. Just as in the condom study described earlier, those participants who were made to feel like hypocrites changed their behavior so that they could feel good about

> In an age where man has forgotten his origins and is blind even to his most essential needs for survival, water along with other resources has become the victim of his indifference.
> —Rachel Carson, *The Silent Spring*, 1962

> God gave Noah the rainbow sign,
> No more water, the fire next time.
> —"Home in the Rock," Negro spiritual

The recent interest in recycling is an effective way for urban areas to reduce litter.

themselves. In this case, they took very brief showers. Indeed, the procedure was so effective that the average time students in this condition spent showering was reduced to three and a half minutes.

**Conserving Energy.**  It may be possible to draw on other social psychological techniques to increase environmentally sound behaviors. Consider the case of energy conservation. As a nation, the United States consumes far more energy, per capita, than any other nation on earth. Historically, we have felt perfectly content using as much energy as we needed, assuming that the planet had an infinite supply of oil, natural gas, and electric power. But this is not true. We have already depleted many of our national oil reserves, and we must import much of our oil from other countries.

It's imperative that we conserve energy. Let's take private homes as an example. By taking such simple measures as increasing ceiling, wall, and floor insulation, plugging air leaks, using more efficient light bulbs, and maintaining furnaces properly, the typical American energy consumer could reduce the amount of energy used to heat, light, and cool his or her home by 50 to 75 percent (Williams & Ross, 1980). The technology needed to increase energy efficiency currently exists, and is well within the financial means of most homeowners. Not only would this technology save energy, but it would also save the individual homeowner a great deal of money. Yet despite the fact that the societal and financial advantages of conservation have been well publicized, the vast majority of homeowners have not taken action. How come? Why have Americans been slow to act in a manner that is in their economic self-interest? This lack of compliance has puzzled economists and policymakers, because they have failed to see that the issue is partly a social psychological one.

In Chapter 5, we noted that people's attention is typically directed to those aspects of their environment which are most salient and vivid (i.e., those aspects which are particularly noticeable). Elliot Aronson and his colleagues (Aronson, 1990; Aronson & Yates, 1985; Coltrane, Archer, and

Aronson, 1986; Stern & Aronson, 1984) reasoned that energy conservation in the home is not a particularly vivid problem, and thus people do not spend much time thinking about it. The bill for natural gas and electricity comes only once a month and is spread out over dozens of appliances; thus, the homeowner has no clear idea which of the many appliances are using the most energy. It is as if you were buying food in a supermarket where the prices of individual items were unmarked and you were billed only at the end of the month. How would you know what to do to save money on your purchases? Perhaps if the sources of home energy consumption were made more vivid, people would take action.

To test this hypothesis, Elliot Aronson and his students (Aronson & Gonzales, 1990; Gonzales, Aronson, and Costanzo, 1988) worked with several energy auditors in California. As in many states, California utility companies offer a free service wherein an auditor will come to people's homes and give them a customized assessment of what needs to be done to make their homes more energy efficient. What a deal! The problem was that less than 20 percent of the individuals requesting audits were actually following the auditors' recommendations.

To increase compliance, the Aronson research team trained the auditors to present their findings in a more vivid manner. For example, let's consider weather stripping: For most people, a small crack under the door didn't seem like a huge drain of energy, so when an auditor told them they should put in some weather stripping, they thought, "Yeah, big deal." Aronson and his students told the auditors to make this statement more vivid:

> Look at all the cracks around that door! It may not seem like much to you, but if you were to add up all the cracks around and under each of these doors, you'd have the equivalent of a hole the size and circumference of a basketball. Suppose someone poked a hole the size of a basketball in your living room wall. Think for a moment about all the heat you'd be losing from a hole that size—that's money out the window. You'd want to patch that hole in your wall, wouldn't you? That's exactly what weather stripping does. And that's why I recommend you install weather stripping.

Similar attempts were made to make other problems more vivid—for example, referring to an attic that lacks insulation as a "naked attic" that is like "facing winter not just without an overcoat, but without any clothing at all."

The results were striking. The percentage of homeowners who followed the vivid recommendations jumped to 61 percent. This study demonstrates that people will act in a manner that is sensible in terms of national goals and their own economic self-interest, but if old habits are involved, the communication must be one that is vivid enough to break through those established habits.

**Reducing Litter.**  Compared to other environmental problems, littering may not seem to be all that serious a matter. Although billboards implore us to "Keep America Beautiful," most people seem to think it isn't a big deal to leave their paper cup at the side of the road instead of in a trash barrel. Unfortunately, those paper cups add up. Littering has increased steadily in California over the past fifteen years, to the point where $100 million of tax money is spent cleaning it up—every year (Cialdini, Kallgren, and Reno,

> And willful waste, depend upon't, brings, almost always, woeful want!
> —Ann Taylor (1782–1866)

BEGIN

① Aunt Clara gives person ugly, itchy sweater.

② Sweater is thrown away.

③ Bag is carted to dump

④ After 10,000 years, dump becomes Earth again.

⑤ Grass grows on the site.

⑥ Grass is eaten by sheep.

⑦ Wool is taken from sheep and fashioned into ugly, itchy sweater.

IT NEVER ENDS

*Drawing by Roz Chast; © 1988 The Four Elements, Harper & Row, NY.*

1991). The stuff we discard is polluting our water systems, endangering wildlife, and costing us millions of dollars.

Littering is another classic social dilemma. Sometimes it's a pain to find a trash can, and from an individual's point of view, the addition of one more paper cup to the side of the road is not going to make much difference. As with all social dilemmas, the problem is that if everyone thinks this way, everyone suffers. How can we get people to act less selfishly when they have that paper cup in hand?

According to Robert Cialdini, Raymond Reno, and Carl Kallgren, the answer is to remind people of the social norms against littering (Cialdini, Kallgren, and Reno, 1991; Cialdini, Reno, and Kallgren, 1990; Reno, Cialdini, and Kallgren, 1993). The phrase "social norm," which has a long history in social psychology and sociology, actually has several meanings. Cialdini and his colleagues (1991) suggest that two of these meanings are critical to understanding when people will litter. First, there are **injunctive norms,** referring to our perceptions of what other people approve of. Regardless of what other people really are doing, injunctive norms pertain to the kinds of things that are socially sanctioned by others. For example, we may be in an environment where many people are littering, but know that there is an injunctive norm against littering—most people disapprove of it.

Second, there are **descriptive norms,** referring to people's perceptions of what most people are actually doing, regardless of what they ought to be doing. Even if there were no injunctive norms against littering, people might be reluctant to litter if they saw that no one else was doing so. As we saw in Chapter 7, we often use observations of other people's behavior to decide on the proper course of action in a particular situation.

Focusing people's attention on either of these norms reduces littering. For example, Raymond Reno and his colleagues (1993) conducted a field

**injunctive norms:** socially sanctioned behaviors—that is, people's perceptions of what behaviors are approved of by others

**descriptive norms:** people's perceptions of how other people are actually behaving in a given situation, regardless of what behaviors are socially sanctioned

experiment to investigate the power of injunctive norms. As people left a local library and approached their cars in the parking lot, an accomplice walked by them, picked up a fast-food bag that had been discarded on the ground, and put the bag in the trash. In a control condition, no bag was on the ground, and the accomplice simply walked by the library patrons. When the patrons got to their car, they found a handbill on their windshield. The question was, How many of these people would litter by throwing the handbill on the ground? Reno and colleagues hypothesized that seeing the accomplice pick up the fast-food bag would be a vivid reminder of the injunctive norm—littering is bad, and other people disapprove of it—and hence would lower their own inclination to litter. They were right: In this condition, only 7 percent of the people tossed the handbill on the ground, compared to 37 percent in the control condition.

What is the best way to communicate descriptive norms against littering? The most straightforward way, it would seem, would be to clean up all the litter in an environment, to illustrate that "no one litters here." In general, this is true: The less litter there is in an environment, the less likely people are to litter (Krauss, Freedman, and Whitcup, 1978; Reiter & Samuel, 1980). There is, however, an interesting exception to this finding. Cialdini and colleagues (1990) figured that seeing one piece of litter on the ground, spoiling an otherwise clean environment, would be a better reminder of descriptive norms than seeing a completely clean environment. The single piece of trash sticks out like a sore thumb, reminding people that no one has littered here—except one thoughtless person. In comparison, if there is no litter on the ground, people might not even think about what the descriptive norm is. Ironically, then, littering may be more likely to occur in a totally clean environment than in one where there is a single piece of litter.

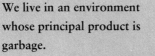

We live in an environment whose principal product is garbage.
—Russell Baker, 1968

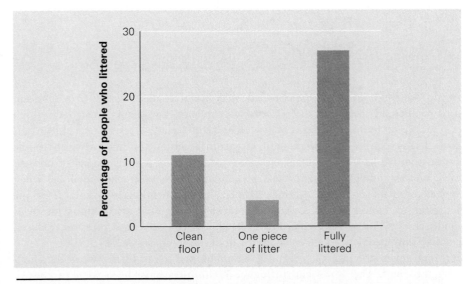

**FIGURE 14.8 Descriptive norms and littering.** Who littered the least: people who saw that no one else had littered, people who saw one piece of litter on the floor, or people who saw several pieces of litter? As shown in the figure, it was people who saw one piece of litter. Seeing the single piece of litter was most likely to draw people's attention to the fact that most people had not littered, making people less likely themselves to litter. (Adapted from Cialdini et al., 1990)

To test this hypothesis, the researchers stuffed students' mailboxes with handbills and then observed, from a hidden vantage point, how many of the students dropped the handbills on the floor (Cialdini et al., 1990). In the first condition, the researchers cleaned up the mailroom so that there were no other pieces of litter to be seen. In the second condition, they placed one very noticeable piece of litter on the floor: a hollowed-out heel of a watermelon. In the third condition, they not only put the watermelon rind on the floor but also spread out dozens of discarded handbills. As predicted, the lowest rate of littering occurred in the condition where there was a single piece of trash on the floor (see Figure 14.8). A single violation of a descriptive norm—the watermelon rind—highlighted the fact that most people had not littered. Now that people's attention was focused on the descriptive norm against littering, virtually none of the students littered. The highest percentage of littering occurred when the floor was littered with lots of handbills; here it was clear that there was a descriptive norm in favor of littering, and many of the students followed suit.

Thus, drawing people's attention to both injunctive and descriptive norms can reduce littering. Of the two kinds of norms, Robert Cialdini and his colleagues suggest that injunctive norms work better. Descriptive norms work only if everyone cooperates—for example, by keeping an environment relatively free of litter. This method is not perfect, however; if trash starts accumulating, then the descriptive norm becomes "See, lots of people litter here!" and littering will increase. In contrast, Raymond Reno and his colleagues (1993) found that reminding people of the injunctive norm works in a wide variety of situations, regardless of how clean the environment is. Once we are reminded that "people disapprove of littering," we are less likely to litter in virtually all circumstances.

## SUMMARY

In this chapter, we examined two main contributions social psychology makes to the areas of health and the environment. The first concerns a basic principle of social psychology—namely, that to understand why people behave the way they do in a particular situation, we have to view that situation through their eyes, understanding how they interpret it. This principle applies to an understanding of **stress**. To understand whether an event like getting married, becoming ill, or living under crowded conditions will be stressful, we have to examine how people interpret and explain it. One key interpretation is how much **perceived control** people have over the event. The less control people believe they have, the more likely it is that the event will cause them physical and psychological problems. For example, if people in high **density** settings feel that they have a low level of control (i.e., they believe it is difficult to escape to a less dense setting), they will feel

more **crowded**, with negative consequences. Crowding can also be aversive if it leads to **sensory overload**, which occurs when other people place a severe demand on our attentional system. In addition, the way in which people explain the causes of negative events is critical to how an event is interpreted, and thus how stressful it will be. When bad things happen, **learned helplessness** results if people make **stable, internal,** and **global attributions** for these events. Learned helplessness leads to depression, reduced effort, and difficulty in learning new material.

Second, we examined some of the ways in which social influence techniques have been used to change people's behavior so that it is more healthy (e.g., practicing safer sex) and better for the environment (e.g., conserving water, saving energy, not littering). This is not easy, because many harmful health habits are difficult to change, and many environmental problems are the result of **social dilemmas,** wherein actions that are beneficial for individuals are, if performed by most people, harmful to everyone. Using proven techniques to change people's attitudes and behaviors, however, social psychologists have had some success in getting people to act in healthier and more environmentally sound ways. One technique is to arouse dissonance in people by making them feel that they are not practicing what they are preaching—for example,

that even though they believe in water conservation, they are taking long showers. Another is to remind people of both **injunctive** and **descriptive norms** against environmentally damaging acts, such as littering. Focusing people's attention on injunctive norms against littering—the idea that throwing trash on the ground is not a socially accepted behavior—was found to be especially effective.

## SUGGESTED READINGS

Cohen, S., Evans, G. W., Stokols, D. S., & Krantz, D. S. (1986). *Behavior, health, and environmental stress.* New York: Plenum. An in-depth discussion of stress and human health, with a focus on studies the authors conducted on the effects of aircraft noise on children.

Seligman, M. E. P. (1990). *Learned optimism.* New York: Springer-Verlag. An interesting book on optimism and learned helplessness theory, by one of its originators.

Stokols, D., & Altman, I. (1987). *Handbook of environmental psychology.* New York: Wiley. A collection of articles by researchers in environmental psychology, covering a wide array of topics in the field.

Taylor, S. E. (1985). *Health psychology.* New York: Random House. A textbook that takes a broad look at psychological issues in health, including stress, coping, health habits, and how people respond to the medical care system.

Taylor, S. E. (1989). *Positive illusions: Creative self-deception and the healthy mind.* New York: Basic Books. A readable book that examines the relationship between people's illusions about themselves and the social world and their physical and mental health. Includes an in-depth discussion of many of the issues covered in this chapter, including perceived control and learned helplessness.

# Chapter 15
## Law and Business

ou be the jury. How would you vote, after hearing the following testimony, taken from an actual case in Texas? The night was cold and dark, in November 1976, when police officer Robert Wood and his partner saw a car driving with its headlights off. After signaling the car to pull over, Wood walked up to the driver's side, intending only to tell the driver to turn on his lights. He never got the chance. Before Wood could even speak, the driver shot Wood, killing him instantly. Wood's partner emptied her revolver at the car as it sped away, but the killer escaped.

A month later, the police picked up a suspect, sixteen-year-old David Harris. Harris admitted that he had stolen a neighbor's car and revolver the day before the murder, and that these were the car and gun involved in Wood's killing. He denied, however, that he was the one who shot Wood. He said he had picked up a hitchhiker by the name of Randall Adams, and had let Adams drive. It was Adams, he claimed, who reached under the seat, grabbed the revolver, and shot the officer.

When the police questioned Randall Adams, he admitted that he had gotten a ride from David Harris, but said that Harris had dropped him off at his motel three hours before the murder occurred. It was Harris's word against Adams's—until the police found three eyewitnesses who corroborated Harris's story. Emily and Robert Miller testified that they were driving by just before Officer Wood was shot. Though it was very dark, they said they got a good look at the driver of the car, and both identified him as Randall Adams. "When he rolled down the window that's what made his face stand out," said Robert Miller. "He had a beard, mustache, kind of dishwater blond hair" (Morris, 1988). David Harris was clean-shaven, and at the time of the murder, Randall Adams did indeed fit Miller's description, as seen in the photo on this page. Michael Randell, a salesman, also happened to be driving by right before the murder, and claimed to have seen two people in the car.

**Randall Adams (left) and David Harris (right).** The fact that eyewitnesses said the murderer had long hair and a mustache was the main reason Adams was convicted of murdering Officer Wood.

He too said the driver had long hair and a mustache.

Who do you think committed the murder? The real jury believed the eyewitnesses and convicted Adams, sentencing him to death. However, as Adams languished in jail, waiting for the courts to hear his appeals, several experts began to doubt that he was guilty. New evidence came to light (largely because of a documentary film made about the case, Errol Morris's *The Thin Blue Line*), and it is now almost certain that David Harris was the murderer. Harris was later convicted of another murder, and while on death row, strongly implied that he, not Randall Adams, had shot Officer Wood. An appeals court overturned Adams's conviction. He was a free man—after spending twelve years in prison for a crime he did not commit.

If Adams was innocent, why did the eyewitnesses say that the driver of a car had long hair and a mustache? And why did the jury believe them? How common are such miscarriages of justice? In the first half of this chapter, we will discuss the answers to these questions, focusing on the role social psychological processes play in the legal system.

## Social Psychology and the Law

Let's begin with a brief review of the American justice system. When someone commits a crime and the police arrest a suspect, a judge or a grand jury decides whether there is enough evidence to press formal charges. If so, lawyers for the defense and the prosecution gather evidence and negotiate with each other. As a result of these negotiations, the defendant often pleads guilty, to a lesser charge. About a quarter of the cases go to trial, where a jury or a judge decides the defendant's fate. There are also civil trials, where one party (the plaintiff) brings a complaint against another (the defendant) for violating the former's rights in some way.

All of these steps in the legal process are intensely social psychological. For example, first impressions of the accused and of the witnesses have a powerful effect on police investigators and the jury; attributions about what caused the criminal behavior are made by police, lawyers, jurors, and the judge; prejudiced beliefs and stereotypical ways of thinking affect those attributions; attitude change and persuasion techniques abound in the courtroom, as lawyers for each side argue their case and jurors later debate with one another; and biases in social cognition affect the jurors' decision making when deciding guilt or innocence. Social psychologists have studied the legal system a great deal in recent years, both because it offers an excellent applied setting in which to study basic psychological processes and because of its immense importance in daily life. If you, through no fault of your own, become the accused in a court trial, what do you need to know to convince the system of your innocence?

We will begin our discussion with eyewitness testimony, the most troubling aspect of the Randall Adams case we just presented. In Chapter 5, we saw that whereas people do form accurate impressions of others, systematic biases can come into play, leading to serious misunderstandings. A closely related question is this: How accurate are people at identifying someone who has committed a crime? Do some of the same biases people bring to social perception apply to eyewitness identification and testimony as well?

## Eyewitness Testimony

The American legal system assigns a great deal of significance to eyewitness testimony. If an eyewitness fingers you as the culprit, you are quite likely to be convicted, even if there is considerable circumstantial evidence indicating that you are innocent. Randall Adams was convicted largely because of the eyewitnesses who identified him, even though in other ways the case against him was weak: He had no criminal record; he had just found steady employment; and he had no reason to be concerned about being pulled over by the police—he was only a hitchhiker (if, indeed, he really was in the car at the time of the shooting). In comparison, David Harris did have reason to fear the police: He had stolen the car and was in possession of a stolen, loaded handgun. Given these facts, why would Randall Adams gun down a police officer? Doesn't David Harris seem a more logical suspect? Despite the implausibility of the Adams-as-murderer scenario, and despite the lack of physical evidence linking Adams to the scene of the crime, the eyewitness testimony that Adams was driving the car was enough to convict him.

Systematic experiments have confirmed that jurors rely heavily on eyewitness testimony when deciding whether someone is guilty. Unfortunately, jurors also tend to overestimate the accuracy of eyewitnesses (Leippe, Manion, and Romanczyk, 1992; Lindsay, Wells, and Rumpel, 1981; Loftus, 1979; Wells, Lindsay, and Ferguson, 1979). Rod Lindsay and his colleagues (1981) conducted a clever experiment that illustrates both of these points. The researchers first staged the theft of a calculator in front of unsuspecting students; they then saw how accurately the students could pick out the "thief" from a set a six photographs. In one condition, it was difficult to identify the thief because he had worn a knit cap pulled over his ears and was in the room for only twelve seconds. In the second condition, the thief had worn the knit cap higher on his head, revealing some of his hair, so that it was moderately difficult to identify him. In the third condition, the thief

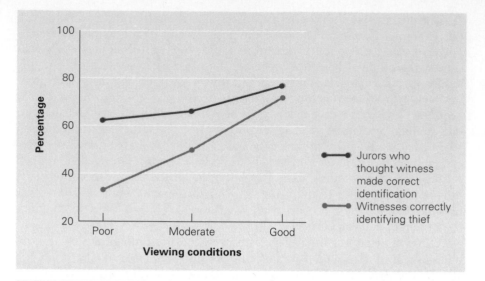

**FIGURE 15.1  The accuracy of eyewitness identification**. The accuracy of eye-witness identification depends on the viewing conditions at the time the crime was committed. As in this study, however, most jurors believe that witnesses can correctly identify the criminal even when viewing conditions are poor. (Adapted from Lindsay et al., 1981)

had worn no hat and stayed in the room for twenty seconds, making it relatively easy to identify him. The first set of results is as we'd expect: The more visual information available about the thief, the higher the percentage of students who correctly identified him in the photo lineup (see the bottom line in Figure 15.1). In the next stage of the experiment, a researcher playing the role of lawyer questioned the students about their eyewitness identifications, just as a real lawyer would cross-examine witnesses in a trial. These question-and-answer sessions were videotaped. A new group of participants, playing the role of jurors, watched the videotapes of these cross-examinations, and rated the extent to which they believed the witnesses had correctly identified the thief. As seen by the top line in Figure 15.1, these jurors overestimated the accuracy of the witnesses, especially in the condition where the thief was difficult to identify.

Why do jurors believe witnesses more than they should? One reason is that they assume the more confident an eyewitness is, the more accurate he or she must be. For example, imagine that you heard testimony from these witnesses: One says, "That's definitely the guy who came into the room and took the calculator. There's absolutely no doubt in my mind—I'd recognize him anywhere." The other eyewitness says, "Well, gee, I'm really not sure, because it all happened so quickly. If I had to guess, I'd say that it was suspect 2, but I'm really not sure." Who would you be more likely to believe? The eyewitness who was more confident, of course! The U.S. Supreme Court concurs with this reasoning, ruling that the amount of confidence witnesses express is a good indicator of their accuracy (*Neil v. Biggers*, 1972).

The only problem—and it is a big one—is that numerous studies have shown that a witness's confidence is not strongly related to how accurate he or she is (Bothwell, Deffenbacher, and Brigham, 1987; Smith, Kassin, and Ellsworth, 1989). The reason is that the things that make us confident are

Eyewitness testimony has a far greater effect on jurors than it should, given that it is often inaccurate. If the eyewitness speaks with great confidence on the witness stand, his or her word virtually ensures a guilty verdict from the jury.

not necessarily the same things that make us accurate. For example, things that happen after people have witnessed a crime, such as rehearsing their testimony before a trial, make them more confident, but have no effect on the accuracy of their identifications. In addition, there are things that influence accuracy, such as the viewing conditions when the crime occurred, that do not always influence confidence. This was the case in the Lindsay and colleagues (1981) experiment, where the witnesses in the "hard-to-identify" condition (in which the thief wore the cap over his ears) had as much confidence in their identifications as the witnesses in the other conditions, even though they were considerably less accurate (see Figure 15.1). Thus, just because a witness is confident does not mean that he or she is accurate.

How accurate are eyewitnesses to real crimes? While it's impossible to say exactly what percentage of the time eyewitnesses are accurate, there is reason to believe that they often make mistakes. Randall Adams was convicted because of eyewitnesses who mistakenly thought he was driving the car, and he spent more than a decade in prison as a result. Researchers have documented more than 1,000 cases of such wrongful arrests as these, and in a remarkably high proportion of these cases, the wrong person was convicted because an eyewitness mistakenly identified him or her as the criminal (Brandon & Davies, 1973; Wells, 1992).

**Biases in Memory Processing.** The problem is that our minds are not like videocameras that can record an event, store it over time, and play it back later, all with perfect accuracy. Think back to our discussion of social perception in Chapters 4 and 5, where we saw that a number of distortions in social cognition and attribution can occur. Because eyewitness identification is a form of social perception, it is subject to similar problems, particularly ones involving memory. In order for someone to be an accurate eyewitness, he or she must successfully complete three stages of memory processing: **acquisition, storage,** and **retrieval** of the events witnessed. At any given time, people notice and pay attention to only a fraction of the informa-

> No subjective feeling of certainty can be an objective criterion for the desired truth.
> —Hugo Münsterberg, 1908

**acquisition:** the process by which people notice and pay attention to information in the environment; because people cannot perceive everything that is happening around them, they acquire only a subset of the information available in the environment

**storage:** the process by which people store in memory information they have acquired from the environment

**retrieval:** the process by which people recall information stored in their memories

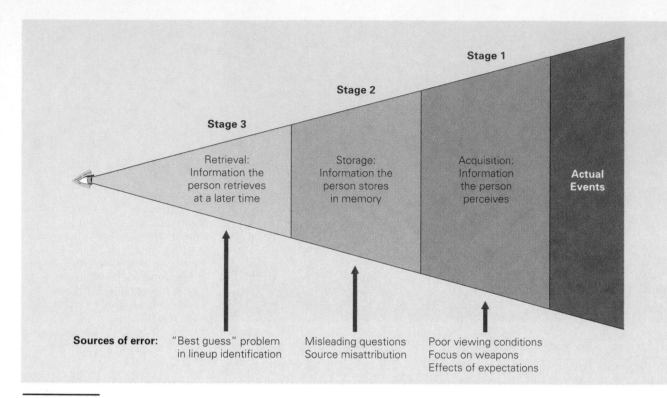

Stage 1

Stage 2

Stage 3

Retrieval:
Information the
person retrieves
at a later time

Storage:
Information the
person stores
in memory

Acquisition:
Information
the person
perceives

Actual
Events

Sources of error:    "Best guess" problem
in lineup identification

Misleading questions
Source misattribution

Poor viewing conditions
Focus on weapons
Effects of expectations

**FIGURE 15.2 Acquisition, storage, and retrieval.**

tion in the surrounding environment, and acquisition refers to that subset of information which is perceived. Of this information, a still smaller subset is actually stored in memory. Of the information that is stored in memory, only a subset can be retrieved at a later time (see Figure 15.2). Eyewitnesses can be inaccurate because of problems at any of these three stages.

**Acquisition.** No one doubts that people accurately perceive a great deal of information about the world around them. Nonetheless, our ability to take in information is limited, particularly when we observe unexpected, complex events. The psychologist Hugo Münsterberg (1908), for example, described the following event, which occurred at a scientific meeting attended by psychologists, lawyers, and physicians: In the middle of the meeting, a clown burst into the room, followed closely by a man with a revolver. The two men shouted wildly, grabbed each other, then fell to the ground in a fierce struggle. One of them fired a shot; then both men ran out of the room.

All the witnesses were asked to write down an exact account of what they had just seen (which was actually an event staged by two actors). These accounts were surprisingly inaccurate. Most of the witnesses omitted or wrote mistaken accounts of about half the actions they had observed. Nor were they very accurate about the duration of the incident—though the two men were in the room for about twenty seconds, the witnesses' estimates ranged from a few seconds to several minutes. John Yuille and Judith Cutshall (1986) found similar results in the accounts of thirteen witnesses to an actual robbery, one in which the thief was killed. Twenty-four percent of the eyewitnesses' descriptions of the people involved were incorrect; 18

Imagine that you are on this street corner, and suddenly witness a hold-up across the street. A thief robs a man of his wallet, and is gone in a matter of seconds. How accurate do you think your description of the thief would be?

percent of their descriptions of what occurred were incorrect; and 11 percent of their descriptions of the objects (e.g., the weapon) were incorrect.

A number of factors influence the amount of information people take in, such as how much time they have to watch an event and the nature of the viewing conditions. As obvious as this sounds, people sometimes forget how these factors limit eyewitness reports of crimes. Crimes usually occur under the very conditions that make acquisition difficult: quickly, unexpectedly, and under poor viewing conditions, such as at night. These conditions certainly describe the scene of the murder of Officer Wood. Eyewitnesses were driving down a dimly lit road, past a pulled-over car, when the unexpected happened—shots rang out and a policeman crumpled to the ground. How well could they see? How much information could they take in in the few seconds it took to drive by? We should also remember that if eyewitnesses are the victims of the crime, they will be terribly afraid and focus their attention on any weapon they see—a factor that limits how accurately they can identify the criminal (Brigham, Maass, Snyder, and Spaulding, 1983; Christianson, 1992; Deffenbacher, 1983; Loftus, Loftus, and Messo, 1987).

The information people notice and pay attention to is also influenced by what they expect to see. Consider our friend Alan, a social psychologist who is an expert on social perception. One Sunday, Alan became concerned when his neighbor, a frail woman in her eighties, did not appear for church. After knocking on her door repeatedly and receiving no response, Alan jimmied open a window and searched her house. Soon, his worst fears were realized: The woman was lying dead on the floor of her bedroom.

Shaken, Alan went back to his house and telephoned the authorities. The police spent a great deal of time in the woman's house, after which a detective came over and asked Alan increasingly detailed questions, centering on whether he had noticed any suspicious activity around his neighbor's house. Alan was confused by this line of questioning, and finally burst out, "Why are you asking me these questions? Isn't it obvious that my neighbor died of old age? Shouldn't we be notifying her family?" Now it was the detective's turn to look puzzled. "Aren't you the one who discovered the body?" he asked. Alan said he was. "Well," said the detective, "didn't you notice that her bedroom had been ransacked, that there was broken glass everywhere, and that there was a belt tied around her neck?"

It turned out that Alan's neighbor had been strangled by a man who had come to spray her house for insects. There had been a fierce struggle, and the fact that the woman was murdered could not have been more obvious. But Alan saw none of the signs. He was worried that his elderly neighbor had passed away. When he discovered that she had in fact died, the farthest thing from his mind was that she had been murdered. As a result, he saw what he expected, and failed to see what he did not expect. When the police later showed him photographs of the crime scene, he felt as though he had never been there. He recognized almost nothing.

Alan's experiences are consistent with our discussion in Chapter 4 of how people use theories and schemas. We have many theories about the world and the people in it, and these theories influence what we notice and remember. Claudia Cohen (1981), for example, showed people a videotape of a woman eating dinner and participating in an informal birthday celebration. Half the participants were told that the woman was a librarian, whereas the other half were told that she was a waitress. The participants' memories for what they had seen in the videotape were affected by the expectations, or stereotypes, they had for occupations and social class. For instance, those who thought the woman was a librarian said she had been wearing glasses (she was not) and that she was drinking wine (it was beer), because these behaviors fit their stereotype of a librarian.

**Storage.**  We have just seen that several variables limit what people perceive, and thus what they are able to store in their memories. Once a piece of information is in memory, it might seem like it stays there, unaltered, until we recall it at a later time. Many people think that memory is like a photograph album. We record a picture of an event, such as the face of a robber, and place it in the memory "album." The picture may not be perfect—after all, few of us have photographic memories. Further, it might fade a bit over time, because memories, like real photographs, fade with age. It seems unlikely, however, that the picture can be altered or retouched, such that things are added to or subtracted from the image. If the robber we saw was clean-shaven, surely we will not pencil in a mustache at some later time. Thus, the fact that the witnesses who testified at the Randall Adams trial remembered that the driver of the car had long hair and a mustache seems like pretty incriminating evidence for Randall Adams.

Unfortunately, the way in which our memories actually work is not so simple. People can get mixed up about where they heard or saw something, so that memories in one "album" get confused with memories in another. As a result, people can have quite inaccurate recall about what they saw. This is the conclusion reached by Elizabeth Loftus and her colleagues after years of research on **reconstructive memory,** defined as a cognitive process whereby memories for an event become distorted by information encountered after the event has occurred (Loftus, 1979; Loftus & Hoffman, 1989). According to Loftus, information that we obtain after witnessing an event can change our memories of the event.

In one of her studies, she showed students thirty slides depicting different stages of an automobile accident. The contents of one slide varied; some

> When an actual perceptual fact is in conflict with expectation, expectation may prove a stronger determinant of perception and memory than the situation itself.
> —Gordon Allport and Leo Postman, 1947

**reconstructive memory:** the process whereby memories for an event become distorted by information encountered after the event has occurred

Students saw one of these pictures and then tried to remember whether they had seen a stop sign or a yield sign. Many of those who heard leading questions about the street sign made mistaken reports about which sign they had seen. (From Loftus, Miller, and Burns, 1978)

students saw a car stopped at a stop sign, whereas others saw the same car stopped at a yield sign (see the photos on this page). After the slide show, the students were asked several questions about the car accident they had "witnessed." The key question varied how the traffic sign was described. In one version, the question asked, "Did another car pass the red Datsun while it was stopped at the stop sign?" In the other version, the question asked, "Did another car pass the red Datsun while it was stopped at the yield sign?" Thus, for half the participants the question described the traffic sign as they had in fact seen it. But for the other half, the wording of the question subtly introduced new information—for example, if they had seen a stop sign, the question described it as a yield sign. Would this small change (akin to what might occur when witnesses are being questioned by police investigators or attorneys) have an effect on people's memories of the actual event?

All the students were shown the two pictures reproduced on this page, and asked which one they had originally seen. Most people (75 percent) who were asked about the sign they had actually seen chose the correct picture; that is, if they had seen a stop sign and were asked about a stop sign, most of them correctly identified the stop-sign photograph (note that 25 percent made a crucial mistake on what would seem to be an easy question). However, of those who got the misleading question, only 41 percent chose the correct photograph (Loftus, Miller, and Burns, 1978).

In subsequent experiments, Loftus and her colleagues have found that misleading questions can change people's minds about how fast a car was going, whether broken glass was at the scene of an accident, whether a traffic

source misattribution: making a mistake about the source of our memories (e.g., believing a man looks familiar because we saw him at the scene of a crime, when in fact he looks familiar because we saw his picture in the newspaper)

light was green or red, and—of relevance to the Randall Adams trial—whether a robber had a mustache (Loftus, 1979). Her studies show that the way in which the police and lawyers question witnesses can change the witnesses' reports about what they saw. (There is some suspicion that in the Randall Adams case, the police may have led the witnesses by asking questions that implicated Adams and not Harris. At the time of the murder, Harris was a juvenile and could not receive the death penalty for killing a police officer; Adams was in his thirties, and could. According to this reasoning, Adams was a "better" suspect in the eyes of the police). But, we might ask, do misleading questions alter what is stored in eyewitnesses' memories, or do the questions change only what these people are willing to report, without retouching their memories?

Though some controversy exists over the answer to this question (Belli, 1989; Loftus & Hoffman, 1989; McCloskey & Zaragoza, 1985; Smith & Ellsworth, 1987; Tversky & Tuchin, 1989), most researchers endorse the following position: Misleading questions cause a problem called source misattribution (Johnson, Hashtroudi, and Lindsay, 1993; Lindsay & Johnson, 1989). People who saw a stop sign but received the misleading question about a yield sign now have two pieces of information in memory, the stop sign and the yield sign. This is all well and good, as long as they remember where these memories came from: the stop sign from the accident they saw earlier, and the yield sign from the question they were asked subsequently. The problem is that people often get mixed up about where they heard or saw something, causing them to believe that the yield sign must be familiar because they saw it during the slide show. This process is similar to the misattribution effects we discussed in Chapter 5, wherein people are unsure about what has caused their arousal. It's easy to get confused about the source of our memories as well.

The implications for legal testimony are sobering. Eyewitnesses who are asked misleading questions often report seeing things that were not really there. In addition, eyewitnesses might be confused as to why a suspect looks familiar. It is likely, for example, that the eyewitnesses in the Randall Adams trial saw pictures of Adams in the newspaper before they testified about what they saw the night of the murder. When asked to remember what they saw that night, they might have become confused because of source misattribution. They remembered seeing a man with long hair and a mustache, but they may have gotten mixed up about where they had seen his face before.

**Retrieval.** Suppose the police have arrested a suspect and want to see if you, the eyewitness, can identify the person. It is common practice for the police to arrange a lineup at the police station, where you will be asked whether one of several people is the perpetrator. Sometimes the police show photographs to witnesses; other times they use lineups of actual suspects and foils (people known not to have committed the crime). In either case, if a witness identifies a suspect as the culprit, the suspect is likely to be charged and convicted of the crime. After all, the argument goes, if an eyewitness saw the suspect commit the crime and then picked the suspect out of a lineup later, that's pretty good evidence that the suspect is the guilty party.

Just as there are problems with acquisition and storage of information, so too can there be problems with how people retrieve information from their memories. A number of things other than the image of a person that is

Give us a dozen healthy memories, well-formed, and . . . we'll guarantee to take any one at random and train it to become any type of memory we might select—hammer, screwdriver, wrench, stop sign, yield sign, Indian chief—regardless of its origin or the brain that holds it.

—Elizabeth Loftus and Hunter Hoffman, 1989

stored in memory can influence whether eyewitnesses will pick someone out of a lineup. Witnesses often choose the person in a lineup who most resembles the criminal, even if the resemblance is not very strong. Suppose, for example, that a nineteen-year-old woman committed a robbery and the police mistakenly arrest you, a nineteen-year-old woman, for the crime. They put you in a lineup and ask witnesses to pick out the criminal. Which do you think would be more fair: if the other people in the lineup were a twenty-year-old man, a three-year old child, and an eighty-year-old woman, or if the other people were all nineteen-year-old women? In the former case, the witnesses might pick you out only because you are the one who most resembles the actual criminal (Buckhout, 1974). In the latter case, it is much less likely that the witnesses will mistake you for the criminal, because everyone in the lineup is the same age and sex as the culprit (Wells, 1992; Wells & Luus, 1990).

"That's him! That's the one! . . . I'd recognize that silly little hat anywhere!"

To avoid this "best guess" problem wherein witnesses pick the person who looks most like the suspect, social psychologists recommend that police follow these five steps:

1. Make sure that everyone in the lineup resembles the suspect.

2. Do not tell the witnesses that the person suspected of the crime is in the lineup, because doing so greatly increases the likelihood that the witnesses will identify someone as the culprit, even if everyone in the lineup is innocent (Malpass & Devine, 1981).

3. Do not always include the suspect in an initial lineup. If a witness picks out someone as the culprit from a lineup that includes only foils, then you will know the witness is not reliable (Wells, 1984).

4. Present pictures of people sequentially instead of simultaneously, because doing so makes it more difficult for witnesses to compare all the pictures, choosing the one that most resembles the criminal, even when the criminal is not actually in the lineup (Lindsay & Wells, 1985).

5. Present witnesses with both photographs and sound recordings of people's voices. Witnesses who both see and hear members of a lineup are much more likely to identify the person they saw commit a crime than people who only see the pictures or only hear the voice recordings are (Melara, DeWitt-Rickards, and O'Brien, 1989).

To summarize, eyewitness testimony is not nearly as accurate as most people think. Several factors can bias the acquisition, storage, and retrieval of what people see, leading to false identifications. In the legal system of some countries, a suspect cannot be convicted on the basis of a sole eyewitness; at least two independent witnesses are needed. Adopting this more stringent standard in the United States might mean that some guilty people go free, but it would avoid many false convictions.

> Take nothing on its looks;
> take everything on evidence.
> There's no better rule.
> —Charles Dickens, *Great Expectations*, 1861

## Detecting Deception

There is yet another reason eyewitness testimony can be inaccurate: Even if witnesses have very accurate memories for what they saw, they might deliberately lie when on the witness stand. After Randall Adams was tried and convicted, evidence came to light suggesting that some of the eyewitnesses who testified against him had lied. For example, the daughter of one of the eyewitnesses had been arrested for armed robbery; this witness may have struck a deal with the police, agreeing to say what they wanted her to say, in

On the eve of his confirmation to the Supreme Court, Justice Clarence Thomas was accused of sexual harassment by a former employee, Anita Hill. He vehemently denied the charges. Is there some way that experts could tell whether Clarence Thomas or Anita Hill was lying? Unfortunately, there is no foolproof method of detecting deception.

> If falsehood, like truth, had only one face, we would be in better shape. For we would take as certain the opposite of what the liar said. But the reverse of truth has a hundred thousand shapes.
> —Montaigne, *Essays*, 1595

return for lenient treatment of her daughter. If so, why couldn't the jurors tell that she was lying when she said she saw Randall Adams at the wheel of the car right before the murder?

Consider also the controversy over Supreme Court Justice Clarence Thomas's confirmation. On the eve of the Senate confirmation vote, charges came to light that Judge Thomas had sexually harassed a former employee, Anita Hill. For the next several days, most Americans were riveted to their television sets, watching Professor Hill level her charges and Judge Thomas rebut them. Who was telling the truth? Or was each telling the truth as he or she saw it? U.S. senators, as well as the nation as a whole, were deeply split over whom to believe.

As we discussed in Chapter 5, several studies have tested people's ability to detect deception. When people watch videotapes of actors who are either lying or telling the truth, their ability to tell who is lying is only slightly better than chance, (i.e., only slightly better than pure guessing; DePaulo, Stone, and Lassiter, 1985). But surely some people must be very good at detecting deception; after all, some jobs require exactly that skill. For example, law enforcement officials, most of whom have spent years with suspects who concoct stories professing their innocence, may be much more skilled than the average person at seeing through these stories to the underlying truth.

To find out, Bella DePaulo and Roger Pfeiffer (1986) showed videotapes of people lying and telling the truth to a group of federal law enforcement officers, including members of the armed forces, the U.S. Customs Service, and the Secret Service. Some of these officers were new recruits, and others were veterans with an average of eight years in law enforcement. The results were surprising. Regardless of their amount of experience, the officers were no more accurate at telling who was lying than a group of college students

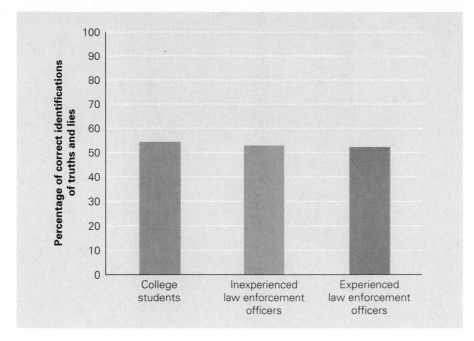

FIGURE 15.3 **Does experience in law enforcement improve the ability to detect deception?** Experienced law enforcement officers were no better at telling who was lying than were inexperienced law enforcement officers or college students. (Adapted from DePaulo & Pfeiffer, 1986)

were, as shown in Figure 15.3. Similar results were found in a study by Paul Ekman and Maureen O'Sullivan (1991), who tested police detectives, judges, psychiatrists, and federal employees who administer lie-detector tests. The moral is this: If someone is motivated to tell a lie, he or she can usually get away with it. Even the experts will have trouble telling who is lying and who is telling the truth.

**The Lie-Detector Test.** If people are not good at detecting liars with their own eyes and ears, perhaps machines can do the job for them. The lie-detector machine, called a **polygraph**, monitors people's physiological responses, such as their heart rate, breathing rate, and amount of perspiration. The assumption is that when people lie, they become anxious, and that this anxiety can be detected by increases in heart rate, breathing rate, and so on. But do polygraphs really work? Anita Hill trusted them enough to take a lie detector test; the results indicated that she was telling the truth when she said Judge Thomas had sexually harassed her. Many employers, including the federal government, trust polygraphs as well, requiring people to take lie-detector tests before being hired.

A great deal of controversy over the accuracy of polygraph tests exists among psychological researchers, and the test has both strong supporters (e.g., Raskin, 1986) and steadfast critics (e.g., Lykken, 1984). Given this disagreement, and given how widespread polygraph tests have become, the U.S. Congress asked the Office of Technology and Assessment in 1983 to write a review of the scientific evidence regarding the polygraph's validity. Several social psychologists have also reviewed this evidence (Ekman, 1992; Saxe, Dougherty, and Cross, 1985), and have reached similar conclusions. First, under optimal conditions (e.g., an experienced examiner), the polygraph can reveal whether someone is lying or telling the truth at levels better than chance. But that doesn't mean the machine is perfect. Even under optimal conditions, the test can be inaccurate, and it often has high error rates. The

**polygraph:** a machine that measures people's physiological responses (e.g., their heart rate); when these machines are used in lie detection, polygraph operators attempt to tell if someone is lying by observing how that person responds physiologically while answering questions

"He says he's having a heart attack, I say he's lying . . ."

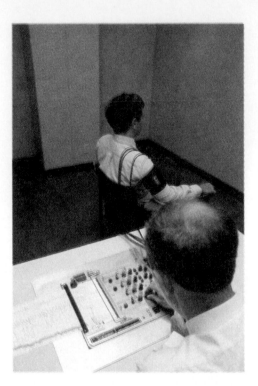

Though polygraphs can detect whether someone is lying at levels better than chance, they are by no means infallible.

Another breakthrough from A. T. & T.

Most psychologists doubt that a foolproof test of whether someone is lying will ever be developed.

error rates vary somewhat, depending on the technique used to administer the test. A recent review by Paul Ekman (1992), averaging across all the different techniques, estimates that the polygraph typically misidentifies about 15 percent of liars as truth-tellers and about 15 percent of truth-tellers as liars.

Thus, if someone fails a lie-detector test administered by an experienced examiner, the chance is better than fifty-fifty that the person was in fact lying. But such a result is not, like Pinocchio's nose, an infallible sign of deceit. Suppose, for example, that you are an honest employee working in a convenience store. The owners tell you that someone has been stealing money from the cash register, and they want you to take a lie-detector test to prove your innocence. "If you are innocent," they say, "what do you have to fear?" What you have to fear is the 15 percent chance that the machine will say you are guilty when you are not. Would you be willing to take a 15 percent chance of losing your job and being arrested for a crime you did not commit? Because of this high rate of error, most states do not allow the results of polygraph tests to be used in court. And in 1988, Congress passed the Employee Polygraph Protection Act, which bars the use of lie-detector machines by private employers, except under special circumstances (e.g., employees who have direct access to drugs can be tested).

It would be nice if there were a foolproof method of telling whether someone is lying or not. Controversies like the one between Anita Hill and Clarence Thomas could be easily resolved. The police could settle a suspect's claim that he or she was home eating a sandwich when the crime was committed, and business owners could find out for sure whether their employees had their hands in the till. But many psychologists doubt that such a test will ever be developed; the nuances of human behavior are too rich and complex to allow foolproof tests of honesty.

## Juries: Group Processes in Action

Ultimately, what decides whether witnesses are telling the truth is not a polygraph but a judge or jury. Juries are of particular interest to social psychologists, because the way they reach verdicts is directly relevant to social psychological research on group processes and social interaction. The right to be tried by a jury of one's peers has a long tradition in English and American law. Trial by jury was an established institution in England at the beginning of the seventeenth century, and the people who founded the first permanent English settlement in North America, at Jamestown, Virginia, carried this tradition with them (though this right was not accorded to Native Americans or other nonwhites, or to a few rebellious English settlers who were summarily hanged). In the United States today, everyone has the right, under most circumstances, to be tried by a jury.

Despite this tradition, the jury system has often come under attack. Sometimes juries reach the wrong verdict, as did the one that convicted Randall Adams of murdering Officer Wood. As argued by a former dean of the Harvard Law School, "Why should anyone think that 12 persons brought in from the street, selected in various ways, for their lack of general ability, should have any special capacity for deciding controversies between persons?" (Kalven & Zeisel, 1966, p. 5). In support of this argument, Harry Kalven, Jr., and Hans Zeisel (1966) found that judges who presided over criminal jury trials disagreed with the verdict rendered by the jury a full 25 percent of the time.

The jury system has its staunch supporters, of course, and few people argue that it should be abolished. The point is that it is not a perfect system, and that there are ways we might expect it to go wrong, based on research in social psychology. Problems can arise at each of three phases of a jury trial: the way in which jurors use information they obtain before the trial begins (pretrial publicity), the way in which they process information during the trial, and the way in which they deliberate in the jury room, after all the evidence has been presented.

> Tis with our judgements as our watches, none go just alike, yet each believes his own.
>
> —Alexander Pope (1688–1744)

**Effects of Pretrial Publicity.** Because the murder of Officer Wood in Texas received considerable attention in the media, it is possible that the jury, before the trial began, was biased by what they had read in the newspapers. The press reported that a key eyewitness had picked Randall Adams out of a police lineup, but this information was untrue and was never presented to the jury during the trial. Nonetheless, two jurors mentioned during the deliberations that they believed the eyewitness had picked Adams out of the lineup (*Dallas Morning News*, May 4, 1987).

Even when the information reported by the media is accurate, it is often stacked against a suspect for a simple reason—the press gets much of its information from the police and the district attorney, who are interested in presenting as strong a case as they can against the suspect. Thus, it's not surprising that the more people hear about a case in the media, the more they believe that the suspect is guilty.

Geoffrey Kramer, Norbert Kerr, and John Carroll (1990) showed that emotional publicity that arouses public passions, such as lurid details about a murder, is particularly biasing. They contacted people who had just finished serving on juries in Michigan, and asked them to watch a videotaped trial of

> A court is no better than each
> . . . of you sitting before me
> on this jury. A court is only as
> sound as its jury, and a jury is
> only as sound as the [people]
> who make it up.
>
> —Harper Lee, *To Kill a*
> *Mockingbird*, 1960

a man accused of robbing a supermarket. Before the jurors viewed the trial, the researchers exposed them to emotional publicity (reports that a car matching the one used in the robbery struck and killed a seven-year-old girl after the robbery), factual publicity (a report that the suspect had an extensive prior criminal record), or no publicity. After watching the trial and deliberating in twelve-member mock juries, the participants rated whether they would vote to convict the suspect. The emotional publicity biased jurors the most, significantly increasing the percentage of jurors who gave guilty verdicts—even though the jurors knew they were not supposed to be influenced by any information they learned before viewing the trial.

Judges and lawyers have a variety of options to try to remedy this problem. First, lawyers are allowed to question prospective jurors before the trial (a process called *voir dire*, which translates as "see speak"). The lawyers ask people whether they have heard anything about the case, and if so, whether they feel they can render an unbiased verdict. In the study we just reviewed, Kramer and his colleagues (1990) put the jurors through a *voir dire* process, removing from the study any jurors who said that because of the pretrial publicity, they could not form an unbiased opinion. Nonetheless, the emotional publicity still influenced the verdicts given by the remaining jurors.

Second, judges can instruct jurors to disregard what they have heard in the media. Several studies have shown, however, that these instructions do little to erase the effects of pretrial publicity, and may even increase the likelihood that jurors use it (Kramer et al., 1990). One reason this can happen is that it's very difficult to erase something from our minds once we have heard it. In fact, as mentioned in Chapter 6, the more we try not to think about something, the more that very thing keeps popping into consciousness (Wegner, 1989, 1992, in press). To illustrate this point, stop reading for a minute and try your best not to think about a white bear. If you are like most people, the more you try to suppress thoughts about white bears, the more such thoughts and visual images will intrude into your consciousness.

Another problem with pretrial publicity is that linking a person's name with incriminating events can cause negative impressions of the person, even if the media explicitly deny any such connection. Daniel Wegner, Richard Wenzlaff, Michael Kerker, and Ann Beattie (1981), for example, found that when research participants read a headline denying any wrongdoing on someone's part—such as "Bob Talbert Not Linked with Mafia"—they had a more negative impression of the person than participants who read an innocuous headline—such as "Bob Talbert Arrives in City." The mere mention of Bob Talbert and the Mafia in the same headline was enough to plant seeds of doubt in readers, despite the headline's explicit denial of a connection. Thus, media reports can have unintended negative effects, and once there, these effects are hard to erase. The best solution is to include in a trial only those jurors who have heard nothing about the case. In highly publicized cases, finding such jurors can be difficult, necessitating a change of venue, whereby the trial is moved to a new location where there has been little publicity.

**Information Processing During the Trial.** How do individual jurors think about the evidence they hear during a trial? As we saw in Chapter 4, people often construct theories and schemas to interpret the world around them, and the same is true of jurors (Smith, 1991). Nancy Pennington and Reid Hastie (1990, 1992) suggest that jurors decide on one story that best

Stop reading, close your eyes, and try not to think about this white polar bear. . . . How successful were you? Likewise, prominent pretrial media coverage of a case may not be easy for jurors to block out of their minds when they are hearing the case.

explains all the evidence. They then try to fit this story to the possible verdicts they are allowed to render. If one of those verdicts fits well with their preferred story, they are likely to vote to convict on that charge.

This explanation has important implications for how lawyers present their cases. Lawyers typically present the evidence in one of two ways. In the first, called the story order, they present the evidence in the sequence events occurred, corresponding as closely as possible to the story they want the jurors to believe. In the second, called the witness order, they present witnesses in the sequence they think will have the greatest impact, even if this means that events are described out of order. For example, a lawyer might save his or her best witness for last, so that the trial ends on a dramatic, memorable note, even if this witness describes events that occurred early in the alleged crime.

If you were a lawyer, in which order would you present the evidence? You probably can guess which order Pennington and Hastie (1990, 1992) hypothesized would be the most successful. If jurors are ultimately swayed by the story or schema they think best explains the sequence of events, then the best strategy should be to present the evidence in the story order and not the witness order. To test their hypothesis, Pennington and Hastie (1988) asked mock jurors to listen to a simulated murder trial. The researchers varied the order in which the defense attorney and the prosecuting attorney presented their cases. In one condition, both used the story order, whereas in another condition, both used the witness order. In other conditions, one attorney used the story order, whereas the other used the witness order.

The results provided clear and dramatic support for the story order strategy. As seen in Table 15.1, when the prosecutor used the story order and the defense used the witness order, the jurors were most likely to believe the prosecutor—78 percent voted to convict the defendant. When the prosecutor used the witness order and the defense used the story order, the tables were turned—only 31 percent voted to convict. Pennington and Hastie (1990)

| Percentage of people voting to convict the defendant | | |
|---|---|---|
| | Defense Evidence | |
| Prosecution Evidence | Story Order | Witness Order |
| Story order | 59% | 78% |
| Witness order | 31% | 63% |

**TABLE 15.1 How should lawyers present their cases?** Lawyers can present their cases in a variety of ways. This study found that the story order works the best, in which lawyers present the evidence in the order that corresponds most closely to the "story" they want the jurors to believe. (Adapted from Pennington & Hastie, 1988)

speculate that one reason the conviction rate in felony trials in America is so high—approximately 80 percent—is that in real trials, prosecutors usually present evidence in the story order, whereas defense attorneys usually use the witness order. To those of our readers who are budding lawyers, remember this when you are preparing for your first trial.

**Deliberations in the Jury Room.** You may have noticed that our discussion so far has left out a crucial part of the jury process: the part where the jury retires to the jury room and deliberates before deciding on the verdict. Even if most jurors are inclined to vote to convict, there might be a persuasive minority who change their fellow jurors' minds. Sometimes this can be a minority of one, as in the classic movie *Twelve Angry Men*. When this film begins, a jury has just finished listening to the evidence in a murder case, and all the jurors except one vote to convict the defendant. But over the course of the next ninety minutes, the lone holdout, played by Henry Fonda, persuades his peers that there is reason to doubt that the young Hispanic defendant is guilty. At first, the other jurors pressure Fonda to change his mind (using techniques of normative and informational conformity, as discussed in Chapter 7), but in the end, reason triumphs and the other jurors come to see that Fonda is right.

As compelling as this movie is, research indicates that it does not reflect the reality of jury deliberations (Kalven & Zeisel, 1966; MacCoun, 1989; Stasser, Stella, Hanna, and Colella, 1984). In the Randall Adams trial, for example, a majority of the twelve-person jury (seven men and five women) initially voted to convict Adams. After eight hours of deliberations, the majority prevailed: The holdouts changed their minds, and the jury voted unanimously to convict Adams. This tendency for juries to go with the initial majority is common. Harry Kalven, Jr., and Hans Zeisel (1966) interviewed the members of more than 200 juries in actual criminal trials. In the vast majority of the cases (97 percent), the jury's final decision was the same as the one favored by a majority of the jurors on the initial vote. Thus, just as we saw in Chapter 7 on conformity, majority opinion usually carries the day, bringing dissenting jurors into line.

In this classic movie, Henry Fonda convinces all of his fellow jurors to change their minds about a defendant's guilt. In real life, however, such cases of a minority in a jury convincing the majority to change its mind are rare.

If jury deliberation is stacked toward the initial, majority opinion, should we just abandon the deliberation process, letting the jury's initial vote determine a defendant's guilt or innocence? For two reasons, this would not be a good idea. First, forcing juries to reach a unanimous verdict makes them consider the evidence more carefully, rather than simply assuming that their initial impressions of the case were correct (Hastie, Penrod, and Pennington, 1983). Second, even if minorities seldom succeed in persuading the majority to change their minds about guilt or innocence, minorities often do change people's minds about how guilty a person is. In criminal trials, juries usually have some discretion about the type of guilty verdict they can reach. In a murder trial, for example, they often can decide whether to convict the defendant of first-degree murder, second-degree murder, or manslaughter. Nancy Pennington and Reid Hastie (1990) found that people on a jury who have a minority point of view often do convince the majority to change their minds about the specific verdict to render. Thus, while a minority are unlikely to convince a majority to change their verdict from first-degree murder to not guilty, they might be able to convince the majority to change the verdict to second-degree murder.

In sum, social psychological research indicates that the American legal system can go wrong in a number of ways: Juries rely heavily on eyewitness testimony, when in fact such testimony is often in error; determining when witnesses are telling the truth is very difficult, even with the use of polygraphs; and since juries are groups of people who try to reach consensus by discussing, arguing, and bargaining, the kinds of conformity pressures and group processes we discussed in Chapters 7 and 9 can lead to faulty decisions. By illuminating these problems in their research, however, social psychologists can help to initiate change in the legal system—change that will lead to greater fairness and equity for all participants.

We turn now to another applied area that has interesting connections to social psychology: the business world. For most of us, encounters with the business world are even more frequent than encounters with the legal system (unless, of course, you are caught embezzling from your employer). We live in an intensely consumer-oriented society. As President Calvin Coolidge said back in 1925, "The chief business of the American people is Business." We buy things; we talk about buying things; we think about buying things—at this very moment, there is undoubtedly some product that you really want to buy. Besides playing our role as consumers from cradle to grave, many of us are (or will be) on the other side of the business transaction as well, working for organizations that manufacture products or provide services for consumers. Just as we saw in our discussion of the law, many aspects of social psychology theory and research are pertinent to the business world. In particular, we will focus on three areas of business—consumer behavior, personnel selection, and organizational leadership—in which social psychologists have applied basic research to real-world situations.

> You can tell the ideals of a nation by its advertisements.
> —Norman Douglas

## Consumer Behavior

From the viewpoint of most businesses, each of us is a potential customer who can make or break a product. In the United States, manufacturers spend in excess of $100 billion a year on advertising, all in an attempt to convince us to use their products. In this section, we will see how successful these efforts are.

**Advertising.** In Chapter 8, we examined the ways in which advertising is used to change people's attitudes about products and services. For example, we discussed techniques that appeal to people's emotions as well as techniques that rely on facts and data. Most of the research we presented was conducted in the laboratory with college students (not in real-world settings, with people of different ages), and focused on changes in attitudes (not on changes in actual consumer behavior). This section of the chapter addresses the more applied question of how successful advertising is at influencing buying behavior in everyday life. Are advertisements just minor annoyances that seldom influence our behavior, or are they powerful determinants of our consumer decisions?

Few would argue that advertising is so powerful that we respond like robots, marching to the store to buy whatever we are told. On the other hand, some disturbing questions about its effects have been raised. Advertisements for tobacco products are banned from television, and many argue that ads for alcoholic beverages should be banned as well—presumably because these ads are effective enough to increase the use of tobacco and alcohol (Jacobson & Hacker, 1985). In 1990, Congress passed the Children's Television Act, which limits the amount of advertising aimed at children that can be shown during certain hours of the day. The act was passed because parents and legislators firmly believed that children were highly susceptible to the seductive lures of advertising.

Is there cause for such concerns? To find out whether advertising truly increases sales, it is necessary to conduct carefully controlled studies. The best evidence that advertising works comes from studies using what are called **split cable market tests.** In this type of research, advertisers work in conjunction with cable television companies, showing a target commercial to a randomly determined group of people. The advertisers see whether these people are more likely to buy the product than those who did not view the commercial. They keep track of what people buy by giving potential consumers special ID cards that are scanned at checkout counters. The advertisers (or researchers) can then determine whether people who saw the commercial for brand X actually buy more of brand X—the best measure of advertising effectiveness.

Magid Abraham and Leonard Lodish (1990) have conducted more than 300 split cable market tests. Their findings indicate that advertising does work, particularly for new products. About 60 percent of the advertisements for new products lead to an increase in sales, compared to 46 percent of the advertisements for established brands. These researchers also found that the effective ads for new products increased sales by an average of 21 percent. Although this figure might seem modest, it translates into millions of dollars when applied to a national advertising campaign. Further, these effective ads worked quickly, increasing sales substantially within the first six months they were shown.

Nonetheless, advertisers are always on the lookout for ways to make their ads more effective. One technique that has been tried is **subliminal messages,** defined as words or pictures that, while not consciously perceived, may influence people's judgments, attitudes, and behaviors on an unconscious level. A majority of the public believe that these messages can shape their attitudes and behaviors, even though they do not know the messages have entered their minds (Zanot, Pincus, and Lamp, 1983). Given the near-hysterical claims that have been made about subliminal advertising, it is important to discuss whether it really works.

**Subliminal Messages.** If there were an Advertising Hall of Infamy, a strong candidate for membership would be the owner of a marketing firm named James Vicary. In the late 1950s, Vicary convinced a movie theater in New Jersey to try a novel approach to selling drinks and popcorn. Imagine you happened to go to the theater that day to see *Picnic*, a popular movie at the time. Unbeknownst to you or the other patrons, you see more than the movie: Messages are flashed on the screen at speeds so quick that they are not consciously perceived, messages that urge you to "drink Coca-Cola" and "eat popcorn." Vicary claimed that these messages registered in the audience members' unconscious minds, and caused them to develop a sudden hankering for a soda or snacks. Coca-Cola sales at the concession counter increased by 18 percent, he said, whereas popcorn sales increased by 58 percent.

When Vicary revealed what he had done, the public reaction was swift. Journalists blasted Vicary's sneaky attempt to boost sales. Minds have been "broken and entered," decried the *New Yorker* (1957, p. 33), and the *Nation* called it "the most alarming and outrageous discovery since Mr. Gatling invented his [machine] gun" ("Diddling the Subconscious," 1957, p. 206). The Federal Communications Commission banned the use of such messages on radio and television, fearing that a kind of mind control like that described in George Orwell's novel *1984* was just on the horizon.

This was hardly, however, the last attempt to influence people with subliminal messages. According to Wilson Bryan Key (1973, 1989), who has

**split cable market tests:** a technique used to test the effectiveness of advertising, whereby advertisers, in conjunction with cable television companies and grocery stores, show a commercial to a randomly determined group of people, and then see whether these people are more likely to buy the product than those who did not see the commercial

> Profits can be obtained either by producing what consumers want or by making consumers want what is actually produced.
> —Henry Simons, 1948

**subliminal messages:** words or pictures that are not consciously perceived, but are purported to influence people's judgments, attitudes, and behaviors

There is no scientific evidence that implanting hidden sexual images in advertisements boosts sales of the product. The public has become so wary of this subliminal technique, however, that some advertisiers have begun to poke fun at it in their ads.

In the field of marketing . . . the trend toward selling [has] reached something of a nadir with the unveiling . . . of so called subliminal projection. That is the technique designed to flash messages past our conscious guard.
—Vance Packard, 1958

written several best-selling books on hidden persuasion techniques, advertisers routinely implant sexual messages in print advertisements, such as the word *sex* in the ice cubes of an ad for gin, and male and female genitalia in everything from pats of butter to the icing in an ad for cake mix. Although these messages are not consciously perceived, Key argues that they put people in a good mood and make people pay more attention to the ad—all of which may increase the likelihood that people will purchase the product.

Subliminal messages are not just visual; they can be auditory as well. In the past decade, a large market has arisen for audiotapes that contain subliminal messages to help people lose weight, stop smoking, improve their study habits, raise their self-esteem, and even shave a few strokes off their golf scores. In 1988, Americans bought more than 5 million of these self-help tapes, and sales in 1990 were estimated to be $50 million (*Newsweek*, July 30, 1990). But are subliminal messages effective? Do they really make us more likely to buy consumer products, or help us to lose weight or stop smoking?

It is important to note that few of the proponents of subliminal advertising have conducted controlled studies to back up their claims. James Vicary did not have a control group who saw the same movie on the same day but with no subliminal messages about Coca-Cola and popcorn. In fact, Vicary reportedly later admitted that he had made up his claims to boost business (Weir, 1984). Similarly, Wilson Bryan Key did not conduct controlled studies comparing the impact of ads with hidden sexual messages with the impact of the same ads without such messages. Fortunately, many controlled studies of subliminal perception have been conducted, allowing us to evaluate the sometimes hysterical claims that are made.

Simply stated, there is no evidence that the type of subliminal messages used in everyday life has any influence on people's behavior. Hidden commands to eat popcorn do not cause people to line up at the concession stand in greater numbers than they would normally do, and the subliminal commands on self-help tapes do not (unfortunately!) help us to quit smoking or lose a few pounds (Bornstein, 1989; Merikle, 1988; Moore, 1982, 1992; Pratkanis, 1992). Anthony Greenwald and his colleagues (1991), for example, performed a careful test of the effectiveness of subliminal self-help tapes. Half the participants listened to tapes that, according to the manufacturer, contained subliminal messages designed to improve memory (e.g., "My ability to remember and recall is increasing daily"), whereas the others listened to tapes that had subliminal messages designed to raise self-esteem (e.g., "I have high self-worth and high self-esteem"). Neither of the tapes had any effect on people's memory or self-esteem. It would be nice if we could improve ourselves simply by listening to music peppered with subliminal messages, but alas, this study (and others) shows that subliminal tapes are no better at magically solving our problems than patent medicines or visits to an astrologist.

Interestingly, research participants in the Greenwald study thought the subliminal tapes were working even though they were not. The researchers were a little devious, in that they correctly informed half the participants about which tape they had, but misinformed the others (e.g., half the people who got the memory tape were told that it was designed to improve their memories, whereas the other half were told it was designed to improve their self-esteem). Those who thought they had listened to the memory tape believed their memories had improved, and those who thought they had listened to the self-esteem tape believed their self-esteem had improved, regardless of which tape they actually listened to. This finding explains why subliminal tapes are a $50 million business. Even though they don't work, people think they do.

When we said that subliminal messages are ineffective, you may have noticed a qualification: They do not work when used in everyday life. There is, though, evidence for such effects in carefully controlled laboratory studies. For example, John Bargh and Paulo Pietromonaco (1982) flashed words on a computer screen so quickly that the words could not be consciously perceived by the viewers. Half the participants "saw" hostile words, such as *unkind* and *insult*, whereas the others saw neutral words, such as *people* and *water*. Everyone then read a paragraph about a fellow named Donald, who had behaved in ways that could be interpreted as either hostile or independent (e.g., he refused to give blood to the Red Cross). Participants who had seen the hostile words were more likely to interpret Donald's actions as hostile than participants who had seen the neutral words were. Several other researchers have found similar effects in the laboratory, showing that subliminally flashed words made a concept or attitude more accessible in people's minds and hence influenced how they later interpreted ambiguous information (e.g., Baldwin, Carrell, and Lopez, 1990; Bornstein, 1992; Bornstein, Leone, and Galley, 1987; Devine, 1989; Fazio, Sanbonmatsu, Powell, and Kardes, 1986).

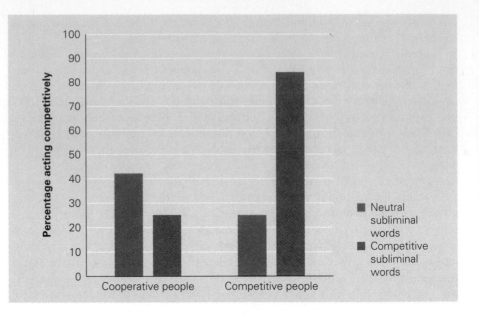

**FIGURE 15.4  The influence of subliminal words on competition.** Flashing competitive words to people at subliminal levels increased the extent to which they acted competitively, if they were competitive people to begin with. The subliminal words had little effect on people who were cooperative to begin with. (Adapted from Neuberg, 1988)

It is frightening to think that our behavior can be influenced by information we do not even know we have seen. Before a new wave of hysteria about mind control begins, however, we should mention some key qualifications. First, no evidence indicates that subliminal messages can get people to act counter to their wishes, values, or personalities. Steven Neuberg (1988) demonstrated this point in a study similar to the one where participants judged how hostile Donald was. Neuberg flashed to participants subliminal words that were neutral or had to do with competitiveness. Everyone then played a Prisoner's Dilemma game with another participant. (As we discussed in Chapter 9, in this game people can choose to take a cooperative stance, maximizing both their own and their partner's gains, or a competitive stance, maximizing their own gains at the expense of their partner.)

Neuberg was interested in whether those who saw the competitive words would act more competitively in the Prisoner's Dilemma game than those who saw the neutral words. The answer was yes, but only if people had a competitive streak to begin with. (Neuberg had previously assessed whether the participants had a general cooperative or competitive orientation.) As you can see in Figure 15.4, if people were competitive types to begin with, seeing the subliminal words about competitiveness served as an extra prod, making them act competitively in the Prisoner's Dilemma game. If people were cooperative types to begin with, seeing the competitive words had no effect on their behavior. As shown in Figure 15.4, cooperative people who saw competitive words responded somewhat more cooperatively, though this difference was not statistically reliable.

The findings of this study are important, because they show that subliminal messages influence behavior only if people are predisposed to act that way in the first place. The people who were cooperative, inclined to act generously toward their fellow humans, could not be forced to reverse course and act competitively simply by having competitive words flashed at them at subliminal levels. Interestingly, however, if people were competitive to begin with, the subliminal words did push them in the direction of even greater competitiveness.

Ads that convey overt, easily perceived messages are more influential than those that contain subliminal messages. For example, many ads blatantly link their product with sex or violence, and these images may have more impact than sexual images hidden in ice cubes or cake icing.

Could subliminal techniques like Neuberg's be applied to everyday life? There is reason to doubt that they could, due to other limitations of successful demonstrations of subliminal effects. All of these demonstrations were conducted under carefully controlled laboratory conditions that would be difficult to reproduce in everyday life. To ensure that the subliminal words register, researchers have to make sure that the illumination of the room is just right, that people are seated just the right distance from a viewing screen, and that nothing else is occurring to distract them as the subliminal words are flashed.

Ironically, the hoopla surrounding subliminal messages has obscured a significant fact about advertising: Ads are more powerful when we can consciously perceive them. Ample evidence demonstrates that the ads we encounter in various forms of media do have substantial effects on our behavior, even though they do not use subliminal messages. Further, such ads influence more than just our consumer behavior. Advertisements transmit cultural stereotypes in their words and images, subtly linking a product with a desired image (e.g., Marlboro ads linking cigarettes with the rugged, macho Marlboro Man; beer ads linking beer consumption with sex).

Ads can reinforce and perpetuate stereotypical ways of thinking about groups of people. Until recently, ads always showed groups of whites (token individuals of color are now mixed into the group); couples are always heterosexual; families are traditional, nuclear ones with a mom, dad, and two or so kids (of each gender); and so on. You would think that divorced families, the elderly, people of color, lesbians and gay men, the physically disabled, and others just didn't exist. Probably most pervasive in advertising imagery is the portrayal of gender stereotypes. Men are doers; women are observers. Erving Goffman (1976), in his book *Gender Advertisements*, offers fascinating examples of how the models in ads are typically posed so that their nonverbal behavior (e.g., their gestures, body position, facial expressions, and eye gaze) is powerful, nonemotional, and active if they are male and passive, submissive, and highly expressive if they are female.

Even more disturbing is the recent trend in some ads, such as those for Newport cigarettes or Guess? clothing, that links the product with sexual hostility and violence (Leo, 1991). For example, a series of Newport cigarette ads depict women who are being pulled by a horse collar, are about to be slammed with a pair of cymbals, or are carried off on a pole like a dead animal. The violence toward women shown in such ads is in no way subliminal; such obvious and overt images are much more powerful than anything hidden in ice cubes or cake icing. Thus, even if effects for subliminal messages in advertisements are eventually documented, those effects are unlikely to be any stronger, or any harder to resist, than the effects of the more overt, consciously perceived kinds of advertising (Wilson & Brekke, 1993).

**Compliance Techniques: Getting People to Buy Your Product.**   Businesses do not rely solely on advertising to get you to buy their products. Most companies invest heavily in sales forces, whose job it is to convince you that their product is the best one on the market. You have probably come across a high-pressure salesperson before, perhaps when you bought a car or a stereo system. Unless you were truly alert and on your guard, we bet you bought the product the salesperson was pushing. How do these salespeople do it? What techniques do they use?

Let's take as an example a ubiquitous form of sales—selling magazine subscriptions door to door. What techniques are likely to be successful at convincing people that they should subscribe to lots of magazines? Over the years, salespeople have developed many ideas about what works and what doesn't. We will discuss two strategies that have proved to be effective in controlled experiments: the "door-in-the-face" and "foot-in-the-door" techniques. A familiarity with these techniques should not only help you in your sales attempts, but also make you better able to identify and resist such techniques when they are used on you.

The first technique works like this: First, ask people to subscribe to a large number of magazines, knowing full well that they will probably refuse. "Excuse me," you might say. "I've got some great deals here. How would you like to subscribe to ten magazines?" Once people have refused, you immediately become more reasonable. "Well," you might say, "do you think you could subscribe to one or two?" This approach is called the **door-in-the-face technique,** because the first request is purposefully so large that people will want to slam the door shut. Several studies show that it works well in getting people to agree to the second, more reasonable request.

For example, Robert Cialdini and his colleagues (1975) decided to see if they could get students to volunteer to chaperon problem adolescents on a two-hour trip to the zoo. When they approached students on a college campus, only 17 percent agreed to this request. In another condition, before asking people to go on the zoo trip, the experimenter made a very large request. "We're currently recruiting university students to work as volunteer, nonpaid counselors at the County Juvenile Detention Center," the experimenter said. "The position would require two hours of your time per week for a minimum of two years. Would you be interested in being considered for one of these positions?" (Cialdini et al., 1975, p. 208). Not surprisingly, no one agreed to such a large time commitment. When students refused, the experimenter said, "Well we also have another program you might be interested in," and went on to ask if they would chaperon the zoo trip. Students in this group were three times more likely to agree to the smaller request—50 percent agreed to go on the zoo trip (see Figure 15.5).

**door-in-the-face technique:** a technique to get people to comply to a request, whereby people are presented first with a large request, which they are expected to refuse, and then with a smaller, more reasonable request, to which it is hoped they will acquiesce

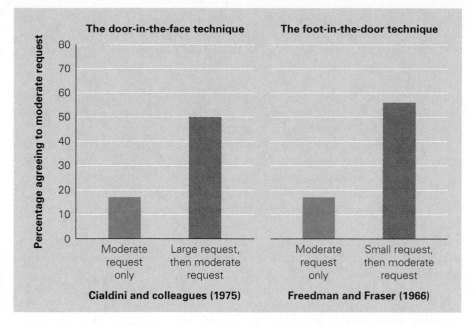

Percentage agreeing to moderate request

Moderate request only · Large request, then moderate request

Moderate request only · Small request, then moderate request

**Cialdini and colleagues (1975)**    **Freedman and Fraser (1966)**

**FIGURE 15.5  Two ways to increase compliance with a request.** Both the door-in-the-face and the foot-in-the-door techniques increase compliance to a moderate request. But which technique is likely to lead to the most *long-term* compliance, whereby people agree to repeated moderate requests? See the text for the answer. (Adapted from Cialdini et al., 1975; Freedman & Fraser, 1966)

Why does the door-in-the-face technique work? The answer is the *reciprocity norm* discussed in Chapter 7—that is the obligation people feel to treat others in the same way they have been treated, such as returning the favor when someone does something nice for them. When a person making a request backs down from an extreme request to a moderate one, it puts pressure on us to reciprocate by moderating our position too—from an outright "No" to a "Well, OK, I guess so." We feel as if the requester is doing us a favor by changing his or her position, trying to meet us halfway; because of the reciprocity norm, we then feel obligated to return the favor and appear reasonable too.

This explanation for why the door-in-the-face technique works also highlights some of its limitations. First, the person making the request must be viewed as reasonable and legitimate. If the person appears to be a manipulator who is just trying to sell us something, we feel less obligated to return the favor by agreeing to a smaller request (Patch, 1986). Second, the two requests have to come from the same person. The Cialdini research group (1975) illustrated this point in another condition of their experiment, where one person made the initial, extreme request and a different person, supposedly from a different organization, made the second, smaller one.

Apparently Calvin has used the door-in-the-face technique a few too many times.

Because it wasn't the same person who was backing down from a large request to a small one, the participants did not feel any pressure to reciprocate by moderating their stance, and thus were not more likely to agree to go on the zoo trip.

Third, the power of the door-in-the-face technique is likely to be relatively short-lived. Once people have agreed to the smaller request, they have met their obligation by meeting the requester halfway; therefore, they will not be more likely to agree to subsequent requests.

Suppose, for example, that your goal is to get people to buy magazine subscriptions from you on a regular basis. Once you have retreated from your request for ten subscriptions to a more reasonable request for one or two, and your customer has met you halfway by agreeing, his or her obligation is over. If you ask for another subscription next month, he or she may well feel exploited, thinking, "This person sure is pushy. You'd think I'd get a break after being so reasonable last time." If you want to get long-term compliance, it is better to use a different approach, called the **foot-in-the-door technique**.

The expression *foot-in-the-door* comes from salespeople who discovered that they were more likely to make a sale (the big request) if they could get the customer to agree to an initial, smaller request, such as letting them into his or her home to display their products. This technique is thus the opposite of the door-in-the-face method. Does it work? To find out, Jonathan Freedman and Scott Fraser (1966) tested whether homeowners would agree to put up a large, obtrusive sign in their front yards that said Drive Carefully. When

**foot-in-the-door technique:** a technique to get people to comply to a request, whereby people are presented first with a small request, which virtually everyone agrees to, and then with a larger request, to which it is hoped they will also acquiesce

Once we've agreed to let a salesperson demonstrate the product in our home, we are more prone to buy it.

someone came to their door and asked the homeowners to do this, only 17 percent agreed. But what if they had agreed earlier to a smaller request? The researchers first asked a different group of homeowners to sign a petition indicating that they were in favor of safe driving. Just about everyone agreed to this innocuous request. Two weeks later, a different individual approached these homeowners and asked them to put the sign in their front yard. Though the sign was just as big and obtrusive to these people as to those in the control group, who had not been contacted earlier, they were more than three times more likely to agree to put it in their front yard (see Figure 15.5).

The foot-in-the-door technique works because of the self-justification processes we discussed in Chapter 3. When people agreed to the small request, they justified doing so by viewing themselves as the kind of person who helps out on important community issues. Once this self-image was in place, it made people more likely to agree to the second, larger request, even when it came two weeks later. Thus, if you want to get long-term compliance, it is better to instill the relevant self-image in people with the foot-in-the-door technique. If you are collecting money for the American Heart Association and want your neighbors to donate on a long-term basis, first ask them for a small amount, such as 50¢ or $1. If they agree, they will come to view themselves as the kind of people who give to this worthy cause, increasing the likelihood that future donations will be forthcoming. There is, of course, a limit to this approach. Getting your neighbor to donate 50¢ probably won't get him or her to make contributions to the American Heart Association to the exclusion of other charities. However, it will make him or her more likely to agree to a larger request than if you had not first asked for the smaller amount (see Burger, 1986; Cialdini, 1988; DeJong, 1979; Dillard, Hunter, and Burgoon, 1984).

## Personnel Selection: Entry into the Business World

So far, we have seen how social psychological principles apply to consumer behavior. We turn now to the application of social psychological research to entry into the business world, such as getting a job and rising to a leadership position in an organization. Let's begin with a discussion of how hiring decisions should be made. Imagine that you are the personnel director of a large department store. There are several sales openings at your store, and it is up to you to decide who to hire. What kind of information would you solicit from the applicants? Once you have this information, how would you use it to make up your mind?

To answer these questions, we need to know what variables will predict who will be a good employee. This is not a trivial question. Using the wrong kind of information to select people is obviously unfair to the applicants and costly for the employer (Hunter & Hunter, 1984). Research on personnel selection shows that many organizations rely heavily on one source of information: the job interview. This won't come as a surprise, since most people believe that a great deal of useful information can be gained by interviewing job applicants. Most employers agree; in fact, it is extremely rare for organizations to hire someone sight-unseen. The only kind of information used more frequently than job interviews is a review of applicants' résumés and application materials (Ash, 1981). As we shall see, however, the research suggests that information learned about an applicant in an interview is actually a poor predictor of how well he or she will do on the job (Arvey & Campion, 1982; Hunter & Hunter, 1984; Mayfield, 1964; Ulrich & Trumbo, 1965; Whetzel, McDaniel, and Schmidt, 1985; Zedeck & Cascio, 1984).

Michael Carrier and his colleagues (1990), for example, examined the **validity** of the job interview as a predictor of later job performance in the hiring of life insurance agents. Surprisingly, the impressions of experienced interviewers bore little correspondence to how well the applicants eventually did on the job. For example, the correlation between the interviewers' ratings and how much life insurance the agents sold in the first year was a tiny .02. (You'll recall from Chapter 2 that a correlation can range from zero to ± 1.00; when a correlation is zero, there is no relation between one variable and the other.) The correlations found in this research were so close to zero that knowing the interviewers' ratings allowed neither the researchers nor the employers to predict how well each applicant would do on the job. Hunter and Hunter (1984) reviewed several studies of this type, and found that the average correlation between interview performance and job performance was an unimpressive .14.

One reason that the validity of the job interview is so low is that interviewers often focus on the wrong kinds of information. Unfortunately, some interviewers are biased by such inappropriate information as an applicant's gender, race, or age—information that is, in fact, illegal to use (Arvey, 1979; Glick, Zion, and Nelson, 1988; Ralston, 1988). As we saw in Chapter 13, self-fulfilling prophecies can result when a prejudiced interviewer acts in a more distant and hostile way to a minority applicant, causing the applicant to respond in a nervous and less effective manner. Failing to realize that it was his or her behavior that made the applicant nervous, the interviewer thinks, "Ah, just as I thought—this person is unqualified." Similarly, interviewers who feel warmth and liking for a job applicant during the interview are likely to interpret the applicant's behavior in a particularly positive light—even if that behavior is relatively unimpressive. Thus, interviewers' first impressions affect their behavior, which in turn affects interviewees' behavior. Note, too, the incredible latitude an interviewer has during the interview—he or she is totally in charge. An interviewer could ask different questions of one versus another interviewee, thereby unconsciously biasing the process (Binning, Goldstein, Garcia, and Scattaregia, 1988; Neuberg, 1989; Snyder & Swann, 1978; Word, Zanna, and Cooper, 1974).

One way to avoid these two problems—interviewers focusing on the wrong kinds of applicant information and their biasing the process by inappropriate questioning—is to use for all applicants a predetermined list of questions. This technique, called a **structured interview,** improves the validity of the interview to a small degree (Wiesner & Cronshaw, 1988; Wright, Lichtenfels, and Pursell, 1989).

A fundamental question, however, concerns the ability of an interview to predict job performance even when the interviewer is well trained and unbiased. Although there is some disagreement about this question, many researchers feel that the interview is simply too small a slice of someone's life to yield useful information. After all, an interviewer has only an hour or less to try to determine how qualified an applicant is, and many applicants are likely to be so nervous that they come across as less qualified than they really are.

---

**validity:** how well a test or assessment technique (e.g., a job interview) predicts what it is supposed to predict (e.g., performance on the job)

**structured interview:** a job interview technique whereby the interviewer asks all the applicants the same questions from a predetermined list; the questions concern only the applicants' qualifications for the job

Thus, even with improved interviewing techniques, the information gleaned from an interview is not a particularly good predictor of job performance. But what kinds of information should an organization use to choose its employees? Fortunately, other types of information are much better predictors, as seen in Table 15.2. The data in this table are averaged over many different studies that looked at performance on many different kinds of entry-level jobs. The best predictor of job performance was found to be applicants' performance on standardized tests of their job-related abilities. (The numbers in the table are correlations, such that the more they approach the maximum value of 1, the better the variable predicted job performance.) For example, tests of motor skills are the best predictors of who will be the best operators of heavy equipment, and tests of cognitive abilities are the best predictor of who will be the best managers or salespeople (Hunter & Hunter, 1984). The second-best predictor is how well people do in a job tryout, where they actually do the job for a short period.

Although the research reported in Table 15.2 is well known to many organizations, it has not had much impact on their use of the job interview. Why do they continue to use job interviews, you might ask, when the evidence clearly indicates that little useful information can be gleaned from them? The answer is twofold. First, some companies use interviews as a way of selling themselves to qualified applicants, rather than as a way of evaluating applicants. And second (probably the more common reason), business managers simply can't accept the fact that interviews are invalid, because they have the illusion that they learn a lot about an applicant from an interview. The cause of this illusion? Our old friend the *fundamental attribution error*, discussed in Chapter 5: the assumption that people's behavior is a direct reflection of the kind of person they are, with an accompanying underestimation of the extent to which the situation influences their behavior.

As applied to a job interview, this attributional error means that interviewers assume that an applicant's behavior during an interview truly reflects his or her personality and qualifications, and that these in turn will predict

| What predicts job performance? | |
|---|---|
| **Predictor** | **Correlation with Job Performance** |
| 1. Standardized tests of ability | .53 |
| 2. Job tryout | .44 |
| 3. Check on applicant's references | .26 |
| 4. Previous experience | .18 |
| 5. Interview of the applicant | .14 |
| 6. Academic achievement (grades) | .11 |
| 7. Amount of education | .10 |
| 8. Interest in the job | .10 |
| 9. Age of applicant | -.01 |

**TABLE 15.2 Personnel selection: What predicts how well people will do on the job?** These data are compiled from dozens of studies that correlated information about applicants with later job performance in a range of entry-level jobs. The higher the number, the better the variable predicted job performance. (Adapted from Hunter & Hunter, 1984)

how well the applicant will perform on the job. If the applicant behaves nervously, the interviewer concludes that he or she must be a nervous person who lacks the necessary interpersonal skills to deal with clients or customers. This attribution could be completely erroneous. Perhaps the applicant appeared nervous because of the situation—job interviews make most of us far more nervous than we'd ever be on the job. Perhaps the interviewer caused the applicant's nervous behavior, by asking intimidating questions in an unfriendly manner. Either way, the fundamental attribution error looms large: If the applicant acts nervous, the interviewer is likely to make a dispositional attribution.

Consider, for example, the reaction one of us had to a woman who was interviewing for a faculty job in our department. During the interview, she seemed highly intelligent but somewhat stiff and formal. "She is brilliant," we concluded, "but not exactly someone who would liven up a party. She probably works so hard that she never relaxes and has fun." Our faculty offered her the job and she accepted. The next time we saw her was the beginning of the next semester, at a beginning-of-the-year party. We were astonished to see a relaxed, witty, informally dressed woman who was in the midst of telling a very funny joke to a colleague. Could this possibly be the same person as the serious, humorless woman in the tailored suit we had met a few months before?

Why were we surprised to see the professor act so differently from the way she had during her interview? Because we had committed the fundamental attribution error, of course! What had changed radically over the few months was not the woman, but the situation in which we saw her. Thus, despite how much we might seem to be learning about a person during a job interview, we would do well to remember the extent to which the situation dictates how people behave.

## Leadership: Reaching the Top of the Business World

Instead of being in charge of personnel selection, imagine now that you are an executive in a company, trying to decide which of your employees would make the best supervisors. You have many dedicated workers, but you want to find the ones who will be the most effective at leading and inspiring others to work to the best of their abilities. How should you decide whom to promote?

**The Great Person Theory.**   The question of what kind of person makes the best leader has intrigued psychologists, historians, and political scientists for ages. One of the best-known ways of trying to answer this question is the **great person theory**, which argues that leaders are born, not made. This theory maintains that there are certain key personality traits that make a person a good leader, and if you don't have them, you're out of luck. "The history of the world is but the biography of great men," wrote Thomas Carlyle in 1841. Ralph Waldo Emerson (1929) echoed this view, arguing that "there is properly no history, only biography."

If the great person theory is true, then we ought to be able to isolate the key aspects of personality that make someone a great leader. Is it a combination of intelligence, charisma, and courage? Is it better to be introverted or extraverted? Should we add a measure of ruthlessness to the mix as well, as Niccoló Machiavelli described in 1513, in his famous treatise on leadership,

**great person theory:** the theory that there are certain key personality traits that make a person a good leader, regardless of the nature of the situation facing the leader

*The Prince*? Or do highly moral people make the best leaders? Psychologists, political scientists, and historians have studied the personalities of leaders in governmental, business, and educational organizations to see what common threads can be found.

Having gotten to the very end of our book, however, you probably know that personality is not the whole story in any arena of life. One of the most important themes of social psychology is that to understand social behavior, it is not enough to consider personality traits alone—we must take the social situation into account as well. Given this premise, and given that the great person theory does not add the social situation to the equation, it is not surprising that the theory has not fared very well.

The relationships between personal characteristics and leadership that researchers have discovered are summarized in the text accompanying the photos on the next page. Some modest relationships have been found; for example, leaders tend to be slightly more intelligent than nonleaders, and to be more driven by the desire for power. What is most telling from the summary, however, is the absence of strong relationships. Many personality factors do not correlate with leadership effectiveness, and those relationships which have been found tend to be modest. For example, Simonton (1987) gathered information about one hundred personal attributes of all U.S. presidents, such as their family backgrounds, educational experiences, occupations and personalities. Only three of these variables—height, family size, and the number of books a president published before taking office—correlated with how effective the presidents were in office (as rated by historians). The other ninety-seven characteristics, including personality traits, were not related to leadership effectiveness at all.

**Considering Personal and Situational Factors.** The inadequacy of the great person theory does not mean that personal characteristics are completely irrelevant to good leadership. Instead, being good social psychologists, we should consider both the nature of the leader and the situation in which he or she is leading. This view of leadership states that it is not enough to be a great person; you have to be the right person at the right time in the right situation. A business leader, for example, can be highly successful in some situations but not in others. Consider Steve Jobs, who, at the age of twenty-one, founded the Apple Computer company with Stephen Wozniak. Jobs was anything but an "MBA" type of corporate leader. A product of the 1960s counterculture, he turned to computers only after sampling LSD, traveling to India, and living on a communal fruit farm. In the days when there were no personal computers, Jobs's offbeat style was well suited to starting a new industry. Within five years, he was the leader of a billion-dollar company.

Jobs's unorthodox style was ill-suited, however, to the fine points of managing a large corporation in a competitive market. The problems facing a large, multinational company were very different from the creative problems of development that Jobs was so talented at solving. Apple began to suffer in competition with other companies, and in 1985 Jobs was forced to leave Apple by John Sculley, a man who Jobs himself had hired to run the company (Patton, 1989).

Thus, to understand who the best leader will be, we have to take into account both the personal characteristics of the leader and the nature of the

Mario Cuomo, Governor of New York

**Intelligence** There is a modest but positive relationship between intelligence and leadership effectiveness (Simonton, 1985; Stogdill, 1974).

**Morality** An examination of historical records showed that in a sample of 600 monarchs, the ones who became the most eminent were those who were either highly moral or highly immoral (Simonton, 1984). This suggests that there are two roads to eminence: having great moral virtue or having Machiavellian deviousness.

Queen Victoria of Great Britain

**Motivation** Leaders who have a strong power motive (self-direction, a concern for prestige, abundant energy) are somewhat more likely to be effective (McClelland, 1975; Sorrentino & Field, 1986; Winter, 1987)

Col. Muammar al-Qaddafi of Libya

**Family Size** U.S. presidents who came from small families are more likely to have become great leaders, as rated by historians (Simonton, 1987).

Franklin Delano Roosevelt, 32nd U.S. president

Abraham Lincoln, 16th U.S. president

**Height** There is a modest correlation between a man's height and the likelihood that he will become the leader of a group (Stogdill, 1974). In the United States, the taller candidate has won every presidential election but two: Richard Nixon versus George McGovern in 1972 and Jimmy Carter versus Gerald Ford in 1976. (In 1992, Bill Clinton had a quarter-inch height advantage over George Bush.) Once in office, tall presidents, such as Abraham Lincoln, are more likely to be great leaders, as rated by historians (Simonton, 1987).

**Personality Traits** Surprisingly little evidence shows that such traits as dominance, charisma, and self-confidence predict who will become leaders (Stogdill, 1974; Hollander, 1975).

Malcolm X, Minister of The Nation of Islam

Some modest relationships between personal characteristics and leadership performance have been found, but in general, it is difficult to predict how good a leader someone will be from his or her personality alone.

situation confronting the leader. By far the best-known theory of leadership that considers both the person and the situation is Fred Fiedler's (1967, 1978) **contingency theory of leadership.** Fiedler makes the assumption that there are two kinds of leaders, those who are task-oriented and those who are relationship-oriented. The **task-oriented leader** is primarily concerned with getting the job done, whereas the **relationship-oriented leader** is more concerned with the feelings of and relationships between the workers.

Fiedler measures these orientations in an interesting way—namely, by asking leaders to evaluate the one worker with whom they find it most difficult to work (the least preferred co-worker, or LPC). Leaders who give the LPC negative ratings are assumed to be task-oriented. Getting the job done is so important to these people that they view any worker who gets in their way in very negative terms. Leaders who give the LPC positive ratings are assumed to be relationship-oriented. Though the LPC is not performing well, these leaders are able to see his or her good side, as if they are saying, "Job performance isn't everything—this person has some good qualities."

Which type of leader is more effective? According to Fiedler's theory, to answer this question we need to consider the nature of the situation—specifically, the amount of control and influence a leader has over the group. In "high-control" work situations, the leader has excellent interpersonal relationships with subordinates, his or her position in the company is clearly perceived as powerful, and the work needing to be done by the group is structured and well defined. In "low-control" work situations, the opposite holds—the leader has poor relationships with subordinates; his or her job position is shaky in terms of perceived power, and the work needing to be done is not clearly defined.

The crux of Fiedler's contingency theory is that task-oriented leaders are most effective in situations that are either very high or very low in control, whereas relationship-oriented leaders are most effective in situations that are moderate in control (see Figure 15.6). When situational control is very low, the task-oriented leader is best at taking charge, imposing some order on a confusing, ill-defined work environment. In this kind of setting, a relationship-oriented leader, who pays attention to people's feelings and relationships, may make his or her subordinates feel good, but not much work is going to get done. A leader who takes control, without worrying about hurting people's feelings, will be most successful.

When situational control is moderate, the relationship-oriented leaders do best. Under these conditions, the wheels are turning fairly smoothly, but some attention to the squeakiness caused by poor relationships and hurt feelings is needed. The leader who can soothe such feelings will be most successful. When situational control is very high, the task-oriented leader is again best at directing the group. Here people are happy and everything is running smoothly, and there is no need to worry about people's feelings and relationships. The leader who pays attention only to the task will get the most accomplished.

Fiedler's contingency theory has been tested with numerous groups of leaders, including business managers, college administrators, military commanders, and postmasters. Although the theory has been controversial, the dozens of studies that have tested it have generally been supportive, conforming well to the pattern shown in Figure 15.6 (Peters, Hartke, and Pohlmann, 1985; Strube & Garcia, 1981).

**contingency theory of leadership:** the theory that leadership effectiveness depends both on how task-oriented or relationship-oriented the leader is and on the amount of control and influence the leader has over the group

**task-oriented leader:** a leader who is concerned primarily with getting the job done, and less so with the feelings of and relationships between the workers

**relationship-oriented leader:** a leader who is concerned primarily with the feelings of and relationships between the workers

> Leadership cannot really be taught. It can only be learned.
> —Harold Geneen, 1984

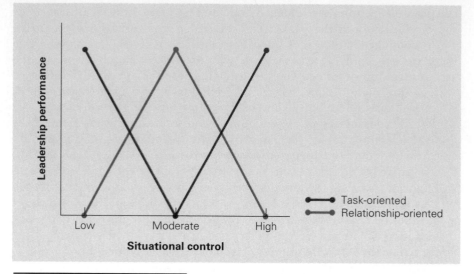

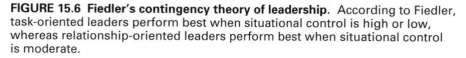

**FIGURE 15.6 Fiedler's contingency theory of leadership.** According to Fiedler, task-oriented leaders perform best when situational control is high or low, whereas relationship-oriented leaders perform best when situational control is moderate.

Fiedler's contingency theory allows us to predict not only how effective a leader will be but also the amount of stress the leader will experience: If the fit between the type of leader and the type of situation is poor, the leader will be ineffective, and will experience a considerable amount of discomfort and stress, whereas if the fit is good, the leader will experience relatively little stress. Martin Chemers and his colleagues (1985) tested this hypothesis with a group of college administrators, measuring whether the administrators were task-oriented or relationship-oriented leaders, and whether their work situations were high, moderate, or low in control. Which administrators do you think reported feeling the most job stress and the most health problems, and which missed the most days of work? As shown in Figure 15.7, Fiedler's contingency theory did a good job of providing the answer: Task-oriented leaders reported that their jobs were most stressful when they were in charge of groups that were moderate in situational control, and relationship-oriented leaders reported the most job stress when they were in charge of groups that were either low or high in situational control.

**Gender and Leadership.** Despite the support for Fiedler's contingency theory, clearly it considers only some of the personal and situational variables that contribute to good leadership (Hollander, 1985; McCann, 1992; Peters et al., 1985). One attribute of leaders that has received a good deal of research attention is their gender. Stereotypes about the leadership styles of women and men abound. Women are thought to care more about the feelings of their co-workers and to be more interpersonally skilled than men. Men are often characterized as controlling, Machiavellian leaders who don't even notice what their co-workers are feeling, much less care about those feelings. Is there any truth to these stereotypes?

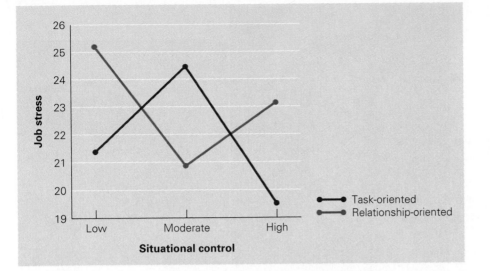

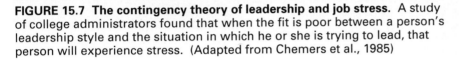

**FIGURE 15.7  The contingency theory of leadership and job stress.** A study of college administrators found that when the fit is poor between a person's leadership style and the situation in which he or she is trying to lead, that person will experience stress. (Adapted from Chemers et al., 1985)

To find out, Alice Eagly and her colleagues have performed several meta-analyses of the literature (Eagly & Johnson, 1990; Eagly & Karau, 1991; Eagly, Makhijani, and Klonsky, 1992). As we discussed in an earlier chapter, a meta-analyses is a statistical technique whereby the effects of a variable, such as gender, can be measured across many studies. Eagly has examined hundreds of studies to answer questions about leadership style and effectiveness in women versus men.

Her review found that in some areas, the stereotypes about leadership style were supported, but in others, they were not. First, consistent with the stereotype, women tended to lead more democratically than men (Eagly & Johnson, 1990). Eagly and Johnson (1990) suggest that this occurs because women tend to have better interpersonal skills than men, allowing them to seek input from group members when making a decision, and to gracefully disregard this input when necessary.

Inconsistent with the stereotype, however, was the finding that men and women leaders in organizations did not differ in the extent to which they adopted the task-oriented versus relationship-oriented style of leadership we discussed earlier. Eagly and Johnson (1990) suggest that this is the case because most organizations train or choose leaders according to the attributes that are best for the job. If a task-oriented leader is needed, either a man or a woman can be trained or selected to meet this need. The same applies to situations where relationship-oriented leaders are needed.

We do not mean to imply that sex discrimination in the business world is nonexistent. Even if men and women are both chosen for task-oriented and relationship-oriented leadership roles, men might still be chosen more often than women for both kinds of roles. Further, there may be differences in how leaders are evaluated, depending on the kinds of leadership roles they occupy.

Businesses want plans and controls. The new workers want options and individual treatment. Indeed, this may be the ultimate challenge that women initiate in the workplace.

—Ellen Goodman, 1989

Sandra Day O'Connor, Supreme
Court Justice

Corazan Aquino, former president of the Phillippines

Margaret Thatcher, former prime
minister of Great Britain

Women leaders tend not to be evaluated any differently from male
leaders, as long as their leadership style is stereotypically "feminine"
(interpersonally oriented, democratic). Women who adopt a stereotypically "masculine" style (autocratic, directive) are evaluated less favorably
than male leaders who adopt the same style—especially by men.

> Old-fashioned ways which no
> longer apply to changed con-
> ditions are a snare in which
> the feet of women have
> always become entangled.
> —Jane Addams, 1907

An old adage says that, because of sex discrimination, a woman has to
be "twice as good as a man" in order to advance. To find out if this is true,
Alice Eagly, Mona Makhijani, and Bruce Klonsky (1992) reviewed more
than sixty studies. The encouraging news is that they found only a very slight
tendency for women to be evaluated less positively than men. However,
under certain circumstances a fair amount of discrimination against women
leaders still exists. If a woman's style of leadership is stereotypically "masculine," in that she is autocratic, "bossy," and task-oriented, she is evaluated
more negatively than men who have the same style (Eagly et al., 1992). This
is especially true if it is men who are doing the evaluating. For example, Doré
Butler and Florence Geis (1990) had male and female accomplices assume
leadership roles in groups of students attempting to solve a business problem.
Both the male and the female leaders were assertive but cordial, taking
charge of the group discussion. The question was, how did the other
members of the group react to these assertive leaders?

The results were discouraging. When a man took charge of the group
and acted assertively, the group members reacted favorably. When a woman
acted in the same fashion, the group members reacted much more negatively.
And consistent with Eagly and colleagues' (1992) review of the literature, it
was the male members of the group who reacted the most negatively to the
female leaders.

It appears that many men are uncomfortable with women who use the
same leadership techniques that men typically use. This response on the part

of male colleagues and bosses puts women in a bind. As we have seen, there are circumstances where a take-charge, autocratic type of leader will be the most successful. If women adopt this leadership style, they may receive criticism and negative performance ratings instead of the praise and success their male colleagues receive when using the same style. As in every aspect of life, stereotypes and prejudice limit the ability of individuals to perform to their fullest abilities. Such a loss is experienced not only by the individual but by the business organization as well. As American business moves into the twenty-first century, it is imperative that attributes like gender, race, and religion no longer bar talented workers from contributing to the marketplace.

## SUMMARY

In the first part of this chapter, we saw that many social psychological principles predict how people respond in the legal arena. Because of the limitations of people's memory, eyewitness testimony is often inaccurate. A number of factors bias the **acquisition, storage,** and **retrieval** of what people observe, sometimes leading to the false identification of criminals. For example, research on **reconstructive memory** indicates that **source misattribution** can occur, wherein people become confused about where they saw or heard something. Jurors often place a great deal of faith in eyewitness testimony, even though jurors are not very good at telling when someone is lying. Because **polygraphs** are also imperfect measures of lie detection, false testimony by eyewitnesses and others sometimes goes undetected. Jurors are susceptible to the same kinds of biases and social pressures we documented in earlier chapters. They are sometimes biased by pretrial publicity, even when trying to put it out of their minds, and jurors with minority views are often pressured into conforming to the view of the majority.

In the second part of the chapter, we saw how social psychological principles help us understand people's behavior in the business world. For example, advertising is a specific type of persuasive communication and in general is quite effective at influencing people's choice of consumer products, as indicated by **split cable market tests.** One kind of advertising, however, which contains words or pictures that are supposedly perceived unconsciously—in other words, **subliminal messages**—has not been shown to influence consumer behavior. Under controlled laboratory conditions, subliminal messages can influence how people interpret another person's ambiguous behaviors, but there is no evidence that subliminal messages have been used successfully in real-world marketing campaigns. In addition to advertising, manufacturers hire salespeople to convince the public to buy their products. We examined two sales techniques that have proved to be very successful: the **door-in-the-face** and the **foot-in-the-door techniques.** The door-in-the-face technique works because of the reciprocity norm, whereby people feel obligated to "return the favor" when a salesperson retreats from a large to a small request. The foot-in-the-door technique leads to long-term compliance, by causing people to view themselves as the sort of person who helps out.

We also discussed how people in the business world decide whom to hire, and we examined who make the best leaders. The best predictor of how well job applicants will do on the job is their performance on standardized tests. Surprisingly, the job interview is a poor predictor of job performance. **Structured interviews,** which ask all applicants the same predetermined questions, do somewhat better, but are still low in **validity.** However, many people still believe that the job interview is a good predictor of performance, because of an illusion that people's behavior reflects the kind of person they are, or the *fundamental attribution error.*

Once people are hired, who make the most effective leaders? There is little support for the **great person theory,** which argues that there are key personality traits that make a person a good leader, regardless of the nature of the situation facing the leader. Leadership effectiveness is a function of both the kind of person a leader is and the nature of the work situation. Research on Fiedler's **contingency theory of leadership** has found that leadership performance depends both on whether a leader is **task-oriented** or **relationship-oriented** and on whether the work environment is high or low in situational control. We also discussed gender differences in leadership style and leadership effectiveness. Unfortunately, sex discrimination still exists; women leaders who act in stereotypically male ways are devalued, particularly by men.

## SUGGESTED READINGS

Cialdini, R. (1993). *Influence: Science and practice* (3rd ed.). New York: HarperCollins. An extremely readable and entertaining account of research on conformity and compliance, with applications to business and all other aspects of everyday life.

Fiedler, F. E., & Garcia, J. E. (1987). *Leadership: Cognitive resources and performance*. A description of research on leadership by prominent researchers in the field. Special attention is given to how leaders' cognitive abilities influence their performance.

Kassin, S. M., & Wrightsman, L. S. (1988). *The American jury on trial: Psychological perspectives*. New York: Hemisphere. A comprehensive look at the psychological issues involved at all levels of jury trials, from jury selection to jury verdicts.

Loftus, E., & Ketcham, K. (1991). *Witness for the defense: The accused, the eyewitness, and the expert who puts memory on trial*. New York: St. Martin's. An account of the role of memory biases in eyewitness identification, by one of the leading researchers in this area.

Pratkanis, A. R., & Aronson, E. (1991). *Age of propaganda: The everyday use and abuse of persuasion*. New York: Freeman. An engaging account of how our attitudes are shaped by the mass media. The effectiveness of different kinds of advertising are discussed, including the use of subliminal messages.

# GLOSSARY

**accessibility:** the ease with which different thoughts and ideas can be brought to mind; an idea that is accessible is already on our minds, or can easily be brought to mind. [4]

**accountability:** the likelihood that you will be held responsible for your actions. [9]

**acquisition:** the process by which people notice and pay attention to information in the environment; because people cannot perceive everything that is happening around them, they acquire only a subset of the information available in the environment. [15]

**actor/observer difference:** the tendency to see other people's behavior as dispositionally caused, while focusing more on the role of situational factors when explaining one's own behavior. [5]

**additive task:** a group task in which performance depends on the sum of each individual's effort (e.g., the total noise made by a group of cheerleaders). [9]

**affective component of an attitude:** the emotions and feelings people associate with an attitude object. [8]

**affectively based attitude:** an attitude based more on people's feelings and values than on beliefs about the nature of the attitude object. [8]

**aggressive action:** a behavior aimed at causing either physical or psychological pain. [12]

**aggressive stimulus:** an object that is associated with aggressive responses (e.g., a gun) and whose mere presence can increase the probability of aggression. [12]

**altruism:** any act that benefits another person but does not benefit the helper, and often involves some personal cost to the helper. [11]

**altruistic personality:** those aspects of a person's makeup which are said to make him or her likely to help others in a wide variety of situations. [11]

**amygdala:** an area in the core of the brain that is associated with aggressive behaviors. [12]

**anchoring/adjustment heuristic:** a mental shortcut that involves using a number or value as a starting point, and then adjusting one's answer away from this anchor; people often do not adjust their answer s ufficiently. [4]

**anxious/ambivalent attachment style:** an attachment style characterized by a concern that others will not reciprocate one's desire for intimacy, resulting in higher-than-average levels of anxiety. [10]

**applied research:** studies designed specifically to solve a particular social problem; building a theory of behavior is usually secondary to solving a specific problem. [2]

**arbitration:** a system of conflict resolution in which a neutral third party imposes a decision on the disputing parties, after hearing both of their arguments. [9]

**archival analysis:** a form of systematic observation whereby the researcher observes social behavior by examining the accumulated documents, or archives, of a culture (e.g., diaries, novels, magazines, and newspapers). [2]

**attachment styles:** the expectations people develop about relationships with others, based on the relationship they had with their primary caregiver when they were infants. [10]

**attitude:** an enduring evaluation—positive or negative—of people, objects, and ideas. [8]

**attitude accessibility:** the strength of the association between an object and a person's evaluation of that object; accessibility is measured by the speed with which people can report how they feel about an issue or object. [8]

**attitude inoculation:** making people immune to attempts to change their attitudes by initially exposing them to small doses of the arguments against their position. [8]

**attribution theory:** a description of the way in which people explain the causes of their own and other people's behavior. [5]

**autobiographical memory:** memories about one's own past thoughts, feelings, and behaviors. [6]

**availability heuristic:** a mental rule of thumb whereby people base a judgment on the ease with which they can bring something to mind. [4]

**avoidant attachment style:** an attachment style characterized by a suppression of attachment needs, because attempts to be intimate have been rebuffed; people with this style find it difficult to develop intimate relationships. [10]

**base rate information:** information about the frequency of members of different categories in the population. [4]

**basic research:** studies that are designed to find the best answer to the question of why people behave the way they do and that are conducted purely for reasons of intellectual curiosity. [2]

**basking in reflected glory:** trying to enhance our image by associating ourselves with successful or famous people.

**behavioral component of an attitude:** people's actions toward an attitude object. [8]

**behaviorally based attitude:** an attitude based on observations of how one behaves toward the attitude object. [8]

**behaviorism:** a school of psychology maintaining that to understand human behavior, one need only consider the reinforcing properties of the environment—that is, how positive and negative events in the environment are associated with specific behaviors. [1]

**belief in a just world:** a form of defensive attribution wherein people assume that bad things happen to bad people and that good things happen to good people. [5]

**biased sampling:** making generalizations from samples of information that are known to be biased or atypical. [4]

**blaming the victim:** our tendency to blame individuals (make dispositional attributions) for their victimization, typically motivated by a desire to see the world as a fair place. [13]

**bookkeeping model:** information inconsistent with a stereotype that leads to a modification of the stereotype. [13]

**brainstorming:** a technique designed to improve group decisions by encouraging the free exchange of ideas and the elimination of criticism. [9]

**bystander effect:** the finding that the greater the number of bystanders who witness an emergency, the less likely any one of them is to help. [11]

**category-based expectancies:** expectations about people based on the groups to which they belong, such as expecting someone to love going to parties because he or she belongs to a party-loving fraternity or sorority. [5]

**catharsis:** the theory that "blowing off steam"—by doing something physically exerting, watching others engage in aggressive behaviors, or actually engaging in direct aggression—relieves built-up aggressive energies and hence reduces the likelihood of further aggressive behavior. [12]

**causal theory:** a theory about the causes of one's own feelings and behaviors, many of which we learn from our culture (e.g., "absence makes the heart grow fonder"). [6]

**central route to persuasion:** the case whereby people elaborate on a persuasive communication, listening carefully to and thinking about the arguments; this occurs when people have both the ability and the motivation to listen carefully to a communication. [8]

**classical conditioning:** the case whereby a stimulus that elicits an emotional response is repeatedly experienced along with a neutral stimulus that does not, until the neutral stimulus takes on the emotional properties of the first stimulus. [8]

**cognitions:** thoughts, feelings, beliefs, or pieces of knowledge. [3]

**cognitive component of an attitude:** people's beliefs about the properties of an attitude object. [8]

**cognitive dissonance:** a drive or feeling of discomfort originally defined as being caused by holding two or more inconsistent cognitions, and subsequently defined as being caused by performing an action that is discrepant from one's conception of oneself as a decent and sensible person. [3]

**"cognitive misers:"** the idea that people have developed efficient mental shortcuts and rules of thumb to help them understand the social world, because they have a limited capacity to process all of the social information impinging on them. [4]

**cognitively based attitude:** an attitude based primarily on people's beliefs about the properties of the attitude object. [8]

**communal relationships:** relationships in which people's primary concern is being responsive to the other person's needs. [10]

**companionate love:** the feelings of intimacy and affection we feel for another person when we care deeply for the person but do not necessarily experience passion or arousal in his or her presence. [10]

**comparison level:** people's expectations about the level of rewards and punishments they are likely to receive in a particular relationship. [10]

**comparison level for alternatives:** people's expectations about the level of rewards and punishments they would receive in an alternative relationship. [10]

**conformity:** a change in behavior due to the real or imagined influence of other people. [7]

**conjunctive task:** a group task in which performance depends on how well the least talented member does (e.g., how fast a team of roped-together mountain climbers can climb a mountain). [9]

**consensus information:** information about the extent to which other people behave the same way toward the same stimulus as the actor does. [5]

**consistency information:** information about the extent to which the behavior between one actor and one stimulus is the same across time and circumstances. [5]

**construal:** the way in which people perceive, comprehend, and interpret the social world. [1]

**contagion:** the rapid transmission of emotions or behaviors through a crowd. [7]

**contingency theory of leadership:** the theory that leadership effectiveness depends both on how task-oriented or relationship-oriented the leader is and on the amount of control and influence the leader has over the group. [15]

**conversion model:** information inconsistent with a stereotype that leads to a radical change in the stereotype. [13]

**correlational method:** the method whereby two or more variables are systematically measured, and the relationship between them (i.e., how much one can be predicted from the other) is assessed. [2]

**correspondent inference theory:** the theory that we make internal attributions about a person when there are (a) few noncommon effects of his or her behavior and (b) the behavior is unexpected. [5]

**counterattitudinal advocacy:** the process that occurs when a person states an opinion or attitude that runs counter to his or her private belief or attitude. [3]

**covariation assessment:** judgment as to the extent to which two variables are correlated; that is, predicting one variable (e.g., a person's friendliness) from another variable (e.g., his or her gender). [4]

**covariation model:** the idea that we make causal attributions about a person's behavior by observing the things that covary with his or her behavior; for example, the extent to which the person's clumsy dancing occurs only with certain partners. [5]

**cover story:** a description of the purpose of a study, given to participants, that is different from its true purpose; cover stories are used to maintain psychological realism. [2]

**crowding:** the subjective feeling of unpleasantness due to the presence of other people. [14]

**debriefing:** explaining to participants, at the end of an experiment, the purpose of the study and exactly what transpired. [2]

**deception:** misleading or concealing from participants the true purpose of a study, or the events that will actually transpire. [2]

**defensive attributions:** explanations for behavior that avoid feelings of vulnerability and mortality. [5]

**dehumanization:** the act of seeing victims as nonhumans (e.g., "gooks" instead of fellow human beings); dehumanization lowers inhibitions against aggressive actions and makes continued aggression easier and more likely. [12]

**deindividuation:** the loosening of normal constraints on behavior, leading to an increase in impulsive and deviant acts. [9]

**density:** the number of people who occupy a given space. [14]

**dependent variable:** the variable a researcher measures to see if it is influenced by the independent variable; the researcher hypothesizes that the dependent variable will depend on the level of the independent variable. [2]

**descriptive norms:** people's perceptions of how other people are actually behaving in a given situa-tion, regardless of what behaviors are socially sanctioned. [14]

**diffusion of responsibility:** the phenomenon whereby each bystander's sense of responsibility to help decreases as the number of other witnesses increases. [11]

**discounting:** underestimating the effects of one cause of our behavior when another cause is conspicuous and salient. [6]

**discrimination:** unjustified negative or harmful action toward a member of a group, simply because of his or her membership in that group. [13]

**disjunctive task:** a group task in which performance depends on how well the most talented member does (e.g., a group of people trying to solve a difficult math problem). [9]

**display rules:** culturally determined rules about the nonverbal behaviors that are appropriate to display. [5]

**distinctiveness information:** information about the extent to which one particular actor behaves in the same way to different stimuli. [5]

**door-in-the-face technique:** a technique to get people to comply to a request, whereby people are presented first with a large request, which they are expected to refuse, and then with a smaller, more reasonable request, to which it is hoped they will acquiesce. [15]

**downward social comparison:** comparing ourselves to people who are worse than we on a particular trait or ability, in order to feel better about ourselves. [6]

**elaboration likelihood model:** the theory that there are two ways in which persuasive communications can cause atti-tude change; the central route occurs when people are moti-vated and have the ability to pay attention to the arguments in the communication; the peripheral route occurs when people do not pay attention to the arguments but are instead swayed by surface characteristics (e.g., who gave the speech). [8]

**emblems:** nonverbal gestures that have well-understood definitions within a given culture; they usually have direct verbal translations, such as the OK sign. [5]

**empathy:** the ability to put oneself in the shoes of another person—to experience events and emotions (e.g., joy and sadness) the way that person experiences them. [11]

**empathy-altruism hypothesis:** the theory holding that when we feel empathy for a person, we will attempt to help him or her, regardless of what we have to gain. [11]

**equity theory:** the theory holding that people are happiest with relationships in which the rewards and costs a person experiences and the contributions he or she makes to the relationship are roughly equal to the rewards, costs, and contributions of the other person. [10]

**Eros:** the instinct toward life, posited by Freud. [12]

**exchange relationships:** relationships governed by the need for equity (i.e., for an equal ratio of rewards and costs). [10]

**experimental method:** the method of choice to study cause-and-effect relationships; the researcher randomly assigns participants to different conditions and ensures that these conditions are identical except for the independent variable (the one thought to have a causal effect on people's responses). [2]

**external attribution:** the inference that a person is behaving a certain way because of something about the situation he or she is in; the assumption is that most people would respond the same way in that situation. [5]

**external justification:** a person's reason or explanation for his or her dissonant behavior that resides outside the indi-vidual (e.g., if a person does something in order to receive a large reward or avoid a severe punishment). [3]

**external validity:** the extent to which the results of a study can be generalized to other situations and to other people. [2]

**extrinsic motivation:** engaging in an activity because of external rewards or pressures, not because we enjoy the task or find it interesting. [6]

**facial feedback hypothesis:** the hypothesis that people's facial expressions can determine the emotions they experi-ence. [6]

**factorial design:** an experimental design in which there is more than one independent variable; each independent variable has more than one version, or "level"; and all possible combinations of these levels occur in one study. [2]

**fear-arousing communications:** persuasive messages that attempt to change people's attitudes by arousing their fears. [8]

**field experiments:** experiments conducted in real-life settings, rather than in the laboratory. [2]

**foot-in-the-door technique:** a technique to get people to comply to a request, whereby people are presented first with a small request, which virtually everyone agrees to, and then with a larger request, to which it is hoped they will also acquiesce. [15]

**frustration-aggression theory:** the theory that frustration— the perception that you are being prevented from obtaining a goal—will increase the probability of an aggressive response. [12]

**fundamental attribution error:** the tendency to over-estimate the extent to which people's behavior is due to their internal, dispositional factors, and to under-estimate the role of situational factors. [1, 5]

**gain-loss effect:** the finding that we like people the most if we feel we have gained in their estimation of us (i.e., if they initially disliked us but now like us), and that we dislike people the most if we feel we have lost their favor (i.e., if they initially liked us but now dislike us). [10]

**Gestalt psychology:** a school of psychology stressing the importance of studying the subjective way in which an object appears in people's minds, rather than the objective, physical attributes of the object. [1]

**global attribution:** the belief that the cause of an event is due to factors that apply in a large number of situations (e.g., your intelligence, which will influence your performance in many areas), as opposed to the belief that the cause is specific and applies in only a limited number of situations (e.g., your music ability, which will affect your performance in music courses but not in other courses). [14]

**great person theory:** the theory that there are certain key personality traits that make a person a good leader, regardless of the nature of the situation facing the leader. [15]

**GRIT, or graduated and reciprocated initiatives in tension-reduction:** a strategy for reducing conflict in real-life situations, in which you (a) communicate your willingness to cooperate, (b) act cooperatively,(c) reciprocate any cooperative acts your opponent makes, but (d) if your opponent acts aggressively, retaliate with the same level of aggression. [9]

**group polarization:** the tendency for groups to make decisions that are more extreme than the initial inclinations of its members. [9]

**groupthink:** a kind of thinking in which maintaining group cohesiveness and solidarity is more important than considering the facts in a realistic manner. [9]

**hostile aggression:** an act of aggression stemming from feelings of anger and aimed at inflicting pain. [12]

**hostile media phenomenon:** the finding that opposing partisan groups both perceive neutral, balanced media presentations as hostile to their side, because the media have not presented the facts in the one-sided fashion the partisans "know" to be true. [4]

**hydraulic theory:** the theory that unexpressed emotions build up pressure and must be expressed to relieve that pressure. [12]

**idiosyncrasy credits:** the credits a person earns, over time, by conforming to group norms; if enough idiosyncrasy credits are earned, the person can, on occasion, behave deviantly without retribution from the group. [7]

**illusory correlation:** the tendency to see relationships, or correlations, between events that are actually unrelated. [4, 13]

**implicit personality theory:** schemas that people use to group various kinds of personality traits together; for example, many people believe that if someone is kind, he or she is generous as well. [5]

**impression management:** consciously or unconsciously orchestrating a carefully designed presentation of self that will create a certain impression, that fits our goals or needs in a social interaction. [6]

**in-group:** the group with which an individual identifies and feels he or she is a member of. [13]

**in-group bias:** especially positive feelings and special treatment for people we have defined as being part of our in-group, and negative feelings and unfair treatment for others simply because we have defined them as being in the out-group. [13]

**independent variable:** the variable a researcher changes or varies to see if it has an effect on some other variable; this is the variable the researcher thinks will cause a change in some other variable. [2]

**individual differences:** the aspects of people's personalities that make them different from other people. [1]

**informational social influence:** the influence of other people that leads us to conform because we see them as a source of information to guide our behavior; we conform because we believe that others' interpretation of an ambiguous situation is more correct than ours. [7]

**informed consent:** explaining to participants the nature of the experiment before it begins, and obtaining their consent to participate in the experiment. [2]

**ingratiation:** the use of strategies (e.g., offering praise, flattery, and positive feedback) to manipulate people or gain their favor. [6, 10]

**injunctive norms:** socially sanctioned behaviors—that is, people's perceptions of what behaviors are approved of by others. [14]

**institutionalized racism:** racist attitudes that are held by the vast majority of us because we are living in a society where stereotypes and discrimination are the norm. [13]

**institutionalized sexism:** sexist attitudes that are held by the vast majority of us because we are living in a society where stereotypes and discrimination are the norm. [13]

**instrumental aggression:** aggression as a means to some goal other than causing pain. [12]

**instrumental conditioning:** the case whereby behaviors that people freely choose to perform increase or decrease in frequency depending on whether they are followed by positive reinforcement or punishment. [8]

**insufficient punishment:** the dissonance aroused when individuals lack sufficient external justification for having resisted a desired activity or object, usually resulting in individuals devaluing the forbidden activity or object. [3]

**integrative solutions:** solutions to conflicts that find outcomes favorable to both parties. [9]

**interjudge reliability:** the level of agreement between two or more people who independently observe and code a set of data; by showing that two or more judges independently come up with the same observations, researchers ensure that the observations are not the subjective, distorted impressions of one individual. [2]

**internal attribution:** the belief that the cause of an event is due to things about you (e.g., your own ability or effort), as opposed to factors that are external to you (e.g., the difficulty of a test). [5, 14]

**internal justification:** reducing dissonance by changing something about oneself (e.g., one's attitude or behavior). [3]

**internal validity:** making sure that nothing else besides the independent variable can affect the dependent variable; this is accomplished by controlling all extraneous variables and by randomly assigning people to different experimental conditions. [2]

**interpersonal conflict:** tension between two or more individuals or groups who have incompatible goals. [9]

**intrapersonal conflict:** tension within one individual due to two or more incompatible goals (e.g., a parent's desires to stay home with his or her children and to pursue a career). [9]

**intrinsic motivation:** engaging in an activity because we enjoy it or find it interesting, not because of external rewards or pressures. [6]

**introspection:** the process whereby people look inward and examine their own thoughts, feelings, and motives. [6]

**investment model:** the theory holding that people's commitment to a relationship depends on their satisfaction with the relationship in terms of rewards, costs, and comparison level; their comparison level for alternatives; and how much they have invested in the relationship that would be lost by leaving it. [10]

**the jigsaw classroom:** a classroom setting designed to reduce prejudice and raise the self-esteem of children by placing them in small, desegregated groups and making each child dependent on the other children in his or her group to learn the course material and do well in the class. [13]

**judgmental heuristics:** mental shortcuts people use to make judgments quickly and efficiently. [4]

**justification of effort:** the tendency for individuals to increase their liking for something they have worked hard to attain. [3]

**kin selection:** the idea that behaviors that help a genetic relative are favored by natural selection. [11]

**learned helplessness:** the state of pessimism that results from explaining a negative event as due to stable, internal, and global factors; learned helplessness causes depression, reduced effort, and difficulty in learning new material. [14]

**the looking-glass self:** seeing ourselves through the eyes of other people, and incorporating their views into our self-concept. [6]

**lowballing:** an unscrupulous strategy whereby a salesperson induces a customer to agree to purchase a product at a very low cost, subsequently claims it was an error, and then raises the price; frequently the customer will agree to make the purchase at the inflated price. [3]

**mass psychogenic illness:** the occurrence, in a group of people, of similar physical symptoms with no known physical cause. [7]

**mediation:** allowing a neutral third party to help the disputing parties resolve a conflict. [9]

**mere exposure:** the finding that the more exposure we have to a stimulus, the more apt we are to like it. [10]

**mindless conformity:** obeying internalized social norms without deliberating about one's actions. [7]

**minimal groups:** meaningless groups formed by grouping strangers on the basis of trivial criteria; minimum group members still display in-group biases, however. [13]

**minority influence:** the case where a minority of group members influence the behavior or beliefs of the majority. [7]

**misattribution of arousal:** attributing one's arousal to the wrong source, resulting in a mistaken or exaggerated emotion. [6]

**mixed-motive conflict:** conflict in which both sides can gain by cooperating, but in which an individual can gain even more by competing against his or her partner. [9]

**modern racism:** prejudice revealed in subtle, indirect ways because people have learned to hide prejudiced attitudes in order to avoid being labeled as racist. [13]

**mundane realism:** the extent to which an experiment is similar to situations encountered in everyday life. [2]

**mutual interdependence:** a situation where two or more groups need each other and must depend on each other in order to accomplish a goal that is important to each of them. [13]

**negative correlation:** a relationship between two variables wherein increases in the value of one variable are associated with decreases in the value of the other variable. [2]

**negative-state relief hypothesis:** the idea that people help in order to alleviate their own sadness and distress. [11]

**negotiation:** a form of communication between opposing sides in a conflict, in which offers and counteroffers are made and a solution occurs only when it is agreed on by both parties. [9]

**noncommon effects:** effects produced by a particular course of action that could not be produced by alternative courses of action. [5]

**nonsocial group:** a group in which two or more people are in the same place at the same time but are not interacting with each other (e.g., fans at a baseball game). [9]

**nonverbal communication:** the way in which people communicate, intentionally or unintentionally, without words; nonverbal cues include facial expressions, tone of voice, gestures, body position and movement, the use of touch, and eye gaze. [5]

**norm of reciprocity:** the assumption that others will treat us the way we treat them (e.g., if we help someone, he or she will help us). [11]

**normative conformity:** the tendency to go along with the group in order to fulfill their expectations and gain acceptance. [13]

**normative social influence:** the influence of other people that leads us to conform in order to be liked and accepted by them; this type of conformity results in public compliance with, but not necessarily private acceptance of, the group's beliefs and behaviors. [7]

**observational method:** the technique whereby a researcher observes people and systematically records measurements of their behavior. [2]

**out-group:** a group with which an individual does not identify. [13]

**out-group homogeneity:** the perception that those in the out-group are more similar (homogeneous) to each other than they really are, as well as more similar than the members of the in-group. [13]

**overconfidence barrier:** the finding that people usually have too much confidence in the accuracy of their judgments; people's judgments are usually not as correct as they think they are. [4]

**the overjustification effect:** the case whereby people view their behavior as caused by compelling extrinsic reasons, making them underestimate the extent to which their behavior was caused by intrinsic reasons. [6]

**participant observation:** a form of systematic observation whereby the observer interacts with the people being observed, but tries not to alter the situation in any way. [2]

**passionate love:** the feelings of intense longing, accompanied by physiological arousal, we feel for another person; when our love is reciprocated, we feel great fulfillment and ecstasy, but when it is not, we feel sadness and despair. [10]

**perceived control:** the belief that we can influence our environment in ways that determine whether we experience positive or negative outcomes. [14]

**perceptual salience:** information that is the focus of people's attention; people tend to overestimate the causal role of perceptually salient information. [5]

**peripheral route to persuasion:** the case whereby people do not elaborate on the arguments in a persuasive communication but are instead swayed by peripheral cues. [8]

**perseverance effect:** the finding that people's beliefs about themselves and the social world persist even after the evidence supporting these beliefs is dis-credited. [4]

**personal relevance:** the extent to which a topic has important consequences for people's well-being. [8]

**persuasive communication:** communication (e.g., a speech or television ad) advocating a particular side of an issue. [8]

**pluralistic ignorance:** the phenomenon whereby bystanders assume that nothing is wrong in an emergency, because no one else looks concerned. [11]

**polygraph:** a machine that measures people's physiological responses (e.g., their heart rate); when these machines are used in lie detection, polygraph operators attempt to tell if someone is lying by observing how that person responds physiologically while answering questions. [15]

**positive correlation:** a relationship between two variables wherein increases in the value of one variable are associated with increases in the value of the other variable. [2]

**postdecision dissonance:** dissonance is inevitably aroused after a person makes a decision. In this situation, dissonance is typically reduced by enhancing the attractiveness of the chosen alternative and devaluing the rejected alternatives. [3]

**prejudice:** a hostile or negative attitude toward a distinguishable group of people, based solely on their membership in that group. [13]

**primacy effect:** the process whereby our first impression of another person causes us to interpret his or her subsequent behavior in a manner consistent with the first impression. [4]

**priming:** the process by which recent experiences increase a schema's accessibility. [4]

**private acceptance:** conforming to other people's behavior out of a genuine belief that what they are doing or saying is right. [7]

**probability level (p-value):** a number, calculated with statistical techniques, that tells researchers how likely it is that the results of their experiment occurred by chance (due to the failure of random assignment) and not because of the independent variable(s); the convention in science, including social psychology, is to consider results significant if the probability level is less than five in one hundred that the results might be due to chance factors and not the independent variables studied. [2]

**process loss:** any aspect of group interaction that inhibits good problem solving. [9]

**propinquity effect:** the finding that the more we see and interact with people, the more likely they are to become our friends. [10]

**prosocial behavior:** any act performed with the goal of benefiting another person. [11]

**psychological realism:** the extent to which the psychological processes triggered in an experiment are similar to psychological processes occurring in everyday life; psychological realism can be high in an experiment, even if mundane realism is low. [2]

**public compliance:** conforming to other people's behavior publicly, without necessarily believing in what we are doing or saying. [7]

**random assignment to condition:** making sure that all participants have an equal chance of taking part in any condition of an experiment; through random assignment, researchers can be relatively certain that differences in their participants' personalities or backgrounds are distributed evenly across conditions. [2]

**random selection:** a way of ensuring that a sample of people is representative of a population, by making sure that everyone in the population has an equal chance of being selected for the sample. [2]

**rationalization trap:** the potential for dissonance reduction to produce a succession of self-justifications which ultimately result in a chain of stupid or immoral actions. [3]

**reactance theory:** the idea that when people feel their freedom to perform a certain behavior is threatened, an unpleasant state of reactance is aroused; people can reduce this reactance by performing the threatened behavior. [8]

**realistic conflict theory:** the theory that limited resources lead to conflict between groups and result in increased prejudice and discrimination. [13]

**reasons-generated attitude change:** attitude change resulting from thinking about the reasons for one's attitudes; people assume that their attitudes match the reasons that are plausible and easy-to-verbalize. [6]

**reciprocity norm:** a social norm, which states that receiving anything positive from another person requires you to reciprocate (or behave similarly)in response. [7]

**reconstructive memory:** the process whereby memories for an event become distorted by information encountered after the event has occurred. [15]

**relationship-oriented leader:** a leader who is concerned primarily with the feelings of and relationships between the workers. [15]

**relative deprivation:** the perception that you (or your group) have less than you deserve, less than you have been led to expect, or less than people similar to you have. [12]

**replication:** repeating a study, often with different subject populations or in different settings. [2]

**representativeness heuristic:** a mental shortcut whereby people classify something according to how similar it is to a typical case. [4]

**retrieval:** the process by which people recall information stored in their memories. [15]

**scapegoating** the tendency for individuals, when frustrated or unhappy, to displace aggression onto groups that are disliked, visible, and relatively powerless. [13]

**schemas:** cognitive structures people have to organize their knowledge about the social world by themes or subjects; schemas powerfully affect what information we notice, think about, and remember. [4]

**secure attachment style:** an attachment style characterized by trust, a lack of concern with being abandoned, and the view that one is worthy and well liked. [10]

**self-affirmation theory:** a theory suggesting that people will reduce the impact of a dissonance arrousing threat to their self-concept by focusing on and affirming their competence on some dimension unrelated to the threat. [3]

**self-awareness:** focusing our attention on our feelings, attitudes, and values. [9]

**self-awareness theory:** the idea that when people focus their attention on themselves, they evaluate and compare their behavior to their internal standards and values. [6]

**self-concept:** the contents of the self; that is, our perception of our own thoughts, beliefs, and personality traits. [3, 6]

**self-esteem:** people's evaluations of their own self-worth—that is, the extent to which they view themselves as good, competent, and decent. [1]

**self-evaluation maintenance theory:** the theory that one's self-concept can be threatened by another individual's behavior, and that the level of threat is determined by both the closeness of the other individual and the personal relevance of the behavior. [3]

**self-fulfilling prophecy:** the case whereby people (a) have an expectation about what another person is like, which (b) influences how they act toward that person, which (c) causes that person to behave in a way consistent with people's original expectations. [4]

**self-handicapping:** creating obstacles and excuses for our-selves, so that if we do poorly on a task, we have ready-made excuses. [6]

**self-justification:** the tendency to justify one's actions in order to maintain one's self-esteem. [3]

**self-perception theory:** the theory that when our attitudes and feelings are uncertain or ambiguous, we infer these states by observing our behavior and the situation in which it occurs. [6]

**self-persuasion:** a long-lasting form of attitude change that results from attempts at self-justification. [3]

**self-presentation:** the attempt to present who we are, or who we want people to believe we are, through our words, nonverbal behaviors, and actions. [6]

**self-promotion:** the process whereby people try to impress other people by describing their talents and exhibiting their knowledge. [6]

**self-schemas:** organized knowledge structures about ourselves, based on our past experiences, that help us understand, explain, and predict our own behavior. [6]

**self-serving attributions:** explanations for one's successes that credit internal, dispositional factors, and explanations for one's failures that blame external, situational factors. [5]

**self-verification theory:** the tendency to seek con-firmation of one's self-concept, whether the self-concept is positive or negative. In some circumstances, this tendency can conflict with self-enhancement and self-justification. [3]

**sensory overload:** the situation in which we receive more stimulation from the environment than we can pay atten-tion to or process. [14]

**social cognition:** how people think about themselves and the social world; more specifically, how people select, inter-pret, remember, and use social information to make judg-ments and decisions. [1, 4]

**social comparison theory:** the idea that we learn about our own abilities and attitudes by comparing ourselves to other people. [6]

**social dilemma:** a situation in which the most beneficial action for an individual will, if chosen by most people, have harmful effects on everyone. [14]

**social exchange theory:** the theory holding that how people feel about a relationship depends on their perceptions of the rewards and costs of the relationship, the kind of relationship they deserve, and their chances for having a better relationship with someone else. [10, 11]

**social facilitation:** the arousal that results when other people are present and our performance can be evalu-ated; this arousal enhances our performance on simple tasks but impairs our performance on complex tasks. [9]

**social groups:** groups in which two or more people are interacting with each other and are interdependent, in the sense that to fulfill their needs and goals they must rely on each other. [9]

**social impact theory:** the theory that conforming to social influence depends on the strength, immediacy, and number of other people in a group. [7]

**social learning theory:** the theory that we learn social behavior (e.g., aggression) by observing others and imitating them. [12]

**social loafing:** the relaxation that results when people are in a group and their individual performance cannot be evalu-ated; this relaxation impairs performance on simple tasks but enhances performance on complex tasks. [9]

**social norms:** the implicit or explicit rules a group has for the acceptable behaviors, values, and beliefs of its members. [7]

**social perception:** the study of how we form impressions of and make inferences about other people. [5]

**social psychology:** the scientific study of the way in which people's thoughts, feelings, and behaviors are influenced by the real or imagined presence of other people. [1]

**social-role theory:** the theory that sex differences in social behavior are due to society's division of labor between the sexes; this division leads to differences in gender-role expec-tations and sex-typed skills, which are responsible for differ-ences in men's and women's social behavior. [5]

**sociobiology:** the application of evolutionary theory to social behavior. [11]

**source misattribution:** making a mistake about the source of our memories (e.g., believing a man looks familiar because we saw him at the scene of a crime, when in fact he looks familiar because we saw his picture in the newspaper. [15]

**split cable market tests:** a technique used to test the effectiveness of advertising, whereby advertisers, in conjunction with cable television companies and grocery stores, show a commercial to a randomly determined group of people, and then see whether these people are more likely to buy the product than those who did not see the commercial. [15]

**stable attribution:** the belief that the cause of an event is due to factors that will not change over time (e.g., your intelligence), as opposed to unstable factors that will change over time (e.g., the amount of effort you put into a task). [14]

**stereotype:** a generalization about a group of people in which identical characteristics are assigned to virtually all members of the group, regardless of actual variation among the members. [13]

**storage:** the process by which people store in memory information they have acquired from the environment. [15]

**stress:** the negative feelings and beliefs that occur whenever people feel they cannot cope with demands from their environment. [14]

**structured interview:** a job interview technique whereby the interviewer asks all the applicants the same questions from a predetermined list; the questions concern only the applicants' qualifications for the job. [15]

**subjective norms:** people's beliefs about how other people they care about will view the behavior in question. [8]

**subliminal messages:** words or pictures that are not consciously perceived, but are purported to influence people's judgments, attitudes, and behaviors. [15]

**subtyping model:** information inconsistent with a stereotype that leads to the creation of a new substereotype to accommodate the information without changing the initial stereotype. [13]

**systematic observation:** a form of the observational method whereby the observer is a trained social scientist who sets out to answer questions about a particular social phenomenon by observing and coding it according to a prearranged set of criteria. [2]

**target-based expectancies:** expectations about a person based on his or her past actions, such as expecting someone to go to the beach on vacation because he or she has always gone to the beach in the past. [5]

**task-oriented leader:** a leader who is concerned primarily with getting the job done, and less so with the feelings of and relationships between the workers. [15]

**testosterone:** a hormone associated with aggression. [12]

**Thanatos:** according to Freud; an instinctual drive toward death, leading to aggressive actions. [12]

**theory of reasoned action:** a theory holding that the best predictors of people's planned, deliberate behaviors are people's attitudes toward the specific behavior and their subjective norms. [8]

**thought suppression:** an effort not to think about something; research shows that the more people try not to think about something, the more that very thought pops into their minds. [6]

**tit-for-tat strategy:** a means of encouraging cooperation by acting cooperatively at first, but then always responding the way your opponent did (cooperatively or competitively) on the previous trial. [9]

**triangular theory of love:** the idea that different kinds of love consist of varying degrees of three components: intimacy, passion, and commitment. [10]

**two-factor theory of emotion:** the idea that emotional experience is the result of a two-step self-perception process in which people first experience physiological arousal and then seek an appropriate explanation for it; if they attribute the arousal to an emotional source, they experience that emotion (e.g., if people attribute their arousal to someone pointing a gun at them, they experience fear). [6]

**ultimate attribution error:** our tendency to make dispositional attributions about an entire group of people. [13]

**unrealistic optimism:** a form of defensive attribution wherein people think that good things are more likely to happen to them than to their peers, and that bad things are less likely to happen to them than to their peers. [5]

**upward social comparison:** comparing ourselves to people who are better than we are on a particular trait or ability, in order to determine the standard of excellence. [6]

**urban-overload hypothesis:** the theory suggesting that people living in cities are likely to keep to themselves in order to avoid being overloaded by all the stimulation they receive. [11]

**validity:** how well a test or assessment technique (e.g., a job interview) predicts what it is supposed to predict (e.g., performance on the job). [15]

**Yale Attitude Change Approach:** the study of the conditions under which people are most likely to change their attitudes in response to persuasive messages; researchers in this tradition focus on "who said what to whom"—that is, on the source of the communication, the nature of the communication, and the nature of the audience. [8]

**zero-sum conflict:** conflict in which one side's gain is always the other side's loss, as in athletic contests. [9]

# REFERENCES

Abelson, R. P. (1976). Script processing in attitude formation and decision making. In J. S. Carroll & J. W. Payne (Eds.), *Cognition and social behavior* (pp. 13–32). Hillsdale, NJ: Erlbaum.

Abelson, R. P., Kinder, D. R., Peters, M. D., & Fiske, S. T. (1982). Affective and semantic components in political person perception. *Journal of Personality and Social Psychology, 42,* 619–630.

Abraham, M. M., & Lodish, L. M. (1990, May–June). Getting the most out of advertising and promotion. *Harvard Business Review,* pp. 50–60.

Abramson, L. Y., Seligman, M. E. P., & Teasdale, J. D. (1978). Learned helplessness in humans: Critique and reformulation. *Journal of Abnormal Psychology, 87,* 49–74.

Adorno, T. W., Frenkel-Brunswick, E., Levinson, D. J., & Sanford, R. N. (1950). *The authoritarian personality.* New York: Harper & Row.

Aiello, J. R., Thompson, D. E., & Brodzinsky, D. M. (1983). How funny is crowding anyway? Effects of room size, group size, and the introduction of humor. *Basic and Applied Social Psychology, 4,* 193–207.

Ainsworth, M. D. S., Blehar, M. C., Waters, E., & Wall, S. (1978). *Patterns of attachment: A psychological study of the strange situation.* Hillsdale, NJ: Erlbaum.

Ajzen, I., & Fishbein, M. (1980). *Understanding attitudes and predicting social behavior.* Englewood Cliffs, NJ: Prentice Hall.

Akert, R. M. (1992). *Terminating romantic relationships: The role of personal responsibility and gender.* Unpublished manuscript, Wellesley College.

Akert, R. M. (1993). The effect of autobiographical memories on the current definition of self. Unpublished manuscript, Wellesley College.

Akert, R. M., Chen, J., & Panter, A. T. (1991). *Facial prominence and stereotypes: The incidence and meaning of faceism in print and television media.* Unpublished manuscript. Wellesley College.

Akert, R. M., & Panter, A. T. (1988). Extraversion and the ability to decode nonverbal communication. *Personality and Individual Differences, 9,* 965–972.

Allen, V. L. (1965). Situational factors in conformity. In L. Berkowitz (Ed.), *Advances in experimental social psychology* (Vol. 2, pp. 133–175). New York: Academic Press.

Allen, V. L., & Levine, J. M. (1969). Consensus and conformity. *Journal of Personality and Social Psychology, 5,* 389–399.

Alloy, L. B., & Abramson, L. Y. (1988). Depressive realism: Four theoretical perspectives. In L. B. Alloy (Ed.), *Cognitive processes in depression* (pp. 223–265). New York: Guilford.

Alloy, L. B., Abramson, L. Y., & Viscusi, D. (1981). Induced mood and the illusion of control. *Journal of Personality and Social Psychology, 41,* 1129–1140.

Alloy, L. B., & Tabachnik, N. (1984). Assessment of covariation by humans and animals: The joint influence of prior expectations and current situational information. *Psychological Review, 91,* 112–149.

Allport, G. (1954). *The nature of prejudice.* Reading, MA: Addison-Wesley.

Allport, G. W. (1985). The historical background of social psychology. In G. Lindzey & E. Aronson (Eds.), *The handbook of social psychology* (Vol. 1, pp. 1–46). Reading, MA: Addison-Wesley.

Amabile, T. M. (1983). Brilliant but cruel: Perceptions of negative evaluators. *Journal of Experimental Social Psychology, 19,* 146–156.

Amabile, T. M., Hennessey, B. A., & Grossman, B. S. (1986). Social influences on creativity: The effects of contracted-for reward. *Journal of Personality and Social Psychology, 50,* 14–23.

Amato, P. R. (1983). Helping behavior in urban and rural environments: Field studies based on a taxonomic organization of helping episodes. *Journal of Personality and Social Psychology, 45,* 571–586.

American Psychological Association. (1992). Ethical principles of psychologists and code of conduct. *American Psychologist, 47,* 1597–1611.

Amir, Y. (1969). Contact hypothesis in ethnic relations. *Psychological Bulletin, 71,* 319–342.

Amir, Y. (1976). The role of intergroup contact in change of prejudice and ethnic relations. In P. Katz (Ed.), *Towards the Elimination of Racism*. New York: Pergamon Press.

Anderson, C. A., & Anderson, D. C. (1984). Ambient temperature and violent crime: Tests of the linear and curvilinear hypotheses. *Journal of Personality and Social Psychology, 46*, 91–97.

Anderson, C. A., Lepper, M. R., & Ross, L. (1980). The perseverance of social theories: The role of explanation in the persistence of discredited information. *Journal of Personality and Social Psychology, 39*, 1037–1049.

Anderson, C. A., & Sechler, E. S. (1986). Effects of explanation and counterexplanation on the development and use of social theories. *Journal of Personality and Social Psychology, 50*, 24–34.

Anderson, C. A., & Sekides, C. (1990). Thinking about people: Contributions of a typological alternative to associationistic and dimensional models of person perception. *Journal of Personality and Social Psychology*.

Andersen, S. M., & Bem, S. L. (1981). Sex typing and androgyny in dyadic interaction: Individual differences in responsiveness to physical attractiveness. *Journal of Personality and Social Psychology, 41*, 74–86.

Andersen, S. M., & Klatzky, R. L. (1987). Traits and social stereotypes: Levels of categorization in person perception. *Journal of Personality and Social Psychology, 53*, 235–246.

Ann Landers, Dear (1990, April 1). *Washington Post*, p. F7.

Ann Landers, Dear (1991, September 10). *Boston Globe*, p. 52.

Archer, D., & Akert, R. M. (1977a). How well do you read body language? *Psychology Today*, October, pp. 68–69, 72, 119–120.

Archer, D., & Akert, R. M. (1977b). Words and everything else: Verbal and nonverbal cues in social interaction. *Journal of Personality and Social Psychology, 35*, 443–449.

Archer, D., & Akert, R. M. (1980). The encoding of meaning: A test of three theories of social interaction. *Sociological Inquiry, 50*(3–4), 393–419.

Archer, D., & Akert, R. M. (1984). Problems of context and criterion in nonverbal communication: A new look at the accuracy issue. In M. Cook (Ed.), *Issues in person perception* (pp. 114–144). London and New York: Methuen.

Archer, D., & Akert, R. M. (in press). *The interpretation of behavior: Verbal and nonverbal factors in person perception*. Cambridge: Cambridge University Press.

Archer, D., & Gartner, R. (1976). Violent acts and violent times: A comparative approach to postwar homicide rates. *American Sociological Review, 41*, 937–963.

Archer, D., & Gartner, R. (1984). *Violence and crime in cross-national perspective*. New Haven, CT: Yale University Press.

Archer, D., Iritani, B., Kimes, D. D., & Barrios, M. (1983). Face-ism: Five studies of sex differences in facial prominence. *Journal of Personality and Social Psychology, 45*, 725–735.

Archer, R. L., Hormuth, S. E., & Berg, J. H. (1979, September). *Self-disclosure under conditions of self-awareness*. Paper presented at the meeting of the American Psychological Association, New York.

Arendt, H. (1965). *Eichmann in Jerusalem: A report on the banality of evil*. New York: Viking.

Argyle, M. (1975). *Bodily communication*. New York: International Universities Press.

Arkin, R. M. (1981). Self-presentational styles. In J. T. Tedeschi (Ed.), *Impression management theory and social psychological research* (pp. 311–333). New York: Academic Press.

Arkin, R. M., & Baumgardner, A. H. (1985). Self-handicapping. In J. H. Harvey & G. Weary (Eds.), *Basic issues in attribution theory and research* (pp. 169–202). New York: Academic Press.

Arkin, R. M., & Maruyama, G. M. (1979). Attribution, affect, and college exam performance. *Journal of Educational Psychology, 71*, 85–93.

Arms, R. L., Russell, G. W., & Sandilands, M. L. (1979). Effects on the hostility of spectators of viewing aggressive sports. *Social Psychology Quarterly, 42*, 275–279.

Aron, A., Aron, E. N., & Smollan, D. (1990). The Inclusion of Other in the Self (IOS) scale and the structure of interpersonal closeness. *Journal of Personality and Social Psychology, 63*, 596–612.

Aronson, E. (1969). The theory of cognitive dissonance: A current perspective. In L. Berkowitz (Ed.), *Advances in experimental social psychology* (Vol. 4, pp. 1–34). New York: Academic Press.

Aronson, E. (1990). Applying social psychology to prejudice reduction and energy conservation. *Personality and Social Psychology Bulletin, 16*, 118–132.

Aronson, E. (1992a). *The social animal*. New York: Freeman.

Aronson, E. (1992b). The return of the repressed: Dissonance theory makes a comeback. *Psychological Inquiry, 3*, 303–311.

Aronson, E., & Bridgeman, D. (1979). Jigsaw groups and the desegregated classroom: In pursuit of common goals. *Personality and Social Psychology Bulletin, 5*, 438–446.

Aronson, E., & Carlsmith, J. M. (1962). Performance expectancy as a determinant of actual performance. *Journal of Abnormal and Social Psychology, 65*, 178–182.

Aronson, E., & Carlsmith, J. M. (1963). Effect of severity of threat in the devaluation of forbidden behavior. *Journal of Abnormal and Social Psychology, 66*, 584–588.

Aronson, E., & Carlsmith, J. M. (1968). Experimentation in social psychology. In G. Lindzey & E. Aronson (Eds.), *The handbook of social psychology* (Vol. 2, pp. 1–79). Reading, MA: Addison-Wesley.

Aronson, E., Ellsworth, P., Carlsmith, J. M., & Gonzales, M. (1989). *Methods of research in social psychology* (2nd. ed.). New York: Random House.

Aronson, E., Fried, C., & Stone, J. (1991). Overcoming denial and increasing the intention to use condoms through the induction of hypocrisy. *American Journal of Public Health, 81*, 1636–1638.

Aronson, E., & Gonzales, M. (1990). The social psychology of energy conservation. In J. Edwards (Ed.), *Social influence processes and prevention*. New York: Plenum Press.

Aronson, E., & Gonzalez, A. (1988). Desegregation, jigsaw, and the Mexican-American experience. In P. A. Katz & D. Taylor (Eds.), *Towards the elimination of racism: Profiles in controversy*. New York: Plenum.

Aronson, E., & Linder, D. (1965). Gain and loss of esteem as determinants of interpersonal attractiveness. *Journal of Experimental Social Psychology, 1*, 156–171.

Aronson, E., & Mettee, D. (1968). Dishonest behavior as a function of differential levels of induced self-esteem. *Journal of Personality and Social Psychology, 9,* 121–127.

Aronson, E., & Mills, J. (1959). The effect of severity of initiation on liking for a group. *Journal of Abnormal and Social Psychology, 59,* 177–181.

Aronson, E., Stephan, C., Sikes, J., Blaney, N., & Snapp, M. (1978). *The jigsaw classroom.* Beverly Hills, CA: Sage.

Aronson, E., & Thibodeau, R. (1992). The jigsaw classroom: A cooperative strategy for reducing prejudice. In J. Lynch, C. Modgil, & S. Modgil (Eds.), *Cultural Diversity in the Schools.* London: Falmer Press.

Aronson, E., & Worchel, P. (1966). Similarity versus liking as determinants of interpersonal attractiveness. *Psychonomic Science, 5,* 157–158.

Aronson, E., Willerman, B., & Floyd, J. (1966). The effect of a pratfall on increasing interpersonal attractiveness. *Psychonomic Science, 4,* 227–228.

Aronson, E., & Yates, S. (1985). Social psychological aspects of energy conservation. In D. Hafemeister, H. Kelly, & B. Levi, (Eds.), *Energy sources: Conservation and renewables* (pp. 81–91). New York: American Institute of Physics Press.

Aronson, J. M., & Jones, E. E. (1992). Inferring abilities after influencing performance. *Journal of Experimental Social Psychology, 28,* 277–299.

Arvey, R. D. (1979). Unfair discrimination in the employment interview: Legal and psychological aspects. *Psychological Bulletin, 86,* 736–765.

Arvey, R. D., & Campion, J. E. (1982). The employment interview: A summary and review of recent literature. *Personnel Psychology, 35,* 281–322.

Asch, S. E. (1951). Effects of group pressure upon the modification and distortion of judgment. In H. Guetzkow (Ed.), *Groups, leadership and men.* Pittsburgh, PA: Carnegie Press. Asch, S. E. (1955). Opinions and social pressure. *Scientific American, 11,* 32.

Asch, S. E. (1956). Studies of independence and conformity: A minority of one against a unanimous majority. *Psychological Monographs, 70,* (9, Whole No. 416).

Asch, S. E. (1957). An experimental investigation of group influence. In *Symposium on Preventive and Social Psychiatry* (pp. 15–17). Walter Reed Army Institute of Research. Washington, DC: U.S. Government Printing Office.

Asch, S. E. (1959). A perspective on social psychology. In S. Koch (Ed.), *Psychology: A study of science* (Vol. 3, pp. 363–383). New York: McGraw-Hill.

Asendorf, J. (1987). Videotape reconstruction of emotions and cognitions related to shyness. *Journal of Personality and Social Psychology, 53,* 542–549.

Ash, R. A. (1981). Comparison of four approaches to the evaluation of job applicant training and work experience. *Dissertation Abstracts International, 42,* 4606B.

Ashmore, R. D., & DelBoca, F. K. (1976). Psychological approaches to understanding intergroup conflict. In P. A. Katz (Ed.), *Towards the Elimination of Racism.* Elsmford, NY: Pergamon Press.

Axelrod, R. (1984). *The evolution of cooperation.* New York: Basic Books.

Axsom, D. (1989). Cognitive dissonance and behavior change in psychotherapy. *Journal of Experimental Social Psychology, 25,* 234–252.

Ayres, I. (1991). Fair driving: Gender and race discrimination in retail car negotiations. *Harvard Law Review, 104,* 817–872.

Azrin, N. H. (1967, May). Pain and aggression. *Psychology Today,* pp. 27–33.

Baldwin, M. W., Carrell, S. E., & Lopez, D. F. (1990). Priming relationship schemas: My advisor and the Pope are watching me from the back of my mind. *Journal of Experimental Social Psychology, 26,* 435–454.

Bandura, A. (1973). *Aggression: A social learning analysis.* Englewood Cliffs, NJ: Prentice Hall.

Bandura, A. (1986). *Social foundations of thought and action.* Englewood Cliffs, NJ: Prentice Hall.

Bandura, A., Ross, D., & Ross, S. (1961). Transmission of aggression through imitation of aggressive models. *Journal of Abnormal and Social Psychology, 63,* 575–582

Bandura, A., Ross, D., & Ross, S. (1963). Imitation of film-mediated aggressive models. *Journal of Abnormal and Social Psychology, 66,* 3–11.

Bar-Tal, D., & Saxe, L. (1976). Perceptions of similarly and dissimilarly attractive couples and individuals. *Journal of Personality and Social Psychology, 33,* 772–781.

Bargh, J. A., & Pietromonaco, P. (1982). Automatic information processing and social perception: The influence of trait information presented outside of conscious awareness on impression formation. *Journal of Personality and Social Psychology, 43,* 437–449.

Barker, R., Dembo, T., & Lewin, K. (1941). Frustration and aggression: An experiment with young children. *University of Iowa Studies in Child Welfare, 18,* 1–314.

Baron, L., & Straus, M. A. (1984). Sexual stratification, pornography, and rape. In N. M. Malamuth & E. Donnerstein (Eds.), *Pornography and sexual aggression*(pp. 186–209). New York: Academic Press.

Baron, R., & Rodin, J. (1978). Personal control as a mediator of crowding. In A. Baum, J. S. Singer, & S. Valins (Eds.), *Advances in environmental psychology* (Vol. 1, pp. 145–190). Hillsdale, NJ: Erlbaum.

Bartlett, D. C. (1932). *Remembering.* Cambridge: Cambridge University Press.

Baron, R. A. (1972). Reducing the influence of an aggressive model: The restraining effects of peer censure. *Journal of Experimental Social Psychology, 8,* 266–275.

Baron, R. A. (1976). The reduction of human aggression: A field study on the influence of incompatible responses. *Journal of Applied Social Psychology, 6,* 95–104.

Baron, R. A. (1988). Negative effects of destructive criticism: Impact on conflict, self-efficacy, and task performance. *Journal of Applied Psychology, 73,* 199–207.

Baron, R. A. (l990). Countering the effects of destructive criticism: The relative efficacy of four interventions. *Journal of Applied Psychology, 75,* 235–245.

Baron, R. A., & Richardson, D. R. (1992). *Human Aggression* (2nd ed.). New York: Plenum Press.

Baron, R. S. (1986). Distraction/conflict theory: Progress and problems. In L. Berkowitz (Ed.), *Advances in experimental social psychology* (Vol. 19, pp. 1–40). Orlando, FL: Academic Press.

Basu, J. E. (1989). Why no one's safe: Effects of smog on residents in Los Angeles Basin. *American Health*, *8*, 64.

Bateson, N. (1966). Familiarization, group discussion, and risk taking. *Journal of Experimental Social Psychology*, *2*, 119–129.

Batson, C. D. (1991). *The altruism question: Toward a social-psychological answer*. Hillsdale, NJ: Erlbaum.

Batson, C. D., Batson, J. G., Griffit, C. A., Barrientos, S., Brandt, J. R., Sprengelmeyer, P., & Bayly, M. J. (1989). Negative-state relief and the empathy-altruism hypothesis. *Journal of Personality and Social Psychology*, *56*, 922–933.

Batson, C. D., Bolen, M. H., Cross, J. A., & Neuringer-Benefiel, H. E. (1986). Where is the altruism in the altruistic personality? *Journal of Personality and Social Psychology*, *50*, 212–220.

Batson, C. D., Coke, J. S., Jasnoski, M. L., & Hanson, M. (1978). Buying kindness: Effect of an extrinsic incentive for helping on perceived altruism. *Personality and Social Psychology Bulletin*, *4*, 86–91.

Batson, C. D., Duncan, B. D., Ackerman, P., Buckley, T., & Birch, K. (1981). Is empathic emotion a source of altruistic motivation? *Journal of Personality and Social Psychology*, *40*, 290–302.

Batson, C. D., Dyck, J. L., Brandt, J. R., Batson, J. G., Powell, A. L., McMaster, M. R., & Griffit, C. (1988). Five studies testing two new egoistic alternatives to the empathy-altruism hypothesis. *Journal of Personality and Social Psychology*, *55*, 52–77.

Battle for your brain, The. *Consumer Reports* (1991, August), pp. 520–521.

Baum, A., & Valins, S. (1977). *Architecture and social behavior: Psychological studies of social density*. Hillsdale, NJ: Erlbaum.

Baum, A., & Valins, S. (1979). Architectural mediation of residential density and control: Crowding and the regulation of social contract. In L. Berkowitz (Ed.), *Advances in experimental social psychology* (Vol. 12, pp. 131–175). New York: Academic Press.

Baumeister, R. (1987). How the self became a problem: A psychological review of historical research. *Journal of Personality and Social Psychology*, *52*, 163–176.

Baumeister, R. (Ed.) (1993). *Self-esteem: The puzzle of low self-regard*. New York: Plenum.

Baumeister, R. F., & Jones, E. E. (1978). When self-presentation is constrained by the target's knowledge: Consistency and compensation. *Journal of Personality and Social Psychology*, *36*, 608–618.

Baumgardner, A. H., Lake, E. A., & Arkin, R. M. (1985). Claiming mood as a self-handicap. *Personality and Social Psychology Bulletin*, *11*, 349–357.

Baxter, L. A. (1986). Gender differences in the heterosexual relationship rules embedded in break-up accounts. *Journal of Social and Personal Relationships*, *3*, 289–306.

Beaman, A. L., Barnes, P. J., Klentz, B., & McQuirk, B. (1978). Increasing helping rates through informational dissemination: Teaching pays. *Personality and Social Psychology Bulletin*, *4*, 406–411.

Beaman, A. L., Klentz, B., Diener, E., & Svanum, S. (1979). Objective self-awareness and transgression in children: A field study. *Journal of Personality and Social Psychology*, *37*, 1835–1846.

Becker, B. J. (1986). Influence again: Another look at studies of gender differences in social influence. In J. S. Hyde & M. C. Linn (Eds.), *The psychology of gender: Advances through meta-analysis* (pp. 178–209). Baltimore, MD: Johns Hopkins University Press.

Becker, M. H., & Josephs, J. G. (1988). AIDS and behavioral change to reduce risk: A review. *American Journal of Public Health*, *78*, 394–410.

Bell, P. A. (1980). Effects of heat, noise, and provocation on retaliatory evaluative behavior. *Journal of Social Psychology*, *110*, 97–100.

Bell, P. R., & Jamieson, B. D. (1970). Publicity of initial decisions and the risky shift phenomenon. *Journal of Experimental Social Psychology*, *6*, 329–345.

Belli, R. F. (1989). Influences of misleading postevent information: Misinformation interference and acceptance. *Journal of Experimental Psychology: General*, *118*, 72–85.

Bem, D. J. (1967). Self-perception: An alternative interpretation of cognitive dissonance phenomena. *Psychological Review*, *74*, 183–200.

Bem, D. J. (1972). Self-perception theory. In L. Berkowitz (Ed.), *Advances in experimental social psychology* (Vol. 6, pp. 1–62). New York: Academic Press.

Berger, P. L. (1963). *Invitation to sociology: A humanistic perspective*. Garden City, NY: Anchor Books.

Berger, P. L., & Luckmann, T. (1967). *The Social Construction of Reality: A Treatise on the Sociology of Knowledge*. Garden City, NY: Anchor Books.

Berglas, S., & Jones, E. E. (1978). Drug choice as a self-handicapping strategy in response to noncontingent success. *Journal of Personality and Social Psychology*, *36*, 405–417.

Berkowitz, L. (1962). *Aggression: A Social Psychological Analysis*. New York: McGraw-Hill.

Berkowitz, L. (1968, September). Impulse, aggression, and the gun. *Psychology Today*, pp. 18–22.

Berkowitz, L. (1971). *Control of aggression*. Unpublished manuscript, University of Wisconsin.

Berkowitz, L. (1978). Whatever happened to the frustration-aggression hypothesis? *American Behavioral Scientist*, *21*, 691–708.

Berkowitz, L. (1981, June). How guns control us. *Psychology Today*, pp. 11–12.

Berkowitz, L. (1983). Aversively simulated aggression. *American Psychologist*, *38*, 1135–1144.

Berkowitz, L. (1987). Mood, self-awareness, and willingness to help. *Journal of Personality and Social Psychology*, *52*, 721–729.

Berkowitz, L. (1988). Frustrations, appraisals, and aversively stimulated aggression. *Aggressive Behavior*, *14*, 3–11.

Berkowitz, L. (1989). Frustration-aggression hypothesis: Examination and reformulation. *Psychological Bulletin*, *106*, 59–73.

Berkowitz, L. (1993). *Aggression*. New York: McGraw-Hill.

Berkowitz, L., & Frodi, A. (1979). Reactions to a child's mistakes as affected by her/his looks and speech. *Social Psychology Quarterly*, *42*, 420–425.

Berkowitz, L., & Green, J. A. (1962). The stimulus qualities of the scapegoat. *Journal of Abnormal and Social Psychology*, *64*, 293–301.

Berkowitz, L., & LePage, A. (1967). Weapons as aggression-eliciting stimuli. *Journal of Personality and Social Psychology*, *7*, 202–207.

Berkowitz, L., & Troccoli, B., (1990). Feelings, direction of attention, and expressed evaluations of others. *Cognition and Emotion, 4,* 305–325.

Berman, J. S., & Kenny, D. A. (1976). Correlational bias in observer ratings. *Journal of Personality and Social Psychology, 34,* 263–273.

Berry, D. S., & McArthur, L. Z. (1986). Perceiving character in faces: The impact of age-related craniofacial changes in social perception. *Psychological Bulletin, 100,* 3–18.

Berscheid, E. (1983). Emotion. In H. H. Kelley, E. Berscheid, A. Christensen, J. H. Harvey, T. L. Huston, G. Levinger, E. McClintock, L. A. Peplau, & D. R. Peterson (Eds.), *Close relationships.* New York: Freeman.

Berscheid, E. (1985). Interpersonal attraction. In G. Lindzey & E. Aronson (Eds.), *The handbook of social psychology* (pp. 413–484). New York: Random House.

Berscheid, E. (1988). Some comments on love's anatomy: Or, whatever happened to old-fashioned lust? In R. J. Sternberg & M. L. Barnes (Eds.), *The psychology of love* (pp. 359–374). New Haven, CT: Yale University Press.

Berscheid, E., Boye, D., & Walster (Hatfield), E. (1968). Retaliation as a means of restoring equity. *Journal of Personality and Social Psychology, 10,* 370–376.

Berscheid, E., & Peplau, L. A. (1983). The emerging science of relationships. In H. H. Kelley, E. Berscheid, A. Christensen, J. H. Harvey, T. L. Huston, G. Levinger, E. McClintock, L. A. Peplau, & D. R. Peterson (Eds.), *Close relationships* (pp. 1–19). New York: Freeman.

Berscheid, E., Snyder, M., & Omoto, A. M. (1989). Issues in studying close relationships: Conceptualizing and measuring closeness. In C. Hendrick (Ed.), *Close relationships: Review of personality and social psychology* (Vol. 10, pp. 63–91). Newbury Park, CA: Sage.

Berscheid, E., & Walster (Hatfield), E. (1978). *Interpersonal attraction.* Reading, MA: Addison-Wesley.

Bertenthal, B. I., & Fisher, K. W. (1978). Development of self-recognition in the infant. *Developmental Psychology, 14,* 44–50.

Bickman, L. (1974). The social power of a uniform. *Journal of Applied Social Psychology, 4,* 47–61.

Binning, J. F., Goldstein, M. A., Garcia, M. F., & Scatteregia, J. H. (1988). Effects of preinterview impressions on questioning strategies in same- and opposite-sex employment interviews. *Journal of Applied Psychology, 73,* 30–37.

Blaskovich, J., Ginsburg, G. P., & Veach, T. L. (1975). A pluralistic explanation of choice shifts on the risk dimension. *Journal of Personality and Social Psychology, 31,* 422–429.

Blau, P. M. (1964). *Exchange and power in social life.* New York: Wiley.

Bodenhausen, G. V. (1988). Stereotypic biases in social decision making and memory: Testing process models of stereotype use. *Journal of Personality and Social Psychology, 55,* 726–737.

Bodenhausen, G. V., & Lichenstein, M. (1987). Social stereotypes and information-processing strategies. The impact of task complexity. *Journal of Personality and Social Psychology, 52,* 871–880.

Bodenhausen, G. V., & Wyer, R. (1985). Effects of stereotypes on decision making and information processing strategies. *Journal of Personality and Social Psychology, 48,* 267–282.

Boggiano, A. K., Barrett, M., Weiher, A., McClelland, G. J., & Lusk, C. M. (1987). Use of the maximal-operant principle to motivate children's intrinsic interest. *Journal of Personality and Social Psychology, 53,* 866–879.

Bond, C., DiCandia, C., & McKinnon, J. R. (1988). Response to violence in a psychiatric setting. *Personality and Social Psychology Bulletin, 14,* 448–458.

Bond, C. F., & Titus, L. J. (1983). Social facilitation: A meta-analysis of 241 studies. *Psychological Bulletin, 94,* 264–292.

Borgida, E., & Howard-Pitney, B. (1983). Personal involvement and the robustness of perceptual salience effects. *Journal of Personality and Social Psychology, 45,* 560–570.

Bornstein, R. F. (1989). Subliminal techniques as propaganda tools: Review and critique. *Journal of Mind and Behavior, 10,* 231–262.

Bornstein, R. F. (1992). Inhibitory effects of awareness on affective responding: Implications for the affect-cognition relationship. In M. S. Clark (Ed.), *Emotion: Review of personality and social psychology* (Vol. 13, pp. 235–255). Newbury Park, CA: Sage.

Bornstein, R. F., Leone, D. R., & Galley, D. J. (1987). The generalizability of subliminal mere exposure effects: Influence of stimuli perceived without awareness on social behavior. *Journal of Personality and Social Psychology, 53,* 1070–1079.

Bossard, J. H. S. (1932). Residential propinquity as a factor in marriage selection. *American Journal of Sociology, 38,* 219–224.

Bothwell, R. K., Deffenbacher, K. A., & Brigham, J. C. (1987). Correlation of eyewitness accuracy and confidence: Optimality hypothesis revisited. *Journal of Applied Psychology, 72,* 691–695.

Bouchard, T. J. (1972). Training, motivation, and personality as determinants of the effectiveness of brainstorming groups and individuals. *Journal of Applied Psychology, 56,* 324–331.

Bouchard, T. J., Barsaloux, J., & Drauden, G. (1974). Brainstorming procedure, group size, and sex as determinants of the problem-solving effectiveness of groups and individuals. *Journal of Applied Psychology, 59,* 135–138.

Bower, G. H., & Hilgard, E. R. (1981). *Theories of learning* (5th ed.). Englewood Cliffs, NJ: Prentice Hall.

Bowlby, J. (1969). *Attachment and loss: Vol. 1. Attachment.* New York: Basic Books.

Bowlby, J. (1973). *Attachment and loss: Vol. 2. Separation: Anxiety and anger.* New York: Basic Books.

Bowlby, J. (1980). *Attachment and loss: Vol. 3. Loss.* New York: Basic Books.

Boyden, T., Carroll, J. S., & Maier, R. A. (1984). Similarity and attraction in homosexual males: The effects of age and masculinity-femininity. *Sex Roles, 10,* 939–948.

Brandon, R., & Davies, C. (1973). *Wrongful imprisonment: Mistaken convictions and their consequences.* London: Allen & Unwin.

Bransford, J. D., & Johnson, M. K. (1973). Considerations of some problems of comprehension. In W. G. Chase (Ed.), *Visual information processing* (pp. 383–438). New York: Academic Press.

Breckler, S. J. (1984). Empirical validation of affect, behavior, and cognition as distinct components of attitude. *Journal of Personality and Social Psychology*, 47, 1191–1205.

Breckler, S. J., & Wiggins, E. C. (1989). On defining attitude and attitude theory: Once more with feeling. In A. R. Pratkanis, S. J. Breckler, & A. G. Greenwald (Eds.), *Attitude structure and function* (pp.407–427). Hillsdale, NJ: Erlbaum.

Brehm, J. W. (1956). Postdecision changes in the desirability of alternatives. *Journal of Abnormal and Social Psychology*, 52, 384–389.

Brehm, J. W. (1966). *A theory of psychological reactance*. New York: Academic Press.

Brehm, J. W., & Cohen, A. R. (1962). *Explorations in cognitive dissonance*. New York: Wiley.

Brehm, S. S. (1992). *Intimate relationships* (2nd ed.). New York: McGraw-Hill.

Brewer, M. B. (1979). In-group bias in the minimal intergroup situation: A cognitive-motivational analysis. *Psychological Bulletin*, 86, 307–324.

Brewer, M. B., & Miller, N. (1984). Beyond the contact hypothesis: Theoretical perspectives on desegregation. In N. Miller & M. B. Brewer (Eds.), *Groups in Contact: The Psychology of Desegregation*. New York: Academic Press.

Brigham, J. C. (1980). Limiting conditions of the "physical attractiveness stereotype": Attributions about divorce. *Journal of Research in Personality*, 14, 365–375.

Brigham, J. C., Maass, A., Snyder, L. S., & Spaulding, K. (1983). The effect of arousal on facial recognition. *Basic and Applied Social Psychology*, 4, 279–293.

Bringle, R. G. (1981). Conceptualizing jealousy as a disposition. *Alternative Lifestyles*, 4, 274–290.

Brock, T. C., Edelman, S., Edwards, S., & Schuck, J. (1965). Seven studies of performance expectancy as a determinant of actual performance. *Journal of Experimental Social Psychology*, 1, 295–310.

Brophy, J. E. (1983). Research on the self-fulfilling prophecy and teacher expectations. *Journal of Educational Psychology*, 75, 631–661.

Brown, J. D. (1990). Evaluating one's abilities: Shortcuts and stumbling blocks on the road to self-knowledge. *Journal of Experimental Social Psychology*, 26, 149–167.

Brown, R. (1965). *Social psychology*. New York: Free Press.

Brown, R. (1986). *Social psychology: The second edition*. New York: Free Press.

Browning, D. L. (1983). Aspects of authoritarian attitudes in ego development. *Journal of Personality and Social Psychology*, 45, 137–144.

Bruch, H. (1973). *Eating disorders*. New York: Basic Books.

Bruch, H. (1978). *The golden cage*. Cambridge, MA: Harvard University Press.

Buck, R. (1984). *The communication of emotion*. New York: Guilford Press.

Buckhout, R. (1974). Eyewitness testimony. *Scientific American*, 231, 23–31.

Burger, J. M. (1981). Motivational biases in the attribution of responsibility for an accident: A meta-analysis of the defensive-attribution hypothesis. *Psychological Bulletin*, 90, 496–512.

Burger, J. M. (1986). Increasing compliance by improving the deal: The that's-not-all technique. *Journal of Personality and Social Psychology*, 51, 277–283.

Burnstein, E., & Vinokur, A. (1977). Persuasive argumentation and social comparison as determinants of attitude polarization. *Journal of Experimental Social Psychology*, 13, 315–332.

Burnstein, E., & Worchel, P. (1962). Arbitrariness of frustration and its consequences for aggression in a social situation. *Journal of Personality*, 30, 528–540.

Burr, W. R. (1973). *Theory construction and the sociology of the family*. New York: Wiley.

Burt, M. R. (1980). Cultural myths and supports for rape. *Journal of Personality and Social Psychology*, 38, 217–230.

Busby, L. J. (1975). Defining the sex-role standard in commercial network television programming directed at children. *Journalism Quarterly*, 51, 690–696.

Butler, D., & Geis, F. L. (1990). Nonverbal affect responses to male and female leaders: Implications for leadership evaluations. *Journal of Personality and Social Psychology*, 58, 48–59.

Buunk, B. (1982). Anticipated sexual jealousy: Its relationship to self-esteem, dependency, and reciprocity. *Personality and Social Psychology Bulletin*, 8, 310–316.

Buunk, B., & Hupka, R. B. (1987). Cross-cultural differences in the elicitation of sexual jealousy. *Journal of Sex Research*, 23, 12–22.

Byrne, D. (1961). Interpersonal attraction and attitude similarity. *Journal of Abnormal and Social Psychology*, 62, 713–715.

Byrne, D. (1971). *The attraction paradigm*. New York: Academic Press.

Byrne, D., & Clore, G. L. (1970). A reinforcement model of evaluative processes. *Personality: An International Journal*, 1, 103–128.

Byrne, D., Clore, G. L., & Smeaton, G. (1986). The attraction hypothesis: Do similar attitudes affect anything? *Journal of Personality and Social Psychology*, 51, 1167–1170.

Byrne, D., & Nelson, D. (1965). Attraction as a linear function of positive reinforcement. *Journal of Personality and Social Psychology*, 1, 659–663.

Cacioppo, J. T., Marshall-Goodell, B. S., Tassinary, L. G., & Petty, R. E. (1992). Rudimentary determinants of attitudes: Classical conditioning is more effective when prior knowledge about the attitude stimulus is low than high. *Journal of Experimental Social Psychology*, 28, 207–233.

Cafferata, P., & Tybout, A. M. (Eds.). (1989). *Cognitive and affective responses to advertising*. Lexington, MA: Lexington Books.

Calder, B. J., & Staw, B. M. (1975). Self-perception of intrinsic and extrinsic motivation. *Journal of Personality and Social Psychology*, 31, 599–605.

Calhoun, J. B. (1973). Death squared: The explosive growth and demise of a mouse population. *Proceedings of the Royal Society of Medicine*, 66, 80–88.

Callaway, M. R., & Esser, J. K. (1984). Groupthink: Effects of cohesiveness and problem-solving procedures on group decision making. *Social Behavior and Personality*, 12, 157–164.

Calvert, J. D. (1988). Physical attractiveness: A review and reevaluation of its role in social skill research. *Behavioral Assessment*, 10, 29–42.

Campbell, D. T. (1967). Stereotypes and the perception of group differences. *American Psychologist*, 22, 817–829.

Campbell, D. T., & Stanley, J. C. (1967). *Experimental and quasi-experimental designs for research*. Chicago: Rand McNally.

Campbell, E. Q., & Pettigrew, T. F. (1959). Racial and moral crisis: The role of Little Rock ministers. *American Journal of Sociology*, 64, 509–516.

Campbell, J. (1980). Complementarity and attraction: A reconceptualization in terms of dyadic behavior. *Representative Research in Social Psychology*, 11, 74–95.

Campos, J. J., & Sternberg, C. (1981). Perception, appraisal, and emotion: The onset of social referencing. In M. E. Lamb & L. R. Sherrod (Eds.), *Infant social cognition: Empirical and theoretical considerations* (pp. 273–314). Hillsdale, NJ: Erlbaum.

Cannon, W. B. (1942). "Voodoo" death. *American Anthropologist*, 44, 169–181.

Cantor, N., & Kihlstrom, J. F. (1987). *Personality and social intelligence*. Englewood Cliffs, NJ: Prentice Hall.

Cantril, H. (1940). *The invasion from Mars: A study in the psychology of panic*. New York: Harper & Row.

Carlsmith, J. M., & Anderson, C. A. (1979). Ambient temperature and the occurrence of collective violence: A new analysis. *Journal of Personality and Social Psychology*, 37, 337–344.

Carlson, J., & Davis, D. M. (1971). Cultural values and the risky shift: A cross-cultural test in Uganda and the United States. *Journal of Personality and Social Psychology*, 20, 392–399.

Carlson, M., Charlin, V., & Miller, N. (1988). Positive mood and helping behavior: A test of six hypotheses. *Journal of Personality and Social Psychology*, 55, 211–229.

Carlson, M., & Miller, N. (1987). Explanation of the relationship between negative mood and helping. *Psychological Bulletin*, 102, 91–108.

Carlyle, T. (1841). *On heroes, hero-worship, and the heroic in history: Six lectures*. New York: Appleton.

Carnevale, P. J. (1986). Strategic choice in mediation. *Negotiation Journal*, 2, 41–56.

Carretta, T. R., & Moreland, R. L. (1982). Nixon and Watergate: A field demonstration of belief perseverance. *Personality and Social Psychology Bulletin*, 6, 446–453.

Carrier, M. R., Dalessio, A. T., & Brown, S. H. (1990). Correspondence between estimates of content and criterion-related validity values. *Personnel Psychology*, 43, 85–100.

Cartwright, D. (1979). Contemporary social psychology in historical perspective. *Social Psychology Quarterly*, 42, 82–93.

Carver, C. S. (1975). Physical aggression as a function of objective self-awareness and attitudes toward punishment. *Journal of Experimental Social Psychology*, 11, 510–519.

Carver, C. S., DeGregorio, E., & Gillis, R. (1980). Ego-defensive attribution among two categories of observers. *Personality and Social Psychology Bulletin*, 6, 44–50.

Carver, C. S., & Scheier, M. F. (1981). *Attention and self-regulation: A control-theory approach to human behavior*. New York: Springer-Verlag.

Cash, T. F., & Derlega, V. J. (1978). The matching hypothesis: Physical attractiveness among same-sex friends. *Personality and Social Psychology Bulletin*, 4, 240–243.

Chaiken, S. (1980). Heuristic versus systematic information processing and the use of source versus message cues in persuasion. *Journal of Personality and Social Psychology*, 39, 752–766.

Chaiken, S. (1987). The heuristic model of persuasion. In M. P. Zanna, J. M. Olson, & C. P. Herman (Eds.), *Social influence: The Ontario Symposium* (Vol. 5, pp. 3–39). Hillsdale, NJ: Erlbaum.

Chaiken, S., Liberman, A., & Eagly, A. H. (1989). Heuristic and systematic information processing within and beyond the persuasion context. In J. S. Uleman & J. A. Bargh (Eds.), *Unintended thought* (pp. 212–252). New York: Guilford Press.

Chapman, L. J. (1967). Illusory correlation in observational report. *Journal of Verbal Learning and Verbal Behavior*, 6, 151–155.

Chapman, L. J., & Chapman, J. P. (1967). Genesis of popular but erroneous psychodiagnostic observations. *Journal of Abnormal Psychology*, 72, 193–204.

Chassin, L., Presson, C. G., & Sherman, S. J. (1990). Social psychological contributions to the understanding and prevention of adolescent cigarette smoking. *Personality and Social Psychology Bulletin*, 16, 133–151.

Cheek, J. M., & Buss, A. H. (1981). Shyness and sociability. *Journal of Personality and Social Psychology*, 41, 330–339.

Cheek, J. M., & Melchoir, L.A. (1990). Shyness, self-esteem, and self-consciousness. In H. Leitenberg (Ed.), *Handbook of social and evaluation anxiety*. New York: Plenum Press.

Chemers, M. M., Hays, R. G., Rhodewalt, F., & Wysocki, J. (1985). A person-environment analysis of job stress: A contingency model explanation. *Journal of Personality and Social Psychology*, 49, 628–635.

Cheng, P. W., Holyoak, K. J., Nisbett, R. E., & Oliver, L. M. (1986). Pragmatic versus syntactic approaches to training deductive reasoning. *Cognitive Psychology*, 18, 293–328.

Christensen, L. (1988). Deception in psychological research: When is its use justified? *Personality and Social Psychology Bulletin*, 14, 664–675.

Christian, J. J. (1963). The pathology of overpopulation. *Military Medicine*, 128, 571–603.

Christianson, S. (1992). Emotional stress and eyewitness memory: A critical review. *Psychological Bulletin*, 112, 284–309.

Cialdini, R. B. (1988). *Influence: Science and practice* (2nd ed.). New York: HarperCollins.

Cialdini, R. B. (1988). *Influence: Science and practice*. Glenview, IL: Scott, Foresman.

Cialdini, R. B., Borden, R. J., Thorne, A., Walker, M. R., Freeman, S., & Sloan, L. R. (1976). Basking in reflected glory: Three (football) field studies. *Journal of Personality and Social Psychology*, 34, 366–375.

Cialdini, R. B., Darby, B. L., & Vincent, J. E. (1973). Transgression and altruism: A case for hedonism. *Journal of Experimental Social Psychology*, 9, 502–516.

Cialdini, R. B., & Fultz, J. (1990). Interpreting the negative mood-helping literature via "mega"-analysis: A contrary view. *Psychological Bulletin*, 107, 210–214.

Cialdini, R. B., Kallgren, C. A., & Reno, R. R. (1991). A focus theory of normative conduct: A theoretical refinement and reevaluation of the role of norms in human behavior. In M. P. Zanna (Ed.), *Advances in experimental social psychology* (Vol. 24, pp. 201–234). San Diego, CA: Academic Press.

Cialdini, R. B., Reno, R. R., & Kallgren, C. A. (1990). A focus theory of normative conduct: Recycling the concept of norms to reduce littering in public places. *Journal of Personality and Social Psychology, 58,* 1015–1026.

Cialdini, R. B., Schaller, M., Houlihan, D., Arps, K., Fultz, J., & Beaman, A. L. (1987). Empathy-based helping: Is it selflessly or selfishly motivated? *Journal of Personality and Social Psychology, 52,* 749–758.

Cialdini, R. B., Vincent, J. E., Lewis, S. K., Catalan, J., Wheeler, D., & Darby, B. L. (1975). Reciprocal concessions procedure for inducing compliance: The door-in-the-face technique. *Journal of Personality and Social Psychology, 31,* 206–215.

Cialdini, R. L., Cacioppo, J., Basset, R., & Miller, J. (1978). Low-ball procedure for producing compliance: Commitment then cost. *Journal of Personality and Social Psychology, 36,* 463–476.

Clark, K., & Clark, M. (1947). Racial identification and preference in Negro children. In T. M. Newcomb & E. L. Hartley (Eds.), *Readings in social psychology* (pp. 169–178). New York: Holt.

Clark, M. S. (1984). Record keeping in two types of relationships. *Journal of Personality and Social Psychology, 47,* 549–577.

Clark, M. S. (1986). Evidence of the effectiveness of manipulations of communal and exchange relationships. *Personality and Social Psychology Bulletin, 12,* 414–425.

Clark, M. S., & Isen, A. M. (1982). Toward understanding the relationship between feeling states and social behavior. In A. H. Hastorf & A. M. Isen (Eds.), *Cognitive social psychology* (pp. 73–108). New York: Elsevier.

Clark, M. S., & Mills, J. (1979). Interpersonal attraction in exchange and communal relationships. *Journal of Personality and Social Psychology, 37,* 12–24.

Clark, M. S., Mills, J., & Corcoran, D. M. (1989). Keeping track of needs and inputs of friends and strangers. *Personality and Social Psychology Bulletin, 15,* 533–542.

Clark, M. S., Ouellette, R., Powell, M. C., & Milberg, S. (1987). Recipient's mood, relationship type, and helping. *Journal of Personality and Social Psychology, 53,* 94–103.

Clark, M. S., & Waddell, B. (1985). Perception of exploitation in communal and exchange relationships. *Journal of Social and Personal Relationships, 2,* 403–413.

Clark, R. D. III, & Maass, A. (1988). The role of social categorization and perceived source credibility in minority influence. *European Journal of Social Psychology, 18,* 347–364.

Clark, R. D. III, & Word, L. E. (1972). Why don't bystanders help? Because of ambiguity? *Journal of Personality and Social Psychology, 24,* 392–400.

Clarke, A. C. (1952). An examination of the operation of residual propinquity as a factor in mate selection. *American Sociological Review, 27,* 17–22.

Cline, V. B., Croft, R. G., & Courrier, S. (1973). Desensitization of children to television violence. *Journal of Personality and Social Psychology, 27,* 360–365.

Cody, M. J. (1982). A typology of disengagement strategies and an examination of the role intimacy reactions to inequity and relational problems play in strategy selection. *Communication Monographs, 49,* 148–170.

Cohen, A. R. (1962). An experiment on small rewards for discrepant compliance and attitude change. In J. W. Brehm & A. R. Cohen (Eds.), *Explorations in cognitive dissonance* (pp. 73–78). New York: Wiley.

Cohen, C. E. (1981). Person categories and social perception: Testing some boundary conditions of the processing effects of prior knowledge. *Journal of Personality and Social Psychology, 40,* 441–452.

Cohen, C. E. (1983). Inferring the characteristics of other people: Categories and attribute accessibility. *Journal of Personality and Social Psychology, 44,* 34–44.

Cohen, D. (Ed.). (1977). *Psychologists on psychology.* New York: Taplinger.

Cohen, D. J., Whitmyer, J. W., & Funk, W. H. (1960). Effect of group cohesiveness and training upon group thinking. *Journal of Applied Psychology, 44,* 319–322.

Cohen, L. J. (1981). Can human rationality be experimentally demonstrated? *The Behavioral and Brain Sciences, 4,* 317–370.

Cohen, S. (1978). Environmental load and the allocation of attention. In A. Baum, J. S. Singer, & S. Valins (Eds.), *Advances in environmental psychology* (Vol. 1, pp. 1–29). Hillsdale, NJ: Erlbaum.

Cohen, S., Evans, G. W., Krantz, D. S., & Stokols, D. (1980). Physiological, motivational, and cognitive effects of aircraft noise on children. *American Psychologist, 35,* 231–243.

Cohen, S., Evans, G. W., Krantz, D. S., Stokols, D., & Kelly, S. (1981). Aircraft noise and children: Longitudinal and cross-sectional evidence on adaptation to noise and the effectiveness of noise abatement. *Journal of Personality and Social Psychology, 40,* 331–345.

Cohen, S., Glass, D. C., & Singer, J. E. (1973). Apartment noise, auditory discrimination, and reading ability in children. *Journal of Experimental Social Psychology, 9,* 407–422.

Cohen, S., Tyrrell, D. A. J., & Smith, A. P. (1991). Psychological stress in humans and susceptibility to the common cold. *New England Journal of Medicine, 325,* 606–612.

Cohen, S., & Williamson, G. M. (1991). Stress and infectious disease in humans. *Psychological Bulletin, 109,* 5–24.

Cole, B. L. (1991, September 15). I greet each day as a gift. *Parade Magazine,* pp. 20–21.

Colligan, M. J., & Murphy, L. R. (1979). Mass psychogenic illness in organizations: An overview. *Journal of Occupational Psychology, 52,* 77–90.

Colligan, M. J., Pennebaker, J. W., & Murphy, L. R. (Eds.). (1982). *Mass psychogenic illness: A social psychological analysis.* Hillsdale, NJ: Erlbaum.

Collins, N. L., & Read, S. J. (1990). Adult attachment, working models, and relationship quality in dating couples. *Journal of Personality and Social Psychology, 58,* 644–663.

Coltrane, S., Archer, D., & Aronson, E. (1986). The social-psychological foundations of successful energy conservation programs. *Energy Policy, 14,* 133–148.

Condon, J. W., & Crano, W. D. (1988). Inferred evaluation and the relation between attitude similarity and interpersonal attraction. *Journal of Personality and Social Psychology, 54,* 789–797.

Conway, M., & Ross, M. (1984). Getting what you want by revising what you had. *Journal of Personality and Social Psychology, 47,* 738–748.

Cook, S. W. (1984). Cooperative interaction in multiethnic contexts. In N. Miller & M. Brewer (Eds.), *Groups in Contact: The Psychology of Desegregation.* New York: Academic Press.

Cook, S. W. (1985). Experimenting on social issues: The case of school desegration. *American Psychologist, 40,* 452–460.

Cooley, C. H. (1902). *Human nature and social order.* New York: Scribner's.

Cooper, J. (1980). Reducing fears and increasing assertiveness: The role of dissonance reduction. *Journal of Experimental Social Psychology, 47,* 738–748.

Cotton, J. L. (1981). *Ambient temperature and violent crime.* Paper presented at the Midwestern Psychological Association convention in Chicago.

Cotton, J. L. (1986). Ambient temperature and violent crime. *Journal of Applied Social Psychology, 16,* 786–801.

Cottrell, N. B., Wack, K. L., Sekerak, G. J., & Rittle, R. (1968). Social facilitation in dominant responses by the presence of an audience and the mere presence of others. *Journal of Personality and Social Psychology, 9,* 245–250.

Courtright, J. A. (1978). A laboratory investigation of groupthink. *Communication Monographs, 45,* 229–246.

Crocker, J. (1981). Judgment of covariation by social perceivers. *Psychological Bulletin, 90,* 272–292.

Crocker, J., Hannah, D. B., & Weber, R. (1983). Personal memory and causal attributions. *Journal of Personality and Social Psychology, 44,* 55–56.

Crocker, J., & Major, B. (1989). Social stigma and self-esteem: The self-protective properties of stigma. *Psychological Review, 96,* 608-630.

Crosby, F., Bromley, S., & Saxe, L. (1980). Recent unobtrusive studies of black and white discrimination and prejudice: A literature review. *Psychological Bulletin, 87,* 546–563.

Crouse, B. B., & Mehrabian, A. (1977). Affiliation of opposite-sexed strangers. *Journal of Research in Personality, 11,* 38–47.

Croyle, R., & Cooper, J. (1983). Dissonance arousal: Physiological evidence. *Journal of Personality and Social Psychology, 45,* 782–791.

Croyle, R. T., & Jemmott, J. B. III. (1990). Psychological reactions to risk factor testing. In J. A. Skelton & R. T. Croyle (Eds.), *The mental representation of health and illness* (pp. 121–157). New York: Springer-Verlag.

Crutchfield, R. A. (1955). Conformity and character. *American Psychologist, 10,* 191–198.

Csikszentmihalyi, M. (1975). *Beyond boredom and anxiety.* San Francisco: Jossey-Bass.

Csikszentmihalyi, M. (1979). The concept of flow. In B. Sutton-Smith (Ed.), *Play and Learning.* New York: Gardner Press.

Csikszentmihalyi, M., & Figurski, T. J. (1982). Self-awareness and aversive experience in everyday life. *Journal of Personality, 50,* 15–28.

Curtis, R. C., & Miller, K. (1986). Believing another likes or dislikes you: Behaviors making the beliefs come true. *Journal of Personality and Social Psychology, 51,* 284–290.

Curtiss, S. (1977). *Genie: A psycholinguistic study of a modern-day "wild child".* New York: Academic Press.

Dabbs, J. M., Jr., Ruback, R. B., Frady, R. L., Hopper, C. H., & Sgoutas, D. S. (1988). Saliva testosterone and criminal violence among women. *Personality and Individual Differences, 7,* 269–275.

Darley, J. M., & Akert, R. M. (1991). *Biographical interpretation: The influence of later events in life on the meaning of and memory for earlier events.* Unpublished manuscript.

Darley, J. M., & Akert, R. M. (1993). *Biographical interpretation: The influence of later events in life on the meaning of and memory for earlier events.* Unpublished manuscript, Princeton University.

Darley, J. M., & Batson, C. D. (1973). From Jerusalem to Jericho: A study of situational and dispositional variables in helping behavior. *Journal of Personality and Social Psychology, 27,* 100–108.

Darley, J. M., & Fazio, R. H. (1980). Expectancy confirmation processes arising in the social interaction sequence. *American Psychologist, 35,* 867–881.

Darley, J. M., Fleming, J. H., Hilton, J. L., & Swann, W. B., Jr. (1988). Dispelling negative expectancies: The impact of interaction goals and target characteristics on the expectancy confirmation process. *Journal of Experimental Social Psychology, 24,* 19–36.

Darley, J. M., & Gilbert, D. T. (1985). Social psychological aspects of environmental psychology. In G. Lindzey & E. Aronson (Eds.), *Handbook of social psychology* (3rd ed., Vol. 2, pp. 949–991). New York: Random House.

Darley, J. M., & Gross, P. H. (1983). A hypothesis-confirming bias in labeling effects. *Journal of Personality and Social Psychology, 44,* 20–33.

Darley, J. M., & Latané, B. (1968). Bystander intervention in emergencies: Diffusion of responsibility. *Journal of Personality and Social Psychology, 8,* 377–383.

Darwin, C. (1872). *The expression of emotions in man and animals.* London: John Murray.

Darwin, C. R. (1859). *The origin of species.* London: Murray.

Davidson, A. R., & Jaccard, J. J. (1979). Variables that moderate the attitude-behavior relation: Results of a longitudinal survey. *Journal of Personality and Social Psychology, 37,* 1364–1376.

Davies, R. (1988). *The lyre of Orpheus.* New York: Penguin Books.

Davis, K. E., & Jones, E. E. (1960). Changes in interpersonal perception as a means of reducing cognitive dissonance. *Journal of Abnormal and Social Psychology, 61,* 402–410.

Davis, M. H., & Stephan, W. G. (1980). Attributions for exam performance. *Journal of Applied Social Psychology, 10,* 235–248.

Davitz, J. (1952). The effects of previous training on post-frustration behavior. *Journal of Abnormal and Social Psychology, 47,* 309–315.

Dawes, R. M. (1980). Social dilemmas. *Annual Review of Psychology, 31,* 169–193.

Dawkins, R. (1976). *The selfish gene.* New York: Oxford University Press.

Deaux, K., & Emswiler, T. (1974). Explanations of successful performance of sex-linked tasks: What is skill for male is luck for the female. *Journal of Personality and Social Psychology, 29,* 80–85.

Deaux, K., & Major, B. (1987). Putting gender into context: An interactive model of gender-related behavior. *Psychological Review, 94,* 369–389.

Deci, E. L., & Ryan, R. M. (1985). *Intrinsic motivation and self-determination in human behavior.* New York: Plenum.

Deffenbacher, K. (1983). The influence of arousal on reliability of testimony. In S. Lloyd-Bostock & B. Clifford (Eds.), *Evaluating witness testimony* (pp. 235–251). London: Wiley

DeJong, W. (1979). An examination of self-perception mediation of the foot-in-the-door effect. *Journal of Personality and Social Psychology, 37,* 2221–2239.

DeJong, W., & Winsten, J. A. (1989). *Recommendations for future mass media campaigns to prevent preteen and adolescent substance abuse.* Unpublished manuscript, Center for Health Communication, Harvard School of Public Health.

Dennett, D. C. (1991). *Consciousness explained.* Boston: Little, Brown.

DePaulo, B. M. (1983). Perspectives on help-seeking. In B. M. DePaulo, A. Nadler, & J. D. Fisher (Eds.), *New directions in helping: Help seeking* (Vol. 2, pp. 3–12). New York: Academic Press.

DePaulo, B. M. (1992). Nonverbal behavior and self-presentation. *Psychological Bulletin, 111,* 203–243.

DePaulo, B. M., Kenny, D. A., Hoover, C. W., Webb, W., & Oliver, P. (1987). Accuracy of person perception: Do people know what kinds of impressions they convey? *Journal of Personality and Social Psychology, 52,* 303–315.

DePaulo, B. M., & Pfeiffer, R. L. (1986). On-the-job experience and skill at detecting deception. *Journal of Applied Social Psychology, 16,* 249–267.

DePaulo, B. M., & Rosenthal, R. (1979). Telling lies. *Journal of Personality and Social Psychology, 37,* 1713–1722.

DePaulo, B. M., Stone, J. I., & Lassiter, G. D. (1985). Deceiving and detecting deceit. In B. R. Schlenker (Ed.), *The self and social life* (pp. 323–370). New York: McGraw-Hill.

DePaulo, B. M., Tang, J., Webb, W., Hoover, C., March, K., & Litowitz, C. (1989). Age differences in reactions to help in a peer tutoring context. *Child Development, 60,* 423–439.

Dermer, M., & Thiel, D. L. (1975). When beauty may fail. *Journal of Personality and Social Psychology, 31,* 1168–1176.

Desmond, E. W. (1987, November 30). Out in the open. *Time,* pp. 80–90.

Deutsch, F. M., & Lamberti, D. M. (1986). Does social approval increase helping? *Personality and Social Psychology Bulletin, 12,* 149–157.

Deutsch, M. (1973). *The resolution of conflict: Constructive and destructive processes.* New Haven, CT: Yale University Press.

Deutsch, M., & Gerard, H. G. (1955). A study of normative and informational social influence upon individual judgment. *Journal of Abnormal and Social Psychology, 51,* 629–636.

Deutsch, M., & Krauss, R. M. (1960). The effect of threat upon interpersonal bargaining. *Journal of Abnormal and Social Psychology, 61,* 181–189.

Deutsch, M., & Krauss, R. M. (1962). Studies of interpersonal bargaining. *Journal of Conflict Resolution, 6,* 52–76.

Devine, P. G. (1989a). Automatic and controlled processes in prejudice: The roles of stereotypes and personal beliefs. In A. R. Pratkanis, S. J. Breckler, & A. G. Greenwald (Eds.), *Attitude structure and function* (pp. 181–212). Hillsdale, NJ: Erlbaum.

Devine, P. G. (1989b). Stereotypes and prejudice: Their automatic and controlled components. *Journal of Personality and Social Psychology, 56,* 5–18.

Dickerson, C., Thibodeau, R., Aronson, E., & Miller, D. (1992). Using cognitive dissonance to encourage water conservation. *Journal of Applied Social Psychology, 22,* 841–854.

Diddling the subconscious: Subliminal advertising. (1957, October 5). *Nation,* p. 206.

Diehl, M., & Stroebe, W. (1987). Productivity loss in brainstorming groups: Toward the solution of a riddle. *Journal of Personality and Social Psychology, 53,* 497–509.

Diener, E. (1980). Deindividuation: The absence of self-awareness and self-regulation in group members. In P. B. Paulus (Ed.), *Psychology of group influence* (pp. 209–242). Hillsdale, NJ: Erlbaum.

Diener, E., & Wallbom, M. (1976). Effects of self-awareness on antinormative behavior. *Journal of Research in Personality, 10,* 107–111.

Dietz, P. D., & Evans, B. E. (1982). Pornographic imagery and prevalence of paraphilia. *American Journal of Psychiatry, 139,* 1493–1495.

Dillard, J. P., Hunter, J. E., & Burgoon, M. (1984). Sequential-request persuasive strategies: Metaanalysis of foot-in-the-door and door-in-the-face. *Human Communications Research, 10,* 461–488.

Dion, K. (1972). Physical attractiveness and evaluations of children's transgressions. *Journal of Personality and Social Psychology, 24,* 207–213.

Dion, K., Berscheid, E., & Walster (Hatfield), E. (1972). What is beautiful is good. *Journal of Personality and Social Psychology, 24,* 285–290.

Dodd, D. K. (1985). Robbers in the classroom: A deindividuation exercise. *Teaching of Psychology, 12,* 89–91.

Dodge, M. K. (1984). Learning to care: Developing prosocial behavior among one- and two-year-olds in group settings. *Journal of Research and Development in Education, 17,* 26–30.

Dollard, J. (1938). Hostility and fear in social life. *Social Forces, 17,* 15–26.

Dollard, J., Doob, L., Miller, N., Mowrer, O. H., & Sears, R. R. (1939). *Frustration and aggression.* New Haven, CT: Yale University Press.

Donnerstein, E. (1980). Aggressive erotica and violence against women. *Journal of Personality and Social Psychology, 39,* 269–277.

Donnerstein, E., & Berkowitz, L. (1981). Victim reactions in aggressive erotic films as a factor in violence against women. *Journal of Personality and Social Psychology, 41,* 710–724.

Donnerstein, E., & Donnerstein, M. (1976). Research in the control of interracial aggression. In R. G. Green & E. C. O'Neal (Eds.), *Perspectives on aggression.* New York: Academic Press.

Donnerstein, E., Linz, D., & Penrod, S. (1987). *The question of pornography: Research findings and policy implications.* New York: Free Press.

Dovidio, J. F., Evans, N., & Tyler, R. B. (1986). Racial stereotypes: The contents of their cognitive representations. *Journal of Experimental Social Psychology, 22,* 22–37.

Dovidio, J. F., Piliavin, J. A., Gaertner, S. I., Schroeder, D. A., & Clark, R. D. III. (1991). The arousal: Cost-reward model and the process of intervention. In M. S. Clark (Ed.), *Review of personality and social psychology* (Vol. 12, pp. 86–118). Newbury Park, CA: Sage.

Druckerman, D. (1968). Ethnocentrism in the inter-nation simulation. *Journal of Conflict Resolution, 12,* 45–68.

Duck, S. (1982). A typography of relationship disengagement and dissolution. In S. Duck (Ed.), *Personal relationships 4: Dissolving personal relationships.* London: Academic Press.

Duke: The ex-Nazi who would be governor. (1991, November 10). *New York Times,* pp. 1, 26.

Dunn, D. S., & Wilson, T. D. (1990). When the stakes are high: A limit to the illusion of control effect. *Social Cognition, 8,* 305–323.

Dunning, D., Griffin, D. W., Milojkovic, J., & Ross, L. (1990). The overconfidence effect in social prediction. *Journal of Personality and Social Psychology, 58,* 568–581.

Duryea, E. J., & Okwumabua, J. O. (1988). Effects of a preventive alcohol education program after three years. *Journal of Drug Education, 18,* 23–31.

Dutton, D. G., & Aron, A. P. (1974). Some evidence for heightened sexual attraction under conditions of high anxiety. *Journal of Personality and Social Psychology, 30,* 510–517.

Duval, S., & Wicklund, R. A. (1972). *A theory of objective self-awareness.* New York: Academic Press.

Duval, S., & Wicklund, R. A. (1975). *A theory of objective self-awareness.* New York: Academic Press.

Eagly, A. H. (1987). *Sex differences in social behavior: A social role interpretation.* Hillsdale, NJ: Erlbaum.

Eagly, A. H., Ashmore, R. D., Makhijani, M. G., & Longo, L. C. (1991). What is beautiful is good, but . . . : A meta-analytic review of research on the physical attractiveness stereotype. *Psychological Bulletin, 110,* 109–128.

Eagly, A. H., & Carli, L. L. (1981). Sex of researchers and sex-typed communications as determinants of sex differences in influenceability: A meta-analysis of social influence studies. *Psychological Bulletin, 90,* 1–20.

Eagly, A. H., & Chaiken, S. (1975). An attribution analysis of communicator characteristics on opinion change: The case of communicator attractiveness. *Journal of Personality and Social Psychology, 32,* 136–244.

Eagly, A. H., & Chaiken, S. (1993). *The psychology of attitudes.* Fort Worth, TX: Harcourt Brace Jovanovich.

Eagly, A. H., & Crowley, M. (1986). Gender and helping behavior: A meta-analytic review of the social psychological literature. *Psychological Bulletin, 100,* 283–308.

Eagly, A. H., & Johnson, B. T. (1990). Gender and leadership style: A meta-analysis. *Psychological Bulletin, 108,* 233–256.

Eagly, A. H., & Karau, S. J. (1991). Gender and the emergence of leaders: A meta-analysis. *Journal of Personality and Social Psychology, 60,* 685–710.

Eagly, A. H., Makhijani, M. G., & Klonsky, B. G. (1992). Gender and the evaluation of leaders: A meta-analysis. *Psychological Bulletin, 111,* 3–22.

Eagly, A. H., & Steffen, V. J. (1986). Gender and aggressive behavior: A meta-analytic review of the social psychological literature. *Psychological Bulletin, 100,* 309–330.

Eagly, A. H., & Wood, W. (1991). Explaining sex differences in social behavior: A meta-analytic perspective. *Personality and Social Psychology Bulletin, 17,* 306–315.

Ebbesen, E. B., & Bowers, R. J. (1974). Proportion of risky to conservative arguments in a group discussion and choice shift. *Journal of Personality and Social Psychology, 29,* 316–327.

Ebbesen, E., Duncan, B., & Konecni, V. (1975). Effects of content of verbal aggression: A field experiment. *Journal of Experimental and Social Psychology, 11,* 192–204.

Economos, J. (1989). Altruism, nativism, chauvinism, racism, schism, and jizzum. *Behavioral and Brain Sciences, 12,* 521–523.

Edwards, K. (1990). The interplay of affect and cognition in attitude formation and change. *Journal of Personality and Social Psychology, 59,* 202–216.

Edwards, W. (1968). Conservatism in human information processing. In B. Kleinmutz (Ed.), *Formal representation of human judgment* (pp. 17–52). New York: Wiley.

Eibl-Eibesfeldt, I. (1963). Aggressive behavior and ritualized fighting in animals. In J. H. Masserman (Ed.), *Science and psychoanalysis, Vol. VI. Violence and war.* New York: Grune & Stratton.

Eisenberg, N., & Fabes, R. A. (1991). Prosocial behavior and empathy: A multimethod developmental perspective. In M. S. Clark (Ed.), *Review of personality and social psychology* (Vol. 12, pp. 34–61). Newbury Park, CA: Sage.

Ekman, P. (1965). Communication through nonverbal behavior: A source of information about an interpersonal relationship. In S. S. Tomkins & C. E. (Eds.), *Affect, cognition, and personality* (pp. 390–442). New York: Springer-Verlag.

Ekman, P. (1985). *Telling lies.* New York: Norton.

Ekman, P. (1992). *Telling lies: Clues to deceit in the marketplace, politics, and marriage* (rev. ed.). New York: Norton.

Ekman, P., & Friesen, W. V. (1969). The repertoire of nonverbal behavior: Categories, origins, usage, and coding. *Semiotica, 1,* 49–98.

Ekman, P., & Friesen, W. V. (1971). Constants across cultures in the face and emotion. *Journal of Personality and Social Psychology, 17,* 124–129.

Ekman, P., & Friesen, W. V. (1975). *Unmasking the face.* Englewood Cliffs, NJ: Prentice Hall.

Ekman, P., Friesen, W. V., & Ellsworth, P. (1982a). Does the face provide accurate information? In P. Ekman (Ed.), *Emotion in the Human Face* (pp. 56–97). Cambridge, England: Cambridge University Press.

Ekman, P., Friesen, W.V., & Ellsworth, P. (1982b). What are the similarities and differences in facial behavior across cultures? In P. Ekman (Ed.), *Emotion in the Human Face* (pp. 128–143). Cambridge: Cambridge University Press.

Ekman, P., Friesen, W. V., O'Sullivan, M., Chan, A., Diacoyanni-Tarlatzis, I., Heider, K., Krause, R., LeCompre, W. A., Pitcairn, T., Ricci-Bitti, P. E., Scherer, K., Tomita, M., & Tzavras, A. (1987). Universals and cultural differences in the judgments of facial expressions of emotions. *Journal of Personality and Social Psychology*, *53*, 712–717.

Ekman, P., & O'Sullivan, M. (1991). Who can catch a liar? *American Psychologist*, *46*, 913–920.

Elig, T. W., & Frieze, I. H. (1979). Measuring causal attributions for success and failure. *Journal of Personality and Social Psychology*, *38*, 270–277.

Elliot, G. R., & Eisdorfer, C. (1982). *Stress and human health: Analysis and implications of research.* New York: Springer.

Elms, A. C., & Milgram, S. (1966). Personality characteristics associated with obedience and defiance toward authoritative command. *Journal of Experimental Research in Personality*, *1*, 282–289.

Emerson, R. W. (1929). *The complete works of Ralph Waldo Emerson.* New York: Wm. H. Wise.

Emery, R. E., Matthews, S. G., & Wyer, M. M. (1991). Child custody mediation and litigation: Further evidence on the differing views of mothers and fathers. *Journal of Consulting and Clinical Psychology*, *59*, 410–418.

Emery, R. E., & Wyer, M. M. (1987). Divorce mediation. *American Psychologist*, *42*, 472–480.

Emswiller, T., Deaux, K., & Willits, J. E. (1971). Similarity, sex, and requests for favors. *Journal of Applied Social Psychology*, *1*, 284–291.

Eron, L. D. (1982). Parent-child interaction, television violence, and aggression of children. *American Psychologist*, *37*, 197–211.

Eron, L. D. (1987). The development of aggressive behavior from the perspective of a developing behaviorism. *American Psychologist*, *42*, 425–442.

Falck, R., & Craig, R. (1988). Classroom-oriented, primary prevention programming for drug abuse. *Journal of Psychoactive Drugs*, *20*, 403–408.

Faranda, J. A., Kaminski, J. A., & Giza, B. K. (1979). *An assessment of attitudes toward women with the bogus pipeline.* Paper presented at the American Psychological Association convention.

Fazio, R. H. (1989). On the power and functionality of attitudes: The role of attitude accessibility. In A. R. Pratkanis, S. J. Breckler, & A. G. Greenwald (Eds.), *Attitude structure and function* (pp. 153–179). Hillsdale, NJ: Erlbaum.

Fazio, R. H. (1990). Multiple processes by which attitudes guide behavior: The MODE model as an integrative framework. In M. P. Zanna (Ed.), *Advances in experimental social psychology* (Vol. 23, pp. 75–109). San Diego: Academic Press.

Fazio, R. H. (in press). Attitudes as object-evaluation associations: Determinants, consequences, and correlates of attitude accessibility. In R. Petty, & J. Krosnick (Ed.), *Attitude strength: Antecedents and consequences.* Hillsdale, NJ: Erlbaum.

Fazio, R. H., Effrein, E. A., & Falender, V. J. (1981). Self-perceptions following social interaction. *Journal of Personality and Social Psychology*, *41*, 232–242.

Fazio, R. H., Powell, M. C., & Williams, C. J. (1989). The role of attitude accessibility in the attitude-to-behavior process. *Journal of Consumer Research*, *16*, 280–288.

Fazio, R. H., Sanbonmatsu, D. M., Powell, M. C., & Kardes, F. R. (1986). On the automatic activation of attitudes. *Journal of Personality and Social Psychology*, *50*, 229–238.

Fazio, R. H., & Zanna, M. P. (1981). Direct experience and attitude-behavior consistency. In L. Berkowitz (Ed.), *Advances in experimental social psychology* (Vol. 14, pp. 162–202). New York: Academic Press.

Fazio, R. H., Zanna, M. P., & Cooper, J. (1977). Dissonance and self-perception: An integrative view of each theory's proper domain of application. *Journal of Experimental Social Psychology*, *13*, 464–479.

Feeney, J. A., & Noller, P. (1990). Attachment style as a predictor of adult romantic relationships. *Journal of Personality and Social Psychology*, *58*, 281–291.

Feldman-Summers, S., & Kiesler, S. B. (1974). Those who are number two try harder: The effect of sex on attributions of causality. *Journal of Personality and Social Psychology*, *38*, 846–855.

Feshbach, N. (1978, March). *Empathy training: A field study in affective education.* Paper presented at the meetings of the American Educational Research Association, Toronto, Ontario, Canada.

Feshbach, N., & Feshbach, S. (1969). The relationship between empathy and aggression in two age groups. *Developmental Psychology*, *1*, 102–107.

Feshbach, S. (1971). Dynamics and morality of violence and aggression: Some psychological considerations. *American Psychologist*, *26*, 281–292.

Festinger, L. (1954). A theory of social comparison processes. *Human Relations*, *7*, 117–140.

Festinger, L. (1957). *A theory of cognitive dissonance.* Stanford, CA: Stanford University Press.

Festinger, L. (1980). Looking backward. In L. Festinger (Ed.), *Retrospections on social psychology* (pp. 236–254). New York: Oxford University Press.

Festinger, L., & Aronson, E. (1960). The arousal and reduction of dissonance in social contexts. In D. Cartwright & A. Zander (Eds.), *Group dynamics* (pp. 214–231). Evanston, IL: Row, Peterson.

Festinger, L., & Carlsmith, J. M. (1959). Cognitive consequences of forced compliance. *Journal of Abnormal and Social Psychology*, *58*, 203–211.

Festinger, L., & Maccoby, N. (1964). On resistance to persuasive communications. *Journal of Abnormal and Social Psychology*, *68*, 359–366.

Festinger, L., Riecken, H. W., & Schachter, S. (1956). *When prophecy fails.* Minneapolis: University of Minnesota Press.

Festinger, L., Schachter, S., & Back, K. (1950). *Social pressures in informal groups: A study of human factors in housing.* New York: Harper & Bros.

Festinger, L., & Thibaut, J. (1951). Interpersonal communication in small groups. *Journal of Abnormal and Social Psychology*, *46*, 92–99.

Fiedler, F. (1967). *A theory of leadership effectiveness.* New York: McGraw-Hill.

Fiedler, F. (1978). The contingency model and the dynamics of the leadership process. L. Berkowitz (Ed.), *Advances in experimental social psychology* (Vol. 11, pp. 59–112). Orlando, FL: Academic Press.

Fincher, J. (1981, October). Presumed guilty: The ordeal of Robert Dillen. *Reader's Digest*, pp. 104–109.

Finckenauer, J. O. (1979). *Juvenile awareness project, evaluation report no. 2.* Unpublished manuscript, Rutgers University.

Fischhoff, B. (1975). Hindsight≠foresight: The effect of outcome knowledge on judgment under uncertainty. *Journal of Experimental Psychology: Human Perception and Performance, 1,* 288–299.

Fishbein, M., & Ajzen, I. (1975). *Belief, attitude, intention, and behavior: An introduction to theory and research.* Reading, MA: Addison-Wesley.

Fisher, J. D., & Nadler, A. (1974). The effect of similarity between donor and recipient on recipient reactions to aid. *Journal of Applied Social Psychology, 4,* 230–243.

Fiske, S. T. (1989). *Interdependence and stereotyping: From the laboratory to the Supreme Court (and back).* Invited address, American Psychological Association, New Orleans.

Fiske, S. T., & Taylor, S. E. (1991). *Social Cognition* (2nd. ed.). New York: McGraw-Hill.

Flink, C., & Park, B. (1991). Increasing consensus in trait judgments through outcome dependency. *Journal of Experimental Social Psychology, 27,* 453–467.

Flowers, M. L. (1977). A lab test of some implications of Janis' groupthink hypothesis. *Journal of Personality and Social Psychology, 35,* 888–897.

Fong, G. T., Krantz, D. H., & Nisbett, R. E. (1986). The effects of statistical training on thinking about everyday problems. *Cognitive Psychology, 18,* 253–292.

Ford, C. S., & Beach, F. A. (1952). *Patterns of sexual behavior.* New York: Ace Books.

Forgas, J. P., & Bower, G. H. (1987). Mood effects on person-perception judgments. *Journal of Personality and Social Psychology, 53,* 53–60.

Forsterling, F. (1989). Models of covariation and attribution: How do they relate to the analogy of analysis of variance? *Journal of Personality and Social Psychology, 57,* 615–625.

Four year study of girls shows concern over weight (A). *Boston Globe* (1992, January 5; West Weekly Section), pp. 1, 4.

Frager, R. (1970). Conformity and anticonformity in Japan. *Journal of Personality and Social Psychology, 15,* 203–210.

Frank, J. D. (1978). *Psychotherapy and the human predicament: A psychosocial approach.* P. E. Dietz, Editor. New York: Schocken Books.

Freedman, D., Pisani, R., Purves, R., & Adhikari, A. (1991). *Statistics* (2nd ed.). New York: Norton.

Freedman, J. (1965). Long-term behavioral effects of cognitive dissonance. *Journal of Experimental and Social Psychology, 1,* 145–155.

Freedman, J. L., & Fraser, S. C. (1966). Compliance without pressure: The foot-in-the-door technique. *Journal of Personality and Social Psychology, 4,* 195–202.

Freud, S. (1930). *Civilization and its discontents* (Joan Riviere, Trans.). London: Hogarth Press.

Freud, S. (1933). *New introductory lectures on psycho-analysis.* New York: Norton.

Friedman, L. (1977). *Sex-Role Stereotyping in the Mass Media: An Annotated Bibliography.* New York: Garland Press.

Friesen, W. V. (1972). *Cultural differences in facial expressions in a social situation: An experimental test of the concept of display rules.* Unpublished dissertation, University of California, San Francisco.

Funder, D. C., & Colvin, C. R. (1988). Friends and strangers: Acquaintanceship, agreement, and the accuracy of personality judgment. *Journal of Personality and Social Psychology, 55,* 149–158.

Furnham, A., & Gunter, B. (1984). Just world beliefs and attitudes toward the poor. *British Journal of Social Psychology, 23,* 265–269.

Gaertner, S. L., & Dovidio, J. F. (1986). The aversive form of racism. In J. F. Dovidio & S. L. Gaertner (Eds.), *Prejudice, Discrimination, and Racism: Theory and Research.* New York: Academic Press.

Gallo, P. S., Jr. (1966). Effects of increased incentives upon the use of threat in bargaining. *Journal of Personality and Social Psychology, 4,* 14–20.

Gallup, G. G., (1977). Self-recognition in primates: A comparative approach to the bidirectional properties of consciousness. *American Psychologist, 32,* 329–338.

Gallup, G. G., & Suarez, S. D. (1986). Self-awareness and the emergence of mind in humans and other primates. In J. Suls & A.G. Greenwald (Eds.), *Psychological Perspectives on the Self* (Vol. 3, pp. 3–26). Hillsdale, NJ: Erlbaum.

Gangestad, S. W. (1989). Uncompelling theory, uncompelling data. *Behavioral and Brain Sciences, 12,* 525–526.

Garfinkle, H. (1967). *Studies in Ethnomethodology.* Englewood Cliffs, NJ: Prentice Hall.

Garner, D. M., Garfinkel, P. E., Schwartz, D., & Thompson, M. (1980). Cultural expectations of thinness in women. *Psychological Reports, 47,* 483–491.

Gavanski, I., & Hoffman, C. (1987). Awareness of influences on one's own judgments: The roles of covariation detection and attention. *Journal of Personality and Social Psychology, 52,* 453–463.

Geen, R., & Quanty, M. (1977). The catharsis of aggression: An evaluation of an hypothesis. In L. Berkowitz (Ed.), *Advances in experimental social psychology* (Vol. 10, pp. 1–36). New York: Academic Press.

Geen, R., Stonner, D., & Shope, G. (1975). The facilitation of aggression by aggression: A study in response inhibition and disinhibition. *Journal of Personality and Social Psychology, 31,* 721–726.

Geen, R. G. (1989). Alternative conceptions of social facilitation. In P. B. Paulus (Ed.), *Psychology of group influence* (2nd ed., pp. 15–51). Hillsdale, NJ: Erlbaum.

Gerard, H. B. (1953). The effect of different dimensions of disagreement on the communication process in small groups. *Human Relations, 6,* 249–271.

Gerard, H. B., & Mathewson, G. C. (1966). The effects of severity of initiation on liking for a group: A replication. *Journal of Experimental Social Psychology, 2,* 278–287.

Gerard, H. B., Wilhelmy, R. A., & Conolley, E. S. (1968). Conformity and group size. *Journal of Personality and Social Psychology, 8,* 79–82.

Gerbner, G., Gross, L., Morgan, M., & Signorielli, N. (1980). The "mainstreaming" of America: Violence profile no. 11. *Journal of Communication, 30*(3), 10–29.

Gerdes, E. P. (1979). College students' reactions to social psychological experiments involving deception. *Journal of Social Psychology, 107,* 99–110.

Gergen, K. J. (1971). *The concept of self.* New York: Holt, Rinehart, & Winston.

Gergen, K. J., Gergen, M. M., & Barton, W. H. (1973). Deviance in the dark. *Psychology Today*, 7, 129–130.

Gerstein, L. H., & Tesser, A. (1987). Antecedents and responses associated with loneliness. *Journal of Social and Personal Relationships*, 4, 329–363.

Gibbons, F. X. (1978). Sexual standards and reactions to pornography: Enhancing behavioral consistency through self-focused attention. *Journal of Personality and Social Psychology*, 36, 976–987.

Gilbert, B. (1990, April). Earth Day plus 20, and counting. *Smithsonian*, 21, 47–55.

Gilbert, D. T. (1989). Thinking lightly about others: Automatic components of the social inference process. In J. S. Uleman & J. A. Bargh (Eds.), *Unintended thought* (pp. 189–211). New York: Guilford Press.

Gilbert, D. T. (1991). How mental systems believe. *American Psychologist*, 46, 107–119.

Gilbert, D. T. (1993). The assent of man: Mental representation and the control of belief. In D. M. Wegner & J. W. Pennebaker, (Eds.), *The handbook of mental control* (pp. 57–87). Englewood Cliffs, NJ: Prentice Hall.

Gilbert, D. T., & Osborne, R. E. (1989). Thinking backward: Some curable and incurable consequences of cognitive busyness. *Journal of Personality and Social Psychology*, 57, 940–949.

Gilbert, D. T., Pelham, B. W., & Krull, D. S. (1988). On cognitive busyness: When person perceivers meet persons perceived. *Journal of Personality and Social Psychology*, 54, 733–740.

Gilbert, G. M. (1951). Stereotype persistence and change among college students. *Journal of Abnormal and Social Psychology*, 46, 245–254.

Gilovich, T. (1991). *How we know what isn't so: The fallibility of human reasoning in everyday life*. New York: Free Press.

Glass, D. (1964). Changes in liking as a means of reducing cognitive discrepancies between self-esteem and aggression. *Journal of Personality*, 32, 531–549.

Glass, D. C., & Singer, J. E. (1972). *Urban stress: Experiments on noise and social stressors*. New York: Academic Press.

Gleicher, F., & Petty, R. E. (1992). Expectations of reassurance influence the nature of fear-stimulated attitude change. *Journal of Experimental Social Psychology*, 28, 86–100.

Glick, P., Zion, C., & Nelson, C. (1988). What mediates sex discrimination in hiring decisions? *Journal of Personality and Social Psychology*, 55, 178–186.

Godfrey, D. K., Jones, E. E., & Lord, C. G. (1986). Self-promotion is not ingratiating. *Journal of Personality and Social Psychology*, 50, 106–115.

Goethals, G. R. (1986). Social comparison theory: Psychology from the lost and found. *Personality and Social Psychology Bulletin*, 12, 261–278.

Goethals, G. R., & Darley, J. M. (1977). Social comparison theory: An attributional approach. In J. M. Suls & R. L. Miller (Eds.), *Social comparison processes: Theoretical and empirical perspectives* (pp. 259–278). Washington, DC: Hemisphere/Halsted.

Goffman, E. (1955). On face-work: An analysis of ritual elements in social interaction. *Psychiatry*, 18, 213–231.

Goffman, E. (1959). *Presentation of self in everyday life*. Garden City, NY: Doubleday Anchor Books.

Goffman, E. (1967). *Interaction ritual*. Garden City, NY: Doubleday.

Goffman, E. (1971). *Relations in public*. New York: Basic Books.

Goffman, E. (1976). *Gender Advertisements*. New York: Harper & Row.

Gold, J. A., Ryckman, R. M., & Mosley, N. R. (1984). Romantic mood induction and attraction to a dissimilar other: Is love blind? *Personality and Social Psychology Bulletin*, 10, 358–368.

Goldberg, P. (1968, April). Are women prejudiced against women? *Trans-Action*, pp. 28–30.

Goldstein, J. H., & Arms, R. L. (1971). Effect of observing athletic contests on hostility. *Sociometry*, 34, 83–90.

Goleman, D. (1982, January). Make-or-break resolutions. *Psychology Today*, p. 19.

Gologor, E. (1977). Group polarization in a non-risk-taking culture. *Journal of Cross-Cultural Psychology*, 8, 331–346.

Gonzales, M. H., Aronson, E., & Costanzo, M. (1988). Using social cognition and persuasion to promote energy conservation: A quasi-experiment. *Journal of Applied Social Psychology*, 18, 1049–1066.

Goodman, N. G. (Ed.). (1945). *A Benjamin Franklin reader*. New York: Thomas Y. Crowell.

Granberg, D., & Brown, T. (1989). On affect and cognition in politics. *Social Psychology Quarterly*, 52, 171–182.

Greeley, A., & Sheatsley, P. (1971). The acceptance of desegregation continues to advance. *Scientific American*, 225(6), 13–19.

Greenberg, J. (1983). *Difficult goal choice as a self-handicapping strategy*. Unpublished manuscript, Ohio State University.

Greenberg, J., & Pyszczynski, T. (1985). The effect of an overheard slur on evaluations of the target: How to spread a social disease. *Journal of Experimental Social Psychology*, 21, 61–72.

Greenberg, J., Pyszczynski, T., & Paisley, C. (1984). The role of extrinsic incentives in the use of test anxiety as an anticipatory attributional defense: Playing it cool when the stakes are high. *Journal of Personality and Social Psychology*, 47, 1136–1145.

Greenberg, J., Pyszczynski, T., & Solomon, S. (1982). The self-serving attributional bias: Beyond self-presentation. *Journal of Experimental Social Psychology*, 18, 56–67.

Greenberg, J., Pyszczynski, T., & Solomon, S. (1986). The causes and consequences of the need for self-esteem: A terror management theory. In R. F. Baumeister (Ed.), *Public self and private self* (pp. 189–212). New York: Springer-Verlag.

Greenberg, L. (1979). Genetic component of bee odor in kin recognition. *Science*, 206, 1095–1097.

Greene, D., Sternberg, B., & Lepper, M. R. (1976). Overjustification in a token economy. *Journal of Personality and Social Psychology*, 34, 1219–1234.

Greenwald, A. G. (1980). The totalitarian ego: Fabrication and revision of personal history. *American Psychologist*, 35, 603–618.

Greenwald, A. G., & Ronis, D. L. (1978). Twenty years of cognitive dissonance: Case study of the evolution of a theory. *Psychological Review*, 85, 53–57.

Greenwald, A. G., Spangenberg, E. R., Pratkanis, A. R., & Eskenazi, J. (1991). Double-blind tests of subliminal self-help audiotapes. *Psychological Science, 2,* 119–122.

Griffin, D. W., Dunning, D., & Ross, L. (1990). The role of construal processes in overconfident predictions about the self and others. *Journal of Personality and Social Psychology, 59,* 1128–1139.

Griffin, D. W., & Ross, L. (1991). Subjective construal, social inference, and human misunderstanding. In L. Berkowitz (Ed.), *Advances in experimental social psychology* (Vol. 24, pp. 319–359). San Diego, CA: Academic Press.

Griffitt, W., & Veitch, R. (1971). Hot and crowded: Influences of population density and temperature on interpersonal affective behavior. *Journal of Personality and Social Psychology, 17,* 92–98.

Griffitt, W., & Veitch, R. (1974). Preacquaintance attitude similarity and attraction revisited: Ten days in a fall-out shelter. *Sociometry, 37,* 163–173.

Grusec, J. E. (1991). The socialization of altruism. In M. S. Clark (Ed.), *Review of personality and social psychology* (Vol. 12, pp. 9–33). Newbury Park, CA: Sage.

Grusec, J. E., Kuczynski, L., Rushton, J. P., & Simutis, Z. M. (1979). Modeling, direct instruction, and attributions: Effects on altruism. *Developmental Psychology, 14,* 51–57.

Guerin, B. (1986). Mere presence effects in humans: A review. *Journal of Experimental Social Psychology, 22,* 38–77.

Guetzkow, H. (1968). Some correspondence between simulation and "realities" in international relations. In M. A. Kaplan (Ed.), *New approaches to international relations.* New York: St. Martin's Press.

Gustafson, R. (1989). Frustration and successful vs. unsuccessful aggression: A test of Berkowitz' completion hypothesis. *Aggressive Behavior, 15,* 5–12.

Hackman, J. R., & Morris, C. G. (1978). Group process and group effectiveness: A reappraisal. In L. Berkowitz (Ed.), *Group processes* (pp. 57–66). New York: Academic Press.

Hagestad, G. O., & Smyer, M. A. (1982). Dissolving long-term relationships: Patterns of divorcing in middle age. In S. Duck (Ed.), *Personal relationships 4: Dissolving personal telationships.* London: Academic Press.

Haggard, E. A., & Issacs, F. S. (1966). Micromomentary facial expressions as indicators of ego mechanisms in psychotherapy. In L. A. Gottschalk & A. H. Auerback (Eds.), *Methods of research in psychotherapy* (pp. 154–165). New York: Appleton-Century-Crofts.

Halberstam, D. (1972). *The best and the brightest.* New York: Random House.

Hall, J. A. (1979). *A cross-national study of gender differences in nonverbal sensitivity.* Unpublished manuscript, Northeastern University.

Hall, J. A. (1984). *Nonverbal sex differences: Communication accuracy and expressive style.* Baltimore, MD: Johns Hopkins University Press.

Hamill, R. C., Wilson, T. D., & Nisbett, R. E. (1980). Ignoring sample bias: Inferences about populations from atypical cases. *Journal of Personality and Social Psychology, 39,* 578–589.

Hamilton, D. L. (1970). The structure of personality judgments: Comments on Kuusinen's paper and further evidence. *Scandinavian Journal of Psychology, 11,* 261–265.

Hamilton, D. L. (1981a). Cognitive representations of persons. In E. T. Higgins, C. P. Herman, & M. P. Zanna (Eds.), *Social cognition: The Ontario Symposium* (Vol. 1, pp. 135–159). Hillsdale, NJ: Erlbaum.

Hamilton, D. L. (1981b). Illusory correlation as a basis for stereotyping. In D. L. Hamilton (Ed.), *Cognitive Processes in Stereotyping and Intergroup Behavior.* Hillsdale, NJ: Erlbaum.

Hamilton, D. L., & Gifford, R. K. (1976). Illusory correlation in interpersonal perception: A cognitive basis of stereotypic judgments. *Journal of Experimental Social Psychology, 12,* 392–407.

Hamilton, D. L., & Sherman, S. J. (1989). Illusory correlations: Implications for stereotype theory and research. In D. Bar-Tal, C. F. Graumann, A. W. Kruglanski, & W. Stroebe (Eds.), *Stereotypes and prejudice: Changing conceptions.* New York: Springer-Verlag.

Hamilton, W. D. (1964). The genetical evolution of social behavior. *Journal of Theoretical Biology, 7,* 1–52.

Hansen, C. H., & Hansen, R. D. (1988). Finding the face in the crowd: An anger superiority effect. *Journal of Personality and Social Psychology, 17,* 917–924.

Harackiewicz, J. M. (1979). The effects of reward contingency and performance feedback on intrinsic motivation. *Journal of Personality and Social Psychology, 37,* 1352–1363.

Harackiewicz, J. M. (1989). Performance evaluation and intrinsic motivation processes: The effects of achievement orientation and rewards. In D. Buss & N. Cantor (Eds.), *Personality psychology: Recent trends and emerging directions* (pp. 128–137). New York: Springer-Verlag.

Hardin, G. (1968). The tragedy of the commons. *Science, 162,* 1243–1248.

Harkins, S. G., & Szymanski, K. (1987). Social loafing and social facilitation: Old wine in new bottles. In C. Hendrick (Ed.), *Group processes and intergroup relations* (Vol. 9, pp. 167–188). Newbury Park, CA: Sage.

Harkness, A. R., DeBono, K. G., & Borgida, E. (1985). Personal involvement and strategies for making contingency judgments: A stake in the dating game makes a difference. *Journal of Personality and Social Psychology, 49,* 22–32.

Harries, K. D., & Stadler, S. J. (1988). Heat and violence: New findings from Dallas field data, 1980–1981. *Journal of Applied Social Psychology, 18,* 129–138.

Harris, B. (1986). Reviewing 50 years of the psychology of social issues. *Journal of Social Issues, 42,* 1–20.

Harris, M. (1974). Mediators between frustration and aggression in a field experiment. *Journal of Experimental and Social Psychology, 10,* 561–571.

Harris, M. B., Benson, S. M., & Hall, C. (1975). The effects of confession on altruism. *Journal of Social Psychology, 96,* 187–192.

Hart, D., & Damon, W. (1986). Developmental trends in self-understanding. *Social Cognition, 4,* 388–407.

Hartshorne, H., & May, M. A. (1929). *Studies in the nature of character: Studies in service and self-control* (Vol. 2). New York: Macmillan.

Harvey, J. H., Flanary, R., & Morgan, M. (1986). Vivid memories of vivid loves gone by. *Journal of Personal and Social Relationships, 3,* 359–373.

Hassebrauck, M. (1988). Beauty is more than "name" deep: The effect of women's first names on ratings of physical attractiveness and personality attributes. *Journal of Applied Social Psychology, 18*, 721–726.

Hastie, R. (1980). Memory for behavioral information that confirms or contradicts a personality impression. In R. Hastie, T. M. Ostrom, E. B. Ebbesen, R. S. Wyer, D. L. Hamilton, & D. E. Carlston (Eds.), *Person memory: The cognitive basis of social perception* (pp. 141–172). Hillsdale, NJ: Erlbaum.

Hastie, R., Penrod, S. D., & Pennington, N. (1983). *Inside the jury.* Cambridge MA: Harvard University Press.

Hastorf, A., & Cantril, H. (1954). They saw a game: A case study. *Journal of Abnormal and Social Psychology, 49*, 129–134.

Hatfield, E. (1988). Passionate and companionate love. In R. J. Sternberg & M. L. Barnes (Eds.), *The psychology of love* (pp. 191–217). New Haven, CT: Yale University Press.

Hatfield, E., Greenberger, E., Traupmann, J., & Lambert, P. (1982). Equity and sexual satisfaction in recently married couples. *Journal of Sex Research, 18*, 18–32.

Hatfield, E., & Sprecher, S. (1986a). *Mirror, mirror: The importance of looks in everyday life.* Albany: State University of New York Press.

Hatfield, E., & Sprecher, S. (1986b). Measuring passionate love in intimate relationships. *Journal of Adolescence, 9*, 383–410.

Hatfield, E., & Walster, G. W. (1978). *A new look at love.* Reading, MA: Addison-Wesley.

Hays, R. B. (1984). The development and maintenance of friendship. *Journal of Social and Personal Relationships, 1*, 75–98.

Hazan, C., & Shaver, P. (1987). Romantic love conceptualized as an attachment process. *Journal of Personality and Social Psychology, 52*, 511–524.

Hazelwood, J. D., & Olson, J. M. (1986). Covariation information, causal questioning, and interpersonal behavior. *Journal of Experimental Social Psychology, 22*, 276–291.

Hearold, S. (1986). A synthesis of 1043 effects of television on social behavior. In G. Comstock (Ed.), *Public communication and behavior*, (Vol. 1). Orlando, FL: Academic Press.

Heider, F. (1958). *The psychology of interpersonal relations.* New York: Wiley.

Henley, N. M. (1977). *Body politics: Power, sex, and nonverbal communication.* Englewood Cliffs, NJ: Prentice Hall.

Hennessey, B. A., Amabile, T., & Martinage, M. (1989). Immunizing children against the negative effects of reward. *Contemporary Educational Psychology, 14*, 212–227.

Hennessey, B. A., & Zbikowski, S. M. (1993). Immunizing children against the negative effects of reward: A further examination of intrinsic motivation focus sessions. *Creativity Research Journal, 6*, 297–307.

Henrick, S. S., & Henrick, C. (1986). A theory and method of love. *Journal of Personality and Social Psychology, 50*, 392–402.

Hepworth, J. T., & West, S. G. (1988). Lynchings and the economy: A time-series reanalysis of Hovland and Sears (1940). *Journal of Personality and Social Psychology, 55*, 239–247.

Hersch, S. M. (1970). *My Lai 4: A report on the massacre and its aftermath.* New York: Vintage Books.

Heunemann, R. L., Shapiro, L. R., Hampton, M. C., & Mitchell, B. W. (1966). A longitudinal study of gross body composition and body conformation and their association with food and activity in the teenage population. *American Journal of Clinical Nutrition, 18*, 325–338.

Hewstone, M., & Jaspars, J. (1987). Covariation and causal attribution: A logical model of the intuitive analysis of variance. *Journal of Personality and Social Psychology, 53*, 663–672.

Higgins, E. T. (1989). Knowledge accessibility and activation: Subjectivity and suffering from unconscious sources. In J. S. Uleman & J. A. Bargh (Eds.), *Unintended thought* (pp. 75–123). New York: Guilford Press.

Higgins, E. T., & Bargh, J. A. (1987). Social cognition and social perception. *Annual Review of Psychology, 38*, 369–425.

Higgins, E. T., Rholes, W. S., & Jones, C. R. (1977). Category accessibility and impression formation. *Journal of Experimental Social Psychology, 13*, 141–154.

Higgins, R. L., & Harris, R. N. (1988). Strategic "alcohol" use: Drinking to self-handicap. *Journal of Social and Clinical Psychology, 6*, 191–202.

Hill, C. T., Rubin, Z., & Peplau, L. A. (1976). Breakups before marriage: The end of 103 affairs. *Journal of Social Issues, 32*, 147–168.

Hill, M. (1982). Group versus individual performance: Are N + 1 heads better than one? *Psychological Bulletin, 91*, 517–539.

Hippler, H. J., Schwarz, N., & Sudman, S. (Eds.). (1987). *Social information processing and survey methodology.* New York: Springer-Verlag.

Hobbes, T. (1986, original published in 1651). *Leviathan.* Harmondsworth, England: Penguin Press.

Hoffman, C., Lau, I., & Johnson, D. R. (1986). The linguistic relativity of person cognition: An English-Chinese comparison. *Journal of Personality and Social Psychology, 51*, 1097–1105.

Hollander, E. P. (1958). Conformity, status, and idiosyncracy credits. *Psychological Review, 65*, 117–127.

Hollander, E. P. (1960). Competence and conformity in the acceptance of influence. *Journal of Abnormal and Social Psychology, 61*, 361–365.

Hollander, E. P. (1985). Leadership and power. In G. Lindzey & E. Aronson (Eds.), *Handbook of social psychology* (3rd ed., Vol. 2, pp. 485–537). New York: Random House.

Holmes, T. H., & Rahe, R. H. (1967). The social readjustment rating scale. *Journal of Psychosomatic Research, 11*, 213–218.

Homans, G. C. (1961). *Social behavior: Its elementary forms.* New York: Harcourt, Brace, & World.

Hornstein, H. A., LaKind, E., Frankel, G., & Manne, S. (1975). Effects of knowledge about remote social events on prosocial behavior, social conception, and mood. *Journal of Personality and Social Psychology, 32*, 1038–1046.

Houston, D. A., & Fazio, R. H. (1989). Biased processing as a function of attitude accessibility: Making objective judgments subjectively. *Social Cognition, 7*, 51–66.

Hovland, C. I., Janis, I. L., & Kelley, H. H. (1953). *Communication and persuasion: Psychological studies of opinion change.* New Haven, CT: Yale University Press.

Hovland, C. I., Lumsdaine, A. A., & Sheffield, F. D. (1949). *Experiments on mass communication*. Princeton, NJ: Princeton University Press.

Hovland, C. I., & Sears, R. R. (1940). Minor studies in aggression: VI. Correlation of lynchings with economic indices. *Journal of Psychology, 9*, 301–310.

Hovland, C. I., & Weiss, W. (1951). The influence of source credibility on communication effectiveness. *Public Opinion Quarterly, 15*, 635–650.

Huesmann, L. R. (1982). Television violence and aggressive behavior. In D. Pearly, L. Bouthilet, & J. Lazar (Eds.), *Television and behavior: Vol. 2. Technical reviews* (pp. 220–256). Washington, DC: National Institute of Mental Health.

Hull, J. G. (1981). A self-awareness model of the causes and effects of alcohol consumption. *Journal of Abnormal and Social Psychology, 90*, 586–600.

Hull, J. G., & Young, R. D. (1983). Self-consciousness, self-esteem, and success-failure as determinants of alcohol consumption in male social drinkers. *Journal of Personality and Social Psychology, 44*, 1097–1109.

Hunt, G. T. (1940). *The wars of the Iroquois*. Madison: University of Wisconsin Press.

Hunter, J. E., & Hunter, R. F. (1984). The validity and utility of alternative predictors of job performance. *Psychological Bulletin, 96*, 72–98.

Hurley, D., & Allen, B. P. (1974). The effect of the number of people present in a nonemergency situation. *Journal of Social Psychology, 92*, 27–29.

Hutchinson, R. R. (1983). The pain-aggression relationship and its expression in naturalistic settings. *Aggressive Behavior, 9*, 229–242.

Hyman, J. J., & Sheatsley, P. B. (1956; 1964). Attitudes toward desegregation. *Scientific American, 195*(6), 35–39, and *211*(1), 16–23.

Ickes, W., & Layden, M. A. (1978). Attributional styles. In J. H. Harvey, W. Ickes, & R. F. Kidd (Eds.), *New directions in attribution research* (Vol. 2, pp. 119–152). Hillsdale, NJ: Erlbaum.

Ickes, W., Patterson, M. L., Rajecki, D. W., & Tanford, S. (1982). Behavioral and cognitive consequences of reciprocal versus compensatory responses to preinteraction expectancies. *Social Cognition, 1*, 160–190.

Ickes, W., Robertson, E., Tooke, W., & Teng, G. (1986). Naturalistic social cognition: Methodology, assessment, and validation. *Journal of Personality and Social Psychology, 51*, 66–82.

Ingham, A. G., Levinger, G., Graves, J., & Peckham, V. (1974). The Ringelmann effect: Studies of group size and group performance. *Journal of Experimental Social Psychology, 10*, 371–384.

Insko, C. A., Schopler, J., Hoyle, R. H., Dardis, G. J., & Graetz, K. A. (1990). Individual-group discontinuity as a function of fear and greed. *Journal of Personality and Social Psychology, 58*, 68–79.

Isen, A. M. (1987). Positive affect, cognitive processes, and social behavior. In L. Berkowitz (Ed.), *Advances in experimental social psychology* (Vol. 21, pp. 203–253). New York: Academic Press.

Isen, A. M., & Levin, P. A. (1972). Effect of feeling good on helping: Cookies and kindness. *Journal of Personality and Social Psychology, 21*, 384–388.

Isenberg, D. J. (1986). Group polarization: A critical review and meta-analysis. *Journal of Personality and Social Psychology, 50*, 1141–1151.

Izard, C. (1969). The emotions and emotion constructs in personality and culture research. In R. B. Cattell (Ed.), *Handbook of modern personality theory* (pp. 496–510). Chicago: Aldine.

Izard, C. (1977). *Human emotions*. New York: Plenum.

Jackson, J. (1981, July 19). Syndicated newspaper column.

Jackson, J. M., & Williams, K. D. (1985). Social loafing on difficult tasks: Working collectively can improve performance. *Journal of Personality and Social Psychology, 49*, 937–942.

Jacobs, P., & Landau, S. (1971). *To serve the devil* (Vol. 2, p. 71). New York: Vintage Books.

Jacobson, M., & Hacker, G. (1985, May 6). The case for curbing alcohol advertising. *Broadcasting*, p. 19.

Jacobson, N. S., Waldron, H., & Moore, D. (1980). Toward a behavioral profile of marital distress. *Journal of Consulting and Clinical Psychology, 48*, 696–703.

James, W. (1890). *The principles of psychology*. New York: Holt.

James, W. (1910). *The principles of psychology* (Vols. 1–2). London: Macmillan.

"Jammy man" actor's plight. (1988, October 18). *New York Times*, p. A25.

Janis, I. L. (1967). Effects of fear arousal on attitude change: Recent developments in theory and experimental research. In L. Berkowitz (Ed.), *Advances in experimental social psychology* (Vol. 3, pp. 166–224). New York: Academic Press.

Janis, I. L. (1972). *Victims of groupthink*. Boston: Houghton Mifflin.

Janis, I. L. (1982). *Groupthink* (2nd ed.). Boston: Houghton Mifflin.

Janoff-Bulman, R., Timko, C., & Carli, L. L. (1985). Cognitive biases in blaming the victim. *Journal of Experimental Social Psychology, 21*, 161–177.

Jeavons, C. M., & Taylor, S. P. (1985). The control of alcohol related aggression: Redirecting the inebriate's attention to socially appropriate conduct. *Aggressive Behavior, 11*, 93–101.

Jecker, J., & Landy, D. (1969). Liking a person as a function of doing him a favor. *Human Relations, 22*, 371–378.

Jellison, J. M., & Riskind, J. A. (1970). A social comparison of abilities interpretation of risk-taking behavior. *Journal of Personality and Social Psychology, 15*, 375–390.

Jennings, D. J., Amabile, T. M., & Ross, L. (1982). Informal covariation assessment: Data-based versus theory-based judgments. In D. Kahneman, P. Slovic, & A. Tversky (Eds.), *Judgment under uncertainty: Heuristics and biases* (pp. 211–230). New York: Cambridge University Press.

Jepson, C., & Chaiken, S. (1990). Chronic issue-specific fear inhibits systematic processing of persuasive communications. *Journal of Social Behavior and Personality, 5*, 61–84.

Job, R. F. S. (1988). Effective and ineffective use of fear in health promotion campaigns. *American Journal of Public Health, 78*, 163–167.

Johnson, B. T., & Eagly, A. H. (1989). Effects of involvement on persuasion: A meta-analysis. *Psychological Bulletin, 106*, 290–314.

Johnson, B. T., & Eagly, A. H. (1990). Involvement and persuasion: Types, traditions, and evidence. *Psychological Bulletin, 107*, 375–384.

Johnson, D. M. (1945). The phantom anesthetist of Mattoon: A field study of mass hysteria. *Journal of Abnormal and Social Psychology, 40*, 175–186.

Johnson, D. W., & Johnson, R. T. (1987). *Learning together and alone: Cooperative, competitive, and individualistic learning* (2nd ed.). Englewood Cliffs, NJ: Prentice Hall.

Johnson, D. W., & Johnson, R. T. (1989). *A meta-analysis of cooperative, competitive, and individualistic goal structures.* Hillsdale, NJ: Erlbaum.

Johnson, L. B. (1971). *The vantage point: Perspectives of the presidency, 1963–69.* New York: Holt, Rinehart, and Winston.

Johnson, M. K., Hashtroudi, S., & Lindsay, D. S. (1993). Source monitoring. *Psychological Bulletin, 114*, 3–28.

Johnson, R. D., & Downing, R. L. (1979). Deindividuation and valence of cues: Effects of prosocial and antisocial behavior. *Journal of Personality and Social Psychology, 37*, 1532–1538.

Johnson, T. E., & Rule, B. G. (1986). Mitigating circumstance information, censure, and aggression. *Journal of Personality and Social Psychology, 50*, 537–542.

Jones, C., & Aronson, E. (1973). Attribution of fault to a rape victim as a function of the respectability of the victim. *Journal of Personality and Social Psychology, 26*, 415–419.

Jones, E., & Kohler, R. (1959). The effects of plausibility on the learning of controversial statements. *Journal of Abnormal and Social Psychology, 57*, 315–320.

Jones, E. E. (1964). *Ingratiation: A social psychological analysis.* New York: Appleton-Century-Crofts.

Jones, E. E. (1979). The rocky road from acts to dispositions. *American Scientist, 34*, 107–117.

Jones, E. E. (1990). *Interpersonal perception.* New York: Freeman.

Jones, E. E., & Berglas, S. (1978). Control of attributions about the self through self-handicapping strategies: The appeal of alcohol and the role of underachievement. *Personality and Social Psychology Bulletin, 4*, 200–206.

Jones, E. E., & Davis, K. E. (1965). From acts to dispositions: The attribution process in social psychology. In L. Berkowitz (Ed.), *Advances in experimental social psychology* (Vol. 2, pp. 219–266). New York: Academic Press.

Jones, E. E., Davis, K. E., & Gergen, K. J. (1961). Role playing variations and their informational value for person perception. *Journal of Abnormal and Social Psychology, 63*, 302–310.

Jones, E. E., Gergen, K. J., & Jones, R. G. (1963). Tactics of ingratiation among leaders and subordinates in a status hierarchy. *Psychological Monographs, 77* (3, Whole No. 566).

Jones, E. E., & Harris, V. A. (1967). The attribution of attitudes. *Journal of Experimental Social Psychology, 3*, 1–24.

Jones, E. E., & McGillis, D. (1976). Correspondent inferences and the attribution cube: A comparative reappraisal. In J. H. Harvey, W. J. Ickes, & R. F. Kidd (Eds.), *New directions in attribution research* (Vol. 1, pp. 389–420). Hillsdale, NJ: Erlbaum.

Jones, E. E., & Nisbett, R. E. (1972). The actor and the observer: Divergent perceptions of the causes of behavior. In E. E. Jones, D. E. Kanouse, H. H. Kelley, R. E. Nisbett, S. Valins, & B. Weiner (Eds.), *Attribution: Perceiving the causes of behavior* (pp. 79–94). Morristown, NJ: General Learning Press.

Jones, E. E., & Pittman, T.S. (1982). Toward a general theory of strategic self-presentation. In J. Suls (Ed.), *Psychological perspectives on the self* (pp. 231–262). Hillsdale, NJ: Erlbaum.

Jones, E. E., Rhodewalt, F., Berglas, S., & Skelton, J. A. (1981). Effects of strategic self-presentation on subsequent self-esteem. *Journal of Personality and Social Psychology, 41*, 407–421.

Jones, E. E., Rock, L., Shaver, K. G., Goethals, G. R., & Ward, L. M. (1968). Pattern of performance and ability attribution: An unexpected primacy effect. *Journal of Personality and Social Psychology, 10*, 317–340.

Jones, E. E., & Sigall, H. (1971). The bogus pipeline: A new paradigm for measuring affect and attitude. *Psychological Bulletin, 76*, 349–364.

Jones, E. E., & Wortman, C.B. (1973). *Ingratiation: An attributional approach.* Morristown, NJ: General Learning Press.

Josephson, W. D. (1987) Television violence and children's aggression: Testing the priming, social script, and disinhibition prediction. *Journal of Personality and Social Psychology, 53*, 882–890.

Judd, C. M., & Park, B. (1988). Out-group homogeneity: Judgments of variability at the individual and group levels. *Journal of Personality and Social Psychology, 54*, 778–788.

Jussim, L. (1986). Self-fulfilling prophecies: A theoretical and integrative review. *Psychological Review, 93*, 429–445.

Kahn, M. (1966). The physiology of catharsis. *Journal of Personality and Social Psychology, 3*, 278–298.

Kahneman, D., & Tversky, A. (1973). On the psychology of prediction. *Psychological Review, 80*, 237–251.

Kahneman, D., & Tversky, A. (1983). Can irrationality be intelligently discussed? *The Behavioral and Brain Sciences, 6*, 509–510.

Kalick, S. M. (1977). *Plastic surgery, physical appearance, and person perception.* Unpublished doctoral dissertation, Harvard University.

Kalven, H., Jr., & Zeisel, H. (1966). *The American jury.* Boston: Little, Brown.

Karabenick, S. A., Lerner, R. M., & Beecher, M. D. (1973). Relation of political affiliation to helping behavior on Election Day, November 7, 1972. *Journal of Social Psychology, 91*, 223–227.

Karlins, M., Coffman, T. L., & Walters, G. (1969). On the fading of social stereotypes: Studies in three generations of college students. *Journal of Personality and Social Psychology, 13*, 1–16.

Kassarjian, H., & Cohen, J. (1965). Cognitive dissonance and consumer behavior. *California Management Review, 8*, 55–64.

Katz, A. M., & Hill, R. (1958). Residential propinquity and marital selection: A review of theory, method, and fact. *Marriage and Family Living, 20*, 237–335.

Katz, D. (1960). The functional approach to the study of attitudes. *Public Opinion Quarterly, 24*, 163–204.

Katz, D., & Braly, K. W. (1933). Racial stereotypes of 100 college students. *Journal of Abnormal and Social Psychology, 28*, 280–290.

Kauffman, D. R., & Steiner, I.D. (1968). Conformity as an ingratiation technique. *Journal of Experimental Social Psychology, 4*, 404–414.

Kelley, H. H. (1950). The warm-cold variable in first impressions of persons. *Journal of Personality, 18*, 431–439.

Kelley, H. H. (1955). The two functions of reference groups. In G. E. Swanson, T. M. Newcomb, & E. L. Hartley (Eds.), *Readings in social psychology* (2nd ed., pp. 410–414). New York: Holt.

Kelley, H. H. (1967). Attribution theory in social psychology. In D. Levine (Ed.), *Nebraska symposium on motivation* (Vol. 15, pp. 192–238). Lincoln: University of Nebraska Press.

Kelley, H. H. (1972). Attribution in social interaction. In E. E. Jones, D. E. Kanouse, H. H. Kelley, R. E. Nisbett, S. Valins, & B. Weiner (Eds.), *Attribution: Perceiving the causes of behavior* (pp. 1–26). Morristown, NJ: General Learning Press.

Kelley, H. H. (1983). Love and commitment. In H. H. Kelley, E. Berscheid, A. Christensen, J. H. Harvey, T. L. Huston, G. Levinger, E. McClintock, L. A. Peplau, & D. R. Peterson (Eds.), *Close relationships* (pp. 265–314). New York: Freeman.

Kelley, H. H., & Stahelski, A. J. (1970). Social interaction basis of cooperators' and competitors' beliefs about others. *Journal of Personality and Social Psychology, 16*, 66–91.

Kelley, H. H., & Thibaut, J. W. (1978). *Interpersonal relations: A theory of interdependence.* New York: Wiley.

Kelly, J. G., Ferson, J. E., & Holtzman, W. H. (1958). The measurement of attitudes toward the Negro in the South. *Journal of Social Psychology, 48*, 305–312.

Kenny, D. A., & La Voie, L. (1982). Reciprocity of interpersonal attraction: A confirmed hypothesis. *Social Psychology Quarterly, 45*, 54–58.

Kenny, D. A., & Nasby, W. (1980). Splitting the reciprocity correlation. *Journal of Personality and Social Psychology, 38*, 249–256.

Kenrick, D. T, & MacFarlane, S. W. (1986). Ambient temperature and horn honking: A field study of the heat/aggression relationship. *Environment and Behavior, 18*, 179–191.

Kerckhoff, A. C., & Back, K. W. (1968). *The June bug: A study of hysterical contagion.* New York: Appleton-Century-Crofts.

Kerckhoff, A. C., & Davis, K.E. (1962). Value consensus and need complementarity in mate selection. *American Sociological Review, 27*, 295–305.

Key, W. B. (1973). *Subliminal seduction.* Englewood Cliffs, NJ: Signet.

Key, W. B. (1989). *Age of manipulation: The con in confidence and the sin in sincere.* New York: Holt.

Kiesler, C. A., & Kiesler, S. B. (1969). *Conformity.* Reading, MA: Addison-Wesley.

Kihlstrom, J. F. (1987). The cognitive unconscious. *Science, 237*, 1445–1452.

Killen, J. D. (1985). Prevention of adolescent tobacco smoking: The social pressure resistance training approach. *Journal of Child Psychology and Psychiatry, 26*, 7–15.

Killian, L. M. (1964). Social movements. In R. E. L. Farris (Ed.), *Handbook of modern sociology* (pp. 426-455). Chicago: Rand McNally.

Kim, M. P., & Rosenberg, S. (1980). Comparison of two structural models of implicit personality theory. *Journal of Personality and Social Psychology, 38*, 375–389.

Kinder, D. R., & Sears, D. O. (1981). Prejudice and politics: Symbolic racism versus racial threats to the good life. *Journal of Personality and Social Psychology, 40*, 414–431.

King, A. S. (1971, September). Self-fulfilling prophecies in training the hard-core: Supervisors' expectations and the underprivileged workers' performance. *Social Science Quarterly*, pp. 369–378.

Kipnis, D. M (1957). Interaction between members of bomber crews as a determinant of sociometric choice. *Human Relations, 10*, 263–270.

Knapp, M. L. (1980). *Essentials of nonverbal communication.* New York: Holt, Rinehart, & Winston.

Knapp, M. L., & Comadena, M. E. (1979). Telling it like it isn't: A review of theory and research on deceptive communications. *Human Communication Research, 5*, 270–285.

Knox, R., & Inkster, J. (1968). Postdecision dissonance at post time. *Journal of Personality and Social Psychology, 8*, 319–323.

Kobak, R. R., & Hazan, C. (1991). Attachment in marriage: Effects of security and accuracy of working models. *Journal of Personality and Social Psychology, 60*, 861–869.

Koditz, T. A. & Arkin, R. M. (1982). An impression management interpretation of the self-handicapping strategy. *Journal of Personality and Social Psychology, 43*, 492–502.

Koestler, A. (1959). The initiates. In R. Crossman (Ed.), *The god that failed.* New York: Bantam.

Kogan, N., & Doise, W. (1969). Effects of anticipated delegate status on level of risk taking in small decision making groups. *Acta Psychologica, 29*, 228–243.

Kogan, N., & Wallach, M. A. (1964). *Risk-taking: A study in cognition and personality.* New York: Holt.

Kohn, A. (1986). *No contest.* Boston: Houghton Mifflin.

Kolb, D. A., Rubin, I. M., & McIntyre, J. M. (1984). *Organizational psychology: An experiential approach to organizational behavior* (4th ed.). Englewood Cliffs, NJ: Prentice Hall.

Koriat, A., Lichtenstein, S., & Fischhoff, B. (1980). Reasons for confidence. *Journal of Experimental Psychology: Human Learning and Memory, 6*, 107–118.

Korte, C. (1980). Urban-nonurban differences in social behavior and social psychological models of urban impact. *Journal of Social Issues, 36*, 29–51.

Kramer, G. P., Kerr, N. L., & Carroll, J. S. (1990). Pretrial publicity, judicial remedies, and jury bias. *Law and Human Behavior, 14*, 409–438.

Krantz, D. S., Grunberg, N. E., & Baum, A. (1985). Health psychology. *Annual Review of Psychology, 36*, 349–383.

Krauss, R. M., & Deutsch, M. (1966). Communication in interpersonal bargaining. *Journal of Personality and Social Psychology, 4,* 572–577.

Krauss, R. M., Freedman, J. L., & Whitcup, M. (1978). Field and laboratory studies of littering. *Journal of Experimental Social Psychology, 14,* 109–122.

Kremer, J. F., & Stephens, L. (1983). Attributions and arousal as mediators of mitigation's effects on retaliation. *Journal of Personality and Social Psychology, 45,* 335–343.

Kressel, K., & Pruitt, D. G. (1989). A research perspective on the mediation of social conflict. In K. Kressel & D. G. Pruitt (Eds.), *Mediation research: The process and effectiveness of third party intervention* (pp. 394–435). San Francisco: Jossey-Bass.

Krosnick, J. A., & Abelson, R. P. (1991). The case for measuring attitude strength in surveys. In J. Tanur (Ed.), *Questions about survey questions* (pp. 177–203). New York: Russell Sage.

Krosnick, J. A., & Alwin, D. F. (1989). Aging and susceptibility to attitude change. *Journal of Personality and Social Psychology, 57,* 416–425.

Kruglanski, A. W. (1989). The psychology of being "right": The problem of accuracy in social perception and cognition. *Psychological Bulletin, 106,* 395–409.

Kruglanski, A. W., & Freund, T. (1983). The freezing and unfreezing of lay-inferences: Effects on impressional primacy, ethnic stereotyping, and numerical anchoring. *Journal of Experimental Social Psychology, 19,* 448–468.

Kruglanski, A. W., & Mayseless, O. (1990). Classic and current social comparison research: Expanding the perspective. *Psychological Bulletin, 108,* 195–208.

Kuhn, T. S. (1962). *The structure of scientific revolutions.* Chicago: University of Chicago Press.

Kulik, J., & Brown, R. (1979). Frustration, attribution of blame, and aggression. *Journal of Experimental Social Psychology, 15,* 183–194.

Kunda, Z. (1990). The case for motivated reasoning. *Psychological Bulletin, 108,* 480–498.

Kunda, Z., & Nisbett, R. E. (1986). The psychometrics of everyday life. *Cognitive Psychology, 18,* 195–224.

Kunz, P. R., & Woolcott, M. (1976). Season's greetings: From my status to yours. *Social Science Research, 5,* 269–278.

Kuo, Z. Y. (1961). Genesis of the cat's response to the rat. In *Instinct* (p. 24). Princeton, NJ: Van Nostrand.

Kuusinen, J. (1969). Factorial invariance of personality ratings. *Scandinavian Journal of Psychology, 10,* 33–44.

Kuykendall, D., & Keating, J. P. (1990). Altering thoughts and judgments through repeated association. *British Journal of Social Psychology, 29,* 79–86.

Kytle, C. (1969). *Ghandi, soldier of nonviolence: His effect on India and the world today.* New York: Grosset & Dunlap.

Laird, J. D. (1974). Self-attribution of emotion: The effects of expressive behavior on the quality of emotional experience. *Journal of Personality and Social Psychology, 33,* 475–486.

Laird, J. D., & Bressler, C. (1992). The process of emotional experience: A self-perception theory. In M. S. Clark (Ed.), *Review of personality and social psychology* (pp. 213–234). Newbury Park, CA: Sage.

Lamm, H., & Kogan, N. (1970). Risk taking in the context of intergroup negotiation. *Journal of Experimental Social Psychology, 6,* 351–363.

Lamm, H., Schaude, E., & Trommsdorff, G. (1971). Risky shift as a function of group members' value of risk and need for approval. *Journal of Personality and Social Psychology, 20,* 430–435.

Lammers, H. B., & Becker, L. A. (1980). Distraction: Effects on the perceived extremity of a communication and on cognitive responses. *Personality and Social Psychology Bulletin, 6,* 261–266.

Landers, A. (1973). Syndicated newspaper column. April 8, 1969. Cited by L. Berkowitz in, The case for bottling up rage. *Psychology Today,* September, pp. 24–31.

Langer, E. J. (1975). The illusion of control. *Journal of Personality and Social Psychology, 32,* 311–328.

Langer, E. J. (1989). Minding matters: The consequences of mindlessness-mindfulness. In L. Berkowitz (Ed.), *Advances in experimental social psychology* (Vol. 22, pp. 137–174). San Diego, CA: Academic Press.

Langer, E. J., Blank, A., & Chanowitz, B. (1978). The mindlessness of ostensibly thoughtful action: The role of "placebic" information in interpersonal interaction. *Journal of Personality and Social Psychology, 36,* 635–642.

Langer, E. J., & Rodin, J. (1976). The effects of choice and enhanced personal responsibility for the aged: A field experiment. *Journal of Personality and Social Psychology, 34,* 191–198.

Langer, P. A. (1986). *Preventing domestic violence against women.* Washington, DC: U.S. Department of Justice, U.S. Government Printing Office.

LaPiere, R. T. (1934). Attitudes vs. actions. *Social Forces, 13,* 230–237.

Latané, B. (Ed.). (1966). Studies in social comparison: Introduction and overview. *Journal of Experimental Social Psychology, Supplement 1,* 1–5.

Latané, B. (1981). The psychology of social impact. *American Psychologist, 36,* 343–356.

Latané, B. (1987). From student to colleague: Retracing a decade. In N. E. Grunberg, R. E. Nisbet, J. Rodin, & J. E. Singer (Eds.), *A distinctive approach to psychological research: The influence of Stanley Schachter* (pp. 66–86). Hillsdale, NJ: Erlbaum.

Latané, B., & Dabbs, J. M. (1975). Sex, group size, and helping in three cities. *Sociometry, 38,* 108–194.

Latané, B., & Darley, J. M. (1968). Group inhibition of bystander intervention. *Journal of Personality and Social Psychology, 10,* 215–221.

Latané, B., & Darley, J. M. (1970). *The unresponsive bystander: Why doesn't he help?* Englewood Cliffs, NJ: Prentice Hall.

Latané, B., & Nida, S. (1981). Ten years of research on group size and helping. *Psychological Bulletin, 89,* 308–324.

Latané, B., Williams, K., & Harkins, S. (1979). Many hands make light work: The causes and consequences of social loafing. *Journal of Personality and Social Psychology, 37,* 822–832.

Latané, B., & Wolf, S. (1981). The social impact of majorities and minorities. *Psychological Review, 88,* 438–453.

Lau, R. R., & Russell, D. (1980). Attributions in the sports pages: A field test of some current hypotheses about attribution research. *Journal of Personality and Social Psychology, 39,* 29–38.

Laughlin, P. R. (1980). Social combination processes of cooperative problem-solving groups as verbal intellective tasks. In M. Fishbein (Ed.), *Progress in social psychology* (Vol. 1, pp. 127–155). Hillsdale, NJ: Erlbaum.

Lazarsfeld, P. (Ed.). *Radio and the printed page.* New York: Duell, Sloan & Pearce.

Lazarus, R. S. (1966). *Psychological stress and the coping process.* New York: McGraw-Hill.

Lazarus, R. S., & Folkman, S. (1984). *Stress, appraisal, and coping.* New York: Springer-Verlag.

LeBon, G. (1895). *The crowd.* London: F. Unwin.

Lee, D. (1959). *Freedom and culture.* Englewood Cliffs, NJ: Prentice Hall.

Lee, J. A. (1973). *The colors of love: An exploration of the ways of loving.* Don Mills, Ontario: New Press.

Lee, J. A. (1977). A typology of styles of loving. *Personality and Social Psychology Bulletin, 3,* 173–182.

Lee, J. A. (1988). Love-styles. In R. J. Sternberg & M. L. Barnes (Eds.), *The psychology of love* (pp. 38–67). New Haven, CT: Yale University Press.

Lehman, D. R., Lempert, R. O., & Nisbett, R. E. (1988). The effects of graduate training on reasoning. *American Psychologist, 43,* 431–442.

Leippe, M. R., Manion, A. P., & Romanczyk, A. (1992). Eyewitness persuasion: How and how well do fact finders judge the accuracy of adults' and children's memory reports? *Journal of Personality and Social Psychology, 63,* 181–197.

Leishman, K. (1987, February). Heterosexuals and AIDS. *The Atlantic Monthly.*

Leo, J. (1991, July 15). Hostility among the ice cubes. *U.S. World and News Reports,* p. 18.

Lepper, M. R., & Greene, D. (1978). *The hidden costs of reward.* Hillsdale, NJ: Erlbaum.

Lepper, M. R., Greene, D., & Nisbett, R. E. (1973). Undermining children's intrinsic interest with extrinsic reward: A test of the overjustification hypothesis. *Journal of Personality and Social Psychology, 28,* 129-137.

Lerner, M. J. (1980). *The belief in a just world: A fundamental decision.* New York: Plenum.

Lerner, M. J., & Simmons, C. H. (1966). Observers' reaction to the innocent victim: Compassion or rejection? *Journal of Personality and Social Psychology, 4,* 203–210.

Leung, K. (1987). Some determinants of reactions to procedural models for conflict resolution: A cross-national study. *Journal of Personality and Social Psychology, 53,* 898–908.

Leventhal, H. (1970). Findings and theory in the study of fear communications. In L. Berkowitz (Ed.), *Advances in experimental social psychology* (Vol. 5, pp. 119–186). New York: Academic Press.

Leventhal, H., Watts, J. C., & Pagano, F. (1967). Effects of fear and instructions on how to cope with danger. *Journal of Personality and Social Psychology, 6,* 313–321.

Levi, P. (1986). *Survival in Auschwitz; and The Reawakening: Two memoirs.* New York: Summit Books.

Levine, J. M., & Russo, E. M. (1987). Majority and minority influence. In C. Hendrick (Ed.), *Group processes: Review of personality and social psychology* (Vol. 8, pp. 13–54). Newbury Park, CA: Sage.

Levine, R. A., & Campbell, D. T. (1972). *Ethnocentrism: Theories of Conflict, Ethnic Attitudes, and Group Behavior.* New York: Wiley.

Levinger, G. (1964). Note on need complementarity in marriage. *Psychological Bulletin, 61,* 153–157.

Levinger, G., Senn, D. J., & Jorgensen, B. W. (1970). Progress toward permanence in courtship: A test of the Kerckhoff-Davis hypothesis. *Sociometry, 33,* 427–433.

Levitas, M. (1969). *America in crisis.* New York: Holt, Rinehart, and Winston.

Levy, J. S., & Morgan, T. C. (1984). The frequency and seriousness of war: An inverse relationship? *Journal of Conflict Resolution, 28,* 731–749.

Levy, S. (1979). Authoritarianism and information processing. *Bulletin of the Psychonomic Society, 13,* 240–242.

Levy-Leboyer, C. (1988). Success and failure in applying psychology. *American Psychologist, 43,* 779–785.

Lewicki, P. (1986). *Nonconscious social information processing.* Orlando, FL: Academic Press.

Lewin, K. (1943). Defining the "field at a given time." *Psychological Review, 50,* 292–310.

Lewin, K. (1948). *Resolving social conflicts: Selected papers in group dynamics.* New York: Harper.

Lewin, K. (1951). Problems of research in social psychology. In D. Cartwright (Ed.), *Field theory in social science* (pp. 155–169). New York: Harper & Row.

Lewis, C. S. (1952). *Mere Christianity.* New York: Macmillan.

Lewis, M. (1986). Origins of self-knowledge and individual differences in early self-recognition. In J. Suls & A. G. Greenwald (Eds.), *Psychological perspectives on the self* (Vol. 3, pp. 55–78). Hillsdale, NJ: Erlbaum.

Lewis, M., & Brooks, J. (1978). Self-knowledge and emotional development. In M. Lewis & L. Rosenblum (Eds.), *The development of affect* (pp. 205–226). New York: Plenum.

Leyens, J. P., Camino, L., Parke, R. D., & Berkowitz, L. (1975). Effects of movie violence on aggression in a field setting as a function of group dominance and cohesion. *Journal of Personality and Social Psychology, 32,* 346–360.

Lichtenstein, S., Fischhoff, B., & Phillips, L. D. (1982). Calibration of probabilities: The state of the art to 1980. In D. Kahneman, P. Slovic, & A. Tversky (Eds.), *Judgment under uncertainty: Heuristics and biases* (pp. 306–334). New York: Cambridge University Press.

Liebert, R. M., & Baron, R. A. (1972). Some immediate effects of televised violence on children's behavior. *Developmental Psychology, 6,* 469–475.

Lindsay, D. S., & Johnson, M. K. (1989). The eyewitness suggestibility effect and memory for source. *Memory and Cognition, 17,* 349–358.

Lindsay, R. C. L., & Wells, G. L. (1985). Improving eyewitness identifications from lineups: Simultaneous versus sequential lineup presentation. *Journal of Applied Psychology, 70,* 556–564.

Lindsay, R. C. L., Wells, G. L., & Rumpel, C. M. (1981). Can people detect eyewitness-identification accuracy within and across situations? *Journal of Applied Psychology, 66,* 79–89.

Lindskold, S. (1978). Trust development, the GRIT proposal, and the effect of conciliatory acts on conflict and cooperation. *Psychological Bulletin, 85,* 772–793.

Lindskold, S., & Han, G. (1988). GRIT as a foundation for integrative bargaining. *Personality and Social Psychology Bulletin, 14,* 335–345.

Linville, P. W., Fischer, G. W., & Salovey, P. (1989). Perceived distributions of characteristics of in-group and out-group members: Empirical evidence and a computer simulation. *Journal of Personality and Social Psychology, 57,* 165–188.

Linz, D., Donnerstein, E., & Penrod, S. (1984). The effects of multiple exposure to filmed violence against women. *Journal of Communication, 34,* 130–137.

Linz, D., Donnerstein, E., & Penrod, S. (1988). Effects of long-term exposure to violent and sexually degrading depictions of women. *Journal of Personality and Social Psychology, 55,* 758–768.

Littlepage, G. E. (1991). Effects of group size and task characteristics on group performance: A test of Steiner's model. *Personality and Social Psychology Bulletin, 17,* 449–456.

Livesley, W. J., & Bromley, D. B. (1973). *Person perception in childhood and adolescence.* New York: Wiley.

Lloyd, S. A., & Cate, R. M. (1985). The developmental course of conflict in dissolution of premarital relationships. *Journal of Social and Personal Relationships, 2,* 179–194.

Lloyd Morgan, C. (1961). C. Lloyd Morgan. In C. Murchison (Ed.), *History of psychology in autobiography* (Vol. 2, pp. 237–264). New York: Russell & Russell. (Original work published 1930)

Loftus, E. F. (1979). *Eyewitness testimony.* Cambridge, MA: Harvard University Press.

Loftus, E. F., & Hoffman, H. G. (1989). Misinformation and memory: The creation of new memories. *Journal of Experimental Psychology: General, 118,* 100–104.

Loftus, E. F., Loftus, G. R., & Messo, J. (1987). Some facts about "weapons focus." *Law and Human Behavior, 11,* 55–62.

Loftus, E. F., Miller, D. G., & Burns, H. J. (1978). Semantic integration of verbal information into a visual memory. *Journal of Experimental Psychology: Human Learning and Memory, 4,* 19–31.

Loftus, E. F., & Palmer, J. C. (1974). Reconstruction of automobile destruction: An example of the interaction between language and memory. *Journal of Verbal Learning and Verbal Behavior, 13,* 585–589.

London, P. (1970). The rescuers: Motivational hypotheses about Christians who saved Jews from the Nazis. In J. R. Macaulay & L. Berkowitz (Eds.), *Altruism and helping behavior* (pp. 241–250). New York: Academic Press.

Lord, C. G., Lepper, M. R., & Preston, E. (1984). Considering the opposite: A corrective strategy for social judgment. *Journal of Personality and Social Psychology, 47,* 1231–1243.

Lord, C. G., Ross, L., & Lepper, M. (1979). Biases assimilation and attitude polarization: The effects of prior theories on subsequently considered evidence. *Journal of Personality and Social Psychology, 37,* 2098–2109.

Lore, R. K., & Schultz, L. A. (1993). Control of human aggression. *American Psychologist, 48,* 16–25.

Lorenz, K. (1966). *On aggression* (M. Wilson, Trans.). New York: Harcourt, Brace, & World.

Lott, A. J., & Lott, B. E. (1961). Group cohesiveness, communication level, and conformity. *Journal of Abnormal and Social Psychology, 62,* 408–412.

Lott, A. J., & Lott, B. E. (1974). The role of reward in the formation of positive interpersonal attitudes. In T. Huston (Ed.), *Foundations of interpersonal attraction.* New York: Academic Press.

Lowry, D. T., Love, G., & Kirby, M. (1981). Sex on the soap operas: Patterns of intimacy. *Journal of Communication, 31,* 90–96.

Lykken, D. T. (1984). Polygraphic interrogation. *Nature, 307,* 681–684.

Lynn, M., & Shurgot, B. A. (1984). Responses to lonely hearts advertisements: Effects of reported physical attractiveness, physique, and coloration. *Personality and Social Psychology Bulletin, 10,* 349–357.

Lysak, H., Rule, B. G., & Dobbs, A. R. (1989). Conceptions of aggression: Prototypes or defining features? *Personality and Social Psychology Bulletin, 15,* 233–243.

Maass, A., & Clark, R. D. III. (1984). Hidden impact of minorities: Fifteen years of research. *Psychological Bulletin, 95,* 428–450.

Maccoby, E. E., & Jacklin, C. N. (1974). *The psychology of sex differences.* Stanford, CA: Stanford University Press.

MacCoun, R. J. (1989). Experimental research on jury decision-making. *Science, 244,* 1046–1050.

Maclean, N. (1983). *A river runs through it.* Chicago: University of Chicago Press.

Madaras, G. R., & Bem, D. J. (1968) Risk and conservatism in group decision making. *Journal of Experimental Social Psychology, 4,* 350–366.

Maier, N. R. F., & Solem, A. R. (1952). The contribution of a discussion leader to the quality of group thinking: The effective use of minority opinions. *Human Relations, 5,* 277–288.

Main, M., Kaplan, N., & Cassidy, J. (1985). Security in infancy, childhood, and adulthood: A move to the level of representation. In T. Bretherton & E. Waters (Eds.), *Growing points of attachment theory and research. Monographs of the Society for Research on Child Development, 50,* 66–104.

Major, B. (1980). Information acquisition and attribution process. *Journal of Personality and Social Psychology, 39,* 1010–1023.

Malamuth, N. M. (1981). Rape fantasies as a function of exposure to violent sexual stimuli. *Archives of Sexual Behavior, 10,* 33–47.

Malamuth, N. M. (1986). Predictors of naturalistic sexual aggression. *Journal of Personality and Social Psychology, 50,* 953–962.

Malamuth, N. M., & Briere, J., (1986). Sexual violence in the media: Indirect effects on aggression against women. *Journal of Social Issues, 42*(3), 75–92.

Malamuth, N. M., Check, J., & Briere, J. (1986). Sexual arousal in response to aggression: Ideological, aggressive, and sexual correlates. *Journal of Personality and Social Psychology, 50,* 330–350.

Malamuth, N. M., & Donnerstein, E. (1983). The effects of aggressive-pornographic mass media stimuli. In L. Berkowitz (Ed.), *Advances in experimental social psychology* (Vol. 15, pp. 103–136). New York: Academic Press.

Malpass, R. S., & Devine, P. G. (1981). Eyewitness identification: Lineup instructions and the absence of the offender. *Journal of Applied Psychology, 66,* 482–489.

Mandler, G. (1975). *Mind and emotion*. New York: Wiley.

Maracek, J., & Mettee, D. R. (1972). Avoidance of continued success as a function of self-esteem, level of esteem certainty, and responsibility for success. *Journal of Personality and Social Psychology, 22*, 90–107.

Markus, H. (1977). Self-schemata and processing information about the self. *Journal of Personality and Social Psychology, 35*, 63–78.

Markus, H. (1980). The self in thought and memory. In D. H. Wegner & R. R. Vallacher (Eds.), *The self in social psychology* (pp. 102–130). New York: Oxford University Press.

Markus, H., & Kitayama, S. (1991). Culture and the self: Implications for cognition, emotion, and motivation. *Psychological Review, 98*, 224–253.

Markus, H., & Nurius, P. (1986). Possible selves. *American Psychologist, 41*, 954–969.

Markus, H., & Sentis, K. (1982). The self in social information processing. In J. Suls (Ed.), *Psychological perspectives on the self* (Vol. 1, pp. 41–70). Hillsdale, NJ: Erlbaum.

Markus, H., & Zajonc, R. B. (1985). The cognitive perspective in social psychology. In G. Lindzey & E. Aronson (Eds.), *Handbook of social psychology* (Vol. 1, pp. 137–230). Hillsdale, NJ: Erlbaum.

Marlowe, D., & Gergen, K. J. (1970). Personality and social behavior. In K. J. Gergen & D. Marlowe (Eds.), *Personality and social behavior* (p. 1–75). Reading, MA: Addison-Wesley.

Marshall, G. D., & Zimbardo, P. G. (1979). Affective consequences of inadequately explained physiological arousal. *Journal of Personality and Social Psychology, 37*, 970–988.

Maslach, C. (1979). Negative emotional biasing of unexplained arousal. *Journal of Personality and Social Psychology, 37*, 953–969.

Mayfield, E. C. (1964). The selection interview—A re-evaluation of published research. *Personnel Psychology, 17*, 239–260.

McAlister, A., Perry, C., Killen, J., Slinkard, L. A., & Maccoby, N. (1980). Pilot study of smoking, alcohol, and drug abuse prevention. *American Journal of Public Health, 70*, 719–721.

McArthur, L. (1972). The how and what of why: Some determinants and consequences of causal attribution. *Journal of Personality and Social Psychology, 22*, 171–193.

McArthur, L. Z. (1990). *Social perception*. Pacific Grove, CA: Brooks/Cole.

McArthur, L. Z., & Baron, R. M. (1983). Toward an ecological theory of social perception. *Psychological Review, 90*, 215–238.

McArthur, L. Z., & Resko, G. B. (1975). The portrayal of men and women in American television commercials. *Journal of Social Psychology, 97*, 209–220.

McCallum, D. M., Harring, K., Gilmore, R., Drenan, S., Chase, J., Insko, C. A., & Thibaut, J. (1985). Competition between groups and between individuals. *Journal of Experimental Social Psychology, 21*, 301–320.

McCann, S. J. H. (1992). Alternative formulas to predict the greatness of U.S. presidents: Personological, situational, and zeitgeist factors. *Journal of Personality and Social Psychology, 62*, 469–479.

McCarthy, J. F., & Kelly, B. R. (1978). Aggressive behavior and its effect on performance over time in ice hockey athletes: An archival study. *International Journal of Sport Psychology, 9*, 90–96.

McCauley, C. (1989). The nature of social influence in groupthink: Compliance and internalization. *Journal of Personality and Social Psychology, 57*, 250–260.

McClelland, D. C. (1975). *Power: The inner experience*. New York: Irvington.

McClintock, C. G., & Liebrand, W. B. G. (1988). Role of interdependence structure, individual value orientation, and another's strategy in social decision making: A transformational analysis. *Journal of Personality and Social Psychology, 55*, 396–409.

McCloskey, M., & Zaragoza, M. (1985). Misleading postevent information and memory for events: Arguments and evidence against memory impairment hypotheses. *Journal of Experimental Psychology: General, 114*, 1–16.

McConahay, J. B. (1981). Reducing racial prejudice in desegregated schools. In W. D. Hawley (Ed.), *Effective school desegregation*. Beverly Hills, CA: Sage.

McConahay, J. B. (1986). Modern racism, ambivalence, and the Modern Racism Scale. In J. F. Dovidio & S. L. Gaertner (Eds.), *Prejudice, discrimination and racism: Theory and Research*. New York: Academic Press.

McFarland, C., & Ross, M. (1987). The relation between current impressions and memories of self and dating partners. *Personality and Social Psychology Bulletin, 13*, 228–238.

McGrath, J. E. (1984). *Groups: Interaction and performance*. Englewood Cliffs, NJ: Prentice Hall.

McGuire, W. J. (1964). Inducing resistance to persuasion. In L. Berkowitz (Ed.), *Advances in experimental social psychology* (Vol. 1, pp. 192–229). New York: Academic Press.

McGuire, W. J. (1968). Personality and susceptibility to social influence. In E. F. Borgatta & W. W. Lambert (Eds.), *Handbook of personality theory and research* (pp. 1130–1187). Chicago: Rand McNally.

McGuire, W. J. (1985). Attitudes and attitude change. In G. Lindzey & E. Aronson (Eds.), *Handbook of social psychology* (3rd ed., Vol. 2, pp. 233–346). New York: Random House.

McGuire, W. J., & McGuire, C. V. (1981). The spontaneous self-concept as affected by personal distinctiveness. In M. D. Lynch, A. A. Norem-Hebeisen, & K. J. Gergen (Eds.), *Self-concept: Advances in theory and research* (pp. 147-171). Cambridge, MA: Ballinger.

McGuire, W. J., McGuire, C. V., Child, P., & Fujioka, T. (1978). Salience of ethnicity in the spontaneous self-concept as a function of one's ethnic distinctiveness in the social environment. *Journal of Personality and Social Psychology, 36*, 511–520.

McGuire, W. J., & Padawer-Singer, A. (1976). Trait salience in the spontaneous self-concept. *Journal of Personality and Social Psychology, 33*, 743–754.

Mead, G. H. (1934). *Mind, self, and society*. Chicago: University of Chicago Press.

Mead, M. (1977). Jealousy: Primitive and socialized. In G. Clanton & L. G. Smith (Eds.), *Jealousy* (pp. 115–127). Englewood Cliffs, NJ: Prentice Hall.

Medalia, N. Z., & Larsen, O. N. (1969). Diffusion and belief in a collective delusion: The Seattle windshield pitting epidemic. In R. Evans (Ed.), *Readings in collective behavior* (pp. 247–258). Chicago: Rand McNally.

Meindl, J. R., & Lerner, M. J. (1985). Exacerbation of extreme responses to an out-group. *Journal of Personality and Social Psychology, 47,* 71–84.

Melara, R. D., DeWitt-Rickards, T. S., & O'Brien, T. P. (1989). Enhancing lineup identification accuracy: Two codes are better than one. *Journal of Applied Psychology, 74,* 706–713.

Menninger, W. (1948). Recreation and mental health. *Recreation, 42,* 340–346.

Merikle, P. M. (1988). Subliminal auditory messages: An evaluation. *Psychology and Marketing, 5,* 355–372.

Merton, R. K. (1948). The self-fulfilling prophecy. *Antioch Review, 8,* 193–210.

Messick, D. M., & Brewer, M. B. (1983). Solving social dilemmas: A review. In L. Wheeler & P. Shaver (Eds.), *Review of personality and social psychology* (Vol. 4, pp. 11–44). Beverly Hills, CA: Sage.

Mettee, D., & Aronson, E. (1974). Affective reactions to appraisal from others. In T. L. Huston (Ed.), *Foundations of interpersonal attraction.* New York: Academic Press.

Mettee, D., Taylor, S. E., & Friedman, H. (1973). Affect conversion and the gain-loss effect. *Sociometry, 36,* 505–519.

Meyer, J. P., & Pepper, S. (1977). Need compatibility and marital adjustment in young married couples. *Journal of Personality and Social Psychology, 35,* 331–342.

Michaels, J. W., Blommel, J. M., Brocato, R. M., Linkous, R. A., & Rowe, J. S. (1982). Social facilitation and inhibition in a natural setting. *Replications in Social Psychology, 2,* 21–24.

Michaelson, L. K., Watson, W. E., & Black, R. H. (1989). A realistic test of individual versus group consensus decision making. *Journal of Applied Psychology, 74,* 834–839.

Milgram, S. (1961). Nationality and conformity. *Scientific American, 205,* 45–51.

Milgram, S. (1963). Behavioral study of obedience. *Journal of Abnormal and Social Psychology, 67,* 371–378.

Milgram, S. (1970). The experience of living in cities. *Science, 167,* 1461–1468.

Milgram, S. (1974). *Obedience to authority: An experimental view.* New York: Harper & Row.

Milgram, S. (1976). Obedience to criminal orders: The compulsion to do evil. In T. Blass (Ed.), *Contemporary Social Psychology: Representative readings* (pp. 175–184). Itasca, IL: F.E. Peacock Publishers.

Milgram, S. (1977) . *The individual in a social world.* Reading, MA: Addison-Wesley.

Milgram, S., & Sabini, J. (1978). On maintaining urban norms: A field experiment in the subway. In A. Baum, J. E. Singer, & S. Valins (Eds.), *Advances in environmental psychology* (Vol. 1, pp. 9-40). Hillsdale, NJ: Erlbaum.

Mill, J. S. (1974). *A system of logic ratiocinative and inductive.* Toronto: University of Toronto Press. (Original work published 1843)

Millar, M. G., & Tesser, A. (1986). Effects of affective and cognitive focus on the attitude-behavior relationship. *Journal of Personality and Social Psychology, 51,* 270–276.

Miller, C. (1972). *Women in Policing.* Washington, D.C.: Police Foundation.

Miller, C. E., & Anderson, P. D. (1979). Group decision rules and the rejection of deviates. *Social Psychology Quarterly, 42,* 354–363.

Miller, C. T. (1982). The role of performance-related similarity in social comparison of abilities: A test of the related attributes hypothesis. *Journal of Experimental Social Psychology, 18,* 513–523.

Miller, D. T., & Ross, M. (1975). Self-serving biases in the attribution of causality: Fact or fiction? *Psychological Bulletin, 82,* 213–225.

Miller, J. G. (1984). Culture and the development of everyday social explanation. *Journal of Personality and Social Psychology, 46,* 961–978.

Miller, N., & Bugelski, R. (1948). Minor studies in aggression: The influence of frustrations imposed by the in-group on attitudes expressed by the out-group. *Journal of Psychology, 25,* 437–442.

Miller, N., & Campbell, D. T. (1959). Recency and primacy in persuasion as a function of the timing of speeches and measurements. *Journal of Anormal and Social Psychology, 59,* 1–9.

Mills, J. (1958). Changes in moral attitudes following temptation. *Journal of Personality, 26,* 517–531.

Mills, J., & Clark, M. S. (1982). Communal and exchange relationships. In L. Wheeler (Ed.), *Review of personality and social psychology* (Vol. 2, pp. 121–144). Beverly Hills, CA: Sage.

Minard, R. D. (1952). Race relations in the Pocohontas coal field. *Journal of Social Issues, 8,* 29–44.

Mischel, W. (1968). *Personality and assessment.* New York: Wiley.

Mita, T. H., Dermer, M., & Knight, J. (1977). Reversed facial images and the mere-exposure hypothesis. *Journal of Personality and Social Psychology, 35,* 597–601.

Montemayor, R., & Eisen, M. (1977). The development of self-conceptions from childhood to adolescence. *Developmental Psychology, 13,* 314–319.

Moore, J. S., Graziano, W. G., & Millar, M. G. (1987). Physical attractiveness, sex role orientation, and the evaluation of adults and children. *Personality and Social Psychology Bulletin, 13,* 95–102.

Moore, T. E. (1982). Subliminal advertising: What you see is what you get. *Journal of Marketing, 46,* 38–47.

Moore, T. E. (1992). Subliminal perception: Facts and fallacies. *Skeptical Inquirer, 16,* 273–281.

Moreland, R. L., & Zajonc, R. B. (1982). Exposure effects in person perception: Familiarity, similarity, and attraction. *Journal of Experimental Social Psychology, 18,* 395–415.

Morris, E. (Director). (1988). *Thin blue line* [film]. New York: HBO Videos.

Morris, W. N., & Miller, R. S. (1975). The effects of consensus-breaking and consensus-preempting partners on reduction of conformity. *Journal of Experimental Social Psychology, 11,* 215–223.

Morsbach, H. (1973). Aspects of nonverbal communication in Japan. *Journal of Nervous and Mental Disease, 157,* 262–277.

Moscovici, S. (1980). Toward a theory of conversion behavior. In L. Berkowitz (Ed.), *Advances in experimental social psychology* (Vol. 13, pp. 209–239). Orlando, FL: Academic Press.

Moscovici, S. (1985). Social influence and conformity. In G. Lindzey & E. Aronson (Eds.), *Handbook of social psychology* (Vol. 2, pp. 347–412). New York: Random House.

Moscovici, S., & Nemeth, C. (1974). Minority influence. In C. Nemeth (Ed.), *Social psychology: Classic and contemporary integrations* (pp. 217–249). Chicago: Rand McNally.

Moyer, K. E. (1976). *The psychobiology of aggression.* New York: Harper & Row.

Moyer, K. E. (1983). The physiology of motivation: Aggression as a model. In C. J. Scheier & A. M. Rogers (Eds.), *G. Stanley Hall Lecture Series* Vol. 3. Washington, DC: American Psychological Association.

Mullen, B. (1986). Atrocity as a function of lynch mob composition: A self-attention perspective. *Personality and Social Psychology Bulletin, 12,* 187–197.

Mullen, B., & Baumeister, R. F. (1987). Group effects on self-attention and performance: Social loafing, social facilitation, and social impairment. In C. Hendrick (Ed.), *Group processes and intergroup relations* (Vol. 9, pp. 189–206). Newbury Park, CA: Sage.

Mullen, B., & Johnson, C. (1988). *Distinctiveness-based illusory correlations and stereotyping: A meta-analytic integration.* Unpublished manuscript, Syracuse University.

Mullen, B., Johnson, C., & Salas, E. (1991). Productivity loss in brainstorming groups. *Basic and Applied Social Psychology, 12,* 3–24.

Münsterberg, H. (1908). *On the witness stand: Essays on psychology and crime.* New York: Doubleday, Page.

Mussen, P., & Eisenberg-Berg, N. (1977). *Roots of caring, sharing, and helping: The development of prosocial behavior in children.* San Francisco: W. H. Freeman.

My Lai: An American tragedy. *Time*(Dec. 5, 1969), pp. 26–32.

Myers, D. G. (1982). Polarizing effects of social interaction. In H. Brandstatter, J. H. Davis, & G. Stocher-Kreichgauer (Eds.), *Contemporary problems in group decision-making* (pp. 125–161). New York: Academic Press.

Myers, D. G., & Arenson, S. J. (1972). Enhancement of dominant risk tendencies in group discussion. *Psychological Reports, 30,* 615–623.

Nadler, A. (1991). Help-seeking behavior: Psychological costs and instrumental benefits. In M. S. Clark (Ed.), *Prosocial behavior: Review of personality and social psychology* (Vol. 12, pp. 290–311). Newbury Park, CA: Sage.

Nadler, A., & Fisher, J. D. (1986). The role of threat to self-esteem and perceived control in recipient reactions to help: Theory development and empirical validation. In L. Berkowitz (Ed.), *Advances in experimental social psychology* (Vol. 19, pp. 81–123). New York: Academic Press.

Nahemow, L., & Lawton, M. P. (1975). Similarity and propinquity in friendship formation. *Journal of Personality and Social Psychology, 32,* 205–213.

Nathanson, S. (1987). *An eye for an eye? The morality of punishing by death.* Totowa, NJ: Roman & Littlefield.

Neil v. Biggers, 409 U.S. 188 (1972).

Neisser, U. (1976). *Cognition and reality: Principles and implications of cognitive psychology.* San Francisco: Freeman.

Nel, E., Helmreich, R., & Aronson, E. (1969). Opinion change in the advocate as a function of the persuasibility of his audience: A clarification of the meaning of dissonance. *Journal of Personality and Social Psychology, 12,* 117–124.

Nemeth, C. (1972). A critical analysis of research utilizing the prisoner's dilemma paradigm for the study of bargaining. In L. Berkowitz (Ed.), *Advances in experimental social psychology* (Vol. 6, pp. 203–234). New York: Academic Press.

Nemeth, C. J. (1986). Differential contributions of majority and minority influence. *Psychological Review, 93,* 23–32.

Nemeth, C. J., & Chiles, C. (1988). Modeling courage: The role of dissent in fostering independence. *European Journal of Social Psychology, 18,* 275–280.

Nemeth, C. J., Mayseless, O., Sherman, J., & Brown, Y. (1990). Exposure to dissent and recall of information. *Journal of Personality and Social Psychology, 58,* 429–437.

Neuberg, S. L. (1988). Behavioral implications of information presented outside of awareness: The effect of subliminal presentation of trait information on behavior in the Prisoner's Dilemma game. *Social Cognition, 6,* 207–230.

Neuberg, S. L. (1989). The goal of forming accurate impressions during social interactions: Attenuating the impact of negative expectancies. *Journal of Personality and Social Psychology, 56,* 374–386.

*New Yorker* (1957, September 21), p. 33.

*New Yorker* (1991, November 4), p. 106.

Newcomb, T. M. (1947). Autistic hostility and social reality. *Human Relations, 1,* 69–86.

Newcomb, T. M. (1961). *The acquaintance process.* New York: Holt, Rinehart, & Winston.

Newcomb, T. M. (1963). Persistence and regression of changed attitudes: Long-range studies. *Journal of Social Issues, 19,* 3–14.

Newtson, D. (1974). Dispositional inferences from effects of actions: Effects chosen and effects forgone. *Journal of Experimental Social Psychology, 10,* 489–496.

Newtson, D. (1990). Alternatives to representation or alternative representations: Comments on the ecological approach. *Contemporary Social Psychology, 14,* 163–174.

Nichols, J. G. (1975). Casual attributions and other achievement-related cognitions: Effects of task outcome, attainment value, and sex. *Journal of Personality and Social Psychology, 31,* 379–389.

Nicholson, N., Cole, S. G., & Rocklin, T. (1985). Conformity in the Asch situation: A comparison between contemporary British and U.S. university students. *British Journal of Social Psychology, 24,* 59–63.

Nietzsche, F. W. (1918). *The genealogy of morals.* New York: Modern Library.

Nisbett, R. E., Caputo, C., Legant, P., & Marecek, J. (1973). Behavior as seen by the actor and by the observer. *Journal of Personality and Social Psychology, 27,* 154–164.

Nisbett, R. E., Fong, G. T., Lehman, D. R., & Cheng, P. W. (1987). Teaching reasoning. *Science, 238,* 625–631.

Nisbett, R. E., Krantz, D. H., Jepson, C., & Kunda, Z. (1983). The use of statistical heuristics in everyday inductive reasoning. *Psychological Review, 90,* 339–363.

Nisbett, R. E., & Ross, L. (1980). *Human inference: Strategies and shortcomings of human judgment.* Englewood Cliffs, NJ: Prentice Hall.

Nisbett, R. E., & Valins, S. (1972). Perceiving the causes of one's own behavior. In E. E. Jones, D. E. Kanouse, H. H. Kelley, R. E. Nisbett, S. Valins, & B. Weiner (Eds.), *Attribution: Perceiving the causes of behavior* (pp. 63–78). Morristown, NJ: General Learning Press.

Nisbett, R. E., & Wilson, T. D. (1977a). Telling more than we can know: Verbal reports on mental processes. *Psychological Review, 84,* 231–259.

Nisbett, R. E., & Wilson, T. D. (1977b). The halo effect: Evidence for unconscious alteration of judgments. *Journal of Personality and Social Psychology, 35,* 250–256.

Nixon, R. M., *In the arena: a memoir of victory, defeat, and renewal.* New York: Simon and Schuster.

Nolen-Hoeksema, S., Girgus, J. S., & Seligman, M. E. P. (1986). Learned helplessness in children: A longitudinal study of depression, achievement, and explanatory style. *Journal of Personality and Social Psychology, 51,* 435–442.

Nowak, A., Szamrej, J., & Latané, B. (1990). From private attitude to public opinion: A dynamic theory of social impact. *Psychological Review, 97,* 362–376.

Oakes, P. J., & Turner, J. C. (1980). Social categorization and intergroup behavior: Does minimal intergroup discrimination make social identity more positive? *European Journal of Social Psychology, 10,* 295–301.

Ohbuchi, K., Kamdea, M., & Agarie, N. (1989). Apology as aggression control: Its role in mediating appraisal of and response to harm. *Journal of Personality and Social Psychology, 56,* 219–227.

O'Leary, A. (1990). Stress, emotion, and human immune function. *Psychological Bulletin, 108,* 363–382.

Olson, J. M., & Zanna, M. P. (1993). Attitudes and attitude change. *Annual Review of Psychology, 44,* 117–154.

Olweus, D. (1991). Bully/victim problems among school children: Basic facts and effects of a school-based intervention program. In D. Pepler & K. Rubin (Eds.), *The development and treatment of childhood aggression* (pp. 411–448). Hillsdale, NJ: Erlbaum.

Olzak, S., & Nagel, J. (1986). *Competitive Ethnic Relations.* New York: Academic Press.

Orbell, J. M., van de Kragt, A. J. C., & Dawes, R. M. (1988). Explaining discussion-induced comparison. *Journal of Personality and Social Psychology, 54,* 811–819.

Osborn, A. F. (1957). *Applied imagination.* New York: Scribner.

Osgood, C. E. (1962). *An alternative to war or surrender.* Urbana, IL: University of Illinois Press.

Osherow, N. (1988). Making sense of the nonsensical: An analysis of Jonestown. In E. Aronson (Ed.), *Readings about the social animal* (pp. 68–86). New York: W. H. Freeman.

O'Sullivan, C. S., & Durso, F. T. (1984). Effects of schema-incongruent information on memory for stereotypical attributes. *Journal of Personality and Social Psychology, 47,* 55–70.

Otten, C. A., Penner, L. A., & Waugh, G. (1988). That's what friends are for: The determinants of psychological helping. *Journal of Social and Clinical Psychology, 7,* 34–41.

Overmier, J. B., & Seligman, M. E. P. (1967). Effects of inescapable shock upon subsequent escape and avoidance learning. *Journal of Comparative and Physiological Psychology, 63,* 23–33.

Packard, V. (1957). *The hidden persuaders.* New York: D. McKay.

Palazzoli, M. P. (1974). *Anorexia nervosa.* London: Chaucer.

Pallak, M. S., & Pittman, T. S. (1972). General motivation effects of dissonance arousal. *Journal of Personality and Social Psychology, 21,* 349–358.

Park, B., & Rothbart, M. (1982). Perception of out-group homogeneity and levels of social categorization: Memory for the subordinate attributes of in-group and out-group members. *Journal of Personality and Social Psychology, 42,* 1051–1068.

Parke, R. D., Berkowitz, L., Leyes, J. P., West, S. G., & Sebastian, R. J. (1977). Some effects of violent and nonviolent movies on the behavior of juvenile delinquents. In L. Berkowitz (Ed. ), *Advances in experimental social psychology* (Vol. 10, pp. 135-172). New York: Academic Press.

Patch, M. E. (1986). The role of source legitimacy in sequential request strategies of compliance. *Personality and Social Psychology Bulletin, 12,* 199–205.

Patterson, A. (1974, September). *Hostility catharsis: A naturalistic quasi-experiment.* Paper presented at the annual convention of the American Psychological Association, New Orleans.

Patton, P. (1989, August 6). Steve Jobs out for revenge. *New York Times Magazine,* pp. 23, 52, 56, 58.

Paulus, P. B., Dzindolet, M. T., Poletes, G., & Camacho, L. M. (1993). Perception of performance in group brainstorming: The illusion of group productivity. *Personality and Social Psychology Bulletin, 19,* 78–89.

Paulus, P. B., McCain, G., Cox, V. (1981). Prison standards: Some pertinent data on crowding. *Federal Probation, 15,* 48–54.

Pedersen, D. M. (1965). The measurement of individual differences in perceived personality-trait relationships and their relation to certain determinants. *Journal of Social Psychology, 65,* 233–258.

Pennebaker, J. W. (1982). *The psychology of physical symptoms.* New York: Springer-Verlag.

Pennebaker, J. W. (1990). *Opening up.* New York: Morrow.

Pennebaker, J. W., & Sanders, D. Y. (1976). American graffiti: Effects of authority and reactance arousal. *Personality and Social Psychology Bulletin, 2,* 264–267.

Pennington, N., & Hastie, R. (1988). Explanation-based decision making: Effects of memory structure on judgment. *Journal of Experimental Psychology: Learning, Memory, and Cognition, 14,* 521–533.

Pennington, N., & Hastie, R. (1990). Practical implications of psychological research on juror and jury decision making. *Personality and Social Psychology Bulletin, 16,* 90–105.

Pennington, N., & Hastie, R. (1992). Explaining the evidence: Tests of the Story Model for juror decision making. *Journal of Personality and Social Psychology, 62,* 189–206.

Peplau, L. A., & Perlman, D. (1982). Perspectives on loneliness. In L. A. Peplau & D. Perlman (Eds.), *Loneliness: A sourcebook of current theory, research, and therapy.* New York: Wiley.

Perrin, S., & Spencer, C. (1981). Independence or conformity in the Asch experiment as a reflection of cultural or situational factors. *British Journal of Social Psychology, 20,* 205–209.

Peters, L. H., Hartke, D. D., & Pohlmann, J. T. (1985). Fiedler's contingency theory of leadership: An application of the meta-analysis procedures of Schmidt and Hunter. *Psychological Bulletin, 97,* 274–285.

Peterson, C., & Seligman, M. E. P. (1984). Causal explanations as a risk factor for depression: Theory and evidence. *Psychological Review, 91,* 347–374.

Peterson, C., Seligman, M. E. P., & Vaillant, G. E. (1988). Pessimistic explanatory style is a risk factor for physical illness: A thirty-five-year longitudinal study. *Journal of Personality and Social Psychology, 55,* 23–27.

Peterson, R. D., & Bailey, W. C. (1988). Murder and capital punishment in the evolving context of the post-Furman era. *Social Forces, 66,* 774–807.

Pettigrew, T. F. (1958). Personality and sociocultural factors and intergroup attitudes: A cross-national comparison. *Journal of Conflict Resolution, 2,* 29–42.

Pettigrew, T. F. (1969). Racially separate or together? *Journal of Social Issues, 25,* 43–69.

Pettigrew, T. F. (1979). The ultimate attribution error: Extending Allport's cognitive analysis of prejudice. *Personality and Social Psychology Bulletin, 5,* 461–476.

Pettigrew, T. F. (1981). Extending the stereotype concept. In D. L. Hamilton (Ed.), *Cognitive processes in stereotyping and intergroup behavior.* Hillsdale, NJ: Erlbaum.

Pettigrew, T. F. (1985). New black-white patterns: How best to conceptualize them? *Annual Review of Sociology, 11,* 329–346.

Petty, R. E., & Brock, T. C. (1981). Thought disruption and persuasion: Assessing the validity of attitude change experiments. In R. E. Petty, T. M. Ostrom, & T. C. Brock (Eds.), *Cognitive responses in persuasion* (pp. 55–79). Hillsdale, NJ: Erlbaum.

Petty, R. E., & Cacioppo, J. T. (1981). *Attitudes and persuasion: Classic and contemporary approaches.* Dubuque, IA: William C. Brown.

Petty, R. E., & Cacioppo, J. T. (1986). *Communication and persuasion: Central and peripheral routes to attitude change.* New York: Springer-Verlag.

Petty, R. E., Cacioppo, J. T., & Goldman, R. (1981). Personal involvement as a determinant of argument-based persuasion. *Journal of Personality and Social Psychology, 41,* 847–855.

Petty, R. E., & Krosnick, J. A. (1993). *Attitude strength: Antecedents and consequences.* Hillsdale, NJ: Erlbaum.

Petty, R. E., Wells, G. L., & Brock, T. C. (1976). Distraction can enhance or reduce yielding to propaganda: Thought disruption versus effort justification. *Journal of Personality and Social Psychology, 34,* 874–884.

Philipsen, G., Mulac, A., & Dietrich, D. (1979). The effects of social interaction on group idea generation. *Communication Monographs, 46,* 119–125.

Phillips, D. P. (1983). The impact of mass media violence on U.S. homicides. *American Sociological Review, 48,* 560–568.

Phillips, D. P. (1986). Natural experiments on the effects of mass media violence on fatal aggression: Strengths and weaknesses of a new approach. In L. Berkowitz (Ed.), *Advances in experimental social psychology* (Vol. 19, pp. 207–250). Orlando, FL: Academic Press.

Piliavin, I. M., Piliavin, J. A. & Rodin, J. (1975). Costs, diffusion, and the stigmatized victim. *Journal of Personality and Social Psychology, 32,* 429–438.

Piliavin, I. M., Rodin, J., & Piliavin, J. (1969). Good Samaritanism: An underground phenomenon? *Journal of Personality and Social Psychology, 13,* 289–299.

Piliavin, J. A., Dovidio, J. F., Gaertner, S., & Clark, R. D. III. (1981). *Emergency intervention.* New York: Academic Press.

Piliavin, J. A., & Piliavin, I. M. (1972). The effect of blood on reactions to a victim. *Journal of Personality and Social Psychology, 23,* 253–261.

Pines, A., & Aronson, E. (1983). Antecedents, correlates, and consequences of romantic jealousy. *Journal of Personality, 51,* 108–136.

Pittman, T. S., & Heller, J. F. (1987). Social motivation. *Annual Review of Psychology, 38,* 461–489.

Pleban, R., & Tesser, A. (1981). The effects of relevance and quality of another's performance on interpersonal closeness. *Social Psychology Quarterly, 44,* 278–285.

Polanyi, M. (1958). *Personal knowledge: Toward a post-critical philosophy.* New York: Harper & Row.

Porter, J. R. (1971). *Black child, white child: The development of racial attitudes.* Cambridge, MA: Harvard University Press.

Porter, J. R., & Washington, R. E. (1979). Black identity and self-esteem, 1968–1978. *Annual Review of Sociology.* Stanford, CA: Annual Reviews.

Potter, S. (1971). *One-upmanship.* New York: Holt, Rinehart, & Winston.

Povinelli, D. J. (1993). Reconstructing the evolution of mind. *American Psychologist, 48,* 493–509.

Powledge, F. (1991). *Free at last? The civil rights movement and the people who made it.* Boston: Little, Brown.

Pratkanis, A. R. (1992). The cargo-cult science of subliminal persuasion. *Skeptical Inquirer, 16,* 260–272.

Pratkanis, A. R., & Aronson, E. (1991). *Age of propaganda: The everyday use and abuse of persuasion.* New York: Freeman.

Prentice-Dunn, S., & Rogers, R. W. (1989). Deindividuation and the self-regulation of behavior. In P. B. Paulus (Ed.), *Psychology of group influence* (2nd ed.). Hillsdale, NJ: Erlbaum.

Priest, R. F., & Sawyer, J. (1967). Proximity and peership: Bases of balance in interpersonal attraction. *American Journal of Sociology, 72,* 633–649.

Proust, M. (1934). *Remembrance of things past* (C. K. Scott-Moncrieff, Trans.). New York: Random House.

Pruitt, D.G. (1971). Choice shifts in group discussion: An introductory review. *Journal of Personality and Social Psychology, 20,* 339–360.

Pruitt, D. G., & Kimmel, M. J. (1977). Twenty years of experimental gaming: Critique, synthesis, and suggestions for the future. *Annual Review of Psychology, 28,* 363–392.

Pryor, J. B. (1980). Self-reports and behavior. In D. M. Wegner & R. R. Vallacher (Eds.), *The self in social psychology* (pp. 206–228). New York: Oxford University Press.

Pryor, J. B., Gibbons, F. X., Wicklund, R. A., Fazio, R. H., & Hood, R. (1977). Self-focused attention and self-report validity. *Journal of Personality, 45,* 513–527.

Pyszczynski, T. A., & Greenberg, J. (1987). Toward an integration of cognitive and motivational perspectives on social inference: A biased hypothesis-testing model. In L. Berkowitz (Ed.), *Advances in experimental social psychology* (Vol. 20, pp. 297–340). San Diego, CA: Academic Press.

Pyszczynski, T. A., Greenberg, J., & LaPrelle, J. (1985). Social comparison after success and failure: Biased search for information consistent with a self-serving conclusion. *Journal of Experimental Social Psychology, 21*, 195–211.

Quattrone, G. A. (1982). Behavioral consequences of attributional bias. *Social Cognition, 1*, 358–378.

Quattrone, G. A. (1986). On the perception of a group's variability. In S. Worchel & W. G. Austin (Eds.), *Psychology of Intergroup Relations* (second edition). Chicago: Nelson Hall.

Quattrone, G. A., & Jones, E.E. (1980). The perception of variability within ingroups and outgroups: Implications for the law of small numbers. *Journal of Personality and Social Psychology, 38*, 141–152.

Rajecki, D. W., Kidd, R. F., & Ivins, B. (1976). Social facilitation in chickens: A different level of analysis. *Journal of Experimental Social Psychology, 12*, 233–246.

Ralston, S. M. (1988). The effect of applicant race upon personnel selection decisions: A review with recommendations. *Employee Responsibilities and Rights Journal, 1*, 215–226.

Ramsey, S. J. (1981). The kinesics of femininity in Japanese women. *Language Sciences, 3*, 104–123.

Rapoport, A., & Chammah, A. M. (1965). *Prisoner's Dilemma: A study in conflict and cooperation.* Ann Arbor: University of Michigan Press.

Raps, C. S., Peterson, C., Jonas, M., & Seligman, M. E. P. (1982). Patient behavior in hospitals: Helplessness, reactance, or both? *Journal of Personality and Social Psychology, 42*, 1036–1041.

Raskin, D. C. (1986). The polygraph in 1986: Scientific, professional, and legal issues surrounding applications and acceptance of polygraph evidence. *Utah Law Review*, 29–74.

Reagan, R. (1990). *An American Life.* New York: Simon and Schuster.

Rehm, J., Steinleitner, M., & Lilli, W. (1987). Wearing uniforms and aggression: A field experiment. *European Journal of Social Psychology, 17*, 357–360.

Reifman, A. S., Larrick, R., & Fein, S. (1988). *The heat-aggression relationship in major-league baseball.* Paper presented at the American Psychological Association convention in San Francisco.

Reis, H. T., Wheeler, L., Speigel, N., Kernis, M. H., Nezlek, J., & Perri, M. (1982). Physical attractiveness in social interaction II: Why does appearance affect social experience? *Journal of Personality and Social Psychology, 43*, 979–996.

Reiter, S. M., & Samuel, W. (1980). Littering as a function of prior litter and the presence or absence of prohibitive signs. *Journal of Applied Social Psychology, 10*, 45–55.

Reitzes, D. C. (1952). The role of organizational structures: Union versus neighborhood in a tension situation. *Journal of Social Issues, 9*, 37–44.

Reno, R., Cialdini, R., & Kallgren, C. A. (1993). The transsituational influence of social norms. *Journal of Personality and Social Psychology, 64*, 104–112.

Rheingold, H. L. (1982). Little children's participation in the work of adults: A nascent prosocial behavior. *Child Development, 53*, 114–125.

Rhodewalt, F., & Davison, J. (1984). *Self-handicapping and subsequent performance: The role of outcome valence and attitudinal certainty.* Unpublished manuscript, University of Utah.

Richmond, V. P., McCroskey, J. C., & Payne, S. K. (1991). *Nonverbal behavior in interpersonal relations.* Englewood Cliffs, NJ: Prentice Hall.

Richter, C. P. (1957). On the phenomenon of sudden death in animals and man. *Psychosomatic Medicine, 19*, 191–198.

Rigby, K. (1988). Sexist attitudes and authoritarian personality characteristics among Australian adolescents. *Journal of Research in Personality, 22*, 465–473.

Rim, Y. (1963). Risk-taking and the need for achievement. *Acta Psychologica, 21*, 108–115.

Riordan, C. A. (1978). Equal-status interracial contact: A review and revision of a concept. *International Journal of Intercultural Relations, 2*, 161–185.

Rodin, J. (1985). The application of social psychology. In G. Lindzey & E. Aronson (Eds.), *Handbook of social psychology* (3rd. ed., Vol. 2, pp. 805–881). New York: Random House.

Rodin, J. (1986). Aging and health: Effects of the sense of control. *Science, 233*, 1271–1276.

Rodin, J., & Langer, E. J. (1977). Long-term effects of a control-relevant intervention with the institutional aged. *Journal of Personality and Social Psychology, 35*, 897–902.

Rogers, R. (1983). Cognitive and physiological processes in fear appeals and attitude change: A revised theory of protection motivation. In J. T. Cacioppo & R. E. Petty (Eds.), *Social psychophysiology: A sourcebook* (pp.153–176). New York: Guilford Press.

Rogers, R., & Prentice-Dunn, S. (1981). Deindividuation and anger-mediated interracial aggression: Unmasking regressive racism. *Journal of Personality and Social Psychology, 41*, 63–73.

Rohrer, J. H., Baron, S. H., Hoffman, E. L., & Swander, D. V. (1954). The stability of autokinetic judgments. *Journal of Abnormal and Social Psychology, 49*, 595–597.

Rosch, E., & Lloyd, B. (1978). (Eds.) *Cognition and Categorization.* Hillsdale, NJ: Erlbaum.

Rosen, S., Bergman, M., Plester, D., El-Mofty, A., & Satti, M. (1962). Prebycusis study of a relatively noise-free population in the Sudan. *Annals of Otology, Rhinology, and Laryngology, 71*, 727–743.

Rosenbaum, M. E. (1986). The repulsion hypothesis: On the nondevelopment of relationships. *Journal of Personality and Social Psychology, 51*, 1156–1166.

Rosenberg, L. A. (1961). Group size, prior experience, and conformity. *Journal of Abnormal and Social Psychology, 63*, 436–437.

Rosenberg, M. J., Davidson, A. J., Chen, J., Judson, F. N., & Douglas, J. M. (1992). Barrier contraceptives and sexually transmitted diseases in women: A comparison of female-dependent methods and condoms. *American Journal of Public Health, 82*, 669–674.

Rosenberg, S., Nelson, S., & Vivekananthan, P. S. (1968). A multidimensional approach to the structure of personality impressions. *Journal of Personality and Social Psychology, 9*, 283–294.

Rosenhan, D. L. (1970). The natural socialization of altruistic autonomy. In J. R. Macaulay & L. Berkowitz (Eds.), *Altruism and helping behavior* (pp. 251–268). New York: Academic Press.

Rosenhan, D. L. (1973). On being sane in insane places. *Science*, 179, 250–258.

Rosenthal, A. M. (1964). *Thirty-eight witnesses*. New York: McGraw-Hill.

Rosenthal, R. (1974). *On the social psychology of the self-fulfilling prophecy: Further evidence for Pygmalion effects and their mediating mechanisms*. New York: MSS Modular Publications.

Rosenthal, R., & DePaulo, B. M. (1979). Sex differences in accommodation in nonverbal communication. In R. Rosenthal (Ed.), *Skill in nonverbal communication: Individual differences* (pp. 68–103). Cambridge, MA: Oelgeschlager, Gunn, & Hain.

Rosenthal, R., Hall, J. A., DiMatteo, M. R., Rogers, P. L., & Archer, D. (1979). *Sensitivity to nonverbal communication: The PONS test*. Baltimore, MD: Johns Hopkins University Press.

Rosenthal, R., & Jacobson, L. (1968). *Pygmalion in the classroom: Teacher expectation and student intellectual development*. New York: Holt, Rinehart, & Winston.

Ross, L. (1977). The intuitive psychologist and his shortcomings: Distortions in the attribution process. In L. Berkowitz (Ed.), *Advances in experimental social psychology* (Vol. 10, pp. 173–220). Orlando, FL: Academic Press.

Ross, L., Amabile, T. M., & Steinmetz, J. L. (1977). Social roles, social control, and biases in social perception. *Journal of Personality and Social Psychology*, 35, 485–494.

Ross, L., Lepper, M. R., & Hubbard, M. (1975). Perseverance in self perception and social perception: Biased attributional processes in the debriefing paradigm. *Journal of Personality and Social Psychology*, 32, 880–892.

Ross, L., & Nisbett, R. E. (1991). *The person and the situation*. New York: McGraw-Hill.

Ross, M. (1976). The self-perception of intrinsic motivation. In J. H. Harvey, W. J. Ickes, & R. F. Kidd (Eds.), *New directions in attribution research* (Vol. 1, pp. 121–141). Hillsdale, NJ: Erlbaum.

Ross, M. (1989). Relation of implicit theories to the construction of personal histories. *Psychological Review*, 96, 341–357.

Ross, M., & Conway, M. (1985). Remembering one's own past: The construction of personal histories. In R. Sorrentino & E. T. Higgins (Eds.), *Handbook of motivation and cognition* (pp. 122–144). New York: Guilford Press.

Ross, M., & McFarland, C. (1988). Constructing the past: Biases in personal memories. In D. Bar-Tel & A. Kruglanski (Eds.), *The social psychology of knowledge* (pp. 299–314). New York: Cambridge University Press.

Ross, M., & Olson, J. M. (1981). An expectancy-attribution model of the effects of placebos. *Psychological Review*, 88, 408–437.

Rothbart, M., & John, O. P. (1985). Social categorization and behavioral episodes: A cognitive analysis of the effects of intergroup contact. *Journal of Social Issues*, 41(3), 81–104.

Rothbart, M., & Park, B. (1986). On the confirmability and disconfirmability of trait concepts. *Journal of Personality and Social Psychology*, 50, 131–142.

Rotton, J., & Frey, J. (1985). Air pollution, weather, and violent crimes: Concomitant time-series analysis of archival date. *Journal of Personality and Social Psychology*, 49, 1207–1220.

Rousseau, J. J. (1930). *The social contract and discourses*. New York: Dutton.

Rubin, J., & Brown, B. (1975). *The social psychology of bargaining and negotiation*. New York: Academic Press.

Rubin, Z. (1970). Measurement of romantic love. *Journal of Personality and Social Psychology*, 16, 265–273.

Rubin, Z. (1973). *Liking and loving: An invitation to social psychology*. New York: Holt, Rinehart, & Winston.

Rubin, Z, Peplau, L. A., & Hill, C. T. (1981). Loving and leaving: Sex differences in romantic attachments. *Sex Roles*, 7, 821–835.

Ruble, D. N., & Feldman, N. S. (1976). Order of consistency, distinctiveness, and consistency information and causal attribution. *Journal of Personality and Social Psychology*, 34, 930–937.

Rudolfsky, M. P. (1972). *The unfashionable human body*. New York: Doubleday.

Rule, B. G., Taylor, B. R., & Dobbs, A. R. (1987). Priming effects of heat on aggressive thoughts. *Social Cognition*, 5, 131–143.

Rusbult, C. E. (1980). Commitment and satisfaction in romantic associations: A test of the investment model. *Journal of Experimental Social Psychology*, 16, 172–186.

Rusbult, C. E. (1983). A longitudinal test of the investment model: The development (and deterioration) of satisfaction and commitment in heterosexual involvements. *Journal of Personality and Social Psychology*, 45, 101–117.

Rusbult, C. E. (1991). *Commitment processes in close relationships: The investment model*. Paper presented at the annual meeting of the American Psychological Association, San Francisco.

Rusbult, C. E., Johnson, D. J., & Morrow, G. D. (1986). Impact of couple patterns of problem solving on distress and nondistress in dating relationships. *Journal of Personal and Social Psychology*, 50, 744–753.

Rusbult, C. E., & Zembrodt, I. M. (1983). Responses to dissatisfaction in romantic involvements: A multidimensional scaling analysis. *Journal of Experimental Social Psychology*, 43, 1230–1242.

Rushton, J. P. (1975). Generosity in children: Immediate and long-term effects of modeling, preaching, and moral judgment. *Journal of Personality and Social Psychology*, 31, 459–466.

Rushton, J. P. (1989). Genetic similarity, human altruism, and group selection. *Behavioral and Brain Sciences*, 12, 503–559.

Russell, B., & Branch, T. (1979). *Second wind: The memoirs of an opinionated man*. New York: Ballantine Books.

Russell, G. W. (1983). Psychological issues in sports aggression. In J. H. Goldstein (Ed.), *Sports violence*. New York: Springer-Verlag.

Russell, J. A., Ward, L. M., & Pratt, G. (1981). Affective quality attributed to environments: A factor analytic study. *Environment and Behavior*, 13, 259–288.

Ryle, G. (1949). *The concept of mind*. London: Hutchinson.

Sacks, O. (1985). *The man who mistook his wife for a hat and other clinical tales*. New York: Harper & Row.

Sadik, N. (1991). World population continues to rise. *The Futurist, 25,* 9–14.

Sadker, M., & Sadker, D. (1985, March). Sexism in the schoolroom of the '80s. *Psychology Today,* pp. 54–57.

Sakurai, M. M. (1975). Small group cohesiveness and detrimental conformity. *Sociometry, 38,* 340–357.

Salovey, P., Mayer, J. D., & Rosenhan, D. L. (1991). Mood and helping: Mood as a motivator of helping and helping as a regulator of mood. In M. S. Clark (Ed.), *Prosocial behavior: Review of personality and social psychology* (Vol. 12, pp. 215–237). Newbury Park, CA: Sage.

Salovey, P., & Rodin, J. (1985). Cognitions about the self: Connecting feeling states and social behavior. In P. Shaver (Ed.), *Self, situations, and social behavior: Review of personality and social psychology* (Vol. 6, pp. 143–166). Beverly Hills, CA: Sage.

Salovey, P., & Rodin, J. (1989). Envy and jealousy in close relationships. In C. Hendrick (Ed.), *Close relationships: Review of personality and social psychology* (pp. 221–246). Newbury Park, CA: Sage.

Salovey, P., & Rodin, J. (1991). Provoking jealousy and envy: Domain relevance and self-esteem threat. *Journal of Social and Clinical Psychology, 10,* 395–413.

Samuels, S. M., & Ross, L. (1993). Reputations versus labels: The power of situational effects in the Prisoner's Dilemma Game. Unpublished manuscript, Stanford University.

Sanders, G. S. (1983). An attentional process model of social facilitation. In A. Hare, H. Bumberg, V. Kent, & M. Davies (Eds.), *Small groups.* London: Wiley.

Saxe, L., Dougherty, D., & Cross, T. (1985). The validity of polygraph testing: Scientific analysis and public controversy. *American Psychologist, 40,* 355–366.

Schachter, S. (1951). Deviation, rejection, and communication. *Journal of Abnormal and Social Psychology, 46,* 190–207.

Schachter, S. (1959). *The psychology of affiliation.* Stanford, CA: Stanford University Press.

Schachter, S. (1964). The interaction of cognitive and physiological determinants of emotional state. In L. Berkowitz (Ed.), *Advances in experimental social psychology* (Vol. 1, pp. 49–80). New York: Academic Press.

Schachter, S. (1977). Nicotine regulation in heavy and light smokers. *Journal of Experimental Psychology: General, 106,* 5–12.

Schachter, S., & Singer, J. E. (1962). Cognitive, social, and physiological determinants of emotional states. *Psychological Review, 69,* 379–399.

Schachter, S., & Singer, J. E. (1979). Comments on the Maslach and Marshall-Zimbardo experiments. *Journal of Personality and Social Psychology, 37,* 989–995.

Schafer, R. B., & Keith, P. M. (1980). Equity and depression among married couples. *Social Psychology Quarterly, 43,* 430–435.

Scheier, M. F., Matthews, K. A., Owens, J., Magovern, G. J., Lefebvre, R. C., Abbott, R. A., & Carver, C. S. (1990). Dispositional optimism and recovery from coronary artery bypass surgery: The beneficial effects of physical and psychological well-being. *Journal of Personality and Social Psychology, 57,* 1024–1040.

Schlenker, B. R. (1980). *Impression management: The self-concept, social identity, and interpersonal relations.* Monterey, CA: Brooks/Cole.

Schmidt, D. E., & Keating, J. P. (1979). Human crowding and personal control: An integration of the research. *Psychological Bulletin, 86,* 680–700.

Schmitt, B. H., Gilovich, T., Goore, N., & Joseph, L. (1986). Mere presence and social facilitation: One more time. *Journal of Experimental Social Psychology, 22,* 228–241.

Schneider, D. J. (1973). Implicit personality theory: A review. *Psychological Bulletin, 79,* 294–309.

Schneider, D. J., Hastorf, A. H., & Ellsworth, P. C. (1979). *Person perception* (2nd ed.). Reading, MA: Addison-Wesley.

Schoeneman, T. J., & Rubanowitz, D. E. (1985). Attributions in the advice columns: Actors and observers, causes and reasons. *Personality and Social Psychology Bulletin, 11,* 315–325.

Schofield, J. W. (1986). Causes and consequences of the color-blind perspective. In J. F. Dovidio & S. L. Gaertner (Eds.), *Prejudice, discrimination, and racism.* Orlando, FL: Academic Press.

Schroeder, D. A., Dovidio, J. F., Sibicky, M. E., Matthews, L. L., & Allen, J. L. (1988). *Journal of Experimental Social Psychology, 24,* 333–353.

Schroeder, D. H., & Costa, P. T., Jr. (1984). Influence of life event stress on physical illness: Substantive effects or methodological flaws? *Journal of Personality and Social Psychology, 46,* 853–863.

Schuler, E. A., & Parenton, V. J. (1943). A recent epidemic of hysteria in a Louisiana high school. *Journal of Social Psychology, 17,* 221–235.

Schulz, R. (1976). Effects of control and predictability on the physical and psychological well-being of the institutionalized aged. *Journal of Personality and Social Psychology, 33,* 563–573.

Schulz, R., & Hanusa, B. H. (1978). Long-term effects of control and predictability-enhancing interventions: Findings and ethical issues. *Journal of Personality and Social Psychology, 36,* 1202–1212.

Schuman, H., & Kalton, G. (1985). Survey methods. In G. Lindzey & E. Aronson (Eds.), *Handbook of social psychology* (3rd ed., Vol. 1, pp. 635–697). New York: Random House.

Schwartz, S. H., & Gottlieb, A. (1976). Bystander reactions to a violent theft: Crime in Jerusalem. *Journal of Personality and Social Psychology, 34,* 1188–1199.

Schwarz, N., Bless, H., Strack, F., Klumpp, G., Rittenauer-Schatka, H., & Simmons, A. (1991). Ease of retrieval as information: Another look at the availability heuristic. *Journal of Personality and Social Psychology, 61,* 195–202.

Scott, J. P. (1958). *Aggression.* Chicago: University of Chicago Press.

Sears, D. O. (1981). Life stage effects on attitude change, especially among the elderly. In S. B. Kiesler, J. N. Morgan, & V. K. Oppenheimer (Eds.), *Aging: Social change* (pp. 183–204). New York: Academic Press.

Secord, P. F., & Backman, C. W. (1964). *Social psychology.* New York: McGraw-Hill.

Segal, M. W (1974). Alphabet and attraction: An unobtrusive measure of the effect of propinquity in a field setting. *Journal of Personality and Social Psychology, 30,* 654–657.

Seligman, M. E. P. (1975). *Helplessness: On depression, development, and death*. San Francisco: Freeman.

Seligman, M. E. P., & Maier, S. F. (1967). Failure to escape traumatic shock. *Journal of Experimental Psychology, 74*, 1–9.

Seligman, M. E. P., & Schulman, P. (1986). Explanatory style as a predictor of productivity and quitting among life insurance agents. *Journal of Personality and Social Psychology, 50*, 832–838.

Selye, H. (1956). *The stress of life*. New York: McGraw-Hill.

Selye, H. (1976). *Stress in health and disease*. Woburn, MA: Butterworth.

Shaffer, D. R. (1986). Is mood-induced altruism a form of hedonism? *Humboldt Journal of Social Relations, 13*, 195–216.

Sharan, S. (1980). Cooperative learning in small groups. *Review of Educational Research, 50*, 241–271.

Sharp, F. C. (1928). *Ethics*. New York: Century Company.

Shaver, K. (1970). Defensive attribution: Effects of severity and relevance on the responsibility assigned for an accident. *Journal of Personality and Social Psychology, 14*, 101–113.

Shaver, P. R., Hazan, C., & Bradshaw, D. (1988). Love as attachment: The integration of three behavioral systems. In R. J. Sternberg & M. L. Barnes (Eds.), *The psychology of love* (pp. 68–99). New Haven, CT: Yale University Press.

Shaver, P. R., Schwartz, J., Kirson, D., & O'Connor, C. (1987). Emotion knowledge: Further exploration of a prototype approach. *Journal of Personality and Social Psychology, 52*, 1061–1086.

Shavitt, S. (1989). Operationalizing functional theories of attitude. In A. R. Pratkanis, S. J. Breckler, & A. G. Greenwald (Eds.), *Attitude structure and function* (pp. 311–337). Hillsdale, NJ: Erlbaum.

Shavitt, S. (1990). The role of attitude objects in attitude function. *Journal of Experimental Social Psychology, 26*, 124–148.

Shaw, M. E. (1971). *Group dynamics: The psychology of small group behavior*. New York: McGraw-Hill.

Sheehan, S. (1982). *Is there no place on earth for me?* Boston: Houghton Mifflin.

Sheppard, B. H., Hartwick, J., & Warshaw, P. R. (1988). The theory of reasoned action: A meta-analysis of past research with recommendations for modifications and future research. *Journal of Consumer Research, 15*, 325–343.

Sherif, M. (1936). *The psychology of social norms*. New York: Harper & Row.

Sherif, M., Harvey, O. J., White, J., Hood, W., & Sherif, C. (1961). Intergroup conflict and cooperation: The robber's cave experiment. Norman: University of Oklahoma, Institute of Intergroup Relations.

Sherif, M., & Sherif, C. W. (1969). *Social psychology*. New York: Harper & Row.

Sherman, I. W., & Berk, R. A. (1984). The specific deterrent effects or arrest for domestic assault. *American Sociological Review, 49*, 261–272.

Sherman, L. W. (1992). The influence of criminology on criminal law: Evaluating arrests for misdemeanor domestic violence. *Journal of Criminal Law and Criminology, 83*, 1–45.

Sherrod, D. R. (1974). Crowding, perceived control, and behavioral aftereffects. *Journal of Applied Social Psychology, 4*, 171–186.

Sherrod, D. R., & Cohen, S. (1979). Density, personal control, and design. In A. Baum & J. R. Aiello (Eds.), *Residential crowding and design* (pp. 217–227). New York: Plenum.

Shettel-Neuber, J., Bryson, J. B., & Young, L. E. (1978). Physical attractiveness of the "other person" and jealousy. *Personality and Social Psychology Bulletin, 4*, 612–615.

Shotland, R. L., & Straw, M. K. (1976). Bystander response to an assault: When a man attacks a woman. *Journal of Personality and Social Psychology, 34*, 990–999.

Shupe, L. M. (1954). Alcohol and crimes: A study of the urine alcohol concentration found in 882 persons arrested during or immediately after the commission of a felony. *Journal of Criminal Law and Criminology, 33*, 661–665.

Sigall, H., & Aronson, E. (1969). Liking for an evaluator as a function of her physical attractiveness and nature of the evaluations. *Journal of Experimental Social Psychology, 5*, 93–100.

Sigall, H., & Ostrove, N. (1975). Beautiful but dangerous: Effects of offender attractiveness and nature of the crime on juridic judgment. *Journal of Personality and Social Psychology, 31*, 410–414.

Sigall, H., & Page, R. (1971). Current stereotypes: A little fading, a little faking. *Journal of Personality and Social Psychology, 18*, 247–255.

Silver, L. B., Dublin, C. C., & Lourie, R. S. (1969). Does violence breed violence? Contributions from a study of the child abuse syndrome. *American Journal of Psychiatry, 126*, 404–407.

Silverstein, B., Perdue, L., Peterson, B., & Kelly, E. (1986). The role of the mass media in promoting a thin standard of bodily attractiveness for women. *Sex Roles, 14*, 519–532.

Silverstein, B., Peterson, B., & Perdue, L. (1986). Some correlates of the thin standard of bodily attractiveness for women. *International Journal of Eating Disorders, 5*(5).

Simonton, D. K. (1984). *Genius, creativity, and leadership: Historiometric inquiries*. Cambridge, MA: Harvard University Press.

Simonton, D. K. (1985). Intelligence and personal influence in groups: Four nonlinear models. *Psychological Review, 92*, 532–547.

Simonton, D. K. (1987). *Why presidents succeed: A political psychology of leadership*. New Haven, CT: Yale University Press.

Simpson, G., & Yinger, J. M., (1885). *Racial and cultural minorities*. New York: Plenum Press.

Simpson, J. A. (1987). The dissolution of romantic relationships: Factors involved in relationship stability and emotional distress. *Journal of Personality and Social Psychology, 53*, 683–692.

Simpson, J. A. (1990). Influence of attachment styles on romantic relationships. *Journal of Personality and Social Psychology, 59*, 971–980.

Simpson, J. A., Rholes, W. S., & Nelligan, J. S. (1992). Support seeking and support giving within couples in an anxiety-provoking situation: The role of attachment styles. *Journal of Personality and Social Psychology, 62*, 434–446.

Singer, J. E., Baum, C. S., Baum, A., & Thew, B. D. (1982). Mass psychogenic illness: The case for social comparison.

In M. J. Colligan, J. W. Pennebaker, & L. R. Murphy (Eds.), *Mass psychogenic illness: A social psychological analysis* (pp.155–169). Hillsdale, NJ: Erlbaum.

Singer, M. (1990). Talk of the town. *The New Yorker*, January 29, 25–26.

Sirois, F. (1982). Perspectives on epidemic hysteria. In M. J. Colligan, J. W. Pennebaker, & L. R. Murphy (Eds.), *Mass psychogenic illness: A social psychological analysis* (pp. 217–236). Hillsdale, NJ: Erlbaum.

Skinner, B. F. (1938). *The behavior of organisms*. New York: Appleton-Century-Crofts.

Slavin, R. E., (1980). Cooperative learning and desegregation. Paper presented at the American Psychological Association convention.

Sloan, J. H., Kellerman, A. L., Reay, D. T., Ferris, J. A., Koepsell, T., Rivara, F. P., Rice, C., Gray, L., & LoGerfo, J. (1988). Handgun regulations, crime, assaults, and homicide: A tale of two cities. *New England Journal of Medicine, 319,* 1256–1261.

Slovic, P., Fischhoff, B., & Lichtenstein, S. (1976). Cognitive processes and societal risk taking. In J. S. Carroll & J. W. Payne (Eds.), *Cognition and social behavior* (pp. 165–184). Hillsdale, NJ: Erlbaum.

Slovic, P., & Lichtenstein, S. (1971). Comparison of Bayesian and regression approaches to the study of information processing in judgment. *Organizational Behavior and Human Performance, 6,* 649–744.

Slusher, M. P., & Anderson, C. A. (1989). Belief perseverance and self-defeating behavior. In R. Curtis (Ed.), *Self-defeating behaviors: Experimental research, clinical impressions, and practical implications* (pp. 11–40). New York: Plenum.

Smith, D. D. (1976). The social content of pornography. *Journal of Communication, 26,* 16–24.

Smith, K. D., Keating, J. P., & Stotland, E. (1989). Altruism reconsidered: The effect of denying feedback on a victim's status to empathic witnesses. *Journal of Personality and Social Psychology, 57,* 641–650.

Smith, M. B., Bruner, J., & White, R. W. (1956). *Opinions and personality.* New York: Wiley.

Smith, R. E., Wheeler, G., & Diener, E. (1975). Faith without works: Jesus people, resistance to temptation, and altruism. *Journal of Applied Psychology, 5,* 320–330.

Smith, S. S., & Richardson, D. (1983). Amelioration of deception and harm in psychological research: The important role of debriefing. *Journal of Personality and Social Psychology, 44,* 1075–1082.

Smith, T. W., Snyder, C. R., & Perkins, S. C. (1983). The self-serving function of hypochondriacal complaints: Physical symptoms as self-handicapping strategies. *Journal of Personality and Social Psychology, 42,* 314–321.

Smith, V. L. (1991). Prototypes in the courtroom: Lay representation of legal concepts. *Journal of Personality and Social Psychology, 61,* 857–872.

Smith, V. L., & Ellsworth, P. C. (1987). The social psychology of eyewitness accuracy: Misleading questions and communicator expertise. *Journal of Applied Psychology, 72,* 294–300.

Smith, V. L., Kassin, S. M., & Ellsworth, P. C. (1989). Eyewitness accuracy and confidence: Within- versus between-subjects correlations. *Journal of Applied Psychology, 74,* 356–359.

Snyder, C. R., & Higgins, R. L. (1988). Excuses: Their effective role in the negotiation of reality. *Psychological Bulletin, 104,* 23–35.

Snyder, C. R., Irving, L. M., & Anderson, J. R. (1991). Hope and health. In C. R. Snyder, & D. R. Forsyth (Eds.), *Handbook of clinical and social psychology* (pp. 285–305). New York: Pergamon.

Snyder, C. R., Smith, T. W., Augelli, R. W., & Ingram, R. E. (1985). On the self-serving function of social anxiety: Shyness as a self-handicapping strategy. *Journal of Personality and Social Psychology, 48,* 970–980.

Snyder, M. (1982). When believing means doing: Creating links between attitudes and behavior. In M. P. Zanna, E. T. Higgins, & C. P. Herman (Eds.), *Consistency in social behavior: The Ontario Symposium* (Vol. 2, pp. 105–130). Hillsdale, NJ: Erlbaum.

Snyder, M. (1984). When belief creates reality. In L. Berkowitz (Ed.), *Advances in Experimental Social Psychology* (Vol. 18, pp. 247–305). Orlando, FL: Academic Press.

Snyder, M., & Ickes, W. (1985). Personality and social behavior. In G. Lindzey & E. Aronson (Eds.), *Handbook of social psychology* (3rd ed., pp. 883–947). New York: Random House.

Snyder, M., & Swann, W. B., Jr. (1978). Hypothesis-testing procedures in social interaction. *Journal of Personality and Social Psychology, 36,* 1202–1212.

Snyder, M., Tanke, E. D., & Berscheid, E. (1977). Social perception and interpersonal behavior: On the self-fulfilling nature of social stereotypes. *Journal of Personality and Social Psychology, 35,* 656–666.

Snyder, M., & Uranowitz, S. W. (1978). Reconstructing the past: Some cognitive consequences of person perception. *Journal of Personality and Social Psychology, 36,* 941–950.

Soames, R. F. (1988). Effective and ineffective use of fear in health promotion campaigns. *American Journal of Public Health, 78,* 163–167.

Solomon, L. Z., Solomon, H., & Stone, R. (1978). Helping as a function of number of bystanders and ambiguity of emergency. *Personality and Social Psychology Bulletin, 4,* 318–321.

Sontag, S. (1978). *Illness as metaphor.* New York: Farrar, Straus, & Giroux.

Sontag, S. (1988). *AIDS and its metaphors.* New York: Farrar, Straus, & Giroux.

Sorenson, T. C. (1966). *Kennedy.* New York: Bantam.

Spencer, S. J., Josephs, R. A., & Steele, C. M. (in press). Low self-esteem: The uphill battle for self-integrity. In R. F. Baumeister (Ed.), *Self-esteem and the puzzle of low self-regard* (pp. 21–36). New York: Wiley.

Srull, T. K. (1981). Person memory: Some tests of associative storage and retrieval models. *Journal of Experimental Psychology: Human Learning and Memory, 7,* 440–462.

Stahyl, S. M., & Lebedun, M. (1974). Mystery gas: An analysis of mass hysteria. *Journal of Health and Social Behavior, 15,* 44–50.

Stangor, C., & Ruble, D. N. (1989). Strength of expectancies and memory for social information: What we remember depends on how much we know. *Journal of Experimental Social Psychology, 25,* 18–35.

Stasser, G., Stella, N., Hanna, C., & Colella, A. (1984). The majority effect in jury deliberations: Number of supporters versus number of supporting arguments. *Law and Psychology Review, 8,* 115–127.

Stasser, G., Taylor, L. A., & Hanna, C. (1989). Information sampling in structured and unstructured discussions in three- and six-person groups. *Journal of Personality and Social Psychology, 57,* 67–78.

Stasser, G., & Titus, W. (1985). Pooling of unshared information in group decision making: Biased information sampling during discussion. *Journal of Personality and Social Psychology, 48,* 1467–1478.

Stasser, G., & Titus, W. (1987). Effects of information load and percentage of shared information on the dissemination of unshared information during group discussion. *Journal of Personality and Social Psychology, 53,* 81–93.

Stasson, M., & Fishbein, M. (1990). The relation between perceived and preventive action: A within-subject analysis of perceived driving risk and intentions to wear seatbelts. *Journal of Applied Social Psychology, 20,* 1541–1557.

Staub, E. (1974). Helping a distressed person: Social, personality, and stimulus determinants. In L. Berkowitz (Ed.), *Advances in experimental social psychology* (Vol. 7, pp. 293–341). New York: Academic Press.

Steblay, N. M. (1987). Helping behavior in rural and urban environments: A meta-analysis. *Psychological Bulletin, 102,* 346–356.

Steele, C. M. (1988). The psychology of self-affirmation: Sustaining the integrity of the self. In L. Berkowitz (Ed.), *Advances in experimental social psychology* (Vol. 21, pp. 261–302). New York: Academic Press.

Steele, C. M. (1992, April). Race and the schooling of black Americans. *Atlantic Monthly,* pp. 68-78.

Steele, C. M., & Josephs, R. A. (1990). Alcohol myopia: Its prized and dangerous effects. *American Psychologist, 45,* 921–933.

Steele, C. M., Hoppe, H., & Gonzales, J. (1986). *Dissonance and the lab coat: Self-affirmation and the free choice paradigm.* Unpublished manuscript, University of Washington.

Steele, C. M. & Liu, T. J. (1981). Making the dissonance act unreflective of the self: Dissonance avoidance and the expectancy of a value affirming response. *Personality and Social Psychology Bulletin, 7,* 383–387.

Steele, C. M. & Liu, T. J. (1983). Dissonance processes as self affirmation. *Journal of Personality and Social Psychology, 45,* 5–19.

Steele, C. M., & Southwick, L. (1985). Alcohol and social behavior I: The psychology of drunken excess. *Journal of Personality and Social Psychology, 48,* 18–34.

Steele, C. M., Spencer, S. J., & Josephs, R. (1992). *Seeking self-relevant information: The effects of self-esteem and stability of the information.* Unpublished manuscript, University of Michigan.

Steele, C. M., Spencer, S. J., & Lynch, M. (1993). Self-image resilience and dissonance: The role of affirmational resources. *Journal of Personality and Social Psychology, 64,* 885–896.

Steele, C. M., Spencer, S. J., & Lynch, M. (in press). Dissonance and self-affirmation resources: Resilience against self-image threats. *Journal of Personality and Social Psychology.*

Steffen, V. J. (1990). Men's motivation to perform the testicle self-exam: Effects of prior knowledge and an educational brochure. *Journal of Applied Social Psychology, 20,* 681–702.

Steinbeck, J. (1988/1961). *Travels with Charley: In search of America.* New York: Penguin Books.

Steiner, I. D. (1972). *Group process and productivity.* New York: Academic Press.

Steiner, I. D., & Rajaratnam, N. A. (1961). A model for the comparison of individual and group performance scores. *Behavioral Science, 11,* 273–283.

Stephan, W. G. (1978). School desegregation: An evaluation of predictions made in Brown vs. Board of Education. *Psychological Bulletin, 85,* 217–238.

Stephan, W. G. (1985). Intergroup relations. In G. Lindzey & E. Aronson (Eds.), *Handbook of Social Psychology* (Vol. 2, pp. 599–658). New York: Random House.

Stern, M., & Hildebrandt, K. A. (1986). Prematurity stereotyping: Effects on mother-infant interaction. *Child Development, 57,* 308–315.

Stern, P. C., & Aronson, E. (1984). *Energy use: The human dimension.* New York: W. H. Freeman and Company.

Sternberg, R. J. (1986). A triangular theory of love. *Psychological Review, 93,* 119–135.

Sternberg, R. J. (1988). *The triangle of love.* New York: Basic Books.

Sternberg, R. J., & Grajek, S. (1984). The nature of love. *Journal of Personality and Social Psychology, 47,* 312–329.

Stich, S. (1990). *The fragmentation of reason: Preface to a pragmatic theory of cognitive evaluation.* Cambridge, MA: MIT Press.

Stich, S., & Nisbett, R. (1980). Justification and the psychology of human reasoning. *Philosophy of Science, 47,* 188–202.

Stogdill, R. M. (1974). *Handbook of leadership.* New York: Free Press.

Stokols, D., & Altman, I. (1987). *Handbook of environmental psychology.* New York: Wiley.

Stone, J., Aronson, E., Crain, A. L., Winslow, M. P., & Fried, C. B. (in press). Inducing hypocrisy as a means of encouraging young adults to use condoms. *Personality and Social Psychology Bulletin.*

Storms, M. (1973). Videotape and the attribution process: Reversing actors' and observers' points of view. *Journal of Personality and Social Psychology, 27,* 165–175.

Storms, M. D., & McCaul, K. D. (1976). Attribution processes and emotional exacerbation of dysfunctional behavior. In J. H. Harvey, W. J. Ickes, & R. F. Kidd (Eds.), *New directions in attribution research* (Vol. 1, pp. 143–164). Hillsdale, NJ: Erlbaum.

Storms, M. D., & Nisbett, R. E. (1970). Insomnia and the attribution process. *Journal of Personality and Social Psychology, 16,* 319–328.

Stouffer, S. A., Suchman, E. A., DeVinney, L. C., Star, S. A., & Williams, R. M., Jr. (1949). *The American soldier: Adjustment during army life* (Vol. 1). Princeton, NJ: Princeton University Press.

Strack, F., Martin, L. L., & Stepper, S. (1988). Inhibiting and facilitating conditions of the human smile: A nonobtrusive test of the facial feedback hypothesis. *Journal of Personality and Social Psychology, 54,* 768–777.

Strauss, M. A., & Gelles, R. J. (1980). *Behind closed doors: Violence in the American family*. New York: Anchor/Doubleday.

Street, W. R. (1974). Brainstorming by individuals, coacting and interacting. *Journal of Applied Psychology, 59*, 433–436.

Stretch, R. H., & Figley, C. R. (1980). Beauty and the boast: Predictors of interpersonal attraction in a dating experiment. *Psychology, A Quarterly Journal of Human Behavior, 17*, 34–43.

Strube, M., & Garcia, J. (1981). A meta-analysis investigation of Fiedler's contingency model of leadership effectiveness. *Psychological Bulletin, 90*, 307–321.

Suls, J., & Fletcher, B. (1983). Social comparison in the social and physical sciences: An archival study. *Journal of Personality and Social Psychology, 44*, 575–580.

Suls, J. M., & Miller, R. L. (Eds.). (1977). *Social comparison processes: Theoretical and empirical perspectives*. Washington, DC: Hemisphere/Halstead.

Summers, G., & Feldman, N. S. (1984). Blaming the victim versus blaming the perpetrator: An attributional analysis of spouse abuse. *Journal of Social and Clinical Psychology, 2*, 339–347.

Swann, W. B., Jr. (1984). Quest for accuracy in person perception. A matter of pragmatics. *Psychological Review, 91*, 457–477.

Swann, W. B., Jr. (1990). To be adored or to be known? The interplay of self-enhancement and self-verification. In R. M. Sorrentino & E. T. Higgins (Eds.), *Motivation and cognition* (pp. 404–448). New York: Guilford Press.

Swann, W. B., Jr., & Ely, R. J. (1984). A battle of wills: Self-verification versus behavioral confirmation. *Journal of Personality and Social Psychology, 46*, 1287–1302.

Swann, W. B., Jr., Hixon, G., & De La Ronde, C. (1992). Embracing the bitter "truth": Negative self-concepts and marital commitment. *Psychological Science, 3*, 118–121.

Swann, W. B., Jr., & Pelham, B. W. (1988). *The social construction of identity: Self-verification through friend and intimate selection*. Unpublished manuscript, University of Texas–Austin.

Swap, W. C. (1977). Interpersonal attraction and repeated exposure to rewarders and punishers. *Personality and Social Psychology Bulletin, 3*, 248–251.

Sweeney, P. D., Anderson, K., & Bailey, S. (1986). Attributional style in depression: A meta-analytic review. *Journal of Personality and Social Psychology, 50*, 974–991.

Swim, J., Borgida, E., Maruyama, G., & Myers, D. G. (1989). Joan McKay vs. John McKay: Do gender stereotypes bias evaluations? *Psychological Bulletin, 105*, 409–429.

Tajfel, H. (1982a). *Social identity and intergroup relations*. Cambridge, England: Cambridge University Press.

Tajfel, H. (1982b). Social psychology of intergroup relations. *Annual Review of Psychology, 33*, 1–39.

Tajfel, H., & Billig, M. (1974). Familiarity and categorization in intergroup behavior. *Journal of Experimental Social Psychology, 10*, 159–170.

Tajfel, H., & Turner, J.C. (1979). An integrative theory of social contact. In W. Austin & S. Worchel (Eds.), *The Social Psychology of Intergroup Relations*. Monterey, CA: Brooks/Cole.

Tanford, S., & Penrod, S. (1984). Social influence model: A formal integration of research on majority and minority influence processes. *Psychological Bulletin, 95*, 189–225.

Tavris, C. (1989). *Anger: The misunderstood emotion*. New York: Touchstone/Simon & Schuster.

Taylor, D. W., Berry, P. C., & Block, C. H. (1958). Does group participation when using brainstorming facilitate or inhibit creative thinking? *Administrative Science Quarterly, 2*, 23–47.

Taylor, S. E. (1981). A categorization approach to stereotyping. In D. L. Hamilton (Ed.), *Cognitive Processes in Stereotyping and Intergroup Relations*. Hillsdale, NJ: Erlbaum.

Taylor, S. E. (1985). *Health psychology*. New York: Random House.

Taylor, S. E. (1989). *Positive illusions: Creative self-deception and the healthy mind*. New York: Basic Books.

Taylor, S. E., & Brown, J. (1988). Illusion and well-being: A social psychological perspective on mental health. *Psychological Bulletin, 103*, 193–210.

Taylor, S. E., & Crocker, J. (1981) Schematic bases of social information processing. In E. T. Higgins, C. P. Herman, & M. P. Zanna (Eds.), *Social cognition: The Ontario Symposium* (Vol. 1, pp. 89–134). Hillsdale, NJ: Erlbaum.

Taylor, S. E., & Fiske, S. T. (1975). Point of view and perceptions of causality. *Journal of Personality and Social Psychology, 32*, 439–445.

Taylor, S. E., Lichtman, R. R., & Wood, J. V. (1984). Attributions, beliefs about control, and adjustment to breast cancer. *Journal of Personality and Social Psychology, 46*, 489–502.

Taylor, S. E., & Lobel, M. (1989). Social comparison activity under threat: Downward evaluation and upward contacts. *Psychological Review, 96*, 569–575.

Taylor, S. P., & Leonard, K. E. (1983). Alcohol and human physical aggression. In R. Geen & E. Donnerstein (Eds.), *Aggression: Theoretical and empirical reviews*. New York: Academic Press.

Taylor, S. P., & Sears, J. D. (1988). The effects of alcohol and persuasive social pressure on human physical aggression. *Aggressive Behavior, 14*, 237–243.

Tedeschi, J. T. (Ed.). (1981). *Impression management theory and social psychological research*. New York: Academic Press.

Teger, A. I., & Pruitt, D. G. (1967). Components of group risk taking. *Journal of Experimental Social Psychology, 3*, 189–205.

Tesser, A. (1980). Self-esteem maintenance in family dynamics. *Journal of Personality and Social Psychology, 39*, 77–91.

Tesser, A. (1988). Toward a self-evaluation maintenance model of social behavior. In L. Berkowitz (Ed.), *Advances in experimental social psychology* (Vol. 21, pp. 181–227). Orlando, FL: Academic Press.

Tesser, A., & Brodie, M. (1971). A note on the evaluation of a computer date. *Psychonomic Science, 23*, 300.

Tesser, A., & Cornell, D. P. (1991). On the confluence of self processes. *Journal of Experimental Social Psychology, 27*, 501–526.

Tesser, A., & Paulus, D. (1983). The definition of self: Private and public self-evaluation management strategies. *Journal of Personality and Social Psychology, 44*, 672–682.

Tesser, A., & Smith, J. (1980). Some effects of friendship and task relevance on helping: You don't always help the one you like. *Journal of Experimental Social Psychology, 16*, 582–590.

Tetlock, P. E. (1983). Accountability and the perseverance of first impressions. *Social Psychology Quarterly, 46*, 285–292.

Tetlock, P. E. (1985). Accountability: A social check on the fundamental attribution error. *Social Psychology Quarterly, 48*, 227–236.

Thibaut, J. W., & Kelley, H. H. (1959). *The social psychology of groups.* New York: Wiley.

Thibodeau, R., & Aronson, E. (1992). Taking a closer look: Reasserting the role of the self-concept in dissonance theory. *Personality and Social Psychology Bulletin, 18*, 591–602.

Thomas, M. H., Horton, R., Lippincott, E., & Drabman, R. (1977). Desensitization to portrayals of real-life aggression as a function of exposure to television violence. *Journal of Personality and Social Psychology, 35*, 450–458.

Thomas, W. I. (1928). *The child in America.* New York: Alfred A. Knopf.

Thompson, L. (1990). Negotiation behavior and outcomes: Empirical evidence and theoretical issues. *Psychological Bulletin, 108*, 515–532.

Thompson, L. (1991). Information exchange in negotiation. *Journal of Experimental Social Psychology, 27*, 161–179.

Thompson, S. C. (1981). Will it hurt less if I can control it? A complex answer to a simple question. *Psychological Bulletin, 90*, 89–101.

Thornton, D., & Arrowood, A. J. (1966). Self-evaluation, self-enhancement, and the locus of social comparison. *Journal of Experimental Social Psychology*, (Suppl. 1), 40–48.

Thornton, W. (1984). Defensive attribution of responsibility: Evidence for an arousal-based motivational bias. *Journal of Personality and Social Psychology, 46*, 721–734.

Toch, H. (1965). *The social psychology of social movements.* Indianapolis: Bobbs-Merrill.

Toch, H. (1980). *Violent men* (rev. ed.). Cambridge, MA: Schenkman.

Traupmann, J., Petersen, R., Utne, M., & Hatfield, E. (1981). Measuring equity in intimate relations. *Applied Psychology Measurement, 5*, 467–480.

Triplett, N. (1898). The dynamogenic factors in pace making and competition. *American Journal of Psychology, 9*, 507–533.

Trivers, R. (1985). *Social evolution.* Menlo Park, CA: Benjamin-Cummings.

Trolier, T. K., & Hamilton, D. L. (1986). Variables influencing judgments of correlational relations. *Journal of Personality and Social Psychology, 50*, 879–888.

Trope, Y., & Bassok, M. (1983). Information-gathering strategies in hypothesis-testing. *Journal of Experimental Social Psychology, 19*, 560–576.

Tucker, J. A., Vuchinich, R. E., & Sobell, M. B. (1981). Alcohol consumption as a self-handicapping strategy. *Journal of Abnormal Psychology, 90*, 220–230.

Turner, C. W., Hesse, B. W., & Peterson-Lewis, S. (1986). Naturalistic studies of the long-term effects of television violence. *Journal of Social Issues, 42*(3), 51–74.

Turner, F. J. (1932). *The significance of sections in American history.* New York: H. Holt and Company.

Tversky, A., & Kahneman, D. (1973). Availability: A heuristic for judging frequency and probability. *Cognitive Psychology, 5*, 207–232.

Tversky, A., & Kahneman, D. (1974). Judgment under uncertainty: Heuristics and biases. *Science, 185*, 1124–1131.

Tversky, A., & Kahneman, D. (1983). Extensional versus intuitive reasoning: The conjunction fallacy in probability judgment. *Psychological Review, 90*, 293–315.

Tversky, B., & Tuchin, M. (1989). A reconciliation of the evidence on eyewitness testimony: Comments on McCloskey and Zaragoza. *Journal of Experimental Psychology: General, 118*, 86–91.

Ulrich, L., & Trumbo, D. (1965). The selection interview since 1949. *Psychological Bulletin, 63*, 100–116.

Uranowitz, S. W. (1975). Helping and self-attributions: A field experiment. *Journal of Personality and Social Psychology, 31*, 852–854.

Valins, S. (1966). Cognitive effects of false heart-rate feedback. *Journal of Personality and Social Psychology, 4*, 400–408.

Vallone, R. P., Griffin, D. W., Lin, S., & Ross, L. (1990). The overconfident prediction of future actions and outcomes by self and others. *Journal of Personality and Social Psychology, 58*, 582–592.

Vallone, R. P., Ross, L., & Lepper, M. R. (1985). The hostile media phenomenon: Biased perception and perceptions of media bias in coverage of the Beirut massacre. *Journal of Personality and Social Psychology, 49*, 577–585.

Van Overwalle, F., & De Metsenaere, M. (1990). The effects of attribution-based intervention and study strategy training on academic achievement in college freshmen. *British Journal of Educational Psychology, 60*, 299–311.

Vance, C. S. (1986, August 2/9). The Meese Commission on the road. *The Nation*, pp. 65, 76.

Vanneman, R. D., & Pettigrew, T. (1972). Race and relative deprivation in the urban United States. *Race, 13*, 461–486.

Voissem, N. H., & Sistrunk, F. (1971). Communication schedules and cooperative game behavior. *Journal of Personality and Social Psychology, 19*, 160–167.

Vonnegut, K. (1963). *Cat's Cradle.* New York: Delacorte Press.

Wagner, R. C. (1975). Complementary needs, role expectations, interpersonal attraction, and the stability of work relationships. *Journal of Personality and Social Psychology, 32*, 116–124.

Wagstaff, G. (1982). Attitudes to rape: The "just world" strikes again? *Bulletin of the British Psychological Society, 35*, 277–279.

Wallach, M. A., Kogan, N., & Bem, D. J. (1962). Group influences on individual risk taking. *Journal of Abnormal and Social Psychology, 65*, 75–86.

Walster, E. (1966). Assignment of responsibility for an accident. *Journal of Personality and Social Psychology, 3*, 73–79.

Walster, E., Aronson, V., Abrahams, D., & Rottman, L. (1966). Importance of physical attractiveness in dating behavior. *Journal of Personality and Social Psychology, 5*, 508–516.

Walster, E., & Festinger, L. (1962). The effectiveness of "overheard" persuasive communication. *Journal of Abnormal and Social Psychology, 65*, 395–402.

Walster, E., Walster, G. W., & Berscheid, E. (1978). *Equity: Theory and research.* Boston: Allyn & Bacon.

Walster, E., Walster, G. W., Piliavin, J., & Schmidt, L. (1973). "Playing hard to get": Understanding an elusive phenomenon. *Journal of Personality and Social Psychology, 26,* 113–121.

Walster, E., Walster, G. W., & Traupmann, J. (1978). Equity and premarital sex. *Journal of Personality, 36,* 82–92.

Warren, B. L. (1966). A multiple variable approach to the assortive mating phenomenon. *Eugenics Quarterly, 13,* 285–298.

Washburn, S., & Hamburg, D. (1965). The implications of primate research In I. DeVore (Ed.), *Primate behavior: Field studies of monkeys and apes* (pp. 607–622). New York: Holt, Rinehart, & Winston.

Watson, D. (1982). The actor and the observer: How are their perceptions of causality divergent? *Psychological Bulletin, 92,* 682–700.

Watson, D., & Pennebaker, J. W. (1989). Health complaints, stress, and distress: Exploring the central role of negative affectivity. *Psychological Review, 96,* 234–254.

Watson, J. (1924). *Behaviorism.* Chicago: University of Chicago Press.

Watson, J. (1950). Some social and psychological situations related to change in attitude. *Human Relations, 3,* 15–56.

Watson, R. I. (1973). Investigation into deindividuation using a cross-cultural survey technique. *Journal of Personality and Social Psychology, 25,* 342–345.

Wattenberg, M. P. (1987). The hollow realignment: Partisan change in a candidate-centered era. *Public Opinion Quarterly, 51,* 58–74.

Weatherly, D. (1961). Anti-Semitism and the expression of fantasy aggression. *Journal of Abnormal and Social Psychology, 62,* 454–457.

Webber, R., & Crocker, J. (1983). Cognitive processes in the revision of stereotypic beliefs. *Journal of Personality and Social Psychology, 45,* 961-977.

Wegner, D. (1986). Transactive memory: A contemporary analysis of the group mind. In B. Mullen & G. R. Goethals (Eds.), *Theories of group behavior* (pp. 185–208). New York: Springer-Verlag.

Wegner, D. M. (1989). *White bears and other unwanted thoughts: Suppression, obsession, and the psychology of mental control.* New York: Viking.

Wegner, D. M. (1992). You can't always think what you want: Problems in the suppression of unwanted thoughts. In M. P. Zanna (Ed.), *Advances in experimental social psychology* (pp. 193–225). San Diego, CA: Academic Press.

Wegner, D. M. (in press). Ironic processes of mental control. *Psychological Review.*

Wegner, D. M., Wenzlaff, R., Kerker, M., & Beattie, A. E. (1981). Incrimination through innuendo: Can media questions become public answers? *Journal of Personality and Social Psychology, 40,* 822–832.

Weinberg, R. S., Richardson, P. A., & Jackson, A. (1983). Effect of situation criticality on tennis performance of males and females. *Newsletter of the Society of the Advancement of Social Psychology, 9,* 8–9.

Weiner, B., Amirkhan, J., Folkes, V. S., & Verette, J. A. (1987). An attributional analysis of excuse giving: Studies of a naive theory of emotion. *Journal of personality and Social Psychology, 52,* 316–324.

Weinstein, N. D. (1980). Unrealistic optimism about future life events. *Journal of Personality and Social Psychology, 39,* 806–820.

Weir, W. (1984, October 15). Another look at subliminal "facts." *Advertising Age,* p. 46.

Weiss, J., & Brown, P. (1977). *Self-insight error in the explanation of mood.* Unpublished manuscript, Harvard University.

Weiss, R. S. (1973). *Loneliness: The experience of emotional and social isolation.* Cambridge, MA: MIT Press.

Wells, G. L. (1984). The psychology of lineup identifications. *Journal of Applied Social Psychology, 14,* 89–103.

Wells, G. L. (1992). *What do we know about eyewitness identification?* Unpublished manuscript, Iowa State University.

Wells, G. L., & Luus, C. A. E. (1990). Police lineups as experiments: Social methodology as a framework for properly conducted lineups. *Personality and Social Psychology Bulletin, 16,* 106–117.

Wells, G. L., Lindsay, R. C. L., & Ferguson, T. J. (1979). Accuracy, confidence, and juror perceptions in eyewitness identification. *Journal of Applied Psychology, 64,* 440–448.

West, S. G., Gunn, S. P., & Chernicky, P. (1975). Ubiquitous Watergate: An attributional analysis. *Journal of Personality and Social Psychology, 32,* 55–62.

Wheeler, L., Koestner, R., & Driver, R. (1982). Related attributes in the choice of comparison others: It's there, but it isn't all there is. *Journal of Experimental Social Psychology, 18,* 489–500.

Whetzel, D. L., McDaniel, M. A., & Schmidt, F. L. (1985, August). *The validity of the employment interview: A review and meta-analysis.* Paper presented at the annual meeting of the American Psychological Association, Los Angeles.

White, G. L. (1980). Physical attractiveness and courtship progress. *Journal of Personality and Social Psychology, 39,* 660–668.

White, G. L. (1981a). A model of romantic jealousy. *Motivation and Emotion, 5,* 295–310.

White, G. L. (1981b). Some correlates of romantic jealousy. *Journal of Personality, 49,* 129–147.

White, R. K. (1977). Misperception in the Arab-Israeli conflict. *Journal of Social Issues, 33,* 190–221.

Whitly, B. E., & Frieze, I. H. (1985). Children's causal attributions for success and failure in achievement settings: A meta-analysis. *Journal of Educational Psychology, 77,* 608–616.

Whittaker, J. O., & Meade, R. D. (1967). Social pressure in the modification and distortion of judgment: A cross-cultural study. *International Journal of Psychology, 2,* 109–113.

Whorf, B. L. (1956). *Language, thought, and reality.* New York: Wiley.

Wicker, A. W. (1969). Attitudes versus actions: The relationship between verbal and overt behavioral responses to attitude objects. *Journal of Social Issues, 25,* 41–78.

Wicklund, R. A. (1975). Objective self-awareness. In L. Berkowitz (Ed.), *Advances in experimental social psychology* (Vol. 8, pp. 233–275). New York: Academic Press.

Wicklund, R. A. (1982). Self-focused attention and the validity of self-reports. In M. P. Zanna, E. T. Higgins, & C. P. Herman (Eds.), *Consistency in social behavior: The Ontario Symposium* (Vol. 2, pp. 149–172). Hillsdale, NJ: Erlbaum.

Wicklund, R. A., & Frey, D. (1980). Self-awareness theory: When the self makes a difference. In D. Wegner & R. Vallacher (Eds.), *The self in social psychology* (pp. 31–54). New York: Oxford University Press.

Wiedenfeld, S. A., O'Leary, A., Bandura, A., Brown, S., Levine, S., & Raska, K. (1990). Impact of perceived self-efficacy in coping with stressors on components of the immune system. *Journal of Personality and Social Psychology, 59,* 1082–1094.

Wiesner, W. H., & Cronshaw, S. F. (1988). The moderating impact of interview format and degree of structure on the validity of the employment interview. *Journal of Occupational Psychology, 61,* 275–290.

Wilder, D. A. (1981). Perceiving persons as a group: Categorization and intergroup relations. In D. L. Hamilton (Ed.), *Cognitive processes in stereotyping and intergroup behavior.* Hillsdale, NJ: Erlbaum.

Wilder, D. A. (1984). Intergroup contact: The typical member and the exception to the rule. *Journal of Experimental Psychology, 20,* 177–194.

Wilder, D. A. (1986). Social categorization: Implications for creation and reduction of intergroup bias. In L. Berkowitz (Ed.), *Advances in Experimental Social Psychology* (Vol. 19, pp. 291–355). New York: Academic Press.

Wilder, D. A., & Shapiro, P. N. (1989). Role of competition-induced anxiety in limiting the beneficial impact of positive behavior by an out-group member. *Journal of Personality and Social Psychology, 56,* 60–69.

Williams, K., Harkins, S., & Latané, B. (1981). Identifiability as a deterrent to social loafing: Two cheering experiments. *Journal of Personality and Social Psychology, 40,* 303–311.

Williams, R. H., & Ross, M. H. (1980, March–April). Drilling for oil and gas in our houses. *Technology Review,* pp. 24–36.

Williams, R. L. (1983, December). For the all-too-common cold, we are perfect, if unwilling, hosts. *Smithsonian,* pp. 47–55.

Williamson, G. M., & Clark, M. S. (1989). Providing help and desired relationship type as determinants of changes in moods and self-evaluations. *Journal of Personality and Social Psychology, 56,* 722–734.

Wills, T. A. (1981). Downward social comparison principles in social psychology. *Psychological Bulletin, 90,* 245–271.

Wills, T. A., Weiss, R. L., & Patterson, G. R. (1974). A behavioral analysis of the determinants of marital satisfaction. *Journal of Consulting and Clinical Psychology, 42,* 802–811.

Wilson, D. K., Purdon, S. E., & Wallston, K. A. (1988). Compliance in health recommendations: A theoretical overview of message framing. *Health Education Research, 3,* 161–171.

Wilson, E. O. (1975). *Sociobiology: The new synthesis.* Cambridge, MA: Belknap Press of Harvard University Press.

Wilson, E. O. (1978). *On human nature.* Cambridge, MA: Harvard University Press.

Wilson, J. Q., & Herrnstein, R. J. (1985). *Crime and human nature.* New York: Simon & Schuster.

Wilson, T. D. (1985). Strangers to ourselves: The origins and accuracy of beliefs about one's own mental states. In J. H. Harvey & G. Weary (Eds.), *Attribution in contemporary psychology* (pp. 9–36). New York: Academic Press.

Wilson, T. D. (1990). Self-persuasion via self-reflection. In J. M. Olson & M. P. Zanna (Eds.), *Self-inference processes: The Ontario Symposium* (Vol. 6, pp. 43–67). Hillsdale, NJ: Erlbaum.

Wilson, T. D., & Brekke, N. C. (1993). *Mental contamination and mental correction: Unwanted influences on judgments and evaluations.* Unpublished manuscript, University of Virginia.

Wilson, T. D., Dunn, D. S., Bybee, J. A., Hyman, D. B., & Rotondo, J. A. (1984). Effects of analyzing reasons on attitude-behavior consistency. *Journal of Personality and Social Psychology, 47,* 5–16.

Wilson, T. D., Dunn, D. S., Kraft, D., & Lisle, D. J. (1989). Introspection, attitude change, and attitude-behavior consistency: The disruptive effects of explaining why we feel the way we do. In L. Berkowitz (Ed.), *Advances in experimental social psychology* (Vol. 19, pp. 123–205). Orlando, FL: Academic Press.

Wilson, T. D., & Hodges, S. D. (1992). Attitudes as temporary constructions. In A. Tesser & L. Martin (Eds.), *The construction of social judgment* (pp. 37–65). Hillsdale, NJ: Erlbaum.

Wilson, T. D., & Kraft, D. (1993). Why do I love thee? Effects of repeated introspections about a dating relationship on attitudes toward the relationship. *Personality and Social Psychology Bulletin, 19,* 409–418.

Wilson, T. D., & LaFleur, S. J. (1992). *Effects of analyzing reasons on the accuracy of self-predictions.* Unpublished manuscript, University of Virginia.

Wilson, T. D., Laser, P. S., & Stone, J. I. (1982). Judging the predictors of one's own mood: Accuracy and the used of shared theories. *Journal of Experimental Social Psychology, 18,* 537–556.

Wilson, T. D., & Lassiter, D. (1982). Increasing intrinsic interest with the use of superfluous extrinsic constraints. *Journal of Personality and Social Psychology, 42,* 811–819.

Wilson, T. D., & Linville, P. W. (1982). Improving the academic performance of college freshmen: Attribution therapy revisited. *Journal of Personality and Social Psychology, 42,* 367–376.

Wilson, T. D., & Linville, P. W. (1985). Improving the performance of college freshmen using attributional techniques. *Journal of Personality and Social Psychology, 49,* 287–293.

Wilson, T. D., Lisle, D. J., Schooler, J., Hodges, S. D., Klaaren, K. J., & LaFleur, S. J. (1993). Introspecting about reasons can reduce post-choice satisfaction. *Personality and Social Psychology Bulletin, 19,* 331–339.

Wilson, T. D., & Stone, J. I. (1985). Limitations of self-knowledge: More on telling more than we can know. In P. Shaver (Ed.), *Review of personality and social psychology* (Vol. 6, pp. 167–183). Beverly Hills, CA: Sage.

Winch, R. (1958). *Mate selection: A study of complementary needs.* New York: Harper & Row.

Winter, D. G. (1987). Leader appeal, leader performance, and the motive profiles of leaders and followers: A study of American presidents and elections. *Journal of Personality and Social Psychology, 52,* 196–202.

Wiseman, F. (Director). (1967). *Titicut follies* [Film]. Cambridge, MA: Zipporah Films.

Wolf, S. (1985). Manifest and latent influence of majorities and minorities. *Journal of Personality and Social Psychology, 48,* 899–908.

Woll, S. (1986). So many to choose from: Decision strategies in videodating. *Journal of Social and Personal Relationships, 3,* 43–52.

Wood, J. V. (1989). Theory and research concerning social comparisons of personal attributes. *Psychological Bulletin, 106,* 231–248.

Wood, J. V., Taylor, S. E., & Lichtman, R. R. (1985). Social comparison in adjustment to breast cancer. *Journal of Personality and Social Psychology, 49,* 1169–1183.

Wood, W. (1982). Retrieval of attitude-relevant information from memory: Effects on susceptibility to persuasion and on intrinsic motivation. *Journal of Personality and Social Psychology, 42,* 798–810.

Word, C. O., Zanna, M. P., & Cooper, J. (1974). The non-verbal mediation of self-fulfilling prophecies in interracial interaction. *Journal of Experimental Social Psychology, 10,* 109–120.

Wortman, C. B., & Brehm, J. W. (1975). Response to uncontrollable outcomes: An integration of reactance theory and the learned helplessness model. In L. Berkowitz (Ed.), *Advances in experimental social psychology* (Vol. 8, pp. 277–336). New York: Academic Press.

Wright, J. C., & Murphy, G. L. (1984). The utility of theories in intuitive statistics: The robustness of theory-based judgments. *Journal of Experimental Psychology: General, 113,* 301–322.

Wright, P. M., Lichtenfels, P. A., & Pursell, E. D. (1989). The structured interview: Additional studies and meta-analysis. *Journal of Occupational Psychology, 62,* 191–199.

Wrightsman, L. S. (1987). *Psychology and the legal system.* Pacific Grove, CA: Brooks/Cole.

Wyer, R. S., & Srull, T. K. (1989). *Memory and cognition in its social context.* Hillsdale, NJ: Erlbaum.

Wyer, R. S., Jr. (1988). Social memory and social judgment. In P. R. Solomon, G. R. Goethals, C. M. Kelley, & B. R. Stephens (Eds.), *Perspectives on memory research.* New York: Springer-Verlag.

Yamaguchi, K., & Kandel, D. B. (1984). Patterns of drug use from adolescence to young adulthood: III. Predictors of progression. *American Journal of Public Health, 74,* 673–681.

Yuille, J. C., & Cutshall, J. L. (1986). A case study of eye-witness memory of a crime. *Journal of Applied Psychology, 71,* 291–301.

Zahn-Waxler, C., Radke-Yarrow, M., & King, R. A. (1979). Child rearing and children's prosocial initiations toward victims of distress. *Child Development, 50,* 319–330.

Zajonc, R. B. (1965). Social facilitation. *Science, 149,* 269–274.

Zajonc, R. B. (1968). Attitudinal effects of mere exposure. *Journal of Personality and Social Psychology, 9,* Monograph Suppl. No. 2, Part 2.

Zajonc, R. B. (1980). Compresence. In P. B. Paulus (Ed.), *Psychology of group influence* (pp. 35–60). Hillsdale, NJ: Erlbaum.

Zajonc, R. B., Heingartner, A., & Herman, E. M. (1969). Social enhancement and impairment of performance in the cockroach. *Journal of Personality and Social Psychology, 13,* 83–92.

Zajonc, R. B., & Sales, S. M. (1966). Social facilitation of dominant and subordinate responses. *Journal of Experimental Social Psychology, 2,* 160–168.

Zanna, M., & Cooper, J. (1974). Dissonance and the pill: An attribution approach to studying the arousal properties of dissonance. *Journal of Personality and Social Psychology, 29,* 703–709.

Zanna, M., & Cooper, J. (1976). Dissonance and the attribution process. In J. H. Harvey, W. Ickes, & R. F. Kidd (Eds.), *New directions in Attribution research* (Vol. 1, pp. 199–217). New York: Erlbaum.

Zanna, M., Goethals, G. R., & Hill, J. (1975). Evaluating a sex-related ability: Social comparison with similar others and standard setters. *Journal of Experimental Social Psychology, 11,* 86–93.

Zanna, M., & Rempel, J. K. (1988). Attitudes: A new look at an old concept. In D. Bar-Tal & A. W. Kruglanski (Eds.), *The social psychology of attitudes* (pp. 315–334). New York: Cambridge University Press.

Zanot, E. J., Pincus, J. D., & Lamp, E. J. (1983). Public perceptions of subliminal advertising. *Journal of Advertising, 12,* 39–45.

Zebrowitz-McArthur, L. (1988). Person perception in cross-cultural perspective. In M. H. Bond (Ed.), *The cross-cultural challenge to social psychology* (pp. 245–265). Newbury Park, CA: Sage.

Zedeck, S., & Cascio, W. F. (1984). Psychological issues in personnel decisions. *Annual Review of Psychology, 35,* 461–518.

Zillmann, D. (1978). Attribution and misattribution of excitatory reactions. In J. H. Harvey, W. J. Ickes, & R. F. Kidd (Eds.), *New directions in attribution research* (Vol. 2, pp. 335–370). Hillsdale, NJ: Erlbaum.

Zillmann, D., & Bryant, J. (1984). Effects of massive exposure to pornography. In N. M. Malamuth & E. Donnerstein (Eds.), *Pornography and sexual aggression.* New York: Academic Press.

Zimbardo, P. G. (1970). The human choice: Individuation, reason, and order versus deindividuation, impulse, and chaos. In W. J. Arnold & D. Levine (Eds.), *Nebraska Symposium on Motivation: 1969* (Vol. 17, pp. 237–307). Lincoln: University of Nebraska Press.

Zimbardo, P. G., Weisenberg, M., Firestone, I., & Levy, B. (1965). Communicator effectiveness in producing public conformity and private attitude change. *Journal of Personality, 33,* 233–255.

Zubek, J. P. (Ed.). (1969). *Sensory deprivation: Fifteen years of research.* New York: Appleton-Century-Crofts.

Zuckerman, M. (1978). Actions and occurrences in Kelley's cube. *Journal of Personality and Social Psychology, 36,* 647–656.

Zuckerman, M., DePaulo, B. M., & Rosenthal, R. (1981). Verbal and nonverbal communication of deception. In L. Berkowitz (Ed.), *Advances in experimental social psychology* (Vol. 14, pp. 1–59). New York: Academic Press.

# CREDITS

Unless otherwise acknowledged, all photographs are the property of Scott, Foresman and Company. Page abbreviations are as follows: (T) top, (C) center, (B) bottom, (L) left, (R) right, (INS) inset, (BG) background.

## CHAPTER 1

**Text and art: p. 15:** Fig. 1.2. From "Effects of reputations and labels in the Prisoner's Dilemma Game: 'Person' versus 'situation' factors" by S. M. Samuels & L. Ross, 1993. Reprinted by permission.

**Photos and cartoons: p.1:** Bob Daemmrich/Uniphoto; **p.2:** Joe Cornish/Tony Stone Images; **p.3:** Kaestner/Uniphoto; **p.4:** AP/Wide World; **p.13:** Collection, The Museum of Modern Art, New York; **p.14:** Greg Smith (Salsa)/TIME Magazine; **p. 14INS:** Waco Tribune Herald/Sygma; **p.18TL:** Archives of the History of American Psychology, University of Akron; **p.18TC:** American Psychological Association; **p.18TR:** American Psychological Association; **p.18BL:** American Psychological Association; **p.18BC:** Courtesy of The Pennsylvania State University Archives; **p.18BR:** Archives of the History of American Psychology, University of Akron; **p.19:** AP/Wide World; **p.20:** The Bettmann Archive; **p.22:** The Kobal Collection; **p.25:** Innervision; **p.26:** Sidney Harris; **p.27:** Canadian Public Health Association.

## CHAPTER 2

**Text and art: p. 57:** Fig. 2.4. From "Aggressive erotica and violence against women" by E. Donnerstein, *Journal of Personality and Social Psychology*, 1980, 39, pp. 269–277. Copyright © 1980 American Psychological Association. Adapted by permission. **p. 66:** Fig. 2.5. From "Ethical principles of psychologists in the conduct of research" from *American Psychologist*, 1992, 47, pp. 1597–1611. Copyright © 1992 American Psychological Association. Extracted and adapted by permission.

**Photos and catoons: p. 32:** AP/Wide World; **p. 35:** Sidney Harris; **p. 38:** Susan Lapides/Design Conceptions; **p. 41L:** Innervisions; **p. 41R:** Charles Gatewood/The Image Works; **p. 45L:** *Literary Digest*; **p. 45R:** *Literary Digest*; **p. 47:** Cheryl Woike Kucharzak; **p. 60:** Joel Gordon Photography.

## CHAPTER 3

**Text and art: p. 88:** Fig. 3.4. From "Reducing fears and increasing assertiveness" by J. Cooper, *Journal of Experimental Social Psychology*, 1980, 47, p. 206. Reprinted by permission of Academic Press, Inc., and the author. **p. 91:** Fig. 3.5. From "Opinion change in the advocate as a function of the persuasibility of this audience" by E. Nel, et al., *Journal of Personality and Social Psychology*, 1969, 12, pp. 117–124. Copyright © 1969 American Psychological Association. Reprinted by permission. **p. 93:** Fig. 3.6. Adapted from "Inducing hypocrisy as a means of encouraging young adults to use condoms" by J. Stone, et al., 1993. Reprinted by permission of J. Stone. **p. 96:** Fig. 3.7. From "Effects of the severity of threat on the devaluation of forbidden behavior" by Aronson & Carlsmith, *Journal of Abnormal and Social Psychology*, 1963, 66, p. 586. Copyright © 1963 American Psychological Association. Reprinted by permission. **p. 99:** Fig. 3.8. From "Liking a person as a function of doing him a favor" by J. Jecker & D. Landy, *Human Relations*, 1969, 22, p. 376. Reprinted by permission of Plenum Publishing Corporation and the author. **p. 103:** Fig. 3.9. From "Dissonance and the pill . . ." by M. Zanna & J. Cooper, *Journal of Personality and Social Psychology*, 1974, 29, p. 706. Copyright © 1974 American Psychological Association. Reprinted by permission. **p. 109:** Fig. 3.12. Adapted from "Dissonance and the lab coat: Self-affirmation and the free choice paradigm" by C. M. Steele, H. Hopp, and J. Gonzales, 1986. Reprinted by permission of the author.

**Photos and cartoons: p. 71:** SuperStock, Inc.; **p. 72:** Lewis Portnoy/Uniphoto; **p. 74:** Brenner/Photo Edit; **p. 82:** D&I MacDonald/The Picture Cube; **p. 83:** Antman/The Image Works; **p. 86:** Larry Kolwoord/The Image Works; **p. 99:** The Historical Society of Pennsylvania; **p. 101:** AP/Wide World; **p. 102:** AP/Wide World; **p. 111:** Terry Ashe/TIME Magazine.

## CHAPTER 4

**Text and art: p. 124:** Fig. 4.2. From "Category accessibility and impression formation" by E. T. Higgins, et al., *Journal of Experimental Social Psychology*, 1977, Vol. 13, pp. 141–154. Reprinted by permission of Academic Press, Inc., and E. T.

Higgins. **p. 129:** Fig. 4.3. From "Pattern of performance and ability attribution" by E. E. Jones, et al., *Journal of Personality and Social Psychology*, 1968, 10, pp. 317–340. Copyright © 1968 American Psychological Association. Reprinted by permission. **p. 130:** Fig. 4.4. From "Perseverance in self perception and social perception . . ." by L. Ross, et al., *Journal of Personality and Social Psychology*, 1975, 32, pp. 880–892. Copyright © 1975 American Psychological Association. Reprinted by permission. **p. 139:** Fig. 4.7. From "Effects of knowledge about remote social events . . ." by H. A. Hornstein, et al., *Journal of Personality and Social Psychology*, 1975, 32, pp. 1038–1046. Copyright © 1975 American Psychological Association. Adapted by permission. **p. 145:** Fig. 4.8. From "Ignoring sample bias: Inferences about populations from atypical cases" by C. R. Hamill, T. D. Wilson, and R. E. Nisbett, *Journal of Personality and Social Psychology*, 1980, 39, pp. 578–589. Copyright © 1980 American Psychological Association. Adapted by permission. **p. 152:** Fig. 4.9. From "The effects of graduate training on reasoning" by D. Lehman, R. Lempert, and R. Nisbett, *American Psychologist*, 1988, Vol. 43, No. 6, pp. 431–442. Copyright © 1988 American Psychological Association. Reprinted by permission. **p. 153:** Fig. 4.10. From "Teaching reasoning" by R. E. Nisbett, et al., *Science*, Vol. 238, pp. 625–631. Copyright © 1987 American Association for the Advancement of Science. Reprinted by permission of AAAS and the author.
**Photos and cartoons: p. 114:** SuperStock, Inc.; **p. 116:** Sygma; **p. 119:** The Kobal Collection; **p. 121L:** J. A. Warner from "The Darker Brother"; **p. 121R:** J. A. Warner from "The Darker Brother"; **p. 138:** Comstock Inc.; **p. 143L:** E. R. Degginger; **p. 143R:** Joe Sohm/The Image Works; **p. 146:** Hans Namuth.

## CHAPTER 5
**Text and art: p. 168:** Fig. 5.1. From "A multidimensional approach to the structure . . ." by S. Rosenberg, et al., *Journal of Personality and Social Psychology*, 1968, 9, pp. 283–294. Copyright © 1968 American Psychological Association. Reprinted by permission. **p. 171:** Fig. 5.2. From "The linguistic relativity of person cognition . . ." by C. Hoffman, et al., *Journal of Personality and Social Psychology*, 1986, 51, pp. 1097–1105. Copyright © 1986 American Psychological Association. Reprinted by permission. **p. 182:** Fig. 5.5. Adapted from "The attribution of attitudes" by E. E. Jones & V. A. Harris, *Journal of Experimental Social Psychology*, 1965, No. 3, pp. 1–24. Reprinted by permission of Academic Press, Inc., and E. E. Jones. **p. 183 & p. 184:** Figs. 5.6 & 5.7. From "Point of view and perceptions of causality" by S. E. Taylor & S. T. Fiske, *Journal of Personality and Social Psychology*, 1975, 32, pp. 439–445. Copyright © 1975 The American Psychological Association. Reprinted by permission. **p. 186:** Material from "Dear Ann Landers," *Boston Globe*, September 10, 1991. Reprinted by permission of Ann Landers and Creators Syndicate. **p. 187 & p. 188:** Figs. 5.8 & 5.9. Adapted from "Videotape and the attribution process: reversing actors' and observers' points of view" by M. D. Storms, *Journal of Personality and Social Psychology*, 1973, 27, pp. 165–175. Reprinted by permission of American Psychological Association and the author. **p. 193:** Fig. 5.10. From "Friends and strangers: Acquaintanceships, agreement, and the accuracy of personality judgment" by D. C. Funder & C. R. Colvin, *Journal of Personality and Social Psychology*,

1988, 55, pp. 149–158. Copyright © 1988 American Psychological Association. Adapted by permission. **p. 203:** From "The development of self-conceptions from childhood to adolescence" by R. Montemayor and M. Eisen, *Developmental Psychology*, 1977, 13, p. 318. Copyright © 1977 American Psychological Association. Reprinted by permission.
**Photos and cartoons: p. 156:** Bonnie Kamin/Comstock Inc.; **p. 158:** McAnn-Erickson; **p. 161:** Dr. Paul Ekman/Human Interaction Laboratory; **p. 162:** Dr. Paul Ekman/Human Interaction Laboratory; **p. 163:** Laurence Wylie; **p. 165:** Robin Akert; **p. 169:** Steve Vidler/Leo de Wys; **p. 173:** Tom Abbott/Leo de Wys; **p. 176L:** AP/Wide World; **p. 176R:** N. Sapieha/Stock Boston; **p. 190ALL:** Focus On Sports.

## CHAPTER 6
**Text and art: p. 205:** Fig. 6.1. From "Self-awareness and aversive experience in everyday life" by M. Csikzenmihalyi & T. Figurski, *Journal of Personality*, 1982, 50, pp. 15–28. Reprinted by permission of Duke University Press. **p. 207:** Fig. 6.2. "Self-awareness theory" from *Attention and Self-Regulation: A Control Theory Approach to Human Behavior* by C. S. Carver & M. F. Scheier. Copyright © 1981 Springer-Verlag, Inc. Reprinted by permission. **p. 211:** From *A Benjamin Franklin Reader* edited by N. G. Goodman, 1945. Reprinted by permission of HarperCollins Publishers. **p. 214:** Fig. 6.3. From "Self-perceptions following social interaction" by R. H. Fazio, et al., *Journal of Personality and Social Psychology*, 1981, 41, pp. 232–242. Copyright © 1981 American Psychological Association. Adapted by permission. **p. 219:** Fig. 6.4. From "Overjustification in a token economy" by D. Greene, et al., *Journal of Personality and Social Psychology*, 1976, 34, pp. 1219–1234. Copyright © 1976 The American Psychological Association. Reprinted by permission. **p. 221:** Fig. 6.5. From "Immunizing children against the negative effects of reward: A further examination of intrinsic motivation training techniques" by B. A. Henessey & S. M. Zbikowski, *Creativity Research Journal*, 1991. Copyright © 1991 Ablex Publishing Corporation. Reprinted with permission from Ablex Publishing Corporation. **p. 227:** Fig. 6.7. From "Some evidence for heightened sexual attraction under conditions of high anxiety" by D. G. Dutton & A. P. Aron, *Journal of Personality and Social Psychology*, 1974, 30, pp. 510–517. Copyright © 1974 American Psychological Association. Reprinted by permission. **p. 232:** Fig. 6.8. From "Self-recognition in primates . . ." by G. G. Gallup, *American Psychologist*, 1977, 32, pp. 329–338. Copyright © 1977 American Psychological Association. Adapted by permission.
**Photos and cartoons: p. 198:** Tim Gibson/Envision; **p. 201L:** Robin Akert; **p. 201R:** From the Personal Collection of R. M. Akert; **p. 202:** HarperCollins Archives; **p. 204:** Danilo Boschung/Leo de Wys; **p. 218:** Focus On Sports; **p. 226:** L. Fisher/Masterfile; **p. 236L:** Smith/Sygma; **p. 236R:** F. Lee Corkran/Sygma.

## CHAPTER 7
**Text and art: p. 250:** Fig. 7.1. From *The Psychology of Social Norms* by M. Sherif. Copyright © 1936 Harper & Brothers. Copyright renewed 1963 Muzafer Sherif. Reprinted by permission of HarperCollins Publishers. **p. 252:** "Radio listeners in panic . . .," *The New York Times*, October 31, 1938. Copyright © 1938 The New York Times Company. Reprinted

# NAME INDEX

167, 183, 184, 187, 197, 234, 239, 499, 503, 542, 549, 553, 577
Taylor, S. P., 462
Taynor, J., 500
Teasdale, J. D., 554
Tedeschi, J. T., 235
Teger, A. I., 352
Tesser, A., 104, 105, 106, 107, 109, 208, 212, 372, 377, 411, 448
Tetlock, P. E., 135, 151
Thew, B. D., 253
Thibaut, J., 261, 357, 360, 393, 420
Thibodeau, R., 20, 75, 289, 534, 571
Thiel, D. L., 379
Thomas, Lewis, 5
Thomas, M. H., 474
Thomas, W. I., 248
Thompson, D. E., 566
Thompson, L., 364
Thompson, M., 262, 263
Thompson, S. C., 26
Thoreau, Henry David, 12, 529
Thornton, D., 233
Thornton, W., 192
*Time*, 32, 247, 418
Titus, L. J., 328, 329
Titus, W., 346, 347
Toch, H., 265, 488
Toffler, Alvin, 559
Traupmann, J., 396, 404
Triplett, N., 328
Trivers, R., 502
Troccoli, B., 485
Trolier, T. K., 148
Trommsdorff, G., 353
Trope, Y., 135
Trumbo, D., 608
Tuchin, M., 588
Tucker, J. A., 238
Turner, C. W., 470
Turner, F. J., 245
Turner, J. C., 283, 504
Tversky, A., 137, 140, 141, 150, 155
Tversky, B., 588
Twain, Mark, 244, 261, 268, 303
Tybout, A. M., 542
Tyler, R. B., 507
Tyrrell, D., 547

Ulrich, L., 608
Uranowitz, S. W., 33, 430
*USA Today*, 286, 558
Ustinov, Sir Peter, 373
Utne, M., 396

Vaillant, G. E., 556
Valins, S., 217, 225, 564
Vallone, R., 78, 127, 151
Vance, C. S., 32
van de Kragt, A. J. C., 569
Vanneman, R. D., 522
Van Overwalle, F., 556
Veach, T. L., 353
Veitch, R., 386, 463
Verette, J. A., 487
Vincent, J., 436
Vinokur, A., 353
Vivekananthan, P. S., 168

Voissem, N. H., 363
Vonnegut, Kurt, 504
Vuchinich, R. E., 238

Waddell, B., 405
Wagner, R. C., 387
Wagstaff, G., 518
Waldron, H., 394
Wall, S., 408
Wallach, M. A., 351, 352
Wallas, Graham, 307
Wallbom, M., 206
Wallston, K. A., 28
Walster, E., 101, 170, 191, 379, 389, 392, 395, 404, 405, 407. *See also* Hatfield, E.
Walster, G. W., 395, 398, 404
Walter, E., 292
Walters, G., 508
Ward, L. M., 128
Warner, Charles Dudley, 311
Warren, Earl, 496
Warshaw, P. R., 318
Washington, R. E., 497
*Washington Post*, 418
Waters, E., 408
Watson, D., 186, 546
Watson, J., 527
Watson, J. B., 16
Watson, R., 336
Watson, W. E., 342
Wattenberg, M. P., 302
Watts, J. C., 299
Weatherly, D., 524
Webber, R., 513, 514
Wegner, D. M., 106, 212, 594
Weiher, A., 218
Weiner, B., 487
Weinstein, 191
Weir, W., 600
Weiss, J., 209
Weiss, R. L., 394
Weiss, R. S., 372
Weiss, W., 291, 292
Wells, G. L., 296, 297, 581, 583, 589
Wenzlaff, R., 594
Wesley, John, 527
West, S. G., 186, 522
Wheeler, G., 433
Wheeler, L., 233, 406
Whetzel, D. L., 608
Whitcup, M., 575
White, G. L., 378, 406, 411
White, R. K., 520
White, R. W., 302, 303
Whitley, B. E., 190
Whitmyre, J. W., 348
Whittaker, J., 270
Whorf, B. L., 170
Wicker, A., 315
Wicklund, R. A., 113, 206, 208, 338
Wiedenfeld, S. A., 550
Wiesner, W. H., 608
Wiggins, E. C., 302
Wilde, Oscar, 377
Wilder, D. A., 503, 504, 532, 533, 534
Wilhelmy, R. A., 268
Willerman, B., 34, 36, 394

Williams, C., 315
Williams, K. D., 333, 334, 335
Williams, R. H., 572
Williams, R. L., 148
Williamson, G. M., 405, 435, 548
Willis, T. A., 234
Wills, T. A., 394
Wilson, D. K., 28
Wilson, E. O., 419, 420
Wilson, J. Q., 462
Wilson, McLandburgh, 557
Wilson, T. D., 7, 46, 144, 145, 148, 151, 180, 209, 210, 211, 212, 314, 383, 384, 555, 556, 604
Winch, R., 387
Winslow, M. P., 92, 93, 558
Winsten, J. A., 301
Winter, D. G., 612
Wiseman, F., 37–38
Wolf, S., 268, 269, 273
Woll, S., 378
Wood, J. V., 232, 234
Wood, W., 307
Woolcott, M., 266
Worchel, P., 388, 466
Word, C. D., 608
Word, C. E., 133
Word, C. O., 519
Word, L. E., 445
Wortman, C. B., 237, 563
Wright, J. C., 148
Wright, P. M., 608
Wrightsman, L. S., 542, 618
Wyer, M. M., 365, 366
Wyer, R., 516
Wyer, R. S., Jr., 122, 507
Wylie, 163

Yamaguchi, K., 311
Yates, S., 572
Yinger, J. M., 522
Young, R. D., 208
Yuille, J. C., 584

Zahn-Waxler, C., 430
Zajonc, R. B., 23, 34, 119, 167, 228, 328, 329, 331, 332, 376, 566
Zanna, M. P., 103, 133, 216, 233, 239, 287, 288, 302, 308, 519, 608
Zanot, E. J., 599
Zaragoza, M., 588
Zbikowski, S. M., 220, 221
Zebrowitz-McArthur, L., 185
Zedeck, S., 608
Zeisel, H., 593, 596
Zembrodt, I. M., 412
Zillmann, D., 225, 476
Zimbardo, P. G., 97, 224, 337, 339
Zion, C., 608
Zubek, J. P., 257
Zuckerman, M., 165, 179

# SUBJECT INDEX

Philosophy, vs. social psychology, 8–9
Physical attractiveness
    and liking, 377–84
    and long-term relationships, 406–7
Pluralistic ignorance, 444
Polarization, group, 351–54
Politeness pattern, 167
Politics
    Bush vs. Dukakis campaign (1988),
        285–86
    change in views on, 135
    Clinton campaign (1992), 286
    David Duke in, 236–37
Polls, political, 44–45
    bias avoided in, 143–44
Polygraph, 591–92
Pornography, and violence against women,
    32, 40–42, 48, 56–57, 475–76
Positive correlation, 44
Postdecision dissonance, 78–85, 108
Powell, Colin, 513, 514
Praise, and attraction, 388–89
Preconceptions, 126
Prejudice, 493, 494–98
    affective component of, 304, 498
    causes of, 502
        attributional biases, 515–20
        conformity to norms, 265, 525–29
        and eye-color experiment, 502–3
        and realistic conflict theory, 520–25
        social cognition, 503–14
    and discrimination, 501–2
    and Willie Horton ads, 286
    Marshall's experience of, 493–94
    reducing of, 529–36
    and stereotypes, 494–95, 498–501,
        507–11
    and illusory correlation, 511–13
    revising of, 513–15
    study on, 314–15, 317
    See also Biases
Presentation of self, 234–38
Presidential Commission on Obscenity and
    Pornography (1970), 32, 475
Presidential elections
    of 1936 (Literary Digest survey), 44
    of 1988, 285–86
    of 1992, 286
Pretrial publicity, 593–94
Primacy effect, 128
Priming, of schemas, 122–25
Prisoner's Dilemma, 12–15, 356–60
    and subliminal messages, 602
Private acceptance, 249
Probability level (p–value), 55
Problem-solving skills, and expression of
    anger, 487–88
Process loss, 343, 345
Product-rating experiments, on cognitive
    dissonance, 81, 108–9
Profile of Nonverbal Sensitivity
    (PONS), 164
Propinquity effect, 373–77
Proselytizing, 79–80
Prosocial behavior, 419
    and care for caveman dwarf, 424
    and consequences for receiver, 448–50
    encouraging of, 450–52

mixed motives in, 428–29
and NYC indifference, 473
personal determinants of
    altruistic personality, 429–33
    gender, 433–35
situational determinants of
    and bystander effect, 439–46
    urban vs. rural environment, 438–39
and social exchange theory, 420–24
and sociobiology, 419–20, 424, 429,
    447, 502
See also Bystander intervention
Psychogenic illness, mass, 253–55
Psychological realism, 58
Psychological stress. See Stress
Psychology, Gestalt, 16–17
Public compliance, 249
Punishment
    and aggression, 477–79
    insufficient, 92–95
Puritans, and self-awareness, 203

Quayle, Dan, 126, 455
Questionnaire experiment, on emotional
    arousal, 222–24
Questions, misleading, 587–88
Quizzes
    on correlation and causation, 50
    on social psychology, 34
    on statistical reasoning, 152

Racetrack, and cognitive dissonance, 82
Racism and race
    institutionalized, 526
    modern, 528–29
    and post-prizefight homicides, 472–73
    See also Prejudice; Segregation
Random assignment to condition, 55, 63
Random numbers table, 55
Random selection, 44
Rape
    blaming victim of, 191–92, 518
    and pornography, 48, 56, 475
Rational behavior, vs. rationalizing, 77–78
Rationalizing behavior, 77–78
    postdecision, 85
    and rationalization trap, 111–12
Reactance theory, 312–13
Reagan, Ronald, 126
Realism
    mundane, 58
    psychological, 58
Realistic conflict theory, 520–25
Reasoned action, theory of, 316
Reasoning. See Inferences; Social cognition
Reasons-generated attitude change, 211–12
Recency effects, 128
Reciprocation, and aggression, 467
Reciprocity, 421
    as norm, 266–67, 420, 605
Reconstructive memory, 586
Record album experiment, on cognitive dis-
    sonance, 108
Reduced accountability, and deindividua-
    tion, 336, 337–38
Reduced self-awareness, and deindividua-
    tion, 336, 338–39
Reflected glory, 237

Reinforcement, 16
Relation-oriented leader, 613
Relationships, 396–97
    and self-evaluation maintenance
        theory, 107
    See also Dating relationship; Friendship;
        Love and long-term relationships
Relative deprivation, 466
Relevance, personal, 294–97
Reliability, interjudge, 40
Replication, 61–62
Representativeness heuristic, 139–41
Research
    applied, 63–64
    basic, 63–64
Research methods. See Methods of social
    psychology
Responsibility
    diffusion of, 37, 445–46
    and Milgram on evil acts, 282
Retrieval (information), 583, 588–89
Review-reading experiment, on praise, 388
Rewards, and overjustification effect,
    217–20
Riot
    and expectations, 466
    in Los Angeles, 455–56
    and Reginald Denny, 423
Risky shift, 351–52
Romantic relationships. See Dating
    relationships; Love and long-term
    relationships
Rural environment, and prosocial behavior,
    438–39
Russell, Bill, 218
Ryan, Leo, 4, 243

Salespeople, compliance techniques of,
    604–7
    lowballing, 82–84
Salience, perceptual, 182–84, 186–88
Sampling, biased, 143–47
    in 1936 Literary Digest poll, 44–45
Saying-is-believing paradigm, 88–92, 290
Scapegoats, 523–25
"Scared straight" program, 313–14
Schatzki, Michael and Jeanne, 561–62
Schemas, 118–22
    accessibility and priming of, 122–25
    and attribution, 180
    causal theory, 209–10
    disconfirming of, 134–35
    and implicit personality, 170
    inaccuracy from, 194
    and judgmental heuristics, 142
    revising of, 125–31
    and self-fulfilling prophecy, 131–34
    self-schemas, 228–30
Schlesinger, Arthur, 349–50
School desegregation, 530–31, 534–36
Scully, John, 611
Seattle windshield-pitting epidemic,
    246, 253
Secure attachment style, 408
Segregation, in U.S. South, 264–65, 525,
    526, 528
    and cognitive-dissonance experiment,
        77–78